The first person to invent a car that runs on water…

… may be sitting right in your classroom! Every one of your students has the potential to make a difference. And realizing that potential starts right here, in your course.

When students succeed in your course—when they stay on-task and make the breakthrough that turns confusion into confidence—they are empowered to realize the possibilities for greatness that lie within each of them. We know your goal is to create an environment where students reach their full potential and experience the exhilaration of academic success that will last them a lifetime. *WileyPLUS* can help you reach that goal.

Wiley**PLUS** is an online suite of resources—including the complete text—that will help your students:

- come to class better prepared for your lectures
- get immediate feedback and context-sensitive help on assignments and quizzes
- track their progress throughout the course

"I just wanted to say how much this program helped me in studying … I was able to actually see my mistakes and correct them. … I really think that other students should have the chance to use *WileyPLUS*."
Ashlee Krisko, *Oakland University*

www.wiley.com/college/wileyplus

80% of students surveyed said it improved their understanding of the material.*

Prepare & Present

Create outstanding class presentations using a wealth of resources, such as PowerPoint™ slides, image galleries, interactive simulations, and more. Plus you can easily upload any materials you have created into your course, and combine them with the resources Wiley provides you with.

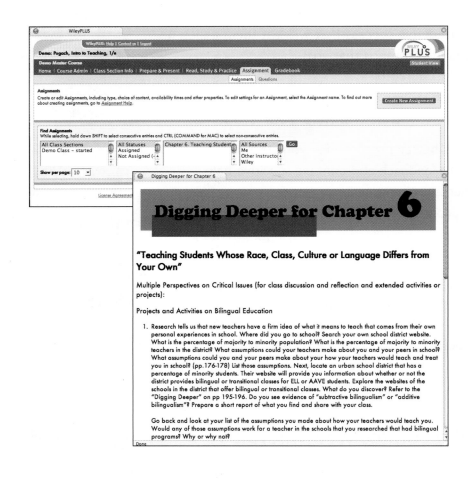

Create Assignments

Automate the assigning and grading of homework or quizzes by using the provided question banks, or by writing your own. Student results will be automatically graded and recorded in your gradebook. *WileyPLUS* also links homework problems to relevant sections of the online text, hints, or solutions—context-sensitive help where students need it most!

---

* Based on a spring 2005 survey of 972 student users of *WileyPLUS*

Track Student Progress

Keep track of your students' progress via an instructor's gradebook, which allows you to analyze individual and overall class results. This gives you an accurate and realistic assessment of your students' progress and level of understanding.

Now Available with WebCT and Blackboard!

Now you can seamlessly integrate all of the rich content and resources available with *WileyPLUS* with the power and convenience of your WebCT or BlackBoard course. You and your students get the best of both worlds with single sign-on, an integrated gradebook, list of assignments and roster, and more. If your campus is using another course management system, contact your local Wiley Representative.

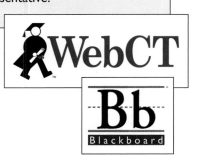

"I studied more for this class than I would have without *WileyPLUS*."

Melissa Lawler, *Western Washington Univ.*

For more information on what *WileyPLUS* can do to help your students reach their potential, please visit

www.wiley.com/college/wileyplus

76% of students surveyed said it made them better prepared for tests. *

TO THE STUDENT

You have the potential to make a difference!

Will you be the first person to land on Mars? Will you invent a car that runs on water? But, first and foremost, will you get through this course?

WileyPLUS is a powerful online system packed with features to help you make the most of your potential, and get the best grade you can!

With Wiley**PLUS** you get:

A complete online version of your text and other study resources

Study more effectively and get instant feedback when you practice on your own. Resources like self-assessment quizzes, tutorials, and animations bring the subject matter to life, and help you master the material.

Problem-solving help, instant grading, and feedback on your homework and quizzes

You can keep all of your assigned work in one location, making it easy for you to stay on task. Plus, many homework problems contain direct links to the relevant portion of your text to help you deal with problem-solving obstacles at the moment they come up.

The ability to track your progress and grades throughout the term.

A personal gradebook allows you to monitor your results from past assignments at any time. You'll always know exactly where you stand.

If your instructor uses *WileyPLUS*, you will receive a URL for your class. If not, your instructor can get more information about *WileyPLUS* by visiting www.wiley.com/college/wileyplus

"It has been a great help, and I believe it has helped me to achieve a better grade."
Michael Morris, *Columbia Basin College*

69% of students surveyed said it helped them get a better grade.*

EDUCATIONAL PSYCHOLOGY
Reflection for Action

Angela M. O'Donnell
Rutgers, The State University of New Jersey

Johnmarshall Reeve
The University of Iowa

Jeffrey K. Smith
Rutgers, The State University of New Jersey

WILEY

JOHN WILEY & SONS, INC

Chapter Opening Graphics, from left to right:
PhotoDisc, Inc./Getty Images
PhotoDisc, Inc./Getty Images
PhotoDisc, Inc./Getty Images
Corbis Digital Stock
PhotoDisc, Inc./Getty Images
Corbis Digital Stock

Chapter Opening Photos:
Chapter 1: Media Bakery
Chapter 2: ©Ellen B. Senisi/The Image Works
Chapter 3: Media Bakery

Chapter 4: Punchstock
Chapter 5: Media Bakery
Chapter 6: Media Bakery
Chapter 7: Dynamic Graphics, Inc./Creatas
Chapter 8: Digital Vision
Chapter 9: PhotoDisc, Inc./Getty Images
Chapter 10: Corbis Digital Stock
Chapter 11: Chapter 9: PhotoDisc, Inc./Getty Images
Chapter 12: Corbis Digital Stock
Chapter 13: Andrew W. Levine/Photo Researchers, Inc.
Chapter 14: Benelux Press/Index Stock

Publisher: *Jay O'Callaghan*
Executive Editor: *Christopher Johnson*
Acquisition Editor: *Robert Johnston*
Senior Development Editor: *Nancy Perry*
Senior Production Editor: *Valerie A. Vargas*
Executive Marketing Manager: *Jeffrey Rucker*
Marketing Consultant: *Laura McKenna*
Creative Director: *Harry Nolan*
Cover Design: *Brian Salisbury*
Cover Photo: *Bohemdn Nomad Picturemakers/CORBIS*
Text Design Credit: *GGS Book Services*
Senior Illustration Editor: *Sandra Rigby*
Senior Photo Editor: *Lisa Gee*
Editorial Assistant: *Katie Melega*
Media Editor: *Alexander Sasha Giacoppo*
Production Management: *Caterina Melara/Preparé Inc.*

This book was set in 10.5/12 Minion by Prepare and printed and bound by Courier Kendallville, Inc. The cover was printed by Courier Companies.

This book is printed on acid free paper. ∞

Library of Congress Cataloging in Publication Data

O'Donnell Angela M.
    Educational psychology: reflection for action / Angela M. O'Donnell, Johnmarshall
Reeve, Jeffrey K. Smith.

        p. cm.

    Includes bibliographical references and index.

    ISBN-13: 978-0-471-45662-9 (pbk.: alk. paper)
    ISBN-10: 0-471-45662-4 (pbk. : alk. paper)
        1. Educational psychology. I. Reeve, Johnmarshall. II. Smith, Jeffrey K. III. Title.

    LB1051.O343 2005
    370.15--dc22   2005054657

Printed in the United States of America

    10 9 8 7 6 5 4 3 2 1

About the Authors

Angela M. O'Donnell is a Professor in the Department of Educational Psychology at Rutgers University. She received her PhD in Experimental Psychology from Texas Christian University and has master's degrees in both Experimental Psychology and Special Education. She is a Fellow of the American Psychological Association and is the President of Division 15 of APA. She received the Early Career Award of Division 15 in 1996 and the New Jersey Psychological Association's Distinguished Teacher Award in 2001. Professor O'Donnell serves on numerous editorial boards of journals in educational psychology. She was Secretary of Division C of the American Educational Research Association and served as Program Chair for Division C. Her research interests are in the areas of collaborative learning and learning strategies. She has published extensively on the cognitive processes involved in specific types of cooperative learning and the use of visual organizers to support cognitive processing.

Johnmarshall Reeve is a Professor in the Department of Psychological and Quantitative Foundations at the University of Iowa. He received his PhD from Texas Christian University and completed postdoctoral work at the University of Rochester. Professor Reeve's research interests center on the empirical study of all aspects of human motivation and emotion with a particular emphasis on the motivating styles teachers use in the classroom to support students' high-quality motivation and engagement. He has published two dozen articles on motivation in journals such as the *Journal of Educational Psychology, Motivation and Emotion,* and *The Elementary School Journal.* For this work, he received the Thomas N. Urban Research Award from the FINE Foundation. He has also published two books, including *Understanding Motivation and Emotion* and *Motivating Others: Nurturing Inner Motivational Resources.* He currently sits on two editorial boards and serves as the Associate Editor for *Motivation and Emotion.*

Jeffrey K. Smith is a Professor in the Department of Educational Psychology at Rutgers University. He received his bachelor's degree from Princeton University and his PhD from the University of Chicago. He has been a member of the faculty at Rutgers since 1976 and has served as Chair of the Department of Educational Psychology. In addition to his work at Rutgers, he served from 1988 to 2005 as Head of the Office of Research and Evaluation at The Metropolitan Museum of Art. Professor Smith's research interests include psychological factors involved in assessment, classroom assessment and grading, and the psychology of aesthetics. He has published over 50 articles and reviews in these areas and has written or edited five books. Professor Smith is the co-editor of the *Bulletin of Psychology and the Arts* and former editor of the journal *Educational Measurement: Issues and Practice.* He currently sits on the editorial board of four journals and is a former member of the National Advisory Board of Buros' *Mental Measurement Yearbook.* He has won awards for teaching, research, and public service.

Preface

The day-to-day work of teachers is not unlike that of researchers. Teachers ask questions that arise from experience. They frame the questions in such a way that they can gather information from research, peers, mentors, parents, and other professionals who will help them answer the question. They need to judge the *trustworthiness* of the information they gather and decide on the best answer to their questions, given the available information.

The Goal of Educational Psychology: Reflection for Action

This book will help preservice teachers develop the skills necessary to become *reflective practitioners* who can frame questions about their classrooms and use a "scientist-practitioner" approach to answer those questions. It does so by highlighting a set of guiding questions about important topics for the classroom, providing an example of a situation that provokes a question for the teacher and describing the theories and empirical findings that might be drawn on to respond to the situation. It links theories and research to practical issues in the classroom through illustrations of "what kids say or do" and through counterintuitive examples of how research contributes to answering classroom questions. Finally, the book models how theory, research findings, and other sources can be drawn upon to provide plausible answers to these questions. Students are guided through a process of reflection (summarized as the acronym **RIDE**) on classroom questions. This critical thinking process involves **R**eflection, **I**nformation Gathering, **D**ecision Making, and **E**valuation that enables students to make reflection an everyday practice.

RIDE

Author Team

The three authors of this text are experts in learning, motivation, and assessment, respectively. Each of us is writing in our special area of substantial experience, providing an advantage over the typical text, in which chapters are written by a single author whose expertise most likely does not fully extend to the range of content needed in an educational psychology text.

Diversity

We have chosen to address issues of diversity as part of the various chapters and not to include a single stand-alone chapter that is typical of other texts. We believe that diversity is a consideration that runs throughout the topics that are under consideration and not a separate set of concerns. It must be valued and addressed in every aspect of the classroom teacher's activity. In addition, we believe this treatment reflects the day-to-day realities of classroom teachers, in which student diversity is increasingly common.

In *Educational Psychology: Reflection for Action,* we provide students with:

1. A clear description of the theoretical principles in psychology that have relevance for education, along with an analysis of their current research support.
2. Practical guidance about how to link theory and practice in the context of classrooms. We illustrate the opportunities for and limits of application of theoretical principles to classroom practice.
3. Learning tools to help preservice teachers develop skills they can build on throughout their teaching careers.

Content and Organization

The textbook consists of three major parts that address:

● Development and motivation
● Learning and teaching
● Assessment

These sections represent the essential content that students must know as they prepare to become teachers.

Part I: Development and Motivation

The first part of the text is concerned with how students develop and how and why they might be motivated to learn. We consider both developmental and motivational ideas here. This particular organization differs from most other texts in providing a theoretical rationale for the students' perspective in the teaching/learning process. Teachers working with children and adolescents need an understanding of both the developmental factors that underlie when students learn and the motivational issues that underlie why students learn. A chapter in this section addresses important concerns related to individual differences in learning that are particularly important because most teachers work in classrooms with students of dramatically differing ability.

Part II: Learning and Teaching

The second part is concerned with learning and teaching and the contexts in which these processes occur. Behavioral, cognitive, social constructivist, and sociocultural theories are addressed, and their implications for instruction and for learning are included. This section also includes a chapter that considers the conditions necessary in a classroom for effective learning and includes a specific chapter on using peer learning.

Part III: Assessment

The third part addresses the question, How do we know students have learned? As teachers experience an increased emphasis on statewide testing, the importance of this topic for them cannot be understated. The chapter on standardized assessment includes specific information on how to translate the results of such assessments into classroom practice.

Chapter 1: Introducing Educational Psychology and Reflective Practice

Educational psychology is the scientific study of psychology in education. Its goals are to understand learners and to promote their learning. The first part of Chapter 1 explains how a focus on these two goals helps teachers better understand all aspects of the teaching-learning process. To do so, we first identify the most pressing concerns that beginning teachers have and illustrate how beginning teachers quiet these concerns by developing teaching efficacy, teaching expertise, and reflective teaching. The second part of the chapter discusses issues of student diversity and students with special needs. The final part of the chapter addresses the role of theory and research in educational psychology.

Chapter 2: Cognitive Development

As infants grow into children and as children grow into adolescents, three interrelated developmental processes unfold: (a) brain development, (b) cognitive development, and (c) language development. Biology and maturation underlie all three developmental processes, but biology provides learners only with developmental potential. Chapter 2 identifies and discusses the school-related experiences that help learners realize their developmental potentials. Exposure to richly stimulating and complex classroom environments and exposure to teachers who guide students' learning provide the essential ingredients that enrich students' brain, cognitive, and language development.

Chapter 3: Social Development

Chapter 3 highlights the role that relationships play in students' social development, and it offers numerous illustrations as to how teachers can help students develop socially. Social development reflects the extent of a person's social competence, peer popularity, trust, initiative, competence, identity, moral development, prosocial orientation, and healthy self-concept. The extent to which students develop socially depends in part on the quality of the relationships in their lives, including the relationships they have with their teachers. The chapter identifies the aspects of a relationship that allow it to be a high-quality relationship. It also discusses specific social-developmental outcomes, aggression, and self-concept.

Chapter 4: Individual Differences among Learners

Chapter 4 is concerned with individual differences among students. The first part of the chapter focuses on intelligence or ability. It describes how the concept of intelligence evolved and introduces a number of theories of intelligence. The next part of the chapter discusses extremes of intelligence and how talent is developed. Some instructional strategies for managing variation in students' ability are then described. The second part of the chapter focuses on learners with special needs and the effects of socioeconomic status on children's success in school.

Chapter 5: Motivation to Learn

Chapter 5 defines motivation and explains how it works—where it comes from, how it changes, what it predicts, and why educators care so deeply about increasing it. This chapter explains self-efficacy, mastery motivational orientation, optimistic attributional style, hope, goal setting, achievement goals, and effective self-regulation. The chapter also explains self-doubt, helpless motivational orientation, pessimistic attributional style, lack of goals, and little capacity for self-regulation. The compound theme that runs throughout the chapter is, first, that student motivation reflects the quality of their thinking and, second, teachers can support students' motivation by helping them think in constructive ways.

Chapter 6: Engaging Students in Learning

Chapter 6 focuses on students' engagement during learning activities. We define engagement, explain why it is important, and identify sources of engagement and instructional strategies for promoting it. The chapter discusses intrinsic motivation, extrinsic rewards, and types of extrinsic motivation. We also discuss three psychological needs that create a desire to be engaged: (a) autonomy, (b) competence, and (c) relatedness. We also discuss curiosity, interest, and positive affect as ways to spark students' engagement. Finally, we explain the roots of disengagement by focusing on anxiety, self-worth protection, and self-handicapping, and we discuss ways to calm students' anxieties and fears.

Chapter 7: Behavioral Learning Theory

Chapter 7 focuses on students' behavior. We ask how students learn the behaviors, skills, and self-regulatory abilities they need to function well in school and in life. To understand how students learn such things, we first define learning and explain how it occurs. We then introduce the basic principles of the behavioral approach to learning. These principles serve as a foundation for understanding and discussing the everyday problems that teachers face in trying to increase the frequency of desirable behaviors and decrease that of undesirable behaviors. We also describe the types of instruction that have been inspired by behavioral learning principles.

Chapter 8: Cognitive Theories of Learning

Chapter 8 focuses on the structures and processes of learning from a cognitive perspective, with special emphasis on information-processing theory. Throughout the chapter, we pay particular attention to how we can understand the needs of exceptional children from a cognitive perspective. We first describe the relationship between cognitive and constructivist theories of learning. Other sections describe the basic processes of encoding and retrieval and the limitations of various components of the information-processing system, such as working memory. Each section also includes the instructional implications of those components. The final section of the chapter addresses complex cognition.

Chapter 9: Effective Teachers and the Process of Teaching

The focus of Chapter 9 is on teachers and teaching, and on how thoughtful learning can be fostered by high-quality teaching. Teachers' knowledge of the subject matter they are teaching and their beliefs about themselves, their students, and the processes of learning and teaching have important influences on classroom practices and problems. This chapter illustrates these differences and tracks the instructional process from beginning to end, discussing planning as a key factor in good teaching, examining teacher-centered approaches to instruction, exploring particular teaching tactics to enhance students' learning, and examining the effective use of homework.

Chapter 10: Social Constructivism and Learning in Community

Chapter 10 focuses on social learning, social constructivism, and learning in community. The ability to learn from observing others is a key element of theories that emphasize the importance of the social context in which learning occurs. The chapter provides examples of instructional use of scaffolding, including the use of technology to scaffold students' learning. Examples of instruction that are influenced by social constructivist or sociocultural theories of learning are also described. The chapter describes how learning can go beyond the classroom and how teachers can take advantage of cultural institutions and other available resources.

Chapter 11: Managing Learning in Classrooms

Chapter 11 looks at the opportunities, problems, and concerns associated with creating and managing successful learning communities in classrooms. We begin with the skeleton, discussing concerns that teachers face in designing the physical environment of classrooms. Then we move into the areas that bring the bare bones to life: creating a learning community, establishing and enforcing norms and rules for behavior, and managing the multidimensional aspects of day-to-day classroom life. Teachers differ in how they answer the questions of classroom management, based on their needs and the needs of their students.

Chapter 12: Learning from Peers

Chapter 12 explains the mechanisms and processes through which peer learning can lead to the acquisition of skills and knowledge in widely differing classroom situations. Peer learning techniques are discussed in the context of both one-on-one tutoring and larger, heterogeneous groups. We also consider key issues in the use of peer learning in the classroom, including the quality of students' discourse, the kinds of tasks that teachers may choose, the role of the teacher in using peer learning, peer mediation, and assessing the outcomes of peer learning.

Chapter 13: Classroom Assessment

Chapter 13 examines the critical issues of classroom assessment: purposes, assessment options, evaluation of results, and the relationship between assessment and instruction. Classroom assessments can let students understand what the teacher thinks is of value in the class and how they are progressing. They let teachers learn how well students are doing in the class. They can also let teachers learn about the efficacy of their teaching. Carefully considered and well-constructed assessments promote the notion that classroom assessment is not just assessment *of* learning; it is assessment *for* learning.

Chapter 14: Standardized and Standards-Based Assessments

In Chapter 14, standardized and standards-based assessments are described. We examine what these tests are, what they are used for, and how they are developed. A variety of different types of standardized tests are described. We also explore the history of such tests and how to understand and interpret the scores, as well as issues related to interpreting scores for students with limited English proficiency or students with special needs. Finally, we consider controversies associated with standardized testing, such as bias in testing and high-stakes testing.

Learning Tools:
A Look inside the Chapters

To help meet the needs of preservice teachers taking this course, we have included the following pedagogical features in each chapter.

Understanding the Context
Reflection for Action R I D E

The opening of each chapter contains an example of a teaching and learning setting, either in the form of actual work or a description of a classroom situation (see the next page for an example). It provides the basis for the students to engage in Reflection for Action that helps students develop the ability to reflect critically on their work, removed from the immediacy of the particular situation.

The sample of classroom life presented in the opening is referred to throughout the chapter, encouraging students to use what appears in that section of the chapter to think about the opening segment.

At the end of each chapter, a more structured and fully realized analysis is presented to students to think through the problem in a systematic and scholarly fashion (see below for description).

Each invitation for students to engage in reflection for action is denoted in the text with the icon shown here: R I D E

Guiding Questions

Following the Reflection for Action piece, we present a set of guiding questions. These questions form the utility basis for what is to be presented in the chapter, because they tie important classroom issues that will resonate with students to the theories and empirical findings presented in the chapter.

Example: **Chapter 10**

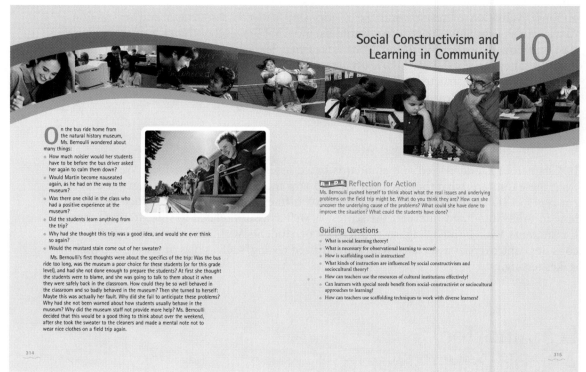

Learning the Material

What Kids Say and Do

Samples of children's work or conversation serve as a watershed between theory and practice and a venue for their integration. Teachers depend on students' work to reason about students' achievement and progress, and the availability of such work can be an important contribution to preservice teacher development.

Example: **Chapter 3**

What Kids Say and Do

Three Students' Answers to "Who Am I?"

Mark:	Julie:	Latisha:
6-year-old	9-year-old	16-year-old
first grader	fourth grader	high school student
My name is Mark.	My name is Julie.	I am a human being.
I have brown eyes.	I am a girl.	I am a girl.
I have brown hair.	I am friendly.	I am ambitious.
I am 6.	I am a truthful person.	I am liberal.
I am tall.	I am always nervous.	I am a Libra.
I am a boy.	I am a very good pianist.	I am sometimes shy.
I am a student.	I am Methodist.	I have some problems but
I am a fast runner.	I am friendly.	can handle them.
		I am moody.

Uncommon Sense

Situations and/or conclusions that are frequently believed by preservice teachers but that are not supported by research are presented for discussion. As an example, students believe that positive reinforcement is always a good practice but are surprised to find that incidents of poor behavior increase in classrooms in which positive reinforcement is provided for good behavior and bad behavior is always ignored. This feature attempts to make students aware of their own misconceptions about predicting and explaining behavior.

Example: **Chapter 13**

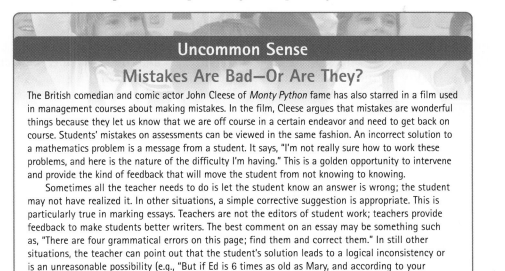

Uncommon Sense
Mistakes Are Bad—Or Are They?

The British comedian and comic actor John Cleese of *Monty Python* fame has also starred in a film used in management courses about making mistakes. In the film, Cleese argues that mistakes are wonderful things because they let us know that we are off course in a certain endeavor and need to get back on course. Students' mistakes on assessments can be viewed in the same fashion. An incorrect solution to a mathematics problem is a message from a student. It says, "I'm not really sure how to work these problems, and here is the nature of the difficulty I'm having." This is a golden opportunity to intervene and provide the kind of feedback that will move the student from not knowing to knowing.

Sometimes all the teacher needs to do is let the student know an answer is wrong; the student may not have realized it. In other situations, a simple corrective suggestion is appropriate. This is particularly true in marking essays. Teachers are not the editors of student work; teachers provide feedback to make students better writers. The best comment on an essay may be something such as, "There are four grammatical errors on this page; find them and correct them." In still other situations, the teacher can point out that the student's solution leads to a logical inconsistency or is an unreasonable possibility (e.g., "But if Ed is 6 times as old as Mary, and according to your answer Mary is 34, how old would that make Ed?").

Wrong answers are a window into the student's cognitive processes. Take a look in.

Taking It to the Classroom

Guidelines for practical issues in classrooms appear throughout each chapter. The vast majority of students who take educational psychology plan to be teachers. How-to guidelines will help preservice teachers link the theoretical principles they read about in the text to appropriate solutions to classroom problems they will soon face in the classroom. These guidelines will also function as a useful reference when readers engage in their student teaching experiences.

Example: **Chapter 13**

Taking It to the Classroom
Marking Student Papers: Being Objective, Specific, and Growth-Oriented

Less desirable comments	More desirable comments
A lot of errors in this area.	See whether you can find four grammatical errors in this section and correct them.
This paragraph is poorly worded and unclear.	I think this paragraph makes the reader work too hard. See whether you can tighten it.
This is hardly your best work.	This looks a little hurried. It doesn't show the care I saw in your last paper.
This is not what we discussed in class.	You're off target somewhat here.
You can't reach the right answer if you are sloppy in your calculations.	You've got the idea, but check your work.
Awkward construction.	Reread this sentence and see whether it says what you want it to.
Redo this.	Try this again.
Excellent job here.	Your use of metaphor here is strong.
Great, I love this.	Think of how much more effective this argument is than in the paper you did last week.

Integrated Primary and Secondary Applications

Integrated into each chapter is content specific to both primary education and secondary education, including the middle school level. It is difficult in a single textbook to provide adequate treatment of content across all age groups. We believe, however, that it is important to deliberately include discussion of the applicability of theories and research to both primary and secondary age groups.

Integrated Content on Diversity

Content related to issues of diversity is distributed among all chapters and not confined to a single chapter. In texts with separate chapters on diversity, the content is often separated from the issues of instruction/assessment and motivation. However, K-12 classrooms are significantly more diverse than even a decade ago. We believe that by integrating the content on diversity into those chapters, preservice teachers may have a better grasp of what diversity among their students will mean for their teaching.

Integrated Content on Students with Special Needs

Frequently, content about individual differences is separated into a single chapter in a text. As with issues of diversity, the content related to individual differences is often separated from the issues of instruction/assessment and motivation. By integrating the content on individual differences into those chapters, preservice teachers may have a more realistic expectation of what differences among their students will mean for their teaching on a day-to-day basis.

Integrated Content on Technology

Technology has become an increasingly important component of many classrooms at both the elementary and secondary levels. Whether it is the use of simulations to present biology or physics labs, computer-generated manipulables for elementary math instruction, or architectural layouts of classrooms for arranging furniture in a kindergarten class, teachers need to know about technology. Consistent with our overall approach to instruction, we have chosen to integrate this material across chapters, showing its importance in the particular area under consideration.

Margin Notes

Students are given many access points to understanding the theory and applications in the chapter.

What Does This Mean to Me?
An SAT verbal score of 650 is a z-score of roughly $+1.5$ (1.5 standard deviations above the mean). Check that against the figure of the normal curve in Figure 14.4, and you can see that this is higher than roughly 93% of the scores.

How Can I Use This?
Check out an electronic book (e-book) from your library and ask yourself what instructional uses it affords that a traditional printed book does not.

RIDE Look at Ms. Baldwin's debate assessment at the beginning of the chapter. What skills and knowledge would lead to the highest marks on this assessment? Are they closely related to how you would have taught this material?

Appendix

PRAXIS™ exam, INTASC Principles

Special margin notes refer students to the Appendix, where they can see the how the contents of the chapter corresponds to the Principles of Learning and Teaching (PLT) of the PRAXIS II™ exam and the INTASC principles.

Appendix
Learning from Others
Students can learn from others through observation learning, and vicarious experience (*PRAXIS™*, I. A. 1, *INTASC*, Principle 2).

Putting It Together R I D E

Reflection for Action End-of-Chapter Activity

A **Reflection for Action** activity consolidates the concepts of each chapter as it models how theory, research findings, and other sources can be drawn upon to provide plausible answers to the question. Students practice *reflecting* on the situation before them, *gathering information* to help them interpret it, *making decisions* on how to handle the situation, and *evaluating* their decisions.

Example: **Chapter 10**

End-of-Chapter Review and Expansion

Each chapter ends with a **Summary,** list of **Key Terms,** and several **Exercises** for thought, discussion, and research.

Supplements: The Teaching and Learning Package

Educational Psychology: Reflection for Action and WileyPLUS

To support diverse teaching and learning, *Educational Psychology: Refection for Action* is available with *WileyPLUS*, a powerful online tool animated by the principles of the textbook that provides instructors and students with a suite of teaching and learning resources in one easy-to-use Web site.

For the Instructor

Prepare and present. *WileyPLUS* offers a wealth of Wiley-provided electronic resources to help professors prepare dynamic class presentations, including an electronic version of the text, detailed PowerPoint slides, text-related video segments, an Instructors Resource Manual, and a Test Bank.

Custom assignments. Professors may create, assign, and grade homework or quizzes by using a Wiley-provided question/assignment bank. Professors may also integrate their own tests or quizzes into this component of *WileyPLUS*.

Automatic monitoring of student progress. An instructor's grade book allows careful tracking and analysis of individual and overall class results.

Flexible course administration. *WileyPLUS* can easily be integrated with another course management system, gradebook, or other course resources.

For the Student

Feedback and support. *WileyPLUS* provides immediate feedback on student assignments (many of which are illustrated by brief video clips) and a wealth of support materials that will help students develop their conceptual understanding of the class material and increase their ability to solve problems.

Study and practice. This feature links directly to text content, allowing students to review the text immediately while studying and completing homework assignments. Pre- and postchapter quizzes integrated in the e-book help students target topics or concepts that require additional work.

Assignment locator. This area allows students to store all tasks and assignments for this course in one convenient location, making it easy for them to stay on task.

Student gradebook. Grades are automatically recorded, and students can access these results at any time.

Reflection, Information Gathering, Decision Making, and Evaluation. Students have the opportunity to work collaboratively on a variety of text-related assignments in order to internalize the process of moving from reflection to action.

- **Video Case Studies.** Produced by CaseNEX, these video clips help students to connect the concepts introduced in class to the complex "real world" school environment. By encouraging students to reflect on what works and collaborate on the design of solutions to instructional challenges, they prepare for decision making and action.

- **Classroom Challenges.** In each chapter, practicing teachers and administrators discuss common classroom dilemmas. Using the tools provided by the text, students are asked to devise and support appropriate solutions.

- **Gather Information Online.** A wealth of author-selected, chapter-specific web sites offer the student the opportunity to dig deeper into important teaching issues.

- **Evaluation and Assessment Practice.** Students interact with samples of children's actual work, taken from elementary and secondary schools around the country, making an initial evaluation of a child's work and then comparing it to the teacher's assessment. In this way, students see best practices modeled and also gain a more sophisticated understanding of the assessment process.

For more information, please view our online demo at www.wiley.com/college/wileyplus. You will find additional information about the features and benefits of *Wiley PLUS*, how to request a "test drive" of *WileyPLUS* for *Educational Psychology: Reflection for Action*, and how to adopt it for class use.

Additional Instructor Resources

Instructor's Manual

Designed to help instructors maximize student learning, the Instructor's Manual presents the authors' teaching philosophy, offers teaching suggestions for each chapter of the text, provides several sample syllabi, suggests ways to organize course materials, and offers ideas for teaching each chapter.

Test Bank

The Test Bank is a comprehensive testing package that allows instructors to tailor examinations according to chapter objectives, learning skills, and content. It includes traditional types of questions (i.e., true-false, multiple-choice, matching, computational, and short-answer), as well as open-ended problems. All questions are cross-referenced to chapter objectives and to level of difficulty.

Computerized Test Bank

The Computerized Test Bank allows instructors to create and print multiple versions of the same test by scrambling the order of all different types of questions found in the Test Bank. Instructors can modify and customize test questions by changing existing problems or adding their own.

PowerPoint Slides

The electronic lecture aids professors in visually presenting the key concepts found in each chapter of the text. Intended as a lecture guide, the PowerPoint slides present material in concise, "bulleted" format that enables easy note taking.

The Wiley Faculty Network

The Wiley Faculty Network is a faculty-to-faculty network promoting the effective use of technology to enrich the teaching experience. The Wiley Faculty Network facilitates the exchange of best practices, connects teachers with technology, and helps to enhance instructional efficiency and effectiveness. The network provides technology training and tutorials, including *Wiley PLUS* training, online seminars, peer-to-peer exchanges of experiences and ideas, personalized consulting, and sharing of resources. For more information about the Wiley Faculty Network, please contact your Wiley representative, go to www.WhereFacultyConnect.com, or call 1-866-4FACULTY.

Additional Student Resources

Educational Psychology: Reflection for Action Tutorial Web Site
www.wiley.com/college/odonnell

The *Educational Psychology: Reflection for Action* **Web site** provides a wealth of support materials that will help students develop an understanding of course concepts and increase their ability to solve problems. On this Web site students will find Web Quizzing and other resources. This site is *free* to students.

Acknowledgments

During the course of development of *Educational Psychology*, the authors benefited greatly from the input of ancillary authors, focus group participants, and manuscript reviewers. The constructive suggestions and innovative ideas of the following people are greatly appreciated.

ANCILLARY AUTHORS

Jim O'Kelly, *Rutgers, the State University of New Jersey:* Instructor's Resource Manual

James Persinger, *Emporia State University:* Instructor's Test Bank

Mary Tallent Runnels, *Texas Tech University:* Instructor's PowerPoint Slides

Anna Lowe, *Loyola University-Chicago:* Student Study Guide

FOCUS GROUP PARTICIPANTS

Mary Frances Agnello
Texas Tech University

Larry Alferink
Illinois State University

James Allen
College of Saint Rose

Woan-Jue Jane Benjamin
Mansfield University

Sandra Bonura
Chapman University

Scott Brown
University of Connecticut

Li Cao
State University of West Georgia

Felicia A. Dixon
Ball State University

Terri Edwards
Northeastern State University

Janet Ferguson
Canisius College

Terry Fogg
Minnesota State University–Mankato

Linda Garavalia
University of Missouri–Kansas City

Robert Hagstrom
Northern Arizona University

Michael Heikkinen
Boise State University

Barbara Hofer
Middlebury College

Brent Igo
Clemson University

Joseph Kush
Duquesne University

Micheline Malow-Iroff
CUNY—Queens College

Pamela Manners
Troy State University

Jeff Miller
California State University, Dominguez Hills

P. Karen Murphy
The Pennsylvania State University–University Park

Joe Nichols
Indiana University-Purdue University–Fort Wayne

Naomi Jeffrey Petersen
Indiana University–South Bend

Nanette Schonleber
Chaminade University of Honolulu

Bruce Smith
Henderson State University

Rosemarie Stallworth-Clark
Georgia Southern University

Jessica Summers
University of Missouri

Phillip Tanner
Northern Arizona University

Alice K. H. Taum
University of Hawaii

Taunya Tinsley
Slippery Rock University of Pennsylvania

Selma Vonderwell
University of Akron

Miriam Witmer
Millersville University

REVIEWERS

Frank D. Adams
Wayne State College

Irene Aiken
University of North Carolina–Pembroke

Funsho Akingbala
St. Edward's University

Joyce Alexander
Indiana University–Bloomington

Padma Anand
Slippery Rock University

Maria Avgerinou
St. Xavier University

Bambi Bailey
Midwestern State University

Jacques Benninga
California State University–Fresno

Shani Beth-Halachmy
National Louis University

Camille Branton
Delta State University

Roger Briscoe
Indiana University of Pennsylvania

Joy Brown
University of North Alabama

Donna Browning
Mississippi State University

Steven Burgess
Southwestern Oklahoma State University

Melva Burke
East Carolina University

Carolyn Burns
Eastern Michigan University

Renee Cambiano
Northeastern State University

Jerrell C. Cassady
Ball State University

Edward Coates
Abilene Christian University

Allen Colebank
Fairmont State University

Chuck Conjar
Hartford Community College

Anne Cook
University of Utah

Philip Cooker
University of Mississippi

Kai Cortina
University of Michigan–Ann Arbor

Krista Cournoyer
Rhode Island College

Andrea Cummings
Georgia State University

Michael G. Curran
Rider University

Gypsy M. Denzine
Northern Arizona University

Robert DiGiulio
Johnson State College

Jerome B. Dusek
Syracuse University

Diane Dusick
University of Southern California

David Estell
Indiana University–Bloomington

Sue Evans
University of Arizona

Daniel Fasko
Bowling Green State University

Harriet Fayne
Otterbein College

Larry Flick
Oregon State University

Terry Fogg
Minnesota State University–Mankato

Michael Gilchrist
Auburn University–Montgomery

Adina Glickman
Stanford University

Jennifer Goeke
Rutgers University

J. Rachel Green
Northeastern State University

Cheryl Greenberg
University of North Carolina–Greensboro

Laurie Hanich
Millersville University

Joyce Hemphill
University of Wisconsin–Madison

K. C. Holder
Eastern Oregon University

David Holliway
Marshall University

Steve Hoover
St. Cloud State University

Sherri Horner
Bowling Green State University

John Hummel
Valdosta State University

Jenefer Husman
Arizona State University–Tempe

Karen Huxtable-Jester
University of Texas–Dallas

Young Hwang
California State University–San Bernardino

Brent Igo
Clemson University

Joyce Juntune
Texas A&M University

Thomas Kampwirth
California State University–Long Beach

Douglas Kauffman
University of Oklahoma–Norman

Frank Keane
Fayetteville State University

Brad Kuhlman
St. Cloud State University

Patricia Lanzon
Henry Ford Community College

Sandra Lloyd
University of Texas–El Paso

Edward Lonky
SUNY–Oswego

Anna Lowe
Loyola University–Chicago

Pamela Manners
Troy State University

Eric Mansfield
Western Illinois University

David Matrone
Central Michigan University

Nancy McBride
University of Nevada–Reno

Catherine McCartney
Bemidji State University

Rita McKenzie
Buena Vista University

Sharon McNeely
Northeastern Illinois University
Alice H. Merz
Indiana University-Purdue University–Fort Wayne
P. Karen Murphy
The Pennsylvania State University–University Park
Vicki Napper
Weber State University
Ruth Nash-Thompson
Edinboro University of Pennsylvania
Judi Neufeld
Lander University
Joe Nichols
Indiana University-Purdue University–Fort Wayne
Cynthia Northington
William Paterson University
Christine Nucci
Florida Memorial College
James O'Kelly
Rutgers University
Ann Pace
University of Missouri–Kansas City
Ann Pardi
SUNY—Buffalo
Helen Patrick
Purdue University–West Lafayette
James Persinger
Emporia State University
Evan Powell
University of Georgia
Judith Puncochar
University of Minnesota
Shelley Randall
Bloomsburg University of Pennsylvania
Melinda Ratchford
Belmont Abbey College
Aaron Richmond
University of Nevada–Reno
Lawrence Rogien
Boise State University
Paul Rooney
University of California–Davis
Jeff Sandoz
University of Louisiana–Lafayette
Gene Schwarting
Fontbonne University
Ray Scolavino
University of Wisconsin–Milwaukee

Mary Seaborn
Indiana Wesleyan University
Marvin Seperson
Nova Southeastern University
Lawrence Sidlik
Arizona State University–West
Audrey Skrupskelis
University of South Carolina–Aiken
Bruce Smith
Henderson State University
Delany Smith
Freed-Hardeman University
Robert Sorrells
Central Washington University
Rayne Sperling
The Pennsylvania State University
Ken Springer
Southern Methodist University
Hillary Steiner
Florida State University
Mary Tallent-Runnels
Texas Tech University
Kellie Tanner
Northern Arizona University
Juli Taylor
University of Wisconsin–Stout
Jennifer L. Titus
Tarleton State University
Y. I. Tomes
Eastern Washington University
Michael Verdi
California State University–San Bernardino
Craig Vivian
Monmouth College
Brenda Walling
East Central University
Jann Weitzel
Lindenwood University
Tony Williams
Marshall University
Sid Womack
Arkansas Tech University
Jamie Wood
Pittsburg State University
Martie Wynne
Loyola University–Chicago
Ming Zhang
Central Michigan University

We would first like to thank all the students and teachers from whom we have learned so much over the years. Their insights and concerns have been important to us as we wrote this text.

As the authors of *Educational Psychology: Reflection for Action*, we would like to acknowledge that we are but part of a remarkable team of individuals responsible for the development of this work. The words are ours, but the enthusiasm and dedication for the project, along with endless hours of editing, rewriting, reviewing, revising, and designing are shared with our colleagues at John Wiley and Sons. This has been a true collaboration from the very beginning, and we want to acknowledge our heartfelt gratitude to our friends at Wiley for their professionalism, encouragement, good humour, expertise, and willingness to nudge when necessary. We could not have asked for a better group of people to work with on this endeavour.

The book began with Brad Hanson, who was dedicated to the notion that a text written by scholars in three key areas of educational psychology would provide a new and exciting perspective. His boundless enthusiasm and energy were contagious, and we agreed to venture forth. At every point, Brad was there for us—with encouragement, ideas, and good cheer. His belief in us as an author team exceeded our own.

Optimism was the spirit throughout the Wiley organization. We received great encouragement and support throughout from Debbie Wiley, Bonnie Lieberman, Joe Heider, Anne Smith, and Barbara Heaney. During the development of the book, Jay O'Callaghan and Christopher Johnson stepped into leadership roles in the organization, and from the perspective of the author team, the transition was seamless. We are indebted to them for going out of their way to ensure that our efforts did not miss a beat.

Great ideas are only ideas unless they are realized. We feel we are truly privileged to have been able to work with Nancy Perry as our development editor. She knows this book better than we do. We could say that she is the "fourth author" of *Educational Psychology: Reflection for Action.* Nancy coordinated our efforts, attended to countless details, kept us on track and on schedule (not a simple task), and never lost sight of the vision for the book. At one of our meetings about halfway through our work, one of us said, "Wouldn't it be great if we could have Nancy with us on all of our work?" This book would not have been completed without her.

Sheralee Connors and Carolyn Smith not only provided meticulous editing of our chapters (any remaining flaws are solely ours), they taught us much about how to write clearly and succinctly. The book is better and we are better writers because of their care with our work and our egos in the editorial process.

We are very proud of the "look and feel" of *Educational Psychology: Reflection for Action.* For that, we thank Harry Nolan and his remarkable design team. Lisa Gee has blended creativity with relentlessness at finding great photographs to bring our abstract ideas to classroom life. Sandra Rigby found just the right style for our illustrations and supervised the artists with care. Valerie Vargas and Caterina Melara have done an excellent job in realizing the layout and design of the book. This text is not only a text, but also a host of supplemental materials. Robert Jordan has been great to work with on the development of these materials.

Since the beginning of our efforts, we have been dedicated to the notion that this book helps the people who teach educational psychology and the people who learn it. That requires not only our own ideas about educational psychology, but those of our colleagues in the field. Jeffrey Rucker, Carl Kulo, Laura McKenna, and Sasha Giacoppo have been exceptionally helpful in bringing the concerns of faculty and students to us and providing with invaluable feedback from the field on our efforts.

One of the truly outstanding features of working with John Wiley and Sons is the commitment to follow through on details that permeates the organization. We have had the good fortune to work with Masha Maizel and Lindsay Lovier and in our day-to-day interactions and found them to be conscientious, professional, and unfailingly responsive. It's been a pleasure to get to know these talented young people who are on their way to great careers in publishing.

We'd like to thank Lisa Smith for her advice, support, and encouragement. Her insights on teaching undergraduates and faith in us as a group are greatly appreciated. Thanks to Leah Smith, Kaitlin Wolf, and Benjamin Smith for providing us with a rich source of anecdotes and experiences to draw upon.

We'd also like to thank our dear friend and colleague, James O'Kelly for his contributions to our work all along the journey. He not only produced the teacher's manual, he contributed scholarly material as well as anecdotes about 5 year olds; he provided verisimilitude and reality checks; and occasionally we called on him for counselling and general wisdom. Jim is a great educator and a great friend.

A wonderful group of teachers helped us in the development of one of the key elements of the book, the RIDE component. Some of these teachers also provided example responses to the scenarios presented at the end of each chapter for students to engage in further practice. Many thanks to Stephanie D'Andrea, Tyler W. Post, Shannon Neville, Michael Lawrence, Gayle Wargo, and Barbara Goldko, Deborah Kris, Megan Schramm-Possinger, and Debra Brock. Nicole diDonato did a great job on helping coordinate material with regard to Praxis and INTASC standards.

We end our acknowledgements where we began our work—smiling, shaking hands, and saying "Thank you" to Brad and Nancy.

Brief Contents

Contents

14 Standardized and Standards-Based Assessments   464

Appendix: Looking at the Praxis II™ Principles of Learning and Teaching Assessment and the INTASC Principles   500

Glossary   510

References   520

Name Index   560

Subject Index   568

How many people ask themselves at 3 P.M. on Monday, "Why in the world am I doing this?" and at 8:30 A.M. on Tuesday they can answer their own question with a smile? Nobody knows the pride I have when I talk to old friends and rather than saying, "I have a job," I say with delight, "I am a teacher!"

—ELEMENTARY SCHOOL TEACHER IN COLORADO

My job is creeping into every aspect of my life. How many people can pick up a box of corn flakes and have it trigger an idea for a lesson plan about government regulation? . . . Teaching stimulates my creative juices like nothing I have ever experienced.

—HIGH SCHOOL TEACHER IN KANSAS

Working with my special education students has been particularly rewarding. Rosie, an autistic child, talks to me now and can say her name. Possibly she could have reached these milestones in another classroom, but it happened in mine. What greater joy can a teacher feel than to witness a child's successes?

—KINDERGARTEN TEACHER IN MINNESOTA

I still cannot get used to how much my heart soars with every student's success, and how a piece of my heart is plucked away when any student slips away.

—MIDDLE SCHOOL TEACHER IN WYOMING

Welcome to the study of educational psychology. As you begin, you probably have a well-informed perspective on teaching and learning. After all, you have spent more than 2,500 days in school, sat through over 18,000 classes, and closely observed about 100 different teachers. So you have probably learned a thing or two. Most of what you have learned, however, has been from the perspective of a student. In a few short years, the roles will reverse, and you will step into the role of the teacher.

As you follow in the footsteps of the first-year teachers quoted here (from DePaul, 1998), consider Ms. Newby, a first-year teacher. Like Ms. Newby, you will understandably be nervous. Still, the show must go on. If you were to offer her some advice, what might you recommend?

Introducing Educational Psychology and Reflective Practice

R I D E Reflection for Action

Ms. Newby is nervous. She wants to leave her nervousness behind and become a confident expert. She wonders what she can do to empower herself even before her first day in the classroom. What can Ms. Newby do? How can she ready herself for opening day?

Guiding Questions

- What is educational psychology?
- What primary concerns do beginning teachers have?
- What is reflective teaching, and how is it different from technical teaching?
- How can teachers recognize, adapt, and respond to diverse learners and students with special needs?
- How do educational psychologists use theory and research?

CHAPTER OVERVIEW

Educational psychology is the scientific study of psychology in education. Its goals are to understand learners and to promote their learning. In pursuing these two goals, educational psychology helps teachers like Ms. Newby prepare themselves for that first year in the classroom. We begin the chapter by explaining how a focus on these two goals helps teachers better understand all aspects of the teaching-learning process. In so doing, we identify the most pressing concerns that beginning teachers have, and illustrate how beginning teachers quiet these concerns by developing teaching efficacy, teaching expertise, and reflective teaching. We then address the idea that all students are different by introducing and discussing the issues of student diversity and students with special needs. In the final part of the chapter, we address the role of theory and research in educational psychology.

Educational Psychology
- A Focus on Learning
- Teaching Expertise

Concerns of Beginning Teachers
- Teaching Efficacy
- Metaphors for Teaching
- The Payoff: Deeply Enjoying Your Work

Reflective Teaching
- Reflection for Action
- A Model of Reflective Teaching: RIDE

Student Diversity and Students with Special Needs
- Diverse Learners
- Students with Special Needs

How Educational Psychologists Use Theories and Research
- What Is a Theory?
- Research Methods
- Critical Thinking

Educational Psychology

All teachers go through classroom episodes that leave them wondering whether they really know their students as well as they think they do. In this book, you have an ally in the endeavor to understand students as learners. This book is about how people learn and how teachers can help them learn. It seeks to deepen your understanding of all aspects of the teaching-learning process and, in doing so, improve your capacity to help others learn. To accomplish these goals, this book pursues two objectives.

1. To understand learners. As you proceed through this book, you will gain knowledge about learners and how they learn.

2. To foster learning. This book seeks to enhance your understanding of the teaching-learning situation and, hence, your capacity to help others learn.

Educational psychology came into existence as a field of study through the writings of early psychologists, including E. L. Thorndike (1903, 1910, 1913), William James (1912), and others. These pioneers showed how psychological theories, such as the early learning theories, applied to educational settings. The field has grown dramatically in its 100 years, but **educational psychology** remains "the scientific study of psychology in education" (Wittrock, 1992, p. 129).

Contemporary educational psychology has a twofold mission: Enhance theoretical knowledge and improve educational practice. Theoretical knowledge revolves around understanding basic psychological processes, such as how learning occurs, where aggression comes from, and what the nature of motivation is. To enhance their theoretical knowledge, educational psychologists ask many Why? questions, such as:

educational psychology The scientific study of psychology in education.

- Why do readers forget so much of what they read?
- Why are some adolescents unusually aggressive?
- Why are students so eagerly engaged in a learning activity one day yet so unengaged the next?

Once educational psychologists understand the educational phenomenon with which they work, they turn to the practical mission of trying to improve educational practice. Improving practice revolves around using theoretical knowledge to enhance practically any aspect of the teaching-learning process. To improve educational practice, educational psychologists ask many How? questions, such as:

- How can teachers improve students' social skills?
- How can schools prevent teenagers from dropping out?
- How can teachers improve non–English-speaking students' reading abilities?

To gain satisfactory answers to these questions, educational psychologists apply scientific research methods to collect the data they need to build their theoretical knowledge and to offer evidence-based answers to improve the teaching-learning process. We discuss these research methods in the final part of this chapter. Also, we offer an appendix in this book to help readers see how our discussion of educational psychology reflects PRAXIS™ content and INTASC principles.

A Focus on Learning

The focus of educational psychology is learning (Renninger, 1996). **Learning** is a relatively permanent change in behavior or knowledge as a result of experience. This focus might seem obvious, but it is actually rather complicated because learning depends on so many factors.

Learning depends on the quality of instruction. It depends on students' motivation and how engaged they are when trying to learn. It also depends on students' developmental readiness to learn. Learning also occurs better under some conditions than it does under other conditions. Once learning occurs, how do teachers know that students have learned—how can teachers assess learning? Assessment informs the learning process and affirms that learning has taken place. Addressing these issues not only requires a sophisticated understanding of learning itself, but it further requires a sophisticated understanding of the multitude of factors that affect learning, including teaching, development, motivation, educational environments, and assessment. This book includes a separate chapter on all of these topics. Overall, the payoff for one's investment of effort in the study of educational psychology is a better understanding of learning and how to promote it (Shuell, 1996).

> learning   A relatively permanent change in behavior or knowledge as a result of experience.

Teaching Expertise

Teaching is one person's interpersonal effort to help others acquire knowledge, develop skill, and realize their potential. To accomplish these goals, teachers explain, demonstrate, listen, guide, support, assess, offer feedback, and otherwise structure a learning opportunity to help learners advance from a state of having less knowledge, skill, and potential to a state of enhanced knowledge, skill, and potential. How well this transformation occurs depends in part on the teacher's expertise. Most beginning teachers are all too conscious of their lack of expertise. Their novice status is just one of the things that makes the first years of teaching challenging. Educational psychologists have studied both beginning teachers and expert veterans to determine how beginners become experts.

> teaching   The interpersonal effort to help learners acquire knowledge, develop skill, and realize their potential.

As they begin their teaching careers, preservice teachers routinely emulate the effective teachers they observed as students (Calderhead & Robson, 1991). Thus, an admired role model is typically the starting point for a beginning teacher's idea about what constitutes good teaching. With actual classroom experience, however, preservice teachers' ideas evolve. Most of the time, beginning teachers become experts by advancing through the following four phases (Kagan, 1992):

1. Decreased focus on self-as-teacher; increased focus on the needs of learners
2. Enhanced knowledge about learners
3. Automation of classroom routines and procedures
4. Growth in problem-solving skills

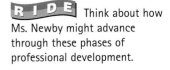 Think about how Ms. Newby might advance through these phases of professional development.

For an illustration of how these phases of professional growth unfold in the lives of most teachers, consider what Ms. Newby's experiences are likely to be. In her first year of teaching, she will constantly ask herself the question, Am I a good teacher? She will worry about what her colleagues, her students, her departmental chair, her principal, and students' parents think of her. In her second year, her focus will probably shift toward her students and what they need. She will ask herself whether her students are learning and how she can help them learn further. During this same year, she will probably discover ways to transform the once-frequent classroom crises into rare events. By her third year of teaching, she will not even have to think about how to cope with classroom crises because her solutions to problems such as dealing with disruptive behavior and making transitions will become fairly automatic. Instead of just reacting to the various kinds of problems that arise during instruction, Ms. Newby will begin to anticipate them, and she will be able to call on a large repertoire of tried-and-true solutions to solve them, often before they have a chance to occur.

These four areas of professional growth highlight two key differences between beginning and expert teachers. First, as reflected in the first two steps, novice teachers focus strongly on themselves as teachers, whereas expert teachers focus strongly on their students as learners. Second, as reflected in the last two steps, novice teachers often possess an oversimplified picture of what constitutes classroom practice. This view of teaching as a one-size-fits-all approach to instruction is typically anchored by a concern with solving problems associated with classroom management. Experts, on the other hand, have acquired a wealth of classroom experience and professional reflection that allows them to automate classroom routines and procedures. They manage classroom situations in ways that are context- and student-specific—the opposite of a one-size-fits-all approach. In a sense, experts operate on automatic pilot. They can retrieve the knowledge and strategies they need in a given teaching situation with minimal cognitive effort. The more they are able to do so, the more time and energy they have available for developing the rich problem-solving skills they need to meet the individual needs of their students (Berliner, 1986).

In addition, expert teachers distinguish themselves in another important way—by their vast knowledge. Here is a sampling of what expert teachers know (Shulman, 1987):

- Broad and deep subject matter knowledge (English literature, algebra)
- How-to instructional strategies (how to capture students' interest)
- Knowledge about learning environments (how to organize students for group work)
- Knowledge about educational materials (curriculum, testing materials)

Concerns of Beginning Teachers

Beginning to teach is exciting and rewarding. Finally, you have the opportunity to put your ideas and plans into practice. Now you have a chance to influence students. But, it is also not easy being a beginning teacher. To illustrate the point, here are the remembrances of Jim, a first-year fifth-grade teacher:

> I came up here thinking, "Elementary education, what an easy degree." I worked with kids all the time, so I wondered what the big mystery was about it. (Bondy & McKenzie, 1999, p. 136)[1]

Two weeks into his teaching career, Jim noticed some unexpected problems:

> I am constantly, constantly having to discipline the entire class. . . . It's a constant battle to maintain order, and it's exhausting. The energy I use in management takes away from the energy I have for curriculum. (p. 139)

The problems grew to include concerns about motivation or lack thereof:

> I got really frustrated at their lack of passion. So I told them, "You know, it really frustrates me to stand up here and see you just slouching in your seats looking at me, half of you not really paying

[1] Quotations from Bondy E., McKenzie J. "Resilience Building and Social Reconstructionist Teaching: A First-Year Teacher's Story," *Elementary School Journal* 100:2 (1999): pp. 136, 139, 140. Published by the University of Chicago Press.

TABLE 1.1

Beginning Teachers' Top Concerns

Area of concern	Examples
Classroom discipline	• How can I best cope with students' misbehavior? • What can I do to prevent acts of aggression before they occur? • Should I set classroom rules at the beginning of the year, or should the students make their own rules?
Motivating students	• How can I engage students more during learning activities? • What is intrinsic motivation, and can I trust it to promote learning? • How should I react to students who protest with "I can't"?
Special needs	• What are the benefits and costs of an inclusive classroom? • How can I best teach slow learners? • Will I be able to accommodate my instruction to students with special needs?
Assessment and grading	• What criteria should I use to develop a grading system? • Should I use portfolios to assess students' work? • How can I assess students' progress?

attention. . . . The things we talk about in here give you the knowledge, but you've got to care, you've got to care about something." (p. 139)

Unfortunately, the problems did not stop there. One month into his career, Jim felt near despair about his students' disrespectful comments to one another:

The thing that really distracts me is the lack of respect they show, not just to me, but to each other. (p. 140)

Beginning teachers face a host of doubts and uncertainties, as do their students. To appreciate which problems beginning teachers consider to be most pressing, researchers asked elementary and secondary school teachers from nine different countries to report the most serious concerns they encountered during their first three years of teaching (Veenman, 1984). Two dozen concerns emerged, but the most attention-getting problems were classroom discipline, motivating students, dealing with special needs, and assessing students' work. Concrete examples of these concerns appear in Table 1.1.

Voicing beginning teachers' concerns is important because teaching success, teaching satisfaction, and professional development are all tied to finding ways to solve these problems (Caprara et al., 2003). Beginning teachers often question their adequacy as teachers. They worry about their professional survival, and they want desperately to be evaluated positively by the principal, their students, parents, and fellow teachers (Bullough, 1989). Finding solutions to the problems listed in Table 1.1 is one way of developing oneself as a teacher. In fact, professional development can be viewed as the successful progression from first being overwhelmed by these problems to later being able to solve them consistently and effectively (Borich, 1988; Fuller & Brown, 1975).

Another way to appreciate the concerns first-year teachers have is to ask them to keep a daily journal. In such a journal, teachers write about their goals, experiences, frustrations, and points of progress. Table 1.2 offers the themes voiced by one elementary-grade teacher's daily reflections: her role as a teacher, beliefs about learning, students' growth trajectories, assessment issues, motivation, and the school realities that limit her capacity to be successful.

What Does This Mean to Me?
Do you have any of the same concerns of beginning teachers listed in Table 1.1?

 Could a sense of uncertainty as to how she will solve teaching problems such as those in Table 1.1 explain why Ms. Newby feels nervous?

How Can I Use This?
One way to track your professional progress as a teacher is to reflect on how well you have found ways to solve these concerns.

TABLE 1.2

Journal Themes from a First-Year Middle School Math Teacher

1. My role as a teacher	I need to seek knowledge myself.
	I always need to ask—why? why? why?
2. What learning is	To be useful, knowledge must be owned by the student, rather than by the teacher. Students learn when they combine what they already know with their classroom experiences.
3. Developmental growth	Students grow as learners. Students grow as human beings.
4. Questions of assessment	Do students' questions reflect their knowledge and quality of learning? If so, should I grade students on the number and type of questions they ask?
5. Motivation	Students should rely on intrinsic, not extrinsic, motivation.
	Students want a sense of community in the classroom.
6. My school reality	I have six classes a day. I teach 30 students per class. How can I reach 180 different students each day?

Teaching Efficacy

Too often, the first year of teaching is a dramatic one. Beginning teachers feel considerable anxiety and doubt over their ability to cope with the teaching situation. In fact, so potentially overwhelming is the transition from teacher education to full-time responsibility that it is sometimes referred to as *the reality shock.* To counter these feelings of anxiety and doubt, beginning teachers need to develop a sense of coping confidence, or teaching efficacy. **Teaching efficacy** is a teacher's judgment of his or her capacity to cope with the teaching situation in ways that bring about desired outcomes (Tschannen-Moran & Hoy, 2001).

Beginning teachers generally have lower teaching efficacy than do veteran teachers (Hoy & Woolfolk, 1993). This is partly true because beginning teachers realize the gap between thinking you can cope well with teaching situations and actually coping well (i.e., teaching efficacy vs. teaching expertise). It is fairly easy to perceive that one has both high efficacy and high expertise when classroom situations are simple and routine. The disparity between perceived efficacy and actual expertise becomes apparent when things go wrong (Bandura, 1997). It is during times of unexpected difficulties and setbacks that teachers become most aware of their capacity to cope with all aspects of the teaching situation. For a sampling of which classroom situations most commonly test teachers' sense of efficacy, Table 1.3 lists items from a Teaching Efficacy questionnaire.

As shown in the table, three teaching domains define most of what constitutes the emotional struggle between feeling efficacious and feeling overwhelmed: classroom management, student engagement, and instructional strategies. Notice how well these three teaching situations correspond to the four concerns voiced by beginning teachers in Table 1.1. Teachers need a sense of efficacy—a sense of *I can do this*—for classroom management to solve problems of classroom discipline. They need a sense of efficacy for student engagement to solve problems of student motivation. They need a sense of efficacy for instructional strategies to solve a range of instructional concerns, including how to assess students' learning and how to adjust their lessons to deal with students' individual differences and special needs.

Striving to develop a sense of teaching efficacy is well worth the effort. Compared with teachers with relatively low efficacy, teachers with high efficacy are more enthusiastic during teaching (Allinder, 1994; Guskey, 1984), more committed to teaching (Coladarci, 1992; Evans & Tribble,

teaching efficacy A teacher's judgment of, or confidence in, his or her capacity to cope with the teaching situation in ways that bring about desired outcomes.

Chapter Reference
Chapter 9 presents an extended discussion of teaching efficacy.

Beginning teachers worry most about how they will solve day-to-day problems associated with discipline, motivation, assessment, and students' special needs. (Media Bakery)

TABLE 1.3

Questionnaire Items to Assess Teaching Efficacy

Factor 1: Efficacy for classroom management

1. How much can you do to control disruptive behavior in the classroom?
2. How much can you do to get children to follow classroom rules?
3. How much can you do to calm a student who is disruptive or noisy?
4. How well can you keep a few problem students from ruining an entire lesson?

Factor 2: Efficacy for student engagement

5. How much can you do to get students to believe they can do well in schoolwork?
6. How much can you do to help your students value learning?
7. How much can you do to motivate students who show low interest in schoolwork?
8. How much can you do to foster student creativity?

Factor 3: Efficacy for instructional strategies

9. To what extent can you use a variety of assessment strategies?
10. To what extent can you provide an alternative explanation or example when students are confused?
11. To what extent can you craft good questions for your students?
12. How much can you do to adjust your lessons to the proper level for individual students?

Note. The above items are from the Ohio State Teacher Efficacy Scale (OSTES).

Source: Reprinted from *Teaching and Teacher Education,* Vol. 17, Tschannen-Moran, M., & Hoy, A. W., "Teacher efficacy: Capturing an elusive construct," 783–805, Copyright 2001, with permission from Elsevier.

1986), and more likely to stay in the profession (Glickman & Tamashiro, 1982). Also, during instruction, teachers with high efficacy invest greater effort and spend more time planning and organizing instructional activities (Allinder, 1994). When things go wrong, they persist in the face of setbacks rather than give up. They are also less critical of the errors their students make (Ashton & Webb, 1986). For all these reasons, this is the sort of teacher you want to become, because teachers with high efficacy are better able to foster positive outcomes for their students, including gains in students' thinking (Anderson, Greene, & Loewen, 1988), motivation (Midgley, Feldlaufer, & Eccles, 1989), and achievement (Ashton & Webb, 1986; Ross, 1992).

Metaphors for Teaching

Visualize yourself in the role of a full-time teacher, and ask yourself how you would complete the following phrase: "The teacher as a _____." In the blank, write a metaphor to capture the spirit of what you would like to accomplish in the classroom. Some possible responses might include *entertainer, coach, lion tamer, choreographer, party host, circus master, traffic cop, ship captain,* and *air traffic controller* (Bullough, 1991; Carter, 1990; Marchant, 1992). For purposes of illustration, Table 1.4 lists the metaphors generated by one group of high school teachers.

Generating metaphors for teaching can help teachers improve their classroom practice in three ways (Tobin, 1990). First, metaphors facilitate reflection. By generating metaphors, teachers gain greater personal understanding of how they view themselves as teachers (Berliner, 1990; Bullough, 1991). As a case in point, elementary school teachers often generate a metaphor that emphasizes the caring and nurturing aspects of teaching (e.g., the teacher as gardener or facilitator.). Secondary school teachers often generate a metaphor that emphasizes the dispensing of knowledge (e.g., the teacher as information giver or ship captain.).

Second, a metaphor can serve as a standard by which teachers can evaluate their current practice. By treating teaching metaphors as standards, they can identify points of conflict that might exist between their teaching ideals and their actual practice. For instance, one beginning teacher adopted the metaphor of *gardener,* which he explained as:

> I see my role as teacher being most importantly one of providing the very best climate in the classroom for the maximum growth and development of each student . . . who needs more or less light, more or less water, or who needs to have weeds pulled up from around them (Bullough, 1991, p. 45).

What Does This Mean to Me?
What metaphor for a teacher would you use?

TABLE 1.4
Teaching Metaphors for Eight High School Teachers

Teacher	Years experience	Subject matter taught	Metaphor for "The teacher as _____"
Amy	0	Social studies	Motivator
Betsy	4	History, psychology	Chameleon
Cal	5	Geography, history	Cowboy
Don	5	Geography, history	Boat captain
Evelyn	7	Spanish	Ringmaster
Francine	7	Journalism	Gardener
Gregory	9	Biology	Team leader
Howard	9	Economics	Coach

Source: Reprinted from *Teaching and Teacher Education,* Vol. 12, Stofflett, R. T., "Metaphor development by secondary teachers enrolled in graduate teacher education," 577–589, Copyright 1996, with permission from Elsevier.

During his first year of teaching, this teacher decided to audiotape several class periods. After listening to the tapes, the *gardener* felt deeply disturbed. What he heard was not the nurturing gardener he conceptualized himself to be but, instead, a teacher who engaged in lengthy monologues that imposed his own agenda on a group of passive listeners. Rather than living up to the standard of a gardener, his teaching reflected curricular demands for content coverage, the need to achieve high standardized test scores, and the accepted norms at his school about what constitutes effective teaching (teaching as telling). By reflecting on the metaphors they hold, teachers may realize, as this teacher did, that their metaphors are inadequate to help them cope effectively with their actual classroom conditions.

> **How Can I Use This?**
>
> Generating a metaphor of your own can give you an ideal to strive for, a standard to judge your current way of teaching, and an opportunity to reflect on yourself as a teacher.

Third, generating a new metaphor can help initiate a desired change in one's current way of teaching. If one's current way of teaching is personally unsatisfactory, one can generate a potentially more appropriate metaphor that represents an ideal goal to strive for. For instance, a teacher might seek to change an adversarial *traffic cop* metaphor to a more collaborative *protector of the learning environment* (Marshall, 1990). In the example provided earlier, the *gardener* developed a second, complementary metaphor. He began to think of teaching as a conversation and himself as a *dialogist*. In this way, a well-chosen metaphor can serve as a conceptual springboard from which to expand and to improve one's way of teaching (Tobin, 1990).

The Payoff: Deeply Enjoying Your Work

Is all this work to anticipate beginning teachers' concerns, develop high teaching efficacy, and generate teaching metaphors worth it? If so, what is the payoff? Experienced teachers report that their efforts to develop expertise are unambiguously worth the sweat and tears. As one teacher explains, effective teaching can be highly rewarding (Brunetti, 2001, p. 60):

> . . . [seeing] one of these kids [from] two years ago and watching him graduate. These kids were going nowhere; they weren't even going to school. We couldn't get 'em to spend two days in class together in a row, and now they're graduating. Any they're graduating because of me. That's the most rewarding of all.

When done well, teaching can be highly rewarding—not only for students but for teachers as well (Brunetti, 2001, p. 56):

> I just love what I do. It's fun. I was out for long periods of time because I had serious eye problems . . . drove the doctors crazy because I wanted the operation right away so I could get back to the classroom.

Reflective Teaching

Teaching is a profession filled with uncertainties. Fortunately, some teaching situations can be approached with rather routine knowledge. Given a familiar set of circumstances, teachers can use their experience and knowledge to provide effective instruction. For instance, given a student's misbehavior, the teacher might implement a time-out procedure. This represents **technical teaching** because a familiar problem surfaced, and the teacher implemented

technical teaching Relying on routine knowledge and tried-and-true solutions to manage classroom problems.

a tried-and-true solution. In many teaching situations, however, surprises surface. For instance, the teacher might be surprised if the time-out increased, rather than decreased, the student's subsequent misbehavior. Classroom surprises force teachers to examine the assumptions they hold about their strategies.

A teaching surprise leads the teacher to reflect on what is happening, why it is happening, and what adjustments need to be made (Schon, 1987). When instruction does not go off as planned, the teacher wonders, What is happening here? How did I get into this mess? What went wrong? How can I get the class back on track? These are reflective questions. Unlike instances of technical teaching, these classroom situations do not lend themselves to tried-and-true solutions. Instead, **reflective teaching** involves generating conjectures to explain a surprising event in the teaching situation, then gathering the information needed to make a decision about what would constitute the most effective course of action.

Figure 1.1 illustrates the two broad ways that teachers translate what they know about teaching into classroom solutions. In any given teaching situation, teachers use their experience and knowledge about the teaching situation to provide students with a constructive learning experience. As they help students learn, teachers encounter predictable classroom events that call for routinely scripted action—that is, for technical teaching—and they encounter surprising classroom events that call for conjectures—that is, reflective teaching (Dewey, 1933; Schon, 1983, 1987; Zeichner & Liston, 1996).

Throughout this book, many instances of technical teaching will be offered. For instance, Chapter 5 offers a number of tried-and-true instructional strategies to motivate students during instruction. Chapter 12 offers a number of tried-and-true instructional strategies to implement cooperative learning. This is very helpful information to the teacher, because teaching is a profession that plays itself out in the preparation and implementation of instructional strategies. However, teaching is also a profession in which events do not always unfold as planned, and teachers find themselves needing to revise and adjust their instructional strategies. In appreciation of the need for reflective teaching, the next section highlights the role that reflection plays in improving the teacher's day-to-day decision making in the classroom. The "Uncommon Sense" box on this page explains how textbooks further assist the teacher's day-to-day decision making in the classroom.

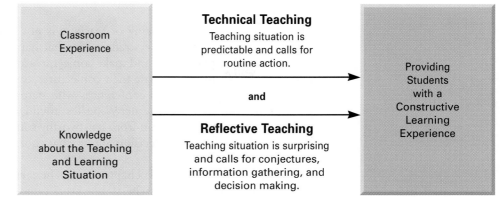

Figure 1.1. Two Modes of Teaching: Technical and Reflective

reflective teaching   Generating conjectures to explain a surprising event in the teaching situation, then gathering the information needed to make a decision about what would constitute the most effective course of action to pursue.

Uncommon Sense

You Learn to Teach by Teaching—Or Do You?

As preservice teachers become beginning teachers and beginning teachers become veterans, most say that they learned how to teach by teaching and by watching others teach (Calderhead, 1989; Zahorik, 1987). Few say that they learned how to teach by reading a textbook (Hall & Loucks, 1982). In addition, teaching is a profession with an absence of absolute truths (Broudy, 1980; Floden & Clark, 1988). In a field that lacks universal truths, textbooks cannot provide all the answers. So why read a textbook such as *Educational Psychology*?

When your turn comes to step into the classroom, your instructional practice will express your underlying beliefs. Teacher beliefs are a tacit collection of assumptions about students, learning, classrooms, and the subject matter to be taught (Kagan, 1992). Textbooks help teachers develop these beliefs. Reading a textbook can also be instrumental in developing your classroom skill. Like the surgeon who amasses large amounts of knowledge before performing his or her first operation, teachers need to explore, develop, examine, and refine a knowledge-based foundation for teaching. In doing so, textbooks can help teachers anticipate classroom problems, understand why they occur, generate possible solutions, and forecast which solutions are likely to be successful and which other solutions are likely to be unsuccessful (Floden & Clark, 1988).

Reflection for Action

The day-to-day decision making of teachers is not unlike that of researchers. From their classroom experiences, teachers reflect on what happened and why it happened; they ask questions, seek explanations, and make conjectures and educated guesses about what is happening and why. To substantiate their conjectures, teachers gather information. They talk to peers, observe mentors, hold conferences with parents, read research reports, subscribe to professional journals, surf Internet Web sites, attend workshops, review videotapes and CDs, and generally seek information from trustworthy sources. With information in hand, teachers can make an informed decision about what course of action is most likely to constitute effective practice.

As we will see later in this chapter, researchers engage in essentially the same reflective process. Teachers and researchers, however, typically begin their reflective practice at different starting points, as illustrated in Figure 1.2. Teachers typically start with a classroom observation, such as noticing how high-stakes tests are affecting their students' anxiety. They reflect by asking, What am I seeing here? What is this anxiety an example of? From this reflection, conjectures arise: Perhaps this is an example of putting too much pressure on students, or perhaps it is an example of insufficient preparation. Researchers typically start with a theory, such as a general theory of anxiety. They reflect by asking, Why does this event occur? What does the theory say is the cause of anxiety? From this reflection, hypotheses arise: Perhaps anxiety is caused by time pressure; perhaps it arises from individual differences within students' personalities. Aside from these different starting points, however, teachers and researchers think in similar ways. As shown in the figure, once begun, reflection produces the fruits of information gathering, decision making, and evaluation (Crocker, 1981).

> **What Does This Mean to Me?**
> Is teaching too demanding to permit teachers to be reflective about their work?

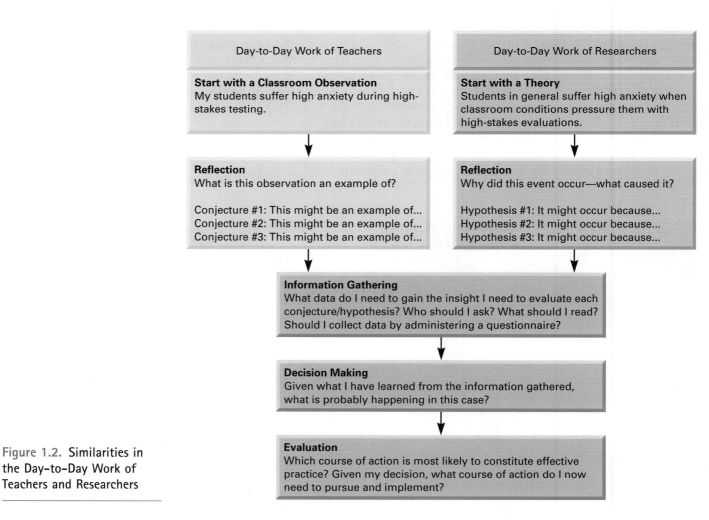

Figure 1.2. Similarities in the Day-to-Day Work of Teachers and Researchers

A Model of Reflective Teaching: RIDE

This book will help preservice teachers become more reflective practitioners. The beginning of each chapter will present a vignette—a brief scenario of a classroom problem—that requires reflective teaching. In this chapter, the opening vignette concerned Ms. Newby and her sense of unease about teaching. In each vignette to come, you will be asked to reflect on the event by using the key concepts described in the chapter. Throughout the reading of the chapter, your task is to propose conjectures as to what the event is an example or illustration of. At the end of each chapter, we present an analysis of the event under the heading of *Reflection for Action*. *Action* is teaching, and *reflection* is thinking what is happening and why it is happening. The goal will be to generate at least three conjectures, then identify the information you need to collect to make a decision about which conjecture best explains and solves the problem.

The model of reflective teaching that we propose is similar to the general problem-solving process that takes place in formal research. As shown in Figure 1.3, the model consists of four sequential components: reflection (R); information gathering (I); decision making (D); and evaluation (E). To illustrate the RIDE model, consider once again the situation depicted in the chapter's opening vignette:

Ms. Newby is nervous. She wants to leave her nervousness behind and become a confident expert. She wonders what she can do to empower herself even before her first day in the classroom. What can Ms. Newby do? How can she ready herself for opening day?

The first objective of reflective teaching is to identify what the event illustrates; that is, what is Ms. Newby's nervousness a manifestation of? Using the concepts highlighted in this chapter, at least three possibilities emerge to help answer the following question.

Appendix
Reflective Teaching
The RIDE scenarios throughout the text are intended to assist you in becoming a reflective practitioner (*PRAXIS*™, IV. A3; *INTASC*, Principle 9).

The Event	Reflection R	Information Gathering I	Decision Making D	Evaluation E
Ms. Newby is nervous. She wants to become a confident expert. What can she do?	**Conjecture #1** Perhaps Ms. Newby's nervousness is a manifestation of low teaching efficacy.	She could complete a questionnaire like the one in Table 1.3 to assess her level of efficacy in terms of her capacity to cope with difficult classroom situations.	If her questionnaire responses show low teaching efficacy, then the problem might be her fear of being overwhelmed by difficult teaching situations.	How close is the relationship between her nervousness and her score on the measure of teaching efficacy? Do gains in efficacy correspond closely with drops in nervousness?
	Conjecture #2 Perhaps Ms. Newby's nervousness is a manifestation of her lack of a potent teaching metaphor to embrace.	She could interview a couple of master teachers to ask what teaching metaphors they use. She could then contrast these metaphors with her own.	If her conversations with the two master teachers provide her with empowering metaphors, then the problem might be the lack of a potent teaching metaphor.	How close is the relationship between her nervousness and her lack of a potent teaching metaphor? Does the embracing of an empowering metaphor correspond closely with a drop in nervousness?
	Conjecture #3 Perhaps Ms. Newby's nervousness is a manifestation of being ill prepared in terms of her knowledge about teaching.	She could read articles from her favorite professional journal to gain knowledge, insights, and instructional strategies to use.	If the information in the professional journal is able to enhance her knowledge, insight, and instructional strategies, then the problem might be her lack of preparedness.	How close is the relationship between her nervousness and her lack of knowledge of the teaching situation? Do gains in knowledge correspond closely with drops in nervousness?

Figure 1.3. RIDE Model

What Theoretical/Conceptual Information Might Assist in Interpreting and Remedying this Situation? Consider the following:

Teaching Efficacy

Ms. Newby might be nervous because she has low teaching efficacy. It might be the case that because Ms. Newby has low teaching efficacy, she, in turn, is nervous about teaching.

Teaching Metaphor

Ms. Newby might lack a potent metaphor to guide her classroom activity. To empower herself and overcome her nagging nervousness, she might embrace a potent metaphor to place her into a more empowering role.

Teaching Knowledge

Ms. Newby might be nervous because she does not yet feel sufficiently prepared for her first day in the classroom. Her nervousness might be a signal that she currently possesses insufficient knowledge about learners, teaching, and the teaching-learning situation in general.

Reflection Reflection is the first and most important step in the RIDE model. A surprising classroom event or problem has occurred, and the teacher needs to interpret and understand what has happened and why it has happened. As described above and as presented in Figure 1.3, three conjectures might emerge: low teaching efficacy; lack of a potent teaching metaphor; and lack of knowledge about the teaching situation. Generating these conjectures is the most crucial aspect of the RIDE model, because if these conjectures are intellectual dead ends, the teacher will not be able to cope effectively. In a real sense, the purpose of each chapter in this book is to help teachers generate highly plausible conjectures to classroom problems.

Appendix
Sources of Information

Many sources of helpful information exist to assist your decision-making in the classroom (*PRAXIS™*, IV. A1; *INTASC*, Principle 9).

Information Gathering In this step, one gathers information to help determine which of the three conjectures is most plausible. Teachers have access to a wide range of information sources, including colleagues, mentors, master teachers, departmental chairs, principals, parents, one's own students, research reports, professional journals, Web sites, inspirational films, instructional videotapes and CDs, workshops, past experiences, and theories such as those featured throughout this book. As one gathers information, one also needs to consider what information he or she can trust (e.g., Is my colleague a good source of information for this particular teaching situation? Is the theory about this phenomenon based on solid evidence?). In the example presented in Figure 1.3, we offer three possible sources of information: (a) completing a questionnaire such as the one featured in Table 1.3; (b) conversing with master teachers to ask what metaphors they embrace; and (c) reading through a favorite journal to gain knowledge and insight about teaching.

Chapter Reference
Chapter 5 presents the mastery-modeling program to enhance one's sense of efficacy.

Decision Making During this step, the goal is to decide how best to understand and interpret the teaching situation one faces, given the available information. In a classroom context, a teacher will never have access to all the information necessary to make a definitive decision. Any decision will always be tentatively prudent and may need to be revisited at a later date. In the example presented in Figure 1.3, the teacher would (a) examine the questionnaire responses to score his or her existing level of teaching efficacy, (b) weigh the advantages and sense of personal fit of the recommended teaching metaphors, and (c) consider the practical value of the knowledge and insights offered in the pages of the professional journal.

Evaluation The questionnaire responses, conversations with master teachers, and journal readings will yield important information. With this information in hand, Ms. Newby is in a position to evaluate the strength of the relationship between these three sources of information and her nervousness about teaching. If her score on the teaching efficacy measure is low, she may sense a close relationship between low efficacy and high nervousness. If she feels inspired and empowered by a potent metaphor, she may sense her nervousness slip away and be replaced by a greater sense of confidence or leadership. If the journal information provides satisfying answers to her questions of what she might do during class, the root of the nervousness is probably a lack of knowledge. Frequently, the information collected points the teacher in the right direction.

Student Diversity and Students with Special Needs

Each year, schools become more diverse. Today, about 40% of the 48 million students enrolled in public schools in the United States are minority students. Seventeen percent of public school students live in poverty. Eight percent speak little or no English in the home. Approximately 13% of these 48 million students have special needs that interfere with their ability to learn. These percentages vary from state to state; Table 1.5 provides the statistics for each state.

TABLE 1.5

State-by-State Information Summarizing Student Diversity and Special Needs

State	Minority students %	Children in poverty %	Non–English-speaking students %	Students with special needs %
Alabama	40	22	1	13
Alaska	40	11	15	13
Arizona	49	19	16	11
Arkansas	29	22	3	13
California	65	20	25	11
Colorado	33	12	10	10
Connecticut	31	10	4	13
Delaware	40	14	3	14
District of Columbia	95	29	11	17
Florida	48	19	8	15
Georgia	46	18	4	12
Hawaii	80	15	9	12
Idaho	15	17	7	12
Illinois	41	15	7	14
Indiana	17	12	4	16
Iowa	10	11	3	15
Kansas	22	14	4	13
Kentucky	12	20	1	15
Louisiana	51	26	2	13
Maine	4	15	1	16
Maryland	48	10	4	13
Massachusetts	24	15	5	15
Michigan	27	14	3	13
Minnesota	18	9	6	13
Mississippi	53	26	1	13
Missouri	21	17	1	15
Montana	14	20	5	13
Nebraska	18	13	4	16
Nevada	46	15	11	11
New Hampshire	5	8	2	14
New Jersey	41	11	4	16
New Mexico	66	26	21	20

(continued)

TABLE 1.5

State-by-State Information Summarizing Student Diversity and Special Needs *(continued)*

State	Minority students %	Children in poverty %	Non–English–speaking students %	Students with special needs %
New York	45	21	7	15
North Carolina	40	17	4	14
North Dakota	11	16	n/a	13
Ohio	20	16	1	12
Oklahoma	36	20	6	14
Oregon	21	16	8	13
Pennsylvania	22	14	n/a	13
Rhode Island	27	16	6	20
South Carolina	45	19	1	15
South Dakota	14	15	3	13
Tennessee	28	18	n/a	16
Texas	59	22	15	12
Utah	15	10	9	11
Vermont	4	12	1	13
Virginia	37	12	4	14
Washington	27	13	n/a	12
West Virginia	6	24	1	18
Wisconsin	20	11	3	14
Wyoming	13	18	3	13

Note. n/a, not available; Minority students represents all PreK-to-12 students not classified as White, non-Hispanic; Children in poverty represents all PreK-to-12 students living in families with annual incomes under $16,895; non-English-speaking students represents all PreK-to-12 students who receive English Language Learner (ELL) services; students with special needs represents all PreK-to-12 students who have individualized education programs (IEPs).

Source: Aggregated data from the Digest of Education Statistics Tables and Figures 2003, National Center for Education, U.S. Department of Education, available at *http://nces.ed.gov//programs/digest/index.asp.*

Given the diversity and special needs in schools, we recognize that all students are different. The recent trends in state and national policy (e.g., No Child Left Behind), however, are to establish academic goals and standards that apply equally to all students and to teach students with special needs in their regular classrooms. Given these trends, the approach taken in this book is to integrate issues of diversity and special needs within the content of each chapter. What this book does not offer is a separate chapter on diversity and special needs. By embedding discussions of diversity and special needs within the content of each chapter, our goal is to help preservice teachers develop the awareness and skills they will need to recognize, adapt, and respond to the diverse learners and students with special needs they will be teaching.

Chapter Reference
Chapter 4 discusses the full range of individual differences among learners.

Diverse Learners

The United States is a pluralistic society composed of identifiable ethnic groups. In schools, the meaning of diversity extends well beyond just ethnic and cultural groups to include diversity with respect to characteristics such as language, socioeconomic status, abilities, and even gender.

Two principles generally define a school's response to diversity. The first is equality, which is an explicit commitment to the ideal that all students are created equal and deserve the same high quality of instruction. Equality is a widely embraced ideal, and this is true irrespective of people's ethnic or cultural background (Schuman et al., 1997). With its emphasis on equality, multicultural education is an outgrowth of the civil rights social movement (Sleeter, 1996). In this context, equality means recognizing and removing barriers that undermine a high-quality education, such as low teacher expectations, poverty (hence, free lunch programs), or differential access to programs and areas of study. The second is accommodation. Instead of forcing students of diverse backgrounds and characteristics to fit into a one-size-fits-all environment, schools commit to an open-armed embrace and appreciation for differences among students. As one case in point, consider how teachers can benefit by appreciating and embracing students' different cultural beliefs about the nature of learning.

Children and adolescents from Western (United States) and Eastern (Asia) cultures typically harbor different beliefs about learning (Li, 2001, 2003). Among U.S. students, learning is largely a process of acquiring external knowledge. Knowledge exists "out there," and students can acquire it, at least in proportion to the extent to which they possess internal characteristics such as intelligence and ability. U.S. students also believe that learning takes place in school and in response to the teaching of others. Among Asian students, learning is largely the means by which one cultivates self-perfection. Knowledge is something they must have, even in the face of hardships. Figure 1.4 graphically displays how students in U.S. classroom who are from the United States and China view learning (Li, 2003).

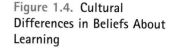

Figure 1.4. Cultural Differences in Beliefs About Learning

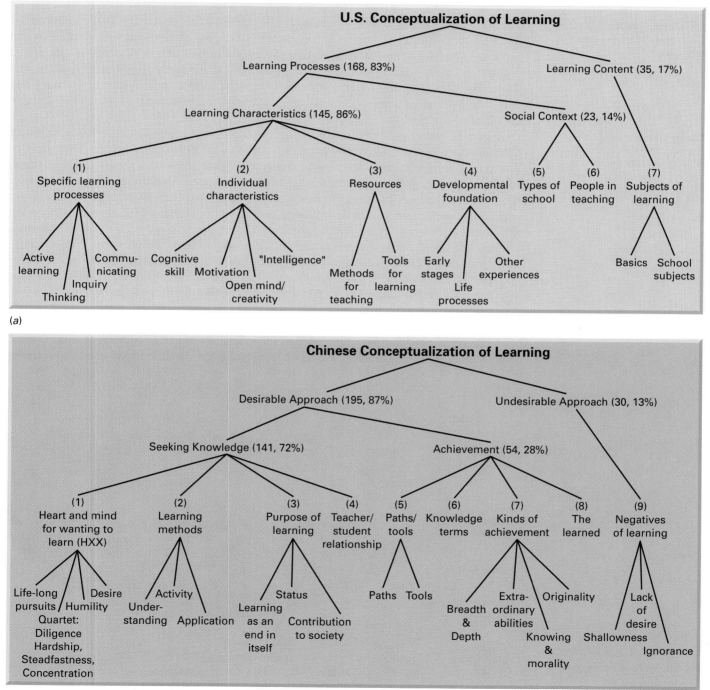

(a)

(b)

Source: (a) Li, J. (2003). U.S. and Chinese cultural beliefs about learning. *Journal of Educational Psychology, 95,* 258–267. Copyright © 2003 by the American Psychological Association. Reprinted with permission. (b) Assistant Professor Jin Li, "Chinese Conceptualization of Learning," *Ethos,* Vol. 29, No. 2: 111–137. © 2001, American Anthropological Association. All rights reserved. Used by permission.

Like all aspects of diversity, cultural differences in beliefs about learning affect what students expect from their teachers and how students react to teachers' instructional strategies. Emphasizing mental processes (intelligence) and an external body of knowledge leads teachers to call attention to what is out there to be known, how the student can acquire it, and how classrooms should be constructed to put learners and knowledge together. In contrast, an emphasis on personal causation leads teachers to emphasize attitudes toward learning. From this point of view, learning is not meant to be fun but instead is a disciplined activity that presents challenges and difficulties, and can even be considered an ordeal for developing one's character (Chao, 1996; Lee, 1996). Overall, this brief review makes the point that one single approach to instruction is likely to prove to be inadequate in a culturally diverse classroom.

Students with Special Needs

Chapter Reference
Chapter 4 discusses mental retardation.

The Individuals with Disabilities Education Act (IDEA), first enacted in 1977, reauthorized in 1997, and reauthorized again in December 2004, gave all students with disabilities the right to a free and appropriate education. Today, about 6.8 million students in U.S. public schools receive special education services, a number that represents about 13% of all students. Two-thirds of the students who receive special services have a specific learning disability or speech or language impairment. Among these students, about 80% struggle specifically with reading.

Chapter Reference
An extended discussion of ADHD appears in Chapter 4.

Figure 1.5 provides a graphical breakdown of this diverse group of students. About half of all students with special needs have a specific learning disability, such as dyslexia. These disabilities generally interfere with learning by undermining the student's capacity to listen, think, speak, read, write, spell, or perform mathematical calculations. About one in five students who receive special services has a speech or language impairment that adversely affects his or her educational performance, such as stuttering or a voice impairment. Mental retardation is the third most prevalent category, and it represents a lower than average general intellectual functioning. The fourth most prevalent category includes all emotional disturbances, including anxiety, depression, schizophrenia, and an inability to maintain positive interpersonal relationships with peers (i.e., conduct disorder). Additional categories include autism (severe difficulties with verbal and nonverbal communication and social interaction); orthopedic impairments, such as cerebral palsy; hearing impairments, including deafness; visual impairments, including blindness; traumatic brain injury; developmental delay; and general health impairments.

One special need that is not included in the official list of special needs is attention deficit hyperactivity disorder (ADHD). ADHD is a neurological condition that involves problems

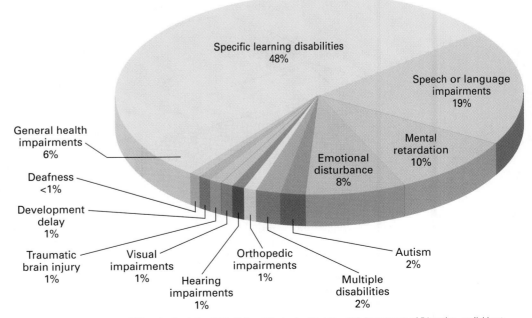

Figure 1.5. Thirteen Categories of Special Needs for Students Who Receive Services under the Individuals with Disabilities Education Act

Source: Data from the Digest of Education Statistics, 2003, National Center for Education, U.S. Department of Education, available at http://nces.ed.gov/programs/ digest/d03/tables/dt052.asp.

What Kids Say and Do

Behaviors Associated with ADHD

Students with attention deficit hyperactivity disorder (ADHD) engage in a range of behaviors that can make the daily rigors of school challenging for them, including:

Verbally disrupting class, such as by talking loudly, by talking excessively, or by yelling out such comments as "This is stupid!"

Blurting out answers to questions instead of listening completely to the question or waiting to be called on

Physically disrupting class, such as by interrupting others or by breaking a pencil out of frustration

Fidgeting; excessive motor activity; acting as though driven by a motor

Unable to settle back into the rhythm of class after recess

Having difficulty sustaining attention for the duration of a task, especially tasks that require extended mental effort; failing to finish schoolwork

Having difficulty attending to details in directions; making careless mistakes

Having difficulty following the rules, waiting turns, or completing required tasks

Chapter Reference
Chapter 2 explains the brain-based origins of two specific learning disabilities—dyslexia and aphasia.

with inattention, impulsivity, and self-regulation that are developmentally inconsistent with the student's age (Barkley, 1997), as exemplified by the "What Kids Say and Do" box on this page. The behaviors listed in the box do not constitute a learning disability in and of themselves, though ADHD is sometimes included under the *General health impairments* category (one reason why this category is as large as it is). More typically, about one-third of students with ADHD have one of the other learning disabilities, usually either a specific learning disability or an emotional disturbance (Cantwell & Baker, 1991; Zentall, 1993). The critical question in determining whether ADHD constitutes a special need is whether it interferes with the student's learning (because it sometimes does not).

By law, schools are required to provide all students with special needs an **individualized education program** (IEP). In preparing an IEP, a committee of school personnel—for example, several of the student's teachers, a special education teacher, the school counselor, and a school administrator—review the student's special needs to develop an instructional plan unique to that student. The IEP will identify the students' strengths and needs, but its basic function is to provide a blueprint for that student's instructional needs during the academic year, a blueprint not only in the academic domain but also in the social, physical, and self-management domains as well. In essence, the IEP outlines how teachers are to plan, manage, deliver, and evaluate their instruction of a student with a special need.

As can be extracted from the list of recommendations provided in the "Taking It to the Classroom" box at the top of next page, what makes special education *special*—that is, different from mainstream education—is partly that it features one-on-one instruction and partly that it is more explicit, intense, supervised, and tailored to reflect students' progress or lack thereof (Torgensen, 1996). The overarching goal of teaching students with special needs is to use explicit, intense, supportive, supervised, and need-based instruction to alleviate some of the obstacles to learning that these students face on a daily basis. Without extra support, students with special needs typically experience poor academic outcomes. As a group, they tend to perform far lower than their peers without special needs on achievement tests, and they are more likely to drop out of school (Marder, 1992). The overall nationwide graduation rate for students with special needs, for instance, is only 32%.

Chapter Reference
Chapter 4 provides an example of an individualized education program (IEP).

individualized education program (IEP) An educational and behavioral intervention plan for a student with special needs.

A teacher interacting with a high-school student with cerebral palsy, an orthopedic impairment. (Mitch Wojnarowicz/ The Image Works)

Taking It to the Classroom

Providing Instruction for Students with Special Needs

In addition to providing instruction consistent with IEPs, teachers in inclusive classrooms might also consider the following approaches to instruction (Gersten & Vaughn, 2001; Vaughn & Linan-Thompson, 2003):

- Individualize instruction.
- Rely on direct and explicit instructional practices.
- Meticulously arrange or structure the learning environment.
- Provide external supports, such as calculators, tape-recorded textbooks, adaptive furniture, special lighting or acoustics.
- Closely monitor students' progress and provide systematic feedback.
- Teach skill-based strategies, such as how to generate questions while reading.

Another group of learners with special needs are students in gifted programs. To identify giftedness in children and adolescents, the following criteria can be helpful (Sternberg & Zhang, 1995). Excellent performance must be:

- Well above the performance of peers of the same age and same degree of instruction
- Rare among these same peers
- Demonstrated on a reliable and valid assessment instrument
- Useful or productive in some way
- Of societal value or worth

The first three qualities reflect exceptional performance in a normative sense—that is, excellence compared to one's peers. The last two qualities show how educational and societal concerns emphasize skill domains such as those that underlie intellectual activity (reading, writing, mathematics), artistic activity (music, art, graphic arts), and physical activity (sports, dance). The overarching goal of special education for gifted students is to provide opportunities for enrichment so that these students can develop their creative and productive talents (Colangelo & Davis, 2003). Specific recommendations for how to enrich one student's artistic talent appears in the "Taking It to the Classroom" box below.

Chapter Reference
Chapter 4 discusses giftedness and talent development.

Taking It to the Classroom

Do You Know Jack? Supporting Talent Development

Jack is a gifted artist. Jack has always been interested in drawing, painting, and making crafts of various kinds. He has not been encouraged by his parents or grandparents, but his teacher has noticed this artistic talent as a strength. For instance, each time Jack writes a story or makes an entry into his journal, he adds a beautiful illustration. What practical and immediate approaches can you take to assist Jack?

- When reacting to Jack's products, adopt an accepting rather than a judging style.
- When talking about Jack's artistic products, focus the conversation around his ideas and interest.
- If Jack produces simple or quick drawings, offer him a challenging topic to draw or paint.
- Encourage Jack to create art rather than just copy or reproduce what he sees.
- Introduce Jack to other artists, especially artists of his own age who share his interest.
- Introduce the giftedness criterion of *usefulness* to Jack and ask how he might extend his art to achieve a degree of usefulness.
- Introduce the giftedness criterion of *social value* to Jack and ask how he might extend his art to achieve a degree of societal worth.

How Educational Psychologists Use Theories and Research

One benefit a study of educational psychology offers preservice teachers is a greater awareness of the principles that underlie learning. One principle, for instance, is that immediate and accurate feedback is critical for learning. Another is that students learn more cooperatively than they do individually. Another is that motivation is a prerequisite for learning. These principles—and others—do not just emerge from the minds of educational psychologists. Instead, they have deep intellectual roots, and the ground in which these principles grow consists of theory and research, the twin tools of educational psychology.

What Is a Theory?

Like all educators, educational psychologists spend a great deal of time observing and trying to understand how students learn and develop. To understand what they see, educational psychologists develop theories. Theories are designed to explain how and why a specific phenomenon functions the way it does. The proposed theory may or may not be accurate, so the educational psychologist uses the theory to create a hypothesis, or prediction, about what should happen if the theory is valid. With an hypothesis in hand, a research study is carried out to collect the data needed to evaluate the accuracy of the hypothesis. If the findings support the theory's prediction, researchers gain confidence in their theory.

A **theory** is an intellectual framework that can be used to identify and explain the relationships that exist among naturally occurring, observable phenomena (Fiske, 2004). One such naturally occurring phenomenon that educators struggle to understand is test anxiety. Figure 1.6 illustrates what a theory of test anxiety might look like. According to this figure, test anxiety is a multidimensional experience that includes an emotional component (worry), a cognitive component (thoughts of failure), and a physiological component (e.g., heart rate acceleration). The theory further proposes that three variables causally explain the rise and fall of students' test anxiety—time limits, high stakes, and external evaluation. The theory also posits that level of anxiety causally predicts students' test performance and test avoidance. Each individual line in the figure with an arrow on the end is important because each represents a separate hypothesis—a testable prediction—to determine the validity or accuracy of the theory.

theory An intellectual framework that organizes a vast amount of knowledge about a phenomenon so that educators can understand and explain better the nature of that phenomenon.

> **How Can I Use This?**
>
> Can you use the information in Figure 1.6 to suggest one strategy a teacher might implement to decrease students' level of anxiety?

With a better understanding of the nature of an educational phenomenon, the theory should help educators gain new insights that their day-to-day experience might not afford. For instance, much of the impetus behind the movement toward alternative assessment (e.g., using portfolios instead of multiple-choice tests to assess students' learning) comes from a deliberate effort to minimize the sort of anxiety-provoking testing conditions that appear on the left-hand side of the figure. A good theory should also offer recommendations that

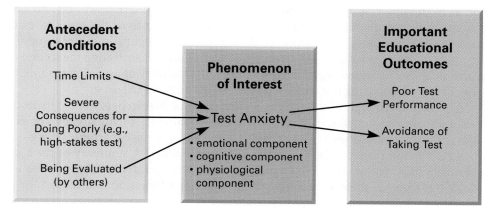

Figure 1.6. A Sample Theory (of Test Anxiety)

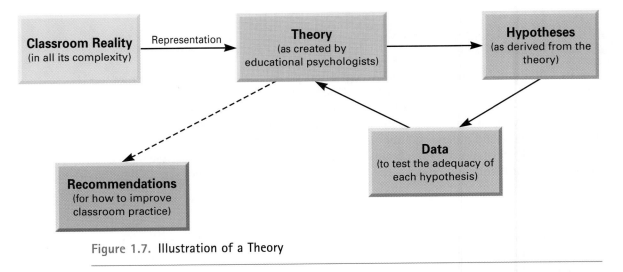

Figure 1.7. Illustration of a Theory

educators can use to solve classroom problems. In this spirit, Figure 1.7 illustrates the function and utility of a theory (Trope, 2004). Many educational phenomena are difficult to understand, and a theory serves the role of explaining or representing classroom reality. To test the validity of a theory, researchers generate hypotheses, carry out a research study, and use their data to determine the adequacy of the hypothesis (and the theory). If practitioners find the theory useful and if the theory helps them better understand some aspect of the classroom reality, they can use the theory to generate evidence-based strategies to improve their classroom practice.

Research Methods

The means through which educational psychologists test, evaluate, and revise their theories is research. In conducting research, they use one or more of the following methods: descriptive studies, correlational studies, experimental studies, and action research.

descriptive studies   A research method used to describe the educational situation as it naturally occurs—what typically happens, how teachers teach, and how students learn and develop.

Descriptive Studies.   **Descriptive studies** describe the educational situation as it naturally occurs. Their purpose is to describe the classroom experience and illustrate the way events typically unfold—what happens, how teachers teach, and how students learn and develop. The kinds of questions that researchers attempt to answer through descriptive research include the following:

● What strategies do first-year teachers use to motivate students?
● What do adolescents think is the purpose of school?
● What obstacles do teachers encounter when implementing cooperative learning?

To answer these questions, researchers typically record what they observe in the classroom, then analyze those data in ways that describe what occurred. The researchers might visit the classroom and tally the frequency with which teachers engage in a particular behavior, as in the first research question above (Newby, 1991). Alternatively, researchers might audiotape or videotape an educational experience, then analyze the tapes to extract the meaning or significance of what occurred. Or researchers might administer a questionnaire or conduct interviews. This interviewing strategy was used in answering the second research question above, because researchers learned that the majority of adolescents think the purpose of school is to hang out with their friends (Bacon, 1993).

Consider an example of a descriptive research study. Researchers wanted to describe the processes of how the goal of becoming a teacher emerges (Schutz, Crowder, & White, 2001). To describe this process, they interviewed 49 preservice teachers, asking questions such as, What influenced you to want to become a teacher? A summary of the biographical stories provided by five of these preservice teachers appears in Table 1.6. For instance, Molly was inspired to become a teacher through her admiration and respect for her elementary art teacher.

TABLE 1.6

Five Preservice Teachers' Explanations of Why They Decided to Become a Teacher

Participant, age	When did you decide?	Grade level and subject interest	What influenced you to want to become a teacher?
Molly, 22	Elementary school	Kindergarten to 12th-grade art	My elementary school art teacher was such an influence to me, I looked up to her as an artist and her ability to pass this to others.
Jane, 19	Elementary school	High school math	I don't know for sure except the fact that I've always liked to help others. When I was little I used to teach my two younger sisters everything I learned. I just like to learn and to teach others what I know.
James, 23	High school	High school history	I found that I liked working with kids. I liked teaching. My favorite players were those who couldn't play, I really enjoyed watching them progress. I enjoyed the fact that I helped them achieve something. I was proud of the player that the boys made fun of when he cleared the bases with a double at the end of the season. When I saw how good he felt about himself, it was then I decided I wanted to become a teacher.
Kerry, 20	High school	Elementary education	Being able to teach my own Sunday school class. I became aware that these children were the basis of our society. I felt that if I wanted them to learn things correctly, I had better teach them and do my part.
Ann, 21	College	Elementary education	I always thought about it but I wasn't quite sure. I then took a career exploration class and did a field experience with my old third-grade teacher. The minute I walked in my old school, I knew I wanted to become a teacher.

Source: Schutz, P. A., Crowder, K. C., & White, V. E. (2001). The development of a goal to become a teacher. *Journal of Educational Psychology, 93*, 299–308. Copyright © 2001 by the American Psychological Association. Reprinted with permission.

Descriptive research often identifies patterns in participants' behavior or experience. In the study just described, researchers heard 49 different stories, but they were able to identify a half-dozen recurring themes that explained how the goal of becoming a teacher emerges (with a brief description and the percentage of teachers nominating each):

Altruism	They desire to help society and children (20%).
Past experiences	Early teaching activity stimulated their interest (19%).
Past teachers	A teaching role model encouraged them to teach (18%).
Personal characteristics	They had the personal characteristics of a teacher (13%).
Parents or family	A family member encouraged them to teach (10%).
Love of children	They wanted to be around children (7%).

What Does This Mean to Me?
Why do you want to become a teacher? When did you make this decision?

Based on their analysis of what these preservice teachers told them, the researchers continued to try to extract meaning from the interviews. In doing so, they uncovered a three-step process that most teachers-to-be go through. First, the person was exposed to a teaching-type experience, as through teaching Sunday school. Second, the teacher-to-be experienced a positive critical incident—a moving and meaningful experience—during that early teaching encounter. Finally, the teacher-to-be translated this positive critical event into the conscious intention to become a professional teacher.

correlational studies A research method used to measure two naturally occurring variables and summarize the nature and magnitude of their relationship in numerical form.

Correlational Studies. **Correlational studies** measure separate variables and summarize in numerical form the nature of the relationship that exists between them. The purpose of correlational research is to articulate the nature and magnitude of the relationship between two naturally occurring variables. The sorts of questions that researchers attempt to answer through correlational research include the following:

- What is the relationship between hours of homework and extent of achievement?
- What is the relationship between class size and student achievement?
- Do bullies have low self-esteem?

Correlational studies begin by measuring the two variables of interest. That is, researchers find ways to measure variables such as bullying and self-esteem. Using these numbers, they calculate the relationship between two variables, which is summarized by a number called the *correlation coefficient.*

correlation coefficient A statistical value that ranges from −1 to +1 to describe both the direction and extent of relationship between two variables.

The **correlation coefficient** (denoted by the letter *r*) is a statistical value that describes both the *direction* and the *magnitude* of the relationship between two variables. Correlation coefficients can range between −1 and +1. The sign (− or +) before the number indicates the direction of the relationship. A relationship between variables can be positive or negative, or there may be no relationship at all. For example, if students' achievement increases as they increase their hours of homework, the relationship is positive, and the value of *r* will be some positive number between 0 and +1, depending on the strength of the relationship between homework and achievement. If student achievement decreases as class size increases, the relationship is negative, and the value of *r* will be some negative number between 0 and −1, depending on the strength of the inverse relationship between class size and achievement. Finally, the relationship between two variables can be nonexistent; that is, the value of one variable predicts nothing about the value of the second variable. For example, if knowing a student's level of self-esteem tells you nothing about how much of a bully he or she is, there is no relationship between the two variables, and the correlation coefficient is zero ($r = 0$).

The absolute value of the number in the correlation coefficient, regardless of whether it is positive or negative, reveals the magnitude, or strength, of the relationship. Values closer to either +1 or −1 indicate strong relationships; they mean that changes in one variable are highly related to changes in the other. Values close to zero indicate weak relationships; they mean that changes in one variable are unrelated to changes in the other.

Consider an example of a correlational research study. Researchers wondered which variables affect students' mathematical proficiency (Byrnes, 2003). They asked nearly 10,000 high school seniors to complete a mathematics test covering geometry, statistics, and algebra. They also asked students about the seven variables listed in Table 1.7. Then they calculated correlation coefficients to summarize the relationship between math proficiency—as measured by each student's score on the math test—and each of these seven variables. As shown in the table, each of the first five variables showed a positive correlation with math proficiency. Notice that some variables (e.g., algebra courses taken) had a stronger positive relationship with math proficiency (as denoted by the higher *r* value) than did other variables (e.g., extent of calculator usage). The sixth variable—relevance of math—showed practically no relationship to math proficiency (*r* is near zero). The seventh variable—math is fact learning—showed a negative correlation, because the more that students thought math was about memorizing facts and formulas, the lower they scored on the proficiency test.

The insights gained from this correlational study can help educators think about possible intervention efforts to boost math proficiency. However, it is important to note that correlational studies show only that two variables are related to one another. They stop short of showing that changes in one variable will lead to a subsequent change in the other. Correlation identifies a relationship, but it does not establish a causal relationship. From the data in Table 1.7, we cannot conclude that taking more algebra courses will lead to gains in students' math proficiency. The causal inference is not warranted because high math proficiency might very well cause the student to take more algebra courses. Or some other variable—such as having excellent mathematics teachers—might cause high scores on both variables. To address the issue of causality, another type of research method is required—the experiment.

TABLE 1.7

Correlations Between Math Achievement and Seven Educational Variables

Educational variable	Correlation with 12th-grade math achievement r (9,499)
Algebra courses taken	.58*
Number of courses taken in algebra and calculus	
Geometry courses taken	.51*
Number of courses taken in geometry and trigonometry	
Extent of homework	.25*
Number of pages of math homework completed each day	
Calculator usage	.30*
"How often do you use a calculator?"	
Liking of math	.37*
Agreement with "I like math"	
Relevance of math	.03
Agreement with "Math is useful for solving everyday problems"	
Math is Fact learning	−.36*
Agreement with "Math is mostly memorizing facts"	

*$p < .05$.

Source: Adapted from Byrnes, J. P. (2003). Factors predictive of mathematics achievement in White, Black, and Hispanic 12th graders. *Journal of Educational Psychology, 95,* 316–326.

Experimental Studies. Only through **experimental studies** can researchers infer a cause-and-effect relationship between two variables. In an experiment, researchers distinguish between two types of variables: independent and dependent. *Independent variables* are hypothesized to cause the change in the dependent variables. The researchers manipulate the independent variable, meaning that they purposely create controlled changes in it. For instance, they might create a high level of the variable and a low level of the same variable. They would then expose research participants to different levels of the independent variable and measure to see whether scores on the dependent variable are different as a function of the level of the independent variable. If so, the value of the *dependent variable* depends on the presence or amount of the independent variable. Consider three research questions that can be answered through the experimental method. In each question, notice how the first variable (independent variable) can be manipulated by the researcher, and the second variable (dependent variable) is measured at a later time to see whether it has been affected:

experimental studies   A research method used to test for a cause-and-effect relationship between two variables.

- Does participation in a Head Start program accelerate preschool children's academic performance?
- Will exposure to an expert model improve students' subsequent writing skills?
- Do time-outs decrease students' misbehavior?

In a typical experimental study, researchers start with an hypothesis. An **hypothesis** is a prediction about how the results of a study will turn out. In the first example above, researchers might predict that a relationship exists between participating in a Head Start program and children's subsequent school achievement. If so, they would propose an hypothesis such as the following: Preschool students who participate in a Head Start program score higher on a subsequent test of their academic performance than comparable preschool children who do not participate in the Head Start program.

hypothesis   A prediction, derived from a theory, of how the results of a research study will turn out.

With an hypothesis in hand, the next step is to identify a sample of participants to investigate. The researchers randomly assign half the sample to the **experimental group** and the other half to the **control group**. Participants in the experimental group are exposed to the independent variable, and participants in the control group are not. Random assignment to conditions is important because it ensures that the two groups will be virtually the same in all characteristics other than the independent variable—characteristics such as age, intelligence, socioeconomic status, and so forth. After some predetermined length of time has

experimental group   The group of participants in an experimental study who are randomly assigned to receive exposure to the independent variable.

control group   The group of participants in an experimental study who are randomly assigned not to receive exposure to the independent variable.

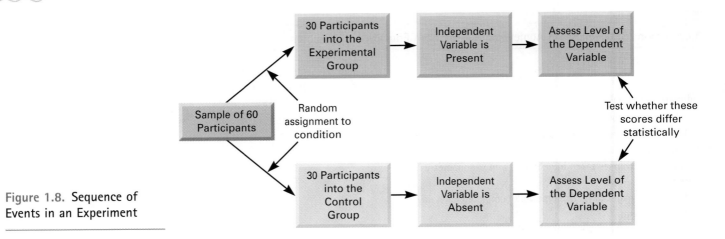

Figure 1.8. Sequence of Events in an Experiment

passed, researchers assess the level of the dependent variable for all participants. The last step in the experiment is to perform a statistical test to see whether the two groups differ in their levels of the dependent variable. The purpose of the statistical test is to make an objective, numbers-based decision as to whether the presence of the independent variable did or did not cause a difference in participants' scores on the dependent variable. Figure 1.8 graphically summarizes this sequence of steps.

Consider an example of an experimental study. Researchers hypothesized that a middle school student's style of walking would influence his teacher's perception of his aggression, achievement, and need for special education (Neal et al., 2003). To test their hypothesis, researchers prepared four different videotapes:

1. A European-American male walking to class with a stroll movement
2. An African-American male walking to class with a stroll movement
3. A European-American male walking to class with standard (no stroll) movement
4. An African-American male walking to class with standard (no stroll) movement

This study actually featured two independent variables: ethnicity and the presence or absence of a stroll. It also included three dependent measures: perceived aggressiveness, perceived achievement, and perceived need for special education. Irrespective of the student's ethnicity, males with strolls were rated as more aggressive, less achieving, and more in need of special education services than were males without strolls. That is, the student's style of walking caused a change in his teachers' perceptions of his likely aggression, achievement, and need for special education. In a rather alarming way, the findings show how teachers can mistake cultural differences (movement style) for cognitive and behavioral disabilities.

Action Research. The three research methods presented thus far make it sound as though only educational psychologists can conduct research. Research, however, is a part of every teacher's day-to-day experience. In fact, the motto underlying **action research** is *teacher-as-researcher*. As the motto implies, teachers themselves carry out action research, and it takes place within teachers' actual classrooms (Oberg & McCutcheon, 1987; van Manen, 1990). The kinds of questions that teachers attempt to answer through action research include the following:

- Do students enjoy being in my class?
- What do my students actually do during their independent study time?
- Which instructional strategy works best for my lower achieving students?

As these research questions imply, action research constitutes whatever research projects teachers undertake to understand better and improve on their own classroom practice. The goal of such research is not to build and refine general scientific theory but to build and refine the teacher's own theory of teaching and approach to instruction. In action research, teachers do not simply import the theories of educational psychology into their classrooms.

action research   A research method carried out by teachers in their own classrooms to inform and refine their personal theories of teaching and classroom practice.

Instead, they conduct research to see which ideas might be useful for the specific needs of their students. In a typical action research project, a teacher will (Kemmis & McTaggart, 1988; Tripp, 1990):

1. Identify a problem.
2. Formulate a plan, using his or her personal theory of teaching.
3. Collect and analyze data to see whether the plan worked.
4. Reflect on what has been learned.
5. Use the new-and-improved personal theory of teaching to revise the plan and repeat steps 2, 3, and 4.

Consider an example of an action research study. A third-grade teacher taught her classes competently—classes began on time, transitions were smooth and quick, and students were consistently on task (Rogers, Noblit, & Ferrell, 1990). But she felt that something important was missing—the atmosphere in her classroom was not quite right. After taking a close look at what she was doing in the classroom, she planned to spend more one-on-one time with her students, which she hoped would improve the classroom atmosphere. *Spend more one-on-one time with each student* was her *action*. To assess her action, she kept a nightly journal recording how much time she spent with each child. After a week of doing so, it became apparent that keeping a journal was an ineffective method because she could not remember all the interactions that took place during the day. Her reformulated plan was to keep a large wall chart with the names of the children listed in rows and the number of interactions listed in columns. Each time she interacted one-on-one with a student, she handed the student a sticker, and the child posted it on the chart beside his or her name. One week later, the chart revealed the data the teacher needed to answer her research question, How much one-on-one time do I spend with my students?

By using action research, the teacher did not confirm or disconfirm a general theory. Instead, the action research project created the opportunity for her to reflect on her personal theory of teaching, asking herself questions such as, What do I believe is good teaching? and What do my students need from me? Through her action research, the teacher improved on both her personal theory and her actual classroom practice. As you read the chapters to come, you will gain information that will help you make similar classroom decisions and, when necessary, conduct your own action research, as discussed in the "Taking It to the Classroom" box on the next page.

A teacher implements her action research plan—spend more one-on-one time with each student. (Media Bakery)

Taking It to the Classroom

Implementing Action Research in Your Classroom

To conduct action research in your own classroom, first identify a problem to be solved. Then carry out the following four steps: planning, acting, monitoring, and reflecting (Kemmis & McTaggart, 1988; Dicker, 1990).

1. **Planning**

   Once a problem has been identified, state a plan of action to address it. If attendance is poor, make a plan to increase it.

2. **Acting**

   Translate the plan into action. Recognizing the unique circumstances within your classroom, implement your plan to increase attendance.

3. **Monitoring**

   Collect the data necessary to assess whether the plan is working. You might keep a journal, writing down points of progress and difficulty after each class. Students might also keep a journal—they could be given five minutes at the end of class to write their reactions to the implemented plan. Alternatively, you might make a tape recording, perhaps taping one class before the plan is implemented and another after its implementation.

4. **Reflecting**

   Classroom events rarely unfold as planned. Adjustments almost always need to be made. During reflection, the teacher-as-researcher critiques the plan, revises it, and thinks of new ways to bring the plan to fruition.

Critical Thinking

For teachers, the role of research is to provide objective, data-based evidence to help answer the questions they care about most. Consider a few claims:

- The smaller the class size, the more students learn.
- The best way to motivate students is to offer attractive rewards.
- Girls learn more in same-sex classes than they do in mixed-sex classes.

Are all these statements true? Are only some of them true? The role of research is to ask (and answer) the question, Does this claim have support—is there enough evidence to back it up and accept the claim as a generally true statement?

The best way to discuss critical thinking is to talk first about uncritical thinking. To the uncritical mind, what people say, do, and experience is accepted as right and true. To the critical mind, however, claims about what works in education need to be evaluated and the evidence examined.

When teachers search for answers to questions about teaching and learning, common sense is a popular starting point. Common sense is typically supplemented by personal experience. For instance, the claim that students learn more in small classes is consistent with common sense. Personal experience can add insight as the teacher reflects on whether his or her own class size numbers have been an important influence on students' learning. Teachers can also engage in discussions with colleagues, mentors, and master teachers to ask what they think about this claim. These are all helpful sources of information, but they all share the same shortcoming: They are all opinions—all subjective ways of knowing.

The role of research is to provide a second opinion—one that is objective and dependent on data collected from research. In adding research to one's thinking, the teacher's capacity for critical thinking increases. Returning to the class size claim, it is appropriate to ask what research can add to what a teacher already knows from common sense, personal experience, and conversations with trusted colleagues. Suppose that these sources suggest that, yes, smaller classes support higher achievement, and they do so because teachers change their approach to instruction to make it more individualized. The problem with this explanation, however, is that does not seem to be true. Teachers generally do not change their teaching styles when moving from larger to smaller classes (Bohrnstedt, Stecher, & Wiley, 2000; Molnar, Smith, & Zahorik, 2000). Instead, as class size decreases, research shows that students become more engaged, both academically and socially. Academically, students are more attentive and more on task, they participate more, and they show greater initiative and effort. Socially, students are more likely to follow rules, interact constructively with the teacher, collaborate more with their peers, and engage in less disruptive behavior. All eight of these reasons—four for academic engagement and four for social engagement—explain why smaller classes yield higher achievement (Finn, Pannozzo, & Achilles, 2003). Such a research finding does not contradict teachers' common sense, personal experience, and peer discussions; rather, it adds to it. It does so by holding a subjective way of knowing up to the light of critical thinking and asking, Are you sure?

When teachers develop their critical thinking—when they supplement their subjective ways of knowing with objective, data-based ways of knowing—they can go beneath the surface of their ideas. Personal experience is no longer sacred but instead needs to be put to objective test. When tested, personal experience is sometimes confirmed, sometimes challenged, and sometimes outright contradicted. It is always, however, enriched. Even the teacher who "already knows" that smaller class size benefits students can walk away from a research report on class size with new insights and a deeper understanding of *why* small class size produces benefits. The "Uncommon Sense" box on this page provides another illustration of the benefits of critical thinking.

Uncommon Sense

Music Training Produces Math Whiz Kids—Or Does It?

Math whiz kids are often gifted musicians. Just as Einstein played the violin, excellence in music seems to pave the way to excellence in math. Before we enroll all of our children in music lessons, however, it is worth asking whether research confirms or contradicts this conclusion.

When researchers look at scores on achievement tests, they find that students with musical training do tend to score higher in math than do students without musical training (Cheek & Smith, 1999). But correlation means association, not causation. For causation, we need to dig deeper. We need an experiment. One experiment randomly assigned some children to take piano lessons for 36 weeks, and a control group of similar children took (nonmusical) drama lessons (Schellenberg, 2004). The children who took piano lessons did not score significantly higher on later math achievement tests than did children in the control group.

What can we conclude? Personal experience, Einstein anecdotes, and correlational data suggest a music-math link. But experimental studies do not. Thinking critically, the conclusion seems to be that although the two variables are related, they are not causally related. Instead, they seem to grow out of other shared variables, such as parental support, high expectations, general intelligence, or a love of all things school-related. To nurture math whiz kids, educators do not need to provide music lessons so much as they need to encourage influences such as parental support, high expectations, general intelligence, and appreciation for school-related activities.

SUMMARY

● **What is educational psychology?**

Educational psychology is the scientific study of psychology in education. Its twofold mission is to understand learners and to foster their learning. Educational psychologists seek to understand all aspects of the teaching-learning process, and they use this knowledge to improve educational practice.

● **What primary concerns do beginning teachers have?**

Beginning teachers have many concerns, but the four at the top of the list are classroom discipline, motivating students, dealing with special needs, and assessing students' work. As teachers find ways to solve these concerns, they develop teaching efficacy—the belief that they can cope effectively with the full range of problems within the teaching situation. Growing teaching efficacy allows teachers to silence their doubt and, consequently, maintain high enthusiasm, stay committed to teaching, and produce gains in students' thinking, motivation, and achievement.

● **What is reflective teaching, and how is it different from technical teaching?**

Teachers can approach some teaching situations with routine knowledge and tried-and-true solutions. This approach represents technical teaching. In many situations, however, surprises surface that lead teachers to think critically about the teaching situation. Teachers ask, What is happening here? What went wrong? How can I get the class back on track? These are reflective questions. Reflective teaching involves generating conjectures to explain and solve the surprising event. To model the process of reflective teaching, the chapter introduced the RIDE model: reflection, information gathering, decision making, and evaluation.

● **How can teachers recognize, adapt, and respond to diverse learners and students with special needs?**

Each year, schools become more diverse. Given such diversity, all students are different. Because teachers need to apply standards that apply equally to all students, teachers need to recognize, adapt, and respond constructively to students' diversity and special needs to help them overcome the unique obstacles they might face. The example of how students from different cultural backgrounds harbor different beliefs about learning illustrates the point that no single approach to instruction will prove adequate in a culturally diverse classroom. The IDEA gave all students with disabilities the right to a free and public education. Because this is so, regular classroom teachers need to be aware of their students' disabilities and provide learning environments that meet the needs of all students.

● **How do educational psychologists use theory and research?**

The twin tools of educational psychology are theory and research. A theory is an intellectual framework to organize a vast amount of knowledge about a phenomenon so as to understand it better and explain its nature. Theories explain how a phenomenon works, but data are needed to test whether the hypotheses generated by the theory are accurate. In carrying out their research, educational psychologists use one or more of the following methods: descriptive studies, correlational studies, experimental studies, and action research. Descriptive studies describe the educational situation as it naturally occurs. Correlational studies identify the nature and magnitude of a relationship that exists between two naturally occurring variables. Experimental studies are designed to test for a casual relationship between two variables, with the causal variable representing the independent variable and the effect variable representing the dependent variable. Action research represents the teacher-as-researcher and is undertaken by teachers to understand better and improve their own classroom practice. Findings from research can help teachers develop their critical thinking skills.

KEY TERMS

action research, p. 26
control group, p. 25
correlation coefficient, p. 24
correlational studies, p. 24
descriptive studies, p. 22
educational psychology, p. 4

experimental group, p. 25
experimental studies,
    p. 25
hypothesis, p. 25
individualized education
    program (IEP), p. 19

learning, p. 5
reflective teaching, p. 11
teaching, p. 5
teaching efficacy, p. 8
technical teaching, p. 10
theory, p. 21

EXERCISES

1. *Generating Metaphors for Teaching*

   Generate a half-dozen metaphors to complete the following sentence: The teacher as
   _____. Once you have several different metaphors to choose from, select one
   that best describes the way you think about yourself as a teacher. Reflect on what that
   metaphor implies about your own views of teaching and learning. Ask yourself whether
   this metaphor represents an ideal role for you as a teacher. If not, can you generate another metaphor that successfully captures the essence of your ideal teaching role?

2. *Digging Up the Roots of Teaching Anxiety*

   Many, perhaps all, teachers suffer some doubt and anxiety about their teaching. Often
   this sense of anxiety is a diffuse one, as the teacher says, "I'm anxious about teaching, but
   in general I'm not sure why." Try this exercise to pinpoint the source of any anxiety you
   currently feel about teaching. Rate yourself on the following three questions, which correspond to the dimensions of teaching efficacy listed in Table 1.3. Use a 1-to-7 scale in
   which 1 means *not at all confident,* and 7 means *highly confident.* How confident are you
   that you will be able to control disruptive behavior in the classroom? How confident are
   you that you will be able to motivate a student who shows low interest? How confident
   are you that you will be able to adjust your lesson to meet the individual needs of all your
   students? By working through this exercise, you can begin to isolate the underlying
   source of your teaching anxiety.

3. *Reflecting on Your Own Theory of Learning*

   Using the word *learning* as your focus, brainstorm common words and phrases that
   come to mind. Generate a dozen different words or phrases that you think are associated with learning. To get you started, here are some possibilities: learn by doing; hands on;
   memory; self-reflection; perseverance; instruction; Socratic method; brain; interest. With
   your list in hand, group the words into clusters of shared meaning. For instance, *hands
   on* and *learn by doing* might fall under the general heading of *active learning.* Give a name
   to the clusters or themes you identify. Then compare your resulting diagram with the
   ones shown for U.S. and Chinese students in Figure 1.4.

4. *Types of Research*

   The chapter identified four types of research methods that are commonly used in educational psychology: descriptive, correlational, experimental, and action. Visit a university library—in person or electronically—to find a journal that features research-based
   articles on some topic related to teaching and learning. You will know it is a research-
   based journal if you see tables and figures of data as you flip through its pages. One such
   journal, for instance, might be the *Journal of Educational Psychology.* Read through several different articles to see whether you can determine what type of research method the
   investigators used. If you locate and flip through the September 2004 issue of the *Journal
   of Educational Psychology,* the first article is a correlational study. The second is an experiment. The third article is a descriptive study.

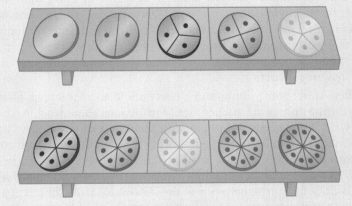

Source: Gettman, D. (1987). Basic Montessori. New York: St. Martin's Press. Reprinted with permission.

This apparatus is a fractions activity (Gettman, 1987). It helps elementary school students understand the concept of fractions—the division of a whole into equal parts. How might you, the teacher, help students develop such a concept? One way might be to use a hands-on approach. You could invite the children to play with the fraction inserts laying side by side in the tray. Using the attached knobs, the children could pick up the inserts, manipulate them, and investigate which inserts fit into the trays and which do not. Through such exploration, students could discover the concept of fractions.

A second way might be to sit beside the children and tutor them. You could plan a lesson in advance. It might begin with an explanation of what fractions are and continue with coaching and mentoring to show them how to use the tray as a tool to understand fractions. Once the children start to show signs that they have the hang of it, you could put your hands in your lap and let them understand the concept in their own way. You could even ask them to explain the concept of fractions to you.

Cognitive Development

2

R I D E Reflection for Action

What is the most effective instructional approach to help students learn concepts such as fractions? Does learning through exploration and self-discovery work best? Does learning through social guidance work best? Which instructional approach would help an elementary school child understand such a concept? Would this approach also work with a child with special needs?

Guiding Questions

- How does education enrich brain development?
- How does Piaget explain cognitive development?
- What are the stages of cognitive development?
- How can teachers apply Piaget's theory in the classroom?
- How does Vygotsky explain sociocognitive development?
- How can teachers apply Vygotsky's theory in the classroom?
- How does language develop?
- How can teachers use their knowledge of cognitive development when working with diverse learners and students with special needs?

CHAPTER OVERVIEW

As infants grow into children and children grow into adolescents, three interrelated developmental processes unfold: brain development, cognitive development, and language development. Biology and maturation underlie all three processes, but biology provides learners with only their developmental potential. For a student's brain, cognitive, and language development to be fully realized, appropriate growth-promoting experiences must also occur. This chapter identifies and discusses the school-related experiences that help learners realize their developmental potentials. The first part of the chapter shows that brain development depends on exposure to richly stimulating learning environments. The second part discusses cognitive development from two perspectives—Piaget's four-stage model and Vygotsky's apprenticeship model. The third part of the chapter discusses language development by explaining how language develops, including a second language.

Brain Development
- Brain Structure and Function
- How Experience (Education) Affects Brain Development

Cognitive Development
- Adaptation and Schemas: Piaget's Theory
- Stages in Cognitive Development
- Applications of Piaget's Theory
- Limitations of Piaget's Theory

Sociocognitive Development
- Cognitive Development as an Apprenticeship: Vygotsky's Theory
- Scaffolding in the Zone of Proximal Development

Sociocognitive Development *(continued)*
- Instructional Conversations
- Role of Language in Cognitive Development
- Cultural Tools
- Importance of Peers
- Applications of Vygotsky's Theory
- Which Theory Should Teachers Apply?

Language Development
- How Language Develops
- Language Disabilities and Brain Functioning
- Technology Support for Young Readers and Students with Special Needs
- Bilingualism and Second-Language Acquisition

Brain Development

The human brain, an organ the size of a coconut and with the texture of cold butter, is the part of the body that learns, thinks, remembers, and solves problems. To study how the brain learns, neuroscientists identify its parts or structures (Kandel, Schwartz, & Jessell, 1991). Once they have done this, their next step is to identify each structure's underlying function or purpose. Educators take a special interest in the study of the brain at this point because they desire to understand how the brain contributes to educational phenomena, such as learning, planning, problem solving, memory, intelligence, language, motivation, and emotion. Figure 2.1 identifies the brain structures associated with these functions.

Brain Structure and Function

Consider how the brain regulates the two functions of memory and emotion. Regarding memory, the **hippocampus** processes a person's new experiences. Only after the hippocampus processes and makes sense of new information is a memory created and eventually stored as long-term knowledge. As a case in point, when a student manipulates the fractions activity described at the beginning of the chapter, the hippocampus's dense network of neurons processes the resulting sensory information (sights, sounds, touch, maybe even smells from the wooden tray); holds that sensory information in memory for a brief time; and while doing so, works to forge new connections between these new experiences and knowledge that is

hippocampus Grape-shaped structure in the limbic area of the brain involved in memory formation and storage.

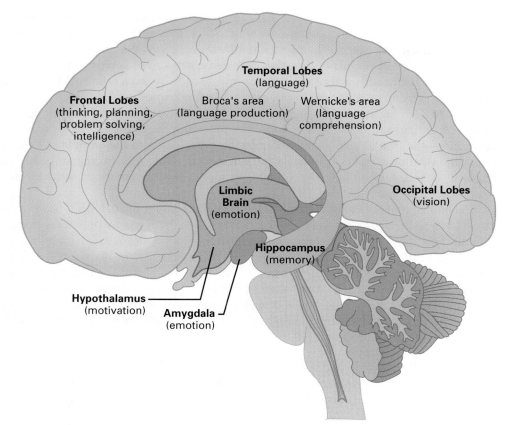

Figure 2.1. Brain Structures and Their Functions

already stored in the brain. Generating connections (synapses) between what is new and what is already known is the basis of learning and memory, as shown in Figure 2.2.

Memories are groups of neurons that fire together in the same pattern each time they are activated. The forging of a memory begins when a neuron is activated by an initial stimulus. If it is stimulated to fire fast enough, that neuron will set off its neighboring neuron, as denoted by the star in Figure 2.2a. If the cells fire in synchrony enough times, a connection is formed between them. The dashed lines represent a lack of connections with the third neuron. Through future encounters with the initial stimulus, the bonded pair of neurons will gain enough strength to trigger their neighboring neurons, as represented by the two stars in Figure 2.2b. If this stimulation happens frequently enough, all three neurons bond together. This pattern of connections represents a memory.

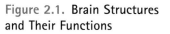 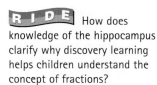 How does knowledge of the hippocampus clarify why discovery learning helps children understand the concept of fractions?

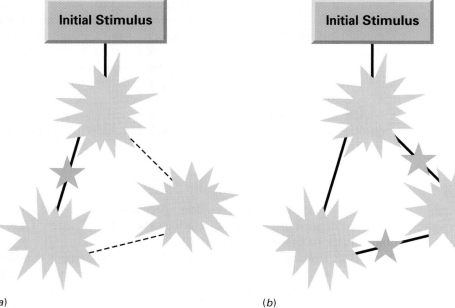

(a)   (b)

Figure 2.2. A Model of How a Learning Experience Becomes a Memory

amygdala Almond-shaped structure in the limbic area of the brain involved in the activation of negative emotions.

Fear and anxiety are two emotions that can interfere with learning. The **amygdala** generates these negative emotions, because the amygdala is the brain's warning system. Students sometimes encounter potentially threatening classroom events (e.g., public speaking, bullies). Perceived threat stimulates the amygdala's dense network of neurons and, once stirred to action, instantaneously activates a complex fear reaction by accelerating the heart, tensing the muscles, freezing action, and producing a *fear face* expression (Davis, 1992; Davis & Whalen, 2001). The amygdala is very sensitive; when activated, it can sidetrack attention, paralyze learning, and derail reason. More optimistically, the brain's center of reason and rationality—the frontal lobe—sends neural projections down to the amygdala. This communication pathway makes it possible for students' thinking to calm the amygdala's fear response. In fact, the ability to use thoughts to soothe negative emotions is the essence of *emotional intelligence* (Goleman, 1995).

neurons Nerve cells that receive and transmit the neural impulses underlying thinking.

The human brain does not fully mature until around the age of 20. It does, however, possess at birth all the neurons it will ever have (Rakic, 1991). **Neurons** are nerve cells that make all brain functions possible, including those introduced in Figure 2.1. The brain has about 100 billion neurons (Carter, 1998). Impressive as that number is, the brain forges about 100 *trillion* connections that join neurons together, as depicted in Figure 2.2. That means that the average neuron connects with about 1,000 of its neighboring neurons. Some connections exist at birth, but most connections between neurons depend on learning. These connections are forged in the following manner (Greenough & Black, 1992; Greenough, Black, & Wallace, 1987; Nelson & Bloom, 1997):

- Exposure to a stimulating learning environment will stimulate neurons.
- When stimulated, neurons reach out to neighboring neurons (by growing *dendrites*, the part of the neuron that extends out like branches off a tree to connect to neighboring neurons).
- With repeated stimulation, the number of connections between neurons increases.

glia cells Cells that support neurons and provide the waxy coating that surrounds nerve fibers.

myelinization The process carried out by glia cells to insulate neurons with a protective coating to prevent damage and increase the speed of communication between neighboring neurons.

The more neurons reach out and connect with one another, the more they need support from the glia cells. **Glia cells** support neurons (*glia* literally means "glue"), and the brain has about 50 times more glia cells than it does neurons. One supportive function of glia cells is to provide neurons with myelin, the waxy coating that surrounds nerve fibers the same way plastic coats an electric wire. This insulation, called **myelinization,** protects neurons from damage and greatly speeds up the transmission of nerve impulses from one neuron to the next.

Glia cells undergo a dramatic growth spurt from birth through adolescence. Practically all the growth in the size of an infant's brain is due to glia cell growth, and this growth explains why infants become increasingly adept at standing and walking. At birth, neurons are not myelinated, but the growth spurt in glia cells and the ensuing process of myelinization allow for faster and more reliable communication between neurons. Myelinization also explains adolescents' ever-increasing attention span. Adolescents have a greater attention span than do children because the neurons in the frontal lobe undergo steady myelinization throughout childhood (Fischer & Rose, 1995). Myelinization helps explain why adolescents are so much better than children in the abilities of thinking ahead, controlling impulses, answering hypothetical questions, and understanding the consequences of their actions (Nelson & Bloom, 1997). If neurons become demyelinated, serious disease occurs, including muscular dystrophy, multiple sclerosis, and amyotrophic lateral sclerosis (Lou Gehrig's disease; Kandel et al., 1991).

How Experience (Education) Affects Brain Development

Stimulated neurons reach out and connect with other stimulated neurons, whereas inactive and understimulated neurons degenerate and die out (Huttenlocher, 1994). The result is that experience leaves a unique mark on brain development.

plasticity The brain's capacity for structural change as the result of experience.

The concept that unites experience (e.g., education) and brain development is neural **plasticity,** which is essentially the brain's capacity for structural change as the result of experience (Greenough et al., 1987). The sensitivity of the developing brain to experience can be seen, for example, in blind students who read Braille. The area of the brain that senses touch from the right index finger is much larger in people who are blind than it is in people who see because the index finger is used to read Braille and because areas of the brain are allocated in proportion to the individual's mental activities (Schwartz & Begley, 2002). The same effect occurs among musicians. Among a group of lifelong violinists, researchers found that the part of their brains that controls the hand movements involved in playing a stringed instrument became larger (Elbert et al., 1995). More specifically, the area of the brain that controls the very active four fingers of the left hand was larger than the area that controls the less active fingers of the right hand and was also larger than the corresponding brain area in nonmusicians.

If practice affects brain development in musicians and people who are blind, it seems reasonable to ask whether schooling affects brain development. Certainly, schooling boosts intelligence, reasoning ability, learning strategies, and talent. Further, education-based intervention programs, such as Head Start, which are designed to provide preschool children with stimulating and complex environments, produce educational gains. But do interventions such as formal schooling and Head Start actually change the structure and function of the brain? Those who study the brain have concluded that they do, though the effect is probably small (Greenough et al., 1987).

Instead of causing brain structures to grow, the main reason educational programs produce academic gains is that stimulating environments give the brain a great deal of information to process, store, remember, and later use to solve problems. This greater reservoir of stored knowledge shows up in brain development not as a larger brain but instead as greater neuronal interconnectivity. Thus, the brain activity depicted in Figure 2.2 explains how schooling enhances brain development better than does having larger brain structures. Experience (or education) provides the developing brain with the stimulation it needs to link more and more neurons together.

Cognitive Development

As children make their way through the school curriculum, they become ever more capable and sophisticated in their thinking. In examining the mental processes that emerge during cognitive development, we will consider two theoretical approaches. Both explain how students become sophisticated thinkers, and both offer concrete advice for teachers who are trying to develop their students' thinking.

In the first approach—Piaget's theory—students are viewed as naturally curious explorers who constantly try to make sense of their surroundings. By manipulating objects and by exploring what is new and unfamiliar, they discover and adapt to the world around them. From this point of view, cognitive development occurs as low-level mental structures are enriched and transformed into higher level structures. By examining Piaget's theory, educators learn what to expect in terms of children and adolescents' thinking across different grade levels. Knowing this, teachers can offer students developmentally appropriate activities and classroom environments that are stimulating, interesting, and complex enough to develop students' higher order thinking.

In the second approach—Vygotsky's theory—students are viewed as young apprentices who benefit from the relationships they have with competent mentors. Through social guidance and cooperative dialogue, students acquire skills and knowledge. From this point of view, cognitive development is the gradual acquisition of skills, knowledge, and expertise. By examining Vygotsky's theory, educators learn that cognitive growth is a socially mediated activity that occurs in a context of social interaction. Knowing this, teachers can offer students social guidance to help them develop the kind of thinking they need to become effective participants in their culture.

Adaptation and Schemas: Piaget's Theory

Jean Piaget was a Swiss psychologist who conducted a lifelong study of children's cognitive development. He observed children and adolescents in natural situations and posed problems for them to solve. Upon hearing their solutions, Piaget would ask them to explain their reasoning. From this reasoning, Piaget learned how young people think and understand the world around them.

Appendix

Learning Theories

As children grow and become adolescents, they become increasingly sophisticated in their thinking skills. Piagetian and Vygotskian theories describe how this occurs (*PRAXIS™*, I. A. 1, *INTASC*, Principle 2).

One problem Piaget posed was the flower problem. As shown in the "What Kids Say and Do" box on this page, the flower problem introduces five daisies and two carnations bunched together into a single vase. Children are asked to observe and manipulate the flowers until they feel comfortable with them. The child's reasoning reveals his or her underlying mental operations. Six-year-old Jenny evidently lacks the mental capacity for two-dimensional classification, instead relying on what her eyes tell her, says that there are more daisies than flowers. Ten-year-old Maria evidently understands what Jenny does not—namely, that objects can be grouped two-dimensionally into classes and subclasses in which the class (flowers) is greater than any of its subclasses (daisies).

What Kids Say and Do

Two Children Solve the Flower Problem

Teacher: Here are a bunch of pretty flowers. As you look them over, which would say is true—are there more daisies than flowers, more flowers than daisies, or are there about the same number of daisies and flowers?

Six-year-old Jenny

"More daisies.

See how many there are!"

Ten-year-old Maria

"More flowers.

There are many daisies, but there are even more flowers."

(Photo By Johnmarshall Reeve)

Piaget studied cognitive development because he viewed intelligence as a basic life process that helps the person adapt to the environment. Hence, the function of thought—its purpose—is to facilitate adaptation. **Adaptation** is the inborn process of adjusting to the demands of the environment. A person adapts when he or she copes with challenges, solves problems, and attains sophisticated ways of thinking. Adaptation occurs through the cognitive processes of assimilation and accommodation, and the motivational process of disequilibrium, as explained below.

The basic building blocks for thinking are schemas (or schemes). **Schemas** are the basic structure for organizing information. Piaget identified three types of these basic cognitive structures. **Behavioral schemas** are mental representations of physical actions. Actions such as grasping, banging, shaking, or kicking are behavioral schemas infants use to explore, respond to, and make sense of the objects around them. Possessing a repertoire of such behavioral schemas, the infant is better able to understand the objects around her. **Symbolic schemas** are language-based mental representations of objects and events. By interacting with animals and by writing letters, children come to understand concepts such as cats and sentences. Possessing a repertoire of such symbolic schemas, children can think about objects and their properties. As development progresses, symbolic schemas become more numerous and more complex. For instance, an early symbolic schema of *sentence* soon differentiates into several types of sentences, such as the basic sentence, the run-on sentence, and the incomplete sentence. Much of what is meant by cognitive development is growth in the number and complexity of one's symbolic schemas.

The third type of schema is the operational schema, which Piaget referred to as an *operation*. An **operation** is a mental action; it is a mental manipulation carried out to solve a problem or to reason logically. Classification is an operation ten-year-old Maria was able to use to reason logically about the flower problem. All mental operations are reversible acts; that is, they can be carried out in one's mind in either one direction or the opposite direction. Addition is a mental operation that involves adding objects together. Subtraction is the reversal of addition; it is the same mental operation, carried out in the opposite direction (Piaget, 1970). Much of what is meant by cognitive development is how sophisticated one's operations are, because operations can be nonexistent, concrete, or abstract, as discussed later in the chapter.

Assimilation. Adaptation occurs through assimilation and accommodation. **Assimilation** is a process of incorporation in which some outside event is brought into a person's way of thinking. It occurs when students find that their existing schemas are adequate to make sense

---

adaptation Adjusting to the demands of the environment.

schemas The basic structure for organizing information.

behavioral schemas Mental representations of physical actions.

symbolic schemas Language-based representations of objects and events.

Chapter Reference
Chapter 8 discusses schemas as key knowledge structures involved in memory.

operation A mental action or a mental manipulation carried out to solve a problem or to reason logically.

assimilation An incorporation process in which an outside event is brought into one's way of thinking.

of what they observe. Assimilation involves adaptation to the extent that the student must grow or expand an existing schema to make room for the new information. Children have schemas for *cat,* adolescents have schemas for *rap music,* and teachers have schemas for *standardized tests.* Assimilation occurs when children make sense of a new four-legged creature by calling it a *cat,* adolescents make sense of a new song by calling it *rap music,* and teachers make sense of the Iowa Test of Basic Skills by calling it a *standardized test.* Through assimilation, schemas grow—in number and in complexity.

Accommodation. A different adaptive process, called *accommodation,* occurs when students find that they must modify or change a schema if they are going to be able to understand what is new. **Accommodation** is a modification process in which an existing schema is changed or modified to make sense of something that is new and different. It occurs when a lower level schema is transformed into a higher level one, as might typically happen when the child's schema for *cat* proves inadequate to the catlike animal encountered at the zoo (a leopard). When a student's existing schema proves inadequate, one of two things must occur: The student can modify the existing schema or can create a new schema for leopards. Accommodation occurs when students modify their schemas into new and better ways of thinking or when they create a whole new schema by copying the thinking of a model (De Lisi & Golbeck, 1999).

accommodation A modification process in which low-level schemas are transformed into higher level schemas.

Disequilibrium. According to Piaget (1954), learning is always an interaction between the student and the environment. The student enters into a learning activity with an existing way of thinking—that is, with schemas, expectations, and predictions about what should happen during the learning experience (see box A in Figure 2.3). Classroom activities, in turn, provide objects and events to be understood and problems to be solved. As learning activities unfold, the student observes what actually happens (see box B in Figure 2.3). For instance, a high school student might come to an English literature class with a schema that poems are short, rhyme, and are about love. The English teacher, however, might present a poem that is long, does not include rhyme, and is about a social issue. The resulting mismatch between *what I expected to happen* versus *what actually happened* is shown in box C in Figure 2.3 as cognitive conflict, or disequilibrium.

Disequilibrium is a state of cognitive conflict that arises when one's existing way of thinking is not confirmed by experience. It typically results in an openness to experience, as in "I want and need more information to make sense of this." Equilibrium, in contrast, follows after accommodation has produced a state of cognitive congruence in which one's way

What Does This Mean to Me?
Would you describe your learning experience in reading this chapter as one of assimilation, accommodation, or both?

disequilibrium A state of cognitive conflict in which one's existing schema or way of thinking is not confirmed by experience.

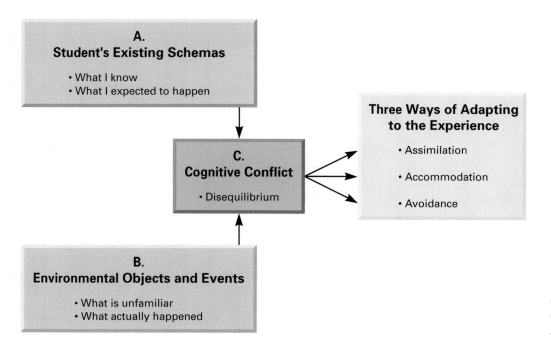

Figure 2.3. Origins and Consequences of Cognitive Conflict

of thinking adequately reflects one's experience. It typically results in a closed way of thinking, as in "Okay, now I understand this; I'm satisfied." (Piaget, 1971). Adaptation is essentially this process of moving from a state of disequilibrium to a state of equilibrium.

In sum, assimilation and accommodation account for growth and developmental change in schemas. It is the motivational process of disequilibrium that initiates these cognitive processes. The contribution that teachers can make to this learning process is to provide environmental objects and events that engender cognitive conflict (represented in box B in Figure 2.3). As shown in Figure 2.3, a third possibility is that students respond to the cognitive conflict with frustration, avoidance, and abandonment of the effort to think. With avoidance, the student does not profit from the learning experience, and adaptation does not occur. Instead, negative emotions—frustration, anxiety, confusion—overwhelm the desire to accommodate the information to be learned, and the student avoids the learning opportunity by ignoring it, physically or mentally walking away from it, or reacting with a playful response that makes light of the inability to understand (De Lisi & Golbeck, 1999).

Stages in Cognitive Development

According to Piaget, cognitive development unfolds in a structured sequence consisting of four stages: sensorimotor, preoperational, concrete operations, and formal operations. In this view, each stage of development represents a qualitatively different level of cognitive growth. Notice the word *operation* within the name of the stages, because cognitive development revolves around acquiring ever more sophisticated operational schemas. Table 2.1 summarizes the primary schemas that students rely on during each stage as well as the major developments that occur during each stage. The table also provides the ages and grade levels commonly associated with each stage.

TABLE 2.1

Piaget's Hypothesized Stages of Cognitive Development

Approximate age and grade level	Stage	Primary schemas	Major developments
0–2 Infancy	Sensorimotor	During infancy, behavior is sensory (touching) and motor (grasping). Infants do not think conceptually but instead use their sensory and motor capacities to gain a basic understanding of their environment and construct sensorimotor coordinations.	Infants internalize behavioral schemas. Through object permanence, infants learn that objects continue to exist when they are out of sight.
2–7 Preschool; early elementary school	Preoperational	Children use symbolism (language, images) to represent various aspects of their environment. Thought is prelogical, perception bound, and egocentric.	Language develops rapidly. Children become imaginative in play.
7–11 Late elementary school	Concrete operations	Children acquire mental operations and apply them to solve concrete problems in front of them.	No longer misled by physical appearances, children use their mental operations to reason.
11 years and older; middle school and high school	Formal operations	Adolescents think about thinking. They use mental operations to consider unseen hypotheses and solve abstract problems.	Adolescents become capable of systematic, deductive, and inferential reasoning, which allows them to consider many possible solutions to a problem and choose the most appropriate one.

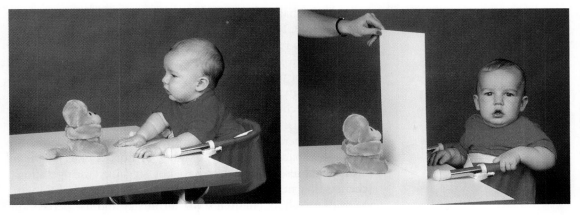

Infants who have not yet mastered object permanence cannot remember hidden environmental objects (i.e., out of sight, out of mind). (Doug Goodman/ Photo Researchers)

Sensorimotor Stage. Cognitive development begins in infancy with the sensorimotor stage. This is a period during which infants coordinate their sensory experiences with their motor capacities and, in doing so, create behavioral schemas. Soon after birth, the infant advances from merely exercising innate reflexes to interacting with the environment through the following five substages:

- *Primary circular reactions* (1–4 months): By chance, infants discover that some actions—such as sucking and arm waving—are satisfying. They then repeat these behavioral schemes over and over (hence, they are circular).

- *Secondary circular reactions* (4–8 months): Infants discover that some actions have interesting effects on the environment (e.g., squeezing a noise-producing ball).

- *Goal-directed behavior* (8–12 months): Intentions replace reflexes. The infant grasps an object, then shakes it intentionally to produce a noise.

- *Tertiary circular reactions* (12–18 months): Curiosity leads the infant to experiment with objects to discover new and interesting properties. Knowing that the rattle makes a pleasing sound, the infant experiments to see what additional effects it might produce if dropped (bounces) or mouthed (tastes bad).

- *Symbolic problem solving* (18–24 months): Infants begin to construct symbolic images of environmental objects. The emergence of symbolic operations marks the end of the sensorimotor stage, as illustrated by the mastery of object permanence.

Object permanence is the understanding that objects in the environment continue to exist even when they cannot be seen or detected by other senses. Adults who leave their houses know that their houses are still there even when they are out of sight. Such a capacity to hold an object in one's memory is an acquired cognitive skill. If you show a one-year-old infant an attractive stuffed animal, then hide it behind some object, such as a curtain, the infant acts as though the stuffed animal had disappeared (i.e., out of sight, out of mind). Two-year-olds, however, can remember that the object still exists and can use mental inferences (guesses, hypotheses) to guide their search for the toy. Because they have a symbolic representation of the object in memory, infants can understand that objects have a permanence that is independent of their behavior. This intellectual achievement—the understanding of object permanence—shows that infants now possess symbolic schemas, mental representations of the world around them.

object permanence
Understanding that objects continue to exist even when they cannot be seen or detected by other senses.

Preoperational Stage. In the preoperational stage, children create symbolic schemas to represent the objects and events in the world around them. A *symbol* is a word or image that stands for something else (DeLoache, 1987, 1991). For instance, the word-symbol *cat* represents the furry pet with four legs, a tail, and a purring sound. Piaget used the term **semiotic function**, or symbolic function, to refer to this new cognitive ability. The most striking use of mental symbols is language, and children's use of language increases very rapidly during this stage.

semiotic function   The symbolic function in which a mental symbol (word) represents an environmental object.

A second hallmark of the preoperational stage is pretend play (Piaget, 1951). During pretend play, children use one object, such as a broom, to represent another object, such as a horse. Such play fosters cognitive development. Preschool children who engage in a good deal of pretend play perform better on tests of their language, creativity, cognitive development, and social maturity than do preschool children who engage in less pretend play (Connolly & Doyle, 1984).

The preoperational stage is mostly characterized by immature cognitive capacity, at least by adult standards. *Preoperational* means that preschool children have not yet gained the operational schemas they need in order to think logically. Instead of thinking logically, preschool children think intuitively and use perception, not reason, to understand the world and to solve problems, just as six-year-old Jenny did in the flowers problem. Another illustration of perception-bound thinking can be illustrated by the three-mountain task shown in Figure 2.4. The preoperational child sits in one chair and looks at the mountains from one perspective while a teddy bear sits in a second chair that offers a different view of the mountains. The child is first asked to describe what the view looks like from his or her perspective. Next, the child is asked to describe what the view looks like from the teddy bear's perspective. Preoperational thinkers will say that the teddy bear sees the mountains from the same view as does the child (e.g., the biggest mountain is still on the left-hand side). In other words, the preoperational child shows an inability to take the perspective of the teddy bear.

Source: Kowalski, R. N., & Westen, D. *Psychology*, Fourth Edition. © 2005 John Wiley & Sons. Reprinted by permission of John Wiley & Sons, Inc.

Figure 2.4. The Three-Mountains Problem

Concrete Operations Stage. An operation is an internal mental activity that allows the child to revise or alter a symbol or image to reach a logical conclusion (Flavell, Miller, & Miller, 1993). Mental manipulations allow the elementary school child's thinking to become dynamic (rather than static), decentered (rather than centered on only one dimension), and logical (rather than perceptual). Table 2.2 summarizes and defines seven capacities of concrete-operational thinking: **animism**, **centration**, **transductive reasoning**, **egocentrism**, **reversibility**, **classification**, and **seriation**.

As elementary-grade children manipulate objects that might be grouped into different categories, they begin to recognize that objects vary on more than one dimension and thus may be grouped in many different ways. For instance, children mentally classify their treasured objects, such as dolls, Beanie Babies, stamps, stickers, and baseball cards, in many different ways. Collections include objects, therefore providing an ideal means for enriching children's classification operation. By trying to organize their collected objects, children develop the concept of relationships between classes and subclasses, and even subclasses within subclasses. In a card collection, for instance, *baseball cards* is the whole, and *National League* and *American League* might be subclasses.

In the test of conservation of a liquid quantity, the pre-operational thinker believes the tall, skinny glass has more juice than the shorter (but wider) glass. (MR © Ellen B. Senisi/The Image Works)

TABLE 2.2

Comparison of Seven Mental Operations During the Preoperational and Concrete Operational Stages

Concept	Preoperational thought	Concrete-operational thought
Animism	The belief that all things are living (e.g., the sun sets because it is tired).	
	Children assume that moving objects have lifelike qualities. A table hurts if it is scratched.	Children distinguish between animate and inanimate objects and know not to ascribe lifelike qualities to inanimate objects.
Centration	Focusing on an object's most salient perceptual feature, such as its height, while neglecting other important features that are not perceptually salient, such as width and depth.	
	Children rely on perception-bound judgment and focus on a single, salient aspect of an object when trying to solve a problem or answer a question.	Children can discount misleading physical appearances and focus on more than one aspect of an object at a time (e.g., considering not only an object's height but also its width and depth).
Transductive reasoning	A causality belief in which children think that when two events occur simultaneously, one must have caused the other.	
	Relying on transductive reasoning, children assume that when two events occur at the same time, one caused the other.	Children have a better understanding of temporal cause-and-effect relationships.
Egocentrism	Viewing the world from one's own perspective while failing to recognize that other people might have a different perspective or point of view.	
	Children typically assume that others share their point of view. "The world is as it looks to me."	Children are more aware of others' perspectives and understand that they can be different from their own. "The world can be seen both from my perspective and from yours."
Reversibility	The ability to reverse an action by mentally performing its opposite, such as mentally putting a piece of paper back into its original state after it has been torn in half.	
	Children cannot mentally undo an action they have witnessed. They cannot understand that adding $2 + 3 = 5$ can be undone, such that $5 - 2 = 3$.	Children can mentally undo an action they witnessed and return the object back to its original state: 2 beads can be added to 3 to make 5, and 2 can be subtracted from 5 to return to the original 3.
Classification	Grouping objects into categories. An understanding of whole/part relationships among objects, such as understanding that Texas is a part of the whole United States.	
	Children use one-dimensional classifications, because they include all objects that share a common attribute in the same single category.	Children use two-dimensional classifications, because they distinguish between whole classes and underlying subclasses by recognizing that objects have more than one attribute.
Seriation	The ability to order or arrange a set of objects along a quantifiable dimension, such as height or weight of the objects.	
	Lacking the ability to seriate, children given a set of six sticks of varying lengths will arrange them in a random or haphazard way.	Children arrange the objects such as the six sticks of differing lengths in serial order, starting with the shortest and finishing with the longest.

How Can I Use This?

Try one of the tasks in Figure 2.5 with an elementary-grade child and ask: How are the two objects different? How are they the same?

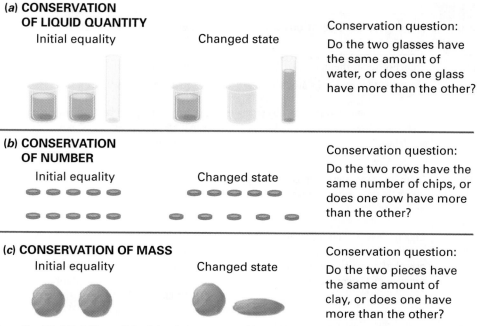

Figure 2.5. Three Piagetian Tests of a Child's Capacity to Conserve

Source: Kowalski, R. N., & Westen, D. *Psychology*, Fourth Edition. © 2005 John Wiley & Sons. Reprinted by permission of John Wiley & Sons, Inc.

Chapter Reference
The implications of seriation for students' self-concepts is discussed in Chapter 3.

conservation   Understanding that appearance alterations (e.g., an object's length, height, or width) do not change the essential properties of an object (e.g., its amount).

With seriation, the concrete-operational child can mentally arrange, or order, a set of objects along a quantifiable dimension, such as height. Understanding operations such as *greater than* (>) and *less than* (<) allows children to arrange objects in a serial order, such as arranging the 20 students in their class in terms of shortest to tallest. Because concrete-operational thinkers can seriate, they begin to recognize that attributes of people can also be arranged on a quantifiable dimension, such as grades, running speed, physical attractiveness, and so forth. Such judgments have important consequences for the child's developing sense of self and self-worth, because seriation makes social comparisons possible. Because of their capacity to seriate, late-elementary school children begin to realize that "I am faster than Joe but slower than Jill and José. Maybe I'm not the fastest after all."

The crucial operational schema that defines the concrete operations stage is **conservation**, the realization that the properties of an object do not change even if its appearance is altered in some way. Lacking the capacity to conserve, preoperational thinkers use their perceptions to judge an object whose appearance has been altered. Concrete-operational children realize that the change in one attribute is compensated by a corresponding change in another attribute. Figure 2.5 shows three illustrations of Piagetian conservation tasks involving the conservation of liquid, number, and mass. In each test of the child's ability to conserve, some perceptual property of the object has been changed—its height, width, or surface area, for instance. Preoperational thinkers follow their eyes and say that each object has changed—more water, more chips, and more clay. Concrete-operational thinkers use the conservation operation to follow their logic and say that the objects contain the same amount, despite an altered appearance. The "Taking It to the Classroom" box on the next page offers six ways teachers can enrich their students' concrete operations.

Formal Operations Stage. As impressive as the cognitive repertoire of concrete-operational thinkers is, operations can be applied only to *concrete* (tangible) objects and events that lie immediately in front of them. With formal-operational thinking, preadolescents and adolescents consider unseen possibilities. They generate hypotheses, and they think logically and systematically about hypotheses, ideas, and possibilities. The *form* in formal operations refers to the capacity to follow the form of an argument and not just its content. Parables, metaphors, ironies, proverbs, analogies, and satire—such as those found in books such as *Animal Farm* and *Gulliver's Travels*—illustrate this feature. Concrete thinkers understand *Animal Farm* to be a story about farm animals, whereas formal thinkers understand the story is a satire on government. With formal-operational thinking, thinking can be independent of concrete reality. For example, actors say, "Break a leg"; parents say, "Money doesn't grow on trees"; and television sportscasters say, "that ball was a frozen rope."

Taking It to the Classroom

Ways to Enrich Concrete Operations

Promote exploration	Provide children with interesting objects to manipulate and explore.
Promote discovery	Instead of telling students about a concept, create the opportunity for them to discover it. To discover *taxonomy*, have children explore leaves of different shapes, colors, and spinal patterns, then ask why some leaves would be grouped together.
Keep discovery going	The teacher's role is to get things started (collect a sample of leaves), then to keep discovery going by supporting students' curiosity and interest. (If a student invents a dubious taxonomy, ask how the student reached that conclusion and point out differences the child does not yet see.)
Ask for predictions	Ask students to predict what might happen next. Before turning the page in a book, first ask the child to predict what might happen next.
Encourage thinking about relationships	As students explore and manipulate objects, ask about relationships: In what ways are these two trees similar to each other? In what ways are they different?
Resist telling or showing students the **right** answer	Resist telling a child something, because telling prevents children from discovering that knowledge by themselves. The problem with telling students answers is that they learn without understanding. Through invention, students learn with understanding.

Most classroom-based tasks involve both real facts and possible hypotheses. In an art class, for instance, the task might be to draw or paint a still life. Concrete-operational thinkers generally draw what is in front of them (flowers, landscapes), whereas formal-operational thinkers think about what is possible (imagined events, abstract art). In a math class, concrete-operational thinkers count beads and coins, whereas formal-operational thinkers reason with abstract concepts such as letters and numbers (e.g., if $4x + 10 = 26$, what does x equal?).

Two ways of thinking hypothetically are inductive and deductive reasoning. With **inductive reasoning**, adolescents reason from a number of specific observations to infer a general conclusion. For instance, Mark may observe that Jeff likes basketball, tennis, and water skiing, and conclude that Jeff probably likes sports in general. Similarly, what should John think upon entering the classroom and observing the following?

inductive reasoning The abstraction of a general principle from a variety of examples.

- The teacher brought cookies.
- The classroom is decorated with balloons.
- Today is Friday.

Going beyond the information in these three observations to infer the conclusion that it's a party represents the exercise of inductive logic. With **deductive reasoning**, adolescents deduce or draw information out of evidence or general premises. For instance:

deductive reasoning Drawing information or hypotheses out of a general premise or a sample of evidence.

- Friday is test day.
- Today is Friday.
- Therefore, we probably have a test today.

The conclusion that *we probably have a test today* is deduced information. Deductive logic goes beyond what is known (Friday is test day; today is Friday) to generate new information. The important point is that adolescents think like the famous detective from literature, Sherlock Holmes, as they use both inductive and deductive thinking to go beyond the information in front of them to generate and deduce new hypotheses.

Systematic problem solving (scientific thinking) represents a formal operation. Concrete-operational thinkers generally use a trial-and-error approach to problem solving as they search haphazardly (unsystematically) for a solution. Formal-operational thinkers are more likely to think systematically during problem solving. To illustrate this difference, consider the pendulum problem in Figure 2.6 (from Inhelder & Piaget, 1958). A weight suspended on a string and set into motion acts as a pendulum. In the pendulum problem, the student is asked to determine which factor explains how fast the pendulum swings. Concrete-operational thinkers are unable to separate the four variables—lengths, weights, elevations, and pushes—to determine or isolate the separate effect of each. For instance, concrete thinkers might change the length of the string but at the same time also change the object's weight and the force of the initial push. Only systematic formal-operational thinkers

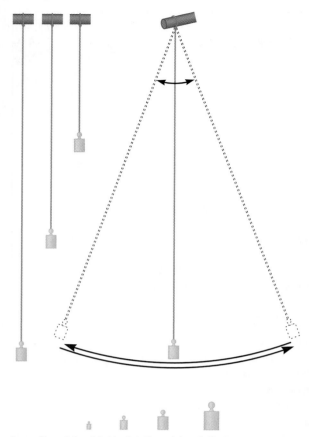

Source: Figure 3 from Inhelder, B. & Piaget, J. (1958). *The Growth of Logical Thinking from Childword to Adolescence.* Copyright © 1958 by Basic Books, Inc. Reprinted by permission of Basic Books, a member of Perseus Books, L.L.C.

Figure 2.6. The Pendulum Problem

who generate and test reasonable hypotheses can come to a conclusion such as the following (Inhelder & Piaget, 1958, p. 75):

. . .after having selected 100 grams with a long string and a medium length string, then 20 grams with a long and a short string, and finally 200 grams with a long and a short, [the student] concludes: "It's the length of the string that makes it go faster or slower; the weight doesn't play any role." She discounts likewise the height of the drop and the force of her push. [Quote from adolescent who solves the problem using formal operations]

The problem in Figure 2.6 may seem artificial, but the same scientific reasoning is used in daily life—by detectives solving a mystery, business owners selecting the best location for a restaurant, or high school seniors deciding which college to attend. In each case, several factors play a possible determining role, and a logical solution requires systematic thinking in which hypotheses are formulated, variables are isolated, confounding factors are controlled, and key influences are identified.

The intellectual transition from concrete to formal operations takes place gradually. Many high school students actually do not use formal operations, or they do so only rarely (Neimark, 1979). Developing formal-operational thinking requires the kinds of cognitive challenges that schools provide (Cole, 1990) in subjects including algebra (e.g., Let $x = 5$. Solve for x in the following equation: $8 = -2x + 2$.), science (e.g., the pendulum problem), literature (e.g., interpreting imagery, satire, metaphors), and politics (e.g., What would happen if a country's political structure changed from socialism to democracy?). Perhaps you are currently enrolled in an introductory philosophy course. If so, glance through the textbook's table of contents, and you will see that the study of logic is basically a training ground for the development and use of formal operations (e.g., inference, deduction, syllogisms, probabilities). Teachers and schooling can clearly help students develop their formal-operational thinking (De Lisi & Staudt, 1980; Fischer, Kenny, & Pipp, 1990), as shown in the "Taking It to the Classroom" box below.

Taking It to the Classroom

Ways to Enrich Formal Operations

Ask for possibilities	Request a statement of all the possibilities relating to a particular event.
Analyze logic	Ask students to state an opinion, such as the opinion that democracy is the best form of government, then to explain why that opinion is valid.
	Help students use inferential and deductive logic.
	Identify and challenge invalid (illogical) arguments, including:
	a. Appeals to the masses (everyone else does it.).
	b. Appeals to pity/feelings (persuasion via emotion, not reason).
	c. Illegitimate appeals to authority (citing a source with no topic expertise in the subject, such as a celebrity's endorsement).
	d. Arguing against the individual (name calling).
Encourage scientific thinking	Create classroom projects that require students to isolate variables, imagine unseen possibilities, and generate hypotheses.
Act as a consultant	As students solve problems, act as a consultant to their exploration, not as an authority who has the answers. As one educator phrased it, "Not a sage on the stage but a guide on the side."
Use peer learning	Because teachers have greater knowledge and status than students do, teachers' answers often come across as definitive. An egalitarian relationship is easier to achieve among peers, so peer learning provides a better opportunity for students to experience cognitive conflict.

Applications of Piaget's Theory

Educators generally react positively to Piaget's ideas (Gallagher & Easley, 1978; Ginsburg & Opper, 1988; Wadsworth, 1996). Here are three applications of Piaget's theory (based on Piaget, 1971, 1973).

1. **Be sensitive to individual differences.** Children differ in their rates of cognitive development. Because this is so, not all children are intellectually ready to learn the same lesson. To be sensitive to differences in students' readiness to learn, plan learning activities for individual students or for small groups of students, rather than for the whole class. For instance, teachers can set up interest areas for students to explore on their own, and they can have students work on personal projects or portfolios of their work.

2. **Motivate by stimulating curiosity.** Students come to school wanting to learn. They come with existing schemas, and they often realize that their current understanding is somehow insufficient. Table 2.3 offers three curiosity-inducing instructional strategies that teachers can use to create motivation-based disequilibrium-creating experiences during instruction: guessing and feedback, suspense, and controversy. With disequilibrium, students are inherently motivated to seek out new knowledge and are open to revising their existing knowledge (Loewenstein, 1994). Thus, curiosity is a natural motivation to learn, one that arises from cognitive conflict.

3. **Promote discovery-based learning.** Piaget advised teachers to avoid instructional strategies that place students in a passive mode of learning (e.g., lecturing, telling, demonstrating, showing). He believed strongly that the mind is *not* a passive receptacle. Instead of being asked to watch and listen to the teacher, students should be encouraged to explore the objects and activities around them (Bruner, 1961). For example, instead of watching a math teacher show on a blackboard how to add and subtract, students should engage in hands-on activities with objects such as beads, coins, and buttons. Similarly, a science teacher might lecture on the metric system, but students would be better served by activities involving measuring themselves, their desks, and any other classroom object of interest. To promote discovery learning, teachers need to provide classroom environments that are rich in stimulation, complexity, and objects of interest—books, computers, art, animals or pets, construction paper, puzzles, libraries, science laboratories, and musical instruments.

Chapter Reference
Using curiosity-inducing strategies to spark students' motivation is discussed further in Chapter 6.

RIDE How would Piaget suggest a teacher help students understand the concept of fractions?

TABLE 2.3

Three Curiosity-Inducing Instructional Strategies

1. **Guessing and feedback**
The teacher asks students a difficult question based on the day's lesson plan. Students then generate an answer by writing it down or saying it aloud. The teacher gives right/wrong feedback. Wrong answers expose students' understanding as inadequate. Students are allowed a second answer, and if this too is incorrect, disequilibrium grows.

- An elementary school teacher brings the topic for discussion into class wrapped in a brown paper bag. She asks students to guess what it might be.
- A history teacher writes the names of five presidents on the board and asks, "What do these presidents have in common? Why should they be grouped together?"

2. **Suspense**
The teacher introduces a learning activity and asks students to try to predict its outcome. Students then collect the data they need to test the validity of their prediction. Students use this outcome-revealing information to assess the adequacy of their prior knowledge.

- One-third book report: Students read the first third of a book and stop to write a brief report consisting of predictions about what will likely happen in the book's remaining pages. As they read, students find out whether their predictions are correct.

- Demonstration: A physics teacher has two objects—a golf ball and a ping pong ball. Students are asked to predict which object will hit the ground first when they are dropped side by side. Students watch the demonstration, hoping that their prediction will be confirmed.

3. **Controversy**
Students are introduced to an issue with more than one possible answer and asked to take a position on that issue. Using these position statements, the teacher divides the students into pairs or small groups and communicates the value of different perspectives, rather than a right or best answer. During the ensuing discussion, students become aware of their peers' differing perspectives, which instigates disequilibrium and the search for additional information to defend their perspective and to critique their peers' perspectives.

- A controversy: Where did the moon come from? Perhaps a textbook offers three different explanations and students debate those explanations.
- An open-ended question: What is the theme of *The Adventures of Huckleberry Finn*?

Limitations of Piaget's Theory

Piaget's ideas have had a lasting impact on the practice of education (Beilin, 1992). But several of his key ideas have been challenged, and these challenges have led to new ways of thinking about cognitive development and the practice of education (Lourenco & Machado, 1996). One limitation is that Piaget sometimes underestimated the intellectual capacities of infants, preschoolers, and elementary school students (Baillargeon, 1987; Bjorklund, 1995). When children are given problems to solve that are simpler and more familiar to them than those used by Piaget, they sometimes show greater problem-solving skills. Under some conditions, even preschoolers can show signs of deductive reasoning (Hawkins et al., 1994).

A second limitation of Piaget's theory concerns his insistence that cognitive development is *qualitatively* different for students of different ages (Bjorklund, 1995). Those who study cognitive development from an information-processing perspective argue that cognitive development unfolds in small *quantitative,* rather than large qualitative, changes (Case & Okamoto, 1996). The idea is that ongoing maturation of the brain and central nervous system explains why older children are more complex thinkers than younger children, as discussed earlier in the section on brain development. Students with more mature brains will be better at sustaining attention, interpreting information, holding information in memory, and thinking abstractly. This greater biological capacity allows adolescents to use more sophisticated *strategies* to solve problems. For instance, adolescents can solve Piagetian tasks like the pendulum problem by remembering what they have and have not done, by processing information faster, by using more efficient problem-solving strategies, and by tapping into their domain-specific prior knowledge (Bjorklund et al., 1997; Case, 1992; Kuhn & Phelps, 1982). Hence, thinking speed, memory capacity, effective strategies, and prior knowledge can—and do—explain advances in cognitive development.

A third limitation concerns the practice of **discovery-based learning**. In science, algebra, and computer programming, for instance, direct instruction in which teachers explicitly teach and show students information often works better than does discovery learning (Klahrl & Nigam, 2004). In addition, **guided discovery** generally produces better learning outcomes than does pure discovery (Mayer, 2004).

A final limitation of Piaget's theory is his relative neglect of the importance of culture and social guidance in the advancement of cognitive development. For Piaget, students developed cognitively when acting as independent explorers who interact in a stimulating environment. However, this view of cognitive development leaves out the important role of social guidance. Often, children's understanding and skills—how to read, how to cook, how to remember, how to plan, how to build something—are socially mediated. That is, students' ways of thinking benefit if they have access to a competent adult as they try to make sense of the world around them. Socially mediated means that children use a competent adult to act as a guide to bridge the gap between an opportunity to learn and the actual experience of learning. The view that cognitive development occurs through guided participation and social interaction is the subject of the next section.

Chapter Reference
The information-processing view of learning and memory is presented in Chapter 8.

discovery-based learning
Students work on their own to grasp a concept or understand a lesson.

guided discovery   Students work under the guidance of a capable partner to grasp a concept or understand a lesson.

Sociocognitive Development

Sociocognitive development is the study of how other people (socio-) guide and develop our thinking (cognitive). To capture the essential flavor of *socio*cognitive development, consider the experience of traveling to a foreign country, one with a different language and different customs from your own. If you have traveled abroad, you probably felt unsure of yourself and wanted to travel with someone who already knew the language and customs rather well. If so, this is how you probably learned your way around: Stay near the trusted guide, watch closely what the guide does, mimic what the guide does, ask the guide whether what you are doing is okay, and attend very closely to any instruction he or she provides. When we find ourselves in uncharted territory, it helps to have a mentor to guide us along the way. For Russian developmental psychologist Lev Vygotsky, students who are asked to learn how to read, play a musical instrument, or solve algebra problems are like travelers in a foreign land who want and benefit from access to a trusted guide.

Cognitive Development as an Apprenticeship: Vygotsky's Theory

About the same time that Piaget was formulating his ideas on cognitive development, Lev Vygotsky was doing the same, though he reached very different conclusions. Vygotsky argued that cognitive development emerges mostly out of the child's social interactions with parents, teachers, peers, and other competent members of society. For Vygotsky, cognitive growth developed from collaborative dialogues with skilled members of the culture (Vygotsky, 1978, 1987).

From this brief introduction, it might already be apparent that Vygotsky's answer to the question, What develops during cognitive development? was different from Piaget's. For Piaget, cognitive development involved enrichment of general operations (e.g., object permanence, conservation) that can be used to solve problems. For Vygotsky, cognitive development involved enrichment of task-specific skills and knowledge (Fischer, 1980). What students need to learn task-specific skills and knowledge is not exploration and discovery but, instead, guided participation.

Guided participation occurs when one engages in learning activities alongside a skilled partner who provides the support and encouragement needed to acquire new skills and new understanding (Rogoff, 1998). Children and adolescents seek out opportunities for social guidance in any number of daily activities, including getting dressed, preparing a nutritious breakfast, crossing the street, working on a computer, learning a sporting activity, learning a foreign language, submitting applications to colleges, and so on. They do so because cognitive processes often occur on the social level before they are internalized and transformed on the individual level. Thus, because learning is so often embedded within social interaction, cognitive development requires an apprenticeship (Rogoff, 1990).

Chapter Reference
Vygotsky's sociocognitive perspective on learning is discussed more completely in Chapters 10 and 12.

guided participation Having one's engagement in a learning activity encouraged, supported, and tutored by a skilled partner.

Scaffolding in the Zone of Proximal Development

A student faces every educational task with a certain range (a bandwidth) of domain-specific competence, as shown in Table 2.4. At the left-hand side of this range is *predevelopment*, a level of competence at which the student is unable to solve problems in that domain, even with assistance. The difficulty of the task overwhelms the student's problem-solving capacities. In the middle of the figure is the **zone of proximal development**, the level at which students can solve problems, provided that they receive sufficient support while doing so. A high school student might be able to write a persuasive 500-word essay, but the extent to which he will be able to do so depends on the teacher's supportive tips and feedback while the student is drafting topic sentences, making transitions between paragraphs, and the like. At the right-hand side of the range is *actual development*, the level at which students are capable of solving problems independently. For example, if a biology teacher asks students to identify a specimen under a microscope, students in the zone of predevelopment will hesitate and stare blankly. Students in the zone of proximal development will express readiness but also require help and support to get through the exercise successfully. Students in the zone of actual development will be fully able to carry out the task on their own.

In Vygotsky's theory, the zone of proximal development is of particular importance because this is the critical zone in which cognitive development grows. Relatively little learning occurs in the zones of either predevelopment or actual development. Instead, learning occurs as teachers help students narrow the gap between their potential development (what they can do with assistance) and their actual development (what they can do alone). How do teachers do this? How do teachers help students achieve that which they cannot yet achieve on their own? For example, how do English teachers advance would-be writers toward

zone of proximal development A level of competence on a task in which the student cannot yet master the task on his or her own but can accomplish that same task with appropriate guidance from a more capable partner.

TABLE 2.4

The Zone of Proximal Development as a Range of Competence

Predevelopment	Zone of proximal development	Zone of actual development
Students lack the competencies needed to learn from the task, even with guidance.	Students can learn from the task if they receive another's expert guidance and support.	Students have the competencies needed to learn from the task on their own.

What Does This Mean to Me?
For a teaching task such as *making a test*, would you place your current competence in the zone of predevelopment, proximal development, or actual development?

With the guidance and support from a capable mentor, students learn complex, culturally-valued skills.
(Dynamic Graphics/Creatas)

scaffolding The guidance, support, and tutelage provided by a teacher during social interaction designed to advance students' current level of skill and understanding.

becoming proficient writers? Essentially, they provide instruction that moves ahead of what students can currently do (Vygotsky, 1987). Teachers ask would-be writers to do what they cannot yet do while simultaneously providing the support they need to do so.

Scaffolding is the guidance, support, and assistance a teacher provides to students during social interaction that allows students to gain skill and understanding. Just like a newly planted tree needs the support of a stake and ropes to hold it upright during its first year of growth, students too need teachers' scaffolding until they gain the skill and understanding that will allow them to learn on their own. Such a scaffold serves at least four functions for a learner:

● It provides support.
● It extends the range of what the learner can do.
● It allows the learner to accomplish tasks that would otherwise not be possible.
● It is used only when needed.

Because students have a difficult time knowing where to begin a new lesson, scaffolding typically begins with the teacher's planning and structuring of the lesson, such as setting up the learning activity, defining the learning goal, and modeling what an idealized performance might look like. Once the lesson begins, scaffolding involves instructional acts, such as providing hints, tips, reminders, examples, directions, challenges, explanations, prompts, and well-timed questions and suggestions. In a nutshell, scaffolding is the teacher's effort to support the student's learning in the zone of proximal development by providing what the student needs most but cannot yet provide for himself—namely, expert planning, strategies, skills, and knowledge.

Chapter Reference
Chapter 10 provides an extensive discussion of scaffolding with several examples and illustrations of what teachers do during scaffolding.

The following is an example of the scaffolding provided by a teacher to an elementary-grade student during a geography lesson:

Teacher:	Here is a map of the United States.
Student:	*(Saying nothing, she just stares at the map, then looks at the teacher.)*
Teacher:	*(Shifting her glance toward the map)* Can you identify any of the states?
Student:	*(The student continues to stare at the map, saying nothing.)*
Teacher:	*(Points to one particular state)* Do you recognize this one?
Student:	Yeah, that's where we live—Texas.
Teacher:	*(Showing excitement)* That's right! What cities are in Texas?
Student:	Dallas and Houston.
Teacher:	*(Taking her hands off the map and placing them in her lap)* Can you show me where Dallas and Houston are on the map?

Student:	*(Pointing to each city)*
Teacher:	What else is in Texas?
Student:	*(The student points to and names additional points of interest. Finally, without any further prodding from the teacher, the student begins to identify other states and other points of interest.)*
Teacher:	*(Adjusts her tutelage by becoming less directive and pausing more often to give the student more chances to talk and take the lead in the learning process.)*

Appendix
Supporting Students' Learning
Teachers need to know a variety of instructional strategies and techniques so that they can support students' learning (*PRAXIS*™, II. A. 2, *INTASC*, Principle 4).

Scaffolding is not just for children. The same process applies equally well for interactions with adolescents, as in the following example of the scaffolding provided by a teacher to a high school student in a mock-restaurant setting during a Spanish class:

Teacher:	You are in a restaurant, and you want to place an order.
Student:	*(Saying nothing, the student sits in the chair in the imaginary restaurant, shrugs, and looks at the teacher.)*
Teacher:	Here comes the waiter; what would you say as a greeting?
Student:	*(The student continues to sit at the table, looking at the teacher, hesitating, and wanting the teacher to take responsibility for the conversation.)*
Teacher:	*(Smiling, pausing, and looking with anticipation at the student, finally asking)* What might a friendly greeting be?
Student:	¿Hola, cómo está usted? *(Hello, how are you?)*
Teacher:	*(Showing excitement)* That's right! What do you say to request a menu?
Student:	¿Puedo ver un menu? *(May I see a menu?)*
Teacher:	*(Backing away from the table so that the student and "waiter" can talk)* Where might the conversation go from there?
Student:	*(Points to the menu item, and says)* La papa al horno, por favor. *(Baked potato, please.)*
Waiter:	¿Y para beber? *(And to drink?)*
Student:	La gaseosa, por favor. *(Soda pop, please.)*
Teacher:	*(Coming back toward the table)* Okay, see whether you can say it all together—greeting, menu request, order.
Student:	*(Turning to the waiter, the student strings together a greeting and an order. Finally, without any further prodding from the teacher, the student begins to engage in a more casual conversation, asking the waiter whether they serve desserts and whether there will be any music during dinner.)*
Teacher:	*(Adjusts her tutelage by asking open-ended questions and pausing more often to give the student more chances to talk and take the lead in the learning process.)*

Instructional Conversations

Scaffolding is a one-on-one process by which teachers assist one student's learning and cognitive development. When teachers apply these same scaffolding principles to a group of learners, the mentoring is called an *instructional conversation*.

Traditional instruction (i.e., direct instruction) typically relies on a one-way conversation in which teachers talk and provide information as students listen and learn. Instructional conversations are different; they are two-way discussions in which a group of learners collectively attempt to make sense of the topic of conversation, often by informing, debating, and persuading one another. Overall, the goal of an instructional conversation is to have students learn within the context of a community of learners (Rogoff, Turkanis, & Bartlett, 2002).

IRE discourse model
Conversation during teaching
that follows an initiate, respond,
evaluate script.

PSQ discourse model
Conversation during teaching that
follows a probe, question, scaffold
script.

Traditional instruction utilizes the **IRE discourse model** (initiate, respond, evaluate), whereas instructional conversations utilize the **PQS discourse model** (probe, question, scaffold). IRE begins as the teacher *initiates* a question—Which planet is closest to the sun?—continues as the student *responds* with an answer—Mercury!—and ends as the teacher *evaluates* the correctness of the response—Yes, that's right. In this *I teach, you learn* model, the teacher provides information and uses IRE discourse to check that students have indeed learned the information. PQS begins as the teacher *probes,* or investigates what students think—What do you think? Can you explain it to me?—*questions* the basis of that thinking—Why do you believe that? What is your evidence?—and *scaffolds* students toward a deeper understanding—What sort of evidence do we need to answer this question? In an instructional conversation, the teacher typically encourages students to reflect on their thinking, develop their logic or reasoning, and obtain the evidence they need to defend or justify their thinking. When teachers use this conversational style, students participate more in their learning, and a community of learners is more likely to emerge.

Traditional, IRE-based classroom conversations are very common (Mehan, 1979), mostly because teachers place a higher priority on covering a lot of content during the lesson than on providing students with opportunities to voice alternative perspectives on the content (Alvermann, O'Brien, & Dillon, 1990). Covering a lot of content is often a necessity, but PQS-based instructional conversations pursue a different goal—namely, to help students reflect on their thinking, gain control over it, and form a community of mutually interested learners.

Classroom teachers find IRE to be relatively easy and PQS to be relatively difficult (Alvermann & Hayes, 1989). To help implement the PQS discourse model, teachers find it useful to come to the class prepared with question frames, such as: Explain why _____. What is a new example of _____? How would you use _____ to _____? How does _____ affect _____? (King, 1989, 1991). Adding PQS-based instructional conversations to one's teaching repertoire is important for three reasons: (a) students generally find instructional conversations more interesting than they find traditional IRE-based conversations; (b) more students get involved and participate in instructional conversations than they do in traditional instruction; and (c) socially shared cognition typically emerges.

socially shared cognition A shared understanding of a problem that emerges during group interaction that would not have been achieved by any individual member of the group acting alone.

Socially shared cognition is meaning, understanding, or a solution to a problem that emerges during a group discussion that would not have been achieved by any individual member alone (Resnick, Levine, & Teasley, 1991). For instance, during a class discussion about the meaning of a literary work, students bring different perspectives and prior knowledge into the conversation as they (and the teacher) probe, question, and scaffold one another's thinking so that all participants gain an understanding of the book that they could not have gained individually. Such a phenomenon supports the Vygotskian truism that, often, two heads are better than one.

Intersubjectivity. Students benefit from expert scaffolding and instructional conversations in two principal ways: intersubjectivity and the transfer of responsibility (Henderson & Cunningham, 1994). **Intersubjectivity** is a unique product that arises from the expert-novice interaction. It occurs as two people converse and come to a shared understanding of how to manage the problem-solving situation (Gauvain & Rogoff, 1989). If the pair is to achieve a measure of intersubjectivity within the relationship, the student must do more than just mimic the expert's language and strategies. Instead, the pair must work collaboratively to formulate a shared focus of attention, shared intentions, shared strategies, mutual engagement, shared emotions—a joint understanding of how to develop skill and solve problems. In short, intersubjectivity is not something the student lacks, nor is it something the teacher has. It is a mutual understanding, a co-construction that acts as an intellectual bridge to extend the student's understanding (Vygotsky, 1987).

intersubjectivity The unique product that arises from social interaction in which the interaction partners come to a shared understanding of how to manage the problem-solving situation.

Transfer of Responsibility. Initially, communication between the teacher and the student is asymmetrical. The teacher selects the activity, models expert performance, sets goals, and explicitly teaches the student. In other words, the teacher takes full responsibility for the task. As the student gains and displays skill and shows fewer nonverbal signs of hesitance and frustration, the teacher begins the subtle process of assessing the student's readiness to take on more responsibility in the endeavor. Transfer of responsibility occurs as the student accomplishes subgoals of the activity, gains skill and understanding, and shows less need for assistance.

In part, transfer of responsibility is initiated by the teacher. The teacher might, for instance, increase the length of pauses in conversation to give the student an opportunity to step in and take more responsibility (Fox, 1988). The teacher might up the ante in terms of performance expectations. The teacher might also begin to replace directive communications with more open-ended questions. In the same spirit, the teacher might ask the student to explain what she is doing and why she is doing it that way. But transfer is also initiated by the student. As students grow their skills and knowledge, they learn how to send signals that they are ready to take on greater responsibility and decision making. Instead of just receiving hints, the student begins to ask for them (Rogoff & Gardner, 1984). The student also shows increased levels of leadership. As the student asks for and takes on more responsibility, the teacher provides fewer instructions and instead spends most of his time monitoring the student's progress and remaining alert for student-initiated cues indicating that the student seeks additional responsibility. Eventually, the student achieves self-regulation, in which she takes on the full responsibility for the task—choosing activities, structuring the task, setting goals, regulating emotion, implementing task strategies, providing self-reminders, deciding when and whether outside help is needed, and basically assuming full responsibility for managing the endeavor. Students who are able to take full responsibility for the task operate within the zone of actual development.

Chapter Reference
Chapter 5 presents an extended discussion of the sociocognitive model as it applies to the capacity for self-regulation.

Role of Language in Cognitive Development

Piaget and Vygotsky came to different conclusions about the role of language in cognitive development. For Piaget, language is a by-product of cognitive development, one that reflects the individual's level of cognitive maturity. Talking to oneself during problem solving, such as muttering while adding numbers, reflects only cognitive egocentrism. Instead of language facilitating cognitive development, mental schema must exist *prior* to the expression of language. In other words, thought precedes language. As a case in point, children use the word *gone* only after they have first mastered object permanence (Gopnik, 1984).

For Vygotsky, language was a social bridge to connect a mentor's advanced development with a novice's immature development. As a social phenomenon, speech is a tool for thinking. The learner first receives the mentor's speech as an external aid, which is then internalized into *inner speech*. Inner speech is verbal thinking. So, in practice, the role of language in cognitive development is to create cognitive development.

Contrasting Piaget's and Vygotsky's views on the role of language in cognitive development raises the question of what role, if any, private speech plays in children's cognitive development. **Private speech** is thought that is spoken aloud, and its purpose is to communicate with oneself for purposes of self-guidance and self-direction while trying to understand and solve a problem (Vygotsky, 1962). Table 2.5 lists three types of private speech that have been shown to contribute positively to children's problem solving and cognitive development: self-guidance, reading aloud, and inaudible muttering (Berk & Garvin, 1984).

private speech   Thought spoken out loud.

TABLE 2.5

Three Types of Private Speech Associated with Gains in Cognitive Development

1. Self-guidance	Remarks about one's own activity that are public but not directed to anyone in particular: "I want to read something. Let's see. I need a book. Where are the books? Oh yeah, there. Now, which one? What did I read last time ...?"
2. Reading aloud	Reading books or other materials aloud, sounding out words, or silently mouthing words: "Sum-time. Sum-e-time. Sum-mer-time."
3. Inaudible muttering	Quiet remarks that cannot be heard by an observer. Child moves his or her lips and makes sounds but the sounds are incomprehensible.

Cultural Tools

Sociocognitive development occurs at two levels (Vygotsky, 1978). The first level is through face-to-face, one-on-one interaction in which a competent member of the culture mentors a less competent member, as discussed earlier. The second level is through the culture's history and technology. Because past members of the culture have developed effective tools for solving problems, students learn more easily when they use these cultural tools. For instance, while learning to read, the would-be reader benefits greatly not only from having a trusted teacher but also from having access to the alphabet, the language, a book, and a library. All these cultural products were invented to help people develop their thinking through reading.

Each culture defines which problems are most important, and each culture creates its own tools for solving these problems. In the United States, for instance, writing papers and making engaging classroom presentations are important problems to be solved, and tools such as computers and PowerPoint software help students become proficient writers and presenters. Literacy and mathematics are also **cultural tools**. With literacy, students develop their ideas through written material; with mathematics, they develop ideas related to numbers and calculations (Nunes, 1999; Rogoff, 2003; Serpell, 1993). Teachers provide students with tools such as books and newspapers to help students solve the problem of understanding printed material and tools such as calculators and statistical software programs to help students solve the problem of understanding and working with numbers. In another culture, the central problems might be farming, tracking prey, or carrying water. Such a culture will provide its members with the tools they need to become skillful in solving these problems.

In any culture, members do not generally learn to use tools through exploration and self-discovery. Rather, they learn to understand, manipulate, and use these tools through a process of social transmission. It is hard to imagine using an unfamiliar tool effectively without first benefiting from the spoken or written words of a mentor. Tools such as the metric system, the periodic table of the elements, maps, and diagrams are typically introduced by a mentor. Such tools are important because they represent the learning and insights gained by the student's predecessors.

Importance of Peers

When it comes to promoting sociocognitive development, peers can be every bit as helpful as teachers. True, peers can be as unskilled and confused as is the novice student, and when novices work together, they are often a source of distraction (Tudge, 1992). However, when novices work with a more able peer, they routinely show the same sort of advances in cognitive development that they show when working with a teacher (Tudge, 1992). Like competent teachers, competent peers can scaffold a student forward (Vygotsky, 1978). This is so because novices pick up new strategies when they observe the performances of their more able peers (Azmitia, 1988). Able peers also make ideal collaborators because they are uniquely sensitive to the novice's zone of proximal development. That is, after the more able peer has learned a skill such as how to solve an algebra problem, he is keenly aware of the critical needs of the novice and can concentrate his guidance on that critical skill area. Hence, able peers are uniquely qualified to offer tailored instruction and guidance to the less able learner.

Piaget also saw peers as important collaborators in students' cognitive development. The nature of their contribution differed, however. For Piaget, peers promote cognitive development by creating cognitive conflict (disequilibrium). For instance, Table 2.3 introduced the curiosity-inducing strategy of controversy to argue that the role of peers is to provide the student with new information to assimilate and contrasting opinions to accommodate. Given a controversy to make sense of, students consider the adequacy of their existing mental structures, experience disequilibrium, and seek to achieve equilibrium through exploration of the pair's differences so as to reconcile the differing views (via assimilation, accommodation). In fact, Piaget argued that peers can induce disequilibrium better than adults can, because disagreements with adults lead to little cognitive conflict when students think adults possess so much more knowledge than they do and should therefore be listened to rather than debated (Tudge & Rogoff, 1989).

cultural tools   Products created and designed by advanced members of a culture to help less advanced members of the culture learn and solve problems.

Appendix
Cultural Experiences
Understanding that individual students come from disparate backgrounds and cultural experiences will assist you in tailoring your instruction to capitalize on those experiences (PRAXIS™, I. B. 6, INTASC, Principle 3).

Chapter Reference
Peer learning is the subject of Chapter 12.

Applications of Vygotsky's Theory

Like Piaget, Vygotsky endorsed an active rather than a passive learner. Also like Piaget, Vygotsky stressed assessing what the student already knows at the beginning of a lesson, then estimating what he or she might be capable of learning (i.e., awareness of the zone of proximal development). Where the two theories differ is in the roles of the teacher, peers, and culture. Vygotsky also offered a new perspective on motivation. With this in mind, here are four classroom applications of Vygotsky's theory.

1. **Teacher as guide, mentor.** Whereas Piaget recommended that students learn by engaging themselves in independent, discovery-based activities, Vygotsky favored a more interventive role for the teacher. The teacher helps by structuring the learning activity, providing instructions, offering guidance, monitoring and correcting the student's progress, staying out in front of students' existing competencies, and gradually turning responsibility for the task over to the student.

   RIDE How would Vygotsky suggest a teacher help students understand the concept of fractions?

2. **Peers as guides, mentors.** A core premise of the Vygotskian approach to instruction is that *two heads are better than one* (Azmitia, 1988). Generally speaking, students who work cooperatively with a more able peer show better subsequent performance and greater problem-solving skills than do students who work alone (Gauvain & Rogoff, 1989; Johnson & Johnson, 1987). The sociocognitive view endorses cooperative learning settings. It also endorses multi-age classrooms, in which younger children (e.g., third graders) benefit from their older and more able peers (e.g., fourth graders). During peer collaboration, it is crucial that the more able peer expose the less able collaborator to a higher level of reasoning (Tudge, 1989).

3. **Culture as guide, mentor.** To see how knowledge and skill can be viewed as occurring within a specific cultural context, consider the following letter. It was written by the leaders of the Indians of the Five Nations in response to a recruitment letter from William and Mary College:

   > You who are wise must know, that different nations have different conceptions of things; and you will therefore not take it amiss, if our ideas of this kind of education happen not to be the same with yours. We have had some experience of it: several of our young people were formally brought up at the colleges of the northern provinces; they were instructed in all your sciences; but when they came back to us . . . [they were] ignorant of every means of living in the woods . . . neither fit for hunting, warriors, or counselors; they were totally good for nothing. We are, however, not the less obliged by your kind offer . . . and to show our grateful sense of it, if the gentlemen of Virginia will send us a dozen of their sons, we will take great care of their education, instruct them in all we know, and make men of them. (Drake, 1834)

   What Does This Mean to Me? Assess your current skill level as a prospective teacher. Did your skill arise from discovery learning? Mentoring? Cultural guidance?

4. **A new view of motivation.** Proponents of discovery learning presume that students are active, interested explorers of their surroundings. This is often the case. They further presume that discovery learning breeds curiosity, interest, and positive emotion. This is only partly true. Learning on one's own can also conjure up a range of negative emotions, such as confusion, frustration, and helplessness (Linn, 1986). If one is to learn, negative emotions need to be managed, and face-to-face scaffolding provides an ideal arena for teachers to do this. Through scaffolding, teachers can help students manage their motivation, mood, and expectations. Whereas Piaget emphasized curiosity and positive emotion as the motivational basis of cognitive development, Vygotsky emphasized perseverance, commitment, and goal setting (Hickey, 1997). This new view of motivation does not argue against interest and curiosity; instead, it adds the idea that learning requires overcoming motivational problems.

Which Theory Should Teachers Apply?

Despite their differences, both the Piagetian and the Vygotskian perspectives on cognitive development offer important contributions to the practice of education. Table 2.6 lists these differences and contributions by identifying each perspective's position on eight issues of interest to teachers.

TABLE 2.6

Summary of Piaget and Vygotsky's Theories of Cognitive Development

Educational issue	Piaget's cognitive-developmental perspective	Vygotsky's sociocognitive-developmental perspective
What develops during cognitive development?	Domain-general mental operations that can be used to solve problems in various contexts.	Domain-specific skill, knowledge, and expertise that is specific to a culturally valued problem.
How does learning occur?	Through discovery, invention. Learning is the internal process of making sense of the external world.	Through social transmission. Learning is a cognitive apprenticeship in which knowledge is passed from more able members of the culture to less able ones.
Is cognitive development universal, or is it culturally specific?	Universal. Cognitive development unfolds in an invariant sequence.	Culturally specific. Students develop skills and understanding that are valued by the culture but do not develop skills and understanding in nonvalued domains.
What is the source of gains in cognitive development?	Rich, stimulating, challenging, and responsive environments. Given these conditions and active, independent exploration, students construct knowledge.	Social interaction and guidance from highly competent members of the culture. Students co-construct knowledge with competent partners through a process of guided participation.
What is the role of the teacher?	To provide students with rich, stimulating, challenging, and responsive environments. Create cognitive conflicts. Ask questions about relationships (same? different?).	To select culturally valued problems to solve, introduce the tools of the culture, provide scaffolding within students' zone of proximal development, probe-question-scaffolding students' thinking during dialogue.
What is the role of peers?	To stimulate cognitive conflict so as to create disequilibrium.	To act as a mentor and guide in much the same ways as the teacher.
How important is language development to cognitive development?	Largely unimportant. Language is a by-product of thought.	Crucial. Language is the most important tool for thought.
Recommended instructional strategies	Discovery-based learning; Montessori classrooms; interest areas; project-based learning; curiosity-inducing strategies.	Scaffolding in the zone of proximal development; dialogue within an instructional conversation; cooperative learning.

As for which theory teachers should apply, it seems that both have merit and that both offer useful recommendations. Some educators recommend that teachers combine the two theories so that Piaget's ideas help teachers formulate instructional strategies to promote disequilibrium and self-discovery, and Vygotsky's ideas help them formulate instructional strategies to promote social guidance and instructional conversations (Glassman, 1994). From this point of view, it is possible to embrace both approaches. In reading this book, for instance, you might ask whether you are exploring an interesting and challenging environmental activity or whether you are benefiting from the social guidance of three veteran authors who are willing to pass along a trick or two. From a different point of view, much can be gained by keeping the theories separate and by weighing their relative merits (Duncan, 1995). Several key differences clearly exist, and there is much to gain in terms of developing teacher beliefs and instructional strategies by debating the relative merits of these approaches to cognitive development.

Language Development

Educators are interested in **language** and its development for three reasons. First, they seek to promote language development because of its facilitating role on cognitive development, as discussed earlier in the chapter. Second, they seek to promote language development for its own sake. By developing language capacities, educators promote valued language-based outcomes, such as literacy, oral communication, vocabulary development, writing composition, and so forth. Third, educators want to develop language in order to help students learn one or more additional languages. This goal includes foreign-language and bilingual education.

language The use of agreed-on rules to combine a small number of symbols (sounds, letters, gestures) to produce a large number of meaningful messages.

How Language Develops

Linguists like to ask this question: If you were to put prelinguistic children on an island alone with no language-speaking adults to teach them, would they still develop a language? This is the essential language question that asks whether language is a naturally inherited process or whether its emergence and development depend on instruction. If language is a naturally inherited process, it should flower naturally as children mature. This can be the case only if children have an innate biological preparedness for language.

Innate Language Acquisition Device. More than 4,000 languages exist today, and any one of them is far too complex to be learned through trial and error or formal instruction. Despite the overwhelming complexity of language, all children learn to talk and by the time they enter school are quite proficient in doing so. This is so because children seem to possess an inborn linguistic processor called a **language acquisition device** (LAD; Chomsky, 1959, 1968) or a *language-making capacity* (LMC; Slobin, 1985). Naturally occurring verbal input appears to be sufficient to activate the LAD so that children learn the language of their culture rather naturally, mostly by listening. What they hear are words and sentences, and what they come to understand and produce are meaning and grammar. Something is going on that allows children to transform words into meaning and sentences into grammar, and it is not formal instruction.

language acquisition device Inborn capacity that enables children to understand grammar and produce language.

To appreciate children's remarkable natural ability to understand language, try the following exercise. Listen to a conversation between people who speak a foreign language with which you are not familiar. As you listen, how do you know which sounds are words? Can you decipher the language's syntax? Can you identify where sentences end? Generally speaking, adults walk away from such an experiment frustrated and bewildered. Children, on the other hand, readily understand what they hear—the sounds, syllables, words, and syntax. The critical period during which the LAD is highly sensitive to language input occurs between 18 months and 6 years of age.

From observations such as these, educators conclude that explicit language teaching by adults is not necessary. With or without explicit instruction, the infant's cries and grunts naturally become babbles, babbles develop into words, words expand into sentences, and sentences become effective communication. The part of language for which people have a biological preparedness is called *syntax*. **Syntax** refers to the structure of language, such as word order and sentence formation rules (e.g., noun-verb-object). Syntax emerges in an orderly and predictable pattern:

syntax The structure of a language, including sentence formation rules, such as noun-verb.

- One-word stage: holophrases, such as "doggie" (1 to $1\frac{1}{2}$ years).
- Two-word stage: telegraphic speech, such as "milk gone" ($1\frac{1}{2}$ to 2 years).
- Conversational stage: Sentence length increases as children learn sentence formation rules (3 years and older).

No matter what language they speak, all children start with single words, or holophrases, usually nouns such as animals, body parts, and toys (Bornstein et al., 2004). They then add verbs to produce two-word speech, or telegraphic speech. By 2 years of age, children universally use about 300 nouns, 100 verbs, and 30 pronouns. Around 4 years of age, children add adjectives, prepositions, and quantifiers to learn grammar and sentence structure—that is, syntax.

In addition, phonology and semantics develop rapidly from age 2 through preschool. **Phonology** refers to sounds and pronunciation (e.g., pronouncing letters and words).

phonology The sounds of a language.

semantics   The meanings of words and sentences.

English-speaking children generally produce simple sounds such as *p*, *n*, and *b* at age 2 and more complex sounds such as *th* by preschool. **Semantics** refers to the meaning of words and sentences. From age 2 to preschool, vocabulary grows rapidly, increasing from about 400 words (age 2) to about 2,000 (preschool age).

Although language qualities such as syntax and phonology are largely innate endowments, other qualities are not. Vocabulary, for instance, is learned. Children constantly point to objects and ask the names of things. They need environmental support—instruction—to learn the meaning of words. They also need environmental support to learn how to engage in the social aspects of speech, such as what gestures mean and how to take turns talking. Reading and writing do not come naturally, either. Reading and writing are one part visual understanding, one part fine motor production, and one part language. The coordination of these systems is required for reading and writing, and formal instruction dramatically helps children accomplish this feat.

Role of a Teacher. Even though children and adolescents learn language rather automatically, educational supports for language development are important. After all, the functional purpose of language is to communicate—to get one's message across and to understand the messages that others are trying to get across (Tomasello, 1992, 1995). Thus, language is constructed through social interaction as students seek ways to make requests, share information, bond with others, make assertions, make denials, and so forth. Social interaction—not just exposure to speech—is therefore important. In particular, children benefit most when they use language during social interactions that are responsive and linguistically complex (Bloom et al., 1996), and they benefit little from passive reception of language, such as when watching television (Snow et al., 1976). In this spirit, the role of the teacher in helping students learn language is to provide many opportunities for language learners to interact socially (Penner, 1987; Rice, 1986), such as the following examples:

- Interact with children in a conversational manner about objects and events that have the child's attention.
- Paraphrase what the child says and add simple elaborations.
- Provide pauses in conversations to give children opportunities to generate language, rather than just be exposed to language.

Language Disabilities and Brain Functioning

The human brain is biologically ready to understand and produce language. Figure 2.7 shows the brain structures in the temporal lobe that underlie language. Wernicke's area, which is near the ear, allows us to understand speech. Broca's area allows us to produce speech. The written aspects of language are perceived in the occipital lobe (see Figure 2.1)—the visual cortex—and relayed to the Wernicke area for processing. Dense communication networks of neurons connect the Wernicke area to both the Broca area and the occipital lobe. With these three areas of the brain and the neural connections between them, people have the brain anatomy to understand and produce spoken and written language.

dyslexia   Reading disability in which words are read from right to left and letters of the same configuration are reversed.

aphasia   Language disability in which the person has difficulty understanding or producing speech.

Understanding how language functions naturally sheds insight into the neural underpinnings of language disabilities. **Dyslexia** is a reading disability in which words are read from right to left (confusing *was* with *saw*) and letters with the same configuration are reversed (*p* and *q*; *b* and *d*). In dyslexia, the areas of the brain in Figure 2.7 fail to work in concert with one another. The problem is that the *pathways* connecting these language structures (the arcuate fasciculus) fail to work. **Aphasia** is a language disability related to trauma in either the Wernicke or Broca areas. With Wernicke's aphasia, the comprehension of language is difficult. With Broca's aphasia, the production of language is not fluent. *Deafness* is also a language disability in that damage to the ear prevents the Wernicke area from being able to process the speech of others. *Blindness* can also be considered a language disability to the extent that damage to the eye or occipital lobe prevents the Wernicke area from processing reading materials.

Genie's Story. *Genie* is the pseudonym given to a young girl who grew up in Los Angeles, California, without access to the normal linguistic input that we all take for granted. Rymer (1993) described Genie as "the most damaged child I've ever seen." She was locked away and isolated from language and social interaction from birth through early adolescence. After being rescued from a domineering and abusive father, 13-year-old Genie entered a hospital and worked daily with a linguist to acquire language. When she entered the hospital, Genie could say only a few words, *stopit* and *nomore*. Two pressing questions were: (a) Could she, as a postpubescent adolescent, learn language? and (b) What did the language areas of her brain look like?

As to whether she could learn language, experts worked with Genie for years. She was able to increase her vocabulary in a rather impressive fashion, but she could not understand grammar and syntax. For Genie, the critical period in which language acquisition needs to occur had passed. Preschoolers learn language easily and quickly, despite the enormous complexity of the task. After puberty, if the language-sensitive areas of the brain have not been stimulated with appropriate linguistic input, people learn language only laboriously, if at all. As to what the language areas of Genie's brain looked like, nonintrusive brain imaging showed that her language areas had atrophied. When she finally did encounter words during her adolescence, Genie processed the words in an area of the brain that only picks up noises—not in the areas of the brain depicted in Figure 2.7.

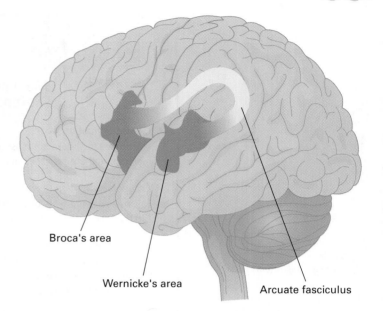

Broca's area

Wernicke's area

Arcuate fasciculus

Figure 2.7. Brain Structures that Make Up the Language Cortex

Technology Support for Young Readers and Readers with Special Needs

Literacy represents the ability to read and write. It is the means through which most education and learning take place. Consequently, the more developed students' language and literacy skills are, the better they function and perform in school (Cummins, 1981). Young children and students with reading disabilities often need technology-based accommodations and external supports to cope successfully with this basic academic task (Lever-Duffy, McDonald, & Mizell, 2005).

Talking Books for Young Readers. CD-ROM storybooks, also known as *talking books,* are digital or computerized versions of traditional picture storybooks (Doty, Popplewell, & Beyers, 2001). Part of the appeal of these electronic texts is that they add multimedia capabilities to the traditional storybook—capabilities such as animation, sound effects, narration, and highlighted text. Many talking books are interactive. With a

> **How Can I Use This?**
>
> Check out an electronic book (e-book) from your library and ask yourself what instructional uses it affords that a traditional printed book does not.

click of the mouse, young readers can listen to a narrator read the text aloud, listen over and over again to the pronunciation of difficult words, see definitions for unfamiliar words, and be entertained by special effects (Labbo, 2000). From a Vygotskian point of view, these technology-embedded features can be considered *electronic scaffolds,* used at the young reader's discretion (McKenna et al., 1996).

Talking books promote young readers' phonological awareness (Chera & Wood, 2003), word recognition (McKenna et al., 1996), and vocabulary development (Higgins & Hess, 1999). Whether talking books promote reading comprehension to a greater extent than do traditional books remains an open question (Matthew, 1997), though talking books do promote reading comprehension when stories are relatively long or complex (Moore & Smith, 1996). The problem with talking books seems to be that their special effects can be so appealing that readers' attention is diverted away from the text material and toward the electronic entertainment of sights and sounds (Trushell, Burrell, & Maitland, 2001). Because multimedia capabilities can act as a two-edged sword, the "Taking It to the Classroom" box on the next page offers some recommendations for elementary school teachers who utilize CD-ROM storybooks (based on McKenna et al., 1996).

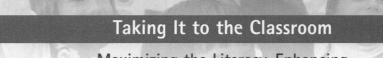

Taking It to the Classroom

Maximizing the Literacy-Enhancing Potential of Electronic Storybooks

- *Choose appropriate books.*

  Electronic storybooks are most appropriate for relatively long and complex stories. Printed text is more appropriate for easily understood material because electronic scaffolds are less needed.

- *Encourage attention to print.*

  The audiovisual effects of electronic storybooks may distract young readers from attending to the text material. It is sometimes prudent to disable certain features of the program.

- *Plan carefully; clarify your goals.*

  Consider using printed material for highly structured reading assignments, and use electronic storybooks during free time. Also use specific features of electronic storybooks to develop specific literacy skills, such as decoding text.

- *Consider different contexts for encounters with books.*

  Introduce a projection device to use an electronic storybook like a big book. Establish reading centers where students can read and explore the electronic storybooks.

Appendix

Supporting Readers with Special Needs

Teachers have a variety of resources (e.g., technology) to support them in adapting their instruction for students with special needs (*PRAXIS*™, I. B. 4; *INTASC*, Principles 1, 3).

Electronic Books for Students with Special Needs. Electronic books can also function as assistive technology to enhance the literacy and classroom participation of students with special needs. Like talking books for young readers, e-books offer literacy-enhancing multimedia features. For instance, e-books offer audio and text-to-speech capabilities (Boyle et al., 2002), extra-large print to students with visual impairments (Cavanaugh, 2002), and highlighted words and text for students with specific reading disabilities, such as dyslexia (Lockard & Abrams, 2004). Figure 2.8 illustrates what these multimedia features look like when integrated into an e-book used by high school students with reading disabilities to define and elaborate on unfamiliar words.

What Does This Mean to Me?

Examine an e-book or Web site with hypertext and ask yourself what role multimedia features play in your reading comprehension.

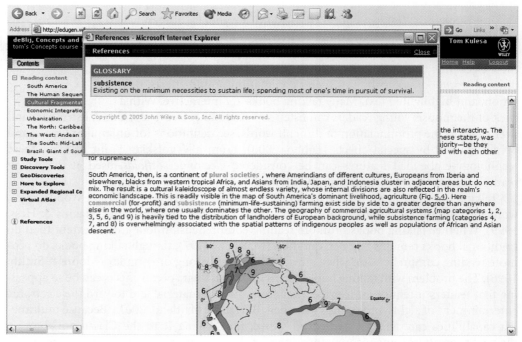

Figure 2.8. Illustration of Assistive Technology to Promote Reading Comprehension for Students with Special Needs

Source: de Blij, H. J., & Muller, P. O. *Concepts and Regions in Geography*, Second Edition. © 2005 H. J. de Blij and John Wiley & Sons, Inc. Reprinted by permission of John Wiley & Sons, Inc.

Text-based scaffolding devices act as embedded resources within reading material to enhance students' reading comprehension and learning (Anderson-Inman & Horney, 1999). Examples of embedded resources within e-books include the following:

- *Transitional resources* that convert text into something more comprehensible to the student, such as speech or definitions.
- *Illustrative resources* that help the reader elaborate on and better understand the text, such as pictures, charts, and video.
- *Summarizing resources* that provide an overview of the text, such as a concept map or a chapter outline.
- *Notational resources* that promote interaction with the text, such as note taking and outlining tools.
- *Enrichment resources,* such as informational sidebars, historical background information, and links to primary resources.

Bilingualism and Second-Language Acquisition

If learning one's native language depends on exposure to linguistic input during a childhood critical period, is the same true for learning a second language? Stated in another way, the language question for second-language acquisition asks whether there is a critical period for second-language learning.

Second-Language Acquisition. The earlier one begins to learn a second language, the greater is his or her chance of developing fluency in that language. For example, one group of researchers studied immigrants from South Korea and China, focusing on when they began to learn English and how successful they were in doing so (Johnson & Newport, 1989). When preschool immigrants tried to learn English, they were able to gain significantly better syntactical competence than were elementary-grade immigrants. Further, the elementary-grade immigrants showed greater fluency than did adolescents. Adolescent immigrants, in turn, were able to gain linguistic competence to a greater degree than were adult immigrants. These data show that second-language proficiency is relatively easy to acquire during childhood, possible but not to the point of native fluency before puberty, and noticeably more difficult after puberty. The "Taking It to the Classroom" box below lists several instructional strategies to support second-language learners' English proficiency.

Appendix
Second Language Learning
Most teachers will encounter students who are learning English as their second language. Knowing some strategies for how to support their learning will be very helpful to you (*PRAXIS*™, I. B. 5; *INTASC*, Principle 3).

What Does This Mean to Me?
If you speak a second language, how much of an accent do you have? If you learned before puberty, you likely sound like a native speaker. If you learned after puberty, you will likely have a noticeable accent. Is this true for you?

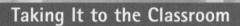

Taking It to the Classroom

Do You Know Jack? Helping Students Learn English

Jack is a student with limited English proficiency. Jack was born in Mexico and has been in this country for 2 years. Though more proficient in Spanish than in English, he speaks English fairly well. Jack was held back a grade during his first year, but he has begun to pick up English rather well. Given his rapid progress, you resist recommending that Jack take an English proficiency class that would require him to leave your regular class. What practical and immediate approaches can you take to assist Spanish-speaking Jack?

- Use synonyms to clarify the meaning of unknown words.
- When necessary, use Spanish to convey a word or concept that Jack doesn't understand, but then continue in English.
- To make English more comprehensible, use concrete materials, visuals, and body-language cues.
- Paraphrase questions and statements to allow for different levels of proficiency.
- Let all students know that there is nothing wrong with an accent, perhaps by playing a recording of famous people with accents.
- Ask Jack to interpret some communication or text that is in Spanish for the rest of the class, therefore showing the value of being bilingual.

These findings raise the practical question of why schools routinely teach foreign languages in high school and college, rather than in elementary school. Research on language acquisition shows that this is clearly a curricular blunder. The best time to acquire a second language is before puberty, not after (Bialystok, 2001). As a rule, a child who is exposed to a language before starting school will develop great proficiency; a child who is exposed to a language before adolescence will develop good proficiency; and an adult who is exposed to a language after adolescence will struggle to develop proficiency.

bilingualism The use of two or more languages in everyday life.

Bilingualism. In the United States, most students speak only English. English is not, however, the first language of 18% of all individuals living in the United States. About 5 million students in the United States public school system speak a language other than English at home. Many states have high percentages of students who speak a language other than English in the home, and many large urban school districts have students who are mostly from non–English-speaking homes.

Bilingualism is the regular use of two (or more) languages, and bilinguals are students who use two (or more) languages in their everyday lives (Grosjean, 1992). A key reason non–English-speaking children and adolescents need a second language is that English is the language of schooling. A pressing question in American education is whether learning two languages (rather than just one, English) hinders the child's proficiency in either language (see the "Uncommon Sense" box below). The practical question is whether students who speak a language other than English in the home would be best served by an English-only classroom.

Evidence shows that learning two languages at the same time during childhood generally results in excellent proficiency in both the classroom language (English) and the native language (Lanza, 1992; Reich, 1986). In fact, there is a benefit to learning two languages, because bilinguals generally outperform monolinguals on tests of language development, concept formation, and nonverbal intelligence (Diaz, 1983, 1985). Findings such as these suggest that students benefit from bilingual education and that the time to acquire a second language is before puberty, not after (Bialystok, 2001).

Uncommon Sense

Non-English-Speaking Children Should Use Only English in the Classroom—Or Should They?

Public opinion polls show that most U. S. citizens favor English-only classrooms. They believe that learning a second language places a mental burden on children. If this is so, the thinking goes, then children need to be relieved of this burden and educated in only the language of the host country, English. Does research support this thinking? Do languages compete with one another? Is bilingualism a mental burden? The research-based answer to these questions seems to be no. Using one's native language in school does not interfere in any meaningful way with the learning of English. This is so because different languages are not stored in different parts of the brain. Rather, learning a second language uses the same cognitive system that learning the first language uses (Francis, 1999; McLaughlin, 1987). Hence, proficiency in one language is highly related to proficiency in a second.

RIDE

REFLECTION FOR ACTION

The Event

A teacher wants to help her students learn a new concept, such as the concept of fractions. Prior to the lesson, the concept is foreign or only vaguely familiar to the majority of her students. What would be an effective instructional approach to help students understand the new concept and grow more sophisticated and capable in their thinking?

Reflection RIDE

Imagine that you are the teacher wanting to help elementary-grade students learn the concept of fractions. Would a disequilibrium-inducing, exploration-based approach work best? The children could pick up the fraction inserts, manipulate them in their hands, move them around to see what fits, and hence discover the concept of fractions. Another way might be to sit beside the children and tutor them. Would such social guidance and teacher mentorship work better?

What Theoretical/Conceptual Information Might Assist in Interpreting and Remedying this Situation? Consider the following:

Create Disequilibrium

A concept such as fractions is best learned by discovering or inventing. Instructional strategies such as exploration, discovery, and making predictions about what might happen next would yield the kinds of experiences children need to develop this concept.

Offer an Apprenticeship

Unfamiliar concepts are best learned through social transmission. Cultural representatives, such as the teacher, already have a sophisticated understanding of such concepts, so an instructional strategy that involves social interaction, guidance, and collaboration would yield the kinds of social experiences children need to develop this concept.

Disequilibrium and Apprenticeship

Perhaps a teacher can use both strategies. Perhaps some students would respond to a hands-on, discovery-based learning experience, and others would respond to a collaborative, mentor-novice experience.

Information Gathering RIDE

You will need several pieces of information. Is the concept of fractions a domain-general mental operation that students can use to solve problems in various contexts, such as math, science, recipes, and economics, or is this concept a domain-specific skill, knowledge, or expertise that is specific to a particular problem? Is students' motivation strong and something to be supported, or is it fragile and something to be soothed? Can you find access to other manipulatives, and can some students act as able peers to tutor the less able students? You might also consult another teacher in the same grade level for his or her perspective on these two instructional methods. A videotape that illustrates a Piagetian or Vygotskian approach to teaching such a lesson could also provide useful information. Several articles and books contain discussions and classroom applications of the Piagetian and Vygotskian approaches as well.

Decision Making `RIDE`

You need to decide what students are to learn—a domain-general concept or a domain-specific skill. You need to decide whether the motivation you are most concerned with is how to promote interest or how to soothe negative emotions, such as confusion and frustration. You will need to decide whether you have the resources that can promote a manipulatives-based lesson or a social guidance-based lesson. From your own teaching philosophy, from your readings of articles and books, and from your conversations with trusted colleagues, you will need to decide whether you prefer a Piagetian exploration-based approach or a Vygotskian social guidance-based approach. You will also need to decide how compatible or incompatible these two approaches are, both in ideology and in practical application.

Evaluation `RIDE`

You will need to monitor and assess the quality of students' understanding, motivation, initiative, and collaboration. You will also need to listen carefully to students' language and activity to gain a sense of whether their thinking is becoming more sophisticated. You will need to evaluate how students are reacting to a purely Piagetian, a purely Vygotskian, or a blended approach. You should have a postlesson assessment measure ready, as well.

Further Practice: Your Turn

Here is a second event for consideration and reflection. In doing so, implement the processes of reflection, information gathering, decision making, and evaluation.

The Event

Mr. Heartland is a high school economics teacher who knows a lot about capitalism, interest rates, and how the economy works. His students, however, do not. By the end of the semester, he wants his students to understand complex concepts such as supply and demand, the stock market, and gross domestic product.

`RIDE` What might this teacher do? How can he help his students develop these concepts? In reflecting on how Mr. Heartland might best foster cognitive development, what approach would you recommend?

SUMMARY

● **How does education enrich brain development?**

The brain is the organ of learning. Exposure to stimulating environments (i.e., education) develops connections between neurons and gives the brain information to store and use in solving problems.

● **How does Piaget explain cognitive development?**

According to Piaget, students are naturally curious explorers who constantly try to make sense of their surroundings. Through exploration, students interact with their surroundings; they discover the world around them and develop three types of schemas—behavioral, symbolic, and operations. New information requires that the student adapt to it, as occurs through the cognitive processes of assimilation and accommodation. Through these processes, students develop simple schemas into more numerous and more complex schemas.

- **What are the stages of cognitive development?**

Four sequential stages provide the structure for cognitive development. During the sensorimotor stage, infants internalize their sensorimotor activities into behavioral schemas. During the preoperational stage, language develops rapidly but thought is prelogical, perception-bound, and egocentric. During the concrete-operational stage, children can use mental operations such as conservation to reason about the objects before them. During the formal-operational stage, adolescents use mental operations to consider unseen hypotheses and solve abstract problems; reasoning is systematic, deductive, and inferential—that is, adultlike and sophisticated.

- **How can teachers apply Piaget's theory in the classroom?**

Piaget's approach offers three recommendations for instruction. First, be sensitive to individual differences—plan learning activities (such as interest areas and portfolio projects) around individuals rather than around the whole class. Second, motivate students by stimulating curiosity and interest and by providing active learning opportunities. Third, promote discovery-based learning. To do so, provide classrooms that are richly stimulating, complex, and interesting, as exemplified by interest areas, project-based learning, and the methods of the Montessori school.

- **How does Vygotsky explain sociocognitive development?**

According to Vygotsky, students are young apprentices who benefit from conversations with competent members of their culture. Through social guidance, they acquire the skills and knowledge they need to solve the problems that are most important in their culture. Cognitive development is the gradual acquisition of new skills and knowledge, and it occurs in the context of guided participation and cooperative dialogue with peers, adults, and cultural tools.

- **How can teachers apply Vygotsky's theory in the classroom?**

Vygotsky's approach offers four recommendations for instruction, each of which relies on social interaction and guided participation to promote cognitive development. First, the teacher acts as a guide, scaffolding students as they work within their zones of proximal development. Second, because two heads are better than one, peers can act as guides and mentors, as exemplified by cooperative learning and multi-age classrooms. Third, culture can guide and scaffold students, such as through the offering of its tools. Fourth, teachers can use scaffolding, the PQS discourse model, and instructional conversations to soothe and support students' motivation during potentially frustrating episodes.

- **How does language develop?**

The essential language question is whether language is a naturally inherited process or whether its development depends on instruction. Children show a remarkable natural ability to understand and use language, presumably because they have an innate language acquisition device. This natural ability extends not only to the child's primary language but to second languages, as well, to support bilingualism. The part of language for which children have a biological preparedness is syntax. Language disabilities, such as dyslexia and aphasia, illustrate how language is impaired when brain structures undermine this otherwise natural process.

- **How can teachers use their knowledge of cognitive development when working with diverse learners and students with special needs?**

Many students enter classrooms with a different language and a different cultural background from those of their teacher and peers. Research on bilingual education shows that learning two languages at the same time generally results in excellent proficiency in both the native language and the classroom language. Reading is a primary means through which most education and learning take place. Students with reading disabilities therefore lack a key resource to enrich their cognitive development. Technologies such as e-books and talking books offer multimedia features that function as accommodations, external supports, and electronic scaffolds, which allow students with reading disabilities to cope more successfully with reading tasks.

KEY TERMS

accommodation, p. 39
adaptation, p. 38
amygdala, p. 36
animism, p. 43
aphasia, p. 58
assimilation, p. 38
behavioral schemas, p. 38
bilingualism, p. 62
centration, p. 43
classification, p. 43
conservation, p. 44
cultural tools, p. 54
deductive reasoning, p. 45
discovery-based learning, p. 48
disequilibrium, p. 39
dyslexia, p. 58

egocentrism, p. 43
glia cells, p. 36
guided discovery, p. 48
guided participation, p. 49
hippocampus, p. 34
inductive reasoning, p. 45
intersubjectivity, p. 52
IRE discourse model, p. 52
language, p. 57
language acquisition device, p. 57
myelinization, p. 36
neurons, p. 36
object permanence, p. 41
operation, p. 38
phonology, p. 57
plasticity, p. 36

PQS discourse model, p. 52
private speech, p. 53
reversibility, p. 43
scaffolding, p. 50
schemas, p. 38
semantics, p. 58
semiotic function, p. 41
seriation, p. 43
socially shared cognition, p. 52
symbolic schemas, p. 38
syntax, p. 57
transductive reasoning, p. 43
zone of proximal development, p. 49

EXERCISES

1. *Toys as Developmentally Appropriate Learning Activities*

   With your knowledge of Piaget's stages of cognitive development, make a trip to a mega toy store to examine the developmental appropriateness of the different toys on the shelves. Many toys will have a suggested age on the package label, but for this field trip, ignore the manufacturer's age recommendations and choose the level of cognitive development at which each toy is most appropriate. Ask yourself questions such as, At what age would this toy be most interesting? Most fun? Also examine which mental operations and cognitive skills are required to interact effectively with each toy. For instance, does this toy stretch and challenge the child's sorting skills? Classification skills? What about operations and knowledge, such as counting, matching, keeping time, vocabulary, labeling objects, pronouncing letters, and so forth? See whether you can find toys that would be most enjoyable for children of the following four ages: 1, 6, 10, and 15. Explain why.

2. *Asking Hypotheticals*

   Concrete-operational thinkers rely on *reality thinking,* whereas formal-operational thinkers rely on *possibility thinking.* Interview several children and adolescents by asking these questions, What would the world be like if human beings were extinct? What would it be like to have a third eye? What would it be like if you lived in the year 2100? Listen to the extent to which their thinking, reasoning, and problem solving reflect reality thinking or possibility thinking. Concrete thinkers will generally find these questions uninteresting, even stupid. Formal thinkers, however, will find these questions interesting, perhaps even asking their teachers to generate new possibilities to think about.

3. *Using Curiosity-inducing Strategies as Motivational Strategies*

   Look over the three curiosity-inducing strategies introduced in Table 2.3: guessing and feedback, suspense, and controversy. As you present information to another person, explicitly use one of these strategies to spark his or her curiosity about the information you are providing. As you use the strategy, closely monitor the other person's sense of curiosity and willingness to obtain more information.

4. *Peer Tutoring*

Provide tutoring for another person in an area in which you are an expert and the other is a novice. As you tutor, monitor closely all the different ways in which you provide social guidance and scaffolding. How subtle or explicit is your scaffolding? After your own tutoring experience, observe a teacher you consider to be a terrific instructor. Watch what this teacher does as he or she provides social guidance and scaffolding. In what ways was your scaffolding the same as the expert's? In what ways was your scaffolding different?

5. *Contrasting Electronic and Printed Books*

Visit a toy store, a bookstore, or a library to locate an e-book (a computer-based version of a printed book that has multimedia features, such as hypertext and drop-down menus) or a talking book (a colorful electronic storybook with multimedia features, such as sound effects and animation). Find a book for which you can also find a regular printed version. Compare the two versions of the book, page by page. Ask yourself what the advantages and disadvantages of the electronic and printed versions are for young readers. Ask yourself what the advantages and disadvantages of the two versions are for students with reading disabilities.

Ms. Hernandez's
fourth-grade class.

(Media Bakery)

Here are 15 members of Ms. Hernandez's fourth-grade class. It is early fall, and Ms. Hernandez has just received this photograph in her mailbox. As she looks at each face, something stirs within her. She becomes determined to build a constructive sense of community with this group of students. She would like to help them become friends. She would like to see her students helping, sharing, and trusting one another. She wants to keep disrespect, put-downs, and acts of aggression out of her classroom. In these early days of September, Ms. Hernandez has noticed some potential obstacles to her goal. One student is hyperaggressive; another has a short temper. Many possess immature social skills. She also has reason to suspect that a couple of her students are neglected at home. Still, as she looks at these smiling faces, she wonders what she can do to help them develop socially.

Social Development

R I D E Reflection for Action

Ms. Hernandez wants to empower her students' social development, and she wants to build a strong sense of community in her classroom. How can she help her students develop the skills they need to make friends and diffuse conflict? What might she do?

Guiding Questions

- What characterizes a high-quality student-teacher relationship?
- What are mental models, and why are they important to social development?
- How can teachers nurture psychosocial development, especially students' initiative, competence, and identity?
- What are the stages of moral development?
- How do social competence and aggression develop?
- How does self-concept develop throughout the school-age years?
- How do students' special needs interfere with their social development?

CHAPTER OVERVIEW

Social development reflects the extent of one's social competence, peer popularity, inter-personal trust, initiative, competence, identity, moral development, prosocial orientation, and healthy self-concept. The extent to which students develop socially depends in part on the quality of the relationships in their lives, including the relationships they have with their teachers and peers. The first part of this chapter identifies the aspects of a relation-ship that allow it to be characterized as a high-quality relationship. The second part discusses specific social-developmental outcomes, such as psychosocial development, social competence, and moral development. A particular emphasis is placed on aggression and the question of what teachers such as Ms. Hernandez can do to help students build the social competencies they need to manage their anger and frustration. The final part of the chapter discusses self-concept. Taken as a whole, the chapter highlights the role that relationships play in students' social development, and it offers numerous illustrations as to how teachers can help students develop socially.

Relationships

- Mental Models—Self and Others
- Quality of Relationships
- Culture, Diversity, and Special Needs
- Trust: The Beginning of Positive Social Development
- Students' Attachment Styles with Teachers
- Attachment for Learners with Special Needs

Psychosocial Development

- Erikson's Framework

Moral Development

- Stages of Moral Development
- The Ethic of Care
- Character and Conscience: Doing the Right Thing for the Right Reason

Aggression and Social Competence

- Aggression
- Video Game Technology and Aggression
- Instrumental and Hostile Aggression
- Social Competence

Self-Concept

- Who Am I?
- Enhancing the Self-Concept

Relationships

Relationships are the soil in which social development grows. Each student who walks through the school's front door brings in a unique history of relationships. The quality of students' past relationships explains a lot about their subsequent social development—why they trust or mistrust others, why they feel competent or incompetent, why they are coop-erative or aggressive, and so forth. In essence, high-quality relationships are the means by which students develop the social competence they need to make friends and be successful in school (Birch & Ladd, 1997; Hamre & Pianta, 2001).

When kindergartners form high-quality relationships with their teachers, they function more positively, both socially and academically (Pianta & Steinberg, 1992). Further, the ben-efits of this relationship continue with the child through elementary school and even into the middle school years (Hamre & Pianta, 2001). Positive early relationships have enduring effects because children uses these high-quality relationships to develop their social skills, learn how to cooperate, learn how cope with frustration, and develop good work habits. This chapter highlights social-developmental outcomes such as these and explains their develop-ment throughout the school-age years.

To capture the flavor of a close versus conflictual child-teacher relationship, Figure 3.1 presents some questionnaire items researchers use to ask teachers to assess how close versus conflictual their relationship is with a student (from Hightower et al., 1986). In general, teachers promote close relationships by being responsive to students' needs and by acting as an all-purpose support system as children and adolescents try to develop the competencies they need to adjust to the varied demands of school.

Close relationship indicators

- If upset, this child will seek comfort from me.
- This child spontaneously shares information about him/herself.

Conflictual relationship indicators

- This child and I always seem to be struggling with each other.
- This child easily becomes angry at me.

Figure 3.1. Questionnaire Items for Kindergarten Teachers to Ask about Their Close vs. Conflictual Relationships with Children

From their daily interactions, children learn what other people think of them, and they learn how other people tend to treat them. Once these expectations are formulated (e.g., "Overall, my experience has taught me that other people are nice and helpful—you can trust them"), children use these expectations to figure out how to respond to the new people they meet. Another term for these expectations is *mental models*.

Mental Models—Self and Others

Mental models are a student's enduring beliefs and expectations about what they are like and what other people are like (Ainsworth et al., 1978; Bowlby, 1982; Bretherton, 1990; Collins et al., 2004; Main, Kaplan, & Cassidy, 1985). *Mental models of the self* represent students' answers to questions such as, Am I lovable? Am I a good person? Am I worthy of other people's attention and care? *Mental models of others* represent students' answers to questions such as, What are other people like? Can you trust other people? Will they be there when you need them? Are others nice and helpful, or are they mostly mean and selfish? (Collins, 1996).

Just as students have a lot of information stored in their memories about what math is like and about what recess is like, they also have a wealth of information stored in their memories about what they are like and what other people are like. Figure 3.2 illustrates the central role that mental models play in understanding and predicting students' social development.

As shown on the left-hand side of the figure, some relationships are of high quality and produce feelings of security, whereas others are of low quality and produce feelings of insecurity. With high-quality relationships, children experience warm, responsive caregivers. Through experience, these children have learned that their caregivers are accessible, dependable, trustworthy, and responsive. They feel secure because they feel loved, accepted, and valued—by parents, teachers, day-care providers, and so forth. With low-quality relationships, children experience cold and unresponsive caregivers. Their experience has taught them that their caregivers are inaccessible, undependable, untrustworthy, and unresponsive. They feel insecure because they feel unloved, rejected, or ignored.

Over time, students transform the history of their interactions with these social partners into mental models of themselves and of others. They may say to themselves, "Because my parents are so warm and caring for me, I must be lovable," or, "My parents are always there

mental models   Students' enduring beliefs and expectations about what they are like and what other people are like.

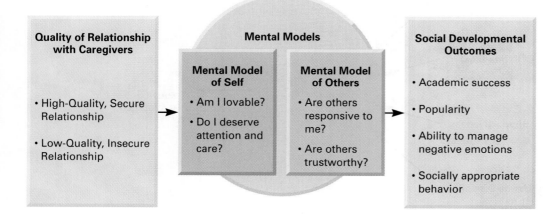

Figure 3.2. Antecedents and Developmental Outcomes of Students' Mental Models of Self and Others

when I need them—I can count on them to be there when I need them." If these experiences are consistent enough, children's mental models become entrenched. Mental models then gain the capacity to affect students' future feelings, thoughts, and behaviors and thus exert a significant effect on their future social development (Belsky & Cassidy, 1994; Rothbard & Shaver, 1994). As shown on the right-hand side of the figure, four key social-developmental outcomes are (a) academic success, (b) popularity, (c) ability to manage negative emotions, and (d) socially appropriate behaviors (Allen et al., 1998; Thompson, 1998, 1999).

Quality of Relationships

relationship   Interaction between two people in which the actions of one person affect the thoughts, feelings, and actions of the other person and vice versa.

A **relationship** involves two people, each affecting the other. The quality of a relationship, therefore, always depends on the contributions of both parties (Kochanska et al., 2004). That said, some ways of relating to students are more likely than others to promote their well-being and social development (Ainsworth et al., 1978; Allen et al., 2003; De Wolff & van Ijzendoorn, 1997; Kochanska, 2002).

What Constitutes a High-Quality Relationship?   Figure 3.3 identifies four characteristics of a high-quality way of relating to students (Reeve, 2005). Although these characteristics overlap, research shows that each contributes to students' social development in a unique and positive way (Allen et al., 2003).

attunement   Sensing and reading another's state of being and adjusting one's own behavior accordingly.

Attunement is sensing and reading a student's state of being and adjusting one's own behavior accordingly (Stern et al., 1983). A synonym for attunement is *sensitivity* (De Wolff & van Ijzendoorn, 1997; Haft & Slade, 1989). When teachers are highly attuned to their students, they know what their students are thinking and feeling, how engaged they are during a learning activity, and whether they understand what they are trying to learn. Highly attuned teachers know these things because they listen closely to what their students say and because they read students' facial expressions and body language to sense and predict what students will do next. They also make a special effort to be aware of what their students want and need. This sensitivity enables the teacher to be highly responsive to students' words, behaviors, needs, preferences, and emotions. It also allows teachers to deal with problems before they occur, because attuned teachers sense the coming storm and diffuse it.

relatedness   The psychological need to establish close emotional bonds and attachments with other people.

Relatedness is a sense of being close to another person; it entails feeling special and important to that person (Furrer & Skinner, 2003). Because it involves a sense of warmth, affection, and acceptance by the other person, relatedness is sometimes referred to as *belongingness* (Goodenow, 1993) or *intimacy* (Berndt, 2004). Establishing a sense of relatedness within the teacher-student (or peer-peer) relationship is important because it gives students a sense of security about themselves and about being with others. This sense of security calms negative emotions that may arise during the school day, such as anxiety, depression, or frustration. It also has an energizing effect that sparks students' enthusiasm and willingness to participate. For these reasons, relatedness is an especially good predictor of students' classroom engagement (Furrer & Skinner, 2003).

Chapter Reference
Chapter 6 discusses both relatedness and supportiveness in depth.

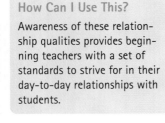

How Can I Use This?
Awareness of these relationship qualities provides beginning teachers with a set of standards to strive for in their day-to-day relationships with students.

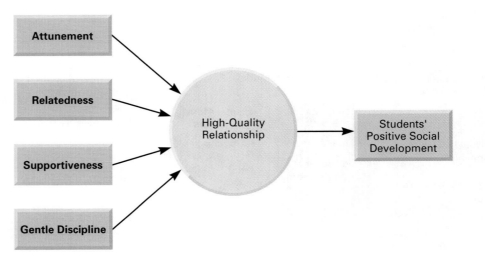

Figure 3.3. Four Characteristics of a High-quality Relationship

Relatedness is a sense of being close to another person. It calms negative emotions and sparks a willingness to participate. (Media Bakery)

Supportiveness is affirmation of the other person's capacity for self-direction. When teachers support their students, they accept students for who they are, express their faith that students can self-regulate their behavior, and assist students as they try to realize the goals they set for themselves. Supportive teachers provide their support in ways that preserve students' autonomy rather than in ways that make students' dependent on the teacher's help (Grolnick, 2003; Noddings, 1984; Reeve, 2005; Rogers, 1969). Supportiveness is important to students' success in school because the more supportive teachers are, the greater students feel in control of their learning and the more engaged they are during learning activities (Ryan & Grolnick, 1986; Reeve, 1996).

supportiveness An affirmation of the other person's capacity for self-direction and contribution to help realize his or her self-set goals.

Gentle discipline is a socialization strategy that involves explaining why a particular way of thinking or behaving is right or wrong. Its opposite is *power assertion,* a socialization strategy that includes forceful commands and a no-nonsense insistence that students comply with the teacher's requests (Kochanska, Aksan, & Nichols, 2003). Gentle discipline is a verbal, relationship-based approach to discipline that begins with a conversation to draw attention to the hurtful effect the student's misbehavior had on others (Grusec & Goodnow, 1994). The teacher then explains why that behavior is wrong and should be changed. The conversation continues with a problem-solving effort as to what action the student might take to undo the harm, such as apologize or share. Students with caregivers who use gentle discipline rather than power assertion show greater social development (Brody & Shaffer, 1982).

gentle discipline A socialization strategy that revolves around explaining why a way of thinking or behaving is right or wrong.

RIDE How can Ms. Hernandez capitalize on these four relationship qualities to promote her students' social development?

What Constitutes a Low-Quality Relationship? Low quality-relationships are those characterized by neglect (indifference, permissiveness, lack of support, lack of involvement) and abuse (insensitivity, rejection, hostility). Children who come to school with a relationship history that includes either neglect or abuse often show delays in their cognitive and social development (Tower, 1996). Neglect in the home can come from poverty, parental depression, divorce, and similar circumstances that take parents away from caring for their children; abuse can come from conflict in the home, parental substance abuse, and a variety of traumatic experiences (Whitbourne et al., 1992). Neglect and abuse lead children to form negative mental models, because they describe themselves as being unlovable (Tower, 1996) and their caregivers as being unresponsive (Gondoli & Silverberg, 1997). Cognitively, these children tend to exhibit poor academic progress, low grades, low scores on standardized tests, and a tendency to be held back a grade (Trickett & McBride-Chang, 1995). Emotionally, these children are prone to anger and chronic emotional difficulties (Newman, 1981). Socially, these children often show a striking absence of social competencies (Trickett & McBride-Chang, 1995). These poor social-developmental outcomes can be seen in students across all grade levels and reflect neglect and abuse not only from parents but from peers and teachers as well (Conger et al., 1993).

> **How Can I Use This?**
>
> Can you use one of the qualities in Figure 3.3 to improve the quality of an existing relationship in your life?

What Does This Mean to Me?
Think of a close relationship in your life. How would you rate the other person in terms of attunement, relatedness, supportiveness, and gentle discipline?

Relationships Are Always Two-Sided. All relationships require work and depend on the constructive contribution of both partners. Some students, such as those with autism or emotional difficulty, may lack the capacity to contribute fully and constructively to a relationship. Other students vary in their willingness to relate to teachers. For instance, some students bring a chronic negative attitude or an array of defiant behaviors into the classroom and, therefore, show an unwillingness to be in relationship with the teacher (Eisenberg, Fabes, et al., 1997; Gallagher, 2002; Kochaska et al., 1997; Tramontana, Hooper, & Selzer, 1988). The more resistance the student shows, the less motivated teachers tend to be to display qualities such as attunement, relatedness, supportiveness, and gentle discipline. On a more optimistic note, the more students display positive emotion and classroom engagement, the more motivated teachers generally are to display the qualities listed in Figure 3.3 (Lay, Waters, & Park, 1989; Skinner & Belmont, 1993).

Culture, Diversity, and Special Needs

Students benefit when teachers provide attunement, relatedness, supportiveness, and gentle discipline. But a student's cultural background will affect how effective these aspects of a relationship will be. Figure 3.3 is based on the assumption that teachers seek to promote students' social development. Sometimes, however, other socialization goals take precedence. Parents in authoritarian families, for instance, emphasize strict discipline to such an extent that their children come to view strict discipline as more appropriate than gentle discipline (Deater-Deckard et al., 1996; Miller, Fung, & Mintz, 1996). Other families might heavily prioritize school success and academic achievement over social success and social development (Schneider & Lee, 1990). Likewise, some cultures strongly value respect for one's elders and, therefore, want to see relationships characterized by adult direction rather than by adult supportiveness.

As society grows more diverse, teachers' knowledge about students' cultural backgrounds grows in importance. Culturally different behaviors are not the same as social skill deficits or behavioral disorders (Feng, 1996). Asian-American students are sometimes believed to display social skill deficits, at least to the extent that they focus on academics and forego opportunities to interact socially with their peers (Reglin & Adams, 1990; Schneider & Lee, 1990). African-American students are sometimes believed to display behavioral disorders, at least to the extent that they enact an energetic, behaviorally intense style (Irvine, 1992). Generally speaking, these behaviors reflect cultural priorities rather than social skill deficits or behavioral disorders. Hence, rather than offering relationships in a cultural void, teachers can promote social development through classroom dialogues about how students can best accomplish social tasks such as the following (Doll, 1996):

- Maintaining a good relationship
- Pursuing equity and justice
- Avoiding trouble with peers and adults

Students with special needs might have a particularly difficult time accomplishing social tasks such as these if they cannot contribute their part to a high-quality relationship. Autistic children and children with emotional disabilities, for instance, often show a difficulty in giving love and affection to interaction partners (i.e., low relatedness). For these students, teachers can help by supplementing their high-quality relationships with the coaching of social skills and the provision of social support as these students engage in peer interactions.

Trust: The Beginning of Positive Social Development

All infants have an emotional need for relatedness, and this need motivates them to seek close, affectionate bonds with their caregivers. Caregivers, in turn, provide varying levels of **care** that produce different degrees of relatedness satisfaction. Some adults provide warm, responsive, sensitive, predictable, and nurturing care, and this high-quality care allows children to form secure **attachments** with them. Other children receive care that leads them to form insecure attachments, because adults are out of synch with the child and provide care that is inconsistent (sometimes loving, sometimes rejecting), impatient, unresponsive, and generally frustrating to the child's need to feel safe and secure. Based on the quality of this

care An emotional concern and sense of responsibility to protect or enhance another person's welfare or well-being.

attachment A close emotional relationship between two persons that is characterized by mutual affection and the desire to maintain proximity with the other.

Check *one* of the following:

_____ I find it relatively easy to get close to others and am comfortable depending on them and having them depend on me. I don't worry about being abandoned or about someone getting too close to me.

_____ I find that others are reluctant to get as close as I would like. I worry that others don't really love me or want to stay with me. I want to merge completely with others, especially love partners, and this desire sometimes scares others away.

_____ I am somewhat uncomfortable being close to others. I find it difficult to trust others completely, difficult to allow myself to depend on them. I become nervous when anyone gets too close to me, and often, others want me to be more intimate with them than I feel comfortable being.

Figure 3.4. Assessing Attachment Classification with a Questionnaire

Source: Hazan, C., & Shaver, P. (1987). Romantic love conceptualised as an attachment process. *Journal of Personality and Social Psychology, 52,* 511–524. Copyright © 1987 by the American Psychological Association. Reprinted with permission.

early care, children develop the kinds of mental models of self and others shown in Figure 3.2 (Mikulincer, 1998).

The basic psychological issue related to a child's mental model of others is trust, whereas the basic psychological issue related to a child's mental model of self is self-esteem.

Trust is one's confidence that the other partner in the relationship cares, is looking out for one's welfare, and will be there when needed (Tschannen-Moran & Hoy, 2000). When students trust their teacher, they know that the teacher will be responsive to their bids for attention, signals of distress, and need for assistance. *Mistrust,* on the other hand, involves being suspicious and expecting to be disappointed. When students mistrust, they stay on alert for signs of betrayal from others. Out of this sense of mistrust flow negative emotions, such as fear, anger, anxiety, and sadness.

In response to how much they trust their caregivers, students develop one of three attachment relationships: secure, resistant, or avoidant (Ainsworth, 1989; Ainsworth et al., 1978). The *secure style* reflects high trust and confidence in the availability of attachment figures in times of need. The *resistant style* reflects a strong desire for relatedness together with mistrust, a fear of rejection, and insecurity about how attachment figures will respond in times of need. The *avoidant style* reflects high mistrust and a preference to maintain one's emotional distance from other people. Figure 3.4 helps clarify the nature of these three attachment styles by providing the beliefs that adolescents with each attachment style might agree with and say aloud during conversation (Hazan & Shaver, 1987). From top to bottom, the three attachment classifications in the table are secure, resistant, and avoidant.

Self-esteem is trust applied to oneself. It is a self-evaluation that one is worthy of a positive or negative evaluation (Baumeister, Tice, & Hutton, 1989). From the perspective of attachment theory (Bartholomew & Horowitz, 1991; Bowlby, 1982), self-esteem in childhood reflects a sense of being worthy of love—a sense of lovability—and it therefore mirrors the warm care received by the child from others. Conversely, the more children feel rejected or ignored by others, the more they come to feel that they are worthless and of little value. Thus, securely attached students have a higher self-esteem than do insecurely attached students (Bylsma, Cozzarelli, & Sumer, 1997; Mikulincer, 1995).

If trust and care are the beginning of positive social development, then mistrust and rejection are the beginning of negative social development. Elementary-grade children are susceptible to childhood depression (Nolan, Flynn, & Garber, 2003), for instance, when they feel rejected by caregivers (My mother makes me feel I'm not loved.) and teachers (The teachers at my school don't like me.). Just as it is a developmental resource to experience trust and high self-esteem, it is a developmental liability for children and adolescents to experience rejection, mistrust, and low self-esteem.

Students' Attachment Styles with Teachers

A child's attachment style is formed during early interactions with primary caregivers. Once the child leaves the home, however, additional relationships emerge to affect his or her mental models of self and others (Ainsworth, 1989; Bowlby, 1988; Howes, 1999). As they encounter caregiving relationships outside the home, children develop relationship-specific

trust Confidence that the other person in the relationship cares, is looking out for your welfare, and will be there when needed.

What Does This Mean to Me?
Which of the three attachment styles describes you best?

self-esteem Trust applied to oneself; an attitude that one is worthy of a positive or a negative self-evaluation.

When children encounter threatening events, it helps to have access to a safe haven, a wise confidant, and a secure base—the teacher. (Stephanie Maze/Woodfin Camp & Associates)

Appendix
Understanding Students' Social Histories

Attachment categories help teachers summarize students' social histories and then offer the types of high-quality relationships students need to grow socially (*PRAXIS™*, I. B. 6, *INTASC*, Principles 1, 2, 3).

beliefs with specific interaction partners, such as one's teacher (Al-Yagon & Mikulincer, 2004). Children therefore develop a mental model of what their parents are like, but they also develop a mental model of what their teacher is like. Even when the attachment figure changes (e.g., from parent to teacher or peer), the basic attachment-related questions remain:

● What does this person do when I am upset?
● Can I trust this person to be available and responsive in times of need?
● With this person's support, what can I accomplish?

Attachment in Childhood. Familiarity with the three attachment styles is important for elementary school teachers because attachment styles explain not only students' trust and self-esteem but also their school functioning, popularity, ability to manage negative emotions, and prosocial/antisocial orientation toward peers (see Figure 3.2). A secure attachment with a teacher provides the child with a *safe haven* to go to when afraid, a strong and wise confidant who can soothe away negative feelings, and a *secure base* from which to explore and investigate the surrounding environment (Bowlby, 1988; Kochanska, Coy, & Murray, 2001). Resistant and avoidant children lack access to such a safe haven, a wise confidant, and a secure base and are, therefore, easily overwhelmed by threatening or distressing events, such as encountering a stranger or having a toy taken away by another child.

In school, teachers rate securely attached children as being more sociable and compliant, having better impulse control, and expressing more positive and less negative emotion; they rate resistantly attached children as more fearful, helpless, tense, and impulsive; and they rate avoidantly attached children as more hostile, aggressive, socially isolated, and disconnected from the purposes of school (Waters, Wippman, & Sroufe, 1979).

Attachment in Adolescence. Adolescents make domain-specific evaluations of their competence, such as "I'm good in school, but not so good in athletics." Through these self-evaluations, they gain a second source of self-esteem beyond their relationship-based childhood mental models of self (Mikulincer, 1995; Park, Crocker, & Mickelson, 2004). Among secure adolescents, self-esteem still tends to be high, as it was in childhood. Among resistant adolescents, self-esteem still tends to be low, as it was in childhood. Because they find little basis for positive self-esteem within their relationships, resistant adolescents often turn to other factors on which they can base their self-esteem, such as their physical appearance, the approval of others, and spirituality. Among avoidant adolescents, self-esteem actually tends to turn positive. This positive self-esteem, however, is rooted in a defensive denial of their need for relatedness, as their peers actually perceive them to be cold and hostile (Bartholomew & Horowitz, 1991). To achieve their high self-esteem, avoidant teenagers use their high level of self-reliance—that is, avoidance of relationships—as a way of evaluating the self positively. The "Taking It to the Classroom" box on the next page provides two telltale signs of supportive teacher.

Attachment for Learners with Special Needs

Children with learning disabilities typically report greater dissatisfaction in their relationship with teachers than do children without learning disabilities (Murray & Greenberg, 2001). Because of this dissatisfaction, they are at risk for socioemotional problems and maladjustment (Culbertson, 1998). These students are also less likely to be securely attached to their teachers. Students with emotional disturbances and students with mild mental retardation are especially likely to report being dissatisfied with their student-teacher relationship.

Teachers, too, report feeling significantly less close to their students with learning disabilities (Al-Yagon & Mikulincer, 2004). Students with learning disabilities are sensitive to the way their teachers relate to them, because they feel that their teachers are less available, less accepting, and more rejecting than do students without learning disabilities.

Taking It to the Classroom

Am I a Supportive Teacher?

One way to assess your own supportiveness toward students is to monitor the extent to which you engage in two relationship-maintaining behaviors during a conflict or intense disagreement: relatedness and autonomy support (Allen & Hauser, 1996; Allen & Land, 1999). With relatedness, the teacher expresses acceptance, shows empathy for the student's point of view, and shows constant signs of engagement—with few signs of disengagement—throughout the conflict and disagreement. With autonomy support, the teacher presents his or her reasoning in an open and flexible way while encouraging the student to do the same. The message is that both points of view have validity and deserve to be heard (as opposed to a more dogmatic "my way or the highway").

Of course, it is tempting to use one's status or position as teacher to override the student's sense of autonomy. It is also tempting to express relationship-disrupting emotions, such as anger or disgust. But doing these things during a disagreement undermines the student's assurance that teacher and student can work together not only to solve a problem but also to maintain the relationship. By supporting relatedness and autonomy during a conflict, the teacher provides the student with a high-quality relationship that functions as a secure base to work through the emotional and cognitive issues in one's life.

For instance, students with learning disabilities frequently *disagree* with the first two of the following statements but *agree* with the third:

- When I need the teacher's help, she is always there.
- The teacher makes me feel welcome in the class.
- The teacher makes me feel that I'm unnecessary in the class.

These data suggest that one reason students with special needs show poorer social development is that they do not believe they receive high-quality relationships from their teachers. When they do receive high-quality relationships from their teachers, however, they are significantly more likely to show meaningful gains in their social, emotional, and academic adjustment (Murray & Greenberg, 2001).

Psychosocial Development

Psychosocial development is a broad term used to describe the quality of a person's development as a function of how other people have treated that person in the past. To make sense of the term, consider each part separately. *Psycho* represents the student's sense of self; *social* represents the quality of the relationships in the person's life; and *development* represents the extent to which one's social development thrives or flounders. Stated differently, teachers (social) affect students' sense of self (psycho), which, in turn, expresses itself through a host of developmental outcomes. For instance, when teachers provide gentle discipline, students tend to develop a positive sense of self and become more likely to interact cooperatively with peers; but when teachers provide harsh discipline, students tend to develop a negative sense of self and become more likely to interact aggressively with peers. (Hoffman, 1975; Kochanska, Aksan, & Nichols, 2003).

psychosocial development A broad term to describe the quality of a person's social development as a function of past relationships in one's life.

Erikson's Framework

The essence of social development is the student's progression toward psychological growth, personal adjustment, a sense of competence, emotional maturity, a prosocial orientation toward others, and a capacity for autonomous functioning (Loevinger, 1976). Perhaps no theory better communicates the role of teachers and schools in students' ongoing social development than Erik Erikson's (1959, 1963, 1964, 1968). As shown in Table 3.1, Erikson described eight developmental turning points (or "crises") that all people face, the approximate age at which each emerges, and the relationships that most influence the resolution of each developmental turning point.

TABLE 3.1

Erikson's Lifespan Developmental Framework

Developmental turning point	Approximate age range	Most important social agents
1. Trust vs. mistrust	Infancy	Caretakers
2. Autonomy vs. shame, doubt	Early childhood	Parents
3. Initiative vs. guilt	Preschool	Parents, siblings, grandparents
4. Competence vs. incompetence	Elementary school	Teachers
5. Identity vs. role confusion	Middle and high school	Role models, peers
6. Intimacy vs. isolation	College	Partners in love, work
7. Generativity vs. stagnation	Teaching career	Students, one's own children
8. Integrity vs. despair	Retirement years	

Erikson argued that social development "has a ground plan" in which development and personal growth proceed through a series of eight successive turning points, as shown in Table 3.1. The phrase *turning point* connotes a crucial period in which the student moves in a direction of either greater strength and adjustment or greater vulnerability and maladjustment. Each turning point is related to all seven others, because a positive resolution at one stage increases the individual's strength and potential to cope with future turning points, whereas a negative resolution leaves the person more vulnerable to later maladjustment. Stages 3–5 emerge during the K-12 years; therefore, they deserve special emphasis. Stage 7 also deserves attention, because it applies to teachers.

Developing Initiative. The developmental turning point that preschool children face above all others involves moving either toward greater initiative or toward hesitance and guilt. **Initiative** is the capacity to use a surplus of energy to plan and constructively carry out a task. Children tap into their reservoir of initiative when they explore the objects around them, draw with crayons, yell at the top of their lungs, and wander outside to see what is out there. As summarized in Figure 3.5, preschool children become increasingly experimental in

initiative The child's capacity to use a surplus of energy to plan and constructively carry out a task.

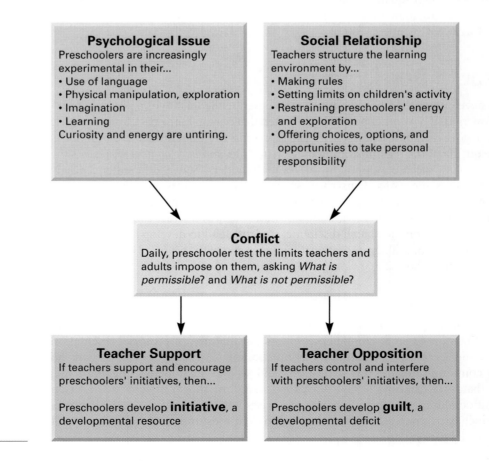

Figure 3.5. The Role of Teachers in Supporting Preschoolers' Initiative

exercising their physical, language, and imagination skills, and their curiosity is endless. Equipped with such energy and curiosity, children test the limits that teachers impose on them to see what is and is not permissible.

The teacher's task during preschool is to provide some direction to students' zest—to nurture initiative while at the same time communicating classroom rules and limits. When teachers find ways to support and encourage preschoolers' curiosity and vigor—even while imposing a structure on classroom activity—children develop initiative, a willingness to explore, and a sense of purpose within their activity. When teachers suppress preschoolers' curiosity, however, children develop guilt, hesitance, and a tendency to sacrifice their initiative so as to live within the limits imposed on them. To find a balance between supporting initiative and setting limits, the "Taking It to the Classroom" box just below offers several useful guidelines.

The developmental turning point in preschool children's lives is moving toward greater initiative or toward hesitance. (Digital Vision)

Taking It to the Classroom

Guidelines for Supporting Preschoolers' Initiative

- Set rules and limits, but offer children some freedom within those limits.
- Explain the "why" behind an imposed rule or limit.
- Explain the "why" behind an instruction not to do something.
- Be tolerant of mistakes and accidents, affirming students' initiative and enthusiasm even while correcting their behavior.
- When children are engrossed in an activity, avoid interrupting them or asking them to change to a different activity.
- Allocate some time during the day for free play.

How Can I Use This?

The next time you impose a restriction on another person, see whether you can do so without undermining that person's sense of initiative.

Developing Competence. The turning point that elementary school students face above all others involves developing a sense of competence rather than incompetence. The "Taking It to the Classroom" box below offers several guidelines for promoting competence in elementary school students. **Competence** is the self-assurance that one can successfully accomplish culturally valued tasks. It involves understanding the relationship between trying hard and

competence The psychological need to be effective as one interacts with the surrounding environment.

Taking It to the Classroom

Guidelines for Supporting Elementary-Grade Children's Competence

- Provide developmentally appropriate challenges to students' skills, and avoid tasks that are too easy or too difficult.
- As students work on these optimally challenging tasks, provide scaffolding—hints, tips, reminders, encouragement, and similar supports for learning.
- After students perform, provide constructive and skill-building feedback.
- Highlight points of progress in the child's skill development.
- Discuss the link between effort, perseverance, and the eventual pleasure of a job well done.
- Take time to recognize the products of a child's work.
- Provide support for discouraged students. For instance, keep samples of their earlier work on hand so they can see that they are indeed making progress.

Psychological Issue
Elementary school children acquire skills and knowledge that are valued by the culture and apply those skills through...
• Behaviors, such as concentration, engagement, perserverance, work habits
• Emotions, such as enjoying the work, feeling interest, feeling useful, feeling satisfied

Social Relationship
Teachers do or do not provide...
• Developmentally appropriate challenges (vs. too easy, too difficult)
• Scaffolding in the zone of proximal development
• Constructive, skill-building feedback
• Praise of a job well done
• Discuss links between child's effort and pleasure of a job well done

Conflict
Daily, elementary-children exercise their skills and strive for mastery and competence in culturally valued tasks such as reading, writing, social skills, art, athletics, asking, *Am I good at this?*

Teacher Support
If teachers support children's strivings for competence, then...

Children develop **competence** (or a work ethic), a developmental resource

Teacher Opposition
If teachers neglect to support these strivings (don't communicate expectations, don't scaffold, don't provide constructive feedback), then...

Children develop **incompetence**, a developmental deficit

Figure 3.6. The Role of Teachers in Supporting Elementary School Students' Competence

Chapter Reference
Chapter 6 discusses competence as a source of motivation.

experiencing the pleasure of a job well done. As summarized in Figure 3.6 above, elementary school students engage themselves in learning a multitude of skills that will be necessary for their lives, including academic skills such as reading, penmanship, and the capacity to enjoy work (Kowaz & Marcia, 1991). Erikson placed particular emphasis on developing a "work ethic," or the emotional capacity to take pleasure in a job well done. When efforts on challenging tasks produce positive feedback and completed tasks, the student begins to develop an enduring sense of competence and mastery. When these same efforts produce negative feedback and a string of unfinished tasks, however, the student begins to develop a sense of incompetence and inferiority.

The developmental turning point in elementary school students' lives is developing a sense of competence or incompetence. (Media Bakery)

The teacher's task during elementary school is to offer students developmentally appropriate challenges, provide positive feedback to communicate a job well done, and engage in ongoing discussions about the relationship between perseverance and the pleasure of work. From this point of view, a lesson in penmanship, singing, or painting is not just about writing, singing, or painting; and playground attempts to hit a softball are about more than merely trying to hit the ball. The content of the day's lesson is important, but elementary school lessons are always embedded within a subtext of developing competence.

Developing Identity. The transition from adolescence into adulthood involves a progressive strengthening of one's sense of identity (Waterman, 1982). Hence, as shown in Figure 3.7, the turning point that secondary school students face above all others is the need to develop a sense of identity within the larger society rather than suffering from role confusion. **Identity** is the sense of being a distinct and productive individual within the larger social framework. Adolescence is a time of exploring occupational and ideological commitments, and students construct a sense of identity when they are able to fit themselves into the adult social system (Baumeister, 1986, 1987; Marcia, 1994). When adolescents search for, find, and eventually commit to a particular set of adult roles and ideological beliefs, they develop a sense of identity; when they fail to do so, they suffer from role confusion and a sense of uncertainty about themselves and their future (Meilman, 1979).

The search for identity begins with awareness of social demands in terms of what one should be as well as social opportunities in terms of what one can be (Grotevant, 1987). The teacher's task during middle and high school is to create classroom (and school-wide) opportunities in which students explore and test their aspirations, personal beliefs, possible future selves, and conceivable occupations. One way to do this is to give adolescents a steady

identity The sense of being a distinct and productive individual within the larger social framework.

Chapter Reference
Chapters 2 and 10 discuss scaffolding in the zone of proximal development, a concept that captures the essence of supporting students' competence.

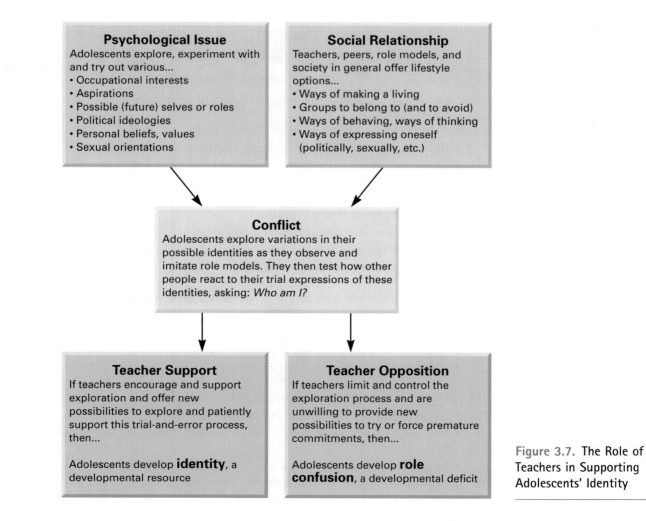

Figure 3.7. The Role of Teachers in Supporting Adolescents' Identity

The developmental turning point in adolescents' lives is developing identity or suffering role confusion.
(Media Bakery)

Appendix
Meeting Students' Developmental Needs

Students' developmental needs vary according to age. Erikson's theory identifies which psychosocial needs are most pressing for student of different ages (*PRAXIS*™, I. B. 1; I. C. 1, *INTASC*, Principles 2, 3, 5).

stream of opportunities to explore and try out for themselves in various aspects of life, such as vocation, personal values, political orientation, and perspectives on marriage and parenting. When presenting such opportunities, teachers need to do so in a classroom climate characterized by openness to change. Overall, the two critical sources of support teachers can provide during this identity-versus-role-confusion struggle is exploration of alternatives and openness to change (Bosma & Kunnen, 2001), as discussed in "Taking It to the Classroom" box on this page.

As students become aware of societal roles, explore these roles, and make decisions about which roles to commit to and which ones to avoid, four identity statuses unfold: diffused, foreclosed, moratorium, and achieved (Marcia, 1966, 1994). With *diffused identity,* the adolescent has not searched, explored, or committed to adult roles. Both exploration and commitment are low. With *foreclosed identity,* the adolescent has not explored, yet has committed to adult roles. Identity foreclosure is common when the adolescent simply takes on and assumes (without exploration) the values, ideology, and occupation of his or her parents. A teenager might say, "My mother was a nurse, my grandmother was a nurse, so I'm going to be a nurse too." With *moratorium,* the adolescent has explored but has not yet committed to adult roles. Exploring roles while withholding personal commitments results in the well-known *identity crisis,* which is a synonym for identity moratorium. With *achieved identity,* the adolescent has actively explored and made personal commitments to a way of life (ideology, occupation). Figure 3.8 summarizes these four identity statuses and indicates the percentages of middle school, high school, and college-age students occupying each of them (Waterman, 1982, 1985). The "What Kids Say and Do" box on the next page reports what adolescents with each status actually said about their own identity search.

Taking It to the Classroom

Guidelines for Supporting Adolescents' Identity

Expand Students' Awareness of Social Opportunities
- Raise awareness of a wide range of identity opportunities.
- Invite guest speakers into the class.
- Identify possible role models to emulate.

Support Exploration of Possible Identities
- Encourage open discussions of ideological possibilities.
- Provide supplemental information for the societal roles in which students express an interest.
- Identify apprenticeship opportunities in the local community.

Communicate Value and Support for School-Based Clubs and Organizations
- Encourage students to explore interest groups.
- Encourage students to join clubs and organizations.
- Understand the positive role that membership in a small club within an otherwise large high school can play in adolescents' identity development.

Support Open-Ended Decision Making about Possible Identities
- Discuss identity struggles in literature, such as Biff's in *Death of a Salesman.*
- Work collaboratively with students to find the resources they need to make decisions about their future.
- Be sensitive to adolescents' familial priorities, especially tension between the family's press for connectedness and the student's desire for individuality.

Extent of personal commitment
to societal roles

Low ◄ - - - - - - - - - - - - ► High

	Extent of Exploration and Investigation of Possible Roles, Options

Low ↑

Identity Diffusion	**Identity Foreclosure**
Exploration: Low Commitment: Low	Exploration: Low Commitment: High
Associated with immature psychosocial development.	Associated with acceptance of what society has to offer.
Middle school 39% students (age 13-16)	Middle school 37% students (age 13-16)
High school 29% students (age 16-18)	High school 36% students (age 16-18)
College 14% students (age 19-21)	College 31% students (age 19-21)
Identity Moratorium	**Identity Achievement**
Exploration: High Commitment: Low	Exploration: High Commitment: High
Associated with questioning of what society has to offer.	Associated with mature psychosocial development and acceptance of what society has to offer.
Middle school 15% students (age 13-16)	Middle school 9% students (age 13-16)
High school 14% students (age 16-18)	High school 21% students (age 16-18)
College 16% students (age 19-21)	College 40% students (age 19-21)

High ↓

Figure 3.8. Four Identity Statuses Related to Occupational Choice (and the Percentages of Students at Different Grade Levels Who Occupy Them)

What Kids Say and Do

Adolescents Speak about Identity Status

A group of high school seniors were asked about their likely occupation after high school in the following way (after each nominated a preferred occupation): So, you might become a(n) _____. Okay, but if something better comes along, how willing would you be to change and give up this occupation?

Achieved Identity

I might, but I doubt it. This is something I've thought about, and I know I want to become an artist. I can't really see what "something better" would be for me.

Moratorium

Maybe. I don't know for sure. If I knew for sure, then I could answer your question better (*laughs*). I would have to look into it—find out more about it. A definite maybe.

Foreclosed Identity

No, not very willing. My parents are happy with it and so am I. It's what I've always wanted to do.

Diffused Identity

Sure. Why not? Who knows what will happen? If something good comes along, I might take it.

Developing Generativity. The primary developmental challenge that experienced teachers face is that of being productive and able to guide the next generation successfully (Erikson, 1963; McAdams et al., 1997; McAdams & du St. Aubin, 1992). (Beginning teachers in their twenties, however, are more likely to be concerned with issues of identity and intimacy than

generativity The sense of being productive in one's work and in looking after and guiding others.

with issues of generativity.) **Generativity** is the sense of being productive in one's work and in looking after and guiding others, particularly one's students and one's own children. It is an active concern for the growth of self and others, a sense of responsibility for sharing skills and knowledge (Bradley, 1997).

In daily life, generativity involves actions such as creative work (e.g., writing, teaching), training those who are less skilled, meeting the needs of one's students, raising one's own children, integrating work with family life to balance self-care with other-care, making contributions to the community (e.g., through volunteer work), and basically "making a difference" in people's lives. Difficulty in achieving a sense of generativity can lead to stagnation and self-indulgence (Levinson, 1986). The springboard to generativity appears to be the experience of career consolidation, in which the teacher gains the self-assurance needed (e.g., through academic tenure) to worry less and less about the self and more and more about the next generation (Vaillant & Milsofsky, 1980). As an overview, the "Uncommon Sense" box on this page discusses the overall developmental goal of positive psychosocial mental health.

What Does This Mean to Me?
Which developmental crisis is currently the most pressing one in your life: Identity? Intimacy? Generativity?

Uncommon Sense

Healthy Development Requires High Trust, Initiative, Competence, Identity, and Generativity—Or Does it?

To develop trust is better than to develop mistrust; to develop autonomy is better than to develop shame; and so on for all eight of Erikson's stages of psychosocial development. It makes sense, then, to assume that the ideal developmental trajectory throughout the lifespan would be the steady accumulation of personal strengths such as trust, autonomy, initiative, competence, identity, intimacy, generativity, and integrity.

According to Erikson (1982), however, it is preferable to develop a certain degree of tension between each stage's polar alternatives, with an emphasis on the more positive alternative. In this way, the student sustains basic trust but does not eliminate mistrust, particularly in situations where mistrust may be more appropriate (e.g., the overly naïve student gets taken advantage of). In addition, human potential needs an internalized system of checks and balances. Initiative needs a conscience to keep it in check (guilt); competence needs a dose of reality (incompetence); and identity needs healthy skepticism (role confusion). In other words, the psychosocial developmental goal is not to eliminate all traces of mistrust, shame, guilt, and so on, so much as it is to develop more trust than mistrust, more initiative than guilt, and so forth through the eight stages.

Moral Development

moral development Students' judgments about what is right and wrong and their reasoning as to why one action is right and another is wrong.

Moral development concerns judgments about right and wrong. It also concerns one's reasoning as to why one action is right and another is wrong. Is it right to share your lunch with a classmate? Is it right to give up your seat on the bus to a classmate? If these things are right, why are they right? Is it wrong to cut in line in front of others? Is it wrong to keep a toy that was supposed to be shared? If these things are wrong, why are they wrong? Students' reasoning as to why some acts are right and others are wrong develops throughout the school years in a predictable pattern.

Stages of Moral Development

According to Lawrence Kohlberg (1975, 1981, 1984), moral reasoning is the application of principles to solve moral dilemmas. The principles that students use to solve moral dilemmas reveal their underlying level of moral development. These principles develop through a series of sequential stages, as shown in Table 3.2. At the preconventional level, children's moral reasoning is immature; the term *preconventional* connotes a period before the development of moral principles. Student in this stage determine right and wrong through a lens of self-interest and an understanding of the personal consequences of their actions. At the *conventional* level, students begin to use principles to reason morally. Conventional reasoning is rooted in social convention, such as doing the right thing so as to live up to

TABLE 3.2

Stages of Moral Development (Kohlberg's Theory)

Preconventional

Understands neither social convention nor moral rules.

Stage 1: Moral judgments are based on a punishment-and-obedience orientation. What is good or right is that which avoids punishment and defers to authority.

Stage 2: Moral judgments are based on what satisfies one's own needs. What is right is what I need; what is wrong is what I get punished for. A pragmatic "you scratch my back and I'll scratch yours" orientation prevails.

Conventional

Understands and embraces social convention.

Values living up to the expectations of the family, group, or culture for its own sake.
Conforms to group norms and acts to maintain them.

Stage 3: Moral judgments are based on a good boy–nice girl orientation. What is good or right is what pleases others and gains their approval.

Stage 4: Moral judgments are based on a law-and-order orientation. What is good or right is doing one's duty, following fixed rules, and acting to maintain the social order.

Postconventional

Understands and embraces moral rules.

Moral rules are defined apart from group norms. Instead of just accepting the social order, the individual adopts his or her own perspective on what is right.

Stage 5: Moral rules are created from socially agreed-upon standards that have been critically examined and revised to meet the needs and values of the society.

Stage 6: Moral rules exist as self-chosen ethical principles, such as justice, equal rights, respect for the individual, fairness, and reciprocity.

the expectations of others. At this level, being good means doing what others approve of. At the *postconventional* level, students understand and embrace moral principles, and these principles are not based on social convention, an authority figure, or a group norm. Instead, what is right is what has stood up to one's own critical examination, been revised, and been determined to be just and fair. The following "What Kids Say and Do" box on this page provides some quotations from high school students who reason at these three levels of moral reasoning when asked whether cheating is wrong.

What Kids Say and Do

Moral Reasoning about Cheating

Question Asked of Tenth- and Eleventh-Grade Students: Most students say that cheating on a test is wrong. Do you agree? If so, could you explain why cheating is wrong?

A Student Using Preconventional Reasoning

Cheating on a test? Yeah, that's wrong. It's bad. You can't just cheat because you want to. If you do, you'd be like a criminal or something.

A Student Using Conventional Reasoning

Duh. I guess it's natural for students to want to cheat—to get ahead, you know. But it is still always wrong to cheat. You have to follow the rules, and that is true regardless of whether you have studied enough or not. That's just the way it is.

A Student Using Postconventional Reasoning

Most of the time cheating is wrong—almost always. Before you say cheating is morally wrong, you've got to consider the whole situation. There is just so much pressure placed on students to excel that cheating might be reasonable. It's wrong, sure, but so is putting so much pressure on students to be #1.

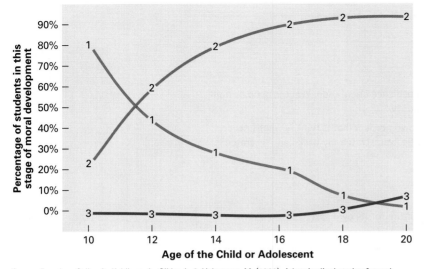

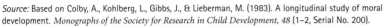

Age of the Child or Adolescent

Source: Based on Colby, A., Kohlberg, L., Gibbs, J., & Lieberman, M. (1983). A longitudinal study of moral development. *Monographs of the Society for Research in Child Development, 48* (1–2, Serial No. 200).

Figure 3.9. Stages of Moral Development for Males Ages 10–36

Chapter Reference
Chapter 2 discusses Piaget's stages of cognitive development.

The level of moral development displayed by males of different ages (10–20 years) appears in Figure 3.9 (Colby et al., 1983). The figure rather strikingly shows that most elementary school students rely on preconventional moral reasoning (10-year-olds: 73%). By middle school, most students rely on conventional moral reasoning (14-year-olds: 62%). By high school, most students continue to rely on conventional moral reasoning (18-year-olds: 84%). Postconventional moral reasoning is rare during the school years. It is also rare in adulthood (Kohlberg, 1984). Based on these data, teachers can expect that most students' moral reasoning will involve either immature moral principles (preconventional) or conventional principles, in which an act is right because "it's what everybody else does."

In many respects, moral reasoning reflects students' cognitive development. As Kohlberg pointed out, "Since moral reasoning clearly is reasoning, advanced moral reasoning depends on advanced logical reasoning; a person's logical stage puts a certain ceiling on the moral stage he can attain" (Kohlberg, 1975, p. 671). Preoperational thinking (to use Piaget's terminology) limits children to egocentric thinking and, thus, cognitively paves the way toward preconventional moral reasoning. Concrete-operational thinking allows the child to overcome egocentrism and recognize other people's points of view. The child understands what others might judge to be good and morally acceptable versus bad and morally unacceptable. Postconventional moral reasoning requires formal-operational thinking, because it is based on abstract principles, not on concrete rules and norms (Schlaefli, Rest, & Thoma, 1985). That said, although many older students rely on formal-operational thinking, few show signs of postconventional moral reasoning. Thus, cognitive development is necessary but not sufficient for moral reasoning (Kuhn et al., 1977; Tomlinson-Keasey & Keasey, 1974).

If they are to advance their moral reasoning to a level that reflects their cognitive development, students need opportunities to discuss moral issues in an open and nonthreatening way. That is, moral reasoning advances through discussions within high-quality relationships and a sense of community in which misdeeds and conflicts are resolved through fairness and perspective taking (Eisenberg, Lennon, & Roth, 1983). Students who are consistently given rationales for why something is right or wrong (i.e., gentle discipline) also show greater advances in their moral development than do students who are disciplined harshly with forceful commands (Brody & Shaffer, 1982; Eisenberg et al., 1983). Thus, to develop moral reasoning requires both cognitive development and supportive social dialogue (Kruger & Tomasello, 1986).

Does Moral Reasoning Predict Moral Behavior? In general, a student's level of moral reasoning as depicted in Table 3.2 predicts his or her helping and sharing behavior (Blasi, 1980; Kohlberg & Candee, 1984; Underwood & Moore, 1982). But the relationship between moral reasoning and moral action is a weak one. This is so because many opportunities to help and share are low-cost situations. When helping or sharing costs the person very little, most people—regardless of their moral development—will lend a helping hand. When the costs of helping are high in terms of time, energy, or money, however, a person's level of moral development does predict whether he or she will help.

In one study, for instance, children could donate an unattractive or an attractive possession to hospitalized children. When they were asked to donate low-cost, unattractive possessions, level of moral reasoning did not predict which children donated their possessions; but when they were asked to donate high-cost, attractive possessions, only children with higher levels of moral reasoning made a donation (Eisenberg & Shell, 1987). Thus, level of moral development predicts moral action, but only when the costs are relatively high. This is so because high costs create moral conflicts (self-interest vs. the needs of others), and for morally immature students, self-interest typically trumps social concern.

The Ethic of Care

In Kohlberg's theory, the highest level of moral reasoning reflects the individual's level of cognitive development and expresses itself in a personal commitment to abstract principles such as justice and fairness. According to a second perspective, however, moral reasoning grows out of relationship concerns. That is, decisions about right and wrong can be based on compassion, social duties and obligations, responsibility to others, and concern for the welfare of others. In short, moral judgments can be based on an *ethic of care* (Gilligan, 1993).

To appreciate how an ethic of care can distinguish among different levels of moral reasoning, Figure 3.10 shows three concentric circles. At the center is a sense of concern, care, and responsibility only for oneself. Self-interest represents the most immature level of moral reasoning—the inner circle. At a more advanced level is the second circle, in which one's range of care expands to include concern for one's in-group, such as friends, family, and "people like me." This level of moral reasoning is more mature than the first because one's ethic of care includes not only oneself but others as well. At the outer boundary is a sense of concern, care, and responsibility for "all people." One's sense of responsibility and compassion extends beyond oneself and one's in-group to include a general *ethic of care*. Thus, according to this view, moral maturity advances from concern for self through concern for one's in-group to concern for all.

Concern, care, and a sense of responsibility for all people. — Moral development as an ethic of care

Concern, care, and a sense of responsibility for one's in-group. — Moral development as care of one's in-group

Concern, care, and a sense of responsibility for one's own welfare. — Moral development as self-interest

Figure 3.10. The Ethic of Care Depicted as Concentric Circles

RIDE How might Ms. Hernandez expand her students' ethic of care to include all class members?

Gender Differences in Moral Development. Carol Gilligan (1993) proposed her relationship-based ethic of care as a theory of moral development because she felt that existing theories were gender biased. She titled her book on this subject *In a Different Voice* because she wanted to voice what she believed to be the female perspective on morality. To formulate her ideas, she began with the assumption that gender socialization leads boys and girls to internalize different moral voices. Boys are encouraged to be independent and assertive and to see moral dilemmas as conflicts of interest. Hence, boys learn a morality of justice. Girls, however, are encouraged to be empathic and concerned about others and to see moral dilemmas as relationship issues. Hence, girls learn a morality of care. Research actually did not support

Caring is an emotional concern and sense of responsibility to protect another's well-being. (Jeffrey Greenberg/Photo Researchers, Inc.)

this assumption, but the theory was nevertheless a milestone in the study of moral development because it argued persuasively that moral development can be based on both a morality of justice and a morality of care—and this is true for *both* boys and girls (Brabeck, 1983).

Character and Conscience: Doing the Right Thing for the Right Reason

When teachers ask students to "do this" or say "don't do that," students tend to comply, at least if they have a positive relationship with the teacher. But students comply for two different reasons (Kochanska, Aksan, & Koenig, 1995), referred to as *situational compliance* and *committed compliance*. With **situational compliance**, students are cooperative but they lack a sincere commitment to the action and, instead, act out of obligation. With **committed compliance**, students eagerly and willingly embrace the request and carry it out in a volitional, self-regulated way rather than in a have-to, teacher-regulated way.

These two types of compliance are negatively correlated, meaning that the more students engage in situational compliance, the less they engage in committed compliance, and vice versa (Kochanska et al., 1995). These two types of compliance have different developmental origins and different implications for students' social competence, morality, and conscience. As shown in Figure 3.11, committed compliance grows out of a high-quality relationship with the teacher. The more teachers show attunement, relatedness, supportiveness, and gentle discipline, the more likely it is that students will respond with committed rather than situational compliance (Kochanska et al., 2001). Students are more likely to show situational compliance when they have a low-quality relationship with the teacher, because the teacher relies only on the assertion of power to gain students' compliance.

Power assertion is a socialization strategy designed to gain compliance through coercion, pressure, forceful insistence, and a negative or critical interaction style; it is associated with situational compliance, impaired self-regulation, and increased aggression (Deater-Deckard et al., 1996; Gershoff, 2002a; Kochanska et al., 2003; McCord, 1985). The problem with power assertion is that it arouses anger and hostility in students, thus generating a resistance against complying with the teacher's wishes. The distinction between these two types of compliance is important, because only committed compliance is associated with ongoing cooperation with the teacher's requests, internalization of rules, gains in moral maturity, and the development of a conscience (Kochanska et al., 1995; Kochanska & Thompson, 1997), as shown in Figure 3.11. Situational compliance is not associated with any gains in students' ongoing social development.

Figure 3.12 frames the chapter's discussion of moral development under the umbrella of character or conscience (Grusec, 1997; Kochanska & Aksan, 2004). At the base of the figure is *moral action,* which represents the absence of aggression and the presence of altruism, committed compliance, and social competence. Above moral action are the three sources that foster prosocial behavior and inhibit aggression. *Moral cognition* is essentially one's thoughts and values about prosocial and antisocial behavior, because it includes the inter-

Sidebar (margin glossary)

situational compliance
Cooperatively carrying out a teacher's "do this" or "don't do that" request with a sense of obligation rather than a sincere commitment to the action.

committed compliance
Cooperatively carrying out a teacher's request to "do this" or "don't do that" with an eager, willing, and sincere commitment to the action.

power assertion   A socialization strategy designed to gain compliance through coercion, pressure, forceful insistence, and a negative or critical interaction style.

Appendix
Social-Emotional-Moral Development

Teachers who support students in one domain of social, emotional, or moral development subsequently enhance students' development in the other two domains of social development as well (*PRAXIS™, I. A. 2, INTASC* Principle 2).

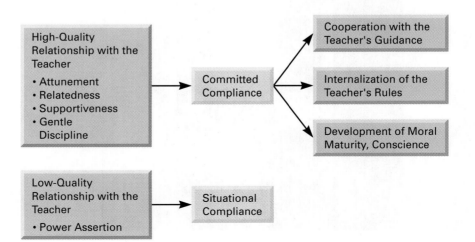

Figure 3.11. Origins and Developmental Implications of Two Types of Compliance

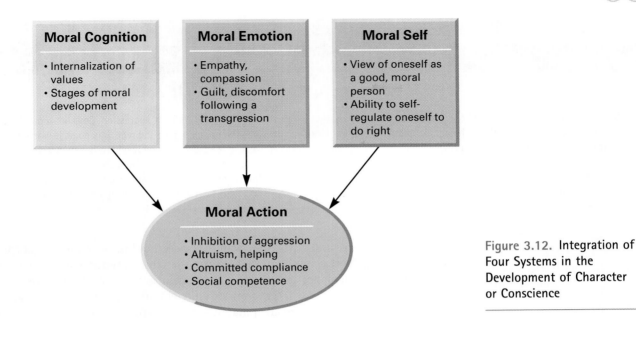

Figure 3.12. Integration of Four Systems in the Development of Character or Conscience

nalization of values and the stages of moral development. *Moral emotions* are those, such as empathy, that foster prosocial action and those, such as guilt and discomfort following a transgression, that inhibit aggression (Kochanska et al., 2002). *Moral self* is the person's mental model in which the self is viewed as a good and moral person who cares for others (Hart & Fegley, 1995). It includes awareness of right and wrong.

The extent to which these four systems are correlated with one another reflects the student's character (Rushton, Brainerd, & Pressley, 1983) or conscience (Kochanska, Padavich, & Koenig, 1996). **Conscience** is the capacity to use one's moral cognition, moral emotions, and moral self to inhibit aggression and to use these same inner resources to initiate altruism and helping. The development of conscience, therefore, is the development of children and adolescents' moral cognition, moral emotions, and moral sense of self. It is helped along by the provision of high-quality teacher-student conversations that help students link their thoughts, emotions, and sense of self to their capacity to do what is right and avoid doing what is wrong (Kochanska & Murray, 2000).

conscience The capacity to use one's moral cognition, moral emotions, and moral self to inhibit aggression and to initiate altruism and helping.

Aggression and Social Competence

Conflicts among students are an inevitable part of classroom life. First, one student insults another. The offended student then persuades friends to exclude the offender from their social activities (as revenge). As these conflicts play themselves out in the classroom, students frequently feel emotions such as anger and frustration. How children and adolescents manage their negative emotions manifests in their displays of aggression and social competence.

Aggression

Aggression is any intentional behavior designed to harm another person or group physically or psychologically (Parke & Slaby, 1983). Students trip each other in the hallway, hit and kick, take each other's possessions, tease and annoy, utter threats such as "I'll beat you up," and call each other names; they spread rumors, tell lies, and defame each other's character; they exclude others from their groups; and they vandalize property (Crick, Bigbee, & Howes, 1996). The "Uncommon Sense" box on the next page lists common aggressive behaviors from both boys and girls. When one student deliberately and intentionally engages in such actions with the purpose of harming another, almost irrespective of how much harm subsequently ensues, the behavior is aggressive. Behavior that causes accidental harm, however, is not aggressive because the harm was not intentional.

aggression Any intentional behavior designed to harm another person or group physically or psychologically.

When teachers are asked why they want to understand the developmental roots of students' aggression, they say it is because they want the sense of security that comes from being able to predict—and hence avoid—danger in their classrooms (Muehlenhard & Kimes, 1999). In that spirit, we too will try to understand why students are aggressive so that teachers can prevent aggression from creeping into their classrooms and finding a home there.

Video Game Technology and Aggression

Many towns have recently suffered deadly shootings by students in their schools, including the 13 murders committed by Eric Harris and Dylan Klebold of Columbine High School. Is it just coincidence that these two boys, like boys who committed violent shootings in other schools, liked to play the video game Doom? One of the Columbine boys customized the Doom game so that it featured two shooters, extra weapons, and defenseless victims—features all too similar to the actual shooting scenario.

Exposure to violent video games does increase viewers' aggression and violence. The more viewers are exposed to violent video games, the more violence they display, and this is true for girls as well as boys and for children as well as teenagers and young adults (Anderson & Bushman, 2001). Exposure to violent video games does more than just stir viewers to violence. It also leads viewers to think more aggressively, feel more aggressively, and experience heightened arousal. Exposure also decreases helping and prosocial behavior.

Why? What role does repeated exposure to violent video games (even violent cartoons) play in the forging of a violence-prone personality in which students become significantly less helpful and significantly more aggressive? Exposure to violence changes how the student thinks. Repeated exposure gives viewers aggressive social expectations (others will be aggressive, not cooperative) and aggressive behavioral scripts (when insulted, one retaliates). Students who take these aggressive social expectations and behavioral scripts into the schools will be more aggressive and less helpful (Anderson, 1983; Anderson & Dill, 2000).

Instrumental and Hostile Aggression

Aggression comes it two types—instrumental and hostile. It is important to distinguish between these types because they have different developmental origins and different classroom remedies (Anderson & Bushman, 2002).

Instrumental Aggression. One type of aggression is **instrumental aggression**, which is strategic behavior to obtain something the aggressor desires, such as a possession, a toy, attention, "my way," or respect from others. During infancy, a developmental period in which aggression hits its peak, instrumental aggression is common, as infants often try to overpower others for toys, possessions, and attention. Among preschoolers, physical acts of aggression generally give way to verbal ones, including teasing, tattling, and name calling. As children enter school, their coping skills during conflict situations expand to include not only physical and verbal aggression but also noncoercive ways of coping, including negotiation. Throughout elementary school, acts of aggression usually give way to these alternative ways of getting what one wants as children develop their social skills.

instrumental aggression
Strategic behavior to obtain something one desires that results in harm inflicted on another person.

What can teachers do to help students make this transition from instrumental aggression to social skill? Approaches involving punishment, behavior modification, and medication generally fall short as intervention strategies, largely because they fail to teach students the social skills they need to resolve conflicts amicably. Two more productive approaches are helping students cope constructively with their anger and building and refining students' prosocial problem-solving skills and strategies (Lochman et al., 1984). Conflicts are difficult situations for children to handle, especially when the conflict makes them feel angry. Teachers can help by showing students how to cope in a way that is both more effective and more prosocial. (This discussion is continued in the section on social competence.)

Hostile Aggression. The second type of aggression is **hostile aggression**, or aggression in which harm is sought as a goal itself. The intent is not to cope but to harm. Hostile aggression is typically impulsive, thoughtless, and driven by anger (Anderson & Bushman, 2002). During infancy, hostile aggression emerges in proportion to the extent to which infants' needs are frustrated—for example, through parental abuse and neglect. Among preschoolers, infantile rage expresses itself through such acts as stubborn defiance, annoying others, and bullying. Some children learn that aggression has value for its own sake, because it enables the child to dominate and control others. Throughout middle and high school, hostile aggression expresses itself in such acts as verbal assault, fighting, property damage, shoplifting, frequent lying, and violent acts such as attacks, strong-arming others, rape, and homicide (Loeber & Hay, 1994). By adolescence, hostile aggression manifests itself in the classroom in three principal ways (Olweus, 1980):

1. Starting fights—unprovoked physical aggression
2. Verbal protests—verbal aggression directed at teachers
3. Verbal hurt—verbal aggression directed at peers

> **hostile aggression**   The anger-driven impulse to inflict intentional harm on another person.

The roots of hostile aggression are (a) having mental models that others are untrustworthy—others are not to be trusted and, in fact, are assumed to be hostile; (b) having friends and a peer group who accept, value, and expect aggression as an interpersonal style; and (c) a disciplinary history with adults who relied on coercion and ridicule (punishment) rather than empathy and perspective taking (gentle discipline) (Olweus, 1980). As for what teachers can do to cope with students' hostile aggression, prevention works better than remediation. Students who actively shun hostile aggression are those who (a) have a history of having their psychological needs met (a mental model that others can be trusted); (b) have friends and peers who discourage, rather than encourage, hostile aggression; and (c) develop strong capacities for empathy and perspective taking.

> **What Does This Mean to Me?**
> Recall a recent display of aggression and judge what type it was—instrumental or hostile? How could you tell?

Constructive Response to Aggression. When students break rules, instigate fights, or cruelly tease their classmates, teachers' most common reaction is to provide discipline immediately following the student's misbehavior. There is little wrong with discipline and classroom management strategies—except for one thing. After years of research, educators now realize that this is not the only, or even the best, approach to curbing aggression.

The long-held view that students' misbehavior should be immediately followed by discipline has given way to a focus on the quality of the teacher-student relationship (Kochanska, 2002; Zhou et al., 2002). This change of emphasis reflects the understanding that the student is an agent in his or her own moral socialization, one who actively processes a teacher's moral messages and exercises a sense of autonomy regarding how to behave (Grusec & Goodnow, 1994; Maccoby, 1992). The quality of the teacher-student relationship is important because it affects the student's willingness to embrace the teacher's rules, values, and requests (Kochanska & Thompson, 1997). The quality of the teacher-student relationship not only affects the student's openness to the teacher's socialization efforts but also determines the effectiveness of specific discipline strategies. Just about any discipline strategy will backfire in the context of a negative, adversarial relationship (Patterson, DeBaryshe, & Ramsey, 1989). It seems reasonable to conclude that teachers need to develop both effective discipline strategies and high-quality relationships with their students.

> **Chapter Reference**
> Chapters 7 and 11 discuss various discipline strategies and classroom management techniques.

Social Competence

Social competence is how skilled children and adolescents are at managing the often frustrating and challenging experiences they have with other people. For example, conflicts with peers often generate anger and frustration; social competence reflects the capacity to respond to the conflict in a socially appropriate manner even while feeling angry and frustrated. The two primary benefits of social competence are the capacity to resolve social conflict amicably and popularity with peers (Eisenberg et al., 1993; Eisenberg, Guthrie, et al., 1997; Hubbard & Cole, 1994).

Several factors explain which students lack social competence (Repetti, Taylor, & Seeman, 2002). Students from homes with high levels of conflict and aggression display much aggression and little social skill during conflict (Crockenberg & Lourie, 1996; Pettit, Dodge, & Brown, 1988). Students living in homes with parents who are cold, unsupportive, or neglectful also exhibit much aggression and little social skill (Brody & Flor, 1998; Weiss et al., 1992). What these students lack is the knowledge and capacity to manage their negative emotions so as to generate constructive, prosocial responses during conflict (Caspi et al., 1995; Caspi et al., 1996). The capacity to manage negative emotions constructively is so central to the concept of social competence that some researchers prefer the term *emotion regulation*. **Emotion regulation** is the capacity to modulate—or calm—upsetting internal emotional reactivity during stressful situations (Thompson, 1994).

 Would greater social competence allow Ms. Hernandez's students to make friends and diffuse conflicts?

emotion regulation   The capacity to modulate or calm internal emotional reactivity during stressful situations.

As highlighted in the "Taking It to the Classroom" box below, teachers can promote students' social competence and emotion regulation in three ways. First, they can use gentle discipline, such as explaining and problem solving, rather than harsh disciplinary strategies. Students who are disciplined gently show greater social competence and prosocial behavior than do students who are disciplined harshly (Weiss et al., 1992). Second, teachers can help students lessen their anger and deepen their empathy toward others by providing them with secure, high-quality relationships (Einsenberg & Fabes, 1998). Although it is true that some students are more empathic than others, it is also true that empathy can be learned, as

---

Taking It to the Classroom

Do You Know Jack? Promoting Social Competence

Jack is easily angered, annoyed, or upset. Jack seems to have a chip on his shoulder. A minor joke at his expense unleashes his fury. If a classmate commits an innocent lapse of etiquette, Jack thinks a major incident has occurred. It is almost to the point where you expect Jack will show his temper at some point during the class. What practical and immediate approaches can you take to assist Jack?

- Separate Jack from classmates who encourage his anger and aggression.
- Create opportunities for Jack to develop friendships with peers who are cooperative, prosocial, and socially competent.
- Expose Jack to a model (peers, videotape, sports figure) who displays high social competence and excellent self-control in potentially aggressive situations.
- Provide Jack with a constructive behavioral script when breaches of etiquette affect him personally (e.g., When others are rude, I will ask them to be polite).
- Provide Jack with a constructive behavioral script when his peers tease him (e.g., When others tease me, I will ignore them).
- Teach Jack nonaggressive, alternative, age-appropriate, and all-purpose ways to deal with situations that distress him, such as negotiation, counting to 10, or withdrawing from the situation.
- Make sure that Jack understands the consequences of his aggression (e.g., loss of friendships, loss of privileges, isolation).
- Reinforce students in the class who demonstrate self-control, helping behavior, and social competence. Make sure that Jack observes the reinforcement.
- Communicate with Jack's parents to share information concerning his progress so they can reinforce Jack at home for demonstrating self-control and social competence.

Taking It to the Classroom

Suggestions for Encouraging Empathy

1. Foster empathy:
   - Let students know what impact their actions have on other people's feelings.
   - Teach them to imagine themselves in the other person's place.
   - Help students understand other people's feelings by reminding them of similar experiences in their own lives.

2. Expect empathy, praise it, and explain how to show it:
   - Let students know that you expect them to be considerate—it is important to you.
   - Recognize occasions when students show empathy for others, and offer your praise and admiration.
   - Explain what actions students can take that would be more considerate.

3. Explain the benefits of empathy:
   - Point out the good feelings that come from caring for others, including a good mood.
   - Point out the relationship benefits that come from caring, including trust and friendship.

discussed in the "Taking It to the Classroom" box on this page (Eisenberg, 1992, 2000; Schulman & Mekler, 1986). When teachers help students feel empathic toward their peers, students respond by showing more prosocial and less antisocial behavior (Carlo et al., 1999). Third, a more indirect strategy is to encourage participation in extracurricular activities. The more students participate in such activities, the more naturally occurring opportunities they have to grow their social competence, and this is especially true for adolescents with low social competence (Mahoney, Cairns, & Farmer, 2003).

Social Competence in Special Education. When teachers are asked what social competencies they consider most important, they generally list cooperating with peers, following directions, maintaining self-control, responding constructively to peer pressure, and avoiding such behaviors as aggression and disrupting the class (Hersh & Walker, 1983; Walker et al., 1992). These competencies are emphasized by both elementary teachers (Lane, Givner, & Pierson, 2004a) and secondary school teachers (Lane, Givner, & Pierson, 2004b). Teachers value these social competencies not only for their own sake but also because they believe that they enable students to succeed in school. Special education teachers frequently place a premium on a narrower band of competencies. They rate cooperation with others and social assertiveness as important, but they rate *maintaining self-control* as the essential social competence for students with special needs (Lane et al., 2004b). Taking this lead from special education teachers, elementary school and secondary school teachers can make the social competence of self-control for their students with special needs a priority.

Self-Concept

Self-concepts are students' mental representations (mental models) of themselves. Accordingly, the **self-concept** is the set of beliefs that a student uses to understand his or her sense of self. Self-recognition begins to appear just before the age of two (Lewis, 1987). With language and a growing number of people to interact with, toddlers develop a verbal sense of self, one characterized by words such as *I, me,* and *mine* (Piaget, 1963; Harter, 1990). Throughout elementary school, children's selves are descriptive and concrete, because they define themselves by their physical qualities and their likes and dislikes. By middle school, students' self-concept gains psychological self-awareness, because it features inner qualities, such as enduring personality traits. By high school, adolescents tend to conceptualize their sense of self in an abstract and differentiated way.

self-concept   Set of beliefs the individual uses to mentally represent or understand his or her sense of self.

What Kids Say and Do

Three Students' Answers to "Who Am I?"

Mark: 6-year-old first grader	Julie: 9-year-old fourth grader	Latisha: 16-year-old high school student
My name is Mark. I have brown eyes. I have brown hair. I am 6. I am tall. I am a boy. I am a student. I am a fast runner.	My name is Julie. I am a girl. I am friendly. I am a truthful person. I am always nervous. I am a very good pianist. I am Methodist. I am friendly.	I am a human being. I am a girl. I am ambitious. I am liberal. I am a Libra. I am sometimes shy. I have some problems but can handle them. I am moody.

Who Am I?

One way to tap into students' developing self-concepts is to ask students of different ages to answer the question, Who am I? Each student generates 20 different self-statements, which can be words, phrases, or sentences. The "What Kids Say and Do" box here features a sampling of such self-statements from three students of different ages.

One pattern to observe in the self-statements of these three students is that self-understanding is descriptive and concrete for the early elementary-grade student (e.g., I have brown eyes), develops into a self-understanding characterized by likes and group memberships for the late-elementary-grade student (e.g., I am a Methodist), and develops further into a self-understanding characterized by unique attributes such as ideological beliefs, sense of morality, interpersonal style, achievement strivings, personal motivations, and abstract personality characteristics (Montemayor & Eisen, 1977; Triandis, 1989). Three patterns govern the development of the self-concept over time: greater realism, greater abstraction, and greater differentiation.

Realism. The self-concept represents beliefs about oneself, and the source of these beliefs in early childhood is one's parents. Accordingly, young children's self-concept is typically wildly optimistic, because young children internalize the glowing self-related statements they hear from their parents (e.g., Oh, you're so smart!). During middle childhood, children gain new perspective on the self via feedback from less-biased interaction partners, such as peers (Markus & Nurius, 1986). Children also begin to attend to and interpret task-related feedback (I couldn't solve the problem; maybe I'm not so good in math after all) and social comparisons of their abilities versus those of their peers (Everyone solved the math problem except me). As a consequence, late-elementary-school students are more realistic in their self-constructions. Interestingly, greater accuracy in one's self-understanding brings not only increased realism but also increased negativism (Stipek & MacIver, 1989), as the self comes to realize that it is probably not the fastest, smartest, prettiest, and strongest self on the planet (as parents sometimes would have it believe). During adolescence, students begin in earnest the lifelong tasks of reflecting on and integrating the vast amount of information they receive from diverse sources in order to develop an understanding of their true self (Harter, 1990).

Abstraction. Changes in cognitive development explain why elementary school children focus mostly on the concrete, observable aspects of self (I have brown hair), whereas high school students focus mostly on abstract qualities and unobservable characteristics (I am ambitious; Harter, 1990). High school students rely on their formal operations to consider their abstract qualities, resolutions of personal struggles, and developmental crises (I want to marry, but I also want to have a career).

Differentiation. Differentiation refers to the number of different domains one incorporates into the self-concept. A child's self-concept advances from a global, undifferentiated self in preschool to a self that is a differentiated, complex, and multidimensional self-view by

What Does This Mean to Me?
Generate five answers to the Who am I? question and rate them in terms of realism, abstraction, and differentiation.

TABLE 3.3	
Twelve Domains of the Differentiated Self-concept	
Mathematics	I find many mathematical problems interesting and challenging.
Verbal	I am an avid reader.
General academic	I like most academic subjects.
Problem solving	I can often see better ways of doing routine tasks.
Physical abilities	I enjoy sports and physical activities.
Appearance	I have a good body build.
Same-sex peers	I am popular with other members of the same sex.
Opposite-sex peers	I make friends easily with members of the opposite sex.
Parents	My parents understand me.
Religion	Continuous spiritual/religious growth is important to me.
Honesty	I am a very honest person.
Emotionality	I tend to be high-strung, tense, and restless.

Source: Items from the 136-item Self-Description Questionnaire (SDQ-III) from Marsh, H. W., & O'Neill (1984). Self description questionnaire III: The construct validity of multidimensional self-concept ratings by late adolescents. *Journal of Educational Measurement, 21,* 153–174. Published by Blackwell Publishing.

high school (Harter, 1990; Marsh & Ayotte, 2003; Marsh & O'Neil, 1984; Montemayor & Eisen, 1977). First graders show their first signs of differentiation by noticing distinctions in their competence in domains such as math versus English (Marsh, Smith, & Barnes, 1983). Throughout the elementary school grades, children's self-concepts continue to differentiate into at least three distinct areas—social, academic, and physical (Harter, 1983; Marsh & Shavelson, 1985)—and sometimes into six areas—relationship with parents, relationship with peers, math, reading, physical abilities, and physical appearance (Marsh, 1990; Marsh, Smith, & Barnes, 1983). By high school graduation day, the 12 differentiated domains listed in Table 3.3 are typical, including the self-view in math, verbal, general academics, problem solving, physical abilities, appearance, same-sex peers, opposite-sex peers, parents, religion, honesty, and emotionality.

The global, one-dimensional self-concept is not a very useful educational construct (Marsh & Craven, 1997). Instead, educators emphasize the multidimensional, hierarchical self-concept (Byrne, 1996; Marsh, 1990; Shavelson & Marsh, 1986). This is so because how good students feel about themselves in subject areas such as math, science, and economics bears little or no relationship to how good they feel about themselves in subjects such as English, history, and foreign languages (Marsh, Byrne, & Shavelson, 1988). For example, educators find little, if any, correlation between a student's math self-concept and his or her verbal self-concept (Marsh & Shavelson, 1985; Marsh et al., 1988). Findings such as these show that by adolescence, students no longer endorse a global self-view but instead understand the domain specificity within the self-concept.

Enhancing the Self-Concept

One goal of education is to promote in students a healthy sense of self—that is, a healthy self-concept (Australian Education Council, 1989). Educators seek to boost students' self-concept for two reasons. First, they believe that enhancing the self-concept is a desirable educational goal in its own right. Second, they believe that an enhanced self-concept will spill over and enhance other valued educational goals, such as academic achievement (Craven, Marsh, & Burnett, 2003).

Enhancing the Self-concept: Why? Educators seek to enhance students' self-concept because they generally believe that doing so will enhance students' academic achievement. When researchers tested whether changes in self-concept predicted students' subsequent grades, they found no such causal effect (Byrne, 1984). Researchers do, however, consistently find that the domain-specific areas of self-concept (math, English, etc.) do correlate with students' achievement in that domain. For instance, the more students achieved in mathematics, the more positive became their math self-concept, whereas their verbal self-concept remained unchanged (Marsh, Byrne, & Yeung, 1999; Marsh & Yeung, 1997a). Domain-specific self-concept beliefs (e.g., "I'm good in math") correlate positively not only with academic achievement in that domain (e.g., math grades, scores on standardized tests) but with other positive educational outcomes as well, including taking course work and putting forth high effort in that domain (Byrne, 1996; Marsh & Yeung, 1997b).

Enhancing the Self-Concept: How? Designing educational interventions to bolster students' self-concept has been both a popular and a frustrating enterprise (Hattie, 1992). When teachers have tried to bolster students' global self-concept by administering a steady stream of praise or positive self-talk, these efforts have been unsuccessful (Burnett, 1999, 2003). Instead, change in students' self-concepts closely *follows* actual achievement gains in specific domains. For example, gains in English self-concept occur mostly in the wake of an achievement experience, such as making a good grade or having a poem accepted by a school publication. One popular intervention program designed to capitalize on this achievement-driven process is the Outward Bound program.

Outward Bound programs are designed to build a positive self-view in adolescents and young adults. The program exists in two versions. The Standard Course is a 26-day residential program comprised of physically and mentally demanding outdoor activities for young adults. This program does not have academic goals, but it is mentioned here because the Standard Course is a well-known program whose goal is to provide the person the sort of achievements that bolster the self-concept.

The Bridging course is a 36-day residential experience comprising academic activities for 13- to 16-year-old underachieving boys. This program has academic goals. It seeks to enhance academic aspects of the self-concept, and the course does generally boost adolescents' achievement in reading and math (Marsh & Richards, 1988). As they improve their reading and mathematics skills, adolescents report enhanced academic self-views after the program is over (Marsh & Richards, 1988). Successful intervention programs such as these show (a) the self-concept is a multidimensional, not a global, phenomenon; (b) intensive intervention programs can boost students' domain-specific skills; (c) as students recognize their skill gains, they change their self-concept accordingly; and (d) these self-concept enhancements endure over time.

Social Comparisons. How well one performs relative to one's peers is a potent source of information for the self-concept. The act of comparing one's personal characteristics, performances, and abilities to the characteristics, performance, and abilities of others is called **social comparison** (Ruble, 1983; Ruble & Frey, 1991; Wood, 1989). Without other students around, it can be difficult for a student to know whether he or she is smart, attractive, athletic, emotional, sensitive, or friendly. It is handy to have other students around to compare how smart or attractive one is with how smart or attractive everyone else appears to be. Social comparison provides especially useful information for students for those abilities about which they are unsure: Am I artistic? Am I a good speaker? Am I a fast reader? As mentioned previously in Chapter 2, early elementary school children lack the capacity to seriate and, therefore, do not use social-comparison information to diagnose their abilities and characteristics. Social-comparison information, therefore, is important only from about the third grade on, and it becomes especially important during adolescence.

Social comparison is an intentional strategy. That is, students seek information about themselves for a reason (Swann, 1999). These reasons include wanting to (a) develop an accurate self-view; (b) enhance the self-view; and (c) learn what excellence is.

When students want to develop an accurate self-view, they compare their characteristics, attributes, and abilities to their peers who share other qualities with them, such as age and gender (Zanna, Goethals, & Hill, 1975). When students want to enhance their self-view (e.g., after failure, rejection), they compare themselves to those they suspect will be less smart, less talented, and the like. Such downward social comparisons allow the student to appear in a favorable light. When students want to learn what excellence is, they compare themselves to others who they suspect possess greater ability than they do (e.g., experts, gifted students, students from higher grades; Gibbon, Benbow, & Gerrard, 1994).

social comparison   The act of comparing one's personal characteristics, performance, and abilities to the characteristics, performances, and abilities of others.

Chapter Reference
Chapter 2 provides a discussion of the cognitive operation of seriation.

What Does This Mean to Me?
The last time you failed at something, what downward social comparisons did you make?

Chapter Reference
Chapter 6 discusses self-worth protection motives within the self-concept.

Self-esteem. Self-esteem is the evaluation of oneself as a person. Whereas self-concept is a description of oneself, self-esteem is an evaluation of oneself (Rosenberg, 1979). Earlier in the chapter, self-esteem was defined as the sense of trust gained from the important people in one's life (e.g., Am I lovable?). So self-esteem is partly evaluated on the emotional basis of how others treat the self (acceptance versus rejection). It is also, however, partly evaluated on the basis of one's competence and achievement in different domains. Accordingly, self-esteem exists as the sum of evaluated domains of the self-concept. Self-esteem is, therefore, high in proportion to which students rate themselves positively across multiple domains of functioning: Am I good in math? Am I good in sports and athletics? Am I popular with members of the opposite sex? Do I make friends easily?

Self-esteem in students with learning disabilities. If self-esteem reflects one's evaluation of his or her abilities in various domains, then students with learning disabilities might be at risk of low self-esteem. By definition, students with learning disabilities have difficulty learning. Because competencies in mathematics, reading, spelling, and writing represent the building blocks of learning, this is unfortunate for the construction of a healthy self-esteem in students with learning disabilities. Research confirms that students with learning disabilities score substantially lower on measures of self-esteem than do equally intelligent students who do not have learning disabilities (Chapman & Boersma, 1991).

RIDE

REFLECTION FOR ACTION

The Event

Ms. Hernandez looks at the photograph shown at the beginning of this chapter. She wants to empower her students' social development, and she wants to build a strong sense of community within her classroom. She wants to see her students trusting each other, forming friendships, sharing, helping, and cooperating with one another; and she wants to diffuse conflicts and keep disrespect, put-downs, and acts of aggression out of her classroom.

Reflection RIDE

Where do positive social-developmental outcomes such as trust, moral development, and social competence come from? Where do negative social-developmental outcomes such as mistrust and aggression come from? How can Ms. Hernandez help her students develop socially? What might she do?

What Theoretical/Conceptual Information Might Assist in Interpreting and Remedying this Situation? Consider the following:

High-Quality Relationships

To what extent does positive social development grow out of having access to high-quality relationships? If she provided greater attunement, relatedness, supportiveness, and gentle discipline, would her students develop social competencies?

Ethic of Care

How can she help her students expand their narrow circle of care that includes only themselves and their best friends to a wider circle that includes care for all class members?

Social Competence

Should Ms. Hernandez concentrate her attention on those classroom situations that involve conflict and aggression? What skills do her students need to handle frustrating interactions, and how can she help them develop the skill to resolve their differences amicably?

Information Gathering RIDE

In what ways do Ms. Hernandez's students express their positive social development? In what ways do they express their negative social development? She will need to collect data on:

- How frequently her students' engage in behaviors such as trusting each other, forming friendships, sharing, helping, cooperating, disrespecting, and aggressing
- The quality of her relationship with students
- Her students' existing ethic of care

To collect these data, she might ask her students to complete a questionnaire. Perhaps a teacher's aid, parent volunteer, or colleague can make observational ratings for her. A conversation with colleagues and master teachers might also shed light on these issues. She might ask her colleagues for suggestions on how to create a caring classroom community. She might also read articles and books about specific topics, such as on empathy development or aggression. Several videotapes on social development exist, and these videotapes frequently address the question of how to help students develop socially.

Decision Making RIDE

Ms. Hernandez needs to decide whether her students simply lack social developmental resources, such as trust and care for others, or whether the problem is deeper in that they not only lack these resources but also possess liabilities, such as tendencies toward aggression and little capacity to regulate negative emotions like anger. She needs to decide whether she has a high-quality relationship with her students and how possible it will be to improve on that relationship. She needs to decide how wide or how narrow her students extend their circle of care—to include only best friends or to include all classmates? She will also need to decide whether she has the time, skill, and access to the resources she will need to teach her students social skills in the same way she teaches her other lessons—with high expectations, modeling, explaining, and practice.

Evaluation RIDE

Ms. Hernandez will need to evaluate the quality of the relationships she provides to her students, the extent of her students' circle of care, and the extent of her students' positive and negative social developmental outcomes. She will need to evaluate how important her relationship to students is—does she notice any increase in their sociability and any decrease in their aggressiveness when she provides attunement, relatedness, supportiveness, and gentle discipline? She will need to evaluate whether her students relate positively to classmates inside their circle of care but negatively to those outside their circle of care. She needs to evaluate whether the improved social competencies she sees in her students reflects committed compliance or only situational compliance.

Further Practice: Your Turn

Here is a second event for consideration and reflection. In doing so, implement the process of reflection, information gathering, decision making, and evaluation.

The Event

Mr. Happyheart is a tenth-grade teacher. For the most part, today has been a good day. His students are learning, and most are actively engaged in the lesson. The classroom calm suddenly comes to a screeching halt as a fight breaks out between two boys. One wrote an insulting remark on the other's desk, and the second boy—after reading it—jumped out of his seat and onto the other boy. Insults and fists start flying.

RIDE   What might this teacher do? Could these events have been prevented? Now that these behaviors have occurred, how might the teacher best cope with the aggression? What would you recommend?

SUMMARY

- **What characterizes a high-quality student-teacher relationship?**

  Relationships are the soil in which social development grows. Therefore, the higher the quality of the relationship between student and teacher, the more positive the student's social development is likely to be. Four qualities define a high-quality relationship: attunement, relatedness, supportiveness, and gentle discipline.

- **What are mental models, and why are they important to social development?**

  Mental models are students' enduring beliefs and expectations about what they are like (Am I a good person?) and what other people are like (Can others be trusted?). These beliefs reflect how other people have treated the student in the past, as represented by the three attachment styles of secure, resistant, and avoidant. Secure attachment reflects high trust in self and others and is associated with positive social-developmental outcomes, such as academic success, popularity, emotion regulation, and prosocial behavior. Resistant and avoidant attachments reflect mistrust in others and are associated with poor social-developmental outcomes.

- **How can teachers nurture psychosocial development, especially students' initiative, competence, and identity?**

  According to Erikson's model, children develop initiative, competence, and identity when teachers find ways to encourage and support these developmental resources. Initiative is the use of surplus energy to plan and constructively carry out a task, and preschool teachers can nurture initiative while at the same time communicating limits. Competence is the self-assurance that one can successfully accomplish culturally valued tasks, and elementary school teachers can nurture competence by offering developmentally appropriate challenges, positive feedback, and discussions about the pleasure of a job well done. Identity is the sense of being a distinct and productive individual within the larger social framework. Middle school and high school teachers can nurture identity by helping students become aware of and explore possible societal roles, such as those related to occupation.

- **What are the stages of moral development?**

  Moral development concerns judgments about what is right or wrong as well as why one action is right and another is wrong. At a preconventional level, children's moral reasoning is immature, and what is right reflects their self-interest. At the conventional level, children's moral reasoning follows social conventions—what is right is what others approve of. At the postconventional level, adolescents' moral reasoning reflects self-chosen principles. Moral development also reflects one's ethic of care. Preconventional children care for the self; conventional children and adolescents extend care to include their in-group of similar others; and postconventional adolescents extend their ethic of care to include all people.

- **How do social competence and aggression develop?**

  Social competence reflects how skilled children and adolescents are at managing the negative emotions they experience during social conflicts so as to produce amicable outcomes. Teachers can promote social competence by using gentle discipline strategies, such as reasoning, and by emphasizing interpersonal skills, such as empathy. Aggression is any intentional behavior that is designed to harm another person or group physically or psychologically. There are two types: instrumental and hostile. With instrumental aggression, which is strategic behavior to obtain a desired object, teachers can help students learn more effective and prosocial ways of getting what they want. With hostile aggression, which is impulsive behavior intended to inflict harm, prevention works better than remediation.

● **How does self-concept develop throughout the school-age years?**

The self-concept is the set of beliefs that students use to understand their sense of self. The self-concept develops throughout the school-age years in a predictable fashion by becoming more realistic, more abstract, and more differentiated. It further develops in response to achievement gains in specific domains and to social comparisons of one's qualities compared to those of one's peers. Whereas self-concept is a description of oneself, self-esteem is an evaluation of oneself.

● **How do students' special needs interfere with their social development?**

All students benefit when their teachers provide them with high-quality relationships characterized by attunement, relatedness, supportiveness, and gentle discipline. Students with special needs, such as autism or an emotional disorder, often have difficulty contributing their part to a relationship. For this reason, interaction partners sometimes feel less close to students with special needs; therefore, they are less likely to develop high-quality relationships with their teachers and peers. Students with special needs also typically report lower self-esteem than students without special needs.

KEY TERMS

aggression, p. 89
attachment, p. 74
attunement, p. 72
care, p. 74
committed compliance,
    p. 88
competence, p. 79
conscience, p. 89
emotion regulation, p. 92
generativity, p. 84
gentle discipline, p. 73

hostile aggression, p. 91
identity, p. 81
initiative, p. 78
instrumental aggression,
    p. 90
mental models, p. 71
moral development, p. 84
power assertion, p. 88
psychosocial development,
    p. 77
relatedness, p. 72

relationship, p. 72
self-concept, p. 93
self-esteem, p. 75
situational compliance, p. 88
social comparison, p. 96
social competence, p. 92
supportiveness, p. 73
trust, p. 75

EXERCISES

1. *Understanding the Elements of a High-quality Relationship*

   Identify a teacher who has an excellent interaction style with students. Ask permission to visit this teacher's class and observe the ensuing student-teacher interactions during instruction. Rate this teacher in terms of attunement, relatedness, supportiveness, and gentle discipline. Do these four factors explain why this teacher has such a positive and constructive relationship with students? Repeat this same exercise with a teacher who has a poor interaction style with students. Does the absence of these four factors explain why this second teacher does not have a positive and constructive relationship with students?

2. *Providing a High-quality Relationship of Your Own*

   Recall a recent interaction you had with someone in which you were in the role of a teacher, such as trying to show a friend how to do something. Recall how that interaction went and how much or how little your friend benefited from your teaching. Think about what role your provision of attunement, relatedness, supportiveness, and gentle discipline played in helping your friend learn. The next time you have another teaching chance, intentionally try to provide high attunement, relatedness, supportiveness, and gentle discipline and notice what changes, if any, occur in the learner.

3. *Assessing Attunement*

   How attuned are you to a student? Find a questionnaire (or construct a brief one of your own) that assesses the student's self-perceptions during a learning activity (e.g., It was fun, I was nervous, I felt competent). After the learning activity is over, ask the other person to complete the questionnaire. Also, independently complete the same questionnaire yourself and try to answer each question the way you think the other person answered it. Place the two completed questionnaires side by side, then compare how much the answers overlapped (high attunement) or diverged (low attunement).

4. *Conducting an Eriksonian Life Review*

Interview a student or a teacher by conducting an Eriksonian life review. A life review is a process in which the person looks back on the developmental influences and milestones that have shaped his or her life. Ask the following questions related to that person's trust, initiative, competence, and identity:

- Who were the most important people who contributed to or interfered with your development?
- In general, would you say that you trust or mistrust other people?
- What memories come to mind when you think about trusting or mistrusting others?
- Recall doing new things, such as starting school or traveling by yourself. As you recall these events, did you show mostly initiative or mostly inhibition? Why?
- Recall a vivid experience in which you received negative feedback, such as an academic failure. How did you react in terms of effort and perseverance? Did you work harder, or did you give up and do something else?
- Who are you? List any five words or phrases that describe who you are in terms of occupation and beliefs.
- Last, looking back, how satisfied versus dissatisfied are you with your life? Have other people mostly supported your development, or have they mostly frustrated and thwarted it?

5. *Who Am I?*

On a single piece of paper, make a list from 1 through 20 down the left-hand side of the page. At the top of the page, write the question, Who am I? Take about 10 minutes to generate 20 different answers to this single question. Use single words, phrases, or complete sentences. After you are done, rate your responses in terms of realism, abstraction, and differentiation.

Flavio Quinto moved on to the final item on the agenda for the faculty meeting: ability grouping. "This year will be the last for ability grouping between classes for math and reading in our elementary schools, at least the way we've traditionally done it. The practice we have of combining all of the classes at the same grade level and reassigning students into separate classes for high, medium, and low achievers for math and reading can't continue. The

(Elizabeth Crews/The Image Works)

superintendent has decided—and the principals' committee agrees—that the benefits no longer outweigh the disadvantages."

Over the past few years, there had been controversy over the district's practice of grouping children for mathematics and reading instruction by ability, determined by scores on a standardized test. Some parents complained that poor children made up the majority of students in the low-ability groups. Others argued that higher achieving students are slowed down when they are placed in the same classes with lower achieving students. These were just a few of the arguments.

The teachers were concerned about this change in policy. Theirs was a very traditional school district. The school had practiced ability grouping for decades. The reading curriculum even used three different programs and sets of books for high-, middle-, and low-achieving students.

After a pause, one of the teachers asked, "And what do the principals suggest that we do instead?" Mr. Quinto replied, "We haven't worked on that yet. We'll need your input."

Individual Differences Among Learners

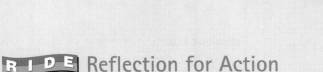

RIDE Reflection for Action

What should the teachers suggest? How will they organize instruction in their classes? What will happen to high achievers if they do not receive the special instruction that enables them to move quickly through the curriculum? Will the low achievers do better without ability grouping? What would you suggest the teachers do? Can you explain why?

Guiding Questions

- How was intelligence understood initially, and how have views of intelligence changed over time?
- How is intelligence measured, and how is it related to achievement?
- How does talent develop?
- What happens when students are grouped by ability?
- In general, how do schools identify children with special needs?
- How are learning disabilities and attention deficit hyeractivity disorder identified?
- How do differences in socioeconomic status and culture affect students' success in school?

CHAPTER OVERVIEW

This chapter is concerned with individual differences among students. The first part of the chapter focuses on intelligence or ability. It describes how the concept of intelligence evolved and introduces a number of theories of intelligence. The next part of the chapter discusses extremes of intelligence and how talent is developed. Some instructional strategies for managing variation in students' ability are then described. The second part of the chapter focuses on prevalent learning needs, including learning disabilities, attention deficit hyperactivity disorder, and limited English proficiency. The chapter concludes with a focus on socioeconomic differences by showing how factors such as poverty affect children's success in school.

Variability in the Classroom

Intelligence
- The History of Intelligence
- Controversies in Intelligence
- Current Thinking on Issues of Intelligence
- How Is Intelligence Measured?

Extremes of Intelligence
- Giftedness
- Mental Retardation

Talent
- Deliberate Practice and the Monotonic-Benefits Assumption
- Effort Becomes Talent
- Early Talent and Developed Talent

Differences in Ability and Instruction
- Between-Class Ability Grouping
- Within-Class Ability Grouping

Learners with Special Needs
- The Law and Special Education
- Identifying Children with Special Needs
- Inclusion

Prevalent Learning Needs
- Learning Disabilities
- Attention Deficit Disorder
- Attention Deficit Hyperactivity Disorders
- Autism and Related Disorders
- Students with Limited English Proficiency

Differences in Socioeconomic Status and Their Role in Learning

Variability in the Classroom

Students are different. Some are good athletes; others are popular. Some have a good idea of their strengths and weaknesses; others do not have a clue. What are your strengths and weaknesses? How do they compare to those of your best friend or your brother or sister? How do you know what your strengths and weaknesses are? How do you think they developed? Were you born with them, or did they develop as you grew? Did you work hard to build up your strong areas, or did you just focus on what you seemed to be good at, or both?

As a teacher, how would you work with a diverse group of students? What is your responsibility in terms of understanding their strengths and weaknesses and making what you teach relevant to their lives?

One of the great things about being a teacher is that no two days are the same, and no two children are the same. The challenge is to acknowledge and celebrate the differences among children, working to maximize the growth in each child. At the same time, the teacher has to adhere to the mandates of the curriculum. There is a natural tension between the aspirations and abilities of students—their dreams and goals—on one hand and the requirements of teaching algebra, or French, or fourth grade, on the other. In his classic work, *The Child and the Curriculum*, John Dewey argues that "the child and the curriculum are simply two limits which define a single process. Just as two points define a straight line, so the present standpoint of the child and the facts and truths of studies define instruction" (Dewey, 1971, p. 11).

Students in today's class-rooms vary in their abilities, motivation, and backgrounds.
(Punchstock)

As Dewey points out, at one end of this continuum are subject areas, which are varied and complex. At the other end are children, who are also varied and complex. Children differ in temperament, enthusiasm, prior knowledge in different subjects, distractibility, self-concept, verbal ability, spatial reasoning, motivation, and on and on. And of course, there is not just one child; there is a whole classroom full of children or adolescents. But as a teacher you should look at this situation not as hopelessly complex but as wonderfully rich. On one hand, you have students who bring a variety of strengths, ambitions, and backgrounds to the task of learning. On the other hand, you have a world of ideas, possibilities, knowledge, and skills to bring to your students. Your task as a teacher is to determine how to work with a roomful of highly diverse students to help them acquire the knowledge, skills, and abilities that you wish them to obtain.

Intelligence

Intelligence is an idea that has been around for thousands of years. Plato identified *reason* as one of the three components of the soul (along with *will* and *appetite*). Aristotle linked intelligence to physiological processes. Charles Darwin wrote extensively about intelligence and greatly influenced his cousin, Francis Galton, a leading early theorist in the field.

Intelligence is a theoretical concept that makes it easier to understand the (psychological) world. Like many such concepts, it has undergone challenges, rejections, and revisions over the course of the past century. Intelligence is the primary characteristic that people have used to measure individual differences, but it is important to keep in mind that there are also emotional and behavioral differences among children in classrooms. Because intelligence is a controversial concept, it is important to understand how it originated and how it has changed over time.

The History of Intelligence

It would be possible to trace the idea of intelligence through antiquity, but a more reasonable starting place might be Europe at the end of the nineteenth century and the beginning of the twentieth. In the late 1870s, the German philosopher and psychologist Wilhelm Wundt founded the first psychological laboratory, emphasizing **physiological psychology** (the study of the relationships among the brain, the nervous system, and behavior, sometimes called *psychophysics*) and making psychology more distinct from philosophy. He is

physiological psychology The study of the relationship between the brain, the nervous system, and behavior.

often referred to as the father of modern psychology. Along with Fechner, Wundt emphasized the importance of the senses and the transmission of information along the nervous system. To study these phenomena, he developed measures of reactions to various stimuli. Although interest in psychophysics would fade in the early twentieth century, Wundt's emphasis on measurement would influence the French psychologist Alfred Binet.

Alfred Binet and Francis Galton   Probably the most important scholars in the early development of the concept of intelligence were Binet and the English psychologist Francis Galton. A younger cousin of Darwin, Galton studied medicine, meteorology, biology, and statistics, among other fields. In addition to his work on intelligence, Galton invented weather maps, the use of fingerprints to identify individuals, and the ideas underlying correlation and regression analysis in statistics (McClearn, 1991). In the field of psychology, he was a pioneer in the area of individual differences. He was obsessed with the measurement of human characteristics and differences among them. He was the first psychologist to use the normal distribution of Gauss as a model for the distribution of human characteristics, and he developed the use of percentiles for reporting scores. His classic work *Hereditary Genius* (Galton, 1869) set forth his theory about the influence of genetics on mental abilities.

Galton's major contribution to psychology may be his focus on individual differences. Why does one person perceive tones more accurately than others; why do some people respond to a stimulus more quickly than others? His interest in mental abilities and genetic influences on them led him to form the Eugenics Society, which argued for selective mating to improve the human race. The ideas associated with the **eugenics** movement are strongly disavowed today.

Alfred Binet came to the study of the mental abilities from a very different perspective. He started out to be a lawyer but shifted to science and ultimately to the study of psychology. In the early 1900s, he was asked to develop a set of measures, or *scales,* that could be used for the placement of low-achieving Parisian students into special schools for children with cognitive disabilities. Along with his assistant, Theodore Simon, he published his first set of scales in 1905. The tasks included in these scales focused on issues that Binet considered to be common sense or practical judgment. He tried them out on a sample of average students to determine which of them could be done by students at various ages. Examples of these tasks include touching various parts of the body on request, determining which of two lines is longer, repeating groups of numbers read by the examiner, and defining everyday words (Nunally, 1967). At higher levels, students were asked to repeat up to seven numbers backward and to find rhymes for multisyllabic words (Fancher, 1985).

If students could answer questions that a typical child could answer at a given age, Binet classified them at that mental level. Thus, if a 12-year-old child could answer the questions for 9-year-olds but not those for 10-year-olds, the child would be classified at the mental level of a 9-year-old. Binet's scales focused on the end product of intelligence rather than on its underlying nature (Nunally, 1967). Binet warned that although his scales seemed appropriate for the students he was working with—that is, students in Paris—he was cautious about the possibility of extending his work beyond that population.

Binet's scales became the basis for all subsequent work in intelligence testing. Psychologists Henry Goddard and Lewis Terman independently brought his work to the United States in the early 1900s. Terman, who taught at Stanford University, developed Binet's scales into what came to be known as the Stanford-Binet intelligence test; Goddard was influential in testing immigrants at Ellis Island and in the development of the Army Alpha and Beta tests, which were used to assess the mental abilities of recruits during World War I. The fifth edition of the Stanford-Binet test was published in 2003.

Intelligence and IQ   What exactly *is* intelligence? This question has been debated since the idea first arose and is still actively debated today. In fact, it is a *hot topic* in both psychology and education. Binet felt that intelligence is "judgment, otherwise called good sense, practical sense, initiative, the faculty of adapting one's self to circumstances" (Binet & Simon, 1916). Goddard's definition was, "that the chief determiner of human conduct is a unitary mental process which we call intelligence" (Goddard, 1920, p. 1). Working with Terman, William Stern suggested that the age level of the tasks a child can perform (**mental age**) could be divided by the child's chronological age to form a ratio of mental age to

---

Chapter Reference
See Chapter 14 for a discussion of the normal distribution and percentiles.

eugenics   A political and scientific movement that argued for selective reproduction of individuals and immigration laws based on intelligence levels.

mental age   The age level associated with the ability to perform certain mental tasks. A mental age of 7 means that a person can perform the tasks of a typical 7-year-old but not those of a typical 8-year-old.

chronological age. When multiplied by 100, this ratio became the child's **intelligence quotient,** or **IQ:**

$$IQ = \frac{\text{mental age}}{\text{chronological age}} \times 100$$

In the early years of IQ measurement, IQ was thought to be a single, overarching ability that could be measured precisely; it was assumed that a two- or three-digit number, the IQ, could be used to represent the measurement. Terman focused on individuals with very high levels of intelligence, whereas Goddard focused on people with lower levels of intelligence. Some psychologists, including Goddard (1920), believed that intelligence is an **innate ability,** or present at birth.

The Development of the Idea of Intelligence At the same time that efforts were being made to measure intelligence, new statistical techniques were being developed. A British psychologist, Charles Spearman, administered a large number of measures of various aspects of mental ability and subjected them to a statistical technique called *factor analysis*. The results of the analysis suggested that intelligence could be viewed as consisting of one broad, or general, factor, which Spearman labeled *g* (for general), plus a variety of individual, or specific, factors (Spearman, 1923, 1927). Psychologists still use *g* as a kind of shorthand for general intelligence.

As factor-analytic techniques progressed, L. L. Thurstone proposed a dramatically different approach (1957) to defining intelligence. Based on an extensive study of schoolchildren in Chicago, Thurstone proposed a model of intelligence consisting of seven **primary mental abilities:**

- Verbal comprehension (ability to understand verbal analogies and comprehend reading passages)
- Word fluency (ability to manipulate words, vocabulary)
- Number facility (speed and accuracy of computation)
- Spatial visualization (ability to do things such as mental rotation of objects)
- Associate memory (ability to remember words or objects presented in pairs)
- Perceptual speed (such as ability to find the number of times a specific letter appears on a printed page)
- Reasoning (ability to solve arithmetic or logical reasoning problems)

This view of intelligence or *primary abilities* is much broader than previous ones. Thus, a child may be strong in word fluency (have a large vocabulary) but not be good at visualizing or in perceptual speed. Thurstone's approach to mental abilities painted a richer picture of the individual, an idea that would appear again later in the development of thinking about intelligence.

Raymond Cattell made a highly useful contribution by proposing the terms *fluid* and *crystallized intelligence* (Cattell, 1963). **Fluid intelligence** refers to the ability to solve problems, figure out what to do when you are not sure what to do, and acquire new skills. **Crystallized intelligence** involves the use of acquired skills and knowledge, such as reading and language skills. Fluid intelligence tends to develop until early adulthood, then declines. Crystallized intelligence, on the other hand, tends to grow throughout adulthood. Note that this does not mean that older adults do not have any fluid intelligence; it just means that they do not have as much as they did when they were younger.

From the early 1900s through the 1960s and 1970s, ideas about intelligence became more elaborate and refined. Still, the notion of intelligence as a single concept that could be represented by an IQ score remained popular, both in the general public and in some circles within the field of psychology.

Controversies in Intelligence

It would be hard to imagine an area of psychology that is more controversial than intelligence. The problem has to do with what is called the **nature/nurture** debate: Is intelligence developed by the individual's experiences within his or her environment, or is it basically genetic in nature and inherited? Early psychologists, such as Galton, Goddard, and Yale psychologist Robert Yerkes, were associated with the eugenics movement. They argued that intelligence is primarily genetic and that governments, therefore, should encourage the reproduction of individuals with higher levels of intelligence and discourage that of individuals with lower levels of intelligence. They also argued for selective immigration laws. In more recent years, arguments have been made concerning racial differences in intelligence and the impact of genetic factors on those differences.

These issues were brought to a head in 1994 with the publication of a highly controversial book, *The Bell Curve,* by Richard Herrnstein and Charles Murray. The authors argued that intelligence, thought of as a single mental ability, is real; that differences among ethnic and racial groups exist; and that intelligence predicts a large number of life outcomes. Perhaps the most eloquent argument against this perspective was presented by anthropologist Stephan Jay Gould in *The Mismeasure of Man* (1981). Gould argued against the notion of intelligence being a single trait as well as against a genetic basis for mental abilities.

Current Thinking on Issues of Intelligence

Building on the earlier work, two new and highly influential theories of intelligence have been proposed in recent years: Robert Sternberg's triarchic theory of intelligence and Howard Gardner's theory of multiple intelligences. The concept of **metacognition,** attributable primarily to John Flavell, has also strongly influenced research and scholarship on mental abilities. These theories and related research have influenced not only how psychologists think about intelligence but also educational practice.

metacognition   Thinking about one's own thinking.

Sternberg's Triarchic Theory of Intelligence

One of the most popular approaches to thinking about intelligence from a practical perspective is Sternberg's **triarchic** theory (Sternberg, 1985, 2000) and his more recent extension of it, which he calls *successful intelligence* (Sternberg, 1997, Sternberg & Grigorenko, 2000). The triarchic theory holds that intelligence has three main facets: *analytical, creative,* and *practical.* The analytical facet is the ability to respond effectively to problems. It has three components: metacomponents, performance components, and knowledge acquisition components. *Metacomponents* have to do with the ability to organize, execute, and evaluate one's cognitive resources in responding to a problem. This is very similar to the idea of metacognition, explained later in this section. *Performance components* are the specific abilities necessary to solve certain kinds of problems: abilities such as those involved in solving an algebra problem or making comparisons between objects. *Knowledge acquisition components* are the abilities involved in new learning—what you would do to memorize new information or perfect a new skill.

triarchic   Comprised of three components, each of which is the top of a hierarchy.

The creative facet of the theory involves generating new ideas, coming up with new approaches, taking a different look at a problem, or combining information in a novel way. This part of the theory has two components: novelty or insight, and **automaticity.** Automaticity is the ability to perform a task without having to think much about it. Ice skating is a good example. When one first learns how to skate, it takes a great deal of cognitive effort just to remain upright. After some practice, however, maintaining balance becomes more automatic, and one can focus on other aspects of skating.

automaticity   The ability to perform a task without having to think much about it.

The practical facet of the theory involves the ability to handle everyday problems and issues. People who are able to adapt to changing aspects of their environment are strong in the practical aspect of intelligence. They are also able to change their environment to meet their needs or to realize that the environment they are in is not the best one for them and to seek out a new environment. The practical facet of the theory might be thought of as "street smarts."

To summarize the triarchic theory, it involves the ability to (a) solve problems, (b) generate new ideas, and (c) put one's ideas and solutions to purposeful use in the environment. A model of the theory is presented in Figure 4.1.

What Does This Mean to Me?
Which of Sternberg's facets is your strongest one? How can you use it to your advantage as a teacher?

Sternberg's Idea of Successful Intelligence

Based on his triarchic theory, Sternberg developed what he calls a theory of successful intelligence. In his words, "Successful intelligence is the ability to succeed in life, given one's own goals, within one's environmental

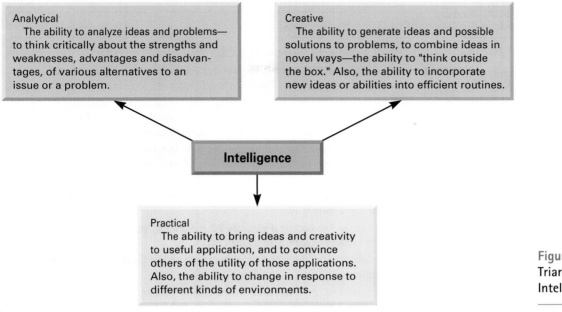

Figure 4.1. Sternberg's
Triarchic Theory of
Intelligence

contexts. Thus successful intelligence is a basis for school achievement, but also life achievement" (Sternberg, 1997 p. 12).

This view of intelligence suggests that educational activities might mean different things for different students and that individuals bring different cognitive strengths and weaknesses to their learning efforts. Teaching designed to promote successful intelligence, according to Sternberg, has four key elements:

1. Teaching for memory learning: the acquisition of information—the who, what, where, when, and how of learning.

2. Teaching for analytical learning: the ability to understand the reasons underlying issues and explain, evaluate, or judge them.

3. Teaching for creative learning: the inventive and creative aspect of learning—letting students explore new ideas of their own imagining.

4. Teaching for practical learning: the practical application of knowledge and skills—making things work in the real world.

Sternberg argues that it is not always necessary to emphasize all four of these elements but that attention to all of them on a regular, ongoing basis will help students enhance their strengths and overcome their weaknesses as they learn about themselves.

Gardner's Theory of Multiple Intelligences Easily the most popular view of intelligence is Howard Gardner's **multiple-intelligences (MI) theory.** Based in part on his observations of schoolchildren and individuals with brain damage, Gardner reasoned that abilities are more separate and isolated than other theories portray them. First presented in 1983 in a now-famous work, *Frames of Mind*, Gardner's theory holds that any concept of intelligence as consisting of a single or small number of overarching abilities is too limiting. As an alternative, Gardner proposes that there are at least eight identifiable forms of intelligence, and possibly more (Gardner, 1993, 1995, 1998, 1999, 2003). Table 4.1 lists and describes these eight forms of intelligence.

Teachers have responded positively to Gardner's theory. It may fit well with their experiences of the different ways in which children learn. It also provides a framework for organizing curricula and assessment and focuses teachers on what children *can* do rather than on what they cannot. Gardner uses a number of criteria to decide whether an ability can be considered intelligence. The main criterion is the ability's contribution to solving genuine problems or difficulties. He has considered additional intelligences, such as **existential intelligence**—concern with larger questions of human existence, such as the meaning of life—but has chosen not to include them in his list of intelligences (Gardner, 1999).

multiple-intelligences (MI) theory
A theory of intelligence that argues that individuals may exhibit multiple intelligences (possibly eight or more).

existential intelligence   Concern with larger questions of human existence, such as the meaning of life.

Appendix
How Students Learn
Various theories of intelligence describe facets of students' learning. You may wish to encourage these varied facets in your classroom (*PRAXIS*™, I. A. 1., *INTASC*, Principle 2).

TABLE 4.1

Gardner's Theory of Multiple Intelligences

According to Howard Gardner, an individual may exhibit the following types of intelligence.

Logical–Mathematical: The ability to understand and use numerical patterns, carry out mathematical operations, and engage in the reasoning associated with logic. This is similar to quantitative ability in many theories of intelligence.

Linguistic: The ability to acquire and use the functions of language to express oneself and to comprehend others. This is similar to verbal ability in traditional theories of intelligence.

Spatial: The ability to recognize and manipulate patterns, spaces, and objects—for example, the ability to rotate objects mentally. This ability is found in some other theories of intelligence, notably, Thurstone's primary mental abilities.

Musical: The ability to recognize and use the components of music (tones, pitches, rhythms, musical phrasing, etc.) in composing or performing music.

Bodily–Kinesthetic: The ability to use the body in a coordinated and productive fashion, such as in athletics, dance, arts and crafts production, dentistry, surgery, etc.

Interpersonal: The ability to interact with others in a positive and productive fashion, to recognize others' feelings, motivations, and intentions.

Intrapersonal: The ability to understand one's own motivations and abilities and use that information to guide one's own life in a productive fashion.

Naturalistic: The most recent addition to the list of intelligences. It involves the ability to understand the natural world, recognizing plant and animal species and the workings of the environment.

How Can I Use This?

What classroom tasks could stimulate the use of Gardner's eight intelligences?

Gardner's theory has been adopted by a number of schools and educators, but it is not without its critics (Smith, 2002). The most consistent criticisms focus on the criteria he uses to identify intelligences, his conceptualization of intelligence, and the absence of empirical support for his conceptualization (Smith, 2002).

Many educators have been very receptive to the ideas behind the theory of multiple intelligences. Some efforts to apply the theory involve either setting up a learning center for each of the intelligences or trying to include all or most of them in lesson plans. Others attempt to identify a child's strengths and emphasize them. Even though Gardner's original work is over 20 years old, its educational implications are still being explored and debated. Perhaps the strongest contribution of MI theory is that it has caused educators to take a different perspective on abilities. If interpersonal skills can be thought of as *intelligence,* rather than just as interpersonal skills, it is important to consider them as part of the educational process. Although other psychologists have considered intelligence to be multifaceted, Gardner's work is revolutionary in its inclusion of athletic and musical ability, and even the ability to understand oneself. It can be argued that these abilities are not really intelligence; it cannot be argued that they are unimportant, and Gardner's work offers a way to evaluate their importance.

entity view of intelligence The belief that intelligence is genetically determined and not alterable.

incremental view of intelligence The belief that intelligence can be improved through effort.

Views of Intelligence People have many different views of the nature of intelligence. Some individuals think that their abilities are determined at birth and cannot be altered in any major way. Carol Dweck describes this as an **entity view of intelligence** (Dweck, 1986, 1999). Others believe that basic abilities can be improved through hard work. This is known as the **incremental view of intelligence.** The idea that ability is fixed seems to change over time; as they grow older, children tend to take a more incremental view (Dweck, 2002). From a teacher's perspective, what is important about these different points of view is that the incremental perspective should be nurtured. If students believe that they can improve their abilities through hard work, they are much more likely to put forth the effort necessary for success in school. If, on the other hand, they feel that their successes and failures are determined by fixed abilities over which they have no control, they are much less likely to strive to succeed.

How Is Intelligence Measured?

What Does This Mean to Me?

Do you have an entity or an incremental view of your own intelligence? What does this mean for how hard you work at tasks?

As discussed earlier, there are many different ways of viewing intelligence. It follows that the types of measures used to assess intelligence differ as well. Another factor in the design of intelligence tests has to do with whether they are intended to be administered to individuals by trained psychologists or educators, or administered to groups. To assess children who may have special needs, individually administered tests are typically used.

Standardized IQ Tests   Two of the most popular individually administered tests are the Wechsler Intelligence Scale for Children, fourth edition (referred to as the WISC IV (2003)) and the Kaufman Assessment Battery for Children, or K-ABC II (2005). The WISC-IV is made up of 13 subtests, of which 6 are combined into a verbal IQ scale and 7 into a performance IQ scale. The subtests on the scales are:

Verbal	Performance
Information	Picture Completion
Similarities	Coding
Arithmetic	Picture Arrangement
Vocabulary	Block Design
Comprehension	Object Assembly
Digit Span	Symbol Search
	Mazes

The K-ABC II is made up of two main scales, a sequential processing scale and a simultaneous processing scale. The sequential processing scale involves working with concepts or objects in order, whereas the simultaneous processing scale involves processing in which order is not a factor.

The subtests on each of these scales are:

Sequential Processing Scale	Simultaneous Processing Scale
Hand Movements	Magic Window
Number Recall	Face Recognition
Word Order	Gestalt Closure
	Triangles
	Matrix Analogies
	Spatial Memory
	Photo Series

The questions (called *items* by measurement specialists) on IQ tests take a wide variety of forms. On most scales, these items rely not so much on the individual's level of knowledge as on his or her ability to do something with the information or situation that is presented. Figure 4.2 provides examples of the types of items that are used in IQ tests.

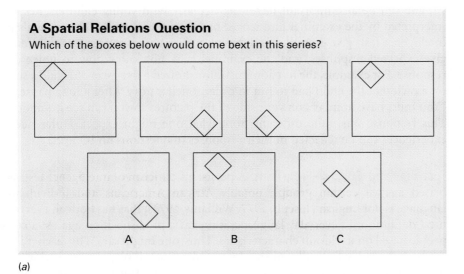

(a)

(continued on page 112)

Figure 4.2. Examples of IQ Test Questions

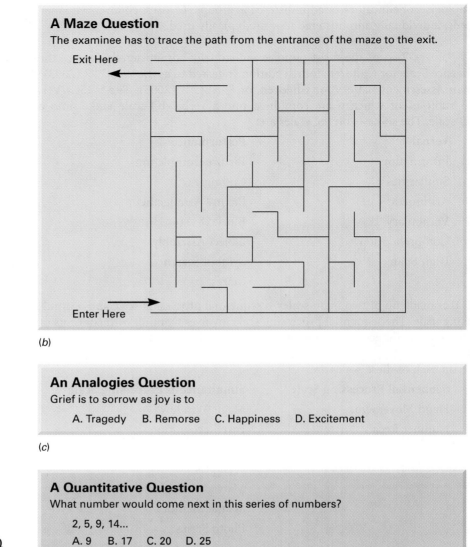

A Maze Question
The examinee has to trace the path from the entrance of the maze to the exit.

Exit Here

Enter Here

(b)

An Analogies Question
Grief is to sorrow as joy is to

    A. Tragedy   B. Remorse   C. Happiness   D. Excitement

(c)

A Quantitative Question
What number would come next in this series of numbers?

    2, 5, 9, 14...
    A. 9   B. 17   C. 20   D. 25

Figure 4.2. Examples of IQ Test Questions *(continued)*

(d)

The effective administration of an individual IQ test requires a good rapport between the examiner and the examinee. The examinee must be willing to show what he or she knows. Fatigue can be an important factor, particularly with young children. Responses must be interpreted by the examiner and scored based on their quality. The manuals provided with intelligence tests give examples of different qualities of responses, but children do not always give expected responses, and the examiner may not know how to judge a very unusual response. For example, the test administrator showed a five-year-old child a series of pictures on a rack that the child had to put in order to tell a story. After a long pause, the child said, "You must have numbers on your side of the pictures so you can see if I'm doing this right." This response was quite different from what one might expect. Differences in children's experiences can be reflected in their responses to questions on IQ tests.

Test Bias and Culture-Free Tests A persistent criticism of intelligence tests is that they are biased against certain groups, notably African Americans and individuals whose first language is not English (Joseph, 1977; Williams, 1974). Bias has both an everyday and a technical definition. In everyday language, it means a predisposition against a certain group of people based on irrelevant characteristics. Thus, one might say, "The teacher is biased against me because I play football and she doesn't like football players." In intelligence testing and other forms of standardized testing, **bias** refers to situations in which the same score would have different meanings for individuals from different groups. For example, if Harold and

bias Systematic unfair treatment of a particular group of individuals.

Maria both get 1140 on their SATs, one should be able to predict that they will do equally well in college. Put another way, if women who score 1140 do better overall in college than men who score 1140, we would conclude that the SATs are biased against men.

Research on most intelligence and other standardized tests has not found this type of evidence for various groups of individuals (Hartigan & Wigdor, 1989; Linn, 1982). Bias, however, can occur either within the test itself or in how the test is used (Shepard, 1982). Measures such as intelligence tests, college admissions tests, and employment tests are all intended to be *part* of a decision-making process. When test scores are weighted too heavily relative to other factors, they can result in decisions that are biased even when the measures used in making them are unbiased.

A number of efforts have been made to develop tests that do not give undue advantage to particular cultural groups; these are known as **culture-free tests.** Raymond Cattell (1940) made some of the earliest efforts to produce a culture-free test. Among the best known of these is the Ravens Progressive Matrices (Raven, 1995), which consists of a series of increasingly complex matrices of shapes: The examinee has to determine which of a series of options would properly complete the matrix. The Ravens test is widely used, but its results show the same differences between whites and minorities as do other measures of intelligence (Veroff, McClelland, & Marquis, 1971).

Measures of New Approaches to Intelligence Having looked at measures based on traditional views of intelligence, it is natural to wonder how the newer approaches, such as Sternberg's or Gardner's models, are measured. Sternberg's triarchic theory is more similar to traditional approaches than is Gardner's multiple intelligences theory. Working with a team of colleagues, Sternberg has been developing the Sternberg Triarchic Abilities Test (Sternberg et al., 2001). The breadth of Gardner's approach to intelligence makes measurement more difficult. Shearer's Multiple Intelligences Developmental Assessment Scales is probably the most fully developed assessment for measuring Gardner's intelligences (Shearer, 2004). (See the "What Kids Say and Do" box above.)

Chapter Reference
Chapter 14 provides a more detailed discussion of test bias.

culture-free tests   Standardized tests that do not include items that might favor one culture over another.

What Kids Say and Do

Messages Received by Children

This "What Kids Say and Do" comes to us from one of our colleagues, who is a developmental psychologist:

It was the first day of third grade and I was walking to school with my best friend, Pete. I said, "Hey, who knows, maybe we'll have the same teacher this year. That would be great." When Pete heard what I said, he began to cry. I said, "Pete, what's the matter? Aren't you feeling good?" Pete's response was, "We're not going to be in the same class, Richard. You're smart. You're going to be in the smart kids' class. I'm dumb. I'm going to be in the dumb kids' class." It would be nice to say that we were in the same class, but we weren't. Pete was right. What kinds of messages do we send to children in school when their self-perception at age 7 is: "You're smart, I'm dumb?"

Extremes of Intelligence

However one views intelligence, or intellectual ability, there are individuals whose performance on measures of intelligence is very strong or very weak. Different individuals have different strengths and weaknesses. Teachers can create a positive climate in their classroom by focusing on what students can do and using these strengths to address areas in which students are having difficulty.

The labels *gifted* and *retarded* have been used to describe people at the extremes of intelligence. There is a tendency to think of people in terms of such labels rather than as individuals with unique strengths and weaknesses. In part, this may be attributable to overreliance

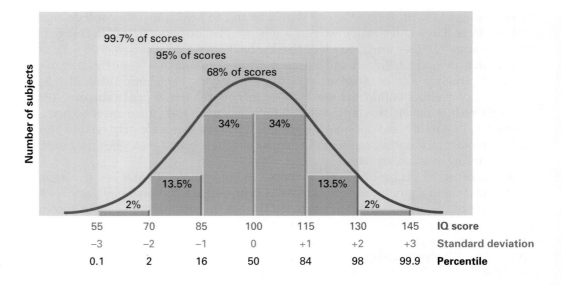

Figure 4.3. A Normal Distribution of IQ Scores

standard deviation   A measure of how far scores vary from the mean.

on the *normal curve,* a bell-shaped frequency distribution, to describe populations of individuals and their characteristics. Extremes of intelligence are identified in part by how far away from an average score is an individual's IQ score. A **standard deviation** is a measure of how far away from the average score a particular score is. A score that is two standard deviations away from the average score is an indicator of extreme intelligence. Definitions of mental retardation typically include an IQ below 70. At the other extreme, definitions of giftedness include an IQ of 130 or greater. Have you ever wondered why these two numbers were chosen? It is basically because they are two standard deviations below and above the mean in the normal curve.

Figure 4.3 shows the normal curve, with IQ scores on the *x* axis. Look at the values of 70 and 130, the typical "cut points" for retardation and giftedness. Does there seem to be anything special about them? Look just to the right and left of those points. Would you imagine that a person with an IQ of 129 is very different in terms of intellectual functioning than one with an IQ of 131? Scores on a standardized IQ test are only one of several criteria used for identifying students who are gifted or have mental retardation.

Chapter Reference
See Chapter 14 for a discussion of statistical concepts such as standard deviation.

Giftedness

Psychologists have long been fascinated by exceptionally talented individuals. Ever since the publication of Galton's *Hereditary Genius* (1869), people with strong abilities or talents have been a focus of research. In education, separate programs for students with strong academic abilities are somewhat more recent. Laws in most states now require gifted education. One of the issues with regard to gifted education is the question of how to determine who is gifted. Most school districts base the decision on a combination of factors, including a measure of academic aptitude or intelligence, performance in school, and recommendations from teachers.

Approaches to gifted education vary widely. Some districts use *pull-out* programs in which gifted students are removed from their regular classes to receive special instruction. Other districts try to incorporate gifted instruction within general education classrooms. Still others accelerate instruction in certain subject areas, such as mathematics or foreign languages. Gifted programs tend to be more common in elementary and middle schools than in high schools. At the high school level, students tend to "sort themselves out" through the selection of courses that interest them. From the perspective of this chapter, it is important to keep in mind that even with a highly reliable measure, there is still a fair amount of error in tests of intelligence or ability. Decisions about a child's future should always be based on several sources of information. When different assessments of a child paint different pictures, it is necessary to obtain more information before making decisions.

 What would the teachers described at the beginning of the chapter do with gifted students once ability grouping was abandoned?

Mental Retardation

The need to identify children with special needs properly and assess the level of those needs was the impetus for the first intelligence test (Binet & Simon, 1916). The American Association on Mental Retardation (AAMR) defines the condition as:

A disability characterized by significant limitation both in intellectual functioning and in adaptive behavior as expressed in conceptual, social, and practical adaptive skills. . . . Mental retardation refers to a particular state of functioning that begins in childhood, has many dimensions, and is affected positively by individualized supports (AAMR, 2002).

The identification of individuals with mental retardation typically includes an IQ score below the 70–75 range. It is important to understand that other factors are involved as well, including how well the individual adapts to new situations, functions in social settings, and handles day-to-day life. The information from this analysis needs to be combined with the test data in order to make an appropriate judgment about the person.

Early research defined different levels of retardation in terms of severity; in contrast, more recent work focuses on the type of support the individual needs. The AAMR describes four levels of support (2002):

- Intermittent: The individual does not need constant, ongoing support, but rather needs support at certain times for certain tasks or transitions in life.

- Limited: The individual needs support in an ongoing and regular fashion, but the degree of support is not extensive.

- Extensive: The individual needs regular, ongoing support that is substantial. Individuals who require this level of support may need assistance in home or work settings on a daily basis.

- Pervasive: This level of support is ongoing and extensive. It is intense and is provided across different environments.

Appendix
Extremes of Intelligence
You are likely to encounter students who vary greatly in their abilities. You will need to know how to accommodate these differences as you plan and implement your instruction (*PRAXIS™*, I. B. 2, I. B. 4, *INTASC*, Principles 1, 3).

Talent

Talent is the capacity to produce exceptional performance. As mentioned previously, test scores are just one measure used to identify exceptional children. Abilities can develop over time. During their school years, students often develop talent in such areas as music, mathematics, science, computers, writing, and athletics. As educators observe talented students in these domains, they frequently attribute the talent to an innate gift. But research shows that talent is often acquired and that practice plays a larger role in its development than is commonly believed (Bloom, 1985; Ericsson, Krampe, & Tesch-Romer, 1993). Figure 4.4 presents a model of how experience and practice contribute to the development of talent.

As shown at the top of the figure, the school curriculum asks students to engage in a variety of activities, such as practicing penmanship, writing essays, working on computers, and playing tennis. Most of the time, students quickly attain a level of proficiency in an activity that is "good enough." After that, their performance becomes routine, and they make little further progress in developing their talent in that domain. For instance, a student may think, "My penmanship is good enough the way it is." The dashed lines in the figure illustrate this normal course of events. Sometimes, however, students wish to increase their ability in a particular domain.

The left side of Figure 4.4 identifies three sources that spark students' desire to increase their talent: enjoyment, valuing, and external support (Csikszentmihalyi, Rathunder, & Whale, 1993). Enjoyment typically arises when the task produces an optimal experience, such as when a student performs a difficult piece of music and has fun doing so. Valuing typically arises from wanting to improve one's skill in the domain for its own sake, such as wanting to improve one's writing skill just to become a better writer, not to make a better grade. External support typically takes the form of having access to resources and social support, such as encouragement from one's teacher. Students with special needs will need a lot of support to engage in these activities.

talent The capacity to produce exceptional performance.

How Can I Use This?
How will you provide opportunities for deliberate practice to students with special needs?

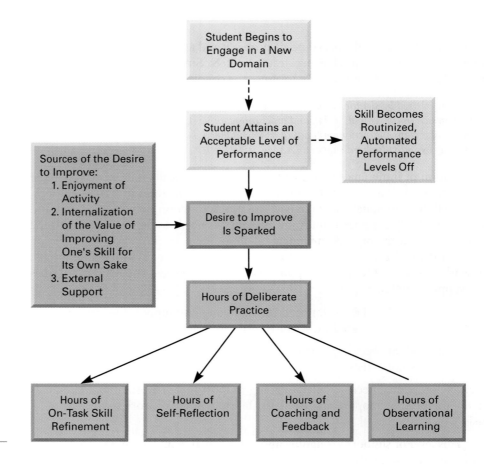

Figure 4.4. Factors That Contribute to the Development of Talent

Deliberate Practice and the Monotonic–Benefits Assumption

deliberate practice Activity that is designed to improve one's skills in a particular area.

The desire to increase one's talent leads one to engage in many hours of deliberate practice. **Deliberate practice** is activity whose main purpose is to attain and improve one's skills (Ericsson et al., 1993; Sosniak, 1985). It is not practice the way we understand it in connection with such activities as playing tennis or playing a musical instrument. Rather, deliberate practice involves repetitive work on a single aspect of the task, such as refining one's grip or finger position on the tennis racket or violin strings. The four boxes at the lower part of Figure 4.4 show what students do during deliberate practice. Some hours are spent on task, directly refining one's skill. During these hours, students invest their full effort as they engage in aspects of the task that they cannot yet do. Other hours are spent in self-reflection. During this "time to think," students engage in mental simulations of what they might do to improve their technique. During self-reflection, performers mentally compare their actual performances against their ideal performance and try to figure out how to close the gap between the two. Other hours of deliberate practice are spent receiving coaching, instruction, and feedback. Improving one's skill and learning how to do what one cannot currently do require the insights and feedback of an expert. Lastly, many hours are spent observing experienced performers. During this observational learning, the student gains exposure to highly skilled models and uses this information to develop new ideas and hypotheses about what to try during their practice time.

monotonic–benefits assumption The argument that there is a one-to-one correspondence between one's effort and one's gains in a skill or ability.

Those who study the development of talent assume that deliberate practice produces **monotonic benefits:** The amount of time an individual spends in deliberate practice is monotonically (one-to-one) related to his or her acquired performance level in that domain (Ericsson et al., 1993; Reingold et al., 2001). This means that the number of hours of deliberate practice is a nearly perfect predictor of performance level, as shown in data such as those graphed in Figure 4.5. The figure plots the hours of weekly practice over the years from age 4 to age 20 for two groups of pianists—amateurs and experts. The amateurs practiced 2 or 3 hours each week for 16 years, and they became good pianists. The experts, however, practiced for about 5 hours per week at age 8, 12 hours at age 14, and about 23 hours at age 18. It is assumed that the number of hours spent in deliberate practice is the transformational event that produces the changes that allow talent to develop.

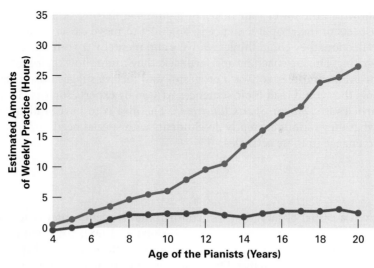

Figure 4.5. Estimated Amount of Time for Practice Alone at the Piano as a Function of Age for Expert Pianists and Amateur Pianists

Source: Ericsson, K. A., Krampe, R. T., & Tesch-Romer, C. (1993). The role of deliberate practice in the acquisition of expert performance. *Psychological Review, 100,* 363–406. Copyright © 1993 by the American Psychological Association. Reprinted with permission.

Effort Becomes Talent

How do hours of deliberate practice produce the wide individual differences that educators observe in students' talents? Deliberate practice alters a student's cognitive capacities and bodily functions (Bloom, 1985; Ericsson, 1998). A less talented chess player, for instance, will survey the pieces on the board, identify the merits of a half-dozen possible moves, then select the best move from among these options. A more talented chess player has acquired much more elaborate chess schemas as a result of many hours of deliberate practice. With each turn, the expert makes an initial survey of the chess patterns, quickly explore as many as 40 or 50 possibilities, evaluate the merits of 5 or so of the best moves, and finally select the best of those. Novice (less talented) and expert (more talented) teachers go through the same process when deciding what to do next in the classroom.

Deliberate practice also changes bodily functions: Piano players develop muscle patterns, such as finger rolls and reverse finger rolls, and long-distance runners grow new capillaries, break down and rebuild their leg muscles, and increase the capacity of their heart and lungs. Through these cognitive and physical means, effort becomes talent. Learners with special needs require a great deal of practice and may need to practice over a longer period.

The process through which writers' hours of deliberate practice help them develop talent illustrates this point. A typical classroom episode unfolds as follows: The teacher tells the students to write a 500-word persuasive essay; the students write their essays; they revise their essays; and finally, the teacher provides some feedback on the quality of the essays. Deliberate practice for talent development would involve a different lesson plan. The teacher might first identify the following writing skills as essential:

- Quality of topic sentences
- Active rather than passive voice
- Strong nouns and verbs
- Vocabulary
- Smooth transitions between paragraphs

The teacher would then highlight one skill to practice, such as the quality of topic sentences. On Monday, the students would write their topic sentences. On Tuesday, they would revise and improve those sentences. At this point, the students would generally feel that their topic sentences are "good enough," so the teacher would have reached the critical point in talent development: encouraging students to improve their topic sentences still further. If the students enjoyed writing, valued writing, and received support for writing, they would then spend Wednesday, Thursday, and Friday engaged in the four aspects of deliberate practice

**What Does This
Mean to Me?**
On what tasks or activities do
you engage in deliberate
practice? What do you do to
be "deliberate" about your
practice?

shown in the lower four boxes of Figure 4.4. During skill refinement, they could revise all aspects of their topic sentence in an effort to move closer to an ideal sentence. During self-reflection, they could think creatively and mentally try out different ways of improving their writing. During coaching and feedback, they could show their sentences to the teacher, peers, or even computer software programs and receive suggestions. During observational learning, they could read topic sentences written by experts such as Hemingway or Joyce, or even articles in *Time* or *Sports Illustrated*. The idea is to have students spend time trying to do what they cannot currently do. Students with special needs will need a great deal of support to engage in these activities.

Early Talent and Developed Talent

Even a casual observation will confirm that students enter school with wide differences in many domains (Howe, Davidson, & Slobada, 1998). Some students are naturally better at math; others are better athletes; and so on. Before students begin investing many hours in deliberate practice, natural talent predicts performance rather well. As the number of hours of practice increases, however, developed talent becomes an ever-better predictor of a student's performance level. At some point—after years of deliberate practice—it becomes an even better predictor of performance than does natural talent (Ericsson et al., 1993; Monsaas, 1985).

Figure 4.6 helps explain the development of talent. During the first phase of talent development, students have not yet engaged in deliberate practice, and natural ability predicts performance very well. This is a period of play in a domain in which activity is spontaneous and motivation is not a problem. The student writes poetry for the fun of it, or the athlete dribbles, shoots free-throws, and plays a game of *horse* for fun. Once students wish to improve their skills, they begin the second phase of talent development and engage in deliberate practice. Such activity requires intense concentration and effort, and motivation can become a problem. With deliberate practice, students see a large and immediate increase in their ability, as shown in Figure 4.6. Much schoolwork involves helping students make the transition from Phase I to Phase II, as illustrated by our earlier example of essay writing. To attain an even higher level of proficiency, Phase III is necessary. This phase features the decision to commit oneself to the domain and engage in many hours of deliberate practice in that domain.

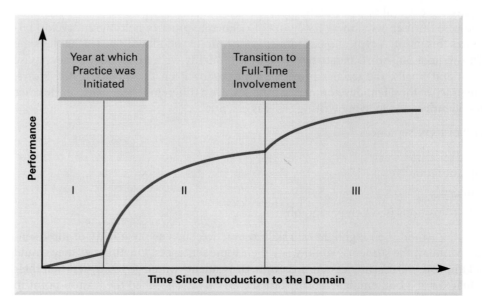

Figure 4.6. Three Phases of Development Toward Adult Expertise

Source: Ericsson, K. A., Krampe, R. T., & Tesch-Romer, C. (1993). The role of deliberate practice in the acquisition of expert performance. *Psychological Review, 100,* 363–406. Copyright © 1993 by the American Psychological Association. Reprinted with permission.

Uncommon Sense

Talent Is Innate—Or Is It?

Many people believe that talent is genetically determined. To some extent, that is true, as students show wide individual differences in their performance across many domains. Math comes easily to some students; language or music comes naturally to others. But people also underestimate the individual's capacity for change and improvement. After all, some gold medalists from the Olympic Games held in the 1950s would not have enough talent to be selected for some of today's high school starting teams (Lehmann, 1998). This is so because talent is also rooted in hours of deliberate practice, instruction, coaching, feedback, and the kinds of activities identified in Figure 4.4. With more and more hours of deliberate practice, the relationship between natural ability and performance decreases whereas that between hours of deliberate practice and performance increases. For an example of this phenomenon, consider the words of three-time Olympic gold medalist Jackie Joyner-Kersee as she remembers her early years of deliberate practice:

(© AP/Wide World Photos)

If I know I've done the work, if I know I've done all the millions and millions of repeats and worked through all my mistakes, then I am confident I can give my best on the one shot that counts (Joyner-Kersee, 1997).

Early talent plays into the model in Figure 4.6 because students who show early promise typically receive more encouragement to pursue deliberate practice. They may also receive more resources, such as books, tutors, and access to transportation so that they can spend time with coaches and attend events related to their area of interest (e.g., concerts, skating competitions). For these reasons, students who show early talent are likely to engage in more hours of deliberate practice over the years than are those who do not show early talent. But research on talent development makes it clear that number of hours of deliberate practice is at least as important as early talent. During deliberate practice, one's skill is constantly reorganized in response to instruction and feedback. The picture that emerges is that talent is not just a matter of genetic individual differences; rather, it reflects a combination of innate capacity, hours of deliberate practice, motivation to improve, and encouragement (van Lieshout & Heymans, 2000). (See the "Uncommon Sense" box above.)

Differences in Ability and Instruction

However you define intelligence or ability, you can be certain that the students in your classroom will vary. Some of the problems of definition come from the varying views of intelligence, with some seeing it as consisting of a narrow set of abilities and others seeing it in broader terms. The word *ability* is often used interchangeably with *achievement,* a use that is problematic because it does not take into account a student's potential. One of the greatest challenges for teachers is to provide appropriate instruction for all the students in their classroom.

From a practical standpoint, teachers must cope with variations in ability or intelligence, however they are defined. A number of options have been explored for managing variations in ability, achievement, or intelligence. One of them is to group children by ability. This is often done by assigning children to classes based on measured ability, a procedure known as **between-class ability grouping.** Low achievers are assigned to one class, average achievers to another, and high achievers to a third. All instruction occurs within these groups. In contrast, children can be assigned to ability groups *within* a class. In this approach, a child may be in the high-achievement group for reading but in the average-achievement group for mathematics. In other words, in **within-class ability grouping,** children are not permanently assigned to a particular group.

Chapter Reference
Chapter 6 explains how to motivate students during uninteresting lessons, which are comparable to deliberate practice.

between-class ability grouping
A procedure in which children are assigned to different classes based on measured ability.

within-class ability grouping
A system in which children are assigned to ability groups within a class.

Between-Class Ability Grouping

Chapter Reference
Chapter 12 provides a fuller discussion of group and peer learning.

Between-class ability grouping occurs when children are assigned to particular classes based on their performance or measured ability. This practice is not common in elementary schools at present. At the high school level, students are often *tracked* into advanced-placement courses, college preparatory courses, and more general courses. In 1990, the Second International Mathematics Study (SIMS) reported that ability grouping was used more frequently in the United States than in other countries that participated in the study (Oakes, 1990).

Ability grouping is controversial. Those who support it argue that gifted students should be educated together because they are not challenged enough in regular classes (Kulik, 1992). Other advocates of ability grouping point to the potential for providing more appropriate curricula and teacher attention to students at the same ability level. Those who oppose ability grouping emphasize the negative effects on low achievers. Students in low-ability tracks have difficulty moving into higher tracks and tend to receive lower quality instruction (Dreeben & Gamoran, 1986; Gamoran & Mare, 1989; Oakes, 1990; Veldman & Sanford, 1984).

Appendix
Promoting Learning for All
You will need to consider your students' various skills, abilities, and interests and design instruction that is appropriate to their needs (*PRAXIS™*, I. B. 4, *INTASC*, Principles 1, 3).

Robert Slavin conducted extensive reviews of the effects of ability grouping in comparison with heterogeneous grouping in both elementary and secondary schools (Slavin, 1987a, 1990). He concluded that there are no advantages associated with ability grouping. Others disagree (Gamoran, 1987; Hallinan, 1990; Hiebert, 1987). The topic thus remains controversial, and the available research has not shown conclusively how ability grouping influences student achievement (Sloane, 2003). A key factor that links grouping and achievement is the quality of the instruction provided (Gamoran, 1987).

The National Association of School Psychologists (NASP) recommends the use of heterogeneous grouping (NASP, 2002). *Multi-age grouping* (also called *nongraded classrooms*), in which classes include children of various ages (e.g., kindergarten through second grade), is one approach of this type. In this approach, children's abilities are less subject to social comparison within their age groups. Research studies show that students in nongraded classrooms perform as well or better than students in traditional classrooms (Anderson & Pavan, 1993; Gutierrez & Slavin, 1992). In addition to positive achievement effects, multi-age classrooms are associated with other gains, such as increases in students' self-esteem and willingness to take responsibility for their own learning (Gutierrez & Slavin, 1992; Mackey, Johnson, & Wood, 1995).

Elizabeth Cohen developed the multiple-abilities treatment to minimize the differentiation among students in a classroom (Cohen, 1994; Cohen & Lotan, 1997). The intent of this program, called *Complex Instruction,* is to promote participation by all students. Students work on complex tasks to which all of them can contribute but none of them can complete alone. Like the other approaches discussed in this section, complex instruction attempts to reduce the focus on a narrow set of skills and increase participation by all students.

 Do the teachers in the account at the beginning of the chapter believe that heterogeneous grouping can be effective?

Within-Class Ability Grouping

Within-class ability grouping involves assigning students in a heterogeneous classroom to homogeneous groups for instruction in specific subjects, such as mathematics and reading. A child is assigned to a reading group, for example, based on his or her current functioning with respect to reading. The same child may be placed in a group at a different level for instruction in mathematics. In an analysis of various studies of within-class ability grouping, Slavin concluded that it can be effective if the instructional pace and materials are adapted to the students' needs (Slavin, 1987b). An important factor in the use of within-class ability grouping is the need for continued assessment so that children can move to another group when their competence increases.

Learners with Special Needs

One might reasonably say that every child has special needs. However, the term *special needs* is used in a specific sense to refer to children who have been identified by the school system as having needs that are significant enough to warrant special educational services. In 1976–1977, the number of students under age 21 who were being served in federally supported programs for individuals with disabilities was 3,694,000. In 1998–1999, the number of students served had grown to 6,055,000. This change represented an increase in number served as a percentage of total enrollment from 8.32% to 13.01%. In the earlier time period, 26% of the students served had specific learning disabilities. In 1998–1999, the percentage had risen to 46% (U.S. Department of Education, 2005). This means that all teachers are likely to encounter students with special needs at some time in their careers.

The Law and Special Education

The Education for All Handicapped Children Act (Public Law 94–142) was passed in 1975. It required states to provide every child between the ages of 3 and 21 with a free and appropriate education, regardless of the severity of the child's handicap. PL 99-457 (1986) extended the requirement for a free and appropriate education to all handicapped children between the ages of 3 and 5. In 1990, the Americans with Disabilities Act extended the rights of individuals with disabilities in areas such as transportation, employment, and telecommunications. PL 94-142 was amended in 1990 by the Individuals with Disabilities Education Act (IDEA), which was reauthorized in 1997 and again in 2004.

The initial law (PL 94-142) required that students be educated in the least restrictive environment possible. The intent was to allow children to be educated with their peers as much as possible. The available options included in-class support, pull-out programs in resource rooms, self-contained classrooms, special day schools, residential schools, and hospitals or home. The further away from the normal classroom a student was placed, the more restrictive the environment was considered to be.

The 2004 IDEA act states that multiple measures must be used to identify children with disabilities and that these measures should be selected so as not to discriminate on a cultural or racial basis. The tests used must be valid and reliable.

Chapter Reference
See Chapter 14 for information about good tests and freedom from bias in testing.

A key change in IDEA 2004 is a statement of the qualifications required of special education teachers. They must demonstrate competence in all the core academic subjects they teach in the same manner as is required for an elementary, middle, or secondary school teacher.

Each child with a disability be provided with an **individualized education program** (IEP) written by a child study team that includes the student's parents or guardians, the student's teachers, a school psychologist, and a special education supervisor. The IEP should include information about:

individualized education program (IEP)   An educational and behavioral intervention plan for a student with special needs.

- The student's current level of performance
- Measurable educational or behavioral goals for the year
- A description of how the child's progress toward meeting the goals will be measured
- A statement of special education and related services, based on scientific research where possible, that will be given to the student
- A description of the student's participation in the regular school program
- An explanation of the child's nonparticipation with nondisabled children in the classroom (if applicable)
- For older students, a description of services that are needed to help the student make a transition toward further education or work in adult life

An example of an IEP is presented in Figure 4.7. Curt is a ninth-grade low achiever who was considered by the district to be a poorly motivated, disciplinary problem student with a "bad attitude". His parents recognized him as a very discouraged, frustrated student who had learning disabilities, especially in language arts.

The IEP team for a student should include no less than one regular teacher of the student, no less than one special education teacher, someone who can interpret the instructional implications of the evaluation, other people with appropriate expertise, and when appropriate, the student. The team also needs to consider special factors, such as the

Unique Educational Needs, Characteristics, and Present Levels of Performance	Special Education, Related Services, Supplemental Aids & Services, Assistive Technology, Program Modifications, Support for Personnel	Measurable Annual Goals & Short-Term Objectives or Benchmarks • To enable student to participate in the general curriculum • To meet other needs resulting from the disability
(including how the disability affects the student's ability to progress in the general curriculum)	(including frequency, duration, & location)	(including how progress toward goals will be measured)
Present Level of Social Skills: Curt lashes out violently when not able to complete work, uses profanity, and refuses to follow further directions from adults.	1. Teacher and/or counselor consult with behavior specialist regarding techniques and programs for teaching skills, especially anger management.	Goal: During the last quarter of the academic year, Curt will have 2 or fewer detentions for any reason. Obj. 1: At the end of the 1st quarter, Curt will have had 10 or fewer detentions. Obj. 2: At the end of the 2nd quarter, Curt will have had 7 or fewer detentions. Obj. 3: At the end of the 3rd quarter, Curt will have had 4 or fewer detentions.
Special Needs: • To learn anger management skills, especially regarding swearing • To learn comply with requests	2. Provide anger management instruction to Curt. Services 3 times/week, 30 minutes. 3. Establish a peer group which involves role playing, etc., so Curt can see positive role models and practice newly learned anger management skills. Services 2 times/week, 30 minutes. 4. Develop a behavioral plan for Curt which gives him responsibility for charting his own behavior. 5. Provide a teacher or some other adult mentor to spend time with Curt (talking, game playing, physical activity, etc.). Services 2 times/week, 30 minutes. 6. Provide training for the mentor regarding Curt's needs/goals.	Goal: Curt will manage his behavior and language in a reasonably acceptable manner as reported by faculty and peers. Obj. 1: At 2 weeks, asked at the end of class if Curt's behavior and language were acceptable, 3 out of 6 teachers will say "acceptable." Obj. 2: At 6 weeks, asked the same question, 4 out of 6 teachers will say "acceptable." Obj. 3: At 12 weeks, asked the same question, 6 out of 6 teachers will say "acceptable."

Study Skills/Organizational Needs:
    How to read text
    Note taking
    How to study notes
    Memory work
    Be prepared for class, with materials
    Lengthen and improve attention span and on-task behavior
 	
Present Level:
Curt currently lacks skill in all these areas.
	1. Speech/lang. therapist, resource room teacher, and content area teachers will provide Curt with direct and specific teaching of study skills, i.e.
	        Note taking from lectures
	        Note taking while reading text
	        How to study notes for a test
	        Memorization hints
	        Strategies for reading text to retain information
	
	2. Assign a "study buddy" for Curt in each content area class.
	
	3. Prepare a motivation system for Curt to be prepared for class with all necessary materials.
	
	4. Develop a motivational plan to encourage Curt to lengthen his attention span and time on task.
	
	5. Provide aide to monitor-on-task behaviors in the first month or so of plan and teach Curt self-monitoring techniques.
	
	6. Provide motivational system and self-recording form for completion of academic tasks in each class.
		Goal: At the end of academic year, Curt will have better grades and, by his own report, will have learnied new study skills.
		Obj. 1: Given a 20-30 min. lecture/oral lesson, Curt will take appropriate notes as judged by that teacher.
		Obj. 2: Given 10-15 pgs. of text to read, Curt will employ an appropriate strategy for retaining info.—i.e., mapping, webbing, outlining, notes, etc.—as judged by the teacher.
		Obj. 3: Given notes to study for a test, Curt will do so successfully as evidenced by his test score.
		
		Goal: Curt will improve his on-task behavior from 37% to 80% as measured by a qualified observer at year's end.
		Obj. 1: By 1 month, Curt's on-task behavior will increase to 45%.
		Obj. 2: By 3 months, Curt's on-task behavior will increase to 60%.
		Obj. 3: By 6 months, Curt's on-task behavior will increase to 80% and maintain or improve until end of the year.

Figure 4.7. **Example of an IEP** *(continued on page 123)*

Source: Bateman, B. D., & Linden, M. A. (1998). *Better IEPS (3rd ed.)*. Longmont, CO: Sopris West Educational Services. Copyright 1998 by Sopris West Educational Services. Reprinted with permission.

Unique Educational Needs, Characteristics, and Present Levels of Performance	Special Education, Related Services, Supplemental Aids & Services, Assistive Technology, Program Modifications, Support for Personnel	Measurable Annual Goals & Short-Term Objectives or Benchmarks • To enable student to participate in the general curriculum • To meet other needs resulting from the disability
(including how the disability affects the student's ability to progress in the general curriculum)	*(including frequency, duration, & location)*	*(including how progress toward goals will be measured)*
Academic Needs/Written Language: Curt needs strong remedial help in spelling, punctuation, capitalization, and usage. **Present Level:** Curt is approximately 2 grade levels behind his peers in these skills.	1. Provide direct instruction in written language skills (punctuation, capitalization, usage, spelling) by using a highly structured, well-sequenced program. Services provided in small group of no more than four students in the resource room, 50 minutes/day. 2. Build in continuous and cumulative review to help with short-term rote memory difficulty. 3. Develop a list of commonly used words in student writing (or use one of many published lists) for Curt's spelling program.	*Goal:* Within one academic year, Curt will improve his written language skills by 1.5 or 2 full grade levels. Obj. 1: Given 10 sentences of dictation at his current level of instruction, Curt will punctuate and capitalize with 90% accuracy (checked at the end of each of each unit taught). Obj. 2: Given 30 sentences with choices of usage, at his current instructional level, Curt will perform with 90% accuracy. Obj. 3: Given a list of 150 commonly used words in writing, Curt will spell with 90% accuracy.
Adaptations to Regular Program: • In all classes, Curt should sit near the front of the class. • Curt should be called on often to keep him involved and on task. • All teachers should help Curt with study skills as trained by spelling/language specialist and resource room teacher. • Teachers should monitor Curt's work closely in the beginning weeks, months of his program.		

Figure 4.7. **Example of an IEP** *(continued)*

student's language needs. Planning for transition services begins when the child is 13, and implementation of the plan in terms of identifying and activating services begins when the child is 16. Members of the IEP team are required to consider the child's strengths, the concerns of his or her parents, the results of the evaluation, and the child's academic, developmental, and functional needs. Under the new law, states may propose to develop multiyear IEP programs covering up to three years in order to provide long-term planning for a child.

A third provision of the initial Public Law 94-142 that remains in effect protects the rights of students and families. The Family Educational Rights and Privacy Act (FERPA; 1974) was written to ensure that schools do not release information about a child's educational records without the permission of his or her parents or guardians. Schools must have procedures for keeping students' records confidential. The aim of this law is to ensure that parents and guardians have access to their child's educational records and that schools do not give that information to others without permission.

Additional protection for students with disabilities is provided by Section 504 of the Rehabilitation Act, which was passed in 1973. This law bars discrimination against people with disabilities in any program that receives federal funds, including public schools. It guarantees that children with disabilities have a right to participate in school activities. Table 4.2 on page 124 provides an overview of the differences between these two laws.

The No Child Left Behind Act of 2001 requires that students with special needs participate in statewide testing and that they meet state standards for achievement. In response to the National Survey of Public School Teachers 2003, 84% of teachers object to the idea that special education students should be expected to meet the same content standards as students of the same age in general education classes (McCabe, 2004).

Chapter Reference
Chapter 14 contains further information about issues of testing students with special needs.

TABLE 4.2

Understanding the Differences Between IDEA and Section 504

	IDEA	Section 504
Purpose of law	Federal statute that governs all special education law in the United States	Federal civil rights statute that requires all schools, public and private, that receive federal financial assistance not to discriminate against children with disabilities
Identification	School districts are required to identify all children in the district who may have a disability. Children living in the district who do not attend public schools are included.	
Eligibility	(a) Child must meet eligibility requirements in one or more of 13 categories or (b) at the discretion of the state and school district, a child aged 3 to 9 may be eligible if he or she is experiencing delays in physical, cognitive, communication, social, emotional, or adaptive development; such delays require special education and related services.	The existence of an identified physical or mental condition (e.g., asthma, ADHD) substantially limits a major life activity. Among these activities are seeing, walking, breathing, working, speaking, learning, and caring for oneself. The school district is allowed to determine whether an impairment "substantially limits" a major life activity. Eligibility is broader under Section 504 than under IDEA.
Evaluation	• Full evaluation by a multidisciplinary team • Requires informed and written consent from parents/guardians • Reevaluation of each child if conditions warrant or if requested by teacher or parents, but at least once every three years • Provides for independent evaluation at district's expense if parents disagree with first evaluation	• Information gathered from a variety of professional sources (e.g., classroom teacher) • Requires notice to parents but not consent (although good practice indicates use of informed consent)
Appropriate Education	• Requires an individual education plan (IEP)	

Source: Adapted from "Understanding the differences between IDEA and Section 504" by Laurie deBettencourt, *Teaching Exceptional Children*, Vol. 34, 2002, 16–23. Copyright 2002 by The Council for Exceptional Children. Adapted and reprinted with permission.

Identifying Children with Special Needs

The identification of children with special needs may begin informally when a teacher sees that a child appears to be having difficulties relative to other children. The child may, for example, have trouble learning to read or have more behavioral problems than is typical. The teacher may begin a prereferral process in which efforts are made to address the child's needs in the classroom. If the problem continues, the child may be referred for a formal evaluation.

Prereferral Processes In response to the rapid increase in the number of students in special education, prereferral intervention teams have become widespread (Buck et al., 2003). These teams (which go by a variety of names, such as pupil assistance committees, teacher intervention teams, or teacher assistance teams) have succeeded in reducing the number of inappropriate referrals for special education services (Kovaleski et al., 1999). Despite variations in how they function, the teams share a number of features (Buck et al., 2003):

- The process focuses on prevention.
- Interventions are designed, employed, and evaluated prior to a formal referral for special education.
- The team uses a problem-solving approach: It reviews information about the child, generates hypotheses about the causes of his or her problems, and designs strategies for intervention. (This process is not unlike the RIDE process you have used throughout this text.)
- The team develops a specific intervention that is implemented by the classroom teacher.
- The team evaluates the effectiveness of the intervention after a specified length of time.

Among the benefits associated with the use of prereferral teams is that a child receives assistance in his or her own class before being considered for special education. The fact that team members collaborate in the interests of the child is also a benefit. Effective interventions at an early stage reduce the number of inappropriate referrals for special education and result in cost savings (Buck et al., 2003).

Referrals If the child's problems persist despite the interventions proposed by the prereferral team, the child may be referred for evaluation for special education services. A school professional may request that a child be evaluated to determine whether he or she has a disability. Parents may also initiate the request for evaluation. The parents or guardians of a child must consent to the evaluation. The evaluation may be conducted by a school psychologist and will include assessments in all areas that are related to the child's suspected disability. The results of the evaluation are used to determine whether the child is eligible for special education services. Parents who disagree with the results of an evaluation can request an independent educational evaluation (IEE). A group of qualified professionals, along with the parents, examine the evaluation results to determine whether the child is eligible for services. If the child is found to be eligible for services under IDEA, the IEP team has 30 days to write an IEP for the child. This process is outlined in Figure 4.8.

Some parents resist having their children declared eligible for special services, because they may be concerned about the negative effects of the special needs label. Special services cannot be provided unless a child is found to be eligible for them, and this includes classifying or labeling the child's needs. Labels can both help and stigmatize a child (Heward & Orlansky, 1992; Keogh & MacMillan, 1996). Teachers can reduce potential problems by modeling respect for students with disabilities and creating a classroom climate in which differences among students are valued.

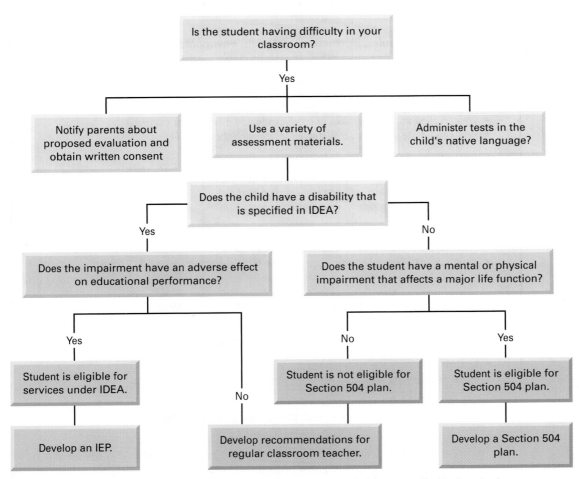

Figure 4.8.
Questions to Ask When Determining Appropriate Services

Source: Adapted from "Understanding the differences between IDEA and Section 504" by Laurie deBettencourt, *Teaching Exceptional Children*, Vol. 34, 2002, 16–23. Copyright 2002 by The Council for Exceptional Children. Adapted and reprinted with permission.

Inclusion

The requirements of IDEA 2004 and Section 504 of the Rehabilitation Act of 1973 have increased the responsibilities of regular classroom teachers in implementing educational programs for classified and at-risk students. (Approximately 75% of the students served under IDEA are in general education classrooms for some part of the school day). The reauthorization of IDEA in 1997 added the regular classroom teacher to the IEP team, because the teacher would have a great deal of responsibility for implementing the program designed by the IEP team. This approach was maintained in the 2004 reauthorization of the law. These increased responsibilities make it necessary to develop strategies to help classified students adapt to a variety of classroom elements. Examples of such strategies are presented in the "Taking It to the Classroom" box below.

Prevalent Learning Needs

With changing laws related to special educations, teachers encounter more students in their classes with special needs. Among the most prevalent kinds of students with special needs are those with learning disabilities and attention deficit disorder.

Taking It to the Classroom

Strategies for the Inclusive Classroom

Establish a positive attitude:

- How can I set a positive tone in the classroom for this student?
- How can I help this student see that his or her efforts will lead to desired academic and social outcomes?

Analyze curriculum, rules, instruction, materials, environment:

Curriculum

- What mandated standards must the student meet?

Rules

- What explicit and implicit rules of conduct should I establish for students?
- How can I make students accountable for following the rules?

Instruction

- What instructional strategies are available to me?
- How can I measure and evaluate student progress?
- What is the role of group work in my classroom?

Materials

- What supplementary instructional materials might I need for this student?
- What role will electronic technologies play in this student's program?

Environment

- Will I need to rearrange the layout of the classroom for this student?
- Will I need to adjust the daily instructional schedule?

Identify student characteristics (i.e., strengths and weaknesses):

- Academic skills
- Social skills
- Learning preferences

Compare student characteristics with the learning environment:

- Identify each significant student characteristic as either a "facilitator," a "barrier," or a "neutral" element within the classroom environment. (For example, poor social skills may be viewed as a barrier to group work.) Following is an example:

(Continued on page 127)

Strategies for the Inclusive Classroom *(continued)*

Category	My Classroom	Facilitators	Neutral	Barriers
Curriculum	State curriculum standards	Conceptual understanding; verbal expression		Reading; writing
Rules	Complete own work			Independent work
	Class on time		X	
	Homework on time			Forgetful
Instruction	Lecture	Auditory skills		
	Independent work			Reading; writing; not a learning preference
	Group work	Learning preference Gets along well w/others		
	Chapter questions	Conceptual understanding		Reading; writing
	Weekly written tests	Conceptual understanding		Reading; writing
Materials				
Environment	Crowded room			
	Auditory distractions			

Select small sets of

- Classroom elements that can be readily modified for the student
- Skills to develop in the student

Collaborate with other professionals who will be involved either directly or indirectly in the student's progress. Among these professionals are:

- School nurses
- Therapists
- Psychologists
- Learning specialists
- Guidance counselors
- Social workers

Review and revise:

- Examine the student's progress toward his or her targeted goals. Which adaptations in the program need to be adjusted? Which ones can be faded or eliminated?

Source: Adapted from: "She will succeed! Strategies for Success in inclusive classrooms" by M. A. Prater, *Teaching exceptional children*, Vol. 35, 2003, 58–64. Copyright 2003 by The Council for Exceptional Children. Adapted and reprinted with permission.

Learning Disabilities

In 1998–1999, more than 2,500,000 children under age 21 were identified as having specific learning disabilities. Less than 1% of children between the ages of 6 and 21 diagnosed with specific learning disabilities were educated outside regular classrooms (U.S. Department of Education, 2000). Forty-four percent of students with learning disabilities spent 80% or more of each school day in their regular classrooms. An additional 39% spent between 40% and 79% of their time in their regular classrooms.

Learning disabilities are invisible. A student's low achievement in school may be an indicator of a learning disability, but not all learning problems are due to disabilities. Learning disabilities can be divided into three broad categories: (a) developmental speech and language disorders, (b) academic skills disorders, and (c) other disabilities (National Institute of Mental Health [NIMH], 2004). Developmental speech and language disorders include disorders of articulation, expressive language, and receptive language. Problems with language are often the earliest indicators of a learning disability. Articulation disorders can be corrected with speech therapy. Problems with expressive language or the communication of ideas or thoughts greatly hinder a child's ability to participate in school activities. Problems with receptive language or comprehending language produced by others are also major obstacles to cognitive development. Speech therapy can be successful in improving certain kinds of children's language difficulties. Achievement skills disorders include difficulties with reading, mathematics, and writing.

The recent reauthorization of IDEA (2004) does not require schools to use a severe discrepancy between current achievement and measured intellectual ability to determine whether a child has a learning disability. The school may instead use an evaluation process to find out whether the child will respond to a scientific, research-based intervention. In other words, the child's response to instruction can become part of the evaluative process.

Attention Deficit Disorder

Attention is needed for taking in information and also producing it when needed. Some students experience difficulty is managing their attention. **Attention deficit disorder** (ADD) is a condition in which children experience persistent difficulties with attention span, impulse control, and sometimes hyperactivity. It is an emotional/behavioral disorder, not a learning disability. Between 3% and 5% of the school-age population is affected by ADD. According to the *Diagnostic and Statistical Manual*, fourth edition, of the American Psychiatric Association (APA, 1994) or DSM-IV, signs of inattention include the following:

- Becoming easily distracted by irrelevant sights and sounds
- Failing to pay attention to details and making careless mistakes
- Rarely following instructions carefully and completely
- Losing or forgetting things such as toys, pencils, books, and tools needed for a task (NIMH, 2004).

Attention Deficit Hyperactivity Disorder

Attention deficit hyperactivity disorder (ADHD) is a condition in which children or adults consistently display inattention, hyperactivity, and impulsiveness. A child who cannot pay attention will have difficulty learning. Any classroom provides challenges to a child who is trying to focus on a learning task. The number of children in the room and the constant interruptions that occur in most classrooms make it difficult for any child to pay attention. For a child with ADHD, the challenge of attending to instruction is much greater. ADD and ADHD differ because of the presence hyperactivity and impulsiveness in ADHD (NIMH, 2004). A hyperactive child is excessively active, may be unable to sit still, and may fidget even when seated. A child with ADHD may also be impulsive. Signs of hyperactivity and impulsivity include the following:

- Feeling restless, often fidgeting with hands or feet, or squirming
- Running, climbing, or leaving a seat in situations in which sitting or quiet behavior is expected
- Blurting out an answer before hearing the whole question
- Having difficulty waiting in line or for a turn

All children exhibit these kinds of behaviors from time to time. DSM-IV contains guidelines for identifying ADHD that include the requirement that the behaviors must appear before the age of 7 and continue for at least 6 months. An important aspect of determining whether a particular disorder exists is that the behavior must be observed over a specified period.

The child's teacher may be the first person to notice that a child is hyperactive and may consult other school personnel about a possible evaluation. A prereferral process such as that described in the preceding section may be the first course of action. Because teachers deal with a variety of children (and experienced teachers have encountered many hundreds of

Chapter Reference
You read about the importance of language for cognitive development in Chapter 2.

attention deficit disorder (ADD) A condition in which children experience persistent difficulties with attention span, impulse control, and sometimes hyperactivity.

Chapter Reference
Chapter 8 provides a fuller description of attention and its importance in learning.

attention deficit hyperactivity disorder (ADHD) A condition in which children or adults consistently display inattention, hyperactivity, and impulsiveness.

children), the teacher will probably have a good idea of what constitutes average behavior for a child of a particular age. Teachers of younger children will also be aware of different developmental patterns and will expect some variation in what constitutes average behavior. When such a teacher identifies a child as significantly different from the average, further analysis is required. A note of caution: Teachers are not immune from expectation effects and may misread a situation. A teacher could ask a colleague to observe a child in order to provide another perspective on the child's behavior. Observational studies of children who are diagnosed as hyperactive support the idea that there are readily observable differences in behavior between children who exhibit the disorder and those who do not (Luk, 1985).

Educational Options   Table 4.3 includes descriptions of behaviors that may be characteristic of a child with ADHD and some general strategies for working with such a child. Children with ADHD vary in the severity of their disorder. Some may be unable to participate effectively in the classroom, whereas many others, given appropriate accommodations, can be very successful. In general, a teacher should try to minimize distractions and help the child regulate his or her behavior. (See the "Taking It to the Classroom" box on page 130).

TABLE 4.3

Behavioral Characteristics and General Strategies for Students with ADHD

Behavior	Characteristics of child	General strategies
Hyperactivity	1. Fidgets with hands/feet 2. Squirms in seat/leaves seat unexpectedly 3. Shows preference for gross motor activities 4. Shows frustration during fine motor tasks	1. Incorporation of gross motor activity and active responses into curriculum (e.g., role play, hands-on activities) 2. Positive attention from peers. 3. Attention and feedback from regular classroom teacher
Impulsivity	1. Inability to delay responding 2. Difficulty waiting for his or her turn in social and academic situations 3. Interrupts/intrudes on others 4. Emotional outbursts/reactions based on feelings, not facts 5. Poor performance on tasks that require planning	1. Cognitive-behavior therapy and self-monitoring of impulses 2. Time-outs 3. Positive reinforcement using tangible or material rewards 4. Response cost/removal punishment
Inattention/ distractibility	1. Difficulty filtering irrelevant sensory information 2. Attraction to "novel" environmental conditions 3. Restriction of activity when experiencing excessive stimulation 4. Initiation of sensation-seeking activity when not sufficiently stimulated	1. Use of varied and interesting tasks (e.g., games, videos) 2. Use of novel qualities (e.g., color, size) to highlight important written task features 3. Moderate levels of noise (e.g., music, fan) during repetitive, familiar, and structured activities
Disorganization	1. Misplaces or loses belongings 2. Difficulty handling materials with multiple pieces 3. Messy desk 4. Difficulty completing tasks and tests within a time framework 5. Overestimates time intervals 6. Haphazard, illegible penmanship	1. Predictable location and labeling of classroom materials 2. Self-talk to monitor organization 3. Use of alternate means of producing responses (e.g., oral, transcribed)

Source: Adapted from "Arranging the classroom with an eye (and ear) to students with ADHD" by Eric Carbone, *Teaching Exceptional Children,* Vol. 34, 2001, 72–81. Copyright 2001 by The Council for Exceptional Children. Adapted and reprinted with permission.

Taking It to the Classroom

Do You Know Jack, the Disorganized?

Jack is disorganized. He often forgets where his materials are. He puts his papers in the wrong folders and binders, and loses them. He brings the wrong books and materials to various classes. He does not finish many of his in-class assignments because of his disorganized approach to them. He loses track of what homework he has, and he brings home the wrong items to do his homework. This disorganized approach affects nearly every aspect of his day at school. What practical and immediate steps can you take to help Jack? Here are some suggestions:

- Talk to Jack's parents about strategies that could help him be more organized.
- Provide Jack with a homework notebook to help him keep track of his assignments.
- Color code his books and notebooks for different subject areas so he can easily see which notebook and book he needs.
- Provide Jack with a list of what he will need for the next day's classes.
- Show Jack good models of how to organize materials.

Chapter Reference
You can read more about teacher expectation effects in Chapter 9.

Chapter Reference
Chapter 7 provides examples of behavior management techniques that might be useful in working with children with ADHD.

Children with ADHD are often treated with medication. A commonly prescribed medication is Ritalin, which is a stimulant. Such medications often reduce children's hyperactivity and improve their ability to pay attention. The use of medication to treat hyperactivity on a continuous basis is quite controversial, however. The NIMH conducted the most extensive study of treatments for ADHD to date: the Multimodal Treatment Study of Children with ADHD (MTA, 1999). Four treatments were compared: (a) medication management alone, (b) behavioral treatments alone, (c) a combination of medication and behavioral treatments, and (d) routine community care. A total of 579 elementary school boys and girls with ADHD were randomly assigned to one of the treatments. All the children were assessed at regular intervals throughout the study. The results showed that long-term combination treatments and medication management alone were superior to intense behavioral treatment and routine community care. The combined treatment was superior on such measures as anxiety, academic performance, oppositionality or defiance, parent-child relations, and social skills.

Autism and Related Disorders

Autism has been a separate category under IDEA since 1990. Autistic children are characterized by extreme social withdrawal, deficiencies in cognitive processes, and language disorders. These symptoms must be present before the child is 3 years old. Approximately 7.5 cases of autism are found per 10,000 children (Hallahan & Kauffman, 2003). Related disorders include pervasive developmental disorder (PDD), which is characterized by abnormal social relations and interactions. Autistic spectrum disorder describes a range of disorders that are indicative of symptoms of autism but may range in severity from mild to severe. No single behavior is always typical of autism and the manifestation of autism is very varied. Among the behaviors that may be present in autistic children are the following (Hallahan & Kauffman, 2003):

- Impaired social responsiveness. The child does not respond to other people in a typical fashion.
- Impaired communication. The child may have impaired verbal and nonverbal communication.
- Stereotypic or ritualistic behavior. The child may exhibit repetitive stereotypic behavior. Examples of stereotypic behavior may include rocking back and forth on one's heels or flapping one's hands.
- Preoccupation with objects and narrow range of interests. Autistic children may play with the same object for extensive periods. They may experience difficulty with changes (Adreon & Stella, 2001).

Teachers who have students in their classes with autistic tendencies will need to provide substantial support to these children. They will need to create a predictable environment and address issues of limited social awareness that these children may have, as well as other difficulties.

Students with Limited English Proficiency

The number of students with limited English proficiency (LEP) has grown substantially. According to estimates in the *Descriptive Study of Services to LEP Students and LEP Students with Disabilities* (Zehler et al., 2003), there were 3,977,819 LEP students in grades K–12 in the United States during the 2001–2002 school year, a 72% increase from the 1991–1992 estimate. These students represent a little over 8% of all students in schools. Spanish is the primary language of 77% of LEP students. Many districts have difficulty identifying LEP, but Zehler et al. (2003) report that an estimated 375,325 LEP students also have special needs.

Clearly, the large number of students who do not speak English proficiently has important implications for teachers. Students' language skills affect every aspect of their learning, including the learning of mathematics. LEP students usually receive either some LEP service in English, extensive LEP services in English, or extensive LEP services with significant native-language use. The study just mentioned found that LEP students scored below grade level in reading and mathematics but that students who completed LEP programs typically were at grade level in these subjects (Zehler et al., 2003).

In a review of federally funded studies dealing with LEP students, 57 studies that focused on instructional services were included. The findings of these studies indicated that student outcomes could be improved by appropriate use of the native language and culture, adequate instruction in particular content areas, and an active learning environment (Special Issues Analysis Center [SIAC], 2003). A trade association, Teachers of English to Speakers of Other Languages (TESOL), has established three main goals and standards for reaching them (TESOL, 1997). These are outlined in Table 4.4. Principles for teaching second-language learners are listed in Table 4.5 on the next page.

Using Technology to Support LEP Students' Learning Technology can be used to help LEP students meet the academic goals and standards set forth by TESOL (1997, see Table 4.4). García (1999) examined the effects of comic strip creation and animation software on the learning processes of bilingual children (Spanish and English) as they learned science and language simultaneously. The addition of visual representations of content being studied was helpful.

TABLE 4.4

ESL Standards for Pre-K–12 Students

Goals	Standards
To use English to communicate in social settings	• Students will use English to participate in social interactions. • Students will interact in, through, and with spoken and written English for personal expression and enjoyment. • Students will use learning strategies to extend their communicative competence.
To use English to achieve academically in all content areas	• Students will use English to interact in the classroom. • Students will use English to obtain, process, construct, and provide subject matter information in spoken and written form. • Students will use appropriate learning strategies to construct and apply academic knowledge.
To use English in socially and culturally appropriate ways	• Students will use appropriate language variety, register, and genre according to audience, purpose, and setting. • Students will use nonverbal communication appropriate to audience, purpose, and setting. • Students will use appropriate learning strategies to extend their sociolinguistic and sociocultural competence.

Source: Teachers of English to Speakers of Other Languages. (1997). *ESL standards for pre-K–12 students.* Alexandria, VA: Author. © 1997 Teachers of English to Speakers of Other Languages. Reprinted with permission.

TABLE 4.5

Principles for Teaching Second-Language Learners

Standards	Specific
Facilitate learning through joint productive activity among teacher and students.	Work on a common task (e.g., design of a Web page) and have opportunities to converse about it.
Develop competence in the language and literacy of instruction across the curriculum.	Use every opportunity to enhance language and literacy skills by having conversation about tasks, asking students to plan and explain activities.
Connect teaching and curriculum to students' experiences and skills of home and community.	Use students' prior knowledge and experience when designing tasks or assignments.
Challenge students toward cognitive complexity.	Have high standards and expectations, use assessments that allow you to provide meaningful feedback.
Engage students through dialogue, especially instructional conversation.	Use conversation to foster thinking skills by questioning, asking for explanations and elaborations of ideas.

Source: Standards from Center for Research on Education, Diversity, and Excellence (2002). Retrieved 7/6/2005, from http://www.crede.org/standards/standards_data.html.

Tools such as e-mail and the World Wide Web can help LEP students continue to develop competence in their first language, a skill that is vital to eventual success in their second language (Thomas & Collier, 2001). (See, however, the "Uncommon Sense" box below.) Padrón and Waxman (1996) argue that technology can be used to engage LEP students in the classroom learning environment, because these learners are often disengaged and have generally experienced more failure than success in learning situations.

Uncommon Sense

The Best Way to Learn a Language Is Through Total Immersion—Or Is It?

Total immersion in a language means that a learner is completely immersed in a language. In other words, all communications are conducted in the language. Examples of immersion programs include ones in which one language (e.g., French) is spoken in a school in the morning and a second language (e.g., English) is spoken in the afternoon. The premise behind the belief that the best way to learn a language is through total immersion is that more time spent on a task leads to better learning. However, it is the quality of the exposure to the language and not merely the quantity of exposure that matters (Crawford, 1998). In order to learn a second language, one must be able to understand what is being taught in that language (Krashen, 1996). A variety of instructional methods can help students learn a second language.

Thomas and Collier (2001) conducted a national study of long-term academic achievement by language minority students. The strongest predictor of achievement in the second language was the amount of formal schooling in the first language. English language learners (ELLs) who were immersed in mainstream classes because their parents refused bilingual or English as a second language (ESL) instruction showed large decreases in reading and math achievement by grade 5. Some programs are more successful than others. Programs in which 90% of instruction is conducted in the child's native language in grades P-2, followed by a gradual transition to English by the fifth grade, are effective. Another effective type of program is 50–50 developmental bilingual programs. In these kinds of programs, children experience bilingual immersion in two languages. Thomas and Collier identified these two kinds of programs as the only ones that helped students reach the 50th percentile in both languages in all subjects. The fewest dropouts also came from these programs.

Differences in Socioeconomic Status and Their Role in Learning

Will the three children described below succeed in school?

Gary is a 7-year-old boy who lives with his siblings and parents in a three-bedrooom house in a low-income neighborhood. He has seven brothers and four sisters. One of his older brothers is in prison. He is often late for school. His clothing is very thin, as though it has been washed too much. His hair sticks out all over. Gary looks forward to lunch at school. His father is an alcoholic, and his mother does not work outside the home. His parents do not allow him to borrow books from the public library because they are afraid that he will damage the books and they will have to pay for them. They rarely spend time with him and never ask him about his schoolwork.

Darren is also 7 years old and is in the same class as Gary. He lives in the same neighborhood. His parents are also poor. He has three siblings, one sister and two brothers. His father works at a store. His mother does not work outside the home. Darren's clothes look warm and comfortable and fit him well. He is always on time for school and usually brings his own lunch. He loves to read and regularly goes to the public library to get books. His mother helps him with his homework every evening, and his father always reads a story to him before he goes to bed.

Miguel is 7 years old and lives in an upper-middle-class suburb. His school is brand new and has Internet access in every classroom. He already reads at the third-grade level. His father and mother both work in professional jobs, and they buy many books and educational toys for him. When he comes home, one of his parents helps him with his homework. His parents are always eager to find out what he learned in school.

A variety of family factors can put children at risk for developmental and learning problems. Poverty is one of the most serious of these. The official poverty rate in 2003 was 12.5%, up from 12.1% in 2002 (U.S. Census Bureau). In 2003, 35.9 million people were living in poverty, 1.3 million more than in 2002. The number of children living in poverty also rose between 2002 and 2003, increasing from 12.1 million to 12.9 million, or almost a full percentage point. A three-year average of poverty levels from 2001 to 2003 indicates that 10.2% of Caucasians, 24% of African Americans, 11% of Asians, and 22% of Hispanic people were considered poor.

Family status is also associated with poverty. Of the families identified as poor in 2003, 5.4% were headed by married couples, 28% had a female householder with no husband present, and 13.5% had a male householder with no wife present. Children born into poverty are at greater risk for developmental problems (Hanson & Carta, 1996). Families who are poor are more likely to live in substandard or unsafe housing and in homes with high levels of stress. The child's experiences in a poor home are less likely to provide the support needed for early learning. Problems that contribute to developmental or learning difficulties include poor nuitrition, neglect, parents with substance abuse problems, child abuse, and violence in the home or neighborhood. Children in lower socioeconomic groups are less likely to have parents who are well educated.

Some researchers have studied the question of why some children in poor environments remain resilient (Werner, 1992). Many children do not succumb to the stresses of a deprived environment and sometimes even thrive (Rak & Patterson, 1996). Among the factors that promote resilience are caring and supportive relationships, high expectations, and opportunities for meaningful participation in school activities (Benard, 1993). It is important to keep in mind that some children in all socioeconomic strata may not experience these three protective factors. At-risk students should be identified on the basis of demonstrated problems in school rather than exclusively on the basis of socioeconomic or sociocultural background (Benard, 1993).

The three children described at the beginning of this section differ in terms of the availability of the three protective factors. Darren is poor, which means that some resources are not available to him. However, he has supportive parents who help him with his homework or read to him, and he goes to the local library. Miguel experiences all three of the protective factors. Gary is the child who is most at risk for school failure, because his home does not protect him from the adverse effects of poverty.

How Can I Use This?

What strategies can you use to provide caring and support, high expectations, and opportunities for participating in your classroom?

RIDE

REFLECTION FOR ACTION

The Event

Mr. Quinto, the school principal, has announced that the school is going to abandon the practice of ability grouping for mathematics and reading. The teachers wonder what they are supposed to do instead.

Reflection RIDE

Imagine that you are one of the teachers. How are you going to teach mathematics and reading to students who are used to working in groups of students with similar ability? Students at the different ability levels have different reading materials and work on different mathematics tasks. How are you going to keep all the children interested? How will you cope with parents of the high achievers who may complain that their children are not getting enough attention?

What Theoretical/Conceptual Information Might Assist in Interpreting and Remedying this Situation? Consider the following.

Intelligence

How is ability for mathematics and reading defined? Would it matter to my instructional decisions whether I subscribed to Gardner's theory of intelligence or Sternberg's?

Talent

How is talent developed? What if I tried to provide practice for students? How can I give them enough deliberate practice to enable them to develop expertise?

Within-Class Ability Grouping

Perhaps I can group students with other children in the class who are close to their level of achievement. Is this a good strategy? How will I know when a child should move to a different group?

Information Gathering RIDE

One of the implications of Gardner's theory of multiple intelligences is that competence can be displayed in a variety of ways. You might want to consider how you decided whether each child was a low, average, or high achiever in reading and mathematics. You might then gather more information about each child's range of skills in those areas. You might consult other teachers about how they plan to respond to the principal's request and discuss the benefits and costs of various strategies. There is an extensive literature on within-class ability grouping that you might consult to find out whether it is a successful teaching strategy and identify potential pitfalls in using it.

Decision Making RIDE

You need to decide whether all the children in your class are going to use the same materials in reading and mathematics. If they are not, you will need to decide how to organize reading and mathematics instruction when students are using different materials and how to allocate your time for instruction in these subject areas. You may need to provide accommodations for some students and modify materials, assignments, or assessments. If you decide to use within-class ability grouping, you will need to decide how to divide your time among the various groups and what kinds of tasks each group will work on. You may choose to use computers to give students additional practice.

Evaluation RIDE

You will need to gather assessment information at regular intervals to determine whether students are making progress. You will also need to evaluate when a child should be moved from one group to another if you choose to use within-class ability grouping.

Here is a second event for consideration and reflection. In doing so, carry out the processes of reflection, information gathering, decision making, and evaluation.

Further Practice: Your Turn

The Event

Jorge is in the seventh grade. Mr. Jackson asks students in his language arts class to write a letter attempting to persuade the school board to allow them to have their own newspaper. After half an hour, he glances over Jorge's shoulder and notices that he has written very little. He reads Jorge's work quickly and notices that the ideas are quite disconnected.

RIDE   Why is Jorge's production so poor? Why are his ideas so disconnected? How can you help him?

SUMMARY

- **How was intelligence understood initially, and how have views of intelligence changed over time?**

  Spearman believed that intelligence could best be understood as consisting of one broad, or general factor, which he labeled g (for general), and a variety of individual, or specific, factors. Thurstone proposed a different approach that involved seven "primary mental abilities": verbal comprehension, word fluency, number facility, spatial visualization, associate memory, perceptual speed, and reasoning. Thurstone's approach to mental abilities painted a richer picture of the individual. Cattell contributed the concepts of *fluid* and *crystallized intelligence*. Modern theories of intelligence include Sternberg's triarchic theory of intelligence, Gardner's theory of multiple intelligences, and the concept of metacognition, attributable primarily to Flavell. Sternberg's triarchic theory has three main facets: analytical, creative, and practical. Sternberg has also developed a theory of successful intelligence. Gardner's theory of multiple intelligences reasons that abilities are more separate and isolated than other theories suggest. Gardner proposed that there are at least eight intelligences, including logical-mathematical, linguistic, spatial, musical, bodily-kinesthetic, naturalistic, interpersonal, and intrapersonal.

- **How is intelligence measured, and how is it related to achievement?**

  Intelligence tests can be administered either to individuals or to groups. Two of the most popular individually administered standardized IQ tests are the WISC-III and the K-ABC. More recent theories, such as Sternberg's and Gardner's, require new ways to measure intelligence. Sternberg has developed the Sternberg Triarchic Abilities Test, and Shearer's *Multiple Intelligences Developmental Assessment Scales* is probably the most fully developed assessment based on Gardner's theory. Measured intelligence is positively correlated with school achievement. This may be because the kinds of skills sampled on an intelligence test are the skills that are valued in schooling. Binet's original task in 1905 was to develop tests that would distinguish between those who were likely to do well in school and those who were not. It is therefore not surprising that measures of achievement and intelligence are related.

- **How does talent develop?**

  Talent is the capacity to produce exceptional performance. The desire to increase one's talent leads one to engage in many hours of deliberate practice. Deliberate practice is activity whose main purpose is to attain and improve one's skills. Students who engage in deliberate practice spent time refining their skills; engaging in self-reflection; receiving coaching, instruction, and feedback; and, finally, observing skilled and experienced performers. Deliberate practice alters a student's cognitive capacities and bodily functions (e.g., muscle patterns). The development of talent proceeds from a period of play in a domain, deliberate practice, and, finally, the decision to commit to the domain and engage in many hours of deliberate practice.

- **What happens when students are grouped by ability?**
  Arguments against between-group ability grouping point to its negative effects on low achievers. Students in low-ability tracks have difficulty moving into higher tracks and tend to receive lower quality instruction. Results for high achievers are less clear.

- **In general, how do schools identify children with special needs?**
  Children who are thought to have special needs are initially screened through a prereferral process that results in an intervention within the child's classroom. If the problems persist, a formal evaluation for special education may be conducted. A team made up of school professionals and the child's parents or guardians meets to determine whether the child is eligible for special services. If the child is found to be eligible for services under IDEA, the team has 30 days to write an IEP for him or her.

- **How are learning disabilities and ADHD identified?**
  There is no objective way to determine whether a child has a learning disability. There are, however, signs that may indicate that the child has a problem that should be investigated. For example, low achievement may be a sign of a learning disability, but not all learning problems are due to disabilities. The recent reauthorization of IDEA (2004) states that schools are not required to use a discrepancy between achievement and intellectual ability in identifying learning disabilities. DSM-IV contains guidelines for identifying ADHD; these include the requirement that the behaviors must appear before the age of 7 and continue for at least 6 months. An important aspect of determining whether a disorder exists is that the behavior must be observed over a specified period. A prereferral process such as that described earlier may be the first course of action. When a teacher identifies a child as significantly different from average, further analysis is required.

- **How do differences in socioeconomic status and culture influence students' success in school?**
  A variety of family factors place children at risk for developmental and learning problems. Poverty is one of the most serious of these. Family status is also associated with poverty: 28% of the families that were identified as poor in 2003 were headed by a single female. Children born into poverty are at greater risk for developmental problems and are more likely to live in substandard or unsafe housing and homes with high levels of stress. A child's experiences in a poor home are less likely to provide the support needed for early learning. Problems that contribute to developmental or learning difficulties include poor nuitrition, neglect, parents with substance abuse problems, child abuse, and violence at home and in the neighborhood. Children in lower socioeconomic groups are less likely to have well-educated parents. Many children, however, do not succumb to the stresses of a deprived environment and sometimes even thrive. Among the protective factors that promote resilience are caring and supportive relationships, high expectations, and opportunities for meaningful participation in school activities.

KEY TERMS

attention deficit disorder (ADD), p. 128
attention deficit hyperactivity disorder (ADHD), p. 128
automaticity, p. 108
bias, p. 112
between-class ability grouping, p. 119
crystallized intelligence, p. 107

culture-free tests, p. 113
deliberate practice, p. 116
entity view of intelligence, p. 110
eugenics, p. 106
existential intelligence p. 109
fluid intelligence, p. 107
incremental view of intelligence, p. 110

EXERCISES

1. *Observation of "Abilities" in the Classroom*

   Visit an elementary or secondary school classroom. Your goal is to identify the abilities that are valued by the teacher or are called upon during the course of a class period. You might look for evidence of Sternberg's triarchic theory of intelligence or Gardner's theory of multiple intelligences.

2. *Resources on Special Needs*

   Identify five Web sites that provide helpful information about students with special needs. Indicate why these sites are useful and the criteria you used to select them.

3. *Poverty and Schooling*

   Create a chart with two columns. In the left-hand column, list the ways in which poverty can affect a child's ability to profit from schooling. You should identify whether you are addressing an elementary school-age child or an adolescent. In the right-hand column, list strategies that could be implemented or resources that could be provided by the school that might limit the impact of the factors listed in the left-hand column.

4. *A Lesson Plan for Deliberate Practice*

   Create a lesson plan for a fifth-grade class in which you provide opportunities for deliberate practice. How will you support learners with LEP or individuals with special needs?

Some of the lessons students try to learn and some of the skills they seek to develop come across as mysteriously coded messages. High school students hear their Spanish teacher voice sophisticated dialogue, and they encounter equally confusing type in the textbook. The same might be said for elementary grade students who watch their teacher write beautiful cursive script on the chalkboard, or middle school students who try to decipher geometry problems. For many lessons and skills, students understand that they will need effort and persistence to progress from bewildered novices to proficient experts. Such effort invariably requires the support of students' motivation.

In preparing today's lesson, Mr. Larsen cannot forget yesterday's. He introduced a difficult concept to his students. Some students showed confidence, tried hard, and regulated their own learning. They set a goal, harnessed their effort, and enthusiastically engaged in the lesson to learn it and learn it well. Other students, however, did not. These students turned anxious, pessimistic, and acted helpless. In the face of the challenging lesson, Mr. Larsen watched as these students' motivation wilted before his eyes. They adopted a negative mood, gave up quickly, and pessimistically muttered, "I'm just not good at this."

As you reflect on Mr. Larsen's teaching situation, consider your own motivational reaction to the coded message on this page. It is a challenging task, one that cannot be deciphered without an investment of your attention, effort, and persistence. How did you react?

To reveal the teacher's secret, solve the coded message.

The Message

Jcokalokcx kr l wtbtbgnkrkob sct
ubltxkxi lxh rzkuu hbabucwjbxo.

The Code

Coded letter   Actual letter

Coded letter		Actual letter
l	=	a
b	=	e
o	=	t
r	=	s
c	=	o
t	=	r
a	=	v
x	=	h

Instructions

The teacher's secret is encrypted as a coded message in which one letter stands for another. Each time you see the coded letter *l*, for instance, replace it with the actual letter *a*. *lto* therefore translates into the word *art*. You have the codes for only 8 letters.
The remaining letters, like the message itself, need to be decoded.

Motivation to Learn

5

RIDE Reflection for Action

Mr. Larsen wants to understand why some students are so negative—so anxious, pessimistic, helpless, and goalless. During today's lesson, he wants to see these students display resilient and constructive motivation. What might he do? How can Mr. Larsen motivate his students to try hard?

Guiding Questions

- What is motivation, and which motivational states are crucial for learners?
- When students are hesitant, what can a teacher do to promote their confidence?
- How can teachers foster in students a constructive, mastery-oriented reaction to failure?
- How can teachers implement a goal-setting program?
- What can a teacher do to transform an anxiety-ridden classroom climate into a culture of eager learners?
- How can teachers help students become self-regulated learners?
- How can teachers support motivation in diverse learners and students with special needs?

CHAPTER OVERVIEW

This chapter defines motivation and explains how it works—where it comes from, how it changes, what it predicts, and why educators care so deeply about increasing it. This chapter explains the ways of thinking that underlie Mr. Larsen's motivated students—strong self-efficacy, a mastery motivational orientation, an optimistic attributional style, hope, goal setting, achievement goals, and effective self-regulation. The chapter also explains the ways of thinking that underlie Mr. Larsen's unmotivated students—self-doubt, a helpless motivational orientation, a pessimistic attributional style, a lack of goals, and little capacity for self-regulation. It further explains how these motivational states apply across grade levels, to diverse learners, and to students with special needs. The twofold theme throughout the chapter is, first, that motivation reflects the quality of students' thinking and, second, teachers can support motivation by helping students think in constructive ways.

Motivation

Self-Efficacy
- Why Self-Efficacy Is Important
- Sources of Self-Efficacy
- Mastery Modeling Programs
- Technology, Socioeconomic Status, and Self-Efficacy
- Self-Efficacy in Students with Learning Disabilities

Mastery Beliefs
- Reactions to Failure
- Learned Helplessness
- Attributions
- Preventing Helplessness, Fostering Mastery
- Hope

Goals
- Difficult, Specific Goals Increase Performance
- Implementation Intentions
- Feedback
- Goal-Setting Programs
- Possible Selves
- Achievement Goals
- Grade-Level Effects on Motivation

Self-Regulation
- Self-Regulatory Processes: Forethought through Reflection
- Promoting Self-Regulation
- Coregulation
- Self-Regulation for Students in Different Grades and for Learners with Special Needs

Motivation

motivation Any force that energizes and directs behavior.

Motivation is the study of the forces that energize and direct behavior. *Energy* means that behavior is strong, intense, and full of effort. *Direction* means that behavior is focused on accomplishing a particular goal or outcome. The study of motivation is, therefore, the study of all the forces that create and sustain students' effortful, goal-directed action.

Table 5.1 identifies 10 important motivational forces. In this chapter, we discuss the 5 found on the left-hand side of the table. Each motivational force—self-efficacy, mastery beliefs, attributions, goals, and self-regulation—represents a way of *thinking* associated with energized and goal-directed action. The motivational states on the right-hand side of the table involve a *need, feeling,* or *striving* that also underlies energized and goal-directed activity. Each of those—psychological needs, intrinsic motivation, extrinsic motivation, positive emotions, and achievement strivings—will be discussed in Chapter 6.

Chapter Reference
Chapter 6 discusses the motivational states on the right side of Table 5.1.

One psychological experience that does not make the list of crucial motivational forces is self-esteem. Self-esteem is a positive evaluation of one's personal characteristics (Rosenberg, 1965). In the "Uncommon Sense" box on page 141, we explain why self-esteem is not a crucial motivation and why motivation researchers do not recommend *boosting self-esteem* as an intervention strategy (Baumeister et al., 2003). In making this point, we hope to take some attention away from self-esteem and direct it instead toward the 10 crucial motivational resources introduced in Table 5.1.

Chapter Reference
Chapter 3 discusses self-esteem further.

TABLE 5.1

Ten Motivational States That Energize and Direct Students' Behavior

Appendix
Understanding Students Motivations

Chapters 5 and 6 help teachers understand the theoretical basis of where motivation comes from and offer instructional strategies to promote students' motivation and engagement (*PRAXIS*™, I. C. 1, *INTASC*, Principle 2).

Five cognitive motivational states discussed in Chapter 5	Five needs, emotions, and strivings discussed in Chapter 6
Self-efficacy An *I can do this* judgment that one can cope effectively with the situation at hand.	*Psychological needs* Conditions within the student that, when nurtured, promote positive emotion, psychological growth, and well-being.
Mastery beliefs A hardy, resistant portrayal of the self during failure that leads to an increase, rather than to a decrease, of effort.	*Intrinsic motivation* Inherent desire to engage one's interests and to exercise and develop one's skills.
Attributions Explanations of why success/failure outcomes occurred.	*Extrinsic motivation* Environmentally created reason (e.g., reward) to engage in a behavior.
Goals What the student is trying to accomplish.	*Positive emotions* Positive feelings, such as curiosity and interest, that attract learners' attention toward learning activities.
Self-regulation Capacity to monitor and evaluate how well one's goal-pursuing efforts are going.	*Achievement strivings* Eagerness to exert high effort when facing a standard of excellence.

To understand students' motivation, consider three points. First, different types of motivation exist. In many teachers' minds, motivation is a unitary construct. Its key feature is its level, or amount. From this point of view, a teacher's focus becomes, How can I foster more (or higher) motivation in my students? But there is more to motivation than how much. Watch as a student studies, paints, or reads a book, and you will see that motivation also

What Does This Mean to Me?
Do different types of motivation explain why you want to become a teacher?

Uncommon Sense

Boosting Self-Esteem Is the Best Way to Motivate Students—Or Is It?

Boosting self-esteem is a popular motivational strategy, one that attempts to motivate students by helping them see the value in themselves. Praise them. Compliment them. Give them some affirmation that they are loved and are important—a sticker, a trophy, or a slogan. Once students feel good about who they are, all sorts of good things will start to happen.

The *self-esteem movement* was essentially launched in 1986, when the state of California decided to boost the self-esteem of all state residents. In doing so, it intended to reduce rates of school failure, unwanted pregnancy, welfare dependence, crime, and drug addiction. Advocates argued that "self-esteem has profound consequences for every aspect of our existence" (Branden, 1984, p. 5) and that virtually all psychological problems could be traced to low self-esteem. Following this lead, several self-esteem-boosting programs were initiated in schools. Empirical research showed that these programs failed to make students' lives better (Baumeister et al., 2003).

Students with high self-esteem do function well in school, whereas students with low self-esteem generally do not (Bowles, 1999; Davies & Brember, 1999). The reason these two variables are correlated, however, is because doing well in school boosts self-esteem (Byrne, 1996; Harter, 1993; Helmke & van Aken, 1995; Shaalvik & Hagtvet, 1990). As Chapter 3 explains, achievement causes self-esteem, but the reverse is not necessarily true. Increases in self-esteem do *not* cause corresponding increases in school performance. In fact, the typical finding is that an intervention to boost self-esteem is likely to *decrease* students' subsequent performances (Forsyth & Kerr, 1999). This is so because self-esteem intervention programs interfere with the natural effort-to-achievement relationship by encouraging students to feel good about themselves regardless of their effort, improvement, or achievement.

What Kids Say and Do

A Class Valedictorian Looks Back at the Quality of Her Motivation

Looking back on my high school career, I can see how extrinsically motivated I was. It has come to haunt me. I was seen as the smart girl in class. One of my best friends turned to competition to see who could be the highest achiever. She would focus solely on beating me in a test score or receiving the class award at the end of the year. I hated the competition, but I did not want to lose. I wanted to be the valedictorian and win all the awards. I was given worksheets upon worksheets for the majority of my classes. I spent hours at night doing tedious work. The whole school system should have taken the pressure off all the awards. It motivated me to do better in my classes but for all the wrong reasons.

varies in its type or quality. As you watch students study, paint, and read, ask, *Why* does this student work so hard? The answer reveals the student's type of motivation.

Understanding types of motivation is important because some types produce better academic functioning than do other types. For instance, as we will see in Chapter 6, intrinsic motivation is different from extrinsic motivation, and as we will see in this chapter, a goal to learn is different from a goal to perform (Ames & Archer, 1988; Ryan & Deci, 2000a). Students who invest their efforts out of intrinsic motivation and with the goal to learn generally show a higher quality of learning than do those who study, paint, and read out of extrinsic motivation and with the goal to perform, for instance. This being the case, teachers need to focus not only on promoting high motivation but also on fostering productive types of motivation. A page from the diary of a class valedictorian helps makes this point in the "What Kids Say and Do" box above.

Third, to flourish, motivation needs supportive conditions. Each day, students walk into classrooms, relationships, and learning activities. The learning environment into which they walk can nurture and support their motivational strivings or it can neglect and frustrate these strivings. When students are surrounded by classroom environments that support and nurture their needs, wants, strivings, and constructive ways of thinking, they show greater engagement and learning.

> **How Can I Use This?**
> How will you motivate students? Which motivational strategies do you currently have high confidence in?

Self-Efficacy

> **self-efficacy** One's judgment of how well he or she will cope with a situation, given the skills one possesses and the circumstances one faces.

Self-efficacy is a person's judgment of how well (or how poorly) he or she will cope with a situation, given the skills one possesses and the circumstances one faces (Bandura, 1986, 1993, 1997). When they possess high efficacy in a given domain—when they feel they have sufficient skills to manage the existing situational circumstances—students believe they *have what it takes* to do well. Students with low self-efficacy doubt their ability to cope, because they believe that the task before them will overwhelm their capacity to cope with it. What students say when they feel inefficacious (overwhelmed) can be seen in the "What Kids Say and Do" box below.

> **Chapter Reference**
> Teacher efficacy was introduced in Chapter 1 and is discussed in detail in Chapter 9.

High self-efficacy is not high ability. A singer might have wondrous vocal talent but may still sing poorly during a recital if he or she is nervous or if the accompanying pianist plays at the wrong tempo. Ability helps performance, but the capacity to cope with the task and circumstances at hand are additionally important. This is so, because *all* performance situations require coping. Whether taking a test, playing a sport, or trying to converse in a foreign language, all performance situations are at least somewhat stressful, unpredictable, and apt to have things go wrong (Bandura, 1997). It is during those times when things go wrong that the importance of self-efficacy becomes apparent. When time runs short, equipment suddenly fails, or the situation takes a surprising turn for the worse, self-efficacy matters most and foreshadows the extent to which the student will be able to turn things around for the better.

What Kids Say and Do

Self-Efficacy and Avoidance

In class, what makes you anxious or afraid? How do you cope? How do you handle the situation?

Having to read aloud . . . in front of the whole class. It's scary. I feel nervous. My stomach hurts. I always, always hope [the teacher] won't ask me to. (fourth-grade student)

Doing hard stuff. It makes me feel dumb. I don't want to do it, so I get someone else to do it for me. (tenth-grade student)

Why Self-Efficacy Is Important

Self-efficacy predicts the quality of students' functioning. Students who doubt their capacity to cope with situational surprises and setbacks experience anxiety (Bandura, 1988), confusion (Wood & Bandura, 1989), negative thinking (Bandura, 1983), bodily tension, and aversive physiological arousal (Bandura et al., 1985). Even highly knowledgeable, highly skilled students may be stricken with self-doubt during a class presentation if they are surprised by a question or unexpectedly asked to make the first presentation of the day. When doubt, anxiety, confusion, negative thinking, and bodily upset dominate their thinking, students become vulnerable to performing dismally. Self-doubt, erratic thinking, and negative emotion are the warning signs that one's performance is on the verge of collapsing and spiraling out of control—the performer panics and "loses it." High self-efficacy is important because it keeps these debilitating thoughts and feelings quiet so that a performer can focus on the task at hand.

As shown in Figure 5.1, self-efficacy beliefs forecast three principal educational outcomes (Bandura, 1986a, 1997): (a) the particular activities and environments students approach versus avoid; (b) how much effort and persistence they put forth; and (c) the quality of their thinking and feeling during the performance.

Selection of Activities. Students continually make choices about what activities to pursue and which environments to spend time in. In general, students seek out, approach, and want to spend time in activities that they feel they can cope with or handle. They avoid activities that they fear might overwhelm their coping capacities (Bandura, 1977a, 1989). Simply put, low efficacy breeds high avoidance. If students believe that taking a math class, learning a foreign language, or socializing at the school dance will overwhelm their coping capabilities, they will actively and intentionally avoid engaging in it. Avoidance guards the self against being in a situation that can potentially overwhelm, stress, confuse, frustrate, or embarrass the self. When students shun an activity out of self-doubt, however, they unwittingly participate in a process that arrests or retards their development (Holahan & Holahan, 1987). Not asking questions in class, not enrolling in an art or math class, or not accepting a social invitation can exert profound, detrimental, and long-term effects on development as avoidance decisions progressively restrict one's range of activities and settings (Bandura, 1982, 1986a; Betz & Hackett, 1986; Hackett, 1985).

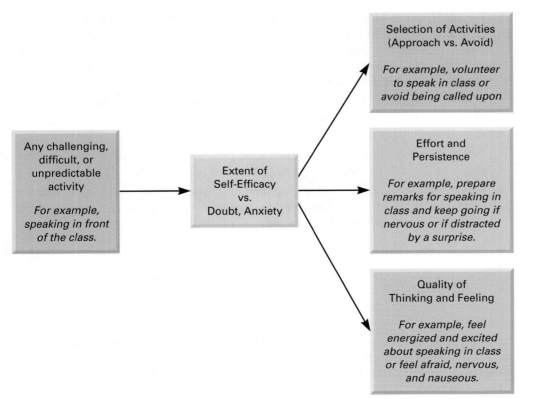

Figure 5.1. Consequences of Strong versus Fragile Self-Efficacy Beliefs

Appendix
Self-Efficacy and Learning
Confidence that they can cope effectively with the task at hand (high self-efficacy) is a key source of motivation that helps students approach the task, learn from it, and acquire skills (*PRAXIS*™, I. C. 1, *INTASC*, Principle 2).

Effort and Persistence. As students engage in a learning activity, their self-efficacy beliefs influence how much effort they exert and how long they continue to exert that effort (Bandura, 1989). Learning is always fraught with difficulties, obstacles, and setbacks, at least to a degree. Difficulties, such as unfamiliar words to pronounce, and setbacks, such as wrong answers, leave students vulnerable to doubt. Such self-doubt leads students to slacken their efforts, settle prematurely on mediocre solutions, or give up altogether (Bandura & Cervone, 1983; Weinberg, Gould, & Jackson, 1979). In contrast, self-efficacy is a motivational resource that students can fall back on during difficult problems to offset doubt and preserve their effort and persistence. The reason self-efficacy plays such a pivotal role in facilitating effort and persistence is not that it silences self-doubt. This is an expected, normal emotional reaction to failure. Instead, self-efficacy leads to *quick recovery* of self-assurance following such setbacks (Bandura, 1986a). It is the resilience of self-efficacy in the face of confusion, failure, and rejection that provides the motivational support students need to maintain their effort and persistence (Bandura, 1989).

Quality of Thinking and Feeling. Students who believe strongly in their efficacy remain remarkably clear-headed in their thinking during stressful episodes, whereas students with doubts think erratically (Bandura & Wood, 1989; Wood & Bandura, 1989). A strong sense of efficacy allows the student to remain *task* focused, asking, "What is the question that I am being asked? What is the feedback telling me? Do I need to alter my strategy?" Self-doubt, on the other hand, distracts decision makers away from the task and toward thinking about deficiencies of the self, declaring, "I'm doing poorly. The audience is going to laugh at me. I'm such a loser." Dwelling on personal deficiencies opens the door to pessimism, anxiety, and depression (Bandura, 1983, 1986a; Bandura, Reese, & Adams, 1982; Bandura et al., 1985). Strong self-efficacy beliefs help keep doubt, anxiety, and distress at bay. Self-efficacy researchers go so far as to say that the root cause of anxiety is low self-efficacy (Bandura, 1983, 1988). If this is true, any sign of anxiety means that self-efficacy is slipping.

Sources of Self-Efficacy

Self-efficacy beliefs are not arbitrary. They have roots. This is an important and practical point because it means that you, as a teacher, can help students build and strengthen their self-efficacy beliefs. As students face challenging and difficult circumstances, they rely on four sources of information to appraise their sense of self-efficacy (Bandura, 1986a; Bandura et al., 1982; Kazdin, 1979; Schunk, 1989, 1991; Taylor et al., 1985):

1. *Personal behavior history.* Memories of what happened in the past when the student tried to carry out the same behavior or cope with the same situation accumulate into a personal behavior history. For example, the last time a child read aloud in class, how effectively was he or she able to do so? Was he or she able to read at a quick pace? To pronounce difficult words?

2. *Vicarious experience.* As they attempt to cope with difficult and potentially overwhelming situations, students closely observe peers and models. If peers can do it, that assures the student that he or she too can do it.

3. *Verbal persuasion.* Pep talks help assure students that they can indeed cope with the situation at hand. The teacher or a classmate may tell the student, "You can do it."

4. *Physiological states.* Before and during their performance, students monitor what their body is telling them in terms of a racing heart versus a calm and steady one. A calm heart communicates a physiological message of confidence.

The most important sources of efficacy are the first two—personal behavior history and vicarious experience (Schunk, 1989). Teachers are well advised to devote most of their attention to these first two sources of self-efficacy information, as seen in the next section.

What Does This Mean to Me?
How strong and resilient is your current self-efficacy for teaching? Which sources of self-efficacy have contributed to your current view?

Mastery Modeling Programs

Empowerment involves possessing the knowledge, skills, and beliefs that students need to exert control over their learning. Empowered students silence their doubts and fears; they persist in the face of adversity; and they think clearly about the what they are doing and how they can do it well. A formal program to empower students with resilient self-efficacy is a

empowerment   Perceiving that one possesses the knowledge, skills, and beliefs needed to silence doubt and exert control over one's learning.

Taking It to the Classroom

How to Implement a Mastery Modeling Program

1. The teacher identifies the component skills that underlie effective coping in a particular situation. Through a questionnaire or interview, the teacher measures students' efficacy expectation on each component skill.

   Example: In a middle school computer course, the teacher first identifies three to five crucial skills that students need if they are to interact competently with the computer (e.g., use drop-down menus, edit a document, scan and import a photograph). The teacher asks students to write down their confidence versus doubt ratings on each of these component skills.

2. The teacher models competent functioning on each component skill, emphasizing those skill areas that students anticipate will be particularly fearsome.

3. Students emulate each modeled skill. The teacher provides corrective feedback as needed.

4. Students integrate these individual skills into one overall performance. During this simulated performance, the teacher introduces only mild obstacles as students enact the full range of their acquired skills in low-stress circumstances.

   Example: After practice and feedback, the teacher asks students to use their new skills, such as first scanning and importing a photograph, then using a drop-down menu to help write a paragraph about a favorite holiday.

5. Students practice in the context of cooperative learning groups. One student performs the activity while peers watch, provide support, and offer encouragement, tips, and reminders about how the performer might cope better. Students take turns until each has performed at least twice.

   Example: Students take turns revising their paragraphs. As they do so, their peers help by showing each other how to use each skill differently and more efficiently.

6. Students perform individually in a realistic situation, one that features authentic obstacles. The teacher provides further modeling and corrective feedback as needed.

   Example: Students are asked to create a two- to three-page presentation on a favorite topic, complete with photographs or illustrations imported from a scanner.

7. Throughout the mentoring, the teacher models confidence, especially in the face of stress.

   Example: As students learn how to control their anxiety, they will feel less vulnerable to being overwhelmed by the computer and thus begin to engage in (rather than avoid) the once feared activity.

mastery modeling program. In such a program, an expert works with a group of novices to show them how to cope effectively with an otherwise fearsome situation. Often, the expert is a teacher or a coach, and the novices are groups of students who are being exposed to lessons and skills that they are not yet familiar with, such as learning about computers, conversing in a second language, or developing talent in music or sport. The "Taking It to the Classroom Box" above outlines the seven steps in a mastery modeling program (based on Ozer & Bandura, 1990):

The mastery modeling program is a formal procedure designed to utilize all four sources of self-efficacy to advance anxious novices toward becoming confident experts. By having students perform each skill and receive corrective feedback (steps 3, 4, and 6), students build efficacy through an accomplished personal behavior history. By watching the expert perform (step 2) and by watching peers perform (step 5), students build efficacy through vicarious experience. By hearing peers' encouragement and tips (step 5), students build efficacy through verbal persuasion. By observing and imitating the teacher's ways of managing performance-debilitating arousal (step 7), students build efficacy through physiological states.

 Could a mastery-modeling program empower Mr. Larsen's anxious students?

In step 5 of a mastery model-
ing program, peers provide
support, encouragement, tips,
and reminders while the
teacher provides corrective
feedback as needed. (Media
Bakery)

Technology, Socioeconomic Status, and Self-Efficacy

Electronic technologies are often new, complex, and apt to change. The key variable that
determines whether students perceive educational technologies as welcomed opportunities
or as fearsome threats is self-efficacy. For instance, when exposed to Internet-based instruction, students with high self-efficacy learn and benefit from the experience, whereas those
with low self-efficacy feel intimidated and learn little (Debowski, Wood, & Bandura, 2001).
Engaging in technology can feel like risk-taking behavior. Thus, before students will
approach, manage, and benefit from educational technology, they first need a firm sense of
efficacy toward that technology (Krueger & Dickson, 1994). The "Taking It to the
Classroom" box on page 147 identifies several ways teachers can help students build a firm
sense of self-efficacy.

   Socioeconomic differences among students leads to inequity of access to electronic
technology. Because technology is often expensive, students from high socioeconomic
families and school districts have greater access to it than do students from low socioeconomic families and school districts. This access disadvantage means that low-income students are less able to use vast amounts of information found in world-class libraries and
available via interactive multimedia instruction. It also threatens to reduce opportunities
for low-income students to cultivate technology-based literacy, skills, and interests.
Technology-based learning is, therefore, limited by at least two key factors: access to technology and the self-efficacy needed to take advantage of its opportunities. Schools and
teachers can play an important role in helping all students—low-income students in particular—gain access to technology and build the sense of efficacy needed to take advantage
of what it has to offer.

Self-Efficacy in Students with Learning Disabilities

Among students with learning disabilities, an interesting self-efficacy phenomenon sometimes occurs, called *calibration* (Klassen, 2002). **Calibration** involves, first, observing what
one's true capabilities are, given recent performances and, second, adjusting one's self-
efficacy beliefs in accordance with that recent personal behavior history. Students with learning disabilities sometimes overestimate their skills. In doing so, they exaggerate and inflate
their self-efficacy beliefs.

   High self-efficacy beliefs are motivational assets, but students with learning disabilities
are often unable to translate their high confidence into effective coping. On writing assignments, for instance, they tend to focus excessively on lower order processes, such as spelling
and grammar, while ignoring higher order demands, such as organizing ideas or writing to
an audience (Wong, Wong, & Blenkinsop, 1989). Competent functioning requires not only
efficacy but also an understanding of task demands.

> **What Does This Mean to Me?**
> Could increased self-efficacy allow females to achieve as much or more than males in domains such as math, science, and technology?

---

calibration An ongoing corrective
process in which the person adjusts
his or her sense of confidence with
a task to reflect most accurately
the quality of his or her recent
performances at that task.

Taking It to the Classroom

Do You Know Jack? Reversing Students' Anxieties

Jack is anxious, very anxious. Jack is not always anxious; he is anxious only in your class. He finds the material particularly difficult, and he feels chronically overwhelmed and confused. Class is just too stressful, so Jack looks for any excuse he can to avoid volunteering or participating. What practical and immediate approaches can you take to assist Jack?

- Talk to Jack and try to isolate what he finds to be the central source of his anxiety.
- Model for Jack what competent functioning in your class looks like and have Jack imitate your competent performance.
- Have one of Jack's able peers model what competent functioning looks like and have Jack imitate his classmate's competent performance.
- Before Jack performs, remind him of a time in the past in which he performed a similar behavior competently.
- Break the coursework into steps and make sure Jack can competently carry out step 1 before going to step 2.
- Form cooperative groups and have all group members offer tips, suggestions, and feedback to each other as they work on the lesson. Emphasize skill development over reproducing right answers.
- Help Jack devise some strategies to regulate his negative thoughts, emotions, and arousal better.

When facing very high self-efficacy beliefs in learners with special needs, it makes little sense to lower their sense of efficacy (Pajares, 1996). Rather, the unique challenge in this situation is to promote students' task analysis. After all, it is surprisingly difficult to answer accurately the question, How sure are you that you can write a good descriptive paragraph? (Graham, Schwartz, & MacArthur, 1993). To answer this question, the would-be writer needs to assess the demands of the assignment and mentally rummage through all four sources of self-efficacy related to writing paragraphs—personal behavioral history, vicarious experience, verbal persuasion, and physiological arousal. From this point of view, teachers can embrace the high efficacy of their students with learning disabilities but focus on students' accurate task analysis, asking, How long do you estimate this writing assignment will take? How many drafts and revisions will be required? What does it take to grab the attention of a reader?

Mastery Beliefs

During most educational endeavors, an outcome is at stake, such as a grade or the respect of one's peers. Before they begin, students forecast how controllable the sought-after outcome is likely to be. For controllable outcomes, students foresee a close relationship between their behavior and the outcome. For example, the student believes if he or she takes good notes and studies for hours, then a positive outcome, such as making an A, will happen. For uncontrollable outcomes, students foresee little or no relationship between their behaviors and outcomes. Good and bad outcomes happen, but not in ways that the student can influence or control. They think, "I'll take the test and see what happens; hopefully, Mr. Jones will give me a break." Students' beliefs as to how much control they have over the outcomes they seek are called *mastery beliefs* (Peterson, Maier, & Seligman, 1993).

Mastery beliefs are different from self-efficacy beliefs. As shown in Figure 5.2, efficacy beliefs explain students' motivation to initiate action or to try, whereas mastery beliefs explain students' motivation to gain control over outcomes. To see the distinction, imagine the thoughts of a student working on a math assignment. Efficacy beliefs concern the question of whether she can generate the needed coping behavior. She wonders, "Can I do this? Will I be able to remember the algebra formulas? If I get stuck, will I be able to get myself unstuck?" Efficacy beliefs help students get started, generate effort, and approach the task. Even students with high self-efficacy, however, can become passive and demoralized when

mastery belief Extent of one's perceived control over a success/failure outcome.

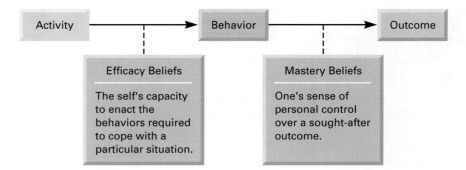

Figure 5.2. Distinction between Efficacy Beliefs and Mastery Beliefs

outcomes are beyond their control. Mastery beliefs concern the question of how much control students have over how the assignment turns out. The student wonders, "What do I need to do to make an A? Will I succeed or fail? Is my grade up to me, or does my grade depend on how difficult the assignment is or how leniently the teacher grades?" Mastery beliefs help students succeed rather than fail.

Reactions to Failure

Many school-related outcomes center on success versus failure, acceptance versus rejection, or winning versus losing. Students with a strong sense of mastery over success, acceptance, and winning respond to an apparent lack of control by remaining task focused and determined to achieve mastery over the outcome, despite the difficulties and setbacks (Diener & Dweck, 1978, 1980). They adjust their behavior and strategies to regain control over the outcome. The opposite of mastery beliefs is helpless beliefs. Students who feel helpless to prevent failure, rejection, and losing respond to an apparent lack of control by giving up and withdrawing, acting as though the outcome were beyond their control (Dweck, 1975; Dweck & Repucci, 1973). Rather than adjusting their behaviors and strategies, they accept the failure (because it is uncontrollable).

When working with easy problems, most students perform well and stay task focused. When outcomes become harder to control, however, the motivational significance of mastery versus helplessness becomes clear. Mastery-oriented students are energized by setbacks or feedback that tells them they are not doing well. Given such feedback, they strive to improve their problem-solving strategies and try even harder than before they received the failure feedback (Dweck, 1999; Mikulincer, 1994). Helpless-oriented students fall apart in the face of setbacks, because they first question and then outright condemn their ability as they feel their control over the outcome slipping farther and farther away. In sum, in hard-to-control situations, mastery-oriented children and adolescents have a hardy sense of self and focus on how to remedy failure (via effort or strategy); helpless-oriented children and adolescents have a fragile sense of self and focus on the punishing aspects of failing (Diener & Dweck, 1978).

The reason mastery-oriented and failure-oriented performers react so differently to failure emanates from their different interpretations of what failure means (Dweck, 1999). Mastery-oriented students do not see failure as an indictment of the self. Instead, they say things like, "The harder it gets, the harder I need to try" and "I love a challenge." For these students, failure feedback is information. Failure tells them that they need more effort, more resources, more enthusiasm, and a new-and-improved strategy. Helpless-oriented individuals, however, view failure as an indictment of the self. They see failure as a sign of personal inadequacy. Helpless-oriented students denigrate their abilities and even their self-worth (Diener & Dweck, 1978). They say things such as, "I'm no good at things like this" and "I guess I'm not very smart." Their problem-solving strategies collapse into simply making wild guesses or picking answers at random. Their emotions quickly turn negative, and they cope via distraction, such as by acting silly (Diener & Dweck, 1978). The self-denigration, negative mood, and immature strategies signal the presence of helplessness, but the telltale sign of helplessness is simply how *quickly* and how *emphatically* the performer gives up (Dweck, 1999).

 Might Mr. Larsen's students be anxious and pessimistic because of their helpless reactions to failure?

What Does This Mean to Me?
Recall a recent failure. How did you react—with increased effort and an improved strategy, or with decreased effort and demoralized affect?

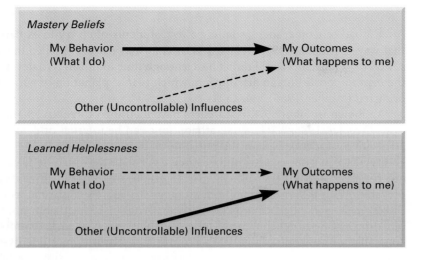

Figure 5.3. Relationship Between Behavior and Outcomes for Students with Mastery Beliefs and for Students with Learned Helplessness

Learned Helplessness

Helplessness is learned (Mikulincer, 1994; Peterson et al. 1993). Through personal experience, students learn the strength of the relationship between their behavior and their outcomes, as shown in Figure 5.3. Imagine a high school student in a biology class who is trying to decide whether to invest effort in the day's lesson. Imagine also the three earlier lessons in which this student invested a good deal of energy to make a good grade by taking notes, asking questions, reading the textbook, and studying late into the night. These efforts comprise *my behavior* in the figure. Over time and through experience, students learn how strong and how predictable the arrow is between *my behavior* and *my outcomes*. If the student comes to believe that there is little to no relationship between how hard she works and the grade she receives, she will begin to feel helpless, because her behavior does not cause her outcomes.

Learned helplessness is the psychological state that results when a student expects that school-related outcomes are beyond his or her control (Mikulincer, 1994; Peterson et al., 1993; Seligman, 1975). Learned helplessness occurs if experience teaches the student that the arrow from *my behavior* to *my outcomes* is weak to nonexistent, whereas the arrow from *other influences* to *my outcomes* is strong and determinate. When learned helplessness occurs, students turn markedly passive and display the three deficits listed in Table 5.2 (Alloy & Seligman, 1979).

learned helplessness The psychological state that results when a student expects that school-related outcomes are beyond his or her personal control.

TABLE 5.2

Motivational Deficits: Three Tell-Tale Signs of Learned Helplessness

Type of deficit	Problem area	Classroom manifestation
Motivation	Unwilling to try	Students say, "Why try?" and "What's the point?"
Learning	Pessimistic learning set	Once students learn that their behavior has little influence over their outcomes, they have a very difficult time relearning which behaviors can and do actually affect their future outcomes.
Emotion	Depressed emotionality	In the face of failure, students show passive, maladaptive, energy-depleting emotions, such as apathy and depression, instead of active, adaptive, energy-mobilizing emotions, such as frustration, anger, and assertiveness.

Attributions

After a bad outcome, such as failing a test, students often try to explain why it turned out that way (Gendolla, 1997; Weiner, 1985). They may reason, "I failed the test because I didn't study" or "I failed because I didn't have enough time to finish." Whatever explanation follows the *because* constitutes an **attribution,** which is an explanation of why a particular outcome occurred (Weiner, 1986).

attribution An explanation of why an outcome occurred.

As shown in Figure 5.4, researchers have identified three key characteristics of attributions (Weiner, 1986, 2004). First, attributions can be internal or external. With an internal attribution, students explain the outcome as caused by forces in the self, such as effort or ability; with an external attribution, students explain the outcome as caused by forces in the environment, such as test difficulty or a noisy room. Second, attributions can be stable or unstable. With a stable attribution, students explain the outcome as caused by enduring forces, such as intelligence or personality; with an unstable attribution, students explain the outcome as caused by ephemeral forces, such as mood or luck. Third, attributions can be controllable or uncontrollable. With a controllable attribution, students explain the outcome as caused by forces under their direct influence, such as effort or strategy; with an uncontrollable attribution, students explain the outcome as caused by forces beyond their control, such as luck or difficult circumstances.

All attributions can be understood within this three-dimensional causal space: internal versus external (locus); stable versus unstable (stability); and controllable versus uncontrollable (controllability). For instance, the attribution of *intelligence* (e.g., I failed because I'm dumb) is internal, stable, and uncontrollable. The attribution of *luck* (e.g., I failed because I

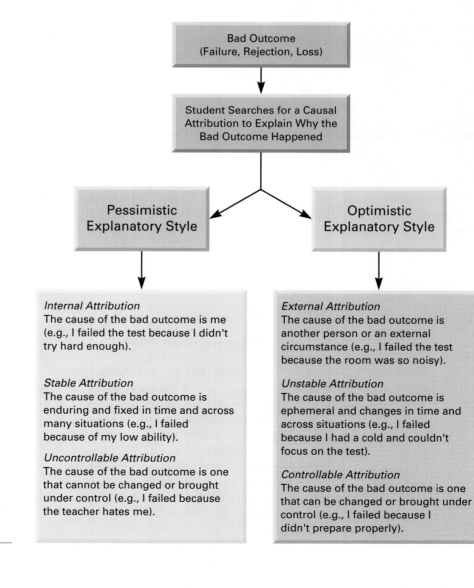

Figure 5.4. Three Attributional Dimensions Underlying the Pessimistic and Optimistic Explanatory Styles

guessed all the wrong answers) is external, unstable, and uncontrollable. The same three-dimensional classification system can be applied to any attribution (effort, strategy, task difficulty, ability, etc.). The reason it is worth a teacher's effort to see students' attributions in this three-dimensional space is because each dimension leads students to formulate a different expectancy regarding their future success. If failure is attributed to a stable influence (e.g., low ability, unfair teacher), students believe that the same outcome will recur in the future. If a failure is attributed to an unstable influence (e.g., low effort, poor strategy), students believe that a different outcome is likely to occur the next time. These forecasts about the likelihood of future successes and failures are the foundation of mastery versus helplessness beliefs. Helpless-oriented thinkers fail and make stable, uncontrollable attributions that lead them to expect a future of chronic failure. They say, "Why try?" Mastery-oriented thinkers fail and make unstable, controllable attributions that lead them to generate the motivation they need to marshal the effort, strategy, preparation, and mentoring they need to remedy the failure.

Explanatory Style. Bad events happen to everyone, but only sometimes do bad events ripen into helplessness. **Explanatory style** is a relatively enduring characteristic that reflects the way students explain why bad events happen to them (Peterson & Barrett, 1987; Peterson & Seligman, 1984). Students generally have a tendency to prefer certain kinds of attributions, and the pattern they habitually make characterizes their explanatory style as either optimistic or pessimistic. An **optimistic explanatory style** is the tendency to explain bad events with attributions that are unstable and controllable, such as, "I lost the contest because I didn't try hard enough." A **pessimistic explanatory style** is the tendency to explain bad events with attributions that are stable and uncontrollable, such as, "I lost the contest because I have low ability." An attribution of low ability is pessimistic because it implies that failure is chronic (stable), and there is little that one can do about it (uncontrollable).

Explanatory style predicts students' behavior in the face of failure. When students with a pessimistic style face educational failures, such as disappointing grades, they typically respond with a passive, fatalistic coping style that leads to decreased effort and even poorer grades (Peterson & Barrett, 1987). If the cause of one's setback is both stable and uncontrollable, it makes sense to withdraw effort and essentially give up—because the poor outcome lies outside the student's control. Students with an optimistic explanatory style, however, see things differently. They see poor outcomes as being under their control and governed by their willful intent. To the extent that they feel that they can change the underlying cause of the poor outcome (i.e., effort is unstable and controllable), it makes sense to act constructively—increase effort, change strategy, prepare in a different way, or gain access to better mentoring and instruction.

Preventing Helplessness, Fostering Mastery

Learned helplessness is both preventable (Altmaier & Happ, 1985; Hirt & Genshaft, 1981; Jones, Nation, & Massad, 1977) and reversible (Miller & Norman, 1981; Orbach & Hadas, 1982). To prevent or reverse helplessness, teachers need to understand its two causes: an unresponsive environment and a pessimistic explanatory style (Peterson et al., 1993). The identification of underlying causes of helplessness suggests two ways to prevent or reverse helplessness: Change the environment's responsiveness; change the student's pessimistic explanatory style.

Changing an Unresponsive Environment into a Responsive One. Sometimes students find themselves in an unresponsive classroom or school, perhaps because of discrimination, favoritism, or a bias of some sort. If teachers and schools wish to cultivate mastery beliefs in their students, they need to make sure that the environments they provide are responsive to students' initiatives and potentially controllable. That said, in most cases, students simply do not know which behaviors actually influence the outcomes they seek (Skinner, Wellborn, & Connell, 1990). Often, students do not really understand what it takes to do well in school, to make good grades, and to have friends. A teacher who shows students the reliable connections between what to do and what subsequently happens helps them build a mastery

explanatory style A personality-like characteristic that reflects the habitual way that students explain why bad events happen to them.

optimistic explanatory style The habitual tendency to explain bad events with attributions that are unstable and controllable.

pessimistic explanatory style The habitual tendency to explain bad events with attributions that are stable and uncontrollable.

motivational orientation (Altmaier & Happ, 1985; Hirt & Genshaft, 1981; Jones et al., 1977). For instance, teachers can hold a classroom discussion to communicate what it takes to do well on the day's assignment or test. Too often, students remain unaware of the keys to success.

Changing a Pessimistic Explanatory Style into an Optimistic One. Students who embrace optimistic explanatory styles for the bad events that come their way are largely immunized against failure's demoralizing effects (Seligman, 1991). Such an immunization process occurs when teachers give students a small dose of failure that is quickly followed by training and coaching to identify the reliable connections between behaviors and outcomes (Klein & Seligman, 1976). A teacher might show students a difficult problem and, after they struggle in vain for a while, reveal the secrets of how to gain control over it. Students say, "Ah, it was solvable after all. I'll figure out the next problem." The logic of giving students an early dose of failure is that the immunization can foster personal control beliefs that are strong enough to prevent the onset of learned helplessness before it has a chance to occur (where there's a will, there's a way).

It is difficult to immunize a student against the demoralizing forces of failure once he or she already embraces a pessimistic explanatory style. For students with an entrenched pessimistic style, attributional retraining is necessary. *Attributional retraining* is essentially teaching students a new way to explain the bad events that happen to them. The teacher can, for instance, attempt to expand the range of possible attributions students use to explain their academic failures (Wilson & Linville, 1982). A student might say, "I failed because I can't read as fast as everyone else; I'm just not a good reader." Given such pessimism, the teacher might offer alternative, and equally valid, attributions to rival and compete against the pessimistic attribution, such as an ineffective strategy, insufficient effort, or a lack of experience in the domain. In attributional retraining, the teacher does not deny or challenge the student's attribution, which might very well be true. Instead, the teacher dilutes the potency of the pessimism by introducing alternative (and valid) explanations. It is important that the teacher's rival attributions be unstable and controllable. To the extent that teachers can help students embrace unstable and controllable attributions for their setbacks, they help students change a pessimistic and maladaptive explanatory style into a more optimistic and adaptive one.

Hope

Like your own reaction to the coded message in the opening vignette, students' motivation to undertake academic challenges can go either way. Under some conditions, students are filled with hope and confidence and act with efficacy and mastery. Under other conditions, students are filled with pessimism and doubt and act with anxiety and helplessness. The study of hope captures much of the essence of this motivational dilemma.

Hope is a motivational wish for a positive outcome that one expects to be able to attain (Snyder, Rand, & Sigmon, 2002; Snyder et al., 1991). When a student says, "I hope to make an A" or "I hope to make the team," he or she expresses both coping confidence (self-efficacy) and optimism about the outcome (mastery beliefs). In other words, hope has two essential ingredients: high self-efficacy and high mastery beliefs. Hope is important because the more hope students feel, the greater is their persistence (Snyder, Shorey, et al., 2002) and performance (Curry et al., 1997). Together, strong efficacy and strong mastery beliefs combine to give students the self-confidence and optimism they need to undertake academic and social challenges with healthy motivation.

Hope is highest when the student sees multiple pathways to a sought-after goal (Snyder et al., 1998). A student who wants to make an A on a homework assignment, for instance, might see the following three paths to an A:

- Collaboration: Work on the assignment with a classmate.
- Computer: Use Internet resources for research.
- Help-seeking: Ask a parent for assistance.

The more viable routes the student can perceive to bring the positive outcome to fruition, the more hope that student will feel. Multiple pathways are important because environmental obstacles inevitably occur to close off one or more of these pathways. A collaboration partner might not be home, one's brother might monopolize the computer, or a

hope   A motivational wish for an outcome that one expects to be fully capable of obtaining.

helping parent might be called away to work. If the student has only one path to a goal, any obstacle that closes off that pathway kills hope—that is, the situation turns hopeless.

Multiple pathways to a goal sustain mastery motivation. Hope also, however, needs high self-efficacy (Snyder et al., 1998). For the student who wants to make an A on her homework, self-efficacy beliefs are important because she will need to cope effectively with the obstacles and setbacks that inevitably arise (I'm not going to let this obstacle stop me). Hope is strong when students know they have access to many routes to success and when they have the coping skills they need to capitalize on those available routes to success. Both mastery and efficacy levels must be reasonably high before a student will experience and maintain hope, because mastery beliefs keep learned helplessness at bay, and self-efficacy beliefs keep doubt and anxiety at bay.

To keep helplessness and anxiety from eroding students' hope, teachers can do two things. First, they can help students generate multiple pathways toward their goals. A student taking a foreign language gains hope when his teacher says that he can try to learn the language through his own efforts but, if he gets stuck, he can also go to the language lab to hear audiotapes or to the classroom computer to use software to practice. Knowing that he can fall back on the language lab and the computer preserves a student's hope for success. Still, the student needs to have a sense of self-efficacy to implement these alternative pathways. So the second thing the teacher can do to build hope is to walk students through a mastery modeling program, as described earlier, to show them how to cope with the language, the language lab, and the computer software program. Equipped with the one-two punch of high efficacy and high mastery, students harbor hope.

Goals

A **goal** is whatever a student is striving to accomplish (Locke, 1996). When a student tries to learn 10 new vocabulary words, read a book by Friday, or achieve a 4.0 GPA, he or she is engaged in goal-directed behavior. Goals generate motivation by focusing students' attention on the *discrepancy* between their present level of accomplishment and their ideal level of accomplishment. As shown in Figure 5.5, the magnitude of the arrow between the present state and the ideal state represents the size of the discrepancy. A discrepancy between *what is* and *what can be* is a fundamental motivational principle (Locke & Latham, 1990, 2002). Its presence creates a desire to act, a desire to change what presently is into what ideally could be.

Figure 5.5 includes four ways of saying the same thing: The student envisions a future outcome that is better than the present state, such as a C average, poor penmanship, not a member of the team, or zero pages read in a book. Therefore, when students ask themselves, What can I do to increase my motivation?, the answer from a goal-setting perspective is very practical: Create an ideal state in your mind. When educators ask, What can I do to motivate my students?, the answer is equally practical: Offer them an ideal state to shoot for.

Generally speaking, students with goals outperform students without goals (Locke, 1996; Locke & Latham, 1990), and the same student performs better with a goal than without a goal. So students who set goals for themselves and students who accept the goals others set for them outperform their no-goal peers.

goal   What the student is trying to accomplish.

Difficult, Specific Goals Increase Performance

Goals enhance performance, but the type of goal one sets determines the extent to which that goal translates into performance gains. The two key characteristics of a goal are how difficult and how specific it is (Locke et al., 1981; Earley, Wojnaroski, & Prest, 1987). Goals need to be difficult, because difficult goals energize the performer more than do easy goals. Goals

Present State	Ideal State
(What is)	(What could be)
C average	B average
Poor penmanship	Good penmanship
Not a member of the team	Member of the team
No pages read in a book	All 200 pages read in a book

Figure 5.5. Four Illustrations of Discrepancies Between What Is (Present State) and What Could Be (Ideal State)

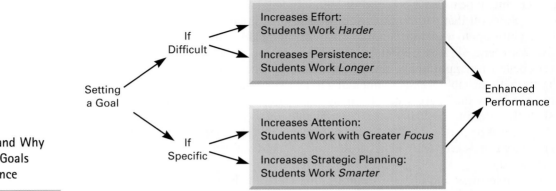

Figure 5.6. How and Why Difficult, Specific Goals Enhance Performance

need to be specific, because specific goals direct students' attention toward the desired course of action better than do vague goals. Figure 5.6 provides a summary of how and why difficult, specific goals enhance performance.

Goal Difficulty. Goal difficulty refers to how hard a goal is to accomplish. *Do your best* and *pass the test* are easy goals. *Make a 90 on the test* and *improve your score by 10 points* are difficult goals, relatively speaking. As goals increase in difficulty, performance increases in a linear fashion (Locke & Latham, 1990; Mento, Steel, & Karren, 1987; Tubbs, 1986). Essentially, difficult goals enhance performance because they require more effort. Effort arises in proportion to what the goal requires: Having no goal stimulates no effort; an easy goal stimulates little effort; a difficult goal stimulates great effort (Bassett, 1979; Locke, 2002; Locke & Latham, 1984, 1990; Earley et al., 1987; Bandura & Cervone, 1983, 1986). Difficult goals also increase the persistence of that effort, because effort continues until the difficult goal is attained (LaPorte & Nath, 1976; Latham & Locke, 1975).

Goal Specificity. Goal specificity refers to how clearly a goal informs students precisely what they are to do. Telling a performer to *do your best* or *study hard* sound like goals, but each is actually an ambiguous statement that does not make clear precisely what the student is to do. Most of the time, translating a vague goal into a specific one involves restating it in numerical terms, such as *make a 90, study for 1 hour, improve 10 points,* or *read pages 1 to 42.* Such specific goals enhance performance because they direct attention and encourage strategic planning. They direct attention toward the task and away from distracters (Kahneman, 1973; Klein, Whitener, & Ilgen, 1990; Locke et al., 1989; Rothkopf & Billington, 1979). They also encourage strategic thinking, as students wonder, How am I going to get this done? (Latham & Baldes, 1975; Terborg, 1976). With specific goals, students become strategic thinkers.

> **How Can I Use This?**
>
> The next time a classmate says, "I'll do my best," encourage him or her to set a difficult and specific goal.

Implementation Intentions

When students fail to realize their goals, part of the problem can be explained by the type of goal. Was it difficult? Was it specific? But there is another critical part of the goal-setting process—namely, forming an implementation intention (Gollwitzer, 1996, 1999; Gollwitzer & Moskowitz, 1996). An **implementation intention** is a plan to carry out one's goal-directed behavior—deciding *in advance* when, where, and for how long goal-directed action will occur.

It is one thing to set a goal, yet another to actually carry it out and accomplish it. All goals take time, but time has a way of opening the door to distractions. An implementation intention links goal-directed behavior to a situational cue, such as a specific time or place, so that goal-directed behavior is carried out automatically, without conscious deliberation or decision making. For example, a student with a goal *to write a 5-page paper* might form an implementation intention that "during study hall on Monday, Tuesday, and Wednesday, I'll write and revise my paper." Once the when-where-how long cue has been chosen and an intention to implement one's goal-directed action has been formed, the mere presence of the anticipated situational cue automatically initiates goal-directed action (Monday's third-period study hall rolls around). If no such intention is formed, third-period study hall comes and goes without the goal-directed action ever taking place.

implementation intention A plan to carry out goal-directed behavior.

Implementation intentions facilitate goal-directed behavior in two ways: getting started and finishing up (Gollwitzer, 1996; Orbell & Sheeran, 2000). Getting started is a problem when students let good opportunities to pursue their goals pass them by, as in "I had all day to read the chapter, but I just never sat down and actually read it." Finishing up is a problem when students suffer interruptions and distractions, as in "I started to read the chapter, but then the phone rang and I never did get back to it."

Feedback

One additional variable is crucial in making goal setting effective—feedback (Erez, 1977). Goal setting enhances performance only in the presence of timely feedback. **Feedback,** or knowledge of results, allows students to keep track of their progress toward a goal (Bandura & Cervone, 1983; Becker, 1978; Erez, 1977; Strang, Lawrence, & Fowler, 1978; Tubbs, 1986).

feedback Knowledge of results.

Without feedback, goal-directed performance is emotionally unimportant. A student-athlete can set a goal of *run a mile in 6 minutes*. But if she never has access to a stopwatch, she has no way to find out whether she is making progress. Feedback is information. It allows performers to judge their current level of performance: "Am I below goal level? At goal level? Above goal level?"

The combination of goals with feedback produces an emotionally meaningful mixture: Goal attainment breeds satisfaction, whereas goal failure breeds dissatisfaction (Bandura, 1991; Matsui, Okada, & Inoshita, 1983). Positive feedback—the news that one is performing at or above goal level—causes satisfaction and positive emotion. Negative feedback—the news that one is performing below goal level—causes dissatisfaction and negative emotion. Either way, effort increases because negative feedback gets students to work harder, and positive feedback gets students to set higher goals (Bandura & Cervone, 1983, 1986).

Goal-Setting Programs

As a teacher, you will often set goals for your students. In general, the point of a goal-setting program is to raise students' performances—to generate higher test scores, to improve attendance, or to have students complete their homework more often. At one level, goal setting is simple. One person sets a goal for another. At another level, however, the overall goal-setting process is more complicated. When a teacher assigns a goal, several conditions must be met before the assigned goal can be expected to improve students' performances. The "Taking It to the Classroom" box below outlines the steps involved in a goal-setting program.

Taking It to the Classroom

Steps in a Goal-Setting Program

Steps in a Goal-Setting Program	What a Teacher Might Say to Implement the Step
1. Specify the objective to be accomplished.	This week in biology, we are going to learn all the parts of a cell.
2. Define goal difficulty.	Try to learn all eight parts of the cell—not *some* parts, but all eight.
3. Define goal specificity.	Be able to locate, spell, and pronounce each part.
4. Specify the time span until performance will be assessed.	Next Monday, we have a test to see how many parts you know.
5. Check on goal acceptance.	Does this sound like a reasonable goal for the week? Any suggestions?
6. Discuss goal attainment strategies.	There are several ways you can learn about the parts of a cell. The textbook provides good pictures, you can make your own drawings, or you can work with a partner and quiz each other.
7. Create implementation intentions.	You have two days to learn the parts of a cell. By the end of Thursday's class, know four parts; by the end of Friday's class, know all eight.
8. Provide performance feedback	At 1:30, I'll hand out a practice quiz that you can use to test your progress.

The first four steps in a goal-setting program involve setting the goal. All goal-setting programs begin with the question, What do you want your students to accomplish? From there, the next step is to ensure that the goal is both difficult and specific, given students' abilities, experiences, and access to resources. In addition, the teacher announces when performance will be assessed. The last four steps in the goal-setting processes help students accept the goal and actually carry it out. The goal needs to be transformed from a teacher-assigned goal into a student-internalized goal, one that has a measure of personal commitment associated with it (Erez & Kanfer, 1983; Erez & Zidon, 1984). To enhance goal acceptance, teachers typically need to negotiate with students and gain their participation in the process (Latham, Erez, & Locke, 1988; Latham & Saari, 1979). The next step is to discuss possible plans, strategies, and implementation intentions to advance students from goal setting to goal attainment. The teacher also needs to provide a steady stream of feedback students can use to assess whether they are performing at, above, or below goal level.

Possible Selves

possible self   A student's long-term goal representing what he or she would like to become in the future.

Possible selves represent students' long-term goals or strivings for what they would like to become (Markus & Nurius, 1986; Markus & Ruvolo, 1989). Some possible selves might include, for instance, honor-roll student, high school graduate, successful artist, counselor, or state champion in a particular sport. Two of the most common possible selves embraced by elementary and middle school students include good student and popular (Anderman, Anderman, & Griesinger, 1999).

An example of how possible selves originate and how they generate daily goals appears in Figure 5.7. Possible selves are almost always social in origin, as students observe successful others (Markus & Nurius, 1986). If the role model is attractive, such as the visiting police officer in Figure 5.7, the student might consider emulating the role model. The individual

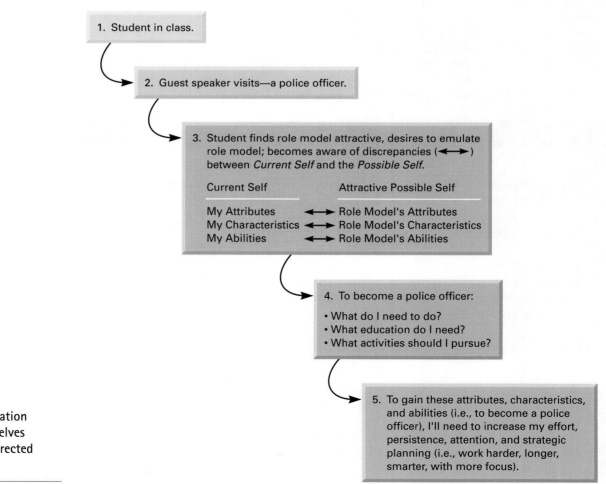

Figure 5.7. Illustration of How Possible Selves Stimulate Goal-Directed Behavior

sees the current self as a *present self* and the role model as a possible future *ideal self*. To figure out how to become the desired future self, the student notices and learns about the attributes, characteristics, and abilities that he or she needs but does not yet possess. The student wonders, "If I am going to become my hoped-for possible self, what do I need to do? What education do I need? What activities should I pursue? How should I behave?" (Cantor et al., 1986; Markus & Nurius, 1986; Markus & Wurf, 1987). The answers to these questions generate goals (I will graduate high school; I will get in shape.). Because of the processes identified in Figure 5.6 (effort, persistence, etc.), students accomplish their short-term goals and gradually acquire the long-term goal of possessing the attributes, characteristics, and abilities of the hoped-for (possible) self (Cross & Markus, 1994; Oyserman & Markus, 1990).

Possible selves play an important motivational role in the classroom, especially for adolescents (Oyserman & Markus, 1990). Without a possible self in a particular subject area, the student lacks an important cognitive basis for wanting to acquire knowledge and skill in that subject (Cross & Markus, 1994). A student who can envision a possible self in that subject, however, sees the events, knowledge, and skills featured as personally important (Cross & Markus, 1994; Markus, Cross, & Wurf, 1990). Thus, for a student enrolled in a foreign-language class who wants to realize possible selves, such as world traveler, French speaker, or foreign-language teacher, the desire to take notes, read books, watch foreign films, and participate in class comes easily. The same can be said for a would-be writer taking an English class, a would-be banker taking a math class, or a future teacher taking an educational psychology class. Consistent with this logic, students with classroom-relevant possible selves have higher grade point averages than do students without such possible selves (Anderman et al., 1999).

Possible selves for students in poverty.

Students who live in poverty often lack role models and mentors who embody the importance of school and what it can do for them in their lives. As a consequence, these students often lack a clear understanding of how current school participation can help their future selves. One group of researchers developed and offered middle school students who lived in poverty a School-to-Jobs intervention program to help develop clear and detailed possible selves. During the after-school intervention, early adolescents worked to identify attractive job-related possible selves, completed problem-solving activities in small groups, and interacted with guest speakers from the community. After the 9-week intervention, students were able to articulate academically oriented possible selves; they identified skills they needed and wanted to develop; and their school engagement improved (Oyserman, Terry, & Bybee, 2002). This research shows that students in poverty often enter school without academically oriented possible selves, though school-related experiences can help them create future selves they would very much like to become.

> **What Does This Mean to Me?**
> Does your possible self of teacher contribute to your interest, motivation, and daily goals in this course?

Possible selves are almost always social in origin. This adolescent might consider becoming an artist by observing this practicing artist. (Media Bakery)

Achievement Goals

achievement goal   What the student is trying to accomplish when facing a standard of excellence.

standard of excellence   Any challenge to the student's sense of competence that ends with a success/failure interpretation.

learning goal   The intention to learn, improve, and develop competence.

performance goal   The intention to demonstrate high ability and prove one's competence.

Certain goals are **achievement goals** because they apply specifically to achievement settings. In an achievement setting, performance is measured against a standard of excellence (Heckhausen, 1967). A **standard of excellence** is any challenge to the student's sense of competence that ends with a success/failure, right/wrong, or win/lose outcome, such as a score on a test, an answer to a question, or the outcome of an election or contest. As shown in Table 5.3, when facing a standard of excellence, students typically adopt one of two achievement goals: learning goals or performance goals (Dweck, 1986; Nicholls, 1979, 1984).

Learning goals focus attention on developing competence and mastering the task. For this reason, learning goals are also called *mastery goals* (Nicholls, 1984). Doing well means improving, learning, and making progress. **Performance goals,** on the other hand, focus attention on demonstrating or proving that one has high ability on the task. Doing well means doing better than others. Overall, with learning goals, students strive to increase, develop, or improve their competence; with performance goals, they strive to demonstrate or prove their ability to an audience of others (Ames & Archer, 1988; Dweck, 1986, 1990; Nicholls, 1984; Spence & Helmreich, 1983).

The fundamental determinant of which type of achievement goal students embrace is their understanding of what constitutes competence (Elliot & McGregor, 2001). Students define competence in two different ways as they ask themselves, Am I good at math? One way to assess competence is to judge the extent to which one has reached a certain maximum capacity in terms of knowledge or skills in that domain. A student is competent with a calculator, for instance, if he knows how to use all the available functions. A second way to assess competence is to judge one's performance relative to the performances of peers. In this case, a student is competent with a calculator to the extent that she performs better on the calculator than does her peers.

Students with different achievement goals want to know different things. Students with learning goals want feedback that they can use to learn and improve, whereas students with performance goals want feedback that they can use to judge their ability and sense of superiority (Butler, 2000). Figure 5.8 on the next page shows a sample of one teacher's feedback on a high school student's writing assignment. A student with a learning goal will likely focus on the teacher's comments and double his effort to improve and develop his writing skills, thinking, "If I can improve on my use of the active voice, develop my paragraphs, and use shorter sentences, then I can improve my writing." A student with a performance goal, however, will likely focus on the letter grade. He will be less interested in the written comments and may even submit later papers or a revision of this paper with the same weaknesses. What the student with a performance goal wants is a means to judge his ability—namely, the letter grade.

The distinction between learning and performance goals is important because the adoption of a learning goal is associated with positive and productive ways of thinking and behaving, whereas the adoption of a performance goal is associated with relatively negative and unproductive ways of thinking and behaving (Dweck, 1999; Dweck & Leggett, 1988; Harackiewicz & Elliot, 1993; Spence & Helmreich, 1983). Students who adopt learning goals—saying to themselves, "In this course, I am going to try to learn as much as I can."—cultivate a self-regulated type of learning in which they seek information in order to acquire,

> **What Does This Mean to Me?**
> What does competence in teaching mean to you—learning and improving or being better than your peers?

TABLE 5.3

Aims of Students with Learning versus Performance Goals

Learning (or mastery) goal	Performance goal
• Improve competence.	• Prove competence.
• Make progress.	• Demonstrate high ability.
• Acquire and develop skills.	• Outperform others.
• Gain understanding.	• Succeed with little apparent effort.
• Overcome difficulties through effortful learning.	• Avoid activities in which one expects to do poorly.

Grade: *C*

Teacher's
Written
Comments:

The paper has a number of strengths.
Your topic sentences in each paragraph were quite good —
brief, clear, and foreshadowing the content of the paragraph
to come. Your spelling was also excellent — no spelling errors.

The paper also has a number of weaknesses.
Here are a couple of key points that you might want to use in
thinking about how you might develop your writing skills in
the future. In almost every sentence, you used the passive
voice. By rewriting these sentences into the active voice, your
writing will become livelier. Also, did you notice that your paper
consisted of only two long paragraphs? I found five separate
ideas in your paper, so a series of five shorter paragraphs
might work better. And, many of your sentences are very long —
one is 36 words and another is 45 words. Long sentences
contain multiple ideas and stress the reader's comprehension.
One way to improve your writing would be to break down
these long sentences into shorter ones.

Figure 5.8. A High School Teacher's Feedback on a Student's Essay

develop, and refine their knowledge and skill (Butler, 2000). As summarized in Figure 5.9, students who adopt learning goals display more positive educational outcomes than do students who adopt performance goals, including greater engagement, more positive functioning, higher quality learning, and more adaptive help seeking (Ames & Archer, 1988; Elliot & Dweck, 1988; Meece, Blumenfeld & Hoyle, 1988; Nolen, 1988; Stipek, & Kowalski, 1989).

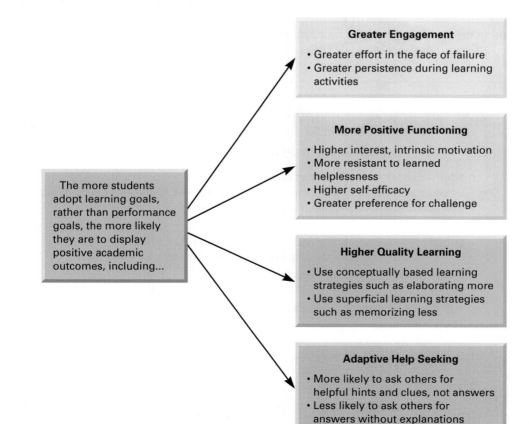

Figure 5.9. Positive Educational Outcomes Associated with the Adoption of Learning Goals

TABLE 5.4

Dimensions of Classroom Climate That Influence Students' Adoption of Learning vs. Performance Achievement Goals

Climate dimension	For teachers who promote learning goals	For teachers who promote performance goals
Success defined as	Improvement, progress	High grades
Value placed on	Effort, learning	Normatively high ability
Reasons for satisfaction	Working hard	Doing better than others
Teacher orientation	How students are learning	How students are performing
View of errors/mistakes	Part of learning	Source of anxiety
Focus of attention	Process of learning	One's performance relative to others' performances
Reasons for effort	Learn something new	Better performance than others'
Evaluation criteria	Progress (grade on effort)	Normative (grade on ability)

Source: Based on Ames, C., & Archer, J. (1988). Achievement goals in the classroom: Students' learning strategies and motivation processes. *Journal of Educational Psychology, 80,* 260–267. Copyright 1988 by the American Psychological Association. Adapted with permission.

Promoting Learning Goals. Teachers influence the type of achievement goals students adopt (Ames & Archer, 1988). For instance, in one study with elementary school children, students were asked to agree or disagree with questions assessing the extent to which their teachers promoted learning goals (The teacher pays attention to whether I am improving) or performance goals (I work hard to get a high grade). The researchers then assessed students' learning strategies, willingness to be challenged, and attitude toward the class. Students with teachers who promoted learning goals used more sophisticated learning strategies, were attracted to challenge rather than threatened by it, and enjoyed the class more (Ames & Archer, 1988). As summarized in Table 5.4, classrooms that promote learning goals have teachers who define success as improvement, value effort, communicate that satisfaction comes from working hard, focus on how students learn, view errors as a natural part of learning, focus on the process of learning, explain the need for high effort while learning something new, and assign grades based on progress or improvement. Additional suggestions on how to promote learning goals appear in the "Taking It to the Classroom" box below.

How Can I Use This?

Use these two checks to determine which type of achievement goals are promoted in the course you are taking: evaluation (improvement vs. "the curve") and recognition (private praise for improvement vs. public praise for beating others).

Taking It to the Classroom

Teacher Discourse to Promote Learning Goals

- *Introduce lessons as learning opportunities.*
  Introduce activities as learning opportunities (This is a chance to develop a new skill), rather than as ability assessments (This is a test of your ability).

- *Focus on understanding.*
  Instead of asking students to produce correct answers, ask students to explain how they arrived at their answers. Encourage students to ask questions when they don't understand.

- *Provide worked-out, step-by-step solutions.*
  Provide correctly worked-out solutions to difficult problems so that students can focus on learning how to solve the problem, rather than on whether their answer is right or their ability is low.

- *Focus on improvement.*
  Give students comments and feedback about their progress, rather than judgments of their ability, such as who scored the highest or performed the best.

- *Support collaborative learning.*
  Encourage students to think of peers as helpful resources for learning, rather than as sources of competition and comparison.

6   6   6   6666666666666666666666 6 6 6

Students Have Achievement Goals of Their Own. Despite the teacher's efforts to establish a learning climate, students harbor goals of their own. Even when teachers enact the classroom strategies outlined in Table 5.4, some students will strive only for high grades and to beat others. Students generally bring performance goals of their own into the classroom when they have the following characteristics: competitiveness; pressure to excel; and parents who communicate conditional approval (Do well and make us proud!) (Church, Elliot, & Gable, 2001; Elliot & McGregor, 2001).

Grade-Level Effects on Student Motivation

Generally speaking, young children come to school with greater interest and self-initiative than do adolescents (Harter, 1981, 1992). By middle school, children often pick up a number of motivational liabilities that can burden them with defensive motivations. For instance, achievement anxiety (test anxiety) is rare in the elementary school grades, moderate and somewhat debilitating in the middle school grades, and common and debilitating in the high school grades (Hill & Wigfield, 1984). Many reasons explain the developmental decline in the quality of students' academic motivation from one grade to the next, but one reason is that the culture of schooling becomes more performance-oriented (Eccles, 1993; Eccles & Midgley, 1989; Eccles, Midgley, & Adler, 1984). With each passing grade, the school culture shifts away from learning for its own sake and toward the products of learning—grades, evaluations, standardized test scores, scholarships, and the like. What this trend means is that primary-school classrooms are more likely to promote learning goals, whereas secondary-school classrooms are more likely to promote performance goals. Hence, high school teachers have a particularly pressing need to create classroom climates that promote learning goals.

Two Types of Performance Goals. Performance goals come in two varieties: approach and avoidance (Elliot, 1999). A performance-approach goal involves striving to show how smart one is and to attain positive judgments from others; a performance-avoidance goal involves striving to not look stupid and to avoid negative judgments from others. To clarify this distinction, Figure 5.10 lists sample items from a questionnaire to assess all three achievement goals. The distinction between types of performance goals is important because students who adopt performance-avoidance goals show the worst educational outcomes (Elliot & Harackiewicz, 1996; Middleton & Midgley, 1997). In a study of sixth-grade math students, those who adopted performance-avoidance goals experienced high anxiety and avoided seeking help from the teacher (to hide their lack of ability).

Multiple Achievement Goals. Adopting a learning goal does not necessarily mean that the student fails to adopt a performance goal; a student can hold multiple achievement goals (Ames & Archer, 1988; Harackiewicz et al., 2000). Hence, students are as likely to have *both* a learning and a performance goal as they are to have *either* a learning or a performance goal (Harackiewicz et al., 1997; Midgley, Anderman, & Hicks, 1995). One reason students often harbor both goals is that teachers (and parents) communicate mixed messages, telling students both to learn and to perform up to externally set standards (Turner et al., 2003).

Mastery Goal
___ An important reason I do my math work is because I like to learn new things.
___ An important reason I do my math work is because I want to get better at it.

Performance-Approach Goal
___ I want to do better than other students in my math class.
___ I would feel successful in math if I did better than most of the other students in the class.

Performance-Avoidance Goal
___ It's very important to me that I don't look stupid in my math class.
___ An important reason I do my math work is so I won't embarrass myself.

Figure 5.10. Questionnaire Items to Assess the Three Types of Achievement Goals

Source: Middleton, M. J., & Midgley, C. (1997). Avoiding the demonstration of lack of ability: An underexplained aspect of goal theory. *Journal of Educational Psychology, 89,* 710–718. Copyright 1997, American Psychological Association. Adapted with permission.

In some ways, students benefit from adopting multiple goals (Harackiewicz et al., 2000). Learning goals promote students' interest, positive affect, and deep understanding of what they are learning, and performance-approach goals promote making good grades and performing well when evaluated (Harackiewicz et al. 1997; Harackiewicz et al., 2000; Turner et al., 2003). No one, however, benefits from adopting a performance-avoidance goal. The dual benefit of harboring both learning and performance-approach goals (high interest, high performance) is limited by two factors: age and ability. Only high school and college students benefit from multiple goals; elementary and middle school students benefit more from learning goals alone (Bouffard, Vezeau, & Bordelau, 1998). For high-ability students— proficient writers, able artists, skilled athletes—multiple goals promote both interest and performance. But when students have less ability—that is, they do not yet have adequate capacities to meet the demands of the activity—learning goals alone are more adaptive (Dweck & Leggett, 1988).

Self-Regulation

All the striving and planning that take place within the goal-setting process occurs over time and need to be monitored and evaluated—that is, regulated. A self-regulated student is one who:

- Sets goals
- Uses effective strategies
- Monitors effectiveness
- Makes adjustments as needed

self-regulation The deliberate planning, monitoring, and evaluating of one's academic work.

Self-regulation is the deliberate planning and monitoring of one's cognitive and emotional processes during the undertaking of academic tasks, such as writing an essay, finishing up homework, or completing a reading assignment in a timely and complete manner (Pintrich & Groot, 1990; Zimmerman, 1989, 2002). As a student engages in an academic task, she sets a goal and makes plans and strategies to accomplish that goal. She also monitors feedback to assess how things are going. All students engage in some such planning and monitoring, but some students do it much better than do others (Winne, 1997). The more students regulate their own learning, the better they do in school. In one study, researchers predicted high school students' academic achievement with 93% accuracy simply on the basis of how extensively students regulated their learning (Zimmerman & Martinez-Pons, 1988).

Self-Regulatory Processes: Forethought Through Reflection

forethought What one thinks about prior to engaging in a task and prior to receiving feedback about the quality of one's performance on that task.

As shown in Figure 5.11, self-regulation is a cyclical process involving forethought, performance, and reflection (Zimmerman, 2000). The quality of students' ongoing forethought, performance, and reflection determines the quality of their self-regulation. **Forethought**

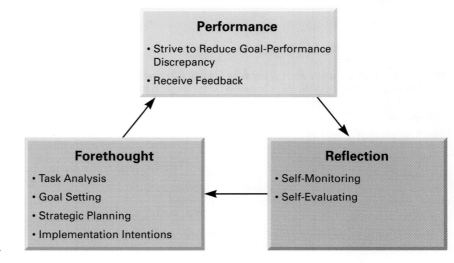

Figure 5.11. Cyclical Phases of Self-Regulation

encompasses task analysis (How difficult? How complex? How interesting?), goal setting, strategic planning, and the formation of implementation intentions. Forethought captures much of the essence of the goal-setting process. Following such forethought, performance begins as the student engages in the task and receives feedback about the quality of his performance. With feedback in hand, **reflection** follows in the form of self-monitoring and self-evaluating. Such reflection allows the student to construct more advanced forethought, and the self-regulation cycle repeats.

Self-monitoring is a self-observational process in which students attempt to keep track of the quality of their ongoing performances (Zimmerman, 2000). The student finds a way to assess performance, such as keeping score, taking notes, or making video or audio recordings of his performances. Such careful, consistent, and objective self-monitoring makes self-evaluation possible. **Self-evaluation** is a judgmental process in which the student compares his or her current performance with the hoped-for goal state (Zimmerman, 2000). A biology student with the goal of making a B on Friday's test, for instance, monitors his study session by testing himself. If he can name 80% of the muscles in the human body, he realizes that he is making progress toward his goal. Together, feedback and self-evaluation open the door to emotional reactions, because students feel good when they make progress and distress when they fail to do so (Carver & Scheier, 1990). Hence, students need to regulate not only their thoughts but their emotions as well.

reflection What one thinks about after engaging in a task and after receiving feedback about the quality of one's performance on that task.

self-monitoring A self-observational process in which students attempt to keep track of the quality of their ongoing performances.

self-evaluation A self-judgmental process in which students compare their current performance with a hoped-for goal state.

Promoting Self-Regulation

Effective self-regulation involves the capacity to carry out the full goal-setting process *on one's own* (Schunk & Zimmerman, 1997; Zimmerman, 1998). It develops gradually through a social learning process, as illustrated in Figure 5.12. On academic tasks that require unfamiliar goals and behaviors, students tend to display novice self-regulatory thinking (e.g., vague goals, no implementation intentions). In such a context, the student is dependent on others (teachers) for guidance. The social learning process begins at an observational level in which the novice observes the verbalizations, strategic planning, self-monitoring, problem-solving, and self-evaluating activities of the expert. It continues with imitation, guidance, corrective feedback, and eventually with the novice's internalization of the expert's way of regulating himself or herself. The novice begins to gain proficiency when he or she internalizes the experts' self-regulatory processes, such as forethought, monitoring, and evaluating.

The effort to become a competent, self-regulated writer illustrates how self-regulation skill is acquired (Zimmerman & Risemberg, 1997). To become proficient, would-be writers need answers to questions such as, If I'm going to become a good writer, what sort of goals do I set, when and where do I write, how do I obtain feedback, and what is good writing, anyway? Through observation of a proficient model, the novice receives preliminary answers to these questions and begins to act on them. Novice writers emulate the expert's style, standards, and even the physical environment in which writing takes place. With internalization, students are increasingly able to ask their mentors more sophisticated questions. They become increasingly able to generate their own planning and goal setting. The once-novice writer begins to set personal goals and engages in self-monitoring and self-evaluating. Eventually, would-be writers reach the point that they no longer need the expert model; they can set their own goals, and they can monitor and evaluate their own work.

Appendix
Capacity for Self-Motivation
Teachers who help students develop self-efficacy, mastery beliefs, hope, goals, and self-regulation capacities help students' future capacity to generate self-motivation (*PRAXIS*™, I. C. 1, 2, and 3, *INTASC*, Principle 5).

Lack of Self-Regulation Skills	**Social Learning Process**	**Acquisition of Self-Regulation Skills**
Unable to regulate one's goals and behaviors in the new domain	1. Observation of expert model 2. Imitation, social guidance, feedback 3. Internalization of goals and standards 4. Self-regulatory process, including self-monitoring, self-evaluating	Now able to regulate one's own goals and behaviors in the domain

Figure 5.12. Summary of the Social Learning Process to Acquire Self-Regulatory Skills

Through observation, imitation, and internalization of a proficient model, the once-novice writer begins to set personal goals and engage in self-monitoring and self-evaluating. (Media Bakery)

Chapter Reference
Chapter 4 discusses talent development.

Progression through the four phases of self-regulation—observation, imitation, self-control, and self-regulation—is only the beginning of expertise. Mastering complex skills such as reading, writing, and music is a time-consuming process that requires not only intensive mentoring but also countless hours of practice (Ericsson, Krampe, & Tesch-Romer, 1993; Ericsson & Charness, 1994). Deliberate practice is crucial, but research on self-regulation shows that students are more likely to develop expertise when they have the benefit of a mentor who models how to plan, monitor, and evaluate the overall goal-setting process.

Coregulation

coregulation A collaborative process in which the teacher and student jointly plan, monitor, and evaluate the academic work of the student.

When students are novices, teachers need to regulate learning activities on their behalf. That is, teachers often need to set the goal, make the plan, communicate a standard of proficiency, articulate the value of the activity, assess the learning, and so on. With observation and imitation, the quality of students' participation changes and becomes more active. In response, the teacher adapts by allowing the student greater autonomy. Eventually, learning becomes a coregulated activity.

During **coregulation,** the quality of the relationship between teacher and student is paramount. Students are more likely to become competent, self-regulated learners when they observe and emulate supportive teachers who provide choices, offer flexible decision making, create opportunities for the student to control task challenge and task difficulty, communicate rich verbal descriptions that answer the student's what, how, why, and when questions, share the responsibility for learning, make time for open-ended activities, and evaluate in nonthreatening and mastery-oriented ways (Perry, 1998; Perry, Nordby, & VandeKamp, 2003; Perry et al., 2002). When students have supportive models to observe, they quickly emulate and internalize the teacher's regulation strategies. Harsh, nonsupportive models take away students' willingness to emulate and internalize what they see. Without supportive models, students lack the critical support they need during the coregulation phase if they are ever to become a sophisticated, self-regulated learner.

Chapter Reference
Coregulation is a sociocultural instructional method. These methods were introduced in Chapter 2 and are elaborated upon in Chapter 10.

Self-Regulation for Students in Different Grades and for Learners with Special Needs

Effective self-regulation needs to be learned. Young, inexperienced students and learners with special needs often need their teachers to provide instruction and external support while learning how to regulate their own behavior.

Grade Level. Schools provide students in the early grades with substantial external support. In the early elementary school grades, teachers provide highly structured learning environments, including the giving of specific directions of what students should do. Little is expected of these students outside the classroom in terms of self-directed learning experiences,

TABLE 5.5
Ten Self-Regulatory Processes Used by Self-Regulated Learners

Self-regulatory process	Example
Goal setting	Make a list of things to accomplish while studying.
Task strategies	Create a mnemonic to remember information.
Imagery	Imagine the consequences of failing to study.
Self-instruction	Rehearse steps in solving a math problem.
Time management	Schedule daily studying and homework time.
Self-monitoring	Keep records of completed assignments.
Self-evaluation	Check work before handing it in to teacher.
Self-consequences	Make TV or telephoning contingent on homework completion.
Environmental structuring	Study in a secluded place.
Help seeking	Use a study partner.

Source: Adapted from Zimmerman, B. J. (1998). Academic studying and the development of personal skill: A self-regulatory perspective. *Educational Psychologist, 33*, 73–86. Adapted with permission.

such as homework or independent study. By the late elementary school grades, teachers begin to assign homework and expect students to show personal responsibility in completing these assignments on their own. By the high school years, teachers expect students to engage in self-initiated studying and to assume full responsibility for completing assignments on their own.

Teachers rarely teach students self-regulatory skills, such as goal setting or self-monitoring (Zimmerman, Bonner, & Kovach, 1996; Zimmerman & Risemberg, 1997). If students are going to develop the self-regulatory skills that each advancing grade expects of them, teachers need to integrate the teaching of self-regulatory skills into their regular classroom lessons (Martinez-Pons, 2002). For a sampling of what skills teachers might teach and model, Table 5.5 provides a range of possible self-regulatory strategies (Zimmerman & Martinez-Pons, 1986, 1988).

Students with Special Needs. Self-regulatory skills predict students' level of academic achievement, and nowhere is this truer than when students face a personal obstacle, such as a learning disability. When an assignment is complex, students with learning disabilities often need added external support. Special education teachers often create self-regulation-boosting prompts that learners with special needs can use to plan, monitor, and evaluate their work. For example, the teacher might provide the student with a set of cue cards in which one card says, *Use exciting, interesting words: Use synonyms for words occurring more than once* (De La Paz, 2001). Notice that such a prompt offers the student a goal (use exciting words), encourages monitoring one's writing (have you used the same word more than once?), and provides an evaluation of what good and bad writing look like. Without these sorts of prompts, students with attention deficit hyperactivity disorder (ADHD) failed to plan, monitor, or evaluate. They also wrote low-quality essays. With the externally provided prompt in hand, the same students generated plans for their writing, monitored what they wrote, evaluated how well they were doing, and wrote higher quality essays.

Effective self-regulation requires planning, anticipating, allocating effort strategically (not impulsively), self-control, self-monitoring, and self-evaluating. Students with ADHD have difficulty with *all* of these skills (Barkley, 1997, 2004). Students with ADHD can therefore be expected to struggle with their academic self-regulation. The types of self-regulatory failures teachers can expect from students with ADHD are a lack of planning and forethought. Thus, students with ADHD have a particularly difficult time with the first crucial phase of effective self-regulation—namely, forethought.

Students with learning disabilities have difficulty with the third phase of effective self-regulation—namely, reflection, as through self-monitoring and self-evaluating their work (Pintrich & Blazevski, 2004). For this reason, students with learning disabilities benefit greatly from external prompts and a teacher's coregulation. With these supports—external prompts and supportive models to learn from—students with learning disabilities are able to better self-regulate themselves during learning activities (Swanson, 2000).

What Does This Mean to Me?
Do you have difficulty completing assignments (papers, readings)? Are you regulated by the self or by deadlines and tests?

RIDE

REFLECTION FOR ACTION

The Event

In preparing today's lesson, Mr. Larsen cannot forget yesterday. He introduced a difficult concept and observed that some students showed confidence, tried hard to learn, and regulated their own learning. Others, however, did not. These students turned anxious, pessimistic, helpless, and quit working at the first sign of failure.

Reflection RIDE

Mr. Larsen wants to understand why some students are so negative—so anxious, pessimistic, helpless, and goalless. During today's lesson, he wants to see these students display resilient and constructive motivation. What might he do? How can Mr. Larsen motivate his students to try hard?

What Theoretical/Conceptual Information Might Assist in Interpreting and Remedying this Situation? Consider the following:

Self-efficacy

Where do confidence and eagerness to try come from? Can he turn students' anxiety into efficacy? Should he take precious class time to implement a mastery modeling program?

Mastery motivation

Perhaps his students act helpless because they do not know how to gain control over the difficult concept. Perhaps they don't know what to do. What if they were presented a series of difficult problems and discussed effective versus ineffective problem-solving strategies?

Goal-setting

Perhaps his students are trying to "do their best" but are not actually doing their best. To help his students work harder, longer, smarter, and with more focus, Mr. Larsen could implement a goal-setting program.

Information Gathering RIDE

What is the problem? How is Mr. Larsen to recognize motivational resources, such as high self-efficacy, mastery motivation, and self-set goals? How is he to recognize motivational problems, such as low self-efficacy, helplessness, and a lack of goals?

- If confident, how do students show their confidence?
- If anxious, how do students express low self-efficacy?
- What do students with mastery-motivational orientations do? How do they explain failure?
- How do students with helpless-motivational orientations behave? How do they explain failure?
- Do Mr. Larsen's students have any goals? Are those goals difficult? Specific?
- Do his students have any plans and implementation intentions to get their work done?

Decision Making `RIDE`

To decide on the best course of action, Mr. Larsen will need at least three kinds of information. First, do students *want* to try? If not, the problem is likely one of low self-efficacy. Students who want to try approach the task, display effort and persistence, and think clearly rather than defensively. Second, are students optimistic and mastery oriented? If not, the problem is likely one of learned helplessness. Students with a mastery-motivational orientation try harder in the face of difficulties and make unstable and controllable attributions. Third, do his students have goals? If not, the problem is likely one of a lack of goals. Students with difficult and specific goals try hard, persist over time, think strategically, and devote their attention to the task at hand.

Evaluation `RIDE`

If Mr. Larsen's information gathering leaves him with the impression that his students approach the lesson with doubt and anxiety, he will need to implement a mastery modeling program to boost his students' self-efficacy. If his information gathering leaves him with the impression that his students are helpless and pessimistic, he will need to discuss how behaviors such as taking notes and forming cooperative learning groups help students gain control over difficult assignments. He might also need to challenge their pessimistic explanatory styles. If his information suggests that his students lack difficult and specific goals, he will need to introduce a formal goal-setting program into the structure of the lesson.

Further Practice: Your Turn

Here is a second event for you to reflect on. In doing so, generate the sequence used above in terms of reflection, information gathering, decision making, and evaluation.

The Event

Looking at the 28 faces in front of her, Mrs. Applesmith can feel the tension in the air. Her students are working on a week-long writing project, and she has noticed that what they care about is making a good grade, doing better than others, and not looking stupid. Few students are actually trying to learn, improve, and develop new skills. Mrs. Applesmith wants to transform this evaluative, competitive, and performance-driven classroom climate into a learning-based culture.

`RIDE` What can Mrs. Applesmith do to create a classroom climate that cultivates learning goals rather than performance goals?

SUMMARY

- **What is motivation, and which motivational states are crucial for learners?**

  Motivation is the study of the forces that energize and direct behavior. Energy means that behavior is strong, intense, and full of effort. Direction means that behavior is focused on accomplishing a particular goal or outcome. The five cognitively based motivational forces emphasized in this chapter were self-efficacy, mastery beliefs, attributions, goals, and self-regulation.

- **When students are hesitant, what can a teacher do to promote their confidence?**

  Self-efficacy represents students' judgments of how well they can cope with a situation, given the skills they possess and the circumstances they face. Self-efficacy beliefs predict students' classroom functioning, especially their approach versus avoidance, extent of effort and persistence, and the quality of their thinking and feeling. Self-efficacy beliefs arise from four sources: personal behavior history, vicarious experience, verbal persuasion, and physiological state. To promote students' self-efficacy beliefs, teachers can implement a seven-step mastery-modeling program.

- **How can teachers foster in students a constructive, mastery-oriented reaction to failure?**

  Mastery beliefs reflect how much personal control students believe they have over the outcomes they seek. When students believe they have little control over their successes and failures, they experience learned helplessness. When they face outcomes that are difficult to control, mastery-oriented students and students with an optimistic explanatory style become energized and increase their effort, whereas helpless-oriented students and students with a pessimistic explanatory style give up trying and self-denigrate their abilities. Hope is a motivational wish for an outcome that one expects to be fully capable of obtaining. For hope to be high, both self-efficacy and mastery beliefs must be reasonably high.

- **How can teachers implement a goal-setting program?**

  A goal is whatever the student is trying to accomplish. Students with goals outperform students without goals. For a goal to enhance performance, it needs to be both difficult and specific, because difficult goals energize students, and specific goals direct their attention toward the desired course of action. In addition, students with goals need implementation intentions and feedback. To help students perform well, teachers can implement an eight-step goal-setting program.

- **What can a teacher do to transform an anxiety-ridden classroom climate into a culture of eager learners?**

  Achievement goals are goals set in achievement settings. Students with learning goals seek to develop their competence: Doing well means improving, learning, and making progress. Students with performance goals seek to prove their competence: Doing well means doing better than others. Learning goals generally lead students toward more productive ways of thinking and behaving. To promote learning goals, teachers can establish classroom climates that define success as improvement, value effort for its own sake, communicate that satisfaction comes from working hard, view errors as a natural part of learning, and assign grades based on progress or improvement.

- **How can teachers help students become self-regulated learners?**

  Self-regulation involves planning, monitoring, and evaluating all aspects of the goal-setting process. With forethought, self-regulated learners analyze the task, create goals, make plans, develop strategies to overcome obstacles, and formulate implementation intentions. With reflection, self-regulated learners monitor feedback, evaluate their progress, reflect on how things are going, and continuously revise their goals, plans, strategies, and intentions as they gain more information about the task and about themselves. Teachers can help students advance from novices to become self-regulating experts through social learning and coregulation processes.

- **How can teachers support motivation in diverse learners and students with special needs?**

  Students with learning disabilities often have inappropriately high self-efficacy beliefs. To appreciate the high demands academic lessons place on them, teachers can help students with learning disabilities make accurate task analyses and hence appropriately calibrate their self-efficacy beliefs with the demanding lessons they face. When students lack possible selves, teachers and school-related programs can help bridge the motivational gap they otherwise see that separates their current schoolwork from their future selves. In terms of self-regulation, students in younger grades and students with special needs show effective self-regulation when teachers provide external prompts and supportive models to emulate.

KEY TERMS

EXERCISES

1. *What Is Motivation?*

   Ask a group of students what motivates them—what helps them put forth effort, persist in the face of difficulty, and seek out challenges? What motives do students spontaneously nominate? Compare the list of motives generated by the group of students you interview with the 10 motives listed in Table 5.1.

2. *Motivating Students*

   Observe a couple of classrooms and pay close attention to those instances in which teachers try to motivate students during learning activities. As you observe, compile a list of the different motivational strategies you observe. Also, note which of these strategies increase students' effort and initiative, and which strategies do not.

3. *Mastery Modeling Program*

   Tutor another person in an activity that is beyond their current skill level (e.g., speak a foreign language; use an unfamiliar computer software program). As you do so, ask about the person's existing anxiety and doubt, then create and implement a mastery-modeling program like the one outlined in the chapter. After the person completes the mastery-modeling program, did you see a substantial increase in that person's confidence and hope, along with an equally substantial drop in his or her anxiety and doubt?

4. *Attributional Retraining*

   Ask a student to explain the underlying cause of a recent failure. Ask why that person thinks he or she failed. As he or she explains what happened and why it happened, listen to the attributions and try to discern the person's characteristic explanatory style. For instance, the person might explain a poor grade by saying that he or she lacks ability in that domain (i.e., a stable-uncontrollable cause). If the attribution seems unnecessarily pessimistic, attempt to expand the possible range of attributions to explain the failure to include an ineffective strategy, insufficient effort, lack of proper training, lack of experience in the domain, and high task difficulty.

5. *Goal-setting Program*

   When a person says he or she would like to perform a particular task better, work with him or her to create a formal goal-setting program that includes the steps outlined in the text. Guide the person through each step (e.g., Is that a difficult goal? Will you need your full capacity to achieve it?). After outlining the full eight-step program, ask whether the other person is confident that the program will yield an enhanced performance.

6. *Quality of Self-regulation*

   Interview a student or a teacher about how he or she completes an important task, such as studying, writing, or teaching. Assess the quality of that person's forethought and reflection by asking about task analysis, self-efficacy, goal-setting, strategic planning, implementation intentions, mood and anxiety, reactions to feedback, self-monitoring, self-evaluation, and general tendency to reflect on what he or she is doing. Once your interview is complete, how would you rate the quality of the person's self-regulation?

Money is an interesting motivator. In the old Jewish fable in the next column, the ruffians first jeered for free. Once the tailor started handing out dimes, the ruffians came to believe they were in it for the money. When the money dried up, so did the motivation to jeer. In schools, the currency is grades. To induce students to read, complete assignments, and participate in class, educators offer grades. Sometimes this leads students to think they are in it for the grade. Without a grade to justify their effort (Will this be on the test?), students' motivation can dry up in the same way that it did for the ruffians.

Money, grades, and other inducements can be powerful motivational forces. Sometimes, however, these external motivators compete with and overwhelm students' own interests and preferences. If students see their inner motivational resources evaporate, they will understandably have a difficult time generating motivation of their own to engage in lessons and activities. This state of affairs leads educators to search for engagement-fostering motivational strategies that do not involve external inducements.

Mrs. Watson is one such teacher. She loves teaching, and she invests herself heavily in the lessons she prepares. However, 20 minutes into the day's lesson, she sees her students staring blankly, participating superficially, and giving only a half-hearted effort.

An Old Jewish Fable

It seems that bigots were eager to rid their town of a Jewish man who had opened a tailor shop on Main Street, so they sent a group of rowdies to harass the tailor. Each day, the ruffians would show up to jeer. The situation was grim, but the tailor was ingenious. One day when the hoodlums arrived, he gave each of them a dime for their efforts. Delighted, they shouted their insults and moved on. The next day they returned to shout, expecting their dime. But the tailor said he could afford only a nickel and proceeded to hand a nickel to each of them. Well, they were a bit disappointed, but a nickel is after all a nickel, so they took it, did their jeering, and left. The next day, they returned once again, and the tailor said he had only a penny for them and held out his hand. Indignant, the young toughs sneered and proclaimed that they would certainly not spend their time jeering at him for a measly penny. So they didn't. And all was well for the tailor.

Engaging Students in Learning

Reflection for Action

When looking back at her students' unengaged faces, what can Mrs. Watson do? Where does disengagement come from, and how can she counteract it? Where does active engagement come from, and what can Mrs. Watson do during her instruction to promote it?

Guiding Questions

- What is engagement, and why is it important?
- What is the difference between intrinsic and extrinsic motivation?
- How can teachers support students' psychological needs?
- How can teachers motivate students during uninteresting activities?
- In what ways can teachers spark students' engagement?
- In what ways can teachers calm students' anxieties and fears?
- How can teachers engage diverse learners and students with special needs?

CHAPTER OVERVIEW

Teachers care deeply about their students' engagement because they know that it predicts how much their students learn and how well they fare in school. In this chapter, we focus on students' engagement during learning activities. In doing so, we define engagement, explain why it is important, explain where it comes from, and identify instructional strategies for promoting it.

One source of engagement is intrinsic motivation, and in this chapter we discuss intrinsic motivation, extrinsic rewards, and how extrinsic rewards affect intrinsic motivation. Psychological needs are another source of engagement, and we present three such needs: autonomy, competence, and relatedness. We also discuss curiosity, interest, and positive affect as ways to spark engagement. Finally, we explain the roots of disengagement by focusing on anxiety, self-worth protection, and self-handicapping, and we explore ways to calm these anxieties, defenses, and fears.

Engagement

Motivation is a private experience. Teachers cannot *see* students' motivation. Instead, what they see during learning activities is how engaged or unengaged their students are. Thus, to understand motivation, it is first necessary to know what is meant by *engagement*.

What Engagement Looks Like

engagement   The extent of a student's behavioral intensity, emotional quality, and personal investment in a learning activity.

Engagement refers to the behavioral intensity, emotional quality, and personal investment in a student's involvement during a learning activity (Connell & Wellborn, 1991; Fredricks, Blumenfeld, & Paris, 2004; Furrer & Skinner, 2003; Wellborn, 1991). To monitor engagement, teachers can keep track of students' behavior, emotion, cognition, and voice, as summarized in Figure 6.1.

behavioral engagement   The extent to which a student displays high attention, strong effort, and enduring persistence on a learning activity.

Behavioral Engagement. When they are highly engaged, students are active and display strong and enduring effort. During activities such as reading, practicing, and extracurricular projects, students express their behavioral engagement through high attention, effort, and persistence (Wellborn, 1991). *Attention* represents the student's concentration and on-

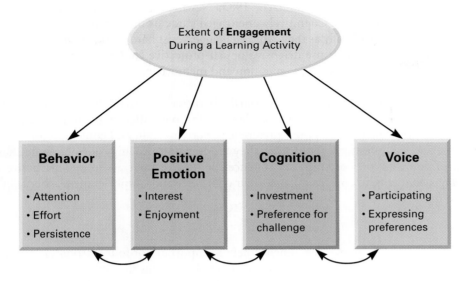

Figure 6.1. Four Interrelated Aspects of Engagement

task focus. With *effort,* students invest a full measure of their capacities in what they are doing, rather than holding back and just going through the motions. With *persistence,* students invest their effort over time, even in the face of difficulties and setbacks. Whether the activity is completing a worksheet or writing a paper, the behaviorally engaged student is on task, working hard, and keeping at the task over time.

Emotional Engagement. Engagement involves more than just paying attention, working hard, and working persistently. It also involves positive emotion (Furrer & Skinner, 2003; Miserandino, 1996). When they are highly engaged, students study and practice hard and long, but they do so within an emotional atmosphere of interest, enthusiasm, enjoyment, and a sense of *wanting to.* In contrast, less engaged students might study or practice hard, but they do so under a cloud of negative emotion—tension, pressure, or stress—an emotional atmosphere of resistance, and a sense of *having to.*

emotional engagement The extent to which a student's task involvement is characterized by positive emotion, such as interest and enjoyment.

Cognitive Engagement. Cognitive engagement expresses itself when students go beyond the basic requirements of the lesson and invest themselves in a committed way (Fredricks et al., 2004). Investing oneself means being strategic and purposive in trying to understand and master the knowledge or skill at hand. Highly cognitively engaged students plan, monitor, and evaluate their activities, using sophisticated learning strategies, such as summarizing

cognitive engagement The extent to which a student mentally goes beyond the basic requirements of a learning activity and invests himself or herself in the learning in a committed way.

When highly engaged, students show not only attention, effort, and persistence but also positive emotion. (Media Bakery)

and elaborating (Corno & Mandinach, 1983; Newmann, Wehlage, & Lamborn, 1992; Pintrich & De Groot, 1990). Cognitively unengaged students might work on the lesson, but they do so rather superficially as they avoid challenge; resist hard work; fail to plan, monitor, and evaluate their activities; use defensive or self-protective coping strategies; and rely on shallow learning strategies, such as repetition and memorizing.

Voice. Highly engaged students show a fourth characteristic—namely, *voice*, an expression of the self during task involvement. Students with voice offer suggestions, recommend activities, express their interests and preferences, participate in and contribute to class discussions, and ask questions about what they are learning (Koenigs, Fiedler, & deCharms, 1977). In doing so, they attempt to influence the flow of the class in a constructive way. Unengaged students, in contrast, silence their own voice and simply let the teacher tell them what to do.

voice A student's expression of self during a learning activity so as to influence constructively how the teacher presents that lesson.

What Does This Mean to Me?
How engaged were you during your last class period? How could you tell?

Why Engagement Is Important. Engagement is important for four reasons. First, it makes learning possible. Learning a second language or developing the skill necessary to play a musical instrument is practically impossible without attention, effort, positive emotion, commitment, and voice. In effect, engagement is a necessary prerequisite for a productive learning experience.

Second, engagement predicts how well students fare in school, especially their achievement and eventual completion of school, as opposed to dropping out (Connell, Spencer, & Aber, 1994). Engagement predicts achievement-related outcomes, such as grades and scores on standardized tests, and it does so across all grade levels (Connell, 1990; Finn & Rock, 1997; Marks, 2000). In one longitudinal study, students' engagement during elementary school predicted their achievement test scores and their decade-later decision to stay in high school or drop out (Alexander, Entwisle, & Dauber, 1993; Alexander, Entwisle, & Horsey, 1997). Thus, engagement contributes to learning the day's lesson, and it contributes to students' longer term school functioning.

Third, engagement is malleable. Therefore, it makes sense to give serious considerations to school-based interventions that aim to enhance it (Finn & Rock, 1997). For instance, engagement increases when teachers (a) relate to students in caring ways (Battistich et al., 1997; Marks, 2000), (b) support students' autonomy or self-determination (Perry, 1998; Reeve, Jang et al., 2004); (c) provide clear structure (Connell, 1990); and (d) offer classroom activities that are interesting, promote a sense of ownership, allow for self-evaluation, and provide opportunities to collaborate with peers (Guthrie & Wigfield, 2000; Newman et al., 1992).

Fourth, engagement gives teachers the moment-to-moment feedback they need to determine how well their efforts to motivate students are working. For instance, when a teacher implements a motivational strategy, he or she can closely monitor the students for changes in their degree of engagement. Engagement is the telltale feedback about students' motivation during the lesson.

How Can I Use This?
The next time you help someone learn something, closely monitor that person's engagement and try to understand why it rises and falls during the lesson.

Teachers can monitor students' engagement to obtain the telltale feedback they need to determine how well their efforts to motivate students are working. (PhotoDisc, Inc./Getty Images)

Two Approaches to Promoting Motivation and Engagement

If engagement is important, how can teachers promote it? To promote engagement, teachers first need to nurture students' underlying motivation. They typically do this in two different ways.

First, adopting a traditional approach, the teacher might try directly to engage students in the learning activity. Several practices illustrate this model:

- The teacher offers an attractive incentive. Students respond by working hard to gain it.
- The teacher sets a goal. Students work hard to perform up to that level.
- The teacher models appropriate behavior. Students emulate what they see.

The logic underlying this frequently used approach is that students' motivation rises and falls in response to what the teacher does or does not do. When teachers offer attractive incentives, set high goals, and model appropriate behavior, students react with heightened motivation and engagement. When teachers do not offer these inducements, students have little to react to, and their motivation and engagement flounder. A graphical depiction of this *teacher directly motivates students* model appears in the upper half of Figure 6.2.

The preceding chapter included several practical illustrations of how teachers can directly motivate their students. For instance, they can set difficult and specific goals (goal setting) or have students observe and imitate an expert model (self-efficacy, self-regulation). Teachers say that this approach has appeal because it puts the teacher in control of students' motivation and engagement. Taking charge and motivating students directly, however, is only one way to motivate students.

Second, a teacher might adopt a **dialectical approach** in which students bring their own motivation into the classroom, and the teacher supports their existing motivation. Several practices illustrate this model:

dialectical approach to motivation The reciprocal, interdependent, and constantly changing relationship between a student's motivation and the classroom conditions that support versus frustrate that motivation.

- Students express an interest. The teacher incorporates that interest into the lesson and offers resources related to it.
- Students suggest a goal. The teacher encourages and supports that goal.
- The teacher listens, responds to questions, and asks students for suggestions.

The logic underlying this approach is that motivation originates within the students themselves. As students express their inner motivation, the teacher reacts. To the extent that teachers can attend to, value, and support students' existing motivation and find ways to build on it, students have the opportunity to become increasingly energized and engaged. A graphical depiction of this *teacher supports students' existing motivation* model appears in the lower half of Figure 6.2.

A unilateral approach: Teacher directly motivates students

Teacher acts → Student reacts → Engagement increases with teacher activity but decreases without it

A dialectical approach: Teacher supports students' existing motivation

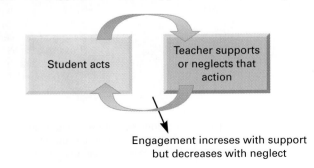

Student acts → Teacher supports or neglects that action

Engagement increases with support but decreases with neglect

Figure 6.2. Two Different Approaches to Motivating Students

Whereas Chapter 5 revolved around the unilateral approach to motivating students, this chapter revolves around the dialectical approach. Within the dialectical approach, three principles of motivation emerge:

Principle 1: Students have motivation of their own. These inner motivational resources explain why students willingly engage in learning activities.

Principle 2: Teachers motivate students when they provide classroom conditions that nurture students' motivation, but they undermine that motivation when they provide conditions that neglect or frustrate students' existing motivation.

Principle 3: How well or how poorly teachers involve and nurture students' motivational resources is reflected in the extent of students' engagement, as shown by the diagonal arrow in the lower right-hand corner of Figure 6.2.

Student–Teacher Dialectic. A dialectical approach to motivation begins with the assumption that the student is inherently active. Inner motivation is the source of that activity (Deci & Ryan, 1985). Different types of inner motivation appear in the left-hand box in Figure 6.3, and their moment-to-moment expression appears as the large upper arrow in the figure. A dialectical approach also assumes that people (teachers, parents, coaches, school administrators, peers), external events (rewards, rules, goals), and the teacher's motivating style (how supportive the teacher is) affect the student and introduce new forms of motivation for the student to internalize. These socialization demands and sources of motivational support or frustration appear as the large lower arrow in Figure 6.3.

Overall, a dialectical approach to motivation emphasizes the reciprocal and interdependent relationship between students' motivation and classroom conditions, such as a teacher's motivating style (Deci & Ryan, 1991; Reeve, Deci, & Ryan, 2004). In dialectic, both the student's motivation and the teacher's motivating style constantly change. The student's motivation changes and grows in response to classroom conditions, as shown by the lower arrow in Figure 6.3. In the same spirit, classroom conditions and the teacher's motivating style change in response to how motivated and engaged students are during the lesson, as shown by the upper arrow in Figure 6.3. The ongoing outcome of the student-classroom

The student engages in classroom activities
as an expression of the self and out of the
desire to interact effectively.

STUDENT MOTIVATION		CLASSROOM CONDITIONS	
Intrinsic Motivation	Interests	**External Events**	**Teacher's Motivating Style**
Internalized Extrinsic Motivation • Identified Regulation	Preferences	• Rewards • Praise, Criticism • Rules	• Autonomy Support • Competence Support • Relatedness Support
	Values	• Expectations • Priorities, Values	• Failure Tolerance
	Curiosity	• Norms	
Psychological Needs • Autonomy • Competence • Relatedness	Positive Affect	• Goals, Challenges • Feedback • Choices	
	Achievement Strivings	• Interesting Activities • Enriched Learning Activities • Grading Practices • Prescriptions ("Do this") • Proscriptions ("Don't do this")	

Figure 6.3. Student–
Classroom Dialectic
Framework

Classroom conditions sometimes involve and
nurture the student's inner resources but at other
times neglect and thwart these resources.

dialectic is an ever-changing synthesis in which the student's inner motivation is nurtured or thwarted by classroom conditions, and classroom conditions introduce new forms of motivation for students to internalize (Deci & Ryan, 1985).

As an example, consider the motivation to read. Interest and curiosity lead a student to seek out and read a book. At the same time, the teacher might also ask the student to read an assigned book. To support the student's interest and curiosity, the teacher might offer interesting books and helpful feedback. Alternatively, the teacher might bypass the student's inner motivation and offer an external motivator—for example, a reward for reading. Wishing to obtain the reward, the student will likely gain a new motive to read—namely, the motivation to gain a reward. This reward might support the student's motivation by helping the student feel competent, or it might thwart the student's motivation the way coins did in the fable at the beginning of the chapter. Either way, the student's motivation for reading will change in response to the teacher's motivating style. Over time, the student's motivation becomes a mixture of inner factors (e.g., curiosity, interest) and socially acquired motives (e.g., obtain rewards).

Engaging Diverse Learners

Low-income minority students experience less educational engagement and are more likely to drop out of school than are their middle- or high-income nonminority counterparts (Rumberger, 1987). To engage themselves in the classroom, low-income minority students need to feel a sense of belongingness and acceptance (Goodenow, 1993). They need to feel understood and welcomed, and have a sense that they play an important role in the school community. The more different students are from their teachers in terms of ethnicity, language, and culture, the more likely it is that students will come to believe that their teachers do not understand them. When students fail to find a place in school where their interests, abilities, and definitions of success are honored, they understandably become increasingly unengaged in classroom activities (Smith & Wilhelm, 2002).

In the "What Kids Say and Do" box below, students in an alternative high school located in the poorest area of a large, urban city explain what they need from their teachers. Each student showed relatively high scores on standardized tests but poor classroom engagement and a low GPA. The quotations communicate that motivation and engagement originate not so much in grades and pressure but in students' inner motivational resources, such as their interest and sense of valuing, as well as in the support teachers provide. Disengagement arose from the students' perception that the teacher was their opponent and enemy, rather than their ally and advocate.

To promote engagement, teachers need to support students' interests, abilities, and definitions of success. Often, however, the approach teachers and schools take is to get tough. One approach, common in an era of standardized tests and teacher accountability, is to pressure students into performing (Gratz, 2000; Thompson, 2001), as through grade-level retention, summer school remediation, and other similar strategies to improve students' abilities

What Kids Say and Do

What Unengaged Students Want Their Teachers to Know

Why I'm Engaged

I read that book, and I started liking reading. . . . It related to me a lot so it was interesting.

The teachers are the biggest thing. . . . when the teachers pay attention to you like you're a student; like you're a person not a grade.

Why I'm Unengaged

You can't get good grades in something you can't stand.

They blackmail you here to get your homework in because if you don't turn it in, you get an after-school detention.

(Neill, 2003). While common, this approach fails to engage reluctant learners because compliance and obedience are poor replacements for the concept of engagement (see Figure 6.1). As one high school student explained, "If you didn't get it [the instruction], you had to spend your whole lunch period in tutoring. So I just . . . stopped doing it. Actually had competitions of who could get the lowest GPA. It was something like 'Oh, I failed anyway, might as well be the best at . . . something.'" (Daniels & Arapostathis, 2005, p. 49).

Compliance and obedience tap into students' behavioral intensity, but they fail in terms of emotional quality, cognitive investment, and personal voice. If teachers are to engage students' positive emotions, cognitive investment, and personal voice, they need to start by making a special effort to identify and affirm students' interests, abilities, and definitions of success.

Intrinsic and Extrinsic Motivation

As you watch students engage themselves in a learning activity, consider why they are engaged. Why is Mark reading that book? Why does Samantha answer questions in class? Why is Lamar a member of the school band?

Any such activity can be enjoyed in two different ways: intrinsically or extrinsically. On the one hand, a student might read a book because doing so produces an intrinsic sense of interest and enjoyment. On the other hand, a student might read a book because doing so produces an extrinsic reward, such as a sticker. *Any* activity, in fact, can be approached from either an intrinsic or an extrinsic motivational orientation (Pittman, Boggiano, & Ruble, 1983; Ryan & Deci, 2000).

Intrinsic motivation is the inherent propensity to engage one's interests and to exercise and develop one's capacities (Deci & Ryan, 1985). It emerges spontaneously out of the individual's needs for autonomy, competence, and relatedness. We discuss these needs in the next section; here, the important point is that intrinsic motivation arises out of students' psychological needs. Thus, to energize intrinsic motivation, teachers need to find ways to involve and nurture students' psychological needs. When teachers are able to do this, students say that the activity is interesting, fun, and enjoyable. Feelings of interest and enjoyment arise as *spontaneous satisfactions* from psychological need satisfaction (Ryan & Deci, 2000).

Intrinsic motivation yields numerous educational benefits. When students are intrinsically motivated, they exhibit healthy, productive functioning, such as initiative, persistence, creativity, high-quality learning, conceptual understanding of what they are learning, and positive well-being (Deci & Ryan, 1987; Ryan & Deci, 2000). For instance, the positive effect of intrinsic motivation on creativity is so robust that Teresa Amabile proposed the following *intrinsic motivation principle of creativity* (Amabile & Hennessey, 1992, p. 55):

> *People will be most creative when they feel motivated primarily by the interest, enjoyment, satisfaction, and challenge of the work itself—rather than by external pressures.*

Extrinsic motivation arises from outside incentives and consequences. Whenever students act to gain a reward, such as high grades, or avoid a punishment, such as a teacher's criticism, their behavior is extrinsically motivated. Students work hard not because they enjoy what they are doing but because they want to receive the reward, such as a marble in the marble jar, bonus points, or their name on the school's honor roll. Extrinsic motivation exists as an *in-order-to* motivation (as in, Do this *in order to* get that). *This* is the behavioral request, whereas *that* is the incentive or consequence. In short, **extrinsic motivation** is an environmentally created reason to initiate or persist in an action.

Extrinsically motivating students to engage in the school curriculum is a widely used strategy (Kohn, 1993). Common positive reinforcers in the classroom include praise, stickers, privileges, tokens, marbles in jars, certificates, attention, high grades, scholarships, honors, trophies, prizes, food, awards, money, and smiles of approval. The benefit of extrinsic motivation is that it recruits willing compliance. Generally speaking, students who are offered an attractive reward to engage in a task are significantly more likely to do so than are students who are not offered a reward.

Often, intrinsically and extrinsically motivated behaviors look the same. Just as the intrinsically motivated student works through math exercises, so does the extrinsically motivated student. It is difficult to know whether students are intrinsically or extrinsically

intrinsic motivation   The inherent propensity to engage one's interests and to exercise and develop one's capacities.

extrinsic motivation   An environmentally created reason to engage in an action or activity.

Chapter Reference
Chapter 7 explains how and why rewards increase students' on-task behavior.

motivated simply by observing them. The essential difference between the two types of motivation lies in what energizes and directs the student's on-task activity. With intrinsically motivated behavior, the motivation emanates from psychological needs and from the spontaneous satisfaction the activity provides (This is fun; I'm good at this). With extrinsically motivated behavior, the motivation emanates from contingent rewards (The teacher promised me 10 extra minutes of recess for doing this).

What Does This Mean to Me? How is your type of motivation affecting the quality of your learning and engagement with this book?

Hidden Costs of Rewards

Research on intrinsic and extrinsic motivation began with an intriguing question: If a person is involved in an intrinsically interesting activity and begins to receive an extrinsic reward for doing it, what happens to his or her intrinsic motivation for that activity? (Deci & Ryan, 1985, p. 43). For example, what happens to a child's motivation if she reads books for fun but then her parents see her reading and say, "Oh, look, Sarah is reading—let's show her how great we think that is and give her $5 for each book she reads!" One might suppose that rewarding Sarah's reading with an attractive prize would increase her motivation to read. It seems like common sense to think that if a student enjoys reading and is also rewarded for doing it, the intrinsic motivation (enjoyment) and extrinsic motivation (money) should work together to produce a sort of supermotivation. Indeed, if you ask teachers to make predictions about what would happen to students' motivation under these circumstances, almost every teacher will predict that it would increase (Hom, 1994).

Supermotivation, however, does not occur. Rather, the imposition of an extrinsic reward for an intrinsically interesting activity typically has a negative effect on future intrinsic motivation (Condry, 1977; Deci, Koestner, & Ryan, 1999; Kohn, 1993). This adverse effect is termed a **hidden cost of reward** (Lepper & Greene, 1978) because our society typically regards rewards as positive contributors to motivation (Boggiano et al., 1987). When people use rewards, they expect to gain the benefit of increasing motivation and behavior, but in so doing they often incur the hidden and unintentional cost of undermining intrinsic motivation (Deci et al., 1999; Kohn, 1993; Lepper & Greene, 1978; Rummel & Feinberg, 1988; Sutherland, 1993).

hidden costs of reward The unexpected, unintended, and adverse effects that extrinsic rewards sometimes have on intrinsic motivation, high-quality learning, and autonomous self-regulation.

Teachers use rewards to motivate students, and they do so for the best of reasons—to increase students' motivation, engagement, and performance. But extrinsic motivation often carries a price in the form of three hidden costs. The first of those hidden costs is a loss of intrinsic motivation. As a case in point, consider the first school-based study to investigate whether extrinsic rewards undermine intrinsic motivation (Lepper, Greene, & Nisbett, 1973). Researchers visited a preschool and introduced a drawing game that the children found very interesting. The researchers observed the amount of time each child played with the drawing game during a free-play period, then children were randomly assigned to one of three groups. In an *expected-reward* group, children were promised an attractive Good Player award if they drew. In a *no-reward* group, children were simply asked whether they wanted to draw. Finally, in an *unexpected-reward* group, children were asked whether they wanted to draw but, after they had done so, were unexpectedly given the Good Player award. One week later, the experimenters returned to assess what had happened to the children's intrinsic motivation to draw. Children in the expected-reward group spent significantly less of their free-play time with the drawing game than did children in the other two groups. In effect, children in the expected-reward group lost some of their intrinsic interest in drawing. The no-reward and unexpected-reward groups showed no such decline.

In thinking about these findings, it helps to ask *why* the children wanted to draw during the second session. Children in the no-reward group drew because they wanted to—drawing was fun, an intrinsically motivating thing to do. Children in the expected-reward group drew in order to get the Good Player award. During their free time, no additional Good Player award was promised, so these children in effect lost their extrinsically motivated reason to draw. They also, unfortunately, lost some of their intrinsic motivation to draw. Children in the unexpected-reward group drew for the same reasons that the children in the no-reward group drew—it was fun and an intrinsically motivated thing to do. Because these children were not induced to draw by an in-order-to promise, their intrinsic motivation was never put at risk.

Putting intrinsic motivation at risk is one cost of extrinsic reward, but there are two additional hidden costs (Deci & Ryan, 1987; Kohn, 1993). Extrinsic rewards also interfere with learning. They typically distract the learner's attention away from the material to be learned and toward getting the reward. As they learn, extrinsically motivated learners are generally passive information processors who attend to rote factual information (getting the right answer) at the expense of conceptual understanding. Extrinsically motivated learners also prefer easy success and quick answers over optimal challenge and the search for a creative solution. Thus, not only do extrinsic rewards put intrinsic motivation at risk, but they also put the quality of students' learning at risk (Benware & Deci, 1984; Harter, 1978; Pittman et al., 1983; Shapira, 1976).

The third hidden cost is that extrinsic rewards interfere with the development of autonomous self-regulation (Lepper, 1983; Ryan, 1993). After a history of always being rewarded for doing their schoolwork, students understandably begin to have difficulty regulating their behavior when not offered rewards for doing their schoolwork. Over time, the presence and absence of rewards, not interest and autonomous self-regulation, come to regulate the student's behavior—whether or not to study, when to study, what to study, how long to study, how hard to study, and so on.

In accepting the idea that extrinsic rewards produce worrisome costs, one might ask whether this is always the case. Extrinsic rewards generally produce these costs, but not always (Cameron, 2001; Deci et al., 1999). In particular, two factors explain when rewards undermine intrinsic motivation, interfere with learning, and derail autonomous self-regulation; those factors are expectancy and tangibility. Expected rewards engender an in-order-to approach to an activity. If teachers can find ways to give students unexpected rewards, these rewards do not produce hidden costs (Greene & Lepper, 1974; Orlick & Mosher, 1978; Pallak et al., 1982). Tangible rewards, such as food prizes, also tend to produce hidden costs; whereas verbal (i.e., intangible) rewards, such as praise, do not (Dollinger & Thelen, 1978).

That extrinsic rewards must be expected and tangible before they produce hidden costs sounds like good news for educators who use rewards. The problem, however, is that schools so often and so routinely use expected and tangible rewards to motivate students. Stickers, tokens, food, prizes, trophies, scholarships, privileges, gold stars, marbles, awards, honor-roll lists, and a dozen other such incentive plans are ubiquitous in schools (Kohn, 1993). In practice, therefore, it is not so comforting to say that only expected and tangible extrinsic rewards produce hidden costs because schools so often present rewards in expected and tangible ways.

Using Extrinsic Motivators Effectively

Not all extrinsic motivation is bad (Covington & Mueller, 2001). The problem lies in *how teachers use rewards*—for what purpose? Figure 6.4 on the next page illustrates cognitive evaluation theory, a theory to help teachers understand the effects that rewards have on students' motivation and engagement. Any extrinsic motivator—praise, money, grades, stickers, surveillance—can be administered either to control behavior or to inform competence. Offering rewards in a controlling way (saying, in effect, "If you do X, you'll get Y") increases compliance, but it also entails the three hidden costs of rewards. Controlling rewards interfere with students' need for autonomy and thus undermine motivation and engagement. Alternatively, offering rewards in an informational way (saying, in effect, "Good job, you're making progress") supports students' engagement without cueing up the hidden costs of rewards. Informational rewards nurture students' need for competence and thus enhance motivation and engagement.

According to **cognitive evaluation theory,** using extrinsic motivators effectively requires that extrinsic rewards be noncontrolling and informational. Extrinsic motivators need to be noncontrolling so as not to interfere with students' need for autonomy, and extrinsic motivators need to be informational so as to support students' need for competence. What teachers say when they give students rewards in controlling versus informational ways can be seen in the "Taking It to the Classroom" box on page 181.

Appendix
Effective Classroom Management
For effective classroom management, teachers need to learn when extrinsic rewards promote, and also when they undermine, students' motivation and engagement (*PRAXIS*™, I. C. 4, *INTASC*, Principle 5).

Chapter Reference
The use of reward and recognition in cooperative groups is discussed in Chapter 12.

cognitive evaluation theory   A theory of motivation that explains how external events such as rewards affect students' psychological needs for autonomy and competence and, hence, their intrinsic motivation.

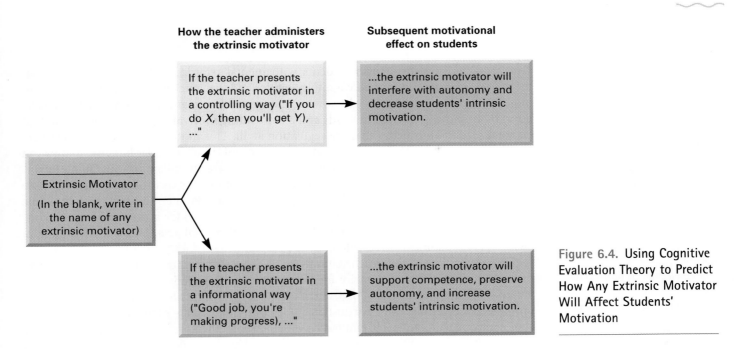

How the teacher administers the extrinsic motivator

Subsequent motivational effect on students

Extrinsic Motivator
(In the blank, write in the name of any extrinsic motivator)

If the teacher presents the extrinsic motivator in a controlling way ("If you do X, then you'll get Y), ..."

...the extrinsic motivator will interfere with autonomy and decrease students' intrinsic motivation.

If the teacher presents the extrinsic motivator in a informational way ("Good job, you're making progress), ..."

...the extrinsic motivator will support competence, preserve autonomy, and increase students' intrinsic motivation.

Figure 6.4. Using Cognitive Evaluation Theory to Predict How Any Extrinsic Motivator Will Affect Students' Motivation

Praise. Consider how one of the most frequently used rewards—**praise**—functions as an extrinsic motivator, sometimes to control students' behavior but other times to nurture their competence (Henderlong & Lepper, 2002; Ryan, Mims, & Koestner, 1983). To communicate a job well done, a teacher might say, "Excellent job, your pronunciation has improved since last week." Alternatively, the teacher might communicate praise in a controlling way, saying, "Excellent job, you did just as you should." Tagging on phrases such as "you should," "you must," "you have to," and "you ought to" conveys pressure, external evaluation, and doing what others tell you to do. In contrast, when praise provides clear, specific, competence-diagnosing feedback, it serves an informative function (Brophy, 1981). We can conclude that the motivational effect of praise lies not so much in the praise itself as in the way it is administered by teachers.

praise Positive verbal feedback.

How Can I Use This?

The next time you give someone a reward, ask yourself, Why am I giving this reward—to control behavior or to inform competence?

Taking It to the Classroom

Communicating Extrinsic Rewards in Controlling vs. Informational Ways

What controlling rewards sound like

If you do X, you'll get Y.

If you want a sticker, you'll have to come to class on time.

In order to earn points for your team, you have to turn your homework in on time.

Commentary:

Notice that each controlling reward bypasses the student's need for autonomy and instead focuses exclusively on gaining compliance.

What informational rewards sound like

Good job, you're making progess.

You're improving your skill so much that you've earned a sticker.

That's good work; you deserve an award.

Commentary:

Notice that each informational reward nurtures the student's need for competence and focuses on the message of a job well done.

How to Motivate Students with Mental Retardation: Intrinsically or Extrinsically?

controlling motivating style
A teacher's enduring tendency to engage students in learning activities by promoting their extrinsic motivation and introjected regulation during the lesson.

Two characteristics distinguish students with mental retardation from students without mental retardation: diminished cognitive abilities and low autonomy. When teachers try to motivate and engage students with low autonomy and low cognitive abilities, they typically do so by employing extrinsic rewards and a **controlling motivating style.** They reason that external regulation is better than no regulation at all. This motivating style allows teachers to control students' behavior but it does so at the cost of thwarting their intrinsic motivation and capacity for autonomous self-regulation. In fact, a steady stream of controlling extrinsic motivators can decrease autonomy to such an extent that the controlling motivating style comes to contribute to students' low engagement and achievement in its own right. Some researchers who study students with mental retardation go so far as to suggest that a controlling motivating style exacerbates the disability of mental retardation itself (Shultz & Switzky, 1993; Silon & Harter, 1985).

Appendix
Motivating Students with Mental Retardation

Like all students, students with mental retardation need and benefit from teachers' instructional strategies that promote their autonomy and instrinsic motivation (*PRAXIS*™, I. B. 4, *INTASC*, Principle 3).

Some special education teachers motivate students with mental retardation by nurturing their inner resources and capacity for autonomous self-regulation (Algozzine et al., 2001; Wehmeyer, Agran, & Hughes, 1998). Instead of asking students to respond to rewards, they promote *self*-determination. For instance, they are taught skills such as self-advocacy and choice making with the goal of empowering them to voice their preferences and choices. In one study, after students with various disabilities learned choice-making and self-advocacy skills, researchers observed them in inclusive classrooms. These students used their self-advocacy and choice-making skills to voice their preferences, communicate better with the teacher, and initiate their classroom activity (Belfiore, Browder, & Mace, 1994; Cooper & Browder, 1998).

What happens when teachers provide autonomy support to students with mental retardation? Like all other students, students with mental retardation who have their autonomy supported rather than their behavior controlled develop a greater sense of autonomy, experience more positive well-being, and achieve higher standardized test scores (Deci et al., 1992). Motivations such as autonomy and intrinsic motivation exist in all students, but these motivations require nutriments from the social environment (i.e., autonomy support from teachers, parents). A teacher's autonomy support nurtures autonomy and intrinsic motivation in students with mental retardation and, in doing so, promotes their learning, adjustment, and well-being (Deci, 2004). It is clearly easier for a teacher to say, "You will get a candy bar if you clean up your desk now" than it is to take the student's perspective and encourage his or her autonomy and self-initiative for cleaning. But autonomy can be supported. When it is enriched, it allows students to develop a greater capacity to regulate their own behavior and display positive outcomes such as engagement, learning, and well-being. This statement is just as true for students with mental retardation as it is for students without mental retardation.

Types of Extrinsic Motivation

External regulation via rewards is only one type of extrinsic motivation. There are two other types, as well (Ryan & Deci, 2000). All three types can be represented on a continuum, as shown in Figure 6.5.

Not At All Autonomous		**Somewhat Autonomous**		**Highly Autonomous**
Amotivation	*Externally Regulated*	*Introjected*	*Identified*	*Intrinsic Motivation*
Lack of any type of motivation— neither intrinsic nor extrinsic	Motivation from an environmentally created reason to act, such as a reward	Motivation from an internalized but pressuring voice, indicating that one must act to avoid guilt or shame	Motivation from internalizing the way of behaving because it is a useful or important thing to do	Motivation from psychological needs that reflects interest and enjoyment
Source of Motivation				
Nothing	Rewards	Guilt/Shame	Importance	Interest

Figure 6.5. Degree of Autonomy (Self-determination) in the Different Types of Motivation

On the far right-hand side of Figure 6.5 is intrinsic motivation, and on the far left-hand side is amotivation (literally, without motivation, or neither intrinsically nor extrinsically motivated). In the middle of the figure are three types of extrinsic motivation—external regulation, introjected regulation, and identified regulation.

According to self-determination theory (Ryan & Deci, 2000, 2002), types of motivation can be distinguished on the basis of how autonomous (or self-determined) each type is. Amotivation is a lack of any sort of motivation—the student is neither intrinsically nor extrinsically motivated. Amotivation is associated with very negative outcomes, such as dropping out of school (Vallerand et al., 1992; Hardre & Reeve, 2003). External regulation represents extrinsic motivation that is not at all autonomous; introjected regulation represents extrinsic motivation that is somewhat autonomous; and identified regulation represents extrinsic motivation that is highly autonomous. Identifying these different types is important because the more autonomous students' extrinsic motivation is, the better they function in school (Gottfried, 1985; Grolnick & Ryan, 1987; Ryan & Connell, 1989). For instance, sixth-grade students who complete their homework because of identified regulation show greater effort, more positive emotion, and higher achievement than do sixth-grade students who complete their homework because of external or introjected regulation (Ryan & Connell, 1989). What students say when they experience each of these different types of motivation can be heard in the "What Kids Say and Do" box below.

What Kids Say and Do

Types of Motivation

Question: *Why Do You Do Your Homework?*

I don't know. Sometimes I do; sometimes I don't. I don't really see what good it does me. (Student with amotivation)

Because that's what I'm supposed to do. (Student with external regulation)

So I won't feel guilty about it. I'd rather just do it and get it over with rather than feel all guilty and worried about it. (Student with introjected regulation)

I do my homework because learning new things is important. (Student with identified regulation)

For fun. I do my homework because it's fun. (Student with intrinsic motivation)

Psychological Needs

A **psychological need** is an inherent source of motivation that generates the desire to interact with the environment so as to advance one's personal growth, social development, and psychological well-being (Ryan & Deci, 2000, 2002). The three psychological needs central to students in school are autonomy, competence, and relatedness (Deci et al., 1991). These needs create a motivational sense of *wanting to* learn, develop, grow, and engage oneself in learning activities. When teachers find ways to integrate these needs into the lessons they teach, they successfully tap into students' natural motivation to learn.

> **psychological need** An inherent source of motivation that generates the desire to interact with one's environment so as to advance personal growth, social development, and psychological well-being.

Autonomy

Autonomy is the psychological need to experience self-direction in the initiation and regulation of one's behavior (Deci & Ryan, 1985). For example, when students feel they are doing something because they want to, they are experiencing high autonomy. Conversely, when they feel they are doing something because they have to, they are experiencing low autonomy. **Perceived locus of causality** (PLOC) is an awkward but important term. It refers to the student's understanding of the source (or locus) of his or her motivated actions (deCharms, 1976). PLOC exists on a continuum that ranges from internal to external. Students experience an internal PLOC when their behavior comes from within themselves—arising from their interests, wants, and desires. Students experience an external PLOC when some outside

> **autonomy** The psychological need to experience self-direction in the initiation and regulation of one's behavior.

> **perceived locus of causality** The person's understanding of whether his or her motivated action is caused by a force within the self (internal) or by some force outside the self that is in the environment (external).

Uncommon Sense

Giving Students Choices Increases Their Autonomy and Intrinsic Motivation—Or Does It?

If autonomy is an important motivational force, it makes sense that teachers should give students many choices. For instance, on a reading assignment the teacher might show students several books and ask them to choose one to read. On a writing assignment, the teacher might write a number of topics on the board and have students choose among them. Most teachers endorse the idea that choices promote motivation (Flowerday & Schraw, 2000), but not all choices are the same. Some choices involve the need for autonomy and promote intrinsic motivation (Zuckerman et al., 1978), whereas others do not (Reeve et al., 2003).

Asking students to choose among predetermined options is by far the most common type of choice teachers give. This is unfortunate, because when offered choices among mandated options (e.g., Do you want to read book *A* or book *B?*), students generally do *not* experience autonomy and intrinsic motivation (Overskeid & Svartdal, 1996; Schraw, Flowerday, & Reisetter, 1998). These types of forced choices bear no motivational fruit (Flowerday, Schraw, & Stevens, 2004). However, when teachers offer students open-ended choices about what to do (e.g., Do you want to read a book?), they *do* experience autonomy and intrinsic motivation (Cordova & Lepper, 1996; Reeve et al., 2003). Choice is motivating when it offers students opportunities to act on their interests and preferences to decide for themselves what to do.

force—a teacher, test, or reward—causes the initiation and persistence of their behavior. With autonomy, students experience an internal PLOC and a high sense of freedom to choose and regulate their actions (Reeve, Nix, & Hamm, 2003). The "Uncommon Sense" box above presents the concept of autonomy in a classroom situation.

autonomy-supportive environment   An interpersonal relationship or classroom climate that involves, nurtures, and satisfies the student's need for autonomy.

R I D E   What role does an autonomy-supportive motivating style play in increasing students' engagement; what role does a controlling style play in decreasing it?

autonomy-supportive motivating style   A teacher's enduring tendency to engage students in learning activities by promoting their intrinsic motivation and identified regulation during the lesson.

How Teachers Support Students' Autonomy. An **autonomy-supportive environment** is a classroom environment that supports students' autonomy; it has the capacity to involve, nurture, and satisfy students' need for autonomy. In autonomy-supportive classroom environments, teachers work hard to identify and support students' interests, preferences, and strivings. The opposite of an autonomy-supportive environment is a controlling one. Controlling environments ignore students' need for autonomy and instead use behavior modification techniques to pressure students to conform to an agenda set by the teacher. Instead of supporting students' autonomy, controlling environments control their behavior. Creating an autonomy-supportive classroom environment involves four essential ingredients (Deci, 1995; Deci et al., 1994; Reeve, 1996; Reeve & Jang, 2005; Reeve et al., 2004; Ryan & La Guardia, 1999), as discussed in the "Taking It to the Classroom" box on page 185.

Why Supporting Autonomy Is Important. The more teachers support students' autonomy and the less they try to control students' behavior, the more positive are students' school-related outcomes. That is, a teacher's **autonomy-supportive motivating style** benefits students' motivation, engagement, and achievement. Compared to students with controlling teachers, students with autonomy-supportive teachers show greater intrinsic motivation, mastery motivation, positive emotion, creativity, conceptual understanding, prosocial behavior, academic performance, and persistence in school (Amabile, 1985; Boggiano et al., 1993; deCharms, 1976; Deci et al., 1981; Deci & Ryan, 1987; Grolnick & Ryan, 1987; Reeve, 2002; Vallerand, Fortier, & Guay, 1997).

Why Are Teachers So Often Controlling? If supporting autonomy is so important, why do teachers so routinely try to control their students' actions? If strategies such as nurturing inner resources and accepting negative affect benefit students, why do teachers, especially beginning teachers (Newby, 1991), so often rely on controlling instructional strategies?

Taking It to the Classroom

How Autonomy-Supportive Teachers Motivate Students

1. **Nurture inner motivational resources.**
   Autonomy-supportive teachers motivate students by supporting their inner motivational resources. To do so, they find ways to coordinate instructional activities with students' psychological needs, interests, and preferences. The idea is to have students' sense of *wanting to* arise out of their own inner motivation. For instance, when asking students to begin a new lesson, teachers can solicit students' suggestions and preferences for how to learn the lesson.

2. **Rely on informational, noncontrolling language.**
   Autonomy-supportive teachers communicate classroom rules, requirements, and expectations with informational and noncontrolling language. Such language avoids rigid, pressuring phrases such as *"have to"* and *"got to"*. For instance, instead of saying, "You've got to work harder" and hence closing down students' autonomy and communication, the teacher might openly invite the student into the problem-solving situation, saying, "I've noticed that your writing doesn't quite have the same spark it did last week; would you like to talk about it?" In this case, the teacher supports both the classroom requirement and the student's autonomy.

3. **Communicate value in uninteresting activities and add rationales to requests.**
   Not all classroom activities can be intrinsically fun. For those activities and requirements that students do not find to be intrinsically interesting undertakings, autonomy-supportive teachers make a special effort to communicate the value within the lesson by offering rationales that explain why the teacher is making such a request. Instead of "because I said so," teachers can provide rationales. To the extent that students hear such a rationale and accept that it does justify their effort, they begin to say to themselves, "Yeah, okay, that makes sense; that *is* something I want to do."

4. **Acknowledge and accept students' expressions of negative affect.**
   Because classrooms have rules, requests, and agendas that are sometimes at odds with students' natural inclinations, students sometimes complain and resist. When teachers acknowledge and accept such feelings, they acknowledge the students' perspectives. Instead of trying to change students' *bad attitude*, teachers can acknowledge students' points of resistance, solicit their problem-solving input, and work collaboratively to transform the learning activity from something not worth doing into something worth doing.

Three reasons explain why some teachers adopt a controlling motivating style. The first is that these teachers believe that controlling strategies are more effective than autonomy-supportive strategies (Boggiano et al., 1987). Controlling strategies can induce compliance, but research makes it clear that students benefit in a number of important ways when teachers support their autonomy (as discussed in the preceding section). What teachers find so appealing about a controlling style is that it allows them to be in control, and it adds structure to the learning environment. But autonomy-supportive classrooms need not lack structure (Ryan, 1993). The optimal classroom environment, from a motivational point of view, is one that is high in both autonomy support and structure.

The second reason teachers are sometimes controlling is that they feel so much pressure from above—from factors outside the classroom that push them toward a controlling style (Pelletier, Seguin-Levesque, & Legault, 2002). The circumstances of the profession dictate that teachers comply with performance standards, accountability pressures, high-stakes testing, curriculum priorities, inflexible state policies, time constraints, large class sizes, and pressure-packed telephone calls from parents. When pressures from above pile up, teachers respond with controlling strategies, such as directives and rigid language, to get students to shape up, produce right answers, and conform to the school's agenda (Deci et al., 1982).

The third reason teachers are often controlling is that they feel so much pressure from below—from factors inside the classroom that pull a controlling style out of them. The biggest such pull teachers feel is student apathy and disengagement (Skinner & Belmont, 1993). When teachers see their students displaying little or no interest, when they skip classes or fail to turn in their homework assignments, teachers shift their approach from nurturing

Appendix
Promoting Intrinsic Motivation
When teachers recognize how to promote students' autonomy and intrinsic motivation, they help students' capacity to become self-motivated learners (*PRAXIS*™, I. C. 3, *INTASC*, Principle 5).

inner motivation to securing behavioral compliance. To gain compliance, teachers are tempted to slip into the habit of using directives and commands, and relying on behavioral modification techniques.

These three reasons explain why teachers often use controlling strategies to motivate their students. Fortunately, however, teachers can learn how to become more supportive, and when they learn to use more autonomy-supportive strategies, their students respond with substantial gains in engagement (deCharms, 1976; Reeve, Jang, et al., 2004).

Competence

competence The psychological need to be effective as one interacts with the surrounding environment.

Competence is the psychological need to be effective as one interacts with the surrounding environment (Deci & Ryan, 1985). Schools challenge students' skills, and competence is the need to develop mastery when challenged. For instance, in a Spanish class, one challenge that students encounter is to understand what Spanish speakers are saying to them; another challenge is to produce the language oneself. As students try to master these challenges, the environment also provides feedback about how well or poorly they are doing, as represented by nods of approval or furrowed brows of confusion. Competence is the psychological need to seek out, take on, and master such challenges. When students involve themselves in mastering optimal challenges, they feel interest and enjoyment, which are the positive emotions that confirm that students are experiencing satisfaction of their underlying need for competence.

The Pleasure of Optimal Challenge. To confirm that students do indeed derive need-satisfying pleasure from optimal challenges, Susan Harter (1974, 1978) gave school-age children a series of problems that varied in difficulty. Some problems were very easy, some easy, others hard, and still others very hard. The experimenter monitored each student's expressed pleasure (through smiling) after solving each problem. A curvilinear (inverted-U) pattern emerged in which students rarely smiled after solving the very easy and easy problems, smiled most after solving the moderately difficult problems, and smiled only mildly following success on the very hard problems. Pleasure was greatest following success during moderate—or optimal—challenge. Easy tasks fail to involve the need for competence; moderately difficult undertakings fully involve the competence need; and very difficult tasks generate too much anxiety and frustration for students to enjoy them, even when they successfully solve them.

challenge–feedback sandwich A learning activity that begins with the presentation of an optimal challenge and ends with informational feedback to communicate how well or how poorly one performed.

How Teachers Support Students' Competence. Optimal challenge is the key classroom condition that involves the need for competence; positive feedback is the key condition that satisfies it. Accordingly, in the classroom, teachers can support students' need for competence by offering **challenge–feedback sandwiches**—that is, lessons that begin with a challenge and end with positive feedback from a job done well. For instance, teachers can

Students smile and derive need-satisfying pleasure from optimal challenge and positive feedback because these conditions best involve and nurture their underlying psychological need for competence. (Media Bakery)

The Solar System

Planets	Sun & Moon	History of Space Exploration	Explorers	General Information
100	100	100	100	100
200	200	200	200	200
300	300	300	300	300
400	400	400	400	400
500	500	500	500	500

Figure 6.6. Classroom Illustration of the Challenge-Feedback Sandwich

challenge students by introducing a difficult math problem; then, during and after the performance, provide feedback about students' improvement, progress, and extent of mastery. It is not so much that the challenge is motivating or that the feedback is motivating; rather, challenge and feedback involve and satisfy the need for competence, and this experience of need satisfaction is what is motivating.

One classroom illustration of how a teacher might implement a challenge-feedback sandwich appears in Figure 6.6. To review recently learned material and to prepare students for an up-coming test, a teacher could create a game similar to Jeopardy®. Students are grouped into teams by the rows they sit in. To begin, a student from row 1 selects a topical box (planets, for 200) and the teacher reads the corresponding question. For instance, for a 200-point level of difficulty, the teacher might read a moderately easy question off a prepared index card such as, Which planet is closest to the earth in miles? Team members then collaborate briefly to provide an answer. A correct answer wins 200 points for the team, which the teacher writes on the chalkboard to keep a running score of how many points each team has accumulated. An incorrect answer loses 200 points, and it also gives the other teams the chance to raise their hands to try to answer the question. A follow-up answer also wins or loses 200 points. Once the question is answered, a student from row 2 selects a different topical box and the procedure repeats until all 25 questions are answered. The winning team might earn bonus points applied to the next day's test. In terms of the challenge-feedback sandwich, the challenges to students' need for competence are the series of increasingly difficult questions, while the feedback is the teacher's right/wrong response, the points won and lost, and the outcome of winning or losing the game.

The problem teachers face when offering challenges and feedback is that students sometimes react with anxiety. When teachers ask students to answer difficult questions, participate in contests, display their artwork, or go to the blackboard to solve a problem, students are as likely to view these events as fearsome threats as they are to see them as attractive challenges. After all, one hallmark of an *optimal challenge* is that success and failure are equally likely outcomes. **Failure tolerance** is the attitude of a teacher who accepts failure and errors as necessary, inherent, and even welcomed parts of the learning process (Clifford, 1988, 1990). It is rooted in the belief that students learn more from their failures than they do from their successes. Therefore, it emphasizes the constructive aspects of failure—identifying its causes, changing strategies, and becoming aware of the need for further instruction (Clifford, 1984).

failure tolerance The attitude of a teacher who accepts failure and error-making as a necessary, inherent, and even welcomed part of the learning process.

Teachers support students' need for competence by offering challenge-feedback sandwiches within a classroom atmosphere of high tolerance for failure. Before students will engage freely in challenging tasks and before they will hear feedback as information rather than as evaluation, the learning climate must tolerate (even value) their failure and errors. It is in this climate of failure tolerance (failure valuing) that students experience an emotional green light to involve their need for competence in the challenges and feedback teachers provide.

flow   A state of concentration in which students become wholly absorbed in an activity.

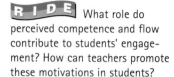 What role do perceived competence and flow contribute to students' engagement? How can teachers promote these motivations in students?

How Can I Use This?

Can you find ways to introduce challenges, goals, and feedback into one of your daily activities so that competence and flow will more likely be experienced?

relatedness   The psychological need to establish close emotional bonds and attachments with other people.

Flow. **Flow** is an absorbing state of concentration in which students become engrossed in the activity at hand (Csikszentmihalyi, 1975, 1990). If you have ever been so wrapped up in a challenging activity that you forgot to eat or failed to realize how much time had passed, you know firsthand what the flow experience is and how it can motivate engagement. The experience of flow goes a long way in explaining why students stick with and develop their talents, such as in music, sports, mathematics, or art (Csikszentmihalyi, Rathunde, & Whalen, 1993).

Flow arises whenever students perceive that the challenges posed by the task match their current skills and competencies, as illustrated in Figure 6.7. The figure is important because it identifies the emotional consequences that arise from the different pairings of challenge and skill. When challenge exceeds skill, students worry that the demands of the task will overwhelm them. When challenge matches skill (i.e., optimal challenge), concentration, involvement, and enjoyment rise as students experience flow. When skill exceeds challenge, students feel bored. Being underchallenged neglects one's need for competence, and that neglect manifests itself as boredom.

The practical implication of flow theory is that *any* activity can be made more enjoyable. Writing papers, debating issues, analyzing a play, completing a worksheet, reviewing material for tomorrow's quiz, and other such activities are rarely at the top of students' lists of must-do activities, but the balance of skill with challenge adds the opportunity to experience flow and deep enjoyment. Consistent with this idea, Csikszentmihalyi found that students actually enjoy doing challenging homework more than they enjoy viewing television (Csikszentmihalyi et al., 1993). Further, students actually experience flow more often in school than they do during their leisure hours (Csikszentmihalyi, 1982). Homework and schoolwork will be more enjoyable to the extent that students find more opportunities for challenge and feedback in these activities than they find while watching television and "hanging out."

Relatedness

Relatedness is the need to establish close emotional bonds and attachments with other people, and it reflects the desire to be emotionally connected to others and interpersonally involved in warm relationships (Baumeister & Leary, 1995; Ryan, 1991; Ryan & Powelson, 1991). Because students have a need for relatedness, they gravitate toward peo-

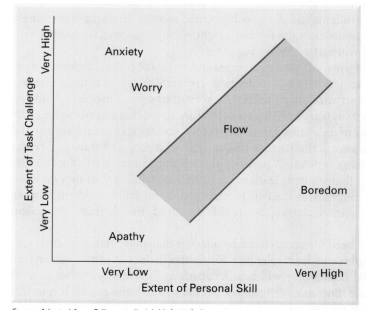

Figure 6.7. Model of Flow

Source: Adapted from Csikszentmihalyi, M. (1975). *Beyond boredom and anxiety: The experience of flow in work and play.* San Francisco: Jossey-Bass. Adapted with permission.

Students' relatedness with the teacher is important because it supports engagement and internalization of the teacher's values and leadership. (Media Bakery)

ple they trust to care for them and away from people they fear will undermine their well-being. What students are looking for in a need-satisfying relationship is an opportunity to open up and relate to another person in an authentic, caring, and emotionally meaningful way (Ryan, 1993).

The primary condition that involves the need for relatedness is social interaction, at least to the extent that such interaction takes place in a relationship characterized by warmth, care, and mutual concern. Merely creating opportunities for students to engage in social interaction will involve their need for relatedness. Satisfaction of that need, however, requires the development of a social bond between the student and the other person. For a relationship to be satisfying, students must perceive that the other person (a) likes them, (b) cares about their welfare, and (c) accepts and values their *true self*, rather than a façade (Baumeister & Leary, 1995; Deci & Ryan, 1991; Ryan, 1993). Social interaction with another person who likes, cares for, and accepts oneself involves and satisfies the relatedness need.

To get a feel for what sort of statements students would agree with when they feel high relatedness at school, here are three items from a questionnaire to assess relatedness involvement and satisfaction (Goodenow, 1993):

- Most teachers at my school are interested in me.
- I am treated with as much respect as other students.
- Sometimes I feel as if I don't belong here (reverse scored).

Why Supporting Relatedness Is Important. Supporting relatedness is important for two reasons. First, students who feel related to their classmates, their teachers, and their school community are more engaged in learning activities (Goodenow & Grady, 1993; Furrer & Skinner, 2003). They also function better in school, because a sense of relatedness makes students more resilient to stress, less likely to drop out of school, and less vulnerable to emotional difficulties, such as depression (Battistich et al., 1997; Osterman, 2000; Ryan, Stiller, & Lynch, 1994).

Second, relatedness to teachers provides the context in which students will internalize their teachers' values (Goodenow, 1993; Grolnick, Deci & Ryan, 1997; Ryan & Powelson, 1991). When students feel emotionally connected to and cared for by their teachers, relatedness is high, and internalization occurs willingly. When deciding whether to do or to believe something, students who feel close to their teachers say, "My teacher wants me to do this; I know [she] wants what is best for me so, okay, I'll do it." When students feel emotionally distant from and neglected by their teachers, relatedness is low, and internalization takes place at a snail's pace, if at all.

What Does This Mean to Me?
Notice the role that relatedness to others has played in the development of your own value system.

Chapter Reference
Chapter 12 highlights students' opportunities to develop relatedness with peers.

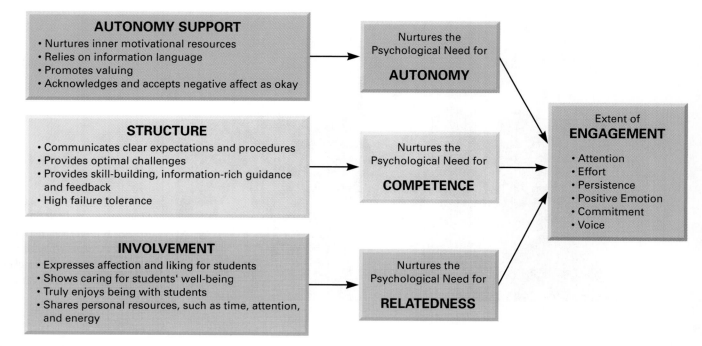

Figure 6.8. A Model of Engagement from Psychological Need Satisfaction

The Engagement Model

From a motivational point of view, high engagement arises from the psychological needs of autonomy, competence, and relatedness (Connell, 1990; Connell & Wellborn, 1991; Skinner & Belmont, 1993; Skinner, Zimmer-Gembeck, & Connell, 1998). The extent to which students feel autonomous, competent, and related in the classroom depends on the extent to which their teachers find ways to involve and support these psychological needs during instruction. Specifically, as shown in Figure 6.8, (a) teacher support for autonomy enhances engagement because it nurtures students' need for autonomy; (b) teacher-provided structure enhances engagement because it nurtures students' need for competence; and (c) teacher involvement enhances engagement because it nurtures students' need for relatedness.

What Makes for a Good Day in School? As discussed earlier, when teachers nurture students' psychological needs, students experience a wide range of positive educational and developmental outcomes. An additional benefit of need-satisfying classrooms is psychological well-being (Reis et al., 2000; Ryan & Deci, 2001; Sheldon, Ryan, & Reis, 1996). Simply put, when students experience a need-satisfying classroom, they say they had a good day. When they experience a classroom that neglects and frustrates their needs, they say they had a bad day.

For instance, as students go about their school day, they engage in a variety of activities, such as attending classes, talking with friends, or playing a musical instrument. Students report having their best, or happiest, days when they experience high levels of autonomy, competence, and relatedness. That is, while in class, talking with friends, or playing an instrument, the more they feel that their behavior emanates from their own intentions (autonomy), the more mastery or flow they feel (competence), and the closer they feel to their teachers and classmates (relatedness), the more positive is their mood, and the greater is their well-being (Kasser & Ryan, 1993, 1996; Sheldon et al., 1996; Sheldon, Elliot, Kim, & Kasser, 2001). These findings are important because they suggest that satisfaction of psychological needs supplies students with the *psychological nutriments* they need to experience good days (Sheldon et al., 1996).

Motivating Students During Uninteresting Lessons

A boring task does not have to remain boring, and students' functioning on relatively uninteresting tasks does not have to be poor (Sansone et al., 1992). After all, few people enjoy brushing their teeth, but most do it every day with care. The "Uncommon Sense" box on page 191 examines whether extrinsic motivation is a useful tool in engaging students in routine activities.

Uncommon Sense

Using Rewards to Motivate Students Is a Good Strategy—Or Is It?

After some reflection, most educators will agree that rewards undermine student functioning when lessons are interesting and fun. What about when lessons are not inherently interesting? Perhaps rewards can motivate students to invest effort on worksheets, repetitive practice, and cleaning their desk space. What student would not like an extra 10 minutes at recess or a sticker for herself or a pizza party for the class? When rewards such as these are at stake, students come to life and eagerly complete even a routine assignment. If students begin a lesson with little intrinsic motivation, extrinsic rewards cannot be so bad, can they? After all, you cannot undermine something that is not there. Nevertheless, just as in other situations, extrinsic motivators interfere with the process of learning and undermine the student's capacity for autonomous self-regulation. Ways to motivate students during uninteresting lessons exist, and these strategies, discussed in the text, promote—rather than undermine—students' inner motivational resources, learning, and autonomous self-regulation.

When a task is uninteresting (from the student's point of view), teachers have two fruitful means of engaging their students: Increase valuing and increase interest. The "Taking It to the Classroom" box below supplements these two core engagement strategies with additional ways to engage otherwise unengaged students.

Increase Valuing. The value of a task stems from its utility (Eccles et al., 1983). Brushing one's teeth and exercising at the gym are valuable because they enable us to attain good health. When students face an uninteresting (but important) lesson, they are often unaware of how that activity can help them attain goals that are important to them. Without the understanding of a lesson's value, students experience a motivational problem. Therefore, the teacher needs to take the time to provide students with a **rationale** to explain why the lesson is worth their effort. The rationales that students find convincing or satisfying are

rationale   A verbal explanation as to why a task is important and worth one's attention, time, and effort.

Taking It to the Classroom

Do You Know Jack? Dealing with Disengagement

Jack is often unengaged. Jack does not participate in classroom activities that are interesting to his classmates. Grades appear to mean little to him. What practical and immediate approaches can you take to assist Jack?

- Ask Jack whether anything is wrong and whether you can help in any way.
- Support Jack's autonomy by integrating his interest or preference into the structure of the day's lesson (e.g., such as through a writing assignment).
- Provide Jack with a goal or optimal challenge to strive for and, as he works, immediate and authentic feedback that tells him how well he is doing.
- When communicating feedback to Jack, use informational language, such as, "You're making progress," rather than controlling language, such as, "Work faster."
- When Jack finds a lesson uninteresting, support his motivation either by explaining why the lesson is useful and truly worth his effort or by suggesting an interest-enhancing strategy, such as setting a goal to strive for.
- Spark Jack's curiosity and exploration with a curiosity-inducing strategy, such as guessing-and-feedback.
- At the beginning of the lesson, induce positive affect by surprising Jack with a small, pleasant gift.
- Place Jack in a role that requires him to be active to fulfill that role, such as a leader, detective, or presenter for his group.
- Adopt a failure-tolerant attitude by communicating to Jack that failure is a useful, constructive, and beneficial aspect of the learning process.

those in which the teacher is able to connect the lesson with the student's future goals and strivings. For instance, preservice teachers generally take a course in educational psychology not because they think the course will be interesting and enjoyable but because they believe it will help them become more effective teachers. Providing rationales works as a motivational strategy because teacher-provided rationales help students preserve their autonomy and generate identified regulation—the self-determined type of extrinsic motivation that is associated with positive functioning (Reeve et al., 2002). Students who sincerely value a lesson truly and willingly want to engage it.

Increase Interest. While students are engaged in relatively boring and uninteresting activities (e.g., doing homework, diagramming sentences, completing worksheets, conjugating verbs in a foreign language), they can engage in a number of strategies to foster interest (Jang, 2003; Sansone et al., 1992; Sansone & Smith, 2000). One interest-enhancing strategy is to create a challenge or a goal to strive for. In trying to master a challenge or accomplish a goal, engagement is as much about mastering the challenge or achieving the goal as it is about the task itself. After all, what is so interesting about athletic activities such as hitting tennis balls, shooting basketballs, or throwing footballs, other than the pursuit of challenging goals? A second interest-enhancing strategy is to change mentally the context of what one is doing—by adding a fantasy context, for instance (Cordova & Lepper, 1996). As a case in point, instead of just reading this book, use your imagination to place yourself in a context of trying to motivate your future students. Preparing oneself to teach future students is likely to be a more interesting activity than simply reading this book. Using this interest-enhancing strategy, a foreign language teacher might invite students to imagine being overseas and trying to communicate as they make their way around town.

How Can I Use This?
Try to increase your interest in this text by creating a goal to strive for or by imagining that you are a teacher trying to motivate students.

Curiosity, Interest, and Positive Affect

To learn something new, students need two things: new information and the motivation to seek out and learn that information. Teachers constantly give students new information, but how can they motivate them to seek it out and learn it? The study of curiosity, interest, and positive affect investigates how teachers can add some emotional punch to information so that students will truly *want* to seek it out and learn it.

To start, try this demonstration: Which of the 48 contiguous United States has the most miles of shoreline? (Alaska and Hawaii are excluded.) Upon first hearing this question, you might not feel motivated to find the answer. But notice what happens as soon as you name a state, then learn that your guess is incorrect. Many people, for instance, will guess Florida. The answer is not Florida. If the answer is not Florida, it must be California, right? No, the answer is not California. Okay, Maine, right? The answer is not Maine. The next guess might be New York, but New York is also incorrect. After learning that their answers are incorrect, most people undergo an interesting motivational shift as "I couldn't care less" slips into something closer to "Okay, now I care; I want to know which state it is." If you have been trying to guess which state has the most shoreline, you have probably experienced an increasing thirst for the answer—an increasing desire to seek out and find some new information. To determine whether your curiosity has increased enough to affect your behavior, let's see whether you are now curious enough to pull an atlas off the shelf or go online to look at a map.

Sparking Curiosity

Curiosity is a cognitively based emotion that occurs whenever students experience a *gap* in their knowledge (Loewenstein, 1994). Students enter learning situations with knowledge and expectancies, and they use this information to make predictions about what will happen. When events unfold in unexpected ways, students experience curiosity. Its cause is, therefore, an *expectancy violation,* as in the following situations:

- I expected X to happen, but then Y actually happened.
- I thought the answer would be X, but it wasn't. Now I'm wondering what the correct answer is.
- I predicted that X would happen, but something else happened instead. I wonder why.

curiosity   A cognitively based emotion that occurs whenever students experience a gap in their knowledge that motivates exploratory behavior to remove that knowledge gap.

Chapter Reference
Chapter 2 presented Piaget's model of curiosity.

Curiosity is important because it motivates engagement-rich exploratory behavior—the search for new information (Berlyne, 1966, 1978; Day, 1982; Loewenstein, 1994; Spielberger & Starr, 1994; Voss & Keller, 1983). When students are curious, they are more likely to ask questions, seek out resources, read books, and ask experts for assistance. Such exploratory behavior puts them in contact with the information they need to close their knowledge gaps. In sum, a knowledge gap causes curiosity; curiosity motivates exploration; and exploratory behavior yields the information students need to learn what will close their knowledge gaps (Berlyne, 1978; Kagan, 1972; Piaget, 1969). Three curiosity-inducing instructional strategies are guessing-and-feedback, suspense, and controversy.

Guessing-and-Feedback. In **guessing-and-feedback,** the teacher first asks students' a difficult question that is relevant to the lesson. In a science class, the teacher might ask, what is room temperature on the Celsius scale? During a geography lesson, a teacher might ask, Which country has more land mass—China or the United States? Students then make guesses about the answer, and the teacher provides feedback about their accuracy. The feedback (No—that's incorrect; it's *not* China) is crucial because it is the means by which teachers make students aware of the gaps in their knowledge. As can be seen during any television quiz show and in popular board games, such as Trivial Pursuit, guessing combined with feedback makes students curious enough to engage in exploratory behavior (Loewenstein, 1994).

> **guessing-and-feedback**
> A curiosity-inducing instructional strategy in which the teacher asks students a difficult question, then announces that students' answers are incorrect so as to reveal a gap in their knowledge.

Suspense. **Suspense** occurs as students await an outcome that they care about (Hitchcock, 1959; Zillman, 1980). Awaiting an outcome gives life to the emotional experiences of hoping for a good outcome and fearing for a bad one. In other words, suspense is hoping for a good outcome and fearing a bad one. The teacher can introduce a demonstration, ask students to write down their predictions, then carry out the demonstration as the students hope that their prediction is correct and fear that it is incorrect. Or the teacher can ask students to cast a vote for the answer they believe to be the correct one. A second-grade teacher can introduce the problem $26 - 17 = ?$; ask students to nominate possible answers, such as 18, 11, or 9; have the students vote for the answer they think is correct; then work out and solve the problem. Solving a problem with a suspense-filled answer on the line is more engaging than is solving a problem that ends with a "so what?" answer.

> **suspense** A curiosity-inducing instructional strategy in which the teacher asks students to predict an outcome before students engage in the work that will reveal that their prediction was right or wrong.

Controversy. **Controversy** arises when the ideas, information, conclusions, or opinions of one person are incompatible with those of another, and the two attempt to reach an agreement (Johnson & Johnson, 1979). The knowledge gap within a controversy is, "Given that I believe *A,* how can you believe *B?*" Searching for information to resolve the controversy constitutes curiosity-inspired exploratory behavior. As one illustration, researchers asked fifth and sixth graders to learn some new information in a small group setting (Lowry & Johnson, 1981). Some students were randomly assigned to work on a class project and critique, argue, and debate one another. Other students worked on the same project but were asked to reach a compromise rather than debate. As expected, students in the controversy group found the topic more interesting; they also read more books about the topic, explored a folder of topic-related information, and scored higher on a later test covering that information.

> **controversy** A curiosity-inducing instructional strategy in which the ideas, conclusions, or opinions of one person are incompatible with those of another, and the two attempt to reach agreement.

> **Chapter Reference**
> Chapter 2 offers additional discussion and examples for each of these curiosity-inducing strategies.

Building Interest

Interest is a topic-specific motivational state that arises from attraction to a particular domain of activity. When piqued, it enhances one's attention, effort, and learning. In the classroom, interest appears in two forms, as summarized in the left-hand side of Figure 6.9 on the next page. **Situational interest** is triggered by external factors and exists as a short-term attraction to a learning activity. For instance, a student might encounter a learning activity, such as a book, field trip, or class project, and notice that it is novel, surprising, or a particularly good fit with his or her needs and goals. That is, something sparks the student's interest, and this short-lived interest sparks spontaneous engagement (Schraw & Lehman, 2001). **Individual interest** is more stable and content-specific (Schiefele, 1999). It develops over time as a personal disposition. With individual interest, the student's unique developmental history creates a clear preference to direct his or her attention and effort toward a particular activity, situation, or subject matter (e.g., music, sports, learning about Mexico).

> **interest** A topic-specific motivational state that arises out of attraction to a particular domain of activity.

> **situational interest** A topic-specific motivational state that is triggered by an external factor that produces a short-term attraction to the learning activity.

> **individual interest** An enduring disposition in which one develops a clear preference to direct attention and effort toward a particular activity, situation, or subject matter.

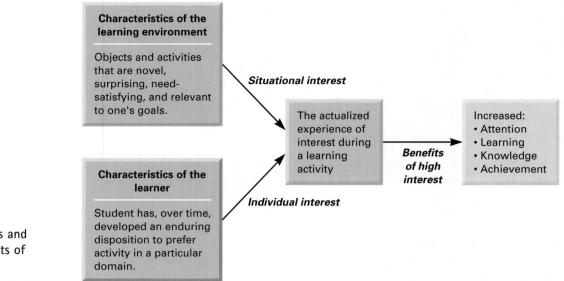

Figure 6.9. Origins and Educational Benefits of Interest

As shown on the right-hand side of Figure 6.9, interest has numerous benefits for learners (Alexander, Kulikowich, & Jetton, 1994; Alexander, Jetton, & Kulikowich, 1995; Hidi, 1990; Renninger, Hidi, & Krapp, 1992; Schiefele, 1991; Schraw & Lehman, 2001; Shirey & Reynolds, 1988). Interest, for instance, directs the learner's attention to the task and away from distractors. It also improves later recall of that material, because interesting material is more deeply processed and more readily remembered than is uninteresting material. Interest in a particular subject also predicts a student's level of achievement in that subject. As shown in Table 6.1, interest correlates with students' achievement across all subject areas, and it does so for both elementary and high school students, and for both males and females (Schiefele, Krapp, & Winteler, 1992).

Several factors explain what happens when students develop an interest. For one thing, something about the presentation of that activity can catch students' interest, such as how novel or surprising it is (Berlyne, 1966). Students also harbor needs and preferences (i.e., inner motivational resources; see Figure 6.3). When classroom activities involve these inner resources, students feel interest; but when classroom activities neglect these resources, students generally feel little or no interest (Danner & Lonky, 1981; Deci, 1992; Gibson, 1988; Malone, 1981). Prior knowledge in a subject area is also a particularly valuable antecedent to

---

TABLE 6.1

Interest–Achievement Correlations for Seven Subject Areas

Subject area	Interest–achievement correlation r
Mathematics	.32
Science	.35
Physics	.31
Biology	.16
Social science	.34
Foreign language	.33
Literature	.17

The numbers in the table represent the average study's correlation (denoted by the symbol r) between students' levels of interest and their achievement in that subject area. Higher numbers represent a stronger association between interest and achievement.

Source: Adapted from Schiefele, U., Krapp, A., & Winteler, A. (1992). Interest as a predictor of academic achievement: A meta-analysis of research. In K. A. Renninger, S. Hidi, & A. Krapp (Eds.). *The role of interest in learning and development.* Hillsdale, NJ: Lawrence Erlbaum Associates. Adapted with permission.

high interest, because interest and knowledge enhance each other. That is, the more knowledge one has about a topic, the more interesting it becomes; and the more interesting it is, the more likely one is to attend to, process, comprehend, and remember (i.e., learn) information about that topic (Alexander et al., 1995; Hidi, 1990; Hidi & Baird, 1986; Kintsch, 1980; Tobias, 1994).

Inducing Positive Affect

Positive affect refers to the everyday experience of feeling good (Isen, 1987). It is the mild, happy feeling students experience when the events in their lives unfold in ways that are better than expected. As unexpected and pleasant events unfold in the classroom—hearing an unexpected compliment, making progress on a project, or seeing an amusing cartoon pop up on an overhead slide—students experience a brief, mild, happy feeling.

> **positive affect** The mild, subtle, everyday experience of feeling good.

Positive affect is important because students who are in a good mood function so much more efficiently and productively than do students who are in a neutral mood. Compared with when they feel neutral, students who feel good are more creative, more efficient in their problem solving, more flexible in their thinking, more thorough in their decision making, more intrinsically motivated, more persistent in the face of failure, more accepting of risk, more cooperative, less aggressive, more sociable, more willing to help others, and more generous (Carnevale & Isen, 1986; Isen, 1987; Isen, Daubman, & Nowicki, 1987; Isen & Levin, 1972).

It is impressive that such a small and unexpected event can have such a substantial and constructive effect on students' thinking, engagement, and sociability. To induce positive affect, teachers do not need to use big, attention-getting, entertainment-like events. Positive affect is subtle. It produces these positive outcomes only when students are unaware of their good mood. It sounds paradoxical, but when students are made aware of their positive feelings (e.g., Oh my, aren't we in a good mood today), positive affect ceases to exert its constructive influence. So instead of entertaining students, the way to induce positive affect is through small, unexpected, and pleasant events, such as giving students a small gift (Isen & Geva, 1987), providing refreshments (Isen et al., 1985), offering a cookie (Isen & Levin, 1972), showing a cartoon (Carnevale & Isen, 1986), giving a "Have a nice day!" card (Wilson et al., 2005), or just asking students to think about positive events (Isen et al., 1985).

> **How Can I Use This?**
>
> Surprise someone with a small gift, such as a compliment or can of soda, then look for any subsequent increase in their creativity or sociability.

Using Technology to Promote Engagement

Technology is widely used in classrooms, and this is as true in elementary school classrooms as it is in high school classrooms. Teachers use computers, Web sites, CD programs, videotapes, e-books, overhead slides, PowerPoint presentations, and so on. One appeal of technology is its potential to promote students' engagement. But not all technology necessarily promotes engagement. Here are four criteria a teacher can use to evaluate any piece of technology in terms of its capacity to motivate and engage students (Keller, 1983):

> A = Attention (or curiosity, interest)
>
> R = Relevance (or value, identified regulation)
>
> C = Confidence (or competence)
>
> S = Satisfaction (or intrinsic and extrinsic motivation)

Attention refers to whether the technology arouses the learner's curiosity and interest. Can the technology spark students' interest and draw in their attention? *Relevance* refers to whether the learner perceives the technology to be connected to his or her personal goals. Is the technology-based lesson relevant to the sort of things students care about? *Confidence* refers to the extent to which the learner expects to be able to master the learning material. Does the technology provide a steady stream of challenges and feedback? *Satisfaction* refers to the learner's intrinsic motivation and reactions to the rewards embedded in the technology. Does the technology have features such as rewarding sound effects following a correct response?

The utility of the ARCS model is its capacity to answer the question, Will students find this technology motivating? According to the ARCS model, to the extent that the technology successfully addresses students' attention, relevance, confidence, and satisfaction, the answer will be yes. As a case in point, one teacher might consider using a computer software game to teach math or phonics skills, and another teacher might consider loading a foreign-language tutorial on the school's computer network. Whether or not students will find the technology motivating and engaging can be estimated in terms of its capacity to meet the ARCS criteria.

Different aspects of technology can stimulate and support different motivational states. Multimedia learning environments that simulate authentic, or real-world, activities can spark curiosity and stimulate interest. Computer programs can offer learners a choice of difficulty levels and, therefore, provide optimal challenges to their skills. Technology is typically highly responsive and, therefore, can provide immediate feedback to nurture competence and flow experiences as well as extrinsic rewards, such as celebratory sound effects. The self-initiated aspects of technology can support learners' autonomy. Multimedia learning environments often embed learning in a context that stimulates interest-enhancing strategies, such as learning within a fantasy context (Cordova & Lepper, 1996; Loftus & Loftus, 1983; Maddux, Johnson, & Willis, 1997; Malone, 1981). Technology-based learning environments can also provide learners with private performance feedback, thus helping to minimize learners' anxiety and needs for self-worth protection and self-handicapping strategies. Teachers can stimulate all these motivational states without technology, but the point is that teachers can use technology to assist themselves in the effort to create conditions under which students will find learning activities motivating and engaging.

Calming Anxiety, Protecting Self-Worth, and Overcoming Fear of Failure

Teachers help students do well in school when they watch for students' motivational resources, but they help students further when they watch for motivational deficits. From a motivational perspective, the root cause of poor learning and underachievement is academic disengagement. Of course, many nonmotivational forces help explain underachievement, factors such as a lack of experience, a lack of resources, or a learning disability. That notwithstanding, it remains true that disengagement explains more than its fair share of poor learning and underachievement.

All too often, disengagement is an intentional decision. Students withhold their effort when they fear that they will be evaluated harshly if they perform poorly. Sometimes students become so fearful of the social and emotional consequences of failure that they would rather not take the risks involved in trying to succeed. Learning, success, and achievement are worthwhile, but in many students' minds, they are not worth the risk of opening the door to experiences such as shame, criticism, embarrassment, and loss of respect. When students decide that preserving their self-worth is more important than learning and achievement, withholding effort becomes an intentional, even strategic, way of coping with academic challenges.

All academic standards of excellence are two-edged swords (Covington & Omelich, 1979). A standard of excellence simultaneously arouses in students both the desire to approach it and do well *and* the desire to avoid it and not embarrass oneself. When facing a standard of excellence, the student feels excitement and hope and anticipates feeling pride in a job well done, yet simultaneously feels anxiety and fear and anticipates feeling shame and humiliation. Thus, as students decide whether to try hard or withhold their effort, they experience an emotional tug-of-war. Figure 6.10 on the next page depicts this emotional conflict: It shows how the anticipation of hope, pride, and enthusiasm motivates approach and engagement, whereas the anticipation of fear, anxiety, and shame motivates avoidance and disengagement.

During adolescence, self-consciousness reaches its peak. Adolescents care deeply about what their peers think of them and their abilities (Gray & Hudson, 1984; Riley, Adams, & Nielson, 1984). With each passing grade, self-consciousness rises, and adolescents gradually accumulate inhibitions against putting forth effort in achievement situations. Three of those inhibitions include fear of being evaluated negatively (achievement anxiety), concern with preserving self-worth (self-worth protection), and desire to present oneself to others in a positive light (self-handicapping) (Baumeister, 1982). These are not motivational resources

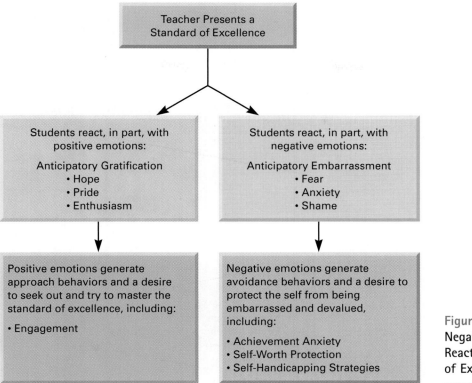

Figure 6.10. Positive and Negative Emotional Reactions to a Standard of Excellence

like the ones included in Figure 6.3. Instead, they are motivational deficits. These sources of inhibition and avoidance begin to rear their ugly heads in late elementary school and grow in strength during middle school, but they blossom into far-reaching, engagement-draining problems during the high school years.

Anxiety is the unpleasant, aversive emotion that students experience in evaluative settings, such as public speaking or taking a test (Dusek, 1980). When students are facing a standard of excellence, anxiety leads them to focus more on the threat of failure than on the hope of success. Anxious students, therefore, display effort-withholding, avoidance-based behaviors, such as making excuses, not participating, skipping classes, and pleading to be allowed to do something else (Smith, Snyder, & Handelsman, 1982). This sensitivity to negative emotion increases with each grade level, such that anxiety exerts little effect on elementary school students, a moderate effect on middle school students, and a rather debilitating effect on high school students (Hill & Sarason, 1966). This is true irrespective of the student's race or gender (Hill, 1980; Willig et al., 1983). The classroom conditions that lead students to feel anxious include external evaluation, high-stakes testing, unrealistic performance demands, external pressures, interpersonal competition, and situations that exceed students' coping capacities (Bandura, 1983; Eccles, Midgley, & Adler, 1984; Hill, 1980, 1984; Lazarus & Folkman, 1984).

Self-worth is an evaluation by others of one's personal worth. Appraisals of self-worth are based largely on three sources of information: perceptions of ability, perceptions of effort, and performance accomplishments (Covington, 1984a, 1984b). Among elementary school children, each of these three sources contributes positively to an evaluation that a person is good and worthy of praise and respect. The solid lines in Figure 6.11 (a) on the next page indicate that an elementary school student's praiseworthiness reflects high ability, high effort, and performance success. The more ability one has, the harder one tries, and the more successes one achieves, the more one deserves an appraisal of high self-worth.

Among adolescents, it is a different story. Adolescents come to understand that people who try hard are to be pitied, not praised. They come to believe that displays of great effort are a telltale sign that the person lacks ability [see the pair of negative signs in Figure 6.11 (b) connecting effort to ability and effort to self-worth]. The adolescent thinks that if someone has to try hard—study hard, prepare for hours, or practice diligently—that person surely

anxiety   The unpleasant, aversive emotion that students experience in evaluative settings.

self-worth   An evaluation by others of one's personal worth.

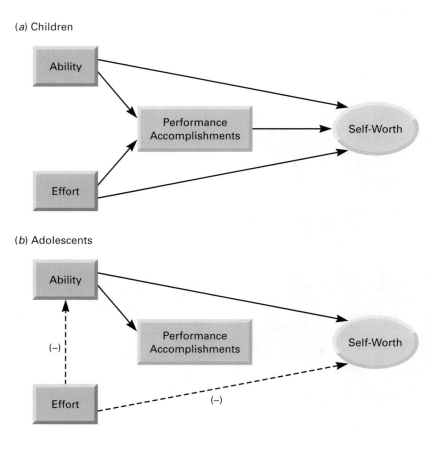

Figure 6.11. Self–Worth Models of Children and Adolescents

must lack the ability that would otherwise allow him or her to breeze through the task with ease (Nicholls, 1978). In other words, great effort is a billboard advertising low ability (Covington, 1984a). A public display of academic engagement thus becomes a threat to the adolescent's self-worth.

self-handicapping   A defensive self-presentation strategy that involves intentionally interfering with one's own performance so as to provide a face-saving excuse for failure in case one does indeed fail.

Self-handicapping is a defensive self-presentation strategy that involves a deliberate effort to interfere with one's own performance so as to provide a face-saving excuse for failure—just in case one does indeed fail (Jones & Berglas, 1978). The goal of self-handicapping is to have others disregard ability as a causal factor in one's poor performance. In doing so, the student protects his or her self-esteem from the potentially damaging effects of failure (McCrea & Hirt, 2001). Often, students who use self-handicapping strategies are those with high ability or high self-esteem—high enough that these self-perceptions need to be protected (Arkin & Baumgardner, 1985; Baumeister, 1982).

The mental calculation that leads to self-handicapping is as follows: "Before I perform and risk failure and humiliation, I will find or create an obstacle to good performance. Then, if I perform poorly, it will be clear to everyone why. The obstacle caused my failure. If I perform well, it will be easy to convince others that my high ability caused not only my success but also my triumph over the obstacle." The sorts of obstacles that students create to handicap themselves include the sick role, stress, anxiety, medication, lack of sleep, a bad mood, lack of practice, lack of preparation, and lack of effort (Baumgardner, Lake, & Arkin, 1985; Covington & Omelich, 1979; Rhodewalt & Fairfield, 1991; Smith, Snyder, & Perkins, 1983; Snyder & Higgins, 1988). The beneficial aspect of self-handicapping is that the self is protected, even immunized, against the possible humiliation of failure. The problem, however, is that sabotaging one's effort undermines performance and makes success less likely and failure more likely.

Anxiety, self-worth, and self-handicapping are problematic, self-defeating solutions to the motivational problem that students wrestle with each time they face a standard of excellence. The best way to help students adopt engagement-promoting solutions to these motivational dilemmas is to take a second look at some of the instructional strategies presented in earlier chapters. First, consider anxiety. Self-efficacy is the antidote to anxiety (Bandura, 1983). Hence, the implementation of a mastery-modeling program can boost students' self-efficacy beliefs so that efficacy overcomes anxiety.

Chapter Reference
Chapter 5 discusses self-efficacy and a mastery-modeling program designed to boost it.

Second, consider protection of self-worth. An incremental self-theory is the antidote to diminished self-worth. Hence, adopting incremental thinking (the harder you work, the smarter you get) and letting go of entity thinking (you either have it or you don't) redefines effort so that it becomes a valued asset rather than a feared liability.

Third, consider the fear of failure. A mastery goal climate is the antidote to self-handicapping strategies. Hence, the implementation of a mastery goal climate places a high social value on effort, improvement, and developing one's competence. It also simultaneously reduces the social value placed on ability and beating others.

Perhaps the strategy that best captures the essence of the effort to calm anxiety, protect self-worth, and overcome the fear of failure is tolerance for failure, discussed earlier in this chapter. Recall that high failure tolerance is a climate in which failure is accepted, valued, even prized as an inherently *useful* and *constructive* aspect of the learning process (Clifford, 1990). This is so because the fundamental motivational problem that is so often embedded in the pursuit of a standard of excellence is this: What will others think of my ability when they see me put forth a great deal of effort on this task? To the extent that students expect others to use great effort as a cue to infer low ability, the motivation to use engagement-depleting defensive strategies will be strong. Tolerance for failure, however, represents a teacher's explicit attempt to solve students' risk-taking dilemma in a way that fosters engagement. To the extent that students find themselves in classrooms that are failure tolerant, they can feel free to engage themselves fully in learning activities without the emotional distress created by anxiety, self-worth judgments, and fear of failure.

Chapter Reference
Chapter 4 distinguishes between incremental thinking and entity thinking.

Chapter Reference
Chapter 5 discusses types of achievement goals and recommendations to promote learning goals over performance goals.

RIDE Can a teacher's high failure tolerance promote engagement by releasing students from the social pressures that breed intentional disengagement?

REFLECTION FOR ACTION

The Event

As we saw at the start of the chapter, Mrs. Watson loves teaching, but she becomes discouraged when her students tune her out and disengage from the lesson she put so much time and heart into preparing. What can she do when they stare blankly, participate superficially, and give only a half-hearted effort?

Reflection **RIDE**

Why are Mrs. Watson's students so disengaged from the lesson? How can she engage them more fully? What instructional strategies might she implement to promote active and enthusiastic engagement?

What Theoretical/Conceptual Information Might Assist in Interpreting and Remedying this Situation? Consider the following:

Autonomous Motivation

Where does autonomous motivation come from? If her students are extrinsically motivated, how can she nurture their autonomy and intrinsic motivation? Would it help if she adopted an autonomy-supportive motivating style?

Competence and Flow

How can she involve her students' need for competence? What if she redesigned her lessons to provide a steady stream of optimal challenges and performance feedback?

Tolerance for Failure

Perhaps her students are disengaged for defensive reasons. What classroom conditions tend to put students on the defensive? How can she establish a classroom climate high in failure tolerance?

Information Gathering RIDE

How does Mrs. Watson know that her students are unengaged? What information does she need to evaluate the quality of her students' motivation? What information does she need to evaluate the quality of her own motivating style? To assess the quality of her students' motivation, she might ask students why they participate in class. To assess the quality of her motivating style, she might videotape a class to assess how much or how little she supports students' autonomy. She might ask a colleague to view the videotape for a second opinion on her motivating style. Are her lessons challenging? How frequently does she provide her students with feedback they can use to monitor their progress? During lessons, do students typically experience flow, boredom, or anxiety? Are her students defensive? Are they holding back out of a sense of anxiety, self-worth protection, or a fear of failing?

Decision Making RIDE

With this information, Mrs. Watson needs to decide the following:

- How engaged versus unengaged her students are
- How autonomously motivated her students are
- Whether her teaching style is autonomy-supportive or controlling
- How challenging and informational her lessons are
- What emotions students' typically experience in class—boredom, flow, or anxiety

She may need to find ways to introduce challenges, feedback, and failure tolerance into her lesson plans. She needs to decide how often students feel flow, interest, and positive affect, and how often they feel anxiety, the need for self-worth protection, and the fear of failure. If students are defensive, she might want to promote students' self-efficacy, incremental self-theories, and mastery goals.

Evaluation RIDE

With each adjustment she makes, Mrs. Watson needs to evaluate how closely her adjustments correspond to rises and falls in her students' engagement. Mrs. Watson needs to evaluate the connections among how engaged her students are, as well as the following:

- The quality of their motivation
- The quality of her motivating style
- The extent to which her instructional strategies spark curiosity, interest, and positive affect or anxiety, self-protection, and the fear of failure

Further Practice: Your Turn

Here is a second event for consideration and reflection. In doing so, implement the process of reflection, information gathering, decision making, and evaluation.

The Event

Mr. Marcus is a little worried about how today's lesson will go. Today's class features a lesson that students in the past have said was difficult and somewhat boring. The lesson, however, is important, even crucial, for students to learn if they are to master the course material and develop the skills they need.

RIDE   What can Mr. Marcus do to add some motivational spark to today's lesson? What can he do to more fully engage his students?

SUMMARY

- **What is engagement, and why is it important?**

  Engagement refers to the behavioral intensity, emotional quality, and personal investment of a student's involvement during a learning activity. To monitor engagement, teachers can keep track of students' behavior, emotion, cognition, and voice. Engagement is important for four reasons: It makes learning possible; it predicts how well students fare in school; it is malleable and therefore open to interventions; and it provides teachers with the moment-to-moment feedback they need to diagnose how well their motivational strategies are working.

- **What is the difference between intrinsic and extrinsic motivation?**

  Intrinsic motivation is the inherent propensity to engage one's interests and to exercise and develop one's capacities. It emerges spontaneously from psychological needs, and it yields numerous educational benefits, such as high-quality learning. Extrinsic motivation is an environmentally created reason to initiate or persist in an action. It emerges from the offering of rewards and generally yields compliance, rather than engagement. Offering extrinsic rewards to engage students sometimes yields hidden and unintended costs, including undermining intrinsic motivation, learning, and autonomous self-regulation. Cognitive evaluation theory shows how teachers can avoid these costs by giving extrinsic rewards in noncontrolling and informational ways.

- **How can teachers support students' psychological needs?**

  All students have three basic psychological needs: autonomy, competence, and relatedness. Autonomy is the need to experience self-direction in the initiation and regulation of one's behavior, and teachers can support autonomy by providing autonomy-supportive environments. Competence is the need to be effective during environmental challenges, and teachers can support competence by providing optimal challenges, positive feedback, and high tolerance for failure. Relatedness is the need to establish close emotional bonds and attachments with others, and teachers can improve students' relatedness by providing opportunities for social interaction within the context of warm, caring relationships.

- **How can teachers motivate students during uninteresting activities?**

  Students find some learning activities uninteresting. Instructional strategies can nevertheless promote autonomy, avoid the hidden costs of rewards, and engage students in learning. One such strategy is to increase students' sense of valuing by providing a rationale to explain why the lesson is truly worth the student's effort. Another strategy is to increase students' interest by offering interest-enhancing strategies, such as creating a goal.

- **In what ways can teachers spark students' engagement?**

  Curiosity, interest, and positive affect can spark students' engagement. Curiosity occurs when students experience a gap in their knowledge, and teachers can spark curiosity with instructional strategies, such as guessing-and-feedback, suspense, and controversy. Interest is a topic-specific, motivational state that arises out of an attraction to a particular domain of activity, and teachers can build students' interest through either situational or individual interest. Positive affect is the mild, subtle, everyday experience of feeling good, and teachers can induce positive affect by offering students a small, pleasant, and unexpected event, such as refreshments.

- **In what ways can teachers calm students' anxieties and fears?**

  Students experience standards of excellence as two-edged swords: challenges to their skills that arouse both the desire to approach them and do well, and the simultaneous desire to avoid them and not embarrass oneself. To reduce anxiety, teachers can implement a mastery-model program. To protect students' self-worth, teachers can emphasize incremental thinking. To avoid self-handicapping strategies, teachers can create a mastery goal climate. The implementation of a failure-tolerant classroom climate best solves students' risk-taking dilemma by calming their anxiety, protecting their sense of worth, and overcoming their fear of failure.

● **How can teachers engage diverse learners and students with special needs?**
Diverse learners' interests and definitions of success sometimes clash with the school's expectations and priorities. When students fail to find a place in school where their interests and preferences are honored, they understandably decrease their engagement, especially when they perceive that teachers are their opponent and enemy rather than their ally and advocate. Special education teachers often dish out a steady stream of extrinsic motivators, because they follow the motto that external regulation is better than no regulation at all. Some special educators, however, take a dialectical approach to motivating students by nurturing their autonomy, intrinsic motivation, and capacity for autonomous self-regulation.

KEY TERMS

anxiety, p. 197
autonomy, p. 183
autonomy-supportive environment, p. 184
autonomy-supportive motivating
    style, p. 184
behavioral engagement, p. 172
challenge-feedback sandwich, p. 186
cognitive engagement, p. 173
cognitive evaluation theory, p. 180
competence, p. 186
controlling motivating style, p. 182
controversy, p. 193
curiosity, p. 192
dialectical approach to motivation, p. 175
emotional engagement, p. 173
engagement, p. 172
extrinsic motivation, p. 178
failure tolerance, p. 187

flow, p. 188
guessing-and-feedback, p. 193
hidden cost of reward, p. 179
individual interest, p. 193
interest, p. 193
intrinsic motivation, p. 178
perceived locus of causality, p. 183
positive affect, p. 195
praise, p. 181
psychological need, p. 183
rationale, p. 191
relatedness, p. 188
self-handicapping, p. 198
self-worth, p. 197
situational interest, p. 193
suspense, p. 193
voice, p. 174

EXERCISES

1. *Monitoring Students' Engagement*
   Use a 1-to-7 scale (1 = not at all; 7 = a great deal) to create a rating sheet to measure the following six aspects of engagement: on-task attention, effort, persistence, positive emotion, personal involvement, and voice. With this rating sheet in hand, observe a classroom and rate the class as a whole on each of these six aspects of engagement. After the class is over, use your ratings to decide whether the students were mostly engaged or mostly unengaged.

2. *Evaluating an Autonomy-supportive Motivating Style*
   Ask a teacher whether you can visit his or her classroom to make some ratings. Use a 1-to-7 rating scale (1 = not used at all; 7 = used very frequently) to score the following four aspects of an autonomy-supportive motivating style: nurtures inner motivational resources; relies on noncontrolling and informational language; promotes valuing and offers rationales; and acknowledges and accepts students' expressions of negative affect. In what ways was the teacher's motivating style related to students' level of engagement?

3. *Providing Rationales*

   Attend a class and write down all the rationales or explanations a teacher offers to explain why students are being asked to follow a rule, enact a procedure, comply with a request, or engage themselves in a learning activity. Some teachers offer no rationales, but many teachers will offer at least one rationale during the lesson. After class, examine each rationale individually and try to revise it so that the rationale becomes a significantly more satisfying, convincing, and engagement-fostering explanation (from the student's point of view).

4. *Providing Challenge and Feedback*

   Ask a teacher whether you can visit his or her classroom to make some ratings. Make two ratings: provides challenges and provides feedback. For the provision of challenge, pay close attention to instances in which the teacher introduces a task. For the provision of feedback, pay close attention to instances in which students are performing or interacting with an assigned task. Are the teacher's offerings of challenge and feedback related to students' experiences of flow, competence, and engagement?

5. *Observing Interest-enhancing Strategies*

   As you engage in a relatively uninteresting activity, pay close attention to anything you do to try to make the activity more interesting. For instance, while exercising, practicing, or driving a long distance, do you use strategies such as setting a goal or imagining you are in a different context? Also, as you read this book, are you doing anything such as drinking a beverage, listening to music, or studying with a friend?

6. *Observing Self-handicapping Strategies*

   Observe any instance in which a person performs in an evaluative setting, such as making a speech in front of an audience. Both before and during the performance, listen carefully for any instances of self-handicapping that the person uses to deflect possible future criticisms of the performance. Particularly listen for handicaps such as fatigue, lack of practice, lack of preparation, or lack of experience. Does it seem as though these self-generated obstacles help or hurt the person's performance?

> "punishment"   "reward system"
>
> "privileges"
> "rules and procedures"
>
> "suspension"   "detention"
> "role models"

"**M**ore ideas, please," asked Allan Duba, director of guidance, as he scribbled another idea on the chalkboard. The principal had appointed him to head a faculty committee whose task was to figure out how to deal with the undesirable behaviors occurring during the middle school lunch periods. Tossing of food ... offensive language ... confrontations between students ... taunting of lunchroom aides—such behaviors were occurring more and more often. It was becoming increasingly difficult for teachers to supervise the lunch period or get students back to their classrooms in an orderly manner.

Behavioral Learning Theory

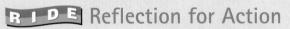

The problem faced by the committee is not an easy one. What should the committee members recommend? Do you think that punishing the students will work? What kind of punishment might be appropriate? Would it be possible to solve the problem without resorting to punishment? What about ignoring what the students are doing? Will it be difficult to get them to change their behavior?

Guiding Questions

- How do teachers who adhere to behavioral, cognitive, and sociocultural approaches describe learning?
- What kinds of learning can be described by behavioral learning theory?
- How do different forms of reinforcement affect behavior and performance?
- How can teachers increase the frequency of desirable behaviors and decrease that of undesirable behaviors?
- How can teachers help students learn self-management?
- How can teachers use behavioral learning principles in instruction?
- How might teachers use behavioral learning theory with diverse learners and learners with special needs?
- What are some limitations of behavioral learning theory?

CHAPTER OVERVIEW

In this chapter, we focus on students' behavior. We ask how students learn the behaviors, skills, and self-regulatory abilities they need to function well in school and in life. To understand how students learn such things, we first define learning and explain how it occurs. We then introduce the basic principles of the behavioral approach to learning. These principles serve as a foundation for understanding and discussing the everyday problems that teachers face in trying to increase the frequency of desirable behaviors and decrease that of undesirable behaviors. We also describe the types of instruction that have been inspired by behavioral learning principles.

Explaining Learning
- Behavioral, Cognitive, and Sociocultural Theories of Learning
- Contrasting Three Theories of Learning
- Kinds of Learning That Can Be Explained by Behavioral Learning Theory

Principles of Behavioral Learning Theory
- Types of Behavioral Learning Theories
- Operant Learning Theory

Reinforcement
- Positive Reinforcers to Strengthen Behaviors
- Negative Reinforcers to Strengthen Behaviors
- Selecting Reinforcers
- Patterns of Reinforcement

Punishment
- Positive Punishers to Suppress Behavior
- Negative Punishers to Suppress Behavior
- Can Punishment Be Used Effectively?

Applied Behavior Analysis

Managing Behavior
- Behavioral Learning Theory and Diverse Learners
- Behavioral Learning Theory and Special Needs Students
- Increasing Desirable Behaviors
- Decreasing Undesirable Behaviors
- Why Do Students Misbehave?
- Promoting Self-Management
- The Fundamental Task of Classroom Management
- Contracts and Contingencies

Influences of Behavioral Learning Theory on Instruction
- Mastery Learning
- Instructional Technology

Limitations of Behavioral Learning Theory

Explaining Learning

On an early October morning, Mrs. Johnson walks down the hall to her first class of the day. She enjoys first period and her students are learning well, but she worries about how they behave toward one another. Too often they are inconsiderate, even rude. She has talked to her students about this, but the put-downs and insults keep coming back like weeds in a garden. So today she has invited the school psychologist to visit her classroom, observe the students' behavior, and offer some recommendations to improve the situation.

The bell rings, class begins, and Mrs. Johnson guides her students through the lesson. As she teaches, the psychologist observes and takes notes. Sure enough, episodes of disrespectful behavior flare up.

At lunch, Mrs. Johnson meets with the psychologist to discuss the students' behavior. She speaks bluntly. She wants to see more behaviors such as supporting, encouraging, sharing, and helping, and fewer behaviors such as insults, put-downs, name calling, and rude gestures. She and the psychologist come up with a plan. They decide that she will reward her students each time they display a desirable, prosocial behavior—supporting, encouraging, sharing, or helping. The reward will be the teacher's approval; she will smile warmly, give positive attention, and offer praise for a job well done. To monitor how well the plan is going, the psychologist promises to visit her class regularly.

Two weeks pass, and the pair are again eating lunch together. This time the psychologist shows Mrs. Johnson a number of charts and graphs. One chart shows how often students engage in desirable behaviors, and Mrs. Johnson is happy to see the line on the chart going up. Another chart shows how often students engage in the undesirable behaviors, and she is even happier to see this line going down. Rewarding desirable, prosocial behaviors has worked. The frequency of desirable behaviors increased, and that of undesirable behaviors decreased. In addition, Mrs. Johnson says that she enjoys her time with these students even more than before.

The two agree that their goal should now be to find out whether the students can manage their own behavior. If so, Mrs. Johnson will no longer need to provide extensive attention every time she sees students behaving appropriately. It is time to determine whether students' newfound prosocial behavior can produce its own, natural consequences of greater friendship and lessened hostility. To see how well students can regulate themselves, the psychologist promises to return in two weeks and create a new set of charts.

Before we begin, consider the perspective of a school psychologist such as the one who visited Mrs. Johnson's class. School psychologists care deeply about students' misbehaviors and social skill deficits, especially when they interfere with learning and interpersonal relations. Careful use of behavioral learning techniques helps school psychologists achieve their goals (Bergan & Caldwell, 1995).

Behavioral, Cognitive, and Sociocultural Theories of Learning

There are numerous theories of learning, and it is important to have a clear understanding of the similarities and differences among them. In this section, we will briefly examine different approaches to learning, focusing on behavioral learning theories. Teachers attempt to create conditions in their classrooms that will promote and facilitate learning. To do this, they must have a theory of learning that guides their decisions about the kinds of learning environments they will create and the kinds of tasks they will assign to students in order to promote learning. Their ideas of what constitutes learning will also influence what they decide to measure in determining whether students have learned what the teacher intends them to learn. This section will also address how individual differences among learners might be viewed from a behavioral learning perspective.

Learning is a process through which relatively permanent changes in behavior or knowledge occur as a result of experience. Through experience, we learn behaviors such as writing our names, driving a car, and teaching a class, and we learn to understand theories of human behavior. In the classroom, teachers provide students with learning experiences. To help students learn particular behaviors and knowledge, they need to provide the kinds of experiences that will facilitate these types of learning. Because the kinds of experiences that foster the learning of behaviors are different from those that foster the learning of knowledge, different approaches to learning have emerged.

Appendix
Understanding Learning
Many theories have attempted to explain learning (*PRAXIS™*, I. A. 1, *INTASC*, Principle 2).

learning   A relatively permanent change in behavior or knowledge that occurs as a result of experience.

Contrasting Three Theories of Learning

The broadest definition of learning involves an interaction between the individual and the environment that results in some permanent change in behavior (overt or covert):

$$\text{Environment} \rightarrow \text{Individual} \rightarrow \text{Behavior}$$

Behavioral, cognitive, and sociocultural theories of learning place different degrees of emphasis on these three components. From a *behavioral viewpoint*, the most important relationship is between the environment and behavior: Changes in the environment will result in changes in behavior. Individual differences are less important to this view of learning, because the goal is to produce desirable behaviors or reduce the frequency of undesirable behaviors. From a behavioral viewpoint, individual differences may be seen as reflecting different histories of conditioning, reinforcement, or punishment.

In contrast, from a *cognitive viewpoint* (including constructivist theories), the individual plays a key role in learning. Two people can perceive the same environment differently, and as a result, the effects of their interactions with their environment on subsequent behavior may vary. For example, two children may watch the same movie; one may be enchanted by it, and the other may respond with fear. Their different reactions reflect not just the stimulus available in the environment (in this case, a movie) but also how that stimulus is understood by each child. Thus, the Individual → Behavior relationship as emphasized over the Environment → Behavior relationship.

A *sociocultural viewpoint* stresses the nature of the environment and its relationship to behavior, but this relationship is quite different from that which might be studied from a behavioral standpoint. The environment is not just the physical environment but includes the history of practice and expertise acquired by a community from which an individual might learn by becoming an apprentice in that community. A sociocultural viewpoint is concerned with the influence of the environment on the individual and his or her behavior.

Teachers pay different degrees of attention to characteristics of the environment, efforts to change the environment, the role of individual differences, and the outcomes of interactions between learners and the environment, depending on which of these theories of learning they favor. A teacher whose theory of learning is grounded in cognitive theory will be interested in children's prior experiences and knowledge, and their individual interpretations of events in the classroom. Another teacher may emphasize a behavioral learning theory and focus on breaking curriculum units down into smaller units to provide opportunities for feedback and reinforcement.

Behavioral learning principles are used in a variety of instructional settings. They are used with children with special needs, in instruction using computer software, and in classroom management. Although more cognitive approaches to instruction are more highly valued at present, behavioral learning theory can make useful contributions to classroom practice.

Kinds of Learning That Can Be Explained by Behavioral Learning Theory

Behavioral learning theory focuses on behavior—the kinds of behaviors that were the concern of Mrs. Johnson and the school psychologist. It also focuses on skills and self-regulatory capacities, as shown in Figure 7.1. Behaviors represent situationally appropriate and desirable actions, such as completing homework assignments, as well as situationally inappropriate and undesirable actions, such as fighting. Skills represent social skills, such as helping others, as well as motor skills, such as playing a musical instrument. Self-regulation represents such actions as goal setting, self-instruction, self-monitoring, self-evaluation, and self-consequences. Behavioral learning theory does not focus on mental knowledge, such as learning information, using memory, understanding concepts, and creating meaning.

What all these behaviors, skills, and self-regulatory abilities have in common is that they represent voluntary, intentional, and purposive ways of trying to adapt to one's environment. Learning these behaviors, skills, and self-regulatory abilities enables one to gain

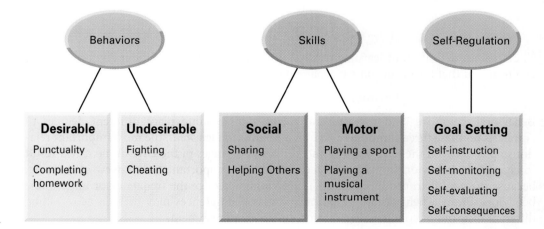

Figure 7.1. The Three Kinds of Learning Explained by Behavioral Learning Theory

rewards and favorable outcomes (e.g., praise, admiration) and avoid punishers and unfavorable outcomes (e.g., criticism, being laughed at). That is, learning behaviors, skills, and self-regulation helps promote students' personal competence, social welfare, and capacity to carry out activities on their own.

Principles of Behavioral Learning Theory

There are several types of behavioral learning theories, each associated with a set of specific principles. Many of these principles can be useful in the classroom.

Types of Behavioral Learning Theories

Early behavioral theorists proposed that learning occurs through a process of **contiguity**—that is, learning is the result of events occurring at the same time. For example, when you enter a store, you may hear a pinging noise. You soon learn to expect that such a noise will occur whenever you enter that store. The two events occur at the same time, and you learn that they are associated with each other.

contiguity A condition in which two events occur at the same time.

The best known contiguity theory is **classical conditioning**, which involves the pairing of a stimulus and a response. Some stimuli, such as loud noise, produce an automatic physiological response, such as a startle reflex. The stimulus leads to the response without any prior learning. The provocative stimulus (loud noise) and consequent response (startle reflex) are termed the **unconditioned stimulus** and the **unconditioned response**. The term unconditioned communicates that the student learns to pair the stimulus and response in a way that is automatic or involuntary.

classical conditioning The association of automatic responses with new stimuli.

unconditioned stimulus A stimulus that, without prior learning, produces an automatic physiological response.

It was the Russian physiologist, Ivan Pavlov who discovered the phenomenon of classical conditioning. He was conducting research on the physiology of digestion. A dog in his laboratory salivated when food was presented to him. The drooling response was automatic. Pavlov began to ring a bell whenever food was presented to the dog, a contiguous pairing of events. Initially, the sound of the bell elicited no response from the dog. Gradually, the dog came to associate the sound of the bell with the food, an unconditioned stimulus (food) that produced an unconditioned response (drooling). The dog soon learned to drool at the sound of the bell. Through experience, the bell had become an *conditioned stimulus*. The once neutral stimulus of the bell gained the capacity to produce a *conditioned response* (drooling) as a result of the contiguous pairing of the two.

unconditioned response A behavior that is produced in response to a stimulus without prior learning. It is typically an automatic physiological response.

conditioned stimulus A stimulus, that with experience, produces a learned or acquired response.

conditioned response A response that is linked to a particular stimulus through conditioning by being paired with the stimulus.

Students may have acquired certain responses through a process of classical conditioning. Most often, the behaviors that are learned are those that were once associated with a strong emotional response. For example, a teacher may pick up a note passed by one eighth-grade student to another and read it aloud to the class. The student whose note is read may experience embarrassment and humiliation. In such circumstances, the student's response is uncontrolled. In future encounters with this teacher, the student may experience embarrassment and withdrawal when the teacher asks for his or her homework assignments. Previously, the request for the homework would not have produced a response of embarrassment.

Associationist theories also depend on the principle of contiguity. When children memorize number facts (e.g., $4 \times 4 = 16$) by rote, they may be simply associating the words. For example, young children may learn songs by simple association of words without perhaps pronouncing the words as intended or without comprehension of what they mean. Frequent pairings of stimuli and responses result in a stronger association between them. In theories of learning that depend on contiguity as the mechanism by which learning occurs, the learner is passive. Events occur, and because they occur together, the learner forms an association between them. The learner does not act on the environment. Instead, the learner rather passively and automatically learns *what goes with what* or what classroom events co-occur. Mrs. Johnson always smiles, the music room is always too hot, chalk on the blackboard squeaks, etc.

An alternative theory of behavioral learning assumes a more active learner. In **operant learning**, the learner acts, or *operates,* on the environment, and depending on what happens as a result, the likelihood of the learner's repeating the behavior will either increase or decrease.

operant learning Actions by a learner, the consequences of which influence further behavior.

Operant Learning Theory

At recess, José and his friends are playing baseball. It is José's turn to bat. He grabs the bat and gets ready for the first pitch. The bat is rather heavy, so he holds his hands about a foot apart. Here comes the first pitch. He swings and misses. Strike one. That did not work, so he moves his hands closer together. Here comes the second pitch. He swings and misses. Strike two.

Eager to make contact with the ball, José moves his hands together. Here comes the third pitch. He swings, and "smack," he hits the ball right over the third baseman's head and runs happily to first base. While standing on the base, he decides that holding his hands apart is no good, whereas holding them together is good. When it is his turn to bat again, José will hold his hands close together.

Most behaviors are learned. We learn how to write our names, ride a bicycle, wait for our turn in line, raise our hand to ask a question, study for a test, and operate a Bunsen burner in chemistry lab. The process through which we learn such behaviors follows a set of principles. Behaviorists such as John B. Watson and B. F. Skinner focused on the objective data of behavior. Skinner's approach was to try to identify relationships between elements of the environment that would predict behavior (Skinner, 1950). His approach has often been described as a *black box* theory with information from the environment going in to the individual who then behaves. But nothing could be said about what occurred in the *black box* of the individual. This approach is in sharp contrast to cognitive approaches that are very interested in what occurs in the individual as he or she receives and actively processes information from the environment.

The Law of Effect   The law of effect was originally proposed by E. L. Thorndike (1913). According to the **law of effect**, behaviors that have good effects tend to become more frequent, whereas behaviors that have bad effects tend to become less frequent. Thus, if a child pets a dog and that petting produces good effects, such as tail wagging and companionship, the child will pet the dog more often. If petting the dog produces bad effects, such as growls and barking, the child will pet the dog less often. The point of the law of effect is that behavior is highly influenced by the effects that follow it.

Consequences   **Consequences** are the good and bad effects that follow a person's behavior. They are important to learning because they influence the future frequency of the behavior. Good consequences influence the person to engage in the behavior more often, whereas bad consequences influence the person to engage in the behavior less often. Consequences that cause a behavior to become more frequent are called *reinforcers*, and consequences that cause a behavior to become less frequent are called *punishers*.

Reinforcement

A **reinforcer**, such as a sticker, a candy bar, or an approving smile, is an environmental event that increases the strength of a behavior. Reinforcers are consequences of behavior that increase the likelihood that the behavior will be performed again. There are two types of reinforcers: positive and negative. A positive reinforcer can involve adding something pleasant to a situation (e.g., a gold star on a homework paper) or removing something unpleasant (e.g., being allowed to rejoin classmates after a time-out). If John's mother wants him to help clean up after dinner, she might either praise him when he helps clean up (a positive reinforcer that adds something pleasant) or stop nagging him when he helps clean up (a negative reinforcer that results in an increase in the desired behavior because the unpleasant stimulus has been removed).

Positive Reinforcers to Strengthen Behaviors

A **positive reinforcer** is any environmental event that, when given, increases the frequency of a behavior. In terms of the law of effect, a positive reinforcer follows the performance of a behavior and increases the probability that the behavior will be performed again. As an example, a teacher might notice that a student used proper punctuation in an essay and,

---

law of effect   The phenomenon in which behavior that produces good effects tends to become more frequent while behavior that produces bad effects tends to become less frequent.

consequences   The good or bad effects that follow a person's behavior.

What Does This Mean to Me?
What kinds of events have you found to be reinforcing or punitive?

reinforcer   A consequence of behavior that increases or strengthens behavior.

positive reinforcer   Any environmental event that, when given, increases the frequency of a behavior.

therefore, places a happy-face sticker on the paper. The giving of the sticker acts as a positive reinforcer if it increases the student's use of proper punctuation in the future. Other common positive reinforcers in the classroom include praise, privileges, tokens, attention, high grades, scholarships, honors, certificates, trophies, prizes, food, awards, money, smiles, public recognition, and positive feedback. When teachers give students a special privilege for being quiet during study time and when schools place students' names on the honor roll for making good grades, they are reinforcing desirable behaviors (being quiet, making high grades) by making sure that those behaviors produce good effects that will strengthen them.

A teacher's affection and approval can positively reinforce and strengthen a student's desirable behavior, such as reading. (Dynamic Graphics, Inc./Creatas)

Undesirable behaviors can also be reinforced, and their frequency of occurrence can increase as a result. As a young child, the nephew of one of the authors was very good at imitating people. A next-door neighbor had a very high-pitched voice, and the boy would imitate him perfectly. His parents laughed when he did this, and he continued to imitate this individual until one day he replied to the neighbor using the same high-pitched voice. His parents were, of course, quite embarrassed because the neighbor thought the boy was making fun of him and was angry. The boy's parents' laughter had served to reinforce his behavior.

Teachers often experience that students have been reinforced previously for negative behaviors. Some children may have been reinforced by other students' approval for disobeying a teacher. It can be very difficult to changes behaviors such as these.

R I D E Why might it be difficult for the committee to change the students' behavior?

Negative Reinforcers to Strengthen Behaviors

A **negative reinforcer** is any environmental event that, when removed, increases the frequency of a behavior. In terms of the law of effect, a negative reinforcer involves the removal of unpleasant events or experiences after a desired behavior has been performed. As an example, a teacher might stare at a student until the student begins working on an assignment. If the student wants the teacher to stop staring at her, she must increase her on-task behavior. The teacher's staring is an unpleasant event, and the teacher stops staring after the student gets to work on the assignment. What is being reinforced is the student's on-task behavior. Other common negative reinforcers in the classroom include nagging, deadlines, surveillance, threats, negative evaluations, ridicule, teasing, laughing (at someone), criticizing, yelling, crying, whining, screaming, pouting, and throwing a temper tantrum. When teachers stop pleading for students to answer their questions, they are attempting to increase (reinforce) the desirable behavior (answering questions) by removing the negative event (pleading).

negative reinforcer Any environmental event that, when removed, increases the frequency of a behavior.

Why Do Rewards Encourage Approach Behavior? A **reward** is anything given in return for another person's service or achievement (Craighead, Kazdin, & Mahoney, 1981). Thus, when a teacher promises students a prize if they will participate more or smiles when students perform well, he or she is giving them an extrinsic reward. Extrinsic rewards are often confused with positive reinforcers, which are defined by their effects on behavior. A focus on rewards highlights the instructional practice of soliciting students' participation or acknowledging their achievement, regardless of whether those rewards actually reinforce behavior. A reward functions as a reinforcer only when the learner values it. Sometimes teachers offer rewards that students do not value; such rewards do not increase the frequency of the desired behavior. For example, a teacher may praise a child publicly for his or her work but the child may instead be embarrassed by this attention. The effect of the praise is punitive rather than reinforcing.

reward Anything given in return for another person's service or achievement.

When they see a sticker attached to their latest homework effort, most children glow with pleasure. When offered the chance to obtain a special privilege, most adolescents perk up

Receiving an extrinsic reward such as a trophy can be very reinforcing to students. (Media Bakery)

with interest. Why? Why do rewards give life to positive emotion and approach behavior or engagement? Like all human beings, students are sensitive to signals of gain and pleasure. The physiological mechanism that makes students sensitive to rewards is release of the neurotransmitter dopamine (Mirenowicz & Schultz, 1994; Montague, Dayan, & Sejnowski, 1996), which triggers the behavioral activation system (BAS; Gray, 1990). Increased activity in the BAS generates positive feelings, such as hope and interest. It also triggers approach behavior, because students will move toward signals of personal gain. Knowing that one will receive a reward for completing a homework sheet may generate positive feelings of anticipation.

The mental event that activates the BAS is the perception that a situation is unfolding in a way that is better than expected (Montague et al., 1996). For instance, expected and predicted classroom situations have little effect on students' BAS. However, when a situation signals that things are taking an unexpected turn for the better, dopamine release and BAS activity increase. Unexpectedly receiving a sticker and becoming aware that one might obtain a special privilege are two examples of situations that have taken a turn for the better. In short, extrinsic rewards encourage approach behavior because they signal that personal gain is imminent (Mirenowicz & Schultz, 1994).

Why Are Extrinsic Rewards Prevalent in Schools? School personnel take note as students display emotional and behavioral responses to extrinsic rewards. To capitalize on such responses, they often identify some desired target behavior and find a way to create a connection between the behavior and the reward. From a motivational (as opposed to behavioral) perspective, teachers use rewards to bolster students' otherwise low motivation (Boggiano et al., 1987). The idea is as follows: If the task itself cannot generate enough motivation for students to engage in it, what is needed is some added external gain that can give students the motivation they lack. For instance, if a poetry assignment fails to motivate students to read, perhaps bonus points for doing the assignment will provide the needed motivation. Hence, extrinsic rewards have motivational value.

Do extrinsic rewards work? It is generally agreed that extrinsic rewards do encourage targeted behaviors, at least when teachers provide them in a sincere and contingent way (Baldwin & Baldwin, 1986; Skinner, 1953). Extrinsic rewards impose a structure on classroom behaviors by encouraging compliance and on-task behavior, and countering random and off-task behavior. When extrinsic rewards are no longer offered in exchange for desired behaviors, however, their effectiveness declines and the once-contingent behavior quickly returns to its previous level.

How Can I Use This?

What alternatives can you think of to motivate behavior without resorting to extrinsic rewards?

Selecting Reinforcers

Not everyone experiences the same consequences in the same way. A teacher may attempt to reinforce a fourth-grader's excellent written work by reading the child's story aloud to the class. The child is likely to derive some pleasure from this. The teacher's goal of reinforcing the child's work will probably be successful. However, if a middle school teacher attempts to reinforce a student's good written work by reading it aloud to the class, the student might experience this action as punitive. Middle school students are very conscious of their peers and may be embarrassed by the teacher's attention, or may be ridiculed by peers as a *teacher's pet*. One way to decide what reinforcers to provide is to ask the students what they would value. Examples of some students' responses are presented in the "What Kids Say and Do" box on the next page.

Patterns of Reinforcement

Students come to class with a history of reinforcement and punishment that influences their behavior in the classroom. You may provide reinforcements and punishments with the goal of increasing the frequency of desirable behaviors or reducing that of undesirable behaviors, and sometimes you may wonder why your strategies are not working. It may be because of patterns of reinforcement and punishment that have been applied to the students' prior behaviors.

Consequences do not always follow behavior. Sometimes a student's on-task behavior goes unnoticed. Not every behavior needs to be followed by reinforcement. Patterns of reinforcement are called *schedules of reinforcement*. These refer to the frequency with which reinforcement is provided. Schedules of reinforcement influence the speed, continuity, and persistence of behaviors. When a behavior is acquired for the first time, it is often under a different schedule of reinforcement than when it is being maintained. **Continuous reinforcement** schedules provide reinforcement after every occurrence of a behavior. In trying to teach autistic children to focus on an aide's face, for example, the aide will provide reinforcement every time the child makes eye contact. Continuous reinforcement can be helpful in learning a new behavior.

Intermittent schedules of reinforcement provide reinforcement only some of the time. Such schedules can be either variable or fixed, as shown in Figure 7.2. A fixed schedule of reinforcement allows the learner to predict when reinforcement will be provided. The schedule can be based on the passage of time (e.g., the first desired behavior after a 5-minute period) or on the number of behaviors performed (e.g., every five homework assignments submitted). When the schedule is based on the passage of time, it is called an **interval schedule**. When the schedule is based on the number of behaviors performed, it is called a **ratio schedule**. During the early acquisition of behaviors, fixed schedules are helpful as they allow the learner to predict when the next reinforcement will occur. They can quickly learn the relationship between the behavior and the consequence.

What Kids Say and Do

What We Find Reinforcing

Kindergarten students
- Being a messenger and leaving the class on my own
- Having lunch with the teacher in the classroom
- A special note home

Fourth-grade students
- Computer time
- Certificate to be the teacher's helper for a week
- Homework passes
- Certificate to select what the teacher brings for a snack for the child

Ninth-Grade Students
- Homework passes
- Chance to retake a quiz
- Pass from doing book report

---

continuous reinforcement Reinforcement that is provided after every performance of a behavior.

interval schedule   A schedule of reinforcement based on time.

ratio schedule   A schedule of reinforcement based on the number of behaviors.

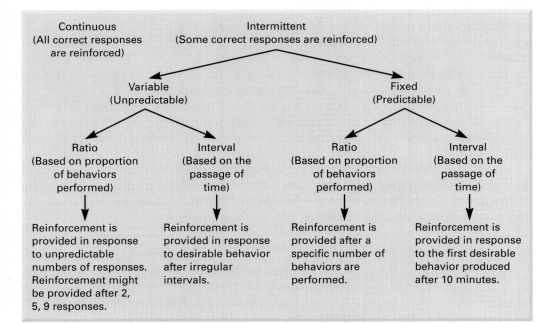

Figure 7.2. Schedules of Reinforcement

Continuous (All correct responses are reinforced)

Intermittent (Some correct responses are reinforced)

Variable (Unpredictable)

Fixed (Predictable)

Ratio (Based on proportion of behaviors performed)

Reinforcement is provided in response to unpredictable numbers of responses. Reinforcement might be provided after 2, 5, 9 responses.

Interval (Based on the passage of time)

Reinforcement is provided in response to desirable behavior after irregular intervals.

Ratio (Based on proportion of behaviors performed)

Reinforcement is provided after a specific number of behaviors are performed.

Interval (Based on the passage of time)

Reinforcement is provided in response to the first desirable behavior produced after 10 minutes.

Variable schedules of reinforcement are unpredictable. For example, if I press my garage door opener, I expect the door to open. Many times, however, it does not open. I may have to press the opener any number of times before it works. Because the door opens some of the time, I continue to press the opener rather than replacing it because it works often enough for my needs. The same pattern of reinforcement happens every day to students in the classroom, as their correct answer, punctuality and offers of kindness are sometimes reinforced and sometimes not.

Effects on Performance   The four schedules of reinforcement (**fixed interval, fixed ratio, variable interval, variable ratio schedules**) have very different effects on behavior. Variable schedules, whether based on the passage of time (interval) or on the number of responses (ratio), result in relatively consistent patterns of responses. Variable ratio schedules result in higher rates of response than do variable interval schedules. If you know that you will be reinforced after performing a certain behavior but don't know how many times you need to perform it before being reinforced, your rate of performance will be higher than it would be if you knew the actual schedule of reinforcement. Persistence in the performance of a behavior is higher when the behavior is reinforced on a variable schedule. If you cannot predict when you will be reinforced, you will likely continue to perform the behavior. For example, if your parents occasionally give you a gift when you get good grades, you may continue to work to keep your grades up in anticipation of future rewards.

Speed of performance is highest under a fixed ratio schedule. For example, if you know that you will get paid for every 10 cans you collect, you will probably work faster to collect cans. Fixed schedules increase predictability and thus give the learner more control over when he or she will receive the reinforcement. These schedules also usually result in a pause in the behavior after the reinforcement has been obtained.

Punishment

Consequences either increase or decrease the frequency of a behavior. **Punishers**, such as time-outs or parking tickets, are consequences that decrease the likelihood that a behavior will occur again in the future. They include presentation (positive) punishers and removal (negative) punishers. The frequency of undesirable behaviors can be decreased by positive punishers—adding something unpleasant to a situation (e.g., detention) or negative punishers—removing something pleasant (e.g., privileges such as time spent on a preferred activity). Table 7.1 provides definitions and examples of each of the four types of consequences: positive reinforcers, negative reinforcers, positive punishers, and negative punishers.

Positive Punishers to Suppress Behavior

A **positive punisher** is any event that, when given, decreases the frequency of a behavior. In terms of the law of effect, a presentation punisher represents bad effects of behavior. As an example, a teacher might reprimand a student who cheated on a test. The teacher gives the reprimand in order to stop the student's cheating. Other presentation punishers that are often used in schools are spanking, detention, assigning extra homework, or sending the student to the principal's office. When a teacher gives a student a disapproving look when the student continually taps a pencil on his desk, the strategy is to punish the undesirable behavior by making sure that it has bad effects that reduce the likelihood that it will occur in the future.

Desirable behaviors may be reduced by inadvertent punishment. A child who is shy and desperate to fit in with peers may experience a teacher's praise and attention in response to an assignment as punitive. The child may be ridiculed by peers or may be embarrassed. The frequency of doing assignments may well decline as a consequence.

Negative Punishers to Suppress Behavior

A **negative punisher** is any event that, when removed, decreases the frequency of a behavior. In terms of the law of effect, a negative punisher represents the termination of a behavior's good effects. For example, a teacher might remove a child from the playground after the child has pushed a classmate to the ground. The teacher takes away the child's playground

---

fixed interval schedule   A schedule of reinforcement based on the passage of a fixed amount of time.

fixed ratio schedule   A schedule of reinforcement based on the number of behaviors performed.

variable interval schedule   A schedule of reinforcement in which reinforcement is provided at irregular intervals based on the passage of time.

variable ratio schedule   A schedule of reinforcement in which reinforcement is provided at irregular intervals based on the number of behaviors performed.

punisher   A consequence of behavior that weakens or decreases behavior.

positive punisher   Any environmental event that, when given, decreases the frequency of a behavior.

negative punisher   Any environmental event that, when taken away, increases the frequency of a behavior.

TABLE 7.1

Definitions and Examples for the Four Types of Consequences

Positive Reinforcer

Definition	Any environmental event that, when given, increases the frequency of a behavior.
Example	The teacher smiles when Sam raises his hand in class. Because he wants to get more smiles from the teacher, he will raise his hand more often in the future.

Negative Reinforcer

Definition	Any environmental event that, when taken away, increases the frequency of a behavior.
Example	The teacher stares coldly at Suzi to encourage her to answer a question. Because she does not like having the teacher stare at her, Suzi will answer questions more often.

Positive Punisher

Definition	Any environmental event that, when given, decreases the frequency of a behavior.
Example	The teacher reprimands John for horsing around during the lesson. Because he does not want to receive any more reprimands, he desists from horsing around.

Negative Punisher

Definition	Any environmental event that, when taken away, decreases the frequency of a behavior.
Example	The teacher places Maria in a time-out for teasing a classmate. Because she does not want to be taken out of the class again, Maria stops teasing her classmates.

How Can I Use This?

If you wanted to teach students a new behavior, what schedule of reinforcement would you select?

privileges in order to punish (decrease) the aggression. This type of negative punisher is called a *response cost,* indicating that each occurrence of the undesirable behavior will cost the student some attractive resource, such as money (a fine or penalty), time on the classroom computer, the chance to watch a movie during the last 15 minutes of class, or a free Saturday morning (as with detention).

A second type of removal (negative) punisher is a time-out from an opportunity for positive reinforcement. Students generally enjoy being with their friends during class, lunch, and recess. A time-out is a procedure in which the teacher directs the student to leave a highly reinforcing environment and go to one that offers little or no reinforcement. In a classroom, a student can be assigned to sit at a distance from other students. School suspensions and expulsions are also removal punishers. When teachers take away points from students who sleep in class and schools suspend students for hitting others, the strategy is to punish these undesirable behaviors (sleeping, hitting) by making sure that they produce bad effects that make them less likely to occur in the future.

The Appeal of Punishers   The benefit to teachers of using punishers is that they can gain students' immediate compliance (Gershoff, 2002b). A verbal reprimand can stop children's horseplay, and peer rejection can stop an adolescent's rudeness. This compliance effect is almost always temporary, however. When the punisher is removed, the undesirable behavior often returns and may even increase. This phenomenon is called *recovery.* As soon as the teacher leaves—and verbal reprimands cease—the child's horseplay returns.

The Problem with Punishers   It is understandable that people use punishers to try to prevent undesirable behaviors from recurring. They see others cheating, hitting, stealing, teasing, name calling, arguing, damaging property, and committing acts of aggression, and they feel that they must do something about it. Usually, that means using a punisher. The punisher might be obvious, such as denial of privileges or a critical remark, or it might be subtle, such as a sigh of disappointment or a cold look. Classroom behaviors such as cheating,

 Could the committee use reinforcement or punishment to help solve the problems in the lunchroom described at the beginning of the chapter?

A trip to the principal's office is a frequently used punishment to teach students that their undesirable behaviors will produce bad effects. (Photo Disc, Inc./Getty Images)

hitting, and stealing cannot be ignored; teachers need to act. Spending a day in a classroom watching teachers interact with misbehaving students will convince almost any observer that punishment is a common strategy. But is it effective? Does the use of a punisher—whether positive or negative—actually suppress undesirable behaviors?

Unlike the single benefit of punishment, the costs are many. Table 7.2 lists four problematic *side effects* of punishment. As shown in the table, using punishers to suppress misbehavior teaches aggression through a modeling effect. The child learns, for instance, that the way to cope with an irritating peer is to punish him or her. Punishment also produces negative emotions. Because punishers are aversive events, they open the door to emotions such as fear, anger, and anxiety and behaviors such as crying and hiding. These negative

---

TABLE 7.2

Four Side Effects of Punishment

Effect of Punishment

1. Punishment teaches aggression.

By using a punisher to suppress another person's behavior, the person administering the punisher is modeling aggression as a means of dealing with undesirable ways of behaving. This effect occurs through observational learning. A student who receives verbal and physical punishment for misbehavior often imitates this way of coping when interacting with others and later tends to use harsh words and behaviors in the hope of suppressing the misbehavior of others.

2. Punishment produces negative emotions.

Punishment is an aversive behavioral strategy. When people receive aversive forms of stimulation, they often feel negative emotions such as fear, anger, distress, and worry. Punished students also report feeling embarrassed or humiliated in a public way. Understandably, students often associate these negative emotions with the person who is punishing them.

3. Punishment undermines the quality of the interpersonal relationship.

People who are punished typically want to escape from the person who is punishing them. They also go out of their way to avoid coming into contact with the person who punishes. Thus, if a teacher uses punishment on students, students may be motivated to stay clear of the teacher.

4. Punishment often exacerbates misbehavior.

Punishment suppresses behavior. But as one person punishes another, the person being punished experiences higher muscle tension, a raising of the voice, and a general increase in vigor of response. Being punished can sometimes throw fuel on the fire of misbehavior by producing shouting, threatening, protesting, and even acts of violence, counterresponse, and revenge. That is, punishment often makes matters worse, not better.

Taking It to the Classroom

Ways to Promote Good Behavior

- Help students achieve academic success.
- Use behavioral contracting.
- Encourage positive reinforcement of appropriate behavior.
- Use individual and group counseling.
- Encourage disciplinary consequences that are meaningful to students and have an instructional and/or reflection component.
- Provide social skills training.

Source: National Association of School Psychologists (2002). *Position statement on corporal punishment in schools.* Retrieved 10 October, 2004 from http://www.nasponline.org/information/pospaper_corpunish.html.

---

emotions are important not only in themselves but also because they undermine the relationship between teacher and student. The final side effect is that punishment often backfires and yields a vigorous protest response. Sometimes, using a punisher is like throwing fuel on the fire of misbehavior. These four side effects of punishment place teachers in a difficult dilemma—they need to stop undesirable behaviors, but the side effects are too troubling to accept. Fortunately, there are viable alternatives to punishment and negative control, such as ignoring behavior, substituting activities, and others.

Corporal Punishment in Schools It may surprise you to know that as many as 22 states allow corporal or physical punishment in schools. In the 1999–2000 school year, more than 300,000 students were paddled in school. The National Association of School Psychologists (NASP) opposes the use of corporal punishment in schools (NASP, 2002), and research on the use of such punishment by parents indicates that it increases immediate compliance but is linked to higher levels of aggression and lower levels of moral internalization (Gershoff, 2002). A disproportionate number of children who experience corporal punishment are minority students or students with disabilities (NASP, 2002). The NASP provides a number of alternative strategies for effective discipline that focus on positive behaviors; these are listed in the "Taking It to the Classroom" box above.

Chapter Reference
Chapter 11 contains many ideas about how to manage classroom behavior.

Can Punishment Be Used Effectively?

Most teachers will agree that punishment and negative control are not the best ways to manage students' behavior. They will say, however, that punishment is still necessary, at least under certain conditions. At the top of the list of those conditions are situations in which misbehavior threatens the safety or well-being of others. A child who hits another child is put into a time-out to protect the victim and the class as a whole.

In one sense, punishment whose goal is to protect others makes sense and is justified. For example, an upper-elementary school student of one of the authors once threw his chair, creating a risk for other students in the room. The student was immediately escorted to the principal's office. Punishment gives teachers a *last resort* to be used when other strategies are unsuccessful. A closer look at what happens in a classroom after a punished troublemaker has been removed (as through time-out, suspension, or expulsion), however, is revealing. More often than not, other students come forward to fill the void left by the absent troublemaker (Noguera, 2003). When this happens, should the teacher punish these students too? As you can see, what teachers need are viable, effective alternatives to punishment, ones that succeed in suppressing undesirable behaviors without producing the harmful side effects identified in Table 7.2. The "Taking it to the Classroom" box on the next page presents an example of how behavioral principles might be used in the classroom.

Taking It to the Classroom

Do You Know Jack? Ignoring Consequences

Jack often seems to ignore or disregard the consequences of his actions. Despite various penalties, punishments, and other negative consequences, he persists in behaving in ways that cause problems both for himself and for others. He does not finish classwork; he teases his peers (or worse); he interrupts the teacher; he behaves immaturely during the change of classes between periods. What can you do to help Jack?

1. Try to find good behaviors to reinforce.

2. Ignore some of the less disruptive behaviors.

3. Observe Jack when he is happy and on task. Note what events or interactions seem to please him.

4. Develop a behavior management plan for Jack (see later in this chapter or in Chapter 11).

5. Try taking Jack's perspective on the problem in an effort to develop some insight. Does he get teased as well? Is he looking for more attention from you?

6. Consult the school psychologist for assistance in developing alternatives for dealing with Jack's behavior.

Applied Behavior Analysis

discriminative stimuli
Antecedent cues that allow the learner to predict the likelihood of reinforcement.

In addition to its consequences, behavior is also influenced by the situational cues that precede it. When particular behaviors are followed by reinforcements in situation A but not in situation B, the cues preceding each behavior signal whether reinforcement is likely or not. These cues become **discriminative stimuli**. A behavior such as petting a dog might have good effects in one situation but bad effects in another. Petting the family's dog might produce tail wags, whereas petting the neighbor's dog might produce growls. As a result, people learn to be sensitive to the situational cues that help them determine whether a behavior is likely to produce good effects (reinforcement) or bad effects (punishment) in a certain situation. In this example, being with the family dog is a cue that petting will produce good effects, whereas being with the neighbor's dog is a cue that petting will produce bad effects. In the same vein, students learn that talking is good during lunch period but bad while taking a test. The point of situational cues is that people learn which behaviors do and do not work in one situation, as well as which behaviors do and do not work in other, different situations.

Because behavior is influenced both by the cues that precede it and by the effects that follow it, the following formulation can be used to summarize two basic principles of behavioral learning theory:

$$A : B \rightarrow C$$

In this formulation, *A* stands for antecedent cues, *B* for behavior, and *C* for consequences. Antecedents come before behavior; consequences occur after behavior. The arrow between *B* and *C* indicates that behavior causes the consequences to happen. Petting the dog causes the dog's good or bad reaction. The colon between the *A* and *B* means that antecedent cues set the stage for—but do not cause—the behavior.

Teachers can observe the kinds of cues that seem to precede desirable or undesirable behaviors. For example, a student may exhibit the undesirable behavior of shouting out answers in class, but only when he or she is seated beside a friend. When the child is seated beside other students, he or she may raise a hand to offer an answer. In this case, observation of the antecedents of the undesirable behavior would allow the teacher to identify the best course of action. The "Taking It to the Classroom" box on the next page provides guidelines for applying behavioral learning principles to classroom problems.

Taking It to the Classroom

Guidelines for Applying Behavioral Learning Principles to Classroom Problems

Phase	Factors to consider
Premodification phase	
Problem identification and definition	• Identify and describe the problem to be resolved and the behavior to be changed. • It is very useful to note antecedent events.
Recording	• Note the contexts in which the behavior occurs and how often it occurs. • Graphs often reveal patterns.
Modification plan	• Focus on a targeted behavior. • Devise a plan based on information revealed by records.
Modification phase	
Modification plan applied	• Ensure that when the targeted behavior occurs, it is followed by an appropriate consequence. • Note: In some cases, the behavior is addressed by changing antecedent conditions.
Recording	• Recording is necessary to determine the plan's effectiveness.
Evaluation	• In most successful interventions, there will be an abrupt change in the number of incidents. • Gradual change usually indicates that a better plan could be designed.
Postmodification phase	
Modification plan removed	• If the plan is successful, discontinue the intervention. • The plan can be considered successful when the student's behavior changes in the desired way and the change is extensive enough to resolve the problem for both the student and the teacher.
Recording	• Monitor the student's behavior after the modification.
Evaluation	• If the targeted behavior returns, decide whether to reapply the original plan or devise a new one. • If the plan is successful, it is a good idea to conduct a periodic "spot check" of behavior, especially if the student displays other undesirable behaviors.

Source: Based on Bergan, J.R., & Caldwell, T. (1995). Operant techniques in school psychology. *Journal of Educational and Psychological Consultation. 6,* 103–110.

Managing Behavior

Managing behavior means setting up conditions that make desirable behaviors more likely to occur and undesirable ones less likely to occur. Such conditions include strategic use of antecedent conditions to cue desirable behaviors and discourage undesirable ones, but for the most part managing behavior involves strategic use of behavioral consequences.

When it comes to managing behavior, students generally like positive control and dislike negative control. Positive control refers to instructional efforts to manage behavior through the use of rewards and positive reinforcement. Negative control refers to instructional efforts to manage behavior through the use of negative reinforcement, positive punishment, and negative punishment. Students also learn better and more efficiently under conditions of positive control than they do under conditions of negative control. All four types of consequences are important determinants of students' learning and behaving, but in practice, effectively managing students' behavior entails a liberal administration of positive reinforcers and minimal use of negative reinforcers, positive punishers, and negative punishers. Before discussing how to increase students' desirable behaviors, let us first wrestle with the problems and shortcomings associated with negative control. Negative control routinely leads to the sort of side effects listed in Table 7.2.

Negative control involves using negative reinforcers to increase desirable behaviors and using positive and negative punishers to suppress undesirable behaviors. Thus, it employs aversive events, such as criticism, threats, deadlines, reprimands, spankings, response costs, and time-outs. Most of the time, negative control means using punishers to suppress undesirable behaviors.

Behavioral Learning Theory and Diverse Learners

Classroom diversity may make it more challenging for beginning teachers to cope with classroom management issues. This may be so for two reasons. First, the more different teachers are from their students, the greater is the likelihood that they will have different definitions of desirable and undesirable behaviors. White, middle-class, female teachers often view being quiet and sitting at one's desk as desirable and appropriate ways of behaving, whereas African American, lower class, male students typically view being assertive and forceful as desirable and appropriate (Irvine, 1990). The greater the diversity, the greater are the chances of misunderstanding. Second, creating a respectful, caring, and productive classroom is always a challenge, and diversity in the classroom, in which students see differences all around them, can make this challenge even greater. Students sometimes interpret difference as inferiority; one student might think that another student speaks the "wrong" language, for instance. On the other hand, when teachers and students value and embrace diversity, they avoid such negative interpretations and develop productive relationships (Weiner, 2003).

Classroom diversity, therefore, places an obligation on teachers to understand their students' cultural, national, and ethnic backgrounds. They can do this by fostering relationships with parents and community representatives, reading and watching videotapes about their students' cultures, and familiarizing themselves with the countries and cultures from which their students have immigrated (Curran, 2003). Armed with such knowledge, they can better interpret and explain students (mis)behavior (Norris, 2003).

Interviews and classroom observations of effective teachers in highly diverse schools reveal three principles of classroom management that work particularly well (Brown, 2003). First, culturally responsive classroom management involves communicating in culturally appropriate ways. One teacher who taught highly language-diverse students, for instance, made a special effort to greet each child in his or her native language. Such an action opens the door to two-way communication in which the minority culture is as valid and respected as is the majority culture. Second, culturally responsive classroom management establishes clear expectations for behavior. In many urban classrooms, establishing clear expectations means being assertive, establishing authority, enforcing rules, reminding students with assurances such as, "I'm here to help you. I'm not going to let you slide! You're not going to get away with acting the wrong way or not doing the work" (Brown, 2003). Third, culturally responsive classroom management revolves around caring for all students. Teachers in diverse classrooms who have well-behaved, highly engaged students offer affection, warmth, and high-quality relationships to all students. What diverse students say when asked to describe caring teachers appears in the "What Kids Say and Do" box on the next page.

Behavioral Learning Theory and Special Needs Students

Teachers can expect that students with special needs will sometimes have a more difficult time displaying desirable behaviors than will students without special needs. To help students with special needs engage in desirable behaviors, develop skills, and carry out self-

Appendix
Awareness of Difference
Differences among students can present challenges to the classroom teacher in managing behavior because of potential misunderstanding (*PRAXIS™*, I. B. 4, *INTASC*, Principle 1).

What Kids Say and Do

Describing Caring Teachers

Here are examples of what middle school students in highly diverse schools say when asked to describe caring teachers:

Caring teachers...

are fair.

ask me what I think.

hold high expectations for what I can do.

Caring teachers do not...

yell.

interrupt me.

criticize me.

hold low expectations for what I can do.

regulated learning, teachers need to give them positive behavioral supports (Soodak, 2003). Behavioral learning theory is still widely used with special needs students. Reinforcement is used in a variety of ways to help students set goals, accomplish goals, and regulate their academic and social behavior.

Under the provisions of the reauthorized Individuals with Disabilities Education Act Improvement (IDEA) (2004), the right of a student with a disability to remain in his or her current educational setting pending an appeal was eliminated for violations that were serious enough to warrant a suspension of more than 10 days. Previously, a student was removed only pending appeal for violations involving drugs, weapons, or other dangerous behavior. The disruption of services to a child with a disability who is moved to a new educational placement may limit the child's progress. Prior to the reauthorization of IDEA in 2004, the school was required to show that the behavior that resulted in disciplinary action was not a manifestation of the child's disability before it could apply the kinds of disciplinary procedures that would be applied to nondisabled students. Under the new law, the burden has been shifted to the parents, who must prove that the behavior for which discipline is being considered was related to the child's disability.

Chapter Reference
Chapter 4 contains an extensive discussion of issues related to students with special needs.

Increasing Desirable Behaviors

Teachers who use behavioral learning principles to increase students' desirable behaviors generally do so in three ways. First, they offer attractive incentives that elicit behaviors. Second, once a desired behavior has begun, they use prompts and behavioral supports to maintain it. Third, after an episode of desired behavior, they use positive reinforcers to strengthen that behavior and encourage its occurrence in the future. As part of this third course of action, they may use **shaping**, or reinforcing gradual approximations of the desired behavior.

shaping   Reinforcement of gradual approximations of the desired behavior.

Incentives An **incentive** is an event that attracts a person toward a particular course of action. Incentives are antecedent conditions; therefore, they always precede desired behaviors. Some common classroom incentives include a smile, a surprise box that contains wrapped gifts from which a child can select, the sound of laughter, or any promise of good things to come. Notice that offering an incentive is a way of sending students the message that attractive consequences will be forthcoming if they engage in the desired behavior. When teachers promise students a reward in order to solicit their learning and participation, they are using the reward as an incentive—an incentive to initiate a teacher-endorsed course of action.

incentive   An environmental event that attracts a person toward a particular course of action.

Prompts and Behavioral Supports   Sometimes students want to engage in a desired behavior but either forget to do so or do not quite know how. Sometimes they need a reminder, as illustrated by the prompt shown in Figure 7.3.

prompts   Physical, verbal, or other assists that help a person perform a desired behavior that he or she would be unlikely to perform without such assistance.

Prompts are physical, verbal, or other assists that help a person perform a desired behavior that he or she might not have performed without such assistance. A teacher might, for instance, provide a student with the first three lines of a poem to get him or her started, or give the child a tip about how to proceed if he or she is stuck or confused. The teacher might also offer a gesture, picture, instruction, suggestion, or hint about how to proceed or how to get back on track. A sign, a note card, a string tied around the finger, or a verbal reminder from a cooperative learning partner, such as, "Okay, now we should paraphrase," are all ways of prompting desired behaviors. After the desired behavior has been prompted and performed, positive reinforcement can be used to strengthen it.

USING FIX-UP STRATEGIES

What to do when I don't understand.

Choose one of these.

- **Ignore and read on.**
- **Guess by context.**
- **Reread to clear up confusion.**
- **Look back at previous information.**
  See if it helps me understand the difficult part.

Source: "Creating Confident and Competent Readers: Transactional Strategies Instruction" by C. P. Casteel, B. A. Isom, and K. F. Jordan, 2000, *Intervention in School and Clinic, Vol. 36,* 67–77. Copyright 2000 by PRO-ED, Inc. Reprinted with permission.

Figure 7.3. A Behavioral Prompt for Readers

Positive Reinforcers   Using positive reinforcers to strengthen desired behaviors can be characterized as a strategy of "catching them being good." When a desired behavior occurs, the teacher gives the student a positive reinforcer—the sooner the better. The purpose is to help the student learn that this particular way of behaving has positive consequences. The more the student associates good effects with the behavior, the more frequently he or she will engage in that behavior.

Punctuality is generally viewed as a desirable behavior. In one study (Hall et al., 1970), teachers gave fifth-grade students a positive reinforcer if they returned promptly from recess and were inside the classroom door before the bell rang. The positive reinforcer was to have their name placed on a wall chart under the heading *Today's Patriots* (the students were learning about eighteenth-century patriots and saw the label as very positive). Figure 7.4 shows how effective the positive reinforcer was in increasing students' punctuality. Before the study (days 1–13), when no positive reinforcer was associated with being in the classroom on time, eight students on average were late returning from recess. During days 14–32, when punctuality earned the student a name on the *Today's Patriots* chart, lateness was rare, and 100% of the students were punctual during days 21–32. During days 33–38, the wall chart was removed so that punctuality no longer earned the status of Patriot, and once again, on each of these days several students were late. Finally, during days 39–43, the wall chart was reinstated, and punctuality rates again returned to 100%. This study shows that giving a positive reinforcer can increase a desired target behavior such as punctuality.

To use positive reinforcement effectively in the classroom, you can do the following:

- Ask students to identify effective reinforcers or observe what they choose to do during their free time.
- Establish a variety of reinforcers, because different children will be reinforced by different consequences.
- Be sure to reinforce behaviors in ways that students value; that is, ensure that the consequences you provide are actually reinforcing.
- Give plenty of reinforcement when students are trying new skills or learning new material.

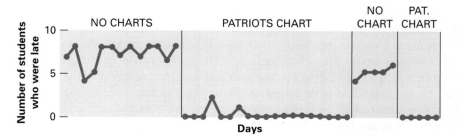

Figure 7.4. Effects of a Positive Reinforcer on Students' Punctuality

Source: Hall, R. V., Cristler, C., Cranston, S. S., & Tucker, B. (1970). Teachers and parents as researchers using multiple baseline designs. *Journal of Applied Behavior Analysis, 3,* 247–255.

Appendix
Positive Behavior

You can encourage and support positive behaviors that will facilitate students' learning and motivation (*PRAXIS*™, I. C. 2, *INTASC*, Principle 5).

- When new behaviors have become established, provide reinforcement on an unpredictable schedule to encourage persistence of those behaviors.
- Try to ensure that all students receive reinforcement.

Praise is frequently used by teachers as a positive reinforcer and when used successful, positive behavior is likely to increase. To use praise appropriately, the teacher should not provide empty compliments. Instead, praise should dependent on the performance of a desired behavior, In giving praise, the teacher should describe what behavior is praiseworthy. Teachers do not always use praise appropriately, however (see the Uncommon Sense box on this page).

Shaping If we waited for a child to perform a complex behavior before reinforcing that behavior, we might not provide much in the way of reinforcement. The child may not yet be able perform such behaviors. For example, cursive writing is difficult for many young children and requires fine motor control and perception. The first time a child writes the letter *a*, it may not resemble what we consider a cursive *a*, and it would not be the desired behavior. However, if we reinforce the child's attempts to write the letter *a* as each one comes closer to the correct form, we are *shaping* the child's behavior. The child is gradually getting closer to performing the behavior at the standard we are aiming for.

Downsides of Rewards From the preceding discussion, the way to increase desired behavior is clear: Offer attractive incentives, provide prompts, and give positive reinforcers when the desired behavior occurs. But just as punishers have troubling side effects, so do incentives and reinforcers. These side effects were discussed in Chapter 6, and we repeat them here. Incentives, rewards, and reinforcers can (a) undermine intrinsic motivation; (b) interfere with learning; and (c) hinder autonomous self-regulation.

Incentives, rewards, and reinforcers are designed to promote extrinsic motivation. Why a student who expects to be rewarded behaves in the desired way is clear—because of the offer of the attractive incentive or reward. So although they are not designed to promote intrinsic motivation, incentives and rewards *do* promote extrinsic motivation and, thus, place intrinsic motivation at risk.

Incentives and rewards can help students learn behaviors and factual knowledge (e.g., the right answer). But when educators want to promote other types of learning, such as conceptual understanding, they need other approaches to instruction; these are discussed in later chapters. Finally, incentives and rewards are intended as ways to regulate desirable and undesirable behaviors. When students learn to depend on incentives, prompts, and rewards to regulate their behavior, these external events can forestall the development of self-regulatory abilities (Joussemet et al., 2004). Educators need to make a special effort to promote students' capacity for self-management. This important topic will be discussed later in the chapter.

Uncommon Sense

Praise Is Always Good—Or Is It?

Praise is often used as a reinforcer in classrooms. Children respond positively to praise from their teachers. It is easy for teachers to use praise as a reinforcer, because it does not require record keeping. But is praising students always a good idea?

Praise is in an attempt to increase the probability that desired behaviors will be repeated. Consequences that are reinforcing are associated with pleasant feelings. Consequences are punitive if the frequency of the undesirable behavior decreases, and receiving a punitive consequence such as criticism is typically associated with unpleasant feelings.

Research on the use of praise and criticism (Meyer, 1992) has found some paradoxical effects. When praise is provided, the recipient often feels that the person providing the praise regards his or her ability as low. In contrast, the recipient of criticism feels that the person providing the criticism regards his or her ability as high. You should be clear and systematic in providing praise, pointing to the behavior that is praiseworthy. Genuine accomplishments should be praised; otherwise, it will not be effective. When providing praise, you should attribute the behavior to the child's efforts and ability.

"That is the correct answer, Billy, but I'm afraid you don't win anything for it."

Decreasing Undesirable Behaviors

Teachers can prevent minor behavior problems from becoming more serious. Punishment produces a mixed response: It gains temporary compliance and thus stops the undesired behavior, but it does so at the expense of four troubling side effects (see Table 7.2). Nevertheless, the use of punishment is quite common. Fortunately, there are a number of effective alternatives to punishment. Let us take a brief look at some of them.

Verbal Reprimands One of the most common types of negative consequences (punishment) is verbal reprimands. Reprimands are a teacher's brief statement to draw attention to misbehavior, such as "no," "don't," "stop that," or "get back to work." Reprimands given in private are likely to be most effective in suppressing undesirable behavior (O'Leary et al., 1970). Some students may find that a scolding by the teacher is actually reinforcing because of the attention they receive, but many find it unpleasant. Depending on the situation, a scolding can be embarrassing as well as unpleasant.

Response Cost The following is an example of the use of response cost. A child in a first-grade class was constantly getting out of her seat without permission. The teacher found this behavior very disruptive, because the child talked to other children and took things from them. He decided to use a response cost system to reduce the incidence of this behavior. He gave the child a jar with 10 marbles in it and told her that she would lose a marble if she got up from her seat without permission. If there were 3 marbles left in the jar at the end of the day, she would receive a reward. As the marbles disappeared, the child became aware of the possible loss of the promised reward. The visible record of her misbehavior gave her a chance to exercise control over her own behavior.

Differential Reinforcement Differential reinforcement is a two-step strategy that captures the essence of the phrase "catch them being good." First, the teacher identifies both the undesired behavior and an alternative, desired way of behaving. For instance, during group work, if a student insults other students, the teacher might identify insults as the undesired behavior and giving encouragement as an alternative, desired behavior. Second, when the desired behavior occurs, the teacher provides a positive reinforcer to strengthen that behavior. At the same time, the teacher ignores the undesired behavior—neither punishing it nor reinforcing it. This differential reinforcement works to suppress the undesired behavior because the alternative way of behaving becomes more frequent and eventually replaces the undesired way of behaving. In other words, if the student encourages his or her peers more, he or she will spend less time insulting. Through differential reinforcement, the teacher plays the constructive role of reinforcer and avoids the negative role of punisher.

Inductive Reasoning Inductive reasoning is a two-step strategy in which the teacher helps the misbehaving student understand the harmful effects of the misbehavior. The teacher holds a conversation with the student to identify and emphasize the suffering caused, intentionally or unintentionally, by the undesired behavior. For instance, if a child *borrowed* another child's pencil, he or she might imagine that little harm had been done. The teacher could describe the harm done to the child who now lacks a pencil and go on to try to induce perspective-taking and empathy for the victim. For instance, the teacher might invite the child to imagine what it would be like to lack a pencil when the class was working on an assignment. The child cannot complete the work in time and may have to stay in at recess to complete the work. In general, inductive reasoning is an effective strategy for coping with misbehavior because it decreases future undesirable behaviors while avoiding harmful side effects and promoting beneficial effects (e.g., greater empathy, increased social skill).

An important extension of inductive reasoning—a third step—is to continue discussing perspective-taking until the child generates a prosocial alternative way of behaving or solving the problem. The teacher might invite the child to answer the question, "Instead of taking Billy's pencil without his permission, what else could you have done that would have allowed you to have a pencil?" Often the child can readily generate prosocial responses, such as, "I could ask his permission" or "I could keep a pencil in my desk" or "We could share his pencil—take turns using it." Teachers who use inductive reasoning believe that *being good* does not simply mean behaving well. It means that students are thinking and learning about their behavior and how it affects others. Through inductive reasoning, the teacher plays the constructive role of counselor and avoids the negative role of punisher. (See the "Taking It to the Classroom" box on the next page for strategies to prevent negative behavior from escalating.)

Observational Learning Experienced teachers can often anticipate misbehavior before it occurs. An experienced teacher, for instance, might anticipate that an elementary school student might shove others to get to the front of the lunch line or that a high school student might ridicule a peer who has difficulty making a classroom presentation. This foreknowledge comes from experience. If the teacher anticipates that such behaviors may occur, he or she can demonstrate what appropriate behavior looks like in these situations. After modeling the desired behavior, the teacher can invite students to imitate it. As students practice the desired behavior, the teacher can coach, refine, and positively reinforce it. Notice that if students are already behaving in the desired way, the teacher is never placed in the position of having to correct their misbehavior. Through observational learning, the teacher serves as a *role model* and avoids the role of *punisher*.

Chapter Reference
Chapter 10 includes a fuller explanation of observational learning.

Scaffolding/Tutoring Sometimes, students misbehave because they do not yet know how to behave in more appropriate ways. Bullies sometimes do not know how to make friends and resort to undesirable behaviors to gain attention and respect. Through scaffolding and tutoring, a teacher can assist students' efforts to learn desirable behaviors. The teacher can provide examples, clues, reminders, hints, tips, challenges—whatever the misbehaving student needs to "get over the hump" and learn more desirable and rewarding ways of behaving. Notice that this sort of coaching also involves the use of prompts and behavioral supports, such as questions, to lead the student to think about the needed content. Through scaffolding, the teacher plays the role of *tutor* or *coach* and avoids the role of *punisher*.

Chapter Reference
Chapters 2, 10, and 12 provide additional information about scaffolding. Different types of scaffolding are described in Chapter 10. Chapter 12 provides more details about tutoring.

Taking It to the Classroom

Preventing Behavioral Escalations

Background

Most classroom problems are minor, and the teacher can easily work with the student to resolve the problem. However, there are times when a relatively minor incident (e.g., arguing, calling out) can escalate into a confrontation between student and teacher. This often results in challenges to the teacher or refusal to comply with the teacher's directives. Other students become anxious or curious onlookers, and instruction comes to a halt. Experts in classroom management recommend that teachers focus on preventing behavioral escalations instead of managing crisis situations once they occur (Shukla-Mehta & Albin, 2003). Following are some guidelines for preventing behavioral escalations in the classroom.

Guidelines for Preventing Behavioral Escalations in the Classroom

Strategy	*Examples/rationale*
Reinforce calm and on-task behaviors.	• Provide positive attention. • Encourage peer approval. • Praise on-task behavior.
Know the triggers.	• Difficult academic tasks • Time pressure • Anxiety about an exam
Do not escalate along with the student.	• Remain calm when provoked. • Disengage from confrontation. • Give student time or space to disengage from confrontation.
Offer opportunities to display responsible behavior.	• Do not make demands on student while he or she is agitated. • Verbally prompt the student regarding appropriate choices. • Debrief student privately to point out consequences and explore suitable alternative behaviors.
Intervene early in the sequence.	Steps: • Recall/identify early problem behaviors in the escalation pattern. • Intervene with deescalation strategies. • Anticipate subsequent problem behaviors and be prepared to continue interventions.
Understand how such incidents ended in the past.	• Teacher should evaluate the effectiveness of a strategy on the basis of its effect on student's previous behavior. ("Is my strategy serving my goal or an undesirable goal?")
Know the function of problem behaviors. (Problem behaviors often have underlying functions or goals.)	• Avoidance of work • Teacher attention • Peer attention
Use good judgment about which behaviors to punish.	• Match consequence to severity of problem behavior. • Avoid using same consequence (e.g., time-out) for all types of problem behaviors.
Teach students socially appropriate behavior to replace problem behavior.	• Teach and reinforce a more responsible behavior (e.g., asking for help) in place of a less desirable behavior (e.g., complaining) when a difficult task is assigned.

Teach academic survival skills and set students up for success.	• Teach effective learning strategies:
	  ○ Note taking
	  ○ Study skills
	• Anticipate mistakes.

Source: Shukla-Mehta, S., & Albin, R.W. (2003). Twelve practical strategies to prevent behavioral escalation in classroom settings. *Preventing School Failure, 47* (3), 156–161. Reprinted with permission of the Helen Dwight Reid Educational Foundation. Published by Heldref Publications, 1319 Eighteenth St., NW, Washington, DC 20036-1802. Copyright © 2003.

Why Do Students Misbehave?

The approach described in the previous paragraph might be summarized as "reinforce, explain, model, or coach desirable behavior so as to reduce and eliminate undesirable behavior." Such strategies replace undesirable behaviors with desirable ones. The question remains, however, as to why students engage in the undesirable behavior in the first place: Why do students misbehave?

One could equally well ask: Why don't students behave properly? The best way to promote on-task attention and desirable behaviors during a lesson is to provide high-quality instruction. That is, regardless of the discipline strategies a teacher employs (positive vs. negative control), teachers who provide interesting activities, ask challenging questions, and know how to engage students in learning will have students who display mostly on-task and desirable behaviors. Teachers who provide boring activities, ask only right-or-wrong factual questions, and do not know how to engage students in learning will have students who display mostly off-task and undesirable behaviors (Jeanpierre, 2004).

In a learning environment, being inattentive, lazy, and uncooperative are undesirable behaviors. If students are to learn, such behaviors must be replaced by more productive, desirable behaviors, such as being attentive and actively engaged. From this point of view, misbehavior is as much a quality of teaching issue as it is one of discipline. This is so because disengagement is a natural response to a lesson that is unchallenging, repetitious, or irrelevant to one's goals. To promote learning and on-task behavior, teachers need to provide effective teaching strategies, high-quality instruction, and a family-like environment in which students feel supported by a caring teacher (Cremin, 1988). Effective classroom management, therefore, requires not only positive control strategies but also high-quality instruction (Newmann, 1992; Noguera, 2003; Wong & Wong, 1998).

Another reason students misbehave is that they find themselves in environments that do not address their needs (Brown, 2003). (See the "Uncommon Sense" box on this page.) An interesting phenomenon occurs when a student's teacher, rather than his or her parents, explains the student's misbehavior. Teachers tend to invoke some shortcoming on the part of the student (e.g., "He doesn't like school," "She's angry"), whereas parents tend to invoke reasons such as boredom and frustration with instruction, the lack of a trusting relationship with the teacher, and school practices that they perceive as unfair and discriminatory (Weiner, 2003). Although this difference in emphasis may be somewhat unfair to the teacher,

> **What Does This Mean to Me?**
> Did you misbehave in high school? Why? What could a teacher have done to prevent this misbehavior?

Uncommon Sense

Zero-Tolerance Policies Solve Problems of Aggression and Violence—Or Do They?

Zero-tolerance policies use exclusionary forms of discipline, such as suspension, when students behave in violent ways. Introduced in the 1990s, they are designed to send a clear and unambiguous message that no aggressive behavior will be tolerated in school (Ayers, Dorhn, & Ayers, 2001). Looking for ways to stop violence, many schools adopted a tough yet simple plan: Evict violent students (i.e., one strike and you're out).

Zero-tolerance policies have four major drawbacks (Noguera, 2003; Skiba & Peterson, 2001). First, they undermine their own purpose by eroding civility within the school. It is hard to promote caring and compassion by using punishment. Second, these policies penalize students who are most in need of emotional connectedness to the school. Third, zero-tolerance policies are rarely applied equally to all students. Students of color and students with disabilities are at the greatest risk of expulsion. Last, students who are suspended rarely change their behavior for the better.

Zero-tolerance policies have the same appeal that any punishment-based strategy has—namely, schools have to do something to protect students who behave properly. The assumption behind this *bad apple theory* is that safety and order can be achieved by removing *bad* individuals and keeping them away from the others, who are presumed to be *good*. Although there is some truth to this belief, it is equally true that aggressive students often abandon their behavioral problems when they are assigned to classes with highly effective teachers (McCarthy & Benally, 2003). The finding that zero-tolerance policies rarely work is uncommon sense because most teachers endorse this *bad apple* theory (Noguera, 2003). Careful analysis reveals, however, that the most common causes of students' misbehavior are classroom factors, such as: (a) being bored and alienated from school, (b) learning from teachers who are disorganized or unmotivated, (c) believing that teachers have very low expectations of what the student can do and accomplish, and (d) having antagonistic relationships with teachers and administrators (Steinberg, 1996). Such findings offer educators a hint of hope, because all these factors are, to some extent, under their control.

Chapter Reference
Chapter 11 provides additional explanations for why students misbehave.

there is some truth in it, because the students who are punished the most are those with the greatest academic, social, economic, and emotional needs (Cartledge & Milburn, 1996; Irvine, 1990; Johnson, Boyden, & Pittz, 2001), particularly students who are low achievers, have learning disabilities, are minorities, are in foster care, or are entitled to free or reduced-price lunches (Meier, Stewart, & England, 1989; Skiba, 2000).

Promoting Self-Management

By using behavioral principles, teachers can influence students' behaviors. Often, however, they want to do more than that. They want to transfer the responsibility for managing behavior away from the teacher and onto the students themselves. In other words, they want to encourage self-management.

Effective self-management is a learned ability. Before students can be expected to manage their own behavior, they need to learn how to do so. Initially, many behaviors are teacher-regulated. For instance, many first-grade students have a difficult time using a quiet voice in class, just as many middle school students have a difficult time doing their homework on time, and many high school students have a difficult time reading assigned books during study hall. To self-manage such behavior, students need to learn the following abilities: (a) plan their behavior and set their own goals (goal setting); (b) provide self-instructions and constructive self-talk (self-instruction); (c) monitor how well or poorly they are behaving (self-observation); (d) evaluate the desirability of their behavior (self-evaluation); and (e) apply self-generated consequences to reinforce their desired behaviors (self-consequences).

Chapter Reference
Chapter 5 discusses how students gain self-regulatory capacities.

Table 7.3 illustrates these aspects of self-management. Whether the person who engages in self-management is a writer, an athlete, a musician, or a student, each of the five regulatory processes contributes to self-management. The student, for instance, engages in self-management by first making a list of what is to be accomplished during the study session (goal setting), verbally prompting and praising desired study behaviors (self-instruction), keeping records of completed assignments (self-monitoring), checking work before handing it in (self-evaluation), and making watching TV or phoning friends contingent on completion of assignments (self-consequences).

How can teachers help students learn such self-regulatory abilities? Obviously, they need to encourage self-management and communicate its value. Some teachers ask students to follow strict routines, whereas others encourage them to be responsible for their own behavior (Bohn, Roehrig, & Pressley, 2004). One effective strategy is to teach students how to carry out a think-aloud analysis (Brown & Pressley, 1994; Pressley et al., 1992). In a think-aloud analysis, the teacher assigns the student a task such as reading a book. At different points in the task (e.g., before reading the book, while reading it, and after reading it), students are to ask themselves questions such as, What is my goal? What specifically will I do? How many pages have I read? Did I do well? What kind of reward do I deserve? Notice that these questions correspond to goal setting, self-instructions, self-monitoring, self-evaluating, and self-consequences, as illustrated in Table 7.3. With experience, students develop these self-regulatory abilities and become increasingly able to manage their own learning and behavior.

Appendix
Promoting a Positive Climate

You can promote positive social behavior, positive relationships, and cooperation about students that will result in more time available for learning (*PRAXIS™*, I. C. 4, *INTASC*, Principle 5).

The Fundamental Task of Classroom Management

The fundamental task of classroom management is to create an inclusive, supportive, caring, engaging, and challenging community in which students frequently engage in desirable, constructive, and prosocial behavior (Good & Brophy, 1997; Weinstein, Curran, & Tomlinson-Clarke, 2003). For a teacher who thinks of classroom management as a system of rules, rewards, and penalties, this view may be puzzling at first. But creating a classroom environment that fully engages students in learning activities is the best antidote to misbehavior. It is also a proactive, preventive strategy, one that promotes and reinforces desirable behavior, rather than a reactive, remedial strategy that controls and punishes undesirable behavior. From this point of view, the ultimate goal of classroom management is not to achieve compliance and control, but rather to provide students with frequent opportunities for learning (Weinstein et al., 2003). The "Taking It to the Classroom" box on the next page offers three suggestions for creating opportunities for students to learn and grow.

Chapter Reference
Chapter 11 provides an extensive discussion of classroom management.

Taking It to the Classroom

Three Suggestions for Creating Opportunities for Students to Learn and Grow

1. *Organize the physical environment in ways that will promote desirable behavior.*
   If the teacher values social interaction, desks should be arranged in clusters so that students can work together, share materials, have face-to-face discussions, and help one another with assignments. If the teacher values being kind to others, he or she can provide a *kindness box* into which students can drop brief notes about acts of kindness they witness; periodically, the teacher can pull a note from the box and read it aloud (Beane, 1999).

2. *Establish expectations for desirable behavior.*
   Effective teachers make certain that students know what is expected of them; they say clearly that students must listen to and respect one another. They also model these behaviors, and they explain why these rules of conduct are important, helpful, and constructive. Throughout the school year, these teachers give students opportunities to practice and develop these ways of behaving, even to the point of teaching classroom behaviors and norms in the same way that they teach academic subjects.

3. *Create caring, inclusive classrooms.*
   Misbehavior such as teasing, insulting, fighting, and bullying stems from disrespect and conflict between students. To prevent such misbehavior before it occurs, teachers can create caring, inclusive communities in their classrooms. One way to achieve this goal is to hold a *morning meeting* in which students greet each other, share news, and participate in a group activity (Kriete, 1999). A similar activity is a *sharing circle* in which students get together to brainstorm and generate solutions to problems such as conflicts that occur on the school bus (Norris, 2003). Notice that the teacher's attention is focused at least as much on promoting high-quality relations between students as it is on promoting specific desirable behaviors or preventing specific undesirable behaviors.

TABLE 7.3

Self-Regulatory Processes Underlying the Effective Self-Management of Writers, Athletes, Musicians, and Students

Self-regulatory processes	Domain			
	Writers	Athletes	Musicians	Students
Goal setting	Setting daily word or page goals	Setting specific and quantifiable daily goals for training	Setting daily practice session goals	Making lists of things to accomplish during study
Self-instruction	Saying aloud what will be written	Self-verbalizing confidence statements—for example, "Let's go!"	Verbally praising or prompting oneself	Rehearsing steps in solving a math problem
Self-monitoring	Keeping records of literary production	Keeping a daily record of goal accomplishment or filming matches for replay	Keeping daily records of performance—for example, stress levels	Keeping records of completed assignments
Self-evaluation	Putting off self-judgments during creation	Breaking game into components and evaluating oneself after each performance	Listening to self-recording, setting realistic standards	Checking work before handing it in
Self-consequences	Putting off pleasurable events until writing is completed	Grading oneself after every match	Refusing to end practice until passage is played flawlessly	Making TV or telephoning contingent on completion of homework

Source: Adapted from Zimmerman, B. J. (1998). Academic studying and the development of personal skill: A self-regulatory perspective. *Educational Psychologist, 33,* 73–86.

The teacher decides which specific behaviors to select for the behavior contract.

The teacher meets with the student to draw up the contract.

The contract should include:
- A listing of student behaviors that are to be reduced or increased
- A statement or section that explains the minimum conditions under which the student will earn a point, sticker, or other token for showing appropriate behaviors
- The conditions under which the student will be able to redeem collected stickers, points, or other tokens for specific rewards
- Bonus and penalty clauses
- Areas for signatures of both teacher and student

Figure 7.5. Creating an Individualized Contract

Source: Wright, J. (2005). Behavior contracts. Retrieved April 25, 2005 from http://www.interventioncentral.org/htmdocs/interventions/behcontr.shtml.

Contracts and Contingencies

One strategy for helping students regulate their behavior is to use behavioral contracts. Contracts can be used to promote new behaviors, increase the rate of performance of a behavior, maintain a skill, decrease undesirable behaviors, or monitor the completion of academic tasks (Downing, 2002). Teachers who wish to use such contracts need to make the decisions illustrated in Figure 7.5. An example of a contract is presented in Figure 7.6

Sometimes teachers manage behavior by means of group contingencies—reinforcements or punishments that apply to the entire class. The goal is to encourage the use of peer pressure to improve behavior. Often, students will be motivated not to let their peers down or to increase the reinforcements available to the group. Students in middle school and high school are particularly concerned about their peers' approval. An example of a group contingency strategy is the "Good Behavior Game" (Barrish, Saunders, & Wolf, 1969). The teacher divides the class into two teams. Each time a rule is broken, the teacher makes a mark beside the name of the team whose member broke the rule. The goal is to have as few marks as possible beside the name of one's team. Research has shown that this approach is effective (Darveaux, 1984, Dolan et al., 1993).

A more recent example of a group contingency program is called *Anchor the Boat* (Lohrman & Talerica, 2004). It involves (a) defining expectations for behavior in positive terms; (b) teaching the expectations, using direct instruction and role-play; and (c) reinforcing students when they have met the criteria for appropriate behavior. A picture of a boat positioned 20 inches above an anchor is attached to a board. If the class engages in 50 or fewer of the undesirable target behaviors during a class period, they earn 2-inch paperclips to make a chain to connect the boat to the anchor. When the chain is complete, they earn a reward.

Lohrmann and Talerica (2004) evaluated this technique in a multi-age classroom that provided learning support for students with learning disabilities. The participants were six boys and four girls. After three days of the intervention, the incidence of undesirable behaviors (talking out of turn, getting out of seats, and incomplete assignments) was reduced. The results were consistent with those of other studies of group contingencies.

The group contingency approach should be used with caution. Romeo (1998) points to a number of potentially negative outcomes: (a) it can model injustice and unfairness; (b) it can create a hostile classroom environment; and (c) other students may become surrogate punishers of children who do not comply with the rules. Students in middle school are particularly vulnerable to the negative effects of peers' disapproval or hostility. Furthermore, some children have poor impulse control and have difficulty regulating their personal behavior unless they receive substantial support. Such children can create problems for other students in a group contingency context, because they may cause the group to lose privileges. In turn, the other students may become hostile toward a difficult student. Teachers should use group contingencies very carefully, especially when the class includes students with special needs.

How Can I Use This?

How can you minimize potential negative effects in using group contingency contracts?

My Contract

My Name: Elizabeth Jones

Grade: 7th Grade

My Goal:

1. Turn in my completed homework on time.

Consequences:

If I meet my goals:

If I complete my homework on time five days in a row, I will get a homework pass for one night.

If I do not meet my goals:

If I do not complete my homework on time on more than one of five days in a row, I will get extra homework for the weekend.

Signatures _____ Student

_____ Teacher

Monday	Tuesday	Wednesday	Thursday	Friday

The teacher will initial each day I am succesful.

Figure 7.6. Example of an Individual Contract

Influences of Behavioral Learning Theory on Instruction

Behavioral learning theory can be used to foster particular kinds of learning. These theories imply that the experience of success is important in instruction because it results in reinforcement and increases the likelihood of continued effort. The focus on opportunities for success also implies that content be broken down in order to maximize opportunities to experience success. Simple skills should be taught before complex skills. Two areas of instruction that have been influenced by behavioral learning theory are mastery learning and instructional technology.

Mastery Learning

In 1968, Benjamin Bloom developed the concept that came to be known as *mastery learning* (Bloom, 1968). The basic principle of mastery learning is that all students can achieve a set of educational objectives with appropriate instruction and enough time to learn.

The curriculum is divided into small units that have specific objectives with formative assessments tied to them. Assessments are given, and further instruction or activities and feedback are provided to help the student overcome problems. Students do not progress to the next unit until he or she has reached a prescribed level of mastery (e.g., 80% correct on a test). Because the material is broken into smaller units, the focus is on success and consequent reinforcement before proceeding to the next unit.

meta-analysis A quantitive review and summary of research on a topic

Many studies of mastery learning programs have been conducted. A series of **meta-analyses** were conducted that synthesized the results of many of those studies (Guskey & Gates, 1986; Guskey & Piggot, 1988; Kulik, Kulik, & Bangert-Downs, 1990). The results of the analyses showed that in general, mastery learning is an effective instructional strategy. Performance on achievement tests improved as a result of mastery learning, as did student attitudes toward learning. The positive results were also found to persist over time (Kulik et al., 1990). Not everyone agrees about the positive effects of mastery learning, however. One analysis concluded that mastery learning had few documented effects (Slavin, 1987). Some of the differences in interpretation of the results of studies occur because researchers do not always include the same studies in their analyses.

Feedback and Knowledge of Results An important component of mastery learning is corrective feedback. One study compared mastery and nonmastery learning to find out how feedback was related to achievement (Wentling, 1973). Four outcomes were examined: immediate achievement, attitude toward instruction, time spent on instruction, and delayed achievement. Participants in both the mastery and nonmastery learning conditions were provided with no feedback, partial feedback in the form of information about the correctness of the response, or complete feedback that included knowledge of the correct response. The results indicated that participants who received partial feedback outperformed those in the nonfeedback and complete-feedback groups on measures of both immediate and delayed achievement. No differences were found in the time spent on instruction or attitudes toward instruction.

In sum, many aspects of mastery learning are influenced by behavioral learning theory. These include the division of content into small units and the use of formative tests that guide the use of corrective feedback and activities. The goal is to foster the experience of success, which is reinforcing and supportive of continued effort. It is useful to keep in mind that although there is much evidence in support of mastery learning as an instructional strategy, mastery learning is not widely used today. Instruction in today's classrooms is influenced more by other theories of learning, such as constructivism or information processing.

Software programs routinely feature positive reinforcers, such as celebratory sights and sounds, to encourage and maintain students' on-task behavior. (Media Bakery)

Instructional Technology

Behavioral learning theory has influenced some aspects of the design of software and computer-assisted instructional programs. Skinner (1958) was the first to propose applying behavioral learning principles to teaching academic skills by using programmed instruction. Content was arranged in small chunks, and progress was organized from simple to complex content. Computer-based instruction involved the use of a computer to deliver programmed instruction and maintain records of progress.

One example of the influence of behaviorism can be seen in software that provides drill and practice (Lockard & Abrams, 2004). A child may be presented with a picture, such as an apple, and asked to make a response, such as selecting the word *apple* from among a number of words. Thus, the child is encouraged to associate the picture with the word *apple*. Success in these kinds of activities may be reinforced by flashing lights, bells, or other signals. The child may persist on the task in pursuit of such reinforcements.

Limitations of Behavioral Learning Theory

Behavioral learning theory cannot adequately explain complex learning. Complex learning is more than the sum of the parts of a task and involves cognitive, metacognitive, and affective or social skills. Behavioral learning theory depends on the segmentation of a curricular unit into small chunks, and students are provided with opportunities to assess their skills. By simplifying the contents, students' opportunities for reinforcement increase. Although this particular approach may assist students in developing specific skills, many curricular content areas cannot be broken down in this way, and measurement of outcomes cannot be assessed so discretely in many domains. Likewise, complex thinking skills cannot be taught in this way because the opportunity to make false starts in solving problems or reasoning about contradictory evidence may not result in positive feedback consistently.

In addition, the negative effects of overreliance on tangible reinforcement or reward may actually decrease motivation and performance. Intrinsic motivation for participation in activities or tasks can be undermined.

Chapter Reference
Chapters 8, 9, and 10 discuss alternative theories of learning that can provide better explanations of complex learning.

RIDE

REFLECTION FOR ACTION

The Event

Mr. Duba is the leader of a committee that has been appointed by the middle school principal to generate ideas and an action plan for reducing misbehavior during lunch period. Members of the committee have contributed ideas about how to solve the problem. Mr. Duba has written some of them on the blackboard. Now it is time for the committee to make some recommendations.

Reflection RIDE

Why are the students behaving badly? How can the committee improve the situation in the lunchroom without also making the students resentful and angry?

What Theoretical/Conceptual Information Might Assist in Interpreting and Remedying This Situation? Consider the three approaches listed below.

Reinforcement of desirable behavior

The committee could recommend creating a system for rewarding good behavior. It might be possible to draw up contracts with different classes, with rewards contingent on improved behavior.

Punishment of undesirable behavior

The committee could recommend sanctions for bad behavior, such as detention, extra homework, or not allowing students who continually break the rules to go on school outings or to the school dance.

Monitoring of antecedents and consequences of behavior

Antecedents precede behaviors. The behavior is followed by consequences that will either increase or decrease the likelihood that the behavior will occur again. Perhaps members of the committee should observe students in the lunchroom and try to identify the antecedents to behaviors, such as throwing food.

Information Gathering RIDE

What is the problem? The problem for the committee is to decide whether to try to improve students' behavior during the lunch period by using reinforcement or by using punishment. The committee should look at the research evidence related to the use of reinforcement and punishment. It will also be important for committee members to observe the situation in the lunchroom and determine whether a few students cause the problems or many students are involved in the disruptive incidents. A careful analysis of the antecedents of disruptive behaviors will be helpful to the committee in deciding how to tackle the problem. It will also be helpful to have more than one member of the committee observe at the same time and compare notes later. Do they observe the same behaviors?

Decision Making RIDE

The committee members may observe in the lunchroom. If they identify that the problems are largely caused by a small number of students who provoke other students, they may decide to reduce the opportunities for the disruptive students to provoke others. They may recommend that the lunch periods be staggered to limit the number of students in the lunchroom at any one time. They may also recommend assigning the disruptive students to different locations in the lunchroom to isolate them from other disruptive students.

If the disruption is not confined to a few students, the committee will need to consider reinforcement and punishment alternatives. Punishment does not extinguish behavior but merely suppresses it. Reinforcement can increase the incidence of positive behaviors but the committee members will need to consider carefully what might be reinforcing to the students. The use of group contingencies (rewards and punishments) might be a useful strategy because middle school students care about the opinions of their peers. Every effort should be made, however, to focus on increasing positive behaviors rather than on punishment. The lunchroom aides might assist with recording incidents of bad behavior, and rewards could be assigned if the number of incidents remains below a certain threshold. The use of group contingencies can have negative outcomes if particular students are unresponsive to peer pressure or are unable to regulate their own behavior adequately (e.g., students with ADHD). Individual contingency contracts can also be used with specific students.

Evaluation RIDE

The lunchroom aides can provide reports of the number of disruptive incidents that occur. A decrease in the frequency of such incidents will indicate that the intervention was successful. If the misbehavior continues at the previous level, the committee will need to reconvene and develop a new strategy.

Further Practice: Your Turn

Here is a second event for you to reflect on. In doing so, generate the sequence used above in terms of *R*eflection, *I*nformation Gathering, *D*ecision Making, and *E*valuation.

The Event

Ms. Jefferson was concerned about her students' lack of interest in reading in the seventh grade. She concluded that they needed more immediate and tangible rewards. She devised a program that would provide rewards for students' reading achievements. Classes in which each child read three books in a month would receive a free pizza party at a local pizzeria. After three months, book borrowing at the school and local libraries had increased dramatically.

RIDE Has Ms. Jefferson succeeded in increasing the frequency of students' reading? What about the quality of their reading?

SUMMARY

- **How do teachers who adhere to behavioral, cognitive, and sociocultural approaches describe learning?**

  Behavioral, cognitive, and sociocultural theories of learning place different emphases on the relationships among the environment, the individual, and behavior. Behavioral learning theories emphasize the connection between the environment and behavior. Cognitive theories emphasize the relationship between the individual and the environment. Sociocultural theories also emphasize the relationship between the environment and the individual, but the environment includes the history of practice and expertise acquired by a community, from which an individual might learn by becoming an apprentice in that community.

- **What kinds of learning can be described by behavioral learning theory?**

  Behavioral learning theory focuses on behavior, skills, and self-regulatory capacities, as shown in Figure 7.1

- **How do different forms of reinforcement affect behavior and performance?**

  Different forms of reinforcement influence the speed with which behaviors are performed, the continuity of the behavior after reinforcement, and the persistence of the behavior. Fixed schedules of reinforcement are the most predictable and are useful in the initial stages of acquiring a behavior. After receiving reinforcement on a fixed schedule, the learner is likely to pause before repeating the behavior. Speed of performance is highest under a fixed ratio schedule of reinforcement because the delivery of reinforcement is predictable, and the learner can control the timing of the behaviors necessary to obtain reinforcement. Variable schedules are unpredictable and result in the greatest persistence of the desired behavior.

- **How can teachers increase the frequency of desirable behaviors and decrease that of undesirable behaviors?**

  Desirable behavior can be increased and undesirable behavior decreased by a combination of reinforcement and punishment. An emphasis on positive behavior management is more likely to be successful than a focus on negative behavior. Positive reinforcements such as praise can be used to increase desirable behaviors. Undesirable behaviors can be decreased by means of such strategies as response cost, differential reinforcement, inductive reasoning about behavior, and the use of contracts.

- **How can teachers help students learn self-management?**

  To effectively manage their own behavior, students need to learn the following capabilities: (a) plan their behavior and set their own goals (goal setting); (b) provide self-instructions and constructive self-talk (self-instruction); (c) monitor how well or how poorly they are behaving (self-observation); (d) evaluate the desirability of their behavior (self-evaluation); and (e) apply self-generated consequences to reinforce desired behaviors (self-consequences).

- **How can teachers use behavioral learning principles in instruction?**

  Behavioral learning theory suggests that the experience of success, positive reinforcement, feedback, and gradual progress are important aspects of learning. Instructional strategies such as mastery learning and many kinds of programmed instruction are strongly influenced by behavioral learning theory.

- **How might teachers use behavioral learning theory with diverse learners and learners with special needs?**

  Behavioral learning principles are frequently used in instructional and behavior management programs for students with special needs (e.g., autistic or emotionally disturbed children). Positive behavioral intervention strategies may also be part of a student's individualized education plan, as required by IDEA 2004. Behavioral learning theory is concerned with the environment and behavior, not with mental states. It is important for a teacher to understand diverse learners' prior histories of reinforcement and punishment.

- **What are some limitations of behavioral learning theory?**

  Behavioral learning theory cannot adequately explain complex learning. Complex learning is more than the sum of the parts of a task and involves cognitive, metacognitive, and affective or social skills. In addition, the negative effects of overreliance on tangible reinforcement or reward may actually decrease motivation and performance.

KEY TERMS

classical conditioning, p. 209
conditioned response, p. 209
conditioned stimulus, p. 209
consequences, p. 210
contiguity, p. 209
continuous reinforcement, p. 213
discriminative stimuli, p. 218
fixed interval schedule, p. 214
fixed ratio schedule, p. 214
incentive, p. 221
interval schedule, p. 213
law of effect, p. 210
learning, p. 207
meta-analysis, p. 232
negative punisher, p. 214

negative reinforcer, p. 211
operant learning, p. 209
positive punisher, p. 214
positive reinforcer, p. 210
prompts, p. 222
punisher p. 214
ratio schedule p. 213
reinforcer, p. 210
reward, p. 211
shaping, p. 221
unconditioned response, p. 209
unconditioned stimulus, p. 209
variable interval schedule, p. 214
variable ratio schedule, p. 214

EXERCISES

1. *Observing the Use of Reinforcements and Punishments*

   Observe a teacher in a classroom. What kinds of reinforcements or punishments does the teacher provide? Make a list of these and classify each as an example of a positive (presentation) or negative (removal) punishment or positive or negative reinforcements.

2. *Reinforcement During the Use of a Computer Game*

   Observe a student playing a computer game. At what points in the game does the student smile or show pleasure? What happens after the student does this? Can you tell what behaviors are being reinforced? Can you tell which consequences are responsible for the students' smiles and sense of pleasure?

3. *Changing Behavior*

   Identify one behavior that you would like to change (e.g., getting up late in the morning). Develop a plan for how you will change this behavior and write it down. Over the course of a week, keep a record of what you did to try to change this behavior. At the end of the week, identify the reinforcers or punishers you used. Were they effective in increasing the frequency of desired behavior or reducing that of undesirable behavior?

4. *Evaluating Education*

   Read B. F. Skinner's "The shame of American education" (1984, *American Psychologist*, *39*, 947–954) and summarize the criticisms that Skinner made of American education. How many of these criticisms are valid in describing the current status of American education?

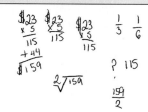

M r. Gomez was going over the problem set for the unit on word problems with fractions on which his class was working. Generally speaking, he was pleased with his students' performance, but there were still a few weaknesses. He thought, "I want them to really understand how to solve these problems—to be confident in their abilities. If I'm teaching this well, and most of the kids are getting it, why aren't they all getting it? What can I do to reach the kids who need help right now?" Mr. Gomez decided to focus his attention on two students who were having trouble. Below is their performance on one particular problem.

The Problem

> The Cinema Club takes the money from their fund drive and puts half of it in the club treasury. They spend one third of it on a trip to the movies, and one sixth of it on supplies. This year their fund drive wash a car wash where they charged $5 to wash a car. They washed a total of 23 cars and got an additional $44 in tips. How much money will they be able to spend on going to the movies?
>
> Be sure to show your work and explain your reasoning in a short paragraph.

Gabby's Answer

```
$5 a car      23 cars
$ 44 in tips          movies

              23+44
1/6  1/3 of 44        What are they doing!!
```

Why didn't they just spend all of the money on the movies—it's a Cinema Club, isn't it? What are they saving for, a trip to a film festival? I'm not sure what I'm supposed to do here. I read the problem several times, but I just got lost and then I got upset. How much money for the movies is a third of the money, but what money are we talking about? Are there two different problems here? If I knew better how to set this up, I think I could do it, but I can't.

Becky's Answer

```
$23   $23   $23      1    1
x 5   x 5   x 5      ─    ─
───   ───   ───      3    6
115   115   115

+ 44
────
$159               ?  115

          ___
        2√159          159
                       ───
                        2
```

Well, I started by trying to figure out how much money they made. I figured once I did that, then I could figure out how much they spent on three things. I multiplied 23 times $5 and got $115 and added $44 and got $159 for the total. But if they put half of the money in the bank, you can't divide $159 in half, so I couldn't figure out what they were supposed to do. I must be doing something wrong, but I checked my math three times and I can't figure out where my error is. I'm sorry but I can't make it work.

Cognitive Theories of Learning

8

Reflection for Action

Wrong answers can often be windows into the cognitive difficulties students are having with a new learning task. What kinds of problems do you see in the work of these two students? What kinds of larger problems do the students' difficulties with these math problems suggest? What kinds of things can you do as a teacher to help these students accomplish their goals in mathematics?

Guiding Questions

- How do cognitive and constructivist theories of learning differ?
- Why are attention, perception, and working memory important for learning?
- How is knowledge represented?
- What are the different kinds of long-term memory?
- How is encoding related to retrieval?
- Why and how do we categorize?
- How can teachers promote complex cognition?
- How can teachers apply cognitive theories of learning in working with diverse students and students with special needs?

CHAPTER OVERVIEW

This chapter focuses on structures and processes of learning from a cognitive perspective, with special emphasis on information-processing theory. The first part of the chapter describes the relationship between cognitive and constructivist theories of learning. Other sections describe the basic processes of encoding and retrieval, and the constraints of various components of the information-processing system, such as working memory, that limit processing. Each section also describes the instructional implications of those components. The final section of the chapter addresses complex cognition. Particular attention is devoted to how we can understand the needs of exceptional children from a cognitive perspective and what teaching strategies might be helpful in reducing the difficulties experienced by all students in classrooms.

Cognitive and Constructivist Theories of Learning

The Information-Processing Model
- Perception
- Attention

Memory Systems
- Sensory Memory
- Short-Term Memory
- Baddeley's Model of Working Memory
- Memory Difficulties of Students with Special Needs
- Long-Term Memory

Encoding, Retrieval, and Forgetting
- Types of Knowledge
- Organization, Practice, and Elaboration
- Mnemonic Strategies
- Imagery and Visual-Learning Strategies
- Retrieval and Forgetting

Categorization
- Teaching Concepts
- Diversity, Culture, and Experience in Developing Concepts and Categories

Complex Cognition
- Metacognition
- Self-Explanation
- Reasoning and Argumentation
- Problem Solving
- Transfer

Cognitive and Constructivist Theories of Learning

In the example that follows, you can see that learning results from the interaction between the student's skills and the kind of instruction that a teacher provides. Jeff Morgan is a student who is having trouble processing information, and his efforts to acquire knowledge are not very successful. In this chapter, you will learn about how information is processed and the kinds of strategies a student can use to acquire knowledge.

Jeff Morgan was excited about taking social studies in his junior year. He really liked the subject matter and had done very well in the course he took in his sophomore year. His teacher last year was exciting, enthusiastic about teaching the content, eager for students to ask questions, and pleased to answer their questions after class. On the first day of the junior year social studies class, Jeff knew things were going to be different. The teacher spoke very rapidly, and the material he taught was not the same as in the textbook. Jeff struggled to take notes. He was not good at spelling, and when he paused to try to spell a word correctly, he could no longer make sense of what the teacher was saying. Unlike last year's teacher, this teacher did not write notes on the board or provide outlines. Jeff hoped that he would get used to the teacher's methods and that things would improve. After two weeks, he looked at his notes. He could hardly make sense of them. There were fragments of ideas that did not seem to be connected. He began to worry about how he would do on exams in this class.

In Chapter 7, we introduced a very general definition of learning as an interaction between the individual and the environment that results in a relatively permanent change in behavior or knowledge. We also saw that a behavioral theory of learning focuses primarily on the relationship between the environment and behavior. In contrast, the relationship between the individual and the environment is the key focus of cognitive theories of learning. From a cognitive perspective, a person does not necessarily view the same environment in the same way as others. For example, two people may see the abbreviation *IRA*. One, who is a reading specialist, may interpret it to mean "International Reading Association." The other, who is nearing retirement, may instead interpret it as "Individual Retirement Account." Although the same environmental stimulus is available to both individuals, they interpret it in different ways as a result of their own experiences and motivations. A cognitive approach to learning explores how individual differences in knowledge and experience influence the way we interpret the environment and, as a result, what we learn from that interaction.

Cognitive theories include a variety of approaches to understanding the relationship between the individual and his or her environment. At the heart of most cognitive approaches to understanding learning is the notion that knowledge is constructed by the learner and affected by the learner's prior experiences. All cognitive theories are constructivist in nature in that they all emphasize the active role of learners in making meaning out of their experience.

Moshman (1982) distinguishes among three types of constructivism: exogenous, endogenous, and dialectical. **Exogenous constructivism** holds that knowledge is derived from the environment. Thus, the learner constructs knowledge by learning to represent the structures that are present in the environment (Moshman 1982). These structures include relationships among objects, information as presented and observed behavior patterns: "Structures of knowledge are adequate or 'true' to the extent that they accurately copy the external structures that they ideally represent" (Moshman, 1982, p. 373). The learner's mental image of a cup, for example, is a *copy* of the physical object. The task of a teacher applying this perspective is to provide the student with a clear and easily understandable representation of knowledge.

Endogenous constructivism is most readily illustrated by Piagetian theory (Moshman, 1982). Piaget recalled an anecdote told to him by a friend who was a mathematician. The friend recalled constructing the concept of numbers when he was about five years old as a result of manipulating pebbles in his garden (Piaget, 1971). The child used his existing cognitive structures (or schemes) to act on the environment. The concept of number was not constructed as a result of interaction with others or because of the nature of the pebbles but instead resulted from the child's coordination of other cognitive structures, such as counting and ordering. The construction of new knowledge thus came from within (endogenous). The learner constructs new knowledge structures from existing structures rather than from internally reconstructing what is present in the environment. From this perspective, the emergence of particular knowledge structures can be predicted. The task of teaching is to arrange the student's environment in such a way as to require the use of existing structures and prompt the creation of new and more sophisticated ones.

The third kind of constructivism is **dialectical constructivism** (Moshman, 1982). From this perspective, a learner acquires knowledge by continually interacting with the environment. The learner acts on the environment, and the feedback from the learner's actions influences new actions. Context matters a great deal. This type of constructivism is perhaps best illustrated by Vygotsky's theory. The source of knowledge is subjective experience in interaction with the individual's environment. This approach to constructivism is addressed in Chapter 10. The current chapter focuses primarily on endogenous constructivism, or information-processing approaches to learning.

exogenous constructivism
Constructed knowledge that mirrors information in the environment.

endogenous constructivism
Construction of new knowledge structures from existing structures rather than from the environment.

Chapter Reference
Piaget's theory was discussed in Chapter 2 and is a good example of endogenous constructivism.

dialectical constructivism The theory that considers knowledge to lie in continual interaction between the individual and the environment. Vygotsky's theory is a good example of this kind of constructivism.

Chapter Reference
Vygtosky's theory was discussed in Chapter 2 and is also included in Chapter 10.

The Information-Processing Model

The learner interacts with the environment and receives information from the environment through the senses. The information-processing approach to learning is an example of endogenous constructivism in which the learner develops internal representations of the

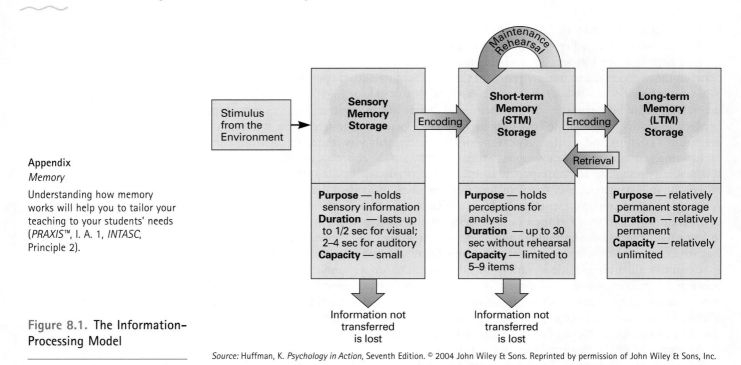

Appendix

Memory

Understanding how memory works will help you to tailor your teaching to your students' needs (*PRAXIS*™, I. A. 1, *INTASC*, Principle 2).

Figure 8.1. The Information-Processing Model

Source: Huffman, K. *Psychology in Action*, Seventh Edition. © 2004 John Wiley & Sons. Reprinted by permission of John Wiley & Sons, Inc.

external world. Perceptual and attentional processes limit the amount of information that is available. Not all the available information can be processed because of the limited capacity of various components of the memory system. Information is processed in working memory and potentially transferred to long-term memory, from which it can be retrieved later. This information-processing system is illustrated in Figure 8.1. In the next few sections of this chapter, we will discuss the components of the information-processing system more fully.

Perception

Perceptual and attentional processes are important to information processing. Students who have difficulty with them are at risk of failure in school. Awareness of these processes and how they affect other aspects of information processing may help teachers develop instructional strategies that will support students as they attempt to learn.

perception   The meaning attached to sensory information.

Perception involves giving meaning to sensory input. One of the difficult things for very young children to learn is that objects have permanence. The face that disappears behind a newspaper when one is playing "peekaboo" remains the same whether it can be seen or not or whether it is turned sideways or not. When children start to recognize letters, we ask them to perform a very complicated task. We ask them to recognize the letters *b, p, d,* and *q* as separate and distinct, even though they are very similar (see Figure 8.2). We also can recognize different kinds of handwriting, as seen in Figure 8.3. The fact that we can learn to do these things suggests how powerful our perception system is.

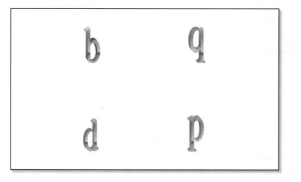

Figure 8.2. Perception of Similarly Shaped Letters

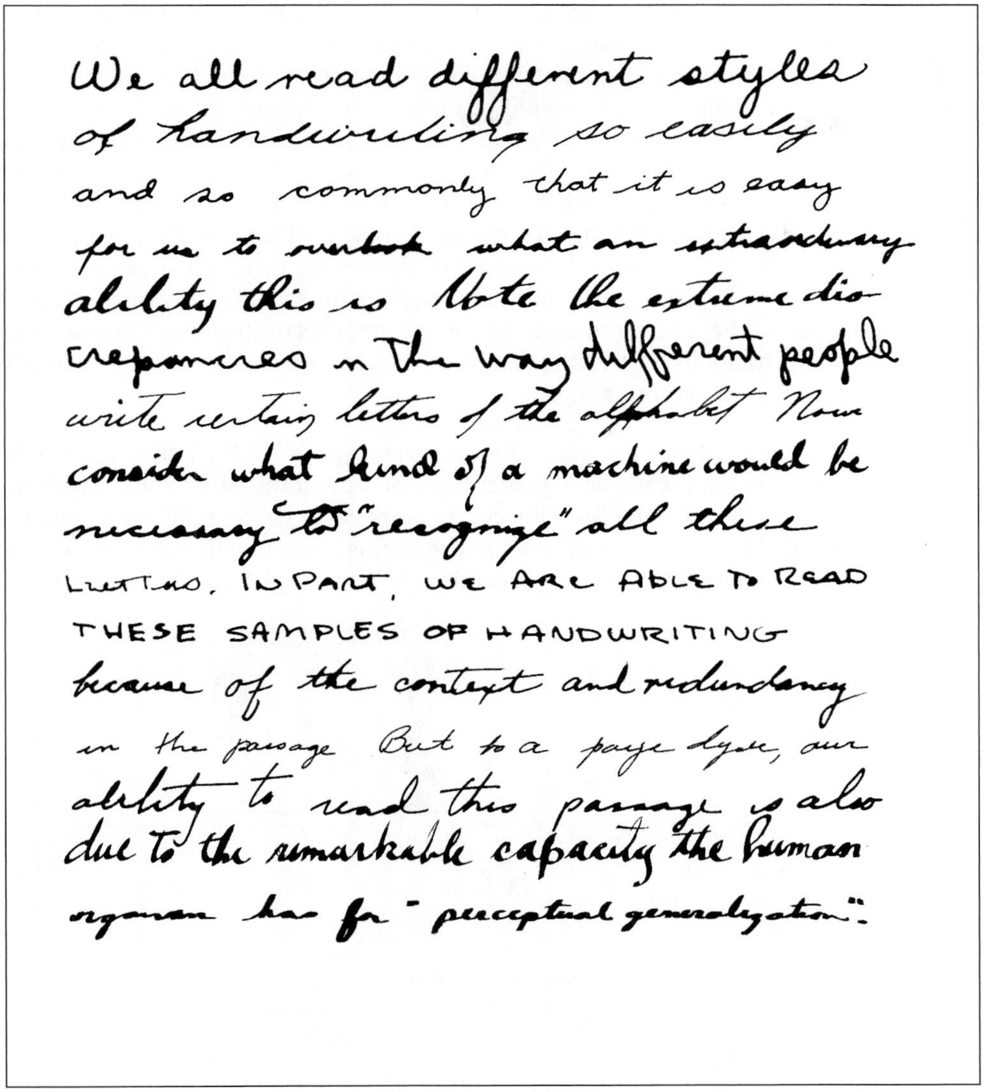

Source: From MAN MACH ENGRG – SEE 51B5501 1st edition by Chapanis. © 1966. Reprinted with permission of Wadsworth, a division of Thomson Learning: www.thomsonrights.com. Fax 800 730-2215.

Figure 8.3. Variations in Handwriting

Recognizing Objects Two approaches are often used to describe how we recognize objects. The first of these is called **feature analysis** or **bottom-up processing** and involves identifying the component features of objects and building a representation of the object from them. An example of feature analysis is phonics, in which sounds associated with individual letters or phonemes are combined to make a word. Only when the features of the word are combined may a student recognize the word. Figure 8.4 presents examples of the letter *A*. If we could recognize objects only through feature analysis, we might recognize only the first

feature analysis Identifying the component features of objects and building a representation of the object from them.

bottom-up processing A process in which a stimulus is analyzed into its components, then assembled into a recognizable pattern, also known as *feature analysis.*

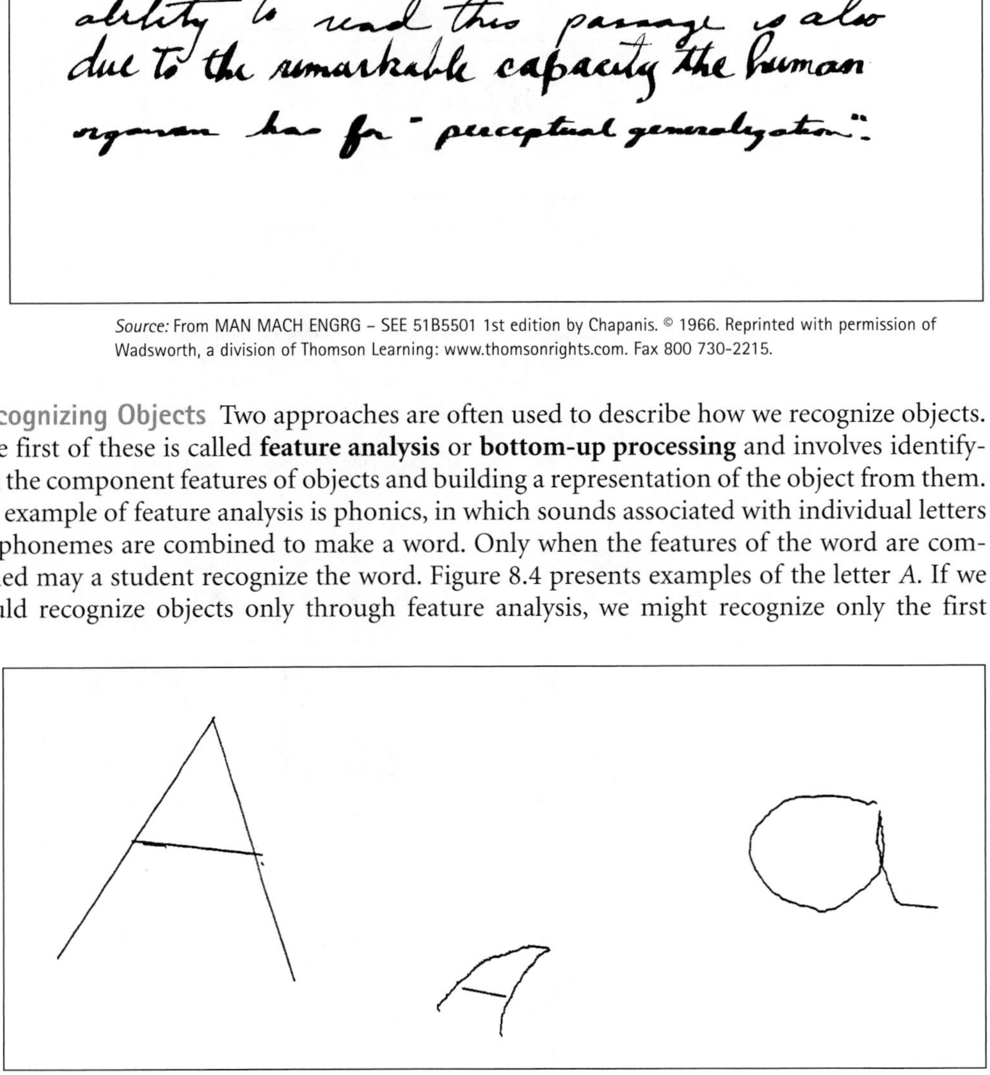

Figure 8.4. Perceiving the Letter *A*

Source: Selfridge, O. G. (1955). Pattern recognition and modern computers. Proceedings of the Western Joint Computer Conference. New York: Institute of Electrical and Electronics Engineers.

Figure 8.5. Context

top-down processing A type of perception in which a person uses what he or she knows about a situation to recognize patterns.

example as an instance of the letter *A*. We would identify individual features (three lines, the angles at which the lines intersect) and assemble them to build a representation of the letter. Using this approach, we would be unlikely to recognize the other two examples.

An alternative approach to recognizing objects is to rely on context and fill in any missing information. This is called **top-down processing**. Figure 8.5 illustrates this approach. Although the letters in Figure 8.5 are incomplete, people typically read the words as THE CAT. Although some of the letters are incomplete, people fill in the missing information. If people relied on feature analysis to recognize the words, they would not recognize them: They could not combine the features effectively because necessary information is missing. Methods for teaching reading that rely on the use of context to infer what words mean use top-down processing.

Object Recognition Relies on Form Some psychologists believed that when viewing objects, the perception of the whole is greater than the sum of the parts. These psychologists were known as Gestalt psychologists. Objects are more easily perceived if they exhibit good form, or *pragnanz*. They also proposed a set of organizing principles that allow us to perceive objects. These are illustrated in Figure 8.6. Among the most important organizing principles

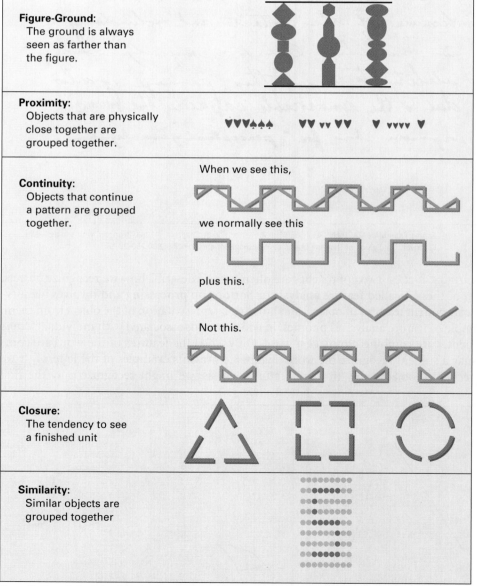

Figure 8.6. Gestalt Principles

Source: Huffman, K. *Psychology in Action*, Seventh Edition. © 2004 John Wiley & Sons. Reprinted by permission of John Wiley & Sons, Inc.

is that of *figure-ground:* The figure is always seen as closer than the ground. We group together elements that appear similar (figure) and distinguish them from those that appear dissimilar (ground). Figure-ground relations are also illustrated in Figure 8.7. You can see either a vase or two faces looking at one another, but not both at the same time.

A second organizing principle is that of *proximity.* When things are close together, they are seen as belonging together (see Figure 8.6). The third principle is that of *continuity:* We prefer continuous forms. In Figure 8.6, you are more likely to see a continuous line than a segmented line. *Closure* is the fourth principle. This principle indicates that we tend to see completed figures rather than incomplete ones and to fill in the missing information (see Figure 8.5). *Similarity* also works as an organizing principle. In Figure 8.6, the green dots are seen to belong to one another and stand apart from the others because of their similarity in size and color. They are perceived in this example as the number 5. Visual displays such as concept maps that that are prepared using Gestalt principles are more effective for learning than displays that do not use these principles (Wallace et al., 1998).

Figure 8.7. What do you see? A vase or two faces?
(Courtesy Kaiser Porcelain, Ltd.)

Attention

Some of the key features of **attention** are illustrated in the following quotation:

> *Everyone knows what attention is. It is the taking possession by the mind, in clear and vivid form, of one out of what seems several simultaneously possible objects or trains of thought. It implies withdrawal from some things in order to deal effectively with others, and is a condition which has a real opposite, in the confused, dazed, scatterbrained state . . . which is called distraction (James, 1890, pp. 403–404).*

attention   Focus that is selective and limited.

This description has a number of noteworthy features: (a) attention involves simultaneous experiences; (b) it is selective, withdrawing from some objects and focusing on others; and (c) lack of attention is characterized by confusion and diffusion. Perceptual processes enable us to organize sensory input, and attentional processes enable us to be selective. Children who suffer from attention disorders or attention deficit/hyperactivity disorders are at risk for school failure. A child who exhibits six of the following characteristics for a period of six months or longer is considered likely to suffer from an attention deficit disorder, according to the *Diagnostic and Statistical Manual of Mental Disorders,* fourth edition, of the American Psychiatric Association (as reported by Centers for Disease Control, 2004):

- Often does not give close attention to details or makes careless mistakes in schoolwork, work, or other activities
- Often has trouble keeping attention on tasks or play activities
- Often does not seem to listen when spoken to directly
- Often does not follow instructions and fails to finish schoolwork, chores, or duties in the workplace (not due to oppositional behavior or failure to understand instructions)
- Often has trouble organizing activities
- Often avoids, dislikes, or doesn't want to do things that take a lot of mental effort for a long period of time (such as schoolwork or homework)
- Often loses things needed for tasks and activities (e.g., toys, school assignments, pencils, books, or tools)
- Often is easily distracted
- Often is forgetful in daily activities

It is easy to see from these symptoms why a child who experiences six or more of these for an extended period of time would be at risk. Pervasive attentional problems can interfere with a child's ability to respond to and benefit from instruction. Most children experience some of the difficulties listed above. Basic processes of attention and perception thus are very important in understanding individual learning and failure to learn.

Because people cannot attend to all the information that is available, they need some means to select the information that is important to them. Various theories have attempted to explain how selective attention works. One of the earliest theories of attention was the *filter theory* (Broadbent, 1958), in which attention was compared to a filter. Sensory information was processed but quickly reaches a bottleneck. Filter theory suggests that attention is

Chapter Reference
Chapter 4 provides additional information about children with attention disorders or attention deficit hyperactivity disorder.

an all-or-none phenomenon. An alternative theory of attention (Treisman, 1960) proposed that attention to one source of information is reduced, but not eliminated, when one pays attention to another source. This is known as an *attenuation model*. You have probably had the experience of being at a party, deeply involved in a discussion with a friend, and suddenly becoming aware that someone at the other end of the room has mentioned your name. A filter model of attention suggests that you would not hear your name being mentioned because your attention is focused entirely on the person with whom you are speaking. An attenuation model suggests that while you are focused primarily on your conversation, some attention remains available for other sources of information.

Attention can also be viewed as a limited resource, similar to a reservoir that can be filled up or emptied. This is known as a *capacity model* (Kahnemann, 1973). Capacity models are concerned with the amount of mental effort needed to perform a task. If two tasks require the same kind of mental effort, they may interfere with each other. You may find it easy to visualize a scene (e.g., your apartment) and describe it in words. Doing two tasks that tap into the same resource can be very difficult. For example, reading a text and counting backward at the same time would be difficult. Both tasks require high mental effort via verbal processing.

Automaticity   As tasks are practiced, they become more automatic and require less attention. Driving and riding a bicycle are examples. If a process is overlearned, however, there may be a tendency to engage in it whether we wish to or not. Automatic processes occur without conscious attention. Sometimes driving is performed automatically. Have you ever driven somewhere while thinking through a problem only to realize upon your arrival that you do not remember the drive. You probably engaged in an automatic process. **Controlled processes**, in contrast, require conscious attention. For example, you are likely to be more deliberate and control your attention when you are driving in bad weather than you might otherwise do. Reading is typically an automatic process. The Stroop Task was used to investigate controlled and automatic processes (Schneider & Shiffrin, 1974). An example is presented in Figure 8.8, where you will find a list of words. Try to name the colors in which the words are printed. In order to *name* the colors, you must prevent yourself from reading the words. This is more difficult when the word refers to a color that is different from the one in which it is printed.

Memory Systems

Imagine what it would be like if you could not remember well. Alan Baddeley describes the case of Clive Wearing, a talented musician who fell ill with a viral infection (Baddeley, 1999). As a result of the encephalitis that developed from the infection, Wearing suffered extensive brain damage. He cannot remember what happened more than a few minutes before. He continues to believe that he has just regained consciousness and keeps a diary in which he constantly records that fact. Wearing has been in this condition since 1985. His case demonstrates how important memory is and how much we take it for granted. When we see examples of great deficiencies in memory, as in patients with Alzheimer's disease, we are reminded of its importance.

A variety of models of memory were proposed in the 1960s. In 1968, Atkinson and Shiffrin developed a model consisting of three different kinds of memory: sensory, short-term, and long-term (Atkinson & Shiffrin, 1968). This model is represented in Figure 8.1 on page 242. The model, though outdated, remains useful to describe the general components of memory.

Sensory Memory

Sensory memory is very brief. Memory for visual information is referred to as *iconic memory*, whereas memory for auditory information is called *echoic memory*. In a famous experiment, George Sperling provided empirical support for the existence of sensory memory. Participants were shown three rows of letters for approximately one-twentieth of a second. After delays of varying length, participants were asked to recall one of the rows. Their recall worsened with longer delays. Based on these findings, iconic memory is thought to last about one-third of a second (Sperling, 1960).

---

automaticity   The ability to perform a task without having to think much about it.

controlled processes   Cognitive processes that require conscious attention.

Red	Yellow	Green
Blue	Red	Yellow
Green	Blue	Red

Source: Westen, D. *Psychology: Brain, Behavior and Culture*, Third Edition. © 2002 John Wiley & Sons. Reprinted by permission of John Wiley & Sons, Inc.

Figure 8.8. The Stroop Test

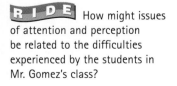 How might issues of attention and perception be related to the difficulties experienced by the students in Mr. Gomez's class?

sensory memory   Brief memories associated with various senses.

Short-Term Memory

Short-Term memory is a temporary memory storage. It has limited capacity and duration. Without active processing of information in short-term memory, the information will be lost.

short-term memory A temporary memory storage.

Capacity and Duration of Short-Term Memory George Miller wrote a classic paper on temporary memory. It was titled "The Magical Number Seven, Plus or Minus Two: Some Limits on Our Capacity for Processing Information" (Miller, 1956). Miller described the capacity of short-term memory storage as 7+ or −2 bits of information. Your telephone number most likely consists of 7 digits. Your social security number consists of 9 digits. Typically, the capacity of an individual's short-term memory is assessed by asking the person to recall a list of numbers such as those in Figure 8.9. An individual is presented with a sequence of digits and asked to repeat them back. (Try this with the list in Figure 8.9.) The length of the sequence is increased until a point is reached at which the individual always fails. The sequence length at which the individual is correct most of the time is considered to be his or her working memory capacity.

(a)	**7 6 3 8 8 2 6**
(b)	7 6 3 8 8 2 6 (20 seconds later)
(c)	**9 1 8** 8 8 2 6 (25 seconds later)

Source: Westen, D. *Psychology: Brain, Behavior and Culture,* Third Edition. © 2002 John Wiley & Sons. Reprinted by permission of John Wiley & Sons, Inc.

Figure 8.9. Digit Span

The duration of short-term memory is about 20 to 30 seconds, if you do not make an effort to rehearse or elaborate on the material. Among the strategies available for keeping information in short-term memory are rehearsal and organization. There are two kinds of rehearsal: maintenance rehearsal and elaborative rehearsal. **Maintenance rehearsal** is what you do when you repeat information over and over without actually altering it. You may do this when you call directory assistance. When you are given the number you require, you repeat it over and over to yourself in order to maintain it in short-term memory. Unfortunately, you actually forget it much of the time. Today, many telephone companies compensate for this deficiency by offering to dial the number for you for a small fee. **Elaborative Rehearsal** involves a deeper form of rehearsal which allows information to be transferred from short- term memory to long-term memory when an individual elaborates on information by connecting the to-be-remembered information to what he or she already knows. One way to reduce the demands on working memory involves **chunking** information, or grouping bits of information. For example, a telephone number may be recalled as two *chunks* (732–7333) rather than as seven separate digits.

maintenance rehearsal A cognitive process in which information in working memory is repeated to oneself frequently.

elaborative rehearsal A way of remembering information by connecting it to something that is already well known.

chunking The grouping of bits of data into larger, meaningful units.

Information is lost from short-term memory through decay and interference. **Decay** occurs when information is not used, and it simply fades from memory. **Interference** occurs when something else gets in the way of your recall. Have you ever gone into the kitchen to get something and found that when you were there, you could not recall what you went in to get? If you have, you have experienced interference.

decay Loss of memories because information is not used.

interference Loss or deficiency of memories because of the presence of other information.

Phenomena Associated with Short-Term Memory. When asked to listen to a list of words and recall them, one typically remembers some of the items at the beginning of the list and those at the end of the list. These are called *primacy* (heard first) and *recency* (just heard) effects. The probability that an item will be recalled depends on its position in the list, a phenomenon known as the **serial position effect** (see Figure 8.10). Recognizing the limits of short-term memory, teachers can keep their instructions brief and provide opportunities for rehearsal.

serial position effect The fact that the likelihood of information being recalled varies according to its position in a list.

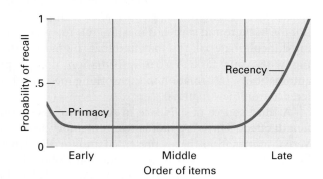

Source: Reprinted from *The psychology of learning and motivation*, Vol. 2, Atkinson, R. C., & Shiffrin, R. N. "Human memory: A proposed system and its control processes," 89–195, Copyright 1968, with permission from Elsevier.

Figure 8.10. Serial Position Effect

Baddeley's Model of Working Memory

working memory   A limited memory system that includes both storage and manipulation functions.

Working memory is a term used to describe a limited, though active, memory system. It differs from short-term memory in that it includes both manipulation functions as well as storage. For example, if you attempt a mental arithmetic problem such as 456×8, you will need to store the information temporarily and keep track of the products of your computation. Thus, you are both storing and manipulating the information. Limited working memory capacity has important implications for learning. (See the "Taking It to the Classroom" box on this page.)

Daneman and Carpenter (1980) devised a task to measure working memory span. Participants were shown sentences and asked to read each one. After reading the final sentence, they were asked to recall the last word in each sentence. An individual's working memory span was the number of words they recalled correctly.

How Can I Use This?

Remember to keep your instructions brief so your students can recall what you want them to do.

Taking It to the Classroom

Do You Know Jack? Solving Word Problems

Jack is having trouble solving word problems in his algebra class. Some problems confuse him because of their wording. Other problems stymie him because he does not know what strategy to use to solve them. Sometimes he uses the wrong mathematical operation to solve the problem. What steps can you take to help Jack overcome this difficulty?

- Have Jack underline key words to help him focus on the important information in the problem.
- Pair him with another student and have them take turns telling each other what the problem is that they are being asked to solve.
- Show Jack how to draw a diagram that may help him keep the important information available to him rather than having him rely on his memory.
- Give Jack worked examples to follow.
- Provide Jack with lots of practice and feedback with similar problems.

The Phonological Loop System   Baddeley proposed that working memory has a number of subsystems that are coordinated by a *central executive* (Baddeley, 1990). The first of these subsystems is the **phonological loop system**, which processes speech or auditory information. It consists of a passive phonological store and an articulatory rehearsal process. Several findings indicate that such a system does indeed exist.

phonological loop   The component of working memory that processes verbal information.

First, people make more errors if the words they are asked to recall are similar in sound to one another. For example, it is harder to recall *man, can, man, map* than it is to recall *pen, day, cow, bar, rig* (Baddeley, 1993, p. 51). This phenomenon is called the **phonological similarity effect**.

phonological similarity effect   People make more errors recalling sets of words if the words they are asked to recall are similar in sound to one another.

Further evidence for the existence of a phonological loop comes from the **unattended speech effect**. When individuals are asked to perform a verbal task (e.g., reading) with speech in the background, performance is impaired. Performance is disrupted whether or not the background speech is meaningful. You may have experienced this effect while studying difficult material. You may find that you have to turn off the radio because it is interfering with your task. Verbal information that is presented auditorially is processed automatically. Information in the working memory store is subject to both decay and interference from new material.

unattended speech effect   Verbal information automatically enters the phonological loop and can interfere with a person's verbal task performance even if that person is not paying attention to the information.

A third source of evidence in support of the phonological loop is found in the **word length effect**. There is a link between memory span and the length of words to be recalled. Verbal information that is presented auditorially gains direct access to the passive phonological store, which retains information in a phonological form.

word length effect   The link between memory span and the length of words to be recalled.

Nick Ellis of the University of Bangor in Wales (Baddeley, 1993) administered a standardized IQ test to Welsh children. Their performance on the digit span was below the norms typically seen among American children (Ellis & Hennelley, 1980). Welsh words take longer to pronounce than their English equivalents. What appeared to be a difference in cognitive functioning between children from the two cultures was actually a difference in word length that affected performance on the digit span test. The results of this research suggest that cultural differences in basic processing should be interpreted with caution.

The Visuospatial Sketchpad   A second subsystem in Baddeley's model is the **visuospatial sketchpad,** which is used for processing visual or spatial material or both. In Figure 8.11 you will see the letter *F*, a stimulus used in one of the tasks invented to explore the spatial and verbal components of recall (Brooks, 1968).

In a study designed to test the processing of these components, participants were shown the letter and asked to keep it in mind. Starting at the bottom left, instructed to say, "Yes" if the corner was at the top or bottom of the letter and "No" if it was not. They found this much harder to do if they were asked to point to the corners as they announced their decisions. In contrast, when participants were shown a sentence such as, "A bird in the hand is not in the bush," and asked to indicate whether each word was a noun or not a noun, their performance was better if the responses were made by pointing rather than by speaking. These results demonstrate that when an individual engages in a visuospatial task such as pointing while performing a visual imagery task, the same processing capacity is being used. If the form of the task (verbal or visual) and that of the response (verbal or visual) are same, performance is impaired.

The Executive System   The central executive system of working memory controls the phonological loop and the visuospatial sketchpad. It is an attentional control system with limited capacity (Baddeley, 1993). Daneman and Carpenter (1983) explored the relationship between working memory and reading comprehension by asking individuals to read passages that contained inconsistencies due to the presence of words with more than one meaning. Here is an example:

> There was a strange noise emanating from the dark house. Bob had to venture in to find out what was there. He was terrified: Rumor had it that the house was haunted. He would feel more secure with a stick to defend himself, so he went and looked among his baseball equipment. He found a bat that was very large and brown and was flying back and forth in the gloomy room. Now he didn't need to be afraid any longer.[1]

When reading this for the first time, most people assume that the *bat* is a baseball bat until information occurring later in the passage contradicts this notion. However, individuals with low working memory spans were able to come to the correct conclusion only 25% of the time. Individuals with high working memory spans are able to keep the initial information in working memory until they encounter the information that clarifies the passage. Additional research suggests that the functioning of the central executive system is the key difference between good and poor comprehenders (Oakhill, 1982, 1984; Oakhill, Yuill, & Parkin, 1986).

Memory Difficulties of Children with Special Needs

It is important for teachers to know that working memory is limited. When instructions are complicated or lengthy, there is a risk that students will not remember them. We may be disappointed when they do not follow instructions, but we may simply have exceeded their working memory's capacity for processing information.

Interruptions are frequent in elementary school classes and include such events as announcements from the administration, telephone calls, and visitors to the classroom. The effects of these distruptions on children's learning have not been studied. It seems reasonable to assume that the constant interruption can produce interference effects. Working memory is involved in such tasks as reading comprehension, writing, problem solving, and mathematics (Swanson & Siegel, 2001). Individuals with a large working memory span utilize cognitive resources more efficiently while reading and as a result have more resources for storage while comprehending the text (Swanson & Siegel, 2001). Students must also retrieve information from long-term memory to include in their writing. Maintaining ideas

[1]Copyright © 1983 by the American Psychological Association. Reproduced with permission.

---

visuospatial sketchpad   The component of working memory that processes visuospatial content.

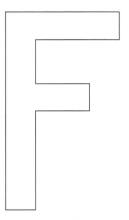

Source: Brooks, L. R. Spatial and verbal components of the act of recall. *Canadian Journal of Psychology, 22, 349–368.* Copyright 1968. Canadian Psychological Association. Reprinted with permission.

Figure 8.11. Brooks Test Using the Letter *F*

R I D E   Think again about the students described at the beginning of the chapter. Are they exhibiting problems of working memory and executive control?

Chapter Reference
The difficulties with working memory that learning-disabled students experience are discussed in Chapter 4.

Taking It to the Classroom

Supporting Working Memory in the Classroom

Here are some guidelines for supporting students' working memory during instruction.

- *Keep directions simple.* Because working memory is limited, students may find it hard to follow complex directions. Simple directions are more likely to be followed correctly because students are more likely to remember what was said.

- *Provide information in both verbal and visual formats.* The working memory system has both verbal and visual processing components. Information that is provided in both visual and verbal formats is easier to process.

- *Teach students to create representations of problems.* Children often have difficulty solving word problems in mathematics. The limitations of working memory can contribute to these difficulties, because children may forget important parts of the problem. Teaching children how to represent what the problem is asking them to do can help. For example, drawing a picture of the problem can be a very useful aid to problem solving.

- *Use tape recorders for children who have difficulties with writing.* Some students' writing may appear very disconnected and unstructured. The difficulties involved in producing writing or typing can interfere with working memory, and the student may simply forget his or her idea while trying to produce text. In such instances, you might have the student audiotape his or her verbally produced story and write it down later or assist the student in writing it down.

What Does This Mean to Me?
Think back to a time in a class when you felt that your working memory was overloaded. What could the teacher have done to make the situation better for you?

and choosing among them while actually producing text can make heavy demands on memory capacity. Some learners have difficulty writing because of limited working memory capacity.

When given a list of words to recall, learning-disabled children remember fewer words than normally achieving peers (Torgesen, 1977). Students with learning disabilities frequently have deficits in working memory (Swanson & Siegel, 2001). In particular, they have difficulty with reading comprehension because of deficits in the phonological loop—that is, the component of working memory that processes verbal information. Difficulties with working memory are problematic on tasks that require a learner to retain information in mind for a short period while also carrying out further activities. This skill is very important in reading tasks in which information that is coming in must be stored temporarily while other information is being processed (Swanson & Alexander, 1997). Difficulties with working memory can also interfere with writing, because efforts to record ideas may interfere with maintenance rehearsal in working memory.

Students and teachers can use a variety of strategies to reduce the demands on working memory. Children often count on their fingers, thus giving themselves a visible record of their cognitive activity rather than relying on memory. Other strategies for supporting working memory include presenting information in **multiple modalities** presenting to various senses, allowing students to record their ideas before writing, or using speech-to-text software to reduce the burden on working memory. (See the "Taking It to the Classroom" box above.)

multiple modalities   Various senses.

Using an external representation can reduce the demands on working memory. (Digital Vision)

Long-Term Memory

The capacity and duration of long-term memory (LTM) are not known, though it is clear that its capacity is very large and its duration is very long. It is also evident that the contents of long-term memory can include all kinds of information. Researchers have described several types of long-term memory. The Atkinson and Shiffrin model (see Figure 8.1 on page 242) was based on the duration of memory. In it, processing was divided among sensory, short-term, and long-term memory. This model was very useful, but it does not provide a complete description of how memory works.

Types of Long-Term Memory There are several ways to distinguish between various kinds of long-term memories. One important distinction is between episodic and semantic memory (Tulving, 1972). **Episodic memory** is memory of events and typically includes sensory information (things seen, heard, or smelled, etc.). Such memories often have heightened emotional content (happy, sad, fearful). You need only consider events of your childhood (e.g., the first day of school) to generate an episodic memory. These memories are embedded in a specific context—a specific time and place.

In contrast, **semantic memory** is memory of verbal information or **declarative knowledge**—that is, knowledge about *what*. It is separate from sensory information and not tied to particular experiences. An example of an item that might be held in semantic memory is the answer to the question, In what city is the National Art Gallery? If you have visited that art gallery, you will have created episodic memories related to the content, and your combined semantic and episodic memory will make this information more memorable and retrievable.

A second distinction is between declarative and procedural memory. **Declarative memory** is like semantic memory: It is memory about what. For example, you might have declarative memories about the structure of a bicycle. **Procedural memory** is memory about *how* to do something. You may remember how to ride a bicycle. These kinds of memory are also called *explicit* and *implicit memory*.

Brain Processes and Memory A number of structures in the medial temporal lobes of the brain (see Figure 8.12) are important for memory. They include the amygdala, the hippocampus and the rhinal cortex that underlies the amygdala and hippocampus. The hippocampus plays a key role in the storage of new memories (Gazzaniga & Heatherton, 2003). The hippocampus and surrounding rhinal cortex are the most important areas for the consolidation of memory (Eichenbaum, 2002; Gazzaniga & Heatherton, 2003). The frontal lobes are also considered important for memory; although people who experience damage to the frontal lobes do not suffer dramatic memory loss, they may have difficulty remembering the order of events. Brain-imaging studies show that when people try to remember a list of words, the frontal lobes light up (Buckner, Kelly, & Petersen, 1999). The frontal lobes are more active when a task requires deeper encoding.

Semantic Memory Semantic memory is memory for meaning and is thought to be organized like a network. Collins and Quillian (1969) proposed the earliest network model of semantic memory. In this model, semantic networks are made up of a network of related propositions. Such a network is analogous to a road map. On a map, cities, towns, and villages are linked to one another through a series of roads that vary in size and frequency of

episodic memory Long-term memory of particular places and events in a person's life.

semantic memory The memory a person has for meaning.

declarative knowledge Factual knowledge that can be expressed through verbal exchange, books, Braille, or sign language; knowing that something is true.

declarative memory Memory for abstract information.

procedural memory Memory for how to do things.

Chapter Reference
Go back to Chapter 2 and examine the picture of the brain on page 35.

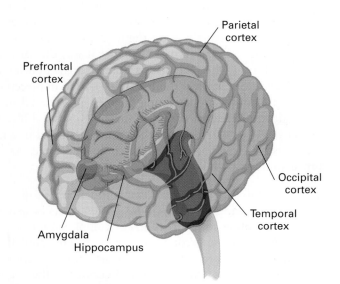

Source: Westen, D. *Psychology: Brain, Behavior and Culture*, Third Edition. © 2002 John Wiley & Sons. Reprinted by permission of John Wiley & Sons, Inc.

Figure 8.12. Major Regions of the Medial Temporal Lobe

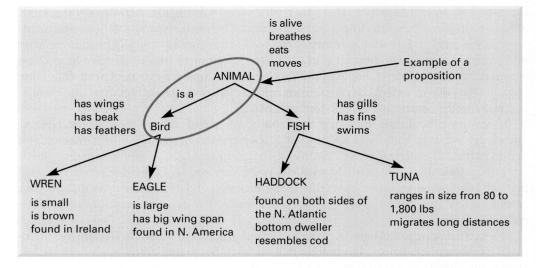

Figure 8.13. Network of Concepts and Example of a Proposition

proposition   The smallest unit of knowledge that can be verified.

use. The same can be said for a semantic network. Figure 8.13 illustrates a network in which the basic unit of a semantic network is a **proposition**, the smallest unit of meaning that can be verified as true or false. A proposition involves linking two concepts by a relationship. For example, the proposition *A bird is an animal* can be verified as true or false. According to Collins and Quillian, it should take longer to verify that *A wren is an animal* than it would to verify that *A bird is an animal* (Collins & Quillian, 1969). The word *wren* is two links away from *animal,* whereas the word *bird* is only one link away. However, based on this model, it should take as long to verify that *A wren is an animal* as it would to verify that *An eagle is an animal.* Most people in the United States will verify the latter proposition more quickly than the former because of familiarity. Connections between ideas also vary in strength and frequency of use. These factors are more important than the actual categorical structures.

Images   When we think about an object that is not present, we experience an image of that object. Responding to a question about an image takes about the same amount of time as responding to a picture (Kosslyn, 1976). In one study, participants were asked to form a mental image of a cat. They were then asked questions such as, Does the cat have a head? and Does the cat have claws? Responses to the latter question took longer, as participants appeared to scan the image. In a related study, participants memorized a fictional map (see Figure 8.14) and were asked to fixate on a specific landmark. A second landmark was mentioned, and participants were asked to imagine a small speck moving from the first landmark to the second. The greater the distance between the two landmarks, the longer it took participants to respond (Kosslyn, Ball, & Reiser, 1978).

In Figure 8.15, two shapes are presented. An individual is asked to determine if the shape on the right is the same as the one on the left. In other words, is the shape on the right a rotated version of the one on the left? To do this task, individuals imagined rotating the shape on the left to determine whether it was the same as the one on the right. Response times are longer when the images were far apart in orientation.

Image information is thought to be stored in piecemeal fashion in long-term memory. Images are created by activating the overall or global shape of the image; elaborations are then added to create a complete image (Kosslyn, 1980, 1983). More detailed images take longer to retrieve. Images are thought to be stored in a nonimage format (Reisberg, 2001) that specifies a *recipe* for constructing the image. As with the processing of language, processing images takes time.

Schemas and Scripts   Semantic memory is organized in complex networks. When people know isolated facts, representations of these facts in semantic memory may not be connected to many other ideas. In contrast, complex understanding of a domain will result in a dense network of interconnected propositions about that domain called a **propositional network**. **Schemas** refer to organized sets of propositions about a topic. From the perspective of endogenous constructivism described at the beginning of the chapter, the learner's schemas may be altered as a result of interacting with the environment. A learner's available schemas influence how he or she interacts with the environment.

propositional network   A set of interconnected pieces of information that contains knowledge for the long term.

schema   The basic structure for organizing information.

Source: Kosslyn, S. M., Ball, T. M., & Reiser, B. J. (1978). Visual images preserve metric spatial information: Evidence from studies of image scanning. *Journal of Experimental Psychology: Human perception and Performance, 4,* 47–60. Copyright © 1978 by the American Psychological Association. Reproduced with permission.

Figure 8.14. Image Scanning with a Fictional Map

A schema that describes the typical sequence of events in a situation is called a **script**, or *event schema.* For example, when you go to a restaurant, you usually expect actions to unfold in a particular way. Sometimes, however, they do not. On a recent occasion, one of the authors went to a restaurant with friends. Before long, the server appeared and asked the people at the table whether they would like drinks. One person asked for a cup of coffee. The server replied that she could not have the coffee now, because that was served after dinner. The server had a different script for how events should unfold than the customer did. This same conflict sometimes occurs between the teacher's classroom script and the students' classroom script.

In the "What Kids Say and Do" box on the next page, you can read the response of a fourth grader named Chloe to a picture prompt that involved her knowledge of a script or event schema. The children in this class were shown a picture of a boy sitting outside an office that was labeled "Main Office." The boy's head was bent down, and he was looking at the floor. His book bag was beside him.

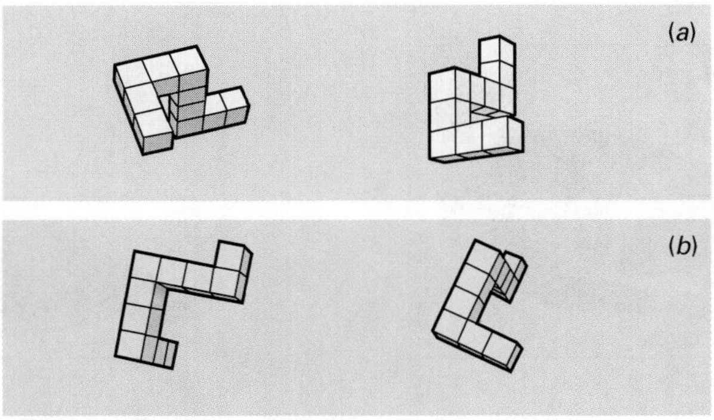

script A schema for the sequence of events in common events, such as ordering food at a fast-food restaurant.

(a)

(b)

Figure 8.15. Mental Rotation

Source: Huffman, K. *Psychology in Action,* Seventh Edition. © 2004 John Wiley & Sons. Reprinted by permission of John Wiley & Sons, Inc.

What Kids Say and Do

Using a Script

"Ouch! That hurt, Billy. I'm telling the principal." Beep went the intercom. "Billy Smith, please come to the office *now!*" Billy went to the main office. He went inside. "The principal will see you in a few minutes. Sit down on the bench." Billy sat down and thought about what he did to Johnny. He said to himself, "My mom is going to kill me." It was now time to speak to the principal about what he had done.

After the conversation, he was suspended for three days. Johnny was doing fine in the hospital, and Billy promised himself that he would never hurt or beat someone up again. A few years later, he forgot about the promise and "Ouch![2]

In this account, Chloe shows knowledge of a schema or script related to being at the principal's office. She knows that a child must have misbehaved in order to be outside the office waiting. She inferred from the picture that the office was that of the principal, rather than another kind of office. Because she identified the office in a particular way, she activated schema-relevant elements of a story: The boy had misbehaved, and there would be consequences for his actions. Chloe also shows her understanding of how scripts allow us to predict actions. At the end of her story, she indicates that Johnny repeated the actions for which he got in trouble.

story grammar   The typical structure of a category of stories.

Another type of script is a **story grammar** that can help students to understand and remember stories (Gagné, Yekovich, & Yekovich, 1993). In the "What Kids Say and Do" box below, Ms. D'Andrea taught her students the following story grammar to help them understand Aesop's fables: title, characters, setting, events, problem, solution, summary, and moral. You can see one child's response to the task of constructing a story grammar.

What Kids Say and Do

Using a Story Grammar for Aesop's Fables

Title	Characters	Setting	3 Events	Problem	Solution	Summary	Moral
The Hare and the Tortoise	The hare and the tortoise	The woods	1. The hare challenges the tortoise to a race. 2. The hare takes a nap during the race. 3. The tortoise wins the race.	The hare thinks that he is the fastest animal in the woods and constantly brags that no one can beat him in a race.	The tortoise accepts the challenge because he has faith that he can win the race.	One day in the woods, a hare was boasting that he was the fastest animal in the woods. No one would take him up on his challenge, until one day a little voice said, "I will." So it was agreed that the hare would race against the tortoise through the woods and back. The hare, thinking he would win the race with no problem, decided to take a nap. All of a sudden, the tortoise passed the hare and won the race.	"Slow and steady wins the race," which means when you take your time, you can accomplish anything.

Source: © Bryan Turton. Used with permission.

[2]Written by Chloe Branch. Used with permission.

Levels of Processing Craik and Lockhart proposed an alternative theory of memory in 1972. It suggested that memory differences are not so much a function of *duration* as of *depth* of processing (Craik & Lockhart, 1972). A classic experiment compared the memory performance of three groups of students as they processed a word list. The first group was asked to determine whether a particular letter was present in a word as it was presented. These students attended to the structure of the word. The second group was asked to decide whether they liked the word when it was presented. Thus, they attended to the content on an affective level. The third group was asked to generate a word that was opposite in meaning to the presented word. These students attended to the meaning of the word. The results showed that students who attended to meaning performed significantly better than those who decided whether they liked a word. The latter group, in turn, did better than the students who only decided whether a particular letter was present. Craik and Lockhart argued that the differences in performance reflected differences in depth of processing.

Craik and Lockhart's concept of **levels of processing** helped shift the emphasis in the study of memory from storage to processing. The Atkinson and Shiffrin model defined memory systems in terms of the storage/duration of memories and described very short stores (sensory and short-term memory) and very long-term stores (long-term memory). It did not permit intermediate memories, such as the memory for course content one might have after cramming for a test. Such information lasts longer than the typical short-term memory storage would predict but is generally not available in long-term memory. The levels-of-processing theory focuses on the likelihood of retrieval as a function of how effortful and meaningful the initial encoding was. The limitation of this work is that it was impossible to measure *depth*. Nevertheless, the emphasis on processing made an enormous contribution to the study of memory.

> **levels of processing theory** A theory that asserts that recall of information is based on how deeply it is processed.

Encoding, Retrieval, and Forgetting

Encoding is the taking in of information. The probability that information will be retrieved or remembered depends on the quality of encoding. Different types of knowledge can be encoded.

Types of Knowledge

The kinds of encoding strategies that students use will vary as a function of the type of knowledge they are acquiring. Declarative knowledge is knowledge about *what*. Examples of declarative knowledge are knowing history facts or being able to name the parts of a cell. **Procedural knowledge** is knowledge about *how*. Knowing how to set up the equipment in the chemistry lab is an example of procedural knowledge. **Conditional knowledge** involves knowledge of both what and how. It involves knowing the necessary information and how to apply it in the right situation.

> **procedural knowledge**
> Knowledge about how to perform tasks.
>
> **conditional knowledge**
> Knowledge that guides a person in using declarative and procedural knowledge.

Organization, Practice, and Elaboration

Remembering is best when information is encoded well. Key processes in good encoding are organization, practice, and elaboration. It is easier to learn organized material than it is to learn disorganized material. For example, Table 8.1 presents two lists of words. List 2 will be easier to learn because it is organized by category: fruits, flowers, and cities. List 1 contains the same information but will be harder to learn because it lacks organization.

Practice helps develop good memory. Material that is used more often is remembered more easily. However, there are different ways of practicing. **Distributed practice** is much more effective than **massed practice**. Distributed practice is done over a period of time, with varying intervals between rehearsals of the information. Rather than studying for an exam the night before, a learner might study for a few hours on alternating days in the week before the test. Distributed practice provides opportunities to practice retrieval after varying lengths of time. Remembering involves using the cues available to assist remembering but also involves generating cues that help remembering. Distributed practice allows students to practice both of these skills. Massed practice, in contrast, involves engaging in extensive practice at one time, such as studying all night before an exam. This can be somewhat effective for an immediate task but is unlikely to lead to long-term recall of information.

> **distributed practice** Practice that is interspersed by unequal intervals.
>
> **massed practice** Intense practice for a single period of time (also known as "cramming").

TABLE 8.1

Organized and Disorganized Lists

List 1	List 2
Geneva	Banana
Orchid	Grape
Orlando	Melon
Geranium	Orange
Melon	Buttercup
Minnesota	Geranium
Orange	Mums
Buttercup	Orchid
Grape	Berlin
Mums	Geneva
Berlin	Minnesota
Banana	Orlando

elaboration A process through which we add and extend meaning by connecting new information to existing knowledge in long-term memory.

Elaboration also helps in encoding and retrieval. When you connect the information you are trying to learn to information you already know or to images or other enhancements of the information to be learned, you are elaborating on the material. Images in particular are powerful aids to memory and are frequently used to elaborate on information. Elaboration helps you extend a network of concepts and the relationships between them. Mnemonic strategies are one example of elaboration.

Mnemonic Strategies

Learning is much easier when information is meaningful. Although higher order thinking skills are important, sometimes facts, concepts, relationships, and the like simply have to be memorized. In such cases, it is helpful to understand the processes through which memory works and what kinds of activities will enhance that process. Students enjoy learning memory tricks and are glad that they have learned them when they see how they can be applied to learning. Strategies for remembering information are known as **mnemonic strategies.**

mnemonic strategies Strategies for remembering nonmeaningful information by making it meaningful.

Acronyms In using the *acronyms* strategy, you would create a word in which each of the letters stands for one of the words to be remembered. For example, in this textbook, you are asked to engage in reflection, information gathering, decision making, and evaluation. The acronym *RIDE* makes this easy to remember. A common acronym is ROY-G-BIV for remembering the colors of the rainbow: **r**ed, **o**range, **y**ellow, **g**reen, **b**lue, **i**ndigo, and **v**iolet.

The Keyword Strategy Among the most helpful mnemonic strategies is the *keyword strategy* for learning vocabulary (particularly in a foreign language). A visual image is used to make a link between a word in the foreign language and its meaning in English. For example, the French word *sortir* means "*to leave*" and is pronounced somewhat like *sort tear* (*tear* as in crying, with apologies to native French speakers). The keyword strategy begins by the learner thinking of something that comes to mind easily when one sees the word *sortir*, For example, *sort tear* might suggest a postal worker sorting so many letters that he is crying. That could be the initial image. Now it has to be modified to put the definition "to leave" into it. This will not be very difficult. The postal worker could be crying, throwing the letters in the air, and leaving the post office. The keyword works by starting with the target word, then going to the image that it prompts—in which the definition is embedded—and retrieving the definition.

Source: Rummel, N., Levin, J. R., & Woodward, M. M. (2003). Do pictorial mnemonic text-learning aids give students something worth writing about? *Journal of Educational Psychology, 95,* 327–334. Copyright © 2003 by the American Psychological Association. Reproduced with permission.

Figure 8.16. Pictorial Mnemonics

Pictorial Mnemonics **Pictorial mnemonics** are an extension of the keyword method (Rummel, Levin, & Woodward, 2003). They are interactive images that combine pictorial and verbal elements. Figure 8.16, for example, shows a pictorial mnemonic for the name *Binet*. The keyword *bonnet* is used to assist memory.

pictorial mnemonics Interactive images that combine pictorial and verbal elements.

The Method of Loci The *method of loci* uses spatial imagery to assist memory. If you need to learn a list of words or concepts, you could visualize yourself walking around a familiar place, such as your apartment, and putting each word in a different place. For example, if you were trying to remember the assignments you needed to complete, you might imagine leaving your assignments in various locations in the apartment. Your assignment for your educational psychology class might be on the kitchen table, your assignment for English beside the TV, and so forth.

Pegword Mnemonics *Pegword mnemonics* requires you to associate each new word with a word on a previously memorized list. For example, suppose that you wish to learn the following list of words: *battleship, volcano, ambulance, policeman, television, computer, calendar, mirror, flashlight, pencil.* First, you would memorize the following rhyme.

One is a bun	Six is a stick
Two is a shoe	Seven is heaven
Three is a tree	Eight is a gate
Four is a door	Nine is a dime
Five is a hive	Ten is a hen

This rhyme is easy to remember because you are depending on similar sounds to help memory. The next step in the strategy is to associate each of the words to be remembered with a line of this rhyme. The first word to be remembered is *battleship*. You now associate battleship with *One is a bun*. You might visualize a battleship between two parts of a hamburger bun.

One = Bun = Battleship

The second word to be memorized is *volcano*. Now you link *volcano* to *Two is a shoe*. You might imagine a shoe with a volcano in it, with lava pouring over the edges of the shoe. The process would continue until you had linked each word with a line of the rhyme. The strategy is very effective for remembering lists of words.

Imagery and Visual-Learning Strategies

A theory that explains why images are helpful in remembering is dual-coding theory (Paivio, 1986). According to this theory, images and words are represented differently, as *imagens* and *logogens*. When the two forms of representations are linked, the memory for the information is stronger. Baddeley's findings on the separate working memory systems for visual and verbal information also support the importance of presenting and learning information in both visual and verbal forms (Baddeley, 1999). Visual strategies such as concept maps and graphic organizers integrate verbal, visual, and spatial information to enhance encoding and retrieval. (See the "Taking It to the Classroom Box" below.)

graphic organizers A visual display of verbal information.

Graphic Organizers A **graphic organizer** is a visual display of verbal information. The term *graphic organizer* includes such devices as concept maps, mind webs, semantic maps, knowledge maps or tables etc. Graphic organizers are intended to help students to comprehend, summarize, and synthesize information. A concept map shows a set of concepts and the relationships between them (see Figure 8.18). A well-designed graphic organizer can represent parts of a whole and show the relationships between those parts. In the example shown in

Taking It to the Classroom

Creating and Enhancing Visual Images from Text

Part of reading comprehension is the creation, modification, elaboration, and enhancement of visual images derived from text. An enjoyable approach to developing this skill involves working on images from the spoken word, not the written word. Consider the following class activity:

Today we are going to listen to a story and picture the story as we go along. Just pay attention to the story and let the images come to your mind. I'll tell you the story and stop and ask questions along the way. Here we go:

"Jack was walking down the street."

In your mind, how old is Jack? (Solicit answers. Most students will consider Jack to be their age.)

"He wished he had brought his cane and a warmer coat."

Now how old is Jack? (Solicit answers again. Some students will make him much older; others will still have him the same age as themselves even though the story now suggests that he should be older.)

Is Jack wearing a coat? (Most students will say no, but clearly he is, because the story says that he wished he had a warmer coat.)

What kind of street is Jack walking down? (Most students will make it a street like the one in front of the school.)

"Smoke was wafting skyward from a farmhouse in the distance."

Now what kind of street is Jack walking down? Is it a windy day or a calm day?

You can continue the story, providing cues like those just described, then checking on those cues. This can be done by reading from a story that is rich in such cues, or even getting books on tape or old-time scary radio stories. The goal is to have the students listen carefully to what the author is saying. Of course, not everyone will come up with the same images, but images should be roughly consistent with what the author is saying. You can also ask students to describe what they have in mind at a certain point, either by writing down their images or by sharing them with the class. Who elaborates on what is being said? Who reports *bare bones* images? This activity can be great fun, and it offers a way to help students with issues of reading comprehension without having to worry about word fluency skills at the same time.

Dinosaurs

What We Know	What We Want to Find Out	What We Learned	How Can We Learn More
Dinosaurs are large. Dinosaurs are dead. They lived a long time ago. There is a movie about dinosaurs.	How long ago did they live? Why did they die? How do we know what they looked like? Who are the people who study dinosuars?	An archeologist has an exciting life. Dinosaurs eat plants, and some eat meat. Some dinosaurs were gigantic, but had small brains. Fossils uncover dinosaur traits.	Research Museums Field trips Archeological digs Videos Internet computer search

Categories of information we expect to use:

A. Size

B. Career

C. Eating habits

D.

E.

F.

G.

Source: Donna Ogle. *K–W–L–H Technique.* Retrieved from the Web site of the North Central Regional Educational Laboratory at http://www.ncrel.org/sdrs/areas/issues/students/learning/lr1kwlh.htm. Reproduced with permission.

Figure 8.17. Sample K–W–L–H

Appendix
Visual Strategies

Using graphic organizers and concept maps in your teaching can help your students understand relationships among concepts they are learning (*PRAXIS*™, II. A. 2, *INTASC*, Principle 4).

Figure 8.17, a fourth-grade teacher used a graphic organizer to help her students use the KWLH strategy, a means of helping students activate existing knowledge. First, the students recall what they *know* about the topic, then they identify what they *want* to know, what they have *learned,* and *how* they can learn more. By providing a graphic organizer, the teacher helps the students comprehend, summarize, and synthesize the day's lesson.

Knowledge Structures Graphic representations can also show the structure of knowledge. In Figure 8.18, three knowledge structures are illustrated. The first is a chainlike structure that clearly shows a sequence of events. Cluster structures show descriptive knowledge about a topic, and hierarchies show the relationships among parts of a system.

Concept Mapping Concept mapping is a strategy in which students create diagrams or pictures to illustrate their understanding of a concept. The teacher can also use concepts maps as teaching aids. Students can be taught to label the relationships between ideas in a concept map. Figure 8.19 includes a list of typical links that might be used to connect ideas. The links are of three types: dynamic, static, and elaborative. Dynamic links show that the information in one node is the outcome of the previous node—for example, driving over nails and glass *results in* flat tires. Static links describe structural relationships between ideas—for example, a poodle is a *type* of dog. Elaborative links extend the information in one node by linking it to another—for example, time is *analogous* to a river. Younger students will experience great difficulty with using a complex set of links such as those found in Figure 8.19. Older students may also experience some difficulty. Therefore, it is best to introduce the various types of links slowly and show clearly how they describe structures of knowledge.

What Does This Mean to Me?
Which are stronger, your verbal skills or your visual skills? How might a graphic organizer help you understand the content of this chapter?

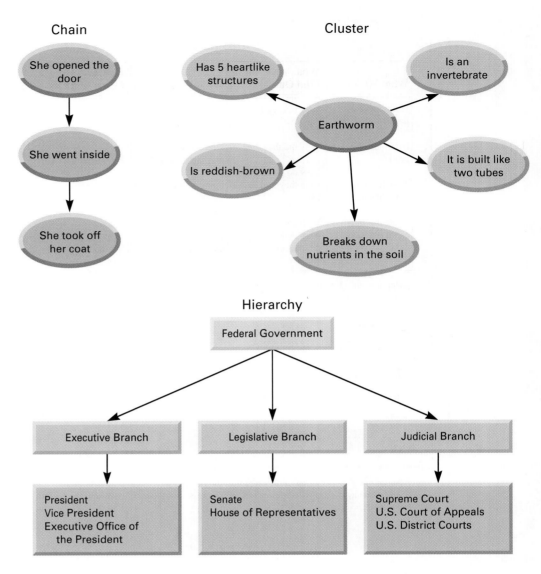

Figure 8.18. Knowledge Structures

Retrieval and Forgetting

recognition memory   Memories are cued, then recognized.

Remembering can occur through either **recognition memory** or **recall**. Recognition simply requires us to respond to information and recognize that we have seen it before. Recognition memory responds to cues. Responding to multiple-choice tests can require recognition memory because the cues provided by the options from which you may choose will provide some assistance to memory. When you recall information, on the other hand, you must generate information without cues. Responding to an essay question, for example, requires that you generate and organize the content. For many people, this kind of remembering is much harder.

recall   Information is retrieved from long-term memory.

spread of activation   The retrieval of bits of information on the basis of their relatedness to each other. Remembering one piece of information stimulates the recall of associated knowledge.

Spread of Activation Retrieval occurs within a semantic network because activation is spread from one node to another. Related ideas are triggered. For example, when you hear the word *butter,* other associations come quickly to mind because of the linked structures in semantic memory. The specific linkages will vary from one person to another. For example, one person may generate *milk* as an associate for *butter,* whereas another may generate *cup.* The person who generates *buttercup* may like flowers; hence, *cup* is more frequently associated with butter. Because of the structure of a network, retrieval can involve reconstructing the links between propositions and ideas. If you are trying to retrieve information during an essay exam, you might recall that there are multiple systems of memory. The fact that you retrieved this idea may then lead you to be able to retrieve other information about the various memory systems.

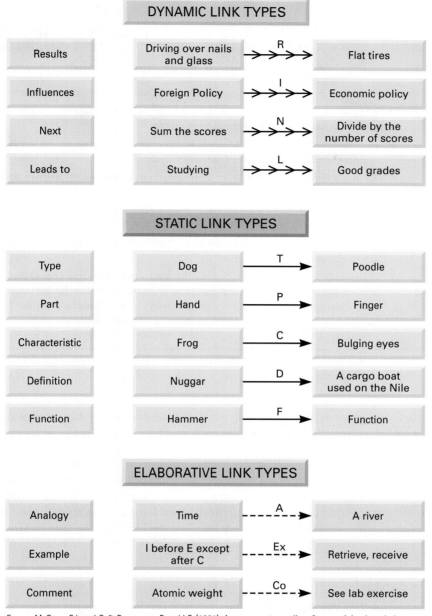

DYNAMIC LINK TYPES

Results	Driving over nails and glass	→R→	Flat tires
Influences	Foreign Policy	→I→	Economic policy
Next	Sum the scores	→N→	Divide by the number of scores
Leads to	Studying	→L→	Good grades

STATIC LINK TYPES

Type	Dog	→T→	Poodle
Part	Hand	→P→	Finger
Characteristic	Frog	→C→	Bulging eyes
Definition	Nuggar	→D→	A cargo boat used on the Nile
Function	Hammer	→F→	Function

ELABORATIVE LINK TYPES

Analogy	Time	--A-->	A river
Example	I before E except after C	--Ex-->	Retrieve, receive
Comment	Atomic weight	--Co-->	See lab exercise

Source: McCagg, Edward C. & Dansereau, Donald F. (1991). A convergent paradigm for examining knowledge mapping as a learning strategy. *Journal of Educational Research, 84 (6)*, 317–324. Reprinted with permission of the Helen Dwight Reid Educational Foundation. Published by Heldref Publications, 1319 Eighteenth St., NW, Washington, DC 20036-1802. Copyright © 1991.

Figure 8.19. Link Types

> **What Does This Mean to Me?**
> Use some of the link types in Figure 8.19 to interrogate your memory of what you have read in this chapter.

Interrogating Memory We can use our knowledge of categories or the kinds of relationships outlined in Figure 8.19 to interrogate our memories. When we cannot recall information about a topic, we can conduct a *relationship-guided search*. A simple acronym for some of the types of links shown in Figure 8.19 is T-PLACE (for type, parts, leads to, analogy, characteristics, examples). If you were to interrogate your memory about a topic such as *famines*, you could ask yourself questions related to the various types of links. For example, what types of famines are there? Those caused by weather conditions, those caused by wars.

Forgetting Forgetting occurs when there is interference or decay. When material is encoded in an organized manner, more cues are encoded, thus making retrieval easier. Also, information that is used more frequently is easier to recall. Material that is not encoded in an organized way and not used often is more likely to be forgotten. This is so because in a propositional network model of memory, retrieval occurs through a process of spreading activation. When one node in a network is triggered, related nodes are also triggered as activation spreads along the links to them. When these links are used often, less activation is

Chapter Reference
Chapter 2 explained and how neurons form and maintain memory.

What Does This
Mean to Me?
Can you explain to yourself
why these principles of
multimedia learning might
be true?

Taking It to the Classroom

Principles of Multimedia Learning

- *Multimedia Principle*: Students learn better from words and pictures than from words alone.
- *Spatial Contiguity Principle*: Students learn better when corresponding words and pictures are presented near each other on the page or screen.
- *Temporal Contiguity Principle*: Students learn better when corresponding words and pictures are presented simultaneously rather than successively.
- *Coherence Principle*: Students learn better when extraneous words, pictures, and sounds are excluded.
- *Modality Principle*: Students learn better from animation and narration than from animation and on-screen text.
- *Redundancy Principle*: Students learn better from animation and narration than from animation, narration, and on-screen text.
- *Individual Differences Principle*: Design effects are stronger for low-knowledge learners than for high-knowledge learners and for high-spatial learners rather than for low-spatial learners. Students who have prior knowledge of the content of a multimedia presentation perform better than those who do not. Furthermore, students with good spatial skills or those who are good at generating and using mental images perform better than those who are less skilled.

Source: Adapted from Mayer, R. (2001). *Multimedia learning* (p. 184). New York: Cambridge University Press. Reprinted with the permission of Cambridge University Press.

needed to generate the connecting node. If the nodes are highly interconnected with many links, forgetting is less likely, but retrieval may take longer. In a curious irony, the more you know, the longer it may take you to verify that you know it.

Forgetting occurs when information is not used. If you have not practiced solving geometry problems for a year, you are likely to have forgotten the steps in doing so. Forgetting also occurs because of interference. If you go to the grocery store having made a mental list of what you need to purchase and you meet a friend, the discussion with your friend may interfere with your recall of your grocery list. (See the "Taking It to the Classroom" box above.)

Categorization

Earlier in the chapter, you saw how attention can be used to narrow the scope of the environmental input we receive. Categorization is another way in which we narrow the range of information available to us. Categorization helps us:

- Reduce complexity
- Identify objects
- Devote less effort to learning
- Decide what actions are appropriate
- Order and relate classes of objects and events

concept An abstraction with which a person categorizes objects, people, ideas, or experiences by shared properties.

Concepts are abstractions that are the result of assigning objects, people, ideas, or experiences to categories. We can most readily distinguish between categories when they differ on a single dimension. For example, triangles can be distinguished from squares or rectangles because triangles have three sides, and squares and rectangles have four sides. Many categories differ in more than one dimension, however, and we learn to distinguish among them by applying logical rules. Examples of rules that allow us to classify objects into categories are illustrated in Figure 8.20.

The *conjunctive rule* is the easiest to learn. It involves using the relationship *and*. For example, a rule that will allow us to classify a shape as a member of a particular category may be that the object must be red *and* square. The *disjunctive rule* uses the relationship *or*. For

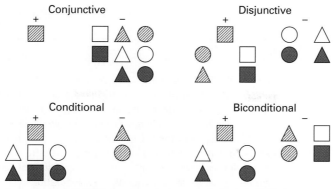

Source: Bourne, L. E. (1970). Knowing and using concepts. *Psychological Review, 77,* 546–556. Copyright © 1970 by the American Psychological Association. Reproduced with permission.

Figure 8.20. Logical Rules for Classification

example, an object may be red *or* square in order to be categorized as a member of a category. The *conditional rule* uses the relationship *if-then*. For example, *if* the object is red, *then* it must be a square to be classified as a member of the category. The *biconditional rule* is the hardest to use. In it, the conditional rule applies in both directions. For example, if the object is red, then it must be a square. If the object is a square, then it must be red.

To understand which instances are members of a concept category, we need to identify **criterial attributes**. These attributes are ones that must be present in order for the instance to be considered a member of the class. The process of including recurring attributes and excluding nonrecurring attributes is called *abstraction*. If a child is attempting to categorize shapes into rectangles or triangles, he or she learns to attend to the number of sides of the object (e.g., three or four) and ignore the varying colors of the shapes.

criterial attributes Attributes that must be presented for an instance to be a member of a particular category.

Concept Attainment Tasks The tasks used by Jerome Bruner and his colleagues (Bruner et al., 1956) in his studies of concept attainment were of two kinds: reception and selection tasks. Reception tasks involve the development of hypotheses about the nature of the target concepts with revisions and alteration to the hypotheses when the data do not fit. In a selection task, an individual is shown a positive instance of a concept, then asked to pick out another instance of that concept. The individual is then told whether the selection was correct. Strategies for completing selection tasks vary. They depend on the individual forming a hypothesis, testing its accuracy, and revising it in coherent ways. Young children are often asked to engage in selection tasks as they learn to classify. Selection strategies include the following:

● Focus gambling, in which the learner focuses on a certain attribute, gambling that it is the correct one. (See the "What Kids Say and Do" box on page 264.)

● Simultaneous scanning, in which the learner keeps all attributes in mind. This strategy has the problem of being too complex and making heavy demands on working memory.

● Successive scanning, in which the learner tests a single hypothesis and persists until it has been proven wrong.

Teaching Concepts

A concept attainment model is often used to teach concepts. Typically, a lesson has four components. First, examples of the concept are presented; then nonexamples are presented. The teacher should lead a discussion of why the examples are good examples of the concepts and the nonexamples are not. If the target concept is *mountain,* children are shown examples and nonexamples. The nonexamples provided could include a hilly landscape and a lighthouse in its surrounding area. The children and their teacher discuss why these are nonexamples. Possible attributes of a mountain that children might identify as missing in the nonexamples include peaks. The teacher would test the children's understanding by providing them with new stimuli and asking them whether they are mountains. The students would test their hypotheses about what attributes make a mountain by answering this question. Errors can occur through **overgeneralization** when a student includes nonexamples in a category or **undergeneralization** when students fail to identify appropriate members of the category.

overgeneralization Inclusion of a nonmember of a category or class in that category of class.

undergeneralization The exclusion of some instances from a category or group even though they are true members of that category or group.

What Kids Say and Do

Focusing on a Single Attribute

Ms. Nowicki taught first grade for many years. For the last week, her class worked on a science unit about *Living Things*. Among the first activities was a task in which the children looked through magazines for pictures of living and nonliving things that they could paste on the appropriate pages in their *Living Things* scrapbooks. The students would later compare their choices and note the shared characteristics of the living things. Ms. Nowicki thought this task would be easy for the children and a good introduction to a discussion of the differences among living things.

When Ms. Nowicki reviewed Anthony's scrapbook, she noticed that he had included a bus and a racing car on a page for living things. When she questioned him about these choices, he claimed that the vehicles were alive because they moved. He insisted on this category for the vehicles, even though he agreed that that they did not have babies, did not need food, and so on.

The timing of the science unit coincided with parent-teacher conferences. Ms. Nowicki mentioned the situation to Mrs. Reynolds, Anthony's mother. "You should've simply told Anthony that vehicles aren't alive and why not—then he'd get it," she stated. Ms. Nowicki replied, "I don't think that's the answer, Mrs. Reynolds. I want to think about this some more. Maybe I should address this situation a different way." "I think you should follow my advice," insisted Anthony's mother.

The next morning, Mrs. Reynolds and Anthony arrived at the classroom a few minutes before the official start of the school day. "Anthony would like to tell you something, Ms. Nowicki," announced Mrs. Reynolds. "Buses and cars aren't alive. Trains and boats aren't, either," he stated. "Now tell Ms. Nowicki why they can move," ordered Mrs. Reynolds. Anthony declared, "They have motors!"

Ms. Nowicki paused for a few moments, and asked, "Is the motor alive, Anthony?" Anthony glanced at his mother, looked back at the teacher, smiled, nodded his head, and said, "Yes!"

Criticisms of Classical Concept Research Not all concepts or categories can be described by defining attributes. Many educations believe that the concept identification tasks seen in Figure 8.20 are very artificial. As the number of attributes increases, the demands on working memory become excessive. For some categories, it is difficult to define a criterial attribute. Such categories are called **natural categories** (Rosch, 1973). For example, it is difficult to identify the attribute that defines *dog*.

natural categories Real-world categories

Natural Categories Real-world or natural categories are hierarchically organized (Rosch et al., 1976). There are three levels in such a hierarchy: superordinate, basic, and subordinate (see Table 8.2). The subordinate level contains the most specific examples of the general or superordinate category. The most important level is the basic level, because the examples at this level are most different from one another. A bus and a car, for instance, are more unalike than are a school bus and a city bus.

TABLE 8.2

Examples of Superordinate, Basic, and Subordinate Categories

Superordinate	Basic level	Subordinate	
Animal	Bird	Robin	Hummingbird
	Dog	Labrador	Poodle
	Fish	Tuna	Haddock
Furniture	Table	Kitchen table	Dining room table
	Lamp	Night lamp	Desk lamp
	Chair	Armchair	Kitchen chair
Vehicles	Car	Sedan	Convertible
	Truck	Pickup truck	Dump truck
	Bus	School bus	City bus

What Kids Say and Do

What Pony?

Children like to categorize as much as adults do. They often categorize according to concepts that are important to them, even if those concepts do not correspond to adult notions.

On a class trip to the zoo, kindergarten teacher Malva Mulrooney eavesdropped on Marisa offering a carrot to a Shetland pony:

Marisa:	Here you go, Mr. Camel.
Mrs. Mulrooney:	"Mr. Camel" is a funny name for a pony. I like that.
Marisa:	What pony?
Mrs. Mulrooney:	This pony, Marisa, the one you're giving that nice carrot too.
Marisa:	(*almost in tears*) This isn't a camel?
Mrs. Mulrooney:	I'm afraid not, dear. It's a beautiful Shetland pony. Tell me, what made you think it's a camel?
Marisa:	Because it's small and brown like the camel in my favorite bedtime book. Camels are small and brown.
Mrs. Mulrooney:	Well, this camel is really a pony. Why don't we call him "Mr. Camel"?
Marisa:	Because his momma probably already gave him his name.
Mrs. Mulrooney:	You're probably right. He really likes that carrot.
Marisa:	Yes, ma'am.

Some members of natural categories are better examples of the category than others. For example, an ostrich is not as good an example of the category *bird* as is a robin. A **prototype** is the best representative of its category. Other members of the category can be more or less similar to the prototype. For example, if the prototype of the category *dog* is an Alsatian, a Labrador retriever would be more similar to the prototype than a dachshund. Members of a category can be described as having **graded membership** in the category, which means that they may be closer or farther away from the prototype for the category. (See the "What Kids Say and Do" box above.)

prototype The best representative of a category.

graded membership The extent to which an object or idea belongs to a category.

Diversity, Culture, and Experience in Developing Concepts and Categories

A child's culture and experience influence the kinds of categories and concepts that he or she develops. One of the authors taught in an elementary school in a very poor inner-city district. She took her class on a field trip to a hilly area that had lots of trees and sheep. The children lived in a housing project, where the landscape was very flat and there were no trees, some grass, but mostly concrete. During the field trip, one of the second graders asked the teacher, "How come the sheep don't fall over?" The teacher looked where the child was pointing and observed a sheep about halfway up a very steep hill. The child had only seen pictures of sheep in books and did not understand that they had knees that could bend. The child's previous experience and categories thus influenced his ideas about how the world works.

Michael Cole (1996) described his experience with an educational project in Liberia in the 1960s. He had been hired as a consultant to help improve the learning of mathematics by children in the Kpelle tribe. Among the things he was told about Kpelle students was that they could not distinguish between geometric shapes because of perceptual problems; they could not classify; and they could not measure. Cole found that the Kpelle measured rice using a *kopi*, a tin that holds one dry pint of rice. They also stored rice in *boke* (buckets), *tins* (tin cans), and bags. There were 24 kopi to a bucket and 48 to a tin, and two buckets were equivalent to one tin. In a study that compared American adults and children with Kpelle adults and children, participants were given four mixing bowls of equal size holding different amounts of rice: 1.5, 3, 4, 5, or 6 kopi. They were shown the tin to be used as a unit of measurement and were then asked to estimate the number of kopi of rice in each bowl.

Appendix
Cultural Differences
Diverse students will vary in their schemas, scripts, and categories of knowledge (*PRAXIS*™, III. B, *INTASC*, Principle 6).

Chapter Reference
The role of culture in cognitive development was discussed in Chapter 2. Further discussion of the effects of culture and community on cognitive processing can be found in Chapter 10.

Kpelle adults were extremely accurate, with an error rate of about 2–3%. The American adults greatly overestimated the amounts. The American children performed like the American adults with smaller amounts and like the Kpelle children with the larger amounts. Cole concluded that people develop cognitive skills in relation to the important activities in their lives. Kpelle children did not have difficulty with concepts of measurement, whatever the cultural differences between them and American children.

Complex Cognition

The preceding sections of the chapter have included discussions of basic information-processing structures and functions. All of these play roles in complex cognitive processes, such as metacognition, reasoning, argumentation, problem solving, and transfer.

Metacognition

metacognition   Thinking about one's own thinking.

Metacognition is the process of thinking about thinking. John Flavell described it as follows: "Metacognition refers to one's knowledge concerning one's own cognitive processes or anything related to them, e.g., the learning-relevant properties of information or data. For example, I am engaging in metacognition if I notice that I am having more trouble learning A than B; if it strikes me that I should double check C before accepting it as fact" (Flavell, 1976, p. 232). Metacognitive knowledge includes knowledge of oneself as a learner, knowledge of strategies for success, and knowledge of when one should use those strategies. You are engaging in metacognition when you realize that you have understood something or have failed to do so.

Metacognition has three basic aspects: planning, monitoring, and evaluating. Planning helps you articulate a goal or purpose for the task you wish to perform. There is an old proverb that states: *No wind helps a ship that sails for no port.* In other words, if you do not know your destination, it is difficult to determine whether you have arrived or how close to your destination you are. Once you have identified a plan, you begin to carry it out. If your goal was to read the first 10 pages of the chapter and you had identified existing knowledge that you thought might be useful, you would proceed to read. As you read, you would monitor whether you understood the material. Many students find themselves at the end of a chapter, feeling very proud that they persisted with the task, but when asked what they read about, they cannot offer an accurate response. Their self-monitoring shut down during their reading, and they failed to notice that they no longer understood the material. (See the "Taking It to the Classroom" box below.)

 Might one or more of the students at the beginning of the chapter be having difficulty with metacognition? How do you know?

Taking It to the Classroom

Guiding Questions for Promoting Metacognitive Thinking

Asking these questions can help students engage in metacognitive thinking:

- How much time and effort will this problem require?
- What do you already know about this problem or argument?
- What is the goal or reason for engaging in extended and careful thought about this problem or argument?
- How difficult do you think it will be to solve this problem or reach a conclusion?
- How will you know when you have reached the goal?
- What critical thinking skills are likely to be useful in solving this problem or analyzing this argument?
- Are you moving toward a solution?

When the task is completed, students should be asked to judge how well the problem was solved or how well the argument was analyzed. Well-structured questions will help them reflect on their learning and may provide insights that will be useful in the future.

Chapter Reference
Chapter 12 describes reciprocal questioning strategies that promote metacognition.

Source: Halpern, D. F. (1998). Teaching critical thinking for transfer across domains. *American Psychologist.* 53, 449–455. Copyright © 1998 by the American Psychological Association. Reproduced with permission.

Self-Explanation

Self-explanations are a means by which students can test their comprehension of material. They are explanations that start with something such as, "Okay, let me see if I understand this." When used effectively, they offer more pathways for retrieving knowledge (Kintsch & Kintsch, 1995) and allow students to assess their competence in a given area. Chi and her colleagues (Chi et al., 1989; Chi et al., 1994) have shown that student self-explanations are useful in physics and biology. Palincsar and Brown (1984) have used a type of self-explanation to develop reading comprehension skills. O'Reilly, Symons, and MacLatchy-Gaudet (1998) demonstrated the greater effectiveness of self-explanations, compared with other instructional interventions with college students in biology. Brewer, Chinn, and Samarapungavan (1998) compared children's explanations with those of scientists. They found that "while children's explanations of the natural world may have very different content from scientists' explanations of the same phenomena, the underlying form of children's explanations is similar in many respects to those of scientists" (p. 134). Teachers can include self-explanations in their instruction by asking students to explain their understandings on a regular basis.

Reasoning and Argumentation

Teachers can promote reasoning and argumentation by having students engage in challenging tasks together. Chinn (in press) defines **argumentation** as discourse among students in which learners take positions, give reasons for those positions, and present counterarguments to each other's ideas when they have different views. Argumentation has four instructional benefits: (a) understanding content, (b) increasing interest and motivation, (c) improving problem-solving skills, and (d) increasing argumentation skills.

The mere fact that children are assigned to groups does not mean that they will engage in meaningful discussions. The quality of the conversations students have together is associated with learning (Webb, 1992). Many factors, such as the nature of the task or the composition of the group, will influence the quality of conversation. For example, children tend to have less abstract conversations about math or technology tasks than they do about language-based tasks (Holden, 1993). Most students need assistance in generating the quality of discourse that is associated with learning. Teachers can promote higher quality discourse by asking students questions that vary in complexity (King, 1991, 1999; King et al., 1998). Asking a student *why* something occurs rather than *what* occurred will result in the student engaging in deeper thinking.

In a study of high-achieving sixth graders working together to solve problems, Barron found that success could not be accounted for by quality of discussion, prior achievement, or the generation of correct solutions (Barron, 2003). Less successful groups ignored or rejected correct proposals made by group members, whereas groups that were more successful discussed correct proposals or accepted them. Chinn and colleagues (Chinn, O'Donnell, & Jinks, 2000) found that fourth graders learned more when they engaged in deeper development of reasons during argumentation. For example, when children were asked to decide which of four conclusions from a science experiment was the best conclusion, they engaged in comparisons of the conclusions and produced more reasons for their decision. In comparison, students who were asked to decide whether the conclusions were good or not had discussions that were quite shallow.

Groups sometimes focus too much on procedural aspects of tasks (Erkens, in press), and even when participants list arguments, they may fail to coordinate their reasons and develop them fully (Andriessen, in press). Successful discourse is coordinated among group members, with participants working together to construct knowledge rather than generating simple lists or arguments (King, 1994, 1999).

Problem Solving

Problems have an initial state (where you are), a desired state (where you would like to be), and a path to follow in order to reach that state. The gap between the initial and desired states is called the *problem space*, and there can be many different paths across the space. Figure 8.21 depicts a physics problem in kinematics that was presented to high school students. The initial state of the problem is that the ball is placed on the ramp. The desired or end state is that the ball lands on the floor. The students must find a way to determine where the ball will land.

argumentation   The process of taking a position, providing reasons for the position, and presenting counterarguments.

Chapter Reference
Learning from and with peers is described in Chapter 12.

Appendix
Promoting Complex Thinking

Providing your students with opportunities to solve problems will allow them to engage in complex thinking (*PRAXIS*™, II. A. 1, *INTASC*, Principle 4).

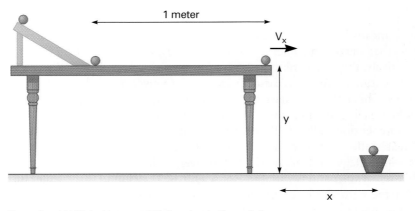

Figure 8.21. Problem Solving

Source: Copyright Michael Lawrence, Ed.D. Reproduced with permission.

Problem solving involves five steps (Bransford & Stein, 1993), which can be remembered using the acronym IDEAL:

- **I**dentifying problems and opportunities
- **D**efining goals and representing the problem
- **E**xploring possible solution strategies
- **A**nticipating, acting
- **L**ooking back

The first step in problem solving is to recognize the nature of the problem. In the example in Figure 8.21, students need to recognize that the problem involves projectile motion and velocity. Experts in a domain typically spend much more time on the initial phases of problem solving than novices do (Bruning, Schraw, & Ronning, 1999). The second step is to define the goals and represent the problem. The problem solver must focus attention and understand the wording of the problem. If the learner has encountered similar problems in the past, he or she may draw on existing problem schemas for the problem.

The third step in problem solving is to explore possible solution strategies. These can include algorithms or heuristics. **Algorithms** are systematic and exhaustive procedures that are guaranteed to produce a solution. For example, if you have forgotten the three-digit combination for the lock on your briefcase, you might begin with 000 and systematically explore all possible combinations until you find the correct one. Alternatively, you could use a heuristic, or shortcut, and knock the lock off with a hammer. **Heuristics** can shorten the time needed to solve a problem, but they are not guaranteed to succeed.

One type of heuristic is **means-end analysis**. The problem solver decides what means would reduce the distance between the initial state and the goal state. For example, if the task is to write an essay for a language arts class, a problem solver might decide that he or she needs to make a detailed outline to help plan the essay. A second frequently used heuristic is *working backward*. This approach starts with the solution and works backward through the problem. For example, if you use this strategy to write a term paper, you might begin by noting the due date for the paper and work backward to determine what you would need in order to meet the due date.

A number of factors can hinder problem solving. One of these is cognitive rigidity, or lack of flexibility in thinking. Individuals who look at a problem from only one perspective are likely to have difficulty solving it because if the solution strategy they attempt does not work, they will have trouble considering alternatives. A specific kind of cognitive rigidity is **functional fixedness.** People who experience functional fixedness are unable to consider alternative uses for an object. For example, someone who is short may be unable to reach a book on the top shelf in a library. A small step is usually available in a library so than an individual can stand on it to reach the upper shelves. If an individual tends toward functional fixedness, he or she might not consider alternatives to using the step to reach the book. A more cognitively flexible individual might ask a tall person for help or use a book from a lower shelf to knock down the desired book.

Noncognitive factors can also interfere with problem solving. Individuals who experience high levels of anxiety may be inhibited during problem solving. Students who have a high fear of failure will be reluctant to run the risk of being wrong.

How Can I Use This?

How could you help a student represent a problem accurately? What strategies would you use?

algorithm   A systematic and exhaustive strategy for solving problems.

heuristic   A rule of thumb or shortcut for solving problems.

means–end analysis   A strategy for reducing the distance between the initial state and the goal state in problem solving.

functional fixedness   Being able to consider only the typical function of an object.

Expert problem solvers have extensive knowledge in a particular domain. They recognize patterns and have access to large stores of information. They have a large repertoire of strategies, and their knowledge is refined, practiced, and organized. They spend more time planning for problem solutions and engaging in problem representation than they spend carrying out solution strategies.

Transfer

The goal of learning is to not only be able to perform a strategy or skill, or to remember something; it is also to be able to apply those skills, strategies, or knowledge in new contexts. This is called **transfer,** the ability to use previously learned skills or information in a new context. There are a number of ways in which to distinguish between types of transfer. **Low road transfer** is the automatic application of previously learned skills (Salomon & Perkins, 1989). An example of low road transfer would be using a pencil rather than a pen to write. In this example, a learner would give no conscious thought to the task and would not need to engage in metacognitive activity, such as monitoring, in order to accomplish the task. **High road transfer** involves deliberative application of knowledge learned in one context to another (Salomon & Perkins, 1989). An example of high road transfer would include trying to identify whether the math problem you are faced with is similar to one you have done before. In this example, you are deliberately searching for prior knowledge that might be useful to solve the current problem. **Positive transfer** occurs when prior knowledge or skill is successfully applied to a new context. For example, individuals easily transfer knowledge of one word processing program to another. **Negative transfer** occurs when learning one skill impairs performance on another. For example, learning one kind of notation for statistics may interfere with one's ability to learn effectively if a different teacher uses different notation.

Transfer does not readily occur. An example of the difficulties associated with transfer can be found in a study conducted by Carraher, Carraher, and Schliemann (1985). They investigated the mathematical strategies used by Brazilian children who worked as street vendors. After recording the nature and accuracy of the computations in which the children engaged while selling their goods, the researchers asked the children to come to their laboratory. The children took a variety of mathematics tests that included the same numbers and mathematical operations as those they had used as street vendors. The results showed that the children were 98% accurate in the practical context of selling but only 37% accurate on the same operations in the laboratory context. This study showed the failure to transfer between real-life context and the classroom context. We are typically concerned about whether what is taught in school will transfer to real-life contexts.

The Cognition and Technology Group at Vanderbilt (CTGV, 1997) developed a set of problem-based curricula called *The Adventures of Jasper Woodbury.* Each *Jasper* adventure was situated in a real-life context and is complex, often including multiple subproblems. In one of the *Jasper* adventures, *Rescue at Boone's Meadow,* the focus is on mathematical concepts of distance, rate, and time. Jasper's friend Larry teaches Emily how to fly a plane. They also discuss their plans for a camping trip to Boone's meadow. As the adventure develops, important embedded data are introduced. These data are facts and numbers that will be needed to solve the problem posed. For the Boone's Meadow problem, the embedded data included information on who knew how to fly an ultralight plane, their weight, the weight of the plane, the plane's payload, and gas consumption etc. The key problem to be solved in this adventure is how to transport a wounded bald eagle as quickly as possible to the veterinarian. By embedded mathematics in a real-life problem context, the CTGV group sought to improve students' ability to transfer their mathematical skills. Evaluations of the Jasper series showed that Jasper students do as well as non-Jasper students on assessments of basic mathematical knowledge but they score better on word problems testing transfer of the knowledge learned through Jasper and on their ability to identify what information needs to be considered in solving complex problems (CTGV, 1997).

Teachers can encourage students to transfer their knowledge and skills by reminding them to look for similarities between the tasks in which they are engaged and ones they have done previously. Students need opportunities to practice new skills. The teacher should provide feedback and remind students to consider the strategies they are using and how these strategies might be useful in the future. Finally, the teacher can provide problems that are very similar to one another (near transfer), then provide problems that are quite varied (far transfer). Students will need help to engage in the metacognitive activity necessary to do far transfer.

Chapter Reference
Problem-based learning is described in Chapter 10

transfer   The ability to use previously learned skills or information in a new context.

low road transfer   The automatic application of previously learned skills.

high road transfer   Deliberate application of previously learned strategy or knowledge to a new problem.

positive transfer   Prior knowledge or skill is successfully applied to a new context.

negative transfer   Prior learning interferes with new learning.

How Can I Use This?

How can you transfer knowledge learned in this course/book to your teaching in an actual classroom?

Chapter Reference
Problem-based learning is discussed in Chapter 10.

R I D E

REFLECTION FOR ACTION

The Event

Recall that some of Mr. Gomez's students were having difficulty with some math problems. The solutions and explanations attempted by students were presented.

Reflection

What kinds of problems were these students having? What have you learned in this chapter that could be applied in these cases? If students are having problems with executive control or metacognition, what might be done to improve their work? What kinds of activities can Mr. Gomez provide for the students to work on that might improve their performance on these kinds of problems and enable them to generalize that learning to other areas and other types of tasks? Is it better to work harder with students on problems of this type or to try to uncover the root cause of their difficulties? (Note: This is not a trick question.)

What Theoretical/Conceptual Information Might Assist in Interpreting and Remedying This Situation? Consider the following:

Working Memory and Executive Control

How would limited working memory or difficulties with executive control influence the children's performance on the math problem? Was there any indication of such difficulties? What kinds of strategies would support students' working memory while they are doing word problems?

Metacognition

Metacognition involves knowledge of oneself as a learner and of strategies for responding to difficulties. Did the students plan, monitor, and evaluate their performance?

Transfer

High road, or consciously controlled transfer, can be distinguished from low road, or more automated transfer. Should the teacher try to have the students practice near or far transfer? Is near transfer more likely to involve low road transfer?

Information Gathering R I D E

There are a number of sources of information about this situation; which ones you use will depend on how the problem is framed. A very good source of information (as is often the case) is the student. How did the student do on similar problems? What might happen if the problem were simplified? If a student's difficulties seem to be due to lack of metacognitive ability, do the same kinds of difficulties show up in other areas of his or her work?

Once you have a better idea of what the problem is, there is the question of what to do about it. Here you might turn to the research literature on instructional techniques for improving working memory, executive control, or whatever the problem might be. It is important to keep in mind that if a broader approach is chosen, it will be necessary to show students how it applies to specific examples of tasks and problems.

Decision Making R I D E

Decision making in this situation involves two phases: diagnosing the problem and selecting a solution. In making a decision, Mr. Gomez needs to think about what he believes to be the most likely cause of a student's difficulties and what he can do about it. He also has to keep in mind that he has a whole class of students to be concerned about. He needs an approach that he can apply within the confines of his instructional setting.

Evaluation R I D E

If Mr. Gomez's approach is successful, he should see improved performance not only on the math problems that triggered his initial concern but on other problems that seem to be stemming from the same underlying difficulty. Of course, success on the math problems alone will be quite rewarding, but Mr. Gomez should watch for possible progress in writing, science experiments, and so forth. The point here is to maintain a broad focus on students' learning. Simply reviewing a specific type of math problem may help students learn to solve that type of problem but will not enable them to generalize that learning to any other kind of math problem, let alone other subject areas.

Further Practice: Your Turn

Here is a second event for consideration and reflection. In doing so, implement the processes of Reflection, Information gathering, Decision making, and Evaluation.

The Event

It happened to Melanie again. Her grades for the marking period did not reflect all the work she had done. Melanie was a serious student in her junior year of high school. She was attentive during her classes. She did her homework and prepared for the tests. But when it came time to take a test, she could not recall the information she had studied. Her grade point average was sinking with each marking period. What further distressed her was that her friends received better grades but spent less time and energy on schoolwork.

R I D E Melanie comes to her home room teacher, Mrs. James, to talk about how she might improve her grades. What can Mrs. James suggest to Melanie that will help her perform better on tests?

SUMMARY

● **How do cognitive and constructivist theories of learning differ?**

Cognitive theories of learning focus on the idea that each person does not necessarily view the same environment in the same way. They explore how individual differences in knowledge and experience influence how we interpret our environment and what we learn as a result. Knowledge is constructed by the learner and influenced by the learner's previous experience. Constructivist theories of learning share the idea that meaning is constructed by the learner. Moshman (1982) distinguished among three types of constructivism: exogenous, endogenous, and dialectical. Exogenous constructivism is characterized by the belief that knowledge is derived from the environment. Endogenous constructivism is most easily illustrated by Piagetian theory: The construction of new knowledge comes from within (i.e., is endogenous). The individual constructs new knowledge structures from existing structures rather than from the environment. Dialectical constructivism is illustrated by Vygotsky's theory, which holds that the source of knowledge is subjective experience in interaction with the environment.

● **Why are attention. perception, and working memory important for learning?**

Perception is important for learning because it involves giving meaning to the sensory input we receive. Gestalt psychologists have proposed a number of organizing principles that allow us to perceive objects. The principles are similarity, symmetry, closure, continuity, and proximity. Attention is important to learning because it involves selection of information, withdrawing from some objects and focusing on others. Lack of attention is characterized by confusion and diffusion. Attentional processes allow us to be selective, and perceptual processes allow us to organize sensory input, two key aspects of learning. Working memory is a limited memory system that includes both storage and manipulation functions. Baddeley's idea of working memory consists of a number of subsystems that are coordinated by a central executive: the phonological loop system, the visuo-spatial sketchpad, and the central executive system, which controls both the loop system and the sketchpad.

Teachers must understand that working memory is limited and that short, concise, and clear instructions are most effective. Limiting the amount of classroom disruption is also important. Working memory is also implicated in such tasks as reading comprehension, writing, problem solving, and mathematics (Swanson & Siegel, 2001). Students with a larger working memory are more successful in the use of cognitive resources during reading comprehension and as a result have more resources for information storage while comprehending text. Teachers must remember that some learners have difficulty with writing because of limitations of working memory.

- **How is knowledge represented?**
  Knowledge is represented in images, propositions, schemas, and scripts. Images and propositions are the basic units for storing visual and verbal information. Schemas represent organized sets of knowledge about a topic and can include both verbal and visual information. Scripts are event schemas. They include the steps needed to complete particular actions, such as dining at a restaurant.

- **What are the different kinds of long-term memory?**
  There are several kinds of long-term memory. Episodic memory is memory for events and can include sensory information. Childhood memories are an example of episodic memory. Semantic memory is memory for verbal information, also known as *declarative knowledge*. Declarative memory is like semantic memory: It is memory about *what*. An example would be a memory about the structure of a bicycle. Procedural memory is memory about how to do something—for example, remembering how to ride a bicycle. These kinds of memory are also called *explicit* and *implicit memory*.

- **How is encoding related to retrieval?**
  The processes of encoding are organization, elaboration, and practice. All three processes can aid in later retrieval of information. When you connect information that you are trying to learn with information that you already know or to images or other enhancements of the information to be learned, you are elaborating on the material and are more likely to remember it. When material is encoded in an organized manner, more cues are encoded, thus making retrieval easier.

- **Why and how do we categorize?**
  Categorization is a way of narrowing the range of information available to us in order to reduce complexity, identify objects, reduce the need for constant learning, decide what actions are appropriate, and order and relate classes of objects and events. This allows us to be more cognitively efficient. Classic approaches to defining categories focused on the use of criterial attributes to assign members to a category. This does not work for natural or real-world categories. Membership in a natural category is best defined by a prototype, or best example, of the category. Other members of the category have graded membership in the category based on their similarity to the prototype.

- **How can teachers promote complex cognition?**
  To promote metacognition in the classroom, the following information should be discussed: the amount of time and effort the problem or argument is worth; what you already know about it; the goal or reason for engaging in extended and careful thought about it; how difficult you think it will be to solve the problem or reach a conclusion; how you will know when you have reached the goal; the critical thinking skills that are likely to be useful in solving the problem or analyzing the argument; and whether you are moving toward a solution. A teacher can promote argumentation by requiring students to articulate and defend positions on topics. Transfer can be encouraged by asking students to look for the similarities between problems.

- **How can teachers apply cognitive theories of learning in working with diverse students and students with special needs?**
  The focus of a cognitive approach to learning is on the relationship between the individual and the environment. Children from different cultural or socioeconomic groups come to school with different experiences and knowledge. Teachers need to tap into what students already know in order to increase their understanding of the content being taught. Students with special needs may have impairments in various aspects of the information-processing system, including perception, attention, working memory, and retrieval. Diverse students may be expected to vary in the content of the knowledge structures they bring to class such as their schemas, scripts, and categories.

KEY TERMS

algorithm, p. 268
argumentation p. 267
attention, p. 245
automaticity, p. 246
bottom-up processing, p. 243
chunking, p. 247
concept, p. 262
conditional knowledge, p. 255
controlled processes, p. 246
criterial attributes, p. 263
decay p. 247
declarative knowledge, p. 251
declarative memory, p. 251
dialectical constructivism, p. 241
distributed practice, p. 255
elaboration, p. 256
elaborative rehearsal, p. 247
endogenous constructivism, p. 241
episodic memory, p. 251
exogenous constructivism, p. 241
feature analysis, p. 243
functional fixedness, p. 268
graded membership, p. 265
graphic organizers, p. 258
heuristic, p. 268
high road transfer, p. 269
interference, p. 247
levels of processing theory, p. 255
low road transfer, p. 269
maintenance rehearsal, p. 247
massed practice, p. 255
means-end analysis, p. 268
metacognition, p. 266

mnemonic strategies, p. 256
multiple modalities, p. 250
natural categories, p. 264
negative transfer, p. 269
overgeneralization, p. 263
perception, p. 242
phonological loop, p. 248
phonological similarity effect, p. 248
pictorial mnemonics, p. 257
positive transfer, p. 269
procedural knowledge, p. 255
procedural memory, p. 251
proposition, p. 252
propositional network, p. 252
prototype, p. 265
recall, p. 260
recognition memory, p. 260
schema, p. 252
script, p. 253
semantic memory, p. 251
sensory memory, p. 246
serial-position effect, p. 247
short-term memory, p. 247
spread of activation, p. 260
story grammar, p. 254
top-down processing, p. 244
transfer, p. 269
unattended speech effect, p. 248
undergeneralization, p. 263
visuospatial sketchpad, p. 249
word length effect, p. 248
working memory, p. 248

EXERCISES

1. *Analyzing What You Know About How You Learn and Remember*

    Find a poem that is more than 12 lines long and try to memorize it. Note the strategies you use to encode information and whether they are effective. What modalities did you use? Did you engage in maintenance or elaborative rehearsal?

2. *Creating a Graphic Organizer or Concept Map*

    Create a graphic organizer or concept map about the attention information presented at the beginning of the chapter (see pags 245–246). Analyze the skills you needed to be able to construct such an organizer or concept map.

3. *Culture, Concepts, and Categories*

    Generate five examples of how cultural background could influence the interpretation of information. For example, the word *pop* means soda to some individuals and a noise to other people.

4. *When a Schema Is a Stereotype*

    A stereotype is a concept that individuals might have that is not completely accurate but is based on generally occurring characteristics. What are some features of a schema that are present in a stereotype you might have of a particular place?

5. *Problems with Memory*

    Identify some things that you find hard to remember (e.g., people's names, formulas, appointments). For example, how difficult a task would it be to learn the names of all your classmates in this course? Develop a plan for how to improve your memory of these items.

Congratulations! You're hired. You are going to teach fifth grade at Monroe Elementary School this fall. You have just received your class schedule and the following list of recommended amounts of time to spend in each subject area per week:

Language Arts	8 hours	Social Studies	3 hours
Mathematics	5 hours	Science	3 hours

One of your first tasks is to make up your weekly class schedule. Remember that children arrive at 8:30 A.M., and you will have to get coats off, recite the Pledge of Allegiance, collect lunch money, and listen to the morning announcements. Also remember that you have to get those coats back on at the end of the day.

Your Fifth-Grade Class Schedule

	Monday	Tuesday	Wednesday	Thursday	Friday
8:30–9:00					
9:00–9:30					
9:30–10:00					
10:30–11:00		Physical Education		Physical Education	Physical Education
11:30–12:00	Lunch	Lunch	Lunch	Lunch	Lunch
12:30–1:00	Music		Music		
1:00–1:30					Library
1:30–2:00					
2:00–2:30		Art	Art		

Effective Teachers and the Process of Teaching

RIDE Reflection for Action

As you create the schedule, consider your main concerns. What are you making sure of and what is less important?

Guiding Questions

- Why are teachers' beliefs important?
- How do teachers' knowledge of subject matter understanding and general knowledge of teaching translate into ways to teach specific material to students?
- How do expert teachers differ from novice teachers?
- What are some general teacher-centered approaches to teaching?
- What kinds of teaching tactics can teachers use?
- How can teachers use homework effectively?
- How can teachers plan to meet the needs of students who have special needs?
- How can teachers develop the expertise necessary for working in culturally diverse settings?

CHAPTER OVERVIEW

The focus of this chapter is on teachers and teaching, and on how thoughtful learning can be fostered by high-quality teaching. We will see that teachers and teaching cannot exist without *someone* and *something* to teach. Teachers' knowledge of the subject matter they are teaching and their beliefs about themselves, their students, and the processes of learning and teaching have important influences on classroom practices and problems. This chapter illustrates these differences through comparisons between novice and expert teachers. The chapter then tracks the instructional process from beginning to end, discussing planning as a key factor in good teaching, examining teacher-centered approaches to instruction, exploring particular teaching tactics to enhance students' learning, and examining the effective use of homework.

What Is Teaching?

Teacher Development
- Beliefs About Teaching and Learning
- Content Knowledge, Pedagogical Knowledge, and Pedagogical Content Knowledge
- Differences in Knowledge Between Experts and Novices
- Online Teacher Communities
- Teachers' Self-Efficacy
- Working in Culturally Different Contexts

Planning
- Instructional Goals
- Using Goals in Classroom Teaching
- Translating Goals into Plans
- Planning for Students with Special Needs

Approaches to Teaching
- Promoting Meaningful Learning
- Discovery Learning
- Direct Instruction

Teaching Tactics
- Providing Explanations
- Providing Feedback
- Asking Questions

Promoting Learning Through Homework
- Benefits of Homework
- A Taxonomy of Homework
- Three Types of Homework
- Homework from the Primary to the Secondary Level: A Developmental Perspective
- Developing Homework Policies
- Homework and Students with Disabilities
- Homework: Cultural and Socioeconomic Differences

What Is Teaching?

Outstanding teaching combines knowledge about the teaching–learning process and a host of other attributes, including:

- Expertise in the subject matter being taught
- Belief in one's ability to teach and students' abilities to learn
- Sensitivity to the needs of different kinds of learners
- Planning and organizational skills
- Interpersonal and leadership skills
- A great deal of hard work

But what do these attributes mean? How do teachers acquire them? How do they work individually or in combination? The attributes of exceptional teaching have long been a focus of researchers in educational psychology as well as related disciplines. This chapter examines what these skills and traits are, and how they work both individually and together

| Child: Interests, motivations, current level of knowledge, skill, and abilities | → | Teacher: The individual responsible for ensuring that the child masters the curriculum | → | Curriculum: The content of what the child is to learn and how to communicate the content |

Figure 9.1. An Initial Model Relating Children, Teachers, and the Curriculum

to result in exceptional teaching. It looks not only at the nuts and bolts of important aspects of teaching, such as planning and homework, but also presents the research on how expert and novice teachers differ, how beliefs about efficacy influence teacher behavior, and the difference between content knowledge and pedagogical content knowledge. It is an inside look into the development of effective teaching.

What do teachers actually do when they are teaching? How can you tell whether someone is teaching or not? Jackson (1968) once asked "If a person were doing all the acts commonly associated with teaching in front of a mirror rather than in front of a class, would it still be considered teaching?" The answer that comes to mind is—of course not. It is immediately followed by the question, Why not? The answer is clear: Teaching is not something one can do alone. It is reciprocal by its very nature: Teaching implies learning; teachers imply students. Students can, of course, be *virtual*, as in the case of an instructional video recording intended for students to see at a later date. By making the videotape, the teacher is intending to promote learning. Thus, **teaching** is an intentional action designed to have an impact on a learner or group of learners. Specifically, teaching is the interpersonal effort to help learners acquire knowledge, develop skill, and realize their potential.

teaching   The interpersonal effort to help learners acquire knowledge, develop skill, and realize their potential.

However, teaching involves more than just an interaction between a teacher and students; teaching also involves content. The content being taught, and the way it is organized—that is, the *curriculum*—is the third component of teaching. There are a variety of ways of thinking about, or representing, the three components of teaching. One approach is linear, with the teacher acting as a mediator between the student and the curriculum (see Figure 9.1).

This view of teaching, however, suggests that the teacher's task is to bring the child to the curriculum, that the only way the child can learn the curriculum is through the intervention of the teacher. A more interactive approach, therefore, is to consider the relationship in terms of a triangle, with the teacher guiding the child's efforts to master the curriculum (see Figure 9.2).

This depiction indicates that the teacher and the child interact and that both are influenced by the curriculum. But it does not suggest that either the child or the teacher can influence the curriculum or make decisions about what is to be learned. Moreover, it suggests that what is to be taught and how it is taught are determined by the curriculum and that the teacher has little or no influence over that process. It does not yet seem satisfactory as a model for teaching and learning in classrooms because the notion of directionality is too confining. Figure 9.3 represents a more interactive approach.

This view of the relationships among child, teacher, and curriculum is more realistic in that it acknowledges that there is some overlap among the three components of the process.

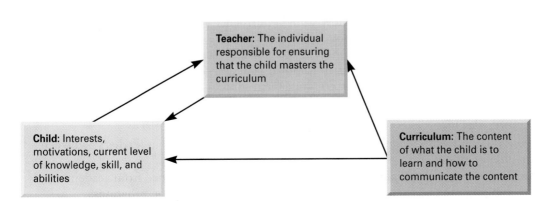

Figure 9.2. Refining the Child/Teacher/Curriculum Model

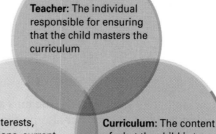

Figure 9.3. An Integrated Model of Child/ Teacher/Curriculum

Figure 9.3 shows that although all three ideas are distinct, the interactions among the three are important. As the educational philosopher John Dewey wrote (Dewey, 1971/1990):

> *Abandon the notion of subject-matter as something fixed and ready-made in itself, outside the child's experience; cease thinking of the child's experience as also something hard and fast; see it as something fluent, embryonic, vital; and we realize that the child and the curriculum are simply two limits which define a single process. Just as two points define a straight line, so the present standpoint of the child and the facts and truths of studies define instruction. It is continuous reconstruction, moving from the child's present experience out into that represented by the organized bodies of truth that we call studies. (p. 11)*

Teacher Development

It takes time to become an effective teacher. In Chapter 1, you read about the concerns of beginning teachers. They often worry about managing the complex activities involved in teaching, such as having mastery of the content they teach, planning, understanding the needs of the diverse students they will teach, and coping with the demands of parents. In this section, we address some of the processes related to teacher development. Key elements that influence teacher development are the beliefs that teachers hold about teaching and learning and their beliefs about their own efficacy in the classroom.

Beliefs About Teaching and Learning

Consider the following two propositions:

1. Students learn best when they are taught in classes in which students at different ability levels are mixed together.
2. To maximize learning, students should be sorted into classes based on their ability or prior achievement.

Which do you believe is true? How did you acquire your belief? What evidence do you have to support your position? How would your belief affect your approach to teaching? What would make you change your current position?

Teachers' beliefs are propositions that individuals believe to be true (Green, 1971). They have been a subject of research in educational psychology for decades. Richardson (1996) argues that teachers' beliefs stem from three main sources:

- Personal experience—the activities, events, and understandings that are a part of everyday life
- Experience with schooling and instruction—the experiences that teachers had when they were students
- Experience with formal knowledge—including knowledge gained from academic subjects and pedagogical knowledge gained in teacher education programs

Thus, what you believe about the efficacy of grouping would depend in part on your own experience in life, what happened to you in school, and what you were taught about grouping in your teacher education courses. In fact, these contentions are supported by research on teachers' beliefs about ability grouping (Hallam & Ireson, 2003).

Beliefs affect the ways in which people process information. A research study whose findings are consistent with one's beliefs, for example, is much more likely to be accepted uncritically than a study that challenges one's beliefs. Beliefs shape expectation of what will happen, and we prepare to respond to events based on those expectations. Teachers act on their beliefs about what good teachers do. A study of preservice teachers showed that their pedagogical beliefs influenced their acceptance of approaches to teaching that were inconsistent with those beliefs (Holt-Reynolds, 1992). Errington (2004) argues that teachers' beliefs are probably the most important factor in determining the success or failure of a new approach to teaching. If you firmly believe in mixed-ability grouping, how receptive would you be to an instructional program based on ability grouping?

Early in their teacher education programs, preservice teachers often describe themselves as supportive of student autonomy in the classroom. However, during student teaching, prospective teachers tend to become more **custodial**, or controlling, in their orientation toward students (Woolfolk & Hoy, 1990). In a three-year study, Simmons and colleagues (1999) examined the beliefs, perceptions, and classroom performance of beginning teachers of secondary school science classes. They found that new teachers held a range of philosophies of education and widely varying knowledge and beliefs about how teachers should teach subject matter, what teachers should do in the classroom, and what students should be doing. They also differed in how they perceived themselves in the classroom. An important finding was that the beginning teachers described themselves as very student-centered, but analyses of observed teaching practices indicated that they were, in fact, very teacher-centered. The beliefs teachers have about themselves and their students may not be accurate.

Teacher educators see changing the beliefs of teachers as essential to educational reform. Classroom experience, particularly the student-teaching experience, has a powerful influence on beliefs about teaching, and once established, those beliefs are highly resistant to change. In a study of elementary school teachers, Wolf and Gearhart (1997) found that it was very difficult to persuade them to change their beliefs about their students' abilities with regard to writing. Richardson (1996) admits that it is difficult to convince teachers to change their beliefs but believes that programs that emphasize an experiential approach in which students have opportunities for reflective field experiences hold promise.

Content Knowledge, Pedagogical Knowledge, and Pedagogical Content Knowledge

Knowledge of subject matter is critical not only at the high school level, where there are history teachers and mathematics teachers, but at the elementary school level as well, where most teachers teach all subjects (Hollon, Roth, & Anderson, 1991; Leinhardt, Putnam, Stein, & Baxter, 1991). Scholars have long debated the value of knowledge about subject matter (**content knowledge**) versus knowledge about how to teach (**pedagogical knowledge**; Newton & Newton, 2001). Lee Shulman (1986, 1987) made a useful contribution to this debate by introducing the concept of **pedagogical content knowledge**. According to Shulman:

> Pedagogical content knowledge identifies the distinctive bodies of knowledge for teaching. It represents the blending of content and pedagogy into an understanding of how particular topics, problems or issues are organized, represented, and adapted to the diverse interests and abilities of learners, and presented for instruction. (Shulman, 1987, p. 4)

Paulsen (2001) points out that pedagogical content knowledge is not the sum of content knowledge and pedagogical knowledge but an understanding of the nexus between the two—that is, of what it takes to translate content knowledge into a set of activities that will help students understand that content. This may consist of coming up with a strong analogy that the students can build on (Hulshof & Verloop, 2002), the ability to break down a complex task into its component parts (Jonassen, Tessmer, & Hannum, 1999), or the realization that students need to engage in activities that will illustrate a common misperception

RIDE How might different teaching beliefs affect how a teacher organizes a class schedule?

custodial A term that refers to an approach to classroom management that views the teacher's role as primarily maintaining an orderly classroom.

content knowledge Knowledge about the subject matter being taught.

pedagogical knowledge Knowledge about how to teach.

pedagogical content knowledge Knowledge about how to make subject matter understandable to students.

RIDE Think back to the opening exercise dealing with scheduling a fifth-grade class. If you were thinking, "I've got to schedule math in the morning because fifth graders tend to be a little sleepy after lunch and too anxious for the day to end later in the afternoon," you were using pedagogical content knowledge.

TABLE 9.1

Examples of Content Knowledge, Pedagogical Knowledge, and Pedagogical Content Knowledge

Content knowledge	Pedagogical knowledge	Pedagogical content knowledge
• Science: The causes of seasons, how gravity works • Math: Factoring quadratic equations, probability • English: Punctuation rules, sonnets • History: The Kansas-Nebraska Act, the Sacco and Vanzetti case	• Development: When children move from concrete-operational to formal-operational thinking • Peer learning: Group structures that work better for social development purposes or work better for learning • Self-regulation: The ability to organize and carry out one's work • Cognition: Overcoming ingrained misperceptions • Classroom organization: Students will have some overlapping and some distinct abilities, interests, and interaction styles	• Knowing that differences in students' backgrounds will require a thorough understanding of the students' current level of knowledge in order to teach them about the Sacco and Vanzetti case • Knowing how to set up groups to work on peer editing of essays • Understanding that science instruction at the elementary school level benefits from larger blocks of time in which activities such as experiments can be completed (even if that means fewer blocks per week)

and lead them to correct it (Berg & Brower, 1991). Table 9.1 illustrates the relationships among the three kinds of knowledge that are important for good teaching.

An example of how content knowledge and pedagogical knowledge come together in terms of pedagogical content knowledge is presented in Figure 9.4. The development and application of pedagogical content knowledge requires the necessary subject matter knowledge, awareness of any pedagogical issues associated with the students being taught, and the ability to bring the two together through appropriate instructional activities.

It is not surprising that experienced teachers have a greater stock of pedagogical content knowledge than do beginning teachers. Fortunately, widespread access to the Internet has made it much easier to share this knowledge. Lederman (2001), for example, has published an online list of literature on teaching science that includes hundreds of entries and is accessible online. Becoming familiar with Web sites that focus on pedagogical content knowledge, lesson

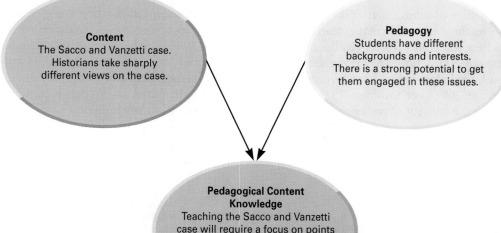

Figure 9.4. Combining Content Knowledge and Pedagogical Knowledge into Pedagogical Content Knowledge

planning, and instructional activities is essential for professional development, especially for new teachers. Examples of these can be found on the Web site that accompanies this book.

www.wiley.com/ college/odonnell

Differences in Knowledge Between Experts and Novices

Take a look at the chessboard in Figure 9.5. Spend about a minute and try to remember where all the pieces are. Then look away and think about how well you could re-create the arrangement of the pieces on the board. Most likely you would not be able to do so because, unless you are a chess expert, it is an extremely difficult task. However, if you *are* a chess expert, it is not difficult at all because the locations of the pieces mean something to a chess expert. It is not just a random arrangement of pieces on squares; it is a specific point in a reasonably well-played game of chess. As is evident from this example, experts see things differently than novices. A person who is knowledgeable about football is likely to be able to predict the next play a team will make. A radiologist will know how to identify a fracture and what subtle differences in an X-rays shading mean.

Research on differences between experts and novices began with the work of Nobel laureate Herbert Simon and his colleague William Chase (Chase & Simon, 1973). They studied differences between experts and novices' perceptions of chessboards, such as the one in the figure. They found that experts processed the information on the board in larger perceptual chunks than did novices. That is, not only is the king seen as occupying a space on the board, but its location is also processed in terms of potential threats against it in its current position and the protection provided by other pieces. This finding has been extended to many other areas, ranging from physics (Chi, Feltovich, & Glaser, 1981) to physical education (Chen, 2002).

Another area in which differences between experts and novices have been studied extensively is teaching (Berliner, 1992, 1994; Livingston & Borko, 1989a). Many studies have compared beginning teachers to experienced ones. They have found that, in general, expert teachers:

- View the classroom as a collection of individuals as opposed to a generic whole (Housner & Griffey, 1985; Kolis & Dunlap, 2004).
- Plan more globally and for longer periods (Livingston & Borko, 1989b).
- Have a more complex view of instructional options (Clermont, Borko, & Krajcik, 1994).
- Run a more smoothly operating classroom (Leinhardt & Greeno, 1986).
- Evaluate student learning more often and in ways that are more closely related to the content of instruction (Newton & Newton, 2001; Sanchez, Rosaes, & Canedo, 1999).
- Attribute failure in a given lesson to problems with planning, organization, or execution rather than to disruptive behavior on the part of students (Gonzalez & Carter, 1996).
- Hold complex ideas about the role of students' existing knowledge and make significant use of it during instruction (Meyer, 2004).

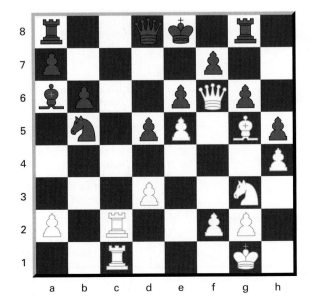

Figure 9.5. Recognizing Chess Patterns

Table 9.2 presents some of the key findings from a review of the literature on expert/novice differences in teaching (Hogan, Rabinowitz, & Craven, 2003).

TABLE 9.2

Differences Between Expert and Novice Teachers

Area	Novice teachers	Expert teachers
Curriculum planning	Plan for the class as a whole.	Differentiate individual differences among students.
	Focus more on short-term planning, with highly structured plans.	Focus on both long-term and short-term planning, with more loosely structured plans.
Instruction	Simpler view of instructional process and fewer instructional strategies.	More complex views of the instructional process; better able to shift among methods.
Teaching routines	Difficulty in shifting from one activity to another.	Smooth transitions between activities.
	Present fewer ideas in a given amount of time.	Present more ideas in a given amount of time.
	Difficulty in questioning for comprehension.	Ease and consistency in probing for comprehension.
Demonstrations	Less variety and detail.	More variety and detail.
	Lack of appreciation of areas of possible misperception or misunderstanding.	Solid appreciation of areas of possible misperception or misunderstanding.
Feedback	Focus more on student interest level than on understanding.	Focus on student comprehension.
Perceptions and reflections	Focus on behaviors and efficacy. Concern with classroom management.	Focus on student learning.
	Less elaborate representation of classroom events/activities.	More elaborate representation of classroom events.
	Effective instruction believed to be focused on clear communication to students.	Effective instruction focused on concepts such as advanced organization, examples and analogies, and assessment of progress.
Classroom management	Focus on solving problems in the here and now.	Focus on anticipating and defining management problems, generating multiple interpretations of behavior and possible approaches.
	More likely to focus on teacher behavior than on student behavior.	More likely to focus on student behavior.
	Attribution of success or failure to problems or lack of problems with students.	Attribution of success or failure to planning, organization, etc.
	Less able to recall events of instruction.	Better able to recall events of instruction.
Communication	Less well organized and thematic.	Organized around a central theme.
	Does not incorporate ongoing evaluation of student progress.	Evaluation of progress incorporated into discourse.

Source: Hogan, T., Rabinowitz, M., & Craven, J. A. (2003). Representation in teaching: Inferences from research of expert and novice teachers. *Educational Psychologist, 38,* 235–247.

Teaching experience alone does not make an expert teacher (Torff, 2003). In an insightful study, Torff (2003) compared three groups of teachers: novices, experienced teachers who were not considered experts, and experienced teachers who were experts. He found that in some areas the experienced teachers resembled the expert teachers (e. g., they were less concerned with presenting a great deal of content-based material). However, in other areas, they were more like novices (e. g., they did not focus on higher order thinking skills).

If just getting more experience is no guarantee of becoming an expert, what can one do to become a more expert teacher? Klein and Hoffman (1993) argue that it is not enough simply to teach prospective teachers the skills, knowledge, and abilities of expert teachers. They believe that various forms of experience are necessary, including personal experience in the area of expertise being developed, supervised experience with a mentor or advisor, role-playing experiences, and vicarious experiences in which one envisions what one would do in certain situations. Experience needs to be combined with active reflection (Artzt & Armour-Thomas, 1999; Ward & McCotter, 2004). A model for the kind of active reflection necessary to gain expertise can be found in the "Reflection for Action" exercises presented throughout this text.

R I D E How would an expert teacher address the problem about scheduling at the beginning of the chapter?

Online Teacher Communities

Teachers are often quite isolated from other adults when teaching. This can be particularly difficult for new teachers who need opportunities to discuss issues and problems and to learn from more experienced teachers. The Internet offers a partial solution by making extensive resources, such as vast stores of lesson plans, teaching ideas, and a variety of online teacher communities, available to assist teachers. One example of an online community is *Tapped In*, which includes educators at every level of the education system from around the world. The goal of *Tapped In* is to assist teachers in supporting one another through peer online networks. Teachers can participate in discussions and mentor other teachers. Another online community, *Proteacher,* has over 30 active discussion boards and a huge number of teaching resources for a variety of subjects. (See the Web site for this text for current Web addresses.)

In Chapter 1, you saw that teachers develop expertise by advancing through the following four phases (Kagan, 1992):

1. Decreased focus on self-as-teacher; increased focus on the needs of learners.
2. Enhanced knowledge about learners.
3. Automation of classroom routines and procedures.
4. Growth in problem-solving skills.

www.wiley.com/ college/odonnell

The availability of online teacher communities can provide ideas and suggestions for how to succeed in these four stages. Many of the online teacher communities provide discussion boards specifically for new teachers. Many of them also deal with the kinds of concerns that beginning teachers have about classroom management, discipline, motivating students, and teaching children with special needs.

Chapter Reference
Chapter 1 provides a description of expertise in teaching and a discussion of the concerns of beginning teachers.

Teachers' Self-Efficacy

One of the most important contributions to psychology in the past 50 years is Bandura's concept of **self-efficacy** (Bandura, 1997). Self-efficacy is a person's belief that he or she can accomplish a task. Bandura (1993) provided an excellent statement of the implications of this belief: "The stronger the perceived self-efficacy, the higher the goal challenges set for themselves and the firmer their commitment to it" (*sic*, p. 119). It is not difficult to see how this concept is related to teaching. Teaching is a highly demanding occupation that requires a commitment to achieve goals in the face of sometimes daunting odds; it requires high levels of mental, physical, and interpersonal energy. Without a strong belief in one's ability to achieve one's instructional goals, it would be easy to give up and pursue a less strenuous career.

self-efficacy One's judgment of how well he or she will cope with a situation, given the skills one possesses and the circumstances one faces.

Taking It to the Classroom

You Don't Know Jack: How Many Jacks Are There?

Mr. Ramsey, the physics teacher, and Ms. Ramón, the Spanish teacher, have just discovered that they both have Jack as a student, although they cannot believe it is the same child. Mr. Ramsey finds Jack a conscientious and attentive student, whereas Ms. Ramón finds Jack to be a constant irritant and a poor student at best in Spanish. What can Ms. Ramón do to find the Jack that appears in Mr. Ramsey's physics class?

- Talk to Jack. Does he like physics? Why?
- Ask Jack about his Spanish class. Does he find it difficult?
- Make an intentional effort to observe Jack during both classes to identify what classroom events bring out his conscientiousness and disruptiveness.
- Develop a behavior contract with him about completing his homework.
- Ask Jack's friend to work with him during class to help him.
- Have him sit at the front of the room so it is easier for him to pay attention.
- Allow him time to practice his Spanish using the language software you have.

---

teaching efficacy A teacher's judgment of, or confidence in, his or her capacity to cope with the teaching situation in ways that bring about desired outcomes.

Chapter Reference
See Chapter 5 for a fuller discussion of self-efficacy.

Not long after Bandura introduced the concept of self-efficacy, researchers began to look at it from the standpoint of teaching (Ashton & Webb, 1986; Gibson & Dembo, 1984; Guskey, 1988; Woolfolk & Hoy, 1990). **Teaching efficacy** is the belief in one's ability to be an effective teacher even with unmotivated students and a challenging teaching environment (Tschannen-Morgan & Woolfolk Hoy, 2001). Research has shown that strong self-efficacy beliefs with regard to teaching lead to improved student achievement (Goddard, Hoy, & Woolfolk Hoy, 2000; Moore & Esselman, 1992; Rosenholz, 1989). In the "Taking It to the Classroom" box on this page, you can see an example of how two teachers feel about their efficacy with respect to the same student.

Developing Self-Efficacy With one-third of new teachers leaving the field within their first three years of teaching (National Commission on Teaching and America's Future, 2003), it is important to understand the role of efficacy in teacher success. Individuals develop self-efficacy as a result of verbal persuasion, personal history, and vicarious experience (see Chapter 5). Teachers can develop a strong sense of self-efficacy if their preparation for teaching includes opportunities to experience successful coping. A mentor can remind a new teacher of what he or she is doing effectively and describe teaching strategies that help the teacher become more effective in the classroom. A new teacher can derive a sense of efficacy by observing other teachers and imitating their behaviors. Finally, a good mentor can provide opportunities for social persuasion related to efficacy. (e. g. "You can do it; Remember when …")

Fostering teacher self-efficacy is complex, and interventions designed to enhance teachers' efficacy have mixed results. Rimm-Kaufman and Sawyer (2003) examined a program for teachers called *Responsive Classroom* that emphasized the development of empathy toward students in elementary school classrooms. They reported an increase in the teachers' sense of self-efficacy. Gordon and Debus (2002) worked with teachers on what they called a "deep learning" approach to teaching at the high school level, but they found no significant differences in self-efficacy between intervention and control groups. Although self-efficacy can flourish in almost any environment, novice teachers benefit from the experience of mastery, a positive school climate, encouragement and support during difficult times, and strong mentoring by more experienced teachers (Brennan, Thames, & Roberts, 1999; Darling-Hammond & McLaughlin, 1996; Jenlink, Kinnucan-Welsch, & Odell, 1996; Yost, 2002; Woolfolk Hoy, 2000). (See the "Uncommon Sense" box on the next page.)

Uncommon Sense

Veteran Teachers Are Not Nervous on the First Day of School—Or Are They?

Jim O'Kelly has a doctorate in education and many years of experience. He is recognized as a skilled teacher and is often asked to mentor new teachers. He has taught kindergarten for many years. In a discussion of the first day of school, Jim related the following story:

You know, I've been teaching kindergarten for 24 years now, and it was only about 3 years ago that I was able to sleep through the night for the week before school started. My wife used to say, "Jim, are you crazy? You've been teaching kindergarten all of your life. You love the kids and they love you. Why are you losing sleep over the beginning of the school year?" I told her that I was about to meet 20 people whom I had never met before and with whom I was about to spend an entire year. Furthermore, their start in school depended on me. They were counting on me, and so were their parents. I didn't know what they would be like this year.

It is normal to be anxious about getting started on a new adventure, and that is what each school year is. Jim lets us know that even a highly experienced teacher is nervous at the beginning of the school year. Experts and novices (and students and parents) may not be so different when it comes to first-day-of-school jitters.

Self-Efficacy and Learners with Special Needs Teacher self-efficacy is particularly important in working with students with special needs. There is a strong tendency for teachers to send troublesome students to be evaluated for **referral** and a high probability that a referred student will become a classified student (Algozzine, Christenson, & Ysseldyke, 1982; Gelzheiser, 1990). Teachers with a high sense of self-efficacy are less likely to refer students for evaluation than are teachers with a low sense of self-efficacy (Soodak & Podell, 1993). If, as the research indicates, referral almost always leads to classification, it follows that classification depends to some degree on the teacher's sense of efficacy in the classroom. (See the "Taking It to the Classroom" box below.)

referral   Educators' shorthand for the recommendation that a child be evaluated for possible special education classification.

Taking It to the Classroom

Self-Efficacy and Special Education Teachers

Brownell (1997) provides some advice for teachers of students with special needs:

- Set high but realistic expectations—if you did not want to work with children who need a great deal of help, you would not be going into special education. But you need to be realistic about what you can accomplish; otherwise, you will be setting yourself up for frequent disappointments. Ask successful colleagues to help you set goals.

- Distinguish between your job and your personal life—you need to be just a person sometimes. A bad day at school should not translate into a bad day as a spouse, parent, or friend.

- Employ professional discretion and personal autonomy—it may sometimes seem as though everything you do as a teacher is predetermined, but in fact you can have a great deal of flexibility if you actively seek it.

- Do not rely on praise—people (your principal, your colleagues, your supervisor) may *or may not* tell you what a great job you are doing. Your professional satisfaction has to stem from the progress you see in your students.

- Track student progress—this is something you almost certainly will ask your students to do. It is a good idea for you to do so, too. If you record your students' progress, it will give you a better sense of perspective when you encounter the rough days that all teachers have from time to time.

- Use best practices—do not forget to be a professional. You should be in constant pursuit of the best practices to apply in your classroom.

Working in Culturally Different Contexts

As discussed earlier, most beliefs that teachers hold about students, learning, and teaching come from their own experiences in life and as students. Because most prospective teachers are white and middle class, their beliefs typically reflect such an orientation. But many of these young people will be teaching in culturally diverse settings, or perhaps in settings that are not very diverse but represent a culture that is different from their own. The issue of teaching in such settings is among the most important ones facing education today (Boyer & Baptiste, 1996). Realizing the importance of the issue, however, is far from having a solid idea of what to do about it. Among the challenges that teachers face in diverse classrooms are these:

- Students with different backgrounds from their own—how to relate to these students, how to understand them

- Students with different backgrounds from those of other students in the class—how to create an environment in which students work well together and care about one another

- Poverty—working with students whose parents have very limited resources and with students whose parents are not present in the home

- Language—working with students who do not speak English (or do not speak it well) and with parents who do not speak English

- Numbers of students with special needs—working in urban school districts, which typically have much higher proportions of students who are classified as having special needs

This list may seem overwhelming, and indeed it would be unwise to underestimate the challenges associated with working with a diverse student body, particularly in a school with large numbers of students in or near conditions of poverty. However, the challenges are accompanied by rewards. A great teacher in a challenging setting can make a huge difference in hundreds of lives over the course of a career. Looking at the issue from the perspective of teacher development, Zimpher and Ashburn (1992) recommend that teacher education programs instill the following beliefs in prospective teachers: (a) belief in the positive aspects of diversity, (b) belief in cooperation, and (c) belief in the value of creating a caring community in the classroom. Taking the perspective of a teacher in a diverse setting, Gay (2003, p. 32) makes the following recommendations for developing a multicultural curriculum:[1]

- Create learning goals and objectives that incorporate multicultural aspects, such as "Developing students' ability to write persuasively about social justice concerns."

- Keep a record to ensure that the teacher includes a wide variety of ethnic groups in curriculum materials and instructional activities in a wide variety of ways.

- Introduce different ethnic groups and their contributions on a rotating basis.

- Include several examples from different ethnic experiences to explain subject matter concepts, facts, and skills.

- Show how multicultural content, goals, and activities intersect with subject-specific curricular standards. (See the "Uncommon Sense" box on the next page.)

Appendix

Influences on Learning

Students' learning is influenced by their experiences (*PRAXIS*™, I. B. 6, *INTASC*, Principles 2, 3).

What Does This Mean to Me?
What might you take for granted that your future students might not?

---

[1] Gay, G. (2003). The importance of multicultural education. *Educational Leadership, 61* (4), p. 32. Copyright © 2003 by Association for Supervision and Curriculum Development. Reprinted by permission. The Association for Supervision and Curriculum Development is a worldwide community of educators advocating sound policies and sharing best practices to achieve the success of each learner. To learn more, visit ASCD at www.ascd.org.

Uncommon Sense

That's True for Everybody—Or Is It?

Did you take it for granted that

- You were going to college?
- You could become what you wanted to become?
- Nobody would ever wonder what you were doing in a particular restaurant, neighborhood, or social setting because of your ethnicity or religious background?
- You would not have to check in advance that the establishment you were going to would have wheelchair access?
- Everyone would understand idiomatic speech in the same way that you do?
- Your academic strengths or weaknesses wouldn't be attributed to your gender or ethnicity?

Although these may or may not be true in your experience, they certainly are not true for everyone.

Planning

Thus far, we have examined the notion of becoming an effective teacher by looking at teachers from a developmental perspective. Now we turn to consider the actual activities and events of successful teaching, the nuts and bolts of being an effective teacher. The remainder of the chapter is an extended walk through the process of teaching, beginning with the planning that goes on before teaching begins, turning to broadly based options for instruction, then to specific teaching tactics, and concluding with an important but often overlooked aspect of effective teaching: homework. We begin at the beginning: determining what is to be taught and planning for instruction.

Outstanding teachers have well-developed planning and organizational skills. As teachers translate instructional goals and objectives into lesson plans, instructional units, and projects and activities, they are beginning the process of teaching. This section begins with instructional goals, then looks at lesson planning, and finally considers the activities that occur in the classroom, where the excitement, the interaction with students, and the reward of watching children make progress take place.

Instructional Goals

It is difficult to know whether progress is being made toward an **instructional goal** if the goal is not clearly defined. Instructional goals have been called *objectives, achievement targets, desired outcomes,* and *standards.* They have been defined in very broad terms and in terms that are so narrow as to be almost microscopic, ranging from "Students will develop a sense of citizenship" to "Students will be able to link 10 state capitals with their states in a matching task in a maximum of 20 seconds." No matter how they are phrased, instructional goals state the desired outcomes of instruction. They are an essential component of the educational process and have been the focus of a great deal of educational research and theory.

Educational Objectives: Bloom's Taxonomy Drawing on the pioneering work of Tyler (1949), who developed **behavioral objectives** in military training, Bloom and colleagues developed a taxonomy of **educational objectives** for use in constructing courses and the assessments to go with them (Bloom et al., 1956). They wrote objectives to reflect what students would be able to do as a result of instruction and classified them according to their level of complexity. The result is widely known as *Bloom's taxonomy.* (The term **taxonomy** is taken from biology, where it is the system of the classification of plants and animals.) Bloom's goal was to organize educational objectives according to the level of cognitive complexity and thought required.

Appendix
Effective Planning

To be a good teacher, you must plan your instruction carefully and link your instructional goals to your teaching strategies (*PRAXIS*™, II. B. 1, 3, *INTASC,* Principles 4, 7).

instructional goal A statement of desired student outcomes following instruction.

behavioral objectives Statements of goals for instruction that clearly set forth what a student will be able to do as a result of the instruction.

educational objectives Explicit statements of what students are expected to be able to do as a result of instruction.

taxonomy A classification of objects according to a set of principles or laws.

What Does This Mean to Me?
Think of a course you are currently taking. What levels of cognitive objectives are identified in the syllabus of the course?

TABLE 9.3

Bloom's Taxonomy of Educational Objectives

Level	Description	Examples
Knowledge	Recall of facts, dates, and general information about a subject.	Identifying the countries in Africa
		Reciting multiplication facts
Comprehension	Understanding information, ideas, or skills.	Being able to understand the material in a paragraph
Application	Applying skills to new situations.	Using an algebra skill such as simultaneous equations to solve a novel math problem
Analysis	In-depth consideration of an idea or concept.	Comparing and contrasting possible causes of the Great Depression
Synthesis	Taking two ideas and concepts and seeing what the intersection or *synthesis* of these ideas would be. This involves generating a new (to the student) idea.	Projecting what would happen if Toni Morrison rewrote the concluding scene from Shakespeare's *Hamlet*
Evaluation	Critical consideration of a concept or theory in some definable context—not simply a judgment of whether one likes or dislikes something and the reasons why. In Bloom's taxonomy, the most sophisticated mental activity.	Evaluating the potential of Piaget's stage theory for explaining conflicts that occur among children on the - playground.

Bloom's taxonomy has been one of the most influential ideas in education over the past half-century (see Table 9.3). Bloom wanted educators to think seriously about what they want to achieve in their classes. He pushed teachers to develop a small set of broad statements about what they want students to be able to do as a result of the planned instruction. By developing a taxonomy that showed what **higher order thinking skills** looked like, he encouraged teachers to make sure that they were not simply requiring students to recall information. In Bloom's model, the goals for a course became a blueprint for developing instruction and assessment.

However, the taxonomy has been the subject of some controversy. One of the problems with the taxonomy, and with the idea of objectives in general, is that it can lead to a somewhat rigid way of thinking about instruction. Teachers may focus on generating objectives based on the taxonomy rather than thinking deeply about the curricular content. In addition, some educators felt that although the first three levels of the taxonomy (knowledge, comprehension, application) seemed reasonable, the three higher levels (analysis, synthesis, evaluation) were either not distinct enough from one another or not very useful in assessing different students' abilities or progress.

Anderson and Krathwohl, colleagues of Bloom's, revised the taxonomy in 2001, reorganizing some of the categories and turning the nouns of Bloom's taxonomic levels into verbs, with the following major results:

higher order thinking skills Skills and abilities that go beyond recall and comprehension, including the ability to apply ideas and concepts, analyze and synthesize information, and evaluate complex information.

Bloom	Anderson
Knowledge	Remembering
Comprehension	Understanding
Application	Applying
Analysis	Analyzing
Evaluation	Evaluating
Synthesis	Creating

This scheme has a logical appeal to it, primarily in employing terms that are more closely related to classroom life, such as *creating* instead of *synthesis*. Further modifications of Bloom's groundbreaking work were to follow.

New Approaches to Goals The use of goals or objectives in planning instruction and assessment has been in and out of favor over the years. Today, instructional goals are once again popular, but in two new forms. The first of these is **standards**, which are discussed later in this section and more fully in Chapter 14. Standards are a set of objectives that define what should be learned in a given subject area by students at specific grade levels.

Another new form of instructional goals is **achievement targets** (Stiggins, 2001). Achievement targets are specific statements of what teachers want to accomplish in a particular lesson or set of lessons. The use of the word *target* implies a goal for the instruction and, therefore, for the assessment that goes with it. Stiggins's (1997) approach, shown in Table 9.4, might be thought of as a set of specifications for what students should learn or do, in contrast to the broader objectives of Bloom's taxonomy. Stiggins's target category of **products**, for example, represents a substantial break from Bloom's thinking. Products are things created by students that reflect their skills and abilities, as well as their ability to create something brand new. Bloom would probably consider products to be forms of assessment rather than an objective or a target; Stiggins believes that the ability to combine those skills and abilities into a successful product is a worthwhile target in itself. Consider, for example, a simple book report. What does a book report represent?

- The underlying skills of being able to comprehend a book one has read, synthesize the ideas contained in the book into a concise report, and communicate those ideas in a clear fashion (Bloom), or
- A goal in and of itself, the ability to produce a report under certain constraints and guidelines that requires pulling together a variety of abilities (Stiggins)

The first of these represents a focus on process skills, whereas the latter focuses on the product. Another key area of difference between Bloom's taxonomy and Stiggins's classification is that Stiggins includes attitudes and dispositions. Because, for example, it does not do a person much good to learn how to read if he or she never reads, for Stiggins the development of positive attitudes is another achievement target. Salomon and Globerson (1987) note that skill may not be enough for learning and transfer. Mindfulness, or the purposeful use of thought and effortful processes, is also necessary for learning and transfer of skills. Unless the tasks in which students are engaged are valued by the students, it is unlikely that they will engage in such effortful processing.

Chapter Reference
See Chapter 14 for a discussion of the use of standards in education.

standards   A comprehensive set of educational objectives organized by subject matter and grade level.

achievement targets   Well-specified statements of what teachers want to accomplish in a particular lesson or set of lessons.

products   Student creations that reflect their skills and abilities as well as their ability to create something new.

TABLE 9.4

Stiggins's Taxonomy

Target	Description	Examples
Knowledge	• Declarative knowledge: facts, terms, concepts, and generalizations • Procedural knowledge: procedures or problem-solving methods	• Declarative: information, facts, dates, relationships, etc. • Procedural: steps involved in a science procedure; the algorithm for a particular mathematics problem
Reasoning	• The process of answering questions through analytical problem solving	• Story problems in mathematics
Skills	• The abilities necessary to put procedural knowledge to use in a fluent fashion and in the appropriate context	• At the elementary school level, the ability to come into school on a winter day, take off outdoor clothes, and get ready for school • At the high school level, the ability to write haiku in the proper form
Products	• Things students create that reflect their current skill and ability levels	• A science experiment lab report • A map detailing U.S. imports and exports
Attitudes and dispositions	• Interests in certain areas; the desire to learn more about a topic	• Purchasing a book about a topic in a lesson • Attendance at a concert

Using Goals in Classroom Teaching

Twenty years ago, teachers were often trained in how to develop and communicate instructional goals and objectives. To a great extent, that is no longer true. The instructional standards movement in assessment at the state and national levels has generated a much more *top-down* model for setting instructional goals. In all likelihood, your instructional goals, objectives, or standards used in your classroom will have been established at the state or national level.

You will still have a number of decisions to make, however, about the kinds of instruction and assessment needed for students to meet the standards set for them. Figure 9.6 provides some examples of instructional goals from various statewide programs. Choose one that is close to the level and subject matter you think you might be teaching, and think about what it means. How specific is it? How would you go about trying to teach the standard? What questions would you have about what might or might not be included as part of that standard or goal?

Consider the standards for eleventh-grade students in Ohio. They seem to be fairly clear and worthwhile objectives for eleventh-grade students. But what kinds of experiences, activities, explorations, explanations, group work, analogies, examples, or experiments would help students understand this material? How should an understanding of how electric motors work (content knowledge) and an understanding of eleventh-grade students in a science class (pedagogical knowledge) be combined to help students gain the knowledge and skills included in the standard (pedagogical content knowledge)? The answer will not be the same for all classrooms. Help, however, is readily available: Curriculum guides have ideas; colleagues and supervisors have suggestions; and veteran teachers offer guidance on the Internet. As a teacher, you will need to make intelligent choices among the options, try them out, and reflect on the results obtained for purposes of expanding and refining your pedagogical content knowledge.

Translating Goals into Plans

Translating instructional goals into lessons and units of instruction is a critical juncture in the process of instruction. Planning for instruction is somewhat similar to planning for other activities, such as a vacation, a party, or how to spend a free Saturday. Planning begins with a set of givens and anticipations.

Planning: An Overview How is planning for instruction like planning a vacation? Each involves:

- Setting objectives or goals
- Choosing a way to achieve those goals
- Making decisions concerning the details of the approach, possibly consulting people who have more experience
- Making changes as the plan is carried out
- Evaluating the plan after it has been carried out in order to be better prepared the next time around

In teaching, there are several layers of plans, with smaller plans nested within larger ones (Sardo-Brown, 1988; Yinger, 1980). A plan for a particular lesson (e. g., a plan for a lesson on the structure of a Shakespearean sonnet) is embedded within a larger plan to teach students various sonnet structures. The plans for teaching about the structures of sonnets may be embedded within a larger unit plan for teaching about common poetic forms. There are various approaches to these subunits. Many elementary school teachers like to take a seasonal approach to the year, emphasizing changes in the seasons and holidays or other events associated with them. With the seasons, they will have units that are often thematic in nature. Thus, there might be a unit on the changing of the leaves or a Valentine's Day unit. Within units, some teachers plan by the day, whereas others plan by the week, then by the day, within the week. Teachers usually look for natural break points in their planning, such as time off for a holiday.

Grade 3 History-Social Science Standards for California Public Schools

3.3 Students draw from historical and community resources to organize the sequence of local historical events and describe how each period of settlement left its mark on the land.

1. Research the explorers who visited here, the newcomers who settled here, and the people who continue to come to the region, including their cultural and religious traditions and contributions.

2. Describe the economies established by settlers and their influence on the present-day economy, with emphasis on the importance of private property and entrepreneurship.

3. Trace why their community was established, how individuals and families contributed to its founding and development, and how the community has changed over time, drawing on maps, photographs, oral histories, letters, newspapers, and other primary sources.

Source: California Department of Education. (1998). *History-social science content standards for public schools*. Retrieved June 2, 2005 from http://www.cde.ca.gov/re/pn/fd/documents/histsocsci-stnd.pdf.

Grade 8 Mathematics Standards for Texas Public Schools

(5) Patterns, relationships, and algebraic thinking. The student uses graphs, tables, and algebraic representations to make predictions and solve problems. The student is expected to

(A) Estimate, find, and justify solutions to application problems using appropriate tables, graphs, and algebraic equations; and
(B) Use an algebraic expression to find any term in a sequence.

Source: Texas Education Agency. (2003). *8th grade TAKS objectives and TEKS student expectations*. Retrieved June 2, 2005 from http://staff.banqueteisd.esc2.net/J_RCanales/scope%20and%20sequence.htm.

Grade 11 Science Standards for Ohio Public Schools

Nature of Matter
1. Explain that elements with the same number of protons may or may not have the same mass and those with different masses (different numbers of neutrons) are called *isotopes*. Some of these are radioactive.

2. Explain that humans have used unique bonding of carbon atoms to make a variety of molecules (e.g., plastics).

Forces and Motion
3. Describe real-world examples showing that all energy transformations tend toward disorganized states (e.g., fossil fuel combustion, food pyramids, and electrical use).

4. Explain how electric motors and generators work (e.g., relate that electricity and magnetism ate two aspects of a single electromagnetic force). Investigate that electric charges in motion produce magnetic fields, and a changing magnetic field creates an electric field.

Source: Ohio Department of Education. (2003). *Academic content standards, K-12 science: Benchmarks and indicators by grade level*. Retrieved June 2, 2005 from http://www.ode.state.oh.us/academic_content_standards/ScienceContentStd/RTF/g_Science_by_Grade_Level.rtf.

Figure 9.6. Samples of Statewide Instructional Goals

Planning on and Planning for: Instructional Time and Scheduling Teachers must regulate their own cognition with respect to teaching. One of the key cognitive processes in which they engage is planning. Teachers have expectations of what may occur in their classrooms based on prior experiences and existing belief systems. Rather than simply react to events in the classroom, teachers need to establish goals and plan specifically for implementing activities that will result in the accomplishment of these goals. This process is an example of problem solving in which teachers engage on a daily basis.

Fifth-Grade Class Schedule					
	Monday	Tuesday	Wednesday	Thursday	Friday
8:30-10:00	Language Arts	Language Arts	Language Arts	Language Arts	Language Arts
10:00-10:15	Recess	Recess	Recess	Recess	Recess
10:15-11:30	Mathematics	Mathematics	Mathematics	Mathematics	Mathematics
11:30-12:15	Phys Ed	Art	Lunch	Phys Ed	Art
12:15-12:45	Lunch	Lunch	Writers' Workshop	Lunch	Lunch
12:45-1:30	Science	Social Studies		Science	Social Studies
1:30-2:00	Music	Phys Ed	Open	Music	Phys Ed
2:00-2:30	Spanish	Spanish		Spanish	Spanish

Figure 9.7. Mrs. Johnson's Class Schedule

Chapter Reference
See Chapter 8 for more information on problem solving.

R I D E Look back to how you developed your plans at the beginning of the chapter. How do your emphases and decisions compare with Mrs. Johnson's? What are the reasons for them?

block scheduling   An approach to scheduling at the middle and high school levels that allows for larger blocks of time to be scheduled for subjects, usually with fewer blocks per week.

When an event is far in the future or might not even occur, the impetus to plan—and to plan realistically—is not as great (except perhaps as a pleasant diversion). The rule here is simple: The more you plan *on* something, the more you plan *for* it. A daily lesson plan for a period that is more than three months away does not really have to be *in the book* right now, but a plan for the day after tomorrow really does. Elementary school teachers must plan about 1,000 hours of instructional time for one group of children (180 school days times 5 to 6 hours a day). High school teachers must plan 150 to 200 hours for each of four or five classes, some of which may be in the same subject and at the same grade level.

Elementary school teachers need to organize the day and the week in their classrooms. They have to make room for *specials,* such as gym, art, and music, which are scheduled for specific times, as well as for lunch and possibly recess. In addition, individual students may be pulled out of class for speech therapy, gifted programs, and the like. Teachers typically come to terms with these interruptions by developing a daily or weekly instructional schedule that lays out when each subject or activity will take place each day. An example of such a schedule is presented in Figure 9.7.

This teacher puts language arts and math in the morning and social studies, science and foreign language (Spanish) in the afternoon. She has allocated an hour and a half each day for language arts and an hour and fifteen minutes for math. Science and social studies each get two hours per week. Clearly, her instructional goals lean more heavily toward language arts and math than to other subjects. Also note that she has left an hour slot open on Wednesdays. This allows her to place other activities in that time slot or use it to catch up if need be. Her planning is now more controlled: She has allocated the available hours to various subject areas, and her planning will take place within the structure she has created.

At the secondary school level, there is no need for this kind of schedule. The times when teachers meet with students are decided well in advance of the school year, and teachers usually have little say in these decisions. Even if a math teacher feels that students learn math better early in the morning than in the afternoon, he or she will still have to have some classes in the afternoon. Another factor that secondary school teachers have to deal with is the amount of time they have for each class each day. In a typical high school, this will probably be 40–50 minutes. Some high schools have **block scheduling**, which structures the academic time for students during a school day in larger blocks of time for particular subjects. For example, science might be taught in two blocks of two hours each instead of five 45-minute classes; the amounts could be much greater.

Within the structures that elementary school teachers create and that secondary school teachers are given, teachers build their plans for the year broadly, for seasons or thematic units somewhat more specifically, and for the upcoming weeks and days even more specifically.

Table 9.5 presents a visual model of the planning process and the issues that need to be considered in developing instructional planning. The results of each day's teaching will lead to changes in the plans for the next day, and sometimes plans at broader levels will have to be adjusted. Flexibility without losing sight of long-term goals is the key. Often, beginning teachers feel that if they do not make it through their plans for the day, the lesson was a failure. Such "failures" probably have more to do with errors in estimating the amount of time it will take to do something than with what went on in the classroom. Veteran teachers are much more likely to evaluate their lessons in terms of students' engagement and responses to the instructional activities that took place.

> **How Can I Use This?**
>
> Are you someone who is highly organized and keeps a tight schedule, or do you tend to be less organized and take things as they come? How might these tendencies translate into teaching?

TABLE 9.5

Levels of Planning for Instruction and Issues Involved in Developing Plans

Level of planning	Specific considerations
Plan for the year in language arts Yearly plans are statements of the overall approach to teaching language arts for the year that clearly address the goals/standards/objectives set for the class.	• Where are my students now? (Test scores, last year's performance, informal assessments) • What resources are available to me? (Expertise, curriculum materials, funds) • What are my students' interests? How can I accommodate diversity in my planning? (Previous year's students, discussions) • What are the overall goals for the year? (Statewide and district standards, my goals, student input) • Are there students with special needs? (What kinds of needs, help available?)
Seasonal plans for the year: Mid-fall Teachers usually like to break the year down into smaller units and relate their lessons to seasonal events and holiday times, such as Thanksgiving and President's Day.	• What is going on this time of year that I can highlight? (Changing leaves, getting colder, Thanksgiving) • Where should we be now in terms of goals? (Experience from previous years, informal assessments) • What seems to be working well with this class? (Student responses, parent/teacher conferences) • Where can I find some good thematic units? (The Internet, teachers' magazines, colleagues)
Instructional units Instructional units are pieces of the planning process that might last for a week or several weeks. They are a cohesive whole made up of a number of parts. A unit in language arts might focus on reading a particular book, working on haiku, or constructing a good paragraph.	• How will students react in terms of motivation in this unit? (Relationship to students' interests) • How will this unit work toward overall goals? (What will students be learning in this unit?) • How will I assess student learning? (Getting the needed information, helping students with self-assessment) • How can I accommodate learners with special needs in this unit? (Modifications, highlighting abilities, getting help from special education teacher)
Daily lesson plans Daily lesson plans are guides for day-to-day activities in the classroom. They include motivational activities, instructional activities, materials needed, and assessments. Beginning teachers tend to be more elaborate and more likely to stick to daily plans than are veteran teachers.	• What should today consist of? (Presenting new material, student activities, group work) • How can I engage student interest? (Student interests, relevance to current events, benefits to students) • How will I know if it is going well? (Informal assessments, student engagement) • What can I do if the lesson "is a disaster"? (Moving on, cycling back, moving to another subject)

www.wiley.com/college/odonnell

Looking at Lesson Plans Individual lesson plans usually have several different elements, including objectives or standards, lists of materials needed, descriptions of activities, and assessment procedures. A variety of Web sites offer lesson plans. You can find some of these in the Web site associated with this text. Examine the lesson plan in Figure 9.8, and ask yourself the following questions:

- What is the teacher trying to accomplish?
- What assumptions does this plan make about the students?
- How does the lesson plan view students as learners?
- Could I teach this lesson from these plans? Would I want to?
- Are the assessment procedures adequate?
- How likely are students to respond positively to this plan?
- How might I improve this plan?
- How difficult would it be to carry out this lesson plan?

TITLE: TEMPERATURE AND WATER DENSITY

AUTHOR: Steve McFarland, Decker Lake Youth Center;
Salt Lake City, UT

GRADE LEVEL: Appropriate for grades 7–8.
OBJECTIVE(s): Students will be able to
1. Explain the density of water as it relates to temperature.
2. Describe the dynamics of ocean currents as they relate to temperature and density.
3. Identify the forces governing convection in liquids.

MATERIALS
Teacher materials—a pair of two -liter plastic soda bottles, two plastic straws, a glue gun with glue sticks, a hot plate, green and red food coloring, a pitcher into which hot liquid can be poured, a bowl large enough to contain a two-liter bottle, crushed ice, and a cutting instrument.

ACTIVITIES AND PROCEDURES
- Cut each two-liter bottle such that each is approximately eight inches tall. Drill or punch one hole about two inches from the bottom, and the other about six inches from the bottom, in each of the bottles. The holes should be one above the other, and just large enough for the plastic straws to fit into snugly.

- Place the straws in the holes horizontally, joining the two bottles at both the two-inch and the six-inch levels. With the glue gun, secure the straws to each bottle opening such that no liquid could leak from the holes.

- Boil about two liters of water, and chill another two liters with ice. Place one of the two-liter bottles in a bowl and add ice inside the bowl but outside the two-liter bottle (this will keep the water that you add to one bottle cold during the demonstration).

- Add red food coloring to the hot water and green to the chilled water. Pour the hot water into one two-liter bottle and cold water into the two-liter bottle that you have prepared with ice.

- Observe as the cold green water travels through the lower straw whille the hot water travels through the upper straw. In the end, each bottle will have a distinct layer of hot res water on top and a cooler green layer of water on the bottom.

TYING IT TOGETHER

Students have difficulty believing that warm water and cold water will actually separate, because in each case they are dealing with just plain water. As the experiment progresses, it becomes apparent that the colder water sinks and the hotter water rises to the top. It also becomes clear that water will move when temperature differences exist. The student no longer has trouble visualizing the concept of ocean currents as they relate to temperature differences. This activity can also be used to help students add to their understanding of the migration patterns and habitats of sea creatures.

Figure 9.8. Example of a Lesson Plan

Source: Copyright by the Columbia Education Center, Portland, OR. Retrieved June 3, 2005 from http://www.col-ed.org/cur/sci/sci212.txt.

Planning for Students with Special Needs

Planning for students with special needs within the context of overall instructional planning poses special challenges. The research in this area suggests that general education teachers at the elementary school level have difficulty adapting their lesson plans for such students or using individualized educational programs (IEPs) in making their decisions (Schumm et al., 1995; Venn & McCollum, 2002). Further, at the middle and high school levels, there is little evidence that differential planning to accommodate the special needs of classified students included in regular classrooms actually occurs (Schumm & Vaughn, 1992; Vaughn & Schumm, 1994).

Planning for classrooms that include students with special needs is certainly more complicated than planning for classrooms without such students, but *not* planning for such students is irresponsible. If you are working with students with special needs, you must decide how to include them in ways that address their needs while fostering the productivity and caring nature of all the students in the class.

In such planning, first consider your instructional goals or objectives. Your task is to bring together the goals and activities you are considering for the class as a whole and the goals and educational assistance required by each special needs student, as documented in the IEP, to form a cohesive instructional plan. This may be challenging, but help is available. Your school's faculty will include special education teachers who are trained to help you with this task. Next, there are written resources and resources on the Web that can help in your planning and even provide practical tips for modifying plans (see the Web site for this text for current URLs). Next, think about the resources you have available for working with students with special needs. You may have an in-class paraprofessional or teacher's aide. You may have resource room help (which will require working with the resource room teacher to coordinate planning). You can give students with special needs extra time to complete assignments or allow them to work on assignments at home with their parents. You can make modifications in assignments that are more in line with the instructional goals for a particular student. You can have students with special needs work with other students, either one on one or in group settings.

The key to planning for inclusion is to keep in mind the goals that have been laid out for students in their IEPs, the resources available to you, and the in-class options and modifications that can be made to maximize growth for each student and for the class as a whole.

Research on Teacher Planning   Research on planning generally shows that as teachers become more experienced, they tend to rely more on routine and do less formal planning (Leinhardt, 1983). This is not to say that teachers do not plan, but it appears that veteran teachers' planning often takes the form of mental rehearsal of what is to be done in class (McCutcheon & Milner, 2002; Morine-Dersheimer, 1979). Teachers often rely on textbooks and curriculum guides as sources of information for planning (McCutcheon, 1980; Smith & Sendelbach, 1979). They focus on what is needed to fill the instructional time available to them (Leinhardt, 1983; Sardo-Brown, 1988; 1990). Teachers are also influenced by external factors, such as district or school requirements or recommendations about how much time to allocate to various subject areas and what areas of the curriculum to emphasize (Sardo-Brown, 1990). Therefore, the extensive approach to planning at all levels that is presented here and in other works on teacher preparation may not be what first-year teachers see when they observe their more experienced peers. Two points are worth mentioning here: It is better to create more detailed plans at first, and it is almost always better to plan well.

Lesson Study   An interesting new approach to looking at planning and the execution of those plans in classrooms comes from Japan and is called *lesson study*. In lesson study, a team of teachers who are teaching the same curriculum work together collaboratively to think about how best to approach the lesson. Then one member of the team teaches the lesson while the other members observe the lesson and collect data and impressions of how the lesson went. They gather together to analyze the data, reflect on the lesson, and discuss what they have learned. The fourth step in the process is to refine and reteach the lesson, perhaps with a different team member, and to consolidate what they have learned about that lesson specifically and what they might generalize to new lessons. This is but a very brief description of this exciting idea. An excellent reference to learn about lesson study is *Lesson Study: A Handbook of Teacher-Led Instructional Change* by Catherine C. Lewis (2002).

Chapter Reference
Chapter 4 presents and discusses an example of an IEP.

www.wiley.com/college/odonnell

R I D E   When organizing classroom schedules, consider accommodations for students with special needs. Some students have difficulty focusing on one subject or sitting in one place for long periods of time.

www.wiley.com/college/odonnell

Planning and Technology Advances in technology can benefit teachers looking for help in planning in several ways. As mentioned earlier in the chapter, there is abundant advice concerning planning on the Internet. There is a Web site for almost any area in which a teacher might develop a lesson. A general search on the Internet using key words such as *teachers' lesson plans* should produce a large number of Web sites. You will need to evaluate carefully the quality of lesson plans you find because, over time, some of these sites become obsolete. The Web site for this text includes a list of useful sites.

Approaches to Teaching

Over the course of their professional development, teachers build up a set of strategies and tactics that they employ in their day-to-day teaching. *Strategies* are broad approaches to teaching and learning. They may include an approach to introducing new or difficult material to children, how to review material before an assessment, or how to organize students into groups for cooperative learning activities. Broad strategies are typically embedded with a general approach to teaching, either a teacher-centered or a student-centered approach. In the sections that follow, we provide an overview of Ausubel's meaningful learning, discovery learning, and direct instruction. Direct instruction and Ausubel's meaningful learning approach are primarily teacher-centered approaches, whereas discovery learning is primarily a student-centered approach.

Chapter Reference
Chapter 10 provides an extensive discussion of student-centered approaches to teaching.

Promoting Meaningful Learning

Ausubel (1965) developed a theory of meaningful learning. Meaning occurs when a learner actively interprets experiences. Ausubel (1961) distinguished between rote and meaningful learning. Rote learning involves verbatim memorization. The information has little connection to what the learner already knows. In contrast, meaningful learning involves connecting new information to what the learner already knows and understands. Three conditions are necessary for meaningful learning: (a) the learner must approach the task at hand with a learning strategy appropriate for extracting meaning; (b) the task must be potentially meaningful to the learner; and (c) the relationship of what the learner knows and the new information must be clear. Ausubel also distinguished between **reception learning** and **discovery-based learning**. In reception learning, "the entire content of what is to be learned is presented to the learner in its final form" (Ausubel, 1961, p. 16). Reception learning is similar to **expository teaching** and requires deductive thinking on the part of the students. The teacher provides an *exposition* of how knowledge of a particular content is structured and organized. The students do not discover this structure for themselves. In discovery learning, learners must integrate information with existing information and reorganize cognitive structures. They *discover* principles by actively engaging in experiences that prompt their exploration of principles underlying these experiences.

reception learning   A type of learning in which the learner acquires the structure of knowledge set forth by the teacher.

discovery-based learning   Students work on their own to grasp a concept or understand a lesson.

expository teaching   A type of teaching in which the teacher provides an exposition of how a particular set of information is structured and organized.

advance organizer   A broad introductory statement of the information that will be presented in a lesson.

comparative organizer   A broad statement that reminds the student of what he or she already knows.

expository organizer   A broad statement of what is to be learned in a lesson.

The teacher begins an expository teaching lesson by introducing an **advance organizer**, which is information about the content to be taught that "serves to bridge the gap between what the learner already knows and what he needs to know before he can meaningfully learn the task at hand" (Ausubel et al., 1978, pp. 171–172). It helps students organize new information that is presented. Advance organizers can be either **comparative organizers** that remind students of what they already know or **expository organizers**. An expository organizer provides students with new knowledge.

An expository lesson involving reception learning begins with the presentation of a concept. The teacher presents a rule, then illustrates it with examples. For example, a high school social studies teacher may be teaching about the origins of war and may begin by presenting the conclusion to be drawn from the lesson: "Wars are caused by a complex set of interacting factors that include economic and social forces, including prior history." This statement is an expository organizer in that it provides the students with an overall statement of the intent of the lesson. One of the misconceptions related to expository teaching is that it is entirely teacher-centered. Clearly, the teacher plays a key role. However, an important aspect of the progress of a lesson is the presentation of examples by both students and teacher to illustrate the general principle under study. Students, for example, might activate prior knowledge of World War I by giving examples of how economic forces helped to cause the war. They might further illustrate some of the social forces that contributed, such as the animosity between various nations. In studying World War II, students will have a framework for encoding new information by relating it to material they already know. They will compare the similarities and differences between the causes of the two wars. The teacher helps the students to connect their examples back to the original advance organizer. Research on the use of advance organizers suggests that they are more effective for learners who lack prior knowledge (West & Fensham, 1976).

Discovery Learning

Discovery learning is characterized by **inductive reasoning**, or the abstraction of general principles from a variety of examples. It involves *bottom-up processing* in contrast to reception learning, which involves *top-down processing*. Students may, for example, attempt to categorize a set of rocks based on criteria they decide on. Their goal is to find the underlying structure of a body of knowledge that would allow them to categorize the rocks correctly on the basis of an underlying principle (e. g., density). Discovery learning often requires support so that it is actually **guided discovery**, in which the teacher provides some direction. In the previous example, the teacher may help students focus on key attributes by asking them to consider which rocks are heavier or bigger. In research on students learning to program in Logo using discovery learning methods, children were found to have difficulty learning even the fundamentals of Logo programming (Dalbey & Linn, 1985; Kurland & Pea, 1985; Mayer, 1988). Left to their own devices to uncover underlying principles related to programming, students are not very successful. There is little evidence that unguided discovery learning is the most effective instructional strategy for the majority of students (Mayer, 2004).

Direct Instruction

Direct instruction, or explicit teaching, is often linked to the work of Rosenshine (1979, 1987). Direct instruction is a systematic form of instruction that is used for mastery of basic skills and facts. Rosenshine (1988; Rosenshine & Stevens, 1986) described six teaching functions that were linked to findings about effective instruction. These functions provide an ordered set of activities in which a teacher can engage that are based on principles abstracted from research. In teaching a lesson, a teacher would do the following:

1. *Review the previous material.* Reviewing prior material allows the teacher to help students activate appropriate schemas for the task at hand. A schema is an organized set of knowledge about a topic. For example, one of the authors of this book asked a 12-year-old whether he had ever heard of Socrates. The boy answered, "Yes, he used to play for Brazil." For the author, Socrates was a philosopher who was the subject of a fine painting in an art gallery. For the child, Socrates was a soccer player. When the teacher reviews previous material, he or she helps ensure that the teacher and students have activated the same organized set of information. The students are thus ready for additional information. Reviewing previous material can also provide the teacher with an opportunity to detect any residual misunderstandings that students may have.

2. *Present new material.* The teacher links the new material explicitly to the material learned previously. He or she communicates goals for the new material and presents it in small segments, providing lots of examples. Many of the features of this kind of instruction are derived from Ausubel's approach to meaningful learning.

3. *Provide guided practice.* The teacher should check students' understanding by asking questions, providing examples that were solved and other problems for practice. The teacher needs to check for misconceptions and misunderstandings and provide additional practice as needed.

The teacher provides support for the students' inquiry as they engage in guided discovery. (PhotoDisc, Inc./Getty Images)

inductive reasoning The abstraction of a general principle from a variety of examples.

guided discovery Students work under the guidance of a capable partner to grasp a concept or understand a lesson.

direct instruction A systematic form of instruction that is used for mastery of basic skills and facts.

What Does This Mean to Me?
What difficulties might discovery learning pose? Would the age of the students matter?

A teacher can use direct instruction to help students master basic skills and facts.

(Bachmann/Photo Researchers, Inc.)

RIDE Consider the schedule you created in the opening exercise of the chapter. Would you change it depending on the type of approach to teaching you adopt? If so, how?

How Can I Use This?

Write an example of each kind of explanation. How are they different? How might these different explanations influence student learning?

4. *Provide feedback.* Provide students with information about the correctness of their efforts and provide corrective information to clarify students' understanding.

5. *Provide independent practice.* A key element in providing guidance as in step 3 is being able to withdraw it. The student needs an opportunity to practice the new skills alone to insure that he or she has mastered the skill. Independent practice can be provided through the use of groups, seatwork, and homework.

6. *Review weekly and monthly.* It is important to review the material in a distributed fashion. Distributed practice or practice at irregular intervals is more effective than massed practice or practice performed once, perhaps just before a test.

Direct instruction may be effective because it presents small amounts of information and provides sufficient practice to attain mastery of the targeted skill. It is also very predictable, which may help some students organize their own learning strategies to fit the task. Direct instruction, however, may not be appropriate for all kinds of tasks, particularly those that do not involve certainty in the outcomes. Many of the same kinds of criticisms that are leveled against behavioral learning theory are leveled against direct instruction. Alternative approaches to instruction are addressed in Chapter 10.

Teaching Tactics

Teachers employ a variety of strategies and tactics in pursuing their instructional goals. They adopt a general strategic approach to teaching and embed specific tactics within that more general approach. Tactics are short-term or local actions with specific purposes. They may include ways to bring students back on task after someone has said something funny or ways to keep the class productively engaged while the teacher works with an individual student.

Providing Explanations

A basic but often overlooked aspect of good instruction is the quality of the explanations teachers present to students (or that students present to themselves). Explanation has a firm scientific and philosophical basis (Hemple & Oppenheim, 1948; Ruben, 1990), but the explanations of teachers and students are of a different nature. Explanations lead students from a state of not understanding something or not being able to do something to a state of understanding or ability to perform. Leinhardt (1993) lists four types of explanations:

1. *Common explanations:* These describe how to do something, such as making a pie.

2. *Disciplinary explanations:* These are explanations from specific disciplines in science and are formal in structure.

3. *Self-explanations:* These are explanations that you might rehearse to yourself to make sure you understand something.

4. *Instructional explanations:* These are provided by teachers, texts, or other materials that are designed to teach.

What makes a good instructional explanation? Context is very important in explanations (Geelan, 2003). As we saw when considering teaching at the beginning of the chapter, instructional explanations involve a person or people receiving the explanation in order to understand something better. Thus, an explanation of why the earth revolves around the sun will be quite different if the intended audience consisted of second graders than it would be if the audience consisted of graduate students in astrophysics. In some respects, though, both explanations should probably share certain characteristics.

Often, a good explanation will call up for the learner some already existing knowledge or skill that is relevant to the present explanation. For example, an explanation in mathematics may make use of colored rods of varying lengths that the students recognize from previous instruction. In earth science, a teacher may start a discussion of molecular movement by asking what happens when someone opens the front door on a cold day.

The beginning of a good explanation is knowing where and how to begin. Leinhardt (1993) refers to the setting that a teacher uses to explain something as a *representation*. For example, the movement of cold and hot air is a representation of molecular movement. Colored rods represent amounts and how they can be combined or divided. A playground fight might be a representation of emotions and their control. Developing a good representation to use as the basis of an explanation requires an accurate sense of what the students already know and often some creativity as well.

Explanations also need to convey clearly what students must learn. Good explanations are presented in a logical fashion and are complete in that they bring the student to the desired knowledge or ability. That is, a good explanation does not get lost along the way to making the point.

Good explanations also take the student's point of view. That is, in developing a good explanation, the teacher needs to anticipate the learning problems that students might face and think of ways to overcome them. The use of high-quality examples and counterexamples is important here. Counterexamples are important in understanding the fundamental nature of a concept. As explained in the "Uncommon Sense" box on this page, counterexamples can be helpful if they are used with care.

Good explanations use analogies and metaphors, often taking them to their limits and beyond. As with good counterexamples, taking a metaphor beyond where it is useful can help students understand the boundaries of a concept. Good explanations check for understanding on a regular basis. Be thoughtful about how you make those checks. Which of the following, for example, is more likely to uncover difficulties?

- Does everyone have this so far?
- If you are with me on this, you should be able to . . .

Appendix
Promoting Learning
Good explanations by the teacher can help students to deepen their understanding of the subject matter (*PRAXIS*™, II. A. 2, *INTASC*, Principle 4).

Uncommon Sense

Counterexamples Should Be Avoided—Or Should They?

The use of examples and counterexamples can help students understand new concepts. When teaching students a new concept—be it symbiosis, estimation, foreshadowing, hegemony, false cognates, or chiaroscuro—it is helpful to indicate what is an example of the concept and what is not.

Consider the concept of metaphor. Which of the following are examples of metaphors and which are not?

- The mountain peak was a silvery pagoda.
- Henry was a steam engine of effort.
- My thoughts were like a kaleidoscope of anxieties and wishes.
- Melinda was the not the prettiest girl in the fourth grade, but she was the most interesting.
- The old woman's fingers were a jumble of twigs.
- Problem 4 is a good example of the utility of estimating answers in advance.

A student who can sort these six examples into three metaphors and three nonmetaphors probably has a good grasp of the concept. Presenting counterexamples helps students understand the boundaries of a concept.

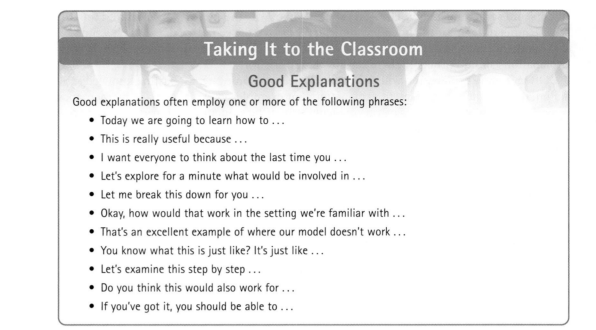

Taking It to the Classroom

Good Explanations

Good explanations often employ one or more of the following phrases:

- Today we are going to learn how to . . .
- This is really useful because . . .
- I want everyone to think about the last time you . . .
- Let's explore for a minute what would be involved in . . .
- Let me break this down for you . . .
- Okay, how would that work in the setting we're familiar with . . .
- That's an excellent example of where our model doesn't work . . .
- You know what this is just like? It's just like . . .
- Let's examine this step by step . . .
- Do you think this would also work for . . .
- If you've got it, you should be able to . . .

Chapter References
Behavioral principles of learning and the effects of reinforcement and punishment are described in Chapter 7. Chapter 4 describes the role of deliberate practice in the development of skill and talent.

Finally, good explanations are flexible. A good explainer needs to know when something is not working and how to change course. Sometimes it is necessary to say simply, "This isn't working. I'll get back to you tomorrow with a better approach." (See the "Taking It to the Classroom" box on this page.)

Providing Feedback

Feedback is a very important aspect of instruction that teachers can use to promote meaningful learning. Mayer (2003) distinguishes among three kinds of learning that feedback can enhance: (a) response learning, (b) concept learning, and (c) skill learning. *Response learning* involves tasks in which the learner provides a simple response to a stimulus. An example of response learning might be saying *cat* when shown a flashcard with the letters C_A_T on it. Feedback in this context provides reinforcement for correct responses. *Concept learning* involves learning a new rule for classification by generating the rule from various examples. An example might be deriving the classification rule "farm animal" when presented with pictures of a cow, a sheep, a pig, and a horse. Feedback in this context is information. *Skill learning* involves acquiring a new procedure, such as double-digit subtraction. Feedback in this context is progress or extent of improvement.

Both behavioral and cognitive theories can explain how feedback promotes learning (Mayer, 2003). Feedback is an important aspect of behavioral approaches to learning, because it represents the consequences of a particular behavior and serves either to reinforce or to punish behavior. Practice with feedback improves performance on response learning

Providing feedback to students is very important in promoting learning as it gives information to students about the quality of their work.
(PhotoDisc, Inc./Getty Images)

tasks (Thorndike, 1931). Deliberate practice, that is, practice sought by the learner (see Chapter 4), is an activity whose main purpose is to attain and improve one's skills (Ericsson, Krampe, & Tesch-Romer, 1993; Sosniak, 1985); it involves repetitive work on a single aspect of the task. The learner actively seeks information about the quality of performance so that subsequent performance can be enhanced.

If feedback served only to reinforce behavior, however, its quality would not go very far toward promoting learning. Research has shown that the quality of the feedback teachers provide in response to students' written work has an important effect on the kind of learning that occurs (Elawar & Corno, 1985; Newell, 1994). Feedback that provides students with information about why they are successful or unsuccessful is more useful for improving performance than feedback that simply provides them with information about results.

Asking Questions

Teachers ask a variety of questions in the course of instruction. Their purposes in asking questions may include focusing students' attention, providing rehearsal of information, stimulating conceptual change, or prompting students to elaborate on information. Teachers often engage in a simple participation approach, in which the teacher asks questions, selected students respond, and the teacher evaluates the responses. This sequence is characteristic of whole-class instruction.

Teachers can base questions on Bloom's taxonomy of cognitive objectives, described earlier (see Table 9.3), in which questions at the lower ends of the taxonomy, which require recall or demonstrations of comprehension, are less cognitively complex than questions that require evaluation. This framework provides a way for teachers to construct the questions they ask according to the cognitive complexity of the answers required. This is important to instruction because the quality of students' reasoning is clearly influenced by the level of the questions they are asked (Chinn, O'Donnell, & Jinks, 2000). In a study of children's reasoning about experiments, students engaged in more complex reasoning when asked to pick the *best* conclusion from among a set of conclusions from an experiment than did students who were simply asked to determine whether the conclusions were adequate (Chinn et al., 2000).

Rosenshine, Meister, and Chapman reviewed 26 intervention studies designed to teach students how to generate questions either before or after they read text. The review considered five procedural prompts that assisted students in asking questions: (a) signal words (e. g., *who, what, where*); (b) generic questions or generic question stems (e. g., *what is a new example of* _____?); (c) main idea; (d) question types that varied in complexity (e. g., the answer is found in a single sentence or requires background knowledge); and (e) story grammar categories (setting, main character). The authors concluded that teaching students how to generate questions resulted in significant gains in comprehension by the students. The most effective prompts were the use of signal words and generic questions and stems.

Chapter Reference
Chapter 12 provides a detailed discussion of how asking questions of varying complexity can promote students' construction of knowledge.

Promoting Learning Through Homework

Teachers' influence on learning extends beyond the classroom. Homework assignments can provide additional practice for or extend the work done in class. Homework is an important component of schooling, and the frequency of its use increases as children move through the school system and into the upper grades. It also represents a fairly large portion of students' lives, particularly in high school. In the 1999 National Assessment of Educational Progress study, students were asked how much time they spent doing homework on a typical night. The results are presented in Table 9.6.

The results show that although quite a few students are not assigned homework, and others do not do the homework they are assigned, most students, even at age 9, do homework on a regular basis. These results are supported by a study carried out at the University of Michigan (Hofferth & Sandberg, 1997). Here, students from ages 9 through 12 reported spending almost four hours a week on homework; whereas students aged 6–8 spent roughly two hours on average (this study did not include high school students). Although there have been numerous reports in the press claiming that children receive too much homework,

TABLE 9.6

Amount of Homework per Night Reported by Percentages of Students of Different Ages

	Age 9 (%)	Age 13 (%)	Age 17 (%)
None assigned	26	24	26
Did not do it	4	5	12
< 1 hour	53	37	26
1–2 hours	12	26	23
> 2 hours	5	8	12

Source: Adapted from U.S. Department of Education (2001). *National assessment of educational progress, 1984 and 1999 long-term trend assessment.* Washington, DC: National Center for Education Statistics.

Parents who provide support to their children when doing homework are more aware of what their children are doing in school. (Blair Seitz/Photo Researchers, Inc.)

Loveless (2003) argues that the amount of homework needs to be viewed within the context of the individual school and the children in that school. He cites a survey by the Public Agenda Foundation indicating that only 10% of parents believe that students get too much homework. Loveless concludes that for most children, the amount of homework does not seem excessive. Despite the data on the lack of excessive homework, some parents believe their children have to do too much homework. Some of the negative response from parents to homework is more related to the extensive extracurricular involvements of students (including work at the high school level) that makes homework difficult to complete than to the actual amount of homework per se. Particularly at the high school level, amount of homework is related to achievement.

Benefits of Homework

Homework can help students develop good study, organizational, and time management skills. The research literature on the effects of homework on achievement indicates that homework is associated with higher achievement at the middle and secondary school levels but not at the elementary school level (Cooper & Valentine, 2001). In fact, more homework often appears to be associated with lower achievement at the elementary school level. How could doing more academic work result in less achievement? Cooper and Valentine suggest several possibilities. For example, less able students may spend more time on the same assignments than do more able students, and elementary school teachers may assign homework to develop study skills rather than to enhance achievement directly.

Cooper and Valentine also identify a number of methodological problems in studying the effectiveness of homework, the biggest one of which is that it is difficult to conduct experiments involving homework. There are very few, if any, studies of homework in which students have been randomly assigned to groups receiving homework or not (or receiving different amounts of homework). Thus, it is hard to disentangle various effects that could influence the results. For example, teachers whose students are struggling with the material being taught may assign more homework. Because those students do not score as well on tests as more able students, it can appear that homework is having a negative effect. This is even more likely to be true at the district level. Many innovative educational practices do not appear to be effective because they are being attempted by low-achieving districts. This is like arguing that diet soda causes people to gain weight because one so often sees people with weight problems drinking diet soda.

Van Voorhis and Epstein (Van Voorhis, 2003; Epstein & Van Voorhis, 2001) have explored the different reasons that teachers assign homework and have developed an interactive program in which parents and students work on homework together. Their TIPS (Teachers Involve Parents in Schoolwork) program (Epstein, 2001) encourages students and parents to work together on learning activities in the home. Their research indicates that this approach increases student achievement.

A Taxonomy of Homework

Research on homework tends to treat all homework as similar, but this is clearly not the case. Teachers assign different types of homework, and these differences can affect student learning in important ways. LaConte (1981) uses a straightforward three-category scheme: practice, preparation, and extension. Epstein and Van Voorhis (2001) list ten categories of purposes for homework: practice, preparation, participation, personal development, parent-child relations, parent-teacher communications, peer interactions, policy, public relations, and punishment. LaConte's approach may be a bit too broad, although there is much to be said for its simplicity. Epstein and Van Voorhis's list is not only much more comprehensive, it also appears to include the underlying purposes of homework. The taxonomy of homework presented below builds on the work of these scholars and is an effort to clarify the options available to teachers. It groups homework according to its function—that is, according to what it is intended to do—and provides specific examples for each category.

Generally speaking, homework allows teachers to extend the instructional day. This time can be used to reinforce material presented in class, to allow students to prepare for the next day's instruction, or to enable students to extend their learning beyond what has been presented in class.

Three Types of Homework

I. Homework based on material taught in class

The purpose of this kind of homework is to reinforce what the teacher has taught. It may be used to make students' responses more automatic (Bloom, 1986).

A. Review

One of the common purposes of homework is to have students review material that has previously been presented. This is often done in preparation for a quiz or a test.

Examples

- Answer questions based on a chapter that has been taught.
- Make an outline of a chapter.
- Review class notes or copy them over and hand them in.

B. Practice

Practice is similar to review, but involves a particular skill or activity that can be applied in a variety of settings.

Examples

- Find the average of a set of numbers.
- Locate the countries of Europe on a map.
- Determine tenses of regular verbs in a foreign language.

C. Rehearsal

One usually associates rehearsal with musical or theatrical performances, but there are other forms of rehearsal as well. Whenever students go over set pieces of material, trying to gain precision and accuracy, they are engaging in rehearsal.

Examples

- Work on pronunciation in a foreign language.
- Rehearse a presentation to the class.
- Give one's address and phone number (kindergarten).

II. Homework based on new material

A second type of homework involves having students work on material that has not yet been presented in class.

A. Preparation

Homework used for this purpose requires students to prepare for an instructional unit in class. The students receive some background information and exposure to instructional content that can be built on during class time. Students may come to class with good questions about concepts they did not understand.

Examples

- Read a section of text material before class.
- Work on math problems that employ new processes.
- Read original materials before a discussion in a history class.

B. Experience

Teachers can also assign homework designed to give students experiences that the teacher can use as a basis for subsequent instruction.

Examples

- Interview the oldest living member of their family as a shared experience for discussing oral history.
- Take a survey of neighbors' preferences for one or another type of cola for a lesson on graph making.
- Generate a list of possible solutions to a problem often encountered by elderly people.

III. Homework that expands on and extends beyond classroom learning

There is usually less emphasis on right or wrong answers in this type of homework. Assessing the quality of the homework and providing constructive feedback will require a rubric, or scoring system.

A. Exploration

Homework involving exploration lets students look at new and different areas of a subject according to their interests and preferences.

Examples

- Pick a country from the continent being studied and make a travel brochure highlighting the special attractions of that country.
- Write a five-page *mini-biography* of a less-well-known figure from the American Revolution.
- Research an endangered species, laying out the nature of the threat to the species and what can be done to help save it.

B. Learning Experience

Learning experience is similar to exploration in that it is open-ended, but this type of homework is more directed or constrained and results in a similar experience for all the students.

Examples

- For kindergarten or first-grade students: Count various items in their home (how many clocks do they have, how many chairs, spoons, etc.).
- Chart the stories on the evening news by category (e.g. politics, economics, sports, celebrities).

C. Expression

Homework involving expression gives students an opportunity to be creative. When developing assignments of this type, it is important for teachers to think about what they are trying to accomplish. Tasks that are generative (that is, tasks in which the student has to generate new information) are more time-consuming and difficult than tasks that require rehearsal of previously learned information.

Examples

- Create a photo essay that emphasizes perspective and vanishing points.
- Demonstrate the use of geometry in designing a school playground.
- Write an editorial about a problem in the school.

Any of these types of homework assignments can be beneficial in a given setting. Even activities that seem like rote memory tasks can be worthwhile. For example, if facts such as the elements of the periodic table, need to be overlearned so that students can call them forth with little effort, homework involving practice will probably be beneficial.

Homework from the Primary to the Secondary Level: A Developmental Perspective

Teachers (and school districts) might do well to look at homework as a developmental process. In addition to being an important adjunct to classroom instruction, homework can also be thought of as the development of the ability to learn on one's own. At the primary level, homework is likely to consist of tasks designed to reinforce and practice material that

What Kids Say and Do

Developing Organizational Skills

Even academically talented young people can have problems with organization. The following is a conversation between an honors student and his father during the second week of the student's senior year.

Alex: Hey, Dad, I have a question for you.

Dad: Alright.

Alex: Okay, well, you know those little calendar-like appointment book things you told me to get?

Dad: Yep.

Alex: Well, I got one.

Dad: Super.

Alex: Okay, well I've got a question about it.

Dad: Yep.

Alex: Well, if I get a homework assignment on say, Thursday, and it's due, say, the next Tuesday, do I write that down on Thursday or Tuesday?

Dad: Well, is it more important to know when you got the assignment or when it's due?

Alex: Oh, good point. Thanks, Dad.

Dad: You bet.

has been presented in class and that will form the building blocks of learning. Primary school children need to know the alphabet, how words rhyme, their arithmetic facts, their phone number, and their address. Moreover, because their academic and cognitive skills are still very much in the formative stages, they would most likely not benefit from homework that extends over long periods of time or requires a great deal of organization and planning. Open-ended and longer term projects, carefully designed and monitored, can certainly be useful and engaging, but generally teachers choose directed-practice types of activities as homework for primary school students.

As students grow older and their skills develop and mature, the potential for longer term, more student-directed homework increases. Because many high school students will go to college after graduating, they need to know how to manage their time on both short- and long-term projects and need to develop strong, regular study habits. Teachers at the high school level might consider the needs these students will have at the college level and design homework assignments and practices that will help students acquire abilities and habits that will serve them well when they enter college. The story presented in the "What Kids Say and Do" box on this page illustrates how pervasive this need is.

Developing Homework Policies

Although students generally view homework as a series of tasks or assignments, teachers need to think of it not only in terms of how each individual assignment affects learning but also in terms of how the program of homework as a whole influences the instructional process in the classroom and the students' overall learning and development. To that end, it is necessary to develop a general homework policy. Homework policies naturally vary according to grade level and subject matter being taught. They usually, however, revolve around answers to common questions. Among the questions you might ask yourself in developing a homework policy are the following:

- How much homework will I assign each night?
- When and how should students hand it in?
- What will I do when students do not do homework?
- How will I respond when students hand in homework late?
- What kind of help can the student seek with the homework?
- What is the proper role of the parent with regard to homework?

Appendix
Extending Learning
You can support student learning by the effective use of homework. Homework can provide a way to connect the classroom and the family (*PRAXIS*™, II. B. 2, III B; *INTASC*, Principles 6, 4).

- What help can students expect from me?
- How will I evaluate the homework?
- How will homework affect grades?
- What should students do if they often have difficulty with homework?

The Web is a good place to look for homework policies that have been adopted by various school districts or individual teachers, as well as for specific ideas for assignments.

Getting Homework Done One of the most severe problems that beginning teachers encounter is getting students to do their homework. Fortunately, teachers can be proactive and use various tactics to increase rates of homework completion:

How Can I Use This?

When you had difficulty completing homework, what seemed to be the major problem? What helped you overcome that problem?

- **Purpose.** Homework should be done for a reason. Relate the type of homework assignment to instructional goals and communicate the purpose clearly to students.
- **Policy.** Establish clear expectations for students and communicate them to students at the beginning of the school year. Make sure that assignments reflect an understanding of students and show respect for them by taking into consideration the children's grade levels, abilities, and support in the home.
- **Design.** Occasionally it is worthwhile to ask, Would I want to do this homework? In creating homework, try to think about who your students are and what their interests are. In particular, if possible, tie homework into the personal lives of your students. This makes the homework more meaningful and interesting, and shows that you care about your students.
- **Support.** Think about what kinds of support are available to students. Remember that students receive different access to help at home. A good idea, particularly for younger or less able children, is to start the assignment in class so that you can help with any problems that might arise. (See the "Taking It to the Classroom" box on this page for an idea on using technology.)
- **Feedback.** Students need to receive feedback about their efforts. To be an effective motivator, feedback must be timely and accurate. "Good job" written quickly on the top of an assignment by a hurried teacher, when in fact the homework was not a *good job,* sends a very clear message: There's no need to work hard because the teacher isn't paying much attention. Feedback that comes two weeks after a student has turned in an assignment says that there are a lot of things more important than this homework. Careful, accurate, and timely responses to homework are essential to students' development and a hallmark of a caring and professional teacher.

Taking It to the Classroom

The Class Homework Site

Some teachers develop homeworkes sites for their classes. These sites post the homework and due dates, and some have extra credit possibilities as well. Sometimes, students take this task up on their own initiative. As part of an effort to help out his classmates, Oswell Smith, a student in the Mamaroneck Public Schools, developed a class homework Web site. Students can ask about what the homework assignment was, get help on difficult problems, and generally be supportive of one another's efforts.

Homework and Students with Disabilities

Students with disabilities must spend time on their schoolwork if they are to learn and develop (Leinhardt, Zigmond, & Cooley, 1981; O'Melia & Rosenberg, 1994), and teachers with classes that include students with disabilities need to consider how to address those students' special homework needs. Should teachers expect them to do the same homework that the other students do, or should they make accommodations for them, as is done in many assessment situations? Answers to these questions will depend on the purposes of the homework (see page 303). Accommodations may need to be made if the teacher's goals for the homework are to be accomplished by students with special needs.

Appendix
Accommodating Differences

You can assist students who have difficulties learning by your careful planning of homework (*PRAXIS*™, I. A. 1, I. B. 4, *INTASC,* Principles 1, 2, 3, 4).

Taking It to the Classroom

Homework Strategies for Students with Disabilities

- *Give clear and appropriate assignments:* Make sure that students know what you expect of them and that they can do the work that is being assigned. Have students begin their homework in class so that any problems that might arise can be cleared up.
- *Make homework accommodations:* Students with disabilities may benefit from fewer and shorter assignments and from additional help (such as a classmate to lend a hand or the use of a calculator where appropriate). They may also need more reminders to complete their work.
- *Ensure clear home/school communication:* Communicate directly with parents about how they can help their students with their homework. Let them know what you would like them to do.
- *Teach study skills:* Students with disabilities and their parents may need some assistance in developing good home-based study skills. The research literature indicates that families of disabled students are somewhat more likely to lack financial resources or not to have strong academic skills themselves (Bryan & Nelson, 1995; Deslandes et al., 1999).
- *Use a homework calendar:* As mentioned earlier, a homework calendar can be helpful for all students, particularly those who do not have strong organizational skills—as is often true of students with disabilities. A useful record-keeping (and reinforcing) practice is to maintain a monitoring chart where you record successfully completed homework assignments with a green marker, incomplete ones with a red marker, and partially complete ones with a yellow marker.

Bryan, Burstein, and Bryan (2001) present a list of promising approaches to working on homework with students with disabilities. One program utilizes homework planning calendars for students and graphs for teachers to record rates of homework completion. These devices were effective for students with disabilities, as well as for other students having problems completing homework (Bryan & Sullivan-Burstein, 1998). A follow-up study two years later found that many teachers were still using the planners and the graphing approach.

Another approach focuses on assisting parents to work on homework with their children. Bryan, Burstein, and Bryan (2001) summarized the results of three studies of the effectiveness of assisting parents of children with disabilities in ways to work with their children (Callahan, Rademacher, & Hildreth, 1998; Rosenberg, 1989; Sah & Borland, 1989; Vinograd-Bausell et al., 1986). They found that when parents utilized the methods they learned in the assistance programs and monitored their children's progress, the children's rates of homework completion and achievement increased.

Five homework strategies for working with students with disabilities are summarized in the "Taking It to the Classroom" box on this page (Warger, 2001).

Homework: Cultural and Socioeconomic Differences

Homework is an area of schooling in which cultural and economic differences among children may have a large impact (Ricciuti, 2004). Some students may not have private space in which to work, and they may not always have someone available for assistance. Other students may have their own computers, access to the Internet, and many other resources. Families may also vary in the degree to which they expect their children to complete homework without assistance; members of some families actively monitor the completion of homework, whereas others regard the task as the child's responsibility. Teachers need to take into account the potential impact of cultural as well as socioeconomic differences when developing homework policies and practices. Among the issues related to cultural diversity, socioeconomic differences, and homework are the following:

- *Economic difficulties* can affect the resources that are available in the home, such as computers, access to the Internet, and reading materials. They can also limit the amount of time a parent can spend with a child on homework. Single parenthood is often associated with economic differences because incomes in single-parent homes are often lower than in two-parent homes. Moreover, many minority single parents are younger mothers who may have had limited educational opportunities themselves.

Thus, their ability to help with homework may be limited. *Teachers need to consider the amount of help that might be available to students at home and adjust homework accordingly. Homework help Web sites, after-school tutoring programs, and in-class help to get homework started are three ways teachers can address this issue.*

- *Extended, blended, and other types of families* need to be considered as well. Some children in single-parent families see both parents regularly. Some children have grandparents or aunts and uncles who play a major role in their rearing. Still other children may have parents and stepparents and live in multiple households. This can play havoc with homework. For example, extended projects might be left at one house and needed at a different house; adults may view their responsibilities with regard to homework differently, and resources (e. g., computers) may be available in one location and not another. *When students appear to be having difficulty with homework, sensitivity to family issues may come into play. Teachers may need to work with some students more with their planning and organizational skills. A homework calendar or notebook may be especially helpful in some cases.*

- *Language differences* can hinder the communication from teacher to parent as well as limit the parents' ability to help on homework. *Finding someone who can help bridge a communication barrier can not only go a long way toward reducing homework problems but also lets parents know how concerned you are about their children's progress.*

- *Cultural differences* frequently go hand in hand with language differences. These differences can range from how parents view education and teachers to what kinds of activities traditionally occur in the home. Some cultures place more emphasis on group activities, whereas others emphasize individuality. *Sensitivity toward cultural differences accompanied with efforts to reach out to parents can go a long way here. Teachers may need to encourage some activities to be completed by the student alone and request that family members participate in other forms of homework.*

RIDE

REFLECTION FOR ACTION

The Event

You are a fifth-grade teacher, and you have been given a class schedule with specific recommendations about how much time to spend on various subjects. On the first day of class, you learn that physical education has been moved to 9 A.M. on three days of the week. You have to reorganize your schedule. How can you create a schedule that will maximize students' learning?

Reflection RIDE

What will happen if the children have physical education first thing in the morning on three days of the week? Will they be able to focus when they return to class? What should you teach first when they return? Should you try to keep subjects in the same time slots as much as possible or not worry about the times when you teach specific subjects? How can you spend the amounts of time you were asked to on the various subjects? What should you do?

What Theoretical/Conceptual Information Might Assist in Interpreting and Remedying This Situation? Consider the following.

Planning

How important are the details of a weekly schedule in terms of organizing your classroom? What goals do you have for the weekly schedule? When is going to be the best time of the day to work on the higher levels of Bloom's taxonomy?

Teachers' Self-Efficacy

How effectively do you think you will manage the class once they return from physical education? Do you think you will be able to sustain their interest during the rest of the school day without having the incentive of physical education available?

Homework

Perhaps you could use homework to enhance what you are doing in the classroom. It might be possible to do some interesting things in the middle of the day and allow students to practice skills at home.

Information Gathering R I D E

You might consult other teachers about how students respond after having physical education first thing in the morning. Are they able to focus? What do experienced teachers typically do right after physical education? You might want to record how much of your lessons you are able to get through when the students have a particular subject at the beginning, middle, or end of the day. Monitoring the frequency of behavior management issues or the kinds of activities that are successful over time may give you a better sense of what you might need to do in reorganizing your schedule. This option would require an action research project (discussed in Chapter 1) to determine what times work best for what instructional content.

Decision Making R I D E

You need to decide when you are going to teach which subjects. The decision you make will represent your instructional goals and sense of teaching self-efficacy for each subject. You also need to decide whether to use homework activities to supplement what you are doing in class and how you might do so. Make certain that you count the minutes allocated to each subject to be certain that they reflect your instructional priorities and those of the district.

Evaluation R I D E

Evaluation is a key factor in this situation. You will need to go back to your weekly schedule and reconsider it once you have one or two weeks' worth of experience. What is working well and what is not? Are students tired or overactive at certain points in the day? Take notes on what is happening in the classroom and review them with a colleague to get suggestions for possible alterations. Do not be afraid to make adjustments at the beginning or during natural breaks in the school year (such as vacations and ends of marking periods).

Further Practice: Your Turn

Here is a second event for consideration and reflection. In doing so, implement the processes of reflection, information gathering, decision making, and evaluation.

The Event

You are in your first year of teaching and things are going pretty well. Your colleague is also a new teacher but is having great difficulty. He has not planned well and does not have clear instructional goals. He also does not seem to have a strategic approach to teaching or specific tactics to teach the daily lessons. His students rarely complete homework. Your colleague has come to you for assistance.

R I D E What key elements of effective teaching and the process of teaching does your colleague seem to lack? How could you help him become a more effective teacher?

SUMMARY

- **Why are teachers' beliefs important?**

  Teachers' beliefs come from personal experience, experience with education, and experiences with formal knowledge. Beliefs shape expectation of what will happen, and we prepare to respond to events based on those expectations. Teachers act on their beliefs about what good teachers do and are probably the most important factor in determining the success or failure of a new approach to teaching. However, the beliefs teachers have about themselves and their students may not be accurate. Teacher educators see changing the beliefs of teachers as essential to educational reform. Classroom experience, particularly the student-teaching experience, has a powerful influence on beliefs about teaching, and once established, those beliefs are highly resistant to change. It is difficult to convince teachers to change their beliefs but programs that emphasize an experiential approach in which students have opportunities for reflective field experiences hold promise.

- **How do teachers' knowledge of subject matter understanding and general knowledge of teaching translate into ways to teach specific material to students?**

  The concept of pedagogical content knowledge developed by Shulman (1986) provides a basis for understanding that knowing the subject matter and knowing how to teach in general do not automatically translate into instructional practice in a given setting. It is important to know how to teach specific material to real students. What types of activities are necessary to bring children to the desired level of knowledge or expertise? The answers vary for each subject and grade level. Fortunately, help is available from subject matter specialists in methods courses during teacher preparation and from colleagues and the Internet once you are in the classroom.

- **How do expert teachers differ from novice teachers?**

  Expert and novice teachers differ along a variety of dimensions. Compared to novices, experts are better able to:

  - View the classroom as a collection of individuals.
  - Plan more globally and for longer periods.
  - Have a more complex view of instructional options.
  - Run a more smoothly operating classroom.
  - Evaluate student learning more often.
  - Attribute failure in a given lesson to problems with planning, organization, and execution.
  - Hold complex ideas about the role of students' existing knowledge and make use of it during instruction.

- **What are some general teacher-centered approaches to teaching?**

  Teacher-centered approaches to teaching include using Ausubel's approach to meaningful learning and direct instruction. These approaches are often contrasted with student-centered approaches, such as discovery learning. Aububel's theory focused on meaningful learning and involved connecting new information to what the learner already knows and understands. Three conditions are necessary for meaningful learning: (a) the learner must approach the task at hand with a learning strategy appropriate for extracting meaning; (b) the task must be potentially meaningful to the learner; and (c) the relationship of what the learner knows and the new information must be clear. Advanced organizers are used to make the connections clearer. Direct instruction is a systematic form of instruction that is used for mastery of basic skills and facts. Rosenshine described six teaching functions that were linked to findings about effective instruction. Direct instruction may be effective because it presents small amounts of information and provides sufficient practice to attain mastery of the targeted skill. It is also very predictable, which may help some students organize their own learning strategies to fit the task. Direct instruction, however, may not be appropriate for all kinds of tasks, particularly those that do not involve certainty in the outcomes.

● **What kinds of teaching tactics can teachers use?**

Teachers can provide high-quality explanations and feedback, and ask good questions. A good explanation requires the learner to use existing knowledge or skill that is relevant to the present explanation. A key element of a good explanation is knowing where and how to begin. Explanations also need to convey clearly what is to be learned. Good explanations take the student's point of view. High-quality examples and counterexamples are helpful. Feedback can promote learning by providing reinforcement or information. The quality of the feedback given to students influences the quality of their learning and performance. An explanation of why students are successful or unsuccessful on their assignments is essential if they are to improve their performance. The kinds of questions that a teacher asks influence the complexity of students' thinking and reasoning. Teachers can use Bloom's taxonomy of cognitive objectives as a guide in asking good questions.

● **How can teachers use homework effectively?**

Effective use of homework requires that teachers have clear instructional goals and explicit reasons for using homework that are related to these goals. Homework can be used to provide practice in skills taught during class or to extend or elaborate on the content of what was covered in class. Teachers must be aware of cultural differences among their students and may need to make accommodations for children who experience language difficulties or have special needs.

● **How can teachers plan to meet the needs of students who have special needs?**

Planning for students with special needs is an increasingly common requirement in regular education classrooms. Such planning should begin with a solid understanding of the student's IEP. Planning flows from the instructional goals and objectives one has established for the class; for students with an IEP, these goals are likely to be different from those for the rest of the class. Then the teacher has to take into consideration the nature of the challenges the student faces and combine that with the available resources. For beginning teachers, help is available from special education personnel in the building and the district, and advice can often be obtained from other teachers who have worked with a particular child. Parents are another source of information and help in developing a program of instruction for special needs children in regular classrooms. Teachers may need to modify homework assignments in order to meet the needs of students with special needs.

● **How can teachers develop the expertise necessary for working in culturally diverse settings?**

To teach well, teachers need to develop a sophisticated understanding of the diverse students they tach, as emphasized in Figure 9.3, that include the use of materials and activities that refer to a wide variety of ethnic groups. When creating instructional goals, they can plan to include examples from the experiences of different ethnic groups to explain subject matter, concepts, and skills. They may also communicate with parents about their expectations with respect to homework and parental participation or support for completing homework.

KEY TERMS

EXERCISES

1. *Pedagogical Content Knowledge*

   Paulsen (2001) says that pedagogical content knowledge is the nexus of knowledge of subject matter and knowledge about how to teach a particular group of students. Imagine that you are going to teach a unit on geography in a seventh-grade practicum experience. The unit focuses on the countries of the European Union and how they work together. As you look through the curricular materials, it seems to you that you have a good grasp of the content, but the material does not seem very exciting. Look back to Chapter 6, "Engaging Students in Learning," and think about how you might develop an instructional approach that would stimulate interest in the learning activity. If the example of the European Union is not a good one for you, think of another topic that might not be exciting for students and apply your pedagogical content knowledge to the development of a lesson plan.

2. *Differences Between Experts and Novices*

   Think of two of your high school teachers. Choose one who was a veteran teacher and excelled at the craft of teaching. For the second one, choose someone who was just starting out as a teacher. Now look at the summary of expert/novice differences in Table 9.2. Compare your two teachers on each of the categories. Which of the differences listed was most evident for the two teachers you are considering? Does it seem that there are one or two areas of dramatic difference, or was the veteran teacher better in almost all respects? Are there any areas in which the novice teacher was better than the experienced teacher? Which areas do you think might be particular strengths and weaknesses for you?

3. *Working in Culturally Different Contexts*

   How much experience do you have interacting with individuals who are different from you in race, ethnicity, or religious background, or in terms of special challenges? Have you spent time in settings in which you were in the minority with regard to any of these aspects? Make a list of significant and ongoing relationships you have with people whose cultural backgrounds are different from yours. What have you learned from these individuals (or settings) that you could apply to working with students who are different from you? Try to focus not just on particulars but also on broader issues of perspective taking, sensitivity, language, and assumptions that should be challenged. If your list is rather short, what can you do to gain broader experience in this area?

4. *Developing Lesson Plans*

   This exercise can be done with a classmate. Each of you should prepare a lesson for a particular curricular goal. Have the lesson plan involve two or three days' worth of classroom work. When you have each developed your lesson plan, answer the following questions:

   • How much time (total clock time) do you think it will take to complete this lesson?

   • What will be the most exciting aspect of this lesson from the perspective of the children?

- What aspect might be somewhat boring for the children?
- How effective do you think this lesson will be in achieving your instructional goals?
- How difficult will it be to carry out this plan?

When you have completed your lesson plans and your answers to the questions, exchange lesson plans with your classmate and answer the questions for his or her plan. Then meet with your classmate to compare your assessments.

5. *Teacher Beliefs and Learners with Special Needs*

   Imagine that you are teaching fifth grade in a self-contained classroom (i.e., you teach all the subject areas). You have a student, Martin, with a learning disability related to reading. Martin seems to be fairly capable academically, but he reads very slowly and often misses important points. His favorite subject is science, but your science program involves a great deal of reading, and Martin is frustrated. What can you do to modify your instruction to make science the exciting and engaging subject that Martin believes it to be? Try to think about this problem in terms of broad categories and resources rather than in the context of day-to-day activities.

On the bus ride home from the natural history museum, Ms. Bernoulli wondered about many things:

- How much noisier would her students have to be before the bus driver asked her again to calm them down?

- Would Martin become nauseated again, as he had on the way to the museum?

- Was there one child in the class who had a positive experience at the museum?

- Did the students learn anything from the trip?

- Why had she thought this trip was a good idea, and would she ever think so again?

- Would the mustard stain come out of her sweater?

(Media Bakery)

Ms. Bernoulli's first thoughts were about the specifics of the trip: Was the bus ride too long, was the museum a poor choice for these students (or for this grade level), and had she not done enough to prepare the students? At first she thought the students were to blame, and she was going to talk to them about it when they were safely back in the classroom. How could they be so well behaved in the classroom and so badly behaved in the museum? Then she turned to herself: Maybe this was actually her fault. Why did she fail to anticipate these problems? Why had she not been warned about how students usually behave in the museum? Why did the museum staff not provide more help? Ms. Bernoulli decided that this would be a good thing to think about over the weekend, after she took the sweater to the cleaners and made a mental note not to wear nice clothes on a field trip again.

Social Constructivism and Learning in Community

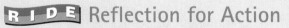

10

Reflection for Action

Ms. Bernoulli pushed herself to think about what the real issues and underlying problems on the field trip might be. What do you think they are? How can she uncover the underlying cause of the problems? What could she have done to improve the situation? What could the students have done?

Guiding Questions

- What is social learning theory?
- What is necessary for observational learning to occur?
- How is scaffolding used in instruction?
- What kinds of instruction are influenced by social constructivism and sociocultural theory?
- How can teachers use the resources of cultural institutions effectively?
- Can learners with special needs benefit from social-constructivist or sociocultural approaches to learning?
- How can teachers use scaffolding techniques to work with diverse learners?

CHAPTER OVERVIEW

This chapter focuses on social learning, social constructivism, and learning in the community. Almost all theories that emphasize the social context in which learning occurs pay attention to the individual's ability to learn from observation. Sociocultural theories of human learning stress the value of scaffolding the learner's efforts. This chapter provides examples of the instructional use of scaffolding, including technology, to support learning. Examples of instruction that are influenced by social-constructivist or sociocultural theories of learning are also described. A second key idea in sociocultural theories of learning is the role of the community in conveying expertise. The chapter describes how learning can go beyond the classroom and how teachers can take advantage of cultural institutions such as museums, art galleries, and parks. These informal learning environments provide an important opportunity to engage the family in the child's learning.

Social Learning, Social Constructivism, and Sociocultural Theory

The previous three chapters introduced behavioral and cognitive approaches to learning. This chapter extends that material. Social learning theory has its roots in behavioral learning theory; it describes how we learn from others, particularly by observing them and imitating their behavior. Social learning theory also includes cognitive elements, because we must encode, retain, and retrieve knowledge of the model's behavior in order to perform that behavior.

According to both social constructivism and sociocultural theory, learners construct knowledge in a social context. In Chapter 8, we introduced the idea that constructivism is not a single theory of learning but includes a number of theories, all of which view learners as active participants in constructing understanding. We distinguished among three kinds of constructivism: exogenous, endogenous, and dialectical (Moshman, 1982). Exogenous constructivism is similar to information processing in that the person creates a representation of what exists in the world. Students construct an understanding of what the teacher presents. Endogenous constructivism is similar to information processing as well as Piagetian constructivism, in which the individual constructs new knowledge from prior knowledge. Learners use prior knowledge to make sense of new information. The third kind of constructivism is dialectical constructivism. Knowledge is constructed as a result of the continual interaction between the individual and his or her social world and environment. This type of constructivism is best illustrated by Vygotsky's theory. The source of knowledge, from this perspective, is subjective experience in interaction with the environment. Social learning theory, social constructivism, and sociocultural theory are all concerned with how we learn from others.

Chapter Reference
An extensive discussion of Piaget and Vygotsky's theories can be found in Chapter 2.

Social Learning Theory

Social learning theory was developed by Albert Bandura. The original theory (Bandura, 1977) was considered a neobehavioral theory because it included concepts such as reinforcement and punishment. However, Bandura's theory added new cognitive elements, in which an observer engages in processes such as attention, encoding, and retrieval of a model's behavior. Chapter 7 illustrated how we learn through direct experience. Consequences follow appropriate and inappropriate behavior, and these consequences help the individual learn how to behave.

In addition to learning from direct experience, we learn through **vicarious experience**—that is, we substitute the experiences of others for our own direct experience. With vicarious experience, we watch what others do. *Vicarious* means that another person acts in our place. For instance, a young child stands on the playground staring at the dangerous-looking swing, not knowing what to do. An older child approaches, sits in the seat, and begins to swing. As the younger child watches, she begins to learn new ways to behave that had not occurred to her before, as well as the consequences of different types of behaviors. Just by watching, she sees how to sit in the seat, how to grip the rope, how to lean back and push off with her feet to get some speed, and to ask others for a push. Also, just by watching, she sees the consequences of all these behaviors. Thus, just by standing and watching, she learns how to swing.

vicarious experience Learning from the experience of another person.

The key characteristic of social learning is its efficiency. If the young child tried to learn how to swing on her own through trial and error, it would likely take her a long time to learn how to swing well. She might swing very poorly at first and possibly fall off. She might also become discouraged. Through social learning, however, she can quickly and reliably learn how to swing well. Think for a minute how fast and effective it can be to learn the following skills by watching others and how slow and cumbersome it can be to learn them through trial and error: how to tie one's shoes, how to operate a camera, how to dress, how to behave with good manners, how to use a computer, and how to converse with a police officer.

In Chapter 7, you saw how the reinforcements and punishments that follow our actions influence our subsequent behavior. Consequences that others experience can also influence our behavior.

Chapter Reference
A detailed description of the basic principles of behavioral learning theory can be found in Chapter 7.

When we observe someone being reinforced for particular behaviors, it may increase the chance that we will perform that behavior in the future. This is called **vicarious reinforcement**. For example, if a teacher smiles approvingly at a child who reports another child's misbehavior, other children are more likely to do the same in the future. If another person is punished for an action, we are less likely to perform the punished behavior. This is called **vicarious punishment**. If the teacher reprimands the child who reports another child for misbehavior, other children will be less likely to report others. Table 10.1 lists four examples of what students can learn vicariously. Teachers can take advantage of this kind of learning by directing students' attention to appropriate models.

vicarious reinforcement If another person is reinforced for a behavior, the likelihood of an observer engaging in that behavior is increased.

vicarious punishment If another person is punished for a behavior, the likelihood of an observer engaging in that behavior is decreased.

Modeling

The girl learning how to swing by watching another child is an example of learning by observing a model (another person) performing a behavior. There are three types of modeling effects: (a) observational learning, (b) inhibitory and disinhibitory effects, and (c) response facilitation (Baldwin & Baldwin, 1986).

Appendix
Learning from Others
Students can learn from others through observation learning, and vicarious experience (*PRAXIS*™, I. A. 1, *INTASC*, Principle 2).

TABLE 10.1
Four Things That Students Learn Through Vicarious Experience

1. New Behaviors

In art class, students initially may have difficulty with painting or sculpting. By watching others, they can imitate what expert painters and sculptors do. In social settings, students might have a hard time knowing how to make friends or how to be popular. By watching popular kids, they can imitate what those kids say and do.

2. New Consequences

Students who have never been on the honor roll can learn what the consequences of such an achievement are by watching what happens to students who make the honor roll. Students also typically learn the consequences of cheating by watching what happens to classmates who cheat. One student can learn how fun computers can be by watching a cooperative learning partner play computer games.

3. Performance Expectations

Students who have little experience on a task do not know what to expect when they are asked to engage in that task. By watching others, they can learn how hard or easy a course is, how likely success and failure are in some endeavor, or what emotions people typically feel during sports, dating, or a class presentation.

4. Self-Talk

By watching others who use optimistic self-statements, students can learn how to talk positively to themselves, learning self-talk such as "I am sure I can do this. I just have to keep trying different ways so I can figure it out." By watching others who use pessimistic self-statements, students can learn how to talk negatively to themselves, learning self-talk such as "I don't think I can do this. I've tried everything, and nothing seems to work."

observational learning Learning by observing other individuals.

Chapter Reference
Shaping and prompting are described more fully in Chapter 7.

Observational Learning **Observational learning** involves the learning of behavior. Observers gather information about a behavior and use it to direct their own actions. Young children learn a great deal through observation and imitation. Parents often model behaviors (e.g., brushing one's teeth) and guide their child in imitating the behavior. Behaviors of a model that are reinforced are more likely to be imitated. Observational learning thus involves both an acquisition stage and a performance stage. To acquire a behavior, a person must attend to the behavior and remember it. Performance involves reproducing the behavior. Continued practice improves the performance of the behavior. Additional shaping and prompting of the behavior may be necessary before it is performed well.

A number of factors influence the likelihood that a behavior will be acquired through observational learning (Baldwin & Baldwin, 1986). The observer must see the model's behavior as positive or useful. If the observer does not see consequences as reinforcing, he or she is unlikely to acquire the behavior. A model that has status or prestige is more likely to be imitated. A second influence on whether the observer will learn from a model is the degree to

A number of factors influence whether a model's behavior will be imitated. A model that has prestige or status such as this grandfather is likely to be imitated. (Corbis Digital Stock)

Taking It to the Classroom

Making Thinking Visible

Following are guidelines for promoting think-alouds so that thinking is visible and can be imitated:

- Tell students that their help is needed to learn more about something that is not well understood.
- Give them something concrete to talk about.
- Ask one student to tell another what he or she is thinking about while performing the task.
- Give plenty of practice at thinking aloud.
- Use probes or questions if a student becomes quiet.

which the model and the observer are similar. Children who experience high self-efficacy are more likely to learn from models (Linnenbrink & Pintrich, 2003). Children are also likely to select models that are similar to themselves. Third, an observer who is engaging in a task is more likely to learn from a model who is engaging in a similar task. Fourth, an observer who attends to a model's behavior closely is more likely to acquire that behavior.

Teachers can help students' observational learning by directing students' attention to what the model is doing and by reinforcing them for paying attention. The visibility of the modeled behavior and the ease with which it can be performed also affect whether the observer will learn the model's behavior. **Cognitive apprenticeships** take advantage of these factors by having the teacher model cognitive strategies and make his or her thinking *visible* (Collins, Brown, & Holum, 1991; Collins, Brown, & Newman, 1989). For example, a teacher may model his or her thinking processes by engaging in a *think-aloud*.

Hallenbeck (2002) presents a teacher who modeled the writing process for a group of learning-disabled students by choosing a topic the students were familiar with: a concession stand fundraising project in which all the students were involved. Students first learned how to brainstorm ideas. In a subsequent lesson, the teacher modeled the color-coding of his brainstormed ideas. Color-coding was the first step in organizing the paper. Using a felt-tipped marker, the teacher used the same color to mark ideas that seemed to belong together. His think-aloud enabled students to understand the process. In the following excerpt, the ideas in quotations were read directly from written work during brainstorming:

> I'm lookin' for things that have to do with the kinds of students involved (in the concessions stand fundraising project). Okay, "officers," I think I'll make that blue dot. That has to do with the students. Uh, "monster cookies, popcorn balls, puppy chow," no, "juice, fruit, popcorn." (Hallenbeck, 2002, p. 233)

The teacher modeled his thoughts about the items he read as he searched for content that had to do with students so he could color-code it in blue. (See the "Taking It to the Classroom" box on this page.)

Inhibitory and Disinhibitory Effects Sometimes the observer does not acquire new behaviors by observing a model. Instead, the chances that a previously acquired behavior will be performed are enhanced, or *disinhibited*. If a teacher tells a student that she will give her extra homework if she gets out of her seat again, then fails to do so, the likelihood that other children will get out of their seats will be increased. The restraint they had shown will be disinhibited because of the teacher's actions. Likewise, if the teacher follows through on her warning and assigns extra homework to the child, other children's willingness to get out of their seats will be *inhibited*. They are not acquiring new behaviors in this situation; instead, the likelihood of their performing a previously learned behavior is increased or decreased.

Response Facilitation Effects Sometimes a model's behavior can serve as a discriminative stimulus for the observer and thus facilitate the observer's response. In other words, the learner may perform a behavior that is already known. Observing others may simply facilitate the learner's performance of the behavior. If, for example, a number of people are looking up into

What Does This Mean to Me?
Think of a teacher you had whom you would like to imitate. What characteristics of the teacher made him or her a worthy model?

cognitive apprenticeship An instructional strategy in which the learner acquires knowledge by modeling the activities of the teacher and is coached by the teacher.

Uncommon Sense

Social Learning Always Has Positive Outcomes— Or Does It?

Friendships do not always have positive effects on social development. During adolescence, some friendships may actually be harmful (Hartup, 1983). Thomas Dishion and his colleagues examined how *deviancy* training predicted future problem behaviors (Dishion, McCord, & Poulin, 1999). *Deviancy training* was defined as positive reactions by peers to discussions about breaking rules or engaging in inappropriate behavior. When boys aged 13–14 experienced deviancy training, they were more likely to use addictive substances (Dishion et al., 1995), report increased delinquency (Dishion et al., 1996), and engage in more violent behavior (Dishion et al., 1997). Peers who participate in interventions designed to reduce problem behavior may in fact encourage such behavior (Dishion, et al., 1999) by providing support for deviant behavior. For example, if in a discussion of the inappropriateness of vandalism, a member of the group describes how his status increased among his peers, the other members of the group may end up seeking peer approval by engaging in the same kind of behavior.

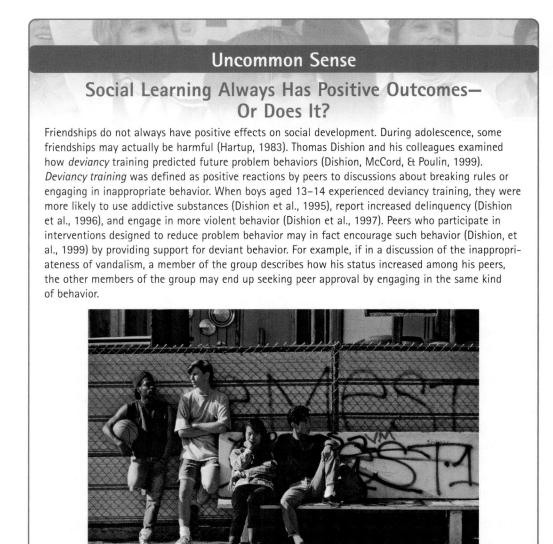

(Corbis Digital Stock)

the sky, the observer is likely to do so too. No new behaviors are acquired. In a classroom context, a student may laugh when other students do because he or she realizes from observing others that it is appropriate to do so. (See the "Uncommon Sense" box on this page.)

Conditions Necessary for Observational Learning

Students can observe without learning. Observational learning only occurs when the learner pays attention to a model's behavior, retains the behavior, can produce the behavior, and is motivated to do so (Bandura, 1986).

- **Attention.** The learner must attend to the important features of a model's behavior in order to learn from it. A teacher can help direct students' attention. For example, a student might be asked to show on the board how he solved a math problem. He might first draw a diagram of his understanding of the problem. The teacher can direct other students' attention to this aspect of his performance and point out how the diagram helped him keep track of important elements of the problem.

- **Retention.** The learner must retain the information that has been observed. A teacher can help students remember by teaching them strategies for retaining information. Examples of such strategies include mental rehearsal or creating acronyms to help in remembering specific steps.

- **Production.** The learner's efforts to imitate the model's behavior may be awkward at first. For example, if you watch a dancer you admire, your efforts to imitate the dancer's steps may be clumsy at first. However, with practice and feedback, your performance of the behavior will come closer and closer to that of the model.

- **Motivation.** A learner can observe a model, attend to specific features of the model's behavior, retain information about the behavior, and be able to produce the behavior. In addition, the learner must be motivated to perform the behavior. Before the learner will perform what has been learned, the learner must see the behavior as important or one that will lead to success or reinforcement.

Modeling and TV Viewing

Television can provide both positive and negative learning experiences. Parents and educators often express concern about whether children may learn to be aggressive or violent by watching television. They also expect that children will learn from instructional programs designed for them.

TV and Aggression The study of what children learn from television has focused primarily on the effects of watching violence on television. Interest in this topic goes back to a classic study conducted by Albert Bandura in 1965. Kindergarten children watched one of three films in which a child (the model) beat up an adult-sized toy called a "Bobo doll." In the first film, the model was rewarded with candy. In the second film, the model was criticized and spanked for the aggressive behavior. In the third film, nothing occurred in response to the model's behavior. After watching one of the films, each child was left alone in a room with some toys, including a Bobo doll, and researchers observed his or her behavior through a one-way mirror. A child who had seen a model being reinforced or not punished was more likely to beat up the Bobo doll—that is, to imitate the aggressive model. Boys were more aggressive than girls.

More recent research suggests that viewing violent television may have a number of negative outcomes. Viewers may engage in increased aggressive behavior, change their attitudes in favor of the use of aggression to solve problems, show decreased sensitivity to violence, and show increased tolerance for violence (Huston et al., 1992). Murray (2001) conducted a preliminary study of how the brain responds to violent and nonviolent imagery. He showed eight children between the ages of 8 and 13 a number of short segments of a violent or nonviolent film (Murray, 2001). The violent segments consisted of two 3-minute scenes of boxing from the movie *Rocky IV.* The nonviolent segments consisted of two 3-minute scenes from a nature program and from a children's literacy program. He found that areas of the brain involved in visual and auditory processing were activated when the children watched both kinds of films. However, watching violent film segments seemed to activate brain areas associated with arousal/attention, detection of threat, encoding and retrieval of episodic memories, and motor programming (Murray, 2001).

Watching violent television can have long-term effects. Huesemann and colleagues conducted a longitudinal study of the relationship between children's exposure to TV violence and their behavior in young adulthood (Huesemann et al., 2003). The participants were between 6 and 10 years old at the time of the initial data collection (1977–1978). In 1992–1995, additional data were collected about the same participants when they were between 20 and 22 years old. The results showed that children's viewing of violence on TV, their identification with same-sex violent TV characters, and their perceptions of the realism of the violence seen were significantly related to their level of aggression as adults. These results were true for both female and male participants and were the same regardless of how aggressive the participants had been as children.

Chapter Reference
The nature of aggression and strategies for promoting prosocial development are described in Chapter 3. Chapter 12 discusses learning from peers as an instructional strategy.

Instructional Benefits and TV Viewing Television viewing can have positive effects. Teachers can use students' television-viewing experiences to increase their understanding of audience. Television advertisements are clearly intended for different kinds of audiences, and the scheduling of particular programs also targets particular kinds of audiences. Stevens (2001) showed that middle school students could identify the intended audience for the television program *Southpark*. Teachers can also use students' television viewing to further

Chapter Reference
Chapter 6 introduced the concept of the dialectical relationship between student and context; see Figures 6.2 and 6.3.

Taking It to the Classroom

Social Learning Theory and Everyday Life

Consider the following everyday activities that involve acquiring skills and knowledge:

- Playing catch
- Riding a bicycle
- Playing chess
- Eating dinner
- Writing a story
- Doing a crossword puzzle
- Meeting people at a party

Which of these activities are learned from others? Which are learned more or less on one's own? Think about one of these activities that is by its nature a social event. Could it be done on one's own? If so, how would it change? Can you play chess by yourself? (You can on the Internet.) When children come to school, they are used to learning in and from social situations. Now think about some of the things that students learn in school. Do they lend themselves more to learning in social situations or to learning individually? How are they affected by modeling?

In thinking about how to develop lessons and activities for the classroom, it is useful to consider the nature of the task and how it might be influenced by social versus individual learning activities and by active modeling by an expert.

their understanding of genre. Various kinds of programs are shown on television (e.g., soap operas, reality shows, documentaries), and discussions of the differences among them can enhance students' understanding of genre (Williams, 2003).

Television can also be used to teach positive skills. Over 99% of homes in the United States have television sets (*Statistical Abstract*, 2000). Mielke (1994) noted that television can be used to address the literacy needs of children with inadequate educational opportunities. Linebarger and her colleagues compared the emergent literacy skills of young children in kindergarten and first grade who viewed 17 episodes of the television program *Between the Lions* with those of children in the same grades who did not (Linebarger et al., 2004). The program incorporates emergent literacy processes (Strickland & Rath, 2000). Teachers in this study were required not to provide additional instruction on the content of the program and asked not to refer to the program in any other instruction. The results of the study showed that the children who viewed the program showed better literacy skills (higher word recognition, standardized test scores, means on letter-sound and phonemic-awareness tasks) than those who did not. These findings did not extend to the children at greatest risk for reading failure. These children may have needed more support from their teachers to benefit from viewing the program. The "Taking It to the Classroom" box on this page provides some ideas about how social learning theory can be used in everyday life.

Social Constructivism and Sociocultural Theory

Social constructivism and sociocultural perspectives on learning include both social and cognitive components. Vygotsky's theory of cognitive development argues for a **dialectical relationship** between the individual and the social context in which the child develops. The individual acts on the social context and changes it, and is subsequently changed by the new social context.

Cognitive processes are modeled in the social world before the child can internalize them (Hogan & Tudge, 1999). Children interact with the adults in their world and gradually acquire the skills available in the community. Table 10.2 compares different constructivist approaches.

dialectical relationship　A relationship in which the participants have mutual influence on one another or in which the actor changes the environment in some way, and that changed environment subsequently changes the actor.

Social constructivist and sociocultural theories of human learning emphasize (a) social participation, (b) authentic tasks in which learning is embedded, and (c) tools to support learning. Both theories place special emphasis on social participation. Learners are social beings who develop competence through participation in valued activities from which meaning can be derived (Wenger, 1998). They integrate new knowledge with existing knowledge and actively interact with their environment. According to Vygotsky (1978), a developing child acquires the skills available in the community by participating in activities with adults. The cognitive skills modeled by skilled members of the community are imitated and eventually internalized.

The tasks in which learners engage are meaningful real-world tasks. In other words, they are **authentic**, and all participants have legitimate roles in performing them (Jonassen, Peck, & Wilson, 1999). For example, students might study the quality of the water in a local river. The Jasper Woodbury problem-solving series (Cognition and Technology Group at Vanderbilt, 1997) presents problems based on real-world situations. In one of Jasper's adventures, students

Chapter Reference
See Chapter 2 for an extensive discussion of Vygotsky's theory. Chapter 12 also includes information about Vygotsky's theory as it relates to learning from peers.

authentic tasks   Tasks that are connected to the real world.

TABLE 10.2

Comparison of the Major Characteristics of Constructivist Perspectives

Major characteristics	Piagetian perspective	Vygotskyan perspective	Social constructivist perspective	Holistic perspective
Goal	Develop logical thinking	Develop self-regulated attention, conceptual thinking, logical memory	Construct and reconstruct contexts, knowledge, and meanings through discourse communities	Student ownership of the learning process
Classroom focus	Spontaneous, student-directed experimentation	Interaction with subject matter concepts to develop advanced cognitive capabilities	Emergence of a community of participants that together re-create knowledge	Real-world communication tasks that build on children's strengths and interests
Role of the teacher	Create and organize challenging experiences; ask probing questions to facilitate learner rethinking	Model, explain, correct, and require the learner to explain	Create discourse communities	Generate and mediate tasks tailored to the needs of each learner in each learning situation
Role of the learner	Manipulate objects and ideas; experience cognitive conflict between one's ideas, experimental results, and teacher's questions; reorganize one's thinking	Interact with the teacher in instruction to develop conscious awareness of and mastery of one's thinking; learn to think in subject matter concepts	Participate in a system of practices that are themselves evolving; participate in the "co-construction" of knowledge	Interact with a variety of learning contexts to learn and communicate actively
Example	Some math and science curricula	Reciprocal teaching	Some elementary school and math classrooms	Whole language

Source: Green, S. K. & Gredler, M. E. (2002). A review and analysis of constructivism for school-based practice. *School Psychology Review, 31,* 53–70. Copyright 2002 by the National Association of School Psychologists, Bethesda, MD. Reprinted with permission of the publisher.

Learners can experience a sense of community and collective efficacy when working on authentic task with experienced members of a community such as this research scientist. (Lawrence Migdale/Photo Researchers, Inc.)

How Can I Use This?

With how will you know with what groups your students identify? In particular, consider how middle and high school students display a sense of collective identity.

collective efficacy   A jointly held belief that the community is effective when working together.

see a video about how architects try to solve a community problem such as designing safe places in which children can play. The video ends with a challenge to design a safe playground for the neighborhood. To solve such problems, students must bring a complex set of skills to the task.

Identification with a community or group is a key element of sociocultural approaches to learning. When individuals participate in a valued activity together, they may experience **collective efficacy**, a jointly held belief that they are effective when they are working together (Bandura, 2000). The processes of identification and the experience of collective efficacy are important motivators for learning.

Sociocultural theories suggest that the tools found in a society (e.g., library corners in classrooms rather than desks bolted together in rows) reflect how the society solves problems and thinks about certain issues (Lebeau, 1998). The artifacts or products created by a community suggest the strategies developed by its members to solve particular problems and support the thinking and activities of its members. For example, most people in the United States know what a dishwasher is. It is a machine in which dishes can be placed after use. When operated, it cleans the dishes. The average American home may have a dishwasher. In such homes, the sink unit consists of a stainless steel basin with faucets embedded in a countertop. In countries where having a dishwasher is the exception rather than the rule, kitchen sinks include the standard basin and faucets but are also designed with a built-in draining board on one side of the basin. It is expected that dishes will be washed by hand and left to dry. The kitchen sink unit includes not only the sink but also a stainless steel draining board with indentations to allow water to drain back into the sink. In contrast, one might never see such a sink unit in an American home because it is expected that a dishwasher may be available. The construction of these sink units reflects how the cultural practices of a community influence the design of objects produced in that community. These, in turn, affect how activities are carried out in that community.

Chapter Reference
See Chapter 2 for a discussion of language as a cultural tool that supports cognitive development.

Development is assisted through the use of tools or artifacts generated by the culture. In Chapter 2, you read that the primary tool by which meaning is communicated among members of a community is language.

Tools such as computers, video cameras, calculators, and mobile phones embody the expertise of their designers and the values of the culture in which they are used. Cognitive activity is distributed, or shared, between the individuals and the tools they use. The tools provide **affordances** or support for particular kinds of cognitive activity. They allow members of the community to act in ways that would not be possible without the tool. For example, a student who uses a calculator does not need to use working memory to engage in mental computations. The student thus frees up cognitive resources that can be devoted to other aspects of the task.

affordance   A property of a tool or artifact that allows a person to act in particular ways that would not be possible without using the tool.

Consider how people's communications and activities have changed as a result of the continued development of the telephone. Early telephone systems had *party lines.* Numerous members of a community had access to the same phone line. These systems made possible not only the intended behaviors of communication but also unintended behaviors, such as eavesdropping on other people's conversations. Telephone booths were originally designed to enable two people to hold a private telephone conversation. This was particularly true in England and other countries, where telephone booths were enclosed boxes in which the person making a phone call could close the door and thus maintain privacy. The advent of cell phones has greatly changed the nature of communications. People can make phone calls whenever they wish and from almost any location. Their phones are not simply devices to allow one person to talk to another but may also include text-messaging systems, access to the Internet, music players, video cameras, and other functions. The cell phone no longer affords privacy as a necessary property of the communication between people as the phone booth once did. In sum, the tools or artifacts produced by a community support certain kinds of thinking and make it possible for its members to engage in activities in which they might otherwise be unable to participate.

> **How Can I Use This?**
>
> Walk into a K–12 classroom and identify the numerous cultural tools in that room, such as the blackboard and wallcharts.

Tools can also serve an important role in communications between the more competent and less competent members of a group. Learners can share knowledge and develop joint understanding more easily if there are visible, tangible objects that can serve as points of reference in solving problems or be used to assist communication. For example, if students in a high school chemistry lab can point to the effects of a chemical reaction, they have a shared representation of what occurred that will permit them to discuss their understanding of what happened.

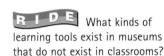 What kinds of learning tools exist in museums that do not exist in classrooms?

In distributed systems, responsibility for a task is shared among participating individuals. The focus is on participants engaging in an activity, and the performance of the group as a whole can exceed that of each individual. Such a system is not simply a division of labor among members but a collaborative activity in which knowledge and expertise are shared: "Cognition in such instances is understood as jointly undertaken by individuals interacting with one another and with surrounding physical, social, and intellectual resources" (Lebeau, 1998, p. 3). The tools available to the group may scaffold its members' performance and support their activity. For example, a group's use of presentation software can help individual students offer new ideas that add to the collective slideshow prepared by the group for presentation to the class.

> **What Does This Mean to Me?**
>
> Can you think of an example of working in a group in which you felt that cognition was distributed?

Examples of instructional forms that are influenced by sociocultural approaches to learning include the computer-supported intentional learning environment (CSILE; Scardamalia, Bereiter, & Lamon, 1994) and communities of learners (Brown & Campione, 1994). (See the "What Kids Say and Do" box on this page.)

What Kids Say and Do

The Benefits of Technology?

This exchange took place between a tutor and a student practicing for the SATs.

Tutor:	So what would you do now?
Student:	Well, we've set this up as a series of simultaneous equations.
Tutor:	That's right.
Student:	And I think the equations are properly laid out.
Tutor:	If so, what would you do next?
Student:	We have to subtract the second equation from the first. This simplifies the problem to—let's see—6 times 8!
Tutor:	And that is....
Student:	Where's my calculator?

Appendix

Prior Experience

Students' prior experience and knowledge vary and influence their learning (*PRAXIS™*, I. B.6, *INTASC*, Principles 1, 2, 3).

The Role of Experience

In Chapter 8, you learned about the role of prior knowledge and experience in cognition. The experiences that children have in their community make an important contribution to their cognitive development (Saxe, 1988). Their activities may help them develop complex understandings. For example, in a study of child street vendors in Brazil, Saxe (1988) found that unschooled child street vendors had developed usable strategies for solving arithmetic and ratio problems involving large numbers. A comparison group of nonvendors had not developed such strategies. The practical experiences of the child vendors had helped them develop strategies for carrying out their daily work.

Similarly, Jurdak, and Shahin (1999) found that child vendors in Lebanon were more effective in using logical mathematical skills in solving problems with transactions or word problems than they were when solving computation problems. Sociocultural theories of learning recognize the crucial role of the cultural practices to which children are exposed in their cognitive and social development.

Instruction is likely to be most effective when it takes account of students' previous experiences and interests. The Algebra Project (2005) is an example of an instructional project that is embedded in students' experience (Moses, 1994). The target students for the Algebra Project are students in underserved rural and inner-city areas, primarily African American and Latino communities. The goal of the project is to help students gain the mathematical skills necessary for college preparatory math classes. The Algebra Project helps students develop mathematical understanding through a process that begins with familiar concrete experiences (e.g., taking a ride on the subway) and moves from there to more abstract mathematics (e.g., the concept of displacements). One of the curricular units developed by the Algebra Project is the African Drums and Ratios Curriculum (Algebra Project, 2005). It is based on the examination of rhythmic concepts and cultural features of African drum traditions. Students learn ideas about pulse, harmonic rhythm, and other rhythmic concepts, which are then used to help them understand such concepts as ratio and proportion, fractions, measurement, and equivalence. Students make their own drums and create percussion compositions. They learn to recognize drum patterns and relationships and represent them in mathematical terms. The curriculum has high interest value for students.

Chapter Reference
The role of interest in motivating students is discussed in Chapter 6.

Efforts have also been made to engage students in learning by situating learning activities within their cultural experience. Eglash (1999) has described the presence of concepts of fractal geometry in many facets of African culture. He has been working with African-American math teachers to find ways to increase minority students' interest in math. In one example of a culturally situated instructional activity, Eglash (2005) describes how African cornrows or braids illustrate four geometric concepts: translation, rotation, reflection, and dilation. Figure 10.1 shows how students might use cornrow braiding to learn fractal geometry.

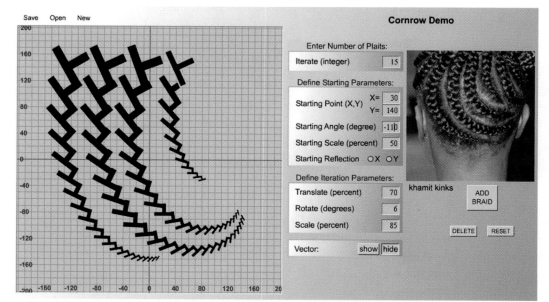

Figure 10.1. Learning Fractal Geometry Using Cornrow Braiding

Source: Eglash, R. Retrieved May 15, 2005, from http://www.ccd.rpi.edu/Eglash/csdt/pr/photos.html. Copyright Ron Eglash. Reproduced with permission.

This and similar instructional approaches try to take advantage of the fact that students are likely to be more motivated when the content of instruction is personally relevant and meaningful to them.

Scaffolding

In Chapter 2, you learned that sociocognitive development occurs at two levels. The first level is face-to-face interaction between less competent and more competent members of a group. The second way is through the culture's history and technology. The more competent member scaffolds the learning of the less competent member. The learner and guide jointly create a zone of proximal development in which the learner is able to perform at a level that he or she could not achieve without assistance. For example, a parent may steady a child's hand as she practices cursive writing, or an older sibling may steady a bicycle as a child learns to ride it.

Scaffolding is more than simply providing help. Wood and his colleagues described scaffolding as "a process that enables a child or novice to solve a problem, carry out a task, or achieve a goal which may be beyond his unassisted efforts" (Wood, Bruner, & Ross, 1976, p. 90). An important aspect of scaffolding is the eventual fading of the support so that the child can perform the task on his or her own. "Once the learner has a grasp of the target skill, the master reduces (or fades) his participation, providing only limited hints, refinements, and feedback to the learner, who practices successively approximating smooth execution of the whole skill" (Brown & Palinscar, 1989, p. 456). A child who is learning to ride a bicycle often begins with the aid of training wheels that provide balance. The child may be further supported by an adult who steadies the bicycle. As the child develops the skills needed to ride the bicycle, the supports are gradually removed. The adult may allow the child to depend solely on the training wheels; eventually these are taken off, and the child rides without support.

The guide who provides scaffolding does so by engaging in three activities: channeling, focusing, and modeling (Pea, 2004). **Channeling** (of the learner's activity) and focusing (of

Chapter Reference
See Chapter 2 for a description of scaffolding. Chapter 12 also provides a description of how scaffolding can be used in the context of learning from peers.

channeling   Providing constraints during the task so that the learner has an increased likelihood of acting effectively.

Scaffolding is more than help. It involves helping a learner perform a task with assistance that the learner could not do alone. (David R. Frazier/Photo Researchers, Inc.)

How Can I Use This?

Examine the sample dialogue between the teacher and the student in Chapter 2. Can you find examples of channeling, focusing, and modeling?

the learner's attention) involve providing constraints during the task so that the learner is more likely to perform it effectively. An example of software designed to channel and focus student learning is *WorldWatcher* (Edelson, Gordon, & Pea, 1999), a tool for displaying and analyzing gridded geographic data in the form of color maps. Students are given access to sets of climate data that are relevant and manageable in size. However, these data sets are constrained in that they are simpler than the complete data would be. The guide focuses the learner's attention by identifying important features of the task. This helps maintain the learner's progress toward completing the task. The guide also models some of the steps involved in completing the task. Earlier in the chapter, we discussed how students can learn from models. The guide who provides scaffolding to a learner takes advantage of this ability by modeling aspects of the task.

Two major steps are involved in scaffolding (Lipscomb, Swanson, & West, 2004): Instructional plans must be developed to lead students from what they already know to a deep understanding of new material, and the plans must be carried out, with the teacher providing support at each step. Applebee and Langer (1983) identified the following five features of appropriate instructional scaffolding.

RIDE In the account at the beginning of the chapter, how could Ms. Bernoulli have used scaffolding to improve the trip the class took to the museum?

1. *Intentionality.* Each instructional activity should help the learner accomplish the task.

2. *Appropriateness.* The task is difficult enough so that the learner needs help.

3. *Structure:* The teacher models strategies and asks questions that are examples of appropriate ways to approach the task.

4. *Collaboration.* The teacher is the learner's partner, not his or her judge. The teacher needs to welcome the learner's efforts and redirect the learner when necessary.

5. *Internalization.* The teacher's support is gradually withdrawn, and the learner can perform the task alone.

The concept of scaffolding is central to Vygotsky's theory and important for classroom teachers. It will be helpful to identify specific acts of instruction that constitute scaffolding. Carefully consider the 18 scaffolding acts listed below under the headings of *planning*—structuring the learning situation for the student and modeling expert skills; *coaching*—social guidance, instruction, and collaboration; and *fading*—the transfer of responsibility for problem solving from the teacher to the ever-more-proficient student (from Wood, Bruner, & Ross, 1976; Rogoff, 1990).

Planning

- Choosing activities—the teacher decides which skills are to be encouraged, such as reading books and writing letters.

- Planning and structuring—setting up the learning situation.

- Selecting task difficulty—modifying or simplifying a complex task to adjust it to the student's current level of readiness and skill.

- Defining the learning goal—"We're going to learn square roots today."

- Scripting task involvement—identifying the sequence of steps required for carrying out the task.

- Modeling the activity for the novice.

Coaching

- Offering tips, hints, pointers, and assistance.

- Suggesting task strategies of which the student is unaware.

- Helping the student maintain pursuit of the goal by calming frustration and supporting interest and effort.

- Offering reminders, prompts—"What happens next?"

- Asking well-timed questions and making well-timed suggestions.
- Explaining why a certain procedure will work best.
- Showing nonverbal cues indicating proficiency and improvement—glances, smiles, and the like.

Fading

- Monitoring the student's need for assistance.
- Decreasing the explicitness of instruction.
- Transferring the center of decision making from the teacher to the collaborative pair, then to the student.
- Pausing more and talking less.
- Listening and answering questions, rather than instructing and directing.

An Instructional Example of Scaffolding Scaffolding can be carried out in a variety of ways. Pea (2004) noted that the term *scaffolding* is used very broadly to describe various kinds of support or help in a learning situation. In its most formal sense, the term refers to a process that includes deliberate fading of teacher support after some time. Informal uses of the concept of scaffolding involve assisting the student's current performance.

Figure 10.2 presents an example of instructional scaffolding. An additional example of scaffolding is the use of procedural facilitation (Scardamalia, Bereiter, & Steinbach (1984) in writing instruction. **Procedural facilitation** is a structured approach to improving students' use of elements of the writing process. The goal is to help students move from knowledge telling to knowledge transformation. In one study, students were given cue cards that contained procedural prompts for each task goal. They were also given specific prompts in the form of starter sentences to help them think about their writing. For example, a cue card might list a task goal as "improving an idea," and the students might be given a specific prompt about how to do this—for example, "I can make my point clearer by. . ." The performance of sixth-grade students who used planning cues and think-aloud modeling strategies was compared to that of a comparison group of sixth graders who used more typical methods of generating ideas and producing text (Scardamalia et al., 1984). Students in the experimental group produced high-quality written compositions and were more reflective than students in the control group.

Scaffolding with Technology

Students need a great deal of assistance in learning how to give appropriate help to peers (Webb & Farivar, 1994). Efforts have been made to scaffold complex cognitive activities by providing support in computer-based environments (Guzdial, 1994). Technology-supported scaffolds can provide task structure or automate aspects of the task (de Jong et al., 1999). They can also be used to reduce the cognitive load involved in the task (Sweller & Chandler, 1994).

Web-Based Inquiry Science Environment Inquiry-based, computer-supported science environments help students learn while doing. Students conduct investigations, interpret the results, and communicate them to others (Reiser et al, 2001; Linn et al., 1994). An inquiry-based environment allows students to engage in scientific processes that are similar to those in which scientists engage, as well as to develop a deep understanding of the nature of science (Tzou et al., 2002).

The Web-based Inquiry Science Environment (WISE) is an online science-learning environment for use by students in grades 4–12 as they learn about and respond to scientific controversies. Software is provided to help students navigate through Web pages that contain content, notes, and hints. Together, these features of the WISE environment guide students as they reflect on the content. An example of a WISE project involves cycles of malaria. Students learn about the nature of the disease, where it is found, and how it is spread. They compare a number of strategies for controlling the spread of malaria. Supports are provided

---

How Can I Use This?

Tutor a novice in a task with which you are very competent. In doing so, use the scaffolding method of planning—coaching—fading. Is this the best way to teach another person a skill?

procedural facilitation A structured approach to improving students' use of elements of the writing process.

Chapter Reference

An additional example of how cue cards can be used to scaffold students' thinking can be found in the description of guided reciprocal questioning in Chapter 12.

Chapter Reference

The limitations of working memory and the potential effects of excessive cognitive load are described in Chapter 8.

MEMORY SNAPSHOT LESSON

Prewriting

Sharing Pictures
- Ask the students to bring a picture to school that they would like to write about. The photograph could be of themselves, a family member, a special pet, an important event, a trip, or anything they have a special memory of.
- In small groups or with the whole class, have students share their photos and discuss why they chose them.

Snapshots and Thoughtshots
- Discuss the concept of snapshots and thoughtshots in writing. Explain that when the students write about their actual photograph, they will be creating a written picture, which can convey the writer's thoughts and feelings. "Writers have a magic camera that they can point at the world and create snapshots that contain smells and sounds as well as colors and light." Bary Lane. *After the End: Teaching and Learning Creative Revision.*

Modeling by the Teacher: Cluster and Open Mind
- Share a photograph that you as a teacher plan to write about. In front of the class, start a cluster in which you generate descriptive language to capture your photograph in words. Then draw an Open Mind in which you draw and record your thoughts and feelings about the memory depicted in the photograph. (An Open Mind is simply a blackline drawing of the outline of a head. Inside the head, use words, pictures, or symbols, and colors to illustrate actions and feelings.)

Prompt
- Provide students with the prompt. Read it out aloud and discuss any questions the students have.

Your task will be to create a written mental snapshot that captures your photograph in words and creates a you-are-there feeling in the reader. Use the "magic camera" of your pen to zoom in on your subject and create rich sensory details (sight, sound, smell, taste, touch, and movement). Remember that you can make your snapshot a "moving picture" by adding action and dialogue. Also, give the reader more panoramic views of thoughts, feelings, and big ideas to create a frame for your specific details.

You will be writing an autobiographical incident about your memory snapshot. An autobiographical incident focuses on a specific time period and a particular event that directly involves you. Your goal is not to tell about your event but to show what happened by dramatizing the event. You may write in the present tense, as though your event were happening now, or in the past tense, to describe your incident as a recollection.

Your memory snapshot paper will have a setting that leaves the reader with a dominant visual impression, a plot or story line, and characters. However, the nature of your memory may cause you to place your emphasis on one of the elements over the others. Throughout your paper, and particularly in your conclusion, you should show (and not tell) the reader why this memory is so significant for you.

Precomposing

- Draw your mental snapshot. Tell the students: "The memory you have in your mind may not be identical to the actual snapshot. Draw the picture of the snapshot in your mind. It may include a number of significant details that are not in your actual photograph. After completing your drawing, write at the bottom of the drawing: *This snapshot memory is significant to me because_____.* Be sure you show the significance of this memory in your writing through the use of your snapshots and thoughtshots."
- Have the students discuss their drawing and the significance of the memory with a partner, then talk about how they might begin their essay, what portion of the memory might be an effective "hook" for the reader.

Modeling

- Before students write, read a model of a memory snapshot piece. have them identify what makes the writing effective. These criteria might become the scoring guide or rubric.

Writing

- Give students ample time to write.

Sharing

- Give the students a memory snapshot response sheet to fill out in pairs or groups of three.
    - The most memorable part of your memory snapshot essay was . . .
    - The words or phrases that were especially vivid and created mental pictures for me were . . . because . . .
    - You made me feel like I was there when . . .
    - One thing I learned about you is . . .

Revising

- Have students revise with an eye toward enhancing snapshots, adding thoughtshots, or showing the significance of the memory.

Editing

- Have students edit for the conventions of English.

Evaluation

- A possible scoring rubric on a 6-point scale might be:
    - Uses rich, sensory/descriptive language (snapshots) to help the reader "picture" the snapshot memory
    - Adds action words and/or dialogue to make the snapshot a "moving picture"
    - Uses thoughtshots to show the characters' thoughts and feelings
    - Clearly demonstrates why the snapshot memory is significant
    - Follows the conventions of written English

Figure 10.2. Scaffolding a Writing Lesson

Source: Curriculum Futures: Preferred Practices. Copyright © 2000. Seventh-Day Adventist North American Division Office of Education. Retrieved May 15, 2005, from http://www.curriculumfutures.org/instruction/a06-06.html. Reproduced with permission.

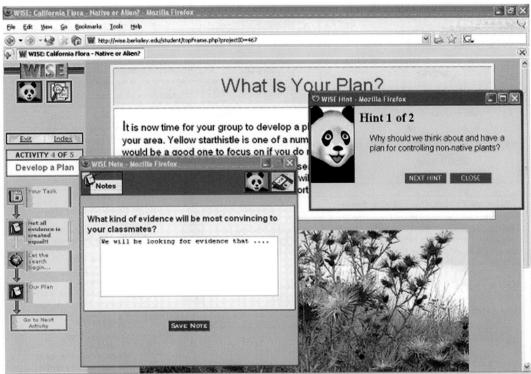

Figure 10.3. A WISE Project Page, with Inquiry Map, a Note, and a Hint

Source: Figure 4.2 in O'Donnell, A., Hmelo-Silver, C, & Erkens, G. (2005) *Collaborative learning, reasoning, and technology.* Mahwah, NJ: Lawrence Erlbaum. Reproduced with permission.

in the form of hints and tools for visualizing data. An example of a WISE environment can be seen in Figure 10.3.

The goals of WISE are to make science accessible by using topics and models that students understand; to make thinking visible by using visualizations and representations; to help students learn from each other by using collaborative tools, online discussions, and group projects; and to promote autonomy with reflection, critique, argument comparison, and design activities. These features focus on authentic tasks, collaborative activity, and meaning.

Biology-Guided Inquiry Learning Environment BGuILE, the biology-guided inquiry learning environment, involves investigations in which students build empirically support-ed explanations from a computer-simulated data set. Scaffolding is provided by features of the environment that offer guidance about what actions to take, the order in which they are to be done, and the required aspects of work products, such as explanations (Reiser, 2002). The BGuILE software serves as the context for investigation, providing access to the primary data and tools for analyzing and explaining them. In addition, informal and structured dis-cussions are interspersed throughout the activities to provide opportunities for reflection and for sharing and critiquing ideas (Reiser, 2002). For example, *The Struggle for Survival,* one of the BGuILE learning environments, helps middle school students learn about the ecosystem and natural selection by investigating a crisis in the Galapagos Islands. The stu-dents' task is to explore what is killing many of the animals on the islands and whether there is a pattern that explains how some of the animals have managed to survive the crisis. The problem gives students a chance to apply and extend their knowledge about species interac-tions, relationships between structure and function, and natural selection (Reiser, 2002). Figures 10.4 and 10.5 present examples of what students see as they work with BGuILE. Figure 10.4 shows the ExplanationConstructor, a computer-based science journal that stu-dents use to construct scientific explanations. As students work on an investigation, they record their primary research questions and other questions as they emerge. They construct explanations and link them to the research questions and evidence that might be used to support the explanations. Figure 10.5 illustrates the artifacts created in the Animal Landlord software (Smith & Reiser, 1998). Using this software, students study examples of animal

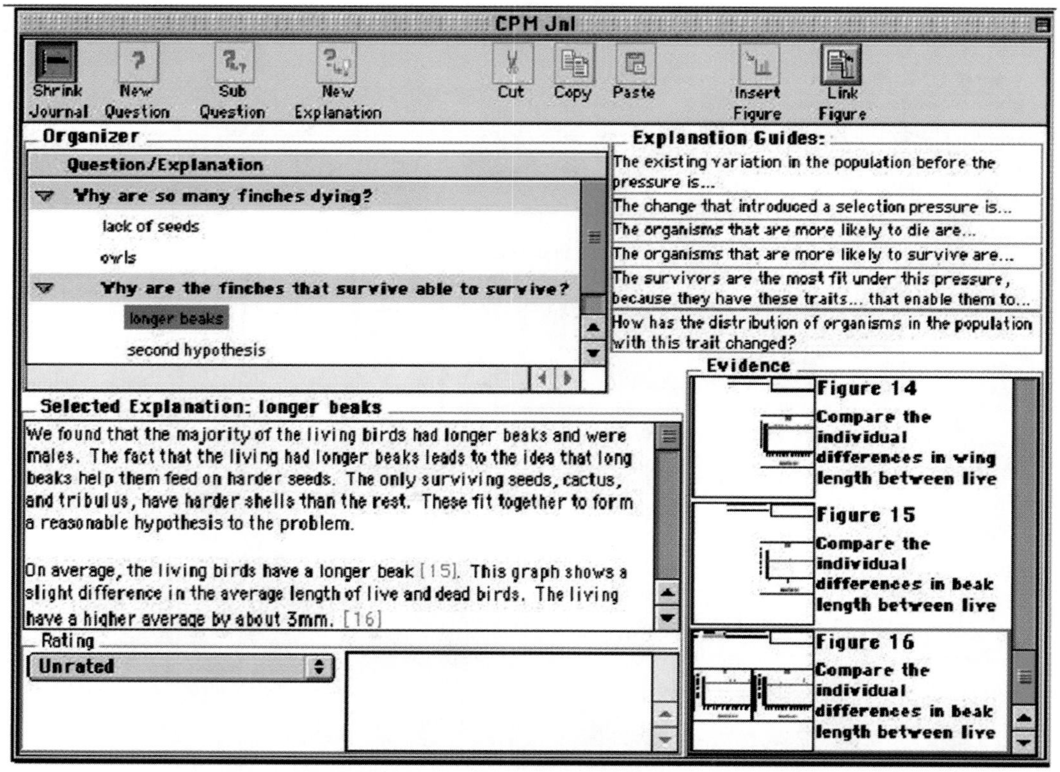

Figure 10.4. The ExplanationConstructor

Source: Figure 1 from Reiser, B. J. (2004). Scaffolding complex learning: The mechanisms of structuring and problematizing student work. *The Journal of the Learning Sciences, 13* (3), 273–304. Reproduced with permission.

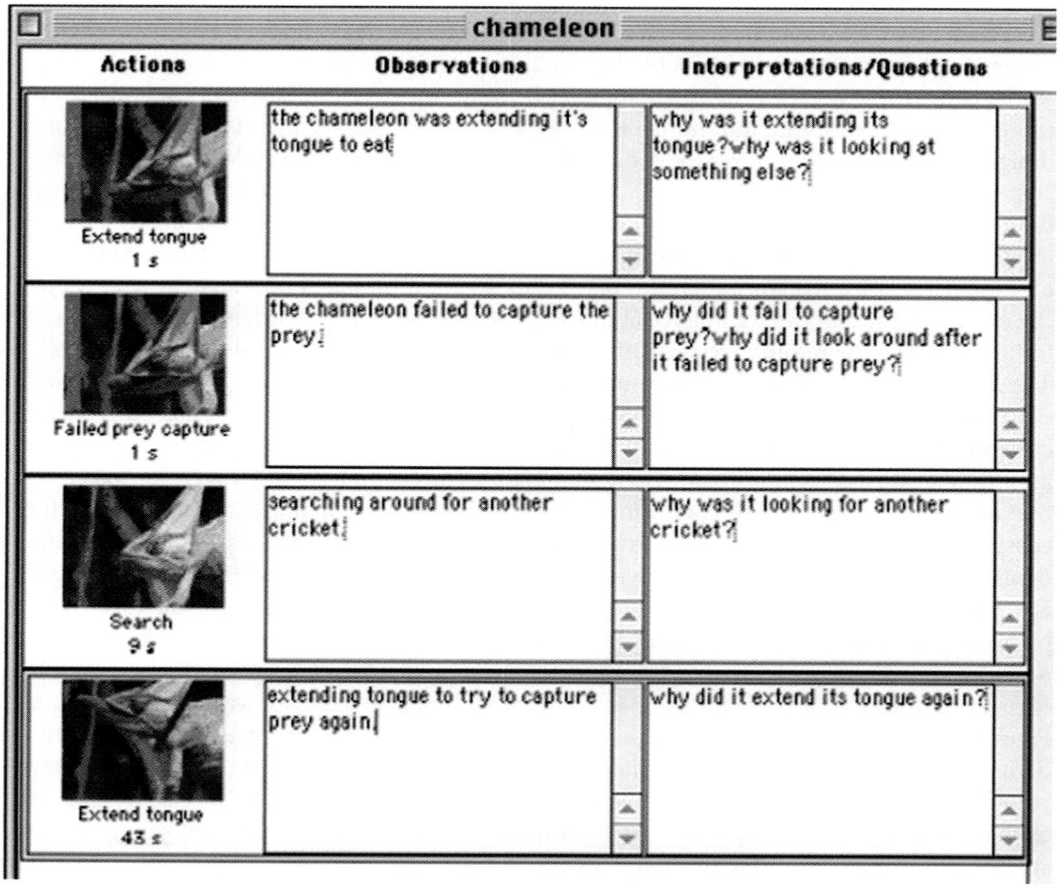

Figure 10.5. Artifacts Constructed in the Animal Landlord

Source: Figure 2 from Reiser, B. J. (2004). Scaffolding complex learning: The mechanisms of structuring and problematizing student work. *The Journal of the Learning Sciences, 13* (3), 273–304. Reproduced with permission.

behavior. They isolate and analyze key components of the animal's behavior. Students select frames from digitized video, categorize the behavior using a behavioral taxonomy, and annotate them with their interpretations.

Much of the research on inquiry-based learning environments focuses on how software tools can scaffold learners' inquiry activities as they complete complex tasks (Reiser, 2002). The software might provide prompts to encourage students or remind them of what steps to take (Reiser, 2002; Davis & Linn, 2000). The availability of graphical organizers or other representational tools can help students plan and organize their problem solving (Reiser, 2002; Quintana et al., 1999). The software can also automate lower level processes and provide representations that help learners track the steps they have taken (Collins & Brown, 1988; Koedinger & Anderson, 1993; Reiser, 2002).

The software makes the methodological aspects of the task explicit by helping students progress through the task and focusing their attention on important conceptual distinctions (Golan, Kyza, Reiser, & Edelson, 2001).

Chapter Reference
The importance of using external representations to support working memory was discussed in Chapter 8.

The second type of research conducted with inquiry-based learning environments examines how students perform on a task before and after using the software (Golan et al., 2001). Research with *Struggle for Survival* shows some initial evidence that high school students working with the unit become better at writing scientific explanations (Reiser et al, 2000; Sandoval, 1998). In particular, the data suggest that after completing the unit, students make fewer unwarranted inferences and are better at formulating coherent explanations (Reiser et al, 2000; Sandoval 1998). Similar results were found with the Animal Landlord software. A comparison of pretest and posttest essay questions also found that the essays on the posttest contained more causal arguments and justified more points than did essays on the pretests (Smith & Reiser, 1998).

Scaffolding for Students with Special Needs

Students with special needs often need a great deal of support when performing academic tasks. One strategy for providing that support is to use assistive technologies. In Section 602 of the recent reauthorization of the Individuals with Disabilities Education Improvement Act (2004), **assistive technology** is defined as "any item, piece of equipment, or product system, whether acquired commercially off the shelf, modified, or customized, that is used to increase, maintain, or improve functional capabilities of a child with a disability." Many assistive-technology tools do not scaffold a student's learning in the way described by Vygotsky. They help the student communicate or participate, but the student remains unable to perform the tasks without assistance.

assistive technology   Any piece of equipment that can improve the functionality of a child with a disability.

How Can I Use This?

When students cannot complete complex instructional activities (e. g., understand an assigned reading) they may feel inadequate. Look for opportunities to use electronic scaffolding and assistive technology to support their progress and learning.

Assistive technology can be used to scaffold the learning of students with special needs by providing supports of various kinds. Students often experience great satisfaction in being able to complete tasks with assistance. (Media Bakery)

One example of assistive technology that can be used to scaffold the learning of students with special needs is text-to-speech software (TTS). TTS uses voice synthesis software to provide oral reading of standard electronic text files, such as documents prepared in a word processor or text on Web pages (Balajthy, 2005). Students who struggle with reading can benefit from using TTS. In a survey of instructors of college students with disabilities, TTS was rated as very useful (Michaels et al., 2002). Research on the use of TTS in support of learning is not very extensive, but preliminary findings are promising. College students with attention deficit disorders and below-grade-level reading scores spent less time reading and were less distracted when using TTS (Hecker et al., 2002). Positive effects on reading comprehension were found in a number of studies (Leong, 1995; Montali, & Lwandowski, 1996; Wise & Olson, 1994).

Text-to-speech software can reduce the demands on working memory experienced by students as they struggle to learn words. Such software assists with word recognition. Students also need assistance with comprehension activities in particular content areas. Teachers may need to provide additional scaffolding for such activities in the form of background knowledge, key questions, or definitions of vocabulary (Balajthy, 2005).

Teachers do not simply rely on technology to provide scaffolding for students with special needs. The teacher plays a key role in providing support and assistance to the student. Chapter 12 provides more details about how peers and teacher support can be utilized to scaffold the learning of students with special needs.

Chapter Reference
The limitations of working memory are described in Chapter 8. Additional information about instructional support for students with special needs can be found in Chapters 4 and 12.

Scaffolding for Students from Diverse Backgrounds

Scaffolding is a useful strategy for working with students from diverse backgrounds. An example is a situation in which there are a number of English language learners (ELL) in a high school science course. Perhaps these students speak English moderately well but not fluently. They are very likely to have difficulty with some of the technical language used in scientific discussions (Buxton, 1998; Minicucci, 1996; Noguchi, 1998). That is, because ELL students learn the syntax and structure of a language mainly through interaction with their peers (Hawkins, 2001), they are often ill equipped to tackle the language of science instruction (and science assessment). This problem is not limited to science classes, but science instruction is a useful example.

Shaw (2002) shows how scaffolding, especially in dealing with the language used in science instruction, can greatly facilitate learning for ELL students. She presents the following suggestions:

1. Assess the difficulty of the language used in the instructional materials. Look for areas where extra assistance might be helpful.
2. Modify your language in discussing complex issues with students.
3. Help students address difficult language issues on their own. For example, work with them to understand the language associated with cause-and-effect relationships.
4. Encourage the use of metacognitive strategies with students. Have them think about what they know and do not know about a subject, and reflect on and summarize what they have learned after instruction.
5. Use graphical organizers to help students to master material.
6. Explicitly teach the vocabulary that students will need to know for an instructional unit.

Appendix
Responsive Teaching
You will need to be able to design instruction that is responsive to your students' needs and prior experiences (*PRAXIS™*, I. B. 4, I. B. 6, II. A. 2, *INTASC*, Principles 1, 2, 3, 4).

Instruction Influenced by Social–Constructivist and Sociocultural Theory

The examples of scaffolded instruction described so far are clearly influenced by social-constructivist and sociocultural theory. Wenger (1998) listed the following implications of these perspectives for human learning:

- A central aspect of human learning is the fact that learners are social beings.
- Knowledge reflects competence in some valued activity.
- The act of knowing involves participating in valued activities.
- Learning should produce meaning.

Examples of instructional strategies that have been influenced by this view of learning include cognitive apprenticeships, reciprocal teaching, and problem-based learning.

Cognitive Apprenticeships

Cognitive apprenticeships are an example of how scaffolding can be used in classrooms. A traditional apprenticeship involves an apprentice learning from a *master* craftsperson. The apprentice learns through observation, coaching, and practice (Lave & Wenger, 1991). The typical apprentice begins by doing simple tasks, gradually becoming more skilled, and finally engaging in the most complex task. A cognitive apprenticeship has much in common with the traditional craft apprenticeship. It includes modeling, coaching, scaffolding, reflection, articulation, and exploration (Brill, Galloway, & Kim, 2001). Earlier in the chapter, you learned that modeling is likely to result in the acquisition of a new behavior when the modeled behavior is visible, easy to observe, and easy to perform. Because cognitive activities lack these qualities, teachers must make explicit efforts to make thinking visible. Teachers can provide a model of how they are solving a problem and have students practice thinking aloud and describing their cognitive processes.

The "What Kids Say and Do" box on the next page presents a story written by Noah, age 12, in which he displays his understanding of scaffolding and apprenticeship.

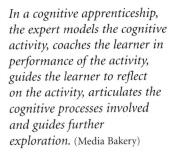

Appendix
Instructional Strategies
It is important for you to be knowledgeable about the appropriate use of a variety of instructional strategies (*PRAXIS*™, II. A. 2, *INTASC*, Principle 4).

In a cognitive apprenticeship, the expert models the cognitive activity, coaches the learner in performance of the activity, guides the learner to reflect on the activity, articulates the cognitive processes involved and guides further exploration. (Media Bakery)

Reciprocal Teaching

Reciprocal teaching is an instructional strategy based on cognitive apprenticeship. Developed by Annemarie Palinscar (Palinscar & Brown, 1984), it was originally designed to improve reading comprehension. It consists of a dialogue between teachers and students regarding segments of text. "The purpose of these discussions is to achieve joint understanding of the text through the flexible application of four comprehension strategies: prediction, clarification, summarization, and question generation" (Palinscar & Klenk, 1991, p. 116). The teacher first models each of these component strategies. When reading a text, he or she summarizes the content of a segment of text, asks a question about the main idea, clarifies any part of the text that is difficult, and predicts what will come next. The teacher then gives students an opportunity to take on some of the responsibility for these strategies by coaching them as they practice the component skills. Gradually, responsibility is shifted from the teacher to the student, and eventually the teacher's involvement in the performance of the strategies is faded. The teacher will continue to monitor the students' performance as they use these cognitive strategies and will provide further coaching if needed.

A summary of 16 research studies on the use of reciprocal teaching provided support for its use as an instructional strategy (Rosenshine & Meister, 1994). Reciprocal teaching has been used with a broad range of students, from third grade through adulthood. It has been successfully used with middle school students who were identified as remedial or special education students (Palinscar & Klenk, 1992).

What Kids Say and Do

Understanding Apprenticeship

The Boy Who Loved Stories
By Noah Rocklin

There once was a boy who loved stories. Any kind of story, books, plays, movies, even the plot of a video game as long as it was a good story.

One day The Boy tried to write a story (which was really just the story he saw on TV last night retold and set in a different place) but, it wasn't as good as the stories he read so he tried again and again and again. After a while he realized he wasn't getting anywhere so he sent his story (or the eighth revision thereof) to ten of his favorite authors so they could offer advice.

In the coming weeks he received nine form letters apologizing about how busy the authors were and one very helpful letter from Gabriel Winters his favorite young author. It made the story better without the affecting the core plot.

The Boy kept sending stories and Gabe, as The Boy came to know him, kept helping until the letters became more like two friends getting each other's comments on a work than a famous author helping out a little kid.

As the years dragged on The Boy graduated from high school and went to a college with a good writing program (as an English major of course). He acted in plays (some of which he wrote), wrote stories for the school paper, but always, always wrote to Gabe.

The Boy graduated and became a man, but he still was The Boy. He got married young, became a well-known author himself and always, always wrote to Gabe. One morning The Boy was eating his breakfast in his new house when the phone rang.

"That's odd," he thought, "I just moved in."

The voice on the phone said, "Hello is this 334-5672?"

"Yes this is. Why are you calling?" asked The Boy.

"Gabriel Winters told me to tell you about his leukemia," stated the voice.

"Oh, my God, how long does he have?" The Boy asked anxiously.

"Until next month I'm...I'm very sorry," the voice said.

"Where is he staying, I need to get there right away."

"At the Mayo clinic, I hope you arrive soon," said the voice solemnly.

The Boy got the first tickets to Rochester he could find. He didn't care about the baby crying, he didn't care about the cramped space, he didn't care about the person kicking his seat, he cared about Gabe and to The Boy that's all that mattered. He arrived at the hospital jetlagged and sure his pocket had been picked at least once, but he had gotten to Gabe and that's all that mattered.

As he walked through the hospital doors he realized this was the first time Gabe and him would meet face-to-face. He found Gabe's room and when he walked in he wasn't sure he was in the right room. The bed's occupant was a small frail man.

"Gabe?" The Boy asked obviously confused.

"Yep," said Gabe also a little confused.

They talked about how they had imagined one another different sizes and about the stories they wrote and the stories they wanted to write and in between The Boy thought, "He's going to be okay no one who has a month to live can seem so... happy." The thought only lasted a millisecond, but it put The Boy's mind at ease and that was good.

The Boy stayed until a little after the funeral and on the way home thought about that one moment where everything was okay. When he arrived home he wrote a book about Gabe and him (changing the names of course). It received good reviews and finally let The Boy move on.

One day The Boy received a letter. It was from a little girl who wanted his advice on her story. The Boy smiled and began to write.

Source: Copyright Noah Rocklin. Reprinted with permission of the author.

Reciprocal teaching illustrates several characteristics of cognitive apprenticeship. First, the teacher models the cognitive strategies to be used, making his or her thinking visible and inviting students to join in. By giving students opportunities to practice each of the strategies under the teacher's guidance, he or she coaches them in the use of the strategies, providing assistance if they are having difficulty with any of them. For example, some students have difficulty summarizing content from a text, and the teacher needs to help them identify the key ideas that must be retained in a summary. Reciprocal teaching also includes other elements of coaching that are considered important, such as providing feedback, hints, and reminders (Brill et al., 2001).

Problem-Based Learning

In **problem-based learning** (PBL), students work in collaborative groups to solve a complex and interesting problem that does not have a single correct answer (Hmelo-Silver, 2004). Students' learning is anchored to the problem posed. An example of a complex problem can be found in *Alien Rescue* (University of Texas at Austin, 2004), a problem-based hypermedia learning environment. The program, presented on a CD, is designed to engage middle school students in solving a complex problem. Students are told that six species of aliens are in Earth's orbit but their spaceship is damaged. The aliens must find new homes on planets that can support their life forms. Students are given the task of selecting the most suitable relocation site for each alien species. They must learn about each species and identify its basic needs. They must also learn about the solar system and the kinds of life that might exist on each of a number of planets. Students take on the role of scientists examining the solar system.

Alien Rescue provides a variety of tools to support learning, including databases of information about the solar system, the aliens, and probe missions carried out by NASA. It also includes a probe design tool, a notebook, tutorials, stories about how experts have handled similar problems, and tools that students can use to present their solutions to the class. With the aid of their teachers, students use technological tools and scientific procedures to help the aliens find new homes that can support them.

The goals of PBL are to engage students in a complex problem-solving process in order to foster the development of (a) flexible knowledge, (b) problem-solving skills, (c) self-directed learning skills, (d) effective collaboration skills, and (e) intrinsic motivation (Hmelo-Silver, 2004). These goals are consistent with the view of learning that is implied by sociocultural and social-constructivist theories. The teacher guides students through a process in which they are presented with the problem scenario, gain an understanding of the problem, and identify the relevant facts. They then generate hypotheses about potential solutions. They identify gaps in their understanding and engage in self-directed learning to fill those gaps. They apply their new knowledge and evaluate their original hypotheses on the basis of what they have learned. Upon completion of a problem, they reflect on what they have learned. This process is depicted in Figure 10.6.

problem-based learning (PBL)
An instructional strategy in which students work in collaborative groups to solve a complex problem that does not have a single correct answer.

Chapter Reference
The general process of solving problems is described in Chapter 9.

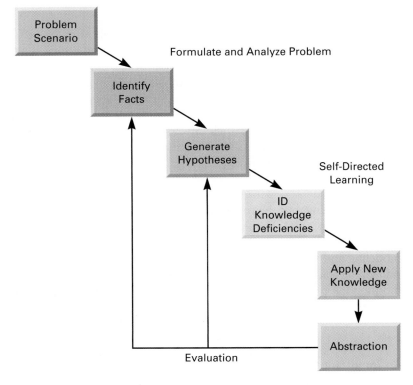

Source: Figure 1 from Hmelo-Silver, C. (2004) *Educational Psychology Review*, Vol. 16. "Problem-based learning: What and how do students learn?" p. 237. With kind permission of Springer Science and Business Media.

Figure 10.6. The Problem-Based Learning Cycle

Facts	Ideas	Learning Issues	Action Plan
Hazardous chemical Near population center	Minimize onsite storage Provide safety training Improve early warning system	What are the safety standards for cyanide storage? What technology is available to safely store hazardous chemicals?	Call EPA to find out standards

Figure 10.7. Example of Using Whiteboard While Determining Cause of Chemical Spill

Source: Figure 2 from Hmelo-Silver, C. (2004) *Educational Psychology Review,* Vol. 16. "Problem-based learning: What and how do students learn?" p. 243. With kind permission of Springer Science and Business Media.

Students engaged in PBL are initially given very little information about a complex problem. They must seek further information from the teacher or facilitator. For example, if the students were working on *Alien Rescue,* they would need to find out what kind of home was needed (air, water, etc) for each alien species. Students work through what they know and what they still need to know, and reevaluate their ideas and their progress toward solving the problem in light of the new information they acquire. Because the problem is complex and students often make false starts or need to revise their hypotheses, it is important for them to record their progress, using a whiteboard to keep track of facts they have uncovered or decisions they have made. Students keep track of (a) facts related to the problem, (b) ideas about solving the problem, (c) learning issues or concepts about which more information is needed, and (d) a plan for action. Figure 10.7 shows what one group of students wrote on a whiteboard as they tried to solve a problem about a chemical spill.

In an example of PBL in the sixth grade, students were assigned the task of designing a zoo. The class was divided into small groups, and each group selected a different climate zone (e.g., equatorial forest) whose animals would be represented at their section of the zoo. Students had to find out what kinds of food, temperature, and space their animals needed. The zoo would have limited space, and students needed to work together to make decisions about the limitations they would impose on their design. For example, they needed to agree on the height of the buildings they would include.

Characteristics of Good Problems To promote flexible thinking effectively, problems must be complex, open-ended, and ill-structured (Barrows & Kelson, 1995; Kolodner, Hmelo, & Narayanan, 1996). For students to be intrinsically motivated by the task, it must also be interesting. Effective problems require knowledge from a variety of domains. When students designed a zoo, for example, they used skills from language arts, mathematics, science, and art. Complex and interesting problems promote discussion and sharing of ideas and enhance the building of knowledge (Hmelo-Silver, 2004). When students need to seek new information as part of the PBL process, they engage in self-directed learning and learn to evaluate the state of their own knowledge.

The Role of the Teacher or Facilitator The purpose of PBL is to engage students in self-directed learning, but the role of the teacher in supporting students as they do so is crucial (Hmelo-Silver, 2004). The teacher can model good strategies, as might be expected in a cognitive-apprenticeship model (Collins et al., 1989). The teacher scaffolds students' learning by modeling and using questioning strategies (Hmelo-Silver, 2002). As students become more skilled, the teacher begins to fade the explicit scaffolding of their activities. The teacher must monitor the progress of a PBL group, encouraging all students to participate and to talk about what they are thinking.

Classroom Communities

An important technique for building learning communities was developed by Ann Brown and Joseph Campione (Brown, 1992; Brown et al., 1993). A central feature of this approach is that students help design their own learning environment, including choosing curricula. The Communities of Learners model (Brown & Campione, 1994) includes the use of

Chapter Reference
Intrinsic motivation and the role of interest in motivation are described in Chapter 6.

Chapter Reference
Questioning strategies are described in Chapter 9; Chapter 12 includes information about helping students ask good questions when working together.

reciprocal teaching (described earlier) and a modified jigsaw arrangement. Students work in small teams to prepare teaching materials. For example, high school students studying human migrations might divide the general topic into smaller ones (flight from war or famine, movement toward economic opportunity, seasonal migrations). The students then regroup into reciprocal teaching seminars in which each student is an expert in one subtopic. (All the children are experts in selected subtopics.)

Chapter Reference
See Chapter 12 for a discussion of *jigsaw* techniques in peer learning.

According to Brown and Campione (1994), the ideal classroom environment has a number of important features:

- *Individual responsibility with communal sharing.* Students must take individual responsibility for their work but share their expertise with others.
- *Ritual, familiar, participant structures.* Students need to know what the participation frameworks are (e.g., reciprocal teaching).
- *A community of discourse.* A key component of a learning community is the building of a community of discourse (Fish, 1980) in which constructive discussions, questioning, and criticism can occur.
- *Multiple zones of proximal development.* Because students are working with several of their peers, they have opportunities to participate in multiple zones of proximal development. For example, a student may serve as the guide for one student's learning but may be the beneficiary of another student's guidance.
- *Seeding, migration, and appropriation of ideas.* Teachers and students *seed* ideas—that is, suggest them. If an idea is adopted by other members of the learning community, it *migrates* and persists over time. Participants can appropriate, or adopt, ideas and language and use them in their own learning.

Learning out of School

Children and adolescents do not learn only in school. In fact, most of their time is spent outside of school. Typically, children and adolescents spend about half the calendar year and less than a third of each day in school. They learn in all kinds of informal settings outside of school. Almost everyone can remember going on trips to art museums, science centers, zoos, newspapers, or other institutions with their school classes. The *class trip* is a key component of American education. It involves a bus trip, having a partner or partners for the day, lunch from somewhere other than the school cafeteria, and perhaps something memorable that took place during the trip—or perhaps not. Even if the institution visited is not very stimulating, the opportunity to take a day off from regular school usually makes the trip worthwhile.

Appendix
Using Outside Resources
You can take advantage of resources outside of school to engage your students and promote learning (*PRAXIS*™, IV. B. 2, *INTASC*, Principles 3, 10).

Libraries are another locale for learning out of school, but they differ from other cultural institutions in the kinds of learning that take place there. *Libraries* can mean public town libraries or school libraries. Obviously, school libraries are not *out of school*, but we will treat them as such because what happens in them is usually more similar to what happens in public libraries than what happens in a typical classroom. Libraries are places where papers are researched, and for some students they are a quiet place to study or do homework.

Learning in Cultural Institutions

Learning in informal settings, such as museums, is very different from learning in structured settings, such as classrooms. Social-constructivist or sociocultural theories of learning are often used to describe the kind of learning that occurs in informal settings (Anderson, Lucas, & Ginns, 2000, 2003). Social interaction, cultural norms, and the use of a wide variety of tools and artifacts characterize learning in these settings. Each type of institution offers different activity or participation structures. For example, a hands-on science museum encourages action by the learner. There are objects to be manipulated, and discussion that may center on what occurs as a result of students' actions. There may be competition among students for a chance to operate a device. In contrast, visitors to an art museum usually are not allowed to touch the objects on display. This results in a more reflective experience. This section of the chapter looks at several kinds of institutions with regard to what is known about learning in each of these settings. The primary purpose here is to look at these issues from the perspective of educational psychology: What kind of learning goes on in these settings, and how can it be enhanced?

Falk and Dierking (2002) discuss three contexts that they consider necessary to understand learning in museums: personal, sociocultural, and physical. Learners in informal settings (including museums) have personal histories of motivation, expectations, existing knowledge, interests and beliefs, and choices. The sociocultural context includes the social facilitation of learning, cultural background and skills, and valued activities within the group. The physical context includes the large-scale environment and the design of the facility. Learning in informal settings is personal and dependent on the context: Learners typically look at what interests them (personal), and the setting provides a different context from their normal classroom environment. Learning in these environments also takes time (Rennie & Johnson, 2004). Because of the complex interactions among the personal, sociocultural, and physical contexts, it is difficult to study how learning occurs in informal settings.

Through the early 1990s, research on class trips to out-of-school learning settings focused on three aspects of such trips: (a) the overall educational value of the trips, (b) the impact of preparing for field trips, and (c) the complexity of learning in these environments (Griffin, 2004). The results indicated that the value of field trips was context-specific and depended on the trip's interest value to the students, the quality of preparation for the trip, and the relevance of the visit to the school curriculum (Griffin, 2004).

Students enjoy visits to museums and other cultural institutions because they provide opportunities to make choices and socialize with peers (Falk & Dierking, 2000; Griffin, 2004). Students with severe learning disabilities can also benefit from a visit to a science center (Brooke & Solomon, 2001). Lebeau and colleagues (2001) identified five elements that positively influence student learning at a science museum: "(1) alignment with accepted science curriculum standards and benchmarks; (b) extension of all contacts through pre- and post-activity connections; (c) integration with other subjects and disciplines; (d) connection of classroom experience to science center experience; and (e) insistence on student production through problem solving, construction, collaboration, and use of creativity" (Lebeau et al., 2001, p. 331).

Cultural institutions in the United States are many and varied. The American Association of Museums reports that there are more than 16,000 museums and other cultural institutions in the nation and that people made 850 million visits to those institutions in 2003 (American Association of Museums, 2003). Many of those visitors were school children on a class trip. Most museums of moderate size or larger have an education department whose main function is to work with teachers and schoolchildren. Its staff will be happy to help you organize and plan a trip to their facility, usually at no cost or a modest cost.

A trip to a cultural institution should not be viewed as simply a day off from school on which you do whatever the institution suggests. You should pick the institution carefully and work with its staff to maximize the benefits of the visit. You should also be proactive in shaping the nature of the experience. In his excellent book on museums, *The Promise of Cultural Institutions,* David Carr (2003) offers some useful guidelines for visiting museums with schoolchildren:

- Children in museums should have sustained encounters with process, ambiguity, collaboration, and mystery, encounters leading to grounded knowledge of how thinking happens.

- Children in museums should have opportunities to interpret open questions about the meanings of evidence. They need to understand that no interpretive vision of the world is perfect, no value is absolute, and no view is necessarily more accurate than others.

- Every child requires time alone to choose and linger, in private. To deny this is to deny the essential nature of the institution.

- Recognizing that the most powerful truths are not those given to us or even those we have discovered whole but those we have crafted for ourselves out of diverse elements over time, children in museums should have opportunities to construct knowledge, rather than receive it.

- Children should come to understand that the museum, both in and behind its public domains, is a system and a structure of knowledge, and that it can be a lifelong resource for the crafting of personal truths. (Carr, 2003, pp. 145–146)

Taking It to the Classroom

Do You Know Jack? Making the Most of a Visit

Jack's art class will be taking a field trip to a nearby city to visit one of the world's great art museums. The museum is hosting a once-in-a-lifetime exhibit of paintings by the Renaissance masters. Jack shows much promise in his understanding of art history. His teacher, Ms. Rainier, wants him to have as rich an experience as possible, but she is concerned that without direct supervision, he will not be as engaged in the learning aspects of the trip as he could be. On the other hand, she does not want to turn a field trip into an unpleasant experience for him. What reasonable steps can Ms. Rainier take to make this a valuable and memorable experience for Jack? Here are some suggestions:

1. Prepare all the students for the trip by discussing the artworks they expect to see.
2. Assign Jack to lead a group of students to report on two paintings, which they will identify before they go to the museum.
3. Have the group develop a set of questions to try to answer while they are at the museum.
4. Allow Jack to develop his group's itinerary for the day.
5. Ask the students to find the *best painting* in the exhibit. They will need to record the names of paintings and why they thought they were good.

What Carr is saying is that museums and other cultural institutions are tools, opportunities for education, and not just places to take the class for a day. The teacher's responsibility is to plan a visit that will link together the class, the institution, and the curriculum. What can the institution provide that cannot be obtained in the classroom? What kinds of experiences can occur there that will solidify, expand, and even *contest* what is being learned in the class? (See the "Taking It to the Classroom" box on this page.)

Teaching with Cultural Institutions

Cultural institutions hold great potential for having a positive impact on the lives of children, but for that potential to be realized, visits to these institutions need to be placed in a proper context. Cultural institutions are sources of awe and wonder; they are places where the *real thing* can be seen, where an actual working model can be examined, where one can imagine the life of a historical person. But to understand the special nature of the experience, one needs appropriate background knowledge (Smith & Carr, 2001). In a study examining people's reactions to actual works of art, as opposed to slides and computer reproductions, Locher and colleagues found that there are more similarities than differences among the three modes of presentation but there is nothing quite like seeing an actual work of art (Locher, Smith, & Smith, 2001).

Teachers can take any of a number of different approaches in working with cultural institutions; the approach chosen depends on the instructional goals that prompted the decision to make the visit. Reasons for visiting cultural institutions might include the following:

- A visit to a historic house may help students better understand the setting of a novel that takes place in the 1880s.
- A visit to a zoo may be focused on looking at differences among various species of reptiles.
- A visit to an exhibit of Islamic art can enhance students' understanding of geometric patterns and forms.
- A visit to a planetarium can enhance students' understanding of the relationships among the orbits of the planets and why seasons change.

These are all examples of using cultural institutions as an adjunct to classroom-based instruction. There are other reasons to go to cultural institutions as well:

- To show children the breadth and depth of cultural and scientific endeavor—to let them see possibilities for careers and contributions to society
- To open their eyes to the potential of self-directed learning by becoming lifelong users of cultural institutions

> ## Taking It to the Classroom
>
> ### Getting Parents to Help
>
> Parents can be a valuable source of assistance in visits to cultural institutions. They may have knowledge about the subject matter of a cultural institution. They may be members of cultural institutions, with insights into what is available there. Class trips are also an opportunity for parents to contribute as chaperones. Send home a note; let parents know what's coming up; and look for opportunities to include parents in the event.

RIDE Think back to Ms. Bernoulli's class trip to the natural history museum described at the beginning of the chapter. Museums are often places where different displays and exhibitions compete for visitors' attention. How does what you have learned about social learning theory relate to the behavior of the children in the museum?

- To give children a chance to discover on their own—to explore the areas of a museum that interest them most
- To promote class cohesiveness and spirit by making the visit to a cultural institution the culmination of a long-term collaborative endeavor in which students research what they will see at the museum.

The success of a visit to a cultural institution will depend on a number of factors, some involving your planning, some involving the nature of the institution and the helpfulness of its staff, some depending on the students themselves, but in all cases the process begins with a clear understanding of what you as the teacher want the class to get out of the experience. (See the "Taking It to the Classroom" box on this page.)

Art Museums Although one might think of art museums as primarily places of learning, many museum professionals see their mission as consisting of collection, preservation, and scholarly research (DeMontebello, 1998). There is an important difference between art museums and many other types of museums: In an art museum, the collection itself is of critical importance; it may or may not be so important in other types of museums. For example, a science museum with an excellent display and explanation of a Foucauldian pendulum or a great hydrology exhibit may offer a valuable educational resource, but the materials themselves probably have no value other than their replacement value. That is, if the exhibit were not working well in terms of its educational function, it could be torn down and replaced with one that does a better job. In contrast, although there are many works of art, only about 35 works by Vermeer exist today. Thus, collecting and preserving great works of art are as important to most art museums as displaying those works and communicating their value to the public, if not more so.

Thus, although most art museums welcome children and encourage visits by school groups, the education of school-age children in art museums requires a different approach than that taken in visits to other cultural institutions. In the first place, art museums are typically quieter and more sedate than other cultural institutions. Art museums see adults as their primary audience, and adults like to view artworks in a quiet setting; the buzz and hustle of a science center is not usually seen in a fine-arts museum. A second difference is that although valuable connections can often be made to curricular topics, many art museums emphasize looking at works of art for their own sake, without worrying about how such a visit can enhance learning that occurs in school.

In choosing to visit an art museum, teachers need to consider carefully what the museum has to offer, as well as the interests and motivation of the children in their class. Will the students get bored and restless? Will the trip be the beginning of a lifelong fascination with art? Will such a visit spark creativity or turn into a frustrating day of rules and limitations?

Zoos, Arboretums, and Other Institutions When thinking of possible sites for class visits, teachers should not limit themselves to traditional notions of what constitutes a cultural institution or a good class trip. There are zoos, arboretums where plants and scrubs are grown for scientific and educational purposes, parks, theatres, music festivals, nature preserves, minor league baseball stadiums, historic landmarks, and many industries that provide excellent opportunities for learning. It is not difficult to locate possible sites on the Web. To see an example of the possibilities, check the wealth of school visit opportunities during a recent year at the Billings Farm & Museum in Vermont, described in the "Taking It to the Classroom" box on the next page.

Taking It to the Classroom

School Visits Options

Billings Farm & Museum

— School Visits —

Billings Farm & Museum presents Vermont farm life as history, science, traditional culture, and human interaction with the environment. Each year, we introduce over 6,300 students of all grade levels to their heritage through the use of our resources:

- **The Working Dairy Farm** -- our Jersey herd, calves, work horses, sheep, and chickens.
- **The Vermont Farm Year in 1890 Exhibits**, emphasize the family responsibilities and activities of farm life in the late 19th century, including the importance of young people.
- **The Restored 1890 Farm House**, features the authentic farm office, familiy living spaces, and creamery -- excellent examples of technology and science to improve farm life of the day.
- **Games and Mini-programs** for students in grades K-2: Hands-on 19th century children's games; Mini program introducing the farm's sheep or chickens.
- **Buttermaking**, an important dairy product during the 1890s. Hands-on for all ages.
- *A Place in the Land*. This powerful award-winning film presents the Billings Farm and its three families, describing their farming, forestry, and sustainability practices for over a century and a half. 30 minutes. Suitable for Grades 4 and up. Please be sure to reserve in advance.
- **Our 8-Minute Video**. *A Thing Worth Doing* describes the evolution of the Billings Farm and responsible land use, with many historic photographs and lively music and voice.
- Visit the **Dairy Bar** for ice cream and the Museum Gift Shop for a selection of mementos and books.

Our education programs are based on inquiry and critical thinking. We use active teaching methods and hands-on, minds-on activities to encourage the discovery of connections between the past and the present, responsibility and learning, skills, and a way of life.

Source: Retrieved May 15, 2005, from http://www.billingsfarm.org/educational.html. Copyright 2005 Billings Farm & Museum in Woodstock, Vermont. Reproduced with permission.

Learning in Libraries Are libraries quiet places where people speak in hushed tones and browse through stacks of books organized by topics? That is how libraries are portrayed in television and movies, and it may be the way they were 20 years ago, but that image is no longer an accurate one. Libraries still have books and periodicals, but they also have computers, instructional videos, and professionals who are trained in the use of the Internet. They are still places where people go to find a quiet place to work that is free from distractions, but they are also places where people go to develop skills and expertise in an ever-broadening array of self-directed learning activities.

Libraries, whether school or public, have immense potential to aid students in their educational efforts. Todd and Kuhlthau (2003) recently completed an extensive survey of 13,000 students in Ohio to find out how they used school libraries and what they thought of them.

Their findings indicate that students are enthusiastic about the learning opportunities offered by libraries. Among other findings, the researchers report that the students said the school library:

- Helped them find different sources of information
- Helped them feel good about asking for information
- Helped them garner more information about their topics than they might otherwise have obtained
- Helped them understand the steps in the research process
- Helped them understand that research takes a lot of work
- Helped them search the Web
- Gave them access to software (PowerPoint, Word, etc.) that helped them with their work
- Helped them get better grades on assignments and projects
- Saved them time on schoolwork
- Provided a study environment in which to do their work efficiently
- Helped take the stress out of learning
- Helped them think about the world around them

Todd and Kuhlthau (2003) also report that African American students were more likely than other students to say that the library helped them develop their reading interests, and that girls were more likely than boys to say that libraries helped them with finding information they needed and using computers more effectively.

Science and History Museums   Science museums and most history museums are designed to be places of learning. They promote learning by engaging students' interests, providing hands-on experiences and a social context in which students can interact with peers and choose what they will examine. Students in a science or history museum typically choose which exhibits they will view; this allows them to follow their own interests. They often group together for discussion, pointing at objects of mutual interest or taking turns manipulating objects. Although there are many features of museums that promote learning, there are also features that hinder it. Science museums can be noisy and full of distractions. Students' attention can be disrupted and opportunities for reflection diminished.

The exhibits in science museums are constructed, or organized, with the goal of facilitating interaction and learning (Allen, 2004). A science museum may have an exhibit that is designed to show how an internal combustion engine works or how hydroelectric energy is produced. A natural history museum may have a diorama designed to show the relationships among several species of prehistoric animals or how a certain species became extinct. Often these exhibits are self-contained. That is, they are designed to engage visitors, introduce them to a topic, explain it, and offer suggestions for future exploration. They are, in a sense, complete from beginning to end. In other exhibits, the museum's best-preserved dinosaur may be displayed without much accompanying text, or an exhibit on visual illusions and tricks of perspective may be presented more for entertainment and engagement than for learning in a formal sense.

The question for the teacher is, What is the best use of this institution for my purposes? As mentioned earlier, a clear understanding of goals is essential to a successful visit. In science and history museums, you can usually anticipate:

- An education staff that will help plan the visit
- Exhibits designed with the goal of educating children
- Introductory and follow-up materials that relate what is in the museum to your curriculum

A Web site that lays out what is at the museum and how to set up your visit is depicted at the end of this chapter.

It is difficult to know what students are learning as they make their way through a museum. Recent research on learning in museums has focused on the kinds of conversations people have while viewing exhibits (Allen, 2002; Leinhardt, Crowley, & Knutson, 2002). Allen examined the conversations of 49 dyads (adult-adult, adult-child) as they viewed a large exhibit at the San Francisco Exploratorium (Allen, 2002). The exhibit was about frogs and consisted of 10 hands-on interactive elements, videos of frog activities, live frogs, an immersion experience involving sitting on a back porch listening to frogs at night, excerpts from children's books, and many other elements. The conversations of the dyads were recorded and later transcribed and coded for evidence of learning. The results showed that 83% of the talk

Chapter Reference
The benefits of student autonomy and choice are described in Chapter 6.

RIDE   Perhaps Ms. Bernoulli might revisit her goals for the class trip to the museum. What did she *want* to accomplish? What did she do to ensure that her goals would be met?

Science museums can promote learning by engaging students' interests and providing authentic, hands-on experiences. (Richard T. Nowitz/Photo Researchers, Inc.)

between members of dyads was related to learning. Five categories of talk related to learning were identified: (a) *perceptual talk* (drawing attention to some element of the exhibit), (b) *conceptual talk* (interpreting the content of the exhibit, including inferences and predictions), (c) *connecting talk* (making connections to existing knowledge), (d) *strategic talk* (talk about how to use the exhibit), and (e) *affective talk* (references to emotions and feelings).

The dyads engaged in a great deal of conceptual talk, and this kind of talk was more frequent when the dyads were discussing the live animals in the exhibit than when they were engaging in hands-on activities. This is not entirely surprising, because involvement in an activity tends to distract individuals from discussions. Adult-child interactions produced less conceptual talk than did adult-adult interactions (Allen, 2002). The conversations often took place as people moved between elements of the exhibit.

The design of exhibits can have an important influence on what occurs when visitors interact with them (Allen, 2004). Exhibits that are created around issues promote a different kind of learning than do more expository exhibits. Issue-based exhibits often provoke controversy and can be emotionally charged (Pedretti, 2004). Pedretti conducted research on exhibitions of this type (2004). One of the exhibits that she studied was called *Mine Games.* The exhibit's designers intended to make science interesting by helping people feel that the issue had some connection to their lives. The exhibit was interactive and involved a simulation game that explored the consequences of building a mine in the imaginary town of Grizzly. Through video and computer simulations, visitors met the town's residents and heard their perspectives on the issues. In the final and unique feature of the exhibit, the *Hot Seat,* visitors sat in a tiered semi-circle and, with the guidance of a mediator, held a discussion of the issue, using information learned from the exhibit. Students who visit such an exhibit have an opportunity to engage in argumentation and reasoning related to its content. Although few exhibits contain a feature like the *Hot Seat,* teachers can use this kind of activity as a follow-up to a museum visit. (See the "What Kid Say and Do" box on this page.)

How Can I Use This?
Historic houses, arboretums, national and state parks, and farms can also be good places for field trips. What other locations could you use for a field trip?

What Kids Say and Do

Personal Connections in Museums

Personal connections are a powerful means for communicating an idea or concept. Think about what you are trying to get across from the perspective of the person who is receiving the message.

Comment books give visitors to a museum a chance to express their reactions, thoughts, and feelings about an exhibition. After an exhibition on dress in the Age of Napoleon, one student asked, "What did 12-year-old girls wear in the Age of Napoleon?"

RIDE

REFLECTION FOR ACTION

The Event

Ms. Bernoulli had a rather trying day at the natural history museum. Her students were normally well behaved in class, but they were not during this visit. They were noisy at the museum and on the bus ride home. During the visit, they did not listen to her instructions or to those of the museum staff. She wondered what had gone wrong and how to make sure that the next visit would be more successful.

Reflection RIDE

Imagine that you are taking your class on a visit to the natural history museum. How would you avoid the problems experienced by Ms. Bernoulli? How can you make the trip an exciting learning experience while at the same time maintaining order? How will you keep the children interested?

What Theoretical/Conceptual Information Might Assist in Interpreting and Remedying the Problems Described in This Situation? Consider the following:

Goals

The goals of the visit were not clear to the students. Ms. Bernoulli had to think about what the trip to the museum was meant to achieve in terms of student learning. Why were they going there? Was it just a day off from school? All her colleagues plan class trips. What do they use them for? How are they supposed to fit in with the curriculum?

Planning

Ms. Bernoulli realized that she had not prepared her class for the visit. The children had little idea of what their day would be like. Moreover, they were in an environment that was completely different from the classroom: Museums are places to explore, roam around, and make choices. Ms. Bernoulli values these ideas as a teacher, but she now realizes that they need to be managed when one is dealing with 23 fifth graders.

Scaffolding

When visiting an unfamiliar learning environment, it helps to have a guide to assist you learn. Ms. Bernoulli realized that she needs to include scaffolds index cards with questions, partners, assistance from museum guides, etc.

Information Gathering RIDE

How can Ms. Bernoulli gather information that will help her understand the field trip, set goals for students' learning, and plan better for the future? First, the field trip has a purpose and she should think about the learning goals and how to achieve them. Second, she can consult colleagues about trips to cultural institutions to assist her planning. What do they do that is effective, and what are some of their "disaster stories?" Also, she can look at some other cultural institutions and see what they do. Finally, she can read some of the research on children's learning in museums to find out what kinds of planning and postvisit activities seem to be most effective. Third, because the museum will be an unfamiliar learning environment for her students, she can assist her students by introducing scaffolding opportunities.

Decision Making RIDE

Fortunately for Ms. Bernoulli, she does not need to take any action right away. She may want to take some disciplinary actions, but she probably will not be going on another field trip in the near future. However, she needs to think about some of the following issues:

- What kind of institution would fit best with what the class is studying? How well does it match the age and nature of her students? What practical aspects of the trip need to be considered (how long will the bus ride be, can the students have lunch at the institution, etc.)?
- How does the institution work with school classes? Many institutions will tailor visits to the needs of the class. Some institutions are highly oriented toward visits by school groups; others are less experienced and less well suited to such visits.
- What should Ms. Bernoulli do to prepare for the visit? She should probably visit the institution on her own first; she should get in touch with the person giving the tour; she should visit the museum's Web site and get the museum's school-group materials so that she can prepare pre- and postvisit activities.
- She needs to set specific goals and objectives for the visit. These will lead to the development of specific activities for the students to engage in while visiting the museum.

Evaluation RIDE

A museum visit is different from other types of school activities. Often, a primary goal of such a visit is to get students excited about the specific museum and about museums in general. Fun, excitement, and engagement are perfectly valid goals. In addition, almost any museum has material that can be linked to instructional goals. For example, in a zoo (or even a natural history museum), the teacher can test students' classification skills by asking what other animals are most closely related to an animal that is new to most students (an ibex, platypus, or wallaby). Islamic art is highly patterned and geometric in nature and can be tied to mathematics instruction. Narrative art can be used to help develop a sense of story in students.

Evaluating the changes one makes in approaching visits to museums, or field trips in general, will depend to some extent on the goals, objectives, and sources of support for such a trip. There are other indicators as well. Is there a "buzz" about the trip in the classroom the day or two afterward? What are students saying about it? It is useful to discuss the visit? This can be done informally during class discussion or through reflections in writing in which the student considers the visit. It will give you an opportunity to reinforce appropriate behavior, gain insight into the best and worst aspects of the day, and make adjustments for future trips. It will also be useful to look for ways to refer to the trip in upcoming lessons. Finally, it can be helpful to have a *discovery* or *exploration* sheet (some museums have these, called *museum hunts*) that can be discussed on the day after the visit. This will give you an idea of the level of students' engagement in the visit and provide a springboard for class discussion.

Further Practice: Your Turn

Here is a second event for you to reflect on. In doing so, generate the sequence used above in terms of reflection, information gathering, decision making, and evaluation.

The Event

Mr. Paine is a high school English teacher. One of his classes is a basic skills class. His students are not very interested in learning to write. Unfortunately, one of the most popular students in the class, Jake, hates writing and is very dismissive of Mr. Paine's efforts. When the students are given time to edit one another's papers, Jake makes disparaging remarks about his peer's writing, the class, and the teacher. Other students have started to imitate Jake's behavior.

RIDE What should Mr. Paine do? Why do the other students imitate Jake? What can Mr. Paine do to utilize Jake as a constructive, rather than destructive role model?

SUMMARY

- **What is social learning theory?**

  Social learning theory was originally developed by Albert Bandura and includes such concepts as reinforcement and punishment. It also includes cognitive elements, because a learner must attend to, remember, and produce behavior that he or she has observed. According to social learning theory, individuals can learn vicariously from the experiences of others. The reinforcements or punishments that follow other people's behaviors will influence the likelihood that the observer will perform those behaviors.

- **What is necessary for observational learning to occur?**

  The learner must attend to the critical features of a model's behavior. The behavior must be remembered. The learner must be able to produce the behavior, although initial efforts to perform it may not be completely correct. Finally, the learner must be motivated to perform the behavior. Vicarious reinforcement or punishment will influence the learner's motivation to perform the behavior.

- **How is scaffolding used in instruction?**

  Scaffolding can be used in a number of ways in instruction. Scaffolded instruction has two key elements: The learner's efforts are supported by a more skilled individual so that the learner can accomplish more than he or she might accomplish alone. With practice and feedback, the learner internalizes the new skill, and support is gradually faded.

- **What kinds of instruction are influenced by social constructivism and sociocultural theory?**

  Potentially, all types of instruction can be influenced by social constructivism and sociocultural theory. Examples of particular instructional strategies that are influenced by social constructivism and sociocultural theory are cognitive apprenticeships, reciprocal teaching, and problem-based-learning. These three strategies all assume that learners construct meaning in a social context and that such construction can be assisted by scaffolding learners' efforts.

- **How can teachers use the resources of cultural institutions effectively?**

  Cultural institutions such as museums, libraries, and zoos are a major source of support for regular classroom instruction and extensions of regular instruction that can make a subject area more exciting. Teachers need to think carefully about what an institution has to offer and how it can be related to what students are learning. Most institutions have education departments that will work closely with teachers to provide an optimal experience.

- **Can learners with special needs benefit from social-constructivist or sociocultural approaches to learning?**

  Behavioral techniques have been shown to be particularly effective for working with students with special needs. Social-constructivist approaches, which employ these techniques, hold strong promise for working with such students. In addition, assistive technology, such as TTS devices, can be a useful adjunct to regular instruction.

- **How can teachers use scaffolding techniques to work with diverse learners?**

  Scaffolding techniques are an excellent way to work with diverse learners. Scaffolding is based on the idea that teachers need to find students' strengths and weaknesses and attempt to build on the strengths and minimize the weaknesses. When working with students with English language difficulties or students whose background in a subject area is weak, scaffolding can help bridge the gap between confusion and understanding.

KEY TERMS

affordance, p. 324
assistive technology, p. 333
authentic tasks, p. 323
channeling, p. 327
cognitive apprenticeship, p. 319
collective efficacy, p. 324
dialectical relationship, p. 322

observational learning, p. 318
problem-based learning (PBL), p. 337
procedural facilitation, p. 329
vicarious experience, p. 317
vicarious punishment, p. 317
vicarious reinforcement, p. 317

EXERCISES

1. *Learning by Observation*

   Have a friend try to teach you some new dance steps. Begin by observing your friend doing the steps, then try them yourself. Reflect on what works well and what does not. Think about the stages necessary for observational learning and talk to your friend about which ones you completed well. What additional help did you need in learning the steps?

2. *Learning or Not?*

   Visit a hands-on science museum or other cultural institution. Select an exhibit and make a list of features you think are helpful to learning and those that are not. Indicate why you have identified each feature as helpful or not.

3. *Scaffolding with Software*

   Select a piece of software that you use often—for example, your word-processing software. Identify characteristics of the software that seem to scaffold your learning or performance. In what sense do these features provide scaffolding? How is the scaffolding faded after use?

4. *Autonomy versus Focus*

   Some of the research you read about in this chapter indicates that students prefer to be able to make choices when visiting a museum. Teachers worry that students will run wild if they do not have focused tasks to carry out during the visit. Give three or four arguments for each of these positions.

5. *Distributed Cognition*

   To gain a better understanding of distributed cognition, participate in an online message board. Notice how many individuals contribute. Does the collective membership of those who post messages know more than any individual participant?

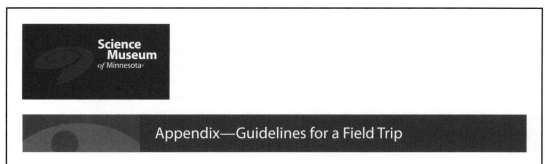

Appendix—Guidelines for a Field Trip

Use our checklist to make sure all of the elements of your successful field trip are in place.

Two weeks before your trip

- **Review your goals** for your visit. Do you want to link into your curriculum and standards, stimulate curiosity, encourage questions and connections, find new areas of interest?
- **Visit the Science Museum** ahead of time.
  - Request a free educator pass. Call (800) 221-9444 or (651) 221-9444 to visit before your field trip.
  - Pick up building maps and handouts at the information kiosk.
  - Make notes about appropriate exhibits, good questions to ask, activity ideas.
  - Talk to museum staff about ideas, questions.
  - Visit the Explore Store to look for books, postcards, posters, other educational items you can use to prepare your students. Teachers get a 10% discount on educational materials.
- **Need extra help?** If you can't schedule a pre-visit, please call to discuss your trip, (651) 221-4554 or (800) 221-9444 x4554. We will answer questions and have information about exhibit changes and field trip suggestions to help plan your trip.
- **Explore this Website** for up-to-date information about programs, exhibitions, and other useful information.
- **Obtain an Explorations gallery guide** to help you structure your trip and integrate classroom activities with museum experiences. For a sample copy e-mail maija@smm.org or click on **Explorations** button below to download the guides in PDF format.
- **Recruit chaperones**. We require one chaperone , 21 or older, for every 10 students. You may bring up to one adult for every five students. Chaperones must remain with their students at all times.
- **Orient chaperones** by sharing your field trip goals.
- Send chaperones copies of **chaperone guidelines**, maps and directions, schedules, student handouts. Include your phone number for chaperone questions.
- **Review your confirmation from the museum**. Make sure all items are correct. Check to see that you've reserved a lunch space if you plan on eating at the museum.

One Week Before Your Trip

- **Check on bus reservation** and schedule.
- **Make copies of the bus driver map** for each driver.
- **Obtain one check**, payable to the Science Museum of Minnesota. Discount coupons are not valid for school groups, but you can use Science Museum memberships. Make a list of membership numbers to give to the box office with your payment.

- **Assemble a packet to bring with you:**
    - copy of the field trip contract
    - bus driver maps
    - list of all students and chaperones
    - group and bus assignments
    - student nametags
    - map of the museum
    - schedule of the day
    - any activity sheets you will use

- **Complete pre-visit classroom activities** that integrate your classroom unit(s) with the museum visit.
- **Review schedule** and plans for the museum trip with your students.
- **Review Museum Manners**. Share behavior expectations and generate your own trip guidelines. Students must stay with their chaperones at all times.

- **Museum Manners**: A few rules to assure a safe and fun trip for everyone (including teachers and chaperones!)
    - Respect others in your group and other museum visitors
    - Use indoor voices
    - No food or drink in museum exhibits
    - No climbing on exhibits
    - Walk in the museum--no running
    - Teachers and chaperones must stay with their groups at all times
- **Confirm Chaperones**, Explain to them your curriculum goals for the trip.

Before Leaving School

- **Meet with chaperones** to review schedule, introduce students, share expectations, museum manners.
- **Get an accurate count of students**, SMM members, chaperones.
- **Collect lunches** in boxes or grocery bags. Label each box or bag with the school and teacher name.
- **Explain to students that backpacks are not allowed in museum exhibit galleries.**

On Arrival

- **Arrive at least 30 minutes** before your first scheduled activity.
- **Give the bus driver the map** and direct to the Education Entrance. Remind the driver to pick up at the same site at the scheduled time of departure.
- **The adult with the payment check should go directly to school box office in the Education Entrance.** Everyone else should follow the museum greeter's directions. The museum greeter will meet you and direct you to lunch and coat storage and help you find your first activity. They will also review museum rules with your group.
- **Store clearly marked lunches** as directed by the museum greeter. Follow directions from the greeter about picking up your lunches at your scheduled lunch time.
- **If you have coats, you may want to leave them on the bus**. Coat storage is somewhat limited.

Enjoy your day! Museum staff are here to assist you.

Source: Retrieved May 15, 2005, from http://www.smm.org/ educationprograms/schoolsandeducators/ FieldTrips/TripCheck.php. Courtesy of the **Science Museum of Minnesota.** Reproduced with permission.

(Courtesy of Teddy Linenfelser, town of Grand Island N.Y. Historian.)

Leah Aronds has just awakened on her first day as a new fourth-grade teacher. She had been dreaming that her classroom looked like the photo here. After a few deep breaths, she realizes that her classroom is not going to look like the photo. Besides the obvious differences in what Ms. Aronds and her students will be wearing, the walls of Ms. Aronds's classroom will not be quite as barren. But some things will be similar. Look at the children's faces. She can expect some of her students to display the eager anticipation shown by the girl in the front row on the right, as well as the tall girl seated in the second row. And the boy in the far back on the right ... he looks as though he is going to be a handful.

Managing Learning in Classrooms

11

R I D E Reflection for Action

Today's classrooms come in all shapes and sizes. They are all fairly barren when not in use. Some stay that way even when teachers are using them; others come alive. Consider these questions: In what kind of classroom would you like to be a student? A teacher? What types of activities are facilitated in classrooms? What types of activities are hindered? How can classroom management be facilitated or hindered through classroom design?

Guiding Questions

- How can classrooms be organized to make it easier to achieve instructional goals?
- How can the first day of school set the tone for the rest of the year?
- How should rules be developed for classrooms?
- How do successful teachers create a learning community in their classrooms?
- How do instructional formats affect classroom management?
- What can be done about problem behaviors that are more serious than occasional rule breaking?
- What is the proper balance between being sensitive to cultural differences and applying the same rules and expectations to all students?
- What kinds of classroom management policies can be used to address the special needs of certain learners?

CHAPTER OVERVIEW

This chapter looks at the opportunities, problems, and concerns associated with creating and managing successful learning communities in classrooms. We begin with the skeleton, discussing some of the concerns that teachers face in designing the physical environment of classrooms. Then we move into the areas that bring the bare bones to life: creating a learning community, establishing and enforcing norms and rules for behavior, and managing day-to-day classroom life. Teachers differ in how they deal with issues of classroom management, based on their needs and those of their students.

Designing the Physical Environment
- The Influence of the Environment on Behavior
- Designing the Elementary School Classroom
- Designing the Middle or Secondary School Classroom
- Addressing Student Diversity and Special Needs Through the Physical Environment
- Using Technology to Design Your Classroom

Designing the Social Environment: Norms and Rules
- The Tension Between Freedom and Structure
- Getting Started
- Establishing Procedures for Routines
- Misbehavior: Informal Correctives and Imposing Penalties
- Conclusions About Establishing Norms and Rules

Managing Day-to-Day Classroom Instruction
- Independent Work or Seatwork
- Small-Group Work
- Whole-Class Instruction
- Special Needs, Diversity, and Instruction

Dealing with Behavior Problems
- Chronic Problems
- Acute Problems
- Personal Problems
- Particular Problems

Designing the Physical Environment

Classrooms are like living organisms (Smith, Smith, & De Lisi, 2001). Their physical structure, furnishings, and state of repair are merely the skeleton, a starting point for classroom design. Classrooms have a life cycle, bursting into action in the fall with chaos, uncertainty, and excitement. By late fall, patterns have been established, and there is a familiar climate in the classroom that lasts through most of the school year, a steady pace and hum of activity. Classrooms have rhythm, flow, and purposes. They have movement and life, moments of joy and despair. Then, in early summer, the activity closes down, and the classroom hibernates, waiting for the beginning of the next school year.

The nature and quality of the activity that occurs in classrooms depend largely on the teacher in charge of the room. Students affect classrooms as well, of course. Some students can have large positive or negative effects on what happens in a classroom, but the key variable is the teacher. The teacher has the power to create a learning community. These communities not only produce learning and growth in children but also promote friendships that can last a lifetime. Teachers serve as models of how to behave in groups. Students' success depends on how well they function within a community: how smoothly they operate and whether they stay focused on the goals of the class.

For 180 days of the year, classrooms are where students live. The only other room where primary or elementary school students spend more time is their bedroom, and they are asleep for most of that time. So it is not surprising that the physical environment of the classroom has many effects on students, effects that we will describe in this section. Consider, too, how much time teachers spend in their classrooms over the course of a career. Making the classroom a positive and welcoming environment is well worth the investment of time and effort it will require.

Elementary and secondary school classrooms differ in a number of important ways. The two most basic differences, obviously, are the age of the children in them and the fact that at the elementary school level, students typically spend the entire day in one classroom, whereas high school students (and most middle school students) move from one classroom to another to take their various courses. Thus, the elementary school classroom is more of a home to students. At the middle and high school levels, the classroom is simply a place to engage in academic work. Because of the magnitude of these differences, we devote separate sections to designing elementary and secondary school classrooms.

The Influence of the Environment on Behavior

Classroom management begins well before the first student enters the room on the first day of school. The influence of physical characteristics of the classroom on achievement is well documented (e.g., Slater, 1968; Tanner, 2000; Tinker, 1939; Weinstein, 1979). The attractiveness of the classroom, the arrangement of the furniture, the quality of the lighting, the ability of the walls to absorb sound, even the nature of the floor coverings have been shown to affect student achievement.

The classroom environment influences behavior, and therefore learning, by determining:

- Where students are located in the room and how close they are to other students
- What students are looking at—other students, the teacher, a computer monitor, a colorful picture, a blank wall, out the window
- How students get from one place to another and who and what they pass on the way there
- Whether students have a comfortable place to read a book or can find art materials easily
- Whether students are feeling inspired or excited by their surroundings, or tired and bored
- Whether students enter a class with eagerness and a sense of anticipation or with feelings of worry and anxiety

In addition to influencing behavior, the classroom environment communicates to students how teachers feel about them and about the tasks of schooling. Does the appearance of the classroom show that the teacher spent a lot of time and effort in thinking about how the classroom will look, or does it look as though the teacher entered the room for the first time on the same day as the students?

Working from a general theory of organizations developed by Fred Steele (1973), Weinstein and Mignano (2003) describe six basic functions of classroom environments:

- **Security and shelter.** Classrooms need to be places where students feel safe and secure, where they know they will not be subject to physical or emotional distress. Because classrooms have very little inherent privacy, students need to have a place in the room that gives them a sense of security and **personal space**, a physical zone that is separate from those of other students and under each student's control. They also need to be as free as possible from the dangers posed by scissors, pencil points, electrical or chemical hazards, or loose objects in much-traveled pathways.
- **Social contact.** The design of the classroom will encourage certain kinds of interactions and discourage others. Teachers must decide how many and what kind of interactions students need to have in order to meet instructional goals.
- **Symbolic identification.** People's home, tell you a great deal about the people who live there: what their interests are, what their tastes are—in short, who they are. What does a classroom say about the students in the class? Does it tell you who they are? Does it reveal anything about them as individuals? Do they have any sense of ownership of this classroom?

How Can I Use This?
Next time you are in a classroom, either as a student or visiting, examine the room to see whether you can identify the influences in this list.

Appendix
Environmental Influences on Behavior
Organizational theory and educational research support the argument that the environment has a strong influence an behavior (*PRAXIS*™, I C. I., *INTASC*, Principle 5).

What Does This Mean to Me?
How do you protect your personal space in rooms where you attend classes?

personal space   An area where an individual feels separate from other individuals and able to be in control.

social contact   Interaction among students.

A well-designed classroom is attractive, safe, and allows multiple activities to occur at the same time. (Media Bakery)

 Look at the photo of a classroom from the 1930s at the beginning of the chapter. Try to rate this classroom in terms of the six functions of classrooms just described. Would it provide the best sense of security and safety? Would it promote growth?

- **Task instrumentality.** A central factor in designing the physical environment of the classroom is the nature of the activities (tasks) that will occur there. Will students be working primarily in groups or by themselves? How much artwork is going to be done? How much seatwork? Will there be an emphasis on silent reading that will require quiet spaces set apart from the rest of the room? Do all the students need to have a clear sight line to the board and the teacher's desk?

- **Pleasure.** Teachers and students spend a great deal of time in classrooms. Classrooms should be pleasing in appearance and create a positive feeling. A mix of colors and textures helps, along with open spaces and *nooks and crannies.* Plants, and even a classroom pet or two (if possible) are welcome additions, particularly at the elementary and middle school levels.

- **Growth.** Young students can grow an amazing amount in the course of a school year. They grow physically, of course, but they also grow cognitively and emotionally, often in ways that are not related to the formal educational goals of the class. A well-designed classroom can promote such growth by providing materials and opportunities that intrigue, excite, and challenge students.

Designing the Elementary School Classroom

Look at the design for a second-grade classroom shown in Figure 11.1. Try to answer the following questions in relation to this design.

- What does this classroom reveal about the person who designed it?
- What will go on in this classroom?
- What kinds of learning and growth will be encouraged?
- What kinds of learning and growth will be hindered?
- What strengths and weaknesses can you spot in this design?
- What kinds of activities would be easy to conduct in this room?
- What kinds of activities would be harder to carry out?

What Does This Mean to Me?
What would you do to improve the arrangement of the classroom in Figure 11.1?

Among the positive aspects of this classroom is that the arrangement of the desks encourages cooperative work. The room has a library center, a separate area for working at the computer, and a table for artwork. Most students would have good sight lines to the teacher and the blackboard. It also looks as though it would be fairly easy to enter the room and find one's seat. On the negative side, it looks as though the cubbies and cabinets might be difficult to get to, particularly if students are using any of the learning centers. Also, if students are actually seated around the desk sets, half of them will be facing away from the teacher.

Well-designed elementary school classrooms meet the six functions in ways that are appropriate for young children. Many elementary schools do not have lockers, for example, so desks and cubbies provide personal space. They should be clearly labeled and easily

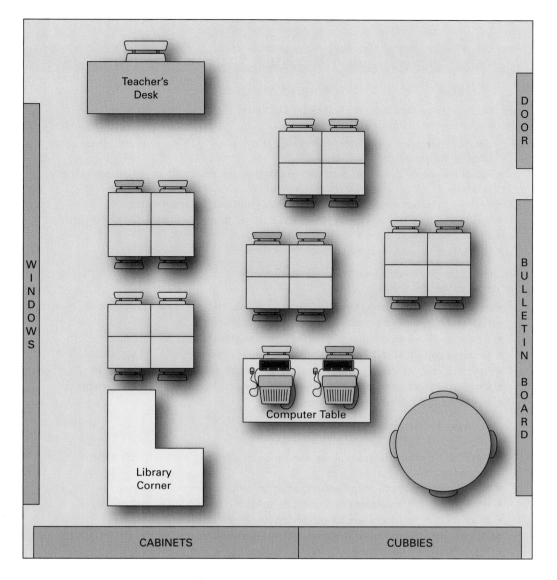

Figure 11.1. Map of a Second-Grade Classroom

accessible, especially at the beginning and end of the day and during **transition times**; otherwise, valuable instructional time could be lost to traffic jams. Frequently used pathways need to be clear and open for young students, who often do not pay as much attention as adults do to where they are going or what they are doing.

One of the tasks of childhood is to learn how to make friends and work with them. Teachers need to think carefully about arrangements of seating, working, and playing areas that will promote positive social interactions. This may mean assigning seats rather than letting children choose their own and rearranging seating when necessary. At the elementary school level, a judicious relocation of children can have a dramatic effect on the atmosphere in the classroom.

Learning centers are found in most elementary school classrooms, especially at the primary level. Library corners, science centers, and art areas can all be important parts of an elementary school classroom. The most recent addition to learning centers is computers. How they will be used needs to be thought through carefully and adjusted from one classroom to another, depending on the number and type of computers available, whether Internet access is available, and how the teacher wants to use these resources. Children in schools in poorer neighborhoods may have far less access to and familiarity with computers at home than children in schools in more affluent neighborhoods.

Much of the work that elementary school students produce is colorful and includes art. Displaying this kind of work on bulletin boards, clotheslines above the students' heads, or windows and doors helps them feel pride in and identify with their classroom, as well as making the room attractive to students. Teachers need to be careful to show each student's

transition times   Times when students are changing from one activity to the next.

learning center   An area of a classroom specifically designed to facilitate exploration of a particular aspect of the curriculum.

Appendix

Designing Classrooms

As children grow, their physical environments need to change to meet their changing physical, emotional, cognitive and social needs (*PRAXIS™*, I. A. 2, *INTASC*, Principle 5).

Taking It to the Classroom

Design Principles

Mrs. Jackson's Design Principles for a First-Grade Classroom
The room arrangement should:

- Generally have wide-open space, with storage that does not interfere with space in the room, because "bigger is better."
- Follow the general rules of the prescribed reading program, with furniture and equipment that is flexible.
- Be "bright and outgoing" as well as feel "homey," with a carpet and a rocker.
- Facilitate partner and group work with desks clustered together, but also facilitate children working on the floor if the activity requires more space than a desk.
- Facilitate social success as well as academic success.

Ms. Abram's Design Principles for a Second-Grade Classroom
The room arrangement should:

- Facilitate hands-on learning through discovery- and inquiry-based teaching with learning centers.
- Facilitate community building among children and teachers.
- Have storage and organizational space that complements the need for floor space.
- Contain alcoves that children can use for small-group activities.
- Have less structured activity than older grades, allowing children to choose activities.
- Vary according the children's development and the curriculum theme or topic of inquiry.
- Include flexible furniture and equipment.

Mr. Bower's Design Principles for a Third-Grade Classroom
The room arrangement should:

- Make full use of all floor and wall space and allow for displaying children's work without wasting space.
- Be acoustically quiet but colorful and exciting to promote interest and learning.
- Permit access to the outdoor environment or "outdoor classroom" to extend activities.
- Provide quality "private" space for teacher/student or teacher/parent conferences.
- Include accessible restrooms and water fountain to minimize interruptions.
- Provide flexible furniture and equipment with space to circulate as children are working.

Source: Lackney, J. A. & Jacobs, P. J. (2004). *Teachers as placemakers: Investigating teachers' use of the physical learning environment in instructional design.* University of Wisconsin School Design Research Studio. Retrieved March 10, 2005, from http://schoolstudio.engr.wisc.edu/placemakers.html. Used with permission.

work and to change the displays frequently so that students can take their work home to their families.

Elementary school classrooms should be forward-looking as well as outward looking. Teachers should consider what developmental challenges (both cognitive and physical) lie ahead for their students and what interests those students might have that are not directly related to the instruction they are receiving in the classroom. An aquarium or terrarium, juggling balls (soft sacks, actually), a telescope or microscope, or materials about careers might spark an interest in a child that will eventually become a vocation or a lifelong avocation.

Lackney and Jacobs (2004) researched the issues that elementary school teachers consider when designing their classrooms. They asked first-, second-, and third-grade teachers what principles they considered important for designing their classrooms. Some of the responses are listed in the "Taking It to the Classroom" box on this page.

Designing the Middle or Secondary School Classroom

The design of middle and secondary school classrooms shares some ideas and concerns with the design of elementary school classrooms, but there are some significant differences. Students typically spend 42–55 minutes a day in a secondary school classroom, as opposed to the whole day. Moreover, typically only one subject is taught in these classrooms, and the demands of that subject dictate the nature of the classroom design. English classes often need to be arranged so that students can readily see one another for purposes of interaction. In addition to facilitating working in groups, in math teachers generally want students to have clear sight lines to the blackboard or projection screen. Science classes obviously need to be arranged so that students can conduct lab work safely. Another consideration for secondary school classrooms is that one teacher may not use the same classroom all day long. Classrooms may be shared by two or more teachers, and arrangements have to be worked out to meet the needs of all the classes meeting in that room.

Middle school classrooms may look more like elementary school classrooms or more like secondary school classrooms, depending on the structure of the classes and the school's instructional philosophy. In many schools, students are grouped into instructional teams and only occasionally move from one classroom to another. In other schools, students travel to each of their classes just as high school students do. Teachers in middle schools often draw ideas from both elementary and secondary school classrooms, as well as bringing their own ideas to bear on the unique challenges and opportunities of teaching middle school students.

Some aspects of classroom design are similar across all the school years. The general functions that Steele (1973) described for organizations apply to secondary school classrooms as much as they do to elementary school classrooms, but they play out differently. As students grow older and are likely to use dangerous chemicals in chemistry classes; power tools in wood, metal, or auto shop courses; and knives in biology labs, issues of security and shelter take on a different meaning. There are other security issues as well. High school and even middle school students may express disagreements or grudges in a physical fashion, sometimes with dramatic **consequences**. Also, particularly at the middle school level, students seem to go through an awkward period during which they are not fully in control of their movements. One way of dealing with this problem is to give students a little more physical space. Students will then be less likely to bump into one another as they walk down aisles to get to their seats and less likely to antagonize one another during instruction.

Social contact among students is not always desirable in instructional settings at the middle and secondary school levels. Much instruction at these levels requires that all the students pay attention to what is happening at the front of the room. Putting desks in rows limits interaction among students and the problems associated with it (Bennett & Blundell, 1983). Today, desks are not bolted down, as they were well into the second half of the twentieth century. It is possible to have desks in rows for some purposes and in groups, semicircles, pairs, or other arrangements for other purposes.

Secondary school classrooms are often rather sterile environments. Many rooms do not look as though anyone lives in them. In such cases, students feel little connection with the room; in Steele's terms, they lack any symbolic identification with the room. Students are likely to think, "This is just a place where I am for a while; it doesn't have anything to do with me." This does not have to be the case. Even if your classroom holds 120 students over the course of a day, you can display items that reflect the kinds of work and interactions that occur there. Even an amusing hat on the skeleton in the biology lab can help students feel more at home.

Efficiency in carrying out tasks is a key feature of the secondary school classroom. Students need to get into the classroom and get to work with a minimum of lost time. If a class loses two minutes a day due to a slow start, this can add up to almost nine days of lost instruction over the course of the year. Establishing and enforcing classroom rules provides much of what is needed to get students on task quickly, but the classroom itself must be ready for the students when they enter. Class arrangements should not provide places where students can gather and chat before the class begins. Students should be easily able to get any supplies they need and get back to their seats quickly. Desks should be arranged so as to focus students' attention naturally where it needs to be focused for the class to begin.

Chapter Reference
Chapter 3 discusses some of the issues involved in social development.

consequences The good or bad effects that follow a person's behavior.

For some instructional needs, such as administering assessments or having students focus on instruction at the front of the room, it can be useful to have student seating organized in rows. (PhotoDisc, Inc./Getty Images)

Remember, however, that one of Steele's (1973) categories of the functions of organizations is pleasure. There is no reason for secondary school classrooms to be unattractive. Plants, posters, mobiles, contrasting colors, and the like make a classroom more attractive and thus contribute to the quality of the interactions that occur within it. A strong effort at the beginning of the year to make a classroom attractive pays off in a more pleasant environment for the rest of the year. Teachers who are not particularly adept in the area of decoration can rely on friends, colleagues, and parents for help in creating an attractive classroom environment.

Steele's final category is growth. Students in middle or high schools often show remarkable physical growth over the course of the school year, but it is really academic growth that is of concern here. Most academic growth is the direct result of the curriculum. But classrooms can also provide opportunities for unplanned growth. Will a friendship develop between two students who are very different simply because they are seated next to each other? Will a student's interest be piqued by a poster or because the student was asked to help contribute to the appearance of the classroom? Will a book that you place in the class library change a student's life? It is hard to know what kinds of growth might occur due more to chance than to deliberate efforts, but a classroom with many things to capture a student's attention holds greater potential for such growth than a barren one.

Addressing Student Diversity and Special Needs Through the Physical Environment

Just as the design of the classroom takes care and consideration, so does the location of students within the classroom. Just as one needs to be careful about the seating arrangements at a wedding reception, some students should not be seated next to certain other students in a classroom. Some students need to be close to the action. Students with special needs may need to be close to the teacher or somewhere where it is quieter or where a paraprofessional can provide extra help unobtrusively. In an experimental study looking at students with emotional/behavioral problems, Kamps and colleagues (1999) found that environmental variables have a strong influence both on increasing positive student behavior and decreasing undesirable behavior.

Students who use wheelchairs need to have wide enough pathways so that they can move where they need to without disrupting the class or feeling embarrassed. Students with physical challenges must be considered carefully in planning art, music, physical education, recess, and lunchtime activities. In thinking about students with special needs, do not hesitate to ask the students or their parents, assistants, or former teachers for advice.

Achieving the right classroom mix requires some trial and error. Sometimes opposites work well together; sometimes they are a recipe for disaster. In an ethnically diverse class, veteran teachers often encourage **cross-ethnic groupings**. At the same time, teachers must be sensitive to students who may feel isolated from friends with whom they feel secure.

Students should be told right away that the seating arrangement established at the beginning of the year may change as the year progresses. They should also understand that the purpose of the class is not social but academic. The most productive arrangement for learning may not be the most socially appealing one. (See the "What Kids Say and Do" box on this page.)

cross-ethnic groupings
Groupings of children from different ethnic groups.

What Kids Say and Do

A Painful Request

Two weeks after rearranging the seats in her eighth-grade honors algebra class, Mrs. Stevens was confronted by Angelo, who had what could have been the saddest face she had ever seen on a child.

Mrs. Stevens:	Angelo, what's the matter? I've never seen such a sad face.
Angelo:	Mrs. Stevens, you have to move my seat. I can't sit next to Maria.
Mrs. Stevens:	I thought you liked Maria.
Angelo:	That's the problem, Mrs. Stevens. If I'm sitting next to Maria, there's no algebra going on in my head.

Using Technology to Design Your Classroom

Designing classrooms and placing students in them is clearly an art, but as with almost all art, it involves a little science as well. Teachers need to think about the kind of learning community they want to build and the instructional tasks that will be carried out in the classroom. Students need to *be* safe and secure and to *feel* safe and secure. The classroom should also be a welcoming and attractive place. Some teachers are naturally better at classroom design than others. Most teachers are willing to share ideas and lend a hand in setting up a colleague's classroom, especially one who is less experienced.

The National Clearinghouse for Educational Facilities is an excellent place to find ideas about how to design a classroom (the Web address for its site can be found on the Web site for this text). A wealth of other resources is available online, including discussion groups, research literature, and software. A simple search on "classroom design" is an excellent way to start. There are also Web resources dealing with classroom design available on the Web site for this text.

www.wiley.com/college/odonnell

Designing the Social Environment: Norms and Rules

Good classroom management skills are important in building a successful career in teaching (Good & Brophy, 2000; Good et al., 1987; Charles, 2002). In fact, Wang, Haertel, and Walberg (1993; 1993/94) argue, based on an extensive analysis of the research literature, that good classroom management has the greatest influence on student learning. The establishment of norms and rules for classroom behavior is an important component of classroom management. The "Taking It to the Classroom" box on the next page provides an example of the need for establishing norms and rules.

When children enter a classroom at the beginning of the year, they enter a physical space that has been designed to encourage desirable behaviors and discourage undesirable ones. But as Mrs. Johnson discovered, they also enter a psychological and social space, and they do not yet know the **social norms** (typical behavior that is considered appropriate), rules, and expectations for that space. Will quiet talking to one's neighbor be permitted? What is the procedure for going to the bathroom? What is the first thing that the student is supposed to do upon entering the classroom? What should students do if they see another student misbehaving?

Walter Doyle (1986) has described six features of classrooms that make them unlike almost any other setting. They may remind you of the idea of a classroom having a life of its own, which we described at the beginning of the chapter (Smith et al., 2001). Doyle's six features of classrooms are:

1. **Multidimensionality.** In classrooms, students do not only read and write, they put on plays, do artwork, argue with one another, care for the class pet, hold elections and debates, conduct science experiments, make recitations in foreign languages, and explore the world through the Internet. Classrooms have to facilitate this multidimensionality.

Appendix
Classroom Rules
Establishing Rules effectively early in the year is the key to a positive classroom community (*PRAXIS*™, I C. 4., *INTASC*, Principle 5).

social norms   Expectations for proper behavior.

multidimensionality   Having more than one characteristic (such as a purpose or an ability) at the same time.

This classroom illustrates the multidimensional nature of middle school life. How many different things are happening here? (Dana White/ Photo Edit)

Taking It to the Classroom

Even the Brightest Kids . . .

Vernita Johnson was a first-year high school English teacher. The principal had assigned her the top honors English class in an effort to "give her one really positive experience in her first year of teaching." It was a noble idea, but it was not working. Six weeks into the school year, Mrs. Johnson was at her wits' end. She was seriously considering quitting at the end of the semester and going to graduate school in any field other than education. These were the brightest kids in the school, yet she found them uncooperative, uninterested, unmanageable, and generally unteachable. They were rude to one another and to her, did not hand in homework on time, and complained about almost every assignment.

At the end of a particularly vexing day, Sander showed up in her doorway. He was not one of the worst-behaving students in the class, but he did not contribute much. Most of the time, he sat and looked at his desk.

"Mrs. Johnson, can I talk with you?" asked Sander, surpassing the total number of words he had spoken in the class to date.

"Certainly, Sander, please come in and have a seat."

"Mrs. Johnson, this class isn't going very well."

She had to suppress a laugh. This was the understatement of all understatements. "No, Sander. It isn't. Do you have any thoughts on why that is?"

Sander paused for an uncomfortably long time. Then he said, "Well, I've been in school with these kids since we were in elementary school, and they're good kids. When your class is over, we all go down the hall to math class, and there aren't any problems there."

"Are you saying this is my fault?"

Another interminable pause, and then, "No. That's just what happens."

"Why did you come see me today, Sander?"

"Because I want this to be a good class. So do the other kids."

Sander had not uttered more than 100 words in the course of this conversation, but he had spoken volumes. First, even with an honors class, there need to be rules and expectations that are consistent with the goals of the course, and they need to be enforced. This has to start at the beginning of the school year. Second, the negative attitude that Mrs. Johnson had developed toward this class may have been unjustified. Maybe the students did want the class to be a good one, but they were not in charge. Third, if she was to salvage the year (and perhaps her teaching career), she needed to make some changes quickly. The first step would be to walk down the hall and have a chat with the honors math teacher.

---

immediacy   In teaching, decisions and actions have to occur in the real time of classroom life, that is, immediately, not at a leisurely pace.

2. **Simultaneity.** Rarely is only one thing going on in a classroom. At the same time that Mrs. Knowles is working with Marissa on initial estimation of long division, a group of students is writing a letter to the mayor to ask that the traffic light near the school stay red longer. Tory and Joaquim are checking out a Web site with information about an upcoming meteor shower, and Martin is trying to paste Lara's desk to the floor. And Mrs. Knowles *knows all of this.* Not only can exceptional teachers handle the multidimensional and simultaneous nature of activities in the classroom, they relish it.

3. **Immediacy.** The French have a saying: *L'esprit d'escalier,* or "the wit of the staircase." It refers to the really clever things people might have said, *had they thought of them at the time.* With thousands of interactions with students each day, *L'esprit d'escalier* could become a teaching motto. Classroom life is a real-time event. Teaching occurs in real time. At the end of the day, a good teacher might come up with a half-dozen better responses to certain situations than the one used at the time. There is no need to be upset about not always coming up with the perfect response. With experience, teachers develop the ability to make good decisions more quickly. This is one of the characteristics that distinguishes veteran teachers from novices.

4. **Unpredictability.** Related to immediacy is the notion of unpredictability. Although in general, teachers have a good sense of what will happen each day, from an instructional perspective they do not know whether a student will come to class with a personal problem that makes him or her act out, or whether a fire drill will occur in the middle of a lesson that is going very well. Teachers have to be calm in the face of

Taking It to the Classroom

When the World Impinges on the Classroom

From time to time, something happens in the world or locally that brings the school day to a halt. Teachers have struggled with the task of talking to students about international tragedies, assassinations of presidents, disasters in space exploration, or local events that had significance for schoolchildren.

When such an event occurs, it is a good idea to talk things over, even if only briefly, with colleagues and supervisors so that the school, as a community, can take a consistent approach. Honesty, compassion, sincerity, willingness to listen and share feelings, and concern for the students should be guiding principles. It is important to keep in mind that how children handle the event depends in part on how it is presented to them and discussed by their teacher.

such unpredictability. See the "Taking It to the Classroom" box on this page for advice on remaining calm in unpredictable situations.

5. **Lack of privacy.** Classrooms are public places. There is no place to hide, especially for the teacher. Stuart Polansky (1986) captures this notion in his highly readable account of high school teaching, *900 Shows a Year: A Look at Teaching from a Teacher's Side of the Desk.* Lack of privacy plays out differently at different levels. Although elementary school teachers need to provide structure and monitoring for students during the entire day, middle and high school teachers are more likely to be the direct focus of the students' attention during each class period. Lack of privacy is a feature of classrooms for students as well as for teachers. In school, students are almost never alone.

6. **History.** Classrooms do not start from scratch each morning. Classroom interactions and their consequences have a history. Brad and Jessica may both fail to turn in homework on the same day. But Brad will be treated differently from Jessica if he has not turned in his homework on four consecutive days and this is the first time she has forgotten her homework all year. A history of events accumulates over the course of the year and affects how the teacher interacts with students and how they interact with one another.

The Tension Between Freedom and Structure

Structure revolves around teachers clearly communicating what they expect students to do to achieve academic, social, and behavioral goals. In most societies and social activities, there is a certain degree of tension between freedom and structure. In highly structured settings where appropriate behavior is well understood, such as going to a movie or participating in a graduation ceremony, people often seek freedom from the regimentation. Thus, they may call out at the film or throw popcorn. They may decorate their mortarboard hats or wear shorts and sandals under their graduation robes. On the other hand, in highly unstructured settings, such as a free Saturday or a trip to a museum, people often seek to impose some structure on the setting. They may decide to work on a stamp collection or a crossword puzzle on a free day. Or they may buy an audio tour in order to make sense of the many different exhibits and displays in a museum (Smith & Wolf, 1996).

It might seem from this analysis that structure and freedom are opposite ends of the same continuum—that high structure means low freedom, and vice versa. But the point is that people value both structure and freedom *at the same time.* Those who study classroom management view structure and freedom as distinct aspects of classroom management strategy. Teachers can impose a highly structured classroom on students and offer them little or no freedom. Or they can impose a highly structured classroom on students and offer them a great deal of freedom by giving them choices, opportunities to be heard, and opportunities to take the initiative within the classroom structure. The worst classroom management strategy is to provide a classroom with little or no structure. This is a permissive environment. Students learn and function better in a highly structured environment. The optimal classroom management environment, however, is one that features both high structure (clear rules, procedures, goals) and considerable freedom within that structure (choices, opportunities).

First impressions are lasting. This teacher has a brightly colored shirt and decorations in the hallway to welcome students on the first day of school. (© Syracuse Newspapers/ Dick Blume/The Image Works)

Initially, a classroom is an unstructured setting. For students to feel comfortable and be productive, some sort of structure must be imposed on that setting. Students need to know what to do, how to do it, when to do it, and how to get help if they need it. The structure should not be stifling; it should set norms and expectations for behavior and impose understandable consequences when those expectations are not met.

Getting Started

For a school year to be successful, it is essential to start setting rules and norms for classroom behavior on the first day of school. As Mrs. Johnson learned the hard way, time spent establishing clear expectations for classroom behavior more than pays off in time saved for learning during the rest of the school year (Evertson & Harris, 2003). Like classroom environments, rules and norms for behavior are different for elementary, middle, and secondary schools, and even for different groups within those schools. Weinstein and Mignano (2003, p. 61) have developed an excellent set of principles for thinking about classroom rules:

- Rules should be reasonable and necessary.
- Rules need to be clear and understandable.
- Rules should be consistent with the instructional goals and with what we know about how people learn.
- Classroom rules need to be consistent with school rules.

Most teachers have a sense of the rules they want for their classrooms, but many find it effective to develop the rules jointly with the class. Needless to say, this requires some informal control on the part of the teacher, especially for younger children, but it is also good to let the children feel a sense of responsibility for how the classroom is run. It is also important to be sure that students understand the specifics of the rules. Exactly what is a violation of the rules and what is not?

The First Day of School No matter what happened the year before, students and their families approach the first day of a new school year filled with hope and some anxiety. The first day of school is critical for the teacher as well, especially the beginning teacher. Whether at the elementary or the secondary level, the first day must be well planned. First impressions are lasting ones. Research findings show clearly that the very beginning of the school year is the most important factor in how the whole year will go. Emmer, Evertson, and Anderson (1980), for example, observed a group of third-grade teachers for the first three weeks of school and found that effective teachers had clear rules for behavior and spent a good deal of time, from Day One, teaching these rules.

Teachers need to clarify on the first day their behavior expectations for the rest of the school year. For younger students, this focus will most likely be on helping them understand the rules. As described in the following sections, it takes a while for younger students to understand fully what is and is not appropriate. Time spent pointing out examples of appropriate and inappropriate behavior will be helpful. At the secondary school level, the issue will more likely be one of testing the rules. Students will be trying to discover what kinds of behavior will *sneak in* just under the limits and what kinds of behavior will be considered *crossing the line*. Burden (2000, p. 96) has developed the following list of guidelines for communicating classroom rules to students:

1. Plan to discuss and teach the rules during the first class session.
2. Discuss the need for the rules.
3. Identify specific expectations that are relevant to each rule; provide examples and stress the positive side of the rules.
4. Inform students of the consequences when rules are followed, as well as when they are broken.
5. Verify understanding.
6. Send copies of your discipline policy to caregivers and to the principal.
7. Post the rules in a prominent location.

8. Remind the class of the rules at times other than when someone has just broken a rule.
9. Review the rules regularly.

The first day is not the day to become the students' friend: The first day is the day to communicate how the class is going to operate and to *nip in the bud* potential problem behaviors. This does not mean that the teacher cannot smile. It just means that the primary task of the day is to work toward establishing the sense of order that will permit the development of a learning community and last for the rest of the school year.

Rules for Elementary School Classrooms Elementary school students are typically more eager to please their teacher than are middle or high school students. This is particularly true of younger children. On the other hand, they know less about what is and is not appropriate classroom behavior. Also, they have more trouble simply understanding rules. Therefore, elementary school teachers need to make sure that rules are understood. They spend more time teaching the rules, demonstrating dos and don'ts, and providing corrective feedback than middle or high school teachers do, but less time dealing with defiant behavior.

Establishing rules requires determining both what the rules should be and what the consequences of not following them should be. It is important to be certain that both the rules and the consequences are reasonable and enforceable. **Detention** is a common punishment for misbehavior, but it works differently in different school systems. In most elementary schools, detention usually means staying in the classroom with the teacher, either after school or at lunchtime. An after-school detention may be inconvenient for parents who are working on a tight schedule.

detention Having a student stay after school or restricting a student's options during free time (such as staying in during recess).

Figures 11.2 and 11.3 show two sets of classroom rules. Figure 11.2 is a set of rules for a kindergarten, and Figure 11.3 is a set of rules for an upper elementary school classroom. It is interesting to see that in the kindergarten, where the children participated in setting the rules, making noise with your shoes was a fairly serious concern, whereas niceness needed to be shown only to friends. Note that the kindergarten rules do not have a set of consequences associated with them.

Mrs. Wade's Classroom Rules

This set of classroom rules were written by and agreed upon by Mrs. Wade's kindergarten class.

- Help Mrs. Wade.
- Don't hit or kick people.
- Play nicely on the playground.
- Be nice to your friends.
- Be quiet in the hallway.
- Raise your hand.
- Don't make fun of people.
- Don't be loud with your shoes.
- Clean up your mess.
- Don't run in the hallway.
- Don't run in the cafeteria.
- Behave.

Figure 11.2. A Set of Kindergarten Rules

CLASSROOM RULES

WHY we have classroom rules: To keep our classroom a positive learning community where everyone can be productive and feel safe and respected.

1. Treat your classmates the way you would like them to treat you.
2. Listen carefully to directions as they are given.
3. Be in your seat and ready to learn when the bell rings.
4. Bring necessary materials to class.
5. When you want to contribute to the discussion, raise your hand to be called on.
6. No hitting, kicking, threatening, throwing of objects, making fun of, or teasing.
7. Follow all school rules as presented in the school handbook.

WHAT the consequences of not following the rules are:

1. A verbal warning that a rule has been broken.
2. A second warning and name written on the board.
3. A conference with the teacher about following rules and a written assignment for the student on how behavior will be improved.
4. Detention and referral to Principal's Office.
5. Conference with student and parents.

FOR A SERIOUS VIOLATION, any of the steps of the consequences may be skipped.

Figure 11.3. A Set of Upper-Elementary School Rules and Consequences

As mentioned earlier, small children tend to be more anxious to please the teacher, so there might not be a need for a formal set of consequences (though in certain classrooms there may be). However, young children do not have as much experience with rules as older students do, and teachers must spend time instructing them in proper behavior. How would the teacher of this kindergarten class go about teaching students the specifics associated with some of these rules, such as "Help Mrs. Wade?"

At the upper elementary school level, however, it is advisable to include clearly stated, enforceable consequences. Note that rules for students in the upper elementary school grades and above should specify consequence for breaking the rules. Teachers must, however, consider whether they are willing to give up part of their lunch periods to spend time with misbehaving students, as this teacher apparently is. The lunchtime detention mentioned here might be problematic in several respects. First, it is also a type of detention for the teacher as well in that she loses her own free time—a break she might welcome in the middle of the day. Second, it is important not to deny the student the opportunity to eat lunch (this detention comes during the recess portion of the lunch period). And third, for some students, taking away a time to go outside and burn off energy might not be an advisable approach to classroom management. (See the "Taking It to the Classroom" box on the next page.)

Taking It to the Classroom

Do You Know Jack? The Reluctant Misbehaver

Jack, an athletic student but a struggling learner, was prone to engage in behavior that would get him into trouble. Seated next to him was Melvin, a much stronger student academically but completely unaware of how irritating his behavior could be. During reading instruction, Jack has been working hard to pay attention while Melvin, who is bored, keeps launching his pencil into the aisle from the edge of his desk. Jack ignores the first several launches, but on about the fifth try, Melvin's pencil hits him in the side of the head. Jack gives out a huge and sincere sigh, picks up Melvin's pencil, and takes a big bite out of the middle. He returns the pieces to Melvin's desk saying, "I think these are yours."

As Jack and Melvin's teacher, what would you do about this situation?

1. Do not laugh, at least not until you make it to the teacher's lounge later in the day.

2. Point out to Jack that the pencil has been in Melvin's hands and on the floor and ask him whether he took that into consideration before putting the pencil in his mouth. Talk to him about more constructive ways to deal with a nuisance such as Melvin.

3. Tell Melvin to stop pestering Jack. Tell him you expect more mature behavior from him and offer some prosocial ways of behaving in that situation.

4. Keep Melvin from getting bored. Melvin needs more challenging work, not as punishment for this incident but to keep him more generally engaged.

Rules for Middle and High School Classrooms Like Vernita Johnson, teachers at the middle and high school levels may find that their students are somewhat less likely to behave appropriately simply to gain the teacher's approval, but that they are better able than younger children to understand rules and consequences. The tone of the rules and consequences will probably have to be somewhat more firm than at the elementary and primary levels. For a beginning teacher, coming up with a list of rules that is comprehensive without reading like the Magna Carta may be challenging. General rules must be considered as well as rules that are specific to particular subjects. Lab or shop courses need different rules than foreign language or math classes. Figures 11.4 and 11.5 show two examples of classroom rules and consequences. Safety is especially important in lab classes, as the teacher in Figure 11.5 emphasizes in her rules.

R I D E Think about a new student joining a classroom in mid-year. How hard would it be to learn classroom rules if they were not made explicit?

Establishing Procedures for Routines

In classrooms, pencils have to be sharpened, assessments handed out, homework turned in, fire drills carried out, and the like. These activities do not need rules, but they do need procedures. Without procedures, time is lost, disturbances occur, and students may feel that they are being treated unfairly. Gaea Leinhardt and her colleagues at the University of Pittsburgh have developed categories of **routines** (Leinhardt et al., 1987), and Weinstein and Mignano (2003) have converted them into a set of practical classroom applications. There are three broad categories of routines: class-running routines, lesson-running routines, and interaction routines.

routines Activities that occur on a regular, ongoing basis and require the same or similar behavior on each occurrence (such as sharpening pencils and going to lunch).

- **Class-running routines:** These involve the everyday, nonacademic business of the classroom, including taking attendance, going to the bathroom, cleaning blackboards, and leaving and entering the room at the beginning and end of the day. Creating effective routines for these types of activities can save teachers and students considerable time and aggravation.

- **Lesson-running routines:** These involve instruction. They specify such things as what students should bring to class every day, how to use language lab equipment, what should be included in homework and how it should be handed in, and procedures for using chemicals in the chemistry lab. The effectiveness of lesson-running routines will directly influence the quality of instruction.

> # Rules for Mr. West's Class
>
> **Our goal is to have a happy and productive classroom where students can learn and Mr. West can teach!**
>
> ## Six Easy to Follow Classroom Rules: *The "B" list!*
>
> 1. Be on time—that's in your seat and ready to go when the bell rings.
> 2. Be respectful—we are all equally important in this class and deserve respect.
> 3. Be ready to learn. Have your homework and other materials out and ready to go.
> 4. Be a follower (of classroom procedures).
> 5. Be safe. Don't create a hazard for yourself or your classmates.
> 6. Be thoughtful. Treat others as you would want to be treated.
>
> ## Consequences *for failing to follow the rules.*
>
> 1st offense: Warning from Mr. West about the behavior and the rule.
> 2nd offense: Conference with Mr. West where the problem is explored.
> 3rd offense: Notification of parents of misbehavior.
> 4th offense: You and your problem go to the Vice Principal's office.

Figure 11.4. A Set of Rules and Consequences at the Middle/Junior High School Level

How Can I Use This?

What procedures used by your teachers seemed to work especially well? Maybe you can adapt them to your own classes.

penalties Consequences for misbehavior, such as loss of privileges, time-out, or a visit to the principal's office.

- **Interaction routines:** These govern talking in the classroom. In a room filled with 30 or so people, talk affects the degree to which students can be heard, concentrate on their work, and engage in class discussions. There will be different routines for different instructional activities. For example, when the teacher is presenting information, students will probably be required to raise their hands if they wish to speak. On the other hand, in a small-group discussion, students need to be able to speak more freely without being impolite to others in the group.

Misbehavior: Informal Correctives and Imposing Penalties

One of the problems that novice teachers frequently run into is establishing and enforcing consequences and **penalties** when students misbehave. Mrs. Johnson, for example, was struggling in this area. Classrooms are filled with students who are engaging in minor infractions of rules or simply not paying attention. These situations call for teacher action that stops the behavior without interrupting the instruction.

We all remember from our own school days some of the more effective methods that our teachers used to keep students in line. Some teachers had a *look* that could stop misbehavior in midstream; others used a mild form of ridicule; still others merely moved toward the misbehaving student.

Something that all teachers need to attend to is who gets the look—or the reprimand, or the punishment—and who does not. Research indicates that boys' misbehavior is more likely than girls' to elicit a response from the teacher and that a student who is weaker

---

Welcome to Miss Gurganus's Class Web Site

Miss Gurganus's Classroom Rules
2003–2004 School Year
Physical Science-Matter

RULES

Each student is to

- Arrive at class each day and on time. When the bell rings, each student should be in his/her seat, ready to learn.
- Come to class prepared. Class binder, agenda planner, and a pencil/pen should be brought to class every day. No passes will be written during class. Pencils and pens may be borrowed for collateral.
- Leave distractions outside the classroom. Coats, hats, cosmetics, food, beverages, and music do not belong in class. Leave them in lockers, bags, or at home.
- Conduct himself/herself responsibility and considerately at all times.
- Follow all safety guidelines and procedures.
- Follow all Lincoln High School rules.

CONSEQUENCES

Failure to follow one of the above rules will usually result in a warning. If the infraction is repeated or is very serious, one or more of the following can be expected:

- change of seat assignment
- time spent in the hall
- phone call home
- referral to the office

Violating a lab safety rule may result in permanent removal from the course

Tardies:

A student is tardy if he/she is not in his/her assigned seat when the bell rings. A student is allowed only two unexcused tardies each quarter. For each unexcused tardy after the second one, five points will be subtracted from the student's class work score.

Figure 11.5. A Set of Rules and Consequences at the High School Level

Source: Kyla Gurganus, Lincoln High School Web site. Retrieved March 25, 2005, from http://lincoln.k12.mi.us/~gurganus/matter_rules.html. Reproduced with permission.

academically is more likely to be punished for an infraction than a good student making the same infraction. Teachers also need to make certain that students who are different from themselves in ethnicity, religion, gender, or ability are receiving fair and equal treatment in terms of misbehavior and the imposition of consequences.

Weinstein and Mignano (2003) have categorized a wide variety of teacher interventions and penalties. Drawing on this work, the following are some options for correcting misbehavior with minimal interruption of the flow of instruction. The "Uncommon Sense" box on the next page discusses which ones teachers choose most frequently.

- Ignoring behavior. Sometimes misbehavior can be ignored in an obvious fashion to communicate that it has been observed and that the teacher considers the flow of instruction more important than one student misbehaving.

- Using facial expressions that let a student know a behavior is not appreciated.

- Making direct eye contact with the miscreant; also known as *the look*.

- Signaling to the offending student with a hand signal or a nod.

- Moving toward the student who is misbehaving.

- Stopping instruction in midsentence. (The pause usually attracts attention.)

- Increasing the volume of instruction noticeably (to let students know there is a disturbance that requires this modification).

off task   Not paying attention to instruction.

Uncommon Sense

Kids Need to Be Brought Back on Task—Or Do They?

Two of the authors of this text teach a course called "Teacher as Researcher" in which students who are preparing to become teachers collect and analyze data on topics of their choice. One group project focused on perhaps the most common form of misbehavior in classrooms: not paying attention, or being **off task.** This research team (Escudero et al., 2002) went into 14 elementary school classrooms (grades 4–6) and observed a complete lesson in mathematics. Their task was to scan the classroom to find a student who was off task. They recorded what kind of off-task behavior the student engaged in and what the teacher did to bring the student back on task. Figure 11.6 shows the percentages of the different kinds of off-task behaviors in which students engaged.

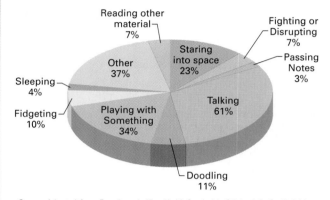

Source: Adapted from Escudero, J., Kim, Y., McGrath, M., Odabasi, P., So, E. & Vera, F. (2002). *What cues cause off-task students to get back on task?* Unpublished manuscript, New Brunswick, NJ: Rutgers University.

Figure 11.6. What Students Do When They Are Off Task

Now look at Figure 11.7 to see what the teachers did to get the students back on task. Somewhat surprisingly, the most frequent behavior that veteran teachers employed to get students back on task was to do nothing. In almost 25% of the cases observed, students got themselves back on task with no action by the teacher. The second most frequent occurrence is to signal to the student, either by nodding or by pointing at the student and the work, that he or she is off task. The *other* category contained a variety of nonverbal and verbal behaviors, including using humor, tapping on the student's desk while passing by, and so forth. Perhaps the most direct intervention that was used with any frequency was simply saying the student's name.

The behavior of the teachers in this study demonstrates that their first priority was keeping the lesson on pace. Novice teachers sometimes expend too much effort dealing with inattention, disrupting the entire class in the process. This research shows that sometimes it might be better not to react immediately when one notices students going off task. Students will often get themselves back on task with no intervention, and when an intervention is needed, it need not disrupt the flow of instruction.

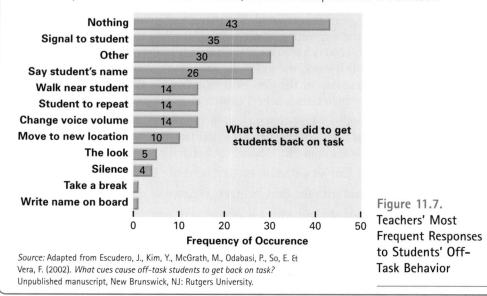

Source: Adapted from Escudero, J., Kim, Y., McGrath, M., Odabasi, P., So, E. & Vera, F. (2002). *What cues cause off-task students to get back on task?* Unpublished manuscript, New Brunswick, NJ: Rutgers University.

Figure 11.7. Teachers' Most Frequent Responses to Students' Off-Task Behavior

- Saying the student's name. This can be done directly or as part of the flow of the instruction, as in, "Let's say, David, for instance, wanted to know . . ."

- Calling on the student. There is a fine line here between bringing the student back into the instruction and making him or her feel "picked on." The difference often lies in how the teacher handles the student's response. Students might feel that they are being treated unfairly, for example, if the teacher calls on them to answer a question they did not hear or cannot answer. A less punitive use of this approach is to call on the student first, then ask the question.

- Using humor. This can be directed toward the class as a whole or toward an individual student. It is important to differentiate between humor and sarcasm, however.

- Using an **I-message** or other indication of disappointment in the student behavior. I-messages involve describing the inappropriate behavior and its effect on the teacher or the class, followed by a statement of the teacher's feelings about the situation. For example, "Danielle, when you start putting things in your backpack before the bell rings, it makes me feel that you don't care about what's happening in class." A less formal approach might be a statement such as, "It's hard for me to explain this properly with other people talking."

- Making a direct request to cease and desist.

- Reminding students that a rule is being broken. This has the additional benefit of letting students know that the teacher knows the rule is being broken.

- Raising the possibility of a penalty if the behavior does not stop.

I-message   A reaction to a behavior that describes the behavior and how it has affected a given situation, and describes the individual's emotional response to the behavior.

What Does This Mean to Me?
Which of these options do you think you would be able to carry out? Which ones should you practice?

Sometimes misbehavior ranges beyond inattentiveness or distracting behavior, and a more significant intervention is necessary. This can be a particular problem for special needs students with behavioral problems. When misbehavior clearly violates class rules and informal correctives do not seem sufficient, penalties might be the next step in maintaining a productive learning community. There are a variety of possible penalties, which Weinstein and Mignano (2003) have organized into categories. These have been adapted to create the list that follows this paragraph. This list should not be interpreted as a hierarchy or a sequence; it is simply a list of possibilities. When they administer penalties, teachers should make a special effort to explain why the student is being penalized and what the student can do to avoid penalties in the future. By explaining the rationale behind the penalty and by offering students a more desirable and productive way of behaving, the teacher's goal is not so much to punish the student as it is to create a learning experience in which the misbehaving student has a chance to internalize the classroom rule and develop a more constructive way of behaving.

If it is necessary to punish a misbehaving student, these guidelines will be helpful:

- Assignment of points toward a penalty. Many teachers have a system in which a student receives a negative mark of some sort for misbehavior. These points have to accumulate for the student to reach the next level of punishment. Typically, improved behavior can reduce the number of points on the student's record.

- Loss of privileges. The privilege lost can be free time, use of the computer, choosing a game for the class to play, or something else that the student values.

- Time out. This means removal from the flow of activity in the classroom for a specified period.

- Written reflections on the problem. Some teachers have students write about what happened, why it happened, what the consequences were, and how they can improve their behavior in the future. The writing assignment may include a letter of apology to an affected student. This is the journal version of having to write, "I will not speak out of turn" 100 times on the blackboard.

- Visits to the principal's office. Nobody wants to go to the principal's office. Teachers should keep in mind that the principal cannot take the time to attend to large numbers of misbehaving children.

- Contact with parents. One of the authors of this text, whose elementary school classroom (as a student) looked a lot like the one described at the beginning of the chapter, remembers his father often saying, "If you're in trouble in school, you're in trouble at home." This was not comforting, but it encouraged model behavior in school. Contacting caregivers should not be used as a threat to students; it should be an admission that the child's behavior is sufficiently out of line that the school and the family need to work together to solve it. To prevent the situation from becoming this serious, teachers may wish to involve students' families in the classroom at a much earlier stage. Teachers need to be careful not to communicate the idea that a student needs to be punished by parents. Positive communication established to promote positive outcomes is the key.

Conclusions About Establishing Norms and Rules

Setting rules, and consequences for not following them, is a critical element of classroom management. Rules need to be taught to students in a conscientious fashion, and teachers must make sure that students—especially younger students—understand them. There are a variety of *tricks* that teachers can use to stop minor misbehaviors before they become major disruptions. Successful teachers blend nonverbal cues, direct requests, humor, and occasionally penalties to keep the class on task. Establishing procedures for running the class, the lesson, and interaction routines is also a nice way to support desired behavior and minimize undesirable behavior.

Beginning teachers do not have to do this all by themselves. Numerous models are available. When this chapter was being written, an Internet search on "classroom rules" produced thousands of Web sites dealing with the topic. In addition, it is advisable for new teachers to ask how other teachers in their school deal with classroom management issues, what kinds of rules students have been required to follow in previous years, and what the most effective classroom routines are.

Managing Day-to-Day Classroom Instruction

Day-to-day instruction can mean many different things. In the classroom from 1937 that is pictured at the beginning of the chapter, it looks as though most instruction will take the form of lectures and explanations by the teacher. Indeed, this is what teaching consisted of for many decades. In some classes, it still is. This approach can be very effective if the teacher's ability to explain is strong. However, most teachers instruct in a variety of formats and settings, using independent (seat) work, small-group work, and whole-class instruction. This section describes those formats and examines the strengths and weaknesses of each.

Independent Work or Seatwork

seatwork Work that is done independently by students at their desks or seats.

Seatwork is independent work on some learning task that is done individually by a student in the classroom. This approach has been in disfavor in recent years because it is assumed to consist of little more than filling in blanks on an endless set of repetitive worksheets. Seatwork, however, does not have to be repetitive or boring. If seatwork is engaging, related to the instructional goals of the class and the student, and geared to the student's cognitive level, it can be a very useful activity. The strength of independent work is that it gives students a chance to work on things they need to do alone: to practice and improve skills, explore new areas, or consolidate what they have learned.

Seatwork has both an instructional and a managerial function (Weinstein & Mignano, 2003). The instructional function has to do with the content and nature of the seatwork, whereas the managerial function stems from the fact that children will be quiet and nondisruptive while doing seatwork, allowing the teacher to focus his or her attention on an individual student or a small group. To make seatwork fulfill both functions, teachers need to keep in mind the potential weaknesses of this approach. For example, if a large number of students are engaged in seatwork, there is a strong possibility that they will finish their work at different times. This can result in students with nothing to do, which is always a

Students sometimes need to develop and reinforce skills through independent seat work. It is important to make sure that this work is productive for students, not just a time filler. (Media Bakery)

problem. In thinking about seatwork, the teacher needs to have an option for students who finish early, such as "When you're finished with this, please work on the geography assignment from yesterday."

Another concern with seatwork is that, because the purpose is to have students work independently, if they get stuck on a problem, the teacher cannot always be there to help them with it. Several options are available for addressing this concern:

- Another student can provide help.
- Students can skip problems that they cannot figure out.
- Students can *hold* their help requests until the teacher is free to help them.
- Independent activities can be assigned that do not call for a series of correct answers. For example, independent work could involve writing in a journal about recently read material or editing a peer's essay.

Seatwork can also be blended with homework by giving students a problem set, allowing some seattime to work on these problems, and assigning as homework the problems that they do not finish in class. This approach has several advantages. First, because every problem done in class means more free time in the evening, there is strong motivation for students to stay on task. Second, if a student has a question about a particular problem, it can be asked while the teacher is available, and misunderstandings can be diagnosed and corrected quickly. Third, if enough problems are assigned, it eliminates the problem of some students finishing their seatwork and not having anything to do.

Another effective approach to seatwork is to have students study for an upcoming assessment. Many students are very poor at studying for exams. If the teacher is going to work with a small group or an individual student, the remaining students can be assigned study material. This studying can be structured so as to teach proper study techniques, such as outlining and condensing material and self-testing.

Small-Group Work

Small-group work might be defined as work done independently by some subset of the entire class. This might be a form of cooperative or collaborative learning (see Chapter 12) or it might be a simple and short-term task that students can work on together, or where they can help one another. This instructional format has a number of strengths, including the following:

- Increased learning
- More interaction among students (Johnson & Johnson, 1989/90)
- Development of friendships (perhaps across gender, racial, and ethnic lines)
- Greater productivity

small-group work Work being done independently by a group of students smaller than the whole class.

Group work has potential weaknesses, as well. Among them are the following:

- Decreased learning (or no increase in learning) in some settings (O'Donnell & O'Kelly, 1994)
- Management problems in the classroom (children working in groups usually increases the noise and activity levels in the classroom which may be a problem in some situations)
- Unequal participation among group members (Cohen 1994)
- Difficulties in assigning grades fairly
- Student disaffection with group-based activities

Working in small groups is a double-edged sword; it offers both strenghts and weaknesses. Effective group work can turn out very well for both the teacher and the students, but group work is often done very poorly. Because it is such a challenging and important aspect of classroom learning today, we devote an entire chapter of this text (Chapter 12) to peer learning. The important point is that group work constitutes one useful option for teachers to consider in their efforts to manage classroom instruction.

Whole-Class Instruction

In many classrooms, particularly at the secondary school level, whole-class instruction dominates instructional time. **Whole-class instruction** simply means that the whole class is participating in the same activity. The activity may be a lecture or explanation by the teacher; it may be a recitation (question by the teacher, answer by a student) or a class discussion. Each of these formats has its own unique strengths and can be very useful if done well. A weakness of much whole-class instruction, however, is that students are often passive in their learning, participating only occasionally at best.

Lecturing and Explaining
Lecturing and **explaining** occur when the teacher is talking to the entire class about a subject, and the students are listening and taking notes. During a lecture, information is being provided, much as it would be in a text format. Lecturing is the predominant mode of instruction in most college courses, especially large classes. More common in K-12 instruction is explanation. The difference between the two is that whereas lecturing is focused on the subject matter and the presentation of information, ideas, and concepts; explanation involves taking apart that information, those ideas and concepts, and putting them back together in such a way as to make them easier to understand. The focus is on the learner at least as much as on the subject matter. A lecture may be the best approach to use if you are trying to get across information that all the students need to know and is not available through other means, but often students need to have things explained to them rather than simply presented in a lecture.

RIDE How does the organization of a classroom encourage or discourage working in small groups?

Chapter Reference
Chapter 12 covers learning in groups.

whole-class instruction Working on instructional material with the whole class at the same time.

lecturing Presentation information to a group of learners as a whole.

explaining Breaking down the concepts and ideas of a lesson to make them easier to understand.

Working in small groups can lead to improved skills, sharing of ideas, and enhance socialization among students. Make sure it is not simply a time to chat about school and friends.
(David Grossman/The Image Works)

This can be thought of in terms of explaining a concept such as Thanksgiving. How could Thanksgiving be explained to the following groups of people?

- A classroom full of kindergarten students
- A group of dignitaries visiting from Thailand (who speak English)
- A friend from Canada

In reflecting on how to go about this, consider:

- How much knowledge people have about this topic at the outset
- What you know and do not know about Thanksgiving
- How much information people have about related concepts
- How much information the group can process at one time
- The best way to convey information to this group
- Good metaphors, analogies, and examples to use

Explanations are almost always more interesting than lectures. Unless a person is truly prepared to listen to a lecture at the level at which it is given, it can be quite boring. If students are bored, they will find relatively more interesting diversions to pass the time. Explanations that are on target, anticipate the students' learning needs, and use bold metaphors and examples that are pertinent to students' lives can be very engaging. When presenting information to the class as a whole, do not lose sight of the need to make sure everyone understands it and to provide opportunities for interaction.

Recitation and Discussion In **recitation,** the teacher asks questions, the students answer, and the teacher evaluates the quality of their responses (this is also called a *drill* or IRE discourse). The idea of recitation is to learn how well the students know the material and whether there are specific areas of misunderstanding or lack of knowledge, and to give students a chance to show what they can do. The focus tends to be on correct answers, which leads to a public evaluation of the quality of the answer and of the student giving the response. Recitation is often criticized because of these two issues, but the recitation format has certain strengths as well. First, sometimes there *are* right answers. For example, if certain chemicals are mixed, either there will be a precipitant or there will not be one. Second, the recitation format is a good way to get an idea of how well the class understands certain concepts. Third, when the class is well prepared for a recitation, it can be a very positive experience. Here are some things that veteran teachers keep in mind when using this format:

recitation An instructional approach where teachers ask closed-ended questions (questions with clear right answers) and students answer them.

- Every student should be called upon for a response. It is easy for some students to get lost in the shuffle. Having a sheet on which to check off names as students participate helps the teacher make sure that everyone is participating, thus avoiding a situation such as the one described in the "What Kids Say and Do" box on the next page. The checklist also silently communicates to students that they will all be expected to participate.

- Pose the question and leave some **wait time** before calling on anyone for an answer. If a particular student is called upon before the question is posed, some of the other students will not try to come up with the answer. If the question is posed before calling on a student, all the students have to think about the question.

wait time The time between when a question is asked in a classroom and when a student is called upon to answer it.

- Look for elements of correctness in responses that are not 100% on target. If a person is way off, some gentle humor can deflect embarrassment. Or simply say, "That's not really what I'm looking for here—who else would like to give this a try?"

- Remember that children from some cultures are not comfortable with public recitation or with receiving public criticism (or even praise). This can be a sensitive issue. It is best not to treat all members of a particular group the same way but instead to try to understand tendencies and look for solutions. Consult a veteran teacher or administrator to find out how teachers approach this issue.

What Kids Say and Do

Helping Out

Andy Mignano, one of the authors of the excellent book on classroom management mentioned earlier, was also the fourth-grade science teacher of a child of one of the authors of this text. When this parent told Andy how much his son, Ben, was enjoying science class, Andy asked, a bit puzzled, "How do you know? He *never* raises his hand in class."

Your author went home and asked his son, "Hey, Buddy, how come you never raise your hand in Mr. Mignano's class?"

"Oh, Dad, Mr. Mignano *knows* I know the material," he replied, "I don't raise my hand so he can find out if the *other* kids know the material."

● Recitation may not be fun, but a quiz show often is. Try turning your recitation into a version of a quiz show that is popular with the students.

Recitation can be an effective way to get an idea of how well the class is doing, but students like to express ideas as well as hunt for right answers. A related format is the class discussion. In class discussions, a topic is raised, and students offer ideas and opinions about it. Discussion questions generally do not have a single right answer, and the teacher does not evaluate students' responses for correctness, as in recitation. Teacher-led discussions can be exciting exchanges; students may come up with new ideas, and the teacher can get a sense of how much the class knows about a topic. The teacher also needs to take steps to avoid certain problems. First, make sure that a few students do not dominate the discussion and that other students contribute. Second, make certain that the topic is one that will generate interest. A common disaster, especially for beginning teachers, is the anticipated 20-minute class discussion that falls flat on its face after 3 minutes. This can be hard to predict. For secondary school teachers who are teaching several sections of the same class, the same topic can generate wildfire in the morning class and not even a spark in the afternoon. Teacher enthusiasm will play a part in how well the discussion goes, but it is hard to predict when a discussion will die out prematurely. The best course is to always have a backup plan.

Our discussion points out certain parallels between lecture and explanation on one hand and recitation and discussion on the other. Lecture and explanation represent two ends of a continuum between a presentation focusing on subject matter and a more student-oriented presentation, a range from "this is what this is about" to "this is how best to understand this." Explanation focuses on the learner; lecture on the topic. Similarly, recitation is directed toward getting right answers based on the material, whereas discussion is directed toward eliciting the ideas and opinions of the participants. Thus, the nature of a discussion is determined more by the group than by the topic, whereas a recitation session is oriented toward the topic. Figure 11.8 summarizes these contrasts.

All the instruction formats we have discussed have both strengths and weaknesses. There is no single approach that is best for all teachers, students, grade levels, or subject areas. Even for a particular teacher, there is no single approach that is best at all times. On the first day of school, for example, most teachers, especially beginning teachers, should use instructional activities that are readily managed, perhaps in a whole-class setting.

Activities that do not involve the whole class usually require more planning and a higher level of energy on the part of the teacher. Organizing instruction to work with groups and individual students should not be viewed as an impossible task but as an opportunity to accomplish more than one thing at a time. A teacher cannot be everywhere at once, but that does not mean that learning should not be going on everywhere at once. It takes planning, careful and enthusiastic action, and reflection on what went well and what did not to develop the ability to blend different teaching formats. When the teacher is working with students individually or with groups, other students must be doing something else. This helps students learn how to work productively on their own or in small groups.

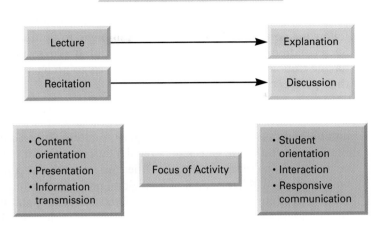

Figure 11.8. A Continuum of Whole-Class Activities

Each teacher has to find the mix of settings and approaches that seems to work best at a particular time. The best advice is always to think through the possibilities of at least two different ways to approach a particular lesson and to look for opportunities to blend different formats.

Special Needs, Diversity, and Instruction

One can see why issues of special needs and diversity must be taken into account in any discussion of classroom instruction simply by looking at the children in a typical classroom. There is diversity in interests, physical ability, ethnicity, language, gender, socioeconomic status, special needs, home life, and a host of other aspects and attributes. How should the teacher deal with these differences in planning instruction? Paul Burden (2003) provides an excellent overview of how to think about diversity as it relates to issues of classroom management. He makes suggestions in four major areas related to developing an **inclusive** and multicultural classroom (pp. 152–158):

inclusive An approach to education in general, whether teaching, working with students, or curriculum, that includes students from different cultures and with different abilities and challenges.

- **Create a supportive and caring environment:** Each student comes to class as a unique individual. If a student speaks a different language, observes different holidays, or has different special interests, celebrate those differences in the classroom. At the same time that those differences are recognized and honored, the same standards have to apply to all the students in the class. All students need to be encouraged, their strengths and weaknesses recognized and incorporated into instruction. This not only promotes academic growth but also shows students that the teacher cares about them. Experienced teachers occasionally look through their class roster and ask, "Am I more positive toward some students than others? Am I treating all the students fairly?" It is easy to slip into a habit of reacting negatively to some students and positively to others for the same or similar behavior.

- **Offer a responsive curriculum:** Make sure that instructional materials are inclusive and free from bias. This can be a particular problem if some materials are old. Even as recently as 10 years ago, instructional materials reflected certain groups in a less-than-positive light. (For example, does the science text describe both male and female scientists, include people with physical challenges, and portray individuals from a variety of cultures?) Web sites are available that provide materials with a multicultural and inclusive orientation.

- **Vary instruction:** Not all children learn equally well from any given approach to instruction. Be sure to use a variety of instructional approaches, including letting children work individually, both in terms of how they learn and, in some cases, what they choose to learn. Do not miss opportunities to include culturally relevant material in your instruction.

- **Provide needed assistance:** Some students need special assistance from time to time. This includes not only special needs children with individual education programs but also students who are struggling with a particular task and students who need a push to achieve a high level of performance. Some children need extra help to follow the norms and rules of the classroom and to fit in with the group as a whole. Such children can be a particular challenge. In working with children who are having trouble, it is almost always useful to try to understand the situation from their perspective.

As a general rule, the teacher should to try to understand who the students are and how they differ from one another, then use that information to benefit the students and the class as a whole. Maintain high expectations for all students while recognizing that they are different. Check on a regular basis to make sure that students have equal opportunities to reach their goals. Other programs that might prove useful, particularly with students with emotional or behavioral problems, include Skillstreaming the Elementary School Child (McGinnis & Goldstein, 1997) and the Affective/Social Skills: Instructional Strategies and Techniques program (Huggins, 1995).

There is a tendency to focus on the problems of students with learning or behavior challenges in terms of what those challenges mean for others (e.g., disruptive behavior, need for additional attention). However, it is often useful to stop and think about life from the perspective of those who are facing the challenges. Bos and Vaughn (2002) have put together an excellent research summary of school life from the perspective of the learning-disabled student. Among their findings are that such students are not well accepted by their peers, have poor conversational skills, are less likely to be chosen in play settings, are more susceptible to peer pressure to engage in inappropriate behavior, and interact less often with their parents and teachers. It is important to remember that students who face these challenges live not only with these difficulties but with the consequences of the difficulties, as well. That is, with fewer friends, less ability to express feelings appropriately, and a greater likelihood to behave inappropriately, all of the developmental social challenges faced by children are exacerbated by these problems.

> **What Does This Mean to Me?**
> If a child from the island nation of Palau is assigned to my class, does that mean I should look up Palau to see what that country is like?

Dealing with Behavior Problems

> **Appendix**
> *Behavior Problems*
> There are a variety of approaches for addressing behavior problems effectively (*PRAXIS™*, II. B. 2, *INTASC*, Principle 5).

Some problems are more serious than occasional misbehavior, acting out, or a class that is rowdy on the Friday afternoon before a holiday. These problems move beyond the realm of classroom rules into serious issues. These issues are of four basic types: chronic problems, acute problems, personal problems, and particular problems.

Chronic Problems

Chronic problems are problems that, although they may not be serious in any one instance, persist over time. This might involve talking out of turn, failure to complete homework, or inability to keep one's hands to oneself. Although these problems may seem small, even trivial, when described on paper, they can be vexing because the usual classroom management techniques are not successful with the students involved. A variety of approaches have been developed for handling chronic misbehavior problems. These include the following:

> **chronic problems** Problems that persist over time, even though they may not be severe.

- **Contingency contracting.** This approach consists of negotiating and agreeing to a contract. The contract calls for appropriate modification of the behavior for a specified period and a reward for successful completion of the contract (the reward is *contingent* on the student's meeting the terms of the contract).

> **contingency contacting** An approach to behavior management that involves a written agreement about behavior that makes rewards and punishments depend on the students' performance of that behavior.

- **Self-management.** This approach involves having a child keep a record of certain behaviors that the teacher wishes to increase (such as raising a hand before speaking in a class discussion) or decrease (such as poking the child in the next seat). Recording desirable or undesirable behaviors in order to become more aware of how frequently they occur should enhance students' self-awareness and self-management skills.

> **self-management** An approach to behavioral modification where students keep a written record of their behavior in an effort to increase desirable behaviors or decrease undesirable ones.

● **Logical consequences.** This is a cognitive approach that involves tying consequences directly to behavior. For example, if a student misbehaves during recess, he or she must spend recess in the classroom. If a student is not working on completing tasks in class, those tasks can be assigned as homework. Vitto (2003) presents some useful suggestions for thinking about appropriate consequences, including asking, Would this consequence cause *me* to change *my* behavior?

These approaches, and other possibilities, are detailed interventions that need to be well understood before being carried out. A list of resources and programs for changing chronic behavior problems can be found at the Web site for this text.

logical consequences An approach to classroom management that lets the natural outcomes of bad behavior serve as the punishment for that behavior.

www.wiley.com/college/odonnell

Acute Problems

Acute problems are problems that do not occur on a regular basis but are serious and demand immediate attention. This might include abusive or defiant behavior, behavior that makes it impossible to go on with the lesson, or behavior that harms or endangers another student or the student who engages in it. Acute problems can occur at any grade level but are more likely to occur at the high school level. Two issues arise in connection with such behavior: how to prevent it and how to deal with it if it occurs.

How Can I Use This?
What is a logical consequence for students who talk to their neighbors too much in class?

Preventing Acute Problems Although some **acute problems** are completely unforeseen, many are escalations of minor issues (Weinstein, 2003). Thus, many acute problems can be prevented simply by not letting minor problems escalate. The key is to be aware of the potential for escalation and to defuse the problem. The tips listed in the "Taking It to the Classroom" box on this page may help prevent many acute problems.

acute problems Problems that occur only infrequently but are severe.

Taking It to the Classroom

Tips for Creating a Peaceful Classroom

This set of principles for working with students in classrooms, compiled by the Center for Adolescent and Family Studies at Indiana University, provides a helpful commonsense way of looking at teaching as a profession.

1. **Have a genuine interest in your students.** Greet students at the door. Learn about their culture(s). Be aware of teen slang terms. Offer praise and encouragement frequently. Attend to students as individuals, not just to the class as a whole.

2. **Communicate classroom rules clearly.** Enforce rules fairly and consistently. Consider each incident's unique circumstances while making discipline-related decisions.

3. **Be objective, not judgmental.** Try to adopt the students' perspective. Look at issues from a variety of perspectives.

4. **Show that you are human.** Be prepared to admit your mistakes. Use humor when appropriate.

5. **Minimize the power differential in everyday communication.** Sitting behind a desk or standing behind a podium can send the message that you want to create some distance between yourself and the students. Avoid language telling students what they must, should, or have to do. Instead, explain the reasons behind your rules, requests, and assignments so that students understand that these really are for their own good.

6. **Address problem behavior directly and immediately.** Unresolved conflicts and issues often recur. Addressing a problem early lessens the chance that it will arise again.

7. **Take a collaborative approach.** Maximize opportunities for student choices within the classroom. Consider the perspective that this is *our* classroom, not *my* classroom. Actively solicit students' opinions and perspectives.

Source: Adapted from Center for Adolescent and Family Studies (1996). Tips for creating a peaceful classroom. *Teacher Talk,* 2(3), Indiana University, Bloomington, IN. Retrieved March 25, 2005, from http://www.education.indiana.edu/cas/tt/v2i3/peaceful.html

It is important to remember that students spend the entire school day with very few opportunities to make choices. Earlier in the chapter, we discussed the tension between freedom and structure. Although students need structure, sometimes they also need a feeling of greater freedom, dignity, and autonomy. If a student behaves in a defiant or disruptive fashion, he or she may be expressing frustration over a lack of choice and control. That frustration may have little or nothing to do with the current situation. (We have all done things that we regretted later because we were upset over a completely different matter.) If, in an attempt to correct the misbehavior, the teacher challenges the student and attempts to exert authority, it may push the student past his or her limits and turn a simple problem into a complex one. This might occur with any student, even one who is usually perceived as a *good* student, so it may come as a surprise to the teacher. When frustrated, it can be hard for the teacher to see that a student is upset and try to understand why so that the problem can be worked out. It is always better to be on guard against such possibilities and to defuse potentially explosive situations before they occur.

Dealing with Acute Problems When a problem becomes acute, a teacher may be angry, intimidated (even fearful), frustrated, and in danger of losing emotional control. The irony here is that it is in these situations that the teacher most needs to be calm, flexible, and in control of his or her emotions. The first priority is to avoid imposing one's own will or trying to *save face.* Instead, it is far better to assess the situation and work to defuse it. Once the situation is calm, order can be reestablished.

If uninvolved students are in danger or are making the problem worse by paying attention to it, the teacher can either ask them to leave the room or tell them to work on something else. This not only removes part of the problem but also communicates to everyone the message that the teacher is in charge.

The next step is to give the problem student some way of escaping from the situation with dignity. A teacher can ask the student to join him or her in the hallway for a minute in a voice that communicates firmness but also sympathy. Once there, the student can present his or her view of the problem. The focus should be on the student's concerns. The teacher can revisit the incident in the classroom when the student is calmer, and a less intense discussion can occur. These steps might not always work; in such cases, the teacher will have to seek help from someone in the school who is trained and responsible for dealing with such situations, such as a principal, counselor, or school psychologist.

When the incident is over, it can be useful for the teacher to discuss it with colleagues. The very act of engaging in a discussion can be helpful emotionally. Moreover, the situation can be analyzed: What went wrong? What other forms of intervention might have been more successful? Finally, the teacher needs to follow up on the situation, talking to the student after things have cooled off—maybe even a day or two later. The incident can be used as an opportunity to help the student work on the underlying problem.

Personal Problems

At all levels, but particularly at the middle and high school levels, students may be dealing with serious problems of mental or physical health. A student might confide in the teacher about a problem—an unwanted pregnancy, an eating disorder, contemplation of suicide, extreme anger toward another student or group of students. Indications of a problem in a piece of written work or artwork might be noticed, or a teacher might overhear a troubling interaction between students. These interactions must be taken very seriously. Although they may be difficult to contemplate, teachers are the first resource available to help deal with such problems.

At the same time, teachers need to remember that they are *not* the school counselor, the school psychologist, or the police. The teacher's role in this process is to work with people who are trained to handle such issues. Many states require that certain observations be reported to the police or other authorities. *It is absolutely essential that teachers understand clearly what their responsibilities are for such reporting.* When in doubt about a given situation, it is critical to find out what these responsibilities are.

In *Principles of Classroom Management: A Professional Decision-Making Model,* James Levin and James F. Nolan (2004) present a set of six warning signs indicating that a student is in distress. The following list is adapted from their work.

1. **Changes in physical appearance.** Changes in dress or grooming habits can be warning signs of deeper problems. Sudden weight loss or gain and problems with teeth can signal eating disorders. Cuts and scarring may indicate self-mutilation.

2. **Changes in activity level.** Students who are frequently tardy or absent, fall asleep in class, or are hyperactive may be expressing symptoms of a wide range of problems.

3. **Changes in personality.** Students who suddenly change from being outgoing and friendly to engaging in outbursts of inappropriate behavior or showing signs of depression need to be watched carefully.

4. **Changes in achievement status.** A decline in a student's performance in class may be a symptom of deeper problems—personal, interpersonal, or even physical.

5. **Changes in health or physical abilities.** If a student appears to be having trouble hearing or seeing, has difficulty speaking, or complains of physical illness, you need to be concerned about the student's overall health.

6. **Changes in socialization.** Children who are isolated and withdrawn and seem to have no or few friends are cause for concern.

Particular Problems

There are particular problems that do not fall neatly into any of the categories discussed thus far. These problems are cheating, bullying, and violence. Cheating and bullying are age-old problems that have recently gained the attention of researchers. Violence is also an age-old problem, one that is all too common in American schools.

Cheating It is sad to say, but cheating is rampant in American schools. Ditman (2000) reports that four of five high achievers in a high school survey admit to having cheated at some point. Evans and Craig (1990) report similar levels of cheating by middle and high school students. In an excellent and highly readable work, *Cheating on Tests: How to Do It, Detect It, and Prevent It,* Cizek (1999) surveys the ways in which students cheat on all types of assessments. He has developed a **taxonomy**, an ordered categorization, of how students cheat. More recently (2003) he has turned this research into a practical handbook for teachers who have discovered that their students are cheating.

taxonomy A classification of objects according to a set of principles or laws.

Although it is difficult to prevent all forms of cheating, there are some simple steps that can minimize the likelihood that cheating will occur:

- Assign seats for exams that are different from the students' regular seats, and if possible, spread students out so that there is space between them, in order to cut down on opportunities for copying from other students' exams.
- If there are several sections of the same course, create multiple forms of exams, or just mix up the order of the choices in the multiple-choice section.
- Give exams that require higher order thinking skills rather than recall of information to reduce the utility of *crib sheets* for the exam. Eliminating hats, gum, cell phones, and PDAs will also cut down on opportunities to use crib sheets.
- Use software that has been specially developed to scan the Internet for plagiarized material in student papers. An alternative is simply to enter a suspicious phrase into a search engine and specify "exact phrase." This is likely to turn up an original source if the material is not orginal.
- Finally, if cheating seems to be a serious problem, use a reference such as one of the books by Cizek.

How Can I Use This?

What are some ways you feel that you could begin a discussion with a student whom you suspect of cheating?

Violence Violence has become a sad and frightening reality in American schools. One research team (Kaufman et al., 1999) found that in the mid-1990s, one in ten schools reported that a serious crime or act of violence had occurred in the school. Although, as a society, only when a tragedy such as the Columbine shootings occurs do we focus on school violence very long, lesser instances of violence occur all too often.

A report issued by the U.S. Secret Service Safe School Initiative (2000) indicates that in most cases, the perpetrators of school shootings felt that they were the victims of bullies (discussed later in the section) or other unfair treatment in school. As teachers, it is important to watch for signs that students are troubled. The warning signs described earlier under the heading of *personal problems* can also indicate that a student may be considering committing a violent act. Teachers may notice troubling signals in students' appearance or behavior, or occasionally in the things they write for assignments. If a teacher is seriously concerned about a particular student, this concern needs to be communicated to a principal, school counselor or psychologist, or perhaps to legal authorities.

Bullying   Bullying often does not appear to be a serious problem for most educators because it tends to occur on school buses, in hallways, on the playground, or after school. In a fascinating study, Barone (1997) found that although 60% of eighth-grade students said that they had been bullied while in middle school, their teachers expected that the percentage would be about 16%. There is clearly a lack of congruence between the magnitude of the problem and its perception by teachers.

Bullying usually involves what Vitto (2003) calls an *imbalance of power*. Students or groups of students who are stronger physically, emotionally, or intellectually, or who are higher in status inflict some sort of hurtful behavior (teasing, taunting, physical abuse) on weaker students or groups of students (Smith & Brain, 2000). This hurtful behavior can turn everyday school life into torture for the victims. Bullies share a number of characteristics, both in terms of personality and in terms of home environment. They want to dominate their victims and show little regard or empathy for them; they tend to have poor academic records; and they are more likely than other students to smoke and consume alcohol (Roberts & Morotti, 2000). They tend to come from homes where aggression and negative attitudes are common (Glover et al., 2000). Different scholars view the problem of bullying differently, but most agree that there are multiple causes of bullying, including social pressures and rewards, personality problems, and family influences (Smith et al., 2004).

Bullying has recently gained the attention of educational researchers, and a number of antibullying programs have been developed. Perhaps the most widely studied program is the Olewus Bullying Prevention Program (Olewus, 1993, 1997), which involves a schoolwide approach to the prevention of bullying. The Olewus program emphasizes direct teaching on the issue of bullying; ongoing communication among school teachers, counselors, and administrators; and a team approach to the problem. Research conducted in Norway, where the program originated, has been quite promising, but efforts to implement the program elsewhere have been less successful (Smith et al., 2004).

www.wiley.com/college/odonnell

The issue for teachers concerns what to do in the classroom about bullying, because it does not usually take place there. The first thing teachers can do is bring the issue out into the open. Teachers need to talk about respect for others' feelings and point out that what is seen as teasing by the instigator is experienced as bullying by the victim. Also, teachers need to monitor potential bullies and clearly communicate to them that such behavior will not be tolerated. Several resources are listed on the Web site that accompanies this text, including such works as *Bully-Proofing Your School: A Comprehensive Approach for Middle School* (Bonds & Stoker, 2000), and *Bullying in American Schools: A Social-Ecological Perspective on Prevention and Intervention* (Espelage & Swearer, 2004).

R I D E

REFLECTION FOR ACTION

The Event

Before children ever enter a classroom, the process of teaching and learning begins when a teacher designs the classroom. Now it is time to think seriously about the classroom you will design. What will it look like? What activities will it encourage or inhibit? How will students react to it?

Reflection   R I D E

How good will you be at designing a classroom? Think about a particular classroom setting, such as a first grade class with 25 6-year-olds or a high school class with 30 students learning about home economics. What do these classrooms need to convey to students. What should they encourage or restrict? Now turn to your future classroom and ask the same questions. Do not just think about this in the abstract. Make a list. Indentify various options and think about the pros and cons.

What Theoretical/Conceptual Information Might Assist in Interpreting and Remedying This Situation? Consider the following.

Considering the Social Environment

What are the norms, rules, and patterns of social interaction you are trying to promote in your classroom? What do you have to pay special attention to in developing the learning community that is going to exist in your classroom? How might you facilitate progress in this area through the design of your classroom?

Influence on Learning and Managing the Classroom

How does classroom design influence learning? Cohen (1994), Morrow and Weinstein (1982), and Evertson and Harris (2003) have looked in detail at how the design of a classroom influences different approaches to learning and management problems.

Symbolic Representation

What does this classroom represent to me and my students? *Looking in Classrooms* by Good and Brophy (2000) offers an excellent vehicle for thinking about such issues.

Information Gathering

Some people are good at design, and others are not. If you are, please keep the ideas presented in the chapter in mind in making your decisions. If you are not, help is available. For practicing teachers, there are books and professional articles, other teachers, Web sites, students, their parents, and others (e.g., friends with some knowledge of design). For the purposes of this assignment, books and articles, Web sites, and friends might be the best sources of information.

Decision Making R I D E

Try out your decision with a simulation. You can do this with a piece of graph paper, a classroom architectural Web site, or furniture purchased at a teachers' supply store. When you have a possible design, check it against your list of things it needs to accomplish. How is it stacking up? Ask a friend who is planning to become a teacher to try the same task, then compare notes. You will quickly realize that classroom design involves trade-offs and compromises. That is fine—it forces you to think hard about what is really important.

Evaluation R I D E

Without having real children in a real setting, it will be difficult to evaluate your classroom, but it would be fun to ask friends who are training to be teachers to give you an evaluation. When you design your actual classroom, remember to evaluate your physical environment on a regular basis to be certain that it is helping you in your teaching.

Further Practice: Your Turn

Now try to imagine how you would deal with a behavioral problem. Lunchtime has arrived, and not a moment too soon. Two of your twelfth-grade English students came into class in the midst of an argument that almost escalated into a physical fight 15 minutes into the period. You were able to get one of the students down to the principal's office during the class and sent the other one there as soon as the period ended. You have a free period for lunch now, but you will see this class again tomorrow.

R I D E What are you going to do now? How should you follow up? What will you do when the students enter your classroom tomorrow? Was your reaction to the situation the best possible one? How would you know?

SUMMARY

- **How can classrooms be organized to make it easier to achieve instructional goals?**

  Good classroom management starts before the beginning of the school year, with the design of the classroom. Classrooms need to be designed in terms of what will take place in them. They need to be organized to support the primary tasks of the class, yet flexible enough to meet multiple demands. They need to provide security and safety while at the same time being pleasant places in which to spend the day.

- **How can the first day of school set the tone for the rest of the year?**

  The first day of school is one of anticipation and anxiety for students and teachers alike (not to mention parents). It is also a critical day in terms of setting the proper tone for the rest of the year. Time spent on the first day introducing and explaining class rules and behavior expectations will be more than repaid later in the year in time available for learning.

- **How should rules be developed for classrooms?**

  During the first few weeks of school, teachers need to establish rules for the classroom and make sure that all the students understand them and the consequences for not complying with them. Teachers may want to involve students in helping to set the classroom rules. For younger students, the challenge will be to make certain that they understand the rules; for older students, the challenge will be to set limits as students try to find out how far rules can be bent.

- **How do successful teachers create a learning community in their classrooms?**

  The goal of setting rules for classrooms, and of classroom design as well, is to create a sense of community. Students should feel that they are all members of a learning community that is working together toward common goals. The establishment of rules and routines for getting work done lets students know what is expected of them, how to get along with one another, and how to get their work done. This structure gives the students the freedom they need to operate within specific limits.

- **How do instructional formats affect classroom management?**

  When students get off task or start to misbehave, one of the first questions teachers should ask is whether their instructional activities are keeping the students engaged. Most classroom instruction combines individual or seatwork, small-group activities, and whole-group instruction, including lecture, explanation, recitation, and discussion. All these formats have both strengths and weaknesses, and teachers must determine the best mix and timing for using them.

- **What can be done about problem behaviors that are more serious than occasional rule-breaking?**

  Behavior problems can arise in classrooms even when they are well managed. Chronic problems, such as not turning in homework or misbehaving on the playground, often need to be addressed with a program of remediation. A variety of such programs are available; they need to be carried out patiently and firmly. Sometimes a situation gets out of hand and calls for immediate attention. Teachers need to respond to acute situations calmly. The personal problems of students can range from mild to heartbreaking. While realizing that they are not counselors or school psychologists, teachers can be a significant source of support—and even inspiration—for a troubled student. It is important to keep an eye out for signs of personal problems as well as potential violence and to inform school counselors, psychologists, or principals when a student is in danger. Two widespread problems also require vigilance on the part of the teacher: cheating and bullying.

- **What is the proper balance between being sensitive to cultural differences and applying the same rules and expectations to all students?**

  The key is to notice that there are differences and that these differences may influence how children behave, how you react to their behavior, and how they respond. There are no quick fixes or golden rules. It is inappropriate to conclude that all students of a certain ethnicity or religion will behave in the same way. It is appropriate to be aware that students may behave differently because of their background and to understand that behavior in the context of the school setting. This is not a situation that can be solved once and for all. It is an attitude toward teaching diverse groups of children that encourages continual learning and reflection on the part of the teacher.

- **What kinds of classroom management policies can be used to address the special needs of certain learners?**

  Once again, there is no easy solution. Teachers have to be sensitive, ask questions, get advice, and make adjustments accordingly. There is a broad literature on students with special needs and many places to get help. Many of the techniques recommended for students with disabilities would work for nondisabled students, as well. In general, students with disabilities need clear instructions and guidelines, help in getting started, frequent feedback and correctives, and a system of record keeping that will help them monitor their progress toward learning and behavioral goals.

KEY TERMS

acute problems, p. 379
chronic problems, p. 378
consequences, p. 359
contingency contracting, p. 378
cross-ethnic groupings, p. 360
detention, p. 365
explaining, p. 374
immediacy, p. 362
I-message, p. 371
inclusive, p. 377
learning center, p. 357
lecturing, p. 374
logical consequences, p. 379
multidimensionality, p. 361

off task, p. 370
penalties, p. 368
personal space, p. 355
recitation, p. 375
routines, p. 367
seatwork, p. 372
self-management, p. 378
small-group work, p. 373
social contact, p. 355
social norms, p. 361
taxonomy, p. 381
transition times, p. 357
wait time, p. 375
whole-class instruction, p. 374

EXERCISES

1. *Classroom Design*

   Design your classroom. Start with a statement of the level and subject areas you are going to teach and what you want your classroom to do for you. Then design your classroom with construction paper cutouts. When you are done, trade your work with one of your classmates and critique each other's work. Then consider the critique you have given and the one you have received. How has the feedback process helped you improve your design and helped you think about how to go about classroom planning?

2. *Instructional Style and Classroom Management*

   Think about your instructional style and approach to classroom management. Make a list of what you think your strengths and weaknesses are in terms of managing a group of children and adolescents. Are you a good organizer, a dynamic personality, patient, strong-willed, good at attending to details, fun to be with, and so forth? Think about how you use your strengths to be an effective classroom manager. If you have a friend in this course whose opinion you value, you might have him or her make the same list about you (and you about that person) to see whether your self-perceptions are shared by others. Then you can explore how your personal characteristics can be turned into management strengths.

3. *Working with Students with Special Needs*

   A student who uses a wheelchair has been assigned to your class. What adjustments will you make to accommodate this student? Find at least two Web sites that provide help in this area and make a list of what you consider to be the three most important accommodations that you can make.

4. *Starting the Year Right*

   The first day of school is critical in setting the tone for the school year. Review the material in the chapter dealing with the first day of school and develop your lesson plans for that day. How will your plans set the right tone for your class?

5. *Linking Motivation to Classroom Management*

   Motivation and classroom management go hand in hand. Go back to Chapters 5 and 6, and review the material on motivation. Which of the theoretical perspectives discussed there seem to be particularly important for classroom management? In what ways?

Ms. O'Neill organized her third-grade class into groups for mathematics. Each group was given a bag of money and asked to find out the total amount of money in the bag. The group you will read about had four members, two boys and two girls. Ms. O'Neill walked by the group and overheard the following interaction:

Maria: 8, 9, 9, and 8 ... how much is it ... 17, right?

Carla: Yeah, that's what I did.

Maria: Yeah, then you carry the 1, that's 9, and 9 is 18.

Wilson: *She wrote, "Oh, W.., I like you."*

Maria: Carry the 1, is 2 ... $2.89.

Andy: *You like her too?*

Maria: $5.00 it says there.

Wilson: *No.*

Maria: Is 2 dollars 80 ... 89 cents.

Carla: 89 cents?

Wilson: *You like, you like Andrea?*

Maria: Wait and that's a ... 4 minus 2 equals 2.

Wilson: *She lives downtown.*

Maria: And 10 minus 7 is 3.

Carla: Okay.

Maria: So, erase the answer, just erase 8 and a 7 ... that's it.

Andy: *I don't want her phone number. I hate ...*

Wilson: *You goin' crazy. You all crazy.*

Andy: *Like this. Me and J ... we the only people that Andrea likes.*

Maria: And then write 13 cents.

Andy: *She don't like you.*

Maria: Wait, you don't have to write the cents.

Carla: Okay, I gotta go.

Wilson: *Then why's she always looking at me?*

Learning from Peers

RIDE Reflection for Action

Maria, Andy, Wilson, and Carla were asked to work together on a math task. Ms. O'Neill hoped that they would learn from one another and help each other understand the task. Are they working together well? Is this group effective? Why do you think so? Do you think they are learning mathematics? Who is most helpful in the group? How might a teacher help students work together? What should you do with this particular group?

Guiding Questions

- How do various theoretical perspectives describe the means by which students can learn from peers?
- How effective is tutoring? What processes are involved?
- What do teachers need to consider when having students work in larger groups?
- What kinds of tasks are suitable for groups of students?
- What is the role of the teacher when using a peer learning strategy?
- Do diverse learners benefit from peer learning?
- Can peer learning be used effectively with students who have special needs?

CHAPTER OVERVIEW

This chapter lays out different theoretical perspectives on peer learning and the means through which peers promote learning. Its purpose is to help you understand how to select a peer learning technique to fit your instructional goals. To help you do so, the chapter explains the mechanisms and processes through which peer learning can lead to the acquisition of skills and knowledge in widely differing classroom situations. The chapter discusses peer learning techniques in the context of both one-on-one tutoring and larger, heterogeneous groups. We also consider key issues in the use of peer learning in the classroom, including the quality of students' discourse, the kinds of tasks that teachers may choose, the role of the teacher in using peer learning, and assessing the outcomes of peer learning.

Perspectives on Peer Learning
- Theoretical Orientations Toward Learning from Peers
- The Social-Motivational Perspective
- The Social-Cohesion Perspective
- Are These Approaches Effective?
- Cognitive-Elaboration Perspectives
- Cognitive-Developmental Perspectives

Tutoring
- Evidence for the Effectiveness of Tutoring
- Processes Involved in Tutoring
- Tutoring Diverse Learners
- Tutoring and Students with Special Needs
- Tutoring for Higher Order Outcomes

Learning in Heterogeneous Groups
- Examples of Cooperative Techniques

Collaboration and Technology
- WebQuests
- Online Mentoring
- Knowledge Forum

Influences on Effectiveness in Heterogeneous Groups
- Gender and Cooperative Groups
- Race, Ethnicity, and Language
- Special Needs and Cooperative Learning
- Status Characteristics

Learning from Peers: Classroom Practices
- Importance of Discourse Quality
- The Role of the Teacher
- Classroom Tasks

Perspectives on Peer Learning

Most people have worked in groups, helped another student with schoolwork, received help with schoolwork, or had some experience with tutoring. All these experiences involve peers working together to improve some aspect of academic performance. Another benefit of peer learning is greater interaction and respect among diverse students. Peer learning is often recommended as a teaching strategy, and both students and teachers can respond well to its use. Many state and national curriculum standards include recommendations about the use of groups and other peer learning situations to enhance critical thinking, conceptual understanding, and other higher order skills. Students often enjoy interacting with one another. Teachers frequently find that the presence of other students can serve as a key instructional resource. Acceptance by peers is linked to many positive outcomes in school, such as satisfaction with school, academic performance, and positive beliefs about academic competence (Hymel, Bowker, & Woody, 1993; Wentzel, 1994; Wentzel & Asher, 1995; Wentzel, Battle, & Looney, 2001). The use of collaborative and cooperative learning in classrooms has the potential to provide the social and emotional support students need from their peers.

Peer learning can be organized in a variety of ways. The tasks assigned, the rewards contingent on completion of the task, and the size and makeup of the group in which children work together influence the success of peer learning. Too often, however, teachers do not

The opportunity to exchange ideas and work with other students can have important social and cognitive outcomes.
(Digital Vision)

connect specific types of peer learning to instructional goals or give enough consideration to issues of assessment.

In the opening vignette, you were asked to decide whether the third-grade group was effective. You have only a brief sample of the children's conversation on which to base your decision. What makes a group effective? Was the group effective as a social unit? Were the children learning? How can groups be formed so that they are effective for both social and cognitive outcomes? This chapter will provide some answers to these questions.

Theoretical Orientations Toward Learning from Peers

Many of the original theories of cooperative learning were strongly influenced by social-psychological principles (Deutsch, 1949). The general principle underlying these theories is **interdependence** (Johnson & Johnson, 1991). Interdependence is a condition in which group members' goal accomplishments are linked together. According to social-motivational theory, cooperation and competition are two sides of the same coin. They are the **goal structure** of the task and characterize the manner in which students relate to others who are also working toward a particular goal. They both focus on the relationships among the goals of the participants in a group activity. In a competitive context, when one individual accomplishes his or her goals, other participants cannot. This is called **negative interdependence**. For example, when one individual is selected as the valedictorian of a high school class, others cannot be selected, because only one person can receive this honor. When one person succeeds, others must fail. This is the essence of competition. In a cooperative context, in contrast, no one can accomplish his or her goals unless everyone does. This is called **positive interdependence**. The success of the group is dependent on everyone in the group succeeding. A soccer team is an example of a cooperatively interdependent group. No one on the team succeeds unless everyone does. Table 12.1 summarizes the kinds of positive outcomes that can result from cooperative learning. The table presents conclusions drawn from a review of more than 300 studies of cooperative, competitive, and individualistic learning. It is important to remember that positive outcomes such as those listed in the table do not occur without careful planning and implementation.

Two different approaches have been taken to creating the kind of interdependence that is necessary for a cooperative group: the social-motivational perspective and the social-cohesion perspective. In describing these perspectives, we give examples of specific techniques associated with each. Later in the chapter we refer back to these techniques to illustrate the kinds of decisions that teachers make when adopting a particular approach and their implications for other aspects of classroom practice.

interdependence   A condition in which group members' goal accomplishments are linked together.

goal structure   The manner in which students relate to others who are also working toward a particular goal.

negative interdependence   A condition that exists when, in order for one person to succeed in accomplishing his or her goals, others must fail to meet their goals.

positive interdependence   A condition that exists when the success of each individual depends on all group members being successful.

TABLE 12.1

Outcomes of Cooperative Learning

Achievement Gains

Cooperative learning is more successful than individual learning.

Cooperative learning is more successful than competition among peers.

Individualistic learning and competitive learning produce similar results.

Additional Gains for Students Engaged in Cooperative Learning

Develop more positive relationships with peers.

Exhibit greater social competence.

Retain information longer.

Show higher levels of reasoning, critical thinking, and metacognition.

Show higher levels of creativity.

Exhibit more positive attitudes toward subject matter.

Source: Johnson, D. W., & Johnson, R. T. (1989). *Cooperation and competition: Theory and research.* Edina, MN: Interaction Book.

The Social-Motivational Perspective

As you read about the various perspectives on peer learning, you will see that each of them fits with certain types of instructional goals. You will also see that many decisions a teacher makes are influenced by his or her perspective on peer learning. A social-motivational approach to creating interdependence relies on the use of rewards or recognition for group productivity. Techniques derived from this perspective include Teams-Games-Tournaments, or TGT (De Vries & Edwards, 1973); Team-Accelerated Instruction, or TAI (Slavin, 1984), Cooperative Integrated Reading and Composition, (CIRC; Madden, Slavin, & Stevens, 1986), and Student Teams Achievement Division, or STAD (Slavin, 1986). The basic premise of these techniques is that students will be motivated to work together and help one another because the group as a whole will be rewarded or will receive recognition. Thus, if one person is not working to help the group, the whole group suffers. Interdependence is created by the use of rewards or the promise of recognition. STAD is one of the most thoroughly researched cooperative learning techniques.

The "Taking It to the Classroom" box on this page summarizes some of the key steps in using STAD. The cooperative aspect typically follows general instruction by the teacher and provides the students with an opportunity to rehearse that material. The teacher makes the key decisions about the content to be taught, the kinds of tests to be given, and the kinds of rewards or recognition that will be used.

Taking It to the Classroom

Implementing STAD

The following is a typical four-step procedure that teachers might use to implement STAD (Student-Teams-Achievement-Divisions) cooperation in their classrooms:

1. Before lesson	Students grouped into four- to six-member heterogeneous teams.	
2. During lesson	The teacher presents the information to be learned, using various instructional strategies (e.g., lecture or videotape presentation).	
3. Peer learning	After students have been exposed to the information, they work together to learn it. For example, the teacher gives the students a worksheet that reviews the lecture material. Students share information to help each other.	
4. After lesson	The teacher gives each student an individual test. The tests are scored based on each student's improvement from a prior test performance. Teams with the highest improvement scores earn a reward of their choice.	

The teacher ensures **individual accountability** through the use of improvement points. Each student is responsible for improving his or her performance. The teacher decides the numbers of improvement points necessary in order to earn specific numbers of team points. For example, students whose test performance exceeds their baseline score by five points may earn three team points. Students who already excel simply need to stay within a specified range of high performance in order to bring the maximum number of points to their team. Team scores are created by adding up the team points generated by each individual.

Rewards or recognition are given to teams with high levels of achievement. Again, teachers must decide how many teams to reward or recognize and how to do so. As described in Chapter 7, the reward should be one that is valued by students. Although there is cooperation among members of a group, the groups compete with other groups in the class. The teacher's goal is to increase the students' motivation. If the success of only one group is acknowledged, some of the benefits of cooperation may be lost in the competition between groups.

Among the important features of the social-motivational approach to peer learning are the use of heterogeneous groups, individual accountability in the form of quizzes, improvement points for calculating overall group performance, and the use of recognition and reward in response to group performance. Interdependence is created and maintained by the use of team points for individual performance. All students are expected to help one another because it is in everyone's interest to gain as many points as possible. The key mechanism promoting interdependence is motivation. The strengths of STAD include successful motivation of all kinds of learners, because each student has a reason to participate. The focus on improvement shifts attention from overall levels of performance to individual accountability for improvement. A weakness of STAD is that it focuses on lower level cognitive objectives. Because students use prepared answer sheets to respond to their peers' efforts to answer questions, the cognitive levels of the tasks may remain quite low, focusing on factual recall and basic comprehension rather than on higher level abilities. It would be very challenging to prepare answer sheets for responses to more open-ended questions.

It is difficult to maintain interdependence if students believe that they are unequal contributors to the group's performance. High-achieving students sometimes believe that working in groups puts them at a disadvantage, even though there is no strong evidence to support this belief (Slavin, 1995). Interdependence can be maintained only if all the participating students believe that they can contribute without risking ridicule or pressure. High-achieving students need to believe that they do not bear all the responsibility for achievement, and lower achieving students need to believe that they can contribute to the group. A key feature of STAD that serves to maintain interdependence is that each student has the same opportunity to contribute to the team score, regardless of his or her actual level of performance. Thus, the high achievers are required to maintain a high level of performance in order to contribute to the group. The average and low achievers need to improve on their previous performances in order to contribute.

Slavin (1986) outlined a number of other cooperative learning techniques, such as TGT, CIRC, and TAI, that all rely on increased motivation as a result of group goals and individual accountability to promote learning. Some of these techniques were developed for specific subject areas, such as mathematics (TAI: Slavin 1984) or reading and writing (CIRC, Madden et al., 1986). The development of CIRC, for example, was based on an analysis of research on how to teach reading and writing. Although a particular technique may be primarily social or primarily cognitive, many cooperative learning techniques include both social and cognitive strategies.

The Social-Cohesion Perspective

A social-cohesion approach to cooperative learning also relies on the principle of interdependence. From this perspective, students are motivated to help one another succeed because they care about one another. David and Roger Johnson, directors of the Center for Cooperative Learning at the University of Minnesota, have conducted research on cooperative learning techniques since the 1970s. They developed the technique known as *Learning Together* (Johnson & Johnson, 1991).

Cooperative learning has five basic elements (Johnson & Johnson, 1991): positive interdependence, face-to-face promotive interaction, individual accountability and personal responsibility, interpersonal and small-group skills, and group processing. In *Learning*

individual accountability Each student is responsible for improving his or her performance.

Chapter Reference
The use of rewards as reinforcers is discussed in Chapter 7. The hidden costs of reward are discussed in Chapter 6.

Together, a great deal of attention is given to the role of social skills. Students may not display the care and concern for others that are central to a social-cohesion approach, and teachers may have to spend much time helping them see others' perspectives and show respect in their responses to others, as well as providing encouragement and feedback. In using *Learning Together,* a teacher selects a lesson and identifies objectives both for the content and for social skills. The teacher must make a number of important decisions about the size of each group, and which students make up a group. He or she must ensure that adequate materials are available and that students are assigned particular roles within the group. The teacher explains the task to the students and establishes positive interdependence among group members. One function of assigning roles within the group is to maintain that interdependence as students work together. The teacher must also establish criteria for evaluating the success of the group and develop a strategy for ensuring that each individual in the group is accountable for his or her performance. As the students work together on the task, the teacher needs to monitor their interactions and note any evidence of expected behaviors (e.g., providing encouragement to others). Once students have completed the assigned task, members of each group work together to discuss how well their group worked.

The focus of the group activity is on team building and the development of social skills. Roles are assigned to individuals (e.g., the *materials manager* is responsible for distributing and collecting materials). The roles are not necessarily cognitive in nature but often involve social management of the group. A group grade is assigned to the completed product. When they have finished their tasks, group members review the aspects of working together that they believed went well and try to identify areas of activity in which they might improve. For example, they might conclude that they asked good questions but did not provide enough encouragement. The strengths of *Learning Together* include its emphasis on social skills, the creation of a caring classroom climate, and students' involvement in evaluating how their groups work. It also stimulates many useful cognitive processes. Figure 12.1 shows that positive interdependence encourages interactions that have many favorable outcomes, such as increased effort, good social relations, and positive psychological adjustment and social competence.

You can see that if, as a teacher, you chose a social-cohesion perspective on cooperative learning, you would engage your students in very different activities (e.g., team building, social skill development) than you would if you chose a social-motivational perspective. If you adopted the latter approach, you would focus more on ways to provide recognition or reward. The tasks you assigned would also differ. If you chose a social-motivational perspective, you might assign tasks that require practice and rehearsal. If you chose a social-cohesion perspective, you might assign more open-ended tasks.

Chapter Reference
Chapter 3 discusses the importance of social competence and positive relationships.

Figure 12.1. **Outcomes of Cooperation**

Source: Johnson, D. W., & Johnson, R. T. (1989). *Cooperation and competition: Theory and research.* Edina, MN: Interaction Book Company. Reproduced with permission.

Grade and Subject: Grade 5 language arts

Content: The novel *Sara, Plain and Tall*

Group Task: Using rotating roles, pairs answer questions on partner worksheets

Grouping	**Positive interdependence**
• Students are assigned to heterogeneous groups. • Pairs are selected by the teacher based on ability. • Pairs work together for a single class period.	• Goal: to create one set of combined answers from the pair • Reward: partner worksheets contribute to grade • Role: assigned roles of Checker and Recorder
Individual accountability	**Interpersonal and cognitive skills**
• Each student has to write an answer for each question before the discussion begins. • Each student is responsible for the pair's combined answer. • Each student is responsible for a particular role within the pair.	• Direct teaching of the skill of criticizing ideas, not people • Guided practice of the skill during the activity
Evaluation and reflection	**Extension activity**
• Each student is evaluated on his or her individual answers and on the pair's combined answer. • There is an individual test on the content of the novel. • Pairs reflect on their contributions using a self- and teammate evaluation form.	• Students who complete the task before other pairs could help other pairs • Pairs who have completed the task could combine all the answers, then give a short oral presentation to the class

Figure 12.2. Analysis of Learning Together Example

Source: From *Classroom Connections: Using and Understanding Cooperative Learning* by ABRAMI. © 1995. Reprinted with permission of Nelson, a division of Thomson Learning: www.thomsonrights.com. Fax 800 730–2215.

Figure 12.2 presents an analysis of an example of *Learning Together*. The teacher of a fifth-grade class assigned the novel *Sara, Plain and Tall*. The academic objective was to have the students discuss and answer questions related to the main characters, the central theme of the story, the actions in the story, and the use of symbolism. The social objective was to have the students criticize ideas but not the students who proposed them.

The tasks on which children work using *Learning Together* can be complex, requiring students to coordinate their efforts in pursuit of a single goal, monitor progress toward that goal, and redirect their efforts if necessary. These are advanced cognitive skills, and if students do not also have good social skills and know how to disagree and question the direction of the group, many kinds of interpersonal issues can arise. Potential weaknesses of the technique include reliance on a group product, a form of assessment that can cause problems if parents or students object. The teacher needs to pay a great deal of attention to creating a classroom culture in which children treat one another with respect and care. Essentially, the teacher must help students develop the desire to help others. This can be quite difficult if the values experienced by children in their homes are also competitive and argue against helping others.

Among the important features of the social-cohesion approach to peer learning are the use of heterogeneous groups, face-to-face interaction, individual accountability, and group processing of the interactions that occur. This approach shares many features with the social-motivational approach, including its reliance on interdependence, its use of heterogeneous groups, and the use of group reward. Deliberate training of students in social skills offsets potentially negative group processes that may result from the heterogeneity of the group's members. The teacher also plays a key role in creating and maintaining a culture of care and respect. Group members' involvement in evaluating the interactions that occurred enhances their awareness of their behavior and contributes to positive interdependence.

metacognition   Thinking about one's own thinking.

The "What Kids Say and Do" box on this page presents the self-assessments of two groups of students working on a cooperative learning task. In this example, how students actually performed on the task is less important than their perceptions of how they worked together and how well they thought things were going. Students develop metacognitive skill slowly, and applying **metacognition** or thinking about one's thinking, to complex social processes takes practice.

Students in Group # 1 were positive in response to the question, What did your group do well? However, when asked how the group could better help them learn, their replies clearly indicated that there were problems. It is important to understand the nature of the question you ask as a teacher. Without asking the second question, What could your group do better to help you learn?, the teacher might not have understood that the students were having some difficulty.

In Group # 2, students did not just say that they were doing well. They were able to explain the processes that were going well (e.g., we take turns and answer questions). There was less conflicting information in the responses of Group # 2's members to the two questions.

What Kids Say and Do

Chapter Reference
A discussion of metacognition can be found in Chapter 8.

Learning to Understand Group Processes

Students in a seventh-grade classroom provided the following comments about how they think they worked together on a cooperative learning task. Two groups evaluated how they worked.

Group 1

What did your group do well?

Sean:	Our group took turns well and was quite organized.
Pablo:	We did everything well.
Isabel:	Well, kinda, we all answered the questions together in the first two sessions.
Stefan:	Our group did well on everything.

What could your group do better to help you learn?

Sean: I think our group could work better together and others could contribute more.

Pablo: Pay attention to what is going on in the group.

Isabel: Well, some people could give other people a chance to answer the questions instead of just saying, "Well, she doesn't know it so I'll go." I thought that, that was very rude and they should learn to give other people at least a minute instead of a second.

Stefan: I think if some people could pay attention to what we are discussing.

Group 2

What did your group do well?

Kirsten: Our group did a lot of things well. We work nicely together and never yell or call names (only if we are fooling around).

Kenisha: Our group did well answering open-minded questions and working as a group.

Brenda: I think so because we work well together and cooperate.

Tonya: My group is good because we work together and take turns answering questions. When we have to solve something and one of us doesn't agree, we try to talk about it.

What could your group do better to help you learn?

Kirsten: Our group sometimes needs to act more serious.

Kenisha: Our group could do better in staying on topic and not making so many weird jokes about it.

Brenda: I do not think that there was really anything the group can do to help me learn but we could be more serious.

Tonya: Our group could stay on topic and stop playing around a lot, but we still learned.

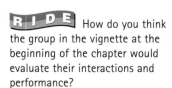 How do you think the group in the vignette at the beginning of the chapter would evaluate their interactions and performance?

Are These Approaches Effective?

Are social-motivational or social-cohesion approaches to peer learning effective? Experiments can be designed to determine whether one instructional intervention is better than another. The results of separate experiments can be combined through **meta-analysis**, a quantitative summary of a number of research studies that test the same hypotheses (e.g., is cooperative learning more effective than individualistic learning?). Meta-analyses of research studies that compared the effectiveness of cooperative, competitive, and individualistic learning conditions show strong support for the effectiveness of cooperative learning (Johnson & Johnson, 1989; see Table 12.1). Many of the studies included in these meta-analyses showed that cooperative learning techniques that reflected either a social-motivational or a social-cohesion perspective were more effective than other methods.

The research literature suggests that including group goals and individual accountability is necessary for successful peer learning. Slavin (1996) examined 52 studies of cooperative learning techniques and found that these techniques were particularly effective when they included group goals and individual accountability. When they did not include these factors, cooperative learning was no more effective than individualistic learning.

Despite the positive effects of cooperative techniques that include group goals and individual accountability, many teachers do not believe in using rewards (Antil et al., 1998) and therefore do not use these techniques exactly as recommended. The research evidence supports the effectiveness of the techniques when they are used as designed. When teachers deviate from the recommended procedures, it is unclear how effective the altered technique is. When teachers choose not to use rewards or recognition when implementing their version of STAD, for example, they are eliminating a key component of the technique that contributes to achievement and positive interaction in heterogeneous groups. If the group incentive required by a social-motivational approach is not replaced by the kinds of effort needed by a social-cohesion approach, problems in group processes and productivity are highly likely. Similarly, efforts to use cooperative learning techniques with students who have learning disabilities can be ineffective if they do not include individual accountability (Jenkins & O'Connor, 2003). Slavin (1992) reported that the positive outcomes of cooperative learning without individual accountability are minimal, and this finding is supported by more recent research by McMaster and Fuchs (2002).

Social perspectives on peer learning do not directly address cognitive processes. A basic assumption of such techniques is that if students are motivated, good things will result. It is true that motivation is an important element of effective learning. However, "will without skill" is unlikely to lead to successful outcomes. A focus on cognitive mechanisms for group learning is quite different from a focus on social-motivational mechanisms. In the next section, we describe several types of peer learning that are influenced by different cognitive or developmental theories.

Cognitive-Elaboration Perspectives

Cognitive-elaboration approaches to peer learning are based on an information-processing approach. Peer interaction is used to amplify, or cognitively elaborate, the performance of basic information-processing activities such as encoding, activation of schemas, rehearsal, metacognition, and retrieval (see Chapter 8).

Encoding involves actively processing incoming information. Students with prior knowledge of a topic are more likely to encode new information effectively because they can link it to information that they already understand. Teachers can help students encode information more effectively by reminding them of what they already know or helping them activate existing **schemas**, or organized sets of knowledge about the topic. **Schemas** are the basic cognitive structures for organizing information. By practicing or rehearsing the information, students process it more deeply, making it easier to retrieve the information later. Performing these activities in the presence of peers will result in deeper processing and more active engagement (O'Donnell, Dansereau, Hythecker et al., 1987). The presence of a peer can help students stay on task, and feedback provided by a peer can help students decide when they need to check their understanding of the content they are trying to explain (O'Donnell & Dansereau, 1992).

meta-analysis A quantitative summary of a research studies that test the same hypotheses.

How Can I Use This?
What aspects of using groups would vary if you chose a social-motivation or social cohesion approach to peer learning?

Chapter Reference
Chapter 8 provides explanations of the cognitive processes promoted by a cognitive-elaboration approach to peer learning.

schema The basic cognitive structure for organizing information.

Taking It to the Classroom

Implementing Scripted Cooperation

The following script is a typical four-step procedure that teachers might use to implement Scripted Cooperation in their classrooms:

1. Before lesson   Students are grouped into pairs. The teacher assigns one student the role of Initiator and the other student the role of Elaborator.

2. During lesson   Both students read the text on their own.

3. Peer learning   After 10 minutes of independent reading time, the Initiator summarizes what was read (without referring to his or her notes). The Elaborator listens, detects errors, then adds new elaborations.

4. After lesson   Together, the Initiator and the Elaborator reflect on their conversation and discuss how the material covered is connected to other things they know.

Scripted Cooperation A learning strategy in which students take turns summarizing materials and criticizing the summaries.

 Would a more structured technique for interaction have helped the group described in the vignette at the beginning of the chapter?

An example of a peer learning strategy that is consistent with a cognitive-elaboration approach is O'Donnell and colleagues' **Scripted Cooperation** (O'Donnell & Dansereau, 1992; O'Donnell, Dansereau, Hall et al., 1987), which is based on information-processing theory. The "Taking It to the Classroom" box on this page summarizes this technique. An important aspect of Scripted Cooperation is that cognitive activities that are typically done by an individual are divided between partners. Students actively elaborate on the information, connecting it to information that they already know and making an active effort to make the new information memorable. The technique improves text processing because it emphasizes cognitive processes that are known to increase learning, such as rehearsal, metacognition, and elaboration.

Research has shown that this is a very effective strategy (O'Donnell & Dansereau, 1992). Not only do students perform better on tests related to the material when they work together, but they also perform better on subsequent tasks when they work alone (O'Donnell, Dansereau, Hall et al., 1987). *Scripted Cooperation* has been used successfully by students as young as third graders (Rottman & Cross, 1990) with reading tasks, and a modified version of the script was used successfully with fifth graders learning to solve math problems (Zuber, 1992). It can also be used with students in high school and college. The technique is highly structured, and with younger children, the teacher must provide numerous opportunities to learn basic skills such as summarizing, error detection, and elaboration. The technique is focused less on what students teach one another than on how the cooperative context can stimulate deeper processing, more focused activity, and a less demanding cognitive load on an individual student.

Noreen Webb's work also stems from a cognitive-elaboration perspective (1989, 1991, 1992). Much of it focuses on students' learning of mathematics. Webb has explored the effects of various types of groupings (i.e., heterogeneous, homogeneous, female-dominated, male-dominated) on achievement. Webb's groups are more open-ended than the dyads that use scripted cooperation. The students decide how to participate, although training in how to do so is usually provided.

Webb and her colleagues found that students who participate actively in a group learn more than students who are passive; those who provide explanations achieve more than those who do not; and higher quality explanations are associated with higher levels of achievement (Webb, 1989, 1991, 1992). High-level explanations are expressions of deeper processing and elaboration of content, and may aid in restructuring existing knowledge.

There are, however, a number of possible difficulties with this approach. First, not all students provide good explanations or are given an opportunity to do so. Typically, the more able students provide more explanations, and the less able or less experienced ones seek help and look for explanations. Webb and her colleagues have attempted to teach students how to seek appropriate help, with mixed success (Webb & Farivar, 1994). There is also the risk of amplifying differences in social status within a classroom. **Status differences** occur when peers see some students as being more valuable and having more to contribute than others.

status differences Differences in status among individuals that influence their participation in group activities.

These differences may occur because of ability or because of more **diffuse status characteristics**, such as race, ethnicity, gender, or language of origin (Meeker, 1981).

Characteristics are considered *diffuse* if they have no direct bearing on task performance but are assumed to indicate greater or lesser capability to perform the task (Meeker, 1981). For example, girls might expect boys to perform certain tasks better than they do even though there may be no differences in performance based on gender. The reverse may also be true. Status differences and their implications are described in more detail later in the chapter.

Figure 12.3 compares social-motivational, social-cohesion, and cognitive-elaboration approaches to peer learning, along with their practical implications.

diffuse status characteristics
Characteristics that have no direct bearing on task performance but are assumed to be indicators of greater or lesser capability to perform the task.

Cognitive-Developmental Perspectives

Peer learning includes cooperative learning, collaboration, and various forms of peer tutoring. Both Piagetian and Vygotskyian theories provide a foundation for peer learning that focuses on development, but they differ in their emphasis on individual cognitive processes or social processes. The three theoretical perspectives described earlier (social-motivational, social-cohesion, and cognitive-elaboration) all depend in part on Piagetian and/or Vygotskyian theories. Both Piaget and Vygotsky stressed a constructivist approach to teaching and learning that involves both individual and social processes. A **constructivist perspective** suggests that individuals create meaning using their prior understandings to make sense of new experiences.

constructivist perspective   A theoretical perspective that stresses the active role of the learner in building understanding and making sense of information.

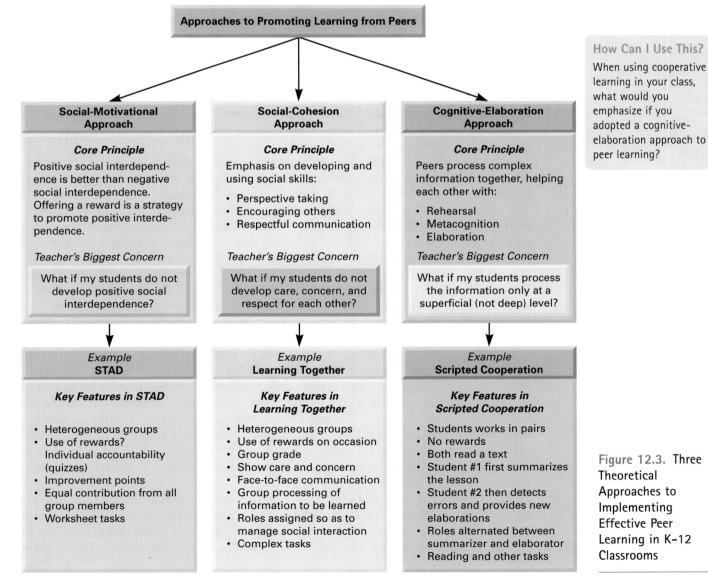

How Can I Use This?
When using cooperative learning in your class, what would you emphasize if you adopted a cognitive-elaboration approach to peer learning?

Figure 12.3. Three Theoretical Approaches to Implementing Effective Peer Learning in K–12 Classrooms

assimilation   An incorporation process in which an outside event is brought into one's way of thinking.

accommodation   A modification process in which low-level schemas are transferred into higher level schemas.

cognitive disequilibrium   The experience of cognitive conflict.

conceptual change teaching   A method of teaching that helps students understand concepts by challenging them to examine their ideas and identify shortcomings in them.

Appendix
Piagets' Contribution
Piaget is one of the theorists who describes how learning occurs and how students construct knowledge. (*PRAXIS*™, 1. A. 1; *INTASC,* Principle 2).

cognitive conflict   Experience of conflict when new information does not agree with existing knowledge.

How Can I Use This?

How would you determine whether a child has experienced cognitive conflict?

Piagetian Theory Piaget developed a constructivist theory of cognitive development in which a child forms new conceptual structures as a result of interactions with his or her environment. Cognitive growth occurs through the process of adaptation and proceeds through the processes of **assimilation** (a process in which an outside event is brought into one's way of thinking) and **accommodation** (a process in which low-level schemas are transformed into higher level schemas). Modifications to existing cognitive structures occur when a structure is changed in some way as a result of experiencing new objects or events. The individual seeks equilibrium or balance in the cognitive system, and when this balance is disrupted, he or she seeks to restore equilibrium Peers may provide opportunities for others to experience **cognitive disequilibrium** or cognitive conflict. For example, students may disagree about the solution of a problem. Through discussions and other activities, they may restore cognitive equilibrium by arriving at new understandings as they work together.

Conceptual change teaching seeks to challenge students' existing concepts so as to create cognitive disequilibrium. Providing students with evidence that contradicts students' initial beliefs will require them to modify cognitive structures on the basis of new information. Through this process of adaptation, students build new cognitive structures.

A general approach to instruction that emerges from this notion is that the teacher first elicits students' expectations about a phenomenon, then gives them opportunities to test their predictions, uncover contradictory evidence, and contrast their expectations with their experiences (Neale, Smith, & Johnson, 1990). Teachers need to create conditions in which students are responsive to the data they gather. For example, in preparing for a unit of instruction on light and shadow, students might be asked to predict where their shadows will fall as they turn their bodies in the sunlight. Some students may respond with the expectation that their shadows will appear in front of their bodies. The teacher can challenge this expectation by providing experiences that contradict it. In this case, if the children are positioned sideways to the sun, their shadows will appear at their sides. The teacher needs to remind them that their predictions about what would happen were different from what actually happened. He or she must then ask them to think about why their predictions were not accurate. At the same time, the teacher should be aware that even though the contradictory information is available, students will not necessarily experience it as creating cognitive conflict. In fact, the new experience or information may simply be assimilated into prior concept with little change in existing cognitive structures.

The intent of this strategy is first to make students aware of their beliefs, then to create cognitive conflict by presenting contradictory experiences. The goal is to have the students take in (assimilate) the new information, then restructure (accommodate) their existing cognitive structures as a result. However, this general approach to instruction may not always work. Accommodation is only one of many possible outcomes that may result when contradictions are presented (De Lisi & Golbeck, 1999). Students may ignore the contradiction between what they expected and what occurred, or they may believe that the actual event is what they anticipated. Chinn and Brewer (1993) showed that students rarely respond effectively to data that contradict their beliefs. In the example of the children's shadows, discussed above, it is best to have other children trace the shadows so that there is an observable record of the event.

Through a combination of predictions, observations, and efforts to reconcile differences, children may experience conceptual change. From a Piagetian perspective, cognitive structures develop as a result of this process of **cognitive conflict** and subsequent restoration of cognitive equilibrium. It is important to keep in mind that, although a teacher may believe that students have experienced cognitive conflict because she has arranged what appear to be contradictory experiences, it does not necessarily follow that they have experienced such conflict. Chinn and Brewer (1993) and De Lisi and Golbeck (1999) describe a variety of responses that children might have to information that conflicts with their existing knowledge. Processes such as cognitive disequilibrium and restoring balance to the cognitive system could occur in social-motivational, social-cohesion, and cognitive-elaboration approaches to peer learning.

Piaget's work has important implications for cooperative learning, mainly because of his ideas about peer influence (De Lisi & Golbeck, 1999). According to Piaget, children are more likely to develop cognitively in contexts in which peers have equal power and all have opportunities to influence one another. When adults work with children, there is an inevitable power structure that is likely to result in children complying with the adult. The risk is that children will simply accept what the more powerful, authoritative adult says without experiencing cognitive conflicts or examining existing beliefs. Even when peers work together without an adult present in the group, power relations may not be equal. Certain children may have more status and power as a function of perceived ability, popularity, and other characteristics, such as gender or race. Children with high status typically have more influence over the interactions that occur in the group. They tend to say more, offer explanations, and provide answers to questions asked by children with lower status. Other children may simply go along with the ideas of these high-status children.

Vygotskyian Theory A second approach to understanding collaboration is associated with Vygotskyian theory. Vygotsky's perspective on development includes both cultural/societal and individual components.

There is a dialectical relationship between the child and the cultural environment: "In the process of development, the child not only masters the items of cultural experience but the habits and forms of cultural behavior, the cultural methods of reasoning" (Vygotsky, 1929, p. 415). Although the social environment provides models of performance and skill, children must still master these skills for themselves. Moshman (1982) refers to this mutual influence between the individual and the environment as **dialectical constructivism;** in this view, knowledge lies in the continual interaction between the individual and the environment.

The characteristics of a student's environment are very important. According to Hogan and Tudge (1999), "The presence or absence of certain types of institutions (e.g., schools), technologies, and semiotic tools (e.g., pens or computers) as well as variations in the values, beliefs, and practices of different cultural groups are interdependent with differences in ways in which children's development proceeds" (p. 41). An example of an effort to provide an environment that is conducive to positive development is the Head Start program. It was founded to improve the quality of the environments available to young children so that their cognitive development could be enhanced. The characteristics of the learner are also important, because traits such as motivation, work ethic, and curiosity affect the degree to which learners work to master the skills they need to participate in their community.

A second key idea concerns what Vygotsky termed the **zone of proximal development**. According to Vygotsky, the zone of proximal development is a level of competence on a task in which the student cannot yet master the task on his or her own but can perform the task with appropriate guidance and support from a more capable partner. Assistance comes from a more competent child or adult who can recognize the learner's current level of functioning and the kind of performance that might be possible, and provide appropriate support. Cognitive development occurs as the child internalizes the processes that take place in the course of interacting with a more competent adult or peer. The child's cognitive structures are reorganized, and in later interactions the child may show evidence of having developed new cognitive structures by explaining his or her thinking or actions.

From a Vygotskian perspective, pairing an adult with a child is most likely to promote cognitive growth. The adult may be expected to have some skill in recognizing the child's current level of functioning and adjusting instruction to support the child's efforts. Webb (1991) noted that the kind of help a learner receives must match his or her needs. One might reasonably expect adults to provide more effectively the level of help needed by a learner. The zone of proximal development is jointly established by the participants (Hogan & Tudge, 1999) and is best accomplished when one partner is aware of the other's current level of functioning and is able to prompt, hint, or otherwise scaffold or support the other partner's developing competence. **Scaffolding** is the guidance, support, and tutelage (e.g., hints, tips, cues, reminders) provided by a teacher during social interaction designed to advance students' current level of skill and understanding.

If adults are not available, more competent peers can support the learning of a less competent student. However, peers need assistance in providing the appropriate level of help. Person and Graesser (1999) have shown, for example, that naïve tutors are not very good at identifying the tutee's current level of functioning and scaffolding the tutee's efforts so that

Appendix
Vygotskys' Contribution
Vygotsky is one of the theorists who describes how learning occurs and how students construct knowledge. (*PRAXIS*™, 1. A. 1; *INTASC, Principle 2*).

dialectical constructivism The theory that considers knowledge to lie in the continual interaction between the individual and the environment.

What Does This Mean to Me?
Can you give an example of an occasion when you experienced dialectical constructivism?

zone of proximal development A level of competence on a task in which the student cannot yet master the task on his or her own but can accomplish that same task with appropriate guidance from a more capable partner.

scaffolding The guidance, support, and tutelage provided by a teacher during social interaction designed to advance the student's current level of skill and understanding.

A learner's competence increases when another person is aware of the learner's current level of functioning and provides appropriate assistance. (PhotoDisc, Inc./ Getty Images)

his or her performance improves. Webb and Farivar (1994) have clearly shown that it is difficult to train young students to identify or act within another learner's zone of proximal development. However, King and her colleagues (King, Staffieri, & Adelgais, 1998) show that with appropriate instructional support, peers can respond effectively to one another's efforts. We return to these issues later in the chapter when we discuss tutoring and strategies for assisting peers. Table 12.2 presents a summary of the different theoretical perspectives described thus far and the mechanisms through which peers can promote learning.

In the preceding sections, we have discussed various theoretical approaches to peer learning. The key difference among these perspectives is the mechanism that allows peer interaction to promote learning. This is important for teachers, because if they do not understand *how* peers promote learning, they will not make appropriate decisions about the size of groups, the kinds of skills needed, how to participate with groups, what kinds of tasks to assign, and other instructional choices. In the next few sections, we will describe strategies for peer learning that range from working in pairs to working in complex heterogeneous groups. We will see how each theoretical approach influences instructional decisions.

What Does This Mean to Me?
Can you explain why different theoretical perspectives on peer learning might influence your decisions in the classroom? Refer to Figure 12.3.

TABLE 12.2

Mechanisms for Promoting Learning from a Variety of Theoretical Perspectives

Theoretical perspective	Mechanisms for promoting learning
Social-motivational	Interdependence created through motivation
Social-cohesion	Interdependence created through care and concern
Cognitive elaboration	Deeper processing of information
Cognitive development—Piaget	Adaptation as a result of cognitive conflict
Cognitive development—Vygotsky	Modeled behavior that is scaffolded and internalized

Peers can support each other's learning by providing help but may need assistance in providing appropriate hints, prompts, or explanations.
(Corbis Digital Stock)

Tutoring

Tutoring is typically conducted by pairing one tutor and one tutee. Many students have little experience working in groups, and new teachers are often reluctant to try group learning because of concerns about **classroom management** (Slavin, 1995). They fear losing control of the classroom or having a noisy room that might draw negative attention from the principal or other teachers. Organizing and managing students is easier when they are working in pairs than when they are working in larger groups, and managing pair learning is also easier than managing learning in more complex groups. There are some tasks (discussed later) that are best carried out by larger groups. However, if neither you nor your students have experience in working with or in groups, it is wiser to start with some simple structures and gradually build up to more complex ones once you are sure that the students have the skills (both cognitive and social) to coordinate their efforts effectively.

Many students benefit from tutoring. Students who experience one-on-one tutoring gain greater understanding of content, report being more motivated, and work faster (Slavin, 1987). According to Bloom (1984), students who receive one-on-one tutoring perform at levels significantly above those achieved by comparable students who experience regular instruction.

Evidence for the Effectiveness of Tutoring

There is a great deal of research evidence supporting the benefits of tutoring (Cohen, Kulick, & Kulick, 1982). Those benefits are particularly evident in studies that were of short duration, employed structured tutoring, focused on lower level skills, used tests developed by the instructor, and typically focused on mathematics. Thirty-eight of the fifty-two studies examined by Cohen et al. (1982) found positive effects for the tutee. More recent evidence in support of tutoring comes from an evaluation of the America Reads tutoring program, a component of the AmeriCorps National and Community Service program. Students who participated in tutorial activities were generally in the low-to-average range in terms of reading skills. Students at all grade levels improved their reading performance over the course of their participation in the program. A number of practices were associated with positive outcomes: (a) Tutors met with their tutees at least three times a week; (b) formal evaluations of tutorial programs were conducted; (c) tutors received training beforehand and additional training during the course of the program; and (d) the programs were moderately or fully implemented as designed.

Tutoring often takes place between more skilled and less skilled students. Typically, the goal is to improve the performance of the less skilled student. Vygotsky's theory of cognitive development is frequently drawn upon to explain the benefits of such tutoring. The tutor's efforts to scaffold the tutee's learning by modeling behaviors, offering prompts' and

tutoring An instructional experience in which one student typically teaches another student who is less skilled.

classroom management Teacher behaviors and management techniques that result in a healthy learning environment, generally free of behavior problems.

Tutoring can provide a variety of benefits for both the tutor and tutee. (Corbis Digital Stock)

providing feedback, are thought to be operating in the tutee's zone of proximal development. Chi and colleagues (Chi et al., 2001) define *scaffolding* as "any kind of guidance that is more than a confirmatory or negative feedback" (p. 473). It includes the kinds of prompts, hints, and splicing of information described by Graesser and colleagues (Graesser & Person, 1994; Graesser, Person, & Magliano, 1995; Person & Graesser, 1999). For example, the tutor might ask, "What's going on here?" to prompt the tutee to describe a process. Tutoring is a skill that can be taught and can be progressively improved with further training and practice.

Structured tutoring in particular is most effective in improving learning. It provides individualized instruction that is consistent across many educational settings (Lindren, Meier, & Brigham, 1991; Slavin & Madden, 1989) and reduces some of the variability in outcomes that occurs as a result of differences among tutors. Tutees' academic achievement increases more if they participate in a structured tutoring program (Lindren et al., 1991).

Tutoring also benefits the tutor (Chi et al., 2001). As they plan, prepare for, and carry out their tasks, tutors improve their understanding of the content they are teaching (Cohen et al, 1982). This is not unexpected. Tutors have opportunities to explain content to another person, and providing explanations has been shown to promote achievement (Webb, 1991, 1992). Moreover, tutors may gain metacognitive experience about their own understanding of the content (Baker & Brown, 1984). In other words, as a tutor tries to explain a concept to a tutee, she may realize that she does not understand it as well as she thought she did. For teachers worried that high-ability students might not receive the same benefits from tutoring that low-ability students receive, high-ability students—when asked which instructional practices seemed most fair to them—selected peer tutoring as the fairest way to help everyone learn (Thorkildsen, 1993).

Processes Involved in Tutoring

We know from the research literature that tutoring helps students; the literature also tells us that tutoring is a process that can be improved in most situations. Naïve tutors may be inhibited by politeness rules (Person et al., 1995). For example, a tutor may be reluctant to tell a tutee that he or she is wrong. Tutors may also provide inappropriate feedback to their tutees (Person & Graesser, 1999). Despite these problems, one-on-one tutoring is effective. Person and Graesser (1999) describe tutoring in terms of five steps:

1. The tutor asks a question (or presents a problem for the student to solve).
2. The student answers the question.
3. The tutor gives feedback on the answer.
4. The tutor and the student collaborate to improve the quality of the answers.
5. The tutor assesses the student's understanding of the answer (Person & Graesser, 1999, pp. 71–72).

Steps 1–3 are typical of the kinds of interactions that may occur between a teacher and a student in the context of whole-class instruction. Steps 4 and 5 rarely occur in that context because of time constraints and the large number of students in most classrooms. Step 4 is the one in which the tutor is most likely to work with the tutee in the zone of proximal development. It is during this step that scaffolding is provided (Chi et al., 2001; Graesser et al. 1995).

In most tutoring situations, the tutor dominates the interaction. McArthur, Stasz, and Zumidzinas (1990) analyzed the activities of tutors and found that 53% of them could have elicited responses from students. Tutees' responses are important because their quality contributes to the effectiveness of the tutoring process (Chi et al., 2001). The efforts of tutees to understand the content being taught, in light of their existing knowledge may be the most valuable aspect of tutoring. However, if tutors are not trained, their instructional efforts will vary. Therefore, it is unlikely that the activities of the tutor alone are responsible for the benefits of tutoring (VanLehn et al., 2003).

Chi and her colleagues (Chi et al., 2001) conducted two studies to examine why tutoring works. The tutors were college students who tutored eighth-grade students about the circulatory system, using a prepared text consisting of 86 sentences. Each sentence was printed on a separate page. The tutor and the tutee worked on one sentence at a time. The tutors' explanations were correlated with student learning, as were the students' responses to scaffolding efforts (e.g., prompts, hints, comprehension questions). In a second study, tutors were trained to prompt tutees for knowledge construction responses, using a set of content-free prompts (e.g., What makes you say that? What happens next?). This procedure is similar to that used by King in her studies of peer tutoring (King, 1991; King et al., 1998), described later in the chapter. The use of prompts resulted in more episodes of deep scaffolding, in which there were longer exchanges between tutors and tutees. Students who were prompted were more constructive overall, displaying more of what they knew and putting more effort into the exchanges.

Figures 12.4 and 12.5 present examples of *shallow* and *deep* scaffolding. In the first episode (Figure 12.4), the tutor and the tutee are working with the statement, "These arteries branch into arterioles and then capillaries." The exchange is described as *shallow* scaffolding because although the tutor asks questions, the questions do not seem to require deep processing. The exchange remains superficial, with the tutor asking questions whose answers do not require complex explanations or reasoning. The key question asked in this episode is, And what would you expect to be passed back and forth? In this question, the tutor provides

Sentence 84) These arteries branch into arterioles and then into capillaries.

S: Like arteries do.
T: Uh-huh.
S: And then.
T: So what would you assume comes next?
S: After capillaries?
T: Uh-huh.
S: Can I look? [pause] Venules. So then, you have venules because they go to the capillaries, to the venules, is that how you say it? To the veins.
T: And we're inside the lungs now?
S: What?
T: Is where this where the picture is inside the lungs?
S: Well this is here. This is where diffusion happens.
T: **And what would you expect to be passed back and forth?**
S: Oxygen and carbon dioxide. Do you want me to put that?
T: You don't have to.
S: O.k.

Note: S = student; T = tutor.

Figure 12.4. An Example of Shallow Scaffolding

Source: Chi, M. T. H., Siler, S. A., Jeong, J., Yamauchi, T., & Hausmann, R. G. (2001). Learning from human tutoring. *Cognitive Science, 25*, 526. Copyright by the Cognitive Science Society.

Sentence 60) If a substance can pass through a membrane, the membrane is permeable to it.

S: So, it explains itself: If something is permeable to something, then that thing can pass through the other thing.
T: So how would the—
S: And if it's impermeable, it can't.
T: **And how would that relate back to the capillary walls?**
S: Well the capillary walls,
T: Can you explain?
S: Well this is how I learned it.
T: Uh-huh
S: In the cell, it's made up of these things and then it has these protein things like this. They're really, really big. And then there's a little substance like oxygen and it can just go through here, but a big substance like sugar which is tons of letters has to go through the protein first.
. . .
T: **And how does, how does that relate to the cell membrane or the capillary?**
S: Well if it's too big, if something's too big, to go into the capillary membrane through the capillary membrane, it can't because the capillary membrane is only one cell thick, but then maybe if it has protein, it can. O.k.
T: O.k.
S: Alright.

Note: S = student; T = tutor.

Figure 12.5. An Example of Deep Scaffolding

Source: Chi, M. T. H., Siler, S. A., Jeong, J., Yamauchi, T., & Hausmann, R. G. (2001). Learning from human tutoring. *Cognitive Science, 25,* 527. Copyright by the Cognitive Science Society.

a description of what happens (something is passed back and forth). All the tutee needs to do is to identify a substance. The tutee in this example commented, "This is where diffusion happens." The tutor could have checked the tutee's understanding of this process by asking, "How does diffusion happen?" Instead, the tutor supplies a statement of what that process is. The tutor does not ask the tutee to explain it, then to work with him to improve the answer and describe what is being diffused.

In contrast, Figure 12.5 is an example of *deep* scaffolding. In the example of *shallow* scaffolding, the tutor and the tutee worked on a sentence that described part of the structure of the circulatory system. The statement itself focused them on a descriptive kind of exchange. In contrast, the interaction in Figure 12.5 focuses on a statement that describes a process. The tutor and the tutee are working on the statement, "If a substance can pass through a membrane, the membrane is permeable to it." The first question asked by the tutor is, How would that relate back to the capillary walls? To answer this question, the tutee must provide a response that shows connected knowledge. When the tutee struggles to respond, the tutor again asks whether the tutee can explain. After the tutee begins to explain, the tutor further probes the tutee's understanding. The tutor is able to draw out a complex explanation by asking high-level questions and prompting the tutee for more information. When tutors ask high-level questions, the result is greater depth of processing by the tutee.

In sum, one-on-one tutoring benefits both tutor and tutee and can be done with varying degrees of effectiveness. The outcomes of tutoring improve when tutors are trained to be less dominant in their interactions with tutees and to provide prompts and scaffold the tutee's learning. In the sections that follow, we will describe some specific examples of tutoring.

What Does This Mean to Me?
Have you ever tutored someone? What was difficult or rewarding about the experience?

Tutoring Diverse Learners

A number of tutoring programs have been developed for use with culturally and linguistically diverse students in urban areas. Two such programs are described in this section. Although they were developed for use with a very diverse group of students who were generally of low socioeconomic status (SES), the techniques can be used with all kinds of learners.

Classwide Peer Tutoring Classwide peer tutoring (CWPT) was developed by researchers at the University of Kansas with the help of classroom teachers. This technique includes elements of both cooperation and competition, and is influenced by a social-motivational perspective on peer learning. Its purpose is to improve overall performance in basic academic skills (Delquadri et al., 1986), particularly for students who are culturally and linguistically diverse and come from poor families. Rather than having less skilled students tutored by more skilled peers, CWPT involves the entire class in tutoring activities. Students are either randomly paired or matched by ability or language proficiency. Students with limited English proficiency are initially paired with students who speak their language but whose English is better.

At the beginning of a week, all the pairs of students are assigned to one of two competing teams. One person serves as a tutor for the first 10 minutes, then the partners switch roles. As in STAD, the teacher presents the content to the whole class and uses the peer tutoring sessions for practice and rehearsal. The tutor asks the tutee a question about an instructional item, such as a math fact or a spelling word. If the tutee answers correctly, he or she is awarded two points. The tutor has an answer sheet so that the answer can be checked. If the answer is incorrect, the tutor provides the correct response, asks the tutee to write or say the correct answer three times (thus providing **positive practice**), and gives the tutee one point for correcting the mistake. (Positive practice involves practicing the correct answer after making a mistake.) If the tutee fails to correct the answer, no points are awarded, and the tutor gives the tutee the answer both orally and visually. The tutor and the tutee are not competing with each other but are contributing to an overall team score. The team is made up of numerous tutor-tutee pairs. The goal is to go through the assigned material at least twice in the allotted time. The more work is completed correctly, the more points the pair contributes to their team. The team with the highest number of points earns recognition or rewards.

> positive practice   Practicing the correct answer after making a mistake.

As the pairs work together, the teacher moves around the classroom and awards bonus points for appropriate tutoring behaviors, such as clear presentation of material, awards points based on performance, and proper use of the error correction procedure, and makes positive comments. Some elements of the Johnsons' social-cohesion approach may be seen in this aspect of the technique in that positive social behaviors are reinforced.

Arreaga-Mayer, Terry, and Greenwood (1998) summarized the research evidence supporting the effectiveness of this particular form of tutoring. They found positive effects of CWPT on a variety of measures of academic achievement, such as reading, spelling, vocabulary, and mathematics (Greenwood, Carta, & Kamps, 1990; Greenwood, Maheady, & Carta, 1991; Mathes & Fuchs, 1993). A four-year study examined the effects of using CWPT with low-SES students on the students' achievement in grades 1 to 4. The performance of these students was compared with that of a control group of children who moved through the same grades and experienced a teacher-designed instructional program. The results showed that CWPT increased student achievement (Greenwood, Delquadri, & Hall, 1989). A follow-up of the students two years later when they were in the sixth grade found that the gains made by those who received CWPT were maintained (Greenwood & Terry, 1993). In addition, compared to students in the control group, fewer members of the CWPT group were placed in special education programs. An additional comparison group was also used, consisting of students from the same school district who were not considered at risk. The parents of students in both the experimental group and the control group of at-risk students had received much less formal education, had lower incomes, and held lower-status jobs than the parents of students in the nonrisk group. Students who had experienced CWPT performed as well as students in the non-risk comparison group on half of the comparisons made.

> **What Does This Mean to Me?**
> Why do you think these tutoring programs were effective?

Using Technology to Improve Implementation Children did not benefit as much from CWPT if they were absent from school, the content was not challenging, or the peer tutoring was of poor quality (Greenwood et al., 1993; Greenwood & Terry, 1993). In an effort to improve the implementation of CWPT, Greenwood and his colleagues developed the Classwide Peer Tutoring Learning Management System (CWPT-LMS: Greenwood et al., 2001; Greenwood et al., 1993), which allows teachers to set up classroom rosters and record outcomes. The system includes a data analysis module that enables teachers to chart individual and classroom progress over time. Tools are available that assist teachers in managing data and sharing, deleting, or modifying program information. The technology allows teachers to monitor the program more effectively and to use data from students to make decisions about instruction.

The CWPT-LMS system was evaluated in the classrooms of five teachers of English language learners (ELL). The results showed that the teachers carried out the program as intended. Both students and teachers were satisfied with the program, and the students made progress in understanding the content being taught.

Reciprocal Peer Tutoring Reciprocal Peer Tutoring (RPT) was originally designed for pairs of low-achieving urban elementary school children (Fantuzzo, King, & Heller, 1992). As in most effective tutoring programs, students receive training before tutoring begins. They are first introduced to the concepts of teamwork, partnership, and cooperation. These efforts are intended to promote a sense of social cohesion. Students learn how to do RPT in two to three 45-minute sessions. RPT sessions occur twice weekly and to date have been applied primarily to the learning of mathematics. Students are assigned to pairs and work on computational problems for the first 20 minutes of a session, during which they play the roles of both teacher and student. The procedure used in RPT is similar to that used in Classwide Peer Tutoring. Student dyads first select a team goal from among a number of available choices. The peer teacher is given a set of flashcards that designate areas in which the student's mathematical skills need improvement. These areas are identified through curriculum-based assessments. Each flashcard has a sample problem on one side and the steps for solving it on the other. The pair is given a worksheet on which they keep track of the number of attempts made to solve the problem. The student tries to solve the problem and receives feedback on the effort. If the student succeeds, he or she is praised. If the student does not, the peer teacher suggests that he or she try the problem again and records the answer in the second column of the worksheet, which is labeled "Try 2." After the first 20 minutes, the two students complete drill sheets, and at the end of the period, they check each other's papers, adding up the total number of problems that were answered correctly. The dyads compare their scores with their team's goals and decide whether they have succeeded. After a specified number of *wins,* student dyads choose rewards from a set of available choices.

Reciprocal peer tutoring combines many elements of both the social-motivational and the social-cohesion perspectives on peer learning. It uses elements of the social-motivational perspective because students are individually accountable for their performance, and teams are rewarded based on their performance. It uses elements of the social-cohesion perspective in its emphasis on preparing students for teamwork and cooperation. The teacher must do a great deal of preparation to provide flashcards and drill sheets for each dyad.

Reciprocal peer tutoring involves both structured interaction and the use of rewards. Are both necessary for this instructional strategy to be effective? Fantuzzo et al. (1992) examined this question in a study of at-risk fourth and fifth graders in an urban elementary school. Students who received both elements of RPT were most successful. These results are similar to those reported by Slavin (1996). Students who experienced structured conditions reported feeling higher levels of academic and behavioral competence. Teachers recognized that students who were eligible for rewards behaved better than students who were not. Overall, peer-assisted learning improves students' on-task behavior during a lesson (Ginsburg-Block & Fantuzzo, 1997). Reciprocal peer tutoring was more effective when parents were supportive (Fantuzzo, Davis, & Ginsberg, 1995; Heller & Fantuzzo, 1993).

Tutoring and Students with Special Needs

Tutoring initially was viewed as a process in which an older or more skilled student tutors a younger or less skilled student. This view was in line with Vygotskyian theory in that a more competent individual was more likely to be able to provide scaffolding to support the creation of a zone of proximal development with a less competent individual. However, techniques such as CWPT, RPT, and structured tutorial interaction show that interactions between peers who are similar in age and ability can achieve similar outcomes.

Students with special needs benefit from tutoring (Cook et al., 1985–1986; Osguthorpe & Scruggs, 1986; Scruggs & Mastropieri, 1998). In general, they also benefit when they have a chance to serve as tutors. For example, students with learning and behavioral problems tutored non–special-needs children in reading for four 20-minute sessions per week (Top, 1984). Both the tutors and the tutees improved their reading skills. Scruggs and Osguthorpe (1986) reviewed 26 studies of the effects of tutoring on the academic performance and social development of tutors and tutees. They concluded that students with mild disabilities can serve as effective tutors for both handicapped and normally achieving peers and that their success depends on careful training and supervision. Tutoring experiences had little effect on students' self-esteem. These results were similar to those found in a meta-analysis of studies in which students with mild disabilities served as tutors (Cook et al., 1985–1986). Peer tutoring in reading for such students is generally effective but is not more effective than teacher-led interventions, such as teacher-led small-group instruction (Mathes & Fuchs, 1994; Mathes et al., 2003).

Peer-Assisted Learning Strategies, or PALS (Fuchs et al., 1997; Mathes et al., 2003) is a technique based on CWPT (Delquadri et al., 1986). Pairs of students work on a skill in which one student is more competent than the other. The main features of this technique include the following:

- The tutor models and gradually fades a verbal rehearsal routine that sets forth a series of steps for solving the problem.

- The teacher provides step-by-step feedback to confirm and praise correct responses, provide explanations, and model strategic behavior for incorrect answers.

- There are frequent verbal and written interaction between tutors and tutees.

- There are opportunities for tutees to apply explanations to subsequent problems.

- The process includes reciprocity, in which both children serve in the roles of tutor and tutee during each session (adapted from p. 27, Fuchs & Fuchs, 1998).

The PALS strategy is influenced by Vygotskyian theory in that it involves the pairing of a higher achieving student with a lower achieving student, along with support for productive interactions. It is successful with mathematics (Fuchs, Fuchs, Yazdian et al., 2002) and reading (Mathes et al., 2003). Learning-disabled students in elementary school classrooms that used PALS were more socially accepted than similar students in classes that did not use PALS, and they enjoyed the same social standing as most of their non–special-needs peers (Fuchs, Fuchs, Mathes et al., 2002).

Appendix

Students as Diverse Learners

Tutoring can be an effective strategy for addressing differences in how students learn. Children with special needs can benefit from being tutored and from providing tutoring to others. (*PRAXIS*™ I B. 2, *INTASC* Principles 2, 3)

Tutoring for Higher Order Outcomes

Both CWPT and RPT were developed for use with learners who are at risk for academic failure as a result of poverty or difficulty with English. Both have been shown to help students succeed academically. The kinds of tasks in which students engage tend to be basic in nature, and assessments target lower level skills. It is possible, however, for students with low skill levels to be involved in tasks that require higher order skills. Examples of techniques that promote such skills are Structured Tutorial Interaction (King et al., 1998) and Complex Instruction (Cohen et al., Lotan, Scarloss, & Arellano, 1999). The role of the task on which peers work and how it fits with particular kinds of peer learning are discussed later in the chapter.

Structured Tutorial Interaction
Tutoring among same-age peers can result in higher order learning. (See the "Taking it to the Classroom" box on the next page for tutoring guidelines). The performances of seventh-grade students assigned to three different peer-tutoring conditions was compared (King et al., 1998). The tutors were the same age as the tutees. The tutors were trained to use one of three strategies for tutoring: (a) explaining material to each other, (b) asking comprehension and thought-provoking questions in addition to explaining, and (c) asking such questions in a particular sequence, as well as explaining. Every student was taught how to explain using the tell-why strategy. They *told* their partners what they knew, explained the *why* and *how* of something, and linked the information to what their partners already knew. The second part of the tutoring strategy required them to *tell why, tell how,* and *use their own words.* The goal of the strategy was to help students

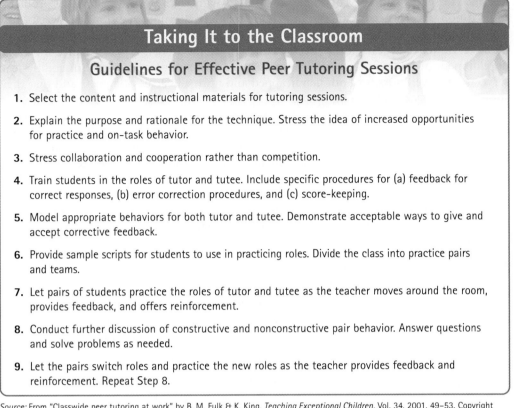

Taking It to the Classroom

Guidelines for Effective Peer Tutoring Sessions

1. Select the content and instructional materials for tutoring sessions.

2. Explain the purpose and rationale for the technique. Stress the idea of increased opportunities for practice and on-task behavior.

3. Stress collaboration and cooperation rather than competition.

4. Train students in the roles of tutor and tutee. Include specific procedures for (a) feedback for correct responses, (b) error correction procedures, and (c) score-keeping.

5. Model appropriate behaviors for both tutor and tutee. Demonstrate acceptable ways to give and accept corrective feedback.

6. Provide sample scripts for students to use in practicing roles. Divide the class into practice pairs and teams.

7. Let pairs of students practice the roles of tutor and tutee as the teacher moves around the room, provides feedback, and offers reinforcement.

8. Conduct further discussion of constructive and nonconstructive pair behavior. Answer questions and solve problems as needed.

9. Let the pairs switch roles and practice the new roles as the teacher provides feedback and reinforcement. Repeat Step 8.

Source: From "Classwide peer tutoring at work" by B. M. Fulk & K. King, *Teaching Exceptional Children,* Vol. 34, 2001, 49–53. Copyright 2001 by The Council for Exceptional Children. Reprinted with permission.

elaborate on ideas, explain their thinking rather than merely describe information, and connect the material to what they already knew. Students were also trained to ask comprehension and *thinking* questions. An example of a thinking question is: How is the circulatory system of the earthworm different from that of the grasshopper? (O'Donnell, 2003). We saw from Chi and colleagues' analysis of shallow and deep scaffolding that different kinds of questions elicit different qualities of thinking and response. Students in the question sequence group learned to ask comprehension questions, following up with a probing question if the answer was not complete. An example of a probing question is How do the valves in the heart work —Can you say more?. If the answer was incorrect, they asked a *hint* question. Finally, they asked a thinking or knowledge-building question. An example of a hint question is: Why are the chambers of the heart important?

Students who asked questions, explained, and sequenced their questions and those who asked questions and explained performed better on inference and integration tasks than did those who engaged in explanation alone. They had no advantage on tests of literal comprehension. Eight weeks after the initial study, students in the two tutoring groups that included inquiry maintained their advantage on tests of inference and integration. This study shows that peer tutoring need not be limited to lower level tasks or outcomes but can be used to promote higher level knowledge.

Learning in Heterogeneous Groups

Many cooperative learning techniques were designed for use with groups of four to six students. Typically, these groups are heterogeneous with respect to academic achievement and other characteristics, such as race, gender, and ethnicity. Larger groups can be used for both simple and complex tasks. Such groups can also be either tightly or loosely structured. In this section, we will first describe some commonly used cooperative techniques (in addition to STAD and Learning Together, described earlier).

Chapter Reference
See Chapter 4 for information about homogeneous grouping of students based on ability.

Learners in heterogeneous groups have the opportunity to learn from students who differ in their skills and interests.
(Richard T. Nowitz/Photo Researchers, Inc.)

Examples of Cooperative Techniques

A variety of cooperative techniques are described here. There are many more that could be included. As you read these examples, pay attention to the kinds of tasks for which the technique can be used, the role of the teacher, and the underlying view of peer learning. Each technique has a **participation structure** or rules that define how to participate in an activity.

Structural Approaches

The structural approach to cooperative learning provides flexible structures for interaction that can be fitted to a variety of tasks (Kagan, 1993). Kagan's structures (1989/1990) can be used to develop a sense of belonging to a team as well as to improve communication skills and mastery of content. In general, the structures for interaction are easily integrated into ongoing instruction. One of Kagan's structures that is easy to implement is the *Think-Pair-Share* technique. Before a lesson begins, students are grouped into pairs, sitting side by side. The teacher presents the lesson, which might be a lecture or demonstration, or might involve hands-on activities. After about 15 minutes, the teacher writes a question on the board or overhead transparency that requires students to reflect on some aspect of the material just presented. For example, a reflective question for a ninth-grade social studies class might be, What caused the American Civil War? Each student tries to answer the question, then each pair of students discusses their answers with one another. They share their answers with the class. The teacher may conduct a whole-class discussion to hear different points of view.

Jigsaw

One of the original cooperative learning techniques is *Jigsaw* (Aronson et al., 1978). Students are divided into heterogeneous four-person groups and assigned topics on which they are to become experts. For example, if a group is learning about the rain forest, each of its members will be responsible for becoming an expert on a particular subtopic (e.g., birds and animals of the rain forest, people who live in the rain forest, plants, and the destruction of the rain forest). Each student has different reading material. Students with the same *expert topic* meet to discuss their topic. The *expert* groups consist of members of different teams. Their task is to learn as much as possible about their topic. They then return to their groups and teach the material to the other members of the group. Each student in turn teaches the group about his or her subtopic. Later, students take individual quizzes on the material, and individual grades are assigned.

In this technique, every student must participate. Each member of a group has access to materials that others in the group do not and is responsible for communicating that information to the others. Some students may have difficulty mastering the material and may be ineffective in communicating it to others in their group. From a cognitive-elaborative perspective, each student will process information more actively because of the need to *teach* it to others. The teacher needs to see that students in expert groups make sure all the experts have mastered the material.

---

participation structures The rules that define how to participate in an activity. Such rules may be formal as well as informal.

> **Expert Sheet**
> **The Blackfoot**
>
> To read: pages 3–9 and 11–12
>
> ***Topics***
>
> 1. How were Blackfoot men expected to act?
> 2. What is a group, and what does it do? What are the most important groups for the Blackfoot?
> 3. What did Blackfoot bands and clubs do?
> 4. What were the Blackfoot customs and traditions?

Figure 12.6. Expert Sheet for Jigsaw

Source: From Robert E. Slavin, *Cooperative Learning*, 2e. Published by Allyn and Bacon, Boston, MA. Copyright © 1995 by Pearson Education. Reprinted by permission of the publisher.

Jigsaw II In *Jigsaw* II (Slavin, 1986), each student reads the same material. Students are assigned to expert groups and given an expert *sheet* to guide their study. Slavin (1995) describes a *Jigsaw* II with a social studies unit about the Blackfoot Indian tribe that is used to teach about groups, group norms, and leadership. An expert sheet might be similar to the one shown in Figure 12.6. Students who have been assigned the same expert topic meet in groups to discuss it, using the expert sheet to guide their learning.

Each student then returns to his or her team and teach the topic to its members. The teacher can provide outlines to guide the discussions, in which each expert presents the information to the rest of the group. Students take individual quizzes, and teams are rewarded in the same way as in STAD. Slavin's redesign of Jigsaw has the advantage of simplifying the preparation of materials.

Group Investigation Sharan and Hertz-Lazarowitz (1980) developed a technique known as *Group Investigation* that consists of six stages. Its key components (Sharan & Sharan, 1992) are interaction, investigation, interpretation, and intrinsic motivation. In the first stage, the teacher chooses a general topic to fit with the curriculum goals for the class. This topic is split into a number of subtopics. Students then organize themselves into research groups, each of which will focus on a particular subtopic. The teacher must ensure that there are adequate resources for students to use in the investigative part of the project. For example, an eighth-grade social studies teacher might assign the topic of famines. The students might organize their research around various countries that have experienced famines: Ethiopia, Ireland, North Korea, Somalia, Sudan, and Ukraine.

In Stage II, students plan their research and decide how they are going to gather the information. They may write down a set of questions to be answered. In Stage III, they carry out the research, with each student contributing to the effort. In Stage IV, the students share the information they have gathered and plan a presentation to the class. They identify the ideas they wish to communicate and develop a strategy for presenting them to the other groups in the class. Each group chooses a representative who works with other representatives to plan an overall strategy for the presentation. In Stage V, the students make their presentations; in Stage VI, the teacher and students evaluate them. They may, for example, jointly construct a test based on the content of the presentations to be given to the entire class. Students conducting a group investigation need to show high levels of self-regulated learning, coordination, and metacognition.

Evaluations of group investigation are typically done by comparing students who participated in group investigations with students who experienced whole-class instruction. They have found that most students in group investigation classes outperform their peers in comparable classes (Lazarowitz & Karsenty, 1990; Sharan & Shachar, 1988; Sharon & Shaulov, 1990). The assessments contain questions that require students not only to provide factual information but also to interpret information and apply it to new problems.

Structured Controversies Students often have difficulty expressing disagreement. Children and adolescents who are shy are unlikely to contradict the class or group leader. They may worry about having the wrong answer or appearing *stupid* to their peers. The ability to argue is an important skill. According to Johnson and Johnson (1995), academic controversy

TABLE 12. 3

Structured Controversies

Step 1	Students research a position, learn the relevant information, and prepare a persuasive "best case possible" for the position.
Step 2	Students present the best case possible for the position in as persuasive and convincing a way as possible.
Step 3	Students engage in an open discussion in which they argue forcefully for their position and rebut attacks on it.
Step 4	Students reverse perspectives and present the opposing position as accurately, completely, persuasively, and forcefully as they can.
Step 5	Students drop all advocacies, create a synthesis or integration of the opposing positions, and reach a consensus as to the best reasoned judgment that may be made about the issue.

Source: Figure 1, Johnson, D. W., & Johnson, R. T. (1995). *Creative controversy: Intellectual challenge in the classroom.* Edina, MN: Interaction Book Company. Reproduced with permission.

occurs when students disagree about ideas, information, opinions, theories, and conclusions. The controversy is resolved as students reach a consensus on a particular position. In the technique known as *Structured Controversy,* the teacher guides students through the steps outlined in Table 12.3.

Students are placed in a four-person cooperative learning group, which is then divided into two pairs. A high school class might be asked to consider whether pollution regulations for cars should be eased. One pair of students is to make the case for keeping the regulations as they are, and the other pair is to make the case for easing them. All the students will do research to support their positions. At each step of the process, the teacher plays an important role. The students may need assistance in finding useful information and distinguishing between good arguments and strong opinions. The students present their positions to one another, with each pair taking turns. They then engage in an open discussion of the ideas that have been presented, trying to convince one another of their point of view. The pairs then switch sides and present the opposing arguments. This causes them to focus on the arguments themselves and makes it easier to achieve consensus. The group then develops a report that summarizes the arguments for each perspective and the group's decision as to which position is best. Students need good social skills to engage in a structured academic controversy. It is important that they not criticize one another personally but instead criticize the arguments being made. (See the "Taking It to the Classroom" box below.)

Taking It to the Classroom

Promoting Productive Interaction

- *Encouraging Respect*
  Discuss with students how they like to be treated and how they do not like to be treated. Have them explain how they might feel if others treat them badly. In some situations, you might ask students to draw up a contract stating how they will treat one another and have each of them sign it and keep a copy.

- *Encouraging Good Thinking*
  Encourage students to be critical of ideas and not of the people who propose them. You could assign one student to record ideas as they are proposed so that they can be discussed later. This will help the group avoid reacting to specific students.

- *Encouraging a Focus on Learning*
  Encourage students to consider different ideas so they that can improve on the arguments they might make. Remind them that it is better to change their minds and adopt a better position than to stick with a bad idea.

Appendix
Teaching Heterogeneous Students

The use of cooperative learning techniques is one approach to teaching heterogeneous students who differ in gender, ability, race, and ethnicity. (*PRAXIS*™ I B. 4, *INTASC* Principles 1, 3)

Collaboration and Technology

Changes in technology and widespread use of the Internet have made it possible to devise new forms of cooperative and collaborative learning. Some of these involve groups of students using online resources together, whereas others involve communication without face-to-face interaction. In this section, we discuss webQuests, online mentoring, and Computer-Supported Intentional Learning Environments (CSILE).

WebQuests

WebQuests use a central question based on a real-world issue and ask students to solve the problem or answer the question. Using the World Wide Web, students can contact experts and access searchable databases, current news reports, and other materials. In many WebQuests, students take on specific roles within a cooperative group and develop expertise (similar to Jigsaw I and II) in a particular aspect of the topic. The students can post their solutions or answers on a Web site for comments and evaluation. An example of a WebQuest is one designed by eTeachers (2005) for high school social studies students. It is based on the Chinese Cultural Revolution; the question asked is, How did China's Cultural Revolution affect the lives of ordinary Chinese at home and abroad? The WebQuest provides background information. Students take on individual roles within a cooperative group: Student, Politician, Dissident, Red Guard, Propagandist, and Housewife. Support is provided for each role in the form of questions that can be used to guide the students' analysis of the problem and collection of information. The students work together to respond to the question. They can then post their response or seek feedback from experts on the topic. This kind of activity not only promotes collaborative learning but also encourages students to learn from the community outside the classroom.

Online Mentoring

Online mentoring takes many forms. It can include one-on-one mentoring or groups of students working with a single mentor. Many online mentoring programs are available. A key consideration in using an online mentoring program is that learners can interact *safely* with adult volunteers. It is important to maintain the learner's privacy, limit access to the learner by undesirable individuals, and establish rules to govern interactions between learners and mentors.

Online mentoring can have many benefits for mentors, students, and teachers. Online communication may be the only way that some volunteers can interact with students because of their work schedules. Students can get more individual attention while working on a project than they might get in the classroom. Online communication gives them opportunities to hone their writing and reading skills. In addition, online mentoring can help students develop a caring relationship with an adult who takes an interest in their work. Teachers can also benefit from the availability of online mentors to provide expertise or resources for various curricular topics.

Knowledge Forum

Knowledge Forum was developed from the Computer-Supported Intentional Learning Environment (CSILE; Scardamalia, Bereiter, & Lamon, 1994), which was designed for use by an entire class of students. Students worked on networked computers in a classroom that was connected to a server and maintained a communal database. The database included text and graphical notes that the students produced and could be accessed by all the students by means of database searches. Any student could add a note or a comment. Only the original writer of a note could delete it. CSILE was evaluated in four classrooms in the same school. Students who had used CSILE performed better on standardized tests of math and language arts than did students in a comparison group (Scardamalia et al., 1994). A study of explanations offered by fifth- and sixth-grade students found that the CSILE students attempted more coherent explanations when asked what they had learned from a particular unit. Knowledge Forum expands on this system and is designed to assist students in *knowledge building:* defining problems, generating hypotheses, collecting and analyzing information, and collaborating.

Chapter Reference
Chapter 10 includes a description of problem-based learning, an instructional strategy that is similar in some ways to WebQuests.

Appendix
Enhancing Learning
You can enhance students' learning by using a variety of resources and materials to support your instruction. Examples of such resources include computers, Internet resources, and other technology. (*PRAXIS*™ II.A.4, *INTASC* Principle 4.)

Influences on Effectiveness in Heterogeneous Groups

Heterogeneous groups have a number of advantages. They give students a chance to work with others who may differ from themselves. When such groups work well, students benefit both academically and socially. However, groups do not automatically work well. Without instruction in the cognitive skills needed for tasks or the social skills needed to coordinate their activities, students tend to work at the most concrete level or give each other only minimal support (Cohen, 1994). Group interaction is influenced by the goals and incentives associated with the assigned task, the nature of the task itself, and individual differences among the participants (O'Donnell & Dansereau, 1992).

Gender and Cooperative Groups

In Chapter 9, you read about the importance of teachers' beliefs and their influence on classroom practices. One area in which teachers appear to have strong beliefs is the role of gender in the classroom, particularly as it relates to interaction in cooperative groups. Many teachers, for example, believe that boys dominate interactions with girls. However, the findings of research on this question are mixed.

Questions of interest with respect to gender include the following: Do girls participate in group interaction at the same rates as boys? Does their participation depend on the balance between boys and girls in the group? Is the participation of boys and girls influenced by the nature of the task they are assigned?

Concerns are often raised about dominance in groups because some students might have limited opportunities to participate in ways that promote learning (Webb, 1989, 1992). Boys and girls in cooperative groups may not participate equally. Many high school teachers use same-gender pairings to limit the degree to which students avoid tasks that they consider gender-specific. One study (Webb, 1984) found that when boys in the group outnumbered girls, the boys dominated the interaction. When girls outnumbered boys, the girls still tended to defer to the boys, even if there was only one. In groups that were balanced with respect to gender, all the students tended to participate equally.

Other studies have found differences in the ways in which boys and girls interact in groups. For example, Underwood and Jindal (1993) found that mixed-gender pairs did not perform as well as same-gender pairs on a computer-based language task. Pairs of boys showed the greatest gains when told to cooperate. Similar results were found by Fitzpatrick and Harman (2000). The kinds of tasks on which children work also play a role. Seven- and nine-year-old children worked in same- or mixed-gender pairs on a language-based computer task and on a noncomputer task (Fitzpatrick & Hardman, 2000). The mixed-gender pairs were less collaborative than the same-gender pairs. Girls in mixed-gender pairs were more assertive during the noncomputer task, whereas boys were more assertive during the computer-based task. Similar gender differences were found by Holden (1993), who examined boys' and girls' contributions to discussions in a language task and in a mathematics/technology task. When boys outnumbered girls in cooperative groups performing a language task, the level of abstract talk contributed by girls was low in comparison to groups whose composition was more balanced. There was little abstract talk in discussions of the mathematics/technology task. Holden concluded that the kind of talk in which students engage varies as a function of the task and the composition of the group.

Tolmie and Howe (1993) found that boys and girls did not differ in performance on a task in which they were asked to predict the trajectories of falling objects but that they did differ in their interactions. Female pairs avoided conflict, focusing instead on what problems they had in common. Male pairs learned most when they discussed the feedback and referred to explanatory factors that might account for differences between predictions and actual events. Mixed pairs were very constrained in their interactions. Table 12.4 presents a summary of the findings we have described.

It is difficult to draw strong conclusions about the role of gender in cooperative groups based on the available evidence. Nevertheless, teachers should be sensitive to the possible influence of gender on group interaction and take it into account when assigning students to groups.

What Does This Mean to Me?
Do you think that gender matters when one is working in a cooperative group? In what ways does it influence group interaction?

What Does This Mean to Me?
Look at Table 12.4. Which of these findings make sense to you? Why?

 What role did gender play in the group interaction recorded in the vignette at the beginning of the chapter?

TABLE 12.4

Summary of Findings on the Role of Gender in Cooperative Groups

Researcher	Year	Findings
Webb	1984	• When boys outnumber girls in a group, boys dominate the interaction.
		• When girls outnumber boys in a group, girls defer to the boys.
Underwood	1993	• Mixed-gender pairs did not perform as well as same-gender pairs on a computer-based language task.
		• Pairs of boys benefited most from directives to cooperate.
Fitzpatrick	2000	• Mixed-gender pairs were less collaborative than same-gender pairs.
		• Girls in mixed-gender pairs were more assertive during a noncomputer task.
		• Boys in mixed-gender pairs were more assertive during the computer task.
Tolmie	1993	• Female pairs avoided conflict, focused on problems experienced.
		• Male pairs learned most when they discussed feedback.
		• Mixed-gender pairs were very constrained in their interactions.
Holden	1993	• When boys outnumbered girls in a group for a language task, girls contributed little abstract talk.
		• There was little abstract talk by either boys or girls on a math/technology task.

Race, Ethnicity, and Language

Cooperative learning is often promoted as an instructional strategy that can be used to integrate children from a variety of backgrounds. Slavin (1995) reviewed a number of studies that examined the effects of cooperative learning on intergroup relations. The findings indicate that children who experience cooperative learning report more cross-racial, cross-ethnic friendships than do children who experience whole-class instruction. It is important to note that although the research is promising, the conclusions drawn from it may not necessarily apply to today's classrooms, because their composition is quite different than it was 20 years ago. Creating positive interdependence would seem to be crucial to the effort to promote positive intergroup relations.

A more recent study examined the effects of a cooperative learning program, Bilingual Cooperative Integrated Reading and Composition (BCIRC), on the Spanish and English reading, writing, and language achievement of second and third graders with limited English proficiency (Calderon, Hertz-Lazarowitz, & Slavin, 1998). The BCIRC program consists of a set of activities that take place before, during, and after reading. They include building background knowledge and vocabulary, making predictions, reading a selection, partner reading and silent reading, story comprehension treasure hunts, story mapping, story retelling, story-related writing, saying words out loud and spelling them, checking the partner's work, putting new vocabulary into meaningful sentences, and tests. Three schools that used BCIRC were included in the study, and the performance of the students who participated in the program was compared to that of students in other schools in the district with similar demographic profiles. Second graders in BCIRC classrooms performed significantly better than students in comparison groups in writing on the Spanish Texas Assessment of Academic Skills. Third graders in BCIRC classrooms outperformed comparison students in reading but not in language. If the third graders had been in BCIRC for two years, they outperformed comparison students on both measures. Third graders in BCIRC classrooms met the criteria for exit from bilingual classes at much higher rates than did students in comparison classes.

Special Needs and Cooperative Learning

Do students with special needs benefit from cooperative learning? Cooperative learning was shown to have significant positive effects in only 50% of the studies reviewed by Tateyama-Sniezek (1990). Techniques that included rewards and methods for making sure that each

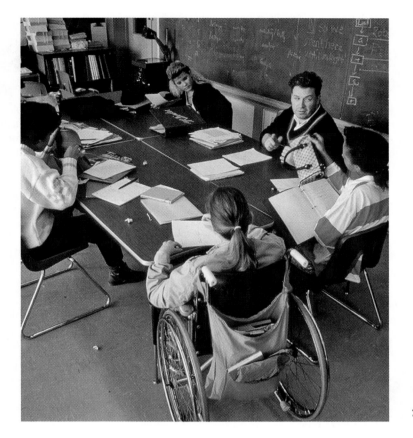

Students with special needs can benefit from working with other students in cooperative groups. (Bob Daemmrich/ The Image Works)

child was responsible for his or her performance had the strongest effects (Stevens & Slavin, 1991). Jenkins and O'Connor (2003) cautioned against drawing firm conclusions from these findings. They point out that more and longer studies are required. In addition, they note that research done to date has not paid enough attention to whether students retain information and/or transfer the skills they acquire to new tasks.

There are, however, some notable successes in using cooperative learning when students with special needs participate in general education classrooms. Stevens and colleagues examined the effectiveness of CIRC with third and fourth graders. They evaluated the effect of the technique over a 12-week and a 24-week period, and found that academically handicapped students achieved more when they were mainstreamed into CIRC classes and received support from a special education teacher who collaborated with the general education teacher (Stevens et al., 1987). In a follow-up study conducted over a two-year period, Stevens and Slavin (1995) showed that students in CIRC classrooms showed higher achievement in vocabulary, comprehension, and language expression than did students in the matched schools. Academically handicapped students in CIRC classrooms showed significantly higher achievement in reading vocabulary, reading comprehension, and language expression than did the students in the pull-out programs.

Some students with learning disabilities prefer not to work in groups (Elbaum, Moody, & Schumm, 1999). In mixed-ability reading groups, the difficulties created by learning disabilities are more visible to classmates. Depending on how the group is structured, the attentional demands of working with a number of others may be too great for these students. Students with learning disabilities may lack the social skills to participate well in a cooperative task (Holder & Fitzpatrick, 1991; Pearl, 1992). However, cooperative learning or other peer learning experiences can improve the classroom social standing of students with learning disabilities (Slavin, 1995). Teachers who wish to use cooperative learning as an instructional strategy need to plan the composition of the groups carefully, design tasks that can be done by students with special needs, and monitor the work of the group closely (see the "Taking It to the Classroom" box on the next page).

How Can I Use This?

What kind of peer learning situation would you use with learning-disabled children? Can you explain your reasoning?

Taking It to the Classroom

Do you Know Jack? Getting the Help He Needs

Jack needs help. Jack, who has a math learning disability, is in middle school. He goes to the resource room to get help with math, but he also participates in general education math classes taught by Mr. Kumar. Jack knows that he has trouble with math, and he feels intimidated when the teacher assigns the class to work in groups. He is afraid that the other students will make fun of him when he cannot do the problems. He does not ask for help because he does not want the others to know how much he is struggling. What can Mr. Kumar do to help Jack?

Mr. Kumar will need to intervene with the whole class to help Jack. Here are some things he can do:

1. Talk to the class about the importance of helping one another.
2. Teach the class communication skills (e.g., paying attention, not talking too loud, and asking one another whether they understand the material).
3. Teach students how to ask for help:
   - Choose someone to help you.
   - Ask for assistance and feedback (e.g., What should I do next? How does this look?).
4. Reward students for helping others (e.g., computer time, choosing library books).
5. Assign Jack to work with other students who are patient and kind.
6. Ask Jack to record on a simple chart the number of times he asks for help.

Status Characteristics

status characteristics
Characteristics of individuals that may signal that they have high or low status.

Some students have high status in the classroom, and their peers defer to them, seek their help, and follow their example. Students with low status seek help and are often ignored, and their contributions may not be valued by their peers. Researchers have studied the cognitive consequences of these kinds of status differences (Cohen, 1982; Cohen & Lotan, 1995, 1997; Cohen, Lotan, & Catanzarite, 1990). When working in groups, higher status students may have more opportunities to engage in the kinds of cognitive activities that promote elaborative processing and higher achievement (Cohen, 1982). Low-status students may not have many such opportunities.

stereotype threat   Concern about being viewed from the vantage point of a negative stereotype or acting to confirm such a stereotype.

Another problem may be posed by **stereotype threat**: "the threat of being viewed through the lens of a negative stereotype or the fear of doing something that would inadvertently confirm that stereotype" (Steele, 1999, p. 46). Minority and female students may perform less well than they are able to perform because of concerns that they might reinforce negative stereotypes about their racial group or gender (Inzlicht & Ben-Zeev, 2003).

Some students can feel left out of group activities or be deliberately excluded by their peers. Teachers need to be on the alert for such problems.

(Ellen B. Senisi/The Image Works)

Who has status in a group? It depends on the culture of the classroom or school. Students who are known to be successful in school often have high status in classrooms where achievement is valued. Other characteristics of students, including athletic ability, popularity, and gender, may also be associated with high status.

Figure 12.7 illustrates some of the ways in which status characteristics operate. In the vignette, the children are discussing the question, Why do people move? Group members are trying to come up with a song in response to the question. Victor disagrees with their interpretation, but he does so quietly. Not until the teacher intervenes and points out the value of his contribution do other students pay attention to his ideas.

Limiting Status Effects in the Classroom Status differences affect interaction, rates of participation, and the kinds of cognitive activities in which students engage (e.g., providing explanations, asking questions). Peer learning techniques that maximize participation by all students can limit the impact of status characteristics. A technique such as *Scripted Cooperation* reduce inequalities in participation because all students must take turns engaging in specified cognitive activities. A cooperative learning technique that involves interdependence among group members can also reduce the effects of status differences. Petersen and colleagues (1991) found that boys gained status over girls in an individualistic learning condition but that in a cooperative condition, there were no perceived differences between boys and girls on measures of achievement, verbal participation in the group, leadership, or status.

In *Complex Instruction*, the teacher chooses a complex task that cannot be completed by a single student alone and to which *all* students can contribute. The teacher begins by discussing what abilities are needed to carry out a task. For example, the class may be asked to design a zoo. The abilities needed include being able to measure, write instructions, and research the housing and food requirements for animals in the zoo; the artistic ability required for creating the actual model; and many other specific abilities. Students come to recognize that no single individual could complete the entire task alone and that each student has something to contribute while also recognizing that some students have many skills. The focus on the specific abilities needed to accomplish the task at hand allows for the inclusion of many children, whereas a narrow focus on traditional academic skills may exclude some children from actively participating. In addition, the focus on what students can contribute to a task encourages them to be task-oriented and to stress abilities rather than deficiencies.

Chapter Reference
See Chapter 4 for a discussion of the theory of multiple intelligences.

"Let's use a tune we all know," suggests Veronica.

"Okay, but what will the song be about?" asks Hector. The group members fall silent for a moment. Carolina, recorder for the day, takes out a piece of paper and a pencil.

"Why don't we use some of the ideas from the song we heard?" Carolina suggests. "How about if we make it about Jose, who wants to come to Hollywood to be a movie star?" Veronica and Hector nod their heads in agreement.

Victor, the fourth member of the group, shrugs his shoulder, looks away, and as usual, mumbles something quietly. "I'm sure this guy didn't have too much fun. Sounds to me like he worked really hard. He fixed the rails and picked tomatoes and mixed cement. For only 50 cents an hour! I'd be tired and disappointed."

Carolina begins to write what she has decided will be the first line of their song. Ms. Garcia, who has been watching the group from a discreet distance, interjects:

"Victor, you listened to the song carefully and you clearly understood the deep message of the lyrics. This is important information for your group. What do you think your group's song should be about?"

"I'm not sure," Victor answers hesitantly. "I just know that my family didn't come here because they wanted to be movie stars. They came because there were no jobs in Mexico. My father says he wanted to work so we could have a better life."

"Maybe we can put those ideas in our song." Veronica is ready to compromise. As they offer examples of how they might do this, Ms. Garcia moves away, now reassured that Victor's contribution will be heard by his group.

Figure 12.7. Status Characteristics

assigning competence The
teacher acknowledges the
contribution of a student to
the completion of a task.

In Figure 12.7, you saw the teacher, Ms. Garcia, intervene in Victor's group to point out how his contribution was valuable to the group. By **assigning competence** to Victor in this context, Ms. Garcia helped the group members accomplish their task and not allow status differences to interfere with the quality of their work.

Learning from Peers: Classroom Practices

The various theoretical perspectives described earlier in the chapter provide frameworks for making decisions when using cooperative or collaborative pairs or groups in the classroom. Three key dimensions of classroom practice are (a) the quality of students' discourse, (b) the role of the teacher in the collaborative classroom, and (c) the tasks selected.

The Importance of Discourse Quality

Appendix
Appreciating Heterogeneous Students

Students who vary in gender, race, ethnicity, and ability or who experience special needs contribute to heterogeneity in the classroom. These differences can enhance learning and you will need to be aware of the influence of these differences on students' learning from particular instructional strategies. (*PRAXIS*™ I B. 2; III. B, *INTASC* Principles 2, 3, 6)

The mere fact that children are assigned to groups does not mean that they will hold meaningful discussions. The kinds of tasks on which they work will influence their talk. Children tend to engage in less abstract talk on mathematics/technology tasks than on language-based tasks (Holden, 1993).

If one adopts a Vygotskyian view of peer learning, intellectual skills must be modeled before a child can internalize them. If the child's reasoning, explanation, or questioning is of very low quality, he or she may gain little practice in higher level thinking in the context of the group. Most students need support in generating the quality of discourse that is associated with learning. Teachers can promote high levels of cognitive activity by asking questions that vary in complexity (King, 1991; King et al., 1998). As can be seen in Table 12.5, asking increasingly complex questions results in higher-quality discourse.

The Role of the Teacher

Teachers' roles are key components of effective peer learning. These roles can be very complex. Different peer learning activities require different stances with respect to students, tasks, and outcomes. Teachers must take into account both the social context in which learning occurs and the cognitive processes that are either supported or hindered in that context. They need to analyze their classrooms to determine whether there may be obstacles that limit the cognitive opportunities available to students or prevent them from making use of those opportunities. Teachers can adopt many roles in relation to the use of peer learning. Table 12.5 presents a summary of these roles. In this section, we look briefly at each of them.

Preparer of Learning Activities A critical role that teachers adopt is that of being a preparer of learning activities. The importance of planning was described in Chapter 9. Teachers identify their instructional goals and select learning tasks for their students that will allow them to accomplish these goals. Teachers need to analyze the complexity of the demands that any particular learning task will place on students' cognitive, emotional, and social resources. For example, if the task is too difficult, students may become easily frustrated and impatient with one another. Alternatively, if the task is too simple, students may become easily bored. As a preparer of learning activities, teachers will provide supports to students (e.g., roles, worksheets, questions, expert sheets) that will assist them as they engage in the task.

Community Builder Most American classrooms are increasingly heterogeneous. The teacher may need to promote the experience of community actively in the classroom and the school so all students feel that they are valued and that the teacher supports their efforts. If they do not feel valued and supported, students may become alienated and have low expectations. As community builder, the teacher develops a context in which students show mutual respect, are willing to help one another, and recognize others' need for help. In adopting this role, the teacher may look to sociocultural theory, Vygotskyian theory, or social-cohesion theory to understand the contribution that community can make to effective learning. Cohen's strategy of assigning competence to students is one way of recognizing the contributions of children with different skills.

Chapter Reference
See Chapter 10 for a discussion of the role of community in learning.

Task Developer Teachers in American classrooms must be aware of state and national standards for educational performance. They need to examine the curricular goals for the classes they teach and design tasks that are appropriate to those goals and might be facilitated by the use of some form of peer learning. They need to understand the students' current level of performance, the desired level of performance, and the kinds of tasks that will promote

TABLE 12.5

Roles for Teachers During Cooperative Work

Teacher role	Teacher activity	Theoretical perspective or technique
Preparer of learning activities	• The teacher selects the learning activity task, including its level of complexity and whether it should offer open-ended problems. • Teacher assigns students their roles and offers role training if needed.	• All approaches
Community builder	• Helps students develop social skills necessary to work together • Emphasizes common purposes • Helps heterogeneous group become a community • Promotes mutual respect • Promotes willingness to help one another • Recognizes others' need for help	• Social-cohesion • Social-cohesion and Social-motivational
Task developer	• Designs group-worthy tasks	• Complex instruction • Group investigation
Model	• Models the use of cognitive and metacognitive strategies • Demonstrates how to engage in constructive social skills, such as encouraging others, taking turns, and elaborating on an idea	• Vygotskyian theory • Reciprocal teaching • Cognitive elaboration
Coordinator of activities	• Assigns students to groups • Manages the classroom; creates a context in which work can be accomplished • Moves between groups and monitors social and cognitive activities	• All approaches

Evaluator	• Provides criteria for evaluation of students' work
	• Leads students in evaluating their own work and group processes
	• Includes measures of individual accountability
	• Give students feedback on:
	  • Use of on-task behavior
	  • Products produced by group
	  • Contributions of individual members
		• Vygotskyian
		
		• Piagetian
		• Cognitive elaboration
		• Social-motivational

the transition from current to desired performance levels. They must understand the use of practice, feedback, examples, alternative representations, and many other features of instruction in order to develop tasks that can be carried out effectively by peers. The focus cannot be simply on *group performance* of a task but on each student's improvement in the skills required by the task.

The Teacher as Model Another role of teachers is that of model. Techniques such as reciprocal peer tutoring emphasize the role of the teacher as the initial model for complex cognitive activity. A skilled teacher is able to make her or his thinking visible, allowing students to practice increasingly complex skills and eventually decreasing the amount of support they need.

Coordinator of Activities Many teachers rely mainly on whole-class instruction, not because they necessarily believe in its efficacy but because they are concerned about managing the learning activities of multiple groups, limiting negative social processes, and "covering the curriculum." (See the "Taking It to the Classroom" box on the next page.)

Taking It to the Classroom

Management Issues to Consider

Here are some guidelines for managing multiple groups:

Getting Students into Groups

Do not have all the students moving at once. Make sure all students know who is in their group and where their group will meet. One strategy is to create four-person groups by handing out four #1 cards, four #2 cards, and so forth. Then call all the #1's together.

Distributing Materials

Designate one person in each group to be the materials person. Each *materials* person can collect and distribute worksheets or other materials to the members of the group. This strategy reduces the number of students moving around the classroom at any one time.

Too Much Noise?

Before asking students to move into groups, decide on a way to reduce the level of noise while they work in groups. Some teachers use *12-inch voices*—one that can be heard only 12 inches away. Others use a card with a large red circle that they can hand to a group if it is too loud.

Getting the Children's Attention Back

Before you assign students to groups, describe the signal you will use when you want them to be quiet and look to you for the next instruction. You might, for example, raise your hand as a signal to be quiet. The students who notice your hand in the air might also be expected to raise their hands so that students around them will notice and quiet down.

What If the Groups Finish Their Work at Different Times?

First make sure that the students who claim to have finished have actually done so. They may have rushed through parts of a task and not understood the material. Have additional questions available that can be used to extend the work.

Evaluator The teacher can choose to evaluate many aspects of a peer learning situation, including students' use of social skills, their on-task behavior, the products they produce, and individual contributions to the group product or other individual products that might be required. The feedback that teachers provide can enhance students' expectations of success or promote explanations of success or failure that are conducive to improved effort and performance. A teacher can also provide feedback that discourages a student and results in negative explanations of poor performance. A summary of how a teacher might play the roles just described appears in Table 12.4.

When more than one person is engaged in a learning task, social processes are involved. In using cooperative groups or other forms of peer learning, the teacher also needs to provide feedback on students' interactions. Cohen and colleagues have shown that when students are given criteria for an acceptable group product and use them to evaluate their work, their interactions improve, and their learning increases (Cohen et al., 2002).

Chapter Reference
Chapter 14 includes extensive information on classroom assessment.

Classroom Tasks

Teachers need to set goals for any task they assign. They may select tasks with the goal of motivating or engaging students, providing a context for social interaction with a student who is having particular difficulties, getting students to learn factual material, or getting them to engage in higher order reasoning and thinking skills. Depending on the goals of the task, the kind of peer learning employed will vary.

Not all tasks require the same level of effort, generate the same level of interest, or require the same cognitive processes. Tasks can be classified along a number of dimensions. The first dimension is complexity. Tasks can be simple and involve simple cognitive strategies, such as rehearsal. Memorizing the names of the capitals of states requires rehearsal. *Basic knowledge acquisition tasks* are those in which content is encoded into the student's memory for later recall. Strategies for helping students master such tasks include teaching them memorization and rehearsal strategies, such as the use of mnemonics, summarization, and elaboration strategies. Techniques such as STAD or Scripted Cooperation can be very useful in helping students perform these tasks effectively.

Other tasks require more complex cognitive skills. Such tasks require students to pose their own questions, explore alternatives, gather information, generate evidence or arguments in support of ideas, and draw conclusions. The techniques that support basic knowledge acquisition and rehearsal are not sufficient to promote these kinds of higher order thinking. Tasks that are more open-ended or require more collaborative knowledge construction call for cooperative techniques that are less structured in order to permit the kinds of interactions that will result in the desired outcomes.

Consider an example: Students in a high school science class could be asked to conduct a chemistry experiment by following the directions in a lab notebook. This task is much simpler and requires lower level cognitive skills than one in which students are asked to design an experiment to determine whether the water from the local lake is safe to drink.

Cohen (1994) distinguishes between individual and group tasks. According to Cohen, a group task is one "that requires resources (information, knowledge, heuristic problem-solving strategies, materials, and skills) that no single individual possesses so that no single individual is likely to solve the problems or accomplish the task objectives without at least some input from others" (p. 8). Such tasks are open-ended and require **problem solving**; students can approach them from a number of vantage points and have multiple opportunities to demonstrate their intellectual competence. These tasks are concerned with important content, require positive interdependence among group members and individual accountability of all members, and include clear criteria for how the group's product will be evaluated (Lotan, 2003). *Group-worthy tasks* (Lotan, 2003) require a great deal of time and expertise on the part of the teacher.

problem solving An activity in which a person uses knowledge to reach a specific goal but in which there is no clearly specified way of reaching the goal.

There are some risks associated with open-ended tasks. Students may be drawn into negative social interactions; some may be easily frustrated if the task is ambiguous; and some will not participate fully. Various strategies, such as the social skills training advocated by the Johnsons, the status interventions proposed by Cohen, and close monitoring of groups, can limit these negative outcomes.

It is important to note that not all students will be ready to assume complex roles and strategies. Students who have not worked in cooperative groups will need training and gradual experience in taking more responsibility for their learning. Likewise, students who have not valued educational achievement in the past will not suddenly become passionate about learning without a major effort to change their values regarding achievement. Techniques such as STAD can be effective in reshaping classroom values so that group success is important. (See the "Uncommon Sense" box below.)

Uncommon Sense

Out-of-School Group Projects Are Always Cooperative—Or Are They?

Classroom time is limited, and it can be difficult to allocate the amount of time needed to carry out a complex group project. Mr. Johnson has worked very hard with his eighth-grade English class to create a climate of mutual respect. He holds a Piagetian view of the contribution of peer learning; that is, he believes that peer interaction is more likely to promote learning if students are equal in status and power. He has assigned students to five-person groups to prepare a computer-based presentation based on Shakespeare's *King Lear*. Each group has to prepare a presentation about Lear's disowning of Cordelia. Members of the group need to meet outside of school hours to discuss their strategy for doing the task, make work assignments, and complete the work.

The students are very busy after school with extracurricular activities and have difficulty arranging a time when they can get together. They need to find somewhere to work, but many of their parents are also very busy, and it is difficult to find a place to work, then arrange for someone to drive everyone to the agreed-upon location. Although the group's members work well together in class and have very trusting relationships, their parents are now involved in this project (and not happy about it). The task is no longer a cooperative one as intended because adults are involved and are putting pressure on their children to get the work done quickly. Mr. Johnson's intention to have students engage in a task that requires deep thought has backfired. By assigning the task to the students to do at home, he introduced elements (parents, transportation, scheduling difficulties) that changed the nature of their collaboration.

R I D E

REFLECTION FOR ACTION

The Event

A group of 4 third graders have been given a bag of money and asked to find out the total amount of money in the bag. Maria, Carla, Andy, and Wilson are talking to one another. Part of their discussion was presented at the beginning of the chapter. Is the group effective? How would you know?

Reflection R I D E

The group is not acting like a group. The two girls, Maria and Carla, are talking to each other and trying to do the task that the teacher assigned. The two boys, Wilson and Andy, are not doing the task and are talking about a girl. They do not interact with the two girls in their group. What is this an example of? It could be an example of poor classroom management, because two of the children are not paying any attention to the task. It could be an example of ineffective instruction, because the teacher did not assign a task that engages the students. It could also be an example of the operation of status characteristics, because the girls do not interact with the boys. It is an example of a dysfunctional group, because the two pairs of students do not interact, and one pair is behaving inappropriately. The students who are working on the task make no effort to engage the other students.

What Theoretical/Conceptual Information Might Assist in Interpreting and Remedying This Situation? Consider the following.

Group Structures

Slavin and the Johnsons describe many of the features of effective group structures. The participants' goals should be interdependent, and each student must be individually accountable for the group's achievement. Perhaps the teacher did not help the students develop a sense of interdependence.

Task Structures

Steiner (1972) describes several types of tasks on which groups work. Some of these tasks are completed by simply having a competent individual solve the problem. Some require coordination of the efforts of several members of a group. Cohen (1994) describes the kinds of cognitive processes that can be promoted using structured and unstructured tasks. The task of finding out how much money is in the bag is a procedural one that is not easily divided among group members.

Classroom Management

The teacher is not attending to the group's interaction and has not noticed the off-task behavior of two of its members. The teacher should draw on theories of reward and scaffolding to correct the problem.

Information Gathering R I D E

How would you decide which of the three possibilities listed above is the correct one? What else would you like to know? The group is not effective in that its four members are not working together. Two members are working on the assigned task, and the other two are off task. It is almost as though there were two parallel conversations going on. You might like to know whether the two off-task children are typically off task. You need to be careful if you determine that the two boys are typically off task. You might attribute the problem to characteristics of the students and not to the nature of the task. It is possible that the teacher always assigns boring tasks that the boys are unlikely to pay attention to, or the tasks might be very easy and not require much effort on the part of the boys, leaving them plenty of time to get into trouble. You might also like to know whether this short segment of conversation is representative of the group's work or just a brief moment of distraction. Depending on the answers to these questions, you might make a different decision about how to solve the problem. If you were the teacher, you might ask the students' previous teacher about their typical behaviors. Do not rely solely on that teacher's comments, because they may color your expectations about these students. You might consult the research literature and find out what it says about task structures that promote more effective engagement. You might also look at the literature on motivation to find out what it says about how to get students engaged in a task.

Decision Making RIDE

What is the best interpretation, given the available information? Without more information, you would conclude that the group is not working well. There are problems with the group's structure. The principles of cooperative learning suggest that heterogeneous groups can work effectively, but group members need to experience interdependence, and each member of the group needs to be individually accountable. The two on-task students in this group make no effort to engage the other students and do not try to redirect them, as might be expected if the students believed that their goals were intertwined. There may also be problems with the task structure. The task does not seem to require contributions by all the group's members, and it therefore facilitates cognitive and social loafing on the part of some of the students. To the extent that the two boys are off task, there is a problem in classroom management, but this problem arises as a consequence of failing to structure the group properly and use a group-worthy task (Lotan, 2003) that would motivate all the members of the group.

Evaluation RIDE

Based on the available information, if you were the classroom teacher, you might decide to assign the students a new task that requires each participant to be involved. You should assign each student a role within the group and require that they all sign a contract that commits them to performing their assigned role. By doing this, you will help them understand the goals of the task and help them become more committed to completing the work. The two students who were on task might encourage the others to perform their assigned roles. You might also find a more interesting task that requires the students to consider alternative solutions to a problem, and you could create a system of individual accountability that would require each student to be responsible for learning.

If you tried a new task or new procedures, would the group function better? You should monitor the group closely to determine whether the students participate more equally. At the end of the period, you might ask the students to assess how well they played their roles and how attentive to the task they were. If you find that the problem of unequal participation remains unsolved, you should engage in a new cycle of reflection, information gathering, decision making, and evaluation.

Further Practice: Your Turn

Here is a second event for you to consider. In doing so, carry out the processes of reflection, information gathering, decision making, and evaluation.

The Event

You have finally decided to have your sixth-grade students work in groups. You have 26 students in your class, 16 boys and 10 girls. Four of them have special needs. The project on which the children will work will take about two weeks. Tommy is often absent because of illness.

RIDE **How many groups will you form? What will the composition of the groups be?**

SUMMARY

- **How do various theoretical perspectives describe the means by which students can learn from peers?**

  Much of the work on cooperative learning is based on a social-motivational perspective and relies on group goals, rewards, and individual accountability to ensure success. Social-cohesion perspectives also rely on positive interdependence among group members for successful peer learning. Interdependence in this case is created by developing social skills and encouraging care and concern for others. Alternative explanations for the efficacy of peer learning can be found in cognitive-developmental and cognitive-elaboration perspectives. The various perspectives on peer learning suggest different mechanisms through which peers may promote learning. The implications for the decisions teachers make vary accordingly. Key decisions involve those related to the size and composition of groups, the tasks on which they work, whether rewards or recognition are provided, and whether there is individual accountability.

- **How effective is tutoring? What processes are involved?**

  Students have the greatest chance to participate when working with a single other student. In larger groups, there are fewer opportunities for each student to participate. It is also easier for teachers to organize pairs of students and maintain control of the classroom environment. This is particularly important if the teacher lacks experience in conducting groups or the students lack experience in working together. There are a variety of strategies for getting students to work effectively in pairs. Many of them involve various forms of tutoring; they include classwide peer tutoring, reciprocal peer tutoring, peer-assisted learning, scripted cooperation, and others. Tutoring is generally effective. Students can be trained in how to prompt their partners' understanding by providing cues or hints and in ways to reduce the tutors' dominance of the dialogue between tutor and tutee.

- **What do teachers need to consider when having students work in larger groups?**

  When students are assigned to larger groups, the composition of the groups must be carefully considered. Techniques for use with larger groups include Jigsaw and Jigsaw II, group investigations, and structured academic controversies. Characteristics such as race, gender, ethnicity, and language of origin can have an effect on group interactions. The research evidence on the effects of gender on interaction is mixed. However, these variables should be considered when forming groups, and group interaction should be closely monitored. Status characteristics may operate in a larger group, with high-status students having more opportunities to participate and to do so in ways that promote learning. Low-status students have limited opportunities. Strategies for minimizing the effects of status characteristics include selecting peer learning techniques that enable all students to participate.

- **What kinds of tasks are suitable for groups of students?**

  Peer learning can be used with a range of tasks. Tasks vary in the complexity of the cognitive processes required, ranging from simple rehearsal strategies to complex higher order reasoning, metacognition, and problem solving. Unstructured tasks permit more creativity but may also lead to negative social processes. Students typically need a great deal of support to engage in higher level thinking. Such support can be provided through the use of questions written and prepared in advance. Teachers can provide students with question stems to help guide their discussions.

- **What is the role of the teacher when using a peer learning strategy?**

  The teacher must play a very active role when using peer learning techniques in the classroom. The teacher's role includes many tasks: preparer of learning activities, building community, designing tasks that are group worthy, providing a model of cognitive activity, coordinating activities, and evaluating groups' products and processes.

- **Do diverse learners benefit from peer learning?**

  Race, ethnicity, and gender may function as diffuse status characteristics and affect the interactions that occur within a group. Teachers need to monitor rates of participation by diverse students for evidence of effects of status characteristics and intervene to increase participation by lower status students. Racial and ethnic minorities are thought to benefit from the use of cooperative learning methods, and intergroup relations are thought to improve as a result. However, few conclusions can be drawn about any benefits that might accrue to diverse learners that do not accrue to other participants in cooperative or other peer learning techniques.

- **Can peer learning be used effectively with students who have special needs?**
  The research evidence on the academic benefits of cooperative learning for students with special needs is mixed. There is stronger evidence that such students benefit both from being tutored and from serving as tutors.

KEY TERMS

accommodation, p. 398
assigning competence, p. 418
assimilation, p. 398
classroom management, p. 401
cognitive conflict, p. 398
cognitive disequilibrium, p. 398
conceptual change teaching, p. 398
constructivist perspective, p. 397
dialectical constructivism, p. 399
diffuse status characteristics, p. 397
goal structure, p. 389
individual accountability, p. 391
interdependence, p. 389
meta-analysis, p. 395

metacognition, p. 394
negative interdependence, p. 389
participation structures, p. 409
positive interdependence, p. 389
positive practice, p. 405
problem solving, p. 421
scaffolding, p. 399
schema, p. 395
Scripted Cooperation, p. 396
status characteristics, p. 416
status differences, p. 396
stereotype threat, p. 416
tutoring, p. 401
zone of proximal development, p. 399

EXERCISES

1. *Why Do You Like Working with Peers?*

   Find a number of students of different ages and ask them why they like working with their peers in a classroom setting. Make notes of their responses and try to categorize the reasons they give. Are the reasons related more to social and emotional processes than to cognitive processes?

2. *Why Do You Dislike Working with Peers?*

   Find a number of students of different ages and ask them why they dislike working with their peers in a classroom setting. Make notes of their responses and try to categorize the reasons they give. Are the reasons related more to social and emotional processes than to cognitive processes?

3. *Difficulties with Group Processes*

   Observe students in an elementary school classroom and a high school classroom in which group work or cooperative learning is being conducted. What difficulties do you see in the group process? Are the students on task? Do they seem to understand what is being asked of them? Do you think they experience positive interdependence?

4. *Classroom Management of Group Work*

   Observe students in an elementary school classroom and a high school classroom in which group work or cooperative learning is being conducted. What aspects of the groups' behavior indicate whether the teacher is an effective classroom manager? What problems do you see? How could they be solved?

5. *Tutoring*

   Pair up with someone in your class and tutor your partner on content from this course. Make notes of the strategies you use to gauge your partner's understanding. What kinds of questions do you ask? What do you learn about your partner's understanding of the material from the answers provided? How do you adjust your strategies?

M r. Antoine, Ms. Baldwin, and Mrs. Chambers have all just finished teaching *The Scarlet Letter* in their ninth-grade English classes. Their classes are filing into their rooms to take the assessments that their teachers have developed. This is what they see:

The Great *Scarlet Letter* Debate

Resolved: "Hester Prynne s treatment by the townspeople was basically fair given the social norms and values of rural Massachusetts at that time."

Pick a partner to work with on this project. Come up to the Great Debate Box and draw a lot that will tell whether you are going to argue to the pros or the cons of this debate, whom you are going to debate against, and when you will be scheduled to debate. Together, develop the arguments that support the position that you have been assigned. You may use the novel and your class notes from our discussion to develop your arguments. You will be graded on the logic of your argument, your ability to support your points from the novel and the writings we have read about the novel, and your speaking ability. You and your partner will receive the same grade for this work.

Chambliss Four-Star Productions Casting Meeting for *The Scarlet Letter*

Congratulations, you have been named Casting Director for Chambliss Four-Star Productions filming of *The Scarlet Letter*. Your task over the next hour is to pick Hollywood stars to portray each of the following characters from *The Scarlet Letter*:

Rev. Arthur Dimmesdale
Hester Prynne
Roger Chillingworth
Pearl

For each character, pick a Hollywood star and write a brief essay explaining why you think the star would be the best person to play the role. In your essay, tell us what you know about the character and the star that makes the star the right person for the role. You may want to discuss other stars that you considered and decided against, and why.

Examination
4th Period English
The Scarlet Letter

Instructions: You will have the entire period to complete this. There are 30 multiple-choice questions, two short essays, and one long esssay. Each multiple-choice question is worth 2 points; the short essays are worth 10 points each, and the long essay is worth 20 points. If you have any questions, please come to my desk to ask them. Please make all your work be your own. Good luck.

1. Who is the protagonist in the novel?
    a. Arthur Dimmesdale
    b. Hester Prynne
    c. Nathaniel Hawthorne
    d. Pearl
    e. The Salem Witch Trials

Classroom Assessment

RIDE Reflection for Action

Each of these assessments might be criticized for one reason or another. What strengths and weaknesses do you find in each of them? After you read the chapter, return to these assessments and answer the questions again. Have your answers changed?

Guiding Questions

- What is the role of assessment in the instructional process?
- How can teachers devise assessments that facilitate instruction and at the same time provide information about students' progress?
- Of the many options teachers have for assessment, which are the best?
- How can a teacher develop a grading system that is fair and that lets students take responsibility for their own learning?
- How can assessment help students learn about their own strengths and weaknesses?
- How can teachers continually improve assessment and grading practices?
- How can teachers create and modify assessments to include learners who face special challenges?
- How do cultural differences among students and their parents affect the process of communicating progress?

CHAPTER OVERVIEW

Classroom assessments are an important form of communication. They inform teachers about student progress. They help students understand what the teacher values in the class and what she thinks of their progress and abilities. When used well, they also give the teacher insight about the efficacy of her teaching and help students develop the skills to assess their own abilities. Carefully considered and well-constructed assessments promote the notion that classroom assessment is not just assessment *of* learning; it is assessment *for* learning. This chapter examines the critical issues of classroom assessment: It looks at reasons for assessment, assessment options, evaluation of results, and the relationship between assessment and instruction. The chapter concludes with a discussion of communicating with parents. In Chapter 14, we will focus on standardized and standards-based assessment; here we will concentrate on assessment used in the classroom.

Assessment for Instruction: Roles, Goals, and Audiences
- Student, Parent, and Teacher Concerns in Assessment
- Other Audiences and Areas of Concern
- Diversity Among Students and Their Parents
- Formative and Summative Assessment

Principles of Assessment and Grading
- Communication
- Fairness
- Growth

Options for Assessment
- Recognition Format
- Generative Format
- Alternative Formats

Developing and Using Assessments
- Determining What to Assess
- Rubrics
- Determining the Best Assessment Format
- Assessing Students with Special Needs
- Administering, Scoring, and Communicating Assessment Results

Interpreting Classroom Assessments
- Comparing Performance with Expectations
- Reflecting on Assessments to Improve Them

Developing a Grading System
- Options for Grading Systems
- Record Keeping for Grading

Communicating with Parents
- Parent/Teacher Conferences
- Maintaining Communication

Assessment for Instruction: Roles, Goals, and Audiences

In everyday life, assessment involves taking stock of the current situation and determining the best course of action for the future. A painter makes a brush stroke or two, then assesses their effect on the overall composition. A lawyer pursues a negotiation for a client, then stops to consider whether the counteroffer is sufficient. A family gathers to weigh the pros and cons of moving to a larger home in a neighboring town.

In education, **assessment** is the process of coming to understand what a student knows and can do. Not only does the teacher gain this information, but in strong assessment programs, the student does as well. Assessing students in classrooms is one of the most important activities that teachers undertake. Assessment reflects the nature of the unique learning community established in each classroom and provides the tangible outcomes of the productivity of that community.

assessment   The process of coming to understand what students know and can do.

Chapter Reference
Chapters 10 and 11 discuss classrooms as communities for learning.

Teachers want students to take pride in their work, to feel a strong sense of responsibility for it, to enjoy the efforts they put into it, and to learn about themselves as a result. When assessments provide the opportunity for students to rise to a challenge, cognitive and emotional growth results. Because of its potential to enhance or detract from instruction, assessment must be carefully considered, planned, and executed. It should address the needs of students, parents, other educators, and the teacher in a fashion that is caring, respectful, and professional. Developing an assessment program takes hard work, considerable thought, openness to new ideas, and the courage to reflect on and be critical of one's own ideas and actions.

Chapter Reference
Chapter 9 includes an extensive presentation of material concerning goals and objectives.

Student, Parent, and Teacher Concerns in Assessment

The fundamental role of assessment in classrooms is to provide feedback to students, their parents, the teacher, other educators, and the larger community. The three primary audiences are students, parents (or guardians), and teachers. Members of each group are likely to have different concerns about assessment.

Student Concerns in Assessment. Questions or concerns that students might have as they approach an assessment include the following.

- Is the test/quiz/activity going to be fun?
- Am I going to do well on it?
- How am I going to do in comparison to other students?
- How will it be graded?
- How will it affect my grade?
- How will it affect what the teacher thinks of me?
- How much work is it going to be?
- If I work hard on it, will I succeed?
- Will being successful be worth the effort?

Of course, students at different levels have different concerns. Young children seek their teacher's approval. A smile, a "good job," a sticker, a star, or a pat on the back can mean everything in the world to a young child. As children grow older, they still desire approval, but they also begin to develop concerns about grades. This development is not always simple, however. As discussed in Chapter 6, some students or even a whole class might wish to avoid publicly demonstrating a strong performance. In other cases, the desire for good grades becomes the primary motivation for students to achieve, crowding out any intrinsic love for learning.

Chapter Reference
Chapter 6 discusses issues of motivation related to achievement and rewards.

Whether an assessment is a cause for anxiety and frustration or an opportunity to show what you know depends on how the assessment setting is constructed by the teacher.
(Mary Kate Denny/Photo Edit)

Parent Concerns in Assessment. Some of the major questions and concerns that parents and caregivers bring to assessments are:

- How is my child doing?
- What can I do to help?
- What are my child's strengths and weaknesses?
- How is my child getting along socially?
- How is my child doing compared to the other children (in the class, in the school, in the nation)?
- Is my child working up to his/her potential?

Teacher Concerns in Assessment. When considering assessment, teachers have to evaluate the progress of individual children as well as the class as a whole. They need to decide whether to move on to the next topic or to spend more time reviewing the current one. They are concerned with how to assess a child with special needs who has an individualized education program (IEP) that requires different assessment procedures from those of the rest of the children in the class. In addition to knowing how well children are doing on a specific task, teachers need to know whether they are developing broad skills that are transferable to a wide variety of tasks. Furthermore, teachers need to help children develop the ability to assess their own strengths and weaknesses. Some questions and concerns that teachers have about assessment are:

- Which assessment option would work best in this situation?
- When should assessment take place—before, during, or after instruction?
- How can this assessment promote students' ability to evaluate their own progress?
- How well does it match the statewide standards or assessments?
- How will I communicate the results to students and parents?
- How much work will it take to construct or select the assessment and to grade it?
- How is this assessment related to others in the class?
- How can students learn that they need to work more in this area without making them feel like failures?
- What if the results are really poor?
- How can this information improve instruction?
- Should this assessment count as part of the students' grades?

Other Audiences and Areas of Concern

Teachers also have to consider their responsibility to other audiences that receive and use assessment information. For example, colleges use high school transcripts to make admissions decisions. What should they expect from a course grade? What should employers expect? Should schools use eighth-grade report cards to determine whom to place in regular or in honors English classes in ninth grade?

There is substantial change and uncertainty in assessment today, not just for classroom assessment, but for annual **standardized assessment** on state-mandated tests as well (Cizek, 2001). State and federal concerns for educational achievement and the funding tied to that achievement have become matters of increasing concern for local school districts. The No Child Left Behind federal legislation mandates not only standardized assessment, but also regular progress of all groups of children on those assessments. State legislators, as representatives of the citizens who pay for schools, have a legitimate interest in how well students are doing (Phelps, 1998). Concerns from outside the school influence classroom decisions on curriculum, time spent in preparation for standardized assessments, and frequently, pressures to have classroom assessments resemble standardized assessments.

Diversity Among Students and Their Parents

Not all students are the same. The student in a high school English class whose world will be crushed if she does not get into the Ivy League school of her dreams is sitting next to the boy who may be the first in his family to go to college. He is wondering whether instead of going

standardized assessment
A measure of student ability in which all students take the same measure under the same conditions.

Chapter Reference
Chapter 14 has extensive coverage on standardized assessment.

to college, he should get a job to help his family. Next to them is a boy with special needs and next to him a girl for whom English is a second language. Their teacher is responsible for assessing each of these students fairly. That teacher must understand that children come from different cultural backgrounds that will influence not only their performances but also their parents' aspirations for them.

Increasingly, teachers work with students who are new arrivals to the United States. Parents who have recently immigrated to the United States may not understand our grading system. They may not realize that homework is expected of students or that parents are expected to be involved in education and may not be aware of what their rights are as parents (Almarza, as cited in Schneider, 2005).

Issues of enculturation and sensitivity to home cultures are important. Talking with parents about goals for their children go can a long way in establishing a strong basis for working with a child. A reference on an assessment to the child's home country tells the child that the teacher is thinking about him or her. Making sure the student understands assessments if the student is not a native English speaker is also essential.

Formative and Summative Assessment

Assessments can serve several purposes in instruction. Michael Scriven (1967) developed one of the most useful ways of distinguishing among assessments. He distinguished between assessments used primarily to help guide instruction and provide feedback to the teacher and the learner, and assessments used for grading or determining the amount of learning on an instructional unit. **Formative assessments** help to *form* future instruction, whereas **summative assessments** *sum up* learning. Formative assessments help us on our way and usually are not used for grading. Summative assessments determine whether a student has achieved the goals of instruction and are usually part of the grading system. When students engage in formative assessment not used as part of the grading system, they realize that the purpose of the assessment is to help them in their learning. Their reactions to this type of assessment are usually much more positive than with summative assessments, which frequently involve a level of anxiety (Wolf & Smith, 1995). Furthermore, formative assessments help students understand their own strengths and weaknesses without the pressures associated with grading. The following can help in differentiating formative and summative assessment:

formative assessment An assessment designed to inform teachers and students about student learning and to help improve instruction.

summative assessment Assessment designed to summarize student achievement.

Formative Assessment

- Given prior to or during instruction
- Information the teacher can use to *form* forthcoming instruction
- Information used to summarize students' strengths and weaknesses
- Not graded

Summative Assessment

- Given after the conclusion of instruction/lesson
- Information the teacher can use to *evaluate* what students have accomplished
- Information used to diagnose what students have accomplished
- Graded

Principles of Assessment and Grading

In developing assessment and grading practices, teachers make a host of choices and decisions, including what to assess, which format to use, how to grade student work, whether an assessment should count for a grade, and how much it should count. The research on classroom assessment shows that teachers' decisions are mixes of ideas and philosophical positions. Cross and Frary (1999) refer to the typical practices of teachers as "hodgepodge grading." In an effort to help teachers develop a coherent and internally consistent approach to assessment and grading, Smith and DeLisi (1998) have devised a set of principles to help teachers make choices about assessment and grading practices. The principles provide a framework for evaluating assessment and grading choices to see whether they are consistent from one choice to the next and with the teacher's instructional goals and teaching philosophy.

Appendix
Characteristics of Assessments

Teachers' choices of assessments should be made based on a set of principles that allow them to use assessments to promote student learning in addition to making judgments about the progress of students (*PRAXIS*™, II. C. 2).

The three principles—communication, fairness, and growth—are equal in importance and, to some extent, conflict with one another because assessment choices, like instructional choices, often involve trade-offs. The principles provide a mechanism for examining trade-offs and deciding how to work toward the best assessment solutions.

Not surprisingly, the principles of assessment and grading begin with the premise that a specific set of instructional goals forms the basis of every teacher's instructional and assessment activities. Classroom assessments and grading practices should flow logically from the goals, objectives, or standards of the teacher and the school district. Briefly, goals are statements of what the teacher wants students to be able to do as a result of instruction. Goals are *not* statements of instructional activities or processes; they are statements of the intended endpoints of instruction. Clearly stated goals for students in a given middle or high school course or across the subject areas at the elementary level are essential as a guide to instructional practice and to assessment (Brookhart, 2001, 1999; Stiggins, 2004).

Communication

Communication involves communication to oneself and communication with students. To communicate effectively, teachers must first understand what they are trying to accomplish in assessment and grading. Therefore, they should make assessment and grading explicit, writing out the decisions as they make them. Later, the teacher can examine them, reflect on them, and share them with others for comments and suggestions.

Once you have made your assessment program explicit, communicate it to the students. Communication is the key to making students take ownership for their own achievement. Grades reflect that achievement. *Grades do not belong to teachers to give out; they are the students' to earn.* Teachers who make clear to students what they expect are much more likely to realize their expectations.

Communication is a two-way street. Just as teachers want to present clear expectations for student performance, students communicate with their teachers. Their performances on assessments, both formal and informal, tell the teacher about their strengths and weaknesses, interests (and lack of same), and concerns. Effective teachers use the communication from students not only to tailor instruction, but also to let students know that they are listening. For example, an assignment on how to search for information can just as easily use a topic of interest to students as not.

Fairness

The second guiding principle of assessment is *fairness*, or the sense that the assessment or grade is just. Students' most frequent complaint about their courses is that the grades or assessments are not fair (Brookhart, 2004). The question of fairness can be broken down into three subcategories: validity, reliability, and freedom from bias. These terms have standard definitions among educational measurement specialists (Feldt & Brennan, 1989; Linn & Gronlund, 1995; Messick, 1989; Nunnally, 1967), but we rework them here to provide a better fit to classroom assessment and grading. They are essentially the same ideas presented in a different light.

Validity.   When measurement specialists talk about **validity**, they are discussing whether an assessment provides useful and accurate information for making decisions (Messick, 1989). Classroom assessment is valid if it reveals student abilities and accomplishments relative to what is being taught. The phrase *what is being taught* is used rather broadly here; besides in-class instruction, it also includes learning that occurs outside the classroom that is part of the instructional process. For example, if a teacher asks students to do research at the library or on the Internet at home, that assignment would be part of *what is being taught*. Moreover, what is being assessed and what is being taught should be closely related to the instructional goals for the class. Goals, instruction, and assessment are tightly interwoven in successful classrooms (Brookhart, 1999, 2001; Stiggins, 2004), and only when they are can a teacher make decisions about how a class is progressing or whether a student has sufficient mastery of a topic to move on to the next topic.

Students are finely attuned to the validity of their assessments. If course content is not assessed, they will question the value of having worked to learn it and will develop similar doubts about future learning. If assessments include content that has not been taught, students will feel that the assessment is unfair.

RIDE   Why is the class reading *The Scarlet Letter?* What is the instructional goal of this unit? Is it concerned with the author's voice, literary style, use of language, historical context, or perhaps the novel's underlying moral implications?

How Can I Use This?

How can you be certain that students understand what you expect of them?

validity   The appropriateness of judgments about students based on assessment information. In classroom assessment, the correspondence between what an assessment measures and what was taught as part of instruction.

RIDE   Look at Ms. Baldwin's debate assessment at the beginning of the chapter. What skills and knowledge would lead to the highest marks on this assessment? Are they closely related to how you would have taught this material?

Reliability. Another aspect of fairness is **reliability**. Reliability is considered an issue of consistency of information (Feldt & Brennan, 1989). That is, a reliable assessment is one that will give much the same results about students if the same test or a very similar one is given again a few days after the first test or if different people grade it. With respect to classroom assessment, reliability means having enough information to make a good judgment about student achievement (Smith, 2003). If a grade is solely based on one short test, even if the test is related to instruction, the amount of information may not be enough to make a good judgment.

Students should have a number of opportunities to show what they can do. Varying the format, or type of assessment has several benefits. First, many students perform better on certain assessment formats than on others. Second, the use of different formats helps students increase their ability to transfer their knowledge and skills and to demonstrate them in new and different venues. Third, teachers find it useful (and more interesting) to have different kinds of student work to evaluate; it is possible to gather information about students using one approach to assessment that might not have been available using a different approach. For example, a student who has difficulty in expressing his or thoughts in writing in English might be able to demonstrate mastery of world history through a multiple-choice assessment.

Freedom from Bias. Freedom from **bias** is another issue in maintaining fairness. Typically, one thinks of bias as an unfair act against individuals who differ in race, gender, physical abilities, native language, or ethnic background. Teachers must be sensitive to these issues in designing assessment and grading practices. If students are going to write on an assigned topic, teachers should consider whether the topic—for example, American football—favors boys over girls or students who have grown up in the United States over immigrants.

Other issues of bias in assessment might not seem obvious at first. For example, if classroom participation is part of assessment, should shy students be at a disadvantage because of a personality characteristic that is unrelated to instructional goals? Bias can also become a critical issue in the grading of homework or the assignment of projects to be completed outside the classroom. When students bring in work from home, the teacher may wonder how much of the assignment was the student's own work and how much help parents, guardians, siblings, or friends provided. Further, is it easier for some students to revise their writing because they have access to good word-processing equipment at home and others do not? In designing a plan for an assessment and grading system, teachers should be sensitive to these issues. They must make very clear to students what they can receive help on and what they must do themselves, and teachers must clearly communicate which activities will count in determining grades.

In sum, fair classroom assessments:

- Are based on instructional goals and the instruction that follows those goals (valid)
- Provide students ample opportunity and variety of assessment formats to show what they can do (reliable)
- Allow all students to demonstrate their achievement equally (validity, reliability, freedom from bias)

Growth

The third of the three assessment principles is growth. A key purpose of schooling is to encourage students to grow—cognitively, emotionally, socially, and physically. As an integral part of instruction, assessment and grading should enhance the instructional process and lead to student growth. In order to facilitate student growth, teachers need to find the right balance between too much assessment and too little. They need to develop assessments that are engaging and rewarding to students. They must provide rapid feedback that is focused on improvement. Teachers should consider whether an assessment is a good instructional device. They should ask, If the assessment is a test, will studying for it enhance learning? If it is a research paper, what skills will be developed by doing the work? If it is a group project, what will all students learn as a result of participating in it?

Teachers should also ask themselves, What is the quality and utility of the information that I will gain about my students as a result of this assessment? If students do not do well on this assessment, will I, and my students, learn about their strengths and weaknesses in relation to this goal? Will this assessment help me determine what further instruction is appropriate? In sum, will it facilitate students' future growth?

reliability Consistency over an aspect of assessment, such as over time and multiple raters. In classroom assessment, having enough information about students on which to base judgments.

bias Systematic unfair treatment of a particular group of individuals.

Chapter Reference
Chapter 14 discusses validity, reliability, and bias in relation to standardized assessment.

Options for Assessment

Chapter Reference
Standardized assessment is
discussed in Chapter 14.

As mentioned earlier, teachers should develop classroom assessments in varied formats. Some options mirror the formats of standardized tests; others derive from classroom-based practice. Each has its own strengths and weaknesses.

Recognition Format

The recognition format requires students to recognize the correct answer from a set of choices. Three types of recognition formats are matching, true/false and multiple choice.

multiple choice   An assessment item format consisting of a stem (question), a right answer, and a set of wrong answers (distracters). Students have to determine the best response to the stem.

Multiple Choice. The most common form of assessment used in U.S. schools is the **multiple-choice** format. Developed for standardized tests because it can be scored quickly and consistently by machine, it continues to be the dominant format of standardized assessment. Teachers who have several sections of a course and dozens of papers to grade might benefit from using this format, but they need to be careful to make sure that the questions are not solely recall of information. Giving students practice in answering multiple-choice assessments can also be helpful to them when they have to take standardized assessments that rely heavily on this format.

stem   The part of a multiple-choice item that asks a question.

distracter   One of the options in a multiple-choice test.

The multiple-choice format consists of a question, or **stem**, followed by a list of options, sometimes called **distracters**, or foils. One of the options is the correct answer, and the remaining options are incorrect. Three-, four-, and five-option multiple-choice tests are the most common. The stem of the multiple-choice item can end in a question mark, or it can simply be an incomplete sentence that could be completed by any of the distracters. (Measurement specialists call test questions **items**, in part because not all test questions are actually questions.) The task of the student is to indicate which of the distracters is the correct choice. The question, Who is the protagonist in *The Scarlet Letter?* presented at the beginning of the chapter, is a simple example of the multiple-choice format. The stem can be a simple question based on a fact from the instructional unit, or it might require comprehension of information from the unit or an inference based on the unit:

item   A test or assessment question, referred to as an *item* because not all test questions are actually questions.

- *When did the Civil War begin?* (Basic fact)
- *What was the major economic advantage the Union had over the Confederacy?* (Comprehension of information)
- *What would have happened to Reconstruction if Lincoln had not been assassinated?* (Inference from information in unit)

The stem of a multiple-choice question can also include information on which the question is based, such as:

Paul and Marie wanted to invite some friends over for a party. They thought that they would need three slices of pizza for each guest. If there are eight slices in a pizza, and if they have eight friends over, how many pizzas will they need?

Once the stem, or question, has been written, the next step is to write an answer that is unambiguously correct or the best choice among alternatives (if there are several possible ways to construct a correct answer). A set of three or four plausible but clearly incorrect distracters then needs to be constructed. In mathematics items, this is usually accomplished by working through the problem in such a way that it includes a conceptual or mathematical error.

Paul and Marie wanted to invite some friends over for a party. They thought that they would need three slices of pizza for each guest. If there are eight slices in a pizza, and if they have eight friends over, how many pizzas will they need?

- a.   *3* (Would be enough for guests, but not for Paul and Marie)
- b.   *4* (Correct answer)
- c.   *5* (A reasonable "guesstimate")
- d.   *8* (The number of guests. Some students will just try to pick something from the problem.)

In verbal items, a good approach is to consider the correct answer and vary one or more of the characteristics of that answer to generate incorrect answers.

When did the Civil War begin?

a. *1861* (Correct answer)
b. *1816* (Reversal of last two digits)
c. *1917* (Beginning of WWI for the United States)
d. *1865* (End of the Civil War)

One of the advantages of the multiple-choice format is that the teacher can control the difficulty of the item. Difficulty can come from a challenging stem or from the options. Consider the following:

Who was the 17th President of the United States?

Difficult answer set:
a. *Andrew Johnson*
b. *Abraham Lincoln*
c. *Millard Fillmore*
d. *Ulysses S. Grant*

Easier answer set:
a. *Andrew Johnson*
b. *Thomas Jefferson*
c. *George Washington*
d. *William Clinton*

Also keep in mind that, with some time and effort, multiple-choice items can be developed to assess **higher order thinking skills** that require higher levels of cognitive processing in students. The following item requires some sophistication on the part of the student:

What would have happened to Reconstruction if Lincoln had not been assassinated?

a. *It would have occurred very much the way it did.* (Addresses the question but a poor choice)
b. *The Confederacy would have reformed to fight again.* (A possibility and therefore attractive but clearly wrong)
c. *It would have been more successful because of Lincoln's popularity.* (Correct answer)
d. *Because Lincoln opposed Reconstruction, it would not have happened.* (Directly answers the question but facts are wrong)

In sum, the multiple-choice format allows teachers to control closely what they are assessing and is useful for assessing discrete pieces of knowledge or understanding. It needs to be developed carefully but is easily and rapidly scored (even without an electronic scanner). However, it does not permit the student to be very creative or imaginative. In addition, a student who does not know the answer to an item can guess the answer; he or she has a one-in-four chance of getting a four-option multiple-choice item correct. Some students take unusual and often not helpful approaches to answering multiple choice questions (see the "Taking It to the Classroom" box below). Multiple-choice items can also be used to assess higher order thinking skills, but creating such items requires substantial thought and work.

higher order thinking skills Skills and abilities that go beyond recall and comprehension, including the ability to apply ideas and concepts, analyze and synthesize information, and evaluate complex information.

 Look at Mr. Antoine's assessment at the beginning of the chapter. What does that multiple-choice question say regarding what Mr. Antoine thinks is important about *The Scarlet Letter?* Use the example about Lincoln and create multiple-choice items for a work of literature that are more challenging and reflective of a higher set of expectations than Mr. Antoine's question.

Taking It to the Classroom

Do You Know Jack? Multiple Choice or Multiple Guess?

Jack has a strange approach to multiple-choice questions. He answers them by looking at the choices first. He picks the two that seem to look the best to him, then reads the question to make a decision between his two options. His older brother told him this was the best way to do it. What can you do to convince Jack to keep all options open until he has read the question?

- Walk through a multiple-choice test with Jack, asking him to explain his approach as he answers several multiple-choice questions with you.
- Let Jack confront the illogic of his approach as he goes through the questions.
- If he does not see his problem, point it out with a more direct approach. Show him that there is usually no way to spot a right or wrong answer without first looking at the question.

matching An assessment item format that involves generating two sets of objects that are to be linked together, such as states and their capitals.

Matching. **Matching** items are very popular with teachers. They have a gamelike quality that is appealing. In the matching format, two lists of concepts are presented side by side, and the student has to match the concept on the left with the corresponding concept on the right. Sometimes the nature of the required relationship is obvious; in other cases, the teacher specifies it, as in the following example:

Match the state with its capital city.

Nebraska	Springfield
North Dakota	Trenton
Illinois	Bismarck
New Jersey	Lincoln

The matching item is similar to the multiple-choice item in that students are required to recognize the correct answer rather than to generate the correct answer themselves. It requires a set of concepts, all of which are of the same type and have another specific concept associated with them. States and their capitals, parts of the body and their functions, and new vocabulary words and their definitions are all examples of concepts that can readily be assessed using the matching format. In the state capital example above, the teacher might want to consider omitting the capitals and requiring the students to fill in blanks. Consider for a minute how different these two formats would be. The matching format has limited applicability in most settings, but the puzzlelike nature of matching items can afford a nice break in an assessment, particularly for younger children.

True/False. Another traditional approach to assessment is the true/false item. It consists of a factual statement that the student has to judge as true or false. The primary advantages of the true/false format are the number of items that can be included on the test (because it does not take long to answer them) and ease of scoring. For some types of information, the true/false format can be effective. For example:

Circle one.

The capital of North Dakota is Springfield.   T   F

This is a simple declarative statement that is false, and it assesses the student's knowledge of state capitals (or at least one of them).

However, two significant problems arise with true/false items. First, if students do not know the answer to the item, they still have a 50/50 chance of getting the item right. Second, some statements are not clearly true or false. For example:

Circle one.

The assassination of Archduke Ferdinand led to the start of World War I.   T   F

This, too, is a simple declarative statement, but it is not one on which all historians agree. For these reasons, it is probably better to avoid using true/false questions.

Generative Format

Items that require a student to generate an answer, or *generative* items, provide an alternative format for assessments. Two basic types of generative items are constructed response, or short answer, and essay.

Appendix

Types of Assessments

It is useful to understand the strengths and limitations of different types of assessments. You should keep in mind that the assessments you choose should align with your instructional goals (*PRAXIS*™, II. C. 1, *INTASC*, Principle 8).

constructed response A type of assessment format in which the student has to provide the answer to the question; more commonly referred to as *short answer*.

Constructed Response (Short Answer). **Constructed response** is the term that measurement specialists use for what most people refer to as short-answer items. Students have to *construct* the answer rather than simply select it from a list as in multiple-choice items. Constructed-response items can take many forms. One very common use is the simple math problem. It can take the form of a story problem to which the student has to generate an answer, such as the following:

At 2 p.m., a 2-meter pole casts a 0.3-meter shadow. If there is a second pole next to it that is 10 meters high, how long a shadow will it cast?

Here is a simple calculation problem:

$$7\frac{7}{8}$$
$$-5\frac{3}{8}$$

Another version of the constructed-response format is the following:

In Niall's Saga, *what are the two underlying themes of the narrative?*

The constructed-response format is probably the one that teachers use most often. It is fairly easy to write constructed-response items, and they can be used in a wide variety of applications. Another advantage of the constructed-response format is that it requires the student to produce (i.e., construct) the correct response rather than simply to identify it, as in the multiple-choice format. Constructed-response items require *recall* rather than *recognition* of information.

Constructed-response questions seem like the simplest and most straightforward type of assessment format because they mimic questions asked in class. The teacher poses a question, and the student answers it. For many questions, the constructed response format looks like a multiple-choice question without the choices. However, because there are no choices, care must be taken in creating constructed-response questions. For example, one can devise either a question that has a number of possible correct answers or a question that does not make sense without the options. Consider the following:

Which of the following is a prime number?

This question makes sense only if it is followed by a set of options. Or consider:

For what is William Henry Harrison known?

There are a number of possible answers to this question. Harrison is known for being the hero of the battle of Tippecanoe; his presidency was very brief due to his early death; and he was also known simply for being President of the United States. If these responses are all acceptable, the question will work well. But if a teacher really wanted to be certain that students knew that Harrison died early in his presidency, he or she would have to rephrase the question more precisely or turn it into a multiple-choice item.

Constructed-response questions should focus on unambiguous instructional content and should be specific enough that a student who knows the answer will get it right. Imprecisely worded questions can mislead students. If the question confuses students, no one can determine why they did not answer it correctly.

Essay Tests.   The essay format is a favorite of high school English teachers but is also widely used at earlier grades and in most subjects. Essay tests are rightly considered to be appropriate for meeting a variety of assessment needs. Further, the very act of writing an essay is a useful instructional activity. Practice in writing is practice in thinking.

The essay item requires the student to compose an essay in response to a question or *prompt*, which is the statement of what students must write. The tests on *The Scarlet Letter* handed out by Ms. Baldwin and Mrs. Chambliss and presented at the beginning of the chapter show two possible prompts for essays. The essay question can be graded on the information provided in the response, the quality of the writing in the essay, or other factors of concern to the teacher. Consider the following essay question and what it requires a student to do.

The first ten amendments to the United States Constitution are called The Bill of Rights and are considered to be a mainstay of our rights and freedoms as citizens. Some legal scholars have argued that we should eliminate the third amendment concerning the quartering of troops in private homes during peacetime. What is your opinion on this question? Write an essay of roughly 200 words defending your decision. Be sure to consider both the positive and negative effects of eliminating this amendment.

The strength of the essay format lies in what it requires of students. A well-constructed essay question requires students to consider the implications of the question, pull together the knowledge they have related to the question, and construct an essay presenting their points and supporting details. The essay format also gives the teacher considerable latitude in the construction of the assessment.

Because it takes a great deal of time for a student to complete an essay item, an assessment can contain relatively few of them. Thus, what is gained in depth of response can come at the cost of breadth. In addition, essay items conflate, or intertwine, several skills (such as organizational ability, recall of information, and the ability to make a good argument) that the teacher may want to assess separately. Students who write well, for example, are likely to do better on an essay test than students who do not write well. Even poor handwriting can interfere with performance on an essay test. Finally, teachers must spend a great deal of time grading essay tests and giving appropriate feedback to students. Essay testing has undergone substantial change in recent years, particularly with regard to the use of *rubrics*, scoring guides for essays (Danielson, 1997; Taggart et al., 2001). The use of rubrics is discussed later in the chapter.

As in all assessments, writing a good essay item begins with reflection on the instructional goal that is being assessed. One then constructs a prompt that requires the student to engage the instructional goal in a meaningful and important fashion. The teacher needs to think about what an excellent answer would include and how it would reflect the instructional goal.

The essay prompt must give students enough information about what a good essay must contain without at the same time providing the information or skills that the teacher is trying to assess. The teacher needs to remember that the open-ended nature of the essay question can leave the student anxious unless sufficient direction is provided in the question. Consider, for example, the following two versions of an essay question:

VERSION 1

In the mid-1400s, Johann Gutenberg developed a process for mass production of books through the use of movable type. Explain how the development of movable type influenced European society. Be sure to consider economic as well as religious developments.

VERSION 2

How did the development of movable type affect economic life in Europe? Write a three- to four-paragraph essay (roughly 300 words) examining the economic consequences of this invention, starting with its first uses and expanding its impact over the remainder of the century. Focus your essay on the changes that occurred in the European economy as a result of movable type. Discuss the economic and social context in Europe at the time of the development. The essay is worth twenty points on the exam. Fifteen points will be given to the quality of the content of your answer, and five points will be awarded based on the quality of the writing and grammar, punctuation, and spelling.

The first version is a reasonable essay prompt, but the second version gives a much clearer sense of what is expected of students and how they will be graded.

Student writing can be developed through prompts that include creativity and imagination along with demonstration of knowledge of instructional content. The prompt below allows students to use their imaginations. The teacher using this assignment chose not to count the responses toward the students' grades because she felt that although she wanted to encourage creativity on the students' part, she did not feel it fair to count that as part of a grade.

We have been studying Greek gods and goddesses. Now it is your turn to "invent" a Greek god or goddess. Use what you know about Greek mythology to create a god or goddess. Determine what characteristics your god or goddess has and why. Present your god or goddess, locate him or her in the Pantheon of gods (to whom is this god or goddess related?), and tell a story that involves your god or goddess. Your presentation should be about 200 words long. I will provide feedback on demonstrated knowledge of Greek mythology, creativity, and good essay-writing techniques.

Alternative Formats

authentic assessment An assessment that is tightly related to the instruction that the students have received or to tasks that are relevant in real life.

alternative assessment A generic term referring to assessments that are different from traditional approaches, such as multiple choice and constructed response.

The past decade has seen the development of a variety of new formats for assessment (Hargreaves, Earl, & Schmidt, 2002; Shepard, 2000). It might be more appropriate to say that experts in formal measurement have *discovered* a number of formats that teachers have been using for some time. These formats have been given many different names, including **authentic assessment** and the choice used here, **alternative assessment**. These approaches are more student-oriented than traditional assessments and less concerned with the formal characteristics of assessment formats. They also tend to relate more closely both to instruction and to real-life applications of the knowledge and skills involved. Types of alternative assessments include performance assessments, portfolios, journals, and informal assessments.

Performance Assessments. The term **performance assessment** covers a wide array of assessment possibilities, but they can be grouped into two categories: those that involve a *performance* and those that result in a *product.*

Some performance assessments are literally real-time performances. Students must demonstrate proficiency or create and deliver a performance of some type; activities include class presentations, recitations in a foreign language, skits, and laboratory demonstrations in a science class.

This type of assessment has several advantages. First and foremost is the fidelity of the assessment to the skill being assessed. For example, the best way to determine whether students are pronouncing *l'œil* correctly is to have them pronounce it. Second, advocates of performance assessment argue that it causes students to prepare for the assessment in ways that are especially conducive to learning. Third, performance assessments tend to be more engaging for students.

The disadvantages to performances include difficulties in scoring, **objectivity** (fairness in grading), and correspondence between what is desired and what is obtained in the assessments. For example, if a talented student presents a speech that is well delivered, creative, and engaging but is somewhat off the assignment that had been given, how are you going to grade it? Furthermore, with respect to objectivity, are you grading everyone fairly, or are you (perhaps unknowingly) biased toward or against some students (perhaps a student with behavior problems)? Performance anxiety might also be a problem in this type of assessment because some students are very reluctant to engage in any kind of performance in front of their classmates. Remember that performances also occur in real time; if each student is to be assessed during a performance or a demonstration of ability, this can occupy an incredible amount of class time.

In the second type of performance assessment, students are given a task and must create a **product**, such as a travel promotion for visiting their home town or a report on the result of a titration experiment. (Assessing students as they conduct the experiment would be the other type of performance assessment.) In this type of performance assessment, the concept of performance does not mean a real-time performance but rather the demonstration of competence in accomplishing a goal or completing a project. Figure 13.1 presents a typical math performance assessment for fourth grade.

The strengths of this type of assessment are similar to those of real-time performances. In addition, more types of products are available to assign, and time limitations are less of a concern. The weaknesses are similar as well (except for performance anxiety), but there is one additional and important difficulty: As with any homework, if a performance assess-

performance assessment An assessment in which students generate a product or an actual performance that reflects what they have learned.

objectivity Not a having a direct interest or bias.

> **What Does This Mean to Me?**
> Do you think that you might tend to *play favorites* when you are assessing students' performance?

products Student creations that reflect their skills and abilities as well as their ability to create something new.

Performance assessments engage students, encourage creativity, and tie closely to instructional goals. (Dennis MacDonald/Photo Edit)

Mrs. Rinaldi's Fourth-Period Math Class

Imagine that you have been assigned the task of painting this classroom. You are going to do it over a weekend at the end of next month. By a week from Friday, you have to present the Board of Education with a plan and a budget for painting the room. You and one friend are going to do the painting, and you will be paid $7.50 an hour for your work. The custodian has cloths to lend you so that you will not spill paint on the desks and counters. Other than that, you must purchase all your materials and come up with a detailed plan for your work. You are to hand in the following:

1. A list of the activities that must take place in order to paint the room and a schedule of when they will occur.
2. A description of the type of paint and color or colors you wish to use and an explanation of why you made these choices.
3. A budget to cover all your expenses and a rationale for that budget.

Your report to the Board should be word-processed, should be free of errors, and should provide a convincing case that you can do the job. Good luck!

Figure 13.1. Thinking "Inside the Room": A Geometry and Planning Task

www.wiley.com/college/odonnell

ment involves work conducted outside the classroom, it is difficult to know whether the student alone completed the work. Help from family members and friends can interfere with the fairness of the assessment. Performance assessment is a rapidly developing field in education today. The Web site associated with this text includes an up-to-date list of Web sites discussing the most current work in performance assessment. The "Taking It to the Classroom" box on the next page presents ideas for developing alternative and performance assessments.

An excellent way to begin thinking about building a performance assessment is to view it not as an assessment per se but as an aspect of instruction related to instructional goals (Smith, Smith, & DeLisi, 2001). This idea actually works for a variety of assessment formats. Frequently, a strong instructional activity that involves independent work can be transformed into an assessment that has good instructional value as well. For example, having students plan for a trip to a different country as part of a social studies unit can have a rubric for grading developed for it. This will help students understand the nature of the project and provide the teacher with insight concerning their ability to seek out reference information. Consider the following:

EXAMPLE 1

In our science lessons, we have learned how to identify four trees that are common in our town: oak, maple, pine, and spruce. Take a walk down the block you live on, and tally the number of each of these types of trees that you see as well as each tree that is not one of these. Graph your results using the bar graph we have learned in our mathematics lessons. Using your graph, answer the following questions:

1. *What is the most common tree in your neighborhood?*
2. *What is the least common tree in your neighborhood?*
3. *Are there more oaks, maples, pines, and spruce combined in your neighborhood, or more other types of trees?*

Taking It to the Classroom

Developing Alternative Assessments

Developing alternative assessments can be a bit daunting at first. Here is a list of 10 ideas to use to get started.

1. Start by thinking not about assessment but by thinking about instruction. What good instructional activities do you have? Can any of them be turned into an alternative assessment? Develop your assessments as you develop your instruction.

2. Don't worry if an assessment is not alternative enough. Focus on the quality of the assessment, not how it would be described.

3. Use the Web. The Internet has thousands of Web sites with an enormous collection of alternative assessment ideas. Look not only for ideas that fit your purposes directly, but also for other ideas that you can adapt to your needs.

4. Think about developing clear rubrics from the beginning. The rubric for an assessment should provide a definition of the assessment as well as your scoring system.

5. Share your work with colleagues. Ask them what they have that works well and ask then for suggestions on your work.

6. Your first efforts may not be brilliant. Do not get discouraged. At first, alternative assessments may take more time and may not deliver exactly what you want. You will get better with each new effort.

7. Keep a portfolio of your work. Maintain in the portfolio both the task and some student examples. Keep some of the best work but also work that was weak that helped you diagnose student difficulties.

8. Make the assessment worth the students' effort. Let them know what you expect from them and how their work will be graded. Make it an important part of their grade if appropriate.

9. Consider having students grade each others' work as well as assessing their own. Alternative assessments are a great way to develop self-assessment skills in students.

10. Be reflective. At the end of an assessment activity, think about what went well and what did not. Takes notes and keep them in your assessment portfolio. Ask the students what they thought of the assessment. And keep trying!

EXAMPLE 2

Imagine that you are in charge of encouraging economic development in our town. You are going to a convention to promote our town to real estate agents. Make a display that you would be able to use at the convention. Use the three-fold poster board that you have been given to present your display. Also, develop a five-minute presentation on why people would like to move to our town. Be sure to include what industry and business opportunities are available as well as quality-of-life issues. You may want to contact local government offices in developing your poster and presentation.

These examples are both excellent beginnings for performance assessments. Consider the two tasks and the differences between them. The first performance assessment is an example of a performance as product. Students will hand in the results of their efforts. The second performance assessment requires both a product and a performance. (The teacher could plan a mini-convention at which students could exhibit their materials and give their presentations.) Further, the first assessment is more specifically defined and closed-ended. That is, there is only one right way to complete it. The appearance of the graphs and the quality of students' answers may differ, but a scoring mechanism for the first task would be fairly easy to generate. The second task is far more open-ended, allowing more latitude for student creativity. Because it is more complex both in the task and in the presentation, it will be more difficult to score than the first example.

Both assessments may have developed from instructional activities. Example 1 may have followed a series of math exercises completed in class. It would then serve as a *capstone* activity, allowing the teacher to see how well the students had learned the graph-making and interpretation lesson. (As a class activity, after students hand in their graphs, the data could be accumulated, and the class as a whole could graph the data.)

It is more difficult to determine what Example 2 is measuring. It might be related to instruction in research techniques, with the project designed to measure a student's ability to seek out and organize information about the positive aspects of a town. Or it might measure whether students have learned the positive aspects of their own town. Either set of understandings and abilities is potentially useful, as long as the project reflects what has occurred during instruction, and the basis for evaluation is made clear to the students.

portfolio A collection of students' work over time that allows for assessment of the development of their skills.

Portfolios. **Portfolios** are collections of students' work. The concept of a portfolio originated in the field of art and spread to advertising and graphic design, where job seekers use their portfolios to demonstrate their abilities to potential employers. In classroom assessment, portfolios involve the collection of students' work over the course of a given period of time (e.g., a unit, a semester, or a year). This allows for an examination of the progress that a student has made in a given area. The audience for a student's portfolio might include the teacher, the student, the student's parents or guardians, or other concerned individuals. Portfolios are particularly effective for student/teacher and parent/teacher conferences about student progress.

The contents of portfolios can vary greatly. A high school writing portfolio might include several drafts or just a few representative works to show how well the student has mastered the writing process over time. An elementary school math portfolio might include samples that demonstrate the student's progress in problem-solving ability. Portfolios can include photographs, artwork, and notes from teachers to students as well as student work. Some teachers keep portfolios for several years and present them to students when they graduate from high school or move from one school to the next.

Some educators argue that portfolios are not assessments in and of themselves but rather materials on which to base assessments. Some consider a portfolio little more than a *folder* for keeping a student's work, something that teachers have always done (Smith et al., 2001). This does not minimize the potential value of the portfolio. Portfolios let students compare what they were doing earlier in the year to what they can do in the present. This helps students develop the ability to assess their own strengths and weaknesses, an invaluable learning tool.

It is not necessary to put everything into a portfolio; in fact, it is probably detrimental, because it would soon become overwhelming. Instead, teachers develop a system for inclusion that will allow for the examination of growth over time. In some instances, all drafts of a piece of important writing are included in the portfolio, but not usually for all writing. All final products might be included, certainly in the case of substantial products. Preliminary notes for a project can give a student, upon reflection, a concrete example of how his or her thinking changed over the course of the project. This can be useful when brainstorming on subsequent projects. In a math class, students can follow the development of their own thinking on a certain topic and consider how this might be helpful as they work on their current math problems. Letting students join in the process of deciding what should and should not be included in their portfolios is usually a good idea, because it promotes a sense of responsibility for one's own achievements.

journal A running set of thoughts, responses to prompts, and reflections that students have concerning their learning in a particular area.

Journals. Student **journals** offer great potential for gaining insight into the thought processes, ideas, concerns, and overall development of student abilities. A journal is a learning diary and can be structured in a number of ways. Some are free-form recordings of students' thoughts about their learning. Others include specific prompts, or requests, for the student to make entries in a journal. Teachers can choose to review them on a regular basis or give students the option of handing them in when they choose to do so.

Journals lie at the intersection of teaching and assessment. Teachers use them widely and for a variety of purposes (Trice, 2000). When students explain what they know, their understanding and difficulties with their understanding become clearer to them. When journals are designed to be shared with teachers, they can provide a rich source of information about how well the class and individual students are doing and where their difficulties lie.

Informal Assessments. The assessment approaches presented so far are designed in advance. Another type of assessment is ongoing, fluid, and essential to teachers in making instructional decisions. Teachers use **informal assessment** to determine whether students understand a concept by asking probing questions or posing problems for them to solve. Equally important is the ability to evaluate the questions that students ask. What level of understanding and interest do they represent? Are the students exhibiting a solid understanding, or do they seem lost? What happens when the teacher changes the situation slightly and asks students to apply what they have learned?

Garnering useful information about students' progress during instruction is one hallmark of an exceptional teacher. This type of assessment informs teachers' decisions about when to move on to the next topic, who might need extra help, and who can afford to take a few minutes to help a classmate. It can help the teacher determine whether a particular instructional approach is working well or not at all.

The use of classroom participation and contribution as an informal part of an assessment and grading system has both strengths and weaknesses. Participation and contribution enhance instruction overall and teach students how to be good citizens in the classroom and in other settings. Classroom discussions can also be a rich source of informal assessment information for teachers to use in determining how well the class as a whole is progressing. However, they include a potential bias against students who are reluctant to speak up in class, for example, because of shyness, cultural differences, or disinclination to appear too smart to their classmates. Further, it is often hard to reconcile, basing part of a student's grade on an assessment that is not part of the instructional goals for the class (few instructional goals include participation). Usually, teachers count participation toward grades because without it, students would participate less and learn less. Thus, counting participation facilitates growth (one of the principles of grading and assessment) but has strong potential to be biased and not directly related to instructional goals.

How can teachers encourage participation while minimizing the drawbacks of counting it as part of a grade?

- First, do not think of it as *participation*; think of it as *contribution*. Provide students with a variety of options for contributing to the class. Positive participation in classroom instruction is but one form of student contribution. They might also work with peers who are having problems in a certain area or bring in newspaper clippings or other illustrative materials, such as specimens of plants for a biology class.

- Second, limit the proportion of a grade that can be earned by participation, and inform the students what it is. Many teachers find that 5% of the total grade is sufficient to encourage contributions to the class.

- Third, develop a system for rewarding students that minimizes potential bias. Do not rely solely on your own judgment at the end of the grading term. (See the "Taking It to the Classroom" box below for a creative example of a rewards system.)

> informal assessment Classroom assessment activities used to get a quick and rough idea of student progress.

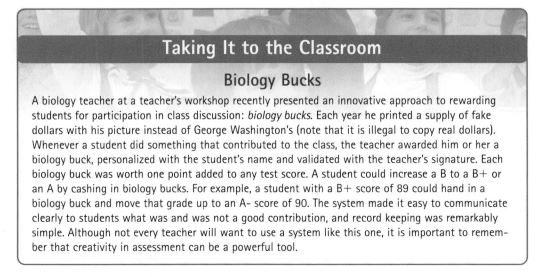

Taking It to the Classroom

Biology Bucks

A biology teacher at a teacher's workshop recently presented an innovative approach to rewarding students for participation in class discussion: *biology bucks*. Each year he printed a supply of fake dollars with his picture instead of George Washington's (note that it is illegal to copy real dollars). Whenever a student did something that contributed to the class, the teacher awarded him or her a biology buck, personalized with the student's name and validated with the teacher's signature. Each biology buck was worth one point added to any test score. A student could increase a B to a B+ or an A by cashing in biology bucks. For example, a student with a B+ score of 89 could hand in a biology buck and move that grade up to an A- score of 90. The system made it easy to communicate clearly to students what was and was not a good contribution, and record keeping was remarkably simple. Although not every teacher will want to use a system like this one, it is important to remember that creativity in assessment can be a powerful tool.

Developing and Using Assessments

Good assessments begin with a clear understanding of what is to be assessed. Then teachers have to determine the best format, how they will grade the assessments, how to take into consideration students with special needs, and how to address the diversity of the classroom. Another consideration in developing classroom assessments is to think about what students will be doing either to complete the assessment (for example, in the case of performance assessments) or to prepare for the assessment (in the case of in-class tests). Are these activities also good instructional experiences?

Determining What to Assess

The impetus for determining what to assess comes from the instructional goals for the class. With the advent of No Child Left Behind and standards-based instruction and assessment that exist in all states, teachers typically work from instructional standards that are state-mandated. But now the teacher needs to turn the standard into a more specific **achievement target** (Stiggins, 2004), a clear statement of what to assess. Consider this standard from the NJ ASK (New Jersey Assessment of Student Knowledge) in mathematics:

A Mathematics Instructional Standard

The students should be able to represent data using an appropriate graph and make inferences based on organized data and displays.

This is a reasonable standard. It seems perfectly clear and appropriate. But a number of issues lurk just beneath the surface:

- How good a graph should the student be able to make?
- Should the data be relevant to students? Should it be a frequency distribution or a cross-tabulation?
- How can this standard be developed into instructional/assessment materials so that students will be engaged in the activities?
- What is the basis for grading? What are the possible instructional ramifications of the results?

These questions are not criticisms of the standard, nor are they intended to demonstrate that the standard will be difficult to address in the classroom. They are issues that naturally concern teachers in the development of instruction and classroom assessment.

Test Blueprints. When developing an assessment, particularly one involving traditional assessment formats, such as multiple choice, constructed response, and essay, teachers rough out a table of specifications, or **test blueprint**, of what to include. The blueprint can be as simple and straightforward as an outline or it can be more sophisticated, such as the **content/behavior matrix** shown in Figure 13.2 (Bloom, Hastings, & Madaus, 1971). A content behavior matrix is a form of test blueprint that crosses behaviors with subject headings to provide a matrix of possible instructional objectives.

The content/behavior matrix in Figure 13.2 is particularly helpful in that it enables teachers to see all the possible areas for writing test questions. Not every possible cell has to have questions in it, however. If a particular combination of a content area and a cognitive behavior has not been taught, it should not be tested. The content/behavior matrix not only helps in test construction but also provides a useful way to reflect on instruction up to the point of the test. It can even lead teachers to a deeper understanding of their instruction ("I really haven't spent much time on this topic, have I?" or "This has turned out to be the real emphasis of this unit"). A good starting point for a test blueprint is the set of district or state standards for the unit being taught. The test blueprint is, in reality, a restatement and expansion of the goals for the unit, essential not just for assessment but for instruction as well.

A content/behavior matrix, with degrees of emphasis assigned, allows for the construction of an assessment in which the number of questions and the scoring weights given to those questions are based on the test blueprint. This ensures that the test reflects the most important elements of instruction.

Students can also use the test blueprint as a guide as they study (Smith and De Lisi, 1998). When students have a blueprint to study from, they can use their study time more

---

achievement targets Well-specified statements of what teachers want to accomplish in a particular lesson or set of lessons.

Chapter Reference
Chapter 9 discusses achievement targets.

test blueprint A statement of what a test will comprise, often in outline form.

content/behavior matrix A method for specifying what is to be assessed by making a matrix with expected student behaviors on one axis and the content on which that behavior will be observed on the other axis.

Content/Behavior Matrix in World History: World War I

Content/Behavior	Europe at the turn of the century	Relationships among European leaders	The beginnings of war	The reaction of the United States
Knowledge of people, facts, and dates	6 items	5 items	4 items	5 items
Understanding causes	0 items	2 items	5 items	3 items
Explaining/predicting outcomes	2 items	4 items	0 items	4 items

Figure 13.2. Content/Behavior Matrix

efficiently. At the elementary level, a test blueprint can be a simple communication to students to help them prepare for a unit test.

Ms. Wade's "Be Ready" Sheet for Thursday's Geography Test

1. *Be able to identify all the countries of Europe.*
2. *Know all of their capitals.*
3. *Know which countries were formerly in the Soviet Union.*
4. *Be able to explain the European Union and how it came to be.*

Rubrics

When using an alternative assessment, such as a group project, journal entry, or performance assessment, it is particularly important to think carefully about what is being assessed. When educators ignore consideration of the underlying purpose of an assessment, the resulting assessments tend to lack reliability and validity (Baxter & Glaser, 1998; Shavelson, Baxter, & Pine, 1991). The need to be clear about the content of the assessment (what is being assessed) and the scoring of the assessment has led to the development of **rubrics**. (The word *rubric* comes from religious writings, in which headings, notes, and commentary were frequently written in red ink. Rubric has the same root as the word *ruby*.)

Rubrics are specifications for how to score assessments, particularly assessments that do not lend themselves to simple right-or-wrong scoring. They are different from test blueprints in that they do not specify what is to be assessed but rather how to score what is being assessed. However, thinking about scoring issues also helps the teacher define the nature of the assessment. For example, when planning an assessment that involves a class presentation, the teacher needs to determine how important the presentational style (as opposed to the content of the presentation) will be, how much the visual aids will count, and what the consequences will be for taking more than the allotted amount of time. In thinking about these issues, the teacher is defining the nature of the assessment.

A rubric typically consists of a set of **criteria** (statements about what is expected) combined with specifications for what levels of performance are required for various scores. This might be combined with a clear statement of what the assignment is (although some rubrics contain just the scoring criteria). Rubrics should clearly state the observable outcomes expected of students. They should describe what students should know and be able to do. Moreover, they should be defined in terms that students who are engaged in the assessment can readily understand.

Look at the example of a rubric for grading middle school science reports on boats and buoyancy presented in Figure 13.3. Does the rubric set clear expectations? As you can see, the rubric not only specifies the scoring but also defines the assignment. Rubrics assist in assessment and instruction by making clear what is to be learned.

Rubrics also assist in creating valid assessments. Look at Figure 13.3 again. In this rubric, attractiveness, spelling and grammar, and timeliness will garner as many points as research, procedure, and conclusion. Is this truly desirable for this particular assignment? It may be, but it is important to understand the choices made in developing rubrics. A topic should not appear in a rubric just because it is easy to define and specify but because it supports the instructional goals.

rubrics Explications of the criteria for a performance assessment or an essay that include specifications for how various levels of performance are to be graded.

criteria Specifications of what is expected of a student on an assessment.

Determining the Best Assessment Format

Appendix
Using Assessments
You should develop and use assessments that will allow you to understand students' current levels of performance and will allow you to design further instruction to help them progress to the next level (*PRAXIS™*, II. C. 4; II C. 5, *INTASC*, Principle 2, 8).

As you have seen, the various assessment options each have strengths and weaknesses. Therefore, consider the appropriateness of various alternatives to a specific assessment goal. For example, if the objective is to have students develop their own ideas in relation to an assigned task, an essay or a performance assessment is appropriate. Students should understand that the generation and execution of good ideas related to the task are important. If, on the other hand, a unit requires that students acquire and comprehend a large amount of information, a multiple-choice or short-answer test can provide a good sample of how much they have learned.

Another consideration is the time and effort needed to build the assessment, administer it, grade it, and communicate the results to the students. Essay tests have many attractive features, but grading them and providing feedback to students takes a great deal of time. Because feedback to students must be timely, teachers pressed for time or with large classes might consider an alternative form of assessment. Although it is desirable to try to develop the best possible assessment in every situation, veteran teachers understand that teaching decisions almost always involve trade-offs.

Chapter Reference
Chapter 14 discusses standards-based assessment.

	Beginning 1	Developing 2	Accomplished 3	Exemplary 4	Score
Introduction	Does not give any information about what to expect in the report.	Gives very little information.	Gives too much information—more like a summary.	Presents a concise lead-in to the report.	
Research	Does not answer any questions suggested in the template.	Answers some questions.	Answers some questions and includes a few other interesting facts.	Answers most questions and includes many other interesting facts.	
Purpose/Problem	Does not address an issue related to tidepools.	Addresses a tidepool issue which is unrelated to research.	Addresses an issue somewhat related to research.	Addresses a real issue directly related to research findings.	
Procedure	Not sequential, most steps are missing or are confusing.	Some of the steps are understandable; most are confusing and lack detail.	Most of the steps are understandable; some lack detail or are confusing.	Presents easy-to-follow steps that are logical and adequately detailed.	
Data & Results	Data table and/or graph missing information and are inaccurate.	Both complete, minor inaccuracies and/or illegible characters.	Both accurate, some ill-formed characters.	Data table and graph neatly completed and totally accurate.	
Conclusion	Presents an illogical explanation for findings and does not address any of the questions suggested in the template.	Presents an illogical explanation for findings and addresses few questions.	Presents a logical explanation for findings and addresses some of the questions.	Presents a logical explanation for findings and addresses most of the questions.	
Grammar & Spelling	Very frequent grammar and/or spelling errors.	More than two errors.	Only one or two errors.	All grammar and spelling are correct.	
Attractiveness	Illegible writing, loose pages.	Legible writing, some ill-formed letters, print too small or too large, papers stapled together.	Legible writing, well-formed characters, clean and neatly bound in a report cover, illustrations provided.	Word processed or typed, clean and neatly bound in a report cover, illustrations provided.	
Timeliness	Report handed in more than one week late.	Up to one week late.	Up to two days late.	Report handed in on time.	
				Total	

Figure 13.3. Rubric for Grading Science Reports

Typically, assessments should be closely linked to instruction. Sometimes teachers do move away from instruction, but they do so with a purpose. For example, most students have to take a **standards-based assessment** (mandatory assessment typically developed at the state level) at the end of the academic year. Often, teachers will build in some classroom assessment activities using assessment formats that are similar to the ones that will appear on the standards-based assessment.

Assessing Students with Special Needs

Many, if not most, classrooms today include students with special needs. These needs may be physical, cognitive, or affective; you might have a student who is visually challenged or has dyslexia or an emotional disturbance. Students with disabilities grow up to be scientists, authors, governors, diplomats, and highly successful businesspeople, as well as some school-teachers. The accomplishments of other students with disabilities are more modest, but each individual who faces a special challenge desires to live as full and productive a life as possible. There are a host of issues that must be addressed when working with classified students; one of those is assessment.

Individualized Education Programs. A student **classified** as having special needs has an **individualized education program (IEP)**, which is an educational and behavioral plan that specifies the student's annual goals. You can learn about IEPs by looking for the Individuals with Disabilities Act on the Internet (a link to the site can be found on the Web site for this text) and examine the IEP in Chapter 4 again as well. IEP goals are related to the general goals for the class, which have been modified in order to maximize the individual child's growth. Historically, classified students have been exempted from standardized testing, but No Child Left Behind requires that almost all children be included in statewide testing programs.

Teachers first need to review the IEP for classified children in their class. Assessments should be derived from instructional goals; if the goals for a given student are different from those for the rest of the class, it follows that the assessment may be different as well. Frequently the IEP will guide teachers regarding the **accommodations**, or modifications, that they should make for classified students. Table 13.1 lists some of these accommodations.

standards-based assessment Assessments that are generated from a list of educational standards, usually at the state or national level; a form of standardized assessment.

classified   A term used to refer to special education students who have been identified as having a particular disability.

individualized education program (IEP)   An educational and behavioral intervention plan for a student with special needs.

www.wiley.com/college/odonnell

Chapter Reference
Chapter 4 presents an example of an IEP.

accommodations   Modifications made in an assessment for students with disabilities.

TABLE 13.1

Accommodations for Assessing Students with Special Needs

Accommodations related to time
- Providing extra time
- Allowing breaks as needed
- Administering the test in several sessions

Accommodations related to the setting
- Giving the test in a quiet, separate room
- Letting the student take the test at home

Accommodations related to the presentation of the assessment
- Large print or magnification
- Having the test read aloud
- Using a helper
- Simplified directions

Accommodations related to the response format
- Letting the student write on the test instead of an answer sheet
- Letting the student use a computer or word processor
- Letting the student say answers rather than write them

Modifications of the assessment
- Simplifying the tasks according to the student's needs
- Allowing the student to use a dictionary or other resource

Classroom Assessments for Students with Special Needs. Any element in the list of accommodations presented in Table 13.1 can be used in classroom assessment procedures. Often, however, it is necessary to think beyond this list and consider what a given assessment means for a student who has different instructional goals from those of the rest of the class. Here creativity, sensitivity, and communication with colleagues, school professionals, family members, and students are essential. Appropriate solutions will vary from one situation to the next. Information about working with students with disabilities is also available at the Web site for the National Center on Educational Outcomes (the link is provided on the Web site for this text).

www.wiley.com/college/odonnell

Administering, Scoring, and Communicating Assessment Results

Once an assessment has been developed, a new phase begins. The teacher has to administer and score the assessments and provide feedback to students. These may seem almost like clerical activities, but they can be done well or poorly, and the impact on students can be substantial.

Administering Assessments. Although as educators we want assessments to be engaging and appealing to students, students need to take assessments seriously, and, without engendering undue anxiety about the outcome, teachers need to make sure that they do. For in-class assessments, set aside a specific time and inform students of the schedule. When appropriate, specify time limits and follow them, but be sure to allow enough time for students to complete their work without feeling rushed. Classrooms should be quiet for in-class assessments and distractions minimized. Students should have a clean area to work on their assessment, and the necessary equipment (pens, pencils, erasers, rulers, calculators) should be readily available.

For projects or presentations, whether completed in class or out of class, rules and expectations need to be explicit. Communicate due dates to students as well as the consequences associated with failure to meet the deadline. Do not, however, establish a rule without considering possible exceptions and what to do about them. If points are to be deducted for overdue projects, what will happen, for example, if a student is ill or there is a death in the family? What about less serious impediments to progress ("We had to go to my grandmother's for her birthday")? If a project is to be completed largely outside of the classroom, the teacher should make clear the kinds of assistance that a student can appropriately receive.

Younger students are less able to allocate their time wisely than are older students. It is frequently helpful to build intermediate checkpoints into a longer project, such as the due dates for an outline and for a rough draft or for a schematic of a poster. We can all remember the last-minute panic of a neglected project. Help your students keep such experiences to a minimum.

Giving Feedback. When an assessment is handed back to students, it is a communication about how well they did on the particular assessment and how well they are doing in the class in general. Waiting for an assessment to be returned can be a source of anticipation, apprehension, or even anxiety for students. The communication itself can produce pride, excitement, disappointment, clarity, or confusion. If the assessment is a paper-and-pencil assessment (and the vast majority of formal and informal assessments in school are), this process begins with what a teacher writes on a paper. The effect on the student between "You missed the point here" and "This isn't exactly what I was looking for" is very different. The first communication finds fault with the student's response. The second accepts the response while indicating that there was an alternative closer to the mark. With forethought and awareness of some principles for marking papers, communications to students can engender a sense of self-efficacy and cognitive growth.

Be objective and specific. Students cannot learn from their mistakes or their successes unless they receive objective feedback about their efforts (Elawar & Corno, 1985; Sadler, 1989). This feedback must accurately reflect how well the student has done. In the abstract, it is easy to think that one would always grade accurately, not being overly generous or harsh about a certain answer on an assessment, but this can be difficult for teachers in individual cases. For example, if the student is Miriam, who has worked very hard to master the material, it may be difficult to mark as wrong an answer that is nearly correct. It may seem the kind thing to do, but it may not help Miriam understand material that she needs to know.

Uncommon Sense

Mistakes Are Bad—Or Are They?

The British comedian and comic actor John Cleese of *Monty Python* fame has also starred in a film used in management courses about making mistakes. In the film, Cleese argues that mistakes are wonderful things because they let us know that we are off course in a certain endeavor and need to get back on course. Students' mistakes on assessments can be viewed in the same fashion. An incorrect solution to a mathematics problem is a message from a student. It says, "I'm not really sure how to work these problems, and here is the nature of the difficulty I'm having." This is a golden opportunity to intervene and provide the kind of feedback that will move the student from not knowing to knowing.

Sometimes all the teacher needs to do is let the student know an answer is wrong; the student may not have realized it. In other situations, a simple corrective suggestion is appropriate. This is particularly true in marking essays. Teachers are not the editors of student work; teachers provide feedback to make students better writers. The best comment on an essay may be something such as, "There are four grammatical errors on this page; find them and correct them." In still other situations, the teacher can point out that the student's solution leads to a logical inconsistency or is an unreasonable possibility (e.g., "But if Ed is 6 times as old as Mary, and according to your answer Mary is 34, how old would that make Ed?").

Wrong answers are a window into the student's cognitive processes. Take a look in.

Feedback should also be specific. Students need to know exactly what they have done well or poorly (Brookhart, 2001; Guskey, 2001). Merely telling students that they have done a good job is not enough to engender learning, particularly when the students can see that almost everyone else in the class has received the same response. Keep in mind that being specific does not necessarily mean providing the right answer. (See the "Uncommon Sense" box on this page for types of feedback.)

Focus on the positive and on growth. A paper that is returned with only criticisms on it can be very discouraging. If the teacher does not notice the really well-written paragraph that the student has struggled with or the math problem on which the student has worked through several false starts to reach a correct answer, the student may begin to wonder whether all the effort was worthwhile. Learning is the process of moving from one state to another. Therefore, whenever possible, try to think about students' past work in comparison to their current work. Students need to see and be reminded of the progress they are making, and portfolios can be valuable for this purpose. Two similar papers may mean very different things. Although they should receive the same grade (if they are being graded), the comments written on them might be quite different. For Martine, this paper may represent real progress, whereas for Edouard, it might be a disappointing effort. (See the "Taking It to the Classroom" box on this page for types of feedback.)

What Does this Mean to Me?

How have you reacted to comments on papers from your teachers and professors?

Student Conferences. Without full and rich communication from a knowledgeable and concerned teacher, students are left on their own to interpret the success or failure of their efforts and can draw the wrong conclusions about their work. The best way to communicate with students is by means of a conference, or conversation. Conferences allow for finding common ground, for misunderstandings to be cleared up, for elaboration of issues and concerns. They let the student respond to the feedback given by the teacher. Teachers often use conferences to discuss essays or other major projects, but it can also be very useful to talk with students about their performance on a test, even a multiple-choice test. The goal of a conference is to help students better understand their efforts, whether positive or negative. It can also help the teacher better understand the student's progress and decide on the next set of learning steps.

Conferences involve communication in both directions. Avoid simply presenting opinions, pointing out weaknesses, and probing for information. Provide reactions, but also ask students for theirs. Stiggins (2004) does an excellent job of describing student/teacher conferences that are informative, positive, and student-centered. He recommends that teachers prepare for the conference by reviewing student work. Focus on listening, and make the conferences relatively brief—a few minutes might do.

Taking It to the Classroom

Marking Student Papers: Being Objective, Specific, and Growth-Oriented

Less desirable comments	More desirable comments
A lot of errors in this area.	See whether you can find four grammatical errors in this section and correct them.
This paragraph is poorly worded and unclear.	I think this paragraph makes the reader work too hard. See whether you can tighten it.
This is hardly your best work.	This looks a little hurried. It doesn't show the care I saw in your last paper.
This is not what we discussed in class.	You're off target somewhat here.
You can't reach the right answer if you are sloppy in your calculations.	You've got the idea, but check your work.
Awkward construction.	Reread this sentence and see whether it says what you want it to.
Redo this.	Try this again.
Excellent job here.	Your use of metaphor here is strong.
Great, I love this.	Think of how much more effective this argument is than in the paper you did last week.

Interpreting Classroom Assessments

Appendix

Interpreting Assessments

The results of assessments are best understood in light of your instructional goals and help you focus on the kind of useful information that can be gleaned from the assessments (*PRAXIS*™, II. C. 6, *INTASC*, Principle 8).

Following some simple procedures can help ensure that assessments truly inform instruction. The first step in interpreting classroom assessments is to reflect once again on the purpose of the assessment. How closely is the content and format related to the instruction that it is designed to assess? Is there other information that can be gleaned from it (such as development of writing skills in an essay based on a social studies unit)? Keeping the overall purpose in mind prevents teachers from focusing on the readily accessible aspects of an assessment and losing sight of its overall goal. For example, when grading essays, teachers sometimes start grading primarily for grammar and lose sight of the development of ideas contained in that essay. On a mathematics assessment, it is possible to focus too heavily on computational issues and not enough on whether the student seems to understand the broader instructional ideas.

Just a few minutes in a one-to-one setting in a student conference can reap great rewards in terms of teacher understanding and student enthusiasm.

(Andrew W. Levine/Photo Researchers, Inc.)

Comparing Performance with Expectations

Children do not always perform as teachers expect they will on assessments. Surprises and disappointments are due in part to the students' performance and in part to the teacher's expectations. Expectations develop fairly naturally once a teacher has worked with a group of students. Although it is very important not to let such expectations affect the grading of student papers, they should affect the interpretation of the assessment and the communication to the student. The work that a student hands in at any given point in time is part of an ongoing thread of work that must be revisited from time to time to assess that student's growth properly. Remember, growth is one of the underlying principles of assessment. (See the "What Kids Say and Do" box below.)

What Kids Say and Do

Points of Departure

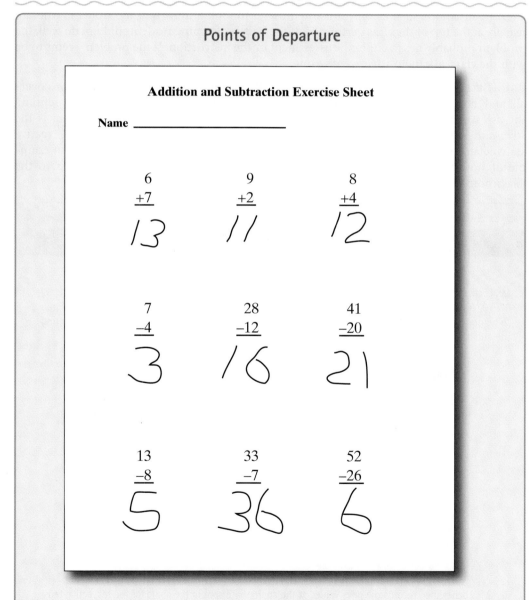

This is a math assessment from a young boy with moderate learning difficulties. It shows that he has acquired a good command of the addition problems and most of the subtraction problems. However, he still has some difficulty with subtraction problems in which the subtracting value is greater than the ones digit in the subtracted value. To understand the kind of performance this represents for this student (progress, no change, or decline), the teacher should have a very good idea of his recent progress and know what to expect.

Looking at Assessment Results for the Class as a Whole and Individuals. In looking at assessments, teachers need to consider both the class as a whole and individual students. At the high school level, teachers do this when assigning letter grades to assessments. At the elementary school level, looking both at individual students and the class as a whole can help teachers decide whether the class needs to review certain concepts or is ready to move on to new material.

When the class in general does not do well on a particular aspect of an assessment, there could be a variety of explanations. First, perhaps the problem lies in the assessment itself. Did the students understand the instructions? Was there a mistake, a typographical error, or a possibility for misinterpretation? Second, perhaps the problem has to do not with the students but with the instruction. If there is nearly unanimity on a wrong response, it might be time to take a serious look at how the instruction was delivered with respect to this content. Finally, the problem may in fact have to do with the students. Perhaps they did not understand the expectations for performance, or there was simply a general letdown in performance. In situations such as this, it is often useful to look at how well the students who are usually at the top of the class performed. If the best-performing students did not do well, the problem probably lies in either the assessment or the instruction. If the problem seems to be with the class, ask them what went wrong.

Data-Based Determinations of Next Steps. Evaluating how well the class performs overall and how well individual students perform is also useful for revising and refining the assessment. A useful tool for summarizing information from assessment data is the *stem-and-leaf diagram*. This tool was invented by John Tukey (1975), a remarkably creative statistician who is also credited with coining the computer terms *bit* and *software*. An example of how to construct a stem-and-leaf diagram is presented in the "Taking it to the Classroom" box on this page.

Taking It to the Classroom

Using a Stem-and-Leaf Diagram

Mr. Locher has 23 scores from an assessment he has given: 78, 64, 94, 83, 80, 91, 84, 86, 83, 57, 88, 97, 62, 79, 70, 75, 82, 80, 93, 91, 89, 86, and 90. He wants to get an idea of how his class scored as a group, so he organizes them using a stem-and-leaf diagram. He begins by drawing a vertical line and entering the numbers from the tens column on the left of the line; this is the stem (Figure 13.4, Graph A).

Graph A	Graph B	Graph C	Graph D
9	9	9 ǀ 7	9 ǀ 7
9	9	9 ǀ 41310	9 ǀ 01134
8	8	8 ǀ 6896	8 ǀ 6689
8	8	8 ǀ 304320	8 ǀ 002334
7	7 ǀ 8	7 ǀ 895	7 ǀ 589
7	7	7 ǀ 0	7 ǀ 0
6	6	6	6
6	6	6 ǀ 42	6 ǀ 24
5	5	5 ǀ 7	5 ǀ 7

Mr. Locher then records the ones values at the appropriate spot in the chart for the respective tens values; these are the leaves. Graph B shows the first score in the list, 78, in its place in the middle part of the figure. Mr. Locher enters the remaining scores in the same fashion, which produces Graph C. He finalizes the stem-and-leaf diagram by arranging the numbers within a row from lowest to highest, as in Graph D. He can now examine the distribution of scores without losing any of the original values. Note that because there are no scores in the 65–69 range, he has left a blank space in the graph. Mr. Locher can now see at a glance that on this assessment, only one student did exceptionally well (a 97); a number of students had solid to strong scores (80–94); and a few had difficulty with the assessment (57, 62, 64).

The results discussed in the box suggest that most students have a fairly solid understanding of the material but that some are struggling. In addition, many students may be having difficulty with one or two aspects of the unit. The teacher can investigate this by looking at the performance of the class on the various sections of the assessment and deciding to review some of the material with all of the class and to work more intensively with a few students.

Reflecting on Assessments to Improve Them

Once the assessment and feedback process has been completed, it is time to reflect on the assessment itself. In the first years of teaching, teachers feel they never have time to reflect on anything, but it is worthwhile to make the effort. Consider the following set of questions as a guide:

- How do the results look as a whole?
- What did I expect? Were there surprises?
- What was particularly difficult for students? For example, why did students pick a certain wrong option on a multiple-choice test?
- What seemed to confuse students? For example, are there items that students who really seemed to know the material got wrong? Why did some of the best students miss the idea behind an essay question?
- Did any of the students take an especially novel and/or useful approach to a performance assessment that I can incorporate next time around?
- How did the students respond to the assessment? Did they find it useful?
- How can I improve this assessment? Should I make changes in the instructions? In the actual tasks?

Good assessment practices now can help you in future years as well. Accumulate good assessments; measurement specialists call this an **item bank** or a **test bank**. Storing assessments electronically along with notes on what worked well and what needs to be revised saves a great deal of time later on. Remember to make revisions each year to ensure that the assessment matches the instruction for *that* year.

item bank A collection of test or assessment items for use in future assessments. Also called *test bank*.

Developing a Grading System

Grading occurs to some degree at all educational levels, but it differs markedly from the elementary to the secondary school levels. At the primary, elementary, and, to some extent, middle school levels, grading is mainly formative. At the secondary school level, grading is far more summative in nature and often plays a critical role in students' attainment of their college aspirations. The specific system teachers develop can have profound effects on both the affective and the cognitive growth of their students.

Teachers need to develop a system for grading that allows them to keep track of the progress of all their students and lets students know how well they are doing on an ongoing basis. Recall the three principles of grading and assessment described earlier in the chapter: communication, fairness, and growth. Keeping these principles in mind will help ensure that the grading system will be fair and encourage students' best efforts.

Options for Grading Systems

A remarkable number of options and alternatives are available (Brookhart, 2004; Guskey, 1994). Because grading systems differ substantially at different educational levels, it is useful to look at the options that are best suited to each level.

Grading Options at the Primary Level. At the primary level, grading is concerned primarily with the development of the skills, learning behaviors, attitudes, and dispositions that will be necessary for student success in later years. Grading systems can be quite elaborate, as can be seen in the example presented in Figure 13.5. Each area of development, such as social skills, work habits, and the academic areas, is associated with a series of behaviorally oriented statements. These statements are rated by the teacher; other ratings may include:

- Exceeds expectations
- Meets expectations
- Needs improvement

New Carrington Elementary School						
Pupil Progress Report	**Student Name** _____					

Rubric for Effort in Class Activities			**Rubric for Progress in Standards**			
O	Consistently Outstanding		M	Displays Complete Mastery		
G	Good Effort Most of the Time		P	Progressing Toward Mastery		
N	Needs Improvement		N	Not Near Mastery at This Time		

English Language Arts	1	2	3	4	Final
Reading					
Sounding out words					
Fluency Reading					
Working with text					
Extending meaning beyond text					
Mathematics					
Number Sense and Operations					
Knows numbers up to 1000					
Knows addition and subtraction facts					
Basic comprehension of fractions					
Measurement					
Can measure common objects with ruler					
Can tell time					
Understand basic concept of weight					

Classroom Behavior (Only Effort Marks Here)				
Takes responsibility for own behavior				
Works well with classmates				
Follows directions				
Hands in homework on time				
Follows rules and routines of the class				
Sustains effort to complete assignments				

Figure 13.5. Primary School Report Card

It may seem odd that the youngest children get the most detailed and complicated report cards. But young children's abilities and knowledge change dramatically from year to year. By the time children have completed their primary school years, kindergarten through third grade, they will have learned to read at a basic level and do mathematics through simple word problems and multiplication tables; they will be able to work together with other children and will understand the rules of proper school behavior; their vocabulary will have increased by thousands of words; and they will have figured out which bus to get on to come home. The changes that occur during this relatively short period are probably greater than those that will occur at any other time of their lives (except perhaps the five years before they entered school). A detailed grading and reporting system is entirely appropriate. The grades that students receive on report cards should always be based on real evidence from the classroom, not on impressions at the end of a marking period. Keeping good records for each child on a regular basis greatly facilitates accurate and productive communication on report cards.

Grading Options at the Upper Elementary and Middle School Levels. At the upper elementary and middle school levels, a shift usually occurs in grading and reporting systems. Letter grades are usually introduced in third or fourth grade, although they are often accompanied by comments about behavior and student growth as well. Work habits and social skills are also rated. This can be seen as a transitional report card, moving from the formative report cards of the primary years to the summative report cards of the secondary level. At the upper elementary level, grades may not be seen as critical, but they set patterns and expectations and

Student report card
MARTINSDALE REGIONAL HIGH SCHOOL
HOME OF THE *PURPLE MARTINS*

Student Name: Henry Melton

Student ID: 100334

Grade: 10

Comment Codes:

1. Excellent Work	5. Behavior problems
2. Homework Missing	6. Improving
3. Needs to try harder	7. Conference needed
4. Absent or tardy often	8. Poor attitude

Marking System (Note: Plusses and minuses may be given for grades A-D.)

A	Superior Performance
B	Above Average
C	Average
D	Below Average
F	Failing

Ref#	Title	Teacher	Period	Marking Period 1	2	3	4	Final
017	English 10 Honors	Arrone	1	A- 1				
043	Geometry CP	Fermat	2	B				
003	French 4	Velez	3	B 3				
093	Chemistry I	Chandra	5	C 2				
105	U.S. History	Johnson	7	B-				
607	Choral Music	Sills	9	B				

Term GPA: 2.90   Cumulative GPA: 3.12

Absent: 2 days Tardy: 0

Figure 13.6. High School Report Card

are sometimes used to determine access to special courses (e.g., advanced math courses) and gifted-and-talented programs. At the middle school level, some students will be taking high school level courses; almost all students will have different teachers for each subject, and the transition to a high school type of report card will have been made in most districts.

Grading Options at the Secondary Level. At the high school level, grading has become rather complicated in recent years. With the increased emphasis on applicants' high school record for college admissions, the importance of high school grades has grown markedly (Smith, 2003). Traditionally, high schools have used a grading system based on a five-point scale corresponding to the A–F grading system. The points possible are A = 4, B = 3, C = 2, D = 1, and F = 0. Decimals are used for plus or minus grades (e.g., B+ = 3.2). The numerical values are combined into a grade point average, and the averages are ranked from highest to lowest to produce class rankings.

Most colleges use grade point averages or class rankings as an important factor in admissions decisions. In addition, admission to honor societies and the selection of valedictorians and salutatorians are determined by class rank. In recent years, many high schools have adopted systems in which additional points are given for performance in honors courses. In some high schools, it is possible to have a grade point average above 4.0 and still not be in the top 10% of the class. Each year, it seems, newspapers carry stories about students suing high schools over the selection of the valedictorian or how the grade point average was calculated in a given situation. For each story that reaches the news, dozens are battled out in the principal's office or a school board meeting. Grading at the secondary level is a serious matter.

Most reporting systems at the high school level are fairly similar. Figure 13.6 presents an example of a high school report card. As can be seen, the report card presents term and cumulative grade point averages.

Record Keeping for Grading

Good record keeping is the mark of a professional in almost any field; in teaching, it is absolutely critical. A high school math teacher with more than 100 students in a given year would find it impossible to keep track of their progress and assign grades fairly without a strong record-keeping system. A kindergarten teacher who observes a child reaching out to help another child for the first time wants to keep a record of that for a parent/teacher conference. If it were just one child and one event, the teacher could rely on memory. But with 24 children and hundreds of events, she must have a system for keeping track of this valuable information.

Record Keeping with Technology. For centuries, grade books were the standard mechanism for record keeping, and they are still the most widely used method. However, electronic record books are replacing paper grade books. The Web site for this text lists some excellent resources in this area, although a teacher can benefit from the same flexibility and

Student Name	Start of Semester Comments	Knowledge of Math Facts/ Concepts		Mathematical Thinking			Homework Checks	End of Marking Period Comments
				Concept Tests	Journal Entries			
		Quiz 1 20	Quiz 2 20	1 50	1	2		
Adams, Nancy	Made good progress last marking period	18	20	44	3	3	YYYYNNYYYY	Working hard, progress continues. Need to focus on concepts.
Blanco, Maritizia	Still uncertain of some facts	14	14	42	2	2	YYNNNYYYYY	Picked up strongly near end of marking period. Increased parent support?
Caperton. Maurice	Very strong in all regards	19	19	48	3	2	YYYYYYYYYY	Continues excellent work. Maybe provide opportunities for enrichment.
Denali, Brooke	Needs to build confidence	17	15	41	2	2	YNYNYYYYYY	Still shaky on confidence level. Needs to experience success.
Hortons, Justin	Ability is there, but careless	13	14	44	2	1	NNYNYYNYYY	Needs a bit of a wakeup call. Enlist parent support. Emphasize potential.
Jackson, Renaldo	Needs a lot of review on facts	13	12	38	3	2	NNNYNNNYN	Still a lot of difficulty. May want to enlist school-based support on this.

Figure 13.7.
Record Keeping with a Spreadsheet

organization by using any standard spreadsheet program or even a basic word-processing program. Figure 13.7 shows an example of a simple but effective use of a spreadsheet program for record keeping.

Helping Students Develop a Sense of Responsibility for Their Grades. As discussed earlier, one of the goals of a good assessment and grading system is to encourage students to take responsibility for their grades. To do this, they must fully understand the grading system and be kept up to date on their progress. This requires that students' work be graded and returned to them quickly and with appropriate comments. Teachers can help students keep track of their progress by providing students with a summary of their grades at several points during the marking system. This does not have to be more involved than letting students look at their record to date (but make sure they cannot look at other students' as well).

Teachers often assign more graded work toward the end of the marking period, leaving students in the dark about how well they are doing until late in the period. Regular evaluation, rapid and thorough feedback, and open communication are the mechanisms through which students can take responsibility for their grades.

Chapter Reference
Chapter 14 presents a practical approach to determining what levels of performance on an assessment should be graded A, B, and so on.

Communicating with Parents

Imagine that the parent of Justin Traub, a fourth-grade student, is going to a parent/teacher conference. Compare the following two possible scenarios.

Conference 1

The teacher is writing at her desk as Mr. Traub stands in the doorway. Mr. Traub is not certain whether to walk in, knock on the open door, or just announce himself. A student desk is in front of the teacher's desk. Twenty seconds later, Ms. Wolf looks up.

Ms. Wolf: Come in, please.

Mr. Traub: Thank you. *(He is not certain where he is supposed to sit, but the desk in front of the teacher's desk seems to be the best choice.)*

Ms. Wolf: Let's see. We're running a little late. You must be, let me see, Mr. Traub, Justin's father.

Mr. Traub: Yes. Good evening.

Ms. Wolf: Well, Justin. I have his materials here somewhere. Yes, here they are. Just a second. Well. Justin's not off to what I would call a terrific start. Although he seems quite good in math for the most part, he's really quite a weak writer. This is something that needs a lot of attention. He does have quite a sense of humor.

Conference 2

The teacher comes to the doorway to greet Mr. Traub. There is a table with three chairs around it that are big enough for adults to sit in. On the table is a set of student materials. There is also a coffee pot with a plate of Danish pastry nearby.

Ms. Wolf: Hi, good evening. I'm Mrs. Wolf, Justin's teacher. Please come in and have a seat.

Mr. Traub: Thank you. I'm Jack Traub, Justin's dad.

Ms. Wolf: Would you like some coffee and Danish? I'd join you, but in all honesty, you're my fifth conference of the night.

Mr. Traub: No thanks, I just ate.

Ms. Wolf: It's great having Justin in my class. He's got such a great sense of humor.

Mr. Traub: He doesn't display it too often, I hope.

Ms. Wolf: I rein him in from time to time, but he's got a pretty good sense of boundaries. I've got some of his work for you to look at. I thought we'd start with math; Justin is really progressing beautifully here. Here's his most recent assessment. Look at how he details all his responses.

Mr. Traub: He talks a lot about being a scientist when he grows up. He says that way he'll get to do exciting stuff and not have to write a lot.

Ms. Wolf: Writing *is* something we need to work on. I try to have students write in the areas of their interest. Perhaps we can find out which of the sciences Justin is most interested in and work on writing skills in that area.

Mr. Traub: You know, he really loves astronomy . . .

Same child, same parent, same information, different Ms. Wolf: Which one would you like to have teaching *your* child?

Most beginning teachers are not parents themselves. Communicating with parents about student progress frequently means talking to people who might be closer to their parents' generation than their own. This can be a bit daunting and, unfortunately, sometimes causes beginning teachers to avoid communicating with parents. Parents and teachers are partners in the enterprise of helping children learn, and parents are more nervous about conferences than teachers are.

Feedback on how well their child is doing in school is highly important to most parents. The girl who seems to fade into the background in a class, sometimes performing well, sometimes not, is the light of her parents' lives. A student who seems listless and bored may be car-

www.wiley.com/college/odonnell

Parent/teacher conferences provide the opportunity to learn more about students and to share hopes and concerns for students. (Bob Daemmrich/ The Image Works)

ing for several younger siblings after school. A boy who is a behavior problem in school may be a model child at home. A teacher has a classful of students; parents sometimes only one.

Parent/Teacher Conferences

Appendix

Parents and Assessment Results

The results of your classroom assessments can provide you with important information that you will share with parents or guardians. Such communications will be an important part of your ongoing relationships with parents/guardians in working together to best help students. Awareness of the background of the family will help you to maximize the value of these communications (*PRAXIS*™, II. C. 6; III B, *INTASC*, Principles 6, 8).

The primary form of teacher-to-parent communication is the regularly scheduled parent/teacher conference. This is a very important interaction from several perspectives (Smith et al., 2001). First, it opens up communication between the parent and the teacher. Second, it is a communication between the teacher and the community. During parent/teacher conferences, a teacher might be talking to dozens of sets of parents or other caregivers. The success or failure of these conferences reflects on the role of the teacher in the community. Comments about them are almost certain to be passed on to a principal, supervisor, or board member. Following some simple rules can ensure successful parent/teacher conferences.

Successful teachers consider the classroom their home and parents their guests. They know who is coming into the room and make certain they feel welcome. More than anything else, the teacher wants parents to know he or she is on the child's side. Teachers and parents are a team working in the best interests of their child. If parents believe that the teacher likes their child and has the child's best interests at heart, they will be much better able to hear and process teacher perceptions of the child's strengths and weaknesses. If they sense that a teacher does not like their child or considers the child a burden, they will be defensive (and appropriately so). The teacher's first task, so to speak, is to bring the parents over to the teacher's side of the desk. It is wise (perhaps critical) to start on a positive note. Tell a story that puts the child in a good light. Focus first on the student's area of greatest strength. Keep in mind that even if the student is only average in this area, *it is the student's greatest strength* and, therefore, potentially the most important area of development for that student. Bring up issues that need to be worked on after you have developed rapport with the parents, and frame these not as problems but as areas for growth that you, the parents, and the student can work on together.

Note that the people coming for a conference about Heather Jackson may not be "the Jacksons." They may be Heather's mother and stepfather. Heather's mother may be using her maiden name. Neither of them may be Jacksons. There are probably records that include the names of each student's caregivers, or you can ask students who will be coming to the conference. When uncertainty arises, the following greeting should work: "Good evening. I'm Heather's teacher, Carmen Monroe. Please come in." This gives visitors a chance to explain who they are as they introduce themselves.

Parents' time is valuable. If it is necessary to finish notes from the conference with the previous set of parents, ask for the parents' indulgence, and finish up quickly. And do not forget to smile. (See the "Taking It to the Classroom" box below.)

Taking It to the Classroom

What Makes a Good Conference?

Good parent/teacher conferences usually contain the following:

- A warm greeting for parents as soon as they come into the room
- A place for parents to sit (Anticipate that some of the parents are large; do not make them sit in a chair designed for a 6-year-old.)
- A welcoming demeanor on the part of the teacher
- A positive beginning
- An attitude of being *on the student's side*
- Notes on what the teacher wants to be sure to discuss
- Readily available student records and examples of student work (Note that if student work is displayed in the classroom, all students should be represented.)
- Specific, objective examples of problem areas that need to be addressed
- No comparisons to other students (even indirectly, such as, "Justin is the best math student in the class")
- An effort to work toward concrete suggestions and recommendations

Maintaining Communication

Many parents are eager to help their children in their schoolwork but are not sure what to do. During the parent/teacher conference, teachers need to gauge the parents' ability and willingness to work with their children. One approach is to set forth some options and see how the parents respond. For example, a parent with a strong mathematical background could help the child with math homework, and you could discuss with the parent the nature of that help. Another is to ask parents what thoughts or concerns they may have about how their child is progressing. The parent might provide a perspective on how to go about solving problems that is different from what has been presented in class and may be more helpful to the student. Some parents feel that helping their children with schoolwork is not their responsibility, or they simply do not have the time or academic ability. But most parents would like to contribute; finding a way for parents to work with their children can often be the most productive outcome of a parent/teacher conference.

Once established, the communication link should be maintained. This used to be quite difficult, because time during the workday usually is not available to either the teacher or the parent, and evening calls seem intrusive. Email, however, offers an effective way for parents and teachers to keep in touch. If possible, get parents' email addresses and have one to give to them, perhaps on a business card for safekeeping. Many school districts have a mechanism by which teachers can post homework assignments on the Internet. Teachers do not have enough time to email all students' parents every day or even every week but can achieve much with an occasional message such as, "Just wanted to let you know that I have read Justin's essay on the Hubble telescope, and it shows some real growth in organization and style." It takes less than a minute and could truly brighten a parent's day. It can also help establish or reaffirm a positive parent/teacher relationship. Teachers can also provide the following via email or online (with passwords for parents):

- Course grades (assessments, quizzes, reports)
- Unexcused absences
- Missed assignments
- Disciplinary concerns

Do not put in an email anything that you would not like see repeated or presented to someone else.

The lesson on parent/teacher communication is simple: Get in touch, stay in touch, and work together for the student's benefit.

RIDE

REFLECTION FOR ACTION

The Event

At the beginning of the chapter, you saw assessments on *The Scarlet Letter* from three high school classrooms. You were asked to present a critique of these assessments by determining what they were trying to measure and how you might have gone about the task differently. Now we will look at this question more systematically. Think about those three approaches to assessment, how you would improve them, and more important, what *your* approach would be.

Reflection RIDE

When you set out to construct an assessment, it is essential to begin with the goals or objectives for that assessment. If you do not know what the objective or achievement target (Stiggins, 2004) is, it is hard to evaluate the assessment. The goal or objective of reading literature is a particularly interesting problem. Why did these classes read *The Scarlet Letter*? To be able to say they read a classic piece of literature? To learn about the norms and mores of a different society? To see how an author can take an example from the past and impart lessons for today? To learn about literary style? To learn who Arthur Dimmesdale was?

What Theoretical/Conceptual Information Might Assist in Interpreting and Remedying This Situation? Consider the following.

Instructional Goals

Why do we read great literature? One source of information for thinking about the appropriate assessment approach is the goals or objectives related to the reading in question.

The Principles of Assessment and Grading

Do these assessments fairly represent what was taught in these classes? Does each student have an equal chance of doing well? Did the teacher clearly communicate expectations to the students? Do students know how they are to be graded on these assessments? How do the assessments promote the growth of the students? The principles of assessment and grading (communication, fairness, and growth) provide an excellent framework for assessing the assessments.

Assessment Options

What alternatives are there to the assessments presented at the opening of the chapter? Are the ones presented the best ones for assessing the goals of the instructional unit in relationship to the skills, knowledge, and abilities being taught?

Information Gathering RIDE

The easiest way to see whether the assessments reflect instructional goals and activities would be to visit the teachers and the classrooms. Of course, one could infer these goals and activities from the assessments themselves. It appears that Mr. Antoine is very much concerned about the students knowing the particulars of the novel. Ms. Baldwin's assessment focuses on applying information from the novel in a debate format. This emphasizes understanding broad themes in the novel and seeing how they relate to contemporary issues. Mrs. Chambliss's assessment looks at the issue of character development and appears to be an entertaining task. A potential problem in Mrs. Chambliss's approach is that some of the students may not have a strong background in modern American cinema; this might be particularly true of students from certain religious and ethnic backgrounds.

Decision Making RIDE

Each of the three assessment approaches has strengths and weaknesses.

- Mr. Antoine's approach will probably result in a thorough assessment of whether the students have read and understood the book. If he uses a good blueprint that is distributed to students before the assessment, it will help them to review the work and strengthen their comprehension of it. However, the assessment does not look very engaging and does not push the students to extend themselves in thinking about the novel.

- Ms. Baldwin's approach is novel and exciting, and it will encourage the students to look at the book from a new perspective and seek out other sources of information. However, it will not result in a broad assessment of students' comprehension of the material. Moreover, students who are good at seeking out and organizing information and are good debaters will have a distinct advantage over those who do not have those abilities. Were these skills taught as part of the unit that included reading the novel? Is this assessment fair?

- Mrs. Chambliss's very creative approach would probably be the most fun to do, especially for a film fan. However, it seems to rely heavily on a background in Hollywood cinema, and students may need to obtain outside help.

Each approach has its strengths and weaknesses. Using all three might be desirable, but the assessment would probably be unreasonably long. Perhaps you could use them in intervals throughout the unit. For example, you could break the traditional assessment into several quizzes. Perhaps you could assign and organize the debate at the beginning of the unit, with the actual debates being a cumulative activity. The casting assignment could be a homework assignment for students to do and share by presenting their choices and defending them in an end-of-unit social exchange.

Evaluation R I D E

Once you have made your choice or choices, you need to monitor your students' responses. How well did they seem to comprehend the material (based on the more traditional assessment)? Was the debate a source of excitement or just added work? Should you combine reading the novel with lessons on gathering information and debating the issues? Would it be better to save the debate for a later instructional unit on debates? Did the casting assessment go well, or did only some students participate? Did your approach to assessing students have them buzzing with excitement or dreading the activity? How well did your assessment enhance your instruction, and how much information did it add to your understanding of your students' progress?

Further Practice: Your Turn

Here is a second Reflection for Action task. Imagine that you have just graded an assessment for your class, and constructed a stem and leaf diagram of the results. They are a disaster. The students did much worse than you had expected. Only the two best students in the class did well, although they did very well.

R I D E What might have gone wrong? How can you find out what happened, and how you can avoid repeating this situation?

SUMMARY

- **What is the role of assessment in the instructional process?**

  Assessment is an integral part of the instructional process. Instruction and assessment should flow logically from clearly stated instructional goals, creating a seamless weave of learning and understanding of what has been learned.

- **How can teachers devise assessments that facilitate instruction and at the same time provide the information they need about students' progress?**

  Teachers can use a set of principles (communication, fairness, and growth) in reflecting on their assessment decisions and the consequences of those decisions. The processes are making sure students understand what is expected of them (communication), gathering information pertinent to instruction (validity), gathering enough information to make good decisions (reliability) and using assessment to enhance instruction (growth).

- **Of the many options teachers have for assessment, which are the best?**

  A wide variety of assessment options are available, some traditional and some more recent developments. These options have both strengths and weaknesses and are more or less useful for different purposes. For example, essays help teachers evaluate students' ability to pull material together, organize thoughts, and communicate clearly. However, they may not be as good for determining whether students have acquired a large and complex set of information. Performance assessments often allow students to display their creativity and how well they can apply the skills and knowledge they have acquired.

● **How can a teacher develop a grading system that is fair and that lets students take responsibility for their own learning?**

Grades should be based on assessments that reflect instructional goals and the instruction that has taken place in the classroom. Students should understand clearly what teachers expect of them and how their work will be graded.

● **How can assessment help students learn about their own strengths and weaknesses?**

Assessment provides students with the opportunity to demonstrate their accomplishments both to their teachers and to themselves. When teachers give, mark, and return assessments in a spirit of support for learning and growth, students will have the opportunity to view their strengths as areas to develop and their weaknesses as points for improvement.

● **How can teachers continually improve their assessment and grading practices?**

Continuous improvement requires an open mind, a conscientious and ongoing effort to improve, and the willingness to reflect in a systematic and meaningful way on one's assessment efforts. The principles of communication, fairness, and growth provide a structure for improving assessments. In addition, at any grade level, asking the students what they thought about the assessment will provide useful feedback.

● **How can teachers create and modify assessments to include learners who face special challenges?**

Teachers can make a variety of modifications in their assessments to give learners facing special challenges the opportunity to display their abilities. These modifications include extra time, a distraction-free place to work, and rewritten instructions to facilitate comprehension of the tasks on the assessment.

● **How do cultural differences among students and their parents affect the process of communicating progress?**

Parents and children from diverse cultural backgrounds may have different views of schooling and teachers, different aspirations for their children, and differing opportunities to participate in school events and activities. Teachers need to be sensitive to such differences and keep the lines of communication open. Teachers are accustomed to telling parents about their classrooms and expectations for students. With parents from different cultures, especially recent arrivals to the United States, it is important not to make assumptions about what parents know and to explain the instructional process thoroughly.

KEY TERMS

accommodations, p. 447
achievement targets, p. 444
alternative assessment, p. 438
assessment, p. 428
authentic assessment, p. 438
bias, p. 433
classified, p. 447
constructed response, p. 436
content/behavior matrix, p. 444
criteria, p. 445
distracter, p. 434
formative assessment, p. 431
higher order thinking skills, p. 435
individualized education program (IEP), p. 447
informal assessment, p. 443
item, p. 434

item bank, p. 453
journal, p. 442
matching, p. 436
multiple choice, p. 434
objectivity, p. 439
performance assessment, p. 439
portfolio, p. 442
products, p. 439
reliability, p. 433
rubrics, p. 445
standardized assessment, p. 430
standards-based assessment, p. 447
stem, p. 434
summative assessment, p. 431
test bank, p. 453
test blueprint, p. 444
validity, p. 432

EXERCISES

1. *Using the Principles of Assessment and Grading: Class Participation*

   Review the principles of assessment and grading presented in the chapter and determine how important class participation would be in determining the grades you would give your students. Consider the following:

   a. How will you encourage classroom participation if you do not count participation toward grades?

   b. If you do count participation, how will you take into consideration that some students are shy and do not want to participate?

   c. How will you count participation so that you will have a system that is reliable, valid, and free from bias?

2. *Evaluating Assessment Quality*

   Think about the best assessment activity you have participated in as a student, whether in elementary school, high school, or college. Write down the characteristics of that assessment activity. What made it high in quality? What level of freedom and what constraints were there? Did you know you were doing well or poorly as you were working on the assessment? If you did, how did you know? Now think about the worst assessment you have ever had. What specifically did you dislike about that assessment? How could it have been turned into a positive experience?

3. *Comparing and Contrasting Your Assessments*

   With one or two classmates, choose a topic and grade level for which all of you feel comfortable in developing an assessment, perhaps using a statewide standard. Work out your plans individually, then meet to discuss your efforts. Who has the most creative idea? Whose assessment seems to cover the intended achievement targets best? Discuss how your work reflects your views about students and the content of the material.

4. *Improving Assessments*

   Working with a partner or a small group of classmates, examine several assessments that you have had in your college courses, based on what you have learned from the chapter. For example, look at a midterm examination or a writing assignment. What would you do to improve these assessments? How do they line up with the principles of assessment and grading? What would you do to improve them?

5. *Moving from Standards to Developing Assessments*

   On the Web, find the statewide standards for your state in the areas that you think you might want to teach. (Nearly all state departments of education include statewide standards for each grade level and subject on their Web sites. A link to state departments of education is provided at the companion Web site for this book.) Choose one of your state standards and think about how you might assess that standard. Start by thinking about how you might teach that standard, then work from your instructional activities toward assessments. Try to develop assessment ideas using at least three of the assessment options discussed in the chapter. Even though the standard may seem to lend itself to a particular type of assessment, try to stretch your thinking to develop a second and a third approach.

You are a new teacher in your school district, and you have just received a copy of this memo from the superintendent to your principal, along with the *sticky note* asking you to be a member of the advisory committee. First, this is not really an invitation; it is a directive. It is also a good opportunity for you—as well as a lot of work.

Memo

To: All Principals
From: Dr. Ramirez, Superintendent of Schools
Re: Statewide Testing Results
Date: September 15

Our analysis of the scores from the statewide testing program is complete. Although there are areas in which we are doing well and should take pride, there is also more work to be done. In particular, we see difficulties in fourth-grade language arts, eight-grade science and mathematics, and eleventh-grade mathematics. Additionally, there are problems in various grade levels, especially when we disaggregate the test scores in different subject areas.

You will find attached to this memo an analysis for your school. Please review your results and write an action plan for your school. I think it would be best to form an advisory committee of teachers to participate in the development of your action plan. Dr. Novick, the test coordinator for the district, is available for consultation. We will hold a meeting of the executive staff in three weeks to review and discuss each school's plan.

Judy—
I'd like to have some "new blood" along with some veterans on this committee. Can I count on your participation?
Thanks—Marty

Standardized and Standards-Based Assessments

RIDE Reflection for Action

Faced with a set of assessment scores and a mandate for addressing problem areas from your school, your committee has to come up with an action plan. As you read this chapter, think about the following questions for the committee's work: What exactly is the situation for your school? Where are the strengths and weaknesses? How reliable and valid is the information that you have? What are some realistic options for improvement? How can you contribute to the work of the committee?

Guiding Questions

- What are standardized assessments, and where do they come from?
- How can a teacher make sense of the statistics and scales that come with these measures?
- What is the best way to interpret standardized test scores?
- How concerned should teachers be about issues of reliability and validity?
- How can teachers fairly assess students with learning and physical challenges?
- Is standardized assessment equally fair for students from different cultural backgrounds?

CHAPTER OVERVIEW

Standardized and standards-based tests are as much a fact of life in schools as taking attendance, recess, and water fountains. In this chapter, standardized and standards-based assessments are demystified. We will examine what these tests are, what they are used for, and how they are developed. We will consider the benefits gained from using such assessments as well as the problems associated with them. We will also look at the history of such tests and how to understand and interpret the scores, and we will consider controversies associated with standardized testing.

The Nature and Development of Standardized Assessment

- A Brief History of Standardized Assessments
- School Testing Programs
- Standards-Based Assessment
- College Admissions Testing
- Intelligence Testing
- Selecting Standardized Assessments
- Categories of Assessments

Technical Issues in Assessment

- Statistics Used in Assessment
- Scales
- Norms and Equating
- Setting Passing and Other Proficiency Scores
- Validity and Reliability

Interpreting Standardized Assessments

- Finding the Child in the Data
- Demystifying the Assessment Report
- Combining Standardized Results with Other Information
- Bringing the Child to the Classroom
- Thinking about the Classroom, School, and District Levels
- Looking at Scores for English Language Learners
- Looking at Scores for Students with Special Needs

Controversies in Assessment

- Bias in Testing
- High-Stakes Testing and Its Implications

The Nature and Development of Standardized Assessment

standardized assessment A measure of student ability in which all students take the same measure under the same conditions.

Chapter Reference
Chapter 9 contains an extensive discussion of educational objectives and standards.

Standardized assessments are tests given under standard conditions. That is, all students taking the test are given the same instructions, are tested in similar physical environments, have the same amount of time to complete the test, and have their tests scored in the same fashion. Standards-based assessments are a form of standardized test developed from a set of standards or objectives. Standardized tests serve a variety of purposes, ranging from determining who is most ready for kindergarten to selecting students for admission to college. For the classroom teacher, end-of-year achievement assessments are the most important form of standardized assessment, whether they are supplied by commercial publishing houses (school achievement assessment programs) or administered through a state department of education (standards-based assessments).

Educators refer to tests and assessments in different ways, and the differences are not completely clear. Generally speaking, a test consists of a set of questions that require student responses, which are graded as correct or incorrect, or scored according to a rubric. The point values are summed to create a total score. *Assessment* is a somewhat broader term that can include scores generated by performances or teacher judgments. Thus, a test is a type of assessment. A *measure*, or *measurement*, is any type of quantification of something. It can be a test, an assessment, or a measure of someone's height. Finally, *evaluation* is sometimes used to mean an assessment or a coordinated group of assessments toward a certain purpose (such as a special needs evaluation). Evaluation can also mean the process through which a program or activity is assessed in terms of its value (*evaluation* and *value* have the same root).

A Brief History of Standardized Assessments

Although standardized assessment can trace its history back over 2,000 years to the civil service examinations given in China (Green, 1991), modern testing really began in the late 1800s. Developments occurring during that period (roughly the 1880s to the early 1900s) in Germany, France, England, and the United States led to the forms of standardized testing that exist today. In Germany, the pioneering psychologist Wilhelm Wundt and his students began the serious examination of individual differences among humans. In England, Charles Darwin's cousin and contemporary, Francis Galton, was interested in the inheritance of intelligence. In the United States, James Cattell focused his efforts on vision, reaction time, and memory, among other characteristics.

In France, Alfred Binet worked to develop a series of mental tests that would make it possible to determine the *mental age* of students who were not performing well in public schools so that they might be assigned to the proper school for remedial work. Binet's work led to two fascinating and quite divergent developments. The first was the creation of the **intelligence test**, and Binet is rightly called the father of intelligence testing. His initial measure, intended to assess abilities in children ages 3 to 13, consisted of a series of questions of increasing difficulty and can be considered the first intelligence test (Wolf, 1973). The American psychologist Lewis Terman expanded on Binet's work to create the Stanford-Binet intelligence test, which is still in use today (Terman, 1916).

The second development arising from Binet's work occurred shortly after his death at a relatively young age. A young Swiss researcher named Jean Piaget came to work in the laboratory that Binet had established with his colleague, Theodore Simon. Piaget used many of the tasks and experiments that Binet had developed (such as the conservation task shown in Figure 2.5 on page 44), but he was more interested than Binet in finding out *why* children answered questions the way they did—especially the characteristic mistakes they made. Thus, Binet's work spawned not only intelligence testing but also Piaget's theory of cognitive development.

All testing at this time was done individually with a trained specialist. A student of Lewis Terman, Arthur Otis, was instrumental in the development of group testing, including objective measures such as the famous (or infamous) multiple-choice item (Anastasi & Urbina, 1997). His work led to the development of the Army Alpha and Beta tests, which were used extensively in World War I. From the 1920s through the 1940s, college admissions testing, vocational testing, and testing for aptitudes and personality characteristics all flourished, bolstered by the belief that progress in the quantification of mental abilities could occur in as scientific a fashion as progress in mathematics, physics, chemistry, and biology.

School Testing Programs

School testing programs began in the 1920s with the publication of the first Stanford Achievement Tests (Anastasi & Urbina, 1997). They were originally designed to help school systems look at the *overall effectiveness* of their instructional programs, *not the progress of individual children*. In keeping with the behaviorist approach to education and psychology that prevailed at the time, multiple-choice testing was favored because grading could be done in an objective fashion and machines could be used to score the tests. More programs developed over the decades, and from the 1960s on, the number of children taking standardized, end-of-year tests grew remarkably rapidly (Cizek, 1998). A fairly small number of companies publish the major school testing programs, which include the Iowa Test of Basic Skills, the Metropolitan Achievement Tests, the Stanford Achievement Tests, and the Terra Nova program. Although these programs usually provide tests for grades K–12, the primary focus has traditionally been on grades 2–8, with less emphasis on kindergarten, first grade, and the high school years.

Measurement specialists develop school testing programs by first looking at what schools teach and when they teach it. In recent years, the focus of this process shifted from school district curriculum guides to statewide assessment standards. These standards are examined

Chapter Reference
See Chapter 13 for a discussion of rubrics.

intelligence test   A measure of generalized intellectual ability.

Chapter Reference
Chapter 4 contains an extensive discussion of intelligence and intelligence testing.

Chapter Reference
Chapter 2 discusses Piaget's stages of cognitive development.

Standardized tests go through a number of trials with real children before the final forms are produced. (Media Bakery)

Chapter Reference
See Chapter 13 for a discussion of multiple-choice, constructed-response, and essay formats.

norming study The administration of an assessment to a representative national sample to obtain a distribution of typical performance on the assessment.

standards–based assessment
Assessments that are generated from a list of educational standards, usually at the state or national level; a form of standardized assessment.

www.wiley.com/college/odonnell

and reduced to a common set of objectives, organized by the school year in which they are taught. Often, compromises are necessary because different school systems teach certain things at different times, particularly in mathematics, science, and social studies. Tests are then developed to reflect a common set of objectives. Historically, these tests consisted primarily of multiple-choice questions, but recent editions include more essay and constructed-response items.

The draft versions of tests go through a number of pilot tests to ensure that they have good technical qualities (discussed later in the chapter). The final version is then tested in a major nationwide **norming study**, in which a large group of students (tens of thousands) take the test to see how well a representative national sample performs on the test. The results of the norming study are used to determine scales, such as grade-equivalent scores and percentiles, all of which are discussed later in the chapter.

Standards-Based Assessment

The most recent development in standardized school testing is **standards-based assessment** (Briars & Resnick, 2000; Resnick & Harwell, 2000). This approach to assessment is based on the development of a comprehensive set of standards (which look much like objectives) for each grade level in each subject area. The standards are then used to develop instructional approaches and materials, as well as assessments that are clearly linked to the standards and to each other. The primary distinction between standards-based assessment and the commercial school testing programs described earlier lies in the notion that standards, instruction, and assessment are all linked together, that assessment is not something to be added on once goals and instructional programs have been established. Standards-based assessment programs at the state level are a key element in the federal No Child Left Behind (NCLB) legislation that is so greatly influencing current assessment practices. It would be an excellent idea to look at the statewide assessment program in the state where you are planning to teach. The Web site that accompanies this text includes links to current information on standards-based assessment.

The No Child Left Behind Act. The No Child Left Behind Act (NCLB) became federal law in January of 2002. NCLB mandates that states comply with a series of regulations and meet achievement standards in order to receive federal assistance in education.

One of the primary requirements of the act is that each state develop an annual assessment program and that schools show regular progress toward meeting the goal that all students will reach high standards of achievement by the 2013–2014 school year. Test scores are broken down by variables such as ethnicity, income levels, and disability to examine gains in performance. Initially, the testing must take place in grades 3–8 in reading and mathematics, with science added by 2007. States have some latitude in the nature of the assessment program, but the federal government must approve the plans.

NCLB also requires that English language learners (ELLs) become proficient in English, that all students are taught by highly qualified teachers, and that students will learn in schools that are safe and free from drugs and that promote learning. Schools that do not meet the standards of NCLB will initially receive support from their states to improve, but if improvement does not occur, a series of sanctions will take place that could include replacing the teaching staff and administration of the school.

College Admissions Testing

Whereas school testing programs have been very important in the pre-high school years, college admissions testing has been the primary assessment concern of high school educators and students alike. College admissions testing has been in existence for a long time, but only fairly recently has it taken the form in which it exists today. In the 1920s, the first version of the SAT was used for college admissions testing (Aiken, 2003); in 1947, the test began to look more like the one in use today (Haladyna, 2002). There are two major college admissions testing programs. The older of these is the SAT, which used to stand for Scholastic Aptitude Test but the College Board, which runs the program, changed the name in 1994 to Scholastic Assessment Test. The College Board changed the name again in 2005 to simply the SAT. The SAT provides a verbal score, a quantitative score, and a writing score, each of which has a scale of 200 to 800. Each test has a *mean* (average) of 500 and a *standard deviation* (how far from the mean the scores tend to be) of 100. (Mean and standard deviation are explained further later in the chapter). A companion set of measures assesses abilities in a variety of specific subject areas; scores use the same scale.

The other major college admissions testing program is the ACT Assessment. ACT is an acronym for American College Testing program, but the program is now called the ACT Assessment. It provides scores in English, mathematics, reading, and science reasoning, using a scale of 1–36 that has a mean of roughly 20 and a standard deviation of 4–5. Starting in 2005, there is also a writing assessment that is optional (some colleges will require it; some will not).

Colleges use admissions tests in different ways. Some large state universities combine them with high school grade point averages, using a mathematical formula. The results of the combination determine admissions. Other colleges and universities use the tests in combination with grades, letters of recommendation, extracurricular activities, and personal statements in a more subjective process to arrive at admissions decisions. Some colleges do not use them at all. Considerable controversy exists concerning the use of college admissions tests and the potential biases associated with them. This is undeniably a sensitive issue in American education; we discuss this later in the "Controversies" section later in the chapter. (See the "Uncommon Sense" box on this page.)

Uncommon Sense
Technology Advances Testing—Or Does It?

Recent advances both in computers and in testing methodology have enabled computer administration of exams such as the Graduate Record Examination. Clear advantages to such administration exist, but so do disadvantages.

Among the advantages are the following.

- The test can be given at different times at different places.
- The selection of harder or easier items depending on how well the examinee performs reduces the time necessary to administer the test.
- Students receive their scores as soon as they finish the test.

Disadvantages include the following.

- On most computerized tests, the examinee cannot go back to reconsider a question after entering an answer into the computer.
- Reading passages require the examinee to scroll back and forth through the text.
- Test security is a big problem, because examinees do not all take the test at the same time.
- Some examinees are far less familiar and comfortable with taking exams by computer than are others.

RIDE Think back to the beginning of the chapter, where the superintendent and principal assigned you to a committee to look at your district's test scores. What can you find out about the test? If the test is a commercially available one, such as the ITBS (from Riverside Publishing) or the Terra Nova (from CTB/McGraw-Hill Publishing), you can find reviews of it in the MMY.

www.wiley.com/college/odonnell

Appendix
Types of Assessments
The requirements of the No Child Left Behind act have increases the importance of teachers' knowledge of various types of assessments and the kinds of information they can provide about students' progress (*PRAXIS*™, II. C. 2, *INTASC*, Principle 8).

criterion-referenced Term describing a method for understanding what assessment scores mean by referring them to some arbitrary standard.

norm-referenced Term describing scores that are given meaning by referring them to scores from other individuals or sets of individuals.

Chapter Reference
See Chapter 7 for more on behaviorism.

Intelligence Testing

If college admissions testing is a sensitive issue in American society, intelligence testing is a hypersensitive issue. Intelligence testing has a long and often not very attractive history. It began in the early 1900s with the work of Binet, described earlier, followed by that of Lewis Terman, Henry Goddard, and Charles Spearman in the United States. Originally designed for the admirable purpose of trying to help students with difficulties in learning, intelligence testing has been used for a host of less acceptable purposes, including prohibiting certain groups of people from immigrating to the United States (American Psychological Association, 1999). Today, intelligence testing in education revolves around the testing of students for purposes of special needs classification and selection for gifted and talented programs. The most widely used tests are the Wechsler Intelligence Scale for Children—Revised (WISC-R) and the Kaufman Assessment Battery for Children (K-ABC).

Selecting Standardized Assessments

There are standardized assessments for almost anything imaginable. There are standardized assessments for becoming a welder, for matching disabled people to animals that can help them in their lives (such as seeing eye dogs), or for determining people's lifestyles. You can find these and thousands of other assessments in a remarkable reference work titled *Mental Measurements Yearbook* (MMY; Plake, Impara, & Spies, 2003). MMY is a series of books published by the Buros Institute of Mental Measurements at the University of Nebraska. These books provide critical reviews of standardized assessments in all areas. Professionals in the field write the reviews, which are usually quite rigorous. MMY can be particularly helpful when a school or school district needs a standardized test for a particular reason. The Web site for this text lists the Web site for MMY.

Categories of Assessments

Assessments can be categorized in a variety of ways. Three of the most widely used categorization systems are:

- Norm and criterion referenced
- Achievement, aptitude, and affective measures
- Traditional and alternative assessments

Norm and Criterion Referencing. If you compare a score to a fixed standard, or criterion (90% and above = A, 80%–90% = B, etc.; or *passing* on the road test to get your driver's license), you are making a **criterion-referenced** interpretation of the score. If you compare a score to how well others did on the same test (70th percentile, above average, best in show), you are making a **norm-referenced** interpretation of the score. The concept of criterion versus norm referencing was developed in the early 1960s (Ebel, 1962; Glaser, 1963; 1968; Popham, 1978; Popham & Husek, 1969). The basic idea relates to the interpretation of the score. Consider, for example, that a student has just received a grade of 34 on an end-of-unit assessment in an algebra class. Is that grade good, okay, bad, or a disaster? It is hard to know without some sort of referencing system. If it is a percent-correct score, a 34 does not look very good. But if the test were the ACT with a maximum score of 36 were the maximum possible score, a 34 might be terrific. Another way to think about a score would be to know how it stacked up against the other scores in the class. A 76 might be right in the middle (an okay score), the best in the class (excellent), or near the bottom (time to get some help).

When criterion-referenced tests (CRTs) were first introduced, they were relatively short, focused on a single, well-defined objective or achievement target, and accompanied by a passing score that certified the student as having *mastered* the objective. A CRT was often a one-page multiple-choice or short-answer test. Educators used CRTs in instructional programs that were objective-based and often developed from a behavioral perspective, such as mastery learning.

Today, educators define the difference between criterion-referenced and norm-referenced testing in broader terms: Tests that use norm-based scores to give meaning to the results are norm-referenced tests; those that use an arbitrarily determined standard of performance to give meaning are criterion-referenced assessments.

Uncommon Sense

Aptitude Tests Predict Future Performance—Or Do They?

Recently, the idea of an aptitude test has fallen out of favor in educational circles, as has, to some extent, the distinction between achievement and aptitude tests. Scholars are concerned about whether students have had the opportunity to learn the material on an achievement test (and whether the test really measures achievement or instead measures the opportunity to have learned the material). They also question racial, ethnic, and gender differences in test results and whether tests whose results reveal such differences should be used for admissions and scholarship purposes. People now often talk about *ability* tests as simply a measure of a student's level of academic performance at a given point in time. Without knowing a student's educational history, a score on such a test does not imply a judgment about how the student attained his or present level of performance.

Achievement, Aptitude, and Affective Tests. Another way to classify tests is to decide whether one is assessing past achievement or predicting future achievement. An assessment that tries to measure what a student has been taught is called an *achievement test* (or assessment); one that is trying to predict how well students will do in future instruction is called an *aptitude test*. For example, the SAT, used by many colleges in deciding which applicants to admit, was originally called the Scholastic *Aptitude* Test. Intelligence tests are also used to predict future school achievement.

Assessment is not limited to what people know and can do; it also includes how they learn, how they feel about themselves, how motivated they are, and what they like and do not like. Issues related to an individual's attitudes, opinions, dispositions, and feelings are usually labeled *affective* issues. A large number of **affective assessments** are used in education, including measures of self-efficacy, self-esteem, school motivation, test anxiety, study habits, and alienation. Educational psychologists frequently use affective assessments to help them understand why some students do better in school than others. (See the "Uncommon Sense" box on this page.)

affective assessment An assessment related to feelings, motivation, attitudes, and the like.

Chapter Reference
Chapters 5 and 6 discuss issues such as self-efficacy, self-esteem, and motivation.

Traditional and Alternative Assessments. A third way of categorizing assessments is according to the form they take. When educators talk about traditional assessments, they are usually referring to multiple-choice tests, either standardized or for classroom use. Of course, teachers have used essay and short-answer tests for years; therefore, they might be considered traditional. As discussed in Chapter 13, a number of alternatives to traditional testing methods have evolved over the past 20 years. These include authentic assessment, performance assessment, portfolio assessment, and more broadly, alternative assessment.

Chapter Reference
Chapter 13 presents descriptions of various approaches to classroom assessment.

Summary of Categories of Assessment. You can classify any assessment using the following categories:

- Normative vs. Criterion-referenced
- Formative vs. Summative
- Achievement vs. Aptitude vs. Affective
- Traditional vs. Alternative

For example, a teacher might use an assessment that requires students to make an oral presentation to determine the final grade in a French course; this would probably be a criterion-referenced, summative, achievement, alternative assessment. It would be criterion-referenced because each student would receive a grade that would not depend on how well other students did. It would be summative because it would be used for grading. It would be an achievement assessment because it would measure learning in the course, and it would be alternative because it uses a format that does not rely on paper-and-pencil approximation of a skill but rather measures the skill directly.

How Can I Use This?
How would you classify a multiple-choice midterm examination in a college history course?

Technical Issues in Assessment

Appendix
Understanding Measurement
You will be better positioned to interpret the results from various assessments if you understand some basic concepts in measurement theory and assessment-related issue (*PRAXIS™*, II. C. 5, *INTASC*, Principle 8).

The technical issues involved in assessment can be daunting to educators at all levels; consequently, some educators shy away from them. However, with some foundational knowledge, all teachers can understand and discuss these issues.

Statistics Used in Assessment

Understanding standardized assessment requires a basic knowledge of some rudimentary statistical concepts concerning summarizing and communicating information about a group of scores. The first has to do with the notion of a typical or average score of a group of people, or the *central tendency*. The second has to do with how much the scores differ from one another, or their *variability*. The third concept is the *z-score*, a standardized numbering system for comparing individual scores against the group mean. The fourth concept is the *normal distribution*, also known as the *normal curve* (and sometimes informally called the *bell curve*), which is a useful mathematical representation of groups of scores. A final useful statistical concept, the *correlation coefficient*, is discussed in Chapter 1. It has to do with how closely two scores measured on the same group are related (such as how closely related height and weight are for a particular group of people). These are not complex ideas, but the mathematics underlying them can get complex. The focus in this chapter is on the ideas, not the math.

Chapter Reference
Chapter 1 presents a definition and discussion of the correlation coefficient.

central tendency An indicator of the center of a set of scores on some variable.

mean The arithmetic mean of a set of scores.

Central Tendency: Mean, Median, and Mode. The simplest way to convey information about the scores of a group of people on a test (or any other variable) is to describe what the middle scores are like. This is the **central tendency** of the scores. Using statistics, there are three measures of central tendency: the mean, the median, and the mode. The most widely used of these measures, the **mean**, is simply the arithmetic average of a group of scores. To obtain the mean, add all the scores together and divide by the total number of scores. Figure 14.1 presents a simple example.

The Scores

8	
5	Total = 8 + 5 + 10 + 5 + 7 = 35
10	
5	Mean = $\frac{35}{5}$ = 7
7	

> There are five scores here. Add them and divide by 5, and you have the *mean* of the scores.

Figure 14.1. Calculating the Mean

median The middle score of a set of scores that have been rank-ordered from highest to lowest.

The **median** is the middle score of a set of scores organized from the lowest score to the highest. It is very useful when a group of scores includes some extreme scores that might make the mean appear not to be representative of the set of scores as a whole. For example, the mean age of all the people in a kindergarten class is usually around 7. This is so because the children are around 5, and the teacher could be in her 30s or 40s. Therefore, the mean is not very useful in this case. The median (and the mode) would be 5, a number much more representative of the typical person in the class. Figure 14.2 shows how to obtain the median.

The Scores	The Scores Reordered from Lowest to Highest
8	5
5	5
10	7
5	8
7	10

> There are five scores here. If they are put in order from lowest to highest, the middle score, 7, would be the *median*.

Figure 14.2. Calculating the Median

Uncommon Sense

We Are All Rich!—Or Are We?

Statistics can be used to confuse. If you were sitting in a room with a billionaire and 19 other people who made just a decent salary, *on average* you would all be millionaires. In reality, however, there would just be one billionaire and 20 people who had to work to earn a living. Combining information in an unreasonable fashion is a common way to trick people into believing a situation or to make an argument that otherwise would not stand up. If something seems too good to be true, it probably is.

The **mode** is simply the score that occurs most frequently. Researchers use the mode in describing the central tendency of variables in situations in which the use of decimals seems inappropriate. For example, it is more reasonable to say that the modal family has 2 children, rather than saying that families have 2.4 children on average (Gravetter & Wallnau, 2004). In the example of the kindergarten classroom, the mode would be a good measure of the central tendency. (See the "Uncommon Sense" box above.)

mode The most frequently occurring score in a set of scores.

Variability: Variance and Standard Deviations. In addition to understanding where the center of a group of scores is, it is important to have an idea of their **variability**—that is, how they spread out, or differ from one another. Statisticians use several measures of variability. The focus here is on those that are most widely used and most important for assessment: the *standard deviation* and the *variance*. These both involve a bit more calculation than the measures of central tendency just discussed, but it is more important to understand the underlying concepts.

variability The degree to which scores on an assessment (or other variable, such as height or weight) are spread out.

The **variance** is the average squared distance of each score from the mean. To obtain the variance, subtract each score in a group of scores (perhaps all 10th graders in a school district on a statewide assessment), then square it. Do this for all the scores, then add them and divide by the total number of scores in the group. Figure 14.3 provides an illustration of this.

variance A measure of how much a set of scores is spread out.

The variance is widely used in statistical analysis, but it is not as practical as the standard deviation because the variance is in the form of squared units. That is, it tells you, on average, how far each score is from the mean *squared*. The standard deviation, on the other hand, provides a measure of the spread of the scores in the numbering system of the scores themselves. Calculating the standard deviation is easy once you have the variance: You simply take the square root of the variance to obtain the standard deviation, as shown in Figure 14.3.

Scores	Scores Minus the Mean (Deviations)	Deviations Squared
8	8 − 7 = 1	1
5	5 − 7 = −2	4
10	10 − 7 = 3	9
5	5 − 7 = −2	4
7	7 − 7 = 0	0

The squared deviations sum up to:
1 + 4 + 9 + 4 + 0 = 18
The variance is the sum of the squared deviations divided by the number of scores in the group:
$\frac{18}{5} = 3.6$

The standard deviation (SD) is simply the square root of the variance, or in this case:
$SD = \sqrt{3.6} = 1.897$

Figure 14.3. Calculating the Variance and the Standard Deviation

standard deviation   A measure of how far scores vary from the mean.

The **standard deviation** provides an index of how far from the mean the scores tend to be. If, in a large set of scores, the distribution of scores looks roughly normal (or bell-shaped), about 95% of the scores will fall within 2 standard deviations on either side of the mean. That is, if one goes up 2 standard deviations from the mean, then down 2 standard deviations from the mean, about 95% of the scores will fall between those two values. If a particular set of scores has a mean of 38, a standard deviation of 6, and more or less a normal distribution, about 95% of the scores would fall between 26 (2 standard deviations below the mean) and 50 (2 standard deviations above the mean). If the standard deviation were 15, the bulk of the scores would range from 8 to 68. If the standard deviation were 2, the scores would range from 34 to 42. (More information about the normal curve appears later in the chapter.)

In essence, the standard deviation provides an easy index of the importance of each individual point in a scale. SAT scores have a standard deviation of 100. Going up 10 SAT points is not a very big increase. ACT scores, on the other hand, have a standard deviation of roughly 4–5. Going up 10 points on an ACT score is a huge jump.

Z-scores. Earlier in the chapter, we discussed norm-referenced testing as a way to give meaning to a score by comparing it to those of others who took the same assessment. Determining the mean and the standard deviation of the scores for the assessment can accomplish this. Consider SAT scores again. They have a mean of roughly 500 and a standard deviation of roughly 100. A score of 550 would be one-half of a standard deviation above the mean. We could call that +0.5 standard deviations above the mean. A score of 320 would be 1.8 standard deviations below the mean, or −1.8.

z-score   A standard score that any set of scores can be converted to; it has a mean of 0.0 and a standard deviation of 1.0.

This concept is called a **z-score**; it is simply how many standard deviations away from its mean a given score is. If the score is above the mean, the z-score is positive. If the score is below the mean, the z-score is negative. The calculation for the z-score is simply the score minus its mean divided by its standard deviation. The formula looks like this:

$$z = \frac{(\text{score} - \text{mean})}{\text{standard deviation}}$$

For example, a student gets a score of 85 on a test. The mean for all the students in the class is 76, and the standard deviation is 6. The z-score is:

$$z = \frac{(85 - 76)}{6} = +1.5$$

This means that a raw score of 85 is 1.5 standard deviations above the mean for this group of students. When combined with a working knowledge of the normal curve, presented below, z-scores provide a lot of information. For example, imagine Maria took a physical fitness test that had national norms that were roughly normal (bell-shaped). Maria gets a raw score of 143. Is that score good, bad, or in the middle? If Maria's z-score on the fitness test were +1.0, that would mean she outperformed roughly 84% of the students in the norming group. A z-score of −1.0 would mean she outperformed only 16% of the students. You can see that the raw score does not present much useful information, but the z-scores tells us a lot.

normal distribution   A mathematical conceptualization of how scores are distributed when they are influenced by a variety of relatively independent factors.

Normal Distribution. The bell-shaped curve, often mentioned in conversations about testing and statistics, is more formally known as the **normal distribution**. It is actually a mathematical model or abstraction that provides a good representation of what data look like in the real world, particularly in biology and the social sciences. Technically, the scores are referred to as forming a *normal distribution*, and the mathematical model is the *normal curve*, although the two terms are informally used interchangeably. Many sets of test scores show a roughly normal distribution. The normal curve is depicted in Figure 14.4. Roughly speaking, normal distributions result when a number of independent factors contribute to the value of some variable.

In a perfectly normal distribution, 96% of the scores fall between 2 standard deviations below the mean and 2 standard deviations above the mean. Moreover, 68% of the scores fall between 1 standard deviation above the mean and 1 standard deviation below the mean. This can be seen in Figure 14.4. This figure provides a good reference for thinking about where scores are located in most roughly normal distributions. Many of the scales used in reporting standardized test scores are based on the concept of the z-score.

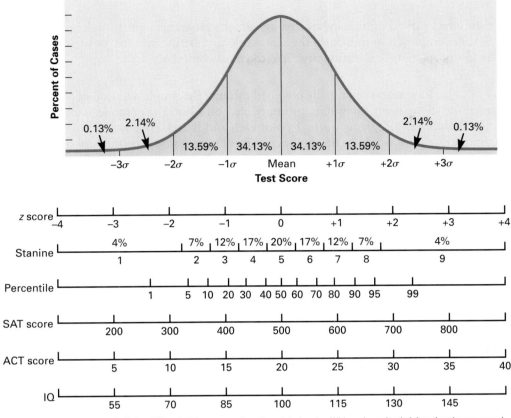

Note: SD stands for standard deviation. SAT and ACT scores are from the original scales. With each year's administration the means and standard deviations change slightly.

Figure 14.4. The Normal Curve and Assessment Scales

Using Statistics to Look at Groups of Scores. When looking at groups of scores, it is advisable to try to look at them from more than one perspective. The results presented on a standards-based assessment may highlight the number of students passing. But you should also look at the distribution of scores as a whole. How many students were close to passing, how many show substantial weaknesses? Are there any scores that have been included in the statistics that seem out of place? For example, are there any zero scores added into the mean? This could just be a student who did not take the assessment for some reason. Also, compare statistics across comparable groups. Are the means and standard deviations similar for all schools in your district? If one school is doing better than others on a given score, or subscale, that could be a clue to finding a particularly effective teaching strategy.

What Does This Mean to Me?
An SAT verbal score of 650 is a z-score of roughly +1.5 (1.5 standard deviations above the mean). Check that against the figure of the normal curve in Figure 14.4, and you can see that this is higher than roughly 93% of the scores.

When looking at a set of test scores, it is important not to lose sight of the individual children who produced them.
(Benelux Press/Index Stock)

Scales

As mentioned earlier, most standardized assessment programs report results using one or more scales employed to transform the scores into numbering systems, or metrics, that are easier to understand. This section describes the most commonly used scales.

raw scores   Scores that are simple sums of the points obtained on an assessment.

Raw Scores. **Raw scores** are usually obtained through the simple addition of all the points awarded for all the items (questions, prompts, etc.) on a test. For example, if an assessment has ten multiple-choice items worth 1 point each and five essays worth 5 points each, the maximum raw score would be 35, and each student's score would be the sum of the points attained on each item. There is, however, one important exception to this definition of a raw score. Occasionally, examinees are penalized for making wrong guesses. For example, the SAT reduces raw scores of examinees for wrong guesses. The penalty is one-fourth of a point on five-choice multiple-choice items and one-third of a point on four-choice multiple-choice items.

The logic behind this penalty is as follows: Examinees should not receive credit for blind guessing. Imagine that a person guessed randomly on 100 five-choice multiple-choice items. One would expect that person on average to get 20 items correct (one-fifth probability on each item times 100 items). That would yield a score of 20. However, on the SAT, that person would also be penalized for guessing wrong on the other 80 items. The penalty is a deduction of one-fourth of a point for each wrong guess. This would result in a deduction of 20 points (one-fourth of a point per wrong guess times 80 wrong guesses). The 20 points deducted would negate the 20 points gained for the correct guesses, leaving the total at zero. Thus, overall, examinees do not gain or lose by guessing randomly. On any particular day with any particular student, however, luck may be running well or poorly. Random guessing could work for or against a particular examinee.

scaled scores   Scores from an assessment that have been transformed into an arbitrary numbering system in order to facilitate interpretation.

Scaled Scores. Raw scores are useful in that they let students know how well they did against a total maximum score. They are not particularly useful in helping students (or teachers or parents) know how good a given score is. Moreover, assessment programs that test students on a yearly basis (such as the SAT or end-of-year standardized school assessment programs) usually construct a new assessment for each new cycle of the assessment. Testing companies try to make the new test produce scores that are as similar, or parallel, to the old one as possible. In testing, *parallel* means that the two tests have highly similar means and standard deviations, and there is a very high correlation between the two tests (usually .80 or above). Even though two tests may be highly parallel, one test may be slightly easier than the other (or perhaps easier in the lower ability ranges and harder in the higher ability ranges). When this happens, a 64 on one test may be equivalent to a 58 on the other. In an effort to make scores more meaningful and to simplify equating scores from one form of a test to another, testing companies report scores in terms of **scaled scores**. Scaled scores are mathematical transformations of raw scores into new scales, or numbering systems.

The first scaled score was the IQ score developed by Lewis Terman (1916). Terman took the French psychologist Alfred Binet's notion of *mental age* (the age associated with how well an examinee could perform intelligence-test tasks) and divided it by the examinee's chronological age to obtain an *intelligence quotient*, or IQ score. (IQ scores are no longer determined in this way.) The SAT (200–800) and ACT (1–36) are scaled scores. Most statewide standards-based assessment programs have scaled scores that they report in addition to levels of performance, such as *proficient* and *advanced proficient*.

percentile   A number that indicates what percentage of the national norming sample performed less well than the score in question.

Percentiles. **Percentiles** are the most straightforward scores other than raw scores. A percentile is the percentage of people who score less well than the score under consideration. For example, if 76% of the people who are tested score below a raw score of 59, the percentile score for a raw score of 59 is the 76th percentile. Percentiles are easy to interpret and are often used to report scores on school testing programs. Do not confuse *percentile* with *percent correct*. A second caution is that percentiles, along with the other scales described here, can drop or increase rapidly if the scale is based on only a few questions. Therefore, when looking at percentiles, always check to see how many questions were included in the scale being reported.

Uncommon Sense

Marian Should Be In Seventh Grade—Or Should She?

Mrs. Roman, a fourth-grade teacher, receives a phone message from the mother of one of her students.

Marian's mom: Mrs. Roman, we just got the standardized test scores back for Marian, and the reading grade-equivalent score is 7.2. We were really pleased to see that and to see that Marian is doing so well. But we were wondering, if Marian is capable of doing seventh-grade work, should we be thinking about having her skip a grade next year? Can we come in and talk about this?

What should Mrs. Roman tell Marian's parents about her test score? First, it is important to understand that Marian took a fourth-grade test. She did very well on the reading portion of the test, as well as would be expected of an average student in the second month of seventh grade. This does not necessarily mean that Marian is ready for seventh-grade work. What it does mean is that she is progressing very well in reading in the fourth grade. What is essential is to make sure that Marian is receiving challenging and interesting assignments and activities in her reading instruction.

Stanines. The U.S. Army developed **stanines** for use in classifying recruits in the armed services during World War II. Stanines (short for "standard nine") are scores from 1 to 9, with 1 being the lowest score and 9 the highest. They are calculated by transforming raw scores into a new scale with a mean of 5 and a standard deviation of 2. They are then rounded off to whole numbers. Therefore, a stanine of 1 would represent a score that is roughly 2 standard deviations below the mean, and a stanine of 6 would be 0.5 standard deviations above the mean. Look at Figure 14.4 to see how stanines work. The utility of the stanine is that it allows communication of a score with a single digit (number). In the days before the widespread use of computers, this was particularly useful, and stanines are still used in assessment programs today for quickly and easily providing an index of how well a student did on a test.

stanines Short for "standard nine," a scaled score that runs from 1 to 9 and has a mean of 5 and a standard deviation of 2.

Grade-Equivalent Scores. A useful but widely misunderstood scale is the **grade-equivalent score**. Grade-equivalent scores are often thought of as indicating how well students should be doing if they are on grade level. This is not true. A grade equivalent score is the mean performance of students at a given grade level. That is, a grade-equivalent score of 5.4 is the performance obtained by an average student in the fourth month of fifth grade (like school years, grade-equivalent years contain only 10 months). But if this is the average performance, is it not the case that about half the students fall below this level? Yes. By the definition of grade equivalent, about half the students will always be below grade level. Do not interpret grade-equivalent scores as where students *ought* to be; instead, interpret them as average scores for students at that point in their school progress. The "Uncommon Sense" box above brings this point home.

grade-equivalent scores Assessment scores that are reported in terms of how well children did in the norming study at various grade levels.

Normal Curve Equivalent Scores. **Normal curve equivalent (NCE)** scores were developed to provide a scale that looks like a percentile but can be used more easily in statistical analyses. NCE scores are transformed scores that have a mean of 50 and a standard deviation of 21.06. This spreads the scores out so that they can be interpreted in roughly the same way as percentile scores. School districts often use NCEs in evaluation reports for programs involving classified students. (See the "Taking It to the Classroom" box on the next page.)

normal curve equivalent (NCE) A scale related to the z-score that has a mean of 50 and a standard deviation of 21.06.

Norms and Equating

Many of the scales discussed so far (e.g., stanines, NCE scores, grade equivalents) involve comparing a student's scores to scores that other students have received. Who are those other students? They are what measurement specialists call the *norming group*, and there are several types. One such group would be a nationally representative sample of students who have taken the test under consideration. Commercially available testing programs, such as the

Appendix

Types of Scores

Standardized assessments report a variety of types of scores. It is helpful to understand the various types of scores when you attempt to interpret the results of these assessments (*PRAXIS*™, II. C. 5, *INTASC*, Principle 8).

Taking It to the Classroom

Summary of Commonly Used Scores

Standardized assessment employs a variety of scores to present information. This table summarizes the definitions of the most common scores and their best usage.

Name	Definition	Best use
Raw score	The total number of points earned on the assessment. This could be simply the total number of items correct or it may include questions scored according to a scoring rubric.	Simply looking at the number of items a student got right or, if a rubric is used, the number of points a student earned. This is often useful in combination with other scores.
Scaled score	An arbitrary numbering system that is deliberately designed not to look like other scores. The SAT, ACT, and IQ scores are examples of scaled scores.	Testing organizations sometimes use scaled scores to equate one form of a test to another.
Percentile	Ranging from 1 to 99, percentiles indicate the percentage of test takers who got a score below the score under consideration. Thus, a raw score of 42 (out of a 50-point maximum) could have a percentile of 94 if the test were a difficult one.	Percentiles are very good for seeing how well a student did compared to other, similar students. It provides a norm-referenced look at how well a student is doing.
Normal curve equivalent score	Ranging from 1 to 99, normal curve equivalent scores (NCEs) are based on the normal curve and have a mean of 50 and a standard deviation of 21.06.	NCE scores were developed to look like percentiles but also have the statistical quality of being a linear scale, which allows for mathematical operations to be carried out on them.
Stanine	Ranging from 1 to 9, stanines (an abbreviation of "standard nine") are based on the normal curve. They have a mean of 5 and a standard deviation of 2, and are also presented rounded off to whole numbers. The U.S. military developed stanines to provide a score that could be presented in a single digit and compared across tests.	Stanines are good for quickly and easily providing an index of how well a student did on a test compared to other students.
Grade-equivalent score	Ranging basically from 1.0 to 12.9, they provide a score that indicates how well a typical student at that year and month of school would have done on the test in question. Imagine that a student had a grade-equivalent score of 5.4 on a given reading test. This would mean that this is how well a typical fifth grader in the fourth month of the school year would have scored.	Grade equivalent scores give a quick picture of how well a student is doing compared to what students in the norming group did at a given grade level. Be cautious about grade equivalent scores when they are far from the level of the test that has been given.
Cut, passing, or mastery score	A score presented usually either as a scaled score or a raw score that indicates that students have exceeded a minimum level of performance on a test. This could be a high school graduation test or a formative test used as part of classroom instruction.	Usually used with criterion referenced assessments, these scores are increasing in importance. They indicate that the student has met the minimal requirements, whether that be for a unit, for high school, or for a driver's license.

 What kinds of scaled scores are used in the statewide assessment program in your state? Most state department of education Web sites will provide information on how to interpret the scales they use. Think back to the introductory material in this chapter. It would be good to go into the committee meeting with the principal understanding what the scaled scores are for your state.

Iowa Test of Basic Skills of Riverside Publishing or the Terra Nova test of CTB/McGraw-Hill, use this approach. They select school districts in such a way as to produce a set of districts that are similar to districts in the nation as a whole. These districts are invited to participate in a *norming study*. If a district declines to participate, another similar district is invited. They continue this process until they have a representative sample. The schools all administer the test under standard testing conditions, even though the districts may or may not actually use the results. The scores of students produced by this norming study give the testing companies the information they need to develop the **norms** for the test. Norms are the information base that the companies use to determine such scales as percentiles and grade equivalents. Norms can also be developed from students who take the test under real conditions. This is how the SAT, ACT, and most statewide testing programs work. The percentiles for these tests are actual percentiles from people who took the test at the same time that the student did, not from a norming study (actually, the SAT and ACT accumulate information over several testings).

Some large school districts and some wealthier school districts use *local norms*. These are norms just for the school district using the test, based on actual administration of the test. Because students within a school district are typically more similar to one another than are students in the entire nation, and because the number of students in a district is much smaller than the number in a norming study, local norms tend to be somewhat unstable. That is, one more answer right or wrong may result in a large jump in a percentile or stanine (there are no local grade-equivalent scores).

> **norms** A set of tables based on a representative national administration of an assessment that makes it possible to show how well particular students did compared to a national sample of students.

Setting Passing and Other Proficiency Scores

When a student is about to take an assessment, one question that is often in the student's mind is, How well do I have to do in order to get the grade I want? If the assessment is the driver's license test, the student is simply interested in passing. If the assessment is the final examination in a course, the student may want to know what the cut score will be for an A. Most assessments have one or more predetermined levels of proficiency associated with them. In classroom assessment, these are the break points between an A and a B, a B and a C, and so forth. In statewide standards-based assessments, there are often two break points: one between passing and not passing, and another between passing and a high level of performance. The scores that determine whether a person passes or fails an assessment are called *passing scores, cut scores,* or *mastery scores.*

Setting **passing scores** on state and national assessments is a fairly sophisticated process that usually involves multiple steps. Setting levels for different grades in a classroom often involves the simple application of the "90 and above is an A . . ." system. With the prevalence of standardized and standards-based assessment in schools, it is important to understand the basic ideas behind how passing scores are set in standardized testing and how you might set standards for different grades in your classroom.

> **passing scores** The scores on an assessment that one needs to obtain or exceed in order to pass the assessment.

Passing Scores in Standardized Assessment.

In standardized assessment, passing scores (sometimes called "cut scores") are set in several basic ways, and new variations on these basic ideas are continually being developed (Impara & Plake, 1995; Plake & Hambleton, 2000). We describe some of these approaches here. The oldest and most common are called the Angoff (1971) approach and the Nedelsky (1954) approach. They share the following ideas.

The Angoff/Nedelsky Approach to Standard Setting.

The Angoff/Nedelsky approaches to standard setting is described in the steps below and summarized in Figure 14.5.

- A number of experts, called *judges*, in the area being tested (e.g., mathematics) are brought together for a standard-setting session.
- The group works with assessment specialists to agree on what general level of competence should determine a passing score (the minimal level of competence that would get a *pass* on the assessment).
- Each judge reviews each item on the assessment with this minimal level of competence in mind.

- Each judge determines how well the *minimally competent* student will perform on each item. For example, a judge may determine that on a 5-point short essay question, a minimally competent person should get at least a 3 on the item. Perhaps, on a 1-point multiple-choice item, the judge determines that the minimally competent person should have about an 80% chance of getting the item right (this is recorded as a 0.8 in the standard-setting system).

- When the judges have assigned point values to how well they think the minimally competent person should do on each item, these values are added together, and the total becomes the estimated passing score for each judge.

- The judges' passing scores are combined to form an overall passing score. There are various ways of doing this, but taking the average of all the judges' scores is a frequently used approach.

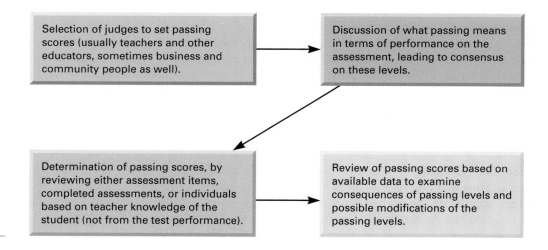

Figure 14.5. Summary of Setting Passing Scores

This approach, or a variation on it, is the most common method used to set passing scores for standardized assessment. As can be seen, the score that is established will depend to a large extent on who is chosen to be on the judging panel and the choice of level of performance considered minimally acceptable. It is important to understand that this process is fundamentally subjective: Although technical issues are involved, the individuals' judgments are the basis for what the passing score should be.

The Student–Based Approach to Standard Setting. A second approach to setting passing scores uses classroom teachers as judges and asks them to make judgments about *students*, not assessments (Tindal & Haladyna, 2002). This is presented below and summarized graphically in Figure 14.6.

- A group of practicing classroom teachers and their students are selected to participate in the standard-setting process.
- The students take the assessment under standard conditions (the conditions under which the test would normally be administered).
- The teachers receive descriptions of the minimal level of competence required for the student to pass the assessment. This may be done in writing, or the teachers may be brought together to discuss what this level means (if two levels, minimal pass and advanced pass, are desired, both levels are discussed).
- Without knowing how well their students did, each teacher rates each student as a *pass* or *not pass* (or on the two levels, if desired), based on knowledge about the student from work in the class.
- All the students who are rated *pass* are put into one group and all those rated *not pass* are put into a second group. The distribution of scores in each group is examined.
- The point where the two curves meet (see Figure 14.6) is the passing score for the assessment. It is the point that best differentiates minimally competent students from students who are not minimally competent, in the judgment of their teachers.

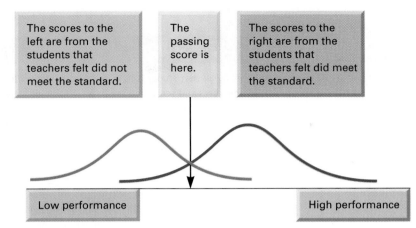

The scores to the left are from the students that teachers felt did not meet the standard.

The passing score is here.

The scores to the right are from the students that teachers felt did meet the standard.

Low performance

High performance

Figure 14.6. Student-Based Approach to Standard Setting

This approach is quite different from the Angoff/Nedelsky procedure, even though this approach also uses judgments to set passing scores. If three levels of performance are needed, the teachers are simply asked to rate their students as *not minimally competent*, *minimally competent*, or *advanced competent*.

The "Taking It to the Classroom" box on the next page shows how you can use these ideas for setting passing scores for setting standards for grading your classroom assessments.

Validity and Reliability

A common statement associated with assessment is, "Of course, we want the assessment to be *valid* and *reliable*." What does this statement mean? The concepts of reliability and validity are simply formal refinements of commonsense notions of what assessments should be. To begin, any assessment might be used in a fashion that is not valid. Validity is technically a characteristic *of the use or interpretation* of an assessment. For example, a science assessment given at the end of a unit of instruction might be a valid indicator of achievement for Mr. Martin's science class but not as valid for Mrs. Jackson's class. Mr. Martin may have focused more on certain aspects of the unit, whereas Mrs. Jackson focused on different aspects. So although people frequently talk about assessments as being valid and reliable, it is important to keep in mind that the validity and reliability of an assessment need to be considered anew for each use. Furthermore, validity and reliability are not absolutes; they are matters of degree. Thus, it is more appropriate to say that the *particular use* of an assessment is *more or less valid*, rather than to say simply that the assessment itself is valid or not.

Validity. **Validity** is the degree to which conclusions about students based on their assessment scores are justified and fair. Validity asks the question, Is the conclusion I am drawing about this student based on this assessment correct? In assessment, validity is the heart of the issue. If an assessment is valid, it actually has to be reliable. The concepts of antique and old provide an analogy. If something is antique, it has to be old, but not all old things are antique (rocks, for example). For standardized assessments, measurement specialists conduct studies to validate empirically that the assessment measures what it is intended to measure. These **validation studies** often include:

- Having experts critically review the items on the assessment to ensure that they measure what is intended (this is called **content validity** evidence)
- Statistically relating the scores from the measure with other, known indicators of the same traits or abilities (this is called **criterion-related validity** evidence)
- Conducting research studies in which the assessments are hypothesized to demonstrate certain results based on theories of what the assessments measure (called **construct validity** evidence)

For example, imagine that a state put a spelling test on its standards-based language arts/literacy test for all fourth grade children. A content validity study might consist of showing the words on the spelling test to fourth grade teachers to see if they agreed that these were words that fourth graders should be able to spell (not too easy, not too hard).

validity   The appropriateness of judgments about students based on assessment information. In classroom assessment, the correspondence between what an assessment measures and what was taught as part of instruction.

validation study   A research study conducted to determine whether an assessment is valid.

content validity   An indicator of the degree to which the items on an assessment appear to fully cover the intended content of the assessment and whether there is any extraneous material.

criterion-related validity   The degree to which an assessment correlates with an independent indicator of the same underlying ability.

construct validity   An indicator of the degree to which an ability really exists in the way it is theorized to exist and whether it is appropriately measured by the assessment.

Taking It to the Classroom

Setting Standards on Classroom Assessments

Teachers set standards all the time. This might be as simple as determining what will be a check, a check-plus, or a check-minus, or as complicated as judging one paper an A— and another a B+. Frequently, teachers choose one of the following standard approaches to assigning letter grades to numerical scores:

Common Number-to-Letter Equivalence Systems

Letter grade	Number grade	System A	System B
A	4.0	93–100	95–100
A—	3.7	90–92	93–94
B+	3.3	87–89	90–92
B	3.0	83–86	87–89
B—	2.7	80–82	85–86
C+	2.3	77–79	83–84
C	2.0	73–76	80–82
C—	1.7	70–72	78–79
D+	1.3	67–69	76–77
D	1.0	63–66	73–75
D—	0.7	60–62	70–72
F	0.0	59 and below	69 and below

There is nothing wrong with using these systems, but they assume that a given percentage correct on an assessment always means the same thing. Some assessments are simply easier than others, even when they are measuring the same objective or achievement target. Consider the following math item from a fifth-grade assessment:

What three consecutive even integers add up to 48?

This is a moderately difficult item. But look what happens when the item becomes a multiple-choice item:

What three consecutive even integers add up to 48?

  a. 8, 10, 12

  b. 16, 16, 16

  c. 15, 16, 17

  d. 14, 16, 18

Now students do not have to generate an answer; they simply have to find a set that adds up to 48 and meets the criterion of consisting of even, consecutive integers. Here is yet another possibility:

What three consecutive even integers add up to 48?

  a. 4, 6, 8

  b. 8, 10, 12

  c. 14, 16, 18

  d. 22, 24, 26

Now all that students have to do is correctly add sets of three numbers and see which set totals 48. The difficulty of the items has been changed substantially, even though ostensibly they all measure the same objective. The point here is that a score of 90 (or 93) may not always represent an A level of performance.

Teachers can *recalibrate* their grading for an assessment by going through a procedure similar to the Nedelsky/Angoff procedure. After developing an assessment, go through it and determine how many points a minimal A student would receive on each item. Add up these points; this becomes the A/B break point. Then do the same thing for the minimally passing student to arrive at the D/F break point. Once these two break points have been determined, the B/C break point and the C/D break point can be determined just by making each grade range roughly equal. For example, this process might yield the following system:

A/B break point	86	*(a difficult test)*
D/F break point	64	

With this information, the B/C break point could be 78 and the C/D break point 71. The point to keep in mind is that the grades associated with an assessment should be the result of a thoughtful process rather than a predetermined system.

Even when grades are disappointing, they contain useful information for improvement and growth. (Blair Seitz/Photo Researchers, Inc.)

A criterion-related validity study might compare the scores obtained on this test to the number of spelling errors students made in their regular written work. A construct validity study might look at how the questions are asked on the test (do students have to pick the correctly spelled word out of a list of four options, or spell the words on their answer sheets after the teacher pronounces them).

More recently, educators have become concerned about the consequences of using a particular assessment. For example, if a college highly values SAT scores as a determining factor in admitting students, what kind of a message does that send to high school students who want to go to that college with regard to how hard they should work on their school subjects? Concerns of this type assess the **consequential validity** of the assessment. In general, the issue of validity has to do with whether an assessment really measures what it is intended to measure and whether the conclusions or inferences that are made about students based on the assessment are justified. In the spelling test example above, the consequential validity question would center on how instruction in language arts/literacy would differ if the test were included or not.

consequential validity Concern for how the assessment will affect the person taking it.

Reliability.

Reliability is the consistency or dependability of the scores obtained from an assessment. Reliability asks the question, Would I get roughly the same score for this student if I gave the assessment again? Imagine a group of high school students were given a grammar assessment in Spanish on a Friday, and the same measure again on Monday (without learning how well they did in between). Correlating the scores between these two assessments would provide a measure of the reliability of the assessment. Reliability is closely related to validity, but it is more limited in scope. In Chapter 13, we defined reliability in classroom assessment as having enough information to make a good judgment about student achievement. The definition presented here is a more formal definition of reliability, applicable to a wider range of assessment issues.

reliability Consistency over an aspect of assessment, such as over time or over multiple raters. In classroom assessment, having enough information about students on which to base judgments.

Chapter Reference
Chapter 13 discusses issues of reliability and validity as they apply to classroom assessment.

As with validity, it is not the assessment itself but the particular application of the assessment that is reliable or not. Moreover, assessments are not either reliable or not reliable; they are either more reliable or less reliable. The essence of reliability is how certain one can be that the assessment would produce the same results on a second administration.

However, reliability is *not* related to the question of whether the assessment is really measuring what it is intended to measure. That is, just because a measure is reliable (i.e., produces consistent results) does not necessarily mean that it is valid (i.e., measures what is wanted or needed). *The SAT math score is just as reliable an assessment of artistic ability as it is of mathematics ability.* It is simply not a *valid* measure of artistic ability. Therefore, measures that do not provide validity evidence may or may not be measuring what you want. You need to carefully examine measures without supporting validity evidence to ascertain whether they are valid for your needs. Reliability is important, but validity is crucial. This point is important because assessments often have reliability evidence but no validity evidence.

The reliability of an assessment is determined in a **reliability study**. The simplest such study is one that assesses *test-retest* reliability by having a group of students take an assessment, then take it again a week or two later. Their scores on the two assessments are correlated, and the result would be the **reliability coefficient**. If the study involves using two different forms of the same test (such as with the SAT), the reliability would be called an *alternate form* reliability.

reliability study A study that is used to determine reliability coefficients.

reliability coefficient An index, ranging from .00 up to 1.00, of how reliable an assessment is.

There are a number of other ways to calculate reliability coefficients. One very common approach is **split-half reliability**. In this approach, the assessment is given once to a group of students. Each student receives two scores, one based on performance on the even-numbered items and another based on performance on the odd-numbered items. These two scores are then correlated and adjusted using a formula that takes into account the fact that only half of the test has been used in obtaining each score. A variation on split-half reliability takes an average of all possible ways of splitting an assessment into two halves; this is **coefficient alpha**, or *Cronbach's alpha*. For multiple-choice assessments, a version of coefficient alpha called *KR-20* is often used. Finally, if a rater or judge is used to score the items on an assessment (such as on an essay assessment or a performance assessment), an index of **inter-rater reliability** is needed. Inter-rater reliability is assessed by having two raters score a set of assessments for a group of students, then correlating the scores produced by the two raters.

split-half reliability A form of reliability coefficient, similar to coefficient alpha, that takes half of the items on an assessment, sums them into a score, then correlates that score with a score based on the other half of the items.

coefficient alpha An approach to assessing reliability that uses a single administration of the assessment and focuses on whether all the assessment items appear to be measuring the same underlying ability; also called *Cronbach's alpha*.

inter-rater reliability A measure of the degree to which two independent raters give similar scores to the same paper or performance.

standard error of measurement
An index of how high or low an individual's assessment score might change on a second testing.

true score The hypothetical true ability of an individual on an assessment.

Teachers often ask how high a reliability coefficient should be. Generally speaking, an assessment that is used to make a decision about a child should have a reliability coefficient of .90 or above. If the assessment is going to be combined with other information, a slightly lower reliability (in the .80s) may be acceptable.

A concept closely related to reliability is very useful in understanding the scores students receive on assessments. This is the **standard error of measurement** (SEM). The SEM provides a way for determining how much variability there might be in a student's score. The best way to think about the SEM is to imagine that a student took the SAT 1,000 times. Each test included different items but measured the same thing. The student would get a somewhat different score on each administration of the test, depending on the specific items on that test, how the student was feeling, whether it was a lucky or unlucky day, and so forth. A plot of these scores would look like a normal distribution. The mean of that distribution is what measurement specialists call the **true score**. The standard deviation of that distribution would be an index of how much the student's score would vary. This standard deviation (of one student taking the test many times) would be the standard error of measurement.

Of course, the SEM is not calculated by making a student take a test 1,000 times. It is usually calculated based on data from a reliability study. The SEM can help us understand how much error there might be in a score. Using the SEM and the normal curve, a teacher can estimate that the true ability of the student will be between one SEM above and below the observed score about 67% of the time, and between two SEMs above and below the observed score about 95% of the time.

An example will make this clear. Imagine that Martin received a 560 on his SAT verbal test. The SEM for the SAT is roughly 30 points. If he took the test again (without doing any additional preparation for it), he would have a two-thirds chance of scoring somewhere between 530 and 590, and a 95% chance of scoring between 500 and 620. That may seem like a large spread in the scores. Indeed it is, and the SAT has a reliability coefficient over .90. As the reliability gets lower, the SEM gets even higher, which is why it is recommended that assessments with low reliability not be used. Think back to the opening activity for this chapter. What evidence is available for the validity and reliability of the standards-based assessment used by your state?

What Does This Mean to Me?
Did your SAT scores (or those of someone who you know) change markedly from one testing to the next? How might the SEM help explain this?

Interpreting Standardized Assessments

Interpreting standardized assessments can be one of the most difficult things that teachers have to do. The difficulty might be attributable partly to the nature of the reports they receive, which can be hard to read, and partly to the love/hate relationship between educators and standardized assessment. That is, at the same time that many educators wish standardized tests would go away, they often put too much faith in them when making decisions about students.

Teachers encounter several problems when looking at standardized test reports. The first is that the teacher sees only the test report, not the actual efforts of students taking the test. On a classroom assessment, the teacher sees the work of each child on each problem or prompt. The teacher is able to gather information about the student on each problem, draw inferences, and make judgments about the student's overall performance on the assessment. With a standardized test, the teacher does not see the work itself, but rather a scaled score of some sort on a label, such as *interpreting text* or *process skills*. What does a score of 189 on *process skills* mean?

A related problem is that teachers do not usually get the results of an assessment until well after it was given. It may be months later; in fact, in some cases it may be after the end of the school year. It is difficult to have an influence on a student who is no longer in your class. Finally, the content of standardized assessments does not always line up directly with what was taught to all of the students. This can be a particular problem in mathematics, where different students can be working on very different material.

The purpose of this section is to see how looking at standardized test results can be a useful part of generating an overall picture of how well students are performing. For most teachers, standardized assessment results are available near the end of the school year. This section assumes that teachers looking at these results are considering students they have

Assessment results provide information about children that needs to be combined with other sources of information to get a useful overall picture of the child's strengths and needs. (Spencer Grant/Photo Researchers, Inc.)

had in their classes during the year. They are assessing the progress those students have made, reflecting on the school year in terms of the each child's growth, and perhaps putting together a summary communication to parents or to the child's teacher for the following school year.

Finding the Child in the Data

The first step in interpreting standardized assessment results is *not* to think of the process as one of interpreting standardized assessment results. Do not think of the task as trying to make sense out of a report; instead, think of it as getting some more information about a child you already know (or, if it is a new student, about a child you will be getting to know). Think of it as a snapshot of a real student, of Margaret. Maybe the picture is a bit blurred, and maybe it is not taken from a great angle. Maybe Margaret hates it. When looking at data from Margaret's standardized assessment results, combine knowledge of Margaret with the assessment results (how well she did on her last classroom project, the kinds of questions she asks, a discussion with her parents at the parent/teacher conference). They are all snapshots of Margaret. None of them by itself gives a true image of Margaret, but in combination, they will get you pretty close to the real child. And that is the goal: *finding the child in the data.*

> **What Does This Mean to Me?**
> A standardized assessment score is a picture of a child on a given day. How does this picture fit with what you know about the child? Where are the consistencies and inconsistencies with your image of the child? How can you reconcile them?

Demystifying the Assessment Report

Assessment reports come in all shapes and sizes. Figures 14.7 and 14.8 present the results of two standardized assessment reports, one from a statewide standards-based assessment and the other from a commercial testing program.

An Eighth-Grade Statewide Assessment. At the top of the report from the New Jersey Statewide Assessment System, there is a set of information that tells:

- Who the child is
- What school and school district he or she comes from
- Gender
- When he or she was born
- Whether he or she has limited English proficiency (LEP)
- Whether he or she is classified for special education (SE)
- Whether he or she is exempt from taking one or more of the assessments (IEP Exempt)
- Whether he or she is in a Title I remedial program (Title I)

There is a tendency to skip over such information, but that is not a good idea. Check this information to make sure that it is correct. For example, if this child is in fact classified LEP and this is not correctly indicated, that is an important mistake that the teacher needs to report.

Below the general information are the summary scores that Marisa received in language arts literacy, mathematics, and science. As can be seen, Marisa passed the mathematics and science portions of the assessment but not the language arts literacy portion. She needed to get a score of 200 on these assessments to pass. Although her mathematics score (224) seems to have been well above the passing score, her science score (200) just passed. Her language arts literacy score (164) seems well below passing. However, because there is no information about the SEM for this assessment, it is difficult to determine the accuracy of these scores.

New Jersey Statewide Assessment System
Grade Eight Proficiency Assessment
Individual Student Report

Name: Marisa Watson

Date of Birth: 08/28/86
Gender: F

LEP:
SE:
IEP Exempt:
Title I:

Test ID No: 0013499866
Answer Folder No: 038257
District/School Student ID No: 81300000000

Content Area	Your Score	Proficiency Level
Language Arts Literacy	164	Partially Proficient
Mathematics	224	Partially Proficient
Science	200	Proficient

Partially Proficient: Score BELOW 200

Proficient: Score AT OR ABOVE 200 but BELOW 250

Advanced Proficient: Score AT OR ABOVE 250

Language Arts Literacy

The Language Arts Literacy section assesses a student's abilities in the following clusters. The number in parentheses is the total number of points possible. A check mark indicates areas of possible strength.

Cluster	Your Score	Just Proficient Mean	
Writing (26)	11.0 out of 26	10.9	✓
Reading (36)	7.5 out of 36	18.6	
Interpreting Text (12)	4.0 out of 12	9.0	
Analyzing/Critiquing (24) Text	3.5 out of 24	9.6	

Mathematics

The Mathematics section assesses a student's abilities in the following clusters. The number in parentheses is the total number of points possible. A check mark indicates areas of possible strength.

Cluster	Your Score	Just Proficient Mean
Number Sense, Concepts & Applications (12)	8.0 out of 12	5.8
Spatial Sense & Geometry (12)	7.0 out of 12	4.9
Data Analysis, Probability, Statistics, & Discrete Mathematics (12)	6.0 out of 12	5.8
Patterns, Functions, & Algebra (12)	7.0 out of 12	6.6
Knowledge (48)	28.0 out of 48	23.0
Problem Solving Skills (26)	15.0 out of 26	11.0

Science

The Science section assesses a student's abilities in the following clusters. The number in parentheses is the total number of points possible. A check mark indicates areas of possible strength.

Cluster	Your Score	Just Proficient Mean
Life Science (19)	9.0 out of 19	8.3
Physical Science (19)	9.0 out of 19	7.6
Earth Science (16)	6.0 out of 16	7.1
Cognitive Skills (27)	8.0 out of 27	10.2
Process Skills (27)	16.0 out of 27	12.8

Figure 14.7. A Standards-Based Report

Source: New Jersey Department of Education. (2001). Middle school statewide assessment. Retrieved June 10, 2005, from http://www.nj.gov/njded/assessment/ms/.

The Measure of Success — TerraNova

TerraNova THE SECOND EDITION

Individual Profile Report

KEN JONES

Grade: 4

Simulated Data

Purpose
This report presents information about this students performance on *TerraNova* CAT. Page 1 describes achievement in terms of performance on the objectives. Together with classroom assessments and classwork, this information can be used to identify potential strengths and needs in the content areas shown.

Birthdate:02/08/92
Special Codes:
ABCDEFGHIJKLMNOPQRSTUVWXYZ
3 59 73   2   1 1 1
Form/Level: C-14
Test Date: 04/24/01   Scoring: PATTERN (IRT)
QM: 31   Norms Date: 2000

Class: JONES
School: WINFIELD
District: GREEN VALLEY

City/State: ANYTOWN, U.S.A.

CTB McGraw-Hill
www.ctb.com   Pg. 1

Obj. No. / Objective Titles	Student	Natl OPI	Diff	Moderate Mastery Range
Reading				
02 Basic Understanding	91	79	12	48-70
03 Analyze Text	92	84	8	52-75
04 Evaluate/Extend Meaning	65	66	-1	50-70
05 Identify Rdg. Strategies	70	74	-4	45-73
Language				
07 Sentence Structure	63	68	-5	45-70
08 Writing Strategies	59	74	-15	50-75
09 Editing Skills	78	63	15	55-75
Mathematics				
10 Number & Num. Relations	71	69	2	47-77
11 Computation & Estimation	83	72	11	45-75
13 Measurement	66	86	-20	45-60
14 Geometry & Spatial Sense	71	72	-1	50-78
15 Data, Stats. & Prob.	61	83	-22	52-78
16 Patterns, Func, Algebra	77	88	-11	44-73
17 Prob. Solving & Reasoning	71	74	-3	52-75
18 Communication	69	68	1	43-73
Science				
19 Science Inquiry	47	74	-27	50-75
20 Physical Science	49	69	-20	52-77
21 Life Science	46	83	-37	45-78
22 Earth & Space Science	52	84	-32	48-73
23 Science & Technology	48	78	-30	52-69
24 Persoanl & Social Persp.	52	56	-4	50-73

Obj. No. / Objective Titles	Student	Natl OPI	Diff	Moderate Mastery Range
Social Studies				
26 Geographic Perspectives	79	91	-12	48-70
27 Historical & Cultural	84	92	-8	52-75
28 Civics & Government	66	65	1	50-70
29 Economic Perspectives	74	70	4	45-73

Objective Performance Index (OPPI) scale: 0, 25, 50, 75, 100

*OPI is an estimate of the number of items that a student could be expected to answer correctly if there had been 100 items for that objective.

Key
Moderate Mastery Range ———
Low Mastery ○
Moderate Mastery ◐
High Mastery ●

Copyright© 2001 CTB/McGraw-Hill. All rights reserved.

Continued on next page ➡

(a)

TerraNova THE SECOND EDITION
CAT COMPLETE BATTERY

Individual Profile Report

KEN JONES

Grade: 4

Simulated Data

Purpose
Page 2 of this report presents norm-referenced information as well as descriptions of the skills and abilities the student demonstrated, and the skills and abilities the student can work toward to show academic growth.
In the descriptions, statements describing written responses refer only to the Multiple Assessments component of the test.

Norm-Referenced Scores	Scale Score	Grade Equiv.	National Stanine	National Percentile	NP Range
Reading	677	5.8	6	65	55-75
–	–	–	–	–	–
–	–	–	–	–	–
Language	657	4.3	5	53	43-60
–	–	–	–	–	–
Mathematics	699	6.8	7	82	74-89
–	–	–	–	–	–
Total Score**	681	5.8	6	72	60-81
Science	671	4.4	5	55	45-66
Social Studies	669	4.7	5	58	48-68
–	–	–	–	–	–

** Total Score consists of Reading, Language, and Mathematics.

National Percentile Scale: 1 10 25 50 75 90 99
National Stanine Scale: 1 2 3 4 5 6 7 8 9

The following are content area descriptions of the kinds of knowledge, skills, and abilities assessed on the *TerraNova* CAT achievement test.

Reading...
The student demonstrated some of the knowledge, skills, and abilities assessed in this content area.
Students read passages of varying degrees of difficulty, including selections from classic and contemporary children's fiction, nonfiction, and poetry. Students show knowledge of grade-level vocabulary and comprehension of passage details and sequence of events. They restate main ideas and themes, compare elements within a text, demonstrate an

(b)

Figure 14.8. A Standardized Test Individual Report

Moving from the overall summary scores, we see that each of the three main scores is broken down into subscales. In language arts literacy, there are writing cluster and reading cluster scores. As is indicated in the descriptive note, the number in parentheses is the maximum number of points Marisa could have received on this part of the assessment (26 in writing, 36 in reading). Marisa received 11 points in writing and 7.5 in reading. Then there is something called the *just proficient mean*, which is a kind of passing score for each subscale on the assessment.

Marisa received an 11 on the writing cluster, and the just proficient mean was 10.9. In reading, Marisa received a 7.5, and the just proficient mean was 18.6. These results suggest that although Marisa is performing fairly well in writing, she is having great difficulty in reading. This is a fairly dramatic finding—one that cannot be disregarded—but what can we make of it? This result needs to be explored. The answer will not be in this printout but may be found in other information about Marisa, such as her class performance, interests, perhaps even how she was feeling on the day of the test. The mathematics and science cluster breakdowns must also be examined to get a full picture of Marisa's performance; strengths need exploration as well as weaknesses. In particular, Marisa's science score is just at the passing level. If she had gotten one more item wrong, she would not have passed this assessment. Examine her cluster scores in mathematics and science to see where her potential strengths and weaknesses lie.

A Commercially Available Elementary School Report. The second report comes from the widely used Terra Nova testing program of CTB/McGraw-Hill. It is for a fourth-grade student and covers the subject areas of reading, language, mathematics, science, and social studies. It is immediately evident that that numerous scores are presented. The majority of the report (Figure 14.8a) deals with what is called *Performance on Objectives*. Scores here are reported on a scale called the *Objectives Performance Index* (OPI). This scale is defined as an estimate of how many items the student would get right if there had been 100 items on that objective. It is roughly equivalent to the percentage correct. The shaded bars represent **mastery levels**, indications of how well the student is doing, in the various subscales. It may be difficult to know how these were determined and what relevance they may have in your classroom. For example, we can see that Ken appears to be doing quite well in Patterns, Functions, and Algebra, but not as well in Data, Statistics, and Probability, according to the Performance on Objectives bars. Probably the best approach to interpreting these scores is to think of the national norming data as a set of baselines for looking at a student. Look at the national average OPI score in each subscale. That is how well the typical student did on that part of the assessment. Now look at how well Ken did. Are the scores above or below the national average? Is the difference substantial? For example, Ken seems to be doing very well in Basic Understanding in Reading (91, compared to the national average of 79). However, he appears to be doing less well on Evaluate/Extended Meaning (58, compared to a national average of 68). The national norms, therefore, provide benchmarks against which a child's score can be compared. In essence, they are a way of letting educators compare children to themselves.

Percentiles, grade equivalents, and stanine scores do this in a simpler fashion because they are directly comparable (a grade equivalent score of 5.6 is greater than one of 5.2; the comparison to the norms has already been made). The second page of the report presents these scores along with confidence bands for the National Percentile Scores (Figure 14.8b). These confidence bands are based on the SEMs (discussed above) for each of the scores. Here we can see that Ken is performing above average in all five areas assessed and that his strongest area appears to be mathematics and his weakest areas appear to be science and social studies.

Combining Standardized Results with Other Information

What conclusions should be drawn about Marisa and Ken? None; at any rate, none yet. Although we have examined the standardized assessment scores for these two students, we need to consider a lot of other information. Remember, these are single snapshots of Marisa and Ken taken on a given day, not complete pictures. This information needs to be combined with other information to arrive at a clearer and more useful evaluation. When information from multiple sources converges, increased confidence can be taken in the interpretation. If the people looking at these results have just spent a year as Marisa and

mastery levels   Levels of proficiency, or mastery, determined for an assessment; related to cut scores and passing scores.

Ken's teachers, a great deal of other information needs to be considered in evaluating these students. For example:

- Do the scores on these assessments match the kinds of performances they displayed in their classroom work?
- Does a score that looks low actually reflect remarkable growth for a student who started the year with substantial difficulties in this area?
- Did the items on the assessment match well with the curriculum taught in the classroom (for example, in science for Ken)?
- Were there personal considerations, such as family problems or minor illness that may have caused the day the assessment was given to have been an unusual one for the student?

The standardized assessment reports are just the beginning of the process of understanding a student's academic achievements; they are not the whole process. The class may have spent the year working on physics and astronomy, whereas the assessment may have addressed a variety of scientific ideas. If Ken is not very interested in science (which, as his teacher, you may know to be the case), perhaps the science score should be taken with a grain of salt. On the other hand, the relatively low score on Evaluate/Extended Meaning in reading may be a disappointment. Perhaps this was an area in which you thought Ken was making solid strides. It is important to remember that the assessment represents the efforts of a student on a particular day. It provides useful information, but information that must be interpreted in the context of what the student has done all year long. This is also true of the student whose classroom performance presents a different picture than his or her standardized test scores (see the "Taking It to the Classroom" box on this page).

Working from the Top Down. The best way to look at standardized assessment results and combine them with other information is to begin with the highest level of information on the report. Most assessments provide a number of primary scores ranging from two (language arts and mathematics) to five or six (science, social studies, sometimes language arts broken into reading and writing). These are the most reliable of the available measures and the best place to begin. Consider the following questions about the child:

- What are the child's strengths and weaknesses, according to the report?
- Do these strengths and weaknesses match what you know about the child?
- Are there any aspects of these scores that do not seem to make sense with regard to this child?

The next level to look at concerns the subscales that are provided within each primary score. If all these look similar, the primary score to which they are related can be considered the child's general ability level. If, however, there are strong discrepancies, this may be a good area for further investigation.

Taking It to the Classroom

Do You Know Jack? Test Taker Par Excellence

Jack does well—very well—on standardized tests. Often, children get test scores that are disappointing to teachers, parents, and the students themselves. Not Jack. Jack's test scores are always a surprise in the other direction: Jack regularly scores in the top 10% and occasionally gets a perfect score on a standardized assessment. But his classroom performance is sloppy, often nonexistent, and generally reflects great indifference to instruction.

What can be done to get Jack's classroom work up to his test performances?

- Have a discussion with Jack about why he is performing poorly in class and why he seems to do so well on standardized tests.
- Have a parent conference to go over Jack's test performance and school performance.
- See whether some more challenging assignments might increase Jack's interest level.
- Check with other teachers about how Jack is doing with them.
- Check Jack's attendance record.
- Allow Jack to choose some activities in which he is interested.

What Kids Say and Do

Making the Data Make Sense

One standard rule for interpreting any score—or, for that matter, any report of data (from a newspaper article or television show, for example)—is that the data have to make sense. If the data do not make sense, be wary of putting too much faith in them. Here is a real example from the experience of one of the authors of this text.

A former graduate student who was a middle school principal called to ask about an assessment score in reading obtained by one of her students. Janell had almost always scored at the 95th percentile or above in every subject area on the commercial standardized assessment. This year was no different, except for the reading score, which placed Janell in the 43rd percentile. Before recommending the student to the child study team for review, the principal wanted to get an expert opinion on the assessment. "Doesn't make sense" was the response. "Bring it down to the university, and I'll have a look at it."

Upon review, an interesting pattern appeared. The answers to each question were given broken down by the subcategory on the assessment (literal comprehension, vocabulary in context, etc.). A plus was used if the item was correct, the letter of the multiple-choice response selected if the item was wrong, and a zero if the item was left blank. On Janell's answer sheet, of 60 questions, 29 were right, 1 was wrong, and 30 were blank. She had gotten only one question wrong but had failed to answer 30 items. Because the items were broken out by subscale, it was not immediately apparent that the 30 blank responses were from items 31–60. In other words, Janell had gotten 29 of 30 correct on the first 30 items and had left the last 30 blank. How could this be?

The principal was able to solve the problem by talking to Janell. Janell told her that on the day of the test she had become ill at lunchtime and had gone home. No one asked her to make up the second half of the test.

In sum, if the data do not make sense, be cautious about how much faith you put in them. There are many more simple mistakes in this world than there are truly amazing results.

Making and Testing Hypotheses about the Child. Looking at the assessment report provides an opportunity to reflect on the progress the child has made during the year. Consider the scores for Ken. It appears that he is not as strong in Evaluate/Extended Meaning as he is in Basic Understanding in Reading. He also is not as strong in Problem Solving and Reasoning as he is in Computation and Estimation in Mathematics. These strengths and weaknesses suggest that Ken is missing some of the more subtle issues in both these areas. This is a general hypothesis about Ken. Is it a reasonable one? This probably cannot be determined just from looking at the assessment results, but a teacher who has had Ken as a student all year long probably has some insight into this hypothesis. Ken's teacher may think, "You know, that's pretty much what I see in Ken as well. He works hard and does well on the literal aspects of most of his work, but he is often reluctant to go beyond the literal to think of the broader possibilities. It almost seems more like a personality characteristic than an academic ability. I wonder what could be done to help bring his abilities out more?" Or the teacher may think, "Those results just aren't consistent with what I see Ken on a day-to-day basis. I need to check out the types of questions that Ken had difficulty with to see what the problem is here. These data don't make sense to me." (See the "What Kids Say and Do" box above.)

Bringing the Child to the Classroom

Once one has looked at an assessment report and developed an overall picture of the student's achievement, the next step is deciding what to do about it. Sometimes this type of analysis results in a summary statement about the child provided to the teacher in the subsequent year; sometimes it is used in a parent/teacher conference. Occasionally, the teacher uses it to plan further instruction for the child during the current school year; such would be the case if the assessment took place in the fall or if the teacher were looking at the results from the previous year's assessment. In this situation, the teacher has to *bring the child to the classroom.*

Bringing the child to the classroom means that the child's strengths, weaknesses, and goals must fit into the environment of the classroom as a whole. If there are 14 students in a self-contained fourth-grade classroom that emphasizes cooperative learning and problem-based instruction, fitting the child into the classroom will mean one thing. If there are 26 students—including 2 with special needs—in a more traditional setting, it will mean something quite different. If the child's parents are very involved in the child's education, their interest may be used to work on areas of need or strength that the teacher cannot address in the classroom. For example, if Ken is indeed having trouble with reading beyond the literal text, his parents might be interested in reading mysteries with him. This would give them an enjoyable vehicle to use in working with their child and helping him develop.

It would be wonderful if each child could get an education tailored to his or her unique needs, but that cannot happen with 20 other equally deserving children in the same classroom. Once the teacher has a good picture of the student and his or her needs, that student has to be brought into the educational and social structure of the classroom. Bringing the child to the classroom thus requires imagination and creativity on the part of the teacher.

Thinking about the Classroom, School, and District Levels

If we only ever had one child to think about, teaching would be a lot easier. But teachers work with classrooms full of children and the group needs to be considered as well as the individual. Teachers can use many of the ideas presented in terms of interpreting scores for individuals for the class as a whole. Overall, what are the strengths of this class, what are the weaknesses? Are there issues that can be a focus for the class as a whole over the course of the year?

Perhaps a group of students appears to be stronger in reading than in mathematics. This might provide the teacher with an opportunity to allocate a little more instructional time to mathematics, and perhaps to assess progress in mathematics within the classroom on a more regular basis.

Another possibility is that there are several students who are having difficulty with a particular aspect of the curriculum. These students might be grouped together for purposes of some special attention. It is important, of course, to reassess progress on a regular basis to make sure that instruction is attuned to students' current needs, and not just where they were at the beginning of the year.

Although teachers focus primarily at the classroom level, they need to recognize that principals are concerned with the school as a whole, and district level personnel need to think about the needs of all the children in the district. Coordination of instruction from one year to the next is a hallmark of a good instructional program. Careful examination of assessment scores across years and grades is an important component of such a program.

Looking at Scores for English Language Learners

Students who do not speak English well, ELL students, sometimes also referred to as LEP students, pose a major problem for the interpretation of assessments. The problem is easy to understand but difficult to solve. Language arts literacy scores may not be measuring the language arts abilities of these students at all but merely measuring their abilities in English. On the other hand, some ELL students speak English fairly well but may have deficiencies in language arts. How can the former situation be separated from the latter?

To begin with, there is research evidence showing that testing accommodations made for ELL students do not reduce the validity of the scores on the assessment (Abedi, Courtney, & Leon, 2003; Abedi & Lord, 2001). Teachers should make sure that ELL students in their class receive accommodations if they are entitled to them. Some state assessment programs have developed alternative forms of assessments for ELL students. Teachers should communicate across grades: A teacher who has an ELL student in third grade can communicate to the fourth-grade teacher about the language abilities of a particular student.

Looking at Scores for Students with Special Needs

Another category that should receive particular attention when one is interpreting assessment results consists of students who have special needs. Some of these students will be exempt from standardized assessments as part of their individualized educational program (IEP), which specifies the instructional goals, methods, and assessments appropriate for the

<aside>
How Can I Use This?

In thinking about what you can do to tailor instruction to the needs of your students, consider the resources you have and try to match them to the students' needs.
</aside>

<aside>
R I D E Think back to the vignette at the beginning of the chapter. Where are the strengths in your district? Where are the weaknesses? Of the students who did not pass the test, how many need a lot of work, and how many need just a little more work?
</aside>

child. However, the federal and many state governments place limits on the number of children who can receive such exemptions. Students with disabilities may be granted certain accommodations in the administration of an assessment (including, but not limited to, extra time, a quiet room, a helper to read to students with limited vision, and/or shorter testing sessions). Another possibility for students with disabilities is to take an alternative form of the assessment that minimizes the impact of the disability (see, e.g., the "DPI Guidelines to Facilitate the Participation of Students with Special Needs in State Assessments" of the Wisconsin Department of Public Instruction, 2002).

Interpreting the results of standardized assessments of students with special needs requires special sensitivity and care, particularly when discussing results with parents. There is a fine line between being sensitive to children's academic challenges and underestimating what they can do. Moreover, what is seen in the classroom environment or what may show up under the pressures of a standardized assessment may be quite different from what parents see in a more supportive and less chaotic home environment. It is particularly important for teachers to look for strengths in working with these students and to see areas in which students are having difficulty as points of departure rather than as areas of weakness.

A major issue in interpreting the scores of students with special needs is the impact of the disability on performance. If a student is easily distracted or unable to concentrate for long periods, an assessment with a long reading passage may be particularly troublesome. Students who are good at mathematical ideas but weak on computation facts may not be able to demonstrate their abilities on multiple-choice mathematics items. Sometimes, assessment results for students with special needs are consistent with teacher expectations; other times, they are baffling. This is one of the reasons why special education is a field of scholarly inquiry unto itself. There are resources available to help teachers work effectively with students with special needs. The Web site accompanying this text includes links to sites where you can find help. Some excellent text resources are also available (see Mastergeorge & Myoshi, 1999; Mercer & Mercer, 2001; Venn, 2004).

Assistive Technology and the Assessment of Learners with Special Needs. Some students require technological assistance to demonstrate their abilities. Assistive technology devices help augment abilities where individuals face special challenges. This is more common than one might think. If you are wearing glasses or contact lenses to read this material, you are using assistive technology. The Florida Alliance for Assistive Services and Technology of the Florida Department of Education lists the following categories of assistive devices and services:[1]

- Augmentative communication devices, including talking computers
- Assistive listening devices, including hearing aids, personal FM units, closed-caption TVs, and teletype machines (TDOS)
- Specially adapted learning games, toys, and recreation equipment
- Computer-assisted instruction, for drawing software
- Electronic tools (scanners with speech synthesizers, tape recorders, word processors)
- Curriculum and textbook adaptations (e. g., audio format, large-print format, Braille)
- Copies of overheads, transparencies, and notes
- Adaptation of the learning environment, such as special desks, modified learning stations
- Computer touch screens or different computer keyboards
- Adaptive mobility devices for driver education
- Orthotics such as hand braces to facilitate writing skills

Controversies in Assessment

Assessment involves evaluating students' progress. Any form of evaluation or assessment holds the potential for controversy, and student assessment is no exception. Some issues in assessment have been controversial for decades; others have appeared within the last 20 years. Some significant current controversies are discussed in this section.

[1] *Source:* Florida Alliance for Assistive Services and Technology. Retrieved June 14, 2005, from FAAST Web site at *http://faast.org/atr k12 rights.cfm*. Used with permission.

Appendix
Careful Use of Assessment Results

The results of assessments completed by students with special needs or those with limited English proficiency should be interpreted with care and sensitivity. It is wise to gather multiple sources of information about students' level of performance (*PRAXIS*™, II. C. 4, *INTASC*, Principles 2, 8).

www.wiley.com/college/odonnell

Assistive devices help special needs students demonstrate the achievements they have made.
(© Mugshots/Corbis Images)

Bias in Testing

Bias in testing has long been a topic of heated debate in the United States (Murphy & Davidshofer, 1994; Thorndike, 1997). Concerns about bias in testing often revolve around the highly verbal nature of some measures. Everyone who has taken the SAT verbal test acknowledges that a strong command of the English language is important in obtaining a good score. But the development of such language proficiency would seem to favor wealthier individuals who have greater access to the kinds of words that appear on the measure. Certainly, individuals who do not speak English as a first language would be at a disadvantage.

However, the situation is far from simple. Even the definition of **test bias** is a subject of debate among scholars. Some believe that whenever an assessment produces different results for members of different racial or ethnic groups, or between genders, that assessment is biased. Measurement specialists use a more refined definition: If individuals from different groups (racial groups, genders, etc.) obtain the same score on an assessment, it should mean the same thing for both individuals. If it does not, that is evidence that the test is biased. For example, if two students, one male and one female, get the same SAT scores, they should be predicted to do similarly well in college. Of course, the prediction is not made for one pair of individuals but for large groups.

test bias The degree to which the scores from an assessment take on different meanings when obtained by individuals from different groups.

Research on college admissions testing indicates that the tests typically do not show bias (Young, 2003). That is, the tests do an equally good job of predicting college performance for students from minority groups as it does for majority students. This finding is contrary to public opinion, but it has been shown to be true in a number of studies. This is not to say that there are no group differences in performance on these measures. Moreover, if colleges weigh the results of admissions tests too heavily, the *admissions process can still be biased even though the assessment is not.* This is somewhat akin to using height as the sole determinant of whom to select for a basketball team. All other things being equal, taller players tend to be

Test bias means that different conclusions are drawn about students from different groups whose abilities are in fact the same. (Media Bakery)

better than shorter players. However, height is not the only factor that determines the quality of basketball players. In the same fashion, admissions test scores are not the only factor that determines success in college. Thus, an admissions system that relies on testing can be biased even though it may be hard to find bias in the measures themselves.

The situation is even more subtle for students who do not speak English as a first language. If a mathematics assessment contains a number of word problems, ELL students may fail to reach a correct answer not because of a deficiency in mathematics ability but because of difficulty understanding exactly what was being asked of them.

High-Stakes Testing and Its Implications

Appendix

High Stakes Testing

Students may feel very pressured by the attention given to high stakes testing in their classrooms and their motivation for learning may be reduced as a result (*PRAXIS™*, I. C. 3, *INTASC*, Principle 5).

The increase in standardized assessment accompanying the federal NCLB Act has had a number of effects on educational practice—some intended, some not. Although the goal of having all children reach high standards of achievement is undoubtedly laudable, there are concerns associated with increased high-stakes standardized assessment that have impact on classroom teachers, including:

- Standardization of curriculum
- Teaching to the test
- Increased emphasis on test performance in classrooms
- Increased reports of cheating on assessments, both by students and by educators

With standardized assessment mandated at each grade level from grades three through eight, school districts must make certain that they are covering the material included in the assessments. As a result, all children are taught the same thing at the same time, regardless of their individual rate of development. This standardization of the curriculum is not the purpose of standards-based instruction (Taylor et al., 2003); rather, it occurs as schools attempt to prepare their students for the assessment that accompanies the adoption of statewide standards. The problem this poses for classroom teachers is that the students in a classroom typically are not all at the same stage of ability or achievement in any given subject area. If they must all take the same test, the teacher must review this material prior to the assessment, thereby interrupting the natural progression of learning for many students.

Education is a complex and multifaceted phenomenon. How children learn, the best conditions for learning, and how to maximize achievement for a class of students are all difficult issues to address. When issues of poverty, learning difficulties, unstable home environments, and limited English ability are thrown into the mix, the situation becomes even more challenging. Over the past several decades, education has increasingly become politicized at both the national and state levels. Governors in every state want to be known as the *education governor* and to be able to claim that their administration has greatly improved education in their states. The problem is that impediments to improving education do not go away simply because people want them to. What is often offered in place of substantive plans for improving education is a call for higher standards and more rigorous assessment of student achievement (see, e.g., National Council on Education Standards and Testing, 1992).

This seems like a worthwhile proposal—who could be opposed to higher standards? The problem is that the mechanisms for meeting the higher standards are left to school districts and ultimately to classroom teachers. The logic here is somewhat tenuous: If students are not achieving enough now, demand more. Smith, Smith, and De Lisi (2001) have compared this stance to working with a high jumper. If the high jumper cannot clear the bar at 6 feet, is it going to do any good to set it at 7 feet? The goal seems noble, but to attain it, something in addition to higher standards is needed.

Concomitant with the increased emphasis on standardized assessment is a greater tendency to *teach to the test*. This phrase refers to the practice of primarily, or even exclusively, teaching those aspects of the curriculum that one knows are going to appear on the standardized assessment. The problem is that those aspects that do not appear on the test will disappear from the curriculum. In its extreme form, students are not just taught only the content that will appear on the test, they are taught that content only in the precise form in which it will appear on the test. For example, if a sixth-grade applied geometry standard is assessed by asking students how many square feet of wallpaper will be needed to paper a room with certain dimensions (including windows and doors), then eventually, in some classrooms, that is the only way in which that aspect of geometry will be taught.

However, as Popham (2001) points out, if the curriculum is well defined and the assessment covers it appropriately, teaching to the test can simply represent good instruction. Of course, this requires teaching the content of the assessment in a such a way that students would be able to use it in a variety of situations, not just to do well on the assessment. Simply put, it is inappropriate to teach the exact items or analogous items to those on the assessment directly to students, but it is perfectly appropriate to teach them the content that will be covered on the assessment.

Teachers cannot afford simply to bury their heads in the sand and hope that all will turn out for the best. Teachers must understand the political, educational, and assessment context in which they work. Teachers can be effective advocates for best practices in education for their students, both in the classroom and in a larger political and social context.

RIDE
REFLECTION FOR ACTION

The Event

At the beginning of the chapter, you were assigned to a committee to consider how to improve the scores of students in your school on the statewide assessment program. Let us examine this issue, using the RIDE process.

Reflection RIDE

First, think about what your role is and what kinds of contributions you can make to this committee. You are a first-year teacher participating on a committee with teachers who are more experienced and have seen a number of innovations in education come and go. To begin with, do not try to be an expert; be a contributor. Listen to and respect more experienced teachers. Next, think about where you can make a contribution. Do your homework. Come to the meeting prepared.

What Theoretical/Conceptual Information Might Assist in This Situation? Consider the following.

The Validity of the Assessment and Curricular Alignment

How well does the district curriculum align with the statewide standards? If the alignment is poor, then the results may not be a valid picture of the students' achievement. However, since the statewide standards are set (fixed), the curriculum may be the thing that has to be adjusted.

Employing Statistical Analysis

What does the distribution of scores for the district look like, not just the percentages of students passing and failing?

Looking for Strengths and Weaknesses

Where do our strengths and weaknesses appear to be? What needs to be addressed? What strengths can be built upon?

Information Gathering

www.wiley.com/college/odonnell

In this chapter, you have learned a great deal about how to look at assessment scores. Find the schoolwide report and examine it carefully before coming to the meeting. What are the school's strengths and weaknesses? How does this year's performance compare to last year's? Are there trends that are consistent over time? How does your school compare to others in the district or to similar schools in the state? The Web site for this text includes links to sites that will help you make such comparisons. You are not the only school facing this kind of problem. What have other schools done to improve scores? Some creative research on the Internet or in teachers' magazines may allow you to attend the meeting armed with good ideas.

Decision Making RIDE

There is a fable about mice being eaten by a cat. They decide to put a bell around the cat's neck so they can hear the cat coming and run away. The problem, of course, is how to get the bell on the cat. Ideas that sound great but cannot be accomplished are sometimes referred to as *belling the cat*. You need ideas that are practical and can be put into effect. In choosing among various options about what to do in your school, the solutions have to be reasonable, given your circumstances and resources.

Evaluation RIDE

Were you able to use your knowledge about standardized assessments to contribute to the committee's ideas, interpretations, and recommendations? The ultimate evaluation will occur when you look at the results for next year and the year after that. However, that is a long time to wait for results. You might want to suggest giving a midyear or even quarterly assessment that resembles the statewide assessment to provide an idea of how you are doing and where adjustments might be made.

Further Practice: Your Turn

Here is a second event for consideration and reflection. In doing so, implement the process of reflection, information gathering, decision making, and evaluation.

The Event

You are teaching fourth grade in your school for the first time. Three weeks before the statewide standardized assessments, you receive a set of materials to use in preparing your students for the test. In reviewing the materials, it seems to you that you are teaching what is going to be on the test in the same format as the test. Although these are not direct questions from the test, you are not sure whether this is ethical.

RIDE *Teaching to the test* is an issue of great concern in American education. On one hand, it seems unfair to expect children to show what they can do on an assessment without a solid understanding of what is expected of them and what will appear on the assessment. On the other hand, if you focus too heavily on what is on the assessment and how it is assessed, will you narrow what your students will learn and the contexts in which they can display their abilities? Will they know how to perform only on the assessment?

SUMMARY

- **What are standardized assessments and where do they come from?**

  Assessment has a fairly short history, with the initial development of standardized assessment evolving from the need to determine appropriate educational placement for students with learning difficulties. Standardized school assessments and college admissions testing are both creations of the first half of the 20th century. Most assessments in use in schools today are required by federal legislation and are based on core curriculum standards developed by committees consisting of educators, businesspeople, and community members. Professional test development companies create most standardized assessments.

- **How can a teacher make sense of the statistics and scales that come with these measures?**

  To understand how standardized assessments are developed and how to interpret the scores, it is necessary to have a rudimentary command of statistics—primarily means, standard deviations, and correlation. The scores associated with standardized assessments are of three main types: scores based on a norming group of students (percentiles, NCE scores, grade-equivalent scores, stanines), scores that are independent of the norming group (SAT scores, scaled scores used in statewide assessment programs), and scores established by panels of experts.

- **What is the best way to interpret standardized test scores?**

  In interpreting standardized assessments, one should begin by thinking about the student, not the assessment. The purpose of looking at standardized assessment scores is to use the information they provide to refine and enhance your understanding of the progress your students have made. Standardized assessments should be combined with knowledge from classroom assessments and your personal knowledge of the student to generate the most complete picture of the student.

- **How concerned should teachers be about the issues of reliability and validity?**

  All assessments should be valid, reliable, and free from bias. *Valid* means that the interpretations based on the scores are appropriate and that the assessment is in fact measuring what it is intended to measure. *Reliable* means that the scores are consistent—that a similar score would be obtained on a second assessment. *Freedom from bias* means that the assessment does not favor one group over another—that the same interpretation of a score would hold, regardless of the race, gender, or ethnicity of a student.

● **How can teachers fairly assess students with learning and physical challenges?**

Accommodations can be made for students who face special challenges that address their needs while maintaining the integrity of the assessment. Extra time, freedom from distractions, and the use of simpler language in math questions are frequently used accommodations. Assistive technology is also appropriate in some situations.

● **Is standardized assessment equally fair for students from different cultural backgrounds?**

This is an issue of great concern for educators. Although research findings suggest that most assessments do not have substantial bias, the assessments can be used in such a way as to produce biased decisions. Special care must be taken in using and interpreting assessment results for students from differing cultural and ethnic backgrounds. At the K-12 level, this often can be seen in using standardized assessments with students who are ELLs.

KEY TERMS

affective assessment, p. 471

central tendency, p. 472

coefficient alpha, p. 483

consequential validity, p. 483

construct validity, p. 481

content validity, p. 481

criterion-related validity, p. 481

criterion-referenced, p. 470

grade-equivalent scores, p. 477

intelligence test, p. 467

inter-rater reliability, p. 483

mastery levels, p. 488

mean, p. 472

median, p. 472

mode, p. 473

normal curve equivalent (NCE), p. 477

normal distribution, p. 474

norms, p. 479

norm-referenced, p. 470

norming study, p. 468

passing scores, p. 479

percentile, p. 476

raw scores, p. 476

reliability, p. 483

reliability coefficient, p. 483

reliability study, p. 483

scaled scores, p. 476

split-half reliability, p. 483

standard deviation, p. 474

standard error of measurement, p. 484

standardized assessment, p. 466

standards-based assessment, p. 468

stanines, p. 477

test bias, p. 493

true score, p. 484

validity, p. 481

validation study, p. 481

variability, p. 473

variance, p. 473

z-score, p. 474

EXERCISES

1. *Understanding Standards, Objectives, and Achievement Targets*

   Go to the Web or another source and find the statewide standards for your state in the areas that you think you might want to teach. (Nearly all state departments of education include statewide standards for each grade level and subject on their Web sites. A link to state departments of education is provided at the companion Web site for this book.) Print out the standards and review them.

   a. What do you think about these standards overall? Do they seem thorough? Are they too detailed or not detailed enough? Do they seem to limit your creativity as a teacher?

   b. If you had to eliminate one of the standards, which one would it be and why? If you could add one, what would it be? The purpose of this activity is to push yourself to think hard about whether the list is a thorough and exhaustive one.

2. *Standards and No Child Left Behind*

How does your state meet the assessment mandates of the NCLB legislation? Go to your state department of education's Web site and find out what the assessment program looks like. Focus on the grade level and/or subject you are planning to teach. What are the standards for the grade and subject? How are the assessments constructed? Are they mostly multiple choice, or do they use authentic assessments? Write a summary of how your state addresses this important issue.

3. *Understanding Scales*

What are the differences between grade-equivalent scores and percentiles? What are the strengths and weaknesses of each? If you could choose only one score to be reported for your students, which one would it be and why?

4. *Making the Data Make Sense*

You are concerned about the test scores you have received for one of your students: They are not consistent with your expectations. What can you do about this now? What are some other sources of information you can turn to in order to assess the situation more fully?

5. *Relating Standardized Assessments to Classroom Assessments*

As a teacher, you will be developing classroom assessments for your students, but they will also be taking standardized assessments. These assessments have become very important in school districts in recent years. What do you think is the proper relationship between classroom assessments and standardized assessments? What types of assessments might you develop that would help your students perform at their best on standardized assessments? Is this goal (optimal performance on standardized assessments) a worthwhile one for your class? Why or why not?

6. *Using Mental Measurements Yearbook*

Research a measurement topic using Mental Measurement Yearbooks. You might start with an assessment your district already uses, or you might pick an area of assessment you are interested in learning more about. You might also be able to find a copy of the assessment in a curriculum library. What can you learn about the validity of the assessment or whether there is evidence of ethnic bias?

Appendix

Looking at the Praxis II™ Principles of Learning and Teaching Assessment and the INTASC Principles

In most states, part of the certification process for becoming a teacher includes an assessment of the aspiring teacher's knowledge, skills, and dispositions. This assessment is often based on what are known as the INTASC (Interstate New Teacher Assessment and Support Consortium) principles and/or involve the Praxis™ assessment developed by the Educational Testing Service.

The INTASC principles are a set of 10 statements that define what the consortium believes are exemplary instructional practices. They involve issues of motivation, collaborative activities, and appropriate assessment practices, among others. INTASC is in the process of developing an instrument that would assess mastery of these principles. It has also been working to develop model policies with respect to teacher preparation, teacher licensure, and professional development that states can use to align their own teaching standards.

Currently, 42 states use at least some part of the Praxis Series™ that consists of three sets of assessments: These are the Praxis I™ for college students wanting to study education to become teachers; The Praxis II™, which includes subject matter assessments as well as an assessment of subject-specific pedagogical skills and knowledge, called the Principles of Learning and Teaching (PLT); and the Praxis III™ for beginning teachers already working in classrooms. Of particular interest here is the PLT assessment, because many of the topics in the assessment parallel those in the text. There are four different levels for the PLT: Early Childhood, K–6, Grades 5–9, and Grades 7–12.

To help you prepare for the PLT and to help you better understand the INTASC principles, we developed a correspondence chart. In the following pages, you can examine the various areas of the PLT and locate in the text where those topics have been discussed. You can do the same for the INTASC principles. Both the Educational Testing Service and the INTASC consortium have Web sites where you can look in depth at these assessments and principles. www.ets.org/praxis/www.ccsso.org/projects/Interstate_New_Teacher_Assessment_and_Support_Consortium

The best way to prepare for any assessment is to test yourself on questions or prompts that are similar to the ones on the real assessment. You can find sample questions for the PLT on the ETS Web site. There are also commercially available practice assessments. Find your strengths and weaknesses, and work on those weaknesses by reviewing the appropriate material on the assessment. Do not hesitate to undertake a serious review. Doctors, lawyers, engineers—professionals in all fields—take special preparation to get ready for certification examinations. Take this preparation seriously—and good luck!

Praxis II™	Educational Psychology	INTASC
I. Students as learners (approximately 35% of test)		
A. Student development and the learning process		Principle #2: The teacher understands how children learn and develop and can provide learning opportunities that support their intellectual, social, and personal development.

Praxis II™	Educational Psychology	INTASC
1. Theoretical foundations about how learning occurs: how students construct knowledge, acquire skills, and develop habits of mind Examples of important theorists		Principle #2 (Knowledge): The teacher understands how learning occurs—how students construct knowledge, acquire skills, and develop habits of mind—and knows how to use instructional strategies that promote student learning.
• Jean Piaget	Chapter 2/ Cognitive development (pp. 37–48) Chapter 12/Piagetian theory (pp. 398–399)	
• Lev Vygotsky	Chapter 2/ Sociocognitive development (pp. 48–56) Chapter 10/ Social constructivism and socio-cultural learning theory (pp. 322–326) Chapter 12/ Vygotskyian theory (pp. 399–400)	
• Howard Gardner	Chapter 4/ Gardner's theory of multiple intelligences (pp. 109–110)	
• Robert Sternberg	Chapter 4/ Triarchic theory of intelligence (pp. 108–109)	
• Albert Bandura	Chapter 5/ Self-efficacy theories (pp. 142–147) Chapter 9/Teacher self-efficacy (pp. 283–285) Chapter 10/ Social learning theory (pp. 317–321)	
Important terms that relate to learning theory:		
• Adaptation	Chapter 2/ Adaptation and schemas (pp. 37–40)	
• Conservation	Chapter 2/ The concrete operations stage (pp. 42–44)	
• Constructivism	Chapter 8/ Cognitive and constructivist theories of learning (pp. 240–241) Chapter 10/Social constructivism and socio-cultural theory (pp. 322–326)	
• Private speech	Chapter 2/ The role of language in cognitive development (pp. 57–58)	
• Scaffolding	Chapter 2/ Scaffolding in the zone of proximal development (pp. 48–51) Chapter 12/ Scaffolding and tutoring (pp. 402–404) Chapter 10/ Scaffolding (pp. 327–329) Chapter 12 (pp. 399–400)	
• Zone of proximal development	Chapter 2/ Scaffolding in the zone of proximal development (pp. 49–51)	
• Learning	Chapter 7/ Behavior learning theory (entire chapter) Chapter 8/ Cognitive learning theories (entire chapter) Chapter 10/ Social constructivism and learning in community (entire chapter)	
• Memory	Chapter 2/ Brain structure and function (pp. 34–37) Chapter 8/ Memory systems (pp. 246–255)	
• Schemas	Chapter 2/ Adaptation and schemas: Piaget's theory (pp. 37–40) Chapter 8/ Schemas and scripts (pp. 253–255)	
• Transfer	Chapter 8/ Transfer (p. 269)	
• Self-efficacy	Chapter 9/ Self-efficacy (pp. 283–285)	

Praxis II™	Educational Psychology	INTASC
2. Human development in the physical, social, emotional, moral, speech/language, and cognitive domains.	Chapter 2/ Cognitive development (entire chapter, includes language development) Chapter 3/ Social development (entire chapter) Chapter 5/ Self-regulation (pp. 162–165) Chapter 8/ Cognitive theories of learning (entire chapter)	Principle #2 (Knowledge): The teacher is aware of expected developmental progressions and ranges of individual variation within each domain (physical, social, emotional, moral, and cognitive), can identify levels of readiness in learning, and understands how development in any one domain may affect performance in others.
B. Students as diverse learners		Principle #3: The teacher understands how students differ in their approaches to learning and creates instructional opportunities that are adapted to diverse learners.
1. Differences in the ways students learn and perform	Chapter 1/ Students with special needs (pp. 15–20) Chapter 4/ Differences in ability and instruction (pp. 119–120) Chapter 4/ Multiple intelligences (pp. 109–110) Chapter 12/ Status characteristics (pp. 416–418)	Principle #2 (Dispositions): The teacher appreciates individual variation within each area of development, shows respect for the diverse talents of all learners, and is commit-ted to help them develop self-confidence and competence. Principle #3 (Knowledge): The teacher understands and can identify differences in approaches to learning performance, including different learning styles, multiple intelligences, and performance modes, and can design instruction that helps use students' strengths as the basis for growth. Principle #3 (Performance): The teacher creates a learning community in which individual differences are respected.
2. Areas of exceptionality in students' learning • Talent/Giftedness • Learning disabilities	Chapter 4 (pp. 114; 115–119) Chapter 4/ Extremes of intelligence (pp. 113–115) Chapter 4/ Learnies with special needs (pp. 120–132) Chapter 4/ Learning disabilities (pp. 127–128) Chapter 5/ Self-efficacy in students with learning disabilities (pp. 146–147)	Principle #3 (Knowledge): The teacher knows about areas of exceptionality in learning— including learning disabilities, visual and perceptual difficulties, and special physical and mental challenges.
• ADHD	Chapter 1/ Students with special needs (pp. 16–20) Chapter 4/ Attention deficit/hyperactivity disorder (pp. 128–130)	
• Functional and mental retardation • Autism	Chapter 4/ Mental retardation (p. 115) Chapter 4 (p. 130)	
3. Legislation and institutional responsibilities relating to exceptional students • Americans with Disabilities Act (ADA); Individuals with Disabilities Education Act (IDEA); Section 504 Protections for Students • Inclusion, mainstreaming, and "least restrictive environment"	Chapter 1/ Individualized education plan (p. 19) Chapter 4/ The law and special education (pp. 121–126) Chapter 4/ The Law and special education (pp. 121–126) Chapter 4/ Inclusion (p. 125)	

Praxis II™	Educational Psychology	INTASC
4. Approaches for accommodating various learning styles, intelligences, or exceptionalities	Chapter 2/ Technology support for young readers and readers with special needs (pp. 59–61) Chapter 6/ Engaging diverse learners (pp. 177–178) Chapter 6/ How to motivate students with mental retardation: intrinsically or extrinsically? (p. 182) Chapter 7/ Behavior learning theory and diverse learners (p. 220) Chapter 7/ Behavior learning theory and special needs students (pp. 220–221) Chapter 9/ Planning with students with special needs (p. 295) Chapter 10/ Scaffolding with students from diverse backgrounds (p. 334) Chapter 10/ Scaffolding for students with special needs (pp. 333–334) Chapter 11/ Managing learning in classrooms (entire chapter) Chapter 12/ Special needs and cooperative learning (pp. 414–415) Chapter 13/ Classroom assessments for students with special needs (pp. 447–448)	Principle #1 (Performance): The teacher can represent and use differing viewpoints, theories, "ways of knowing," and methods of inquiry in teaching of subject matter concepts. Principle #3 (Performance): The teacher identifies and designs instruction appropriate to students' stages of development, learning styles, strengths, and needs.
5. Process of second-language acquisition and strategies to support the learning of students for whom English is not a first language	Chapter 2/ Second Language Acquisition (pp. 61–62)	Principle #3 (Knowledge): The teacher knows about the process of second-language acquisition and about strategies to support the learning of students whose first language is not English.
6. Understanding the influence of individual experiences, talents, and prior learning, as well as language, culture, family, and community values on students' learning	Chapter 2/ Cultural tools (p. 54) Chapter 2/ The importance of peers (p. 54) Chapter 3/ Culture, diversity, and special needs (p. 74) Chapter 4/ Talent (pp. 114–119) Chapter 4/ Difference in ability and instruction (pp. 119–120) Chapter 4/ Inclusion (p. 125) Chapter 4/ Educational options (pp. 119–120) Chapter 4/ The role of socioeconomic status and its role in learning (p. 133) Chapter 9/ Working in culturally different contexts (p. 286) Chapter 9/ Homework and cultural differences (pp. 307–308) Chapter 10/ The role of experience (pp. 326–327) Chapter 10/ Learning outside of school (pp. 339–345) Chapter 13/ Diversity among students and their parents (pp. 430–431)	Principle #1 (Knowledge): The teacher understands how students' conceptual framework for an area of knowledge, conceptions, and misconceptions can influence their learning. Principle #2 (Knowledge): The teacher understands that students' physical, social, emotional, moral, and cognitive development influences learning and knows how to address these factors when making instructional decisions. Principle #3 (Knowledge): The teacher understands how students' learning is influenced by individual experiences, talents, and prior learning, as well as language, culture, family, and community values. Principle #3 (Knowledge): The teacher has a well-grounded framework for understanding cultural and community diversity and knows how to learn about and incorporate students' experiences, cultures, and community resources into instruction. Principle #3 (Disposition): The teacher is sensitive to community and cultural mores. The teacher makes students feel valued for their potential as people and helps them to learn to value each other.

Praxis II™	Educational Psychology	INTASC
C. Student Motivation and the Learning Environment		Principle #5: The teacher uses an understanding of individual and group motivation and behavior to create a reaming environment that encourages positive social interaction, active engagement in learning, and self-motivation.
1. Theoretical foundations of human motivation and behavior	Chapter 3/ Psychosocial development (pp. 77–84) Chapter 5/ Motivation to learn (entire chapter) Chapter 7/ Increasing desirable behavior (pp. 221–224)	Principle #5 (Knowledge): The teacher can use knowledge about human motivation and behavior drawn from the foundational sciences of psychology, anthropology, and sociology to develop strategies for organizing and supporting individual and group work.
2. How knowledge of human motivation and behavior should influence strategies for organizing and supporting individual and group work in the classroom	Chapter 5/ Motivation to learn (entire chapter) Chapter 6/ Engaging students in learning (entire chapter)	Principle #5 (Knowledge): The teacher understands the principles of effective classroom management and can use a range of strategies to promote positive relationships, cooperation, and purposeful learning in the classroom.
3. Factors and situations that are likely to promote or diminish student's motivation to learn and how to help students to become self-motivated	Chapter 5/ Motivation to learn (entire chapter) Chapter 5/ Self-efficacy (pp. 142–147) Chapter 5/ Mastery modeling programs (pp. 144–145) Chapter 5/ Mastery beliefs (pp. 147–149) Chapter 5/ Goals (pp. 153–162) Chapter 6/ Engaging students in learning (entire chapter)	Principle #5 (Knowledge): The teacher recognizes factors and situations that are likely to promote or diminish intrinsic motivation and knows how to help students become self-motivated.
4. Principles of effective classroom management and strategies to promote positive relationships, cooperation, and purposeful learning	Chapter 5/ Mastery modeling programs (pp. 144–145) Chapter 5/ Promoting self-regulation (pp. 163–164) Chapter 6/ Two approaches to producing engagement (pp. 175–177) Chapter 6/ Using extrinsic motivators effectively (pp. 180–181) Chapter 6/ The engagement model (p. 173) Chapter 7/ Managing behavior (pp. 219–230) Chapter 7/ Promoting self-management (pp. 227–228) Chapter 7/ The fundamental task of classroom management (pp. 228–229) Chapter 7/ Feedback and knowledge of results (p. 230) Chapter 9/ Providing feedback (pp. 300–301) Chapter 11/ Managing learning in classrooms (entire chapter) Chapter 13/ Communicating with parents (pp. 456–458)	Principle #5 (Performance): The teacher analyzes the classroom environment and makes decisions and adjustments to enhance social relationships, student motivation and engagement, and productive work.

Praxis II™	Educational Psychology	INTASC
II. Instruction and assessment (approximately 35% of test)		
A. Instructional strategies		Principle #4: The teacher understands and uses a variety of instructional strategies to encourage students' development of critical thinking, problem solving and performance skills.
1. Major cognitive strategies		Principle #4 (Knowledge): The teacher understands the cognitive processes associated with various kinds of learning (e.g., critical and creative thinking, problem structuring and problem solving, invention, memorization, and recall) and how these processes can be stimulated.
• Critical thinking	Chapter 1/ Critical thinking (pp. 28–29) Chapter 12/ Perspectives on peer learning (pp. 388–400)	
• Inductive and deductive thinking	Chapter 2/ The formal operations stage (pp. 44–46) Chapter 7/ Inductive reasoning (p. 225) Chapter 8/ Reasoning and argumentation (p. 267)	
• Problem structuring and problem solving	Chapter 8/ Problem solving (pp. 267–269)	
• Invention	Chapter 11/ Misbehavior: informal correctives and imposing penalties (pp. 368–372)	
• Encoding and Retrieval	Chapter 8 (pp. 225–262)	
2. Major categories, advantages, and appropriate uses of instructional strategies		Principle #4 (Knowledge): The teacher understands principles and techniques, along with advantages and limitations associated with various instructional strategies (e.g., cooperative learning, direct instruction, discovery learning, whole-group discussion, independent study, interdisciplinary instruction).
• Cooperative learning	Chapter 2/ Peers as guides, mentors (p. 54) Chapter 12/ Learning from peers (entire chapter)	
• Direct instruction	Chapter 2 Limitations of Piaget's theory (p. 48) Chapter 9/ Direct instruction (pp. 297–298)	
• Discovery learning	Chapter 2 Limitations of Piaget's theory (p. 48) Chapter 9/ Discovery learning (p. 297)	
• Expository teaching	Chapter 9/ Expository teaching (pp. 296–297)	
• Concept mapping	Chapter 8/ Concept mapping (pp. 258–260)	
• Questioning	Chapter 9/ Asking questions (p. 301) Chapter 12/ The importance of discourse quality (p. 418)	
• Mastery learning	Chapter 7/ Mastery learning (pp. 231–232)	
• Problem-based learning	Chapter 10/ Problem-based learning (pp. 337–338)	
• Reciprocal teaching	Chapter 10/ Reciprocal teaching (pp. 335–336)	
• Whole-group discussions	Chapter 11/ Whole-class instruction (pp. 374–377)	
• Small group discussions	Chapter 12/ Learning in heterogeneous groups (pp. 408–411)	
• Independent work	Chapter 11/ Small group work (pp. 373–374) Chapter 11/ Independent work or seatwork (pp. 372–373)	

Praxis II™	Educational Psychology	INTASC
3. Principles, techniques, and methods associated with major instructional strategies		
• Direct instruction	Chapter 9/ Direct instruction (pp. 297–298)	
• Student-centered models	Chapter 10/ Social constructivism and learning in community (entire chapter)	
4. Methods for enhancing student learning through the use of a variety of resources and materials		Principle #4 (Knowledge): The teacher knows how to enhance learning through the use of a wide variety of materials as well as human and technological resources (e.g., computers, audiovisual technologies, videotapes and discs, local experts, primary documents and artifacts, texts, reference books, literature, and other print resources).
• Computers, Internet resources, Web pages, email	Chapter 10/ Instruction influenced by social-constructivist and sociocultural theory (pp. 334–339) Chapter 9/ Online teaching communities (p. 283)	
• Audiovisual technologies, such as videotapes and CDs	Chapter 10/ Scaffolding with technology (pp. 329–333)	
• Local experts	Chapter 9/ Differences in knowledge between experts and novices (pp. 281–283)	
• Field trips	Chapter 10/ Learning in cultural institutions (pp. 339–341)	
• Libraries	Chapter 10/ Learning in libraries (pp. 343–346)	
• Museums	Chapter 10/ Science and history museums (pp. 346–347)	
B. Planning instruction	Chapter 9/ Planning (pp. 287–296)	Principle #7: The teacher plans instruction based on knowledge of subject matter, students, the community, and curriculum goals.
1. Techniques for planning instruction, including addressing curriculum goals, selecting current topics, incorporating learning theory, subject matter, curriculum development, and student development and interests	Chapter 9/ Planning (pp. 287–296) Chapter 11/ Managing learning in classrooms (entire chapter) Chapter 13/ Classroom assessment (entire chapter)	Principle #4 (Performance): The teacher carefully evaluates how to achieve reaming goals, choosing alternative teaching strategies and materials to achieve different instructional purposes and to meet student needs (e.g., developmental stages, prior knowledge, reaming styles, and interests). Principle #7 (Knowledge): The teacher understands reaming theory, subject matter, curriculum development, and student development and knows how to use this knowledge in planning instruction to meet curriculum goals.
2. Techniques for creating effective bridges between curriculum goals and students' experiences	Chapter 8/ Transfer (p. 269) Chapter 9/ Homework (pp. 301–308) Chapter 9/ Guided discovery (p. 297) Chapter 10/ Modeling (p. 317)	Principle #4 (Performance): The teacher constantly monitors and adjusts strategies in response to learner feedback.

Praxis II™	Educational Psychology	INTASC
C. Assessment strategies		Principle #8: The teacher understands and uses formal and informal assessment strategies to evaluate and ensure the continuous intellectual and social development of the learner.
1. Types of assessments	Chapter 13/ Options for assessment (pp. 434–443) Chapter 14 (pp. 466–471)	Principle #8 (Knowledge): The teacher understands the characteristics, uses, advantages, and limitations of different types of assessments (e.g., criterion-referenced and norm-referenced instruments, traditional standardized and performance-based tests, observation systems, and evaluations of student work) for evaluating how students learn, what they know and are able to do, and what kinds of experiences will support their further growth and development.
2. Characteristics of assessments	Chapter 13/ Principles of assessments and grading (pp. 431–433) Chapter 14 (pp. 472–484)	
3. Scoring assessments	Chapter 13/ Administering, scoring, and communicating assessment results (pp. 448–449) Chapter 13/ Developing a grading system (pp. 453–456)	
4. Use of assessments	Chapter 13/ Developing and using assessments (pp. 444–449)	Principle #2 (Performance): The teacher assesses individual and group performance in order to design instruction that meets learners' current needs in each domain and that leads to the next level of development. Principle #8 (Performance): The teacher appropriately uses a variety of formal and informal assessment techniques (e.g., observation, portfolios of student work, teacher-made tests, performance tasks, projects, student self-assessments, peer assessment, and standardized tests) to enhance her or his knowledge of learners, evaluate students' progress and performances, and modify teaching and learning strategies.
5. Understanding of measurement theory and assessment-related issues	Chapter 13/ Data-based determinations of next steps (pp. 452–453) Chapter 13/ Developing a grading system (pp. 453–456) Chapter 14 (pp. 472–484)	Principle #8 (Knowledge): The teacher understands measurement theory and assessment-related issues, such as validity, reliability, bias, and scoring concerns.
6. Interpreting and communicating results of assessments	Chapter 13/ Communicating with parents (pp. 456–459) Chapter 13/ Administering, scoring, and communicating assessment results (pp. 448–449) Chapter 14 (pp. 484–492)	Principle #8 (Performance): The teacher maintains useful records of student work and performance and can communicate student progress knowledgeably and responsibly, based on appropriate indicators, to students, parents, and other colleagues.

Praxis II™	Educational Psychology	INTASC
III. Communication techniques (approximately 15% of test)		
A. Basic, effective verbal and nonverbal communication techniques	Chapter 2/ Transfer of responsibility (p. 53) Chapter 11/ Taking it to the classroom: tips for creating a peaceful classroom (p. 379) Chapter 13/ Principles of assessment and grading (pp. 431–433) Chapter 13/ Communication (pp. 456–459)	Principle #6: The teacher uses knowledge of effective verbal, nonverbal, and media communication techniques to foster active inquiry, collaboration, and supportive interaction in the classroom. Principle #6 (Knowledge): The teacher recognizes the importance of nonverbal as well as verbal communication.
B. Effect of cultural and gender differences on communications in the classroom	Chapter 9/ Ensure clear home/school communication (pp. 305–306) Chapter 11/ Taking it to the classroom: Tips for Creating a peaceful classroom (p. 379) Chapter 12/ Taking it to the classroom: Do you know Jack? Getting the help he needs (p. 416)	Principle #6 (Knowledge): The teacher understands how cultural and gender differences can affect communication in the classroom.
C. Types of communications and interactions that can stimulate discussion in different ways for particular purposes	Chapter 9/ Providing explanations (pp. 298–300) Chapter 9/ Providing feedback (p. 300) Chapter 9/ Asking questions (p. 301)	Principle #6 (Performance): The teacher knows how to ask questions and stimulate discussion in different ways for particular purposes, for example, probing for learner understanding, helping students articulate their ideas and thinking processes, promoting risk taking and problem solving, facilitating factual recall, encouraging convergent and divergent thinking, stimulating curiosity, helping students to question.
IV. Profession and community (approximately 15% of test)		
A. The reflective practitioner	RIDE scenarios throughout the book Chapter 1/ Reflective teaching (pp. 10–15)	Principle #9: The teacher is a reflective practitioner who continually evaluates the effects of his/her choices and actions on others (students, parents, and other professionals in the learning community) and who actively seeks out opportunities to grow professionally.

1. Types of resources available for professional development and learning
  • Professional literature
  • Colleagues
  • Professional associations
  • Professional development activities
	Chapter 9/ Teacher development (pp. 278–283)	Principle #1 (Disposition): The teacher realizes that subject matter knowledge is not a fixed body of facts but is complex and ever evolving. He or she seeks to keep abreast of new ideas and understandings in the field.
		
		Principle #9 (Knowledge): The teacher is aware of major areas of research on teaching and of resources available for professional learning (e.g., professional literature, colleagues, professional associations, professional development activities).

2. Ability to read, understand, and apply articles and books about current research, views, ideas, and debates regarding best teaching practices		Principle #1 (Knowledge): The teacher understands major concepts, assumptions, debates, processes of inquiry, and ways of knowing that are central to the discipline(s) he or she teaches. Principle #1 (Performance): The teacher can evaluate teaching resources and curriculum materials for their comprehensiveness, accuracy, and usefulness for representing particular ideas and concepts.

Praxis II™	Educational Psychology	INTASC
3. Ongoing personal reflection on teaching and learning practices as a basis for making professional decisions		Principle #1 (Knowledge): The teacher can relate his or her disciplinary knowledge to other subject areas. Principle #9 (Performance): The teacher is committed to seeking out, developing, and continually refining practices that address the individual needs of students.
B. The Larger Community		Principle #10: The teacher fosters relationships with school colleagues, parents, and agencies in the larger community to support students' learning and well-being.
1. Role of the school as a resource to the larger community	Chapter 9/ Teacher development (pp. 278–283) Chapter 10/ Instruction influenced by social constructivism and sociocultural theory (pp. 334–339) Chapter 10/ Learning outside of school (pp. 339–345) Chapter 11/ Managing learning in classrooms (entire chapter)	Principle #10 (Knowledge): The teacher understands schools as organizations within the larger community context and understands the operations of the relevant aspects of the system(s) within which he or she works.
2. Factors in the students' environment outside of school	Chapter 10/ Learning outside of school (pp. 339–345)	Principle #3 (Disposition): The teacher is sensitive to community and cultural mores. The teacher makes students feel valued for their potential as people and helps them to learn to value each other. Principle #10 (Knowledge): The teacher understands how factors in the students' environment outside of school (e.g., family circumstances, community environments, health and economic conditions) may influence students' lives and learning.
3. Develop and utilize active partnerships among teachers, parents/guardians, and leaders in the community to support the educational process	Chapter 9/ Ensure clear home/school communication (pp. 305–306) Chapter 9/ Providing feedback (p. 300) Chapter 11/ Managing learning in classrooms (entire chapter) Chapter 13/ Communicating with parents (pp. 456–459)	Principle #10 (Performance): The teacher makes links with the learners' other environments on behalf of students by consulting with parents, teachers of other classes and activities within the schools, counselors, and professionals in other community agencies. Principle #10 (Performance): The teacher establishes respectful and productive relationships with parents and guardians from diverse home and community situations and seeks to develop cooperative partnerships in support of student learning and well-being.
4. Major laws related to students' rights and teacher responsibilities	Chapter 4/ The law and special education (pp. 121–126)	Principle #10 (Knowledge): The teacher understands and implements laws related to students' rights and teacher responsibilities (e.g., for equal education, appropriate education for handicapped students, confidentiality, privacy, appropriate treatment of students, reporting in situations related to possible child abuse).

Glossary

accommodation A modification process in which low-level schemas are transformed into higher level schemas. (Ch. 2, 12)

accommodations Modifications made in an assessment for students with disabilities. (Ch. 13)

achievement goal What the student is trying to accomplish when facing a standard of excellence. (Ch. 5)

achievement targets Well-specified statements of what teachers want to accomplish in a particular lesson or set of lessons. (Ch. 9, 13)

action research A research method carried out by teachers in their own classrooms to inform and refine their personal theories of teaching and classroom practice. (Ch. 1)

acute problems Problems that occur only infrequently but are severe. (Ch. 11)

adaptation Adjusting to the demands of the environment. (Ch. 2)

advance organizer A broad introductory statement of the information that will be presented in a lesson. (Ch. 9)

affective assessment An assessment related to feelings, motivation, attitudes, and the like. (Ch. 14)

affordance A property of a tool or artifact that allows a person to act in particular ways that would not be possible without using the tool. (Ch. 10)

aggression Any intentional behavior designed to harm another person or group physically or psychologically. (Ch. 3)

algorithm A systematic and exhaustive strategy for solving problems. (Ch. 8)

alternative assessment A generic term referring to assessments that are different from traditional approaches, such as multiple choice and constructed response. (Ch. 13)

amygdala Almond-shaped structure in the limbic area of the brain involved in the activation of negative emotions. (Ch. 2)

animism The belief that all things are living. (Ch. 2)

anxiety The unpleasant, aversive emotion that students experience in evaluative settings. (Ch. 6)

aphasia Language disability in which the person has difficulty understanding or producing speech. (Ch. 2)

argumentation The process of taking a position, providing reasons for the position, and presenting counterarguments. (Ch. 8)

assessment The process of coming to understand what students know and can do. (Ch. 13)

assigning competence The teacher acknowledges the contribution of a student to the completion of a task. (Ch. 12)

assimilation An incorporation process in which an outside event is brought into one's way of thinking. (Ch. 2, 12)

assistive technology Any piece of equipment that can improve the functionality of a child with a disability. (Ch. 10)

attachment A close emotional relationship between two persons that is characterized by mutual affection and the desire to maintain proximity with the other. (Ch. 3)

attention Focus that is selective and limited. (Ch. 8)

attention deficit disorder (ADD) A condition in which children experience persistent difficulties with attention span, impulse control, and sometimes hyperactivity. (Ch. 4)

attention deficit hyperactivity disorder (ADHD) A condition in which children or adults consistently display inattention, hyperactivity, and impulsiveness. (Ch. 4)

attribution An explanation of why an outcome occurred. (Ch. 5)

attunement Sensing and reading another's state of being and adjusting one's own behavior accordingly. (Ch. 3)

authentic assessment An assessment that is tightly related to the instruction that the students have received or to tasks that are relevant in real life. (Ch. 13)

authentic tasks Tasks that are connected to the real world. (Ch. 10)

automaticity The ability to perform a task without having to think much about it. (Ch. 4, 8)

autonomy The psychological need to experience self-direction in the initiation and regulation of one's behavior. (Ch. 6)

autonomy-supportive environment An interpersonal relationship or classroom climate that involves, nurtures, and satisfies the student's need for autonomy. (Ch. 6)

autonomy-supportive motivating style A teacher's enduring tendency to engage students in learning activities by promoting their intrinsic motivation and identified regulation during the lesson. (Ch. 6)

behavioral engagement   The extent to which a student displays high attention, strong effort, and enduring persistence on a learning activity. (Ch. 6)

behavioral objectives   Statements of goals for instruction that clearly set forth what a student will be able to do as a result of the instruction. (Ch. 9)

behavioral schemas   Mental representations of physical actions. (Ch. 2)

between-class ability grouping   A procedure in which children are assigned to different classes based on measured ability. (Ch. 4)

bias   Systematic unfair treatment of a particular group of individuals. (Ch. 4, 13)

bilingualism   The use of two or more languages in everyday life. (Ch. 2)

block scheduling   An approach to scheduling at the middle- and high school levels that allows for larger blocks of time to be scheduled for subjects, usually with fewer blocks per week. (Ch. 9)

bottom-up processing   A process in which a stimulus is analyzed into its components, then assembled into a recognizable pattern, also known as *feature analysis.* (Ch. 8)

calibration   An ongoing corrective process in which the person adjusts his or her sense of confidence with a task to reflect most accurately the quality of his or her recent performances at that task. (Ch. 5)

care   An emotional concern and sense of responsibility to protect or enhance another person's welfare or well-being. (Ch. 3)

central tendency   An indicator of the center of a set of scores on some variable. (Ch. 14)

centration   Focusing on an object's most salient perceptual feature while neglecting important features that are not perceptually salient. (Ch. 2)

challenge-feedback sandwich   A learning activity that begins with the presentation of an optimal challenge and ends with informational feedback to communicate how well or how poorly one performed. (Ch. 6)

channeling   Providing constraints during the task so that the learner has an increased likelihood of acting effectively. (Ch. 10)

chronic problems   Problems that persist over time, even though they may not be severe. (Ch. 11)

chunking   The grouping of bits of data into larger, meaningful units. (Ch. 8)

classical conditioning   The association of automatic responses with new stimuli. (Ch. 7)

classification   Grouping objects (parts) into categories (wholes). (Ch. 2)

classified   A term used to refer to special education students who have been identified as having a particular disability. (Ch. 13)

classroom management   Teacher behaviors and management techniques that result in a healthy learning environment, generally free of behavior problems. (Ch. 12)

coefficient alpha   An approach to assessing reliability that uses a single administration of the assessment and focuses on whether all the assessment items appear to be measuring the same underlying ability; also called *Cronbach's alpha.* (Ch. 14)

cognitive apprenticeship   An instructional strategy in which the learner acquires knowledge by modeling the activities of the teacher and being coached by the teacher. (Ch. 10)

cognitive conflict   Experience of conflict when new information does not agree with existing knowledge. (Ch. 12)

cognitive disequilibrium   The experience of cognitive conflict. (Ch. 12)

cognitive engagement   The extent to which a student mentally goes beyond the basic requirements of a learning activity and invests himself or herself in the learning in a committed way. (Ch. 6)

cognitive evaluation theory   A theory of motivation that explains how external events such as rewards affect students' psychological needs for autonomy and competence and, hence, their intrinsic motivation. (Ch. 6)

collective efficacy   A jointly held belief that the community is effective when working together. (Ch. 10)

committed compliance   Cooperatively carrying out a teacher's request to "do this" or "don't do that" with an eager, willing, and sincere commitment to the action. (Ch. 3)

comparative organizer   A broad statement that reminds the student of what he or she already knows. (Ch. 9)

competence   The psychological need to be effective as one interacts with the surrounding environment. (Ch. 3, 6)

concept   An abstraction with which a person categorizes objects, people, ideas, or experiences by shared properties. (Ch. 8)

conceptual change teaching   A method of teaching that helps students understand concepts by challenging them to examine their ideas and identify shortcomings in them. (Ch. 12)

conditional knowledge   Knowledge that guides a person in using declarative and procedural knowledge. (Ch. 8)

conditioned response   A response that is linked to a particular stimulus through conditioning by being paired with the stimulus. (Ch. 7)

conditioned stimulus   A stimulus, that with experience, produces a learned or acquired response. (Ch. 7)

conscience   The capacity to use one's moral cognition, moral emotions, and moral self to inhibit aggression and to initiate altruism and helping. (Ch. 3)

consequences   The good or bad effects that follow a person's behavior. (Ch. 7, 11)

consequential validity   Concern for how the assessment will affect the person taking it. (Ch. 14)

conservation   Understanding that appearance alterations (e.g., an object's length, height, or width) do not change the essential properties of an object (e.g., its amount). (Ch. 2)

constructed response   A type of assessment format in which the student has to provide the answer to the question; more commonly referred to as *short answer.* (Ch. 13)

constructivist perspective   A theoretical perspective that stresses the active role of the learner in building understanding and making sense of information. (Ch. 12)

construct validity   An indicator of the degree to which an ability really exists in the way it is theorized to exist and whether it is appropriately measured by the assessment. (Ch. 14)

content/behavior matrix   A method for specifying what is to be assessed by making a matrix with expected student behaviors on one axis and the content on which that behavior will be observed on the other axis. (Ch. 13)

content knowledge   Knowledge about the subject matter being taught. (Ch. 9)

content validity   An indicator of the degree to which the items on an assessment appear to fully cover the intended content of the assessment and whether there is any extraneous material. (Ch. 14)

contiguity   A condition in which two events occur at the same time. (Ch. 7)

contingency contacting   An approach to behavior management that involves a written agreement about behavior that makes rewards and punishments depend on the students' performance of that behavior. (Ch. 11)

continuous reinforcement   Reinforcement that is provided after every performance of a behavior. (Ch. 7)

control group   The group of participants in an experimental study who are randomly assigned not to receive exposure to the independent variable. (Ch. 1)

controlled processes   Cognitive processes that require conscious attention. (Ch. 8)

controlling motivating style   A teacher's enduring tendency to engage students in learning activities by promoting their extrinsic motivation and introjected regulation during the lesson. (Ch. 6)

controversy   A curiosity-inducing instructional strategy in which the ideas, conclusions, or opinions of one person are incompatible with those of another, and the two attempt to reach agreement. (Ch. 6)

coregulation   A collaborative process in which the teacher and student jointly plan, monitor, and evaluate the academic work of the student. (Ch. 5)

correlational studies   A research method used to measure two naturally occurring variables and summarize the nature and magnitude of their relationship in numerical form. (Ch. 1)

correlation coefficient   A statistical value that ranges from -1 to $+1$ to describe both the direction and extent of relationship between two variables. (Ch. 1)

criteria   Specifications of what is expected of a student on an assessment. (Ch. 13)

criterial attributes   Attributes that must be presented for an instance to be a member of a particular category. (Ch. 8)

criterion-referenced   Term describing a method for understanding what assessment scores mean by referring them to some arbitrary standard. (Ch. 14)

criterion-related validity   The degree to which an assessment correlates with an independent indicator of the same underlying ability. (Ch. 14)

cross-ethnic groupings   Groupings of children from different ethnic groups. (Ch. 11)

crystallized intelligence   The use of acquired skills and knowledge, such as reading and language skills. (Ch. 4)

cultural tools   Products created and designed by advanced members of a culture to help less advanced members of the culture learn and solve problems. (Ch. 2)

culture-free tests   Standardized tests that do not include items that might favor one culture over another. (Ch. 4)

curiosity   A cognitively based emotion that occurs whenever students experience a gap in their knowledge that motivates exploratory behavior to remove that knowledge gap. (Ch. 6)

custodial   A term that refers to an approach to classroom management that views the teacher's role as primarily maintaining an orderly classroom. (Ch. 9)

decay   Loss of memories because information is not used. (Ch. 8)

declarative knowledge   Factual knowledge that can be expressed through verbal exchange, books, Braille, or sign language; knowing that something is true. (Ch. 8)

declarative memory   Memory for abstract information. (Ch. 8)

deductive reasoning   Drawing information or hypotheses out of a general premise or a sample of evidence. (Ch. 2)

deliberate practice   Activity that is designed to improve one's skills in a particular area. (Ch. 4)

descriptive studies   A research method used to describe the educational situation as it naturally occurs—what typically happens, how teachers teach, and how students learn and develop. (Ch. 1)

detention   Having a student stay after school or restricting a student's options during free time (such as staying in during recess). (Ch. 11)

dialectical approach to motivation   The reciprocal, interdependent, and constantly changing relationship between a student's motivation and the classroom conditions that support versus frustrate that motivation. (Ch. 6)

dialectical constructivism   The theory that considers knowledge to lie in continual interaction between the individual and the environment. Vygotsky's theory is a good example of this kind of constructivism. (Ch. 8, 12)

dialectical relationship   A relationship in which the participants have mutual influence on one another or in which the actor changes the environment in some way, and that changed environment subsequently changes the actor. (Ch. 10)

diffuse status characteristics   Characteristics that have no direct bearing on task performance but are assumed to be indicators of greater or lesser capability to perform the task. (Ch. 12)

direct instruction   A systematic form of instruction that is used for mastery of basic skills and facts. (Ch. 9)

discovery-based learning   Students work on their own to grasp a concept or understand a lesson. (Ch. 2, 9)

discriminative stimuli   Antecedent cues that allow the learner to predict the likelihood of reinforcement. (Ch. 7)

disequilibrium   A state of cognitive conflict in which one's existing schema or way of thinking is not confirmed by experience. (Ch. 2)

distracter   One of the options in a multiple-choice test. (Ch. 13)

distributed practice   Practice that is interspersed by unequal intervals. (Ch. 8)

dyslexia   Reading disability in which words are read from right to left and letters of the same configuration are reversed. (Ch. 2)

educational objectives   Explicit statements of what students are expected to be able to do as a result of instruction. (Ch. 9)

educational psychology   The scientific study of psychology in education. (Ch. 1)

egocentrism   Viewing the world from one's own perspective while failing to recognize that other people might have a different perspective or point of view. (Ch. 2)

elaboration   A process through which we add and extend meaning by connecting new information to existing knowledge in long-term memory. (Ch. 8)

elaborative rehearsal   A way of remembering something by connecting it to something that is already well known. (Ch. 8)

emotional engagement   The extent to which a student's task involvement is characterized by positive emotion, such as interest and enjoyment. (Ch. 6)

emotion regulation   The capacity to modulate or calm internal emotional reactivity during stressful situations. (Ch. 3)

empowerment   Perceiving that one possesses the knowledge, skills, and beliefs needed to silence doubt and exert control over one's learning. (Ch. 5)

endogenous constructivism   Construction of new knowledge structures from existing structures rather than from the environment. (Ch. 8)

engagement   The extent of a student's behavioral intensity, emotional quality, and personal investment in a learning activity. (Ch. 6)

entity view of intelligence   The belief that intelligence is genetically determined and not alterable. (Ch. 4)

episodic memory   Long-term memory of particular places and events in a person's life. (Ch. 8)

eugenics   A political and scientific movement that argued for selective reproduction of individuals and immigration laws based on intelligence levels. (Ch. 4)

existential intelligence   Concern with larger questions of human existence, such as the meaning of life. (Ch. 4)

exogenous constructivism   Constructed knowledge that mirrors information in the environment. (Ch. 8)

experimental studies   A research method used to test for a cause-and-effect relationship between two variables. (Ch. 1)

experimental group   The group of participants in an experimental study who are randomly assigned to receive exposure to the independent variable. (Ch. 1)

explaining   Breaking down the concepts and ideas of a lesson to make them easier to understand. (Ch. 11)

explanatory style   A personality-like characteristic that reflects the habitual way that students explain why bad events happen to them. (Ch. 5)

expository organizer   A broad statement of what is to be learned in a lesson. (Ch. 9)

expository teaching   A type of teaching in which the teacher provides an exposition of how a particular set of information is structured and organized. (Ch. 9)

extrinsic motivation   An environmentally created reason to engage in an action or activity. (Ch. 6)

failure tolerance   The attitude of a teacher who accepts failure and error-making as a necessary, inherent, and even welcomed part of the learning process. (Ch. 6)

feature analysis   Identifying the component features of objects and building a representation of the object from them. (Ch. 8)

feedback   Knowledge of results. (Ch. 5)

fixed interval schedule   A schedule of reinforcement based on the passage of a fixed amount of time. (Ch. 7)

fixed ratio schedule   A schedule of reinforcement based on the number of behaviors performed. (Ch. 7)

flow   A state of concentration in which students become wholly absorbed in an activity. (Ch. 6)

fluid intelligence   The ability to solve problems, figure out what to do when one is not sure what to do, and acquire new skills. (Ch. 4)

forethought   What one thinks about prior to engaging in a task and prior to receiving feedback about the quality of one's performance on that task. (Ch. 5)

formative assessment   An assessment designed to inform teachers and students about student learning and to help improve instruction. (Ch. 13)

functional fixedness   Being able to consider only the typical function of an object. (Ch. 8)

generativity   The sense of being productive in one's work and in looking after and guiding others. (Ch. 3)

gentle discipline   A socialization strategy that revolves around explaining why a way of thinking or behaving is right or wrong. (Ch. 3)

glia cells   Cells that support neurons and provide the waxy coating that surrounds nerve fibers. (Ch. 2)

goal   What the student is trying to accomplish. (Ch. 5)

goal structure   The manner in which students relate to others who are also working toward a particular goal. (Ch. 12)

graded membership   The extent to which an object or idea belongs to a category. (Ch. 8)

grade-equivalent scores   Assessment scores that are reported in terms of how well children did in the norming study at various grade levels. (Ch. 14)

graphic organizers   A visual display of verbal information. (Ch. 8)

guessing-and-feedback   A curiosity-inducing instructional strategy in which the teacher asks students a difficult question and then announces that students' answers are incorrect so as to reveal a gap in their knowledge. (Ch. 6)

guided discovery   Students work under the guidance of a capable partner to grasp a concept or understand a lesson. (Ch. 2, 9)

guided participation   Having one's engagement in a learning activity encouraged, supported, and tutored by a skilled partner. (Ch. 2)

heuristic   A rule of thumb or shortcut for solving problems. (Ch. 8)

hidden costs of reward   The unexpected, unintended, and adverse effects that extrinsic rewards sometimes have on intrinsic motivation, high-quality learning, and autonomous self-regulation. (Ch. 6)

higher order thinking skills   Skills and abilities that go beyond recall and comprehension, including the ability to apply ideas and concepts, analyze and synthesize information, and evaluate complex information. (Ch. 9, 13)

high road transfer   Deliberate application of previously learned strategy or knowledge to a new problem. (Ch. 8)

hippocampus   Grape-shaped structure in the limbic area of the brain involved in memory formation and storage. (Ch. 2)

hope   A motivational wish for an outcome that one expects to be fully capable of obtaining. (Ch. 5)

hostile aggression   The anger-driven impulse to inflict intentional harm on another person. (Ch. 3)

hypothesis   A prediction, derived from a theory, of how the results of a research study will turn out. (Ch. 1)

identity   The sense of being a distinct and productive individual within the larger social framework. (Ch. 3)

I-message   A reaction to a behavior that describes the behavior and how it has affected a given situation, and describes the individual's emotional response to the behavior. (Ch. 11)

immediacy   In teaching, decisions and actions have to occur in the real time of classroom life, that is, immediately, not at a leisurely pace. (Ch. 11)

implementation intention   A plan to carry out goal-directed behavior. (Ch. 5)

incentive   An environmental event that attracts a person toward a particular course of action. (Ch. 7)

inclusive   An approach to education in general, whether teaching, working with students, or curriculum, that includes students from different cultures and with different abilities and challenges. (Ch. 11)

incremental view of intelligence   The belief that intelligence can be improved through effort. (Ch. 4)

individual accountability   Each student is responsible for improving his or her performance. (Ch. 12)

individual interest   An enduring disposition in which one develops a clear preference to direct attention and effort toward a particular activity, situation, or subject matter. (Ch. 6)

individualized education program (IEP)   An educational and behavioral intervention plan for a student with special needs. (Ch. 1, 4, 13)

inductive reasoning   The abstraction of a general principle from a variety of examples. (Ch. 2, 9)

informal assessment   Classroom assessment activities used to get a quick and rough idea of student progress. (Ch. 13)

initiative   The child's capacity to use a surplus of energy to plan and constructively carry out a task. (Ch. 3)

innate ability   The ability a person was born with. (Ch. 4)

instrumental aggression   Strategic behavior to obtain something one desires that results in harm inflicted on another person. (Ch. 3)

instructional goal   A statement of desired student outcomes following instruction. (Ch. 9)

intelligence quotient (IQ)   A method for communicating the level of a person's intelligence. (Ch. 4)

intelligence test   A measure of generalized intellectual ability. (Ch. 14)

interdependence   A condition in which group members' goal accomplishments are linked together. (Ch. 12)

interest   A topic-specific motivational state that arises out of attraction to a particular domain of activity. (Ch. 6)

interference   Loss or deficiency of memories because of the presence of other information. (Ch. 8)

inter-rater reliability   A measure of the degree to which two independent raters give similar scores to the same paper or performance. (Ch. 14)

intersubjectivity   The unique product that arises from social interaction in which the interaction partners come to a shared understanding of how to manage the problem-solving situation. (Ch. 2)

interval schedule   A schedule of reinforcement based on time.

intrinsic motivation   The inherent propensity to engage one's interests and to exercise and develop one's capacities. (Ch. 6)

IRE discourse model   Conversation during teaching that follows an initiate, respond, evaluate script. (Ch. 2)

item   A test or assessment question, referred to as an *item* because not all test questions are actually questions. (Ch. 13)

item bank   A collection of test or assessment items for use in future assessments. Also called *test bank*. (Ch. 13)

journal   A running set of thoughts, responses to prompts, and reflections that students have concerning their learning in a particular area. (Ch. 13)

language The use of agreed-on rules to combine a small number of symbols (sounds, letters, gestures) to produce a large number of meaningful messages. (Ch. 2)

language acquisition device Inborn capacity that enables children to understand grammar and produce language. (Ch. 2)

law of effect The phenomenon in which behavior that produces good effects tends to become more frequent while behavior that produces bad effects tends to become less frequent. (Ch. 7)

learned helplessness The psychological state that results when a student expects that school-related outcomes are beyond his or her personal control. (Ch. 5)

learning A relatively permanent change in behavior or knowledge as result of experience. (Ch. 1, 7)

learning center An area of a classroom specifically designed to facilitate exploration of a particular aspect of the curriculum. (Ch. 11)

learning goal The intention to learn, improve, and develop competence. (Ch. 5)

lecturing Presentation information to a group of learners as a whole. (Ch. 11)

levels of processing theory A theory that asserts that recall of information is based on how deeply it is processed. (Ch. 8)

logical consequences An approach to classroom management that lets the natural outcomes of bad behavior serve as the punishment for that behavior. (Ch. 11)

low road transfer The automatic application of previously learned skills. (Ch. 8)

maintenance rehearsal A cognitive process in which information in working memory is repeated to oneself frequently. (Ch. 8)

massed practice Intense practice for a single period of time (also known as "cramming"). (Ch. 8)

mastery belief Extent of one's perceived control over a success/failure outcome. (Ch. 5)

mastery levels Levels of proficiency, or mastery, determined for an assessment; related to cut scores and passing scores. (Ch. 14)

matching An assessment item format that involves generating two sets of objects that are to be linked together, such as states and their capitals. (Ch. 13)

mean The arithmetic mean of a set of scores. (Ch. 14)

means-end analysis A strategy for reducing the distance between the initial state and the goal state in problem solving. (Ch. 8)

median The middle score of a set of scores that have been rank-ordered from highest to lowest. (Ch. 14)

mental age The age level associated with the ability to perform certain mental tasks. A mental age of 7 means that a person can perform the tasks of a typical 7-year-old but not those of a typical 8-year-old. (Ch. 4)

mental models Students' enduring beliefs and expectations about what they are like and what other people are like. (Ch. 3)

meta-analysis A quantitative review and summary of research on a topic. (Ch. 7) A quantitative summary of a research studies that test the same hypotheses. (Ch. 12)

metacognition Thinking about one's own thinking. (Ch. 4, 8, 12)

mnemonic strategies Strategies for remembering nonmeaningful information by making it meaningful. (Ch. 8)

mode The most frequently occurring score in a set of scores. (Ch. 14)

monotonic-benefits assumption The argument that there is a one-to-one correspondence between one's effort and one's gains in a skill or ability. (Ch. 4)

moral development Students' judgments about what is right and wrong and their reasoning as to why one action is right and another is wrong. (Ch. 3)

motivation Any force that energizes and directs behavior. (Ch. 5)

multidimensionality Having more than one characteristic (such as a purpose or an ability) at the same time. (Ch. 11)

multiple choice An assessment item format consisting of a stem (question), a right answer, and a set of wrong answers (distracters). Students have to determine the best response to the stem. (Ch. 13)

multiple-intelligences (MI) theory A theory of intelligence that argues that individuals may exhibit multiple intelligences (possibly eight or more). (Ch. 4)

multiple modalities Various senses. (Ch. 8)

myelinization The process carried out by glia cells to insulate neurons with a protective coating to prevent damage and increase the speed of communication between neighboring neurons. (Ch. 2)

natural categories Real-world categories. (Ch. 8)

nature/nurture A shorthand term for the debate over whether mental abilities are developed by the individual's environment (nurture) or inherited (nature). (Ch. 4)

negative interdependence A condition that exists when, in order for one person to succeed in accomplishing his or her goals, others must fail to meet their goals. (Ch. 12)

negative punisher Any environmental event that, when removed decreases the frequency of a behavior. (Ch. 7)

negative reinforcer Any environmental event that, when taken away, increases the frequency of a behavior. (Ch. 7)

negative transfer Prior learning interferes with new learning. (Ch. 8)

neurons Nerve cells that receive and transmit the neural impulses underlying thinking. (Ch. 2)

normal curve equivalent (NCE) A scale related to the z-score that has a mean of 50 and a standard deviation of 21.06. (Ch. 14)

normal distribution A mathematical conceptualization of how scores are distributed when they are influenced by a variety of relatively independent factors. (Ch. 14)

norming study The administration of an assessment to a representative national sample to obtain a distribution of typical performance on the assessment. (Ch. 14)

norm-referenced   Term describing scores that are given meaning by referring them to other individuals or sets of individuals. (Ch. 14)

norms   A set of tables based on a representative national administration of an assessment that makes it possible to show how well particular students did compared to a national sample of students. (Ch. 14)

objectivity   Not having a direct interest or bias. (Ch. 13)

object permanence   Understanding that objects continue to exist even when they cannot be seen or detected by other senses. (Ch. 2)

observational learning   Learning by observing other individuals. (Ch. 10)

off task   Not paying attention to instruction. (Ch. 11)

operant learning   Actions by a learner, the consequences of which influence further behavior. (Ch. 7)

operation   A mental action or a mental manipulation carried out to solve a problem or to reason logically. (Ch. 2)

optimistic explanatory style   The habitual tendency to explain bad events with attributions that are unstable and controllable. (Ch. 5)

overgeneralization   Inclusion of a nonmember of a category or class in that category of class. (Ch. 8)

participation structures   The rules that define how to participate in an activity. Such rules may be formal as well as informal. (Ch. 12)

passing scores   The scores on an assessment that one needs to obtain or exceed in order to pass the assessment. (Ch. 14)

pedagogical content knowledge   Knowledge about how to make subject matter understandable to students. (Ch. 9)

pedagogical knowledge   Knowledge about how to teach. (Ch. 9)

penalties   Consequences for misbehavior, such as loss of privileges, time-out, or a visit to the principal's office. (Ch. 11)

perceived locus of causality   The person's understanding of whether his or her motivated action is caused by a force within the self (internal) or by some force outside the self that is in the environment (external). (Ch. 6)

percentile   A number that indicates what percentage of the national norming sample performed less well than the score in question. (Ch. 14)

perception   The meaning attached to sensory information. (Ch. 8)

performance assessment   An assessment in which students generate a product or an actual performance that reflects what they have learned. (Ch. 13)

performance goal   The intention to demonstrate high ability and prove one's competence. (Ch. 5)

personal space   An area where an individual feels separate from other individuals and able to be in control. (Ch. 11)

pessimistic explanatory style   The habitual tendency to explain bad events with attributions that are stable and uncontrollable. (Ch. 5)

phonological loop   The component of working memory that processes verbal information. (Ch. 8)

phonological similarity effect   People make more errors recalling sets of words if the words they are asked to recall are similar in sound to one another. (Ch. 8)

phonology   The sounds of a language. (Ch. 2)

physiological psychology   The study of the relationship between the brain, the nervous system, and behavior. (Ch. 4)

pictorial mnemonics   Interactive images that combine pictorial and verbal elements. (Ch. 8)

plasticity   The brain's capacity for structural change as the result of experience. (Ch. 2)

portfolio   A collection of students' work over time that allows for assessment of the development of their skills. (Ch. 13)

positive affect   The mild, subtle, everyday experience of feeling good. (Ch. 6)

positive interdependence   A condition that exists when the success of each individual depends on all group members being successful. (Ch. 12)

positive practice   Practicing the correct answer after making a mistake. (Ch. 12)

positive punisher   Any environmental event that, when given, decreases the frequency of a behavior. (Ch. 7)

positive reinforcer   Any environmental event that, when given, increases the frequency of a behavior. (Ch. 7)

positive transfer   Prior knowledge or skill is successfully applied to a new context. (Ch. 8)

possible self   A student's long-term goal representing what he or she would like to become in the future. (Ch. 5)

power assertion   A socialization strategy designed to gain compliance through coercion, pressure, forceful insistence, and a negative or critical interaction style. (Ch. 3)

praise   Positive verbal feedback. (Ch. 6)

primary mental abilities   L. L. Thurstone's theory of intelligence as consisting of seven distinct abilities. (Ch. 4)

private speech   Thought spoken out loud. (Ch. 2)

problem-based learning (PBL)   An instructional strategy in which students work in collaborative groups to solve a complex problem that does not have a single correct answer. (Ch. 10)

problem solving   An activity in which a person uses knowledge to reach a specific goal but in which there is no clearly specified way of reaching the goal. (Ch. 12)

procedural facilitation   A structured approach to improving students' use of elements of the writing process. (Ch. 10)

procedural knowledge   Knowledge about how to perform tasks. (Ch. 8)

procedural memory   Memory for how to do things. (Ch. 8)

products   Student creations that reflect their skills and abilities as well as their ability to create something new. (Ch. 9, 13)

prompts   Physical, verbal, or other assists that help a person perform a desired behavior that he or she would be unlikely to perform without such assistance. (Ch. 7)

proposition   The smallest unit of knowledge that can be verified. (Ch. 8)

propositional network   A set of interconnected pieces of information that contains knowledge for the long term. (Ch. 8)

prototype   The best representative of a category. (Ch. 8)

PSQ discourse model   Conversation during teaching that follows a probe, question, scaffold script. (Ch. 2)

psychological need   An inherent source of motivation that generates the desire to interact with one's environment so as to advance personal growth, social development, and psychological well-being. (Ch. 6)

psychosocial development   A broad term to describe the quality of a person's social development as a function of past relationships in one's life. (Ch. 3)

punisher   A consequence of behavior that weakens or decreases behavior. (Ch. 7)

rationale   A verbal explanation as to why a task is important and worth one's attention, time, and effort. (Ch. 6)

ratio schedule   A schedule of reinforcement based on the number of behaviors. (Ch. 7)

raw scores   Scores that are simple sums of the points obtained on an assessment. (Ch. 14)

recall   Information retrieved from long term memory. (Ch. 8)

reception learning   A type of learning in which the learner acquires the structure of knowledge set forth by the teacher. (Ch. 9)

recitation   An instructional approach where teachers ask closed-ended questions (questions with clear right answers) and students answer them. (Ch. 11)

recognition memory   Memories are cued, then recognized. (Ch. 8)

referral   Educators' shorthand for the recommendation that a child be evaluated for possible special education classification. (Ch. 9)

reflection   What one thinks about after engaging in a task and after receiving feedback about the quality of one's performance on that task. (Ch. 5)

reflective teaching   Generating conjectures to explain a surprising event in the teaching situation, then gathering the information needed to make a decision about what would constitute the most effective course of action to pursue. (Ch. 1)

reinforcer   A consequence of behavior that increases or strengthens behavior. (Ch. 7)

relatedness   The psychological need to establish close emotional bonds and attachments with other people. (Ch. 3, 6)

relationship   Interaction between two people in which the actions of one person affect the thoughts, feelings, and actions of the other person and vice versa. (Ch. 3)

reliability   Consistency over an aspect of assessment, such as over time and multiple raters. In classroom assessment, having enough information about students on which to base judgments. (Ch. 13, 14)

reliability coefficient   An index, ranging from .00 up to 1.00, of how reliable an assessment is. (Ch. 14)

reliability study   A study that is used to determine reliability coefficients. (Ch. 14)

reversibility   The ability to reverse an action by mentally performing its opposite. (Ch. 2)

reward   Anything given in return for another person's service or achievement. (Ch. 7)

routines   Activities that occur on a regular, ongoing basis and require the same or similar behavior on each occurrence (such as sharpening pencils and going to lunch). (Ch. 11)

rubrics   Explications of the criteria for a performance assessment or an essay that includes specifications for how various levels of performance are to be graded. (Ch. 13)

scaffolding   The guidance, support, and tutelage provided by a teacher during social interaction designed to advance the student's current level of skill and understanding. (Ch. 2, 12)

scaled scores   Scores from an assessment that have been transformed into an arbitrary numbering system in order to facilitate interpretation. (Ch. 14)

schema   The basic cognitive structure for organizing information. (Ch. 2, 8, 12)

script   A schema for the sequence of events in common events, such as ordering food at a fast-food restaurant. (Ch. 8)

Scripted Cooperation   A learning strategy in which students take turns summarizing materials and criticizing the summaries. (Ch. 12)

seatwork   Work that is done independently by students at their desks or seats. (Ch. 11)

self-concept   Set of beliefs the individual uses to mentally represent or understand his or her sense of self. (Ch. 3)

self-efficacy   One's judgment of how well he or she will cope with a situation, given the skills one possesses and the circumstances one faces. (Ch. 5, 9)

self-esteem   Trust applied to oneself; an attitude that one is worthy of a positive or a negative self-evaluation. (Ch. 3)

self-evaluation   A self-judgmental process in which students compare their current performance with a hoped-for goal state. (Ch. 5)

self-handicapping   A defensive self-presentation strategy that involves intentionally interfering with one's own performance so as to provide a face-saving excuse for failure in case one does indeed fail. (Ch. 6)

self-management   An approach to behavioral modification where students keep a written record of their behavior in an effort to increase desirable behaviors or decrease undesirable ones. (Ch. 11)

self-monitoring   A self-observational process in which students attempt to keep track of the quality of their ongoing performances. (Ch. 5)

self-regulation   The deliberate planning, monitoring, and evaluating of one's academic work. (Ch. 5)

self-worth   An evaluation by others of one's personal worth. (Ch. 6)

semantic memory   The memory a person has for meaning. (Ch. 8)

semantics   The meanings of words and sentences. (Ch. 2)

semiotic function   The symbolic function in which a mental symbol (word) represents an environmental object. (Ch. 2)

sensory memory   Brief memories associated with various senses. (Ch. 8)

serial position effect   The fact that the likelihood of information being recalled varies according to its position in a list. (Ch. 8)

seriation   The ability to order or arrange a set of objects along a quantifiable dimension, such as height. (Ch. 2)

shaping   Reinforcement of gradual approximations of the desired behavior. (Ch. 7)

short-term memory   A temporary memory storage. (Ch. 8)

situational compliance   Cooperatively carrying out a teacher's "do this" or "don't do that" request with a sense of obligation rather than a sincere commitment to the action. (Ch. 3)

situational interest   A topic-specific motivational state that is triggered by an external factor that produces a short-term attraction to the learning activity. (Ch. 6)

small-group work   Work being done independently by a group of students smaller than the whole class. (Ch. 11)

social comparison   The act of comparing one's personal characteristics, performance, and abilities to the characteristics, performances, and abilities of others. (Ch. 3)

social competence   How skilled children and adolescents are at managing the often frustrating and challenging experiences they have with other people. (Ch. 3)

social contact   Interaction among students. (Ch. 11)

social norms   Expectations for proper behavior. (Ch. 11)

socially shared cognition   A shared understanding of a problem that emerges during group interaction that would not have been achieved by any individual member of the group acting alone. (Ch. 2)

split-half reliability   A form of reliability coefficient, similar to coefficient alpha, that takes half of the items on an assessment, sums them into a score, and then correlates that score with a score based on the other half of the items. (Ch. 14)

spread of activation   The retrieval of bits of information on the basis of their relatedness to each other. Remembering one piece of information stimulates the recall of associated knowledge. (Ch. 8)

standard deviation   A measure of how far scores vary from the mean. (Ch. 4, 14)

standard error of measurement   An index of how high or low an individual's assessment score might change on a second testing. (Ch. 14)

standardized assessment   A measure of student ability in which all students take the same measure under the same conditions. (Ch. 13. 14)

standard of excellence   Any challenge to the student's sense of competence that ends with a success/failure interpretation. (Ch. 5)

standards   A comprehensive set of educational objectives organized by subject matter and grade level. (Ch. 9)

standards-based assessment   Assessments that are generated from a list of educational standards, usually at the state or national level; a form of standardized assessment. (Ch. 13, 14)

stanines   Short for "standard nine," a scaled score that runs from 1 to 9 and has a mean of 5 and a standard deviation of 2. (Ch. 14)

status characteristics   Characteristics of individuals that may signal that they have high or low status. (Ch. 12)

status differences   Differences in status among individuals that influence their participation in group activities. (Ch. 12)

stem   The part of a multiple-choice item that asks a question. (Ch. 13)

stereotype threat   Concern about being viewed from the vantage point of a negative stereotype or acting to confirm such a stereotype. (Ch. 12)

story grammar   The typical structure of a category of stories. (Ch. 8)

summative assessment   Assessment designed to summarize student achievement. (Ch. 13)

supportiveness   An affirmation of the other person's capacity for self-direction and contribution to help realize his or her self-set goals. (Ch. 3)

suspense   A curiosity-inducing instructional strategy in which the teacher asks students to predict an outcome before students engage in the work that will reveal that their prediction was right or wrong. (Ch. 6)

symbolic schemas   Language-based representations of objects and events. (Ch. 2)

syntax   The structure of a language, including sentence formation rules, such as noun-verb. (Ch. 2)

talent   The capacity to produce exceptional performance. (Ch. 4)

taxonomy   A classification of objects according to a set of principles or laws. (Ch. 9, 11)

teaching   The interpersonal effort to help learners acquire knowledge, develop skill, and realize their potential. (Ch. 1, 9)

teaching efficacy   A teacher's judgment of, or confidence in, his or her capacity to cope with the teaching situation in ways that bring about desired outcomes. (Ch. 1, 9)

technical teaching   Relying on routine knowledge and tried-and-true solutions to manage classroom problems. (Ch. 1)

test bias   The degree to which the scores from an assessment take on different meanings when obtained by individuals from different groups. (Ch. 14)

test blueprint   A statement of what a test will comprise, often in outline form. (Ch. 13)

theory   An intellectual framework that organizes a vast amount of knowledge about a phenomenon so that educators can understand and explain better the nature of that phenomenon. (Ch. 1)

top-down processing   A type of perception in which a person uses what he or she knows about a situation to recognize patterns. (Ch. 8)

triarchic   Comprised of three components, each of which is the top of a hierarchy. (Ch. 4)

transductive reasoning   A causality belief in which children think that when two events occur simultaneously, one must have caused the other. (Ch. 2)

transfer   The ability to use previously learned skills or information in a new context. (Ch. 8)

transition times   Times when students are changing from one activity to the next. (Ch. 11)

true score   The hypothetical true ability of an individual on an assessment. (Ch. 14)

trust   Confidence that the other person in the relationship cares, is looking out for your welfare, and will be there when needed. (Ch. 3)

tutoring   An instructional experience in which one student typically teaches another student who is less skilled. (Ch. 12)

unattended speech effect   Verbal information automatically enters the phonological loop and can interfere with a person's verbal task performance even if that person is not paying attention to the information. (Ch. 8)

unconditioned response   A behavior that is produced in response to a stimulus without prior learning. It is typically an automatic physiological response. (Ch. 7)

unconditioned stimulus   A stimulus that, without prior learning, produces an automatic physiological response. (Ch. 7)

undergeneralization   The exclusion of some instances from a category or group even though they are true members of that category or group. (Ch. 8)

validation study   A research study conducted to determine whether an assessment is valid. (Ch. 14)

validity   The appropriateness of judgments about students based on assessment information. In classroom assessment, the correspondence between what an assessment measures and what was taught as part of instruction. (Ch. 13, 14)

variability   The degree to which scores on an assessment (or other variable, such as height or weight) are spread out. (Ch. 14)

variable interval schedule   A schedule of reinforcement in which reinforcement is provided at irregular intervals based on the passage of time. (Ch. 7)

variable ratio schedule   A schedule of reinforcement in which reinforcement is provided at irregular intervals based on the number of behaviors performed. (Ch. 7)

variance   A measure of how much a set of scores is spread out. (Ch. 14)

vicarious experience   Learning from the experience of another person. (Ch. 10)

vicarious punishment   If another person is punished for a behavior, the likelihood of an observer engaging in that behavior is decreased. (Ch. 10)

vicarious reinforcement   If another person is reinforced for a behavior, the likelihood of an observer engaging in that behavior is increased. (Ch. 10)

visuospatial sketchpad   The component of working memory that processes visuospatial content. (Ch. 8)

voice   A student's expression of self during a learning activity so as to influence constructively how the teacher presents that lesson. (Ch. 6)

wait time   The time between when a question is asked in a classroom and when a student is called upon to answer it. (Ch. 11)

whole-class instruction   Working on instructional material with the whole class at the same time. (Ch. 11)

within-class ability grouping   A system in which children are assigned to ability groups within a class. (Ch. 4)

word length effect   The link between memory span and the length of words to be recalled. (Ch. 8)

working memory   A limited memory system that includes both storage and manipulation functions. (Ch. 8)

zone of proximal development   A level of competence on a task in which the student cannot yet master the task on his or her own but can accomplish that same task with appropriate guidance from a more capable partner. (Ch. 2, 12)

z-score   A standard score that any set of scores can be converted to; it has a mean of 0.0 and a standard deviation of 1.0. (Ch. 14)

References

Abedi, J., & Lord, C. (2001). The language factor in mathematics. *Applied Measurement in Education, 14,* 219–234.

Abedi, J., Courtney, M., & Leon, S. (2003). *Effectiveness and validity of accommodations for English language learners in large-scale assessments.* CSE Report 608. Los Angeles: National Center for Research on Evaluation, Standards, and Student Testing, University of California.

Abrami, P.C., Chambers, B., Poulsen, C. De Simone, C., d'Appollonia, S., & Howden, J. (1995). *Classroom connections: Using and understanding cooperative learning.* Toronto: Harcourt Brace

Adreon, D., & Stella, J. (2001). Transition to middle and high school: Increasing the success of students with Asperger syndrome. *Intervention in School and Clinic, 32,* 266–271.

Aiken, L. R. (2003). *Psychological testing and assessment,* (11th ed.). Boston: Allyn & Bacon.

Ainsworth, M. D. S. (1989). Attachments beyond infancy. *American Psychologist, 44,* 709–716.

Ainsworth, M. D. S., Blehar, M. C., Waters, E., & Wall, S. (1978). *Patterns of attachment: A psychological study of the strange situation.* Hillsdale, NJ: Lawrence Erlbaum.

Al-Yagon, M., & Mikulincer, M. (2004). Socioemotional and academic adjustment among children with learning disorders: The mediational role of attachment-based factors. *Journal of Special Education, 38,* 111–123.

Alexander, K. L., Entwisle, D. R., & Dauber, S. L. (1993). First-grade classroom behavior: Its short- and long-term consequences for school performance. *Child Development, 64,* 801–814.

Alexander, K. L., Entwisle, D. R., & Horsey, C. S. (1997). From first-grade forward: Early foundations of high school dropout. *Sociology of Education, 70,* 87–107.

Alexander, P. A., Jetton, T. L., & Kulikowich, J. M. (1995). Interrelationship of knowledge, interest, and recall: Assessing a model of domain learning. *Journal of Educational Psychology, 87,* 559–575.

Alexander, P. A., Kulikowich, J. M., & Jetton, T. L. (1994). The role of subject-matter knowledge and interest in the processing of linear and nonlinear text. *Review of Educational Research, 64,* 201–252.

Algozzine, B., Browder, D., Karvonen, M., Test, D. W., & Wood, W. M. (2001). Effects of interventions to promote self-determination for individuals with disabilities. *Review of Educational Research, 71,* 219–277.

Algozzine, B., Christenson, S. & Ysseldyke, J. E. 1982). Probabilities associated with the referral to placement process. *Teacher Education and Special Education, 5,* 19–23.

Allen, J. P., & Hauser, S. T. (1996). Autonomy and relatedness in adolescent-family interactions as predictors of young adults' states of mind regarding attachment. *Development and Psychopathology, 8,* 793–809.

Allen, J. P., & Land, D. (1999). Attachment in adolescence. In J. Cassidy & P. R. Shaver (Eds.), *Handbook of attachment: Theory, research, and clinical applications* (pp. 319–335). New York: Guilford Press.

Allen, J. P., McElhaney, K. B., Land, D. J., Kuperminc, G. P., Moore, C. W., O'Beirne-Kelly, H., & Kilmer, S. L., (2003). A secure base in adolescence: Markers of attachment security in the mother-adolescent relationship. *Child Development, 74,* 292–307.

Allen, J. P., Moore, C. W., Kuperminc, G., & Bell, K. (1998). Attachment and adolescent psychosocial functioning. *Child Development, 69,* 1406–1419.

Allen, S. (2002). Looking for learning in visitor talk: A methodological exploration. In G. Leinhardt, K. Crowley, & K. Knutson (Eds.), *Learning conversations in museums* (pp. 259–303). Mahwah, NJ: Lawrence Erlbaum.

Allen, S. (2004). Designs for learning: Studying science museum exhibits that do more than entertain. *Science Education, 88,* S17–S33.

Allinder, R. M. (1994). The relationship between efficacy and the instructional practices of special education teachers and consultants. *Teacher Education and Special Education, 17,* 86–95.

Alloy, L. B., & Seligman, M. E. P. (1979). On the cognitive component of learned helplessness and depression. *The Psychology of Learning and Motivation, 13,* 219–276.

Altmaier, E. M., & Happ, D. A. (1985). Coping skills training's immunization effects against learned helplessness. *Journal of Social and Clinical Psychology, 3,* 181–189.

Alvermann, D. E., & Hayes, D. A. (1989). Classroom discussions of content area reading assignments: An intervention study. *Reading Research Quarterly, 24,* 305–335.

Alvermann, D. E., O'Brien, D. G., & Dillon, D. R. (1990). What teachers do when they say they're having discussions of content area reading assignments: A qualitative analysis. *Reading Research Quarterly, 25,* 296–322.

Al-Yagon, M., & Mikulincer, M. (2004). Socioemotional and academic adjustment among children with learning disorders: The mediational role of attachment-based factors. *Journal of Special Education, 38,* 111–123.

Amabile, T. M. (1985). Motivation and creativity: Effect of motivational orientation on creative writers. *Journal of Personality and Social Psychology, 48,* 393–399.

Amabile, T., & Hennessey, B. A. (1992). The motivation for creativity in children. In A. K. Boggiano & T. S. Pittman (Eds.), *Achievement and motivation: A social developmental perspective* (pp. 54–76). New York: Cambridge University Press.

American Association of Museums. (2003). Museum Financial Information, 2003. Washington DC: Author.

American Association on Mental Retardation. (2002) *Mental retardation: Definition, classification, and systems of support* (10th ed). Washington, DC: Author.

American Psychiatric Association. (1994). *Diagnostic and Statistical Manual of Mental Disorders* (4th ed.). Washington, DC: Author.

American Psychological Association (1999). Controversy follows psychological testing. *APA Monitor Online, 30*(11). Retrieved August 12, 2005 from http://www.apa.org/monitor/dec99/554.html.

Ames, C. A., & Archer, J. (1988). Achievement goals in the classroom: Student learning strategies and motivational processes. *Journal of Educational Psychology, 80,* 260–267.

Anastasi, A., & Urbina, S. (1997). *Psychological testing,* (7th ed.). Upper Saddle River, NJ: Prentice Hall.

Anderman, E. M., Anderman, L. H., & Griesinger, T. (1999). The relation of present and possible academic selves during early adolescence to grade point average and achievement goals. *Elementary School Journal, 100,* 3–17.

Anderson, C. A. (1983). Imagination and expectation: The effect of imagining behavioral scripts on personal intentions. *Journal of Personality and Social Psychology 45,* 293–305.

Anderson, C. A., & Bushman, B. J. (2001). Effects of violent video games on aggressive behavior, aggressive cognition, aggressive affect, physiological arousal, and prosocial behavior: A meta-analytic review of the scientific literature. *Psychological Science, 12,* 353–359.

Anderson, C. A., & Bushman, B. J. (2002). Human aggression. *Annual Review of Psychology, 53,* 27–51.

Anderson, C. A., & Dill, K. E. (2000). Video games and aggressive thoughts, feelings, and behavior in the laboratory and in life. *Journal of Personality and Social Psychology, 78,* 772–790.

Anderson, D., Lucas, K. B., & Ginns, I. S. (2000). Development of knowledge about electricity and magnetism during a visit to a science museum and related post-visit activities. *Science Education, 84,* 658–679.

Anderson, D., Lucas, K. B., & Ginns, I. S. (2003). Theoretical perspectives on learning in an informal setting. *Journal of Research in Science Teaching. 40,* 177–199.

Anderson, L. W. & Bourke, S. F. (2000). *Assessing affective characteristics in the schools.* Mahwah, NJ: Lawrence Erlbaum Associates.

Anderson, L. W., & Krathwohl (Eds.). (2001). *A taxonomy for learning, teaching, and assessing: A revision of Bloom's taxonomy of educational objectives.* New York: Longman.

Anderson, R. H., & Pavan, B. N. (1993). *Nongradeness: Helping it to happen.* Lancaster, PA: Technomic Publishing.

Anderson, R., Greene, M., & Loewen, P. (1988). Relationships among teachers' and students' thinking skills, sense of efficacy, and student achievement. *Alberta Journal of Educational Research, 34,* 148–165.

Anderson-Inman, L., & Horney, M. (1999). Electronic books: Reading and studying with supportive resources. Available online at http://www.readingonline.org/electronic/ebook/index.html.

Andriessen, J. (2005). Collaboration in computer conferencing. In A. M. O'Donnell, C. E. Hmelo-Silver, & G. Erkens (Eds.), *Collaborative learning, reasoning, and technology.* Mahwah, NJ: Lawrence Erlbaum, 197–231.

Angoff, W. H. (1971). Scales, norms, and equivalent scores. In R. L. Thorndike (Ed.) *Educational Measurement* (2nd ed., pp. 508–600). Washington, DC: American Council of Education.

Antil, L. R., Jenkins, J. R., Wayne, S. K., & Vadasy, P. F. (1998). Prevalence, conceptualizations, and the relation between research and practice. *American Educational Research Journal, 35,* 419–454.

Applebee, A. N., & Langer, J. (1983). Instructional scaffolding: Reading and writing as natural language activities. *Language Arts, 60,* 168–175.

Arkin, R. M., & Baumgardner, A. H. (1985). Self-handicapping. In J. Harvey & G. Weary (Eds.), *Basic issues in attribution theory and research* (pp. 169–202). New York: Academic Press.

Aronson, E., Blaney, N., Stephan, C., Sikes, J., & Snapp, M. (1978). *The Jigsaw classroom.* Beverly Hills, CA: Sage.

Arreaga-Mayer, C., Terry, B. J., & Greenwood, C. R. (1998). Classwide peer tutoring. In K. Topping & S. Ehly (Eds.), *Peer-assisted learning* (pp. 105–119). Mahwah, NJ: Lawrence Erlbaum.

Artzt, A. F., & Armour-Thomas, E. (1999). A cognitive model for examining teachers' instructional practices in mathematics: A guide for facilitating teacher reflection. *Educational Studies in Mathematics, 40,* 211–235.

Ashton, P. T., & Webb, R. B. (1986). *Making a difference: Teachers' sense of efficacy and student achievement.* New York: Longman.

Atkinson, R. C., & Shiffrin, R. M. (1968). Human memory: A proposed system and its control processes. In K. W. Spence & J. T. Spence (Eds.), *The psychology of learning and motivation* (Vol. 2, pp. 89–195). Orlando, FL: Academic Press.

Australian Education Counsel (1989). *The common and agreed national goals of schooling.* Canberra: AGPS.

Ausubel, D. P. (1961). In defense of verbal learning. *Educational Theory, 11,* 15–25.

Ausubel, D. P. (1965). A cognitive structure view of word and concept meaning. In R. C. Anderson & D. P. Ausubel (Eds.), *Readings in the psychology of cognition.* New York: Holt, Rinehart & Winston.

Ausubel, D. P., Novak, J. D., & Hanesian, H. (1978). *Educational psychology: A cognitive view* (2nd ed). New York: Holt, Rinehart & Winston.

Ayers, W., Dohrn, B., & Ayers, R. (2001). *Zero tolerance: Resisting the drive for punishment in our schools.* New York: The New Press.

Azmitia, M. (1988). Peer interaction and problem solving: When are two heads better than one? *Child Development, 59,* 87–96.

Bacon, C. S. (1993). Student responsibility for learning. *Adolescence, 28,* 199–212.

Baddeley, A. (1990). *Human memory.* Needham Heights, MA: Allyn & Bacon.

Baddeley, A. (1993). *Using your memory: A user's guide.* London: Penguin Books.

Baddeley, A. (1999). *Essentials of human memory.* Hove, UK: Psychology Press.

Baillargeon, R. (1987). Object permanence in $3\frac{1}{2}$ and $4\frac{1}{2}$-month-old infants. *Developmental Psychology, 23,* 655–664.

Baker, L., & Brown, A. L. (1984). Metacognitive skills and reading. In P. D. Pearson (Ed.), *Handbook of reading research* (pp. 353–394). New York: Longman.

Balajthy, E. (2005, January/February). Text-to-speech software for helping struggling readers. *Reading Online, 8*(4). Retrieved January 3, 2005 from http://www.readingonline. org/articles/art_index.asp?HREF=balajthy2/index.html.

Baldwin, J. D., & Baldwin, J. I. (1986). *Behavior principles in everyday life* (2nd ed.). Englewood Cliffs, NJ: Prentice Hall.

Baldwin, J. D., & Baldwin, J. I. (1986). *Behavior principles in everyday life* (2nd ed.). Englewood Cliffs, NJ: Prentice Hall.

Bandura, A. (1965). Influence of models' reinforcement contingencies on the acquisition of imitative responses. *Journal of Personality and Social Psychology, 1,* 589–595.

Bandura, A. (1977a). Self-efficacy: Toward a unifying theory of behavioral change. *Psychological Review, 84,* 191–215.

Bandura, A. (1977b). *Social learning theory.* Englewood Cliffs, NJ: Prentice Hall.

Bandura, A. (1982). Self-efficacy mechanism in human agency. *American Psychologist, 37,* 122–147.

Bandura, A. (1983). Self-efficacy mechanisms of anticipated fears and calamities. *Journal of Personality and Social Psychology, 45,* 464–469.

Bandura, A. (1986a). *The social foundations of thought and action.* Upper Saddle River, NJ: Prentice Hall.

Bandura, A. (1986b). Self-efficacy. In *Social foundations of thought and action: A social cognitive theory* (pp. 390–453). Englewood Cliffs, NJ: Prentice Hall.

Bandura, A. (1988). Self-efficacy conception of anxiety. *Anxiety Research, 1,* 77–98.

Bandura, A. (1989). Human agency in social cognitive theory. *American Psychologist, 44,* 1175–1184.

Bandura, A. (1991). Self-regulation of motivation through anticipatory and self-regulatory mechanisms. In R. A. Dienstbier (Ed.), *Nebraska symposium on motivation: Perspectives on motivation* (Vol. 38, pp. 69–164). Lincoln: University of Nebraska Press.

Bandura, A. (1993). Perceived self-efficacy in cognitive development and functioning. *Educational Psychologist, 28,* 117–148.

Bandura, A. (2000). Exercise of human agency through collective efficacy. *Current Directions in Psychological Science, 9,* 75–78.

Bandura, A. (2002). Growing primacy of human agency in adaptation and change in the electronic era. *European Psychologist, 7,* 2–16.

Bandura, A., & Cervone, D. (1983). Self-evaluative and self-efficacy mechanisms governing the motivational effects of goal systems. *Journal of Personality and Social Psychology, 45,* 1017–1028.

Bandura, A., & Cervone, D. (1986). Differential engagement of self-reactive influences in cognitive motivation. *Organizational Behavior and Human Decision Processes, 38,* 92–113.

Bandura, A., & Wood, R. E. (1989). Effect of perceived controllability and performance standards on self-regulation of complex decision making. *Journal of Personality and Social Psychology, 56,* 805–814.

Bandura, A., Reese, L., & Adams, N. E. (1982). Microanalysis of action and fear arousal as a function of differential levels of perceived self-efficacy. *Journal of Personality and Social Psychology, 43,* 5–21.

Bandura, A., Taylor, C. B., Williams, S. L., Mefford, I. N., & Barchas, J. D. (1985). Catecholamine secretion as a function of perceived coping self-efficacy. *Journal of Consulting and Clinical Psychology, 53,* 406–414.

Barkley, R. A. (1997). Behavioral inhibition, sustained attention, and executive functions: Constructing a unifying theory of ADHD. *Psychological Bulletin, 121,* 65–94.

Barkley, R. A. (2004). Attention-deficit/hyperactivity disorder and self-regulation: Taking an evolutionary perspective on executive functioning. In R. F. Baumeister & K. D. Vohs (Eds.), *Handbook of self-regulation: Research, theory, and applications* (pp. 301–323). New York: The Guilford Press.

Barkley, R. A. (1997). Behavioral inhibition, sustained attention, and executive functions: Constructing a unifying theory of ADHD. *Psychological Bulletin, 121,* 65–94.

Barone, F. J. (1997). Bullying in school: It doesn't have to happen. *Phi Delta Kappan, 79,* 80–82.

Barrett, H. (2000). Create your own electronic portfolio: Using off-the-shelf software to showcase your own student work. *Learning & Leading with Technology, 27*(7), 15–22.

Barrish, H. H., Saunders, M., & Wolf, M. M. (1969). Good Behavior Game: Effects of individual contingencies for group consequences on disruptive behavior in a classroom. *Journal of Applied Behavior Analysis, 2,* 119–124.

Barron, B. (1993). When smart groups fail. *Journal of the Learning Sciences, 12,* 307–359.

Barrows, H. S., & Kelson, A. C. (1995). *Problem-based learning in secondary education and the problem-based learning institute* (Monograph 1). Springfield, IL: Problem-Based Learning Institute.

Bartholomew, K., & Horowitz, L. M. (1991). Attachment styles among young adults: A test of a four-category model. *Journal of Personality and Social Psychology, 61,* 226–244.

Bassett, G. A. (1979). A study of the effects of task goal and schedule choice on work performance. *Organizational Behavior and Human Performance, 24,* 202–227.

Bateman, B. D., & Linden, M. A. (1998). *Better IEPS* (3rd ed). Longmont, CO: Sopris West.

Battistich, V., Solomon, D., Watson, M., & Schaps, E. (1997). Caring school communities. *Educational Psychologist, 32,* 137–151.

Baumeister, R. F. (1982). A self-presentational view of social phenomenon. *Psychological Bulletin, 91,* 3–26.

Baumeister, R. F. (1986). *Identity: Cultural change and the struggle for self.* New York: Oxford University Press.

Baumeister, R. F. (1987). How the self became a problem: A psychological review of historical research. *Journal of Personality and Social Psychology, 52,* 163–176.

Baumeister, R. F., Campbell, J. D., Krueger, J. I., & Vohs, K. D. (2003). Does high self-esteem cause better performance, interpersonal success, happiness, or healthier lifestyles? *Psychological Science in the Public Interest, 4,* 1–44.

Baumeister, R. F., Tice, D. M., & Hutton, D. G. (1989). Self-presentational motivations and personality differences in self-esteem. *Journal of Personality, 57,* 547–579.

Baumeister, R., & Leary, M. R. (1995). The need to belong: Desire for interpersonal attachments as a fundamental human motivation. *Psychological Bulletin, 117,* 497–529.

Baumgardner, A. H., Lake, E. A., & Arkin, R. M. (1985). Claiming mood as a self-handicap: The influence of spoiled and unspoiled public identities. *Personality and Social Psychology Bulletin, 11,* 349–357.

Baxter, G. P., & Glaser, R. (1998). Investigating the cognitive complexity of science assessments. *Educational Measurement: Issues and Practice, 17*(3), 37–45.

Beane, A. L. (1999). *The bully-free classroom: Over 100 tips and strategies for teachers K -8.* Minneapolis, MN: Free Spirit.

Becker, L. J. (1978). Joint effect of feedback and goal setting on performance: A field study of residential energy conservation. *Journal of Applied Psychology, 63,* 428–433.

Beilin, H. (1992). Piaget's enduring contribution to developmental psychology. *Developmental Psychology, 28,* 191–204.

Belfiore, P. J., Browder, D. M., & Mace, C. (1994). Assessing choice making and preference in adults with profound mental retardation across community and center-based settings. *Journal of Behavioral Education, 4,* 217–225.

Belsky, J., & Cassidy, J. (1994). Attachment: Theory and evidence. In M. Rutter & D. Hay (Eds.), *Development through life: A handbook for clinicians* (pp. 373–402). Oxford, UK: Blackwell Scientific Publications.

Benard, B. (1993). Fostering resiliency in kids. *Educational Leadership, 51,* 44–48.

Bennett, N., & Blundell, D. (1983). Quantity and quality of working rows and classroom groups. *Educational Psychology, 3,* 93–105.

Benware, C., & Deci, E. L. (1984). Quality of learning with an active versus passive motivational set. *American Educational Research Journal, 21,* 755–765.

Berg, T., & Brower, W. (1991). Teacher awareness of student alternate conceptions about rotational motion and gravity. *Journal of Research in Science Teaching, 2,* 3–18.

Bergan, J. R., & Caldwell, T. (1995). Operant techniques in school psychology. *Journal of Educational and Psychological Consultation, 6,* 103–110.

Berk, L. E., & Garvin, R. A. (1984). Development of private speech among low-income Appalachian children. *Developmental Psychology, 20,* 271–286.

Berliner, D. (1992). The nature of expertise in teaching. In F. Oser, A. Dick, & J. Patry, Eds.), *Effective and responsible teaching* (pp. 227–248). San Francisco: Jossey-Bass.

Berliner, D. (1994). Expertise: The wonders of exemplary performance. In J. Mangieri & C. Block (Eds.), *Creating powerful thinking in teachers and students* (pp. 161–186. Fort Worth, TX: Holt, Reinhart & Winston.

Berliner, D. C. (1986). In pursuit of the expert pedagogue. *Educational Researcher, 15,* 5–13.

Berliner, D. C. (1990). If the metaphor fits, why not wear it? The teacher as executive. *Theory into Practice, 29,* 85–93.

Berlyne, D. E. (1966). Curiosity and exploration. *Science, 153,* 25–33.

Berlyne, D. E. (1978). Curiosity and exploration. *Motivation and Emotion, 2,* 97–175.

Berndt, T. J. (2004). Children's friendships: Shifts over a half-century in perspectives on their development and their effects. *Merrill-Palmer Quarterly, 50,* 206–223.

Betz, N. E., & Hackett, G. (1986). Applications of self-efficacy theory to understanding career choice behavior. *Journal of Social and Clinical Psychology, 4,* 279–289.

Bialystok, E. (2001). *Bilingualism in development: Language, literacy, and cognition.* New York: Cambridge University Press.

Binet, A., & Simon, T. (1916). *The development of intelligence in children.* Baltimore, MD: Williams & Wilkins.

Birch, S. H., & Ladd, G. W. (1997). The teacher-child relationship and children's early school adjustment. *Journal of School Psychology, 35,* 61–79.

Bjorklund, D. F. (1995). *Children's thinking: Developmental function and individual differences* (2nd ed.). Pacific Grove, CA: Brooks/Cole.

Bjorklund, D. F., Miller, P. H., Coyle, T. R., & Slawinski, J. L. (1997). Instructing children to use memory strategies: Evidence of utilization deficiencies in memory training studies. *Developmental Review, 17,* 411–441.

Blasi, A. (1980). Bridging moral cognition and moral action: A critical review of the literature. *Psychological Bulletin, 88,* 1–45.

Bloom, B. (1968). Learning for mastery. *Evaluation Comment, 1*(2), 1–5.

Bloom, B. S. (1984). The search for methods of group instruction as effective as one-to-one tutoring. *Educational Leadership, 41*(8), 4–17.

Bloom, B. S. (1985). *Developing talent in young people.* New York: Ballantine Books.

Bloom, B. S. (1986). Automaticity: "The hands and feet of genius." *Educational Leadership, 43*(5), 70–77.

Bloom, B. S., Engelhart, M. D., Furst, E. J., Hill, W. H., & Krathwohl, D. R.. (Eds.) (1956). Taxonomy *of educational objectives: Handbook I, Cognitive domain.* New York: David McKay.

Bloom, B. S., Hastings, J. T., & Madaus, G. F. (1971). *Handbook on formative and summative evaluation of student learning.* New York: McGraw-Hill.

Bloom, L., Margulis, C., Tinker, E., & Fujita, N. (1996). Early conversations and word learning: Contributions from child and adult. *Child Development, 67,* 3154–3175.

Boggiano, A. K., Barrett, M., Weiher, A. W., McClelland, G. H., & Lusk, C. M. (1987). Use of the maximal-operant principle to motivate children's intrinsic interest. *Journal of Personality and Social Psychology, 53,* 866–879.

Boggiano, A. K., Flink, C., Shields, A., Seelbach, A., & Barrett, M. (1993). Use of techniques promoting students' self-determination: Effects on students' analytic problem-solving skills. *Motivation and Emotion, 17,* 319–336.

Bohn, C. M., Roehrig, A. D., & Pressley, M. (2004). The first day of school in the classrooms of two more effective and four less effective primary grade teachers. *Elementary School Journal, 104,* 269–287.

Bohrnstedt, G. W., Stecher, B. M., & Wiley, E. W. (2000). The California class size reduction evaluation: Lessons learned. In M. C. Wang & J. D. Finn (Eds.), *How small classes help teachers do their best* (pp. 201–225). Philadelphia: Temple University Center for Research in Human Development and Education.

Bonds, M., & Stoker, S. (2000). *Bully-proofing your school: A comprehensive approach for middle schools.* Longmont, CO: Sopris West.

Bondy, E., & McKenzie, J. (1999). Resilience building and social reconstructionist teaching: A first-year teacher's story. *The Elementary School Journal, 100,* 129–150.

Borich, G. D. (1988). *Effective teaching methods.* Columbus, OH: Merrill.

Bornstein, M. H., Cote, L. R., Maital, S., Painter, K., Sung-Yun, P., Pascual, L., Pecheux, M.-G., Ruel, J., Venuti, P., & Vyt, A. (2004). Cross-linguistic analysis of vocabulary in young children: Spanish, Dutch, French, Hebrew, Italian, Korean, and American English. *Child Development, 75,* 1115–1140.

Bos, C. S., & Vaughn, S. (2002). *Strategies for teaching students with learning and behavior problems,* Boston: Allyn & Bacon.

Bosma, H. A., & Kunnen, E. S. (2001). Determinants and mechanisms in ego identity development: A review and synthesis. *Developmental Review, 21,* 39–66.

Bouffard, T., Vezeau, C., & Bordelau, L. (1998). A developmental study of the relation between combined learning and performance goals and students' self-regulated learning. *British Journal of Educational Psychology, 68,* 309–319.

Bourne, L. E. (1970). Knowing and using concepts. *Psychological Review, 70,* 546–566.

Bowlby, J. (1982). *Attachment and loss: Vol. 1. Attachment.* New York: Basic Books (original work published in 1969).

Bowlby, J. (1988). *A secure base: Clinical applications of attachment theory.* London: Routledge.

Bowles, T. (1999). Focusing on time orientation to explain adolescent self concept and academic achievement: Part II. Testing a model. *Journal of Applied Health Behavior, 1,* 1–8.

Boyer, J. B., & Baptiste, Jr., H. P. (1996). The crisis in teacher education in America: Issues of recruitment and retention of culturally different (minority) teachers. In J. Siklua (Ed.), *Handbook of research on teacher education* (2nd ed., pp. 779–794) New York: Simon & Schuster MacMillan.

Boyle, E. A., Washburn, S. G., Rosenberg, M. S., Connelly, V. J., Brinckerhoff, L. C. & Banerjee, M. (2002). Reading SLiCK with new audio texts and strategies. *Teaching Exceptional Children, 35,* 50–55.

Brabeck, M. (1983). Moral judgment: Theory and research on differences between males and females. *Developmental Review, 3,* 274–291.

Bradley, C. L. (1997). Generativity—stagnation: Development of a status model. *Developmental Review, 17,* 262–290.

Branden, N. (1984). *The six pillars of self-esteem.* New York: Bantam Books.

Bransford, J. D., & Stein, B. S. (1993). *The ideal problem-solver: A guide to improving thinking, learning, and creativity* (2nd ed). New York: Worth Publishing.

Brennan, S. W., Thames, W., & Roberts, R. (1999). Mentoring with a mission. *Educational Leadership, 57*(3), 49–52.

Bretherton, I. (1990). Open communication and internal working models: Their role in the development of attachment relationships. In R. A. Thompson (Ed.), *Nebraska Symposium on Motivation: Vol. 36. Socioemotional development* (pp. 57–113). Lincoln: University of Nebraska Press.

Brewer, W. F., Chinn, C. A., & Samarapungavan, A. (2000). Explanation in scientists and children. In F. C. Keil & R. A. Wilson (Eds.), *Explanation and cognition* (pp. 279–298). Cambridge, MA: MIT Press.

Briars, D. J., & Resnick, L. (2000). Standards, assessments—and what else? The essential elements of standards-based school improvement. *CSE Technical Report 528.* Los Angeles: National Center for Research on Evaluation, Standards, and Student Testing.

Brill, J. M., Galloway, C., & Kim, B. (2001). *Cognitive apprenticeship as an instructional model.* Retrieved November 26, 2004, from http://www.coe.uga.edu/epltt/CognitiveApprenticeship.htm.

Broadbent, D. E. (1958). *Perception and communication.* New York: Pergamon.

Brody, G. H., & Flor, D. L. (1998). Maternal resources, parenting practices, and child competence in rural, single-parent African-American families. *Child Development, 69,* 803–816.

Brody, G. H., & Shaffer, D. R. (1982). Contributions of parents and peers to children's moral socialization. *Developmental Review, 2,* 31–75.

Brooke, H., & Solomon, J. (2001). Passive visitors or independent explorers: Responses of pupils with severe learning difficulties at an interactive science center. *International Journal of Science Education, 23,* 941–953.

Brookhart, S. M. (1999). Teaching about communicating assessment results and grading. *Educational Measurement: Issues and Practice, 18(1),* 5–14.

Brookhart, S. M. (2001). Successful students' formative and summative use of assessment information. *Assessment in Education, 8,* 153–169.

Brookhart, S. M. (2004). *Grading.* Upper Saddle River, NJ: Pearson Education.

Brooks, L. R. (1968). Spatial and verbal components in the act of recall. *Canadian Journal of Psychology, 22,* 349–368.

Brophy, J. (1981). Teacher praise: A functional analysis. *Review of Educational Research, 51,* 5–32.

Broudy, H. S. (1980). What do professors of education profess? *Educational Forum, 44,* 441–451.

Brown, A. C. (1992) Design experiments: Theoretical and methodological challenges in creating complex interventions in classroom settings. *Journal of the Learning Sciences, 2,* 141–178.

Brown, A. L., & Campione, J. C. (1994). Guided discovery in a community of learners. In K. McGilley (Ed.), *Classrooms lessons: Integrating cognitive theory and classroom practice* (pp. 229–272). Cambridge, MA: MIT Press.

Brown, A. L., & Palincsar, A. S. (1989). Guided, cooperative learning, and individual knowledge acquisition. In L. B. Resnick (Ed.), *Knowing, learning, and instruction: Essays in honor of Robert Glaser* (pp. 393–451). Hillsdale, NJ: Lawrence Erlbaum.

Brown, D. F. (2003). Urban teachers' use of culturally responsive management strategies. *Theory into Practice, 42,* 277–282.

Brown, R., & Pressley, M. (1994). Self-regulated reading and getting meaning from text: The transactional strategies instructional model. In D. H. Schunk & B. J. Zimmerman (Eds.), *Self-regulation of learning and performance: Issues and educational implications* (pp. 155–179). Hillsdale, NJ: Lawrence Erlbaum.

Brownell, M. (1997). *Coping with stress in the special education classroom: Can individual teachers more effectively manage stress?* ERIC Digest #E545. ERIC Clearinghouse on Disabilities and Gifted Education, Reston, VA.

Bruner, J. S. (1961). The act of discovery. *Harvard Educational Review, 31,* 21–32.

Bruner, J. S., Goodenow, J. J., & Austin, G. A. (1956). *A study of thinking.* New York: John Wiley.

Brunetti, G. J. (2001). Why do they teach? A study of job satisfaction among long-term high school teachers. *Teacher Education Quarterly, 28,* No. 2, 49–74.

Bruning, R. H., Schraw, G. J., & Ronning, R. R. (1999). *Cognitive psychology and instruction* (3rd ed.). Columbus, OH: Merrill.

Bryan, T., & Nelson, C. (1995). Doing homework: Perspectives of elementary and middle school students. *Journal of Learning Disabilities, 27,* 488–499.

Bryan, T., & Sullivan-Burstein, K. (1998). Teacher-selected strategies for improving homework completion. *Remedial and Special Education, 19,* 263–275.

Bryan, T., Burstein, K., & Bryan, J. (2001). Students with learning disabilities: Homework problems and promising practices. *Educational Psychologist, 36(3),* 167–180.

Buck, G. H., Polloway, E. A., Smith-Thomas, A., & Cook, K. W. (2003). Prereferral intervention processes: A survey of state practices. *Exceptional Children, 69,* 349–360.

Buckner, R. L., Kelly, W. M., & Petersen, S. E. (1999). Frontal cortex contributes to human memory formation. *Nature Neuroscience, 2,* 311–314.

Bullough, R. V. (1991). Exploring personal teaching metaphors in preservice teacher education. *Journal of Teacher Education, 42,* 43–51.

Bullough, R. V., Jr. (1989). *First year teacher: A case study.* New York: Teachers College Press.

Burden, P. R. (2000) *Powerful classroom management strategies: Motivating students to learn.* Thousand Oaks, CA: Corwin Press.

Burden, P. R. (2003) *Classroom management: Creating a successful learning community* (2nd ed.). New York: John Wiley & Sons.

Burnett, P. (1999). Children's self-talk and academic self-concepts: The impact of teachers' statements. *Educational Psychology in Practice, 15,* 195–200.

Burnett, P. (2003). The impact of teacher feedback on self-talk and self-concept in reading and mathematics. *Journal of Classroom Interaction, 38,* 11–16.

Butler, R. (2000). What learners want to know: The role of achievement goals in shaping information seeking, learning, and interest. In C. Sansone & J. M. Harackiewicz (Eds.), *Intrinsic and extrinsic motivation: The search for optimal motivation and performance* (pp. 161–194). San Diego: Academic Press.

Buxton, C. (1998). Improving the science education of English language learners: Capitalizing on educational reform. *Journal of Women and Minorities in Science and Engineering, 4* (4), 341–369.

Bylsma, W. H., Cozzarelli, C., & Sumer, N. (1997). Relation between adult attachment styles and global self-esteem. *Basic and Applied Social Psychology, 19,* 1–16.

Byrne, B. M. (1984). The general/academic self-concept nomological network: A review of construct validation research. *Review of Educational Research, 54,* 427–456.

Byrne, B. M. (1996). *Measuring self-concept across the life span: Issues and instrumentation.* Washington, DC: American Psychological Association.

Byrnes, J. P. (2003). Factors predictive of mathematics achievement in White, Black, and Hispanic 12th graders. *Journal of Educational Psychology, 95,* 316–326.

Calderhead, J. (1989). Reflective teaching and teacher education. *Teaching and Teacher Education, 5,* 43–51.

Calderhead, J., & Robson, M. (1991). Images of teaching: Student-teachers' early conceptions of classroom practice. *Teaching and Teacher Education, 7,* 1–8.

Calderon, M., Hertz-Lazarowitz, R., & Slavin, R. E. (1998). Effects of bilingual cooperative integrated reading and composition on students' making the transition from Spanish to English reading. *The Elementary School Journal, 99,* 153–165.

California Department of Education (1998). *History-social science content standards for California public schools.* Retrieved June 2, 2005 from http://www.cde.ca.gov/re/pn/fd/documents/histsocsci-stnd.pdf.

Callahan, K., Rademacher, J. A., & Hildreth, B. L. (1998). The effect of parent participation in strategies to improve the homework performance of students who are at risk. *Remedial and Special Education, 19,* 131–141.

Cameron, J. (2001). Negative effects of rewards on intrinsic motivation—A limited phenomenon: Comments on Deci, Koestner, and Ryan (2001). *Review of Educational Research, 71,* 29–42.

Cantor, N., Markus, H., Niedenthal, P., & Nurius, P. (1986). On motivation and the self-concept. In R. M. Sorrentino & E. T. Higgins (Eds.), *Handbook of motivation and cognition* (Vol. 1, pp. 96–121). New York: Guilford Press.

Cantwell, D. P., & Baker, L. (1991). Association between attention deficit-hyperactivity disorder and learning disorders. *Journal of Learning Disabilities, 24,* 88–95.

Caprara, G. V., Barbaranelli, C., Borgogni, L., & Steca, P. (2003). Efficacy beliefs as determinants of teachers' job satisfaction. *Journal of Educational Psychology, 95,* 821–832.

Carbone, E. (2001). Arranging the classroom with an eye (and ear) to students with ADHD. *Teaching Exceptional Children, 34,* 72–81.

Carlo, G., Fabes, R. A., Laible, D., & Kupanoff, K. (1999). Early adolescence and prosocial moral behavior. II: The role of social and contextual influences. *Journal of Early Adolescence, 19,* 133–147.

Carnevale, P. J. D., & Isen, A. M. (1986). The influence of positive affect and visual access on the discovery of integrative solutions in bilateral negotiation. *Organizational Behavior and Human Decision Processes, 37,* 1–13.

Carr, D. (2003). *The promise of cultural institutions.* Walnut Creek, CA: AltaMira Press.

Carraher, T. N., Carraher, D. W., & Schliemann, A. D. (1995). Mathematics in the streets and in the schools. *British Journal of Developmental Psychology, 3,* 21–29.

Carter, K. (1990). Meaning and metaphor: Case knowledge in teaching. *Theory into Practice, 29,* 109–115.

Carter, R. (1998). *Mapping the mind.* Berkley, CA: University of California Press.

Cartledge, G., & Milburn, J. F. (1996). *Cultural diversity and social skills instruction: Understanding ethnic and gender differences.* Champaign, IL: Research Press.

Carver, C. S., & Scheier, M. F. (1990). Origins and functions of positive affect: A control-process view. *Psychological Review, 97,* 19–35.

Case, R. (1992). *The mind's staircase: Exploring the conceptual underpinnings of children's thought and knowledge.* Hillsdale, NJ: Lawrence Erlbaum.

Case, R., & Okamoto, Y. (1996). The role of central conceptual structures in the development of children's thought. *Monographs of the Society for Research in Child Development, 61,* No. 1–2, Serial No. 246.

Caspi, A., Henry, B., McGee, R. O., Moffitt, T. E. & Silva, P. A. (1995). Temperamental origins of child and adolescent behavior problems: From age three to age fifteen. *Child Development, 66,* 55–68.

Caspi, A., Moffitt, T. E., Newman, D. L., & Silva, P. A. (1996). Behavioral observations at age 3 predict adult psychiatric disorders. *Archives of General Psychiatry, 53,* 1033–1039.

Casteel, C. P., Isom, B. A., & Jordan, K. F. (2000). Creating confident and competent readers: Transactional strategies instruction. *Intervention in School and Clinic, 36,* 67–77.

Cattell, R. B. (1940). A culture-free intelligence test: Part 1. *Journal of Educational Psychology, 31,* 161–179.

Cattell, R. B. (1963). Theory of fluid and crystallized intelligence: A critical experiment. *Journal of Educational Psychology, 54,* 1–22.

Cavanaugh, T. (2002). EBooks and accommodations: Is this the future of print accommodation? *Teaching Exceptional Children, 35,* 56–61.

Center for Adolescent and Family Studies. (1996). *Teacher talk, 2*(3), Indiana University. Retrieved March 25, 2005 from http://www.education.indiana.edu/cas/tt/v2i3/peaceful.html.

Center for Research on Education, Diversity, and Excellence (CREDE). (2002). Retrieved 7/6/2005, from http://www.crede.org/standards/standards_data.html.

Centers for Disease Control. (2004). *Attention-deficit/hyperactivity disorder—Symptoms of ADHD.* Retrieved on 28 October 2004 from http://www.cdc.gov/ncbddd/adhd/symptom.htm.

Chao, R. K. (1996). Chinese and European American mothers' views about the role of parenting in children's school success. *Journal of Cross-Cultural Psychology, 27,* 403–423.

Chapanis, A. (1965). *Man machine engineering.* Belmont, CA: Wadsworth.

Chapman, J. W., & Boersma, F. J. (1991). Assessment of learning disabled students' academic self-concepts with the PASS: Findings from 15 years of research. *Developmental Disabilities Bulletin, 19,* 81–104.

Charles, C. M. (2002). *Building classroom discipline* (7th ed.). Boston: Allyn & Bacon.

Chase, W. G., & Simon, H. A. (1973). Perception in chess. *Cognitive Psychology, 4,* 55–81.

Cheek, J. M., & Smith, L. R. (1999). Music training and mathematics achievement. *Adolescence, 34,* 759–761.

Chen, W. (2002). Six expert and student teachers' views and implementation of constructivist teaching using a movement approach to physical education. *The Elementary School Journal, 102,* 255–272.

Chera, P., & Wood, C. (2003). Animated multimedia "talking books" can promote phonological awareness in children beginning to read. *Learning and Instruction, 13,* 33–52.

Chi, M. T. H., Bassok, M., Lewis, M. W., Reimann, P., & Glaser, R. (1989). Self-explanations: How students study and use examples in learning to solve problems. *Cognitive Science, 13,* 145–182.

Chi, M. T. H., de Leeuw, N., Chiu, M. H., & LaVancher, C. (1994). Eliciting self-explanations improves understanding. *Cognitive Science. 18,* 439–477.

Chi, M. T. H., Feltovich, P. J., & Glaser, R. (1981). Categorization and representation of physics problems by experts and novices. *Cognitive Science, 5,* 121–152.

Chi, M. T. H., Siler, S. A., Jeong, H., Yamauchi, T., & Hausmann, R. G. (2001). Learning from human tutoring. *Cognitive Science, 25,* 471–533.

Chinn, C. A., & Brewer, W. F. (1993). The role of anomalous data in knowledge acquisition: A theoretical framework and implications for science instruction. *Review of Educational Research, 63,* 1–49.

Chinn, C. A., O'Donnell, A. M., & Jinks, T. S. (2000). The structure of discourse in collaborative learning. *Journal of Experimental Education, 69,* 77–97.

Chomsky, N. (1959). A review of B. F. Skinner's *Verbal behavior. Language, 35,* 26–129.

Chomsky, N. (1968). *Language and mind.* San Diego, CA: Harcourt Brace Jovanovich.

Church, M. A., Elliot, A. J., & Gable, S. L. (2001). Perceptions of classroom environment, achievement goals, and achievement outcomes. *Journal of Educational Psychology, 93,* 43–54.

Cizek, G. J. (1998). *Filling in the blanks. Putting standardized testing to the test.* Washington, DC: Thomas B. Fordham Foundation.

Cizek, G. J. (1999). *Cheating on Tests: How to do it, detect it, and prevent it.* Mahwah, NJ: Lawrence Erlbaum.

Cizek, G. J. (2001). More unintended consequences of high-stakes testing. *Educational Measurement: Issues and Practice, 20,* 19–27.

Cizek, G. J. (2003). *Detecting and preventing classroom cheating: Promoting integrity in assessment.* Thousand Oaks, CA: Corwin Press.

Clermont, C. P., Borko, H. & Krajcik, J. S. (1994). Comparative study of the pedagogical content knowledge of experienced and novice chemical demonstrators. *Journal of Research in Science Teaching, 31,* 419–441.

Clifford, M. M. (1984). Thoughts on a theory of constructive failure. *Educational Psychologist, 19,* 108–120.

Clifford, M. M. (1988). Failure tolerance and academic risk-taking in ten- to twelve-year-old students. *British Journal of Educational Psychology, 58,* 15–27.

Clifford, M. M. (1990). Students need challenge, not easy success. *Educational Leadership, 48,* 22–26.

Cognition and Technology Group at Vanderbilt (1997). *The Jasper Project: Lessons in curriculum, instruction, assessment, and professional development.* Mahwah, NJ: Lawrence Erlbaum.

Cohen, E. G. (1982). Expectation states and interracial interactions in school settings. *Annual Review of Sociology, 8,* 209–235.

Cohen, E. G. (1994). Restructuring the classroom: Conditions for productive small groups. *Review of Educational Research, 64*(1), 1–35.

Cohen, E. G., & Lotan, R. A. (1995). Producing equal-status interactions in the heterogeneous classroom. *American Educational Research Journal, 32,* 99–120.

Cohen, E. G., & Lotan, R. A. (1997). *Working for equity in heterogeneous classrooms: Sociological theory in practice.* New York: Teacher's College Press.

Cohen, E. G., Lotan, R. A., & Catanzarite, L. (1990). Treating status problems in the cooperative classroom. In S. Sharan (Ed.), *Cooperative learning: Theory and practice.* New York: Praeger.

Cohen, E. G., Lotan, R. A., Abrams, P. L., Scarloss, B. A., & Schultz, S. E. (2002) Can groups learn? *Teacher's College Record, 104,* 1045–1068.

Cohen, E. G., Lotan, R. A., Scarloss, B. A., & Arellano, A. R. (1999). Complex instruction: Equity in cooperative learning classrooms. *Theory into Practice, 38,* 80–86.

Cohen, P. A., Kulick, J. A., & Kulick, C. C. (1982). Educational outcomes of tutoring: A meta-analysis of findings. *American Educational Research Journal, 19,* 237–248.

Coladarci, T. (1992). Teachers' sense of efficacy and commitment to teaching. *Journal of Experimental Education, 60,* 323–337.

Colangelo, N., & Davis, G. A. (Eds.) (2003). *Handbook of gifted education* (3rd ed.). Boston: Allyn & Bacon.

Colby, A., Kohlberg, L., Gibbs, J., & Lieberman, M. (1983). A longitudinal study of moral development. *Monographs of the Society for Research in Child Development, 48* (1–2, Serial No. 200).

Cole, M. (1990). Cognitive development and formal schooling: The evidence from cross-cultural research. In L. C. Moll (Ed.), *Vygotsky and education* (pp. 89–110). New York: Cambridge University Press.

Cole, M. (1996). *Cultural psychology: A once and future discipline.* Cambridge, MA: The Belknap Press of Harvard University Press.

Collins, A. M., & Quillian, M. (1969). Retrieval time from semantic memory. *Journal of Verbal Learning and Verbal Behavior, 8,* 240–247.

Collins, A., & Brown, J. S. (1988). The computer as a tool for learning through reflection. In H. Mandl & A. Lesgold (Eds.), *Learning issues for intelligent tutoring systems* (pp. 1–18). New York: Springer-Verlag.

Collins, A., Brown, J. S., & Holum, A. (1991). Cognitive apprenticeship: Making thinking visible. *American Educator, 15*(3), 38–39.

Collins, A., Brown, J. S., & Newman, S. E. (1989). Cognitive apprenticeship: Teaching the crafts of reading, writing, and mathematics. In L. B. Resnick (Ed.), *Knowing, learning, and instruction: Essays in honor of Robert Glaser* (pp. 453–494). Hillsdale, NJ: Lawrence Erlbaum.

Collins, N. L. (1996). Working models of attachment: Implications for explanation, emotion, and behavior. *Journal of Personality and Social Psychology, 71,* 810–832.

Collins, N. L., Guichard, A. C., Ford, M. B., & Feeney, B. C. (2004). Working models of attachment: New developments and emerging themes. In W. S. Rholes & J. A. Simpson (Eds.), *Adult attachment: Theory, research, and clinical implications* (pp. 196–239). New York: Guilford Press.

Condry, J. (1977). Enemies of exploration: Self-initiated versus other-initiated learning. *Journal of Personality and Social Psychology, 35,* 459–475.

Conger, R. D., Conger, K. J., Elder, G. H. Jr., Lorenz, F., Simons, R., & Whitbeck, L. (1993). A family process model of economic hardship and adjustment of early adolescent girls. *Developmental Psychology, 29,* 206–219.

Connell, J. P. (1990). Context, self, and action: A motivational analysis of self-system processes across the life-span. In D. Cicchetti (Ed.), *The self in transition: From infancy to childhood* (pp. 61–97). Chicago: University of Chicago Press.

Connell, J. P., & Welborn, J. G. (1991). Competence, autonomy, and relatedness: A motivational analysis of self-system processes. In M. R. Gunnar & L. A. Sroufe (Eds.), *Self processes in development: Minnesota symposium on child psychology* (Vol. 23, pp. 167–216). Chicago: University of Chicago Press.

Connell, J. P., Spencer, M. B., & Aber, J. L. (1994). Educational risk and resilience in African-American youth: Context, self, action, and outcomes in school. *Child Development, 65,* 493–506.

Connolly, J. A., & Doyle, A. (1984). Relation of social fantasy play to social competence in preschoolers. *Developmental Psychology, 20,* 797–806.

Cook, S. B., Scruggs, T. E., Mastropieri, M. A., & Casto, G. C. (1985–1986). Handicapped students as tutors. *The Journal of Special Education, 19,* 155–164.

Cooper, H., & Valentine, J. C. (2001). Using research to answer practical questions about homework. *Educational Psychologist, 36*(3), 143–153.

Cooper, K. J., & Browder, D. M. (1998). Enhancing choice and participation for adults with severe disabilities in community-based instruction. *Journal of the Association for Persons with Severe Handicaps, 23,* 252–260.

Cordova, D. I., & Lepper, M. R. (1996). Intrinsic motivation and the process of learning: Beneficial effects of contextualization, personalization, and choice. *Journal of Educational Psychology, 88,* 715–730.

Corno, L., & Mandinach, E. (1983). The role of cognitive engagement in classroom learning and motivation. *Educational Psychologist, 18,* 88–108.

Covington, M. (1984a). The self-worth theory of achievement motivation: Findings and implications. *Elementary School Journal, 85,* 5–20.

Covington, M. (1984b). Motivation for self-worth. In R. Ames & C. Ames (Eds.), *Research on motivation in education* (Vol. 1, pp. 77–113). New York: Academic Press.

Covington, M., & Omelich, C. L. (1979). Effort: The double-edged sword in school achievement. *Journal of Educational Psychology, 71,* 169–182.

Covington, M. V., & Mueller, K. J. (2001). Intrinsic versus extrinsic motivation: An approach/avoidance reformulation. *Educational Psychology Review, 13,* 157–176.

Craighead, W. E., Kazdin, A. E., & Mahoney, M. J. (1981). *Behavior modification: Principles, issues, and applications.* Boston: Houghton Mifflin.

Craik, F. I. M., & Lockhart, R. S. (1972). Levels of processing: A framework for memory research. *Journal of Verbal Learning and Verbal Behavior, 11,* 671–684.

Craven, R. G., Marsh, H. W., & Burnett, P. (2003). Cracking the self-concept enhancement conundrum: A call and blueprint for the next generation of self-concept enhancement research. In H. W. Marsh, R. G. Craven, & D. M. McInerney (Eds.), *International advances in self-research* (pp. 91–126). Greenwich, CT: Information Age Publishing.

Cremin, L. (1988). *American education.* New York: Harper & Row.

Crick, N. B., Bigbee, M. A., & Howes, C. (1996). Gender differences in children's normative beliefs about aggression: How do I hurt thee? Let me count the ways. *Child Development, 67,* 1003–1014.

Crockenberg, S., & Lourie, A. (1996). Parents' conflict strategies with children and children's conflict strategies with peers. *Merrill-Palmer Quarterly, 42,* 495–518.

Crocker, J. (1981). Judgment of covariation by social perceivers. *Psychological Bulletin, 90,* 272–292.

Cross, L. H., & Frary, R. B. (1999). Hodgepodge grading: Endorsed by students and teachers alike. *Applied Measurement in Education, 12(1),* 53–72.

Cross, S. E., & Markus, H. R. (1994). Self-schemas, possible selves, and competent performance. *Journal of Educational Psychology, 86,* 423–438.

Csikszentmihalyi, M. (1975). *Beyond boredom and anxiety: The experience of play in work and games.* San Francisco: Jossey-Bass.

Csikszentmihalyi, M. (1982). Toward a psychology of optimal experience. *Review of Personality and Social Psychology, 3,* 13–36.

Csikszentmihalyi, M. (1988). The flow experience and its significance for human Psychology. In M. Csikszentmihalyi & I. S. Csikszentmihalyi (Eds.), *Optimal experience* (pp. 15–35). Cambridge, UK: Cambridge University Press.

Csikszentmihalyi, M., & Nakamura, J. (1989). The dynamics of intrinsic motivation: A study of adolescents. In C. Ames & R. Ames (Eds.), *Research on motivation in education* (Vol. 3, pp. 45–71). San Diego: Academic Press.

Csikszentmihalyi, M. (1990). *Flow: The psychology of optimal experience.* New York: Harper & Row.

Csikszentmihalyi, M., Rathunde, K., & Whalen, S. (1993). *Talented teenagers: The roots of success and failure.* New York: Cambridge University Press.

Culbertson, J. L. (1998). Learning disabilities. In T. H. Ollendick & M. Hersen (Eds.), *Handbook of child psychopathology* (pp. 117–156). New York: Plenum Press.

Cummins, J. (1981). The role of primary language development in promoting educational success for language minority students. In California Department of Education. *Schooling and Language Minority Students: A Theoretical Framework,* (pp. 3–50). Sacramento: Author.

Curran, M. E. (2003). Linguistic diversity and classroom management. *Theory into Practice, 43,* 334–340.

Curry, L. A., Snyder, C. R., Cook, D. L., Ruby, B. C., & Rehm, M. (1997). The role of hope in student-athlete academic and sport achievement. *Journal of Personality and Social Psychology, 73,* 1257–1267.

Dalbey, J., & Linn, M. C. (1985). The demands and requirements of computer programming: A literature review. *Journal of Educational Computing Research, 1,* 253–274.

Daneman, M., & Carpenter, P. A. (1980). Individual differences in working memory and reading. *Journal of Verbal Learning and Verbal Behavior, 19,* 450–466.

Daneman, M., & Carpenter, P. A. (1983). Individual differences in integrating information between and within sentences. *Journal of Experimental Psychology: Learning, Memory, and Cognition, 9,* 561–584.

Daniels, E., & Arapostathis, M. (2005). What do they really want? Student voices and motivation research. *Urban Education, 40,* 34–59.

Danielson, C. (1997). *Performance tasks and rubrics: Upper elementary school mathematics.* Larchmont, NY: Eye on Education.

Danner, F. W., & Lonky, E. (1981). A cognitive-developmental approach to the effects of rewards on intrinsic motivation. *Child Development, 52,* 1043–1052.

Darling-Hammond, L., & McLaughlin, M. W. (1995). Policies that support professional development in an era of reform. In *Phi Delta Kappan, 76* 597–604.

Darveaux, D. X. (1984). The Good Behavior Game plus merit: Controlling disruptive behavior and improving student motivation. *School Psychology Review, 13,* 510–514.

Data from the Digest of Education Statistics, 2003, National Center for Education, U.S. Department of Education, available at http://nces.ed.gov/programs/digest/d03/tables/ dt052.asp.

Davies, J., & Bremer, I. (1999). Reading and mathematics attainments and self-esteem in years 2 and 6—An eight-year cross-sectional study. *Educational Studies, 25,* 145–157.

Davis, E. A., & Linn, M. C. (2000). Scaffolding students' knowledge integration: Prompts for reflection in KIE. *International Journal of Science Education, 22,* 819–837.

Davis, M. (1992). The role of the amygdala in conditioned fear. In J. P. Aggleton (Ed.), *The amygdala: Neurobiological aspects of emotion, memory, and mental dysfunction* (pp. 255–305). New York: John Wiley & Sons.

Davis, M., & Whalen, P. J. (2001). The amygdala: Vigilance and emotion. *Molecular Psychiatry, 6,* 13–34.

Day, H. I. (1982). Curiosity and the interested explorer. *Performance and Instruction, 21,* 19–22.

de Jong, Martin, E., Zamarro, J., Esquembre, F., Swaak, J., & van Joolingen, W. R. (1999). The integration of computer simulation and learning support: An example from the physics domain of collisions. *Journal of Research in Science Teaching, 36,* 597–615.

De La Paz, S. (2001). Teaching writing to students with attention deficit disorders and specific language impairment. *The Journal of Educational Research, 95,* 37–47.

De Lisi, R., & Golbeck, S. (1999). Implications of Piagetian theory for peer learning. In A. M. O'Donnell & A. King (Eds.), *Cognitive perspectives on peer learning* (pp. 3–37). Mahwah, NJ: Lawrence Erlbaum.

De Lisi, R., & Staudt, J. (1980). Individual differences in college students' performance on formal operations tasks. *Journal of Applied Developmental Psychology, 1,* 201–208.

De Vries, D. L., & Edwards, K. J. (1973). Learning games and student teams: Their effects on classroom process. *American Educational Research Journal, 10,* 307–318.

De Wolff, M., & van Ijzendoorn, M. H. (1997). Sensitivity and attachment: A meta-analysis on parental antecedents of infant attachment. *Child Development, 68,* 571–591.

Deater-Deckard, K., Dodge, K. A., Bates, J. E., & Pettit, G. S. (1996). Physical discipline among African American and European American mothers: Links to children's externalizing behaviors. *Developmental Psychology, 32,* 1065–1072.

deBettencourt, L. U. (2002). Understanding the differences between IDEA and Section 504. *Teaching Exceptional Children, 34,* 16–23.

Debowski, S., Wood, R. E., & Bandura, A. (2001). Impact of guided mastery and enactive exploration on self-regulatory mechanisms and information acquisition through electronic search. *Journal of Applied Psychology, 86,* 1129–1141.

deCharms, R. (1976). *Enhancing motivation: Change in the classroom.* New York: Irvington.

Deci, E. L. (1992). The relation of interest to the motivation of behavior: A self-determination theory perspective. In K. A. Renninger, S. Hidi, & A. Krapp (Eds.), *The role of interest in learning and development* (pp. 43–70). Hillsdale, NJ: Lawrence Erlbaum.

Deci, E. L. (1995). *Why we do what we do: The dynamics of personal autonomy.* New York: Penguin Books.

Deci, E. L. (2004). Promoting intrinsic motivation and self-determination in people with mental retardation. In H. N. Switzky (Ed.), *International Review of Research in Mental Retardation* (Vol. 28, pp. 1–29). New York: Elsevier Academic Press.

Deci, E. L., & Ryan, R. M. (1985). *Intrinsic motivation and self-determination in human behavior.* New York: Plenum.

Deci, E. L., & Ryan, R. M. (1987). The support of autonomy and the control of behavior. *Journal of Personality and Social Psychology, 53,* 1024–1037.

Deci, E. L., & Ryan, R. M. (1991). A motivational approach to self: Integration in personality. In R. Dienstbier (Ed.), *Nebraska symposium on motivation: Perspectives on motivation* (Vol. 38, pp. 237–288). Lincoln: University of Nebraska Press.

Deci, E. L., Eghrari, H., Patrick, B. C., & Leone, D. R. (1994). Facilitating internalization: The self-determination theory perspective. *Journal of Personality, 62,* 119–142.

Deci, E. L., Hodges, R., Pierson, L., & Tomassone, J. (1992). Autonomy and competence as motivational factors in students with learning disabilities and emotional handicaps. *Journal of Learning Disabilities, 25,* 457–471.

Deci, E. L., Ryan, R. M., & Williams, G. C. (1995). Need satisfaction and the self-regulation of learning. *Learning and Individual Differences, 8,* 165–183.

Deci, E. L., Koestner, R., & Ryan, R. M. (1999). A meta-analytic review of experiments examining the effects of extrinsic rewards on intrinsic motivation. *Psychological Bulletin, 125,* 627–668.

Deci, E. L., Schwartz, A., Sheinman, L., & Ryan, R. M. (1981). An instrument to assess adult's orientations toward control versus autonomy in children: Reflections on intrinsic motivation and perceived competence. *Journal of Educational Psychology, 73,* 642–650.

Deci, E. L., Spiegel, N. H., Ryan, R. M., Koestner, R., & Kauffman, M. (1982). Effects of performance standards on teaching styles: Behavior of controlling teachers. *Journal of Educational Psychology, 74,* 852–859.

Deci, E. L., Vallerand, R. J., Pelletier, L. G., & Ryan, R. M. (1991). Motivation and education: The self-determination perspective. *Educational Psychologist, 26*, 325–346.

DeLoache, J. S. (1987). Rapid change in the symbolic functioning of very young children. *Science, 238*, 1556–1557.

DeLoache, J. S. (1991). Symbolic functioning in very young children: Understanding of pictures and models. *Child Development, 62*, 736–752.

Delquadri, J. C., Greenwood, C. R., Whorton, D., Carta, J. J., & Hall, R. V. (1986). Classwide peer tutoring. *Exceptional Children, 52*, 535–542.

DeMontebello, P. (1998, June). *Museums in a new millennium.* Presentation to the Association of Art Museum Directors. Providence, RI.

DePaul, A. (1998). *What to expect your first year of teaching.* Washington, DC: U.S. Department of Education.

Deslandes, R., Royer, E., Potvin, P., & Leclerc, D. (1999). Patterns of home and school partnership for general and special education students at the secondary level. *Exceptional Children, 65*, 496–506.

Deutsch, M. (1949). A theory of cooperation and competition. *Human Relations, 2*, 129–152.

Dewey, J. (1933). *How we think.* New York: D. C. Heath.

Dewey, J. (1971). *The child and the curriculum.* Chicago: The University of Chicago Press.

Dewey, J. (1990). *The child and the curriculum; The School and Society.* Chicago: The University of Chicago Press.

Diaz, R. M. (1983). Thought and two languages: The impact of bilingualism on cognitive development. In E. W. Gordon (Ed.), *Review of research in education* (Vol. 10, pp. 23–54). Washington, DC: American Educational Research Association.

Diaz, R. M. (1985). Bilingual cognitive development: Addressing three gaps in recent research. *Child Development, 56*, 1376–1388.

Dicker, M. (1990). Using action research to navigate an unfamiliar teaching assignment. *Theory into Practice, 29*, 203–208.

Diener, C. I., & Dweck, C. S. (1978). An analysis of learned helplessness: Continuous changes in performance, strategy, and achievement cognitions following failure. *Journal of Personality and Social Psychology, 36*, 451–462.

Diener, C. I., & Dweck, C. S. (1980). An analysis of learned helplessness: II. The processing of success. *Journal of Personality and Social Psychology, 39*, 940–952.

Dishion, T. J., Capalsi, D. M., Spracklen, K. M., & Li, F. (1995). Peer ecology of male adolescent drug use. *Development and Psychopathology, 7*, 803–824.

Dishion, T. J., Eddy, J. M., Haas, E., Li, F., & Spracklen, K. (1997). Friendships and violent behavior during adolescence. *Social Development, 6*, 207–223.

Dishion, T. J., McCord, J., & Poulin, F. (1999). When interventions harm: Peer groups and problem behavior. *American Psychologist, 54*, 755–764.

Dishion, T. J., Spracklen, K. M., Andrews, D. W., & Patterson, G. R. (1996). Deviancy training in male adolescent friendships. *Behavior Therapy, 27*, 373–390.

Ditman, O. (July/August 2000). Online term-paper mills produce a new crop of cheaters. *Harvard Education Letter, 16*(4), 6–7.

Dolan, L. J., Kellan, S. G., Brown, C. H., Werthamer-Larsson, L., Rebok, G. W., & Mayer, L. S. (1993). The short term impact of two classroom-based preventative interventions on aggressive and shy behaviors and poor achievement. *Journal of Applied Developmental Psychology, 14*, 317–345.

Doll, B. (1996). Children without friends: Implications for practice and policy. *School Psychology Review, 25*, 165–183.

Dollinger, S. J., & Thelen, M. H. (1978). Overjustification and children's intrinsic motivation: Comparative effects of four rewards. *Journal of Personality and Social Psychology, 36*, 1259–1269.

Doty, D. E., Popplewell, S. R., & Byers, G. O. (2001). Interactive CD-ROM storybooks and young readers' reading comprehension. *Journal of Research on Computing in Education, 33*, 374–384.

Downing, J. A. (2002). Individualized behavior contracts. *Intervention in School and Clinic, 37*, 168–172.

Doyle, W. (1986). Classroom organization and management. In M. C. Wittrock (Ed.), *Handbook of research on teaching* (pp. 392–431). New York: Macmillan.

Drake, S. G. (1834). *Biography and history of the Indians of North America.* Boston: Perkins and Hilliard, Gray.

Dreeben, R., & Gamoran, A. (1986). Race, instruction, and learning. *American Sociological Review, 51*(5), 660–669.

Duncan, R. M. (1995). Piaget and Vygotsky revisited: Dialogue or assimilation? *Developmental Review, 15*, 458–472.

Dusek, J. (1980). The development of test anxiety in children. In I. Sarason (Ed.), *Test anxiety: Theory, research, and applications* (pp. 87–110). Hillsdale, NJ: Lawrence Erlbaum.

Dweck, C. S. (1975). The role of expectancies and attributions in the alleviation of learned helplessness. *Journal of Personality and Social Psychology, 31*, 674–685.

Dweck, C. S. (1986). Motivational processes affecting learning. *American Psychologist, 41*, 1040–1048.

Dweck, C. S. (2000). *Self-theories: Their role in motivation, personality, and development.* Philadelphia: Psychology Press.

Dweck, C. S. (2002). The development of ability conceptions. In A. W. J. Eccles (Ed.), *The development of achievement motivation.* San Diego, CA: Academic Press.

Dweck, C. S., & Leggett, E. L. (1988). A social-cognitive approach to motivation and personality. *Psychological Review, 95*, 256–273.

Dweck, C. S., & Repucci, N. D. (1973). Learned helplessness and reinforcement responsibility in children. *Journal of Personality and Social Psychology, 25*, 109–116.

Earley, P. C., Wojnaroski, P., & Prest, W. (1987). Task planning and energy expended: Exploration of how goals influence performance. *Journal of Applied Psychology, 72*, 107–113.

Ebel, R. L. (1962). Content standard test scores. *Educational and Psychological Measurement, 22*, 15–25.

Eccles, J. S. (1993). School and family effects on the ontogeny of children's interests, self-perceptions, and activity choices. In J. E. Jacobs (Ed.), *Nebraska symposium on motivation: Developmental perspectives on motivation* (Vol. 40, pp. 145–208). Lincoln: University of Nebraska Press.

Eccles, J. S., & Midgley, C. (1989). Stage/environment fit: Developmentally appropriate classrooms for early adolescents. In R. E. Ames & C. Ames (Eds.), *Research on motivation in education* (Vol. 3, pp. 139–186). New York: Academic Press.

Eccles, J. S., Adler, T. F., Futterman, R., Goff, S. B., Kaczala, C. M., Meece, J. L., et al. (1983). Expectations, values and academic behaviors. In J. T. Spence (Ed.), *Achievement and achievement motivation* (pp. 75–146). San Francisco: W. H. Freeman.

Eccles, J. S., Midgley, C., & Adler, T. (1984). Grade-level changes in the school environment: Effects on achievement motivation. In J. G. Nicholls (Ed.), *The development of achievement motivation* (pp. 283–331). Greenwich, CT: JAI Press.

Edelson, D. C., Gordin, D., & Pea, R. (1999). Addressing the challenges of inquiry-based learning through technology and curriculum design. *The Journal of the Learning Sciences, 8*, 391–450.

Eglash, R. (1999). *African fractals: Modern Computing and indigenous design.* New Brunswick, NJ: Rutgers University Press.

Eglash, R. (2005). *Culturally situated design tools: Teaching math through culture.* Retrieved 7/12/05 from www.rpi.edu/eglash/csdt.html.

Eichenbaum, H. (2002). *The cognitive neuroscience of memory.* Boston: Oxford University Press.

Eisenberg, N. (1992). *The caring child.* Cambridge, MA: Harvard University Press.

Eisenberg, N. (2000). Emotion, regulation, and moral development. *Annual Review of Psychology, 51*, 665–697.

Eisenberg, N. Fabes, R. A., Bernszweig, J., Karbon, M., Poulin, R., & Hanish, L. (1993). The relation of emotionality and regulation to preschoolers' social skills and sociometric status. *Child Development, 64*, 1418–1438.

Eisenberg, N., Fabes, R. A., Shepard, S. A., Murphy, B. D., Guthrie, I. K., Jones, S., et al. (1997). Contemporaneous and longitudinal prediction of children's social functioning from regulation and emotionality. *Child Development, 68*, 642–664.

Eisenberg, N., & Fabes, R. A. (1998). Prosocial development. In W. Daman & N. Eisenberg (Eds.), *Handbook of child psychology: Social, emotional, and personality development* (Vol. 3, pp. 701–778). New York: Wiley.

Eisenberg, N., & Shell, R. (1987). Prosocial moral judgment and behavior in children: The mediating role of costs. *Personality and Social Psychology Bulletin, 12*, 426–433.

Eisenberg, N., Guthrie, I. K., Fabes, R. A., Reiser, M., Murphy, B. C., Holgren, R., Maszk, P., & Losoya, S. (1997). The relations of regulation and emotionality to resiliency and competent social functioning in elementary school children. *Child Development, 68*, 295–311.

Eisenberg, N., Lennon, R., & Roth, K. (1983). Prosocial development: A longitudinal study. *Developmental Psychology, 19*, 846–855.

Elawar, M. C., & Corno, L. (1985). A factorial experiment in teachers' written feedback on student homework: Changing teacher behavior a little rather than a lot. *Journal of Educational Psychology, 77*, 162–173.

Elbaum, B., Moody, S. W., & Schumm, J. S. (1999). Mixed ability grouping for reading: What students think. *Learning Disabilities Research and Practice, 14*, 61–66.

Elbert, T., Pantev, C., Wienbruch, C., Rockstroh, B., & Taub, E. (1995). Increased cortical representation of the fingers of the left hand in string players. *Science, 270*, 305–307.

Elliot, A. J. (1999). Approach and avoidance motivation and achievement goals. *Educational Psychologist, 34*, 169–189.

Elliot, A. J., & Harackiewicz, J. (1996). Approach and avoidance goals and intrinsic motivation: A mediational analysis. *Journal of Personality and Social Psychology, 70*, 461–475.

Elliot, A. J., & McGregor, H. (2001). Test anxiety and the hierarchical model of approach and avoidance achievement motivation. *Journal of Personality and Social Psychology, 76*, 628–644.

Elliot, E., & Dweck, C. (1988). Goals: An approach to motivation and achievement. *Journal of Personality and Social Psychology, 54*, 5–12.

Ellis, N. C., & Hellelley, R. A. (1980). A bilingual word-length effect: Implications for intelligence testing and the relative ease of mental calculation in Welsh and English. *British Journal of Psychology, 71*, 43–52.

Emmer, E. T., Evertson, C. M., & Anderson, L. (1980). Effective classroom management at the beginning of the school year. *The Elementary School Journal, 80*(5), 219–231.

Epstein, J. L. (2001). *School, family, and community partnerships: Preparing educators and improving schools.* Boulder, CO: Westview.

Epstein, J. L., & Van Voorhis, F. L. (2001). More than minutes: Teachers' roles in designing homework. *Educational Psychologist, 36*(3), 181–193.

Erez, M. (1977). Feedback: A necessary condition for the goal setting performance relationship. *Journal of Applied Psychology, 62*, 624–627.

Erez, M., & Kanfer, F. H. (1983). The role of goal acceptance in goal setting and task performance. *Academy of Management Review, 8*, 454–463.

Erez, M., & Zidon, I. (1984). Effects of goal acceptance on the relationship to goal difficulty and performance. *Journal of Applied Psychology, 60*, 69–78.

Ericsson, K. A. (1998). Basic capacities can be modified or circumvented by deliberate practice: A rejection of talent accounts of expert performance. *Behavioral and Brain Sciences, 21*, 413–414.

Ericsson, K. A., & Charness, N. (1994). Expert performance: Its structure and acquisition. *American Psychologist, 49*, 725–747.

Ericsson, K. A., Krampe, R. T. C., & Tesch-Romer, C. (1993). The role of deliberate practice in the acquisition of expert performance. *Psychological Review, 100*, 363–406.

Erikson, E. H. (1959). Identity and the life cycle. *Psychological Issues, 1,* 1–171.

Erikson, E. H. (1963). *Childhood and society* (2nd ed.). New York: Norton.

Erikson, E. H. (1964). *Insight and responsibility.* New York: Norton.

Erikson, E. H. (1968). *Identity, youth, and crisis.* New York: Norton.

Erikson, E. H. (1982). *The life cycle completed.* New York: Norton.

Erkens, G., Prangsma, M., & Jaspers, J. (2005). Planning and coordinating activities in collaborative learning. In A. M. O'Donnell, C. E. Hmelo-Silver, & G. Erkens (Eds.), *Collaborative learning, reasoning, and technology.* Mahwah, NJ: Lawrence Erlbaum, 233–263.

Errington, E. (2004). The impact of teacher beliefs on flexible learning innovation: Some practices and possibilities for academic developers. *Innovations in Education and Teaching International, 41,* 39–47.

Escudero, J., Kim, Y., McGrath, M., Odabasi, P., So, E., & Vera, F. (2002). *What cues cause off-task students to get back on task?* Unpublished manuscript, New Brunswick, NJ: Rutgers University.

Espelage, D. L., & Swearer, S. M. (2004). *Bullying in American schools: A social-ecological perspective on prevention and intervention.* Mahwah, NJ: Erlbaum.

eTeachers. (2005). *The Chinese cultural revolution WebQuest.* Retrieved May 8, 2005 from http://www.eteachers.com.au/ samples/int/sec/china/studyroom/6cultrev/webcultural.htm.

Evans, E. D., & Craig, D. (1990). Teacher and student perceptions of academic cheating in middle and senior high schools. *Journal of Educational Research, 84,* 44–52.

Evans, E. D., & Tribble, M. (1986). Perceived teaching problems, self-efficacy and commitment to teaching among preservice teachers. *Journal of Educational Research, 80,* 81–85.

Evertson, C., & Harris, A. (2003). *Classroom organization and management program (COMP): Creating conditions for learning.* Nashville, TN: Vanderbilt University.

Falk, J. H., & Dierking, L. D. (2000). *Learning from museums.* Walnut Creek, CA: AltaMira Press.

Falk, J. H., & Dierking, L. D. (2002). *Learning without limits: How free-choice learning is transforming education.* Walnut Creek, CA: AltaMira Press.

Family Educational Rights and Privacy Act of 1974. Retrieved April 10, 2005 from http://www.ed.gov/policy/gen/guid/ fpco/ferpa/index.html.

Fancher, R. E. (1985). The intelligence men: Makers of the IQ controversy. New York: W. W. Norton & Company.

Fantuzzo, J. W., Davis, G. Y., & Ginsberg, M. D. (1995). Effects of parent involvement in isolation or in combination with peer tutoring on student self–concept and mathematics achievement. *Journal of Educational Psychology, 87,* 272–281.

Fantuzzo, J. W., King, J. A., & Heller, L. R. (1992). Effects of reciprocal peer tutoring on mathematics and school adjustment. *Journal of Educational Psychology, 84,* 331–339.

Feldt, L. S., & Brennan, R. L. (1989). Reliability. In R. L. Linn (Ed.), *Educational Measurement* (3rd ed.). New York: Macmillan.

Feng, H. (1996). Social skill assessment of inner city Asian, African, and European American students. *Social Psychology Review, 25,* 228–239.

Finn, J. D., & Rock, D. A. (1997). Academic success among students at risk for school failure. *Journal of Applied Psychology, 82,* 221–234.

Finn, J. D., Pannozzo, G. M., & Achilles, C. M. (2003). The "why's" of class size: Student behavior in small classes. *Review of Educational Research, 73,* 321–368.

Fischer, K. W. (1980). A theory of cognitive development: The control and construction of hierarchies of skills. *Psychological Review, 87,* 477–531.

Fischer, K. W., Kenny, S. L., & Pipp, S. L. (1990). How cognitive processes and environmental conditions organize discontinuities in the development of abstractions. In C. N. Alexander & E. J. Langer (Eds.), *Higher stages of human development: Perspectives on adult growth.* New York: Oxford University Press.

Fischer, K. W., & Rose, S. P. (1995, Fall). Concurrent cycles in the dynamic development of the brain and behavior. *SRCD Newsletter,* 3–4, 15–16.

Fish, S. (1980). *Is there a text in this class: The authority of interpretive communities.* Cambridge, MA: Harvard University Press.

Fiske, S. T. (2004). Mind the gap: In praise of informal sources of formal thinking. *Personality and Social Psychology Review, 8,* 132–137.

Fitzpatrick, H., & Hardman, M. (2000). Mediated activity in the primary classroom: Girls, boys, and computers. *Learning and Instruction, 10,* 431–446.

Flavell, J. (1976). Metacognitive aspects of problem-solving. In L. B. Resnick (Ed.), *The nature of intelligence.* Hillsdale, NJ: Lawrence Erlbaum.

Flavell, J. H., Miller, P. H., & Miller, S. A. (1993). *Cognitive development* (3rd ed.). Englewood Cliffs, NJ: Prentice Hall.

Floden, R. E., & Clark, C. M. (1988). Preparing teachers for uncertainty. *Teachers College Record, 89,* 505–524.

Flowerday, T., & Schraw, G. (2000). Teacher beliefs about instructional choice: A phenomenological study. *Journal of Educational Psychology, 92,* 634–645.

Flowerday, T., Schraw, G., & Stevens, J. (2004). The role of choice and interest in reader engagement. *Journal of Experimental Education, 72,* 93–114.

Forsyth, D. R., & Kerr, N. A. (1999). *Are adaptive illusions adaptive?* Poster presented at the annual meeting of the American Psychological Association, Boston, MA.

Fox, B. A. (1988). *Interaction as a diagnostic resource in tutoring* (Technical Report No. 88-3). Boulder, CO: University of Colorado, Institute of Cognitive Science.

Francis, W. S. (1999). Cognitive integration of language and memory in bilinguals: Semantic representation. *Psychological Bulletin, 125,* 193–222.

Fredricks, J. A., Blumenfeld, P. C., & Paris, A. H. (2004). School engagement: Potential of the concept, state of the evidence. *Review of Educational Research, 74,* 59–109.

Fuchs, D., Fuchs, L. S., Mathes, P. G., & Martinez, E. A. (2002). Preliminary evidence on the social standing of students with learning disabilities in PALS and no-PALS classrooms. *Learning Disabilities Research, 17,* 205–215.

Fuchs, D., Fuchs, L. S., Mathes, P. G., & Simmons, D. C. (1997). Peer-assisted learning strategies: Making classrooms more responsive to academic diversity. *American Educational Research Journal, 34,* 174–206.

Fuchs, L. S., & Fuchs, D. (1998). General educator's instructional adaptation for students with learning disabilities. *Learning Disabilities Quarterly, 21,* 23–33.

Fuchs, L. S., Fuchs, D., Yazdian, L., & Powell, S. R. (2002). Enhancing first-grade children's mathematical development with peer-assisted learning strategies. *School Psychology Review, 31,* 569–583.

Fulk, B. M., & King, K. (2001). Classwide peer tutoring at work. *Teaching Exceptional Children, 34(2),* 49–53.

Fuller, F. F., & Brown, O. H. (1975). Becoming a teacher. In K. Ryan (Ed.), *Teacher education.* Chicago: University of Chicago Press.

Furrer, C., & Skinner, E. A. (2003). Sense of relatedness as a factor in children's academic engagement and performance. *Journal of Educational Psychology, 95,* 148–162.

Gagné, E. D., Yekovich, C. W., & Yekovich, F. R. (1993). *The cognitive psychology of school learning* (2nd ed.). Boston: Little, Brown.

Gallagher, J. M., & Easley, J. A., Jr. (1978). *Knowledge and development: Piaget and education* (Vol. 2). New York: Plenum Press.

Gallagher, K. C. (2002). Temperament and parenting style—adjustment. *Developmental Review, 22,* 623–643.

Galton, F. (1869). *Hereditary genius.* New York: Macmillan.

Gamoran, A. (1987). Organization, instruction, and the effects of ability grouping: Comment on Slavin's best evidence synthesis. *Review of Educational Research, 57,* 341–345).

Gamoran, A., & Mare, R. D. (1989). Secondary school tracking and educational inequality: Compensation, reinforcement, or neutrality. *American Journal of Sociology, 94,* 1146–1183.

García, E. E. (1999). Attributes of effective schools for language minority students. *Education and Urban Society, 20,* 387–398.

Gardner, H. (1985). *Frames of mind.* New York: Basic Books.

Gardner, H. (1993). *Multiple intelligences: The theory in practice.* New York: Basic Books.

Gardner, H. (1995). Reflections on multiple intelligences. *Phi Delta Kappan, 77,* 200–208.

Gardner, H. (1998). Are there additional intelligences? The case for naturalist, spiritual, and existential intelligences. In J. Kane (Ed.), *Education, information, and transformation* (pp. 111–131). Upper Saddle River, NJ: Merrill-Prentice Hall.

Gardner, H. (1999). *Intelligence reframed: Multiple intelligences for the 21st century.* New York: Basic Books.

Gardner, H. (2003). *Multiple intelligences after twenty years.* Paper presented at the annual meeting of the American Educational Research Association, Chicago, IL.

Gauvain, M., & Rogoff, B. (1989). Collaborative problem solving and children's planning skills. *Developmental Psychology, 25,* 139–151.

Gay, G. (2003). The importance of multicultural education. *Educational Leadership, 61(4),* 30–35.

Gazzaniga, M. S., & Heatherton, T. F. (2003). *Psychological science.* New York: W. W. Norton.

Geelan, D. (2003). Teacher expertise and explanatory frameworks in a successful physics classroom. *Australian Science Teachers' Journal, 49(3),* 22–32.

Gelzheiser, L. M. (1990). Reducing the number of students identified as learning disabled: A question of practice, philosophy, or policy? In S. B. Sigmon (Ed.), *Critical voices in special education: Problems and progress concerning the mildly handicapped* (pp. 43–50). Albany, NY: State University of New York Press.

Gendolla, G. H. E. (1997). Surprise in the context of achievement: The role of outcome valence and importance. *Motivation and Emotion, 21,* 165–193.

Gershoff, E. T. (2002a). Corporal punishment by parents and associated child behaviors and experiences: A meta-analytical and theoretical review. *Psychological Bulletin, 128,* 539–579.

Gershoff, E. T. (2002b). Corporal punishment, physical abuse, and the burden of proof: Reply to Baumrind, Larzelere, and Cowan (2002), Holden (2002), and Parke (2002). *Psychological Bulletin, 128,* 602–611.

Gersten, R., & Vaughn, S. (2001). Meta-analyses in learning disabilities: Introduction to the special issue. *Elementary School Journal, 101,* 247–249.

Gettman, D. (1987). *Basic Montessori.* New York: St. Martin's Press.

Gibbon, F. X., Benbow, C. P., & Gerrard, M. (1994). From top dog to bottom half: Social comparison strategies in response to poor performance. *Journal of Personality and Social Psychology, 67,* 638–652.

Gibson, E. J. (1988). Exploratory behavior in the development of perceiving, acting, and the acquiring of knowledge. *Annual Review of Psychology, 39,* 1–41.

Gibson, S., & Dembo, M. H. (1984). Teacher efficacy: A construct validation. *Journal of Educational Psychology, 76,* 569–582.

Gilligan, C. (1993). *In a different voice: Psychological theory and women's development.* Cambridge, MA: Harvard University Press.

Ginsburg-Block, M., & Fantuzzo, J. W. (1997). Reciprocal peer tutoring: An analysis of "teacher" and "student" interactions as a function of training and experience. *School Psychology Quarterly, 12,* 134–149.

Ginsburg, H. J., & Opper, S. (1988). *Piaget's theory of intellectual development* (3rd ed.). Englewood Cliffs, NJ: Prentice Hall.

Glaser, R. (1963). Instructional technology and the measurement of learning outcomes. *American Psychologist, 18,* 519–522.

Glaser, R. (1968). Adapting the elementary school curriculum to individual performances. *Proceedings of the 1967 Invitational Conference on Testing Problems 3–36.* Princeton, NJ: Educational Testing Service.

Glassman, M. (1994). All things being equal: The two roads of Piaget and Vygotsky. *Developmental Review, 14,* 186–214.

Glickman, C., & Tamashiro, R. (1982). A comparison of first-year, fifth-year, and former teachers on efficacy, ego development, and problem solving. *Psychology in Schools, 19,* 558–562.

Glover, D., Gough, G., Johnson, M., & Cartwright, N. (2000). Bullying in 25 secondary schools: Incidence, impact and intervention. *Educational Research, 42,* 141–156.

Goddard, H. H. (1920). *Human efficiency and levels of intelligence.* Princeton, NJ: Princeton University Press.

Goddard, R. D., Hoy, W. K., & Woolfolk Hoy, A. (2000). Collective teacher efficacy: Its meaning, measure, and impact on student achievement. *American Educational Research Journal, 37,* 479–507.

Golan, R., Kyza, E. A., Reiser, B. J., & Edelson, D. C. (2001, March). *Structuring the task of behavioral analysis with software scaffolds.* Paper presented at the Annual Meeting of the National Association for Research on Science Teaching, St. Louis.

Goleman, D. (1995). *Emotional intelligence.* New York: Bantam Books.

Gollwitzer, P. M. (1996). The volitional benefits of planning. In P. M. Gollwitzer & J. A. Bargh (Eds.), *The psychology of action: Linking cognition and emotion to behavior* (pp. 287–312). New York: Guilford Press.

Gollwitzer, P. M. (1999). Implementation intentions: Strong effects of simple plans. *American Psychologist, 54,* 493–503.

Gollwitzer, P. M., & Moskowitz, G. B. (1996). Goal effects on action and cognition. In E. T. Higgins & A. W. Kruglanski (Eds.), *Social psychology: Handbook of Basic principles* (pp. 361–399). New York: Guilford Press.

Gondoli, D. M., & Silverberg, S. B. (1997). Maternal emotional distress and diminished responsiveness: The mediating role of parenting efficacy and parental perspective taking. *Developmental Psychology, 33,* 861–868.

Gonzalez, L. E., & Carter, K. (1996). Correspondence in cooperating teachers' and student teachers' interpretations of classroom events. *Teaching and Teacher Education, 12,* 39–47.

Good, T. L., & Brophy, J. E. (1997). *Looking into classrooms.* New York: Addison-Wesley.

Good, T. L., & Brophy, J. E. (2000). *Looking in classrooms* (8th ed.). New York: Longman.

Good, T. L., Slavings, R., Harel, K., & Emerson, H. (1987). Student passivity: A study of question-asking in K-12 classrooms. *Sociology of Education, 60,* 181–199.

Goodenow, C. (1993). The role of belongingness in adolescents' academic motivation. *Journal of Early Adolescence, 13,* 21–43.

Goodenow, C. (1993). Classroom belongingness among early adolescent students: Relationship to motivation and achievement. *Journal of Early Adolescence, 13,* 21–43.

Goodenow, C., & Grady, K. E. (1993). The relationship of school belonging and friends' values to academic motivation among urban adolescent students. *Journal of Experimental Education, 62,* 60–71.

Gopnik, A. (1984). The acquisition of *gone* and the development of the object concept. *Journal of Child Language, 11,* 273–292.

Gordon, C., & Debus, R. (2002). Developing deep learning approaches and personal teaching efficacy within a preservice teacher education context. *British Journal of Educational Psychology, 72,* 483–511.

Gottfried, A. (1985). Academic intrinsic motivation in elementary and junior high school students. *Journal of Educational Psychology, 77,* 631–645.

Gould, S. J. (1981). *The mismeasure of man.* New York: W. W. Norton.

Graesser, A. C., & Person, N. (1994). Question-asking during tutoring. *American Educational Research Journal, 31,* 104–137.

Graesser, A. C., Person, N., & Magliano, J. (1995). Collaborative dialog patterns in naturalistic one-on-one tutoring. *Applied Cognitive Psychology, 9,* 359–387.

Graham, S., Schwartz, S., & MacArthur, C. (1993). Learning disabled and normally achieving students' knowledge of writing and the composing process, attitude toward writing, and self-efficacy for students with and without learning disabilities. *Journal of Learning Disabilities, 26,* 237–249.

Gratz, D. (2000). High standards for whom? *Phi Delta Kappan, 81,* 681–687.

Gravetter, F. J., & Wallnau, L. B. (2004). *Statistics for the behavioral sciences.* Belmont, CA: Wadsworth/Thompson Learning.

Gray, J. A. (1990). Brain systems that mediate both emotion and cognition. *Cognition and Emotion, 4,* 269–288.

Gray, W. M., & Hudson, L. M. (1984). Formal operations and the imaginary audience. *Developmental Psychology, 20,* 619–627.

Green, K. E. (1991). *Educational testing: Issues and applications.* New York: Garland Publishing.

Green, S. K., & Gredler, M. E. (2002). A review and analysis of constructivism for school-based practice. *School Psychology Review, 31,* 53–70.

Green, T. (1971). *The activities of teaching.* New York: McGraw-Hill.

Greene, D., & Lepper, M. R. (1974). Effects of extrinsic rewards on children's subsequent intrinsic interest. *Child Development, 45,* 1141–1145.

Greenough, W. T., & Black, J. E. (1992). Induction of brain structure by experience: Substrates for cognitive development. In M. R. Gunnar & C. A. Nelson (Eds.), *Minnesota symposia on child psychology: Developmental neuroscience* (Vol. 24, pp. 155–200). Hillsdale, NJ: Lawrence Erlbaum.

Greenough, W. T., Black, J. E., & Wallace, C. S. (1987). Experience and brain development. *Child Development, 58,* 539–559.

Greenwood, C. R., & Terry, B. (1993). Achievement, placement, and services: Middle school benefits of classwide peer tutoring used at the elementary school. *School Psychology Review, 22,* 497–516.

Greenwood, C. R., Arreaga-Mayer, C., Utley, C. A., Gavin, K. M., & Terry, B. J. (2001). Classwide peer tutoring learning management system. *Remedial and Special Education, 22,* 34–47.

Greenwood, C. R., Carta, J. J., & Kamps, D. (1990). Teacher versus peer-mediated instruction. In H. Foot, M. Morgan, & R. Shute (Eds.), *Children helping children* (pp. 177–206). London, UK: John Wiley.

Greenwood, C. R., Delquadri, J. C., & Hall, R. V. (1989). Longitudinal effects of classwide peer tutoring. *Journal of Educational Psychology, 81,* 371–383.

Greenwood, C. R., Finney, R., Terry, B., & Arreaga-Mayer, C. (1993). Monitoring, improving, and maintaining quality implementation of the classwide peer tutoring program using behavioral and computer technology. *Education and Treatment of Children, 16,* 19–47.

Greenwood, C. R., Maheady, L., & Carta, J. J. (1991). Peer tutoring programs in the regular classroom. In G. Stoner, M. R. Shinn, & H. M. Walker (Eds.), *Intervention for achievement and behavior programs* (pp. 179–200). Washington, DC: National Association of School Psychologists.

Griffin, J. (2004). Research on students and museums: Looking more closely at the students in school groups. *Science Education, 88,* S59–S70.

Grolnick, W. S. (2003). *The psychology of parental control: How well-meant parenting backfires.* Mahwah, NJ: Lawrence Erlbaum.

Grolnick, W. S., & Ryan, R. M. (1987). Autonomy in children's learning: An experimental and individual differences investigation. *Journal of Personality and Social Psychology, 52,* 890–898.

Grolnick, W. S., Deci, E. L., & Ryan, R. M. (1997). Internalization within the family: The self-determination perspective. In J. E. Grusec & L. Kuczynski (Eds.), *Parenting and children's internalization of values: A handbook of contemporary theory* (pp. 135–161). New York: Wiley.

Grosjean, F. (1992). Another view of bilingualism. In R. Harris (Ed.), *Cognitive processing in bilinguals* (pp. 51–62). Amsterdam: Elsevier.

Grotevant, H. D. (1987). Toward a process model of identity formation. *Journal of Adolescent Research, 2,* 203–222.

Grusec, J. E. (1997). A history of research on parenting strategies and children's internalization of values. In J. E. Grusec & L. Kuczynski (Eds.), *Parenting and children's internalization of values: A handbook of contemporary theory* (pp. 3–22). New York: Wiley.

Grusec, J. E., & Goodnow, J. J. (1994). The impact of parental discipline methods on the child's internalization of values: A reconceptualization of the current points of view. *Developmental Psychology, 30,* 4–19.

Guskey, T. R. (1984). The influence of change in instructional effectiveness upon the affective characteristics of teachers. *American Educational Research Journal, 21,* 245–259.

Guskey, T. R. (1988). Teacher efficacy, self-concept, and attitudes toward the implementation of instructional innovation. *Teaching and Teacher Education, 4,* 63–69.

Guskey, T. R. (1994). Making the grade: What benefits students. *Educational Leadership, 52*(2), 24–27.

Guskey, T. R. (2000). *Developing grading and reporting systems for student learning.* Thousand Oaks, CA: Corwin Press.

Guskey, T. R. (2001). Helping students make the grade. *Educational Leadership, 59*(1), 20–27.

Guskey, T., & Gates, S. (1986). Synthesis of research on the effects of mastery learning in elementary and secondary classrooms. *Educational Leadership, 43,* 73–80.

Guskey, T., & Piggot, T. (1988). Research on group-based mastery learning programs: A meta-analysis. *Journal of Educational Research, 81,* 197–216.

Guthrie, J. T., & Wigfield, A. (2000). Engagement and motivation in reading. In M. Kamil & P. Mosenthal (Eds.), *Handbook of reading research* (Vol. 3, pp. 403–422). Mahwah, NJ: Lawrence Erlbaum.

Gutierrez, R., & Slavin, R. E. (1992). Achievement effects of the nongraded elementary school: A best evidence synthesis. *Review of Educational Research, 62,* 333–376.

Guzdial, M. (1994). Software-realized scaffolding to facilitate programming for science learning. *Interactive Learning Environments, 4,* 1–44.

Hackett, G. (1985). The role of mathematics self-efficacy in the choice of math-related majors of college women and men: A path analysis. *Journal of Counseling Psychology, 32,* 47–56.

Haft, W. L., & Slade, A. (1989). Affect attunement and maternal attachment: A pilot study. *Infant Mental Health Journal, 10,* 157–172.

Haladyna, T. M. (2002). *Essentials of standardized achievement testing: Validity and accountability.* Boston: Allyn & Bacon.

Hall, G. E., & Loucks, S. F. (1982). Bridging the gap: Policy research rooted in practice. In A. Lieberman & M. W. McLaughlin (Eds.), *Policy making in education* (81st Yearbook of the National Society for the Study of Education, Part 1, pp. 133–158). Chicago: University of Chicago Press.

Hall, R. V., Cristler, C., Cranston, S. S., & Tucker, B. (1970). Teachers and parents as researchers using multiple baseline designs. *Journal of Applied Behavior Analysis, 3,* 247–255.

Hallahan, D. P., & Kauffman, J. M. (2003). *Exceptional learners* (9th ed). Boston: Allyn & Bacon.

Hallam, S., & Ireson, J. (2003). Secondary school teachers' attitudes towards and beliefs about ability grouping. *British Journal of Educational Psychology, 73,* 343–356.

Hallenbeck, M. J. (2002). Taking charge: Adolescents with learning disabilities assume responsibility for their own writing. *Learning Disabilities Quarterly, 25,* 227–246.

Hallinan, M. T. (1990). The effects of ability grouping in secondary schools: A response to Slavin's best-evidence synthesis. *Review of Educational Research, 60,* 501–504.

Halpern, D. F. (1998). Teaching critical thinking for transfer across domains. *American Psychologist. 53,* 449–455.

Hamre, B. K., & Pianta, R. C. (2001). Early teacher-child relationships and the trajectory of children's school outcomes through eighth grade. *Child Development, 72,* 625–638.

Hanson, M. J., & Carta, J. J. (1996). Addressing the challenges of families with multiple risks. *Exceptional Children, 62,* 201–212.

Harackiewicz, J. M., & Elliot, A. J. (1993). Achievement goals and intrinsic motivation. *Journal of Personality and Social Psychology, 65,* 904–915.

Harackiewicz, J. M., Barron, K. E., Carter, S. M., Lehto, A. T., & Elliot, A. J. (1997). Predictors and consequences of achievement goals in the college classroom: Maintaining interest and making the grade. *Journal of Personality and Social Psychology, 73,* 1284–1295.

Harackiewicz, J. M., Barron, K. E., Tauer, J. M., Carter, S. M., & Elliot, A. J. (2000). Short-term and long-term consequences of achievement goals in college: Predicting continued interest and performance over time. *Journal of Educational Psychology, 92,* 316–330.

Hardre, P. L., & Reeve, J. (2003). A motivational model of rural students' intentions to persist in, versus drop out of, high school. *Journal of Educational Psychology, 95,* 347–356.

Hargreaves, A., Earl, L., & Schmidt, M. (2002). Perspectives on alternative assessment reform. *Educational Researcher, 39*(1), 69–95.

Hart & Fegley, (1995). *Child Development, 66,* 1346–1359.

Harter, S. (1974). Pleasure derived by children from cognitive challenge and mastery. *Child Development, 45,* 661–669.

Harter, S. (1978). Pleasure derived from optimal challenge and the effects of extrinsic rewards on children's difficulty level choices. *Child Development, 49,* 788–799.

Harter, S. (1981). A model of mastery motivation in children: Individual differences and developmental changes. In W. A. Collin (Ed.), *Aspects of the development of competence* (Vol. 14, pp. 215–255). Hillsdale, NJ: Lawrence Erlbaum.

Harter, S. (1983). Developmental perspectives on the self-system. In E. M. Hetherington (Ed.) & P. H. Mussen (Series Ed.), *Handbook of child psychology: Socialization, personality, and social development* (Vol. 4, pp. 275–386). New York: Wiley.

Harter, S. (1990). Causes, correlates and the functional role of global self-worth: A life-span perspective. In R. J. Sternberg & J. Kolligian, Jr. (Eds.), *Competence considered* (pp. 67–97). New Haven, CT: Yale University Press.

Harter, S. (1992). The relationship between perceived competence, affect, and motivational orientation within the classroom: Processes and patterns of change. In A. K. Boggiano & T. S. Pittman (Eds.), *Achievement and motivation: A social-developmental perspective* (pp. 77–114). New York: Cambridge University Press.

Harter, S. (1993). Causes and consequences of low self-esteem in children and adolescents. In R. F. Baumeister (Ed.), *Self-esteem: The puzzle of low self-regard* (pp. 87–116). New York: Plenum Press.

Hartigan, J. A., & Wigdor, A. K. (1989). *Fairness in employment testing: Validity generalization, minority issues, and the General Aptitude Test Battery.* Washington, DC: National Academy Press.

Hartup, W. W. (1983). Peer relations. In P. H. Mussen (Series Ed.) & E. M. Hetherington (Vol. Ed.), *Handbook of child psychology: Volume 4: Socialization, personality, and social development* (pp. 103–196). New York: Wiley.

Hattie, J. A. (1992). *Self-concept.* Hillsdale, NJ: Lawrence Erlbaum.

Hawkins, B. (2001). Supporting second language children's content learning and language development in K-5. In M. Celce-Murcia (Ed.). *Teaching English as a second or foreign language* (pp. 367–383). Boston: Heinle & Heinle.

Hawkins, J., Pea, R., Glick, J., & Scribner, S. (1994). "Merds that don't like mushrooms": Evidence for deductive reasoning by preschoolers. *Developmental Psychology, 20,* 584–594.

Hazan, C., & Shaver, P. (1987). Romantic love conceptualized as an attachment process. *Journal of Personality and Social Psychology, 52,* 511–524.

Hecker, L., Burns, L., Elkind, J., Elkind, K., & Katz, L. (2002). Benefits of assistive reading software for students with attention disorders. *Annals of Dyslexia, 52,* 244–272.

Heckhausen, H. (1967). *The anatomy of achievement motivation.* New York: Academic Press.

Heller, L. R., & Fantuzzo, J. W. (1993). Reciprocal peer tutoring and parent partnership: Does parent involvement make a difference? *School Psychology Review, 22,* 517–534.

Helmke, A., & van Aken, M. A. G. (1995). The causal ordering of academic achievement and self-concept of ability during elementary school: A longitudinal study. *Journal of Educational Psychology, 87,* 624–637.

Hemple, C. G., & Oppenheim, P. (1948). Studies in the logic of explanation. *Philosophy of Science 15,* 135–175.

Henderlong, J., & Lepper, M. R. (2002). Effects of praise on children's intrinsic motivation: A review and synthesis. *Psychological Bulletin, 128,* 774–795.

Henderson, R. W., & Cunningham, L. (1994). Creating interactive sociocultural environments for self-regulated learning. In D. H. Schunk & B. J. Zimmerman (Eds.), *Self-regulation of learning and performance: Issues and educational applications* (pp. 255–281). Hillsdale, NJ: Lawrence Erlbaum.

Herrnstein, R. J., & Murray, C. (1994). *The bell curve: Intelligence and class life in American life.* New York: The Free Press.

Hersh, R., & Walker, H. M. (1983). Great expectations: Making schools effective for all students. *Policy Studies Review, 2,* 147–188.

Heward, W. L., & Orlansky, M. D. (1992). *Exceptional children* (4th ed.). Columbus, OH: Charles E. Merrill.

Hickey, D. T. (1997). Motivation and contemporary socio-constructivistic instructional perspectives. *Educational Psychologist, 32,* 175–193.

Hidi, S. (1990). Interest and its contribution as a mental resource for learning. *Review of Educational Research, 60,* 549–571.

Hidi, S., & Baird, W. (1986). Interestingness—A neglected variable in discourse processing. *Cognitive Science, 10,* 179–194.

Hiebert, E. (1987). The context of instruction and student learning: An examination of Slavin's assumptions. *Review of Educational Research, 57,* 337–340.

Higgins, N., & Hess, L. (1999). Using electronic books to promote vocabulary development. *Journal of Research on Computing in Education, 31,* 425–430.

Hightower, A. D., Work, W. C., Cowen, E. L., Lotyczewski, B. S., Spinnell, A. P., Guare, J. C., & Rohrbeck, C. A. (1986). The Teacher-Child Rating Scale: A brief objective measure of elementary children's school problem behaviors and competencies. *School Psychology Review, 15,* 393–409.

Hill, K. T. (1980). Motivation, evaluation, and educational testing policy. In L. J. Fyans (Ed.), *Achievement motivation: Recent trends in theory and research* (pp. 34–95). New York: Academic Press.

Hill, K. T. (1984). Debilitating motivation and testing: A major educational problem, possible solutions, and policy applications. In R. Ames & C. Ames (Eds.), *Research on motivation in education: Student motivation* (Vol. 1). New York: Academic Press.

Hill, K. T., & Sarason, S. (1966). The relation of test anxiety and defensiveness to test and school performance over the elementary-school years: A further longitudinal study. *Monographs of the society for research in child development, 104,* 31 (Whole No. 2).

Hill, K. T., & Wigfield, A. (1984). Test anxiety: A major educational problem and what can be done about it. *The Elementary School Journal, 85,* 105–126.

Hirt, M., & Genshaft, J. L. (1981). Immunization and reversibility of cognitive deficits due to learned helplessness. *Personality and Individual Differences, 2,* 191–196.

Hitchcock, A. (1959, July 13). Interview by H. Brean. *Life,* 72.

Hmelo-Silver, C. E. (2002). Collaborative ways of knowing: Issues in facilitation. In G. Stahl (Ed.), *Proceedings of CSCL 200* (pp. 199–208). Mahwah, NJ: Lawrence Erlbaum.

Hmelo-Silver, C. E. (2004). Problem-based learning: What and how do students learn? *Educational Psychology Review, 16,* 235–266.

Hofferth, S., & Sandberg, J. (1997). Children's time. *Child development supplement—Panel study of income dynamics.* Ann Arbor, MI: Institute for Social Research, University of Michigan.

Hoffman, M. L. (1975). Moral internalization, parental power and the nature of parent-child interaction. *Developmetal Psychology, 11,* 228–239.

Hogan, D. M., & Tudge, J. R. H. (1999). Implications of Vygotsky's theory of peer learning. In A. M. O'Donnell & A. King (Eds.), *Cognitive perspectives on peer learning* (pp. 39–65). Mahwah, NJ: Lawrence Erlbaum.

Hogan, T., Rabinowitz, M., & Craven, J. A. (2003). Problem representation in teaching: Inferences from research of expert and novice teachers. *Educational Psychologist, 38,* 235–247.

Holahan, C. K., & Holahan, C. J. (1987). Self-efficacy, social support, and depression in aging: A longitudinal analysis. *Journal of Gerontology, 42,* 65–68.

Holden, C. (1993). Giving girls a chance: Patterns of talk in cooperative group work. *Gender and Education, 5,* 179–189.

Holder, H., & Fitzpatrick, H. (1991). Interpretation of emotion from facial expressions in children with and without learning disabilities. *Journal of Learning Disabilities, 24,* 170–177.

Hollon, R. E., Roth, K. J., & Anderson, C. W. (1991). Science teachers' conceptions of teaching and learning. In J. Brophy (Ed.), *Advances in research on teaching, 2,* (pp. 145–185). Greenwich, CT: JAI Press.

Holt-Reynolds, D. (1992). Personal history-based beliefs as relevant prior knowledge in coursework: Can we practice what we teach? *American Educational Research Journal, 29,* 325–349.

Hom, H. L., Jr. (1994). Can you predict the overjustification effect? *Teaching of Psychology, 21,* 36–37.

Housner, L. D., & Griffey, D. (1985). Teacher cognition: Differences in planning and interactive decision making between experienced and inexperienced teachers. *Research Quarterly for Exercise & Sport, 56,* 44–53.

Howe, M. J. A., Davidson, J. W., & Slobada, J. A. (1998). Innate talents: Reality or myth? *Behavioral and Brain Sciences, 21,* 399–442.

Howes, C. (1999). Attachment relationships in the context of multiple caregivers. In J. Cassidy & P. R. Shaver (Eds.), *Handbook of attachment: Theory, research, and clinical applications* (pp. 671–687). New York: Guildford Press.

Hoy, W. K., & Woolfolk, A. E. (1993). Teachers' sense of efficacy and the organizational health of schools. *Elementary School Journal, 93,* 355–372.

Hubbard, J. A., & Cole, J. D. (1994). Emotional correlates of social competence in children's peer relationships. *Merrill-Palmer Quarterly, 40,* 1–20.

Huesemann, L. R., Moise-Titus, J., Podolski, C. L., & Eron, L. D. (2003). Longitudinal relations between children's exposure to TV violence and their aggressive and violent behavior in young adulthood: 1977–1992. *Developmental Psychology, 39,* 201–221.

Huggins, P. (1995). *The ASSIST program—Affective/social skills: Instructional strategies and techniques.* Seattle: Washington State Innovative Education Program.

Hulshof, H., & Verloop, N. (2002). The use of analogies in language teaching: Representing the content of teachers' practical knowledge. *Journal of Curriculum Studies, 34,* 77–90.

Huston, A. C., Donnerstein, E., Fairchild, J., Feshbach, N. D., Katz, P. A., Murray, J. P., et al. (1992). *Big world, small screen: The role of television in American society.* Lincoln: University of Nebraska Press.

Huttenlocher, P. R. (1994). Synaptogenesis, synapse elimination, and neural plasticity in human cerebral cortex. In C. A. Nelson (Ed.), *Minnesota symposia on child psychology: Threats to optimal development: Integrating biological, psychological, and social risk factors* (Vol. 27, pp. 35–54). Hillsdale, NJ: Lawrence Erlbaum.

Hymel, S., Bowker, A., & Woody, E. (1993). Aggressive versus withdrawn unpopular children: Variations in peer and self-perceptions in multiple domains. *Child Development, 64,* 879–896.

Impara, J. C., & Plake, B. S. (Eds.) (1995). Standard setting for complex performance tasks (Special Issue). *Applied Measurement in Education, 8*(1).

Individuals with Disabilities Education Act Amendments of 1997. Retrieved April 10, 2005 from http://www.ed.gov/policy/speced/leg/idea/idea.pdf.

Individuals with Disabilities Education Improvement Act of 2004. Retrieved April 10, 2005 from http://thomas.loc.gov/cgi-bin/query/z?c108:h.r.1350.enr.

Inhelder, B., & Piaget, J. (1958). *The growth of logical thinking from childhood to adolescence.* New York: Basic Books.

Inzlicht, M., & Ben-Zeev, T. (2003). Do high-achieving female students underperform in private? The implications of threatening environments on intellectual processing. *Journal of Educational Psychology, 95,* 796–805.

Irvine, J. J. (1990). *Black students and school failure: Policies, practices, and prescriptions.* New York: Greenwillow Books.

Isen, A. M. (1987). Positive affect, cognitive processes, and social behavior. In L. Berkowitz (Ed.), *Advances in experimental social psychology* (Vol. 20, pp. 203–253). New York: Academic Press.

Isen, A. M., & Geva, N. (1987). The influence of positive affect on acceptable level of risk: The person with a large canoe has a large worry. *Organizational Behavior and Human Decision Processes, 39,* 145–154.

Isen, A. M., & Levin, P. F. (1972). Effects of feeling good on helping: Cookies and kindness. *Journal of Personality and Social Psychology, 21,* 384–388.

Isen, A. M., Daubman, K. A., & Nowicki, G. P. (1987). Positive affect facilitates creative problem-solving. *Journal of Personality and Social Psychology, 51,* 1122–1131.

Isen, A. M., Johnson, M. M. S., Mertz, E., & Robinson, G. F. (1985). The influence of positive affect on the unusualness of word associations. *Journal of Personality and Social Psychology, 48*, 1413–1426.

Jackson, P. W. (1968). *Life in classrooms.* New York City: Holt, Rinehart, & Winston.

James, W. (1890). *Principles of psychology.* New York: Holt.

James, W. (1912). *Talks to teachers on psychology: And to students on some of life's ideals.* New York: Holt.

Jang, H. (2003). *Providing a rationale as a motivational model to engage students in an uninteresting lesson: A test of multiple models.* Unpublished dissertation, University of Iowa, Iowa City, IA.

Jeanpierre, B. J. (2004). Two urban elementary science classrooms: The interplay between student interactions and classroom management practices. *Education, 124*, 664–675.

Jenkins, J. R., & O'Connor, R. E. (2003). Cooperative learning for students with learning disabilities: Evidence from experiments, observations, and interviews. In H. L. Swanson, K. R. Harris, & S. Graham (Eds.), *Handbook of learning disabilities* (pp. 417–430). New York: Guilford.

Jenlink, P. M., Kinnucan-Welsch, K., & Odell, S. J. (1996). New directions for professional development: Designing professional development learning communities. In D. J. McIntyre, & D. M. Byrd, (Eds.), *Preparing tomorrow's teachers: The field experience. Teacher education yearbook IV,* (pp. 63–86). Thousand Oaks, CA: Corwin Press.

Johnson, D. W., & Johnson, R. T. (1979). Conflict in the classroom: Controversy and learning. *Review of Educational Research, 49*, 51–69.

Johnson, D. W., & Johnson, R. T. (1987). *Learning together and alone: Cooperative, competitive, and individualistic learning* (2nd ed.). Englewood Cliffs, NJ: Prentice Hall.

Johnson, D. W., & Johnson, R. T. (1989). *Cooperation and competition: Theory and research.* Edina, MN: Interaction Book.

Johnson, D. W., & Johnson, R. T. (1989/90). Social skills for successful groupwork. *Educational Leadership, 47*(4), 29–33.

Johnson, D. W., & Johnson, R. T. (1991). *Learning together and alone: Cooperative, competitive, and individualistic learning.* Englewood Cliffs, NJ: Prentice Hall.

Johnson, D. W., & Johnson, R. T. (1995). *Creative controversy: Intellectual challenge in the classroom.* Edina, MN: Interaction Book.

Johnson, D. W., Johnson, R. T., & Holublec, E. (1993). *Circles of learning: Cooperation in the classroom* (5th ed). Edina, MN: Interaction Book.

Johnson, J. S., & Newport, E. L. (1989). Critical period effects in second language learning: The influence of maturational state on the acquisition of English as a second language. *Cognitive Psychology, 21*, 60–99.

Johnson, T., & Boyden, J. E., & Pittz, W. (2001). *Racial profiling and punishment in U.S. public schools: How zero tolerance policies and high stakes testing subvert academic excellence and racial equity.* Oakland, CA: Applied Research Center.

Jonassen, D. H., Peck, K. C., & Wilson, B. G. (1999). *Learning with technology: A constructivist perspective.* Upper Saddle River, NJ: Merrill/Prentice Hall.

Jonassen, D. H., Tessmer, M., & Hannum, W. H. (1999). *Task analysis methods for instructional design.* Mahwah, NJ: Lawrence Erlbaum.

Jones, B.F., Pierce, J., & Hunter, B. (1989). Teaching students to construct graphic representations. *Teaching Exceptional Children, 46*(4), 20–25.

Jones, E. E., & Berglas, S. (1978). Control of attributions about the self through self-handicapping strategies: The appeal of alcohol and the role of underachievement. *Personality and Social Psychology Bulletin, 4*, 200–206.

Jones, S. L., Nation, J. R., & Massad, P. (1977). Immunization against learned helplessness in man. *Journal of Abnormal Psychology, 86*, 75–83.

Joseph, A. (1977). *Intelligence, IQ, and race—When, how and why they became associated.* San Francisco: R & E Research Associates.

Joussemet, M., Koestner, R, Lekes, N., & Houlfort, N. (2004). Introducing uninteresting tasks to children: A comparison of the effects of rewards and autonomy support. *Journal of Personality, 72*, 139–166.

Joyner-Kersee, J. (1997). *A kind of grace: The autobiography of the world's greatest female athlete.* New York: Warner Books.

Juel, C. (1996). What makes literacy tutoring effective? *Reading Research Quarterly, 31*(3), 268–289.

Jurdak, M., & Shahin, I. (1999). An ethnographic study of the computational strategies of a group of young street vendors in Beirut. *Educational Studies in Mathematics, 40*, 155–172.

Kagan, D. M. (1992). Implications of research on teacher belief. *Educational Psychologist, 27*, 65–90.

Kagan, J. (1972). Motives and development. *Journal of Personality and Social Psychology, 22*, 51–66.

Kagan, S. (1989/1990). The structural approach to cooperative learning. *Educational Leadership, 47*(4), 12–15.

Kagan, S. (1993). *Cooperative learning.* San Juan Capistrano, CA: Kagan Cooperative Learning.

Kahneman, D. (1973). *Attention and effort.* Englewood Cliffs, NJ: Prentice Hall.

Kamps, D., Kravits, T., Stolze, J., & Swaggart, B. (1999). Prevention strategies for at-risk students and students with EBD in urban elementary schools. *Journal of Emotional & Behavioral Disorders, 7*(3), 178–188.

Kandel, E. R., Schwartz, J. H., & Jessell, T. M. (1991). *Principles of neural science.* (3rd ed.). New York: Elsevier.

Kasser, T., & Ryan, R. M. (1993). A dark side of the American dream: Correlates of financial success as a central life aspiration. *Journal of Personality and Social Psychology, 65*, 410–422.

Kasser, T., & Ryan, R. M. (1996). Further examining the American dream: Differential correlates of intrinsic and extrinsic goals. *Personality and Social Psychology Bulletin, 22*, 80–87.

Kaufman, A. S., & Kaufman, N. L. (2005). *KABC-II: Kaufman Assessment Battery for Children* (2nd ed.). Circle Pines, MN: AGS Publishing.

Kaufman, P., Chen, X., Choy, S., Chandler, K., Chapman, C., Rand, M., & Ringel, C. (1999). Indicators of school crime and safety, 1998. *Educational Statistics Quarterly, 1*(1), 42–45.

Kazdin, A. E. (1979). Imagery elaboration and self-efficacy in the covert modeling treatment of unassertive behavior. *Journal of Consulting and Clinical Psychology, 47*, 725–733.

Keller, J. M. (1983). Motivational design of instruction. In C. M. Reigeluth (Ed.), *Instructional design theories and models* (pp. 383–434). Hillsdale, NJ: Lawrence Erlbaum.

Kemmis, S., & McTaggart, R. (1988). *The action research planner* (2nd ed.). Geelong, Victoria, Australia: Deakin University Press.

Keogh, B. K., & MacMillan, D. L. (1996). Exceptionality. In D. Berliner & R. C. Calfee (Eds.), *Handbook of educational psychology* (pp. 311–330). New York: Macmillan.

King, A. (1989). Effects of self-questioning training on college students' comprehension of lectures. *Contemporary Educational Psychology, 14*, 366–381.

King, A. (1991). Effects of training in strategic questioning on children's problem-solving performance. *Journal of Educational Psychology, 83*, 307–317.

King, A. (1994). Guiding knowledge construction in the classroom: Effects of teaching children how to question and how to explain. *American Educational Research Journal, 31*, 111–126.

King, A. (1999). Discourse patterns mediating peer learning. In A. M. O'Donnell & A. King (Eds.), *Cognitive perspectives on peer learning* (pp. 87–115). Mahwah, NJ: Lawrence Erlbaum.

King, A., Staffieri, A., & Adelgais, A. (1998). Mutual peer tutoring: Effects of structured tutorial interaction to scaffold peer learning. *Journal of Educational Psychology, 90*, 134–152.

Kintsch, E. & Kintsch, W. (1995). Strategies to promote active learning from text: Individual differences in background knowledge. *Swiss Journal of Psychology, 54*, 141–151.

Kintsch, W. (1980). Learning from text, levels of comprehension, or: Why anyone would read a story anyway? *Poetics, 9*, 87–98.

Klahrl, D., & Nigam, M. (2004). The equivalence of learning paths in early science instruction. *Psychological Science, 15*, 661–667.

Klassen, R. (2002). A question of calibration: A review of the self-efficacy beliefs of students with learning disabilities. *Learning Disability Quarterly, 25*, 88–102.

Klein, D. C., & Seligman, M. E. P. (1976). Reversal of performance deficits in learned helplessness and depression. *Journal of Abnormal Psychology, 85*, 11–26.

Klein, G. A., & Hoffman, R. R. (1993). Seeing the invisible: Perceptual-cognitive aspects of expertise. In M. Rabinowitz (Ed.), *Cognitive science foundations of instruction* (pp. 203–226). Hillsdale, NJ: Lawrence Erlbaum.

Klein, H. J., Whitener, E. M., & Ilgen, D. R. (1990). The role of goal specificity in the goal-setting process. *Motivation and Emotion, 14*, 179–193.

Kochanska, G, Gross, J. N., Lin, M.-H., & Nichols, K. E. (2002). Guilt in young children: Development, determinants, and relations with a broader system of standards. *Child Development, 73*, 461–482.

Kochanska, G. (2002). Mutually responsive orientation between mothers and their young children: A context for the early development of conscience. *Current Directions in Psychological Science, 11*, 191–195.

Kochanska, G., & Aksan, N. (2004). Conscience in childhood: Past, present, and future. *Merrill-Palmer Quarterly, 50*, 299–310.

Kochanska, G., Aksan, N., & Koenig, A. L. (1995). A longitudinal study of the roots of preschoolers' conscience: Committed compliance and emerging internalization. *Child Development, 66*, 1752–1769.

Kochanska, G., Aksan, N., & Nichols, K. E. (2003). Maternal power assertion in discipline and moral discourse contexts: Commonalities, differences, and implications for children's moral conduct and cognition. *Developmental Psychology, 39*, 949–963.

Kochanska, G., Coy, K. C., & Murray, K. T. (2001). The development of self-regulation in the first four years of life. *Child Development, 72*, 1091–1111.

Kochanska, G., Friesenborg, A. E., Lange, L. A., & Martel, M. M. (2004). Parent's personality and infant's temperament as contributors to their emerging relationship. *Journal of Personality and Social Psychology, 86*, 744–759.

Kochanska, G., & Murray, K. T. (2000). Mother-child mutually responsive orientation and conscience development: From toddler to early school age. *Child Development, 71*, 417–431.

Kochanska, G., Padavich, D. L., & Koenig, A. L. (1996). Children's narratives about hypothetical moral dilemmas and objective measures of their conscience: Mutual relations and socialization antecedents. *Child Development, 67*, 1420–1436.

Kochanska, G., & Thompson, R. A. (1997). The emergence and development of conscience in toddlerhood and early childhood. In J. E. Grusec & L. Kuczynski (Eds.), *Parenting and children's internalization of values: A handbook of contemporary theory* (pp. 53–77). New York: Wiley.

Koedinger, K. R., & Anderson, J. R. (1993). Reifying implicit planning in geometry: Guidelines for model-based intelligent tutoring system design. In S. J. Lajoie & S. J. Derry (Eds.), *Computers as cognitive tools* (pp. 15–45). Mahwah, NJ: Lawrence Erlbaum.

Koenigs, S. S., Fiedler, M. L., & deCharms, R. (1977). Teacher beliefs, classroom interaction, and personal causation. *Journal of Applied Social Psychology, 7*, 95–114.

Kohlberg, L. (1975). The cognitive-developmental approach to moral education. *Phi Delta Kappan*, 670–677.

Kohlberg, L. (1981). *Essays on moral development: Vol. 1. The philosophy of moral development*. San Francisco: Harper & Row.

Kohlberg, L. (1984). *Essays on moral development: Vol. 2. The psychology of moral development*. San Francisco: Harper & Row.

Kohlberg, L., & Candee, D. (1984). The relationship of moral judgment to moral action. In W. Kurtines & J. Gewirtz (Eds.), *Morality, moral behavior and moral development* (pp. 52–73). New York: Wiley.

Kohn, A. (1993). *Punished by rewards: The trouble with gold stars, incentive plans, A's, praise, and other bribes*. Boston: Houghton Mifflin.

Kolis, M., & Dunlap, W. P. (2004). The knowledge of teaching: The K3P3 model. *Reading Improvement, 41*, 97–107.

Kolodner, J. L, Hmelo, C. E., & Narayanan, N. H. (1996). Problem-based learning meets case-based reasoning. In D. C. Edelson & E. A. Domeshek (Eds.), *Proceedings of ICLS 96* (pp. 188–195). Charlottesville, VA: AACE.

Kosslyn, S. M. (1976). Can imagery be distinguished from other forms of internal representation? Evidence from studies of information retrieval times. *Memory and Cognition, 4*, 291–297.

Kosslyn, S. M. (1980). *Image and mind.* Cambridge, MA: Harvard University Press.

Kosslyn, S. M. (1983). *Ghosts in the mind's machine.* New York: W. W. Norton.

Kosslyn, S. M., Ball, T. M., & Reiser, B. J. (1978). Visual images preserve metric spatial information: Evidence from studies of image scanning. *Journal of Experimental Psychology: Human Perception and Performance, 4*, 1–20.

Kovaleski, J. E., Gickling, E. E., Morrow, H., & Swank, P. R. (1999). High versus low implementations of instructional support teams: A case for maintaining program fidelity. *Remedial and Special Education, 20*, 170–183.

Kowaz, A. M., & Marcia, J. E. (1991). Development and validation of a measure of Eriksonian industry. *Journal of Personality and Social Psychology, 60*, 390–397.

Krashen, S. D. (1996). *Under attack: The case against bilingual education.* Culver City, CA: Language Education Associates.

Kriete, R. (1999). *The morning meet book.* Greenfield, MA: Northeast Foundation for Children.

Krueger, N., Jr., & Dickson, P. R. (1994). How believing in ourselves increases risk taking: Perceived self-efficacy and opportunity recognition. *Decision Sciences, 25*, 385–400.

Kruger, A. C., & Tomasello, M. (1986). Transactive discussions with peers and adults. *Developmental Psychology, 22*, 681–685.

Kuhn, D., Kohlberg, L., Langer, J., & Haan, N. (1977). The development of formal operations in logical and moral judgment. *Genetic Psychology Monographs, 95*, 97–188.

Kuhn, D., & Phelps, E. (1982). The development of problem-solving strategies. In H. Reese (Ed.), *Advances in child development and behavior* (Vol. 17, pp. 1–44). New York: Academic Press.

Kulik, C., Kulik, J., & Bangert-Downs, R. (1990). Effectiveness of mastery learning programs: A meta-analysis. *Review of Educational Research, 60*, 265–306.

Kulik, J. A. (1992). An analysis of the research on ability grouping: Historical and contemporary perspectives. *Communicator: The Journal of the California Association for the Gifted, 22*(5), 29–34.

Kurland, D. M., & Pea, R. D. (1985). Children's mental models for recursive Logo programs. *Journal of Educational Computing Research, 2*, 235–244.

Labbo, L. D. (2000). 12 things you can do with a talking book in a classroom computer center. *The Reading Teacher, 53*, 542–546.

Lackney, J. A., & Jacobs, P. J. (2004). *Teachers as placemakers: Investigating teachers' use of the physical learning environment in instructional design.* University of Wisconsin School Design Research Studio. Retrieved March 10, 2005 from http://schoolstudio.engr.wisc.edu/placemakers.html. Madison, WI.

LaConte, R. T. (1981). *Homework as a learning experience. What research says to the teacher.* Washington, DC: National Education Association.

Lane, K. L., Givner, C. C., & Pierson, M. R. (2004a). Teacher expectations of student behavior: Social skills necessary for success in elementary school classrooms. *Journal of Special Education, 38*, 104–110.

Lane, K. L., Givner, C. C., & Pierson, M. R. (2004b). Secondary teachers' views of social competence: Skills essential for success. *Journal of Special Education, 38*, 174–186.

Lanza, E. (1992). Can bilingual 2-year-olds code-switch? *Journal of Child Language, 19*, 633–658.

LaPorte, R. E., & Nath, R. (1976). Role of performance goals in prose learning. *Journal of Educational Psychology, 68*, 260–264.

Latham, G. P., & Baldes, J. J. (1975). The practical significance of Locke's theory of goal setting. *Journal of Applied Psychology, 60*, 122–124.

Latham, G. P., & Locke, E. A. (1975). Increasing productivity with decreasing time limits: A field replication of Parkinson's law. *Journal of Applied Psychology, 60*, 524–526.

Latham, G. P., & Saari, L. M. (1979). Importance of supportive relationships in goal setting. *Journal of Applied Psychology, 64*, 151–156.

Latham, G. P., Erez, M., & Locke, E. A. (1988). Resolving scientific disputes by the joint design of crucial experiments by the antagonists: Application to the Erez-Latham dispute regarding participation in goal setting. *Journal of Applied Psychology, 73*, 753–772.

Lave, J., & Wenger, E. (1991). *Situated learning: Legitimate peripheral participation.* New York: Cambridge University Press.

Lay, K. L., Waters, E., & Park, K. A. (1989). Maternal responsiveness and child compliance: The role of mood as mediator. *Child Development, 60*, 1405–1411.

Lazarowitz, R., & Karsenty, G. (1990). Cooperative learning and students' academic achievement, process skills, learning environment, and self-esteem in a 10th grade biology classroom. In S. Sharan (Ed.), *Cooperative learning: Theory and research* (pp. 123–149). New York: Praeger.

Lazarus, R. S., & Folkman, S. (1984). *Stress, appraisal, and coping.* New York: Springer-Verlag.

Leagerspetz, K. M. J., Bjorkquist, K., & Peltonen, T. (1988). Is indirect aggression typical of females? Gender differences in aggressiveness in 11- to 12-year-old children. *Aggressive Behavior, 14*, 403–414.

Lebeau, R. B. (1998). Cognitive tools in a clinical encounter in medicine: Supporting empathy and expertise in distributed systems. *Educational Psychological Review, 10*, 3–34.

Lebeau, R. B., Gyamfi, P., Wizevich, K., & Koster, E. (2001). Supporting and documenting free-choice in informal science learning environments. In J. Falk (Ed.), *Free-choice science education: How we learn outside of school.* New York: Teachers College Press.

Lederman, N. G. (2001). A partial list of the empirical theoretical literature on subject-specific pedagogy. *School Science & Mathematics, 101*(2), 61–80.

Lee, W. O. (1996). The cultural context for Chinese learners: Conceptions of learning in the Confucian tradition. In D. A. Watkins & J. B. Biggs (Eds.), *The Chinese learner* (pp. 45–67). Hong Kong, China: Comparative Education Research Centre and the Australian Council for Education Research Ltd.

Lehmann, A. C. (1998). Historical increases in expert performance suggest large possibilities for improvement of performance without implicating innate capacities. *Behavioral and Brain Sciences, 21*, 419–420.

Leinhardt, G. (1983, April). *Routines in expert math teachers' thoughts and actions.* Paper presented at the annual meeting of the American Educational Research Association, Montreal, Canada.

Leinhardt, G. (1993). Instructional explanations in history and mathematics. In W. Kintxch (Ed.), *Proceedings of the Fifteenth Annual Conference of the Cognitive Science Society* (pp. 5–16). Hillsdale, NJ: Lawrence Erlbaum.

Leinhardt, G., & Greeno, J. G. (1986). The cognitive skill of teaching. *Journal of Educational Psychology, 78*, 75–95.

Leinhardt, G., Crowley, K., & Knutson, K (2002). (Eds.), *Learning conversations in museums.* Mahwah, NJ: Lawrence Erlbaum.

Leinhardt, G., Putnam, R. J., Stein, M. K., & Baxter, J. (1991). Where subject knowledge matters. In J. Brophy (Ed.), *Advances in research on teaching, vol. 2* (pp. 145–185). Greenwich, CT: JAI Press.

Leinhardt, G., Weidman, C., & Hammond, K. M. (1987). Introduction and integration of classroom routines by expert teachers. *Curriculum Inquiry, 17*(2), 135–175.

Leinhardt, M. F., Zigmond, N., & Cooley, W. W. (1981). Reading instruction and its effects. *American Educational Research Journal, 18*, 343–361.

Leong, C. K. (1995). Effects of online reading and simultaneous DECtalk aiding in helping below average and poor readers comprehend and summarize text. *Learning Disabilities Quarterly, 19*, 101–116.

Lepper, M. R. (1983). Social-control processes and the internalization of social values: An attributional perspective. In E. T. Higgins, D. N. Ruble, & W. W. Hartup (Eds.), *Social cognition and social development.* New York: Cambridge University Press.

Lepper, M. R., & Greene, D. (Eds.) (1978). *The hidden costs of reward.* Hillsdale, NJ: Lawrence Erlbaum.

Lepper, M. R., Greene, D., & Nisbett, R. E. (1973). Undermining children's intrinsic interest with extrinsic rewards: A test of the "overjustification" hypothesis. *Journal of Personality and Social Psychology, 28*, 129–137.

Lever-Duffy, J., McDonald, J. B., & Mizell, A. P. (2005). *Teaching and Learning with Technology* (2nd ed.). Boston: Allyn & Bacon.

Levin, J., & Nolan, J. F. (2004). *Principles of classroom management: A professional decision-making model* (4th ed.). Boston: Pearson.

Levine, M. (2002). *A mind at a time* (pp. 85, 86). New York: Simon & Schuster.

Levinson, D. J. (1986). A conception of adult development. *American Psychologist, 41*, 3–13.

Lewis, C. C. (2002). *Lesson study: A handbook of teacher-led instructional change.* Philadelphia: Research for Better Schools.

Lewis, M. (1987). Social development in infancy and early childhood. In J. D. Osofsky (Ed.), *Handbook of infant development* (2nd ed.). New York: Wiley.

Li, J. (2001). Chinese conceptualization of learning. *Ethos, 29*, 111–137.

Li, J. (2003). U.S. and Chinese cultural beliefs about learning. *Journal of Educational Psychology, 95*, 258–267.

Lindren, D. M., Meier, S. E., & Brigham, T. A. (1991). The effects of minimal and maximal peer tutoring systems on the academic performance of college students. *Psychological Record, 41*, 69–77.

Linebarger, D. L., Kosanic, A. Z., Greenwood, C. R., & Doku, N. S. (2004). Effects of viewing the television program *Between the Lions* on the emergent literacy skills of young children. *Journal of Educational Psychology, 96*, 297–308.

Linenfelser, T. Grand Island's pictures from the past (Vol. 3). Retrieved March 25, 2005 from http://www.isledegrande.com/picpage03.html.

Linn, M. C. (1986). Science. In R. Dillon & R. Sternberg (Eds.), *Cognition and instruction* (pp. 155–197). Orlando, FL: Academic Press.

Linn, M. C., diSessa, A., Pea, R., & Songer, N. (1994). Can research on science learning and instruction inform standards for science education? *Journal of Science Education and Technology, 3*, 7–15.

Linn, M. C., & Slotta, J. D., (2005). Enabling participants in online forums to learn from one another. In A. M. O'Donnell, C. Hmelo-Silver, & G. Erkens (Eds.), *Collaborative learning, reasoning, and technology* (pp. 61–97). Mahwah, NJ: Lawrence Erlbaum.

Linn, R. (1982). Ability testing: Individual differences, prediction, and differential prediction. In A. Wigdor & W. Garner (Eds.), *Ability testing: Uses, consequences, and controversies* (Part II; pp. 335–388). Washington, DC: National Academy Press.

Linn, R. L., & Gronlund, N. E. (1995). *Measurement and assessment in teaching* (7th ed.). Englewood Cliffs, NJ: Prentice Hall.

Linnenbrink, E. A., & Pintrich, P. R. (2003). The role of self-efficacy beliefs in student engagement and learning in the classroom. *Reading and Writing Quarterly: Overcoming Learning Difficulties. 19*, 119–137.

Lipscomb, L., Swanson, J., & West, A. *Scaffolding.* Retrieved July 13, 2005, from http://www.coe.uga.edu/epltt/scaffolding.htm.

Livingston, C., & Borko, H. (1989a). Expert-novice difference in teaching: A cognitive analysis and implications for teacher education. *Journal of Teacher Education, 40*(4), 36–42.

Livingston, C., & Borko, H. (1989b). Cognition and improvisation: Differences in mathematics instruction by expert and novice teachers. *American Educational Research Journal, 26,* 473–498.

Locher, P., Smith, L. F., & Smith, J. K. (2001). Original paintings versus slide and computer reproductions: A comparison of view responses. *Empirical Studies in Arts, 17,* 121–129.

Lochman, J. E., Burch, P. R., Curry, J. F., & Lampron, L. B. (1984). Treatment and generalization effects of cognitive-behavioral and goal-setting interventions with aggressive boys. *Journal of Consulting and Clinical Psychology, 52,* 915–916.

Lockard, J., & Abrams, P. D. (2004). *Computers for the twenty-first century educators* (6th ed.). Boston: Allyn & Bacon.

Locke, E. A. (1996). Motivation through conscious goal setting. *Applied and Preventive Psychology, 5,* 117–124.

Locke, E. A. (2002). Setting goals for life and happiness. In C. R. Synder & S. J. Lopez (Eds.), *Handbook of positive psychology* (pp. 299–312). New York: Oxford University Press.

Locke, E. A., & Bryan, J. F. (1996). Motivation through conscious goal setting. *Applied and Preventive Psychology, 5,* 117–124.

Locke, E. A., & Latham, G. P. (1984). *Goal-setting: A motivational technique that works!* Englewood Cliffs, NJ: Prentice Hall.

Locke, E. A., & Latham, G. P. (1990). *A theory of goal setting and task performance.* Englewood Cliffs, NJ: Prentice Hall.

Locke, E. A., & Latham, G. P. (2002). Building a practically useful theory of goal setting and task motivation. *American Psychologist, 57,* 705–717.

Locke, E. A., Chah, D. O., Harrison, S., & Lustgarten, N. (1989). Separating the effects of goal specificity from goal level. *Organizational Behavior and Human Decision Processes, 43,* 270–287.

Locke, E. A., Shaw, K. N., Saari, L. M., & Latham, G. P. (1981). Goal setting and task performance: 1969–1980. *Psychological Bulletin, 90,* 125–152.

Loeber, R., & Hay, D. F. (1994). Developmental approaches to aggression and conduct problems. In M. Rutter & D. F. Hoy (Eds.), *Development through life: A handbook for clinicians* (pp. 488–516). Malden, MA: Blackwell Scientific.

Loevinger, J. (1976). Stages of ego development. In J. Loevinger (Ed.), *Ego development* (pp. 13–28). San Francisco: Jossey-Bass.

Loewenstein, G. (1994). The psychology of curiosity: A review and reinterpretation. *Psychological Bulletin, 116,* 75–98.

Loftus, G. R., & Loftus, E. F. (1983). *Mind at play: The psychology of video games.* New York: Basic Books.

Lorhmann, S., & Talerica, J. (2004). Anchor the boat: A class-wide intervention to reduce problem behavior. *Journal of Positive Behavior Interventions, 6,* 113–120.

Lotan, R. A. (2003). Group-worthy tasks. *Educational Leadership, 60*(6), 72–75.

Lourenco, O., & Machado, A. (1996). In defense of Piaget's theory: A reply to 10 common criticisms. *Psychological Review, 103,* 143–164.

Loveless, T. (2003). How well are American students learning? With special sections on homework, charter schools, and rural school achievement. *The 2003 Brown Center Report on American Education, 1*(4). Washington, DC: The Brookings Institution.

Lowry, N., & Johnson, D. W. (1981). Effects of controversy on epistemic curiosity, achievement, and attitudes. *Journal of Social Psychology, 115,* 31–43.

Luk, S. (1985). Direct observation studies of hyperactive behavior. *Journal of the American Academy of Child Psychiatry, 24,* 338–344.

Mabry, L. (1999). Portfolios plus: *A critical guide to alternative assessment.* Thousand Oaks, CA: Corwin Press.

Maccoby, E. E. (1992). The role of parents in the socialization of children: An historical overview. *Developmental Psychology, 28,* 1006–1017.

Mackey, B., Johnson, R., & Wood, T. (1995). Cognitive and affective outcomes in a multiage language arts program. *Journal of Research in Childhood Education, 10,* 49–61.

Madden, N. A., Slavin, R. E., & Stevens, R. J. (1986). *Cooperative integrated reading and comparison: Teacher's manual.* Baltimore, MD: Johns Hopkins University, Center for Research on Elementary and Middle Schools.

Maddux, C. D., Johnson, D. L., & Willis, J. W. (1997). *Educational computing: Learning with tomorrow's technologies.* (2nd ed.). Boston: Allyn & Bacon.

Mahoney, J. L., Cairns, B. D., & Farmer, T. W. (2003). Promoting interpersonal competence and educational success through extracurricular activity participation. *Journal of Educational Psychology, 95,* 409–418.

Main, M., Kaplan, N., & Cassidy, J. (1985). Security in infancy, childhood, and adulthood: A move to the level of representation. In I. Bretherton & E. Waters (Eds.), Growing points of attachment theory and research. *Monographs of the Society for Research in Child Development, 50* (1–2, Serial No. 209), 66–104.

Malone, T. W. (1981). Toward a theory of intrinsically motivating instruction. *Cognitive Science, 4,* 333–369.

Marchant, G. J. (1992). A teacher is like a . . . : Using simile lists to explore personal metaphors. *Language and Education, 6,* 33–45.

Marcia, J. E. (1966). Development and validation of ego identity status. *Journal of Personality and Social Psychology, 3,* 551–558.

Marcia, J. E. (1994). The empirical study of ego identity. In H. A. Bosma, T. L. G. Graffsma, H. D. Grotevant, & D. J. de Levita (Eds.), *Identity and development: An interdisciplinary approach* (pp. 67–80). Thousand Oaks, CA: Sage.

Marder, C. (1992). Education after secondary school. In M. Wagner, R. D'Amico, C. Marder, L. Newman, & J. Blackorby (Eds.), *What happens next? Trends in postschool outcomes of youth with disabilities.* The second comprehensive report from the National Longitudinal Transition Study of Special Education Students (pp. 3-1–3-19). Menlo Park, CA: SRI International.

Markus, H., Cross, S., & Wurf, E. (1990). The role of self-esteem in competence. In R. J. Sternberg & J. Kolligian (Eds.), *Competence considered* (pp. 205–225). New Haven, CT: Yale University Press.

Marks, H. M. (2000). Student engagement in instructional activity: Patterns in the elementary, middle, and high school years. *American Educational Research Journal, 37,* 153–184.

Markus, H. R., & Ruvolo, A. P. (1989). Possible selves: Personalized representations of goals. In L. A. Pervin (Ed.), *Goal concepts in personality and social psychology* (pp. 211–241). Hillsdale, NJ: Lawrence Erlbaum.

Markus, H., & Nurius, P. (1986). Possible selves. *American Psychologist, 41,* 954–969.

Markus, H., & Wurf, E. (1987). The dynamic self-concept: A social psychological perspective. *Annual Review of Psychology, 38,* 299–337.

Marsh, H. W. (1990). The structure of academic self-concept: The Marsh/Shavelson model. *Journal of Educational Psychology, 82,* 623–636.

Marsh, H. W., & Ayotte, V. (2003). Do multidimensional dimensions of self-concept become more differentiated with age? The differential distinctiveness hypothesis. *Journal of Educational Psychology, 95,* 687–706.

Marsh, H. W., & Craven, R. G. (1997). Academic self-concept: Beyond the dustbowl. In G. Phye (Ed.), *Handbook of classroom assessment: Learning, achievement and adjustment.* Orlando, FL: Academic Press.

Marsh, H. W., & O'Neill, R. (1984). Self description questionnaire. III: The construct validity of multidimensional self-concept ratings by late adolescents. *Journal of Educational Measurement, 21,* 153–174.

Marsh, H. W., & Richards, G. (1988). The Outward Bound Bridging Course for low achieving high-school males: Effects on academic achievement and multidimensional self-concepts. *Australian Journal of Psychology, 40,* 281–298.

Marsh, H. W., & Shavelson, R. J. (1985). Self-concept: Its multifaceted, hierarchical structure. *Educational Psychologist, 20,* 107–125.

Marsh, H. W., & Yeung, A. S. (1997a). The causal effects of academic self-concept on academic achievement: Structural equation models of longitudinal data. *Journal of Educational Psychology, 89,* 41–54.

Marsh, H. W., & Yeung, A. S. (1997b). Coursework selection: The effects of academic self-concept and achievement. *American Educational Research Journal, 34,* 691–720.

Marsh, H. W., Byrne, B. M., & Shavelson, R. J. (1988). A multifaceted academic self-concept: Its hierarchical structure and its relation to academic achievement. *Journal of Educational Psychology, 80,* 366–380.

Marsh, H. W., Byrne, B. M., & Yeung, A. S. (1999). Causal ordering of academic self-concept and achievement: Reanalysis of a pioneering study and revised recommendations. *Educational Psychologist, 34,* 155–167.

Marsh, H. W., Smith, I., & Barnes, J. (1983). Multitrait-multimethod analyses of the self-description questionnaire: Student-teacher agreement on multidimensional ratings of student self-concept. *American Educational Research Journal, 26,* 333–357.

Marshall, H. H. (1990). Metaphor as an instructional tool in encouraging student teacher reflection. *Theory into Practice, 29,* 128–132.

Martinez-Pons, M. (2002). Parental influences on children's academic self-regulatory development. *Theory into Action, 41,* 126–131.

Mastergeorge, A. M., & Miyoshi, J. N. (1999). *Accommodations for students with disabilities: A teacher's guide.* CSE Technical Report 508. Los Angeles: CRESST/University of California.

Mastropieri, M. A., Scruggs, & Scruggs, T. E. (1998). Enhancing school success with mnemonic strategies. *Intervention in School & Clinic, 33,* 201-208.

Mathes, P. G., & Fuchs, L. S. (1993). Peer mediated reading instruction in special education resource rooms. *Learning Disabilities Research and Practice, 8,* 233–243.

Mathes, P. G., Torgeson, J. K., Clancy-Menchetti, J., Santi, K., Nicholas, K., Robinson, C., & Grek, M. (2003). A comparison of teacher-directed versus peer-assisted instruction to struggling first-grade readers. *Elementary School Journal, 103,* 459–479.

Matsui, T., Okada, A., & Inoshita, O. (1983). Mechanism of feedback affecting task performance. *Organizational Behavior and Human Performance, 31,* 114–122.

Matthew, K. I. (1997). A comparison of the influence of interactive CD-ROM storybooks and traditional print storybooks on reading comprehension. *Journal of Research on Computing in Education, 29,* 263–275.

Mayer, R. (2001). *Multimedia learning* (p. 184). New York: Cambridge University Press.

Mayer, R. E. (1988). *Teaching and learning computer programming.* Hillsdale, NJ: Lawrence Erlbaum.

Mayer, R. E. (2003). *Learning and instruction.* Upper Saddle River, NJ: Merrill Prentice Hall.

Mayer, R. E. (2004). Should there be a three-strikes rule against pure discovery learning? The case for guided methods of instruction. *American Psychologist, 59,* 14–19.

McAdams, D. P., Diamond, A., du St. Aubin, E., & Mansfeld, E. (1997). Stories of commitment: The psychosocial construction of generative lives. *Journal of Personality and Social Psychology, 72,* 721–731.

McAdams, D. P., & du St. Aubin, E. (1992). A theory of generativity and its assessment through self-report, behavioral acts, and narrative themes in autobiography. *Journal of Personality and Social Psychology, 62,* 1003–1015.

McArthur, D., Stasz, C., & Zmuidzinas, M. (1990). Tutoring techniques in algebra. *Cognition and Instruction, 7*(3), 197–244.

McCabe, M. (2004, January). Teachers: Special ed. students should meet own standards. *Education Week, 23,* 20–21.

McCagg, E. C., & Dansereau, D. F. (1991). A convergent paradigm for examining knowledge mapping as a learning strategy. *Journal of Educational Research, 84,* 317–324.

McCarthy, J., & Benally, J. (2003). Classroom management in a Navajo middle school. *Theory into Practice, 42,* 296–304.

McClearn, G. E. (1991). A trans-time visit with Francis Galton. In G. A. Kimble, M. Werheimer, & C. L. White (Eds.), *Portraits of pioneers in psychology* (pp. 1–11). Hillsdale, NJ: Lawrence Erlbaum Associates.

McCord, J. (1995). *Coercion and punishment in long-term perspectives.* New York: Cambridge University Press.

McCrea, S. M., & Hirt, E. R. (2001). The role of ability judgments in self-handicapping. *Personality and Social Psychology Bulletin, 27*, 1378–1389.

McCutcheon, G. (1980). How do elementary teachers plan? The nature of planning and influences on it. *Elementary School Journal, 81*, 4–23.

McCutcheon, G., & Milner, H. R. (2002). A contemporary study of teacher planning in a high school English class. *Teachers and Teaching: Theory and Practice, 8*(1), 81–94.

McGinnis, E., & Goldstein, A. (1997). Skillstreaming the elementary school child: A guide for teaching prosocial skills (rev. ed). Champaign, IL: Research Press.

McKenna, M. C., Reinking, D., Labbo, L. D., & Watkins, J. H. (1996). *Using electronic storybooks with beginning readers* [Instructional Resource]. Athens, GA, and College Park, MD: National Reading Research Center.

McLaughlin, B. (1987). *Theories of second-language learning.* London: Arnold.

McMaster, K. N., & Fuchs, D. (2002). Effects of cooperative learning on the academic achievement of students with learning disabilities: An update on Tateyama-Sniezek's review. *Learning Disabilities: Research and Practice, 17*, 107–117.

Meece, J., Blumenfeld, P., & Hoyle, R. (1988). Students' goal orientations and cognitive engagement in classroom activities. *Journal of Educational Psychology, 80*, 514–523.

Meeker, B. (1981). Expectation states and interpersonal behavior. In M. Rosenberg & R. H. Turner (Eds.), *Social psychology: Sociological perspectives* (pp. 290–319). New York: Basic Books.

Mehan, H. (1979). *Social organization in the classroom.* Cambridge, MA: Harvard University Press.

Meier, K., Stewart, J., & England, R. (1989). *Race, class, and education: The politics of second generation discrimination.* Madison, WI: University of Wisconsin Press.

Meilman, P. W. (1979). Cross-sectional age changes in ego identity status during adolescence. *Developmental Psychology, 15*, 230–231.

Mento, A. J., Steel, R. P., & Karren, R. J. (1987). A meta-analytic study of the effects of goal setting on task performance: 1966–1984. *Organizational Behavior and Human Decision Processes, 39*, 52–83.

Mercer, C. D., & Mercer, A. R. (2001). *Teaching students with learning problems* (6th ed.). Upper Saddle River, NJ: Merrill/Prentice Hall.

Messick, S. (1989). Validity. In R. L. Linn (Ed.), *Educational Measurement* (3rd ed.). New York: Macmillan.

Meyer, J. (2004). Novice and expert teachers' conceptions of learners' prior knowledge. *Science Education, 88*, 970–983.

Meyer, W. (1992). Paradoxical effects of praise and criticism on perceived ability. In W. Stroebe & M. Hewstone (Eds.), *European review of social psychology* (Vol. 3, pp. 259–283). Oxford, UK: John Wiley.

Michaels, C. A., Prezant, F. P., Morabito, S. M., & Jackson, K. (2002). Assistive and instructional technology for college students with disabilities: A national snapshot of postsecondary service providers. *Journal of Special Education Technology ejournal, 17.* Retrieved November 11, 2005 from http://jset.unlv.edu/17.1/michaels/first.html.

Middleton, M. J., & Midgley, C. (1997). Avoiding the demonstration of lack of ability: An underexplained aspect of goal theory. *Journal of Educational Psychology, 89*, 710–718.

Midgley, C., Anderman, E., & Hicks, L. (1995). Differences between elementary and middle school teachers and students: A goal theory approach. *Journal of Early Adolescence, 15*, 90–115.

Midgley, C., Feldlaufer, H., & Eccles, J. (1989). Change in teacher efficacy and student self- and task-related beliefs in mathematics during the transition to junior high school. *Journal of Educational Psychology, 81*, 247–258.

Mielke, K. (1994). *Sesame Street* and children in poverty. *Media Studies Journal, 8*, 125–134.

Mikulincer, M. (1994). *Human learned helplessness: A coping perspective.* New York: Plenum Press.

Mikulincer, M. (1995). Attachment style and the mental representation of the self. *Journal of Personality and Social Psychology, 69*, 1203–1215.

Mikulincer, M. (1998). Attachment working models and the sense of trust: An exploration of interaction goals and affect regulation. *Journal of Personality and Social Psychology, 74*, 1209–1224.

Miller, G. A. (1956). The magical number seven, plus or minus two: Some limits on our capacity for processing information. *Psychological Review. 6*, 81–97.

Miller, I. W., & Norman, W. H. (1981). Effects of attributions for success on the alleviation of learned helplessness and depression. *Journal of Abnormal Psychology, 90*, 113–124.

Miller, P. J., Fung, H., & Mintz, J. (1996). Self-construction through narrative practices: A Chinese and American comparison of early socialization. *Ethos, 24*, 237–280.

Minicucci, C. (1996). Learning science and English: How school reform advances scientific learning for limited English proficient middle school students. *National Center for Research on Cultural Diversity and Second Language Learning, Educational Practice Report: 17.*

Mirenowicz, J., & Schultz, W. (1994). Importance of unpredictability for reward responses in primate dopamine neurons. *Journal of Neurophysiology, 72*, 1024–1027.

Miserandino, M. (1996). Children who do well in school: Individual differences in perceived competence and autonomy in above-average children. *Journal of Educational Psychology, 88*, 203–214.

Molnar, A., Smith, P., & Zahorik, J. (2000). *1999–2000 evaluation results of the Study Achievement Guarantee in Education (SAGE) program.* Milwaukee: University of Wisconsin, School of Education.

Monsaas, J. A. (1985). Learning to be a world class tennis player. In B. S. Bloom (Ed.), *Developing talent in young people* (pp. 211–269). New York: Ballantine Books.

Montague, P. R., Dayan, P., & Sejnowski, T. J. (1996). A framework for mesencephalic dopamine systems based on predictive Hebbian learning. *Journal of Neuroscience, 16*, 1936–1947.

Montali, J., & Lewandowski, L. (1996). Bimodal reading: Benefits of a talking computer for average and less skilled readers. *Journal of Learning Disabilities, 29*, 271–279.

Montemayor, R., & Eisen, M. (1977). The development of self-conceptions from childhood to adolescence. *Developmental Psychology, 13,* 314–319.

Moore, M., & Smith, L. (1996). Interactive computer software: The effects on young children's reading achievement. *Reading Psychology, 17,* 43–64.

Moore, W., & Esselman, M. (1992, April). *Teacher efficacy, power, school climate and achievement: A desegregating district's experience.* Paper presented at the annual meeting of the American Educational Research Association, San Francisco, CA.

Morine-Dersheimer, G. (1979). *Teacher plan and classroom reality.* The South Bay Study, Part 4, Research series number 60. East Lansing, MI: Institute for Research on Learning, Michigan State University.

Morrow, L. M., & Weinstein, C. S. (1982). Increasing children's literature use through program and physical design changes. *Elementary School Journal, 83*(2), 131–137.

Moses, R. P. (1994). Remarks on the struggle for citizenship and math/science literacy. *Journal of Mathematical Behavior, 13,* 107–111.

Moshman, D. (1982). Exogenous, endogenous, and dialectical constructivism. *Developmental Review, 2,* 371–384.

Muehlenhard, C. L., & Kimes, L. A. (1999). The social construction of violence: The case of sexual and domestic violence. *Personality and Social Psychology Review, 3,* 234–245.

Multimodal Treatment Study of Children with ADHD. (1999). A 14-month randomized clinical trial of treatment strategies for attention-deficit hyperactivity disorder (ADHD). *Archives of General Psychiatry, 56,* 1073–1086.

Murphy, K. R., & Davidshofer, C. O. (1994). *Psychological testing: Principles and applications,* (3rd ed.). Englewood Cliffs, NJ: Prentice Hall.

Murphy, P. K., & Edwards, M. (2005, April). *What the studies tell us: A meta-analysis of discussion approaches.* Paper presented at the Annual Meeting of the American Educational Research Association, Montreal.

Murray, C., & Greenberg, M. T. (2001). Relationships with teachers and bonds with school: Social emotional adjustment correlates for children with and without disabilities. *Psychology in the Schools, 38,* 25–41.

Murray, J. P. (2001). TV violence and brainmapping in children. *Psychiatric Times, 18*(10). Retrieved December 9, 2004 from http://www.psychiatrictimes.com/p011070.html.

Museum Financial Information. (2003). Washington DC: American Association of Museums.

National Association of Psychologists. (2002). Position statement on ability grouping. Retrieved October 21, 2004 from http://www.nasponline.org./information/pospaper_ag.html.

National Association of School Psychologists (2002). *Position statement on corporal punishment in schools.* Retrieved October 10, 2004 from http://www.nasponline.org/information/pospaper_corpunish.html.

National Commission on Teaching and America's Future (2003). *No dream denied: A pledge to America's children.* Retrieved February 10, 2005 from http//www.nctaf.org/dream/dream.html.

National Council on Education Standards and Testing. (1992). *Raising standards for American education: A report to Congress, the Secretary of Education, the National Education Goals Panel, and the American people.* Washington, DC: Author.

National Institute of Mental Health. (2004). Attention deficit/hyperactivity disorder. Retrieved October 24, 2004 from http://www.nimh.nih.gov/publicat/adhd.cfm.

Neal, L. I., McCray, A. D., Webb-Johnson, G., & Bridgest, S. T. (2003). The effects of African American movement styles on teachers' perceptions and reactions. *The Journal of Special Education, 37,* 49–57.

Neale, D. C., Smith, D., & Johnson, V. G. (1990). Implementing conceptual change teaching in primary science. *Elementary School Journal, 91,* 109–131.

Nedelsky, L. (1954). Absolute grading standards for objective tests. *Educational and Psychological Measurement, 14,* 3–19.

Neill, M. (2003). The dangers of testing. *Educational Leadership, 60,* 43–46.

Neimark, E. D. (1979). Current status of formal operations research. *Human Development, 22,* 60–67.

Nelson, C. A., & Bloom, F. E. (1997). Child development and neuroscience. *Child Development, 68,* 970–987.

Newby, T. J. (1991). Classroom motivation: Strategies of first-year teachers. *Journal of Educational Psychology, 83,* 195–200.

Newell, G. (1994). The effects of written between-draft responses on students' writing and reasoning about literature. *Written Communication, 11,* 311–347.

Newman, F. M., (1981). Reducing student alienation in high schools: Implications of theory. *Harvard Educational Review, 51,* 546–564.

Newmann, F. (1992). *Student engagement and achievement in American secondary schools.* New York: Teachers College Press.

Newmann, F., Wehlage, G. G., & Lamborn, S. D. (1992). The significance and sources of student engagement. In F. Newmann (Ed.), *Student engagement and achievement in American secondary schools* (pp. 11–39). New York: Teachers College Press.

Newton, D. P., & Newton, L. D. (2001). Subject content knowledge and teacher talk in the primary science classroom. *European Journal of Teacher Education, 24,* 369–379.

Nicholls, J. G. (1978). The development of the concepts of effort and ability, perceptions of academic achievement, and the understanding that difficult tasks require more ability. *Child Development, 49,* 800–814.

Nicholls, J. G. (1979). Development of perception of own attainment and causal attributions for success and failure in reading. *Journal of Educational Psychology, 71,* 94–99.

Nicholls, J. G. (1984). Achievement motivation: Conceptions of ability, subjective experience, task choice, and performance. *Psychological Review, 91,* 328–346.

Noddings, N. (1984). *Caring: A feminine approach to ethics and moral education.* Berkeley, CA: University of California Press.

Noguchi, J. (1998). "Easifying" ESP texts for EFL science majors. *Proceedings of The Japan Conference on English for Specific Purposes.* Aizuwakamatsu City, Fukushima, Japan. (ERIC Document Reproduction Service No. ED 424 776).

Noguera, P. A. (2003). Schools, prisons, and social implications of punishment: Rethinking disciplinary practices. *Theory into Practice, 42,* 341–350.

Nolan, S. A., Flynn, C., & Garber, J. (2003). Prospective relations between rejection and depression in young adolescents. *Journal of Personality and Social Psychology, 85,* 745–755.

Nolen, S. B. (1988). Reasons for studying: Motivational orientations and study strategies. *Cognition and Instruction, 5,* 269–287.

Norris, J. A. (2003). Looking at classroom management through a social and emotional learning lens. *Theory into Practice, 42,* 313–318.

Nunally, J. C. (1967). *Psychometric theory.* New York: McGraw-Hill.

Nunes, T. (1999). Mathematics learning as the socialization of the mind. *Mind, Culture, and Activity, 6,* 33–52.

O'Donnell, A. M., & Dansereau, D. F. (1992). Scripted cooperation in student dyads: A method for analyzing and enhancing academic learning and performance. In R. Hertz-Lazarowitz & N. Miller (Eds.), *Interaction in cooperative groups: The theoretical anatomy of group learning* (pp. 120–141). New York: Cambridge University Press.

O'Donnell, A. M., & King, A. (1999). *Cognitive perspectives on peer learning.* Mahwah, NJ: Lawrence Erlbaum.

O'Donnell, A. M., Dansereau, D. F., Hall, R. H., & Rocklin, T. R. (1987). Cognitive, social/affective, and metacognitive outcomes of scripted cooperative learning. *Journal of Educational Psychology, 79,* 431–437.

O'Donnell, A. M., Dansereau, D. F., Hythecker, V. I., Larson, C. O., Skaggs, L., & Young, M. D. (1987). The effects of monitoring on cooperative learning. *Journal of Experimental Education, 54,* 169–173.

O'Donnell, A., & O'Kelly, J. (1994). Learning from peers: Beyond the rhetoric of positive results. *Educational Psychology Review, 6*(4), 321–349.

O'Donnell, A., Hmelo-Silver, C, & Erkens, G. (2005). *Collaborative, learning reasoning, and technology.* Mahwah, NJ: Lawrence Erlbaum.

O'Leary, K. D., Kaufman, K. F., Kass, R. E., & Drabman, R. S. (1970). The effects of loud and soft reprimands on the behavior of disruptive students. *Exceptional Children, 37,* 145–155.

O'Melia, M. C., & Rosenberg, M. S. (1994). Effects of cooperative homework teams on the acquisition of mathematics skills by secondary students with mild disabilities. *Exceptional Children, 60,* 538–548.

O'Reilly, T., Symons, S., & MacLatchy-Gaudet, H. (1998). A comparison of self-explanation and elaborative interrogation. *Contemporary Educational Psychology, 23,* 434–445.

Oakes, J. (1990). *Multiplying inequalities: The effects of race, social class, and tracking on opportunities to learn mathematics and science* (No. ED 329615). Santa Monica, CA: Rand Corporation.

Oakhill, J. V. (1982). Constructive processes in skilled and less skilled comprehender's memory for sentences. *British Journal of Psychology, 73,* 13–20.

Oakhill, J. V. (1984). Inferential and memory skills in children's comprehension of stories. *British Journal of Educational Psychology, 54,* 31–39.

Oakhill, J. V., Yuill, N., & Parkin, A. (1986). On the nature of the differences between skilled and less skilled comprehenders. *Journal of Research in Reading, 9,* 80–91.

Oberg, A., & McCutcheon, G. (1987). Teachers' experience doing action research. *Peabody Journal of Education, 64,* 116–127.

Ohio Department of Education (2003). *Academic content standards, K-12 science: Benchmarks and indicators by grade level.* Retrieved June 2, 2005 from http://www.ode.state.oh.us/academic_content_standards/ScienceContentStd/RTF/g_Science_by_Grade_Level.rtf.

Olweus, D. (1980). Familial and temperamental determinants of aggressive behavior in adolescent boys: A causal analysis. *Developmental Psychology, 16,* 644–660.

Olweus, D. (1993). *Bullying at school: What we know and what we can do.* Oxford, UK: Blackwell.

Olweus, D. (1997). Bully/victim problems in school: Facts and intervention. *European Journal of Psychology of Education, 12,* 495–510.

Orbach, I., & Hades, Z. (1982). The elimination of learned helplessness deficits as function of induced self-esteem. *Journal of Research in Personality, 16,* 511–523.

Orbell, S., & Sheeran, P. (2000). Motivation and volitional processes in action initiation: A field study of the role of implementation intentions. *Journal of Applied Social Psychology, 30,* 780–797.

Orlick, T. D., & Mosher, R. (1978). Extrinsic rewards and participant motivation in a sport-related task. *International Journal of Sport Psychology, 9,* 27–39.

Osguthorpe, R., & Scruggs, T. E. (1986). Special education students as tutors: A review and analysis. *Remedial and Special Education, 7*(4), 15–26.

Osterman, K. F. (2000). Students' need for belonging in the school community. *Review of Educational Research, 70,* 323–367.

Overskeid, G., & Svartdal, F. (1996). Effects of reward on subjective autonomy and interest when initial interest is low. *Psychological Record, 46,* 319–331.

Oyserman, D., & Markus, H. (1990). Possible selves and delinquency. *Journal of Personality and Social Psychology, 59,* 112–115.

Oyserman, D., Terry, K., & Bybee, D. (2002). A possible selves intervention to enhance school involvement. *Journal of Adolescence, 25,* 313–326.

Ozer, E. M., & Bandura, A. (1990). Mechanisms governing empowerment effects: A self-efficacy analysis. *Journal of Personality and Social Psychology, 58,* 472–486.

Padrón, Y. N., & Waxman, H. C. (1996). Improving the teaching and learning of English language learners through instructional technology. *International Journal of Instructional Media, 23,* 341–354.

Paivio, A. (1986). *Mental representation: A dual coding approach.* New York: Oxford University Press.

Pajares, F. (1996). Self-efficacy beliefs in academic settings. *Review of Educational Research, 66,* 543–578.

Palincsar, A. S., & Brown, A. L. (1984). Reciprocal teaching of comprehension-fostering and comprehension-monitoring activities. *Cognition and Instruction, 1,* 117–175.

Palinscar, A. S., & Klenk, L. J. (1991). Dialogues promoting reading comprehension. In B. Means, C. Chelemer, & M. S. Knapp (Eds.), *Teaching advanced skills to at-risk students* (pp. 112–140). San Francisco: HarperCollins.

Palinscar, A. S., & Klenk, L. J. (1992). Fostering literacy in supportive contexts. *Journal of Learning Disabilities, 25,* 211–225.

Pallak, S. R., Costomiris, S., Sroka, S., & Pittman, T. S. (1982). School experience, reward characteristics, and intrinsic motivation. *Child Development, 53,* 1382–1391.

Park, L. E., Crocker, J., & Mickelson, K. D. (2004). Attachment styles and contingencies of self-worth. *Personality and Social Psychology Bulletin, 30,* 1243–1254.

Parke, R. D., & Slaby, R. G. (1983). The development of aggression. In P. Mussen (Series Ed.) & E. M. Hetherington (Ed.), *Handbook of child psychology: Socialization, personality, and social development* (Vol. 4, pp. 547–641). New York: Wiley.

Patterson, G. R., Debaryshe, B. D., & Ramsey, E. (1989). A developmental perspective on antisocial behavior. *American Psychologist, 44,* 329–335.

Paulsen, M. B. (2001). The relation between research and the scholarship of teaching. *New Directions for Teaching and Learning, 86,* 19–29.

Pea, R. (2004). The social and technological dimensions of scaffolding and related theoretical concepts for learning, education, and human activity. *Journal of the Learning Sciences, 13,* 423–451.

Pearl, R. (1992). Psychosocial characteristics of learning disabled students. In N. Singh & I. Beale (Eds.), *Current perspectives in learning disabilities: Nature, theory, and treatment* (pp. 96–117). New York: Springer-Verlag.

Pedretti, E. G. (2004). Perspective on learning through research on critical issues-based science center exhibitions. *Science Education, 88,* 33–45.

Pelletier, L. G., Seguin-Levesque, C., & Legault, L. (2002). Pressure from above and pressure from below as determinants of teachers' motivation and teaching behavior. *Journal of Educational Psychology, 94,* 186–196.

Penner, S. G. (1987). Parental responses to grammatical and ungrammatical utterances. *Child Development, 58,* 376–384.

Perry, N. (1998). Young children's self-regulated learning and contexts that support it. *Journal of Educational Psychology, 90,* 715–729.

Perry, N. E., Nordby, C. J., & VandeKamp, K. O. (2003). Promoting self-regulated reading and writing at home and school. *Elementary School Journal, 103,* 317–338.

Perry, N. E., VandeKamp, K. O., Mercer, L. K., & Nordby, C. J. (2002). Investigating teacher-student interactions that foster self-regulated learning. *Educational Psychologist, 37,* 5–15.

Person, N. K., & Graesser, A. C. (1999). Evolution of discourse during cross-age tutoring. In A. M. O'Donnell & A. King (Eds.), *Cognitive perspectives on peer learning* (pp. 69–86). Mahwah, NJ: Lawrence Erlbaum.

Person, N. K., Kreuz, R. J., Zwaan, R., & Graesser, A. C. (1995). Pragmatics and pedagogy: Conversational rules and politeness strategies may inhibit effective tutoring. *Cognition and Instruction, 13,* 161–188.

Petersen, R. P., Johnson, D. W., & Johnson, R. T. (1991). Effects of cooperative learning on perceived status of male and female pupils. *The Journal of Social Psychology, 113,* 717–735.

Peterson, C., & Barrett, L. C. (1987). Explanatory style and academic performance among university freshmen. *Journal of Personality and Social Psychology, 53,* 603–607.

Peterson, C., & Seligman, M. E. P. (1984). Causal explanations as a risk factor for depression: Theory and evidence. *Psychological Review, 91,* 347–374.

Peterson, C., Maier, S. F., & Seligman, M. E. P. (1993). *Learned helplessness: A theory for the age of personal control.* New York: Oxford University Press.

Pettit, G. S., Dodge, K. A., & Brown, M. M. (1988). Early family experience, social problem solving patterns, and children's social competence. *Child Development, 59,* 107–120.

Phelps, R. P. (1998). The demand for standardized testing. *Educational Measurement: Issues and Practice, 17,* 5–23.

Piaget, J. (1951). *Play, dreams, and imitation in childhood.* New York: Norton.

Piaget, J. (1954). *The construction of reality in the child.* New York: Basic Books.

Piaget, J. (1963). *Origins of intelligence in children.* New York: Norton.

Piaget, J. (1969). *Psychology of intelligence.* New York: Littlefield, Adams.

Piaget, J. (1970). *Genetic epistemology.* New York: W. W. Norton.

Piaget, J. (1971). *Science of education and the psychology of the child.* New York: Viking Press.

Piaget, J. (1973). *To understand is to invent: The future of education.* New York: Viking Press.

Pianta, R. C., & Steinberg, M. (1992). Teacher-child relationships and the process of adjusting to school. In R. C. Pianta (Ed.), *New directions for child development: Vol. 57. Beyond the parent: The role of other adults in children's lives* (pp. 61–80). San Francisco: Jossey-Bass.

Pintrich, P. R., & Blazevski, J. L. (2004). Applications of a model of goal orientation and self-regulated learning to individuals with learning problems. In L. M. Glidden (Ed.), *International Review of Research in Mental Retardation* (pp. 31–83). San Diego: Elsevier Academic Press.

Pintrich, P. R., & De Groot, E. (1990). Motivation and self-regulated learning components of academic performance. *Journal of Educational Psychology, 82,* 33–40.

Pittman, T. S., Boggiano, A. K., & Ruble, D. N. (1983). Intrinsic and extrinsic motivational orientations: Limiting conditions on the undermining and enhancing effects of reward on intrinsic motivation. In J. Levine & M. Wang (Eds.), *Teacher and student perceptions: Implications for learning* (pp. 319–340). Hillsdale, NJ: Lawrence Erlbaum.

Plake, B. S., & Hambleton, R. K. (2000). A standard setting method designed for complex performance assessments: Categorical assignments of student work. *Educational Assessment, 6*(3), 197–215.

Plake, B. S., Impara, J. C., & Spies, R. A. (2003). *The fifteenth mental measurements yearbook.* Lincoln, NE: The University of Nebraska Press.

Polansky, S. B. (1986). *900 shows a year: A look at teaching from a teacher's side of the desk.* New York: Random House.

Popham, W. J. (1978). *Criterion-referenced measurement.* Englewood Cliffs, NJ: Prentice Hall.

Popham, W. J. (2001). Teaching to the test? *Educational Leadership, 58*(6), 16–20.

Popham, W. J., & Husek, T. R. (1969). Implications of criterion-referenced measurement. *Journal of Educational Measurement, 6,* 1–9.

Prater, M. A. (2003). She will succeed! Strategies for success in inclusive classrooms. *Teaching Exceptional Children.* May/June, pp. 58–64.

Pressley, M., El-Dinary, P. N., Gaskins, I., Schuder, T., Bergman, J., & Almasi, L. (1992). Beyond direct explanations: Transactional instruction of reading comprehension strategies. *Elementary School Journal, 92,* 511–554.

Quintana, C., Eng, J, Carra, A. Wu, H. K., & Soloway, E. (1999). Symphony: A case study in extending learner-centered design through process space analysis. In M. Willians & M. W. Alton (Eds.), *Proceedings of CHI 99 Conference on Human Factors in Computing Systems* (pp. 473–480). New York: ACM Press.

Rak, C., & Patterson, L. (1996). Promoting resilience in at-risk children. *Journal of Counseling and Development, 74,* 368–373.

Rakic, P. (1991). Plasticity of cortical development. In S. E. Brauth, W. S. Hall, & R. J. Dooling (Eds.), *Plasticity of development.* Cambridge, MA: Bradfort/MIT Press.

Reeve, J. (1996). *Motivating others: Nurturing inner motivational resources.* Boston: Allyn & Bacon.

Reeve, J. (2002). Self-determination theory applied to educational settings. In E. L. Deci & R. M. Ryan (Eds.), *Handbook of self-determination theory* (pp. 183–203). Rochester, NY: University of Rochester.

Reeve, J. (2005). Teachers as facilitators: What autonomy-supportive teachers do and why their students benefit. *Elementary School Journal, 105,* 381–391.

Reeve, J., & Jang, H. (2005). *What autonomy-supportive teachers say and do during instruction.* Unpublished manuscript, University of Iowa, Iowa City, IA.

Reeve, J., Deci, E. L., & Ryan, R. M. (2004). Self-determination theory: A dialectical framework for understanding sociocultural influences on student motivation. In D. M. McInerney & S. Van Etten (Eds.), *Big theories revisited: Research on sociocultural influences on motivation and learning* (Vol. 4, pp. 31–60). Greenwich, CT: Information Age.

Reeve, J., Jang, H., Carrell, D., Barch, J., & Jeon, S. (2004). Enhancing high school students' engagement by increasing teachers' autonomy-supportive instructional strategies. *Motivation and Emotion, 28,* 147–169.

Reeve, J., Jang, H., Hardre, P., & Omura, M. (2002). Providing a rationale in an autonomy-supportive way as a strategy to motivate others during an uninteresting activity. *Motivation and Emotion, 26,* 183–207.

Reeve, J., Nix, G., & Hamm, D. (2003). The experience of self-determination in intrinsic motivation and the conundrum of choice. *Journal of Educational Psychology, 95,* 375–392.

Reglin, G. L., & Adams, D. R. (1990). Why Asian American high school students have higher grade point averages and SAT scores than other high school students. *High School Journal, 73,* 143–149.

Reich, P. A. (1986). *Language development.* Englewood Cliffs, NJ: Prentice Hall.

Reingold, E. M., Charness, N., Pomplun, M., & Stampe, D. M. (2001). Visual span in expert chess players: Evidence from eye movements. *Psychological Science, 12,* 48–55.

Reis, H. T., Sheldon, K. M., Gable, S. L., Roscoe, J., & Ryan, R. M. (2000). Daily well-being: The role of autonomy, competence, and relatedness. *Personality and Social Psychology Bulletin, 26,* 419–435.

Reiseberg, D. (2001). *Cognition: Exploring the science of the mind* (2nd ed.). New York: W. W. Norton.

Reiser, B. J. (2002). Why scaffolding should sometimes make tasks more difficult for learners. In G. Stahl, (Ed.) *Computer support for collaborative learning foundations for a CSCL community: Proceedings of CSCL 2002* (pp. 255–264.). Mahwah, NJ: Lawrence Erlbaum.

Reiser, B. J. (2004). Scaffolding complex learning: The mechanisms of structuring and problematizing student work. *The Journal of the Learning Sciences, 13,* 273–304.

Reiser, B. J., Tabak, I., Sandoval, W. A., Smith, B. K., Steinmuller, F., & Leone, A. J. (2001). BGuILE: Strategic and conceptual scaffolds for scientific enquiry in biology classrooms. In S. M. Carver & D. Klahr (Eds.) *Cognition and instruction: Twenty-five years of progress* (pp. 263–305). Mahwah, NJ: Lawrence Erlbaum.

Rennie, L. J., & Johnson, D. J. (2004). The nature of learning and its implications for research on learning from museums. *Science Education, 88,* 5–16.

Renninger, K. A. (1996). Learning as the focus of the educational psychology course. *Educational Psychologist, 31,* 63–76.

Renninger, K. A., Hidi, S., & Krapp, A. (Eds.) (1992). *The role of interest in learning and development.* Hillsdale, NJ: Lawrence Erlbaum.

Repetti, R. L., Taylor, S. E., & Seeman, T. E. (2002). Risky families: Family social environments and the mental and physical health of offspring. *Psychological Bulletin, 128,* 330–366.

Resnick, L., & Harwell, M. (2000). *Instructional variation and student achievement in a standards-based education district.* CSE Technical Report 522. Los Angeles: National Center for Research on Evaluation, Standards, and Student Testing.

Resnick, L., Levine, J. M., & Teasley, S. D. (Eds.) (1991). *Perspectives on socially shared cognition.* Washington, DC: American Psychological Association.

Rhodewalt, F., & Fairfield, M. (1991). Self-handicapping in the classroom: The effects of claimed self-handicaps on response to academic failure. *Basics of Applied Social Psychology, 16,* 397–416.

Ricciuti, H. R. (2004). Single parenthood, achievement, and problem behavior in white, black, and Hispanic children. *Journal of Educational Research, 97*(4), 196–206.

Rice, M. L. (1986). Children's language acquisition. *American Psychologist, 44,* 149–156.

Richardson, V. (1996). The role of attitudes and beliefs in learning to teach. In J. Sikula, T. Buttery, & E. Guyton (Eds.), *Handbook of research on teacher education* (2nd ed., pp. 102–119.) New York: Macmillan.

Riley, T., Adams, G. R., & Nielson, E. (1984). Adolescent egocentrism: The association among imaginary audience behavior, cognitive development, and parental support and rejection. *Journal of Youth and Adolescence, 13,* 401–417.

Rimm-Kaufman, S. E., & Sawyer, B. E. (2003). Primary-grade teachers' self-efficacy beliefs, attitudes toward teaching, and discipline and teaching practice priorities in relation to the responsive classroom approach. *Elementary School Journal, 104,* 321–341.

Roberts, W. B., & Morotti, A. A. (2000). The bully as victim: Understanding bully behaviors to increase the effectiveness of interventions in the bully-victim dyad. *Professional School Counseling, 4,* 148–155.

Rogers, C. E. (1969). *Freedom to learn: A view of what education might become.* Columbus, OH: Merrill.

Rogers, D. L., Noblit, G. W., & Ferrell, P. (1990). Action research as an agent for developing teachers' communicative competence. *Theory into Practice, 29,* 179–184.

Rogoff, B. (1990). *Apprenticeship in thinking: Cognitive development in social context.* New York: Oxford University Press.

Rogoff, B. (1998). Cognition as a collaborative process. In D. Kuhn & R. S. Siegler (Eds.), *Cognition, language, and perceptual development* (Vol. 2). In W. Damon (Series Ed.), *Handbook of child psychology* (5th ed., pp. 679–744). New York: John Wiley & Sons.

Rogoff, B. (2003). *The cultural nature of human development.* New York: Oxford University Press.

Rogoff, B., & Gardner, W. (1984). Adult guidance of cognitive development. In B. Rogoff & J. Lave (Eds.), *Everyday cognition: Development in social context* (pp. 95–116). Cambridge, MA: Harvard University Press.

Rogoff, B., Turkanis, C. G., & Bartlett, L. (2002). *Learning together: Children and adults in a school community.* New York: Oxford University Press.

Romeo, F. (1998). The negative effects of using a group contingency system. *Journal of Instructional Psychology, 25,* 130–134.

Rosch, E. (1973). Natural categories. *Cognitive Psychology, 4,* 328–349.

Rosch, E., Mervis, C. B., Gray, W. D., Johnson, D. M., & Boyes-Braem, P. (1976). Basic objects in natural categories. *Cognitive Psychology, 8,* 382–440.

Rosenberg, M. (1965). *Society and the adolescent self-image.* Princeton, NJ: Princeton University Press.

Rosenberg, M. (1979). *The conceiving self.* New York: Basic Books.

Rosenberg, M. S. (1989). The effects of daily homework assignments on the acquisition of basic skills by students with learning disabilities. *Journal of Learning Disabilities, 22,* 314–323.

Rosenholz, S. (1987). Education reform strategies: Will they increase teacher commitment? *American Journal of Education, 95,* 534–562.

Rosenshine, B. (1979). Content, time, and direct instruction. In P. Peterson & H. Walberg (Eds.), *Research on teaching: Concepts, findings, and implications* (pp. 28–56). Berkeley, CA: McCutchan.

Rosenshine, B. (1987). Explicit teaching. In D. Berliner & B. Rosenshine (Eds.), *Talks to teachers* (pp. 75–92). New York: Random House.

Rosenshine, B., & Meister, C. (1994). Reciprocal teaching: A review of the research. *Review of Educational Research, 64,* 479–530.

Rosenshine, B., & Stevens, R. (1986). Teaching functions. In M. Wittrock (Ed)., *Handbook of research on teaching* (3rd ed., pp. 376–391).

Rosenshine, B., Meister, C., & Chapman, S. (1996). Teaching students to generate questions: A review of the intervention studies. *Review of Educational Research, 66,* 181–221.

Ross, J. A. (1992). Teacher efficacy and the effect of coaching on student achievement. *Canadian Journal of Education, 17,* 51–65.

Rothbard, J., & Shaver, P. R. (1994). Continuity of attachment across the lifecourse: An attachment-theoretical perspective on personality. In M. Sperling & W. Berman (Eds.), *Adult attachment* (pp. 31–71). New York: Guilford Press.

Rothkopf, E. Z., & Billington, M. J. (1979). Goal-guided learning from text: Inferring a descriptive processing model from inspection times and eye movements. *Journal of Educational Psychology, 71,* 310–327.

Rottman, T. R., & Cross, D. C. (1990). *Scripted cooperative reading: Using student-student interaction to enhance comprehension.* Paper presented at the Annual Meeting of the American Educational Research Association, San Francisco.

Ruben, D. H. (1990). *Explaining explanation.* London: Routledge.

Ruble, D. (1983). The development of social comparison processes and their role in achievement-related self-socialization. In E. T. Higgins, D. N. Ruble, & W. W. Hartup (Eds.), *Social cognition and social development: A sociocultural perspective* (pp. 134–157). New York: Cambridge University Press.

Ruble, D., & Frey, K. S. (1991). Changing patterns of comparative behavior as skills are acquired: A function model of self-evaluation. In J. Suls & T. A. Wills (Eds.), *Social comparison: Contemporary theory and research* (pp. 79–107). Hillsdale, NJ: Lawrence Erlbaum.

Rumberger, R. W. (1987). High school dropouts: A view of issues and evidence. *Review of Educational Research, 57,* 101–121.

Rummel, A., & Feinberg, R. (1988). Cognitive evaluation theory: A meta-analytic review of the literature. *Social Behavior and Personality, 16,* 147–164.

Rummel, N., Levin, J. R., & Woodward, M. M. (2003). Do pictorial mnemonic text-learning aids give students something worth writing about? *Journal of Educational Psychology, 95,* 327–334.

Rushton, J. P., Brainerd, C. J., & Pressley, M. (1983). Behavioral development and construct validity: The principle of aggregation. *Psychological Bulletin, 94,* 18–38.

Ryan, R. M. (1991). The nature of the self in autonomy and relatedness. In J. Strauss & G. R. Goethals (Eds.). *The self: Interdisciplinary approaches* (pp. 208–238). New York: Springer-Verlag.

Ryan, R. M. (1993). Agency and organization: Intrinsic motivation, autonomy and the self in psychological development. In J. Jacobs (Ed.), *Nebraska symposium on motivation: Developmental perspectives on motivation* (Vol. 40, pp. 1–56). Lincoln: University of Nebraska Press.

Ryan, R. M., & Connell, J. P. (1989). Perceived locus of causality and internalization: Examining reasons for acting in two domains. *Journal of Personality and Social Psychology, 57,* 749–761.

Ryan, R. M., & Deci, E. L. (2000a). Intrinsic and extrinsic motivations: Classic definitions and new directions. *Contemporary Educational Psychology, 25,* 54–67.

Ryan, R. M., & Deci, E. L. (2000b). Self-determination theory and the facilitation of intrinsic motivation, social development, and well-being. *American Psychologist, 55,* 68–78.

Ryan, R. M., & Deci, E. L. (2001). To be happy or to be self-fulfilled: A review of research and eudaimonic well-being. In S. Fiske (Ed.), *Annual Review of Psychology* (Vol. 52, pp. 141–166). Palo Alto, CA: Annual Reviews.

Ryan, R. M., & Deci, E. L. (2002). An overview of self-determination theory: An organismic-dialectical perspective. In E. L. Deci & R. M. Ryan (Eds.), *Handbook of self-determination research* (pp. 3–33). Rochester, NY: University of Rochester Press.

Ryan, R. M., & Grolnick, W. S. (1986). Origins and pawns in the classroom: Self-report and projective assessments of individual differences in children's perceptions. *Journal of Personality and Social Psychology, 50,* 550–558.

Ryan, R. M., & La Guardia, J. G. (1999). Achievement motivation within a pressured society: Intrinsic and extrinsic motivations to learn and the politics of school reform. In T. Urdan (Ed.), *Advances in motivation and achievement* (Vol. 11, pp. 45–85). Greenwich, CT: JAI Press.

Ryan, R. M., & Powelson, C. (1991). Autonomy and relatedness as fundamental to motivation and education. *Journal of Experimental Education, 60,* 49–66.

Ryan, R. M., Mims, V., & Koestner, R. (1983). Relation of reward contingency and interpersonal context to intrinsic motivation: A review and test using cognitive evaluation theory. *Journal of Personality and Social Psychology, 45,* 736–750.

Ryan, R. M., Stiller, J., & Lynch, J. (1994). Representations of relationships to teachers, parents, and friends as predictors of academic motivation and self-esteem. *Journal of Early Adolescence, 14,* 226–249.

Rymer, R. (1993). *Genie: A scientific tragedy.* New York: HarperCollins.

Sadler, D. R. (1989). Formative assessment and the design of instructional systems. *Instructional Science, 18* (2), 119–144.

Sah, A., & Borland, J. H. (1989). The effects of a structured home plan on the home and school behaviors of gifted learning-disabled students with deficits in organizational skills. *Roeper Review, 12*(1), 54–57.

Salomon, G., & Globerson, T. (1987). Skill may not be enough: The role of mindfulness in learning and transfer. *International Journal of Educational Research, 11,* 623–637.

Salomon, G., & Perkins, D. N. (1989). Rocky roads to transfer: Rethinking mechanisms of a neglected phenomenon. *Educational Psychologist, 17,* 269–334.

Sanchez, E., Rosaes, J., & Canedo, I. (1999). Understanding and communication in expositive discourse: An analysis of the strategies used by expert and pre-service teachers. *Teaching and Teacher Education, 15,* 37–58.

Sandoval, W. A. (1998). *Inquire to explain: Structuring inquiry around explanation construction in a technology supported biology curriculum.* Unpublished Ph.D. dissertation. Evanston, IL: Northwestern University.

Sansone, C., & Smith, J. L. (2000). Self-regulating interest: When, why, and how. In C. Sansone & J. M. Harackiewicz (Eds.), *Intrinsic motivation: Controversies and new directions* (pp. 343–373). New York: Academic Press.

Sansone, C., Weir, C., Harpster, L., & Morgan, C. (1992). Once a boring task always a boring task? Interest as a self-regulatory mechanism. *Journal of Personality and Social Psychology, 63,* 379–390.

Sardo-Brown, D. (1988). Experienced teachers' planning practices: A U. S. survey. *Journal of Education for Teaching, 16,* 57–71.

Sardo-Brown, D. (1988). Twelve middle school teachers' planning. *Elementary School Journal, 89,* 69–87.

Saxe, G. B. (1988). The mathematics of child street vendors. *Child Development, 59,* 1415–1425.

Scardamalia, M., Bereiter, C., & Lamon, M. (1994). The CSILE project: Trying to bring the classroom into World 3. In K. McGilley (Ed.), *Classroom lessons: Integrating cognitive theory and classroom practice* (pp. 201–228) Cambridge, MA: MIT Press.

Scardamalia, M., Bereiter, C., & Steinbach, R. (1984). Teachability of reflective processes in written composition. *Cognitive Science, 8,* 173–190.

Schellenberg, E. G. (2004). Music lessons enhance IQ. *Psychological Science, 15,* 511–514.

Schiefele, U. (1991). Interest, learning, and motivation. *Educational Psychologist, 26,* 299–323.

Schiefele, U. (1999). Interest and learning from text. *Scientific Studies of Reading, 3,* 257–280.

Schiefele, U., Krapp, A., & Winteler, A. (1992). Interest as a predictor of academic achievement: A meta-analysis of research. In K. A. Renninger, S. Hidi, & A. Krapp (Eds.) *The role of interest in learning and development* (pp. 183–212). Hillsdale, NJ: Lawrence Erlbaum.

Schlaefli, A., Rest, J. R., & Thoma, S. J. (1985). Does moral education improve moral judgment? A meta-analysis of intervention studies using the Defining Issues Test. *Review of Educational Research, 55,* 319–352.

Schneider, A. J. (2005). Cultural differences in school expectations for Latino parents. *Parenting*. Retrieved March 20, 2004 from http://missourifamilies.org/features/parenting-articles/index.htm.

Schneider, B., & Lee, Y. (1990). A model for academic success. The school and home environment of East Asian students. *Anthropology and Education Quarterly, 21*, 358–377.

Schneider, W, & Shiffrin, R. M. (1974). Controlled and automatic processing I: Detection, search, and attention. *Psychological Review, 84*,1–66.

Schon, D. A. (1983). *The reflective practitioner*. New York: Basic Books.

Schon, D. A. (1987). *Educating the reflective practitioner*. San Francisco: Jossey-Bass.

Schraw, G., & Lehman, S. (2001). Situational interest: A review of the literature and directions for future research. *Educational Psychology Review, 13*, 23–52.

Schraw, G., Flowerday, T., & Reisetter, M. (1998). The role of choice in reader engagement. *Journal of Educational Psychology, 90*, 705–714.

Schulman, M., & Mekler, E. (1986). *Bringing up a moral child*. Reading, MA: Addison-Wesley.

Schultz, G. F., & Switzky, H. N. (1993). The academic achievement of elementary and junior high school students with behavior disorders and their nonhandicapped peers as a function of motivational orientations. *Learning and Individual Differences, 5*, 31–42.

Schuman, H., Steeh, C., Bobo, L., & Krysan, M. (1997). *Racial attitudes in America: Trends and interpretation*. Cambridge, MA: Harvard University Press.

Schumm, J. S., & Vaughn, S. (1992). Planning for mainstreamed special education students: Perceptions of general classroom teachers. *Exceptionality, 3*, 81–98.

Schumm, J. S., Vaughn, S., Haager, D., McDowell, J., Rothlein, L., & Saumell, L. (1995). General education teacher planning: What can students with learning disabilities expect? *Exceptional Children, 61*, 335–352.

Schunk, D. H. (1989). Self-efficacy and achievement behaviors. *Educational Psychology Review, 1*, 173–208.

Schunk, D. H. (1991). Self-efficacy and academic motivation. *Educational Psychologist, 26*, 207–231.

Schunk, D. H., & Zimmerman, B. J. (1997). Social origins of self-regulatory competence. *Educational Psychologist, 32*, 195–208.

Schutz, P. A., Crowder, K. C., & White, V. E. (2001). The development of a goal to become a teacher. *Journal of Educational Psychology, 93*, 299–308.

Schwartz, J. M., & Begley, S. (2002). *The mind and the brain: Neuroplasticity and the power of the mental force*. New York: HarperCollins.

Scriven, M. (1967) The methodology of evaluation. In R. W. Tyler (Ed.), *Perspectives of curriculum evaluation* (pp. 39–83). Chicago: Rand McNally.

Scruggs, T. E., & Mastropieri, M. A. (1998). Tutoring and students with special needs: In K. Topping & S. Ehly (Eds.), *Peer-assisted learning*, (pp. 165–182). Mahwah, NJ: Lawrence Erlbaum.

Scruggs, T. E., & Osguthorpe, R. (1986). Tutoring interventions within special education settings: A comparison of cross–age and peer tutoring. *Psychology in the Schools, 23*, 187–193.

Selfridge, O. G. (1955). Pattern recognition and modern computers. *Proceedings of Western Joint Computer Conference*. New York: Institute of Electrical and Electronics Engineers.

Seligman, M. E. P. (1975). *Helplessness: On depression, development, and death*. San Francisco: W. H. Freeman.

Seligman, M. E. P. (1991). *Learned optimism*. New York: Alfred A. Knopf.

Serpell, R. (1993). *The significance of schooling life-journeys in an African society*. Cambridge, England: Cambridge University Press.

Shaalvik, E. M., & Hagtvet, K. A. (1990). Academic achievement and self-concept: An analysis of causal predominance in a developmental perspective. *Journal of Personality and Social Psychology, 58*, 292–307.

Shapira, Z. (1976). Expectancy determinants of intrinsically motivated behavior. *Journal of Personality and Social Psychology, 34*, 1235–1244.

Sharan, S., & Hertz-Lazarowitz, R. (1980). A group investigation method of cooperative learning in the classroom. In S. Sharan, P. O'Hare, C. Webb, & R. Hertz-Lazarowitz (Eds.), *Cooperation in education* (pp. 14–46). Provo, UT: Brigham Young University Press.

Sharan, S., & Shachar, H. (1988). *Language learning in the cooperative classroom*. New York: Springer-Verlag.

Sharan, S., & Shaulov, A. (1990). Cooperative learning, motivation to learn, and academic achievement. In S. Sharan (Ed.), *Cooperative learning: Theory and research* (pp. 173–202). New York: Praeger.

Sharan, Y., & Sharan, S. (1992). *Expanding cooperative learning through group investigation*. New York: Teacher's College Press.

Shavelson, R. J., & Marsh, H. W. (1986). On the structure of self-concept. In R. Schwarzer (Ed.), *Anxiety and cognitions*. Hillsdale, NJ: Lawrence Erlbaum.

Shavelson, R. J., Baxter, G. P., & Pine, J. (1991). Performance assessment in science. *Applied Measurement in Education, 4*(4), 347–362.

Shaw, J. (2002). Linguistically responsive science teaching. *Electronic Magazine of Multicultural Education, (4)*1. Retrieved July 13, 2005, from http://www.eastern.edu/publications/emme.

Shearer, C. B. (2004). Using a multiple intelligences assessment to promote teacher development and student achievement. *Teachers College Record, 106*, 147–162.

Sheldon, K. M., Elliot, A. J., Kim, Y., & Kasser, T. (2001). What is satisfying about satisfying events? Testing 10 candidate psychological needs. *Journal of Personality and Social Psychology, 80*, 325–339.

Sheldon, K. M., Ryan, R. M., & Reis, H. T. (1996). What makes for a good day? Competence and autonomy in the day and in the person. *Personality and Social Psychology Bulletin, 22*, 1270–1279.

Shepard, L. (2000). *The role of classroom assessment in teaching and learning*. CSE Technical Report 517. Los Angeles: National Center for Research or Evaluation, Standards and Student Testing.

Shepard, L. A. (1982). Definitions of bias. In R. Berk (Ed.), *Handbook for detecting test bias* (pp. 9–30). Baltimore: Johns Hopkins University Press.

Shirey, L. L., & Reynolds, R. E. (1988). Effect of interest on attention and learning. *Journal of Educational Psychology, 80,* 159–166.

Shuell, T. J. (1996). The role of educational psychology in the preparation of teachers. *Educational Psychologist, 31,* 5–14.

Shukla-Mehta, S., & Albin, R. W. Twelve practical strategies to prevent behavioral escalation in classroom settings. *Preventing School Failure, 47,* 156–161.

Shulman, L. S. (1986). Those who understand: Knowledge growth in teaching. *Educational Researcher, 15*(2), 4–14.

Shulman, L. S. (1987). Knowledge and teaching: Foundations of the new reform. *Harvard Educational Review, 57*(1), 1–22.

Silon, E. L., & Harter, S. (1985). Assessment of perceived competence, motivational orientation, and anxiety in segregated and main-streamed educable mentally retarded children. *Journal of Educational Psychology, 77,* 217–230.

Simmons, P. E., Emory, A., Carter, T., Coker, T., Finnegan, B., Crockett, D., et al. (1999). Beginning teachers: Beliefs and classroom actions. *Journal of Research in Science Teaching, 36,* 930–954.

Skiba, R. J. (2000). When is disproportionality discrimination? The overrepresentation of Blacks in school suspension. In W. Ayers, B. Dorhn, & R. Ayers, R. (2001). *Zero tolerance: Resisting the drive for punishment in our schools* (pp. 165–175). New York: The New Press.

Skiba, R. J., & Peterson, R. L. (2001). School discipline at a crossroads: From zero tolerance to early response. *Exceptional Children, 66,* 335–346.

Skinner, B. F. (1950). Are theories of learning necessary? *Psychological Review, 57,* 193–216.

Skinner, B. F. (1953). *Science and human behavior.* New York: Macmillan.

Skinner, B. F. (1958). Reinforcement today. *American Psychologist, 13,* 94–99.

Skinner, E. A., & Belmont, M. J. (1993). Motivation in the classroom: Reciprocal effects of teacher behavior and student engagement across the school year. *Journal of Educational Psychology, 85,* 571–581.

Skinner, E. A., Wellborn, J. G., & Connell, J. P. (1990). What it takes to do well engagement and school achievement. *Journal of Educational Psychology, 82,* 22–32.

Skinner, E. A., Zimmer-Gembeck, M. J., & Connell, J. P. (1998). Individual differences and the development of perceived control. *Monographs of the Society for Research in Child Development, 63,* (2–3, Whole No. 204).

Slater, B. (1968). Effects of noise on pupil performance. *Journal of Educational Psychology, 59,* 239–243.

Slavin, R. E. (1984). Combining cooperative learning and individualized instruction: Effects on students mathematics achievement, attitudes, and behaviors. *Elementary School Journal, 84,* 409–422.

Slavin, R. E. (1986). *Using student team learning* (3rd ed). Baltimore, MD: The Johns Hopkins University Press.

Slavin, R. E. (1987a). Making Chapter 1 make a difference. *Phi Delta Kappan, 69,* 110–119.

Slavin, R. E. (1987b). Mastery learning reconsidered. *Review of Educational Research, 57,* 172–213.

Slavin, R. E. (1987c). Ability grouping and student achievement in elementary schools: A best evidence synthesis. *Review of Educational Research, 57,* 293–336.

Slavin, R. E. (1987d). Ability grouping and its alternatives: Must we track? *American Educator, 11*(2), 32–36.

Slavin, R. E. (1990). Achievement effects of ability grouping in secondary schools: A best-evidence synthesis. *Review of Educational Research, 60,* 471–499.

Slavin, R. E. (1995). *Cooperative learning* (2nd ed). Boston: Allyn & Bacon.

Slavin, R. E. (1996). Research on cooperative learning and achievement: What we know, what we need to know. *Contemporary Educational Psychology, 21,* 43–69.

Slavin, R. E., & Madden, N. A. (1989). What works for students at-risk: A research synthesis. *Educational Leadership, 46*(5), 4–13.

Sleeter, C. E. (1996). Multicultural education as a social movement. *Theory into Practice, 35,* 239–247.

Sloane, F. C. (2003). *An assessment of Sorenson's model of school differentiation: A multilevel model of tracking in middle and high school mathematics.* Unpublished dissertation, University of Chicago, Chicago.

Slobin, D. I. (1985). Crosslinguistic evidence for the language making capacity. In D. I. Slobin (Ed.), *The crosslinguistic study of language acquisition: Theoretical issues* (Vol. 2). Hillsdale, NJ: Lawrence Erlbaum.

Smith, B. K., & Reiser, B. J. (1998). *National Geographic* unplugged: Designing interactive nature films for classrooms. In C. M. Karat, A. Lund, J. Coutaz, & J. Karat (Eds.), *Proceedings of CHI 98* (pp. 424–431). New York: ACM Press.

Smith, E. L., & Sendelbach, N. B. (1979, April). *Teacher intentions for science instruction and their antecedents.* Paper presented at the annual meeting of the American Educational Research Association, San Francisco, CA.

Smith, J. David, Schneider, B. H., Smith, P. K., & Ananiadou, K. (2004). The effectiveness of whole-school antibullying programs: A synthesis of evaluation research. *School Psychology Review, 33*(4), 547–560.

Smith, J. K. (2003). Reconceptualizing reliability in classroom assessment. *Educational Measurement: Issues and Practice, 22*(4), 82–88.

Smith, J. K., & Carr, D. W. (2001). In Byzantium. *Curator, 44,* 335–354.

Smith, J. K., & DeLisi, R. (1998). Co-principal investigators. Making the grade: Improving postsecondary grading and assessment practices. Final Report, Fund for the Improvement of Postsecondary Education. New Brunswick, NJ.

Smith, J. K., & Wolf, L. F. (1996). Museum visitor preferences and intentions in constructing aesthetic experience. *Poetics: A Journal of Empirical Research in the Arts and Literature, 24,* 219–238.

Smith, J. K., & Wolf, L. F. (2004). The Influence of Test consequence on national examinations. *North America Journal of Psychology, 5,* 13–26.

Smith, J. K., Smith, L. F. & DeLisi, R. (2001). *Natural classroom assessment.* (p. 130). Thousand Oaks, CA: Corwin Press.

Smith, M. K. (2002). Howard Gardner and multiple intelligences. *The encyclopedia of informal education.* Retrieved 4/6/05 from http://www.infed.org/thinkers/gardner.htm.

Smith, M., & Wilhelm, J. (2002). *Reading don't fix no Chevys: Literacy in the lives of young men.* Portsmouth, NH: Heinemann.

Smith, P. K., & Brain, P. (2000). Bullying in schools: Lessons from two decades of research. *Aggressive Behavior, 26,* 1–9.

Smith, T. W., Snyder, C. R., & Handelsman, M. M. (1982). On the self-serving function of an academic wooden leg: Test anxiety as a self-handicapping strategy. *Journal of Personality and Social Psychology, 42,* 314–321.

Smith, T. W., Snyder, C. R., & Perkins, S. C. (1983). The self-serving function of hypochondriacal complaints: Physical symptoms as self-handicapping strategies. *Journal of Personality and Social Psychology, 44,* 787–797.

Snow, C. E., Arlman-Rupp, A., Hassing, Y., Jobse, J., Joosken, J., & Vorster, J. (1976). Mother's speech in three social classes. *Journal of Psycholinguistic Research, 5,* 1–20.

Snyder, C. R., & Higgins, R. L. (1988). Excuses: Their effective role in the negotiation of reality. *Psychological Bulletin, 104,* 23–35.

Snyder, C. R., Harris, C., Anderson, J. R., Holleran, S. A., Irving, L. M., Sigmond, S. T., Yoshinobu, L., Gibb, J., Langelle, C., & Harney, P. (1991). The will and the ways: Development and validation of an individual-differences measure of hope. *Journal of Personality and Social Psychology, 60,* 570–585.

Snyder, C. R., Lapointe, A. B., Crowson, J. J., Jr., & Early, S. (1998). Preferences of high- and low-hope people for self-referential input. *Cognition and Emotion, 12,* 807–823.

Snyder, C. R., Rand, K. L., & Sigmon, D. R. (2002). Hope theory: A member of the positive psychology family. In C. R. Snyder & S. J. Lopez (Eds.), *Handbook of positive psychology* (pp. 257–276). New York: Oxford University Press.

Snyder, C. R., Shorey, H. S., Cheavens, J., Pulvers, K. M., Adams, V. H. III, & Wiklund, D. (2002). Hope and academic success in college. *Journal of Educational Psychology, 94,* 820–826.

Soodak, L. (2003). Classroom management in inclusive settings. *Theory into Practice, 42,* 327–333.

Soodak, L. C., & Podell, D. M. (1993). Teacher efficacy and student problem factors in special education referral. *The Journal of Special Education, 27,* 66–81.

Sosniak, L. A. (1985). Learning to be a concert pianist. In B. S. Bloom (Ed.), *Developing talent in young people.* New York: Ballantine Books.

Spearman, C. (1923). *The nature of "intelligence" and the principles of cognition.* London: Macmillan.

Spearman, C. (1927). *The abilities of man.* New York: Macmillan.

Special Issues Analysis Center. (2003). *Literature review of federally funded studies related to LEP students.* Washington, DC: Office of Bilingual and Minority Languages Affairs.

Spence, J. T., & Helmreich, R. L. (1983). Achievement-related motives and behavior. In J. T. Spence (Ed.), *Achievement and achievement motives: Psychological and sociological approaches* (pp. 10–74). San Francisco: W. H. Freeman.

Sperling, G. (1960). The information available in brief visual presentations. *Psychological Monographs: General and Applied, 74,* 1–29.

Spielberger, C. D., & Starr, L. M. (1994). Curiosity and exploratory behavior. In H. F. O'Neil, Jr. & M. Drillings (Eds.), *Motivation: Theory and research* (pp. 221–243). Hillsdale, NJ: Lawrence Erlbaum.

Stanford-Binet (5th ed.) (2003). Itasca, IL: Riverside Publishing.

Statistical abstracts. (2000). Washington, DC: Government Printing Office.

Steele, C. M. (1999, August). Thin ice: "Stereotype threat" and Black college students. *Atlantic Monthly,* 44–54.

Steele, F. I. (1973). *Physical settings and organization development.* Reading, MA: Addison-Wesley.

Steinberg, L. (1996). *Adolescence* (4th ed). New York: McGraw-Hill.

Steiner, I. D. (1972) *Group Process and Productivity.* New York: Academic press.

Stern, D. N., Spieker, S., Barnett, R. K., & MacKain, K. (1983). The prosody of maternal speech: Infant age and context related changes. *Journal of Child Language, 10,* 1–15.

Sternberg, R. J. (1985). *Beyond IQ: A triarchic theory of human intelligence.* New York: Cambridge University Press.

Sternberg, R. J. (1997). *Successful intelligence.* New York: Plume.

Sternberg, R. J. (2000). Patterns of giftedness: A triarchic analysis. *Roeper Review, 22,* 231–235.

Sternberg, R. J., & Grigorenko, E. L. (2000). *Teaching for successful intelligence.* Arlington Heights, IL: Skylight.

Sternberg, R. J., & Zhang, L. F. (1995). What do we mean by giftedness: A pentagonal implicit theory. *Gifted Child Quarterly, 39,* 88–94.

Sternberg, R. J., Castejon, J. L., Prieto, M. D., Hautamaki, J., & Grigorenko, E. L. (2001). Confirmatory factor analysis of the Sternberg Triarchic Abilities Test in three international samples: An empirical test of the triarchic theory of intelligence. *European Journal of Psychological Assessment, 17*(1), 1–16.

Stevens, L. P. (2001). *Southpark* and society: Instructional and curricular implications of popular culture in the classroom. *Journal of Adolescent and Adult Literacy, 44,* 548–555.

Stevens, R. J., & Slavin, R. E. (1991). When cooperative learning improves the achievement of students with mild disabilities: A response to Tateyama-Sniezek. *Exceptional Children, 57,* 276–280.

Stevens, R. J., & Slavin, R. E. (1995). Effects of a cooperative learning approach in reading and writing on academically handicapped and nonhandicapped students. *The Elementary School Journal, 95,* 241–262.

Stevens, R. J., Madden, N. A., Slavin, R. E., & Farnish, A. (1987). Cooperative integrated reading and composition: Two field experiments. *Reading Research Quarterly, 22,* 433–454.

Stevens, T., Olivarez, Jr., A., Lan, W. Y., & Tallent-Runnels, M. K. (2004). Role of mathematics self-efficacy and motivation in mathematics performance across ethnicity. *Journal of Educational Research, 97*(4), 208–221.

Stiggins, R. J. (1997) *Student centered classroom assessment.* Upper Saddle River, NJ: Prentice Hall.

Stiggins, R. J. (2001). *Student-centered classroom assessment* (3rd ed.). Upper Saddle River, NJ: Merrill/Prentice Hall.

Stiggins, R. J. (2004). *Student-involved assessment for learning*. Upper Saddle River, NJ: Merrill/Prentice Hall.

Stipek, D. J., & Kowalski, P. S. (1989). Learned helplessness in task-orienting versus performance-orienting testing conditions. *Journal of Educational Psychology, 81*, 384–391.

Stipek, D., & MacIver, D. (1989). Developmental change in children's assessment of intellectual competence. *Child Development, 60*, 521–538.

Stofflett, R. T. (1966). Metaphor development by secondary teachers enrolled in graduate teacher education. *Teaching and Teacher Education, 12*, 577–589.

Strang, H. R., Lawrence, E. C., & Fowler, P. C. (1978). Effects of assigned goal level and knowledge of results on arithmetic computation: A laboratory study. *Journal of Applied Psychology, 63*, 446–450.

Strickland, D. S., & Rath, L. K. (2000, August). Between the lions: Public television promotes early literacy. *Reading Online, 4*(2). Retrieved January 3, 2005 from http://www.readingonline.org/articles/art_index.asp?HREF =strickland/index.html.

Sutherland, S. (1993). Impoverished minds. *Nature, 364*, 767.

Swann, W. B., Jr. (1999). *Resilient identities: Self, relationships, and the construction of social reality*. New York: Basic Books.

Swanson, H. L. (2000). What instruction works for students with learning disabilities? Summarizing the results from a meta-analysis of intervention studies. In R. Gersten, E. Schiller, & S. Vaughn (Eds.), *Contemporary special education research: Syntheses of the knowledge base on critical instructional issues* (pp. 1–30). Mahwah, NJ: Lawrence Erlbaum.

Swanson, H. L., & Alexander, J. E. (1997). Cognitive processes as predictors of word recognition and reading comprehension in learning-disabled and skilled readers: Revisiting the specificity hypothesis. *Journal of Educational Psychology, 89*, 128–158.

Swanson, H. L., & Siegel, L. (2001). Learning disabilities as working memory deficit. *Issues in Education, 7*, 1–48.

Sweller, J, & Chandler, P. (1994). Why some material is difficult to learn. *Cognition and Instruction. 12* 185–233

Taggart, G. L., Phifer, S. J., Nixon, J. A., & Wood, M. (2001). *Rubrics: A handbook for construction and use*. Lanham, MD: Scarecrow Press.

Tanner, C. K. (2000). The influence of school architecture on academic achievement. *Journal of Educational Administration, 38*, 309–330.

Tateyama-Sniezek, K. M. (1990). Cooperative learning: Does it improve the academic achievement of students with handicaps? *Exceptional Children, 54*, 426–437.

Taylor, C. B., Bandura, A., Ewart, C. K., Miller, N. H., & DeBusk, B. F. (1985). Capabilities soon after clinically uncomplicated acute myocardial infarction. *American Journal of Cardiology, 55*, 635–638.

Taylor, G. Shepard, L., Kinner, F., & Rosenthal, J. (2003). *A survey of teachers' perspectives on high stakes testing in Colorado: What gets taught, what gets lost*. CSE Technical Report 588. Los Angeles: Center for the Study of Evaluation, University of California.

Teachers of English to Speakers of Other Languages. (1997). *ESL standards for pre-K–12 students*. Alexandria, VA: Author.

Terborg, J. R. (1976). The motivational components of goal setting. *Journal of Applied Psychology, 61*, 613–621.

Terman, L. M. (1916). The measurement of intelligence: An explanation of and a complete guide for the use of the Stanford revision and extension of Binet-Simon intelligence scale. Boston: Houghton Mifflin.

Texas Education Agency. (2003). *8th grade TAKS objectives and TEKS student expectations*. Retrieved June 2, 2005 from http://staff.banqueteisd.esc2.net/J_RCanales/scope%20and %20sequence.htm.

The Algebra Project (2005). Retrieved March 21, 2005 from http://www.algebra.org.

The Rehabilitation Act of 1973. Retrieved April 10, 2005 from http://www.nationalrehab.org/website/history/act.html.

Thomas, W. P., & Collier, V. P. (2001). *A national study of school effectiveness for language minority students' long-term academic achievement*. Retrieved January 30, 2005 from http://www.crede.org/research/llaa/1.1_es.html.

Thompson, R. A. (1994). Emotion regulation: A theme in search of definition. *Monographs of the Society for Research in Child Development, 59* (2–3, Serial No. 240).

Thompson, R. A. (1998). Early sociopersonality development. In W. Damon (Series Ed.), N. Eisenberg (Ed.), *Handbook of child psychology: Social, emotional, and personality development* (Vol. 3, pp. 25–104). New York: Wiley.

Thompson, R. A. (1999). Early attachment and later development. In J. Cassidy & P. R. Shaver (Eds.), *Handbook of attachment: Theory, research, and clinical applications* (pp. 265–286). New York: Guilford.

Thompson, S. (2001). The authentic standards movement and its evil twin. *Phi Delta Kappan, 82*, 358–362.

Thorkildsen, T. A. (1993). Those who can, tutor: High-ability students' conceptions of fair ways to organize learning. *Journal of Educational Psychology, 85*, 182–190.

Thorndike, E. L. (1903). *Educational psychology*. New York: Lemcke & Buechner.

Thorndike, E. L. (1910). The contribution of psychology to education. *Journal of Educational Psychology, 1*, 5–12.

Thorndike, E. L. (1913). *Educational psychology* (3 vols.) New York: Teachers College, Columbia University Press.

Thorndike, E. L. (1913). *Educational psychology Vol. II. The psychology of learning*. New York: Teachers College Press.

Thorndike, E. L. (1931) *Human learning*. New York: The Century Co.

Thorndike, R. M. (1997). *Measurement and evaluation in psychology and education*, (6th ed.). Upper Saddle River, NJ: Merrill.

Thurstone, L. L. (1957). *Primary mental abilities*. Chicago, IL: University of Chicago Press.

Tindal, G., & Haladyna, T. H. (2002). *Large-scale assessment programs for all students*. Mahwah, NJ: Lawrence Erlbaum.

Tinker, M. A. (1939) The effect of illumination intensities upon speed of perception and upon fatigue in reading. *Journal of Educational Psychology, 30*, 561–571.

Tobias, S. (1994). Interest, prior knowledge, and learning. *Review of Educational Research, 64*, 37–54.

Tobin, K. (1990). Changing metaphors and beliefs: A master switch for teaching? *Theory into Practice, 29*, 122–127.

Todd, R., & Kuhlthau, C. (2003). *Student learning through Ohio school libraries.* Retrieved December 15, 2003 from http://www.oelma.org/studentlearning.htm.

Tolmie, A., & Howe, C. (1993). Gender and dialogue in secondary school physics. *Gender and Education, 5*, 191–209.

Tomasello, M. (1992). *First verbs: A case study of early grammatical development.* Cambridge, England: Cambridge University Press.

Tomasello, M. (1995). Language is not an instinct. *Cognitive Development, 10*, 601–609.

Tomlinson-Keasey, C., & Keasey, C. B. (1974). The mediating role of cognitive development in moral judgment. *Child Development, 45*, 291–298.

Top, B. L. (1984). *Handicapped children as tutors: The effects of cross-age, reverse role tutoring on self-esteem and reading achievement.* Provo, UT: Brigham Young University.

Torff, B. (2003). Developmental changes in teachers' use of higher order thinking and content knowledge. *Journal of Educational Psychology, 95*, 563–569.

Torgensen, J. K. (1996). Thoughts about intervention research in learning disabilities. *Learning Disabilities: A Multidisciplinary Journal, 7*, 55–58.

Torgesen, J. K. (1977). Memorization processes in reading-disabled children. *Child Development, 48*, 56–60.

Tower, C. C. (1996). *Understanding child abuse and neglect.* Needham Heights, MA: Allyn & Bacon.

Tramontana, M. G., Hooper, E. P., & Selzer, S. C. (1988). Research on the preschool prediction of later academic achievement: A review. *Developmental Review, 8*, 89–146.

Treisman, A. M. (1960). Contextual cues in encoding listening. *Quarterly Journal of Experimental Psychology, 12*, 242–248.

Triandis, H. C. (1989). The self and social behavior in differing cultural contexts. *Psychological Review, 96*, 506–520.

Trice, A. D. (2000). *A handbook of classroom assessment.* New York: Longman.

Trickett, P. K., & McBride-Chang, C. (1995). The developmental impact of different forms of child abuse and neglect. *Developmental Review, 15*, 311–337.

Tripp, D. H. (1990). Socially critical action research. *Theory into Practice, 29*, 158–166.

Trope, Y. (2004). Theory in social psychology: Seeing the forest and the trees. *Personality and Social Psychology Review, 8*, 193–200.

Trushell, J., Burrell, C., & Maitland, A. (2001). Year 5 pupils reading an "interactive storybook" on CD-ROM: Losing the plot? *British Journal of Educational Technology, 32*, 389–401.

Tschannen-Moran, M., & Hoy, A. W. (2001). Teacher efficacy: Capturing an elusive construct. *Teaching and Teacher Education, 17*, 783–805.

Tschannen-Moran, M., & Hoy, W. K. (2000). A multidisciplinary analysis of the nature, meaning, and measurement of trust. *Review of Educational Research, 70*, 547–593.

Tschannen-Moran, M., & Woolfolk Hoy, A. (2001) Teacher efficacy: Capturing an elusive construct. *Teaching and Teacher Education, 17*, 783–805.

Tubbs, M. E. (1986). Goal-setting: A meta-analytic examination of the empirical evidence. *Journal of Applied Psychology, 71*, 474–483.

Tudge, J. R. H. (1989). When collaboration leads to regression: Some negative consequences of socio-cognitive conflict. *European Journal of Social Psychology, 19*, 123–138.

Tudge, J. R. H. (1992). Processes and consequences of peer collaboration: A Vygotskian analysis. *Child Development, 63*, 1364–1379.

Tudge, J. R. H., & Rogoff, B. (1989). Peer influences on cognitive development: Piagetian and Vygotskian perspectives. In M. H. Bornstein & J. Bruner (Eds.), *Interaction in human development.* Hillsdale, NJ: Lawrence Erlbaum.

Tukey, J. W. (1977). *Exploratory Data Analysis.* Reading, MA: Addison-Wesley.

Tulving, E. (1972). Episodic and semantic memory. In E. Tulving & W. Donaldson (Eds.), *Organization of memory* (pp. 381–403). New York: Academic Press.

Turner, J. C., Meyer, D. K., Midgley, C., & Patrick, H. (2003). Teacher discourse and sixth graders' reported affect and achievement behaviors in two high-mastery/high-performance mathematics classrooms. *Elementary School Journal, 103*, 357–382.

Tyler, R. (1949). *Basic principles of curriculum and instruction.* Chicago, IL: University of Chicago Press.

Tzou, C. T., Reiser, B. J., Spillane, J. P., & Kemp, E. K. (2002, April). *Characterizing the multiple dimensions of teachers' inquiry practices.* Paper presented at the Annual Meeting of the American Educational Research Association, New Orleans, LA.

U.S. Census 2000. Retrieved April 7, 2005 from http://www.census.gov/main/www/cen2000.html.

U.S. Department of Education, Office of Special Education Programs, Data Analysis System, 2002–2003. Washington, DC: Author.

U.S. Department of Education. (2001). *National assessment of educational progress, 1984 and 1999 long-term trend assessment.* Washington, DC: National Center for Education Statistics.

U.S. Department of Education (2005). Retrieved from http://www.ed.gov/rschstat/research/pubs/research.html.

U.S. Secret Service Safe School Initiative. (2000). *An interim report on the prevention of targeted school violence in schools.* Washington, DC: Author.

Underwood, B., & Moore, B. (1982). Perspective-taking and altruism. *Psychological Bulletin, 91*, 143–173.

Underwood, G., & Jindal, N. (1993). Gender differences and cooperation in a computer-based language task. *Educational Research, 36*, 63–74.

University of Texas at Austin (2004). *Alien rescue.* Retrieved May 16, 2005 from http://jabba.edb.utexas.edu/liu/aliendb/home.htm.

Vaillant, G. E., & Milofsky, E. (1980). The natural history of male psychological health. IX. Empirical evidence for Erikson's model of the life cycle. *American Journal of Psychiatry, 137*, 1348–1359.

Vallerand, R. J., Fortier, M. S., & Guay, F. (1997). Self-determination and persistence in a real-life setting: Toward a motivational model of high school dropout. *Journal of Personality and Social Psychology, 72,* 1161–1176.

Vallerand, R. J., Pelletier, L. G., Blais, M. R., Briere, N. M., Senecal, C., & Vallieres, E. F. (1992). The Academic Motivation Scale: A measure of intrinsic, extrinsic, and amotivation in education. *Educational and Psychological Measurement, 52,* 1003–1017.

van Lieshout, C. F. M., & Heymans, P. G. (2000). *Developing talent across the lifespan.* Hove, East Sussex, UK: Psychological Press.

Van Manen, M. (1990). Beyond assumptions: Shifting the limits of action research. *Theory into Practice, 29,* 152–157.

Van Voorhis, F. L. (2003). Interactive homework in middle school: Effects on family involvement and science achievement. *Journal of Educational Research, 96*(6), 323–328.

VanLehn, K., Siler, S. A., Murray, C., & Bagget, W. B. (2003). Human tutoring: Why do only some events cause learning? *Cognition and Instruction, 21,* 209–249.

Vaughn, S., & Linan-Thompson, S. (2003). What is special about special education for students with learning disabilities? *The Journal of Special Education, 37,* 140–147.

Vaughn, S., & Schumm, J. S. (1994). Middle school teachers' planning for students with learning disabilities. *Remedial & Special Education, 15,* 152–161.

Veenman, S. (1984). Perceived problems of beginning teachers. *Review of Educational Research, 54,* 143–178.

Veldman, D. J., & Sanford, J. P. (1984). The influence of class ability level on student achievement and classroom behavior. *American Educational Research Journal, 21,* 629–644.

Venn, J. J. (2004). *Assessing students with special needs.* (3rd ed.). Upper Saddle River, NJ: Merrill Prentice Hall.

Venn, M. L., & McCollum, J. (2002). Exploring the long- and short-term planning practices of Head Start teachers for children with and without disabilities. *The Journal of Special Education, 35,* 211–223.

Veroff, J., McClelland, L., & Marquis, K. (1971). *Measuring intelligence and achievement motivations in surveys.* Ann Arbor, MI: University of Michigan.

Vinograd-Bausell, C. R., Bausell, R. B., Proctor, W., & Chandler, B. (1986). Impact of unsupervised parent tutors on word recognition skills. *Journal of Special Education, 20,* 83–90.

Virginia Education Association and the Appalachia Educational Laboratory (1992). Recommendations for Teachers. Author.

Virginia Standards of Learning Algebra I Blueprint (2003). (pp. 1048, 1069). Richmond, VA: Commonwealth of Virginia Department of Education.

Vitto, J. M. (2003). *Relationship-driven classroom management: Strategies that promote student motivation.* Thousand Oaks, CA: Corwin Press.

Voss, H. G., & Keller, H. (1983). *Curiosity and exploration: Theory and results.* San Diego: Academic Press.

Vygotsky, L. S. (1929). The problem of the cultural development of the child. *Journal of Genetic Psychology, 36,* 415–434.

Vygotsky, L. S. (1962). Thought and language. Cambridge, MA: MIT Press. (Original work published 1934).

Vygotsky, L. S. (1978). *Mind in society: The development of higher psychological processes.* Cambridge, MA: Harvard University Press.

Vygotsky, L. S. (1987). Thinking and speech. In R. W. Rieber & A. S. Carton (Eds.), *The collective works of L. S. Vygotsky* (translated by N. Minick). New York: Plenum Press.

Wadsworth, B. J. (1996). *Piaget's theory of cognitive and affective development: Foundations of constructivism* (5th ed.). White Plains, NY: Longman.

Walker, H. M., Irvin, L. K., Noell, J., & Singer, G. H. S. (1992). A construct score approach to the assessment of social competence: Rationale, technological considerations, and anticipated outcomes. *Behavior Modification, 16,* 448–474.

Wallace, D. S., West, S., Wandell, C., Ware, A., & Dansereau, D. F. (1998). The effect of knowledge maps that incorporate Gestalt principles on learning. *Journal of Experimental Education. 67,* 5–16.

Wang, M. C., Haertel, G. D., & Walberg, H. J. (1993). Toward a knowledge base for school learning. *Review of Educational Research, 63*(3), 249–294.

Wang, J. (1998). Opportunity to Learn: The impacts and policy implications. *Educational Evaluation and Policy Analysis. 20*(3), 137–156.

Wang, J., & Goldschmidt, P. (1999). Opportunity to Learn, language proficiency, and immigrant status: Effects on mathematics achievement. *Journal of Educational Research. 93*(20), 101–111.

Wang, M. C., Haertel, G. D., & Walberg, H.J. (1990). What influences learning? A content analysis of review literature. *Journal of Educational Research. 84,* 30–43.

Wang, M. C., Haertel, G. D., & Walberg, H. J. (1993). Toward a knowledge base for school learning. *Review of Educational Research, 63,* 249–294.

Wang, M. C., Haertel, G. D., & Walberg, H. J. (1993/94). What helps students learn? *Educational Leadership, 51*(4), 74–79.

Ward, J. R., & McCotter, S. S. (2004). Reflection as a visible outcome for preservice teachers. *Teaching & Teacher Education, 20,* 243–257.

Warger, C. (2001). *Five homework strategies for teaching students with disabilities.* ERIC/OSEP Digest E608. Arlington, VA: ERIC Clearinghouse on Disabilities and Gifted Education.

Warton, P. M. (2001). The forgotten voices in homework: Views of students. *Educational Psychologist, 36*(3), 155–165.

Waterman, A. S. (1982). Identity development from adolescence to adulthood: An extension of theory and a review of research. *Developmental Psychology, 18,* 341–358.

Waterman, A. S. (1985). Identity in the context of adolescent psychology. In A. S. Waterman (Ed.), *Identity in adolescence: Processes and contexts: New directions for child development* (Vol. 30). San Francisco, CA: Jossey-Bass.

Waters, E., Wippman, J., & Sroufe, L. A. (1979). Attachment, positive affect, and competence in the peer group. *Child Development, 50,* 821–829.

Webb, N. M. (1984). Sex differences in interaction and achievement in cooperative small groups. *Journal of Educational Psychology, 76,* 33–44.

Webb, N. M. (1989). Peer interaction and learning in small groups. *International Review of Educational Research, 13,* 21–40.

Webb, N. M. (1991). Task-related verbal interaction and mathematics learning in small groups. *Journal of Research in Mathematics Education, 22,* 366–269.

Webb, N. M. (1992). Testing a theoretical model of student interaction and learning in small groups. In R. Hertz-Lazarowitz & N. Miller (Eds.), *Interaction in cooperative groups: The theoretical anatomy of group learning* (pp. 102–119). New York: Cambridge University Press.

Webb, N. M., & Farivar, S. (1994). Promoting helping behavior in cooperative groups in middle school mathematics. *American Educational Research Journal, 31,* 369–395.

Wechsler, D. (2003). Wechsler Intelligence Scale for Children (4th ed). San Antonio, TX: Psychological Corporation.

Wehmeyer, M. L., Agran, M., & Hughes, C. A. (1998). *Teaching self-determination to students with disabilities: Basic skills for successful transition.* Baltimore: Brookes.

Weinberg, R. S., Gould, D., & Jackson, A. (1979). Expectations and performance: An empirical test of Bandura's self-efficacy theory. *Journal of Sport Psychology, 1,* 320–331.

Weiner, B. (1985). An attributional theory of achievement motivation and emotion. *Psychological Review, 92,* 548–573.

Weiner, B. (1986). *An attributional theory of motivation and emotion.* New York: Springer-Verlag.

Weiner, B. (2004). Attribution theory revisited: Transforming cultural plurality into theoretical unity. In D. M. McInerney & S. Van Etten (Eds.), *Big theories revisited: Research on sociocultural influences on motivation and learning* (Vol. 4, pp. 13–29). Greenwich, CT: Information Age.

Weiner, L. (2003). Why is classroom management so vexing to urban teachers? *Theory into Practice, 42,* 305–312.

Weinstein, C. (1979). The physical environment of the school: A review of the research. *Review of Educational Research, 49*(4), 577–610.

Weinstein, C. S. (2003). *Secondary classroom management: Lessons from research and practice* (2nd ed.). Boston: McGraw-Hill Higher Education.

Weinstein, C. S., & Mignano, Jr., A. J. (2003). *Elementary classroom management: Lessons from research and practice* (3rd ed.). Boston: McGraw-Hill Higher Education.

Weinstein, C., Curran, M. E., & Tomlinson-Clarke, S. (2003). Culturally responsive classroom management: Awareness into action. *Theory into Practice, 42,* 269–276.

Weiss, B., Dodge, K., Bates, J. E., & Pettit, G. S. (1992). Some consequences of early harsh discipline: Child aggression and a maladaptive social information processing style. *Child Development, 63,* 1321–1335.

Wellborn, J. P. (1991). *Engaged and disaffected action: The conceptualization and measurement of motivation in the academic domain.* Unpublished doctoral dissertation, University of Rochester.

Wenger, E. (1998). *Communities of practice.* Cambridge, UK: Cambridge University Press.

Wentling, T. (1973). Mastery versus nonmastery instruction with varying test item feedback treatments. *Journal of Educational Psychology, 65,* 50–58.

Wentzel, K. R. (1994). Relations of social goal pursuit to social acceptance, classroom behavior, and perceived social support. *Journal of Educational Psychology, 86,* 173–182.

Wentzel, K. R., & Asher, S. R. (1995). Academic lives of neglected, rejected, popular, and controversial children. *Child Development, 66,* 754–763.

Wentzel, K. R., Battle, A., & Looney, L. (2001, April). *Classroom support in middle school: Contributions of teachers and peers.* Paper presented at the annual meeting of the American Educational Research Association, Seattle, WA.

Werner, E. E. (1992). The children of Kauai: Resiliency and recovery in adolescence and adulthood. *Journal of Adolescent Health, 13,* 262–268.

West, L. H. T., & Fensham, P. J. (1976). Prior knowledge or advance organizers as affective variables in chemical learning. *Journal of Research in Science Teaching, 13,* 297–306.

Whitbourne, S. K., Zuschlag, M. K., Elliot, L. B., & Waterman, A. S. (1992). Psychosocial development in adulthood: A 22-year sequential study. *Journal of Personality and Social Psychology, 63,* 260–271.

Wiggins, G. P. (1999). *Assessing student performance: Exploring the purpose and limits of testing.* Hoboken, NJ: John Wiley and Sons.

Williams, B. T. (2003). What they see is what we get: Television and middle school writers. *Journal of Adolescent and Adult Literacy, 46,* 546–554.

Williams, R. L. (1974). Scientific racism and IQ: The silent mugging of the black community. *Psychology Today, 7*(12), 32–41.

Willig, A. C., Harnisch, D. L., Hill, K. T., & Maehr, M. L. (1983). Sociocultural and educational correlates of success-failure attributions and evaluation anxiety in the school setting for black, Hispanic, and Anglo children. *American Educational Research Journal, 20,* 385–410.

Wilson, T. D., & Linville, P. W. (1982). Improving the academic performance of college freshman: Attribution therapy revisited. *Journal of Personality and Social Psychology, 42,* 367–376.

Wilson, T. D., Centerbar, D. B., Kermer, D. A., & Gilbert, D. T. (2005).The pleasures of uncertainty: Prolonging positive moods in ways people do not anticipate. *Journal of Personality and Social Psychology, 88,* 5–21.

Winne, P. H. (1997). Experimenting to bootstrap self-regulated learning. *Journal of Educational Psychology, 88,* 397–410.

Wisconsin Department of Public Instruction (2002). *DPI guidelines to facilitate the participation of students with special needs in state assessments.* Madison, WI: Wisconsin Department of Public Instruction.

Wise, B. W., & Olson, R. K. (1994). Computer speech and the remediation of reading and spelling problems. *Journal of Special Education Technology, 12,* 207–220.

Wittrock, M. C. (1992). An empowering conception of educational psychology. *Educational Psychologist, 27,* 129–141.

Wolf, L. F., & Smith, J. K. (1995). The consequence of consequence: Motivation, anxiety, and test performance. *Applied Measurement in Education, 8,* 227–242.

Wolf, S. A., & Gearhart, M. (1997). New writing assessments: The challenge of changing teachers' beliefs about students as writers. *Theory Into Practice, 36,* 220–230.

Wolf, T. H. (1973). *Alfred Binet.* Chicago: University of Chicago Press.

Wong, B. Y. L., Wong, R., & Blenkinsop, J. (1989). Cognitive and metacognitive aspects of learning disabled adolescents' composing problems. *Learning Disability Quarterly, 12,* 300–322.

Wong, H. K., & Wong, R. T. (1998). *The first days of school: How to be an effective teacher.* Mountain View, CA: Harry K. Wong Publications.

Wood, D., Bruner, J., & Ross, G. (1976). The role of tutoring in problem solving. *Journal of Child Psychology and Psychiatry and Allied Disciplines, 17,* 89–100.

Wood, J. V. (1989). Theory and research concerning social comparisons of personal attributes. *Psychological Bulletin, 106,* 231–248.

Wood, J. W. (2002). *Adapting instruction to accommodate students in inclusive settings.* Upper Saddle River, NJ: Merrill Prentice Hall.

Wood, R. E., & Bandura, A. (1989). Impact of conceptions of ability on self-regulatory mechanisms and complex decision making. *Journal of Personality and Social Psychology, 56,* 407–415.

Woolfolk Hoy, A. (2000, April). *Changes in teacher efficacy during the early years of teaching.* Paper presented at the annual meeting of the American Educational Research Association, New Orleans, LA.

Woolfolk, A. E., & Hoy, W. K. (1990). Prospective teachers' sense of efficacy and beliefs about control. *Journal of Educational Psychology, 82,* 81–91.

Wright, J. (2005). Behavior contracts. Retrieved April 25, 2005 from http://www.interventioncentral.org/htmdocs/interventions/behcontr.shtml.

Yerkes, R. M. (1941). Man-power and military effectiveness: The case for human engineering. *Journal of Counseling Psychology, 5,* 205–209.

Yinger, R. J. (1980). A study of teacher planning. *Elementary School Journal, 80,* 107–127.

Yost, R. (2002). "I think I can.": Mentoring as a means of enhancing teacher efficacy. *Clearing House, 75,* 195–197.

Young, J. W. (2003). *Validity in college admissions testing.* New York: The College Board.

Zahorki, J. A. (1987). Teachers' collegial interactions: An exploratory study. *Elementary School Journal, 87,* 385–396.

Zanna, M. P., Goethals, G. R., & Hill, J. F. (1975). Evaluating a sex-related ability: Comparison with similar others and standard setters. *Journal of Experimental Social Psychology, 11,* 86–93.

Zehler, A. M., Fleischman, H. J., Hopstock, P. J., Stephenson, T. G., Pendzick, M. L., & Sapru, S. (2003). *Descriptive study of services to LEP students and LEP students with disabilities.* Washington, DC: Office of the Department of Education.

Zeichner, K. M., & Liston, D. P. (1996). *Reflective teaching: An introduction.* Mahwah, NJ: Lawrence Erlbaum.

Zentall, S. S. (1993). Research on the educational implications of attention deficit hyperactivity disorder. *Exceptional Children, 60,* 143–153.

Zhou, Q., Eisenberg, N., Losoya, S. H., Fabes, R. A., Reiser, M., Guthrie, I. K., Murphy, B. C., Cumberland, A. J., & Shepard, S. A. (2002). The relations of parental warmth and positive expressiveness to children's empathy-related responding and social functioning: A longitudinal study. *Child Development, 73,* 893–915.

Zillman, D. (1980). Anatomy of suspense. In P. H. Tannenbaum (Ed.), *The entertainment functions of television* (pp. 133–163). Hillsdale, NJ: Lawrence Erlbaum.

Zimmerman, B. J. (1989). A social cognitive view of self-regulated academic learning. *Journal of Educational Psychology, 81,* 329–339.

Zimmerman, B. J. (1998). Academic studying and the development of personal skill: A self-regulatory perspective. *Educational Psychology, 33,* 73–86.

Zimmerman, B. J. (2000). Attaining self-regulation: A social cognitive perspective. In M. Boekaerts, P. R. Pintrich, & M. Zeidner (Eds.), *Handbook of self-regulation* (pp. 13–39). San Diego, CA: Academic Press.

Zimmerman, B. J. (2002). Becoming a self-regulated learner: An overview. *Theory into Practice, 41,* 64–70.

Zimmerman, B. J., & Martinez-Pons, M. (1986). Development of a structured interview for assessing student use of self-regulated learning strategies. *American Educational Research Journal, 23,* 614–628.

Zimmerman, B. J., & Martinez-Pons, M. (1988). Construct validation of a strategy model of student self-regulated learning. *Journal of Educational Psychology, 80,* 284–290.

Zimmerman, B. J., & Risemberg, R. (1997). Become a proficient writer: A social cognitive perspective. *Contemporary Educational Psychology, 22,* 73–101.

Zimmerman, B. J., Bonner, S., & Kovach, R. (1996). *Developing self-regulated learners: Beyond achievement to self-efficacy.* Washington, DC: American Psychological Association.

Zimpher, N. L., & Ashburn, E. A. (1992). Countering parochialism in teacher candidates. In M. E. Dilworth (Ed.), *Diversity in teacher education: New expectations* (pp. 40–41). San Francisco: Jossey-Bass.

Zuber, R. I. (1992). *Cooperative learning by fifth-grade students: The effects of scripted and unscripted cooperation.* Unpublished doctoral dissertation, Rutgers, The State University of New Jersey, New Brunswick, NJ.

Zuckerman, M., Porac, J., Lathin, D., Smith, R., & Deci, E. L. (1978). On the importance of self-determination for intrinsically-motivated behavior. *Personality and Social Psychology Bulletin, 4,* 443–446.

Name Index

Subject Index